CEDU 쎄듀는 A **C**omprehensive **E**nglish e**DU**cation(종합적 영어교육)의 약자입니다.

저자

김기훈

現 ㈜ 쎄듀 대표이사
現 메가스터디 영어영역 대표강사
前 서울특별시 교육청 외국어 교육정책자문위원회 위원

저서   천일문 / 천일문 Training Book / 천일문 GRAMMAR
첫단추 BASIC / 쎄듀 본영어 / 어휘끝 / 어법끝 / 문법의 골든룰 101
절대평가 PLAN A / 리딩 플랫폼 / ALL쏨 서술형 시리즈
Reading Relay / The 리딩플레이어 / 빈칸백서 / 오답백서
첫단추 / 파워업 / 수능영어 절대유형 / 수능실감 등

쎄듀 영어교육연구센터

쎄듀 영어교육센터는 영어 콘텐츠에 대한 전문지식과 경험을 바탕으로
최고의 교육 콘텐츠를 만들고자 최선의 노력을 다하는 전문가 집단입니다.

오혜정 센터장 • **장정문** 전임연구원 • **오승은** 연구원

마케팅	콘텐츠 마케팅 사업본부
제작	정승호
영업	문병구
인디자인 편집	올댓에디팅
디자인	이연수
영문교열	Stephen Daniel White

수능실감

독해 최우수 문항

최우수

문항

500제

PREFACE

2024학년도 수능은 2018~2023 수능과 마찬가지로 절대평가로 시행됩니다. EBS 연계 비율, 문항 수 및 유형, 난이도 모두 2023학년도와 유사하게 출제될 것으로 예상되고 있습니다. 절대평가가 도입된 이래로 1등급 비율은 2018학년도 10.03%, 2019학년도 5.30%, 2020학년도 7.43%, 2021학년도 12.66%, 2022학년도 6.25%, 2023학년도 수능 7.83%로 나타났습니다.

2022학년도부터 EBS 교재에 나온 지문이 그대로 출제되는 직접연계가 없어지고 간접연계와 비연계 문제로 출제되면서 수능 영어의 난이도는 상승했습니다. EBS 연계 교재의 지문과 소재는 같되 내용이 다른 간접연계 문항들은 마치 실전에서 비연계 문항을 대하는 생소함을 줄 수 있습니다. 그러므로 과거에 비해 **양질의 비연계 문제를 다량으로 풀어야 할 필요성**이 생기게 되었습니다.

본 **수능실감 독해 최우수 문항 500제**는 이러한 요구에 부응하고자 기획된 것입니다. 10년 연속 베스트셀러를 달성한 수능실감 시리즈(2014~2023학년도 대비)에 실린 문항 중 고품질의 최우수 문항들을 선별 수록한 문제집으로서 수능 영어를 치르게 될 수험생들에게는 비연계 및 간접연계 대비에 최적화된 것이라 할 수 있습니다.

수능실감 시리즈 총 2,673개에 달하는 독해 문항들 중에서 상대적으로 더 좋은 평가를 받은 문항들을 1차로 추렸으며, 그중에서 2017~2023학년도 수능 영어의 난이도 또는 그보다 약간 어려운 난이도의 문항들을 2차로 엄선하여 총 500개 문항을 20문항씩 25회로 구성하였습니다. 절대평가 1등급을 위한 국내 최고 품질의 비연계 대비서로서 학생들이 자주 틀리는 주요 유형들을 빠짐없이 수록하였고 그렇지 않은 유형들도 감을 잃지 않도록 적절히 배치하여, 시간 대비 효율성을 더했습니다.

지난 30년간 수능 영어 현장에서 수험생과 같이 호흡하며 보유하게 된 양질의 문제 개발 능력은 쎄듀만의 자부심입니다. 거기에 덧붙여 자세하고 친절한 해설은 수험생 여러분의 문제해결력과 적용력을 한층 업그레이드해주리라 확신합니다. 본 교재를 접한 모든 수험생 여러분의 앞날에 합격의 영광이 있기를 진심으로 기원합니다.

저자

CONTENTS

책속의 책 [정답 및 해설]

○ 답안지의 해당란에 성명과 수험번호를 쓰고, 또 수험번호와 답을 정확히 표시하시오.
○ 문항에 따라 배점이 다르니, 각 물음의 끝에 표시된 배점을 참고하시오. 3점 문항에만 점수가 표시되어 있습니다. 점수 표시가 없는 문항은 모두 2점씩입니다.

---

1. 다음 글의 목적으로 가장 적절한 것은?

Dear Cindy,

I just saw a great story about a group of parents who have formed a babysitting cooperative in their town, and I think it would be a wonderful addition here in Fairview. Here's the way it works: Several caregivers (mothers, fathers, single parents, grandparents) get together and pledge that they will be available to babysit for each other's children. An hour is credited to a member's account for every hour they act as babysitter for another member of the group. The members then can draw upon the hours banked in their accounts when they need babysitting for their own children. As you know, finding a reliable babysitter around here is very difficult, and the good ones are in such demand that it is almost impossible to schedule them. I think that setting up a cooperative can provide high-quality care to our children. I look forward to your reply.

Sincerely,
Karen Diamond

① 어린이 돌봄 서비스의 개선 필요성을 설명하려고
② 어린이 돌봄 협동조합을 구성할 것을 제안하려고
③ 어린이 돌봄 시설에 대한 정부 지원을 호소하려고
④ 어린이 돌봄 단체의 회원 자격 요건을 문의하려고
⑤ 어린이 돌봄 단체 구성을 위한 모임을 안내하려고

2. 다음 글에서 필자가 주장하는 바로 가장 적절한 것은?

The quest for joy and happiness is a universal desire. It is unfortunate, however, that people so often believe that the search will be entirely fulfilled by finding the perfect job, acquiring some new gadget, losing weight, or maintaining an image. The problem inherent in looking outward for sources of happiness is that focusing on what you do not have or what you are not inevitably leads to unhappiness. It is said that the grass is always greener on the other side of the fence. When you have stopped comparing yourself and your assets to others, you will be able to recognize that to others, you are on the more blessed side. Learning to live in the moment and enjoying your personal lot can be a source of profound contentment.

① 남과 비교하지 말고 자신이 가진 것을 즐겨라.
② 현재에 만족하지 말고 더 큰 목표를 추진하라.
③ 남에 대한 관찰을 통해 자기 단점을 극복하라.
④ 경제적 성공보다 내면의 아름다움을 추구하라.
⑤ 타인의 진심 어린 비판을 겸허하게 받아들여라.

3. 다음 글에서 밑줄 친 Both parties win이 의미하는 바로 가장 적절한 것은? [3점]

Contributing to other people's newsletters with articles or inserts is an inexpensive and excellent way to reach new markets and tap into the captured customers of another business. Most newsletter publishers welcome submissions from others because finding content for newsletters is an ongoing challenge. If you provide them with non-competing information, you can easily gain access to another company's newsletter. For example, a massage therapist might submit to a chiropractor's newsletter. The services are similar enough to appeal to the same audience, but different enough to offer distinct services. You can either submit a story, or provide an insert to the newsletter publisher. In the latter case, it works much like a joint mailing. You help defray the cost of mailing the newsletter in exchange for letting your insert ride along. Both parties win.

*insert: 삽입 광고 **chiropractor: 척추 지압 요법사 ***defray: 부담하다

① Newsletter publishers and advertisers share successful marketing tools.
② Contributing to other people's newsletters is both cheap and effective.
③ Publishers can get help from both contributors and the mailing system.
④ Providing an insert benefits both newsletter publishers and contributors.
⑤ Contributing to a newsletter provides the contributor with newsletter access.

4. 다음 글의 주제로 가장 적절한 것은?

In a recent study comparing every Nobel Prize-winning scientist from 1901 to 2005 with typical scientists of the same era, both groups attained deep expertise in their respective fields of study. But the Nobel Prize winners were dramatically more likely to be involved in the arts than less accomplished scientists. A representative study of thousands of Americans showed similar results for creative people — entrepreneurs and inventors. People who started businesses and contributed to patent applications were more likely than their peers to have leisure time hobbies that involved drawing, painting, architecture, sculpture, and literature. Interest in the arts among entrepreneurs, inventors, and eminent scientists obviously reflects their curiosity and aptitude. People who are open to new ways of looking at science and business also tend to be fascinated by the expression of ideas and emotions through images, sounds, and words.

① the importance of arts as a source of creative insight
② the requirements for innovators to collaborate with artists
③ the differences between ordinary and extraordinary people
④ the reasons for encouraging curiosity for inventive thinking
⑤ the necessity of expertise to turn a great idea into an action

5. 다음 도표의 내용과 일치하지 <u>않는</u> 것은?

Percent of Canadian Energy Obtained from Various Sources

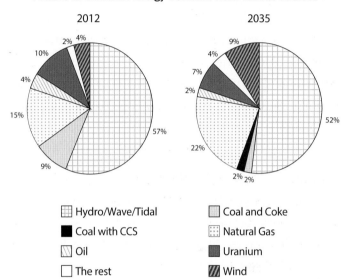

▦ Hydro/Wave/Tidal	▨ Coal and Coke
■ Coal with CCS	▥ Natural Gas
⧄ Oil	▦ Uranium
▢ The rest	▨ Wind

The pie charts above show the percentages of Canada's energy obtained from various sources in 2012 and their predicted shares in 2035. ① We can see that Hydro/Wave/Tidal sources will shrink by five percentage points but remain the dominant source of energy. ② Coal and Coke are predicted to shrink by seven percentage points, while Natural Gas is predicted to grow by the same amount. ③ Wind is predicted to more than double from 4% to 9%, which is the biggest percentage-point increase among all the energy sources. ④ Meanwhile, Coal with CCS, which wasn't used at all in 2012, is predicted to account for 2% of Canada's energy in 2035. ⑤ Uranium and Oil are two sources predicted to shrink over time, with the former dropping by three percentage points and the latter by two.

*coke: 코크스 ((석탄으로 만든 연료))

6. Ole Gunnar Solskjaer에 관한 다음 글의 내용과 일치하지 <u>않는</u> 것은?

Ole Gunnar Solskjaer was born in 1973 in Kristiansund, Norway. Between 1994 and 1996 Solskjaer played for Molde FK, during which he netted 31 goals in 38 matches and attracted the attention of Hamburger SV and Cagliari. But in July 1996 the footballer completed a move to Manchester United. He made his debut as a substitute in the match against Blackburn Rovers, and in his first season he helped the team to win the title with his 18 goals. In the several seasons after Solskjaer joined Manchester United he proved himself an eminent striker, though he appeared on the field as a substitute. In the 2001/02 season he got a regular spot in the starting eleven. He represented Norway and earned 67 caps. He was called up to the national squad for the 1998 FIFA World Cup and Euro 2000.

*cap: 국가 대표 선수, 대표 선수로 출전할 기회

① 1973년에 노르웨이의 Kristiansund에서 태어났다.
② Molde FK팀에서 38경기 동안 31득점을 기록했다.
③ Blackburn Rovers팀에 입단하여 교체선수로 데뷔했다.
④ 2001-2002 시즌에 팀에서 선발 선수 자리를 획득했다.
⑤ 1998년 월드컵에서 노르웨이 국가 대표 선수로 발탁됐다.

7. 다음 글의 밑줄 친 부분 중, 어법상 <u>틀린</u> 것은? [3점]

In *The Odyssey*, Homer's classic work from around 800 B.C., the hero Odysseus faces many perils and tests on his return home from the Trojan War. At one point his ship must pass the Sirens, ① <u>whose</u> haunting voices lure sailors to their death on the rocks near shore. Odysseus wanted to hear the Sirens, so he put wax in his men's ears and tied ② <u>himself</u> to the ship's mast in order that he could safely hear the Sirens' singing without going mad. He knew willpower alone wasn't enough to overcome the Sirens' temptation. Therefore, Odysseus did not perish and emerged on the other side of the Sirens more ③ <u>prepared</u> to complete his journey home. Unlike Odysseus, however, few of us foresee the challenges we will face. As a result, the willpower we assume when we set a goal rarely ④ <u>to match</u> the willpower we display in achieving that goal. Something always comes up to sink our boat. The belief ⑤ <u>that</u> we have a lot of willpower triggers overconfidence.

*mast: (배의) 돛대

8. 다음 글의 밑줄 친 부분 중, 문맥상 낱말의 쓰임이 적절하지 <u>않은</u> 것은? [3점]

We often hear the expression "music is the universal language." By this people mean that even if two people do not speak each other's language, they can at least appreciate music ① <u>together</u>. But like so many popular sayings, this one is only ② <u>partially</u> true. Although all people do have the same physiological mechanisms for hearing, what a person actually hears is influenced by his or her culture. Westerners tend to miss much of the richness of Javanese and Sri Lankan music because they have not been ③ <u>conditioned</u> to hear it. Whenever we encounter a piece of non-

Western music, we hear it (process it) in terms of our own ④ culturally influenced set of musical categories involving scale, melody, pitch, harmony, and rhythm. And because those categories are defined differently from culture to culture, the appreciation of music across cultures is not always ⑤ impossible.

*physiological: 생리적(生理的)인, 생리학(상)의

[9~12] 다음 빈칸에 들어갈 말로 가장 적절한 것을 고르시오.

9. *Apocalypse Now,* a film produced and directed by Francis Ford Coppola, gained popularity, and with good reason. The film is the adaptation of J. Conrad's novel *Heart of Darkness*, which is set in the African Congo at the end of the 19th century. Unlike the original novel, *Apocalypse Now* is set in Vietnam and Cambodia during the Vietnam War. The setting, time period, dialogue, and other incidental details are updated to the then present day, but the fundamental story line and themes of *Apocalypse Now* are the same as those of *Heart of Darkness*. Both describe a physical journey, reflecting the central character's mental and spiritual journey, down a river to confront the deranged Kurtz character, who represents the worst aspects of civilization. By giving *Apocalypse Now* a setting that was _____ at the time of its release, audiences were able to experience and identify with its themes more easily than they would have if the film had been a literal adaptation of the novel. [3점]

*deranged: 비정상적인

① simplistic   ② westernized
③ sophisticated   ④ contemporary
⑤ unconventional

10. Stress is a hot topic in American culture today. Its popularity stems from the need to get a handle on this condition — to deal with stress effectively enough so as to lead a "normal" and happy life. But dealing with stress is _____.
Many people's attitudes, influenced by their rushed lifestyles and expectations of immediate satisfaction, reflect the need to eliminate stress rather than to manage, reduce, or control their perceptions of it. As a result, stress never really goes away; it just reappears with a new face. A bit of reflection will reveal that this is inevitable. Stressful life events, from choosing a major or changing jobs to having a child or losing a family member, will continue to occur throughout any fulfilling life. Dealing with them, not avoiding or ignoring them, is the only solution. For those who refuse this advice, studies show that real bodily harm in the form of heart disease or cancer is the likely outcome. [3점]

① a fact, not a theory
② a theory, not a fact
③ a skill, not a practice
④ an outcome, not a process
⑤ a process, not an outcome

11. In his famous *Art and Illusion*, Ernst Gombrich, influenced as he is by Kant and Wittgenstein, asks, "Does a painter paint what he sees? Or does he see what he paints?" Gombrich, who strongly adheres to the latter view, argues that even when the explicit goal of art is imitation, the process of depiction or representation is always dependent on the artist's preconceptions. Without a set of stereotypes or categories, the visual artist would never succeed in classifying the mirage of impressions he is confronted with and organize his perception into an experience that is orderly, structured, and recognizable. The history of art displays a succession of ever-changing styles and stereotypes. No art, according to Gombrich, _____. [3점]

*mirage: 신기루

① should be sought for its own sake
② can depart from the realm of imitation
③ provides an accurate representation of reality
④ involves an artist's arbitrary interpretation of nature
⑤ tells about the different ways artists envision the world

12. It's tempting to reserve the "giver" label for larger-than-life heroes such as Mother Teresa or Mahatma Gandhi, but being a giver doesn't require extraordinary acts of sacrifice. It just involves a focus on acting in the interests of others, such as by giving help, providing mentoring, sharing credit, or making connections for others. Outside the workplace, this type of behavior is quite common. According to research led by Yale psychologist Margaret Clark, most people act like givers in close relationships. In marriages and friendships, we contribute whenever we can without keeping score. But in the workplace, give and take becomes more complicated. Professionally, people _____. When they help others, they protect themselves by seeking reciprocity. They operate on the principle of fairness, and their relationships are governed by even exchanges of favors. [3점]

*reciprocity: 상호 이익

① translate their inborn selfishness into collective benefits
② divide their interests into collective good and well-being
③ strive to preserve an equal balance of giving and getting
④ tend to be selfish rather than altruistic, pursuing their own interest
⑤ balance their losses against the gains they anticipate from cooperation

13. 다음 글에서 전체 흐름과 관계 <u>없는</u> 문장은?

Accumulation of mercury, especially in its organic form, is a well-recognized problem for populations whose diet includes a high intake of fish. ① However, there is evidence that fish that accumulate mercury also accumulate selenium in equivalent amounts and the simultaneous presence of the selenium is believed to be able to counteract the toxic effects of the mercury. ② A study of a population of Inuit sealers in East Greenland whose daily intake of marine foods was made up of 200g of fish and 180g of seal meat found that blood mercury levels often exceeded 200μg/l, a level regarded as the lowest concentration observed in clinical methyl mercury intoxication. ③ In spite of these high levels of mercury, there were no signs of toxicity. ④ But people who are worried about their exposure to mercury need to limit their seafood intake, particularly of fish that are high on the food chain, such as shark, or white tuna. ⑤ This was attributed to the presence of high levels of selenium in the fish and seal meat consumed by the sealers and their families.

*selenium: ((화학 원소)) 셀레늄 **methyl mercury: 메틸수은

[14~15] 주어진 글 다음에 이어질 글의 순서로 가장 적절한 것을 고르시오.

14.

> The scientific value of wildlife results from the role it serves in the advancement of science. Much of what we know about ecology and behavior came from studying wildlife.

(A) Hence, we reason that if there are sufficient old-growth forests to support a healthy population of spotted owls, then there should be a sufficient amount of forests to meet the needs of other species.

(B) Because spotted owls have large home ranges, they are one of the first species to be affected when old-growth forests become scarce.

(C) Some types of wildlife serve as sentinel species and are used to monitor environmental health. For instance, spotted owls are used by environmentalists to monitor whether we have preserved enough old-growth forests in the Pacific Northwest of the U.S.

*sentinel: 보초병, 감시병

① (A) – (C) – (B) ② (B) – (A) – (C)
③ (B) – (C) – (A) ④ (C) – (A) – (B)
⑤ (C) – (B) – (A)

15.

> A copyright owner may transfer the entire copyright or any part of it to another person, or may grant limited permission to others to copy the work. The transfer of all the exclusive rights in a copyright is commonly known as an *assignment*.

(A) This means that the assignee can give permission to others to copy the work and enforce against infringements. The party that assigns the copyright relinquishes its rights altogether.

(B) It must be made in writing and be signed by the copyright owner or the owner's agent. Once the rights are assigned, the party who receives the assignment is entitled to all of the protection and remedies accorded to the copyright owner by the statute.

(C) For example, a writer who assigns all rights to an article to a magazine can no longer grant permission to others to use the text or sue parties who reproduce the work without his or her permission. [3점]

*relinquish: 양도하다 **statute: 법규

① (A) – (C) – (B) ② (B) – (A) – (C)
③ (B) – (C) – (A) ④ (C) – (A) – (B)
⑤ (C) – (B) – (A)

[16~17] 글의 흐름으로 보아, 주어진 문장이 들어가기에 가장 적절한 곳을 고르시오.

16.

> Although this has helped many companies, some workers have lost their jobs in this country due to the shift in manufacturing sites.

Three major causes of unemployment are: changes in industry and the economy, changes in wages, and changes in government policies. Industrial changes have had a profound effect on the economy. (①) Manufacturing, or blue-collar jobs, have been declining because, with the advent of automation, many jobs have been lost. (②) Before blue-collar workers can be employable again, they must be retrained for new jobs. (③) Meanwhile, largely because of organized labor, wages in Europe, North America, and Japan are quite high when compared with wages of other countries. (④) The problem this creates is that many companies have moved manufacturing jobs to countries, such as Mexico, where wages are much lower. (⑤) Often, the federal government will institute new policies aimed at helping the economy adjust to change, but some economists argue that policies such as unemployment compensation and welfare only serve to promote or prolong unemployment.

17.

> Indeed, there is a sense in which know-how is prior to, and more fundamental than, know-that.

When we discuss knowledge, we often focus on theoretical 'knowledge of the head' and overlook practical 'knowledge of the hand.' (①) Indeed, there seems to be something of a prejudice against the latter. (②) For example, the abstract knowledge of the scientist is generally held in higher esteem than the practical knowledge of the car mechanic or the craftsman. (③) This prejudice may derive from the widespread assumption that our capacity for reason is what distinguishes us from the rest of the animal kingdom. (④) However, it could be argued that our ability to manipulate things is just as unique, and that the hand with its opposable thumb is as good a symbol of human intelligence as the head with its bulging cranium. (⑤) After all, we need basic skills, such as the ability to speak and the ability to manipulate objects, before we can acquire any kind of knowledge.

[3점] *bulging: 불룩 나온 **cranium: 두개골

18. 다음 글의 내용을 한 문장으로 요약하고자 한다. 빈칸 (A), (B)에 들어갈 말로 가장 적절한 것은?

The replacement theory holds that new information entering the memory replaces old information already stored. Studies that support this theory show that misleading information replaces the original memories of people. For instance, one study showed pictures of a car accident to two groups of people. In one group, the researchers asked leading questions to make the people think they had seen a yield sign, when the picture had actually shown a stop sign. Those in the other group were not asked leading questions and therefore remembered seeing the stop sign. When both groups were later gathered together, they were told the purpose behind the experiment and asked to guess if they thought they had been part of the group that was misled. Nearly everyone in the group that was misled claimed that they had truly seen the yield sign and were not deceived. This led researchers to conclude that the implanted memory replaced the actual one.

↓

> According to a psychological study, post-event information has a significant likelihood of _____(A)_____ original memories and producing _____(B)_____ ones which seem genuine.

	(A)		(B)
①	altering	……	distorted
②	reinforcing	……	distorted
③	reinforcing	……	detailed
④	renewing	……	detailed
⑤	altering	……	detailed

[19~20] 다음 글을 읽고, 물음에 답하시오.

Canadian psychologist Joanne V. Wood and colleagues decided to test the effects of "positive self-statements." The researchers asked people with reported low self-esteem to recite the following affirmation: "I am a lovable person." They then measured these people's moods and their feelings about themselves. Across the board, the group with low-esteem felt worse after being made to recite the positive affirmation. On the other hand, people with reported high self-esteem felt better. The psychologists then asked the participants to list negative and positive thoughts about themselves. What was found was that those with low self-esteem were in a better mood when they were allowed to have negative thoughts about themselves. In fact, the subjects were in a better mood thinking negative thoughts than they were when asked to focus on positive affirmations. The researchers suggest that positive praise and affirmations, such as "I am a lovable person," were (a) mismatched with the mindset of those with low self-esteem. This led to feelings of conflict and just feeling bad, which then led to more (b) negative thoughts about themselves.

Is positive thinking worthless then? Wood doesn't think so. She suggests that it could work in situations where people make very (c) general statements that are impossible to argue with or consider in too much detail, or when nothing major is at stake. For example, people may be better off saying "I choose good gifts for people" rather than "I'm a generous person." But as she says, "(d) Unreasonably positive self-statements, such as 'I accept myself completely,' are often encouraged by self-help books. Our results suggest that such self-statements may (e) harm the very people they are designed for: people low in self-esteem."

19. 윗글의 제목으로 가장 적절한 것은?

① Positive Affirmations: Friend or Foe?
② Positive Affirmations Are Contagious!
③ Two Sides of Emotion: Positivity and Negativity
④ Forget Positive Thinking, Just Be More Realistic
⑤ Positive Self-statements Boost Mood and Self-Esteem

20. 밑줄 친 (a) ~ (e) 중에서 문맥상 낱말의 쓰임이 적절하지 <u>않은</u> 것은? [3점]

① (a)　　② (b)　　③ (c)　　④ (d)　　⑤ (e)

1. 다음 글에 드러난 Jeff의 심경 변화로 가장 적절한 것은?

This was a big day in Jeff's swim class. All the students were going to jump from the high diving board into the deep end of the pool. As Jeff walked toward the board, a strange feeling started to grow inside him. It was a lot taller than he'd imagined, and his hands started to feel sweaty. After he got onto the board, he looked around and thought about backing down. The height made his stomach turn. Then he saw his older brother sitting by the pool and smiling at him. This was the motivation Jeff needed. Before he could change his mind, he swallowed hard and determined to jump. It was all over in an instant. Soon, Jeff was back above the water swimming powerfully toward the edge of the pool with a big grin on his face. He felt like he could do anything in the world.

① nervous → confident
② ashamed → surprised
③ jealous → peaceful
④ annoyed → relieved
⑤ anxious → terrified

2. 밑줄 친 human memory is like a compost heap이 다음 글에서 의미하는 바로 가장 적절한 것은?

Our experiences are laid down with the most recent still retaining much detail and structure, but, with time, they eventually break down and become integrated with the rest of our experiences. That's why we often remember them differently from the way they actually happened. Psychologists Dan Simons and Chris Chabris recently surveyed 1,500 US adults and discovered fundamental misunderstandings held by the general public. About two out of three adults (63 percent) thought that memory works like a video camera, recording experiences that can be played back later. Half of the respondents believed that once a memory was formed it was unchanged and reliable. These misconceptions have led to comparison with other ways of storing information that evoke some notion of a permanent store. A common metaphor is to liken human memory to a vast library storing volumes of information, which is wrong. Rather, human memory is like a compost heap.

① our memories are arranged one by one in recorded order
② our memory errors occur due to our environmental changes
③ our memories disappear gradually, but some of them stand out
④ our experiences are often misunderstood in our nervous system
⑤ our memories can easily become mixed up and distorted over time

3. 다음 글의 요지로 가장 적절한 것은?

"Beauty is in the eye of the beholder." While this statement may be true, some works of art remain beautiful in the eyes of many "beholders." Although such masterpieces are unique, they have certain qualities in common. Pablo Picasso's *Three Musicians* can be interpreted only through an understanding of his style. Even the experienced art lover can be unsure as to what he sees. But — comprehend it or not — he is likely to be intrigued by it. Equally appealing is Claude Monet's painting of a Japanese bridge over a pond full of water lilies. Even a brief glance leaves the admirer with no doubt as to what he is viewing. Yet each painting is a masterpiece. Each indefinitely attracts the viewer, drawing his very soul to them. Each expresses an experience common to mankind — not just of a certain era, but of all eras.

① 명작이 되기 위해서는 그 작품만의 독특함이 있어야 한다.
② 예술 작품에 대한 이해는 어느 정도의 학습을 필요로 한다.
③ 명작은 사람들을 매료시키는 공통적인 특성을 가지고 있다.
④ 개인마다, 문화마다 예술 작품에 대한 해석이 다를 수밖에 없다.
⑤ 작가의 개인적 경험이 담겨 있지 않은 작품은 명작이 될 수 없다.

4. 다음 글의 주제로 가장 적절한 것은? [3점]

When children misbehave it can be very easy to react with frustration, resentment or even anger because behavior doesn't happen in a vacuum. Rather than reacting based on our feelings, we can pause to consider our child's true needs in these moments. Why do kids really misbehave? To answer that question, we must first understand the root cause of those annoying, frustrating, and maddening behaviors. When our children are misbehaving in a way that seems really irritating and irrational, it is often a result of a psychological need: social connection. Our children's deepest desire is to have relationship with us and others around them. It's just the way we're hardwired. Belonging refers to the emotional connection and positive attention we need with one another. Without both of these innate needs being met, children will misbehave. Once the connection is made, children are then open to respectful correction.

① roles of parents in enhancing children's social skills
② ways to cope with misbehaving children through discipline
③ understanding a child's misbehavior as a desire for connection
④ relationship between parenting style and children's misbehavior
⑤ reasons why a variety of social connections are good for children

5. 다음 글의 제목으로 가장 적절한 것은?

At Facebook, Randi Zuckerberg told her team that she was changing the name of their group from "Consumer Marketing" to "Creative Marketing." Despite the fact that it seemed like a small change, it had an instant impact on the group. Immediately, the members redefined themselves as a creative hub of the company, even though nobody else in the firm knew about the name change. Within a few days, the team reorganized the space, bringing in new furniture and supplies and designing a media wall to showcase their creative accomplishments. They started coming up with more innovative ideas and suggested new projects that reflected their newly defined role in the company. It became abundantly clear that the team was incredibly creative, but that they hadn't thought that it was their primary role to generate new ideas. The change in their name gave them explicit permission to exercise their imagination.

① Sometimes Sweat the Small Stuff
② You Become What You Call Yourself
③ Creative Vocabulary Creates Creative People
④ Don't Be Afraid to Change for the Consumers
⑤ Redefine Your Role in the Company with Imagination

6. YMCA Lifeguard Classes에 관한 다음 안내문의 내용과 일치하는 것은?

YMCA Lifeguard Classes

Our program will prepare you to give First Aid and CPR, as well as certify you in the basics of lifeguarding. This is your first step to an exciting and rewarding career!

Ages: Students must be aged 17 and over to register for the class.

When: July 11-August 21
· You can choose one of two classes below:
   - Mondays, from 4:00 p.m. – 7:30 p.m.
   - Saturdays, from 10:00 a.m. – 2:00 p.m.

Contact: Email: ccdavies@bulkmail.net
    Phone: 447-349-0010

Cost: It's $300 for non-members; YMCA members receive a 20% discount.
(This includes all course materials, including informational booklets and CPR mask.)

Register: Online at www.lifeguardcert.org, by phone at 447-349-0010, or in person at the downtown YMCA. Please register at least one week in advance. Classes will fill up quickly, so don't wait!

*CPR: 심폐소생술

---

① 18세부터 강좌 신청이 가능하다.
② 일주일에 2번 강의를 들어야 한다.
③ 회원은 60달러 할인을 받는다.
④ 심폐소생 마스크는 따로 구매해야 한다.
⑤ 등록은 시작 일주일 전부터 온라인으로만 받는다.

7. 다음 글의 밑줄 친 부분 중, 어법상 틀린 것은? [3점]

Competitive activities can be more than just performance showcases where the best is recognized and the rest are overlooked. The provision of ① timely, constructive feedback to participants on performance is an asset that some competitions and contests offer. In a sense, all competitions give feedback. For many, this is restricted to information about ② whether the participant is an award- or prizewinner. The provision of that type of feedback can be interpreted as shifting the emphasis to ③ demonstrating superior performance but not necessarily excellence. The best competitions promote excellence, not just winning or "beating" others. The emphasis on superiority is what we typically see as fostering a detrimental effect of competition. Performance feedback requires that the program ④ go beyond the "win, place, or show" level of feedback. Information about performance can be very helpful, not only to the participant who does not win or place but also to those who ⑤ are.

8. 다음 글의 밑줄 친 부분 중, 문맥상 낱말의 쓰임이 적절하지 않은 것은? [3점]

Children recognize books as fiction sooner than television. Apparently, the fact that print does not physically resemble the things and events it symbolizes makes it ① easier to separate its content from the real world. Thus, as many have feared, television, with its presentation of live action, is a more ② tempting medium in transforming fantasy into reality. But what is a negative effect in the presentation of fiction can be a positive one in the presentation of fact. Television can be an extremely compelling medium for teaching children about the ③ imaginary world. In Scandinavia it was found that if eleven-year-olds learn of the same news event from television, parents, teachers, and the newspaper, the ④ majority will rely primarily on television. They consider television the ⑤ best-informed medium, and they say that on television "you can see for yourself what is happening."

[9~12] 다음 빈칸에 들어갈 말로 가장 적절한 것을 고르시오.

9. The ability to detect danger in the posture of others has been studied by the neuroscientist Beatrice Gelder. Her research has demonstrated that the brain of an observer reacts more powerfully to the body language of a person in a posture indicating fear than it does even to a fearful facial expression. Looks of fear can paralyze or, at least, evoke our own potent fear-based reactions. Yet, as powerful as facial expressions are in conveying danger, a person's uptight posture and furtive movements make us even more uncomfortable. Wouldn't you, too, be startled by the sudden recoiling of the hiker in front of you a split second *before* you heard the hissing of a coiled snake? This type of _____ behavior occurs throughout the animal world. If, for example, one bird in a flock on the ground suddenly takes off, all the other birds will follow immediately after; they do not need to know why. [3점]

*furtive: 수상한; 은밀한 **recoil: 움찔하다 ***hissing: 쉿쉿 하는 소리

① imitative   ② emotional
③ calculated   ④ threatening
⑤ unproductive

10. Peter Gollwitzer and colleague Veronika Brandstatter found that using action triggers is quite an effective way to motivate action. Their study showed that a specific psychological commitment can function as a strong action trigger. In one study, they tracked college students who had the option to earn extra credit in a class by writing a paper about how they spent Christmas Eve. But there was a catch: to earn the credit, they had to hand in the paper by December 26. Most students had good intentions of writing the paper, but only 33 percent of them took some time for writing and submitting it. Other students in the study were required to set action triggers — to note, in advance, exactly when and where they intended to write the report (for example, "I'll write this report in the living room on Christmas morning before everyone gets up"). An impressive 75 percent of those students wrote the report. That's a pretty astonishing result for such _____. [3점]

① a writing skill
② a relaxed deadline
③ an unconscious action
④ an unexpected strategy
⑤ a small mental investment

11. Text communication does create problems, even for people who are skilled at it. Lacking sounds and visuals, it is not a rich sensory encounter. You cannot see other people's faces or hear them speak. All the important interpersonal cues provided by voice, body language, and physical appearance disappear, which can dramatically alter how people relate to each other. Without those cues, it is easier to misunderstand the other person. Your online companion might be sick, drunk, or depressed without your knowing it. For some people, the lack of physical presence generated by the cues of voice and appearance might _____. Typed text feels formal, distant, unemotional, and lacking a supportive and empathic tone. In fact, without a visual and auditory connection, you can never be absolutely certain about the other person's identity. This absence of face-to-face cues, which adds a little anonymity, encourages some people to behave inappropriately.

*empathic: 공감의 **anonymity: 익명성

① reduce the sense of intimacy and trust
② increase the feeling of interest and mystery
③ allow for freedom of expression and body language
④ add life to novel forms of text communication
⑤ not be related to the lack of understanding

12. Pet food used to be about selecting a small, medium, or large bag of whatever your local feed or grocery store stocked. Today, choosing pet food from among the hundreds of varieties in the $17 billion United States market can be a complicated task. Beef, duck, vegetables, and salmon are part of today's pet diets. Once created to profit from human food manufacturing waste, the pet food industry now makes products with human-grade ingredients that sell well because people want something better for their beloved animal companions. The number of people purchasing pet food with human-grade ingredients is on the increase. As a result, pets truly do increase the burden on agriculture, because _____. [3점]

*human–grade: (동물 사료가) 사람이 먹는 수준의

① they are no longer eating the "leftover" products
② there is currently no standard for pet food safety
③ the competition between pet food providers is fierce
④ farmers are likely to be restricted by "unpredictability"
⑤ their food is a "luxury" turned into an "everyday" item

13. 다음 글에서 전체 흐름과 관계 <u>없는</u> 문장은?

Seasonal weather conditions are always a concern for greenhouse gardeners. ① The climate determines not only how and when the greenhouse will be used but what type of structure to build in the first place. ② For example, in a cold-weather climate that frequently experiences heavy snowfall, a high-pitched roof might be ideal because it can prevent the build-up of ice and snow by efficiently helping them to slide off. ③ In a location that sees less snowfall but gets cold, strong winds, a sun-heated pit, which is a greenhouse with the majority of the structure housed below ground, might be the best choice, because it is naturally insulated and requires less heat to operate. ④ For this reason, it's a good idea to contact a professional in order to ensure your roof satisfies safety regulations. ⑤ The same type of structure might not be practical for a more temperate area.

*pit: (크고 깊은) 구덩이 **insulate: 단열하다

[14~15] 주어진 글 다음에 이어질 글의 순서로 가장 적절한 것을 고르시오.

14.

In certain circumstances, the defense can introduce witnesses to describe positive characteristics of a defendant that would make it unlikely that he committed a particular crime.

(A) This ironic outcome occurs because the prosecution is allowed to cross-examine character witnesses to try to show that they are not good judges of the defendant's character. During cross-examination, prosecutors might ask a witness whether she knows about previous behaviors by the defendant that contradict her testimony.

(B) Although one might expect this kind of testimony to help the defendant, research shows that positive character evidence has little effect on jurors' guilt judgments or likelihood of conviction. Paradoxically, the use of character evidence may actually increase the likelihood that a defendant will be convicted.

(C) For example, a prosecutor might say, "You said the defendant is kind and gentle. Are you aware that he was removed from high school after injuring another student in a fistfight?" Although jurors are only supposed to use this information to evaluate the credibility of the character witness, it may influence their impressions of the defendant as well. [3점]

*the prosecution: 검찰 측

① (A) – (C) – (B)   ② (B) – (A) – (C)
③ (B) – (C) – (A)   ④ (C) – (A) – (B)
⑤ (C) – (B) – (A)

15.

There are many aspects of sustainability and, even if you decide you want to address all of them, the problem is that buildings are complex collections of various elements. There will always be many different factors to balance.

(A) Studies show that the overall carbon footprint of a super-green building in such a location will be larger than that of a less-than-ideal building in a city center well connected to public transport.

(B) It will not, however, be possible for most users of the building to reach it by public transport or to walk or cycle there. Almost everyone will need to drive.

(C) For example, if you locate a building next to a beautiful park in the middle of nowhere, it will be possible to align it perfectly to take advantage of the sun and to have windows that open because there will be very little noise.

*sustainability: (환경 파괴 없는) 지속 가능성
**carbon footprint: 탄소 발자국((온실 효과를 유발하는 이산화탄소의 배출량))

① (A) – (C) – (B)   ② (B) – (A) – (C)
③ (B) – (C) – (A)   ④ (C) – (A) – (B)
⑤ (C) – (B) – (A)

[16~17] 글의 흐름으로 보아, 주어진 문장이 들어가기에 가장 적절한 곳을 고르시오.

16.

> Buildings could be constructed with a central heating and air-conditioning system that allowed the interior to be climate controlled and thus thermally comfortable at all times.

Humans are remarkably resourceful and our ancestors were able to develop ways to survive quite nicely in every environment on earth. Want to live in the desert, the tundra, or the jungle? No problem. (①) People found ways to work within the limits and constraints of their environments. (②) If it was really hot for part of the year, they didn't have the option to install central air. (③) Instead, they figured out ways to stay cool by creating thermally comfortable microclimates. (④) However, after the discovery of fossil fuels, the need to fit a building into the local climatic environment became less important. (⑤) As a result, many of the traditional ways of staying comfortable have been lost or forgotten. [3점]

*thermally: 온도 면에서 **microclimate: 미기후((微氣候, 주변 다른 지역과는 다른, 특정 좁은 지역의 기후))

17.

> In the business world, you are constantly challenged to get people to do things you want them to do.

A classic example of persuasion occurred when I was attending army boot camp and was talking to my buddy while one of the sergeants was conducting a class on land mines. He abruptly interrupted our conversation and said, "You'd better listen to what I'm telling you, boy, because it could save your life." (①) From that point on, I was all ears because he had persuaded me with a hook: my life. (②) If you're the boss, you can apply manipulative tactics when you tell a subordinate, "Here's a task I want you to do. Don't ask any questions. Just do it." (③) Or you can apply persuasive tactics like, "Here's a task I'd like you to do. Before you get

started, let's first discuss why it's important to you and our organization." (④) Leaders persuade with hooks. (⑤) Idiots manipulate with force.

*boot camp: 신병 훈련소 **sergeant: 부사관

18. 다음 글의 내용을 한 문장으로 요약하고자 한다. 빈칸 (A), (B)에 들어갈 말로 가장 적절한 것은? [3점]

A song does not come to life until performers take it off the written page. For better or for worse, the composer does not know how individuals will interpret his work. Composers make many markings on the written page to communicate their intentions for a song for singers and pianists but those intentions are not always honored. It may seem that clear key and time signatures, tempo and other markings would be enough, but singers and pianists do not always strictly adhere to markings. An authentic performance of a song also depends on the difficulty of the piece and the abilities and limitations of the performers. For example, if a young singer were trying to perform a late Debussy song and had never sung in French, the challenges of the language could prevent her from mastering the nuances of the piece. Vocal deficiencies can draw attention away from the music and to the singer himself; for this reason, it is critically important that singers perform music that is appropriate to their age and abilities and the same is true for pianists.

*key and time signature: 조 및 박자 기호

↓

> Composers are not able to _____(A)_____ their music much after they write it, as each performance depends on a performer's _____(B)_____ of the piece and his or her abilities.

	(A)		(B)
①	control	......	training
②	control	......	reinterpretation
③	criticize	......	training
④	criticize	......	reinterpretation
⑤	copy	......	talents

[19~20] 다음 글을 읽고, 물음에 답하시오.

British Cycling, which was the governing body for professional cycling in England, had recently hired Dave Brailsford as its new director. At the time, British Cycling had endured nearly one hundred years of (a) insignificance with no British cyclist achieving outstanding results. Brailsford had been hired to put British Cycling on a new trajectory. What made him different from previous coaches was his relentless commitment to a strategy that he referred to as the aggregation of (b) small gains. Brailsford began by making slight adjustments you might not expect from a professional cycling team. The bike seats were redesigned to make them more comfortable and alcohol was rubbed on the tires for a better grip. Riders were asked to wear electrically heated jerseys to maintain ideal muscle temperature in order to (c) boost their performance, and biofeedback sensors were used to monitor how athletes responded to a particular workout. But he didn't stop there. The inside of the team truck was painted white, which helped cyclists spot and remove little bits of dust that would normally slip by unnoticed but could (d) upgrade the performance of the finely tuned bikes. Even a doctor was hired to teach riders the best way to wash their hands to reduce the chances of catching a cold. As hundreds of other tiny improvements accumulated, the results came faster than anyone imagined. Five years after Brailsford took over, the British Cycling team (e) dominated the cycling events at the 2008 Olympic Games in Beijing, where they won an astounding 60 percent of the gold medals available.

*trajectory: 궤도, 궤적

19. 윗글의 제목으로 가장 적절한 것은?

① Forget about Goals, Focus on a System Instead
② Perfect Equipment Makes You a Flawless Cyclist
③ Don't Let the Climax of British Cycling Just Be Forgotten
④ How the Invincible Cyclist Turned to the Symbol of Collapse
⑤ Minor Enhancement: a Game Changer in the Fate of British Cycling

20. 밑줄 친 (a) ~ (e) 중에서 문맥상 낱말의 쓰임이 적절하지 <u>않은</u> 것은? [3점]

① (a) ② (b) ③ (c) ④ (d) ⑤ (e)

○ 답안지의 해당란에 성명과 수험번호를 쓰고, 또 수험번호와 답을 정확히 표시하시오.

○ 문항에 따라 배점이 다르니, 각 물음의 끝에 표시된 배점을 참고하시오. 3점 문항에만 점수가 표시되어 있습니다. 점수 표시가 없는 문항은 모두 2점씩입니다.

1. 다음 글의 목적으로 가장 적절한 것은?

Dear the Victoria Food Bank:

On behalf of the Michigan Islanders organization, thank you for your recent correspondence regarding the work of your charity organization, the Victoria Food Bank, and its ongoing need for support. Based on your letter, it is clear that your organization is playing an important role in helping feed the hungry right here in our area and enhancing our region's quality of life. We deeply appreciate that you took the time to bring your efforts to our attention. Regretfully, given the enormous number of daily requests we receive, the Michigan Islanders will be unable to provide your outstanding organization with a contribution at this time for we have reached our maximum donation limit. We are touched and honored, however, that you reached out to our organization as you seek the additional resources that will enable you to move forward. Again, on behalf of everyone at the Michigan Islanders, thank you for your letter and our best wishes for a successful event.

Sincerely,
Mark Foster

① 무료 급식 자선 행사를 홍보하려고
② 무료 급식 단체의 기부 요청을 거절하려고
③ 무료 급식 지원 예산의 확대를 요청하려고
④ 무료 급식 단체에게 예산 위원회 참석을 부탁하려고
⑤ 무료 급식으로 지역 사회에 기여한 것을 감사하려고

2. 다음 글에서 필자가 주장하는 바로 가장 적절한 것은?

Specialization is a fact of life. In order to function in the world, you have to narrow your focus and limit your field of view. When you're trying to generate new ideas, however, such information-handling attitudes can limit you. They not only may force you into restricting your problem too narrowly, they may also prevent you from looking in outside areas for ideas. Indeed, the more divergent your sources, the more original the idea you create is likely to be. Make it a rule to be on the lookout for new and interesting ideas that others have used successfully. Your idea has to be original only in its adaptation to the problem you're working on.

① 창의적인 생각을 위해 다방면에 관심을 가져야 한다.
② 성공하기 위해서 다른 사람의 생각을 모방하지 마라.
③ 자기 자신의 능력의 한계치를 함부로 설정하지 마라.
④ 저작권을 보호받기 위해서는 법 절차를 알아야 한다.
⑤ 남의 존경을 받으려면 자기 지식을 전문화해야 한다.

3. 밑줄 친 The straw that stirs the drink counts for a lot이 다음 글에서 의미하는 바로 가장 적절한 것은? [3점]

Most top university professors disregard duties that take time from research. They see administration as a bore, and everyone wants someone else to be the department chairman. As a result of neglecting responsibility, most academic departments are less exciting places than they should be. Bad department chairmen make foolish choices when they assign the teaching of important courses and the use of precious department space and facilities. The wrong faculty members handle departmental seminars and keep the library buying journals that no one reads. Departmental meetings last far too long without addressing vital issues until there is no oxygen left in the room. The straw that stirs the drink counts for a lot. Being chairman need not consume more than

10 percent of an intelligent professor's time, possibly less than he or she might waste griping about bad decisions made by others.

*gripe about: ~에 대해 불평하다

① The burden of a department chairman has to be lightened.
② An academic department needs a chairman with leadership and efficiency.
③ Some professors think being a department chairman hinders their research.
④ A department chairman's role is to examine the operations of the department.
⑤ A department chairman is responsible for participating in the decision-making.

4. 다음 글의 주제로 가장 적절한 것은? [3점]

We used to think that with age there was a progressive deterioration in brain-cell structure and function. But that widespread assumption has proved wrong. New nerve cells have been found to be generated in the brains of old animals, and we're learning more and more how this amazing property of the aged brain can be manipulated. Low levels of regular exercise, for instance, have been found to significantly enhance neurogenesis in the hippocampus, a brain structure that deals with memory. Moreover, a recent study from my laboratory showed that certain nerve cells in the eyes of old mice are capable of growing new processes. We have also found such growth of nerve cells in the eyes of old people. Then there is the tremendous promise of stem-cell research, which is still in its infancy, for replacing damaged or dysfunctional body organs. We will be able to regenerate parts of the brain that have worn out or been damaged in the course of a lifetime, providing renewed capabilities to those who are currently considered old folks.

*neurogenesis: 신경조직의 형성[발생]

① redefining ageing as a positive growth experience
② discovery of factors affecting the increase of life expectancy
③ possibility of regaining youth by making scientific discoveries
④ natural consequence of deteriorating nerve cells in old animals
⑤ stem-cell research as the most important factor in healthy ageing

5. 다음 도표의 내용과 일치하지 <u>않는</u> 것은?

How Much Do You Like or Dislike the Idea of Drone Delivery?

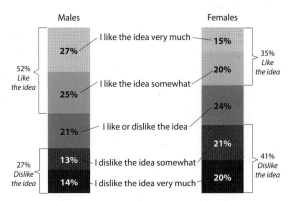

The graph above shows the percentage of U.S. males and females who like or dislike the idea of drone delivery in 2018. ① At 27%, the percentage of men who like the idea of drone delivery very much is less than twice as much as that of women who like it very much, which is 15%. ② One in four men like the idea of drone delivery somewhat, which is greater than the one in five women who replied that they like the idea somewhat. ③ The percent of men who have a neutral stance on drone delivery is three percentage points less than that of women. ④ Over two-fifths of women dislike the concept of drone delivery, which is 15 percentage points higher than men who dislike it. ⑤ The difference between the percentage of women and men who dislike the idea very much is 6 percentage points.

6. Lysippos에 관한 다음 글의 내용과 일치하지 <u>않는</u> 것은?

Lysippos was considered one of the three great Greek sculptors of the 4th century. He began sculpting in his youth by teaching himself. Later, he became the head of the art school of Argos and Sicyon. Unfortunately, scholars today face difficulty in the study of Lysippos because he had such a great number of students who actively tried to imitate his style. As a result, there are many copies of his work, and it can be difficult to identify originals. Art historians have praised Lysippos for his grace and elegance, noting the smaller heads of his figures and great attention to detail. In contrast to the typical Greek sculptures of the time, the works created by Lysippos portray incredibly realistic human forms with detailed eyelids and toenails. It is said that he produced more than 1,500 works, and all of them were in bronze.

① 4세기에 그리스의 위대한 조각가였다.
② Argos and Sicyon 예술학교의 교장이었다.
③ 많은 학생들이 그의 스타일을 모방했다.
④ 사실적인 인간의 형상을 묘사했다.
⑤ 조각 작품의 재료를 다양하게 사용했다.

7. 다음 글의 밑줄 친 부분 중, 어법상 틀린 것은? [3점]

When you look at a flower, you must understand that you don't see the same thing a butterfly sees, and ① <u>that</u> if you switched your eyes with an insect's eyes the floral world would turn into an explosion of madness. Your impossible nighttime living room is a ② <u>completely</u> visible playground to a cat. And if you've ever shined a laser pointer next to a kitten, then surely you've realized something is taking place in its tiny cat head that isn't ③ <u>happening</u> in yours. You know the world is not as it appears, and all it takes is one great optical illusion to prove it. Believing otherwise is too simplistic. The stars are always in the sky, but the light of the sun ④ <u>filtered</u> through the atmosphere makes them impossible to see in the day. If you toss a rock into a pond, and that splash turns the heads of a frog and a fox, ⑤ <u>which</u> they see is not what you see. Each creature's version of reality is unique to its nervous system.

8. 다음 글의 밑줄 친 부분 중, 문맥상 낱말의 쓰임이 적절하지 <u>않은</u> 것은? [3점]

International maritime codes specify that more maneuverable vessels must keep out of the way of less maneuverable vessels. The captains of more maneuverable vessels, such as power-driven boats, are ① <u>responsible</u> for avoiding less steerable vessels, such as sailing ships, and ships engaged in fishing, and vessels not under command. It is easier for powerboats to avoid hitting sailing ships than vice versa. Aviation codes are based on the same principle. The right of way of the sky ranks craft in order of the ease with which they can be ② <u>controlled</u>. Airplanes in normal operation, which are the most easily maneuvered aircraft, have the ③ <u>lowest</u> priority in right of way. Airplanes refueling other aircraft, which are less easily maneuvered, have a ④ <u>lesser</u> right of way than airplanes in normal operation. Balloons, which are still more difficult to maneuver than airplanes refueling other aircraft, have a ⑤ <u>higher</u> priority right of way. Finally, aircraft in distress have the highest priority right of way of all, since an aircraft in distress is very difficult or impossible to control.

*maritime code: 해양법 **maneuverable: 조종할 수 있는
***in distress: 조난당한

[9~12] 다음 빈칸에 들어갈 말로 가장 적절한 것을 고르시오.

9. You might expect that because humans are well equipped to think, they would love to think and would spend all their free time doing it. This is certainly not the case. (If all thinking were fun, people would probably spend much of their free time doing math problems, but they don't.) Researchers have found that often people seem lazy or careless about their thinking. Social psychologists use the term *cognitive miser* to describe people's reluctance to do much extra thinking. Just as a miser tries to avoid spending money, the cognitive miser tries to avoid thinking too hard or too much. Of course, this isn't entirely a matter of laziness. People's capacity to think is limited, and so people must conserve their thinking. There is much evidence that when people's capacity for thinking is already preoccupied, they take even more shortcuts to ＿＿＿＿＿＿＿ further need for thought. [3점]

*miser: 구두쇠

① fulfill   ② create
③ reduce   ④ identify
⑤ perceive

10. Competition seems to interfere with achievement primarily because it is stressful. The anxiety that arises from the possibility of losing interferes with performance. Even if this anxiety can be suppressed, it is difficult to do two things at the same time: trying to do well and trying to beat others. Competition can easily distract attention from the task at hand. Consider a teacher asking her pupils a question. A little boy waves his arm wildly to attract her attention, crying, "Please! Please! Pick me!" Finally recognized, he has forgotten the answer. So he scratches his head, asking, "What was the question again?" The problem is that he has focused on ＿＿＿＿＿＿＿＿＿, not on the subject matter.

① asking the question
② distracting his teacher
③ beating his classmates
④ doing well on an exam
⑤ suppressing his anxiety

11. The correlation observed in English between frequency of usage and etymology is not necessarily true of every language. Some languages — German is a case in point — have traditionally ＿＿＿＿＿＿＿＿＿＿＿＿＿＿＿ for enriching the vocabulary with words for more sophisticated notions or new products. For example, *Übersetzung* is equivalent to the English word "translation," but it literally means "setting over." *Fernsehen* is equivalent to "television" but it literally means "far-seeing." *Lautlehre* is equivalent to "phonology," but it literally means "sound study." That is, in German, native roots are combined to form new compounds having the same meaning as the classical-based compounds. This method of vocabulary enrichment is familiar also in English: *doorbell, horseshoe, lighthouse, shorthand,* and *stronghold* are all compounds containing native elements only. However, compared to German, English has been less inventive in producing new words from native roots; instead, it has added and creatively recycled roots from other languages. [3점]

*etymology: 어원

① looked to adopt figurative meanings
② used the separation of compound words
③ expanded the original meanings of words
④ developed a variety of borrowing languages
⑤ depended on the resources of the language itself

12. Like adults, young children expect names to refer to _____. Susan Gelman once showed her 13-month-old son a button on her shirt and called it "button." He then started to press it, because, though it didn't look much like a button on his electronic toys, he knew what category it belonged to, and that's what you do with a button. For older children, you get the same subtle appreciation of the force of a noun that you find in adults. One four-year-old made the point when describing a violent playmate: "Gabriel didn't just hurt me! He hurt other kids, too! He's a *hurter*! Right, Mom? He's a *hurter*!" The child is presumably stressing that this sort of behavior reflects a deeper aspect of Gabriel's nature. And in an experimental work, Gelman told five-year-olds about a child named Rose who often eats carrots, and added, for half of the children: "She is a carrot-eater." This name has an effect; it caused those children to think of Rose as a more permanent eater of carrots — she will eat them in the future, even if her family discourages it. It is part of her nature. [3점]

① objects that are created with an intention
② objects that share deep hidden properties
③ objects that occupy the same geographical area
④ things that have both similarities and differences
⑤ things for which usefulness are emphasized by parents

13. 다음 글에서 전체 흐름과 관계 없는 문장은?

Technological advances have increased exposure to new food choices by allowing food products to be distributed from one continent to another while reducing the risk of spoilage and contamination. ① Before the nineteenth century, the only methods available for preserving meat were drying, salting, and smoking, none of which were entirely practical since large quantities of food could not be processed or preserved for very long. ② The canning process was developed in 1809 and was a product of the Napoleonic wars; the process allowed heat-sterilized food to be stored for longer periods of time without spoiling. ③ Further methods of processing in the twentieth century involved dehydrating, freezing, and treating with ultrahigh temperatures, increasing shelf life, convenience, and variety of food products. ④ As food distribution continues to expand across the globe, political decisions related to food systems will ultimately affect the cost of food and food selection. ⑤ In addition, refrigeration, vacuum packing, fast freezing, etc. ensured that seasonal items would be available year-round in economically developed societies.

*heat–sterilized: 가열 살균한

[14~15] 주어진 글 다음에 이어질 글의 순서로 가장 적절한 것을 고르시오.

14.

Many animals, including warm-blooded mammals, change body position or posture to help regulate internal temperature. This, too, is a familiar behavior in the cold when animals curl up to conserve heat and groups of animals, such as puppies and kittens, huddle together for protection from the cold.

(A) However, body extension does not work when surrounding temperature is warmer than body temperature, because heat accumulates faster. Hence, physiological strategies, such as sweating, must be called into play.

(B) The same types of postural adjustments are seen in the heat. Extended postures increase heat loss by increasing the surface area of the body exposed to the environment. They are useful to dissipate heat when the environment is hot but still below the body temperature.

(C) Retracted postures lessen heat loss to the environment by decreasing the surface area available to exchange heat. They are favored when surrounding temperature is much colder than body temperature.

*dissipate: 소멸시키다 **retract: 움츠리다

① (A) – (C) – (B)   ② (B) – (A) – (C)
③ (B) – (C) – (A)   ④ (C) – (A) – (B)
⑤ (C) – (B) – (A)

15.

According to one traditional definition, aesthetics is the branch of philosophy that deals with beauty, especially beauty in the arts. Examining the pleasing features of the *Mona Lisa* or a snow-capped mountain, for instance, would fall under aesthetics.

(A) This work is widely admired but not for being beautiful. So a better definition of aesthetics would be that it is the branch of philosophy that studies the ways things please people when experienced.

(B) That definition seems too narrow, however, since works of art and natural objects may attract us with features other than their beauty. Instead of evoking admiration of beauty, artists may evoke puzzlement, shock, and even disgust.

(C) Consider Picasso's *Guernica*, a huge (11-ft.×25.6-ft.) painting in black, white, and grey that he created in response to the slaughter of Spanish civilians by German and Italian warplanes during the Spanish Civil War. Images of dying soldiers and people screaming dominate the canvas.

*slaughter: 대량학살

① (A) – (C) – (B)   ② (B) – (A) – (C)
③ (B) – (C) – (A)   ④ (C) – (A) – (B)
⑤ (C) – (B) – (A)

[16~17] 글의 흐름으로 보아, 주어진 문장이 들어가기에 가장 적절한 곳을 고르시오.

16.

By making your purchases at local businesses, you spread that wealth out to more local people and increase your community's standard of living.

When you buy from large corporations, you support the increasing consolidation of wealth and power in the hands of the few. (①) Chain businesses often take those dollars directly away from smaller local businesses that cannot afford to lose the income. (②) This is because local businesses rely more on local suppliers and service providers, forming a kind of local economic web of interdependence that creates jobs and a thriving community. (③) Therefore, every dollar you spend at a local business helps your community maintain its individual character, uniqueness, and diversity while supporting your neighbors in their quest for the good life. (④) Paying in cash, rather than by credit card, can also help local businesses as they are often the ones least able to afford the hefty fees the credit card companies charge them for each and every transaction. (⑤) Look in the phone book for local alternatives to large corporate chains.

*consolidation: 공고히 하기 **hefty: 과중한, 무거운

17.

Its critics argue that it has resulted in massive environmental damage, destroyed traditional farming practices, increased inequality, and left farmers reliant on expensive seeds and chemicals provided by Western companies.

The introduction of chemical fertilizers and high-yield seed varieties into the developing world, beginning in the 1960s, is known today as the "green revolution." (①) This revolution has had far-reaching consequences. (②) As well as triggering a population boom, it helped to lift hundreds of millions of people out of poverty and supported the historic rebirth of the Asian economies and the rapid industrialization of China and India — developments that are transforming geopolitics. (③) But the green revolution's many other social and environmental side effects have made it extremely controversial. (④) Doubts have also been expressed about the long-term sustainability of chemically intensive farming. (⑤) But for better or worse, there is no question that the green revolution did more than just transform the world's food supply in the latter half of the twentieth century; it transformed the world. [3점]

*geopolitics: 지정학

18.
다음 글의 내용을 한 문장으로 요약하고자 한다. 빈칸 (A), (B)에 들어갈 말로 가장 적절한 것은? [3점]

In an experiment, more than one hundred volunteers were shown two photographs, each of a woman's face. After looking at both pictures for a few seconds, they had to choose the one that looked most attractive to them. Immediately after three such choices, subjects were shown again the face they had just chosen and were asked to explain their choice. They readily complied. On three other trials, the experimentalist, in a sleight of hand, exchanged the picture of the chosen woman with the opposite image. That is, immediately after deciding that woman A was more attractive, a double-card ploy was used to confront subjects with the picture of woman B and they had to explain why they chose her (the two women depicted on the photos were quite distinct). Remarkably, most of the time the subjects were fooled. Only in fewer than 25% of trials were participants aware that their original choice was not honored, that they had been fooled. Most of the time, they ignored the discrepancy between their original conscious decision and what they were told they had decided. And even more remarkably, they proceeded to justify this choice even though it contradicted what they actually did a few seconds earlier.

*a sleight of hand: 날랜 손재주

↓

We tend to unknowingly ____(A)____ our behavior to make it seem that we have ____(B)____ made a choice all along.

	(A)		(B)
①	change	......	accidentally
②	change	......	deliberately
③	overlook	......	symbolically
④	maintain	......	accidentally
⑤	maintain	......	deliberately

[19~20] 다음 글을 읽고, 물음에 답하시오.

The potatoes we planted are descended from wild ancestors growing on the Andean plateau. The Incas figured out how to grow impressive yields of potatoes under the most unlikely conditions, developing an approach that is still in use in parts of the Andes today. A more or less vertical habitat presents special (a) challenges to both plants and their cultivators, because the microclimate changes dramatically with every change in altitude or orientation to the sun and wind. No monoculture could succeed under such circumstances, so the Incas developed a method of farming that is monoculture's exact opposite. Instead of betting the farm on a single plant variety, the Andean farmer, then as now, made a great many bets, at least one for every ecological niche. To Western eyes, the resulting farms look (b) organized; the plots are discontinuous, offering none of the familiar satisfactions of an explicitly ordered landscape. Yet the Andean potato farm represented an intricate ordering of nature that, unlike Versailles in 1999, say, or Ireland in 1845, can withstand virtually anything nature is apt to throw at it. Since the margins and surroundings of the Andean farm were populated by wild potatoes, the farmer's cultivated varieties regularly naturally crossed with their wild relatives, which (c) refreshed the gene pool and produced new hybrids. Whenever one of these new potatoes (d) proves its worth — surviving a drought or storm, say, or winning praise at the dinner table — it is promoted from the margins to the fields and, in time, to the neighbors' fields as well. Artificial selection is thus a continual local process, each new potato the product of an ongoing back-and-forth between the land and its cultivators, mediated by the universe of all possible potatoes: the species' genome. The genetic (e) diversity cultivated by the Incas and their descendants is an extraordinary cultural achievement and a gift of incalculable value to the rest of the world.

*niche: 적소, 적합한 곳

19. 윗글의 제목으로 가장 적절한 것은?

① History of Domestication of the Potato
② Why Potatoes Were Important to the Incas
③ We Are Eating the Same Potatoes Incas Did
④ Evolution of Inca Potatoes Resulted in Diversity
⑤ Potatoes: Gifts of the Andes for Worldwide Cultivation

20. 밑줄 친 (a) ~ (e) 중에서 문맥상 낱말의 쓰임이 적절하지 <u>않은</u> 것은? [3점]

① (a)   ② (b)   ③ (c)   ④ (d)   ⑤ (e)

○ 답안지의 해당란에 성명과 수험번호를 쓰고, 또 수험번호와 답을 정확히 표시하시오.
○ 문항에 따라 배점이 다르니, 각 물음의 끝에 표시된 배점을 참고하시오. 3점 문항에만 점수가 표시되어 있습니다. 점수 표시가 없는 문항은 모두 2점씩입니다.

1. 다음 글에 드러난 'I'의 심경 변화로 가장 적절한 것은?

In fourth grade, I was one of a few kids recruited to move some supplies from our classroom to a neighboring room at my elementary school in Toronto. I was flattered to find myself among people endowed with such responsibility. My classmates envied me for taking the job. Among the items was a glass fishbowl containing a lone goldfish. The vessel was three-quarters full of water, and quite heavy. Concerned that the fish would be placed in the hands of someone who might care less than I did, I volunteered to transport the bowl to its destination, a table next to the sink in the adjoining room. How ironic. I firmly held the bowl in my child's hands and methodically walked out the door, down the hall, and into the new room. As I gingerly approached the table, the bowl slipped from my grasp and smashed on the hard floor. It was a moment of horror that played out in slow motion. Fragments of glass splintered and water splashed across the floor. I stood there stunned. It was like a bad dream.

① frustrated → delighted
② bored → embarrassed
③ calm → annoyed
④ excited → shocked
⑤ lonely → scared

2. 밑줄 친 is like this pin factory on a larger scale이 다음 글에서 의미하는 바로 가장 적절한 것은? [3점]

Adam Smith illustrated and developed his ideas about modern society in his *Wealth of Nations* by using the example of a pin factory. Imagine ten people were tasked with making pins. If each person had to make a whole pin, perhaps each might make ten pins a day. Making a whole pin involves several distinct processes. Let's suppose it involves ten different tasks. If one person had to do all these tasks, there would be time lost as that person moved from one task to another. Furthermore, it would be hard to become skilled at all these different tasks — that would require lots of training and effort. But what if each person in the factory focused on just one of the ten tasks instead? Time would be saved in a myriad of ways, and the factory would be able to produce a lot more pins — though, no person by himself would be making a whole pin. As a result, the factory might produce 10,000 pins per day, whereas it would have produced only 100 without specialization. Modern society is like this pin factory on a larger scale.

① is created by accepting individual differences
② concentrates on enhancing the quality of goods
③ can survive the depletion of the necessary labor force
④ is put in crisis unless it accomplishes consensus goals
⑤ functions well when the division of labor is established

3. 다음 글의 요지로 가장 적절한 것은?

Research on emotion shows that positive emotions wear off quickly. Our emotional systems like newness. They like change. We adapt to positive life circumstances so that before too long, the new car, the new spouse, the new house — they don't feel so new and exciting anymore. But gratitude makes us appreciate the value of something, and when we do so, we extract more benefits from it; we're less likely to take it for granted. In effect, gratitude allows us to participate more in life. We notice the positives more, and that magnifies the pleasures you get from life. Instead of adapting to goodness, we celebrate goodness. We spend so much time watching things — movies, computer screens, sports — but with gratitude we become greater participants in our lives as opposed to spectators.

① 새로운 것을 선호하는 것은 인간의 일반적인 성향이다.
② 긍정적인 감정은 부정적인 감정보다 더 빨리 사라진다.
③ 환경에 익숙해지면 심리적인 긴장을 더는 데 도움이 된다.
④ 감사함이 있으면 긍정적인 것들을 더 많이 경험하게 된다.
⑤ 고마움을 느낄 때는 말로 적극적으로 표현하는 것이 좋다.

4. 다음 글의 주제로 가장 적절한 것은?

In general, searching online for health information can be valid, eye-opening, educational, and even useful. While many doctors roll their eyes when they hear, "I did my research," from a patient, sometimes that research can be sound. If a patient has a rare disease and presents articles about it, many of us will be grateful that we were saved some extra work. But the Web becomes entangled when sites angled with opinions, personal anecdotes, exaggeration, and false claims manipulate the navigator to believe what is posted. People also run into trouble when looking for information online based on preconceived notions. Here comes the Curse of the Original Belief. If you believe that megadosing on vitamin C will prevent colds, you will seek out (and easily find) sites promoting this notion. If you think that juice cleanses are the way to better health and well-being, it's easy to find websites supporting this. If delaying vaccines is your cup of tea, online sources abound. If you're debating whether to eat only organic food, plenty of available information will support this.

*entangle: 뒤얽히게 하다 **angle: 왜곡하다 ***juice cleanse: 해독 주스

① considerations when developing health information online
② patterns of online health information seeking behavior
③ difficulties of searching for valuable health information online
④ advantages and disadvantages of seeking health information online
⑤ tendencies of people to believe that online health information is false

5. 다음 글의 제목으로 가장 적절한 것은? [3점]

Mathematics as taught in school is perceived by most secondary school students as a subject lacking history. The teacher becomes the source of all that has to be learned on the subject, and his task is to convey that knowledge to the student. Usually in the instructional process, the understanding of the process of mathematical creation and of the age-old grappling with mathematical problems is completely lost. Mathematics to most students is a closed subject, located in the mind of the teacher who decides whether answers are correct or not. This situation is particularly harmful to mathematics teaching, more than to teaching in most of the other sciences. Mathematics is by nature an accumulative subject; most of what was created millennia ago — both content and processes — is still valid today. Exposing students to some of this development has the potential to make the subject fun and to humanize it for them.

*grapple with: ～을 해결하려고 노력하다

① Motivate Students Not to Give Up Learning Math
② There Is No Standardized Method for Teaching Math
③ The Application of Various Teaching Methods for Math
④ The Ways Math Education Can Influence Students' Success
⑤ Teach the Development of Math within a Historical Context

6. Conquering Fear에 관한 다음 안내문의 내용과 일치하지 <u>않는</u> 것은?

Conquering Fear
a workshop by Greg Milson

Greg Milson has been a climber for 25 years and is the author of two books. In 2007, he lost both of his arms in a climbing accident on the Matterhorn. In this 90-minute workshop, he'll talk about overcoming physical disability.

Where & When: The Shanty Hall, above the town of Zermatt on Friday, July 28 at 7:30 p.m.
Presentation: The spoken presentation is given in German, but simultaneous translation in 4 languages including English will be available.

Reservations must be made online at www.shantyhall.com by July 27.
(Admission is $18 and space is limited to 200 seats.)
Seating is done on a first-come basis.
Food and drinks are not allowed inside the hall.

---

① 발표자는 등반가이자 작가이다.
② 워크숍의 주제는 신체장애 극복에 관한 것이다.
③ 발표는 영어로 이루어지고 4개 국어로 동시통역된다.
④ 7월 27일까지 온라인 예약을 해야 한다.
⑤ 좌석 배치는 선착순으로 이루어진다.

7. 다음 글의 밑줄 친 부분 중, 어법상 <u>틀린</u> 것은? [3점]

Whatever you do, please don't paste a fake smile on your face. Plastic smiles do ① <u>damage</u> to your soul. We've all known people who've worn silly grins while they talked about something ② <u>sad</u>. This tendency to smile even when you don't feel like it developed in childhood, when our parents persuaded us into smiling for the camera or for other people even though we didn't feel like it. ③ <u>Make</u> kids smile when they aren't up to it sends a message that it's not OK to be authentic. Even in front of the camera it's better to capture genuine irritable faces ④ <u>than</u> false stares. The most fascinating snapshots are truthful, ⑤ <u>those</u> that catch people being real. Fake people plaster on smiles when they'd rather be crying, or they smile when they're angry or sad. Slowly they lose touch with their souls.

8. 다음 글의 밑줄 친 부분 중, 문맥상 낱말의 쓰임이 적절하지 <u>않은</u> 것은?

Uncertainty is a basic fact of life. Despite uncertainty, people must make ① <u>predictions</u> about the world. Will the car you are considering buying be reliable? Will you like the food you order? When you see an animal in the woods, what should you do? One source of information that reduces uncertainty is category membership. Although all Xpress Sportscars are not exactly the same, they are so ② <u>similar</u> that you can predict with some confidence that the new Sportscar you are considering will be reliable. Kansas City style barbecue ribs are not ③ <u>identical</u>, but they taste more similar to one another than they do to roast chicken or tofu dishes. Knowing the category of an entity therefore serves to ④ <u>increase</u> the uncertainty associated with it to the degree that the category members are uniform with respect to the prediction you want to make. This *category-based induction* is one of the main ways that categories are ⑤ <u>useful</u> to us in everyday life.

[9~12] 다음 빈칸에 들어갈 말로 가장 적절한 것을 고르시오.

9. From a medical standpoint, health is viewed as an attribute of the individual. The fields of medicine and public health have traditionally acknowledged environmental causes of illness and assigned risk to specific exposures. In the past decade, biologists, ecologists, and physicians have also developed a concept of ecosystem health. This idea recognizes that humans are participants in complex ecosystems and that their potential for health is _____ to the health function of those ecosystems. An ecosystem-based health perspective takes into account the health-related services that the natural environment provides (e.g., soil production, pollination, and water cleansing) and acknowledges the fundamental connection between a healthy environment and human health. An ecosystem health stance is a nonanthropocentric, holistic world view increasingly shared by biological scientists. [3점]

*pollination: 수분, 가루받이 **nonanthropocentric: 인간 중심적이 아닌

① inferior   ② preferable
③ secondary   ④ proportional
⑤ contributable

10. Researchers have reported various nonverbal features of sarcasm. Most disagree as to whether nonverbal cues are essential to the perception of sarcasm or the emotion that prompts it. Even so, research confirms the finding that nonverbal cues are more credible than verbal cues, especially when verbal and nonverbal cues conflict. Also, nonverbal cues are better indicators of speaker intent. As the nature of sarcasm implies a contradiction between intent and message, nonverbal cues may "leak" and reveal the speaker's true mood as they do in deception. Ostensibly, sarcasm is the opposite of deception in that a sarcastic speaker typically intends the receiver to recognize the sarcastic intent; whereas, in deception the speaker typically intends that the receiver not recognize the deceptive intent. Thus, when communicators are attempting to determine if a speaker is sarcastic, they compare _____ and if the two are in opposition, communicators may conclude that the speaker is being sarcastic.

*sarcasm: 빈정댐, 비꼼 **ostensibly: 표면상으로

① the speaker's mood and nonverbal messages
② sarcastic messages with deceptive ones
③ verbal cues with their own emotions
④ the verbal and nonverbal message
⑤ verbal cues with written language

11. Drawing on their experience in using operant conditioning to train animals for circuses, TV, and film stunts, Kellar Breland and Marian Breland described a number of situations in which their attempts to condition an animal's behavior ran head-on into the animal's built-in instincts. For example, according to the theory of operant conditioning, rewarding a behavior should increase its frequency. However, when the Brelands attempted to train a raccoon to drop two coins in a piggy bank by rewarding this response with food, the raccoon did not cooperate. After the raccoon was rewarded with food for dropping two coins into the bank, it took the next two coins and began rubbing them together, just as they do to remove the shells of newly caught crayfish. Eventually, the coin-rubbing response overpowered the coin-dropping response, and the Brelands had to abandon their attempt to condition the raccoon. The Brelands used this and other examples to emphasize _____. [3점]

*operant conditioning: 조작적 조건 형성 **crayfish: 가재

① the difficulty of domesticating wild animals
② the importance of biologically programmed behavior
③ the possibility of restraining instinct through training
④ the instinctive behavior overwhelmed by reinforcement
⑤ the balance between positive and negative reinforcement

12. One unspoken truth about creativity — it isn't about wild talent so much as it is about productivity. To find a few ideas that work, you need to try a lot that don't. It's a pure numbers game. Geniuses don't necessarily have a higher success rate than other creators; they simply do more — and they do a range of different things. They have more successes *and* more failures. That goes for teams and companies too. It's impossible to generate a lot of good ideas without also generating a lot of bad ideas. The thing about creativity is that at the outset, you can't tell which ideas will succeed and which will fail. So the only thing you can do is try to _____. [3점]

*at the outset: 처음에

① use unconventional ideas to make yourself unique
② fail faster so that you can move onto the next idea
③ borrow from others in order to avoid trial and error
④ recognize the essential merits and attributes of a good idea
⑤ overcome the feeling that too much is better than not enough

13. 다음 글에서 전체 흐름과 관계 없는 문장은?

Fear is directly linked with desire. The stronger we desire something, the more intensely we fear losing it. Urged by various instincts, we strongly want, desire, and need both material and immaterial things. ① These range from life itself and the presence of loved ones to wanting fame, fortune, power, prestige, love, arts, sports, and so on. ② Each of these provides us with a different sort of pleasure and satisfaction, and life becomes richer and highly desirable, and the thought of losing these objects strikes fear in our hearts. ③ Only people who succeed in securing the basic necessities are able to achieve discipline over their possessive instincts. ④ Depending on which we cherish the most, we fear losing that the most intensely. ⑤ Death, in particular, puts an end to these attachments and their related joys, and thus, people normally fear death the most.

*prestige: 명망

[14~15] 주어진 글 다음에 이어질 글의 순서로 가장 적절한 것을 고르시오.

14.

A first-born who has a younger brother or sister gains a double advantage over other babies. For the first year or two of his life he enjoys the full attention of his new parents and is treated royally as an only child.

(A) This means that he has a solid foundation of "self" on which he can now build the limiting factors of social sharing. The result is a self-assured personality that is capable of a genuine mixing-in with others.

(B) He learns how much he is loved without any interruptions or interference. His self-respect blossoms, and he rates himself as being "worthy of love."

(C) But then, before he has the chance to become self-important, along comes baby number two and suddenly he finds that almost all of the parental attention is now focused on this tiny new arrival. He has to come to terms with this, but when he does so, he does not lose his own sense of self-worth.

① (A) – (C) – (B)　　② (B) – (A) – (C)
③ (B) – (C) – (A)　　④ (C) – (A) – (B)
⑤ (C) – (B) – (A)

15.

Within the space of a few decades around the middle of the eleventh century, there was a dramatic shift in the source of fish from around 80 per cent freshwater to 80 per cent saltwater fish like cod, haddock and herring.

(A) With the spread of agriculture, forests were felled and land deep ploughed for crops. Soil erosion soon turned fast-running, cool and clear water into sluggish, warm and turbid water, which species like salmon did not enjoy.

(B) Nor did salmon, and other fish that migrated from sea to rivers to spawn, benefit from the construction of thousands of dams across Europe's rivers to supply power for corn mills and other industries. With their migration routes blocked, freshwater fisheries' production collapsed.

(C) At the time, demand was increasing rapidly thanks to a combination of population growth and urbanization. Fresh fish supplies were in freefall as a result of human-caused habitat change in rivers, lakes and estuaries. [3점]

*turbid: 탁한 **spawn: (물고기·개구리 등이) 알을 낳다
***estuary: 포구, 강어귀

① (A) – (C) – (B)　　② (B) – (A) – (C)
③ (B) – (C) – (A)　　④ (C) – (A) – (B)
⑤ (C) – (B) – (A)

[16~17] 글의 흐름으로 보아, 주어진 문장이 들어가기에 가장 적절한 곳을 고르시오.

16.

> Some who have been instituting telepsychiatric sessions have noticed that rather than being inhibited by this mode of communicating, patients actually feel less inhibited than when speaking to a psychiatrist face to face.

Logic suggests that our increasing reliance on electronic communications might increase social isolation. Indeed, some studies suggest that unlimited access to e-mail actually increases people's sense of loneliness and isolation. (①) But there are others working in the new medium of telemedicine who have found that electronic communications may make it easier for people to interact. (②) In isolated communities, too small to afford full-time medical health providers, telemedicine — diagnosis and treatment with the assistance of videoconferencing technology — is being tried out with success. (③) This may be part of the same phenomenon as the ease that we feel in communicating our deepest burdens to a respected but impersonal confessor. (④) It may be part of the successful principle behind confessing sins to a hidden priest in the Catholic confessional. (⑤) However, in this new age, the person to whom we bare our hearts is not hidden behind oak walls and velvet curtains but behind a glowing, protective computer screen. [3점]

*confessional: 고해 성사실

17.

> And it is not the basic, "general" laws of physics but rather the particular arrangements of the millions of bits of information in our inherited genes that establish these connections.

Many scientists look on chemistry and physics as ideal models of what psychology should be like. (①) After all, the atoms in the brain are subject to the same all-inclusive physical laws that govern every other form of matter. (②) Then can we also explain what our brains actually do entirely in terms of those same basic principles? (③) The answer is no, simply because even if we understood how each of our billions of brain cells work separately, this would not tell us how the brain works as an agency. (④) The "laws of thought" depend not only upon the properties of those brain cells but also on how they are connected. (⑤) To be sure, "general" laws apply to everything, but, for that very reason, they can rarely explain anything in particular. [3점]

18. 다음 글의 내용을 한 문장으로 요약하고자 한다. 빈칸 (A), (B)에 들어갈 말로 가장 적절한 것은?

In many 'Asian' societies people are governed by 'shame', and 'What will others say?', and an external locus of control. There is group pressure to maintain the reputation of the group, for example, the family, the team or the organization. If an individual steps out of line, he/she is concerned about what others may say. There may be feelings of shame or 'loss of face' for the individuals and the group to which he/she belongs. In 'western' societies governed by 'guilt', people are not so concerned about what others will say if they do something wrong. Individuals are raised to answer more to their own conscience and internal sense of right and wrong. Indeed in Judaeo-Catholic societies children are reared with a very strong sense of guilt.

*locus: (존재하는) 장소, 중심지

↓

> Asians who emphasize acting _____(A)_____ within a group are governed by shame, whereas Westerners who follow _____(B)_____ criteria are governed by guilt.

	(A)		(B)
①	securely	......	internal
②	securely	......	external
③	responsibly	......	objective
④	honorably	......	internal
⑤	honorably	......	external

[19~20] 다음 글을 읽고, 물음에 답하시오.

When someone shouts at you, "Look out!" and you jump just in time to avoid being hit by an automobile, you owe your escape from injury to communication by means of noises. You did not see the car coming; nevertheless, someone did, and he made certain noises to communicate his alarm to you. In other words, although your nervous system did not record the danger, you were (a) unharmed because another nervous system did. You had, for the time being, the advantage of someone else's nervous system in addition to your own. Indeed, most of the time when we are listening to the noises people make or looking at the black marks on paper that stand for such noises, we are drawing upon the experiences of others in order to make up for what we ourselves have (b) missed. Obviously the more an individual can make use of the nervous systems of others to (c) supplement his own, the easier it is for him to survive. And, of course, the more individuals in a group make helpful noises at each other, the better it is for all — within the limits, naturally, of the group's talents for social organization. Birds and animals congregate with their own kind and make noises when they find food or become alarmed. In fact, gregariousness as an aid to survival and self-defense is forced upon animals as well as upon man by the necessity of (d) separating nervous systems even more than by the necessity of uniting physical strength. Societies, both animal and human, might almost be regarded as huge (e) cooperative nervous systems.

*gregariousness: 군거성

19. 윗글의 제목으로 가장 적절한 것은?

① The Importance of Physical Strength for Survival
② Using the Nervous Systems of Others for Survival
③ Noise as an Aid for Gathering and Living Together
④ Principles of Perception to Improve Communication
⑤ Language and Survival: How We Imitate Each Other

20. 밑줄 친 (a) ~ (e) 중에서 문맥상 낱말의 쓰임이 적절하지 않은 것은? [3점]

① (a)　　② (b)　　③ (c)　　④ (d)　　⑤ (e)

○ 답안지의 해당란에 성명과 수험번호를 쓰고, 또 수험번호와 답을 정확히 표시하시오.
○ 문항에 따라 배점이 다르니, 각 물음의 끝에 표시된 배점을 참고하시오. 3점 문항에만 점수가 표시되어 있습니다. 점수 표시가 없는 문항은 모두 2점씩입니다.

1. 다음 글의 목적으로 가장 적절한 것은?

Dear Mr. Hagen,

As you know, I have been a tenant in the house you own on Broad Street for the past two years. I have been quite happy with my apartment, and I have never missed a rent payment. I believe I have been a model tenant in all other ways. I would like to continue to live here. Unfortunately, I have just been laid off from my job. I am looking for other employment in the area, and I expect I will find new work within the coming months. Until then, I would like to see if there is a way I could reduce some or all of my monthly rent by performing services for you at the house. I am a capable landscaper and painter, and I would be happy to do whatever jobs around the house you would ask. I would appreciate hearing from you soon.

Thank you.
Steven Abbott

① 주택 임대료 납부 기한 연장을 부탁하려고
② 주택 임대차 계약의 변경에 대해 항의하려고
③ 집주인에게 집을 수리해 줄 것을 요청하려고
④ 건물 임대 계약으로 인한 손해 보상을 요구하려고
⑤ 임대료를 대신해 할 수 있는 일이 있는지 문의하려고

2. 다음 글에서 필자가 주장하는 바로 가장 적절한 것은?

The current food crisis not only deprives vulnerable people of their right to food, but it also benefits huge international corporations that monopolize the food chain. Just ten corporations not only control one-third of the US$ 23 billion commercial seed market, but also 80 per cent of the US$ 28 billion global pesticide market. In order to change the situation for local farmers, we need to change the global paradigm for agricultural policy-making and give absolute priority to investments in small gardens that provide food for individual families and local production, including irrigation, infrastructure, seeds, pesticides, and so on. Peasant farmers and small-scale agriculture have been neglected for too long. The issue of the exclusion of peasants from the development process and the neglect of their rights should be immediately addressed. National governments and international organizations should give absolute priority to investments in small-scale agriculture and local production.

① 소규모 자작농들에게 적합한 새로운 품종을 개발해야 한다.
② 소규모 농업과 현지 생산 부문에 대한 투자를 우선해야 한다.
③ 효율적인 식량 생산을 위하여 자급적 농업을 기업화해야 한다.
④ 농업 분야 연구 개발에 힘쓰는 기업에 우대책을 제공해야 한다.
⑤ 식량의 고른 분배를 위하여 국제기구의 권한이 강화되어야 한다.

3. 밑줄 친 they keep us running on a treadmill이 다음 글에서 의미하는 바로 가장 적절한 것은? [3점]

In adulthood, many child prodigies become experts in their fields and leaders in their organizations. Yet "only a fraction of gifted children eventually become revolutionary adult creators," laments psychologist Ellen Winner. "Those who do must make a painful transition" from a child who "learns rapidly and effortlessly in an established domain" to an adult who "ultimately makes a domain." Most prodigies never make that leap. They apply their extraordinary abilities in ordinary ways, mastering their jobs without questioning defaults and without making waves. In every domain they enter, they play it safe by following the conventional paths to success. They become doctors who heal their patients without fighting to fix the broken systems that prevent many patients from affording health care in the first place. They become lawyers who defend clients for violating outdated laws without trying to transform the laws themselves. Although we rely on them to keep the world running smoothly, <u>they keep us running on a treadmill.</u>

① Geniuses lack the practical skills to function in society.
② The exceptional abilities of prodigies diminish as they age.
③ Prodigies assign easy but tedious duties to ordinary people.
④ Prodigies become non-conformists who make up their own rules.
⑤ Most prodigies don't try to alter the social system.

4. 다음 글의 제목으로 가장 적절한 것은?

Fashions and social pressures shift. Throughout almost the first three-quarters of the 20th century, log houses in the United States, as in Norway, were considered to be rough, primitive, and low-class housing. As a consequence, weatherboards were widely used to mask earlier log construction. However, in the prosperous 1960s, when many individuals were seeking a challenge to the status quo, fashions changed and social pressure relaxed. These changes encouraged persons who wished to ride the crest of changing fashion, to seek out hidden log buildings, to remove the siding, and to enjoy the glow of their visual confirmation of society's rediscovery of its heritage. Needless to say, this was not a widely pursued innovation, but enough affluent people did do so in their quest to maintain their position as societal leaders. As a result, the log house reasserted its position as an American icon, regardless of the ethnic background of its original builders.

*the status quo: 현재 상태 **ride the crest of: ～으로 성공을 구가하다
***quest: 추구

① How Americans Have Improved Log Houses
② The Origin of Log Houses in the United States
③ The Log House: From a Hut to an American Symbol
④ The Log House: A Prestigious, Eco-friendly and Healthy Home
⑤ Basis of Modern Design and the Current Status of Log Houses

5. 다음 도표의 내용과 일치하지 <u>않는</u> 것은?

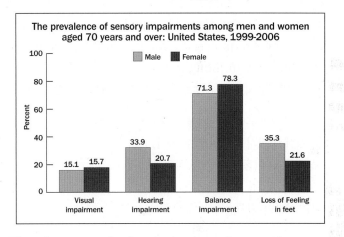

The prevalence of sensory impairments among men and women aged 70 years and over: United States, 1999-2006

The above graph shows the prevalence of sensory impairments among males and females aged 70 years and over from 1999 to 2006 in the United States. ① The least prevalent impairment is vision impairment, with a difference of no more than 0.6 percentage points between men and women. ② Nearly one out of every three men has impaired hearing and about a fifth of women have impaired hearing, which makes it the third most common impairment among both men and women. ③ Women are found to be more likely than men to have a balance impairment, and the gap between the two groups is exactly 7 percentage points. ④ It is more common for men to have loss of feeling in the feet than women, with a difference of roughly 14 percentage points. ⑤ The largest percentage gap between the two groups was found in hearing impairment, followed by loss of feeling in feet.

*prevalence: 발생 비율

6. Sappho에 관한 다음 글의 내용과 일치하지 <u>않는</u> 것은?

Sappho was a well-known lyric poet of ancient Greece. She was born on the Greek island of Lesbos sometime between 630 and 612 B.C. Sappho lived during a time of unstable government on Lesbos. She was temporarily exiled to Sicily between 604 and 594 B.C., for reasons which are not known. Sappho died in 570 B.C. in Lesbos, Greece. During her lifetime she wrote poems expressing love. In the third century B.C., the Library of Alexandria organized Sappho's poetry into nine books, but the surviving portion is very small, containing only one poem in complete form, the "Hymn to Aphrodite." She wrote in a rather difficult Aeolic Greek dialect, and that's the reason why her work was copied less and less over the years. But her poetry is praised for its clarity of language and simplicity of thought.

*Sicily: 시칠리아 ((이탈리아 남쪽의 섬)) **Aeolic: 아이올리스 지방의

① 정치적으로 혼란한 시기에 살았다.
② 고향에서 잠시 추방된 적이 있다.
③ 생애 동안 아홉 권의 시집을 출판했다.
④ 어려운 방언을 사용해 시를 썼다.
⑤ 시어의 명료함과 사고의 단순성으로 칭송받는다.

7. 다음 글의 밑줄 친 부분 중, 어법상 <u>틀린</u> 것은? [3점]

The 2008 winners of the annual awards for sustainable tourism all demonstrate that the best practice in tourism is far-reaching, and ① extends beyond what was once understood to constitute tourism — mainly just planes, hotels, and beaches. As an example, the winner of the poverty reduction award was an initiative ② in which both local farmers and tourists benefit. The hoteliers in this award-winning nation have traditionally imported much of their food while ignoring local farmers ③ who produce was going to waste. Now, 1,000 farmers, most of whom are women, have been helped ④ to supply local hotels. At the same time, the country's travel foundation, one of the funding organizations, and the initiative have launched their own farmyard — to demonstrate best practice and to become a tourist attraction on its own merits. Taking tourists to the farmyard, for example, is one way in which they can see how their contribution to sustainability is ⑤ working.

*hotelier: 호텔 경영자

8. 다음 글의 밑줄 친 부분 중, 문맥상 낱말의 쓰임이 적절하지 <u>않은</u> 것은? [3점]

Robert Putnam, a Harvard political scientist, Cass Sunstein, a respected legal scholar and a former senior official in the Obama administration, and Eli Pariser, the director of MoveOn.Org, are among those who warn that cable and web-based media are creating and reinforcing a series of identity ghettos. Their argument is a variant of the old "selective exposure" thesis: we choose to be exposed only to media that ① reinforce the views that we already have. Their concern is that as people congregate in their own comfortable media enclaves, the opportunity to meet and exchange ideas with those who have different views is ② vanishing. Political activists, hockey fans, and followers of every imaginable show, game, music video, or celebrity all ③ gravitate not to great public spaces, but to the limited and protected confines of their own groups. As Pariser argues, "By definition, a world constructed from the ④ unfamiliar is a world in which there's nothing to learn." For Pariser, the danger is that "you can get stuck in a ⑤ static, ever-narrowing version of yourself — an endless you-loop." In the end, "the user has become the content."

*ghetto: 고립 집단, 빈민가 **enclave: 고립된 장소

[9~12] 다음 빈칸에 들어갈 말로 가장 적절한 것을 고르시오.

9. So far we've overlooked a very important contributor to logical thinking (as well as memory and physical and mental performance in general): _____. Certainly they play a huge role in physical performance. To appreciate this, play a few solitary rounds of darts. Note your performance. Now position a picture of one of your children or a child known to you on the bull's-eye of the board and start again. In the original study testing this rather grim situation, most people were hard-pressed to hit the child's photo — especially if it was of their own child — despite their recognition that it was only a picture. In other words, full intellectual recognition of the distinction between reality and image wasn't sufficient to offset the reluctance to throw a sharp instrument at an image of their child. Most people are similarly reluctant to tear up a piece of paper with a loved one's name written on it. [3점]

*bull's-eye: (과녁의) 중심; 핵심; 명중

① emotions   ② commitments
③ experiences   ④ intuitions
⑤ circumstances

10. To attract the best people and succeed as a business, the authentic organization of the future will need to foster environments where creativity and innovation are at a premium, employees feel engaged and committed, and leadership pipelines are carefully cultivated for future success. In our research, workplaces with those qualities look for _____, hiring people for differences that are more than skin deep. Differences in thought processes, frames of references and skills, among other things. Case in point: Back in the 1980s, the business division of a US publisher had one of the most widely diverse workforces. One senior editor had been part of a Washington think tank and was an expert on Asian culture; another held a PhD in American history; another had worked as a speechwriter for a US president and was an environmental activist. There was also an associate editor who had interned at the *New Yorker* magazine and another who had a background in foreign affairs. Only two of those editors held MBAs — and this was the business division!

① a sense of authenticity
② an unusual kind of diversity
③ a variety of ethnic backgrounds
④ people with overseas experience
⑤ innovative ways to improve teamwork

11. One facet of the nominal fallacy, the error of believing that the label carries explanatory information, is the danger of using common words and _____. This has the often disastrous effect of leading an unwary public down a path of misunderstanding. Words like "theory," "law," "force" do not mean in common discourse what they mean to a scientist. "Success" in Darwinian evolution is not the same "success" as taught by Dale Carnegie. "Force" to a physicist has a meaning quite different from that used in political discourse. The worst of these, though, may be "theory" and "law," which are almost polar opposites — theory being a strong idea in science while vague in common discourse, and law being a much more muscular social than scientific concept. These differences lead to sometimes serious misunderstandings between scientists and the public that supports their work. [3점]

*unwary: 부주의한 **discourse: 담화, 담론 ***muscular: 강력한

① seeking new contexts for them
② giving them a scientific meaning
③ utilizing previous scientific knowledge
④ indicating a clear lack of understanding
⑤ applying them in appropriate analogies

12. Relying solely on the European honeybee for pollination services is a risky strategy because it relies on single-species management. Almond pollination in California depends on the European honeybee and oil palm pollination in Southeast Asia depends on a single imported African beetle. Recent studies highlight the need to compensate for this weakness by protecting pollination against asynchronous annual variations in bee abundance. Different pollinating species also occupy different spatial, temporal, and conditional niches in which only an abundant and varied collection of providers will lead to a high quality and quantity of services. These facts suggest that _____ across agricultural landscapes to ensure pollination services under various conditions and across space and time.

[3점]

*asynchronous: 동시에 존재하지 않는 **niche: (시장의) 틈새

① bee farming should be done under stricter regulations
② import bans on harmful alien species must be enforced
③ rare species should conceive their own survival strategies
④ pollinator multiplicity should be preserved or strengthened
⑤ raising more than two kinds of crops together can be stable

13. 다음 글에서 전체 흐름과 관계 <u>없는</u> 문장은? [3점]

Coaches must understand that when they make a strategy decision, it is a good or bad decision at the time it is made based on the players' abilities, the situation, and the percentages, not on whether the play was successful or unsuccessful! ① Coaches make decisions based on all the factors available to them, and then the players have to execute the play called by the coach. ② How the players perform their skills on a particular play has nothing to do with the wisdom of the coach's decision. ③ To reach a high level of skill, the players may need to perform a skill or game situation thousands of times so that they have multiple opportunities to practise and perform the skills. ④ The coach must make his decision before he knows how the players will perform (known as first guessing), but the fans, parents, and media have the luxury of waiting until a play is over and then determining if the decision was a good or bad one (known as second guessing). ⑤ Fans, parents, and the media are therefore never wrong on a strategy decision!

[14~15] 주어진 글 다음에 이어질 글의 순서로 가장 적절한 것을 고르시오.

14.

Cultural messages shape many communication behaviors, and listening is no exception. In particular, listening behavior appears to be affected by how people in a given culture think about the importance of time.

(A) In contrast, collectivistic cultures such as Korea emphasize social harmony over efficiency. As part of their listening behavior, people in these cultures often pay close attention to nonverbal behaviors and contextual cues to determine the meaning of a speaker's message.

(B) In individualistic cultures, people often think of time as a resource. Americans, for instance, commonly say that "time is money," and they think of time as a commodity that can be saved, spent, and wasted.

(C) People in such cultures typically place a high value on efficiency, and they expect others to do the same. They value direct, straightforward communication, and listeners become impatient with speakers who don't "get to the point."

*collectivistic: 집단주의적인

① (A) – (C) – (B)   ② (B) – (A) – (C)
③ (B) – (C) – (A)   ④ (C) – (A) – (B)
⑤ (C) – (B) – (A)

15.

Hospitals used to be required to perform autopsies on a certain percentage of deaths at their institution as a quality control measure. However, that requirement was dropped years ago.

(A) One is cost — about $2,000 to $3,000 per autopsy. Insurance usually will not cover the procedure. Doctors also are not likely to encourage an autopsy because it might turn up something they missed in life, and families often see autopsies as disrespectful of their loved one.

(B) Some new hospitals do not even have autopsy facilities. Today, autopsies are usually performed only in crimes or unusual deaths. Autopsies are rare with "natural" deaths. There are also several disincentives to performing this type of autopsy.

(C) The biggest disincentive to autopsies, however, is our unending faith in medical technology. Why do an autopsy if tests have already confirmed the cause of death? There is little thought that anything else could have been involved. [3점]

*autopsy: (사체의) 부검

① (A) – (C) – (B)   ② (B) – (A) – (C)
③ (B) – (C) – (A)   ④ (C) – (A) – (B)
⑤ (C) – (B) – (A)

[16~17] 글의 흐름으로 보아, 주어진 문장이 들어가기에 가장 적절한 곳을 고르시오.

16.

> Prior to this realization, a baby's motto seems to be "Out of sight, out of mind."

Realizing that a thing exists even after it disappears from sight is a major accomplishment of babies in their first year of life. (①) For example, a three-month old baby will stare with great interest at an object, but if you hide it behind a piece of paper, they will not try to look for it. (②) By about six months, infants begin to understand that a hidden object is still actually here, somewhere. (③) If a baby of this age drops a toy from her table, she will look for it; she also will look under a cloth for a toy that is partially hidden. (④) By one year of age, most babies have developed an awareness of the permanence of things. (⑤) This is the age at which they love to play peekaboo.

*peekaboo: 숨어 있다가 '까꿍'하며 아이를 놀래주는 장난

17.

> An argument raged over whether the private corporation was trying to establish patents on human genetic sequences, a violation of the norm of openness.

Because scientific research is so often conducted in the interests of national defense or under the sponsorship of private firms that hope to profit from applications of the findings, the norms of common ownership and publication are often suspended. (①) Such situations have led to innumerable conflicts in scientific circles. (②) An outstanding example is the race to publish the complete map and inventory of the human genome — all the sequences of human DNA that constitute our genes. (③) In 2001, two rival groups raced to be the first to complete the research, one in the private sector, the Celera Genomics Corporation, led by J. Craig Venter, and the other a government-funded laboratory headed by Francis Collins. (④) The public laboratory had, or claimed to have, no such business interest. (⑤) Eventually the competing teams compromised and issued a joint publication of the map, but the controversy and legal battles over issuing patents for genetic material have continued. [3점]

*innumerable: 무수한

18. 다음 글의 내용을 한 문장으로 요약하고자 한다. 빈칸 (A), (B)에 들어갈 말로 가장 적절한 것은?

As a teacher, I've often heard my students scolding themselves after receiving a graded test, "I knew the answer to #42 was (b)!" My typical response is that I've never had a student intentionally answer a question incorrectly, so why, if they knew the answer was (b), did they circle (a)? This reminds them gently of a common flaw in human reasoning. It's called *the hindsight bias*: the tendency to believe that our forecasts were more accurate than they actually were. It could be seen after the 2014 World Cup when sports analysts claimed to have predicted the shocking 7-to-1 final victory of Germany over Brazil, as well as after the Cold War when many claimed to have seen that the collapse of Russia had been inevitable. Though harmless on the surface, we must be careful of the hindsight bias. The danger of this bias is that it makes us believe we're better than we really are. It can hinder our learning from our past errors, hence holding back the extent to which we can develop.

↓

> People tend to see events that have already occurred as having been more _____(A)_____ than was actually the case, which _____(B)_____ the ability to improve.

	(A)		(B)
①	inevitable	……	overestimates
②	predictable	……	overestimates
③	predictable	……	limits
④	doubtful	……	limits
⑤	inevitable	……	controls

[19~20] 다음 글을 읽고, 물음에 답하시오.

In 2015, a group of researchers in France fatigued their subjects' executive brains by putting them through a (a) repetitive exercise called the Simon task. In it, participants are shown a set of left and right pointing arrows on a computer screen, one of which is always positioned at the screen's center. Subjects are instructed to press the left or right arrow key on the keyboard, according to the direction at which that central arrow points. The key to the experiment is that, in order to focus on the central arrow, the subjects must suppress the influence of the other arrows. The subjects performed that task over and over without a break for forty minutes. After the Simon task had (b) dulled the subjects' executive faculties, the researchers presented them with a test of their elastic thinking. The subjects were given a few minutes to imagine as many uses as they could for a set of household objects, like a bucket, a newspaper, and a brick. Their answers were scored according to criteria such as the total number of uses the subject was able to imagine and the (c) originality of each idea (as judged by the number of other subjects who had also thought of that use). The scores were then compared with those of a control group who had not first engaged in the Simon task. The researchers found that when a subject's capacity for executive function was (d) renewed, both the total number of imagined uses and their creativity were significantly greater. The lesson is that our elastic thinking capacity may be highest when we feel "burnt out." That's good to know when scheduling your tasks — you could be better at generating imaginative ideas if you do that kind of thinking after working on a chore that involves a period of (e) tedious and focused effort that strains your powers of concentration.

19. 윗글의 제목으로 가장 적절한 것은?

① How to Avoid Creative Fatigue
② Fatigue Can Help Free the Mind
③ How We Can Improve Our Concentration
④ Why We're More Creative When We're Alert
⑤ We Do Little on Tasks When We're Most Tired

20. 밑줄 친 (a) ~ (e) 중에서 문맥상 낱말의 쓰임이 적절하지 않은 것은? [3점]

① (a)　　② (b)　　③ (c)　　④ (d)　　⑤ (e)

○ 답안지의 해당란에 성명과 수험번호를 쓰고, 또 수험번호와 답을 정확히 표시하시오.
○ 문항에 따라 배점이 다르니, 각 물음의 끝에 표시된 배점을 참고하시오. 3점 문항에만 점수가 표시되어 있습니다. 점수 표시가 없는 문항은 모두 2점씩입니다.

1. 다음 글에 드러난 Jean의 심경 변화로 가장 적절한 것은?

Jean's mother ruled her daughter's practice sessions with an iron fist. She cut Jean no slack. Her rule for Jean was an hour of practice, seven days a week. Jean couldn't bear the rigorous schedule of her practice sessions any longer. When it was time for practice, gloom came over her face as she sighed deeply. After realizing how difficult it was for Jean, Jean's piano teacher persuaded her mother to do away with the tight schedule. The mother willingly accepted the advice. As soon as she was able to play the piano on her own terms, she looked forward to her lessons and found great joy in playing. She told her teacher that she really enjoyed playing the piano, so much so that she didn't even realize how quickly time passed when she was playing the piano.

① ashamed → relaxed   ② depressed → delighted
③ joyful → gloomy   ④ pleased → lonely
⑤ scared → confused

2. 밑줄 친 Alternatives are not even imagined가 다음 글에서 의미하는 바로 가장 적절한 것은?

Despite the accumulated frustration and rage brought about by our struggle to adapt ourselves to machines, genuine resistance to the machine is relatively rare. Our preconditioning to favor novelty keeps us fascinated by the machines. Generally people try bravely, even enthusiastically, to accommodate themselves. They are not sure why they are consequently unhappy. They do not blame the machines, for we have convinced ourselves — or been convinced by advertising and promotion — of their marvelous natures and of our great need for them. We have created dependency where none existed, forgetting that we survived and thrived as a species for hundreds of thousands of years without the internal combustion engine or the cell phone. Now too many of us feel lost and inadequate and frightened if the lights go out. We love our machines, after all — as we would a spouse in an enduring bad marriage, whose flaws are so familiar, whose irritating voice is so much a part of the background that it is impossible to conceive its not being there. Alternatives are not even imagined.

*internal combustion engine: 내연 기관

① We continue to study machines to find new life.
② We don't think we can live without using machines.
③ We hesitate to use machines with which we are unfamiliar.
④ We should have other plans in case machines are not available.
⑤ We don't believe that machines are controlling our daily routine.

3. 다음 글의 요지로 가장 적절한 것은?

There is a long-standing debate within psychology as to whether emotions per se are stored in memory. Some investigators argue that emotion cannot be stored in memory but must be reconstructed based on knowledge concerning the circumstances in which the emotion was experienced. According to this view, when asked to remember emotions, people retrieve not the fleeting emotional experience but a redescription of it based on memory for relevant details concerning the event or based on beliefs about how one is likely to have felt. Remembering the circumstances in which an emotion was experienced also may cause people to experience a similar but new emotion in the present, and it is this new emotion that is then reported. As William James put it, "The revivability in memory of the emotions, like that of all the feelings of the lower senses, is very small.... We can produce not remembrances of the old grief or rapture but new griefs and raptures, by summoning up a lively thought of their exciting cause."

*per se: 그 자체로는 **rapture: 환희

① 감정의 기억은 강렬한 것을 제외하고는 대부분 잊게 된다.
② 과거 감정은 현재 상황에 따라 왜곡되고 변형되어 상기된다.
③ 감정의 기억은 그것을 야기했던 상황을 떠올림으로 재구성된다.
④ 감정은 세부사항보다는 대략적인 내용을 바탕으로 떠올려진다.
⑤ 긍정적인 감정은 부정적인 감정보다 오래 기억되는 경향이 있다.

4. 다음 글의 주제로 가장 적절한 것은? [3점]

Many still find it plausible to look at bees and ants as little more than 'reflex machines', lacking an internal representation of the world, or an ability to foresee even the immediate future. Insects are close to 'philosophical zombies': hypothetical beings that rely entirely on routines and reflexes, without any awareness. But perhaps the problem is not that insects lack an inner life, but that they don't have a way to communicate it in terms we can understand. So maybe we misdiagnose animal brains as having machine-like properties simply because we understand how machines work — whereas, to date, we have only a fragmentary and imperfect insight into how even the simplest brains process, store and retrieve information. However, there are now many signs that consciousness-like phenomena might exist not just among humans or even great apes — but that insects might have them, too. If the same behavioral and cognitive criteria are applied as to much larger-brained vertebrates, then some insects are likely to qualify as conscious agents.

*vertebrate: 척추동물

① the potential of insect brains to possess consciousness
② difficulties in pulling back the veil on animal intelligence
③ differences of cognitive system between humans and insects
④ inferiority of insect brains to human brains in communication
⑤ ways to reveal the mystery of whether insects have consciousness

5 다음 글의 제목으로 가장 적절한 것은?

How do people maximize their odds of creating a masterpiece? They come up with a large number of ideas. On average, creative geniuses weren't qualitatively better in their fields than their peers. They simply produced a greater volume of work, which gave them more variation and a higher chance of originality. When the London Philharmonic Orchestra chose the 50 greatest pieces of classical music, the list included six pieces by Mozart, five by Beethoven, and three by Bach. To generate a handful of masterworks, Mozart composed more than 600 pieces before his death at thirty-five, Beethoven produced 650 in his lifetime, and Bach wrote over a thousand. This is also true for Picasso. His list of works includes more than 1,800 paintings, 1,200 sculptures, 2,800 ceramics, and 12,000 drawings, not to mention prints, rugs, and tapestries — only a fraction of which have received acclaim.

*tapestry: 태피스트리((여러 가지 색실로 그림을 짜 넣은 직물))

① Are Great Artists Born or Made?
② The Three Most Beloved Composers
③ Focus on Quality Brings a Masterpiece
④ The More, The Greater the Odds of a Hit
⑤ Perspiration Is Outweighed by Inspiration

6. Longbeach Summer Baseball Camp에 관한 다음 안 내문의 내용과 일치하는 것은?

Longbeach Summer Baseball Camp

ALL KIDS ARE WELCOME!

Come join the fun at Longbeach summer baseball camp!

This baseball camp provides boys and girls with an exciting, healthy environment where they can hit and throw lots of balls, improve their abilities, and develop lasting friendships.

We offer Full-day and Half-day camps for boys and girls, ages 7-13. Campers are grouped based on age.

Period: Monday, May 3 – Friday, May 14 (Two weeks)
Location: Longbeach High School Tennis Courts
Camp Options
Full-day Camp: 9:30 a.m. – 3:00 p.m. ($450)
Half-day Camp: 9:30 a.m. – 12:30 p.m. ($300)
• Kids must be age 10 or older to sign up for the Full-day Camp.
• Please submit your payment by May 2.
(This price includes meals and a training suit.)

- Mornings consist of drilling, conditioning and off court fun. Afternoons will focus on fun competitive games.
- Kids are allowed to bring their own bat and gloves or they may borrow them from the camp at no cost.
- Please note, space in the camp is limited, so registration is on a first-come, first-served basis.

---

① 참가자들의 야구 실력을 기준으로 반이 편성된다.
② 종일 캠프는 반일 캠프보다 참가비가 두 배 더 비싸다.
③ 참가비는 캠프가 시작하는 날까지 전액 납부해야 한다.
④ 배트와 글러브는 대여료를 내고 빌려준다.
⑤ 공간이 제한되어 있어 등록은 선착순으로 마감한다.

---

7. 다음 글의 밑줄 친 부분 중, 어법상 틀린 것은? [3점]

Knowing how the honey bee lives in its natural world is important for a broad range of scientific studies. This is because *Apis mellifera* has become one of the model systems for investigating basic questions in biology, especially ① those related to behavior. ② Whether one is studying these bees to solve some mystery in animal cognition, behavioral genetics, or social behavior, it is critically important to become familiar with their natural biology before designing one's experimental investigations. For example, when sleep researchers used honey bees to explore the functions of sleep, they benefited greatly from knowing that it is only the elderly bees within a colony, the foragers, ③ they get most of their sleep at night and in comparatively long bouts. If these researchers had not known which bees are a colony's soundest sleepers when nightfall comes, then they might ④ have failed to design truly meaningful sleep-deprivation experiments. A good experiment with honey bees, as with all organisms, taps into ⑤ their natural way of life.

*forager: 먹이 조달자 **bout: (활동의) 시간, 기간 ***tap into: ~을 활용하다

8. 다음 글의 밑줄 친 부분 중, 문맥상 낱말의 쓰임이 적절하지 <u>않은</u> 것은? [3점]

Psychiatry is a field that demands a tremendous knowledge of human nature. The psychiatrist must ① gain insight into the mind of the disturbed patient as quickly and accurately as possible. In this field of medicine the practitioner can only diagnose, treat and prescribe effectively when quite sure of what is going on in the patient. ② Superficiality has no place here. Diagnostic errors are soon apparent, whereas a ③ correct understanding of the disorder leads to successful treatment. In other words, our knowledge of human nature is rigorously tested. In everyday life errors in our judgement of another human being are not necessarily linked with dramatic consequences, for these consequences may occur so long after the mistake has been made that the connection between cause and effect is not ④ obscure. We are frequently astonished when terrible misfortunes occur many years after a ⑤ misunderstanding of another person. These unhappy events teach us that it is the duty of every human being to acquire a working knowledge of human nature.

*psychiatry: 정신 의학

[9~12] 다음 빈칸에 들어갈 말로 가장 적절한 것을 고르시오.

9. Several studies have shown that individuals who are ostracized, excluded, or rejected by others behave in ways that will increase their inclusion status (i.e., being included or excluded in a group). These behaviors range from working harder in group settings, to conforming to group perceptions, or being more sensitive to information about others. For example, Williams and Sommer found that women responded to ostracism by increasing their efforts on a subsequent group task. Similarly, Williams, Cheung, and Choi observed that ostracized individuals were more likely than others to conform to the opinions of other people. Thus, these studies show that in response to social rejection, people seek to reconnect themselves with their social worlds. In addition, Gardner, Pickett, and Brewer found that individuals who experience social rejection are more likely to remember socially relevant information. Thus, _____ needs appear to guide the processing and retention of information that is consistent with one's motive.

*ostracize: 배척하다 **retention: 보유

① innovation　　　　　② leadership
③ self-actualization　　④ security
⑤ belongingness

10. Historical linguists study the languages spoken today, and from them make estimates about the ancestral languages from which they descended. Where possible, linguists also work from written records on languages in earlier times. For linguistics (as for genetics), we assume that present data give us the remnants of earlier communities. But the definition of "earlier community" is different in each case. For language, it is assumed that each language has one parent. In genetics a person has more and more ancestors as one goes to earlier generations, while a language has a single ancestor at each stage. The "tree model" of languages presents the range of languages descended from an ancestor, and indicates relationships with other languages descended from the same ancestor. Because of the single-ancestor characteristics of the linguistic "tree model," language gives more evidence on path of early human migration than does genetics, because it _____. [3점]

*remnant: 자취, 나머지

① allows for fewer possibilities
② has traces of historical relics
③ can be transformed by regions
④ is handed down as oral traditions
⑤ has an unchangeable original form

11. Trust is the key element for counselors who work with children. Without an adequate level of trust, the therapeutic relationship will be hindered. Sometimes, because of the importance of this issue, we need _____. In initial sessions, we might allow time for a young child to play freely. If the counselor begins by talking about the child's problems, the child may become stressed and refuse to speak. Instead, children need time to get ready, so counselors working with children need patience. Only when they are ready to open themselves up can children be invited to tell their story. When inviting the child, the counselor doesn't try to hurry the therapeutic process but allows the child opportunities to express themselves and to explore feelings and issues which may be troubling for them. The counselor doesn't question, but instead invites the child to share what they wish.

① to volunteer information on our own
② to show consistency in our behavior
③ to consider the kids as equal beings
④ to amuse kids with fun activities
⑤ to progress very slowly at first

12. Tourism is an important mediator in the development of fusion cuisine, because the mixing of different culinary traditions is often stimulated by people who travel to produce or consume food. This process of mobile food appreciation has been going on for centuries, as has been shown in the analysis of the development of the historical food trade that linked different countries. However, the development of fusion foods can _____. Tourists very often demand food which is "traditional" or "authentic," and yet many tourists are also averse to trying new and unfamiliar foods. One impulse for the development of fusion cuisine in Asia has been the desire to produce food which is more familiar and therefore appetizing to foreign visitors. The flip side is that "rootless" cuisine may also come to be seen as "inauthentic" by visitors searching for unique and original culinary experiences. [3점]

① accelerate the development of overseas tourism
② contribute to the development of food culture
③ satisfy locals' tastes more than tourists'
④ provide a more nutritionally-balanced diet
⑤ hinder the development of native-cuisine experiences

13. 다음 글에서 전체 흐름과 관계 <u>없는</u> 문장은? [3점]

Within the arena of household consumption, research predominantly focuses on direct *rebound effects* among consumers particularly for energy appliances in the home and fuel efficiency in vehicles. ① For example, often large energy savings are predicted when consumers replace traditional incandescent light bulbs with more efficient compact fluorescent bulbs. ② However, these savings rarely reach their predicted targets as research indicates that many consumers, recognizing that the light costs less to operate, appear less thorough about switching it off, resulting in more hours of use, i.e. higher energy consumption. ③ In the same way, the efficiency of cars has improved greatly because the tendency of consumers to buy smaller cars has enhanced the improvement in fuel efficiency. ④ Similarly, studies have indicated that energy savings from efficiency improvements, for example, a more efficient space heating unit or increased levels of insulation, are often then spent on increased heating standards. ⑤ Here, the consumer may gain by operating a warmer home for the same or lower cost than they had previously.

*incandescent light bulb: 백열전구 **fluorescent bulb: 형광등

[14~15] 주어진 글 다음에 이어질 글의 순서로 가장 적절한 것을 고르시오.

14.

We apply a finite set of explanations in many different contexts without considering the subtleties of each situation. This is the "one-size-fits-all" approach to problem solving.

(A) This is moving in the wrong direction of the feedback loop, from knowledge to reality. It is starting with what we already believe and insisting that reality fit it. This is not the same as having core values, which can always be adapted.

(B) The problem comes when those values become so rigid that they no longer work well and are applied arbitrarily without careful consideration. This happens when we don't ask ourselves tough questions and relevant feedback is ignored.

(C) People who take this approach have blind spots, areas where they miss important things about a situation. Not only do their solutions often fail, they may not even recognize those failures, preventing them from learning. Instead, they tend to force the data to fit their preconceived ideas.

① (A) – (C) – (B) ② (B) – (A) – (C)
③ (B) – (C) – (A) ④ (C) – (A) – (B)
⑤ (C) – (B) – (A)

15.

A *lichen* is an organism consisting of a fungus and an alga living together, usually in an interdependent relationship. These hardy species are good biological indicators of air pollution because they continually absorb air as a source of nourishment.

(A) For this reason, scientists discovered SO_2 pollution on Isle Royale, Michigan, in Lake Superior, an island where no car or tall factory chimney has ever existed. They used Evernia lichens to point the finger northwest toward coal-burning facilities in and around the Canadian city of Thunder Bay, Ontario.

(B) A highly polluted area around an industrial plant might have only gray-green crusty lichens or none at all. An area with moderate air pollution might support only orange crusty lichens.

(C) In contrast, areas with clean air can support larger varieties of lichens. Some lichen species are sensitive to specific air-polluting chemicals. Old man's beard and yellow Evernia lichens, for example, can sicken and die in the presence of excessive sulfur dioxide (SO_2), even if the pollutant originates far away. [3점]

*lichen: 이끼, 지의류 **alga: 조류(藻類), 말

① (A) – (C) – (B) ② (B) – (A) – (C)
③ (B) – (C) – (A) ④ (C) – (A) – (B)
⑤ (C) – (B) – (A)

[16~17] 글의 흐름으로 보아, 주어진 문장이 들어가기에 가장 적절한 곳을 고르시오.

16.

> The irony is that teammates *want* the opportunity to challenge each other.

The most effective and innovative teams have regular, intense debates — which has been fun for us to observe. (①) The ability to disagree, without causing offense, is essential to robust communication and problem-solving within teams. (②) Yet when we pose the question to groups of leaders about what's better — a team that's almost always harmonious or one that has conflicts and arguments — the vast majority vote for a team with no disharmony. (③) As long as discussions are respectful and everyone gets the chance to contribute equally, most people thrive on this kind of debate — finding it not only intellectually stimulating but important to getting to the route of problems and working out optimal solutions. (④) Teams feel more bonded and more effective when they regularly engage in challenging discussions, when members are encouraged to argue with one another's ideas and perspectives. (⑤) It's also true even if the debates get a little heated.

*robust: 왕성한 **optimal: 최적의

17.

> That is, all other things equal, a wire of small diameter is more resistant than one of larger diameter.

Electrical resistance (measured in ohms) refers to how easily an electrical current passes through some material. (①) Some substances, such as many metals, are low in resistance, so electrical currents pass easily through them. (②) In contrast, materials such as glass and rubber are high in resistance and thus are poor electrical conductors. (③) The actual resistance of any given material when it is placed in an electrical circuit depends upon its physical properties, e.g. diameter and length in the case of wire. (④) The resistance of an electric wire decreases as the diameter of the wire increases. (⑤) In addition, the resistance of any material increases as its length increases: a 2-foot length of wire is twice as resistant as a 1-foot length of the same wire. [3점]

18. 다음 글의 내용을 한 문장으로 요약하고자 한다. 빈칸 (A), (B)에 들어갈 말로 가장 적절한 것은? [3점]

People hate to lose something more than they like gaining something of equal value. Given this near-universal truth about the human psyche, it may not be surprising that many acts of dishonesty and cheating in the real world are born from fear of losing something we value. Pressure to avoid getting an "F" in a class leads many students to bring cheat sheets into exams more so than does the possibility of getting an "A." Pressure to avoid losing market share tempts those in business to break laws more often than does setting new sales records. Not owing the government additional money is a bigger motivator for cheating on taxes than is getting a bigger refund. Sure, in all these cases gains like the bigger sales figure or the bigger refund may motivate people to cheat, but the point is that they'll never be as motivating as avoiding a loss of equal amount.

*psyche: 마음, 정신

↓

> A greater ____(A)____ to face potential failure, compared with giving up a benefit of similar worth, may ____(B)____ wrongdoing.

	(A)		(B)
①	willingness	……	cause
②	willingness	……	prevent
③	urge	……	trigger
④	unwillingness	……	elicit
⑤	unwillingness	……	interrupt

[19~20] 다음 글을 읽고, 물음에 답하시오.

When we are reading, few of us wonder whether a text was written by hand or word-processed. But experts on writing do not agree: pens and keyboards bring into play very different (a) cognitive processes. Handwriting is a complex task which requires various skills — feeling the pen and paper, moving the writing implement, and directing movement by thought. Children take several years to master this precise (b) muscular exercise: you need to hold the scripting tool firmly while moving it in such a way as to leave a different mark for each letter. Operating a keyboard is not the same at all: all you have to do is press the right key. It is easy enough for children to learn very fast, but above all the movement is exactly (c) identical, whatever the letter. It's a big change. Typing is the result of a singular movement of the body, handwriting is not.

Furthermore, an electronic text does not leave the same mark as its handwritten counterpart. When you draft a text on the screen, you can change it as much as you like but there is no record of your editing. The software does keep track of the changes somewhere, but users cannot access them. With a pen and paper, however, it's all there. Words crossed out or corrected, bits scribbled in the margin and later additions are there for good, leaving a visual record of your work and its creative stages. Some handwriting advocates regret the disappearance of these (d) ornamental effects. It's not just a question of writing a letter: it also involves drawing, acquiring a sense of harmony and balance, with rounded forms. There is an element of dancing when we write, a melody in the message, which adds the (e) impersonal aspect to the text. After all, that's why emoticons were invented: to restore a little emotion to text messages.

19. 윗글의 제목으로 가장 적절한 것은?

① How Can We Preserve Handwriting?
② The Light and Dark Sides of Handwriting
③ Handwriting vs. Typing: Which Is Faster?
④ Why Is the Pen Mightier Than the Keyboard?
⑤ Pens Remember Details Better Than Keyboards

20. 밑줄 친 (a) ~ (e) 중에서 문맥상 낱말의 쓰임이 적절하지 <u>않은</u> 것은? [3점]

① (a)　　② (b)　　③ (c)　　④ (d)　　⑤ (e)

○ 답안지의 해당란에 성명과 수험번호를 쓰고, 또 수험번호와 답을 정확히 표시하시오.
○ 문항에 따라 배점이 다르니, 각 물음의 끝에 표시된 배점을 참고하시오. 3점 문항에만 점수가 표시되어 있습니다. 점수 표시가 없는 문항은 모두 2점씩입니다.

1. 다음 글의 목적으로 가장 적절한 것은?

Dear Mr. Nelson,

I am the activities director at the Patrick White Adventures in Art Camp. I am also a big fan of your Jacksonville Luminaria shop on Main Street and already own several of your beautifully designed luminarias. I know that many boys and girls in the area visit your shop frequently since holiday decorating is one of the hottest retro rages today. I am now planning our program for the next calendar year. I am wondering if you have an hour or so during the third week of November to share your luminary-making artistry with our young people. I could arrange your visit at a time that would be most convenient for you. Will you send an e-mail to johnlee@whiteadven.com or call to 555-1234 when you can? Thank you for considering the idea.

Sincerely,
John Lee

*luminaria: 루미나리아 ((장식용 등))

① 영화에 등장할 장식용 등 협찬을 문의하려고
② 청소년 대상 아트 캠프 프로그램을 홍보하려고
③ 청소년 대상 공예 강좌 일정에 대해 논의하려고
④ 청소년을 위한 장식용 등 만들기 강의를 요청하려고
⑤ 장식용 등 판매 상점의 판촉 광고 제작을 의뢰받으려고

2. 밑줄 친 are careful not to rock the boat가 다음 글에서 의미하는 바로 가장 적절한 것은? [3점]

Yale psychologist Irving Janis showed that just about every group develops an agreed-upon view of things — a consensus reality, the "PC" or politically correct view. Any evidence to the contrary is automatically rejected without consideration, often ridiculed, and may lead to exclusion of the person presenting the un-PC data. So group members are careful not to rock the boat. In his classic book, *Groupthink*, Janis explained how panels of experts made enormous mistakes. People on the panels, he said, worry about their personal relevance and effectiveness, and feel that if they deviate too far from the consensus, they will not be taken seriously. People compete for stature, and the ideas often just tag along. Groupthink causes groups to get locked into their course of action, unable to explore alternatives, because no one questions the established course. The more cohesive the group, the greater the urge of the group members to avoid creating any discord.

*stature: 위상, 지명도

① play a crucial role in encouraging dissent in the group
② try to resolve conflict among the members of the group
③ point out problems in the group's decision-making process
④ are reluctant to voice opinions against the group's thoughts
⑤ make efforts to protect group members from adverse information

3. 다음 글의 요지로 가장 적절한 것은?

Like every other human activity, sport is affected by how humans process information. Committing data to memory and then retrieving it at a later time is a complex process with many opportunities for interference. Distinctive portions of a competition (i.e. controversial decisions, exceptional technical performances, actions following stoppages in play, etc.) are often easily remembered by coaches and spectators alike, while non-critical events are more likely to be forgotten. This form of highlighting, when combined with emotions and personal bias of the coach, may cause a distorted perception of the game in total. Furthermore, our processing system has limitations that make it near impossible to view, assimilate and store all actions that take place within the playing area. These limitations result in the coach focusing attention on a specific area of play (usually what is considered to be the most critical area) with the peripheral action largely ignored.

*peripheral: 주변적인, 지엽적인

① 선수들에 대한 공정한 평가가 팀의 성적과 직결된다.
② 코치의 선수 평가는 평소의 훈련 태도에 의해 영향받는다.
③ 최고의 코치는 경기에서 아무리 사소한 부분도 놓치지 않는다.
④ 코치들은 경기의 모든 사항을 완전히 파악하고 기억할 수 없다.
⑤ 기술적 요소를 적절히 도입하는 것이 경기 진행에 도움이 된다.

4. 다음 글의 주제로 가장 적절한 것은?

In reading a poem, you develop meaning and interpret a story from words filled with both intentional and unintentional ambiguities; you extract such meaning by drawing upon the poem's content, context, and use of poetic devices. When facing complicated questions from a managerial (or any other business function's) stance, having this ability to balance unknowns and generate solutions from nuanced reasonings allows for more imaginative and effective solutions. Relying exclusively on the rigidity of scientific methods would be a flawed approach to nearly all complex issues. Poetry teaches you to wrestle with and simplify complexity. Every business encounters complex problems, and complex questions demand complex solutions. A regular poetry reader is more likely to arrive at such solutions because he or she can derive meaning from vague, dynamic arguments as done when reading poems.

① strict attitudes as a valuable component of business leadership
② simplified poetic approaches as ways to relieve mental distress
③ poetry reading as a tool for improving problem-solving skills in business
④ contrasts and comparisons between poetic thinking and business thinking
⑤ types of poetry that helps business people enhance their thinking abilities

5. 다음 표의 내용과 일치하지 <u>않는</u> 것은?

Trade in Sporting Goods by Type Between EU and Extra-EU Countries, 2014 and 2019

	2014 (million EUR)		2019 (million EUR)		Average annual rate of change(%), 2014-2019	
	Exports	Imports	Exports	Imports	Exports	Imports
Balls	71.5	311.9	71.1	316.4	−0.1	0.3
Boats	3,506.0	1,981.7	6,717.2	3,905.3	13.9	14.5
Gymnastic	900.1	1,770.0	1,332.8	2,441.6	8.2	6.6
Skis	536.4	192.6	647.9	239.7	3.9	4.5
Sporting shotguns	350.8	47.7	365.7	62.0	0.8	5.4
Sports footwear	832.0	2,003.1	1,606.1	3,445.2	14.1	11.5
Sportswear	231.6	714.5	363.0	1,005.9	9.4	7.1

The above table shows the monetary values of the exports, imports and average annual rate of change of sporting goods by type between the European Union (EU) and countries outside the EU (Extra-EU) in 2014 and 2019. ① The export value of Boats was the highest both in 2014 and in 2019, while the highest import value didn't follow the same trend because of the import value of sports footwear in 2014. ② The export value of Skis was less than one tenth of that of Boats in 2019. ③ In the import sector, four sporting goods segments recorded more than 1,000 million EUR in 2019. ④ Sports footwear indicated the largest average annual rate of change in exports from 2014 to 2019, while the rate of change of Sporting shotguns indicated Sporting shotguns increased the slightest in exports by 0.8 percent. ⑤ The average annual rate of change of Balls was the only one which decreased in imports.

6. Tiziano Vecellio에 관한 다음 글의 내용과 일치하지 <u>않는</u> 것은?

Tiziano Vecellio, otherwise known as Titian, was the greatest painter of Venice and the last Titan of the Italian Renaissance. His paintings represented the richness of color and the joy of living, and he sought to depict not only the glory of the human body but also an aura of spirituality. Vecellio was born to a family of poor peasants in the Venetian Alps in 1477. At the age of nine he was sent to Venice and began to study painting there for the first time. Vecellio did portraits of Emperors such as Charles V, Philip II of Spain, and Pope Paul III. In his late years, his productivity was undiminished in quantity and in creative ideas. The great master died of the plague in 1576. He was buried in the church of Santa Maria dei Frari, where two of his most famous works can still be seen.

*the Titan: 거장, 거물

① 인체의 아름다움과 영적인 기운을 묘사하려 했다.
② 베니스에서 처음으로 미술을 공부하기 시작했다.
③ 황제들과 교황의 초상화를 그렸다.
④ 말년에 그의 작품 생산성은 감소했다.
⑤ 그가 안치된 교회에서 여전히 그의 작품을 볼 수 있다.

7. 다음 글의 밑줄 친 부분 중, 어법상 틀린 것은? [3점]

Has your creativity ground to a stop? Instead of letting frustration ① <u>get</u> the better of you, try to sit back and take a few deep breaths. Did you know that drawing a deep breath ② <u>gives</u> your creativity a boost by taking in the negative ions in oxygen? The negatively ③ <u>charged</u> oxygen circulates throughout the brain, refreshing the neurons. Because these negative ions promote alpha waves of longer amplitude in the brain, which ④ <u>are</u> associated with creative thinking, suddenly your creativity receives a boost. So, next time your creative spirit feels burdened, spend two minutes taking deep breaths, breathing in and out every five seconds, and ⑤ <u>repeating</u> the cycle at least 12 times.

*boost: 활력 **amplitude: 진폭

8. 다음 글의 밑줄 친 부분 중, 문맥상 낱말의 쓰임이 적절하지 <u>않은</u> 것은? [3점]

Clearly, danced rituals did not seem like a ① <u>waste</u> of energy to prehistoric peoples. They took the time to fashion masks and costumes; they joyfully burned calories in the execution of the dance; they preferred to record these scenes over any other group activity. Thus anthropologist Victor Turner's attribution of danced ritual to an occasional, marginal, or liminal status seems especially ② <u>justified</u> in the prehistoric case — and more representative of the production-oriented mentality of our own industrial age than of prehistoric priorities. Surely these people knew hardship and were often ③ <u>threatened</u> by food shortages, disease, and wild animals. But ritual, of a danced and possibly ecstatic nature, was ④ <u>central</u> to their lives. Perhaps only because our own lives, so much easier in many ways, are also so ⑤ <u>constrained</u> by the modern imperative to work, we have to wonder *why*.

*liminal: 처음의, 발단의 **ecstatic: 황홀해 하는

[9~12] 다음 빈칸에 들어갈 말로 가장 적절한 것을 고르시오.

9. _____ is an integral part of all art, and sometimes, even where it seems the least likely, one finds a comprehensive communication between the artist and the audience very difficult. For example, not just in abstract painting, but in the most straightforward painting. Just take one of the best-known paintings, the *Mona Lisa*, painted by Leonardo da Vinci. No one mistakes that this painting is the portrait of a woman; that much we know. However, the intriguing smile in this painting is interpreted in so many different ways, in terms of what state of the mind this smile depicts. Therefore, an audience can never be sure exactly what the artist had in mind. This holds true on all levels, and thus, perfect communication cannot occur between most artists and their audiences through their art alone.

*intriguing: 호기심을 자아내는

① Coherence
② Mystery
③ Elaboration
④ Universality
⑤ Subjectivity

10. Appearance creates the first impression customers have of food, and first impressions are important. No matter how attractive the taste, an unpleasant appearance is hard to ignore. As humans, we do "eat with our eyes" because our sense of sight is more highly developed than the other senses. This is not the case with many animals. Dogs, for example, depend mainly on smell to explore their world. Humans, however, have a greatly advanced sense of sight. So messages received from other senses are often ignored if _____. Yellow candy is expected to be lemon-flavored, and if it is grape-flavored, many people cannot accurately identify the flavor. A strawberry ice cream tinted with red food coloring seems to have a stronger strawberry flavor than one that has no added food coloring, even when there is no real difference. [3점]

① the other senses aren't exceptionally developed
② they correspond with what we already know
③ the appearance is overwhelmingly positive
④ they have proven to be unreliable
⑤ they conflict with what is seen

11. The primary perceptual faculty in human beings, as in all primates, is *vision*. Much of the improved understanding of perceptual processes has therefore derived from the neurobiology of visual perception. As Semir Zeki, a principal researcher in the field, has observed, the study of vision is a "profoundly philosophical enterprise," for it constitutes an inquiry into "how the brain acquires knowledge of the external world, which is no simple matter." Until the 1970s, Zeki points out, neurological models of perception were heavily influenced by the mistaken philosophic view, probably traceable to Kant, that "sensing" reality and "understanding" (grasping) it are fundamentally disparate phenomena. Now, however, through sophisticated techniques for studying both normal subjects and patients who have suffered various impairments of brain function, we know that normal perception entails simultaneous "seeing" and "understanding." Specialized areas of the brain not only detect visible attributes such as color, form, and motion but also "identify" and integrate them into a unified, coherent "picture." The integration of visual information that results _____ _____. [3점]

*disparate: 이질적인

① constitutes both sensory perception and recognition of the visual world
② plays an important role to improve accuracy of auditory perception
③ can become cluttered and disorienting — offering no meaningful insight
④ is useful for connecting key ideas in a text and explaining complex topics
⑤ has multiple complex meanings depending on the viewer's knowledge base

12. As with present-day hunter-gatherers, ancient nomadic societies were severely limited to only those objects that they could take with them; thus, they tended to develop simple portable technologies for hunting, gathering, cooking, transportation, and defense. Perhaps surprisingly, life does not seem to have been especially hard for hunter-gatherers. The secrets of their success seem to have been populations that did not exceed the food supply, simple and limited material needs, and the ability to move to another area when the local food supply ran out. Nomadic hunter-gatherer societies have persisted into the twentieth century in such diverse environments as the African desert, the tropical rain forest, and the Arctic tundra. Remoteness might be the key to _____ _____. For the rest of us, our lives now deeply depend on widespread and complex technological systems. [3점]

① developing new technologies for poverty reduction
② strengthening regional cooperation in the area of data collection
③ avoiding conversion to more technologically intensive ways of life
④ adapting to drastic change of external conditions such as natural disasters
⑤ creating an information-based society where technology plays a vital role

13. 다음 글에서 전체 흐름과 관계 <u>없는</u> 문장은?

Without a doubt, abstracting is challenging for people in every discipline. ① Many famous novelists — Mark Twain and Ernest Hemingway, for instance — have written to their editors that they regretted the extreme length of their manuscripts; if they had had more time, the work would have been significantly shorter. ② Winston Churchill is supposed to have said that he could talk for a day with five minutes' notice but needed a day to prepare if he had only five minutes in which to speak. ③ The poet Edwin Arlington Robinson transitioned from writing short verse to lengthy works as he got older, remarking, "I am over sixty now, and short poems are much too difficult." ④ Philosopher Immanuel Kant used to stare out his window at a stone tower to think before he wrote; when trees grew up threatening to block his view, he chopped them down. ⑤ The essence of writing, these individuals claim, is not putting words on the page but learning to recognize and eliminate the unnecessary ones.

[14~15] 주어진 글 다음에 이어질 글의 순서로 가장 적절한 것을 고르시오.

14.

> The importance of the retail sector to the global economy is particularly evident during times of crisis. World leaders, faced with a severe economic downturn, look to consumers for help.

(A) Meanwhile, governments pick up their share through corporate, land, income, and consumption taxes. Consumers are at the heart of all this economic activity.

(B) After 9/11, U.S. President Bush asked Americans to carry on with their lives, not to lose confidence, and to continue spending. Leaders made similar requests in response to the recent global recession, because when consumers stop buying, the economy grinds to a halt.

(C) In contrast, when consumers are confident and spending freely, money flows through retail stores, up the supply chain, and all the way back to the manufacturers, farmers, and other producers, making stops along the way with lawyers, bankers, and other service firms.

*recession: 경기 불황 **grind to a halt: 서서히 멈추다

① (A) – (C) – (B)　　② (B) – (A) – (C)
③ (B) – (C) – (A)　　④ (C) – (A) – (B)
⑤ (C) – (B) – (A)

15.

> When discussing medicinal herbs, the news media often quote skeptical doctors who warn that if you fool around with herbs, you're playing with fire. With herbs, they say, it's impossible to guarantee good dose control.

(A) Drugs offer a precise amount of chemicals, usually measured in milligrams. With herbs, potency can vary with the health of the individual plant, how much time the product spent in storage, and other factors. But warnings about dose control obscure a larger truth.

(B) Dose control means knowing exactly how much of the active ingredient — the chemical that exerts the healing effect — you're getting per dose. To a certain extent, those skeptics are right.

(C) When used as recommended by reputable herbalists, medicinal herbs are almost always less potent than their pharmaceutical counterparts. So with most herbal remedies, the risk of overdose is tiny. In fact, it's virtually nonexistent, according to the latest research. [3점]

*potency: 약효 **herbalist: 한의사, 약초의(醫)

① (A) – (C) – (B)　　② (B) – (A) – (C)
③ (B) – (C) – (A)　　④ (C) – (A) – (B)
⑤ (C) – (B) – (A)

[16~17] 글의 흐름으로 보아, 주어진 문장이 들어가기에 가장 적절한 곳을 고르시오.

16.

> But business is also utilitarian in that pursuing self-interest is thought to maximize the total good, and playing by the established rules of the competitive game is seen as advancing the good of society.

Both self-interest and utility play important roles in organizational decisions, and business people blend these two theories. (①) To the extent that each business pursues its own interests and each business person tries to maximize personal success, business is egotistical. (②) The economist Adam Smith held such a view. (③) He argued that if business is left to pursue its self-interest, the good of society will be served. (④) Indeed, Smith believed that only through egotistical pursuits could the greatest economic good be produced. (⑤) The essence of Smith's position can be seen in *The Wealth of Nations*, in which Smith underscores the interplay between self-interest and the social good. [3점]

17.

> This process takes emphasis off the need to reduce consumption, the increase in which is a major factor in the waste increase in the first place.

The potential for recycling to contribute to sustainable communities has been questioned. Critics point out that the prevailing recycling model is dependent on a market for recyclable materials. (①) In order to be profitable, new products must be manufactured using the recycled material and consumed. (②) Even with increases in recycling rates, without reductions in consumption, the amount of waste sent to landfills and incinerators and the amount of raw materials consumed will continue to increase. (③) The existence of recycling programs is sometimes represented as a defense against the need to reduce consumption. (④) For example, the bottled water industry, which has been criticized on multiple environmental grounds, notes that it encourages the recycling of plastic bottles. (⑤) The majority of recycled plastic beverage bottles, however, are manufactured into other products, and new plastic bottles are made from virgin materials. [3점]

*incinerator: 소각로

18. 다음 글의 내용을 한 문장으로 요약하고자 한다. 빈칸 (A), (B)에 들어갈 말로 가장 적절한 것은?

Although commonsense knowledge may have merit, it also has drawbacks, not the least of which is that it often contradicts itself. For example, we hear that people who are similar will like one another ("Birds of a feather flock together") but also that persons who are dissimilar will like each other ("Opposites attract"). We are told that groups are wiser and smarter than individuals ("Two heads are better than one") but also that group work inevitably produces poor results ("Too many cooks spoil the broth"). Each of these contradictory statements may hold true under particular conditions, but without a clear statement of when they apply and when they do not, aphorisms provide little insight into relations among people. They provide even less guidance in situations where we must make decisions. For example, when facing a choice that entails risk, which guideline should we use — "Nothing ventured, nothing gained" or "Better safe than sorry"?

*aphorism: 경구(警句), 격언

↓

> As aphorisms possess ＿＿＿(A)＿＿＿ meanings, using them to find direction in a ＿＿(B)＿＿ situation may prove difficult.

	(A)		(B)
①	conflicting	……	specific
②	conflicting	……	real-life
③	practical	……	specific
④	practical	……	real-life
⑤	abstract	……	normal

[19~20] 다음 글을 읽고, 물음에 답하시오.

Man lives not, like the beasts of the field, in a world of merely (a) physical things but in a world of signs and symbols. A stone is not merely hard, a thing into which one bumps; but it is a (b) monument of a deceased ancestor. And all this which marks the difference between beasts and humans is because man remembers, preserving and recording his experiences.

The revivals of memory are, however, rarely literal. We naturally remember what interests us because it interests us. The past is recalled not because of itself but because of what it adds to the present. Thus the primary life of memory is (c) emotional rather than practical. Savage man recalled yesterday's struggle with an animal not in order to study in a scientific way the qualities of the animal or for the sake of calculating how better to fight tomorrow, but to escape from the dullness of today by (d) forgetting the event of yesterday. The memory has all the excitement of the combat without its danger and anxiety. To revive it and revel in it is to (e) enhance the present moment with a new meaning, a meaning different from that which actually belongs either to it or to the past. Memory is vicarious experience in which there are all the emotional values of actual experience without its strains and troubles. The triumph of battle is even more vividly felt in the memorial war dance than at the moment of victory. At the time of practical experience man exists from moment to moment, preoccupied with the task of the moment. As he re-surveys all the moments in thought, a drama emerges with a beginning, a middle and a movement toward the climax of achievement or defeat.

*vicarious: 대리의, 간접적인

19. 윗글의 제목으로 가장 적절한 것은?

① Memory Distortion and Its Avoidance
② Why Does Man Revive Past Experience?
③ New Experiences Can Strengthen Old Memories
④ How to Use Signs and Symbols to Improve Memory
⑤ The Influence of Emotion on Learning and Memory

20. 밑줄 친 (a) ~ (e) 중에서 문맥상 낱말의 쓰임이 적절하지 않은 것은? [3점]

① (a)　　② (b)　　③ (c)　　④ (d)　　⑤ (e)

○ 답안지의 해당란에 성명과 수험번호를 쓰고, 또 수험번호와 답을 정확히 표시하시오.

○ 문항에 따라 배점이 다르니, 각 물음의 끝에 표시된 배점을 참고하시오. 3점 문항에만 점수가 표시되어 있습니다. 점수 표시가 없는 문항은 모두 2점씩입니다.

---

1. 다음 글에 드러난 'I'의 심경 변화로 가장 적절한 것은?

In the late afternoon, I left my farmhouse and came into the woods. I vividly remembered my childhood running around excitedly to find fireflies. When the sun went down, a lot of fireflies' flashes greeted me. The green light rose several inches, then swooped down and across the forest. I was gazing at the scene in rapture. I felt as if I had gone back to my childhood. Time had gone so fast, and in the sky above me night's darkness was complete. As I stood to leave the wonderful forest, however, I realized I had to walk in the complete darkness to the farmhouse. Copperheads, the "hooked-tooth twister," concerned me most. These snakes were particularly active on muggy summer nights. I moved slowly, seeing the copperhead's leafy camouflage everywhere in the failing light. My body was tense as I walked through the misty air on my way.

① delighted → lonely
② bored → nervous
③ calm → annoyed
④ relieved → gloomy
⑤ pleased → scared

2. 다음 글에서 필자가 주장하는 바로 가장 적절한 것은?

One reason our children may ignore our instructions is that if we have not been consistent about *following through* on instructions and rules in the past, our children will not assume that we really mean it this time. So they will just wait and see what happens, which buys them more time to do what they feel like doing. The unpredictability of parents' responses leaves a lot of room for subtle testing and outright misbehavior. Even children who are usually cooperative will test in situations where they sense, from their parents' initial reaction, that parents are uncomfortable about *following through*. They may try to "bend the rules" without quite breaking them. This often happens in public, where children can see that the parents' embarrassment is keeping them from *following through*. Sometimes what we think of as being flexible about rules looks to the child as if we're giving in. The more consistently we *follow through*, the more our children will listen to us, take our instructions seriously, and cooperate.

① 자녀에게 지시를 할 때는 상황에 따라 융통성 있게 하라.
② 자녀가 감당할 수 있는 정도로 규칙을 정해 지키게 하라.
③ 자녀에게 지시나 규칙을 적용할 때는 일관성 있게 행하라.
④ 자녀와 좋은 관계를 유지하려면 지시하려는 태도를 버려라.
⑤ 자녀에게 지시할 때는 엄격함과 사랑이 균형을 이루도록 하라.

3. 다음 글에서 밑줄 친 track the complexity of the dance가 의미하는 바로 가장 적절한 것은? [3점]

The advantages of personal contact include experiences we can't consciously register. In a shared space, people plug into what the psychologist Daniel Goleman has called "neural WiFi," "a feedback loop that crosses the skin-and-skull barrier between bodies." When scientists videotape conversations and slow them down to watch frame by frame, they detect synchronies between nonverbal elements

—a shared rhythm very much like the beat that guides an improvisation in jazz. The movements themselves are coordinated to within a fraction of a second—our brains are taking in data on the order of milli- or microseconds. But conscious processing of information happens in the comparatively sluggish scale of seconds. When two people talk to each other, writes Goleman, "our own thoughts can't possibly track the complexity of the dance."

*synchrony: 동시성 **improvisation: 즉흥 연주 ***sluggish: 느린

① repeat personal contact over and over
② affect both verbal and nonverbal factors
③ grasp what the other party intends to say
④ detect synchronies between verbal elements
⑤ catch up with nonverbal clues in conversations

4. 다음 글의 주제로 가장 적절한 것은?

In essence, when a retailer decides to build a larger store, it bets that it can use that extra square footage and expanded inventory to attract the higher volume of customers it needs to generate an acceptable return on investment. In contrast, as retail square footage decreases, so too does the number of products a retailer can carry. Moreover, smaller stores tend to have smaller trade areas and fewer customers. As a result, they have to ensure that the products they carry are well matched to the customers they attract. With limited space, it is difficult to simultaneously appeal to multiple market segments. Therefore, the location decision is especially important and requires the small retailer to emphasize geographic segmentation — that is, as stores get smaller, they generally need to be located closer to the customer segments they target. On the other hand, while larger format stores can carry a greater variety and broader selection of products that appeal to distinct customer segments, they have to attract enough customers from each segment to justify the added cost of that expanded space.

*segmentation: 세분화

① a variety of interrelated tasks for managing customer acquisition
② changes in customer acquisition tactics depending on the store size
③ product differentiation approach to attracting customers into a store
④ necessity of the analysis of existing markets for customer acquisition
⑤ implementation of a segmentation strategy on the basis of the store size

5. 다음 글의 제목으로 가장 적절한 것은?

The bristlecone pine, which has a documented maximum lifespan of over 5,000 years, is one of the longest-lived organisms in the world. But such longevities are attained only by trees that live in the harsh, windswept peaks of the White Mountains in California. Individuals of the same species that live in more protected environments have significantly shorter lives, on the order of about 1,000 years. This lifespan is still extraordinarily long by any standard, but the 80% reduction in longevity is striking. A harsh environment is ideal for extended longevity because it results in fewer parasites and smaller amounts of flammable underbrush, which leads to accidental death. The shortness of the growing season may also play a role, although much evidence suggests that these long-lived trees have an apparently unlimited, or at least a very large, capacity for continuous cell division.

*cell division: 세포 분열

① Why Modern Trees Are Short-Lived
② Longer Lives in a Harsh Environment
③ How to Tell the Age of a Bristlecone Pine
④ Trees Hold the Secret to Human Immortality
⑤ Establish a Protected Place for a Special Tree

6. ABC Battery-powered Car for Kids에 관한 다음 안내문의 내용과 일치하지 <u>않는</u> 것은?

ABC Battery-powered Car for Kids

Your kids can drive their own car!
Children's electric cars are miniature versions of real cars, with motors that run on rechargeable batteries.

Product information
- With real horn and engine sounds, this glossy vehicle gives the most authentic feel of a car.
- It comes with a 12v battery-powered motor that is suitable for riding indoors as well as outdoors but only on flat surfaces.
- Running time 1-2 hours
- Comes with LED lights and MP3 input
- Suitable for kids aged 3-6 years

Safety Information
- Appropriate protective equipment such as a safety helmet and knee and elbow pads should be worn at all times.
- Children should be supervised by an adult at all times when using the vehicle.

---

① 모터는 재충전되는 배터리로 작동한다.
② 실제 차량처럼 경적이 있고 엔진 소리가 난다.
③ 평평하지 않은 실외에서도 탈 수 있다.
④ 이용 가능한 최소 연령은 3세이다.
⑤ 보호 장구를 반드시 착용하고 타야 한다.

7. 다음 글의 밑줄 친 부분 중, 어법상 <u>틀린</u> 것은? [3점]

Although aquaculture occurs in a controlled environment, cases of escapes, contamination, and spread of disease have been documented, all of ① which may harm the natural ecosystem in the surrounding area. For example, studies in Chile have shown that escaped salmonids can colonize their new, nonnative environment, resulting in resource competition and potentially ② altering local ecosystem processes. Shrimp production in Asia and other parts of the world ③ has resulted in the deforestation of mangroves and wetlands in order to create space for shrimp ponds. The cultivation of carnivorous fish depends on the extraction of wild fin-fish that are converted to meal for fish food. In some parts of the world, this has meant depleted stocks for local fishermen, who still depend on these species for a supplement to their diet or for income. Experts have recently recommended that native herbivorous or filter feeders ④ are farmed, rather than nonnative carnivorous species, in order to avoid some of these potential problems. Another suggested solution is to farm exclusively in terrestrial, man-made tanks ⑤ where all stages of production could be managed, including the disposal of waste.

*salmonid: 연어과 어류
**mangrove: 맹그로브((강가나 늪지에서 뿌리가 지면 밖으로 나오게 자라는 열대 나무))
***filter feeder: 여과 섭식(攝食) 동물((물속의 유기물 · 미생물을 여과 섭취하는 동물))

8. 다음 글의 밑줄 친 부분 중, 문맥상 낱말의 쓰임이 적절하지 <u>않은</u> 것은? [3점]

As the sun rises in the morning, sunlight warms the ground, and the ground warms the air in contact with it by conduction. However, air is such a ① <u>poor</u> heat conductor that this process only takes place within a few centimeters of the ground. As the sun rises higher in the sky, the air in contact with the ground becomes even warmer, and there exists a thermal boundary ② <u>separating</u> the hot surface air from the slightly cooler air above. Given their random motion, some air molecules will ③ <u>establish</u> this boundary: The "hot" molecules below bring greater kinetic energy to the cooler air; the "cool" molecules above bring a deficit of energy to the hot surface air. However, on a windless day, this form of heat exchange is slow, and a substantial temperature ④ <u>difference</u> usually exists just above the ground. This explains why runners on a clear, windless, summer afternoon may ⑤ <u>experience</u> air temperatures of over 50°C (122°F) at their feet and only 32°C (90°F) at their waist.

*thermal: 열의 **kinetic: 운동의

[9~12] 다음 빈칸에 들어갈 말로 가장 적절한 것을 고르시오.

9. Investment clubs are small groups of people who pool their money and make joint decisions about investments in the stock market. Which clubs produce high returns, and which produce low ones? It turns out that the worst-performing clubs are primarily social. Their members know each other, eat together, and are connected by bonds of affection. By contrast, the best-performing clubs offer limited social connections and are focused on increasing returns. Dissent is far more frequent in the high-performing clubs. The low performers usually have unanimous votes, with little open debate. The votes in low-performing groups are cast to build social connections rather than to ensure high economic returns. In short, _____ produces significantly lower earnings. [3점]

① greed
② pride
③ impatience
④ overconfidence
⑤ conformity

10. Considering the volume of information that people in our contemporary society must keep track of, a certain amount of notetaking and storing of information in books is unavoidable. But the tendency away from recalling is growing beyond all sensible proportions. One can easily and best observe in oneself that writing things down _____, but some everyday examples may help to illustrate the point. One such example occurs in stores. Today a salesclerk will rarely do a simple addition of two or three items in his or her head, but instead will enter the numbers into a machine. Our schools provide another example. Teachers can observe that the students who diligently record every word of the lecture often do not perform as well at recall as those who trusted their capacity to understand and, hence, can produce at least the essentials. [3점]

① organizes one's tasks and priorities
② avoids temporary failures of memory
③ enhances one's access to information
④ diminishes one's power of remembering
⑤ makes an impression of being thorough

11. Studies have shown that as anger increases, cognitive processing speed goes down, fine motor coordination and sensitivity to pain decrease, and muscle strength often increases. So for some athletes doing some tasks, anger can be beneficial. For example, the defensive lineman who must make his way past a blocker to make a tackle might benefit from having some level of anger. For other tasks, anger would be a hindrance. The quarterback who needs to read the defense before deciding which receiver to throw to would likely perform better if he were not angry. In fact, some research supports this thesis. Players at football positions that require a lot of decision making tend to demonstrate _____.

[3점]

① a preference for logical, rational tasks
② higher levels of anger than their teammates
③ a greater tolerance for pain than other athletes
④ an attitude of superiority over those around them
⑤ lower levels of anger than players at positions that do not

12. In seeking advice, a client acknowledges an inability to deal with a problem. For certain individuals, engaging an advisor therefore represents a loss of status or prestige, because they fear that other persons will judge them less competent or knowledgeable than was first assumed. Experienced managers often resist suggestions that they hire management consultants for this reason. "What can a consultant tell me that I don't already know?" is their common response. Developing-country governments are also sometimes reluctant to acknowledge publicly their reliance on foreign consultants since to do so might diminish the government's status in the eyes of the local population. As a result, a skilled advisor _____ for the actions and decisions of a client. Inexperienced consultants sometimes cannot resist showing off their knowledge and influence, and they occasionally lose their clients as a result. One American advisor who was working on a reform of the tax system in a West African country told many local officials and business executives that he was responsible for "determining the country's new tax policy." When reports of these conversations reached the minister of finance, he fired the American advisor. [3점]

① tends to take an objective and neutral stance
② is willing to express politely whatever he judges
③ knows how to get along with locals to gain their favor
④ emphasizes the positive aspects rather than the negative ones
⑤ tries to maintain a low profile and avoids taking credit publicly

13. 다음 글에서 전체 흐름과 관계 <u>없는</u> 문장은?

Charity began with a focus on giving to the poor. Then, in the 15th century, it expanded to address the environment in which the poor lived. ① In the 19th century, with the influence of business leaders and ideals, the focus was on helping the poor help themselves. ② This progression of ideas and methods in charity work led to one conclusion: Being kind means more than simply showing kindness. ③ For example, a social service organization may reject an unemployed man's request for financial aid and suggest training instead. ④ Organizations rely on training as a way to demonstrate how much they value their employees, which is a benefit to both the company and the employee. ⑤ While this gesture may seem cruel to a depressed man, the counter-argument is that the economic right of the man and his long-term sustainability are more valuable than a one-time aid.

[14~15] 주어진 글 다음에 이어질 글의 순서로 가장 적절한 것을 고르시오.

14.

Archaeology has numerous applications.

(A) Excavations such as that done at the African Burial Ground in New York City give us insight into the living conditions of groups not well represented in the written record. Such knowledge is frequently fundamental to cultural identity. Beyond this, archaeology has sometimes produced technical applications relevant to the current world.

(B) For example, in Israel's Negev Desert, in Peru, and in other locations, archaeological study of ancient peoples has yielded information about irrigation design and raised-field systems that allowed modern people to make more effective use of the environment and raise agricultural yields.

(C) Establishing the archaeological record has often enabled native peoples to regain access to land and resources that historically belonged to them. Work in archaeology is often basic to understanding the history of groups that left little record.

*excavation: 발굴

① (A) – (C) – (B)　　② (B) – (A) – (C)
③ (B) – (C) – (A)　　④ (C) – (A) – (B)
⑤ (C) – (B) – (A)

15.

In addition to efforts to develop natural and more sustainable adhesive materials for commercial use, recent years have seen the emergence of a wide variety of "green adhesives."

(A) Low-temperature hot melt glues, for example, require less energy to melt and apply, and new cardboard and foil-based packaging has also been developed to reduce the landfill waste from plastic tube applicators.

(B) These have attempted to place limits on the amount of volatile organic compounds contained in adhesive products, as these compounds are thought to release hazardous air pollutants posing both health and environmental risks. Other products are designed to save energy and reduce waste.

(C) Efforts to produce and market these have been associated not only with the use of more sustainable raw materials but also with minimizing the environmental impacts of adhesives, particularly with regard to reducing harmful compounds and solvents contained in the adhesives. A number of governments have introduced regulations on the chemical emissions produced when using adhesives. [3점]

*adhesive: 접착성의; 접착제 **volatile: 휘발성의 ***solvent: 용제

① (A) – (C) – (B)　　② (B) – (A) – (C)
③ (B) – (C) – (A)　　④ (C) – (A) – (B)
⑤ (C) – (B) – (A)

[16~17] 글의 흐름으로 보아, 주어진 문장이 들어가기에 가장 적절한 곳을 고르시오.

16.

> As a result, green light is reflected, and this makes the forest seem brighter to human visitors than it does to plants, because plants cannot "see" this colour.

Most of the forest is dark, because only 3 per cent of the sun's light penetrates the canopy. (①) For the plants under the trees this makes it pitch-black. (②) You might not think so when you walk through the forest, but this has to do with the green shade you find there. (③) Trees use the chlorophyll in the leaves to convert light, water and carbon dioxide into sugar. (④) Chlorophyll, however, has a "green gap", which means it can't make use of this wavelength of light. (⑤) As 97 per cent of all the other wavelengths of light have already been absorbed and processed in the canopy, from where the green plants on the forest floor are standing, things literally look gloomy. [3점]

*canopy: 숲의 우거진 윗부분 **chlorophyll: 엽록소

17.

> However, it may be so familiar to so many people that they have become accustomed to its disadvantages and may be able to use it very effectively, despite the disadvantages and inconvenience.

The idea that innovation is linked with meeting the needs of social groups means that the problems innovative people seek to solve are at least partly socially determined. (①) Where there is no social awareness that a problem exists, there may be no drive to produce solutions and thus no innovation. (②) A simple example is the area of the design of everyday objects — tools, for example. (③) A tool may be awkward to use and inefficient, or possibly even dangerous — a hammer is a good example.

(④) The people may even be incapable of imagining that a hammer could be different. (⑤) In this case, there is no social pressure to introduce effective novelty and, in a sense, no problem, no matter how bad the design may be, because society has decided there is no problem.

18. 다음 글의 내용을 한 문장으로 요약하고자 한다. 빈칸 (A)와 (B)에 들어갈 말로 가장 적절한 것은?

Much prosocial behavior is stimulated by others, such as when someone acts more properly because other people are watching. Dogs will stay off the furniture and out of the trash when their owners are present, but they casually break those rules when alone. Humans may have more of a conscience, but they also still respond to the presence or absence of others. Public circumstances generally promote prosocial behavior. Participants in a study by Kay L. Satow sat alone in a room and followed tape-recorded instructions. Half believed that they were being observed via a one-way mirror (public condition), whereas others believed that no one was watching (private condition). At the end of the study, the tape-recorded instructions invited the participant to make a donation by leaving some change in the jar on the table. The results showed that donations were seven times higher in the public condition than in the private condition. Apparently, one important reason for generous helping is to make (or sustain) a good impression on the people who are watching.

*prosocial: 친사회적인

↓

> In the situation where they are _____(A)_____, people tend to behave more _____(B)_____ than they do in the condition where they are not.

	(A)		(B)
①	isolated	……	impulsively
②	isolated	……	generously
③	perplexed	……	slowly
④	watched	……	impulsively
⑤	watched	……	generously

[19~20] 다음 글을 읽고, 물음에 답하시오.

As Pat Darcy says, our brains have evolved to make us happy when we engage in the arts. The exercise of artistic skills predates even the origin of our species. That the exercise of elastic thinking skills such as idea generation, pattern recognition, divergent thinking, and imagination is inherently rewarding is the reason people have always put energy into the arts, despite the (a) lack of material reward (for most). In fact, material recompense can even get in the way of the (b) pleasure we feel in such activities. Consider, for example, how the great Russian writer Fyodor Dostoyevsky responded when a Russian publisher paid him a fairly large advance to write a novel. Note that he had not been given strict guidelines regarding what to write; he had merely been asked to write something engaging in exchange for money. Despite that, in a letter to a friend, Dostoyevsky wrote, "I believe you have never written to order, by the yard, and have never experienced that hellish torture." The hellish torture he referred to wasn't just the great novelist being a drama queen; the prospect of being paid for his work gave Dostoyevsky writer's (c) block.

Dostoyevsky's was not an isolated case. Many recent studies in social psychology suggest that monetizing creative output can (d) disrupt the processes that lead to innovation, saying that offering an extrinsic reward for an intrinsically enjoyable behavior can be counterproductive. That (e) confirms the ideas of traditional psychology, which is full of papers investigating the importance of reward in encouraging or even controlling a person's behavior. Difficulty in original thinking arises, says psychologist Teresa Amabile, "when you try for the wrong reasons."

19. 윗글의 제목으로 가장 적절한 것은?

① Happiness as a Reward for Artistic Work
② Money Rewards Enhance a Writer's Inspiration
③ Putting Rewards in Art: Path Toward Innovation
④ What Is an Effective Way to Increase Artistic Activities?
⑤ Extrinsic Incentives Undermine Artistic Creation Motivation

20. 밑줄 친 (a) ~ (e) 중에서 문맥상 낱말의 쓰임이 적절하지 않은 것은? [3점]

① (a)　　② (b)　　③ (c)　　④ (d)　　⑤ (e)

○ 답안지의 해당란에 성명과 수험번호를 쓰고, 또 수험번호와 답을 정확히 표시하시오.

○ 문항에 따라 배점이 다르니, 각 물음의 끝에 표시된 배점을 참고하시오. 3점 문항에만 점수가 표시되어 있습니다. 점수 표시가 없는 문항은 모두 2점씩입니다.

---

1. 다음 글의 목적으로 가장 적절한 것은?

Dear Coordinator:

My mother, Emma Miller, is presently a patient at Beacon General Hospital. She is recovering from a heart condition, and will be released shortly. Her primary caregiver is my father. Both are in their eighties. For a period of time while she is convalescing, my father will need some in-home care to relieve him for periods of time while he runs errands and does the shopping. I understand that the Office for the Aging administers a program that sends home aides to the elderly for exactly this sort of situation. We would like to arrange for an aide to be with my mother two or three times a week for a period of two hours at a time. Please contact my father, Ron Miller, directly at the number listed to arrange dates and times.

Sincerely,
Laura Hall

*convalesce: 건강을 회복하다

① 노인을 위한 재활 프로그램을 안내하려고
② 입원 환자의 퇴원 수속에 관해 문의하려고
③ 노인을 위한 재택 돌봄 서비스를 신청하려고
④ 저소득층 노인 가구의 가사 지원을 건의하려고
⑤ 돌봄 서비스 담당자에게 만나줄 것을 요청하려고

2. 다음 글에서 필자가 주장하는 바로 가장 적절한 것은?

While it seems that the Court reflecting the will of the people takes us forward as a nation, we get into a dangerous situation if we rely on changing times as justification for making legal decisions. The job of keeping up with changing times should largely be up to the legislature and the administration — regularly elected representatives of the people. They should be in charge of enacting or changing policies as the people demand it. With elections every two or four years and heavy participation with their constituents, those two branches of government are best suited to keep in touch with society. The Court, on the other hand, doesn't have that exposure to the public. If the Court gets in the business of trying to follow the people, it presents a dangerous future. The Court can start determining what is right and wrong, instead of what is legal and illegal. The Court should always try its best to stick to sound legal reasoning when making decisions.

① 법원은 사회 요구와 상관없이 타당한 법적 추론을 유지해야 한다.
② 법관은 새로운 가치를 법적 판단의 근거로 삼을 수 있어야 한다.
③ 의회와 정부는 좀 더 적극적으로 국민의 의사를 반영해야 한다.
④ 사회의 변화 속도에 맞추어 법률 개정이 적기에 이루어져야 한다.
⑤ 법원은 사회에 큰 영향을 줄 가능성이 있는 판결에 신중해야 한다.

3. 밑줄 친 we'll confine ourselves to the planet on which we live가 다음 글에서 의미하는 바로 가장 적절한 것은? [3점]

Many have claimed that, with billions of likely Earthlike planets, civilizations like ours must be common in our galaxy. However, the more we learn, the more unlikely that appears. SETI — the Search for Extraterrestrial Intelligence program — has been scanning the firmament for radio signals over more than forty years, and they have failed to intercept a single coherent message. More fundamentally, complex biological beings did not evolve to traverse the vastness of interstellar space; if interstellar travelers exist they'll be robots capable of "sleeping" over many thousands of years. Remember that stars are separated in distances measured by "light years" and, with light speed at 186,000 miles (300,000 km) in a single second, interstellar travel by living things remains a fantasy. Setting astrobiology ("the science without a subject") aside <u>we'll confine ourselves to the planet on which we live.</u>

*firmament: 창공, 하늘 **traverse: 통과하다, 횡단하다

① we need to focus on SETI rather than on the studies of the earth
② there is definite evidence for the existence of extraterrestrial life
③ the search for extraterrestrial intelligence is quite meaningless
④ we are not ready for contact with extraterrestrial intelligence
⑤ there is a high likelihood of contact with extraterrestrials

4. 다음 글의 제목으로 가장 적절한 것은?

In a battery of studies, Wharton's Cassie Mogilner assigned some subjects to help another person — by writing a note to a sick child, for example, or editing a student's essay. Another group of subjects were instructed to do something else; in one study they wasted time by counting the letter 'e's in Latin text, in a second study they did something for themselves and in a third they simply left the academic lab early. In each experiment the people who lent a hand to others felt as if they had more time than the people who did not. Research shows that giving to others can make you feel more "time affluent" and less time-constrained than if you choose to waste your extra time or spend it on yourself. Next time you need a break from a busy day, don't do something mindless like surf the web. Instead, pick an activity that helps someone else: bring your co-worker a cup of coffee or edit your daughter's school essay.

① Why Helping Others Is Easier Than Helping Yourself
② The Secret to Well-Being: Being More Charitable
③ Time Management: Ability to Realize Your Goals
④ Pressed for Time? Give Some of Yours Away
⑤ Genuine Ways to Help Others in Need

5. 다음 도표의 내용과 일치하지 않는 것은?

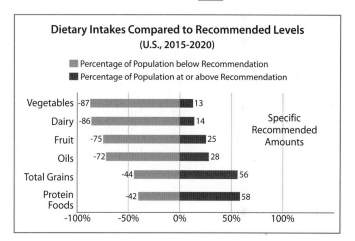

The above graph shows the percentages of the U.S. population's dietary intakes compared to the recommended levels of various food groups from 2015 to 2020. ① Vegetables and Dairy showed the highest and second highest rates for those who failed to meet the recommended level. ② Protein Foods showed the highest percentage of people who consumed more than the recommended intake level, at 58 percent. ③ More than half of the U.S. population exceeded Total Grains and Protein Foods recommendations. ④ For Oils, the percentage of people who ate less than the recommended intake level was lower than those who did not. ⑤ Three-quarters of the U.S. population ate less Fruit than the recommended amount, which was three times higher than the percentage of people who consumed the recommended amount or more.

6. William Butler Yeats에 관한 다음 글의 내용과 일치하지 않는 것은?

William Butler Yeats was born in Dublin, Ireland. His father was a lawyer and a well-known portrait painter. Yeats was educated by his father in London, where his father was studying art, but frequently returned to Ireland as well. His first volume of verse appeared in 1887, but in his earlier period, his dramatic production outweighed his poetry both in bulk and in import. He founded the *Irish Theatre* and served as its chief playwright. His plays usually treat Irish legends; they also reflect his fascination with mysticism and spiritualism. Although a convinced patriot, Yeats deplored the hatred of the Nationalist movement, and his poetry is full of moving protests against it. Yeats is one of the few writers whose greatest works were written after the award of the Nobel Prize. Whereas he received the Prize chiefly for his dramatic works, his significance today rests on his lyric achievement.

① 런던에서 아버지로부터 교육을 받았다.
② 초기에는 시보다는 희곡 작품에 주로 전념했다.
③ 희곡 작품에서 신비한 아일랜드 전설을 주로 다루었다.
④ 노벨상을 받은 이후에는 작품 활동을 그만두었다.
⑤ 희곡 작가보다는 시인으로서 더 평가받는다.

7. 다음 글의 밑줄 친 부분 중, 어법상 틀린 것은? [3점]

Placing organic products into the global market has a number of implications. Global markets are characterized by the strong role ① played by corporations in transport, handling, distribution, marketing and sales. Entering into the same markets as conventional agricultural products is likely to result in organic produce ② being subject to the same economic conditions that have shaped conventional agriculture and made sustainable practices unattractive. Organic producers competing in existing global markets will face economic incentives likely ③ to erode the principles of organic farming. An emerging issue of potentially great concern is challenges brought against nations ④ their trading preferences run counter to such groups as the World Trade Organization. Entry into global markets may offer grounds on which to challenge national subsidies for conventional agriculture, but retaliatory challenges against organic farming are ⑤ likely. A further concern is that global markets are uncertain and often volatile, which has the effect of reducing the security of farming enterprises and can be added to the economic incentives for larger-scale enterprises.

*retaliatory: 보복성(의) **volatile: 불안정한

8. 다음 글의 밑줄 친 부분 중, 문맥상 낱말의 쓰임이 적절하지 않은 것은?

In organizations, there is no simple cause-and-effect relationship between introducing a management technique and getting an improved business result. This ① contrasts with other spheres of activity where simple causal relationships do seem to operate. Hit the nail with the hammer, and it goes into the wood. Show a dog food, and it salivates. This kind of simple cause-and-effect logic can be ② misleading if applied to the complex world of organizations, where it is difficult to trace single effects to single causes. ③ Controllable outside factors can sink a wonderfully designed team (a hurricane just swept the entire inventory out to sea). Or they can rescue one whose design was so bad that failure seemed ④ assured (the firm that was competing for the contract just went belly-up). In organizations, ⑤ multiple causes are operating at the same time and interacting with each over an extended period of time.

*salivate: 침을 흘리다 **belly-up: 죽은; 파산한

[9~12] 다음 빈칸에 들어갈 말로 가장 적절한 것을 고르시오.

9. The economy of life produces astonishing outcomes. Among these is sting autotomy, the horrible process in which a stinging insect self-eviscerates, leaving its stinger embedded in the target's flesh. This suicidal behavior troubled Charles Darwin as he formulated his theory of natural selection. He pondered how killing oneself could promote passing fitness via descendants to future generations. An insect's self-evisceration could provide strong evidence against his theory. Amazingly, even though Gregor Mendel's genetics, much less the modern concept of DNA, were unknown to Darwin, he came up with essentially the correct answer. By facilitating the reproduction of your close relatives, mainly nestmates, your lineage would be passed down via relatives, because of your _____. Sting autotomy maximizes the pain and damage of a sting, thereby aiding in the defense of the colony against large predators.

*autotomy: 자절((일부 동물이 위기를 벗어나기 위해 몸의 일부를 스스로 끊는 일))

**self-eviscerate: 자기 몸의 일부를 떼어 내다

① selfless sacrifice
② drastic revenge
③ passive defense
④ survival instinct
⑤ egotistic motives

10. Global warming, like the extinction of species, soil loss, and all the other signs that the planet is having difficulty sustaining the humanity that lives on it, underscores the global economy's inability to _____. In a market system prices are meant to allocate resources efficiently. When demand exceeds supply, prices can be expected to rise and quickly readjust the balance — attracting more producers into the market and pushing some price-conscious consumers away. Yet this doesn't happen when it comes to the environment. We often get that for "free," no matter how much we consume. As is the case with other free things, the lack of a price signal to regulate our consumption results in us consuming too much, until we exhaust the resource at hand. [3점]

① bounce back from crisis
② grow over the long term
③ produce sustainable energy
④ raise production sufficiently
⑤ put a proper price on nature

11. There are inevitably times when people care more about justice being visited upon the overprivileged and powerful than about becoming better off themselves. Following the 2010 British Petroleum (BP) oil spill in the Gulf of Mexico, BP set about compensating local fishermen with out-of-court settlements totaling several billion dollars. But for one shrimp producer from Grand Isle, Louisiana, this wasn't what he wanted. "I want my day in court," he said. "If they can get off with just paying the money — well, they've got plenty of money, they are not really going to learn a lesson." Viewed unkindly, this is a demand for vengeance. More sympathetically, it shows that principles of justice and fair punishment are as valid within the economy as anywhere else, and cannot be balanced using money alone. Either way, this fisherman was expressing something that is incomprehensible from the rationalist perspective of economics. It is a demand that English political philosopher Thomas Hobbes would have understood — that _____ — but which an increasingly technocratic governing class often can't. [3점]

*vengeance: 복수, 앙갚음

**technocratic: 테크노크라시의((많은 권력이 과학 기술 전문가에게 집중되는))

① the law should let the free market work well
② all people are entitled to a fair and public trial
③ the force of the law should apply to all equally
④ human rights are the basic rights and freedoms
⑤ the law must be both readily known and available

12. When people's processing objectives do not bias the information to which they attend, goal-irrelevant factors may have an impact. One such factor may be _____ at the time the information is received. A study by Bower, Gilligan, and Monteiro is illustrative. Participants under hypnosis were instructed to recall a past experience that made them feel either happy or sad and then to maintain these feelings after they were brought out of their hypnotic state. Then they read a passage about two persons that described both happy events and unhappy events that occurred to them. Finally, they recalled the information they had read. Participants who had been induced to feel happy recalled a greater proportion of positively-valenced events, and a lower proportion of negatively-valenced events, than did participants who were induced to feel sad. [3점]

*hypnosis: 최면　**valenced: 유인가(誘引價)를 갖는

① the conversion of feelings that are changed in the context
② the affective reactions that people happen to be experiencing
③ emotional expressions that have widely been used in one culture
④ passionate responses that get in the way of effective communication
⑤ unexpected behavior that is not related to a person's emotional state

13. 다음 글에서 전체 흐름과 관계 <u>없는</u> 문장은? [3점]

Citizenship education is usually associated with educational institutions, where it is often implemented as a subject matter, but sometimes as cross-curricular approaches, as extracurricular programs or as a broader institutional project that shapes most activities. ① Although schools are important sites of citizenship learning, the acquisition of (and reflection on) citizenship knowledge, skills, attitudes and values constitutes a complex process that spans from cradle to grave, and includes a broad variety of settings. ② For instance, the family, media, community associations, workplaces and social movements are powerful socialization agencies for the development of citizenship values and political competencies. ③ Nevertheless, various subject areas of school curriculum, particularly geography and history, can play a critical role in citizenship education. ④ The 'cradle to grave' metaphor may suggest a chronological sequence, but lifelong citizenship learning is seldom a continuous, uninterrupted and linear accumulation of learning experiences. ⑤ It is a messy complex of learning experiences that complement and contradict each other, challenging some of our prior assumptions and creating significant tensions in our consciousness.

[14~15] 주어진 글 다음에 이어질 글의 순서로 가장 적절한 것을 고르시오.

14.

> Sleep, rather than rest, and 'unconsciousness' (when the term can be used), are certainly to be found in insects.

(A) For example, at night the bee sleeps for about 6-8 hours, when it will often have 'droopy' antennae, and be fairly unresponsive to other bees bumping into it. Although most insects have very good eyes, there are no eyelids, and so we cannot tell from their eyes whether they are asleep.

(B) When the jar stops moving they settle down and are even less responsive than normal to further, gentle shaking of the jar. It is as if their sleep has become deeper in compensation for its loss.

(C) However, as antennae are just as important as eyes, and probably more so, droopy antennae certainly indicate that the animal is not in contact with reality and is not just resting. Bees, for example, can easily be deprived of sleep by keeping them in continuously moving jars, so that the insects have to fly about all the time. [3점]

*droopy: 축 늘어진

① (A) – (B) – (C) 　② (A) – (C) – (B)
③ (B) – (C) – (A) 　④ (C) – (A) – (B)
⑤ (C) – (B) – (A)

15.

> According to Greek mythology, the Oracle at Delphi was consulted to gauge the risk of waging a war. In modern times, the term *Delphi* refers to a group survey technique for combining the opinions of several people to develop a collective judgment.

(A) The opinions of everyone surveyed are summarized in a report and returned to the respondents, who then have the opportunity to modify their opinions. Because the written responses are kept anonymous, no one feels pressured to conform to anyone else's opinion.

(B) If people change their opinions, they must explain the reasons why; if they don't, they must also explain why. The process continues until the group reaches a collective opinion. Studies have proven the technique to be an effective way of reaching consensus.

(C) The technique comprises a series of structured questions and feedback reports. Each respondent is given a series of questions (e.g., what are the five most significant risks in this project?), to which he writes his opinions and reasons. [3점]

*oracle: 신탁(神託), 신의 말씀

① (A) – (C) – (B) 　② (B) – (A) – (C)
③ (B) – (C) – (A) 　④ (C) – (A) – (B)
⑤ (C) – (B) – (A)

[16~17] 글의 흐름으로 보아, 주어진 문장이 들어가기에 가장 적절한 곳을 고르시오.

16.

> You might be inclined to think this means that the body has a built-in clock that controls the length of life by limiting cell reproduction.

What controls the number of times cells divide? (①) The answer may lie with our telomeres, the protective tips on the ends of our chromosomes (a bit like the protective tips on the ends of shoestrings). (②) These tips become shorter each time cells divide. (③) Eventually, when the telomeres have nearly disappeared, the cells stop dividing, causing the cells to age and deteriorate. (④) However, scientists view this process not in this way, but rather as a mechanism that may have developed through evolution to prevent the growth of tumors early in life. (⑤) This mechanism would have been beneficial when human life expectancy was short, but it has become costly as life expectancy has increased, because cells that cannot be replenished will age and become defective over time.

*telomere: 말단소체, 말단소립 **chromosome: 염색체 ***tumor: 종양

17.

> Sometimes, however, a revolution in scientific understanding is needed to conceive of new technologies.

While science and technology are closely related, they are not the same. (①) It is not necessary to have a true scientific understanding of something to develop a technology that works. (②) Trial and error, treating things as black boxes in which the result is known but the process that produces the result is not understood, is sufficient to develop many forms of technology. (③) Such was the shift Einstein brought to physics when he proved matter and energy were interchangeable, which opened up the possibilities of nuclear power. (④) A similar revolution has occurred in biology, with the understanding that living organisms grow and develop through the expression of genes, encoded in DNA, which are built from the same four building blocks. (⑤) This understanding allows us to conceive of ways to re-engineer living organisms and gives rise to genetic engineering and other aspects of modern biotechnology, such as cloning and genomics. [3점]

18. 다음 글의 내용을 한 문장으로 요약하고자 한다. 빈칸 (A), (B)에 들어갈 말로 가장 적절한 것은?

Suppose your company decides to put you in charge of a new project. First, you need to put together a team. So, you arrange to have dinner with Kevin, a possible recruit from a different department of the same company. It's imperative in this situation that you figure out exactly what kind of person he is, so you do your best to form an accurate picture of him. You ask specific questions to draw out his true personality and test if he has the qualities that fit the bill for the new project. Now let's take a moment to imagine another scenario. Let's say that you run into Kevin by accident and decide to have dinner together. You probably would not be trying to figure out what kind of a person he is or what qualities he brings as an employee. Instead, you would simply try to enjoy your time with light conversation. Regardless of what you discuss, you'd probably remember less from this second impromptu dinner.

↓

> The ___(A)___ to form an impression of another can force you to pay closer attention to the information about the person and ___(B)___ the information better.

(A)	(B)	(A)	(B)
① need	convey	② chance	remember
③ need	remember	④ chance	convey
⑤ ability	analyze		

[19~20] 다음 글을 읽고, 물음에 답하시오.

When you are an expert, your deep knowledge is obviously of great value in facing the usual challenges of your profession, but your immersion in that body of (a) conventional wisdom can impede you from creating or accepting new ideas, and hamper you when you are confronted with novelty and change. Such frozen thinking has plagued the careers of scientists and (b) ruined the health of many a business. For example, if you land in the hospital, it's natural to want to be treated by the most experienced physicians on staff. But according to a 2014 study, you'd be better off being treated by the relative (c) novices. The study appeared in the prestigious *Journal of the American Medical Association* (JAMA). It examined ten years of data involving tens of thousands of hospital admissions and found that the thirty-day mortality rate among high-risk acute-care patients was a third lower when the top doctors were out of town — for example, when they were away at conferences. The JAMA study didn't pinpoint the reasons for the decreased death rate, but the authors explained that most errors made by doctors are connected to a tendency to form opinions quickly, based on prior experience. In cases that are not routine, that can be misleading, because the expert doctors may miss important aspects of the problem that are (d) consistent with their initial analysis. As a result, although junior doctors may be slower and less confident in treating run-of-the-mill cases, they can be more open-minded in handling unusual cases or treating patients with (e) subtler symptoms. Just as an experienced golfer can have difficulty altering the much-rehearsed stroke that is encoded in his motor cortex, so too may a professional thinker have difficulty shedding the old ways of thinking lodged in her prefrontal cortex.

*motor cortex: 운동 피질 **prefrontal cortex: 전두엽 피질

19. 윗글의 제목으로 가장 적절한 것은?

① Frozen Thinking: How Can We Deal with It?
② Risks Associated with Weak Critical Thinkers
③ Flexible Thinking in a Constantly Changing World
④ Why Frozen Thinking Is Dangerous to Experts
⑤ The Value of Expert Skills in Medical Science

20. 밑줄 친 (a) ~ (e) 중에서 문맥상 낱말의 쓰임이 적절하지 않은 것은? [3점]

① (a)　　② (b)　　③ (c)　　④ (d)　　⑤ (e)

○ 답안지의 해당란에 성명과 수험번호를 쓰고, 또 수험번호와 답을 정확히 표시하시오.
○ 문항에 따라 배점이 다르니, 각 물음의 끝에 표시된 배점을 참고하시오. 3점 문항에만 점수가 표시되어 있습니다. 점수 표시가 없는 문항은 모두 2점씩입니다.

1. 다음 글에 드러난 'I'의 심경 변화로 가장 적절한 것은?

I began to drive across the high desert to my parental home. The view out of the car window was the same lifeless landscape, an endless reach of uninhabited sand dunes. The monotony of the landscape is sometimes broken by a mirage. I turned on the radio, but slow old songs came out. I felt drowsy and yawned repeatedly. I turned off the radio. However, as I drove up toward the eastern slope of Mt. Timpanogos, the landscape changed dramatically. A gentle breeze bearing the fragrance of mosses and columbine swept around the rocky mountain base. Smelling the subtle scent suddenly altered my mood. This odor evoked a flood of memories of boyhood friends and deeds long since vanished from conscious memory. The association was so strong that I immediately recalled some scenes of my hometown — its gentle airs, its balmy sunshine, its bright and dewy flowers and happy fishing expeditions with my father! I felt as if I were at home.

*dune: (해변의) 모래 언덕

① disappointed → satisfied
② frightened → comfortable
③ regretful → curious
④ bored → pleased
⑤ gloomy → sympathetic

2. 밑줄 친 live life in the emergency lane이 다음 글에서 의미하는 바로 가장 적절한 것은? [3점]

Life is a bit like a highway, with numerous lanes that we can take to go on the journey of our lives. Most of the time, we simply go on without knowing which lane we are on. But there is a lane we need to make a conscious effort to avoid. If you live life in the emergency lane, it brings you a great deal of frustration. An emergency-lane person is always in a hurry, always anxious to get somewhere else. Every decision seems critical, every mistake a potential disaster. Everything seems to be front-page news. Consider for a moment just how silly and pointless it is to be so upset so much of the time. I think the best way out of this is to appreciate the fact that bad things happen. We're going to be cut off in traffic and we're going to lose things and make mistakes and our plans are going to be messed up. But that's life. It's important to accept that life is not going to be easy all the time.

① leave everyone behind
② take things too seriously
③ regret your past decisions
④ follow others without thinking
⑤ miss everything that is meaningful

3. 다음 글의 요지로 가장 적절한 것은?

Change by alternatives is supposed to be the method that works in any democracy. The opposition party puts forward an alternative policy to the governing party and if the electorate prefer the alternative they vote in the opposition at the next electoral opportunity. But, for a variety of reasons, it does not quite work that way. Any party in opposition knows that to get back into power it must not only hold its own supporters but also capture some of the floating voters or other party voters. So the alternatives get less and less different and in the end no true alternative is offered. Furthermore in a complex world the same experts make the economic analyses and so the proposed policies end up by being quite similar. In most democratic countries today it is quite hard to see the real differences in the policies offered by the opposing parties. The similarity will probably get greater as it becomes less possible to undo policies set in motion by previous governments. It is only in countries like the UK where the parties have a historical class base that differences of policy can exist.

*electorate: (전체) 유권자

① 민주주의 국가에서 야당에 의한 정책 대안은 정권을 잡을 수 있는 기회이다.
② 정당의 주요 정책들은 선거용으로 만들어지고 실제로 실행되는 경우는 적다.
③ 오늘날의 민주주의 국가에서 야당과 여당의 정책에서 차이를 찾는 것은 어렵다.
④ 야당과 여당의 정당 정책의 유사성은 유권자로 하여금 정당 선택을 어렵게 한다.
⑤ 정당들은 선거에서 이기기 위해 지지자의 성향에 맞는 극단적인 정책을 제시한다.

4. 다음 글의 주제로 가장 적절한 것은?

When most people think of major consumers of water resources they tend to focus on things that they can see, like showers and lawn sprinklers. However, we have recently come to realize that beef is particularly and unacceptably water-intensive, especially when accounting for the grass and grain required to raise cattle. Home water use is only the tip of the iceberg, and a large majority of the water consumed for beef is hidden from plain view. That is why the advocacy material of vegan and environmental groups often places water usage at the very top of the list of indictments against beef. The figure most commonly cited (also often used in the mainstream press) is that it takes 2,500 gallons of water to produce a single pound of beef (equal to about 20,820 liters per kilogram).

*indictment: 기소

① the problems with feeding grass to cattle
② the necessity of using clean water for cattle
③ some advantages of raising cattle with grain
④ the water-intensive nature of beef production
⑤ how to produce meat using the least resources

5. 다음 글의 제목으로 가장 적절한 것은?

Giacomo Rizzolatti of the University of Parma discovered mirror neurons in a part of the monkey brain responsible for planning movement. These nerve cells fire both when a monkey performs an action (like picking up a peanut) and when the monkey sees someone else do the same thing. Before long, similar systems were found in human brains, too. The surprising conclusion may be that when we see someone do something, the same parts of our brain are activated as if we were doing it ourselves. We may know what other people intend and feel by simulating what they are doing within the same motor areas of our own brains. As Rizzolatti puts it, "The fundamental mechanism that allows us a direct grasp of the mind of others is not conceptual reasoning but direct simulation of the observed events through the mirror mechanism."

① What Triggers Mirror Neurons?
② The Pros and Cons of Mirror Neurons
③ Mirror Neurons: Our Natural Mind Readers
④ Why Is Imitating Others Important in Social Life?
⑤ We Cannot Observe Others Without Mirror Neurons

6. Valentine's with Father-Daughter Dance에 관한 다음 안내문의 내용과 일치하는 것은?

Valentine's
with Father-Daughter Dance

Dates:
Friday, Feb. 8 and Saturday, Feb. 9 6:30-8:00 P.M.

Celebrate Valentine's Day by taking your daughter to the "Daddy Daughter Dance" — an event arranged by the city at Floral Hall.

Formal dress is required.

Light refreshments will be served at the dance hall and all participants will have their photo taken.

The cost is $29 per father/daughter duo, plus $6 for each additional daughter.
Please note that all attendees must be registered and pay in advance through our website.

Sorry moms and sons, this event is father/daughter only. But stay tuned for the city's mother/son dance around Halloween time.

---

① 이틀간 두 시간 동안 진행된다.
② 행사 옷차림은 자유 복장으로 제한이 없다.
③ 홀 내부에서는 어떠한 음식물도 제공되지 않는다.
④ 웹사이트에서 사전에 등록하고 비용을 지불해야 한다.
⑤ 인원이 적을 경우에는 어머니와 아들의 신청을 받는다.

7. 다음 글의 밑줄 친 부분 중, 어법상 틀린 것은? [3점]

Just as conditioning processes sometimes make foods aversive, such processes can also make foods more appetitive. For example, a powerful way to increase our preference for a disliked food is ① to mix it with some food item or sweetener that we strongly prefer. This may be ② how some people grow to like black coffee: They first drink it with cream and sugar and then gradually eliminate the extra ingredients as the taste of the coffee itself becomes pleasurable. Similarly, in one study, college students developed ③ increased preference for broccoli or cauliflower after eating it a few times with sugar. Unfortunately, few parents ④ using such a method to improve their children's eating habits, possibly because they perceive sugar to be unhealthy and do not realize that the sugar can later be withdrawn. Instead, parents often try to entice their children to eat a disliked food by offering dessert as a reward — a strategy that easily backfires in ⑤ that the contrast between the disliked food and the subsequent dessert might result in the former becoming even more disliked.

*aversive: 싫어하는

8. 다음 글의 밑줄 친 부분 중, 문맥상 낱말의 쓰임이 적절하지 않은 것은? [3점]

In oral cultures, knowledge is limited to the collective memory of the group. This puts a serious limitation on the amount that can be known and it makes such knowledge very ① fragile. If the wisdom of the tribe is not committed to memory then it cannot be passed on to the next generation and will be permanently lost. Given this, oral societies tend to ② encode their knowledge in formulaic patterns, such as rhymes, proverbs and clichés, which are easy to memorize. They also tend to be cognitively ③ conservative; for any experimentation or divergence from established ways of thinking puts the wisdom that has been accumulated over generations at risk. On the plus side, members of oral cultures are sometimes ④ capable of prodigious feats of memory. Some scholars speculate that Homer's *Iliad* was originally an oral text which, despite being passed on by word of mouth from one storyteller to the next, was ⑤ destroyed with remarkable fidelity. Indeed, the story itself may have been composed centuries before it was first written down.

*cliché: 상투적인 문구 **prodigious: 놀라운 ***fidelity: 충실함

[9~12] 다음 빈칸에 들어갈 말로 가장 적절한 것을 고르시오.

9. It is essential for innovators to be _____. This is not easy. As human beings we are programmed to seek the approval of those around us. Yet a radical and transformative thought goes nowhere without the willingness to go against convention. "If you have a new idea, and it's disruptive and you're agreeable, then what are you going to do with that?" says Peterson. "If you worry about offending people's feelings and upsetting the social structure, you're not going to put your ideas forward." As the playwright George Bernard Shaw once put it: "The reasonable man adapts himself to the world: the unreasonable one persists in trying to adapt the world to himself. Therefore, all progress relies upon the unreasonable man."

① disagreeable   ② attentive
③ persuasive   ④ inquisitive
⑤ selfless

10. In a culture where screens replace craft, the philosopher-mechanic Matthew Crawford argues, people lose the outlet for self-worth established through _____. One way to understand the exploding popularity of social media platforms in recent years is that they offer a substitute source of aggrandizement. In the absence of a well-built wood bench or applause at a musical performance to point toward, you can instead post a photo of your latest visit to a hip restaurant, hoping for likes, or desperately check for retweets of a clever quip. But as Crawford implies, these digital cries for attention are often a poor substitute for the recognition generated by handicraft, as they're not backed by the hard-won skill required to tame the "infallible judgment" of physical reality, and come across instead as "the boasts of a boy." Craft allows an escape from this shallowness and provides instead a deeper source of pride. [3점]

*aggrandizement: 지위 확대 **quip: 재치 있는 말

① the repetitive processes involved in handiwork
② respect and recognition from others
③ cumulative cultural achievements
④ unambiguous demonstrations of skill
⑤ awareness of improvements on their competence

11. Color defines our world and our emotions. It is usually seen before imagery. Our eyes are attracted to color to such an extent that the color of an object is perceived before the details imparted by its shapes and lines. At first glance, we do not see the different species of trees present in a summer woodland, but rather see the preponderance of green. The artist, architect, and designer, however, are generally concerned with _____. Upon entering a room, we first see the color or colors used in the interior design and then discern the furnishings and artifacts contained within the space. An artwork, be it fine or commercial, is aesthetically pleasing to the viewer when its color usage allows the viewer to see the content of the piece (both color and imagery) together. When this is accomplished, a work's message is conveyed immediately, without a "second look" on the part of the viewer. [3점]

*impart: 전하다 **preponderance: 압도적으로 많음

① making their works as realistic as possible
② light and color than capturing the perfect form
③ having color and imagery perceived simultaneously
④ the way people respond to objects and environments
⑤ making marks that enable the art of visualizing ideas

12. We don't yet know if your level of exercise will affect your gut microbes, whether or not you are pregnant. But the mouse studies have turned up one interesting fact. Forced exercise, as opposed to voluntary exercise, affects the mouse microbiomes differently, particularly with regard to levels of gut inflammation. While we don't yet understand how this all works, it's possible that forced exercise could lead to anxiety, which could lead to an elevation of bacteria that induce or fail to prevent gut inflammation. While this is supposition, it does suggest that you _____, while following the advice of your doctor or midwife for exercise during your pregnancy. But on the whole a little exercise may help change your microbiome and reduce inflammation, which is all to the good. And if you can get outside, you will likely feel better for it. [3점]

*microbiome: 미생물 군집 **inflammation: 염증

① do intensive regular exercise with moderate anxiety
② only do as much exercise as you feel comfortable with
③ exercise on a daily basis to boost your immune system
④ know sore muscles are a sign that you're getting stronger
⑤ always exercise according to your age and physical abilities

13. 다음 글에서 전체 흐름과 관계 <u>없는</u> 문장은?

The news media are hungry for new findings, and reporters often latch onto ideas from the scientific laboratories before they have been fully tested. ① Also, a reporter who lacks a strong understanding of science may misunderstand or misreport complex scientific principles. ② To tell the truth, sometimes scientists get excited about their findings, too, and leak them to the press before they have been through a thorough review by the scientists' peers. ③ As a result, the public is often exposed to late-breaking nutrition news stories before the findings are fully confirmed. ④ For example, the media have reported that oat products lower blood cholesterol, which is well-established by scientific research. ⑤ Then, when the hypothesis being tested fails to hold up to a later challenge, consumers feel betrayed by what is simply the normal course of science at work.

*latch onto: ~을 입수하다 **oat: 귀리

[14~15] 주어진 글 다음에 이어질 글의 순서로 가장 적절한 것을 고르시오.

14.

The impacts of tourism on the environment are evident to scientists, but not all residents attribute environmental damage to tourism. Residents commonly have positive views on the economic and some sociocultural influences of tourism on quality of life, but their reactions to environmental impacts are mixed.

(A) Alternatively, some residents express concern that tourists overcrowd the local fishing, hunting, and other recreation areas or may cause traffic and pedestrian congestion.

(B) Some residents feel tourism provides more parks and recreation areas, improves the quality of the roads and public facilities, and does not contribute to ecological decline. Many do not blame tourism for

traffic problems, overcrowded outdoor recreation, or the disturbance of peace and tranquility of parks.
(C) Some studies suggest that this divide in residents' feelings about tourism's relationship to environmental damage is related to the type of tourism, the extent to which residents feel the natural environment needs to be protected, and the distance residents live from the tourist attractions. [3점]

*tranquility: 고요함

① (A) – (C) – (B)　　② (B) – (A) – (C)
③ (B) – (C) – (A)　　④ (C) – (A) – (B)
⑤ (C) – (B) – (A)

15.

Online consumer research studies confirm that when visitors land on a website, they experience "stay" or "go" moments within the first 10 seconds. If it looks unprofessional or hard to use, they leave and usually won't be back.

(A) Unfortunately, this is often not the case. Quite a few shortsighted entrepreneurs underestimate the negative impact of poorly written copy, amateurish design, and convoluted navigation.
(B) Remember that this is one of those areas where it doesn't pay to be penny wise and pound foolish — it's just too important. Don't annoy or — worse yet — alienate prospective customers because your cousin's friend's aunt's next-door neighbor's brother volunteered to design your website on the cheap.
(C) In other words, your target audience will judge you, your products and services, and your company in a snap — and you're likely to get only one chance to impress them. Given this, all website owners should be doing everything they can to ensure that their online visitors are blown away by their website's look, feel, and navigability. [3점]

*convoluted: 대단히 복잡한

① (A) – (C) – (B)　　② (B) – (A) – (C)
③ (B) – (C) – (A)　　④ (C) – (A) – (B)
⑤ (C) – (B) – (A)

[16~17] 글의 흐름으로 보아, 주어진 문장이 들어가기에 가장 적절한 곳을 고르시오.

16.

It often requires great cleverness to conceive of measures that tap into what people are thinking without altering their thinking, called reactivity.

Researchers in psychology follow the scientific method to perform studies that help explain and may predict human behavior. (①) This is a much more challenging task than studying snails or sound waves. (②) It often requires compromises, such as testing behavior within laboratories rather than natural settings, and asking those readily available (such as introduction to psychology students) to participate rather than collecting data from a true cross-section of the population. (③) Simply knowing they are being observed may cause people to behave differently (such as more politely!). (④) People may give answers that they feel are more socially desirable than their true feelings. (⑤) But for all of these difficulties for psychology, the payoff of the scientific method is that the findings are replicable; that is, if you run the same study again following the same procedures, you will be very likely to get the same results.

*replicable: 반복 가능한

17.

> And when programmers invented "file-sharing" tools around the same time, a shudder ran through the entertainment industries, as they watched their lock hold on distribution suddenly evaporate.

As we live in a world made of software, programmers are the architects. The decisions they make guide our behavior. (①) When they make something newly easy to do, we do a lot more of it. (②) If they make it hard or impossible to do something, we do less of it. (③) When coders made the first blogging tools in the late '90s and early '00s, it produced an explosion of self-expression; when it's suddenly easy to publish things, millions more people do it. (④) In fact, they fought back by hiring their own programmers to invent "digital rights management" software, putting it in music and film releases, making those wares trickier for everyday folks to copy and hand out to their friends; they tried to create artificial scarcity. (⑤) If wealthy interests don't like what some code is doing, they'll pay to create software that fights in the opposite direction. [3점]

*shudder: 전율, 몸서리 **lock hold: 잠금장치

18. 다음 글의 내용을 한 문장으로 요약하고자 한다. 빈칸 (A), (B)에 들어갈 말로 가장 적절한 것은?

Occasionally, governments explicitly discriminate against foreign companies in favor of domestic companies. For instance, in 2005 the government of Argentina (successfully) stimulated consumers to boycott Shell after the company had raised the oil price. In many countries, more subtle 'buy national' campaigns are still implemented in which consuming products from home companies is favored over 'foreign' products. However, with the increasing foreign content of domestic products, and increasingly ambiguous ownership structures of leading companies, the distinction between 'foreign' and 'domestic' has become increasingly challenged. In addition, national and local host governments have good reasons to attract (or retain) large foreign multinational enterprises. International companies affect the macro-economic policies of individual countries particularly through their (potentially) positive impact on trade and investment flows, competition, technology transfer and tax income. In consequence, governments prefer to use incentives rather than sanctions, and non-discrimination principles rather than discriminatory practices in their policies towards multinational enterprises.

↓

> Due to changes in industry itself, rather than _____(A)_____ domestic industries in all cases, the majority of governments now tend to _____(B)_____ manufacturers from abroad.

	(A)		(B)
①	restricting	······	tolerate
②	defending	······	disdain
③	preferring	······	punish
④	restricting	······	support
⑤	preferring	······	welcome

[19~20] 다음 글을 읽고, 물음에 답하시오.

The extraordinary growth of spectator sports, undoubtedly deeply influenced by television and by the way in which sports are the main way of selling goods, is one of the marks of our world. The historian of technology Lewis Mumford suggests that modern sports may be defined as 'those forms of (a) organized play in which the spectator is more important than the player.' They are a spectacle, in many ways closer to drama or ritual than to playing a game. The crowd becomes part of a chorus, emotionally and psychologically blending together, taken for a moment out of their ordinary lives and worries. Even in the privacy of their home, people dress up in their team's colors, and pretend that they are (b) part of the crowd as they watch the television. Being in a crowd makes us brave. We can shout and say things we would normally be too (c) timid to express. It is often the time when we can make our prejudices and passions known, whether for our country, our political opinions, or our hatreds, in a way that as single individuals we find impossible. It is not surprising that when they are watching games and sports, people reveal such (d) refined emotions.

Mass sports and private game-viewing are forms of conspicuous consumption. Many modern societies have a great deal of leisure, and people fill up their spare time — and often demonstrate their new-found affluence — through watching games. Often they do this privately, in the world of computer games and Internet rivalries. The increasing amount of leisure time often created by machines must be filled. So if anything is the new 'religion' of the world, it is a game or sports. More money, emotion and activity are now (e) generated by sports and games than anything else on earth, except war.

19. 윗글의 제목으로 가장 적절한 것은?

① Watching Sports: Now and Then
② Why People Watch Games and Sports
③ What Is the Fascination of Playing Games?
④ Ritual, Identities, and Alternative Lifestyles
⑤ Watching Games Makes You Proud of Yourself

20. 밑줄 친 (a) ~ (e) 중에서 문맥상 낱말의 쓰임이 적절하지 않은 것은? [3점]

① (a)　　② (b)　　③ (c)　　④ (d)　　⑤ (e)

1. 다음 글의 목적으로 가장 적절한 것은?

Every year, university students from all over the country are invited to test their artistic skill in the Concord Film Festival's poster design contest. Thousands of students compete for the top prizes, and winners are chosen by a panel of professional judges. Past years have seen an amazing display of creativity and talent, and this year's competition was no exception. Unfortunately, due to the great number of entries this year, it has been very difficult for our judges to choose only three outstanding posters. As a result, we've decided to announce the winners one week later than originally scheduled. There is no need to worry, however, as prizes and other details will remain unchanged. Winners will still receive recognition and cash prizes, and their work will still be published. Thanks to everyone for supporting this wonderful event.

① 전문 심사위원을 초청하려고
② 대회 참가 수칙을 안내하려고
③ 포스터 대회 참가를 독려하려고
④ 수상자 선정 기준 변경을 공지하려고
⑤ 수상자 발표가 지연된 것을 알리려고

2. 밑줄 친 cognitive processing이 다음 글에서 의미하는 바로 가장 적절한 것은? [3점]

A possible explanation for the value of writing is that it allows people to express themselves. If the driving process is self-expression, one could argue that both verbal and nonverbal forms of expression would provide comparable benefits. It should be noted, however, that traditional research on the venting of emotions has failed to support the clinical value of emotional expression in the absence of cognitive processing. A recent experiment by Anne Krantz and James W. Pennebaker sought to learn if the disclosure of a trauma through dance or bodily movement would bring about health improvements in ways comparable to writing. In the study, students were asked to express a traumatic experience using bodily movement, to express an experience using movement and then write about it, or to exercise in a prescribed manner for three days, ten minutes per day. Whereas the two movement expression groups reported that they felt happier and mentally healthier in the months after the study, only the movement plus writing group evidenced significant improvements in physical health and grade point average.

*grade point average(GPA): 평균 평점

① the systematic process of demonstrating what caused a trauma
② the mental process of putting a traumatic experience into writing
③ the natural process of expressing a traumatic experience nonverbally
④ the dynamic process of converting negative emotions to positive ones
⑤ the logical process of analyzing a trauma through verbal reasoning

3. 다음 글의 요지로 가장 적절한 것은?

Alphabetic literacy, in order to overcome the limitations of method and so achieve its full potential, had to await the invention of the printing press. The original achievement, the Greek alphabet, had solved an empirical problem by applying abstract analysis. But the material means for maximizing the result required the assistance of further inventions and had to await a long time for it. Such necessary combination of technologies is characteristic of scientific advance. To realize that there is energy available when water is converted into steam was one thing. To harness the energy successfully was another, requiring the parallel construction of machine tools capable of producing fine tolerances to fit piston to cylinder, the manufacture of lubricants capable of sealing the fit, the parallel invention of slide-rod mechanisms to control the periods of steam pressure, and of crank and connecting rod to convert the thrust into rotation. The energy of the alphabet likewise had to await the assistance provided by the dawning age of scientific advance in Europe in order to be fully released.

*tolerance: 허용 오차 **lubricant: 윤활유

① 기술이 비약적으로 발전하려면 집단 지성의 힘이 필요하다.
② 기술이 생겨도 쓰임의 용도가 없으면 기술은 발전하지 않는다.
③ 필요에 따라 기술이 생긴 것이 아니라 과학기술이 필요를 만든다.
④ 기술이 힘을 발휘하려면 여러 관련 기술들과 결합되어야 한다.
⑤ 기술은 단계적으로 발전하므로 획기적인 발견이란 불가능하다.

4. 다음 글의 주제로 가장 적절한 것은?

For more than two decades, school reform has been driven by an agenda that appears to be uninformed by even the most basic research into what we now know about the functioning of the brain or the healthy development of the child. Educational leaders and policy makers aren't asking, "What do children need for healthy brain development?" "How do they learn best?" or "When's the optimal time to teach him or her to read or do algebra?" Rather, they seem to be asking, "What do we need this child to be able to do in order to meet our school, local, or national standards?" Most reform has been focused on what to cram into children's heads — and testing them ad nauseam to see what sticks — rather than on developing their brains. What this means is that we do more but accomplish less. Educational reforms fail because they hinge on policies that lower the sense of control of students, teachers, and administrators alike, predictably leading to greater stress, lower student engagement, and ever more teacher dissatisfaction and burnout.

*ad nauseam: 지겹도록 **hinge on: ~에 의존하다

① effects of school reforms on teachers and students
② teachers' role in supporting their students' education
③ reasons why conventional school reforms have failed
④ strategies to improve students' performance in school
⑤ factors that impact school quality and student achievement

5. 다음 도표의 내용과 일치하지 <u>않는</u> 것은?

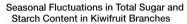

Seasonal Fluctuations in Total Sugar and
Starch Content in Kiwifruit Branches

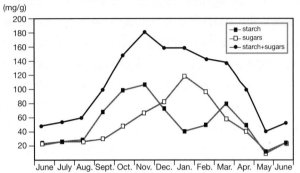

The graph above shows the seasonal changes in the mass of sugars and starch in one gram of kiwifruit branches. ① Starch in kiwifruit branches is at its highest level in November and its lowest level in May. ② Sugars in kiwifruit branches are at their highest level in January, which is the only month the amount of sugars in kiwifruit branches exceeds that of starch. ③ Throughout the year, the period when the amount of starch is greater than that of sugars is longer than the period when sugars exceed starch. ④ There is very little difference in the amount of starch and sugars between May and August. ⑤ The total amount of starch and sugars combined is the highest in November and the lowest in May, which is identical to the case of starch alone.

*starch: 전분, 녹말

6. python에 관한 다음 글의 내용과 일치하지 <u>않는</u> 것은?

Pythons are more closely related to boas than to any other snake family. As far as differences go, however, pythons have an additional bone in their head and more teeth than boas. Pythons can range from 4 to 29 feet long depending on the species. Larger pythons can prey on animals as large as a house cat or a full-grown deer. In Africa, there are pythons that eat gazelles. Despite their size, pythons are rarely dangerous to humans. The python can live up to 30 years. The breeding time is between 60 or 70 days. Python skin is used to make clothing, such as vests, belts, boots and shoes, or fashion accessories such as handbags. Pythons are listed as near threatened, not endangered, because they are hunted for the sale of python skin. In California, the sale of python skin or parts has been outlawed since 1970.

*python: 비단뱀 **gazelles: ((동물)) 가젤(작은 영양)

① 보아 뱀보다 더 많은 이빨을 가지고 있다.
② 종에 따라 몸길이가 25피트나 차이 날 수 있다.
③ 몸집이 큰 것은 고양이나 사슴을 먹기도 한다.
④ 사람을 위험하게 하는 경우는 거의 없다.
⑤ 지나친 사냥으로 멸종 위기 동물에 올라 있다.

7. 다음 글의 밑줄 친 부분 중, 어법상 <u>틀린</u> 것은? [3점]

Being sensitive to understanding what resources students have outside of school ① <u>is</u> extremely helpful when trying to support student learning. Having worked with my own sons on their language arts homework at the primary level, I can see how students ② <u>whose</u> parents are English-language learners are at a severe disadvantage when completing worksheets. If they do not understand or cannot read the directions or do not have the cultural knowledge to help the students with the homework, then these students do not have these resources to assist ③ <u>them</u> in learning. In addition, working or single parents may not have or may not extend the resource of time or energy to students, so these special circumstances may leave these students at a disadvantage with both their daily homework and more extensive projects. ④ <u>Given</u> these dilemmas, it is greatly appreciated when teachers can offer parents practical suggestions on how to help their students. Often, the parents simply do not have all the teaching tips and pedagogical knowledge ⑤ <u>help</u> their child improve their academic skills.

*pedagogical: 교육학의

8. 다음 글의 밑줄 친 부분 중, 문맥상 낱말의 쓰임이 적절하지 <u>않은</u> 것은?

Altruism — unselfish concern for the welfare of others — presents sociobiology and evolutionary theory in general with a very real ① difficulty. For writers like Edward Wilson, the behaviour patterns of species and individuals are totally susceptible to biological explanation; some creatures are altruistic because they are driven by their genes to ② sacrifice themselves for the well-being of others. For example, a small bird will give a warning cry when a predator approaches, and so risk its life to safeguard its fellows. The trouble is that, in Wilson's words, 'fallen heroes do not have children.' If altruism is rooted in genes, the individuals with those genes would ③ disappear. Only those possessing selfish genes would ④ die. However, altruism yet exists: how can evolutionary theory explain this? Wilson suggests that ⑤ continued altruism is due to the evolutionary motivation of genes to defend and protect the species gene pool.

*susceptible to: ~이 가능한

[9~12] 다음 빈칸에 들어갈 말로 가장 적절한 것을 고르시오.

9. The first thing to understand about anxiety is that it's part of our biological heritage. Long before any recorded human history, our ancestors lived in a world filled with life-threatening dangers: predators, hunger, toxic plants, unfriendly neighbors, heights, disease, drowning. It was in the face of these dangers that the human mind evolved. The qualities necessary to avoid danger were the qualities that evolution bred into us as human beings. A good many of those qualities amounted simply to different forms of caution. Fear was protective; one had to be cautious about many things to survive. This cautiousness persists in our present psychological makeup in the form of some of our deepest hatreds and fears. These fears are _____ — we owe a great deal to their existence. [3점]

① harm
② stressors
③ ambiguity
④ communication
⑤ remnants

10. The disciplines that make up the natural sciences can be divided into two classes: those that are historical, and those that are not. For subjects like cosmology, geology, and biology, history is of utmost importance. The goal of much of the activity in these disciplines is to reconstruct the history of the cosmos, the Earth, and the life forms that have inhabited it, respectively. For the mathematician, physicist or chemist, on the other hand, history does not matter. The logical structures mathematicians explore are timeless, and both physics and chemistry deal with properties of the universe that we have every reason to believe are the same today as they ever have been, or ever will be. Thus, in principle, all the open questions in physics and chemistry could be answered this afternoon if the right experiments were done. Moreover, there is no reason to think that the outcomes of those experiments would be any different if they were done by other people, at other times, or in other places. The assumption that the conclusions reached by physicists and chemists _____ is fundamental to the way geologists, biologists and cosmologists use them.

*cosmology: 우주론

① are subject to change based on new findings
② provide accurate estimates of the ages
③ contribute to the work of historians
④ deal with everything in the universe
⑤ are independent of time and place

11. The innate differences we each experience in terms of _____ contribute greatly to how we perceive the world. If you have difficulty hearing when others speak, you will hear only bits and pieces of conversation and make decisions and judgments based upon minimal information. What if your eyesight is poor? Then you will focus on fewer details and your interaction with the world will be affected. If your sense of smell is deficient, you may not be able to discriminate between a safe environment and a health hazard, which would render you more vulnerable. At the opposite extreme, if you are oversensitive to stimulation, you may avoid interacting with your environment and miss out on life's simple pleasures. [3점]

① what preconceptions we hold in our minds
② how we take in and process specific details
③ how well we understand spoken conversations
④ how sensitive we are to different types of stimulation
⑤ what elements of the environment we are vulnerable to

12. Like the downtown office complex, tourism has frequently developed as _____. The strategy of carving out sharply demarcated and defended zones for middle-class consumers of entertainment and leisure came naturally to older cities confronted with problems of crime, poverty, and physical neglect. Creating a "tourist bubble" was tempting — some might say necessary — as a way not only of securing a space for development, but for achieving an efficient application of scarce resources. In a hostile environment, zones of demarcation can solve seemingly insolvable problems of image and social control. Tourists who visit converted cities are unlikely to see the city of decline at all, except on their way from an airport. For tourists, the city can be reduced to a simulacrum, a set piece representing the city in its entirety. Thus, reduced to Harbor Place or the Renaissance Center and Greektown, both Baltimore and Detroit can be presented as gleaming new places to play. [3점]

*demarcate: 경계를 설정하다 **bubble: (외따로 있는) 특별한 장소
***simulacrum: 복제품

① the rock that looks very like gold
② a path not yet trodden by anyone
③ roses growing from a little garden
④ islands of renewal in seas of decay
⑤ the tip of the iceberg in a vast sea

13. 다음 글에서 전체 흐름과 관계 <u>없는</u> 문장은?

The impact of climate change on animals and plants interacts with habitat loss and fragmentation. This is because the main effect of climate change is to shift the area of where any one species can live successfully. ① In a warming world, this habitable space moves either polewards across the landscape, to the North or South, or up in elevation, with species living higher up mountains than ever before. ② This happens because the area where the mean temperature is 15°C, for example, shifts in these directions under global warming. ③ In order to limit the effects of global warming, countries are urged to make a commitment to preventing further rises in temperature that threaten the planet. ④ Survival then depends on whether a particular species can move, and if so, whether there is a suitable pathway for the movements to happen. ⑤ Neither of these things can be assumed, and where habitats become too fragmented, a suitable pathway for organisms to move to other areas becomes less of a realistic possibility.

*fragmentation: 단편화

[14~15] 주어진 글 다음에 이어질 글의 순서로 가장 적절한 것을 고르시오.

14.

Your trash that cannot be recycled or repurposed in some way will need to go in the regular garbage and will likely end up in a landfill. This garbage should normally be all dry and fit in a small bag, or if possible in your area, directly in a trash bin with no bag at all.

(A) They are dry and anaerobic spaces that essentially "mummify" anything contained in them, including plastic. Until it is full and closed, any decomposition that does occur in a landfill creates undesirable methane, a heat-trapping greenhouse gas that is roughly thirty times stronger than carbon dioxide.

(B) You may think that a compostable garbage bag would be the best way to dispose of this rubbish, but the best is really not to use a bag at all if possible. The reason is that landfills are not meant to encourage decomposition.

(C) The release of this material from open landfills contributes to global warming, and thus climate change. Of course, the best is to minimize your waste so you are not sending anything to landfills. [3점]

*anaerobic: (생물) 무산소성[혐기성]의 **decomposition: 분해
***compostable: 퇴비로 바뀔 수 있는

① (A) – (C) – (B)　　　② (B) – (A) – (C)
③ (B) – (C) – (A)　　　④ (C) – (A) – (B)
⑤ (C) – (B) – (A)

15.

You might think that new scientific discoveries, building upon previous knowledge, simply add to our knowledge.

(A) To create the correct new understanding, the old structure has to be dismantled and a new one created in its place. One cannot simply add to the existing knowledge if the new knowledge logically contradicts what had been known before.

(B) The reason that old knowledge is replaced has to do with the fact that nature follows logical rules. The logic of nature has to be consistent and 'hang together'. A single new scientific fact can show that the entire existing logical structure is incorrect.

(C) Often, however, new scientific results don't just add to what we know, but fundamentally change what we know (or what we thought we knew). What we used to believe true becomes false, and new knowledge takes its place. Science often advances by replacing past knowledge with new knowledge, not simply by adding to existing knowledge. [3점]

*dismantle: 해체하다, 분해하다

① (A) – (C) – (B)　　　② (B) – (A) – (C)
③ (B) – (C) – (A)　　　④ (C) – (A) – (B)
⑤ (C) – (B) – (A)

[16~17] 글의 흐름으로 보아, 주어진 문장이 들어가기에 가장 적절한 곳을 고르시오.

16.

> The upright stride was also very helpful, because it allowed arms and hands to be used for a much wider range of purposes (although it became harder to swing around in trees).

The growth of human brains may have been related to increasing tool use. (①) Although humans are not the only animals who use tools, our species has developed this skill to a far greater extent than any other animal. (②) The emergence of tool use was the result of an unprecedented coordination between stereoscopic eyes, brains and limbs, which had first emerged while our human ancestors were still a forest-dwelling species. (③) As a result, humans learned to perform ever more tasks with their hands, even while walking. (④) Today, by contrast, great apes cannot do this; they have to sit still to execute such tasks. (⑤) As a result of these developments, early humans slowly became more powerful with respect to other larger animals. [3점]

*stereoscopic: 입체적으로 보는

17.

> But not all farm plots are equal; regional variations in sunshine, soil, and other conditions meant that one farmer might grow particularly good onions while another grew especially good apples.

Humans have been on Earth for 200,000 years. (①) For the first 99% of this time, we didn't do much of anything but reproduce and survive. (②) This was mainly due to harsh global climatic conditions, which stabilized sometime around 10,000 years ago. (③) People soon thereafter developed farming and irrigation, and they gave up their nomadic lifestyle in order to cultivate and tend stable crops. (④) This eventually resulted in specialization; instead of growing all the crops for his own family, a farmer might grow only what he was best at and trade some of it for things he wasn't growing. (⑤) Because each farmer was producing only one crop, and more than he needed, marketplaces and trading emerged and grew, and the establishment of cities followed. [3점]

18. 다음 글의 내용을 한 문장으로 요약하고자 한다. 빈칸 (A), (B)에 들어갈 말로 가장 적절한 것은?

Regulations covering scientific experiments on human subjects are stringent. Subjects must give their informed, written consent, and experimenters must submit their proposed experiments to rigorous scrutiny by overseeing bodies. Scientists who experiment on themselves can avoid the restrictions associated with experimenting on other people. They can sidestep most of the ethical issues involved: nobody, presumably, is more aware of an experiment's potential hazards than the scientist who devised it. Nonetheless, experimenting on oneself remains deeply problematic. One obvious drawback is the danger involved; knowing that it exists does nothing to reduce it. A less obvious drawback is the limited range of data that the experiment can generate. Human anatomy and physiology vary, in small but significant ways, according to gender, age, lifestyle, and other factors. Experimental results derived from a single subject are, therefore, of limited value; there is no way to know whether the subject's responses are typical or atypical of the response of humans as a group.

*stringent: 엄격한, 엄중한 **scrutiny: 정밀 조사
***anatomy: (해부학적) 구조

↓

> Scientific self-experimentation has the advantage of avoiding _____(A)_____ problems associated with the experiment, but also has the danger involved in it and the limitation that the results do not _____(B)_____ a diverse population.

	(A)		(B)	
①	moral	…	select	
②	moral	…	represent	
③	legal	…	select	
④	legal	…	explain	
⑤	political	…	represent	

[19~20] 다음 글을 읽고, 물음에 답하시오.

If your client is trying to decide between a jacket and a sweater, she might not purchase either if she can't make up her mind. How can you help her decide what she really wants? Recent research shows that decision making is simplified when a consumer considers a third, less attractive option. Akshay Rao, a marketing professor, conducted research that shows that, when a less desirable sweater is considered in the situation above, the shopper could (a) solve her conundrum by choosing the more attractive sweater. Akshay Rao says, "The less appealing sweater plays the role of a decoy that makes the other sweater appear more (b) pleasing than before. In some ways, it is quite straightforward. When a consumer is faced with a choice, the presence of a relatively unattractive option (c) improves the choice share of the most similar, better item."

In fact, subjects had their brains scanned while they made their choices, and the presence of the extra possibility systematically increased preference for the better options. The brain scans showed that when making a choice between only two equally preferred options, subjects tended to display irritation because of the (d) difficulty of the choice process. The presence of the third option made the choice process easier. When considering three options, buyers displayed an (e) increase in activation of the amygdala, an area of the brain associated with negative emotions. There are several implications of this research. Alternatives are routinely encountered in a variety of settings, including Web-based travel markets, and cell-phone plans. In these markets, the addition of irrelevant options is a strategy that reduces negative emotion.

*decoy: 미끼 **amygdala: (뇌의) 편도체

19. 윗글의 제목으로 가장 적절한 것은?

① Why Do Consumers Suffer from Comparison?
② Use the Decoy Effect as a Marketing Strategy
③ The Decoy Effect: How to Make Rational Choices
④ Marketing Tactic: Switch Your Customer's Preference
⑤ The Paradox of Choice: More Attractive Is Less Preferred

20. 밑줄 친 (a) ~ (e) 중에서 문맥상 낱말의 쓰임이 적절하지 <u>않은</u> 것은? [3점]

① (a)　　② (b)　　③ (c)　　④ (d)　　⑤ (e)

○ 답안지의 해당란에 성명과 수험번호를 쓰고, 또 수험번호와 답을 정확히 표시하시오.
○ 문항에 따라 배점이 다르니, 각 물음의 끝에 표시된 배점을 참고하시오. 3점 문항에만 점수가 표시되어 있습니다. 점수 표시가 없는 문항은 모두 2점씩입니다.

1. 다음 글에 드러난 노인의 심경 변화로 가장 적절한 것은?

The flea market sale began and most items went quickly. An elderly man had one old baseball card left on his table. Mark stared at the grey image and then turned the card over. "That's one of my favorites," said the man. "How... how much?" asked Mark. "Fifty dollars," he said. When Mark shook his head and handed back the card, the man's heart sank. "I'm badly in the need of money right now. How about twenty dollars?" the elderly man pleaded. "Look," Mark said. "I know a lot about baseball cards. You need to take it to an antiques dealer. That card is worth at least $1,500." Suddenly the man's eyes widened. He said, with watery eyes, "I will never forget your honesty." Then he clutched the card to his chest, and walked away.

① desperate → grateful
② indifferent → thrilled
③ worried → confident
④ regretful → relieved
⑤ anticipating → sorrowful

2. 다음 글에서 필자가 주장하는 바로 가장 적절한 것은?

All historians understand that they must never, ever talk about the future. Their discipline requires that they deal in facts, and the future doesn't have any yet. A solid theory of history might be able to embrace the future, but all such theories have been discredited. Thus historians do not offer, and are seldom invited, to take part in shaping public policy. They leave that to economists. But what if public policy makers have an obligation to engage historians, and historians have an obligation to try to help? Done right, history could make decision making and policy far more sophisticated and adaptive, and this could invest the study of history with the level of consequence it deserves. We should learn from history, and Santayana's warning continues in force: that those who fail to learn from history are condemned to repeat it.

① 역사가는 과거의 사실을 사실 그대로 전달해야 한다.
② 공공 정책의 의사 결정 과정에 역사가를 참여시켜야 한다.
③ 역사가는 공공 정책의 시행 과정을 기록하고 보존해야 한다.
④ 역사가는 현대의 대중들이 이해하기 쉽게 역사를 전달해야 한다.
⑤ 역사가와 경제학자는 올바른 공공 정책을 수립하기 위해 협력해야 한다.

3. 밑줄 친 If we can't see it, we don't think about it이 다음 글에서 의미하는 바로 가장 적절한 것은? [3점]

Interactions between people and environmental features have spatial dimensions that are often overlooked. Our impact on resource supplies, such as forests, fish stocks, and the various minerals and metals used to make the things that we consume, happens in particular places. Often the environmental impacts of our consumption and waste generation are distanced from us, and we do not experience them directly. The demand for diamonds as a symbol of love in North America, Europe, and Japan is linked to negative and violent impacts in diamond-producing, former European colonies of West Africa. Similarly, although we may fault China for its unabated greenhouse gas emissions, the industrial productivity there, enabled in part by low environmental standards, provides inexpensive goods to consumers around the world. Consumption in richer parts of the world is often both spatially and cognitively distant from its negative impacts, whether it is the mining of materials for batteries in hybrid cars or the dumping of toxic electronic waste in poor countries desperate for a source of income. If we can't see it, we don't think about it.

*unabated: 조금도 수그러들지 않는

① We are not interested in how to solve environmental issues for each country.
② We do not care about environmental issues that are not directly related to us.
③ We don't think about environmental problems caused by poor countries at all.
④ We can't think of a solution to environmental problems until we know the cause.
⑤ A closer look at environmental issues gives us a better understanding about them.

4. 다음 글의 요지로 가장 적절한 것은?

Humans evolved to crave stories. This craving has, on the whole, been a good thing for us. Stories give us pleasure and instruction. They simulate worlds so we can live better in this one. They help bind us into communities and define us as cultures. Stories have been a great boon to our species. But are they becoming a weakness? There's an analogy to be made between our craving for stories and our craving for food. A tendency to overeat served our ancestors well when food shortages were a predictable part of life. But now that we modern desk jockeys are awash in cheap grease and corn syrup, overeating is more likely to fatten us up and kill us young. Likewise, it could be that an intense greed for stories was healthy for our ancestors but has some harmful consequences in a world where books, TVs, and the Internet make stories omnipresent. I think the literary scholar Brian Boyd is right to wonder if overconsuming in a world filled with junk stories could lead to something like a "mental diabetes epidemic."

*boon: 요긴한 것; 혜택 **awash: (양이 많아서) 넘쳐나는

① 도덕적이고 건전한 이야기가 정신 건강에 유익하다.
② 인간은 태생적으로 이야기를 좋아하는 성향이 있다.
③ 무분별하게 이야기에 탐닉하는 것은 정신 건강에 해롭다.
④ 자주 접하는 이야기는 사람의 정서와 감정에 영향을 준다.
⑤ 이야기를 갈망하는 것은 음식을 갈망하는 본능에서 비롯된다.

5. 다음 글의 제목으로 가장 적절한 것은?

A Chicago restaurant owner was having trouble with "no-shows." People would make dinner reservations, but fail to appear for dinner. Additionally, they would not call to cancel their reservations. At this restaurant, it was common for the receptionist to take the reservation by phone and then say, "*Please call if you change your plans.*" For months, the no-show rate at this restaurant was approximately 30%. As part of a behavioral science study, researchers conducted an experiment, whereby they instructed the receptionists to stop saying, "*Please call us if you change your plans,*" and start saying, "*Will you please call us if you change your plans?*" Furthermore, the receptionist was instructed to intentionally pause and wait for the caller to respond. What do you think happened by simply adding two words to the script and ending with a question mark? Amazingly, by making these simple and almost effortless changes, which made callers make a commitment — either yes or no, the no-show rate at this restaurant dropped a whopping 20 percentage points, from 30% to 10%.

*whopping: 엄청 큰

① Different Strategies to Deal with Restaurant No-Shows
② Should Restaurants Charge Customers Who Fail to Show Up?
③ A Restaurant No-Show Solution: Getting Customers to Say Yes
④ A Clear Reservation Policy Helps Reduce the Cost of No-Shows
⑤ An Initial Small Request Makes Customers Feel More Comfortable

6. Annual Holiday Food Drive에 관한 다음 안내문의 내용과 일치하지 <u>않는</u> 것은?

Annual Holiday Food Drive

Dec.10 – 14
Now more than ever&we need your help
to make a difference in our community.

We will be collecting non-perishable food items during the week of December 10. All donations will go directly to Arlington families in need. Please be part of the annual Holiday Food Drive!

Items Needed:
Cereal&boxed pasta&pasta sauce&canned meats& canned fruits & vegetables&peanut butter&rice& cooking oil (PLEASE CHECK EXPIRATION DATE). Public health rules prevent us from accepting any homemade&already opened&or unlabeled food.

Location:
Drop off at Arlington Civic Center&2100 Central St. Mon. 10 a.m. – 9 p.m. Tue. – Fri. 10 a.m. – 6 p.m.
* After hours non-perishable items may be placed in our drop box&located next to the main entrance.

Visit ArlingtonCivicCenter.org for more information!

---

*food drive: 음식 자선 행사

① 월요일부터 금요일까지 5일간 하는 행사이다.
② 상하지 않는 식품을 모아 어려운 이웃에게 보낸다.
③ 가정에서 만든 음식은 밀폐 포장해서 보내야 한다.
④ 첫날은 다른 날보다 세 시간 더 오래 수거한다.
⑤ 수거 시간 이후에는 지정된 수거함에 두면 된다.

7. 다음 글의 밑줄 친 부분 중, 어법상 틀린 것은? [3점]

Higher density living in cities means that fewer people have their own garden spaces and that gardens in modern homes are ① <u>constantly</u> becoming smaller. This is one reason for the importance of maintaining public gardens and ② <u>integrating</u> garden spaces into new developments. Many of the benefits provided by gardens are available for all ③ <u>to enjoy</u> in public gardens and parks and these venues are often the scene of weddings, parties, and family get-togethers of all sorts. Public gardens provide us with opportunities for recreation, contemplation, education, and inspiration. Their importance to the community and to the environment cannot be overstated and will only grow as higher density living ④ <u>deprives</u> more people of private garden spaces. Whether it's as a venue to socialize with friends, play sport, practise yoga, meditate, picnic, explore, play, or learn about the natural world, your local park ⑤ <u>having</u> much to offer, even if you do have your own garden.

8. 다음 글의 밑줄 친 부분 중, 문맥상 낱말의 쓰임이 적절하지 <u>않은</u> 것은? [3점]

For nearly two centuries, people in the United States have plowed or paved over the nation's swamps and marshes. Rich wetland soils make highly productive farmlands, and sites near large rivers or the coast are ① <u>desirable</u> locations for development. These mysterious ecosystems are also home to creatures many people think of as undesirable, such as crocodiles and mosquitoes, which provides another reason to ② <u>eliminate</u> them. California has lost over 90% of its wetlands. Now, nearly two-thirds of the state's native fish are extinct, endangered, threatened, or in decline.

Forested riparian wetlands near the Mississippi River once had the capacity to store about 60 days of river ③ <u>discharge</u> but now can store only about 12 days. Researchers say that the flooding of the Gulf of Mexico coast from Hurricane Katrina in 2005 would have been much less extensive had the region not ④ <u>conserved</u> so much of its wetlands in the past century. Without wetlands, pollutants make their way more ⑤ <u>readily</u> to streams, lakes, and the oceans.

*swamp: 늪 **marsh: 습지 ***riparian: 강가의, 강가에 사는

[9~12] 다음 빈칸에 들어갈 말로 가장 적절한 것을 고르시오.

9. As infants develop, they continue to interpret what is dangerous, as well as learning how to soothe themselves through reading nonverbal cues and eventually, through understanding verbal language. They ask and receive _____ repeatedly from their parents and other caregivers. A toddler seeing snow for the first time might say "Mamma!" with alarm, alternating looking at the snow with looking at her mother, pointing, and showing distress. Her mother reassures her, smiling, "It's just snow, honey." The toddler, having no idea what "snow" means or if it is dangerous, comes to recognize that her mother is not scared from her facial expression and reassuring tone, which she has learned to interpret over time, and concludes that snow is not dangerous.

*toddler: (걸음마를 시작한) 유아

① warnings   ② objectives
③ limitations   ④ reassurance
⑤ confusion

10. How often do we think about the air we breathe, the water we drink, or the soil our agribusiness conglomerates plant our vegetables in? Not often enough. The typical attitude toward natural resources is often _____. Only when someone must wait in line for hours to fill the car gas tank does gasoline become a concern. Only when people can see — and smell — the air they breathe and cough when they inhale does air become a visible resource. Water, the universal solvent, causes no concern (and very little thought) until shortages occur, or until it is so foul that nothing can live in it or drink it. Only when we lack water or the quality is poor do we think of water as a resource to "worry" about. Is soil a resource or is it "dirt"? Unless you farm, or plant a garden, soil is only "dirt." Whether you pay any heed to the soil/dirt debate depends on what you use soil for — and on how hungry you are.

*conglomerate: 복합 기업 **inhale: 숨을 들이쉬다
***pay heed to: ~에 주의를 기울이다

① emotional release
② fast internalization
③ harmless resistance
④ deliberate ignorance
⑤ a continuous concern

11. Poetry, being the language of precision, needs to express ideas and feelings in their most condensed although richest forms. Thus, good poetry by nature must be mercilessly frugal on the usage of words without compromising the content and the meaning. Suppose you have a piece of cloth soaked with water, and you must get it as dry as you can and as soon as you can for one reason or another. The harder you turn and twist this piece of cloth, the more water you extract from it, and the drier it gets, short of ripping the fabric. In a way, poetry is just like that. The more you squeeze letters, words, adjectives, verbs, nouns, and so on while still preserving the integrity of the intended meaning, the better the poetry becomes. Hence, in poetry, _____.

[3점]

① the concept of "less is more" applies
② the meanings of words are rather figurative
③ its form should not be lean and economical
④ "irrationality" is bound to be largely embraced
⑤ many of the words at one's disposal fail to qualify

12. For some reason, sound technology seems to induce a strange sort of deafness among its most advanced pioneers. Some new tool comes along to share or transmit sound in a new way, and again and again its inventor _____. When Thomas Edison invented the phonograph in 1877, he imagined it would regularly be used as a means of sending audio letters through the postal system. Individuals would record their missives on the phonograph's wax scrolls, and then pop them into the mail, to be played back days later. Bell, in inventing the telephone, made what was effectively a mirror-image miscalculation: He envisioned one of the primary uses for the telephone to be as a medium for sharing live music. An orchestra or singer would sit on one end of the line, and listeners would sit back and enjoy the sound through the telephone speaker on the other. So, the two legendary inventors had it exactly reversed: people ended up using the phonograph to listen to music and using the telephone to communicate with friends. [3점]

*phonograph: 축음기 **missive: 편지, 서한(書翰)

① has a hard time imagining how the tool will eventually be used
② fails to monitor public reaction to the invention and improve it
③ wants to show people how his invention improves people's lives
④ impresses the public by suggesting multiple ways to utilize the tool
⑤ tries to develop a device to help the disabled communicate with others

13. 다음 글에서 전체 흐름과 관계 <u>없는</u> 문장은? [3점]

The quality of entertainment is often measured by an audience to the degree that it invokes an emotional response among that audience—this leads to opinion. ① The degree to which we are emotionally affected by entertainment typically influences our opinion of how good or bad we think it is. ② If after watching a stand-up comedian a member of the audience stated 'that was really funny', it would suggest that the person thought the comedian was good, which contains a suggestion of recommendation. ③ By watching a show that is 'labelled' a comedy, this person expected to feel positive emotions, including happiness, amusement, and joy. ④ You can't make a joke without inserting a tragic twist, and you can't be a comedian without holding a small amount of melancholy, for even a short time, over the audience. ⑤ These emotions are then physically transformed by the audience into laughter and applause; a comedian that doesn't invoke an emotional response among the audience that results in laughter and applause is usually considered as being 'not funny' and therefore a 'poor' comedian—or low quality entertainment in the opinion of that audience.

[14~15] 주어진 글 다음에 이어질 글의 순서로 가장 적절한 것을 고르시오.

14.

It is time that often plays a crucial and defining role in environmental economics. Traditional economics can determine efficient ways to allocate resources for producing goods and services.

(A) In the case of many environmental goods, allocation of resources over a long period is critical. For example, while burning fossil fuels and polluting the environment today, we may be creating problems for future generations for years or forever.

(B) Similarly, if we harvest all prawns today, the supply will be gone forever. Our consumption decisions on some environmental goods may be 'irreversible' and may have a profound impact on the well-being of future generations.

(C) The allocation is, however, simplified and confined to a single period of time with the underlying presumption that the production of an additional unit of a commodity today does not prevent producing one tomorrow.

*prawn: 새우

① (A) – (C) – (B)　　② (B) – (A) – (C)
③ (B) – (C) – (A)　　④ (C) – (A) – (B)
⑤ (C) – (B) – (A)

15.

Novice counselors learning active listening techniques often find silences difficult, just as many of us do in social settings. Remember, however, that in an active listening setting your client may be processing some very difficult emotions and struggling to find the right words.

(A) You may be tempted to jump in, usually with a question, which to the client can feel like an intrusion on their thoughts. You may need to learn to be comfortable with silence.

(B) Your client may need space to stop, think and feel. When you are a novice a short silence feels very long. It is unlikely to feel as long to the client as it does to you.

(C) And you may need to learn to trust yourself with this space in the helping relationship. If eventually you need to break the silence then it is probably better to do this with some kind of reflection than it is to ask a question. [3점]

*intrusion: 침해

① (A) – (C) – (B)　　② (B) – (A) – (C)
③ (B) – (C) – (A)　　④ (C) – (A) – (B)
⑤ (C) – (B) – (A)

[16~17] 글의 흐름으로 보아, 주어진 문장이 들어가기에 가장 적절한 곳을 고르시오.

16.

> To accomplish this, food companies began advertising their products regionally and nationally through newspapers and magazines, and locally via circulars, billboards, and in-store promotions.

Throughout the nineteenth century, many Americans grew a substantial portion of their own food on farms or in gardens. Small general stores catered to those who lived in small communities or who desired luxuries unavailable locally. (①) Food was sold mainly as a generic product measured out from unmarked barrels, sacks, and jars. (②) This changed as food production was industrialized. (③) Following the Philadelphia Centennial Exposition, food processors and manufacturers prospered as agricultural surpluses flooded the market and technology lowered the cost of production. (④) The result was the rise of large food manufacturers, who needed to persuade consumers of the superiority of branded products over generic groceries. (⑤) Food advertising became a major source of American opinion and action regarding what, when, and how to eat. [3점]

*cater to: ~의 요구를 채워 주다 **generic: 상표 없는

17.

> The child then tries to get her attention in an effort to restore affect to her emotionally blank face.

A piece of evidence that supports the infant's capacity to understand other people's emotions is provided by the "still-face" test developed by Edward Tronick. (①) In this test, the mother is instructed to distort her affective feedback to her infant by making an expressionless face (a still face) after a period of normal playful exchanges with her child. (②) The child first becomes unpleasantly surprised to see the mother's emotionless expression. (③) When these efforts fail, the child becomes very uncomfortable, distressed, and anxious. (④) Finally, when the mother's face does not change, the child becomes indifferent, detached, and bored. (⑤) Most infants also react physiologically to the mother's still face with an increased heart rate, which Edward Tronick attributed to disruption of the infant's desire to relate to others.

18. 다음 글의 내용을 한 문장으로 요약하고자 한다. 빈칸 (A), (B)에 들어갈 말로 가장 적절한 것은? [3점]

Kawamura, a graduate student at Showa Women's University, documented communications exchanged by a group of thirty who were organizing a party at a bar. "As the date grew nearer, the frequency of messages increased. But only four people showed up on time at the agreed place," Kawamura said. However, dozens of others stayed in touch through voice and text messages while they trickled in. "Kids have become loose about time and place. If you have a phone, you can be late," added Kawamura. Kamide, another graduate student, agreed that it is no longer taboo to show up late: "Today's taboo," Kamide presumed, "is to forget your mobile phone or let your battery die." Later it was discovered that this "softening of time" was noted for the same age group in Norway. "The opportunity to make decisions on the spot has made young people reluctant to divide their lives into time slots, as older generations are used to doing," agreed a Norwegian researcher.

*trickle in: (사람이) 드문드문 오다

↓

> As cell phones have _____(A)_____ the temporal-spatial concept of young people, being late isn't considered _____(B)_____.

	(A)		(B)
①	contracted	……	agreeable
②	contracted	……	unacceptable
③	expanded	……	agreeable
④	expanded	……	unacceptable
⑤	narrowed	……	offensive

[19~20] 다음 글을 읽고, 물음에 답하시오.

John Stuart Mill wondered whether each of us would rather be the pig satisfied or Socrates dissatisfied, and at times it may seem as though a lot of people have chosen the former. But that is only in the short term. Long-term, we have no choice but to be (a) discontented when things are constant and unchanging. The satiety of our appetites, the endless repetition of the same thoughts and feelings will eventually lead us to move on in mind and seek (b) fresh inputs. To begin with, people may readily sacrifice their freedom for comfort, but increasingly the absence of change, the monotony of surroundings and routines will lead to acute discomfort and the search for something new. That is why I am optimistic that people who are fed a constant diet of the same ideas, the same foods, or the same TV programs will eventually come to think differently. It may take time, but change and moving on will be inevitable. People are increasingly switching off and staying away from the familiar and (c) demanding shows and films that lazy television executives and film producers offer. Instead, space has opened up for intelligent and entertaining programs and for independent filmmaking. It is here, at the creative end of the culture that popular success is to be found. The lesson is already being learned in the corporate world, where monopolies try to cope by (d) diversifying their range of services. The increasingly global market has led to a firmer appreciation of the interesting local ones. And I am optimistic that people, through (e) boredom and the need for something new, will seek out better, not worse, experiences.

19. 윗글의 제목으로 가장 적절한 것은?

① Why We Prefer Simple to Complicated
② How Our Brain Handles Novelty and Change
③ Promote Good Desires and Inhibit Bad Desires
④ Human Nature Pursues Novelty beyond Comfort Zone
⑤ We Change Ourselves Only After Basic Needs Are Met

20. 밑줄 친 (a) ~ (e) 중에서 문맥상 낱말의 쓰임이 적절하지 않은 것은? [3점]

① (a)　　② (b)　　③ (c)　　④ (d)　　⑤ (e)

○ 답안지의 해당란에 성명과 수험번호를 쓰고, 또 수험번호와 답을 정확히 표시하시오.
○ 문항에 따라 배점이 다르니, 각 물음의 끝에 표시된 배점을 참고하시오. 3점 문항에만 점수가 표시되어 있습니다. 점수 표시가 없는 문항은 모두 2점씩입니다.

1. 다음 글의 목적으로 가장 적절한 것은?

Dear Mr. Jones:

For many of us, pets are part of the family. They give at least as much as they take. But with this joy comes responsibility; pet owners must speak for their dogs, cats, birds, and other animal coresidents, and ensure that they receive the best possible care. For 12 years, I have been the owner of a dog charm school, and I have prepared a book to publish that can offer pet owners a lot of valuable how-to advice on these subjects. I notice you are the editor for *How to Raise a Pet Dog for Fun and Profit*. Would you consider looking at my publishing plan for a nonfiction, do-it-yourself book, aimed at pet dog owners, that focuses on health, obedience, and grooming? I would greatly appreciate your consideration. A self-addressed stamped envelope is enclosed for your reply.

Thanks,
Kevin Smithers

① 반려견을 훈련하는 방법에 관해 설명하려고
② 반려견 훈련에 도움이 되는 책을 추천하려고
③ 반려견에 관한 책을 저술해 줄 것을 권유하려고
④ 반려견을 돌보는 방법에 대한 정보와 조언을 구하려고
⑤ 반려견 관련 책의 출판 계획을 검토해 줄 것을 요청하려고

2. 밑줄 친 fail to act accordingly가 다음 글에서 의미하는 바로 가장 적절한 것은? [3점]

While we dislike failing in our regular endeavors, games are an entirely different thing, a safe space in which failure is okay, neither painful nor the least unpleasant. The phrase "It's just a game" suggests that this would be the case. And we do often take what happens in a game to have a different meaning from what is outside a game. To prevent other people from achieving their goals is usually hostile behavior that may end friendships, but we regularly prevent other players from achieving their goals when playing friendly games. Games, in this view, are something different from the regular world, a frame in which failure is not the least distressing. Yet this is clearly not the whole truth: we are often upset when we fail, we put in considerable effort to avoid failure while playing a game, and we will even show anger toward those who foiled our clever in-game plans. In other words, we often argue that in-game failure is something harmless and neutral, but we repeatedly fail to act accordingly.

*foil: 저지하다

① try to change our plans for winning a game
② are upset and angry when we fail in a game
③ express our frustration when we are alone
④ stop playing a game when we're satisfied
⑤ tend to forget to learn from our failures

3. 다음 글의 요지로 가장 적절한 것은?

Anyone who has young children knows their love of "why" questions. In the 1920s, psychologist Frank Lorimer observed a four-year-old boy over four days and recorded all the "whys" the child asked during that time. There were forty of them, questions such as *Why does the watering pot have two handles? Why do we have eyebrows?* The act of questioning is so important to our species that we have a universal indicator for it: all languages, whether tonal or nontonal, employ a similar rising intonation for questions. Certain religious traditions see questioning as the highest form of apprehension, and in both science and industry, the ability to ask the right questions is absolutely essential. Chimpanzees, on the other hand, can learn to use rudimentary signing to communicate with their trainers, and even to answer questions, but they never ask them. They are physically powerful, but they are not thinkers.

① 나이가 들수록 어린이들의 질문을 좋아하는 성향은 줄어든다.
② 사물에 대해 호기심을 갖는 것은 인간과 동물이 동일하다.
③ 인간은 언어를 통해 질문하지만 동물은 몸짓으로 묻는다.
④ 어린이가 호기심을 표현하는 방식은 문화에 따라 다르다.
⑤ 질문을 하는 점이 동물과 구별되는 인간만의 특성이다.

4. 다음 글의 주제로 가장 적절한 것은?

In a recent study, researchers compared two groups of volunteers who consumed 90 grams of protein each day, primarily in the form of lean beef. One group ate 30 grams of protein at each meal, while the other group ate 10 grams at breakfast, 15 grams at lunch, and 65 grams at dinner. The volunteers who consumed the evenly distributed protein meals had a twenty-four-hour muscle protein synthesis 25 percent greater than those subjects who ate according to the skewed protein distribution pattern. Better muscle synthesis means a more efficient utilization of calories, and less protein being oxidized and ending up as glucose or fat. So balancing your protein intake throughout the day is key. Add an egg, a glass of mixed vegetable juice, Greek yogurt, or a handful of nuts to get closer to 30 grams of protein in the morning. Do something similar to get to 30 grams for your midday meal, and then consume no more than 30 grams of protein for dinner. Many of my patients are in the best shape of their lives after fifty by simply bringing back the balance that helps them shed the fat, build muscle, and look younger.

*skewed: 편향된 **glucose: 포도당

① reasons why too much protein is bad for health
② physical conditions that can increase protein needs
③ the necessity of spreading out protein intake evenly
④ easy ways to increase the amount of protein in a diet
⑤ the importance of taking in high-protein food for weight loss

5. 다음 표의 내용과 일치하지 <u>않는</u> 것은?

Public's Policy Priorities: 2012-2020
% who say _____ should be a top priority
for the president and Congress

	8 years ago Jan 2012	4 years ago Jan 2016	1 year ago Jan 2019	Now Jan 2020
Terrorism	69	75	67	74
Economy	86	75	70	67
Health care costs	60	61	69	67
Education	65	66	68	67
Environment	43	47	56	64
Poor and needy	52	54	60	57
Jobs	82	64	50	49

The above table shows the U.S. public's thoughts on which issues the president and Congress should prioritize over eight years, from January 2012 to January 2020. ① The percentage of the public who considered defending against terrorism a top priority was the third highest in 2012, but the highest in 2020. ② While an overwhelming share of the public (86%) cited strengthening the economy as a major priority in 2012 and 75% did so four years later, that fell to 67% in 2020. ③ In 2016, 47% of Americans rated protecting the environment as a top priority, but in 2020, more than six in ten did so. ④ Health care costs, education, the environment, and problems of the poor and needy were all issues that had a higher percentage as a top priority in 2019 than in 2020. ⑤ The share of Americans who say improving the job situation is a top priority declined the most sharply among policy priorities from 2012 to 2020, by 33 percentage points.

6. Samuel Clemens에 관한 다음 글의 내용과 일치하지 <u>않는</u> 것은?

Samuel Clemens, known by his pen name Mark Twain, was an American writer, humorist, and lecturer. He was raised in Hannibal, Missouri, a town on the Mississippi River. Many of his stories were inspired by his experiences there. He served an apprenticeship with a printer and then worked as a typesetter, contributing articles to the newspaper of his older brother Orion Clemens. His first story, "The Celebrated Jumping Frog of Calaveras County", was published in 1865. The short story brought international attention and was even translated into French. *The Adventures of Tom Sawyer* (1876) and its sequel *The Adventures of Huckleberry Finn* (1884) tell the adventures of two boys on the Mississippi River. Twain earned a great deal of money from his writings, but he invested in ventures that lost most of it. He began a world tour giving lectures to pay off his debts, and eventually overcame his financial troubles. He died from a heart attack in 1910, aged 74.

① Mark Twain이라는 필명으로 글을 썼다.
② 형이 운영하는 신문사에 기사를 기고했다.
③ 최초의 이야기가 국제적인 주목을 받았다.
④ 많은 돈을 벌었지만 벤처에 투자하여 돈을 잃었다.
⑤ 세계를 돌아다니며 강연을 했지만 빚을 갚지는 못했다.

7. 다음 글의 밑줄 친 부분 중, 어법상 틀린 것은? [3점]

Not all organisms are able to find sufficient food to survive, so starvation is a kind of disvalue often ① <u>found</u> in nature. It also is part of the process of selection ② <u>by which</u> biological evolution functions. Starvation helps filter out those less fit to survive, those less resourceful in finding food for ③ <u>themselves</u> and their young. In some circumstances, it may pave the way for genetic variants to take hold in the population of a species and eventually allow the emergence of a new species in place of the old ④ <u>one</u>. Thus starvation is a disvalue that can help make possible the good of greater diversity. Starvation can be of practical or instrumental value, even as it is an intrinsic disvalue. ⑤ <u>What</u> some organisms must starve in nature is deeply regrettable and sad. The statement remains implacably true, even though starvation also may sometimes subserve ends that are good.

*disvalue: 반(反)가치, 부정적 가치 **implacably: 확고히
***subserve: 공헌하다

8. 다음 글의 밑줄 친 부분 중, 문맥상 낱말의 쓰임이 적절하지 <u>않은</u> 것은?

The term *genius* can be traced back to the Latin word *ingenium*: a natural-born talent. The essence of this talent is seen as ① <u>original</u> productivity, which employs confident intuition to access new areas of creativity. The person who has genius — a brilliant creative power — is also known as a genius. It was not until the Renaissance that people began to describe an artistic creative potential or the source of ② <u>inspiration</u> as genius. The key significance for invention is that the so-called genius develops ideas that no one has had previously and, in the words of Immanuel Kant, that 'genius must be considered the very ③ <u>same</u> of a spirit of imitation'. In addition, Kant established that genius cannot indicate scientifically how it brings about its product, but rather gives the rule as ④ <u>nature</u>. Hence, where an author owes a product to his genius, he does not himself know how he conceived the ideas, nor is it in his power to invent the like at pleasure, or methodically, and communicate the same to others in such precepts as would put them in a position to produce ⑤ <u>similar</u> products.

*precept: 지침, 교훈

[9~12] 다음 빈칸에 들어갈 말로 가장 적절한 것을 고르시오.

9. Unlike conventional marketing activities, like advertising and promotions, that are planned, sports events are inherently unpredictable. Fans, athletes, teams, and companies do not know outcomes. Despite even the most formidable track records of success, one cannot know for certain whether past sport performances will continue or whether expectations will be turned upside down. This very unpredictability separates sports from almost all other corporate marketing activities. Indeed, many business managers find this prospect of uncertainty distinctly uncomfortable and consequently shy away from using sports as a marketing platform. Yet sports fans follow sports partly because outcomes are not guaranteed. Fans have an emotional attachment to their favorite teams and athletes, irrespective (mostly) of their recent performances. If sports were _____ then they would lose credibility, spontaneity would be lost, and they would be no different than a conventional company-directed ad campaign.

① banned
② scripted
③ advertised
④ capitalized
⑤ competitive

10. The fantasies of children and grown-ups, sometimes called daydreams, are always concerned with the future. These 'castles in the air' are the goal of their activity, built up in fictional form as models for real activity. Studies of childhood fantasies show clearly that the striving for power plays the predominant role. Children express their ambition in their daydreams. Most of their fantasies begin with the words 'when I grow up', and so on. There are many adults who live as though they too were not yet grown up. The clear emphasis on the striving for power indicates again that the psyche can develop only when a certain goal has been set; in our civilization, this goal involves social recognition and significance. An individual never stays long with any neutral goal, for the communal life of humankind is accompanied by constant self-evaluation giving rise to the desire for superiority and the hope of success in competition. The fantasies of children almost always _____. [3점]

*communal: 공동의

① reflect their plans to help their community
② reflect a particular identity-forming interest
③ have something to do with their successful experiences
④ involve situations in which the child exercises power
⑤ reveal their lack of ability to recognize reality and fantasy

11. The universality of music is, perhaps, more contentious than that of language because we place greater emphasis on production than listening, with many individuals declaring themselves to be unmusical. In this regard, John Blacking's comments, made in the 1970s, on the contradiction between theory and practice in the middle-class, Western society in which he grew up, remain relevant today. Music was and remains all around us: we hear it when we eat and try to talk in restaurants and airport lounges; it is played all day long on the radio; in fact, there are few occasions when someone is not trying to fill moments of potential silence with music. Blacking remarked that 'society claims that only a limited number of people are musical, and yet it behaves as if all possessed the basic capacity without which no musical tradition can exist — the capacity to listen and distinguish patterns of sound'. He favoured the idea that _____, and noted that the existence of a Bach or a Beethoven was only possible because of the presence of a discriminating audience. [3점]

*contentious: 이론의 여지가 있는

① music and human culture always work together
② audience is a key to success in the music industry
③ there was no such thing as an unmusical human being
④ audience differentiates the best musicians from lesser ones
⑤ musical talent is derived from the repetitive exposure to music

12. Confirmed scientific theories are often referred to as 'laws of nature' or 'laws of physics', but it is important to recognize exactly what is meant by 'law' in this case. This is not the sort of law that has to be obeyed. A scientific law cannot dictate how things should be; it simply describes them. The law of gravity does not require that, having tripped up, I should adopt a prone position on the pavement — it simply describes the phenomenon that, having tripped, I fall. Hence, if I trip and float upwards, I am not disobeying a law, it simply means that I am in an environment (e.g. in orbit) in which the phenomenon described by 'the law of gravity' does not apply, or that the effect of gravity is countered by other forces that enable me to float upwards. The 'law' cannot be 'broken' in these circumstances, and can only be found _____. [3점]

① to have validity if the description contains evidence to support
② to be true or false upon repeated observation of the physical world
③ to be inadequate to give a complete description of what is happening
④ to have discrete and definite evidence regardless of human interpretation
⑤ to be flexible enough to be applied differently depending on the context

13. 다음 글에서 전체 흐름과 관계 없는 문장은?

There are natural cycles of unfortunate events like drought or insect plagues or outbreaks of disease that negatively impact ecosystems and also harm the soil. But there are many more ways in which humans neglect or abuse this important resource. ① One harmful practice is eliminating the vegetation that serves to hold soil in place. ② Sometimes just walking or riding your bike over the same place will kill the grass that normally grows there. ③ Other times land is deliberately cleared to create space for some other use. ④ As soil resources serve as a basis for food security, the international community advocates for its sustainable use. ⑤ Soils can also be contaminated if too much salt accumulates in the soil or if pollutants are allowed to enter the ground.

[14~15] 주어진 글 다음에 이어질 글의 순서로 가장 적절한 것을 고르시오.

14.

As far as we know, the best way to reap the benefits of plants is by consuming them in their natural forms. When new research reveals a benefit of eating particular fruits and vegetables, many people are quick to attribute that benefit to one particular ingredient.

(A) This finding stirred up a lot of interest in beta-carotene (vitamin A) and led many people to start taking vitamin A supplements to reduce their risk of cancer.

(B) For instance, studies have found that consuming fruits and vegetables rich in carotenoids reduces the risk of developing several kinds of cancer.

(C) But fruits and vegetables contain at least forty different carotenoids, often at higher levels than beta-carotene. We cannot just assume that one ingredient will produce the same result in isolation as it will when it is part of a complex package like a plant. It's not just an issue of isolating one component and packaging it in a pill at high doses.

*carotenoid: 카로티노이드 ((적황색 색소))

① (A) – (C) – (B)　　② (B) – (A) – (C)
③ (B) – (C) – (A)　　④ (C) – (A) – (B)
⑤ (C) – (B) – (A)

15.

Research subjects may be at risk if their privacy is compromised. Therefore, subjects expect that researchers will protect their privacy and keep their participation in, and results from, the study confidential.

(A) However, in those situations in which data must be tied to an individual (for example, when data will be collected from the same subjects on many different occasions), every precaution should be taken to safeguard the data and keep them separate from the identities of the participants.

(B) In other words, a coding system should be employed that allows the researcher to identify the individual, but the information identifying them should be kept separate from the actual data so that if the data were seen by anyone, they could not be linked to any particular individual.

(C) In most research studies, there should be no need to connect data to individuals. Thus, in many cases, privacy and confidentiality are not issues, because the participants have anonymity [3점]

① (A) – (C) – (B)　　② (B) – (A) – (C)
③ (B) – (C) – (A)　　④ (C) – (A) – (B)
⑤ (C) – (B) – (A)

[16~17] 글의 흐름으로 보아, 주어진 문장이 들어가기에 가장 적절한 곳을 고르시오.

16.

> Further, assuming that people generally have predominantly positive attitudes about themselves, relationship formation would be facilitated by their having positive evaluations of each other.

Many people are uncertain about how to regard themselves: they are not certain of their abilities, their social stimulus value, or their worth. (①) For these persons, their self-evaluations constitute opinions about which they are concerned and in need of social support. (②) Accordingly, we would expect to find the formation of interpersonal relationships to be facilitated when two individuals hold opinions of each other that are similar to their respective self-evaluations. (③) This creates a situation in which each can reward the other by expressing opinions that validate the accuracy of the other's self-image. (④) Put in everyday terms, this assertion is that a friendship is made more likely if the two persons can honestly say nice things about each other. (⑤) In the strategies of how to "win friends and influence people" this suggests the importance of praise and flattery. [3점]

17.

> Reaching larger user groups in turn means that the price of the product or service can be reduced.

For a technology to become widespread, it must appeal to users with weaker purchasing motivations. (①) Only by expanding beyond the first people who make use of the new technology to the much larger communities can it achieve the returns to scale that allow the developers to recover their initial investments. (②) For example, early cellular telephone users frequently had bills of $1,000 per month for service within their own town. (③) Today such service might cost just $25 per month. (④) Broad adoption also demands new levels of performance, reliability, ease of use, and support. (⑤) Some of this happens naturally as developers learn about the technology and manufacturing becomes more efficient. [3점]

*return to scale: 규모에 대한 수익

18. 다음 글의 내용을 한 문장으로 요약하고자 한다. 빈칸 (A), (B)에 들어갈 말로 가장 적절한 것은? [3점]

Some species have evolved not only a theory of mind but also, distinctly, a theory of relationships — which is evolutionarily advantageous, because recognizing relationships between other individuals helps predict their social behavior. The most basic type of such knowledge is when one animal knows the relative dominance rank of two other animals, not just its own rank with respect to the others. This important ability is widespread, seen in hyenas, lions, horses, dolphins, and, of course, primates, but also in fish and birds. Capuchin monkeys in a fight preferentially seek out allies that they know to be higher ranked than their opponents, and they also seek out allies that they know have closer relationships with them than with their opponents. If two chimpanzees have a fight and a bystander offers consolation to the loser, this can reconcile the two combatants, but only if the bystander has a friendship with the aggressor. All three animals understand what it means for two of them to have a special bond.

*consolation: 위로, 위안 **reconcile: 화해시키다

↓

> Some animals have the ability to comprehend their social relationships, namely the ___(A)___ and social ties between them, which plays a role in dealing with their ___(B)___.

	(A)		(B)
①	grouping	......	conflicts
②	grouping	......	communication
③	ranking	......	conflicts
④	ranking	......	communication
⑤	network	......	interactions

[19~20] 다음 글을 읽고, 물음에 답하시오.

All rituals are grounded in repetition and rigidly fixed action sequences. But they differ from habits in one important way. Rituals lack a direct, immediate reward. Instead, we have to invent a meaning and impose it on them. We lift our glasses to toast, blow out candles on a birthday cake, and wear caps and gowns at graduation. The act of standing silently for a song, singing while candles burn, or wearing a ceremonial costume acts as feedback, reinforcing our belief that something (a) meaningful is taking place — an act of respect for our country, a celebration of another year, or an educational accomplishment.

Furthermore, rituals are a (b) universal human impulse. Native Americans, especially in the Southwest, had rain ceremonies. Japanese have the art of the tea ceremony. Aztecs performed human sacrifices on top of their pyramids. To an objective eye, these rituals are not especially (c) rational and certainly not all are desirable. But researchers are discovering a logic behind them, especially in times of uncertainty and anxiety. Repetition is its own reward. Consider the high-stakes, high-pressure world of elite athletes. A great deal of money, fame, and talent are on the line each time they compete. Winning requires a lot of confidence and some luck. Given the pressures that athletes are under, it is no surprise eighty percent of pros (d) perform superstitious rituals before playing, which range from always eating four pancakes to seeing the number 13 at least once. Players use them to gain a sense of control in this highly (e) predictable environment.

19. 윗글의 제목으로 가장 적절한 것은?

① Superstitious Belief Rooted in the Ritual
② Ritual, Formal Performance and Culture
③ Is It Necessary to Preserve Tradition in Rituals?
④ Ritual Performance: Its Significance and Functions
⑤ A Ritual Is a Means to an End, Not an End in Itself

20. 밑줄 친 (a) ~ (e) 중에서 문맥상 낱말의 쓰임이 적절하지 않은 것은? [3점]

① (a)   ② (b)   ③ (c)   ④ (d)   ⑤ (e)

○ 답안지의 해당란에 성명과 수험번호를 쓰고, 또 수험번호와 답을 정확히 표시하시오.
○ 문항에 따라 배점이 다르니, 각 물음의 끝에 표시된 배점을 참고하시오. 3점 문항에만 점수가 표시되어 있습니다. 점수 표시가 없는 문항은 모두 2점씩입니다.

1. 다음 글에 드러난 Archer의 심경 변화로 가장 적절한 것은?

It was the end of a beautiful summer day, and the sky was slowly turning red. Seeing children playing with their dogs on the beach, Archer thought it had been a good decision to turn down Ethan's offer to go see a musical together. A cool breeze brushed his face, the refreshing smell of oak leaves tickled his nostrils, and the sound of chirping birds filled his ears. He told himself that everything at the campsite on Bondi Beach was perfect, smiling lightly. It was just then that something fell from the sky and touched his hand. Raindrops! The rain was falling harder and harder. Everyone at the campsite started to take down their tents, and Archer was one of them. Ethan's suggestion popped into Archer's head once more when he realized the whole evening was now a mess. Though it was already too late, Archer couldn't stop thinking he should have followed Ethan to the musical hall.

*nostrils: 콧구멍

① relieved → terrified
② contented → regretful
③ delighted → jealous
④ depressed → pleased
⑤ stressed → confident

2. 다음 글에서 필자가 주장하는 바로 가장 적절한 것은?

All the branches of science such as life sciences, botany, zoology, physiology, physics, chemistry, agriculture and geology, etc. are correlated and interrelated with each other. For example, if we are studying a geology lesson on the rocks and minerals of the Earth, then we must be studying the chemical composition, structure and properties of these rocks and minerals. Similarly, in the study of agriculture, the knowledge of rocks and chemicals is involved. The study of rocks and soil helps in choosing different types of soils for different crops. The knowledge of chemistry helps us in determining different types of manures. Therefore, it is always worthwhile to deal with different branches of science in a unified manner for the benefit of students. It is necessary to bring out correlation of one branch of science with another branch to make science education more meaningful and effective.

*manure: 비료, 거름

① 통합 과학을 가르치기 위해 과학자들은 서로 협력해야 한다.
② 학생들은 자기의 전공 분야 이외에 다른 분야도 공부해야 한다.
③ 과학의 여러 분야를 통합된 방식으로 학생들에게 가르쳐야 한다.
④ 세분된 과학의 분야에 각기 다른 유용한 접근법을 적용해야 한다.
⑤ 학생들은 여러 과학 분야보다는 한 분야에 집중해야 한다.

3. 밑줄 친 need a more holistic model이 다음 글에서 의미하는 바로 가장 적절한 것은? [3점]

The calorie argument claims that, based on weight, age, and several other variables, we each need a specific number of calories per day. To lose, gain, or maintain weight in this model, you have two variables: calories consumed and calories expended. According to this theory, to lose weight we simply eat less and move more. To gain weight, we move less and eat more. If we followed this simplified formula, we could eat Twinkies all day and run those calories off on a treadmill. However, common sense tells us this is not health. Sure, counting calories can help some people move in the right direction by eliminating the most egregious diet offenders, but for those who are serious about being healthy, simply counting calories doesn't make the cut. Counting calories does not help manage appetite or eliminate cravings, and these can be serious impediments to weight loss. It also doesn't help manage or reverse diseases. We need a more holistic model.

*egregious: 아주 나쁜 **impediment: 방해(물), 장애

① should have a role model for weight loss
② need to have a long-term perspective of a diet
③ should keep our mind and body in top condition
④ should develop a new, comprehensive weight-loss theory
⑤ must try a traditional way for a successful diet and weight loss

① difficulties of preserving and reviving endangered languages
② necessity of studying endangered languages in the digital age
③ primary objective of the preservation of endangered languages
④ importance of preserving linguistic diversity in the digital world
⑤ saving endangered languages through technology and digital tools

4. 다음 글의 주제로 가장 적절한 것은?

Although the efforts to revive dying languages are admirable, the challenges facing those who would reverse the extinction process are intimidating. Not all of the extinctions are the direct result of hostility and repression from a dominant government, as was the case with American Indians throughout most of U.S. history. But where brutal repression failed to make indigenous languages and culture extinct, intense globalization since the 1980s has been more successful. The recent revolution in communications technology has provided powerful tools (through the airwaves and cyberspace) for the spread of mainstream Western culture and language. Yet, for some endangered languages, the tide is changing through the digital revolution. As Rosenberg points out, digital technology, discussion groups, software companies, and apps are lifelines for language preservation for minority and endangered language communication needs. At one time technology forced some language speakers to adopt the dominant language of their community or nation. Now, new tools create the possibility for revitalizing languages and retaining language speakers of endangered languages.

*intimidating: 위협적인, 겁을 주는 **repression: 억압, 탄압

***indigenous: 고유한, 토착의

5. 다음 글의 제목으로 가장 적절한 것은?

What makes us so adaptable? In one word, culture — our ability to learn from others, to copy, imitate, share, and improve. When humans learned to communicate using oral and, later, written language, ideas, knowledge, and practices — how to make a fishhook, build a boat, fashion a spear, sing a song, carve a god — could replicate and combine like genes. But unlike genes, they could jump from one mind to another across distances of time and space. Culture freed humans from the limitations of their biology; according to evolutionary biologist Mark Pagel, when humans discovered culture, they achieved a momentous shift in the balance of power "between our genes and our minds." Humans became the only species to acquire guidance on how to live from the accumulated knowledge of their ancestors, rather than just from their DNA.

*replicate: 복제하다

① Social Evolution: from Genes to Culture
② Genes Affect Culture, Culture Affects Genes
③ Culture: Human Abilities That Can Transcend Genes
④ Cultural Adaptability and Accumulation of Knowledge
⑤ What Is the Relationship Between Language and Culture?

6. Warwick Castle Family Walk에 관한 다음 안내문의 내용과 일치하는 것은?

Help out your local charities at the
WARWICK CASTLE FAMILY WALK
Sunday 4th October 2020

Support these important local charities:
Age UK Coventry and Age UK Warwickshire, who offer services and support for local older people

- A 3-kilometer walk in the historic grounds of Warwick Castle
- Registration from 9 a.m., walk starts at 10 a.m. sharp
- £6 per person, £3 children under 12 years old
- Includes admission to the Castle and free parking for participants until 12 noon
- Raise £25 for donation and get in free

To book and register your spot
email info@ageukwarks.org.uk
or call 01725 497400

---

① 지역 단체 두 곳이 공동 주최하는 걷기 행사이다.
② 기부금은 지역 아동을 위한 봉사와 지원에 쓰인다.
③ 등록은 오전 10시에 즉시 시작된다.
④ 참가자들은 하루 종일 주차장을 무료로 이용할 수 있다.
⑤ 25파운드의 기부금을 모금해 오면 입장료가 무료이다.

7. 다음 글의 밑줄 친 부분 중, 어법상 틀린 것은? [3점]

Academic work is by its nature never done; while flexibility of hours is one of the privileges of our work, it can easily translate into working all the time or ① feeling that one should. Mary Morris Heiberger and Julia Miller Vick note this paradox: "Despite their heavy workloads, academics have more freedom ② to structure their own time than practically anyone else in the economy. For some people, this is the great advantage of the career path; for others, it is a source of stress." Furthermore, given the time and money ③ required to get a PhD and its uncertain economic returns, it is clear that most of us pursue an academic career for idealistic, rather than pragmatic, reasons. And while believing in ④ that one does is a key aspect of job satisfaction, idealism also can lead to overwork. The irony is that the more committed we are to our vocation, the more ⑤ likely it is that we will experience time stress and burnout.

*pragmatic: 실용적인

8. 다음 글의 밑줄 친 부분 중, 문맥상 낱말의 쓰임이 적절하지 <u>않은</u> 것은? [3점]

Heidegger used the term *Dasein* — "being there" — for the being that exists. He rejected the idea that there is an external world ① separate from a conscious observer. Instead, he developed a *phenomenological* view, in which our understanding of things is always in relation to ② ourselves. For example, if you put on a jumper, it is because the jumper will keep you warm, or you think it will look good on you. It is not because the jumper is made of twisted yarn and is a few millimeters thick. This applies to knowledge, too. We might read a book about politics because it interests us, or because understanding politics helps us make sense of what we see happening around us. We see it in terms of a ③ tool, or satisfying a need. Heidegger saw the *Dasein* (principally the human "being") as completely immersed in and part of the world that defines it. No separation between consciousness and environment is ④ impossible. "Being *there*" means that "there" — our context — is the defining aspect of "being." We are not shut off from the world in an ⑤ enclosed mind — which Heidegger called the "cabinet of consciousness."

*phenomenological: 현상학의 **yarn: 실, 방적사

[9~12] 다음 빈칸에 들어갈 말로 가장 적절한 것을 고르시오.

9. The contamination pathway in the first known case of an outbreak associated with imported mangoes is particularly _____. In 1999, 78 people in 13 US states became ill from a common strain of *Salmonella enterica*; 15 patients were hospitalized and two died. Investigators traced the mangoes back to a farm in Brazil. They discovered that, surprisingly, no Europeans who had consumed mangoes from the same farm were affected. Investigators deduced that the mangoes destined for the US had probably absorbed the microbe as a result of a hot water treatment used to fight off fruit flies. The treatment was required to meet US standards barring produce carrying the Mediterranean fruit fly — standards the Europeans did not impose. The farmer had adopted the hot water treatment to avoid employing cancer-causing pesticides to fight off the fruit flies. But investigators discovered that dipping the mangoes in hot water, then submerging them in cool water before packing initiated a process in which gases inside the fruit contracted, drawing in contaminated water. So steps that the farmer had taken to clear the mangoes of insects without using carcinogens had ultimately provided an entree for the pathogen.

*deduce: 추론하다 **carcinogen: 발암 물질 ***pathogen: 병원균

① diverse
② arbitrary
③ mysterious
④ paradoxical
⑤ experimental

10. According to Thomas Eriksen of the University of Oslo, author of *Tyranny of the Moment*, our modern electronic lifestyle systematically favors fast time activities that require instant, urgent responses (email, cell phone calls, etc.). Such stimuli tend to crowd out slow time activities such as reflection, play and long-term love relationships. This dynamic has a particularly unfortunate effect in academia, which is supposed to be somewhat insulated from the larger society so that students and scholars can think more broadly and with longer range perspectives. But in fact, universities mirror the rest of society, and _____ is as much an issue within the academy as anywhere else. As instrumental, short-term, applied goals take center-stage, our society has less access to the wisdom and complexity that deep, reflective thinking can provide. This is a major loss. [3점]

① the rejection of modern conveniences
② the contempt for fast time activities
③ the dwindling time to think
④ the problem of social isolation
⑤ the underestimation of simple wisdom

11. In some cases development may be necessary for the conservation and/or preservation of natural resources. Establishing a conservation easement in a rural area, for example, typically requires financial resources. Conservation programs can be very costly and many of these costs may be forced on local communities. Thus, it may be more difficult for a very poor area to conserve its natural amenities. There is a large body of literature suggesting that the poor are likely to exploit their natural environment if there are no other opportunities to improve their livelihoods. Thus, many conservation programs today _____ _____ for rural residents in order to build a successful conservation program. In this instance, there is a mutual relationship between the environment and jobs. [3점]

*conservation easement: 보존 지역권

① focus their efforts on maximizing their strengths
② actively arrange a wide variety of helpers and guides
③ provide free and high-quality educational opportunities
④ understand the need to provide economic opportunities
⑤ engage in the creation of literature about the environment

12. It may seem odd to suggest that numbers are a human invention. After all, some might say, regardless of whether humans ever existed, there would still be predictable numbers in nature, be it eight (octopus legs), four (seasons), twenty-nine (days in a lunar cycle), and so on. Strictly speaking, however, these are simply regularly occurring *quantities*. Quantities and correspondences between quantities might be said to exist apart from the human mental experience. Octopus legs would occur in regular groups even if we were unable to perceive that regularity. *Numbers*, though, are the words and other symbolic representations we use to differentiate quantities. Much as color terms create clearer mental boundaries between colors along adjacent portions of the visible light spectrum, numbers create conceptual boundaries between quantities. Those boundaries may reflect a real division between quantities in the physical world, but these divisions _____. [3점]

① allow humans to visualize naturally existing quantities
② blur the difference between the tangible and the abstract
③ orient human mind around a numerical theoretical concept
④ are the standard of measurement for values of that quantity
⑤ are generally inaccessible to the human mind without numbers

13. 다음 글에서 전체 흐름과 관계 <u>없는</u> 문장은?

As an academic discipline, architecture *is* outside of the humanities — so in that sense, there's no question that it is not one of the humanities. Not institutionally at least, even if there is something of a family resemblance. ① Architecture students aren't oriented to thinking, reading, and writing in quite the same way as are students within the humanities. ② What's interesting about architecture is that it has always been unsure as to where to position itself and its own identity as a discipline: it is itself internally divided about whether it is a science, a technological discipline, or a mode of art or aesthetic production. ③ This uncertainty regarding its own identity has led it to be quite open to philosophical and critical theory in a way that is unimaginable for other disciplines, like engineering or medicine, for example. ④ What's important is that we acknowledge architecture as an artistic practice — not as pure science. ⑤ What I can say positively as an outsider is that architecture is a discipline seeking self-definition, and for that self-definition it looks outside of itself, to see what others say about it.

[14~15] 주어진 글 다음에 이어질 글의 순서로 가장 적절한 것을 고르시오.

14.

Labeling people according to our first impressions is an inevitable part of the perception process. These labels are a way of making interpretations. "She seems cheerful." "He seems sincere." "They sound awfully conceited."

(A) Whether the judgment is accurate or not, after you accept your friend's evaluation, it will probably influence the way you respond to the neighbor. You'll look for examples of the insincerity you've heard about — and you'll probably find them.

(B) Suppose, for instance, you mention the name of your new neighbor to a friend. "Oh, I know him," your friend replies. "He seems nice at first, but it's all an act." Perhaps, this appraisal is off-base.

(C) If they're accurate, impressions like these can be useful ways of deciding how to respond best to people in the future. Problems arise, however, when the labels we attach are inaccurate, because after we form an opinion of someone, we tend to hang on to it and make any conflicting information fit our image.

① (A) – (C) – (B) ② (B) – (A) – (C)
③ (B) – (C) – (A) ④ (C) – (A) – (B)
⑤ (C) – (B) – (A)

15.

During the past ten thousand years or longer, man as a whole has been so successful in dominating his environment that almost any kind of culture can succeed for a while, so long as it has a modest degree of internal consistency and does not shut off reproduction altogether. No species of ant or white ant enjoys this freedom.

(A) To a scarcely lesser extent the same is true for social carnivores and primates. In short, animal species tend to be tightly packed in the ecosystem with little room for experimentation or play.

(B) The slightest inefficiency in constructing nests, in establishing odor trails, or in conducting nuptial flights could result in the quick extinction of the species by predation and competition from other social insects.

(C) Man has temporarily escaped the constraint of interspecific competition. Although cultures replace one another, the process is much less effective than interspecific competition in reducing variance. [3점]

*carnivore: 육식 동물 **nuptial flight: 혼인 비행
***interspecific: 종간(種間)의

① (A) – (C) – (B) ② (B) – (A) – (C)
③ (B) – (C) – (A) ④ (C) – (A) – (B)
⑤ (C) – (B) – (A)

[16~17] 글의 흐름으로 보아, 주어진 문장이 들어가기에 가장 적절한 곳을 고르시오.

16.

> That might have suggested it was the presence of danger that determined whether they used magic or not, but that explanation didn't match with other observations.

When the anthropologist Bronislaw Malinowski observed the daily lives of native people living on the Trobriand Islands of the South Pacific, he realized that while the islanders used magic rituals abundantly, they saved them only for certain activities. (①) When they went after the plentiful fish in a sheltered lagoon, for instance, they didn't use magic, but when they fished in the open sea, they did. (②) The islanders used magic to keep insects from destroying their crops, for example, but they didn't in gardening generally. (③) Malinowski realized that what made the difference was control. (④) When the islanders felt their own work and skill would determine success or failure, they did not turn to magic. (⑤) When the outcome involved luck or other factors they couldn't control, they did. [3점]

*lagoon: 석호, 초호((환초로 둘러싸인 얕은 바다))

17.

> Rather, the assumption is that affective experiences are an important component of moral judgment and that the latter involves a complex integration of thoughts, feelings, and experiences.

Social domain theory views emotions and moral judgments as reciprocal processes that cannot be disentangled. (①) This view differs from emotivist or intuitionist approaches to morality, which are principally based on research with adults and give priority to emotional and implicit processes while avoiding reasoning as largely post hoc rationalizations. (②) From the social domain perspective, this treatment of emotions and reasoning as distinct, opposing influences represents a false dichotomy. (③) To borrow from Kant's famous saying, moral reasoning without emotion is empty; emotions without reasoning are blind. (④) Children's affective experiences influence their understanding, encoding, and memory of moral violations and are part of a complex evaluative process. (⑤) Information obtained from observing the affective consequences of acts for others, as well as past or immediate emotional responses to moral situations, may constitute the foundation on which moral understanding is constructed. [3점]

*disentangle: 떼다, (엉킨 것을) 풀다 **post hoc: 사후(事後)의
***dichotomy: 이분법

18. 다음 글의 내용을 한 문장으로 요약하고자 한다. 빈칸 (A)와 (B)에 들어갈 말로 가장 적절한 것은?

In a modern world, we are constantly processing huge amounts of new information, but we often don't realize how our intake of information is affected by how easy it is to comprehend. In a study concerning the level of fluency in processing information, participants were asked to read a recipe for creating a Japanese lunch dish, then to rate the amount of effort and skill they thought the recipe would require and how likely they were to prepare the dish at home. Subjects who were presented with the recipe in a difficult-to-read font rated the recipe as more difficult and said they were less likely to attempt to make the dish. The researchers repeated the experiment, showing other subjects a one-page description of an exercise routine instead of a recipe, and found similar results: subjects rated the exercise as harder and said they were less likely to try it when the instructions were printed in a font that was hard to read.

↓

> If the ___(A)___ of information is difficult to understand, that affects our ___(B)___ about the substance of that information.

	(A)		(B)
①	form	......	judgments
②	level	......	attitudes
③	source	......	beliefs
④	meaning	......	perceptions
⑤	appearance	......	concentration

[19~20] 다음 글을 읽고, 물음에 답하시오.

Recent experiments conducted by Patricia Chen, a researcher of Stanford University suggest that students should (a) self-reflect about how they approach their studies and the available resources. For the experiments, the control group, which consisted of half the class, received just a regular reminder of a statistics exam coming up in a week. The intervention group got the reminder and a 15-minute online survey that made students think about what they expected would be on the exam, what grade they might get, what resources would be best used for preparation and how they would use them. In particular, they were asked to choose from 15 available class resources, like practice questions, readings from the textbook, lecture notes or peer discussions. In the study, students who strategized their resource use before studying (b) outperformed comparable classmates in the control group. They got an average of 3.45% higher in points than those who did not strategize. Why was the intervention so effective? The researchers found that the brief intervention exercise made students more (c) mindless about how they approached their learning. It's not merely about using a greater number of resources for studying. The important point here is using resources more effectively. "(d) Blind effort alone, without directing that effort in an effective manner, doesn't always get you to where you want to go," said Chen. The researchers found that strategic thinking had additional (e) psychological benefits, helping students feel more empowered about their education. Students in the intervention group were also less stressed out about the upcoming exams.

19. 윗글의 제목으로 가장 적절한 것은?

① Fewer Study Resources Make Higher Test Scores
② Why Does Stress Negatively Affect Our Test Results?
③ Irregular Study Habits Help to Improve Student Grades
④ Why "15" Is the Magical Number for Academic Success
⑤ A Self-Administered Study Leads to Improved Exam Scores

20. 밑줄 친 (a) ~ (e) 중에서 문맥상 낱말의 쓰임이 적절하지 <u>않은</u> 것은? [3점]

① (a)   ② (b)   ③ (c)   ④ (d)   ⑤ (e)

1. 다음 글의 목적으로 가장 적절한 것은?

To the Editor:

Our son was involved in a serious multiple-vehicle accident near the Crosstown Shopping Center last week. He sustained only relatively minor injuries, but unfortunately, others were not so lucky. I fully appreciate the fact that a reporter had the right to be there and cover the incident. However, your reporter at the scene, John Stevens, was extremely insensitive to those who were injured. My husband and I had to push our way past your reporter to get to our son. Mr. Stevens continued to ask questions and invade our privacy. We asked him to leave us alone, but he persisted. I teach political science at the college level and fully support freedom of the press, but rude behavior should not be tolerated under any circumstances. Perhaps Mr. Stevens was absent from class the day they were covering courtesy.

Sincerely,
Laura Pottenger

① 보도 기자의 과잉 취재에 대해 항의하려고
② 사고를 취재해준 보도 기자에게 감사하려고
③ 피해를 입힌 쇼핑센터에 배상을 요구하려고
③ 사고 경위에 대한 정확한 조사를 촉구하려고
⑤ 편파적인 보도 내용에 대해 문제를 제기하려고

2. 밑줄 친 government architecture is the mirror of the governments themselves가 다음 글에서 의미하는 바로 가장 적절한 것은? [3점]

When I was a student of architecture in Europe in the mid-30s, I was struck by the observation that the appearance of government buildings in various countries differed greatly. Those built in Italy during the early, comparatively calmer years of the Mussolini regime were relatively light and open, but as the situation in Europe worsened, Italy's position worsened, too; new buildings acquired thicker walls, heavier details and a generally more massive appearance. Similarly, when Hitler came to power in Germany and later fought against the Allied powers to retain his pervasive dominance, the official structures had extremely massive weight, and modern architecture, which is very light in structure and appearance, was forbidden. In Scandinavia, on the other hand, where the King and other ruling personages were secure enough that it was not unheard of for them to be seen on street cars, government architecture had reached an unprecedented stage of apparent fragility. After much thought I finally came to the conclusion that government architecture is the mirror of the governments themselves.

① Great buildings come from powerful governments.
② Local governments should control building regulations.
③ Architecture doesn't always represent political culture.
④ A government building is the space where politics literally take shape.
⑤ A government's stability is apparent in the weight of its buildings.

3. 다음 글의 요지로 가장 적절한 것은?

The goal of a reputable, scholarly biography is simply to provide the facts in a chronological order. In this way, the reader can learn about the subject's life without the distracting input of the biographer and the potentially dangerous influence of subjectivity. This represents the pinnacle of biographical writing, and the manifestation of the subject's life as science. This scientific method implies that subjectivity could and should be eliminated, but is this even a possibility or just a fallacy? An author cannot remain fully detached and impartial to the subject, as if they were not already somehow invested in the matter, or they probably wouldn't have begun to undertake such a task. The biographer will inevitably begin the process with their own interpretations and preconceived notions, and even if they aim to create an objective biography, these notions will inevitably influence their writings.

① 전기 작가는 자신과 관련이 있는 인물을 대상으로 삼는다.
② 전기의 객관성은 과학적인 증거의 제시를 통해서 이루어진다.
③ 전기는 독자의 흥미를 끌기 위해 인물을 왜곡하여 다룰 수 있다.
④ 전기는 인물 전체가 아닌 특정 부분을 강조해 다루기 마련이다.
⑤ 전기 작가의 주관이 들어가 있지 않은 전기는 사실상 불가능하다.

4. 다음 글의 주제로 가장 적절한 것은?

Almost any scientific discovery has a potential for evil as well as for good; its applications can be channeled either way, depending on our personal and political choices. But there's a real danger that rather than campaigning energetically for optimum policies, we will be lulled into inaction by fatalism — by a belief that science is advancing so fast and is so strongly influenced by commercial and political pressures that nothing we do will make any difference. Cynics would go further and say that anything that is scientifically and technically possible will be done — somewhere, sometime — despite ethical and prudential objections and whatever the regulatory regime. Whether this idea is true or false, it's an exceedingly dangerous one, because it engenders a despairing pessimism and demotivates efforts to secure a safer and fairer world.

*be lulled into: ~에 빠지게 하다

① challenges and difficulties of controlling science
② the danger of believing that science is uncontrollable
③ immense potential and disastrous downsides of science
④ reasons why attempts to regulate science is detrimental
⑤ importance of ethical choices on how science is applied

5. 다음 도표의 내용과 일치하지 <u>않는</u> 것은?

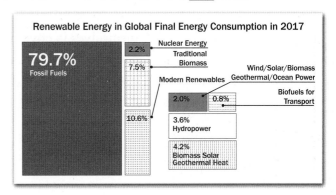

Renewable Energy in Global Final Energy Consumption in 2017

The figure above shows the share of renewable energy in global final energy consumption in 2017. ① In 2017, the share of "Fossil Fuels" consumption in the world's final energy consumption accounted for nearly 80 percent, while that of "Modern Renewable Energy" consumption was about 10 percent. ② The ratio of "Nuclear Energy" consumption in the world's final energy consumption slightly exceeded 2 percent. ③ The consumption of "Traditional Biomass" made up 7.5 percent, which was more than twice as high as the consumption of "Hydropower." ④ In the consumption share of "Modern Renewables," "Biomass/Solar/Geothermal Heat" consumption took the largest share with 4.2 percent, which was larger than the sum of the shares of "Hydropower" and "Biofuels for Transport." ⑤ The consumption of "Wind/Solar/Biomass/Geothermal/Ocean Power" was 2.0 percent, which was more than twice as high as that of "Biofuels for Transport."

*biomass: 생물자원 **geothermal: 지열의

6. Northern Pike에 관한 다음 글의 내용과 일치하지 <u>않는</u> 것은?

The Northern Pike gets its name from its resemblance to the pole-like weapon known as a pike used in the middle ages. Northern Pike are found in fresh water throughout the Northern Hemisphere. They play an important role as predator fish in many bodies of water. They are large eaters and tend to snap at bait quite readily, making them a favorite among fishermen. Their toothy jaws readily grab and hold slippery prey, including frogs, crayfish and even ducklings. Northern Pike are excellent swimmers, despite their large size and heavy weight. They swim, on average, between eight and ten miles per hour. Pike are good at camouflaging themselves in covered areas. Their camouflaging tendencies, along with their ability to remain perfectly still for long periods of time, make Northern Pike the perfect predator.

① 중세의 무기처럼 생긴 모습에서 이름이 붙여졌다.
② 북반구 전역의 담수에서 서식한다.
③ 미끼를 쉽게 물어서 낚시꾼들이 좋아한다.
④ 시속 10마일의 속도로 헤엄칠 수 있다.
⑤ 뛰어난 위장술로 조용히 숨어 상위 포식자를 피한다.

7. 다음 글의 밑줄 친 부분 중, 어법상 <u>틀린</u> 것은? [3점]

The effect and implications of using images of animals in advertising are subtle. Animals ① <u>used</u> to sell products and services that are aimed at children are usually shown as silly or "cute." "Tony the Tiger" is just one example of an animal image ② <u>with which</u> we are all familiar and that has come to be closely associated with a particular food product marketed to children. Tigers, many would argue, should be valued for the wildness and independence ③ <u>that</u> is inherent in their nature, and should not be portrayed as friendly purveyors of breakfast cereal. Most people would view the use of animal images as ④ <u>harmless</u>. However, many advocates of animal rights argue that these images exploit animals, play a role in the perpetuation of a view that trivializes animals, and ultimately ⑤ <u>contributes</u> to a lack of respect for members of other species.

*purveyor: (식료품) 조달업자 **perpetuation: 영속화

8. 다음 글의 밑줄 친 부분 중, 문맥상 낱말의 쓰임이 적절하지 <u>않은</u> 것은? [3점]

A change in the environment can open up new opportunities for some species. Whenever such an opportunity emerges, nature ① <u>tests</u> the variations in traits of existing individuals against it. A portion of the existing species will be genetically equipped to take advantage of those new opportunities. Since each species is ② <u>unique</u> in terms of its food sources, competitors, variations among individuals, and chemical errors, what is an opportunity to one species will not be an opportunity to all species. Those species which cannot take advantage of the opportunity may be ③ <u>transformed</u>. When a specific example of how one animal changed to take advantage of a new opportunity is given, it doesn't mean that every type of animal would also change in that same way. If that took place then all animals would soon become ④ <u>identical</u> — and extinct. It is always the case that just a portion of species ⑤ <u>adapt</u> when an opportunity is presented.

[9~12] 다음 빈칸에 들어갈 말로 가장 적절한 것을 고르시오.

9. Directness and honesty are qualities that our society values highly. We expect people to be who they say they are and tell us the truth about themselves. Before the advent of computers, anyone who used an assumed name was thought to be hiding something disreputable. Inexperienced computer users may continue to feel this way about online contacts. Because so many of the cues that we use to evaluate people are missing in cyberspace, computer users need to understand that virtual meeting places are different from face-to-face contacts. Until we have good reason to know and trust the people behind the instant message pop-up or the chat room screen, we should remain _____ and it is not dishonest to do so.

① anonymous   ② courteous
③ skeptical   ④ committed
⑤ unchanged

10. By the late twentieth century, state-of-the-art hospitals were typically designed around state-of-the-art equipment. The more scanners and X-ray machines a hospital had, and the more sophisticated its biochemical blood and urine tests, the more advanced its care was thought to be. Often, the hospital's physical space appeared to prioritize the care of the equipment rather than the care of the patients. In the early 1970s, one could still find hospitals where the only department that was air-conditioned was the Radiology Department, because the sensitive equipment could not tolerate the summer heat. As reliance on and admiration for medical technology increased in the mid-twentieth century, the comfort of patients was somehow pushed aside and their surroundings were often neglected. Hospital planners assumed that patients could adapt to the demands of technology, rather than the other way around. As a philosopher of technology, Jacques Ellul says of the modern hospital, "_____."
[3점]   *radiology department: 영상의학과, 방사선과

① Vision precedes reality
② Our actions drive progress
③ The means dominate the end
④ Out of massive quantities comes quality
⑤ Knowledge is the mother of civilizations

11. Prior to the Second World War, nation-states regulated their economic and fiscal affairs primarily as domestic matters; however, in the post-war era we have witnessed a huge expansion and intensification of economic interdependence. As a result, the global economy is acutely vulnerable to disruption by the malfunction of any single nation-state's fiscal-political system; a serious malfunction can trigger a chain reaction known commonly as the 'domino effect.' Such a disruptive event occurred in 1997 when Thailand, with a relatively small national economy, suffered a financial collapse which touched off sufficient uncertainty among investors that they pulled their money out of neighbouring Malaysia, Indonesia, and South Korea. The resulting destabilization of these national economies hastened the 'Asian Economic Crisis' and sparked a global recession. Increasingly, national institutions _____ _____; this has prompted an urgent call for effective international regulatory institutions. [3점]

*fiscal: 재정(상)의 **destabilization: 불안정화

① are preferring to do business in Asia
② ignore the financial decisions of others
③ are refusing to invest in small nations
④ cannot handle emerging economic problems
⑤ receive blame for promoting economic inequality

12. Since humans are also animals, arguably much can be gained from learning about the nature of animal warfare — especially the roles of dominance and activity. Much research has followed close observations of humanity's closest relatives, the primates, but that does not imply that _____.
Similarities and analogies can be applied, especially in the tactical methods of warfare, including the chase, deception, camouflage, encirclement, and so on, that animals have evolved and which humans try to mimic. Nevertheless, the human mind also generates purposes, intentions, concepts, and explicit understandings unknown in the animal kingdom (e.g., the suicide bomber). This remains true even if trial-and-error processes in man's military strategy converge on or mimic strategies that have evolved in the natural kingdom. [3점]

*primate: 영장류

① animals' warfare strategies are limited to physical activities
② primates form a social structure similar to that of humans
③ there's not a correspondence between humans and animals
④ all that can be learned from animals applies to human action
⑤ humans have been affected by the warfare strategies of animals

13. 다음 글에서 전체 흐름과 관계 <u>없는</u> 문장은? [3점]

Twenty to thirty years is a long time in the annals of information technology — long enough to allow us to discern a fundamental rift between the inner workings of yesterday's and today's computational tools. ① At the beginning, in the 1990s, we used our brand-new digital machines to implement the old science we knew — in a sense, we carried all the science we had over to the new computational platforms we were then just discovering. ② Now, to the contrary, we are learning that computers can work better and faster when we let them follow a different, nonhuman, postscientific method; and we increasingly find it easier to let computers solve problems *in their own way* — even when we do not understand what they do or how they do it. ③ In a metaphorical sense, computers are now developing their own science — a new kind of science. ④ The increasing diffusion of intelligent tools has already exposed tension between public governance and private governance of platforms. ⑤ Thus, just as the digital revolution of the 1990s (new machines, same old science) generated a new way of making, today's computational revolution (same machines, but a brand-new science) is generating a new way of thinking.

*annals: 역사 **rift: 간극, 균열

[14~15] 주어진 글 다음에 이어질 글의 순서로 가장 적절한 것을 고르시오.

14.

The Romans used many highly flavoured herbs and spices, and it seems that they liked their food to have a highly complex and strong taste. One of the reasons for this might involve, but not overcome, a food safety issue. The Romans used lead to line many of their cooking and storage vessels.

(A) One of the symptoms of lead poisoning is altered taste, often with a metallic taste in the mouth. Perhaps they tried to disguise the metallic taste with strong herbs and spices, or perhaps their sense of taste was so poor due to lead poisoning that the only way that they could taste anything was to make it incredibly highly flavoured.

(B) A lot of their food was quite acid and therefore dissolved the lead. It is clear from studies on Roman bones that they had a high body burden of lead, and indeed many of them must have been suffering from chronic lead poisoning.

(C) Their desire for highly spiced food, for whatever reason, had a good knock-on effect. Many herbs and spices contain antibacterial chemicals, and so their inclusion at high concentrations in Roman food probably reduced pathogen levels.

*line: ~의 안벽을 붙이다

① (A) – (C) – (B)　　② (B) – (A) – (C)
③ (B) – (C) – (A)　　④ (C) – (A) – (B)
⑤ (C) – (B) – (A)

15.

A change in species in an ecosystem can not only disrupt relationships among the organisms in a community, but can also set in motion secondary or indirect effects that can reverberate through a system for centuries.

(A) In places like many national parks around the world, society's goal is to perpetuate diverse, self-renewing natural communities not only for maintenance of vital ecological processes, but also for the recreational and tourist industries they support.

(B) Species can often come and go without affecting large-scale processes, such as soil fertility, plant productivity, or water cycling. From a human perspective, of course, the precise mix of species may matter a great deal.

(C) Eventually this widening circle of disturbance may affect the structure or stability of a community and interfere with larger ecosystem processes. But it would be misleading to claim that every species loss — or every invasion by a non-native creature — threatens systemwide disruptions. [3점]

① (A) – (C) – (B)　　② (B) – (A) – (C)
③ (B) – (C) – (A)　　④ (C) – (A) – (B)
⑤ (C) – (B) – (A)

[16~17] 글의 흐름으로 보아, 주어진 문장이 들어가기에 가장 적절한 곳을 고르시오.

16.

> Anderson wondered what good it would do to leave his grandchildren great wealth if the price of accumulating that wealth was an uninhabitable planet.

About twenty years ago, Ray Anderson, the late CEO of the immensely successful carpet manufacturer, Interface, had what he described as an epiphany. (①) Here he was, with more money than he or his heirs would know what to do with, when he realized that his company was poisoning the environment. (②) Carpet making is (or was) a petroleum-intensive industry and his company's environmental footprint was huge. (③) So Anderson resolved to transform every aspect of his company's operations, moving to achieve a zero footprint goal by 2020. (④) He assumed that the development of new production processes and a commitment to pollution control would cost money — a lot of it. (⑤) But he was willing to sacrifice the bottom line to achieve a social good.

*epiphany: 깨달음, 통찰 **bottom line: 이익, 최종 결과

17.

> But very early the Egyptians found that twelve months of thirty days each could provide a useful calendar of the seasons if another five days were added at the end, to make a year of 365 days.

The rhythm of the Nile was the rhythm of Egyptian life. The annual rising of its waters set the calendar of sowing and reaping with its three seasons: inundation, growth, and harvest. (①) The flooding of the Nile from the end of June till late October brought down rich silt, in which crops were planted and grew from late October to late February, to be harvested from late February till the end of June. (②) The rising of the Nile, as regular and as essential to life as the rising of the sun, marked the Nile year. (③) The primitive Egyptian calendar, naturally enough, was a "nilometer" — a simple vertical scale on which the flood level was yearly marked. (④) Even a few years' reckoning of the Nile year showed that it did not keep in step with the phases of the moon. (⑤) This was the "civil" year, or the "Nile year," that the Egyptians began to use as early as 4241 B.C. [3점]   *inundation: 범람 **silt: 토사

18. 다음 글의 내용을 한 문장으로 요약하고자 한다. 빈칸 (A), (B)에 들어갈 말로 가장 적절한 것은?

It is very important in the information age to understand the difference between knowledge and information. What is accessible by computer and, indeed, what is published in the journals is information. Knowledge is something that has to be constructed in the mind of the expert reader. This is what scholarship is about. Information is, these days, instantly accessible, but knowledge still takes years of dedicated study to acquire. Imagine that a freak accident wiped out an entire field of experts on a subject while all were attending a conference. How long would it take to reconstruct expertise in the field so that research could once again progress? It would probably take many years, despite the fact that their research was all published. To take another example, what do producers of science documentaries for television programmes do when they are researching their subjects? They talk to the experts rather than trying to read the journals. Quite rightly, as that is the only place that knowledge is to be found — inside the heads of the scholars.   *freak: 매우 이상한

↓

> While information means _____ (A) _____ data obtained from various sources, knowledge is the _____ (B) _____ of knowing something, which is accumulated for a certain period of time based on the studies of a person.

	(A)	(B)		(A)	(B)
①	personal	state	②	personal	pattern
③	research	way	④	processed	state
⑤	processed	pattern			

[19~20] 다음 글을 읽고, 물음에 답하시오.

Social psychologist Jack Brehm asked housewives to rate how much they liked a series of household items, such as coffee makers and toasters. For each woman, he took items that she ranked as equally attractive, told her that she could take one of them home, and allowed her to choose. After the choice, each woman was asked to re-rate the items. Brehm found that the ranking of the chosen item went up and the ranking of the others (a) dropped.

There is a simple demonstration of this tendency, the sort one can do in a bar. Take three identical things, such as coasters, and put two of them in front of your subject. Ask him to choose between them. Once he chooses, hand over the chosen object, then bring out the third, and now ask him to choose between the rejected object and the new one. What you'll tend to find is that the rejected object has dropped in value—it is tainted by not having been chosen the first time around, and so the tendency here is to choose the (b) new object. Nobody really knows why this happens. Perhaps it has to do with (c) self-enhancement; we want to feel good about ourselves, and so we pump up the value of our choices and denigrate the road not taken. Or maybe it is an evolved mental trick to make repeated hard decisions easier—once you choose between two close options, your choice will make the difference between the options seem (d) smaller, making it an easier choice in the future. A third proposal is self-perception theory. We assess our own choices as if they were done by another person, and so when I observe myself choosing A over B, I draw the (e) same conclusion that I would if someone else made this choice—A is probably better than B.

19. 윗글의 제목으로 가장 적절한 것은?

① Decision-Making Is Important for Self-Growth
② The Psychology of Why We Prefer Expensive Things
③ What Are Your Values?: Quick Decision-Making Skills
④ People Put Things to Value Because They Want to Own Them
⑤ Why Things You Choose Are More Valuable Than Those You Don't

20. 밑줄 친 (a) ~ (e) 중에서 문맥상 낱말의 쓰임이 적절하지 않은 것은? [3점]

① (a)　　② (b)　　③ (c)　　④ (d)　　⑤ (e)

○ 답안지의 해당란에 성명과 수험번호를 쓰고, 또 수험번호와 답을 정확히 표시하시오.

○ 문항에 따라 배점이 다르니, 각 물음의 끝에 표시된 배점을 참고하시오. 3점 문항에만 점수가 표시되어 있습니다. 점수 표시가 없는 문항은 모두 2점씩입니다.

1. 다음 글에 드러난 'I'의 심경 변화로 가장 적절한 것은?

One time in seventh grade, I was third chair in band, so I decided to challenge Jim, who had first chair. I practiced a piece over and over, and I thought I had a pretty good chance of winning a higher chair. On the audition day I was nervous but confident because all the girls I knew were wishing me good luck and were saying, "Oh, you'll win!" By the time I got to the band room, I felt pretty sure of myself. I played the song and made a few mistakes, but I thought I had done pretty well. Jim went into the band room when I came out, and I could hear his playing through the door. Soon he made a mistake and stopped playing. By this time I was sure I "had it made." When my teacher finally came out of the room, I waited for him to smile and congratulate me. Instead, he said, "I'm sorry, Lee Ann, we'll keep the same seating arrangement." I was at a loss at what to say. I numbly put my clarinet away and stared out the window for a while.

① calm → furious
② gloomy → delighted
③ terrified → relieved
④ satisfied → regretful
⑤ hopeful → disappointed

2. 다음 글에서 필자가 주장하는 바로 가장 적절한 것은?

The need to think about people humanely applies not only to individuals but to groups as well. I was called into a client's firm to help him solve a problem. His company had just completed a crash development project that had required the team to work almost 24 hours a day and 7 days a week for two months. It was an enormous success. But a month later, two of the team members left their jobs to work for a competitor. Why? my client wanted to know. I asked him what the company had done to celebrate the launch. He looked at me, puzzled. Nothing, he said. His team simply resumed their normal working hours. Rather than acknowledging how working those insane hours had affected the team members and their families, the company turned its back on the human impact. It could have offered the team time off, or a bonus, or the chance to work at home one day a week for a month—anything, really, to show their appreciation and gratitude. Little wonder that when no thanks were forthcoming, some team members decided to bolt.

*crash: 단기 집중적인 **bolt: 달아나다

① 과도한 업무 끝에 이룬 성과는 보상이 필요하다.
② 공정한 보상은 직원들의 동기 부여에 효과적이다.
③ 업무량보다는 업무 성과를 반영한 보상이 중요하다.
④ 물질적 보상과 정신적 보상이 함께 이루어져야 한다.
⑤ 과도한 업무는 업무 수행에 부정적인 영향을 미친다.

3. 밑줄 친 I now have something that I can give to everybody가 다음 글에서 의미하는 바로 가장 적절한 것은?

Lincoln was much plagued by people seeking offices or favors. He was unwell one day and not feeling inclined to listen to such requests. One petitioner, however, managed to get into his office. Just as the man was settling down for a lengthy interview, Lincoln's physician entered. Holding out his hands to him, Lincoln asked what the blotches on them were. The doctor instantly diagnosed varioloid, a mild form of smallpox. "It's contagious, I believe?" asked Lincoln. "Very contagious," was the answer. The visitor got to his feet at this point. "Well, I can't stop now, Mr. Lincoln, I just called to see how you were," he said. "Oh, don't be in a hurry," said Lincoln kindly. "Thank you, sir, I'll call again," said the visitor, heading speedily for the door. As it closed behind him, Lincoln said to his physician, "A good thing about this is that I now have something that I can give to everybody."

*plague: 성가시게 하다　**blotch: 반점　***smallpox: 천연두

① I want to share with other people the privilege I enjoy now.
② I'm worried that my disease can be easily passed to others.
③ Fortunately, everyone who comes to me can ask me a favor.
④ Ironically, people won't contact me for fear of infection now.
⑤ My disease won't prevent people from coming to me for favors.

4. 다음 글의 주제로 가장 적절한 것은? [3점]

From birth, children strive to learn about the world around them. Throughout their childhood, books help in this task. Books with pictures are a natural starting point, since visual literacy comes long before a child can decode words on a page. Well before children can read, they can follow the pictures and put together the information they need to ask and answer questions and to grasp a story. For young readers, pictures continue to provide helpful cues to the text. Even for adults, it's said, a picture is worth a thousand words. Today, in a world of screens and images, children expect to learn about their world through pictures. And advances in laser scanning technology and other changes in book production over the last forty years have made it possible to produce relatively inexpensive books with astonishing images on every page. A wealth of attractive and interesting picture books has been the result.

① the value and remarkable progress of picture books
② the problem of increasing prices of picture books
③ advantages of books over technological gadgets
④ reasons picture books limit children's imagination
⑤ the necessity of helping children read picture books

5. 다음 글의 제목으로 가장 적절한 것은?

Stories can be used to misrepresent science. In an article titled "Against storytelling of scientific results," Yarden Katz explains that certain defining features of narrative are antithetical to key ideals and practices of scientific work. But credible science communication and storytelling are not mutually exclusive — they can be great allies. In contrast with straight communication of experimental results, telling individual research stories portrays science as a human-driven endeavour, full of successes, uncertainties, missteps and failures, which in turn promotes transparency. What really matters is what story is being told and by whom. For example, the Intergovernmental Panel on Climate Change (IPCC) uses storytelling to engage a wider range of stakeholders with its findings. The IPCC perceives no conflict between a narrative approach and its mandate to neutrally inform policymaking with the latest science.

① A Scientific Story Tries to Inform, Not Persuade
② Storytelling: A Powerful Tool for Science Communication
③ Individual Stories Are More Convincing Than Sets of Data
④ Storytelling Compromises Objectivity of Scientific Research
⑤ Effective Scientific Presentation: Be a Storyteller, Not a Lecturer

6. LED Table Lamp에 관한 다음 안내문의 내용과 일치하지 <u>않는</u> 것은?

LED Table Lamp

Starting Up
- Place the metal base on the surface of the table and then insert the control panel box into the metal-based slot.
- Insert the power plug into a properly wired electrical outlet.

Operating the Control Panel Buttons
• Power Touch Button
- The lamp is switched to OFF with the green LED button lit.
- For safety and to conserve energy, the lamp will automatically turn off after 10 hours of use.

• Brightness Touch Button
- There are five brightness levels as indicated by the LED indicators on the control panel.
- The next time the desk lamp is switched to ON, the last-used brightness level is used.

• Timer Touch Button (blue LED button is lit when the timer is switched to ON.)
- After one hour, it beeps five times. After another hour, it beeps once and the table lamp switches OFF automatically.

---

① 구매 후 작동시키려면 금속 받침 홈에 제어판을 삽입한다.
② 전원이 꺼지면 전원 버튼에 녹색 불이 들어온다.
③ 안전을 위해 전원은 10시간 이후에 자동 차단된다.
④ 전원을 다시 켜면 마지막으로 설정된 밝기로 켜진다.
⑤ 타이머를 작동하면 1시간 후 자동적으로 꺼진다.

---

7. 다음 글의 밑줄 친 부분 중, 어법상 <u>틀린</u> 것은? [3점]

In England in the early 1900s property owners ① <u>whose</u> land was being eroded by wave action clamored for the Government to take preventive action. Their island was disappearing beneath the sea! They argued so loudly that a Royal Commission was appointed to study the matter. After making a careful survey, the commission reported that over a period of thirty-five years England and Wales lost 4,692 acres and gained 35,444 acres, ② <u>giving</u> a net gain of nearly nine hundred acres a year. This finding seemed to prove that people whose land disappeared ③ <u>complaining</u> more loudly than those whose land was increasing. It must be admitted, however, that the land lost probably was good cliffland on the open coast which disappeared in a spectacular way, whereas the land ④ <u>gained</u> was low, sandy and not particularly valuable. Non-geologists are usually not aware that the very existence of a cliff is warning ⑤ <u>that</u> erosional processes are at work, even though the changes seem to be very slow.

*erode: 침식시키다 **clamor: 아우성치다 ***net gain: 순이익, 순수익

8. 다음 글의 밑줄 친 부분 중, 문맥상 낱말의 쓰임이 적절하지 <u>않은</u> 것은? [3점]

Once formed, oil and natural gas do not necessarily stay trapped in the source rocks of their origin. Instead, they can ① <u>migrate</u> in response to pressure differentials in the surrounding rock. To do so, the source rock must have tiny pores that create pathways for the oil and gas to travel. If the source rock is too ② <u>fine-grained</u>, then the petroleum material remains captured within the source rock. Often, the rock above the petroleum source rock is saturated with water; in this case, the gas and oil, both being lighter than water, ③ <u>ascend</u>. As a consequence, the typical migration route is upward or sideways, and it continues until the oil and gas encounter a barrier in the form of impermeable rock—rock that is too ④ <u>dense</u> to contain the pores and pathways necessary for further migration. Because the gas is lighter than oil, it accumulates above the oil and just beneath the impermeable rock that constitutes a seal and ⑤ <u>accelerates</u> further travel.

*pore: (암석 등의) 작은 구멍; 곰곰이 생각하다　**saturated: 흠뻑 젖은

[9~12] 다음 빈칸에 들어갈 말로 가장 적절한 것을 고르시오.

9. Without _____ there could be no science of any kind. An individual is only itself and cannot explain anything else. It cannot even explain itself! Even though a medical doctor applies her general knowledge to a particular patient, she must know what is common to all possible cases of the same type. Imagine she spent four years in her medical school studying one and only one patient. She would be fine if the only patient she ever had to treat were that one case. But imagine what would happen as soon as a different patient walked into her office. She would be totally helpless in dealing with the new body and would either have to give up her practice or return to medical school to learn about other cases.

① causality　　　　　② evidence
③ universality　　　　④ imagination
⑤ practicability

10. As a professor of medieval history at the University of Strasbourg in the 1920s and the 1930s, before moving to the Sorbonne in Paris in 1936, Marc Bloch encouraged his students to consider the landscape as a historical document. If written texts provided a view into conscious historical processes, topography, he suggested, provided valuable insight into phenomena that were unconscious and invisible, such as social, economic, and political structure. Bloch described rural history as _____. Studying the form of agricultural fields as seen from an airplane, he contended, provided insight into the society that had produced them. Bloch demonstrated these connections as he took his students on field trips into the countryside near Strasbourg to see the elongated fields of Alsace, which he considered to be characteristic of all of northern Europe. According to Bloch, students of history could best understand historical processes by looking at historical processes that were still very much alive. [3점]

*topography: 지형학　**elongate: 길게 늘이다

① gradual geographical change over time
② efforts for conserving agricultural fields
③ a vibrant human interaction with the soil
④ a dilemma of soil conservation and exploitation
⑤ the struggle for a productive agricultural system

11. Psychologists Baba Shiv and Alexander Fedorikhin developed an experiment that looked at the kind of decisions people make when their cognitive systems are occupied, compared to when they have less to think about. In this study, 165 participants on a diet were asked to memorize either a two- or seven-digit number. After they were shown the number briefly, they were asked to memorize it and then select a snack, which was supposed to be a reward for participating in the study. The participants got to choose either a piece of chocolate cake or a salad. Among dieters who had to memorize the two-digit number, 41 percent chose the chocolate cake, while among those who memorized the seven-digit number, 63 percent chose chocolate cake, an increase of 22 percentage points. Those who had to memorize the seven-digit number said their decision was influenced more by their emotional, impulsive side than by their rational, prudent side. The researchers concluded that the group memorizing the longer number _____.

① energized their mind power beyond their absolute limit
② subconsciously resisted an impulse to eat unhealthy food
③ were completely committed to gaining an intrinsic reward
④ had less available brainpower to carefully consider the items
⑤ were encouraged to fight against the impulse to eat more meal

12. Language is often period specific, and historians must be extremely cautious not to read modern definitions into past times and thereby corrupt meaning. Words may have had a specific meaning or use in the past that is far different from current usage. Further, just as modern English has its own jargon and idioms, they were also present in the past. For example, the historical use of the word icon would have religious connotations, while in the twenty-first century the word would often be associated with a clickable image on a computer's desktop. Having the *Oxford English Dictionary* or another etymological dictionary close at hand for reference will help researchers avoid this form of potential misinterpretation. This is especially important because of the instability and sometimes open-ended meaning which words may convey. In order for historians to extract precise meaning from language effectively, it is essential that they have a clear idea of _____. [3점]

*jargon: 특수 용어 **etymological: 어원의

① how language developed grammar in a historical context
② how they understand the modern meaning of words
③ how humans have developed language-based cultures
④ how the past is re-created in the historian's mind
⑤ how these words functioned in the context of their time

13. 다음 글에서 전체 흐름과 관계 <u>없는</u> 문장은?

Each of us tends to remain in a particular long-term disposition; we seem to have a set point for personal happiness that is not easy to change. ① In fact, like other personality traits, personal happiness appears to be strongly influenced by our genes. ② Studies demonstrate that identical twins are significantly more likely to exhibit the same level of happiness than are fraternal twins or other siblings. ③ Behavior geneticists have used these studies to estimate just how much genes matter, and their best guess is that long-term happiness depends 50 percent on a person's genetic set point. ④ Today, the development of genetic science and technology enables us to analyze the genes' behavior in our body. ⑤ What we experience in life can, of course, change our moods for a period of time, but in most cases these changes are temporary.

*fraternal twins: 이란성 쌍둥이

[14~15] 주어진 글 다음에 이어질 글의 순서로 가장 적절한 것을 고르시오.

14.

> While industrial robots offer an unrivaled combination of speed, precision, and brute strength, they are, for the most part, blind actors in a tightly choreographed performance.

(A) Very often these are jobs that involve filling the gaps between the machines, or they are at the end points of the production process. Examples might include choosing parts from a bin and then feeding them into the next machine, or loading and unloading the trucks that move products to and from the factory.
(B) They rely primarily on precise timing and positioning. In the minority of cases where robots have machine vision capability, they can typically see in just two dimensions and only in controlled lighting conditions.

(C) They might, for example, be able to select parts from a flat surface, but an inability to perceive depth in their field of view results in a low tolerance for environments that are to any meaningful degree unpredictable. The result is that a number of routine factory jobs have been left for people. [3점]

*choreograph: (춤 따위를) 짜다, 구성하다 **tolerance: 허용 범위

① (A) – (C) – (B)　　　② (B) – (A) – (C)
③ (B) – (C) – (A)　　　④ (C) – (A) – (B)
⑤ (C) – (B) – (A)

15.

> Most early primate studies assumed that primates were highly territorial and that groups would fight to defend their territories. We now know that most primates are not what we would call "territorial," because areas they use overlap with areas that other groups of the same species use.

(A) This is not to say that if one spends enough time watching primates she won't see two groups coming together over a contested area and putting on a big show for each other — lots of hooting and hollering and maybe even some fighting.
(B) There are conflicts over space, and in most cases groups of the same species tend to avoid being in the same place at the same time (though not always). Researchers have argued that this is a way to minimize the risk of conflict between groups.
(C) These conflicts can result in serious injury or death but rarely do. Just as within groups, between-group conflicts are often resolved via negotiations or avoidance. Or just running away. Severe violence and aggression between groups is rare and seldom results in death. [3점]

*hoot: (동물이) 울부짖다 **holler: 큰 소리를 지르다

① (A) – (C) – (B)　　　② (B) – (A) – (C)
③ (B) – (C) – (A)　　　④ (C) – (A) – (B)
⑤ (C) – (B) – (A)

[16~17] 글의 흐름으로 보아, 주어진 문장이 들어가기에 가장 적절한 곳을 고르시오.

16.

> People in these kinds of careers must be prepared to solve difficult problems by applying their knowledge to new situations.

Each year, the National Association of Colleges and Employers asks employers which abilities they want college graduates to possess. At or near the top of that list each year is "analytical reasoning," a kind of critical thinking skill. (①) Yet accounting majors might ask, "Aren't mathematical and business skills more important for a career as an accountant?" (②) Likewise, nursing majors might suggest that knowledge of medicine is more important for them. (③) Although accountants and nurses obviously need these skills, they must also have a full complement of higher-order thinking skills. (④) In addition, they must be able to decide which new ideas they should accept or reject and be able to justify their decisions. (⑤) On any given day, people in these careers, and most of the careers you may be considering after college, must be able to effectively use critical thinking skills. [3점]

17.

> However, our control over the actions we take on the basis of our perceptions, memories, and emotions is vastly greater.

Our control over our abilities to perceive, remember, and emote has certain concrete limits, which is itself a sign of the fundamental separateness of these abilities from the processes that do the controlling. A color-blind person, for example, cannot simply decide to start seeing colors correctly. (①) An elderly person with a bad memory cannot simply decide to start remembering. (②) A sociopath who fails to feel empathy for the people he harms cannot simply decide to start feeling empathy. (③) Once the color-blind person knows that he sees both red and green as green, he can take steps to ensure that his actions do not endanger himself or others. (④) For instance, even though red and green traffic lights may look the same to him, he can memorize the position of the lights — red on top, green on the bottom — to make sure that he does not cause an accident. (⑤) He can use executive processing to correct for a perceptual deficit.

*emote: 감정을 여과 없이 드러내다

18. 다음 글의 내용을 한 문장으로 요약하고자 한다. 빈칸 (A), (B)에 들어갈 말로 가장 적절한 것은? [3점]

In one study, students completed a difficult intellectual task that required them to manipulate twelve shapes to form a large square. The experimenter who explained the task offered to help them if they encountered difficulty, and then left the room so the students could work on the problem uninterrupted. For some of the students, a small pile of money from the board game Monopoly sat on the corner of their desk — a constant, subtle reminder of money. By the time four minutes had elapsed, almost 75 percent of the students who weren't reminded of the money had asked for help; in contrast, only 35 percent of the students who sat peering at the Monopoly money asked for help after four minutes. A minute later, a student who happened to be walking through the lab ran into a minor disaster when she dropped twenty-seven pencils on the floor. The participants with money unconsciously on their mind picked up fewer pencils than did the students who weren't primed with the concept of money.

↓

> According to the study above, the money not only reminded the students of their _____ (A) _____, but also drove them toward _____ (B) _____.

	(A)		(B)
①	adaptability	......	selfishness
②	adaptability	......	generosity
③	perseverance	......	competitiveness
④	independence	......	selfishness
⑤	independence	......	generosity

[19~20] 다음 글을 읽고, 물음에 답하시오.

All speech is an exercise of power because there is a speaker and a listener. So the more blatant and explicit the message, the more (a) difficult it is to exercise discrimination — that is free will — in receiving the message. An explicit order, as in the army, is the worst: it is flatly coercive, binding, and demanding obedience. On the other hand, the kind of (b) indirect, allusive communication that is a peculiar characteristic of friendship allows ideas to flow and feelings not to be bruised. Someone who is a friend is presented with an opportunity to draw conclusions: "Perhaps you would like to consider..." This approach has several advantages. It (c) avoids infringing the integrity of the other person; acts are apparently entered into with free will, as the contracts of rational individuals. Thus we do not say "You must do this" when asking a friend for a favor, but "I wonder if you could possibly..."

Often the best form of communication with friends is, surprisingly, silence. Friendship is not only about what we do say, but even more importantly about what we do not. True friendship occurs when "information" is conveyed by the (d) absences of words. The striving is to convey as much as possible indirectly, "between the lines." The reason such "negative" communication is important is that it requires a greater closeness than positive communication. The (e) shorter the distance between sender and receiver, the more the need for explicitness and directness. Only when two or more people converse an enormous amount can the much more economical negative communication take place. This strategy is necessary when free and independent individuals are interacting.

19. 윗글의 제목으로 가장 적절한 것은?

① Ways to Improve Communication Skills
② How Can Friends Communicate Effectively?
③ For Better Friendships, Be a Better Listener
④ Communication Skills Make You an Effective Person
⑤ Types of Friendship Are Characterized by Communication

20. 밑줄 친 (a) ~ (e) 중에서 문맥상 낱말의 쓰임이 적절하지 <u>않은</u> 것은? [3점]

① (a)　　② (b)　　③ (c)　　④ (d)　　⑤ (e)

1. 다음 글의 목적으로 가장 적절한 것은?

Dear Mr. Black:

You were recommended to us as someone who specializes in estate planning. My wife and I are both in our eighties. We have recently sold our house and moved to a retirement community in Willow Grove. We are both in good health for our age, but my wife is confined to a wheelchair. At this point in our lives, I would like to see that the money we have is being handled properly. There is one gift of money my wife and I would like to make. Our son Donald passed away almost thirty years ago when he was a student at Willow Grove High School. I would like to endow a college scholarship in his name, but I am unsure of how to do it with my estate. I look forward to hearing from you soon. We would appreciate it if you could meet with us at our apartment.

Sincerely,
Ron Miller

① 상속 재산 처리 문제로 만날 약속을 정하려고
② 재산 관리 업무를 맡아 해줄 것을 부탁하려고
③ 아들을 기념하는 장학 재단 설립을 공표하려고
④ 재산 처리 문제를 도와줄 대리인을 추천하려고
⑤ 재산을 장학금으로 기부하는 방법을 의논하려고

2. 밑줄 친 exercising a particular kind of economy with the truth가 다음 글에서 의미하는 바로 가장 적절한 것은? [3점]

Vagueness is an obstacle to efficient communication. Sometimes people who want to avoid committing themselves to a particular course of action use vagueness as a ploy. For instance, a politician asked how precisely he intends to save money in the public sector might make vague generalisations about the need for improved efficiency, which, while true, don't commit him to any particular way of achieving this. A good journalist would then press for further information about precisely how this efficiency was to be achieved, forcing him to come out from behind this veil of vagueness. Or someone who was late for an appointment but didn't want to admit that this was because he'd stopped for a drink on the way might say 'Sorry I'm late, I had something I needed to do on the way here and it took slightly longer than I expected', deliberately leaving the cause of the delay vague, and exercising a particular kind of economy with the truth.

*ploy: 책략, 계략

① expressing neatly without wasting words or time
② hiding the truth by omitting relevant information
③ emphasizing the details of the affair by changing the topic
④ diverting attention from the true issues to emotional issues
⑤ asking questions about the important points that must be told

3. 다음 글의 요지로 가장 적절한 것은?

Neuroplasticity is the ability of the brain to constantly form and reorganize synaptic connections, which are the linkages between individual neurons. The more a particular connection is used, the stronger it becomes and the easier it is for the person to activate this pathway in the future. The same is true for the synaptic connections responsible for discipline.

Even if the genetic lottery gave you a less-than-ideal prefrontal cortex, you can structure your environment in such a way as to "stretch" what you've been given and improve your self-discipline. It certainly would have been easier to learn the skills when you were younger, just as languages have been proven to be easier to learn when young, but you shouldn't feel discouraged if you struggle with self-discipline in your adulthood. Self-discipline can be consistently exercised to achieve sustainable improvements over time, at any age. As with any skill, the more you practice being disciplined, the better you become at it.

*prefrontal cortex: 전두엽 피질

① 자제력은 나이가 들어갈수록 강해지는 경향이 있다.
② 자제력은 환경적 요인보다 유전적 요인에 좌우되기 쉽다.
③ 자제력은 현대인의 생존과 성공을 좌우하는 필수조건이다.
④ 자제력을 발달시키려면 어린 시절의 훈련이 특히 중요하다.
⑤ 나이에 상관없이 꾸준히 노력하면 자제력은 향상될 수가 있다.

4. 다음 글의 제목으로 가장 적절한 것은? [3점]

In general, the environment changes much faster than biology — agriculture was invented 12,000 years ago and potato chips less than 200 years ago. In contrast, biological systems that regulate our consumption and digestion of food are still very similar to those of our primate ancestors. Our evolved traits that were once advantageous become maladaptive due to changes in the environment. Rapidly increasing rates of obesity, coronary artery disease, hypertension, and even dental cavities can be explained by this mismatch. Another example of a mismatch is the hygiene hypothesis, which suggests that some diseases developed because modern sanitation practices have removed critical bacteria that co-evolved with humans. For example, children who are raised in cities are more likely to develop asthma than children raised on farms. Our vulnerability to asthma is therefore the consequence of a mismatch between our current exposure to bacteria and the dynamics of that exposure in our hunter-gatherer past.

*coronary artery disease: 관상 동맥 질환 **hypertension: 고혈압

① Biological Evolution Lags behind Cultural Change
② Evolutionary Mismatch: The Root of Modern Diseases
③ The Reason We Get Sick: Unexpected Environmental Change
④ Types of Modern Diseases Caused by Our Adaptiveness
⑤ Evolutionary Mismatch and What You Can Do about It

5. 다음 도표의 내용과 일치하지 <u>않는</u> 것은?

2014-2020 Global Games Market

Revenues per Segment with Compound Annual Growth Rates

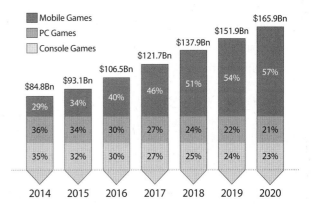

Bn: Billion

The above graph shows the revenues of the global games market per segment from 2014 to 2020. While positions in the market shuffled, there is no doubt that the market as a whole continued to grow rapidly in size. ① The total revenues of the global games market steadily increased from $84.8 billion in 2014 to $165.9 billion in 2020. ② While the proportion of mobile games nearly doubled during this period, PC and console games steadily decreased to about a third. ③ The percentage of PC games and console games combined accounted for less than that of mobile games in 2017. ④ PC games was more popular than console games in 2015, but these segments were then tied for two consecutive years in 2016 and 2017. ⑤ Console games took up a bigger market share than PC games in 2020.

*revenue: 수입

6. black flying fox에 관한 다음 글의 내용과 일치하지 않는 것은?

The black flying fox is among the largest bats in the world, and has a wingspan of more than one meter. It is native to Australia, Papua New Guinea, and Indonesia. They gather into large colonies known as camps, typically in rainforests and eucalyptus open forests. The black flying fox breeds once a year. During the first 4 weeks of its life, the newborn bat totally depends on its mother. After this period, the female begins leaving the baby at the camp every night in order to find food. Although the population of black flying foxes as a whole is not currently endangered, these animals do face some serious threats. For example, in many parts of their range, the bats are hunted for food. Additionally, climate change leads to rising temperatures, which negatively impact the population of this species.

① 양쪽 날개의 폭이 1미터가 넘는다.
② 숲에서 무리를 지어 서식한다.
③ 생후 1개월부터 직접 먹이를 찾으러 다닌다.
④ 많은 지역에서 식용으로 사냥되고 있다.
⑤ 기후 변화가 개체 수를 줄이는 위협이 된다.

7. 다음 글의 밑줄 친 부분 중, 어법상 틀린 것은? [3점]

Even though unemployment is painful to those who have no source of income, ① reducing unemployment is not costless. In the short run, a reduction in unemployment may come at the expense of a higher rate of inflation, especially if the economy is close to full capacity, ② where resources are almost fully employed. Moreover, trying to match employees with jobs can quickly lead to significant inefficiencies ③ because of mismatches between a worker's skill level and the level of skill required for a job. For example, the economy would be wasting resources ④ subsidizing education if people with PhDs in biochemistry were driving taxis or tending bars. That is, the skills of the employee may be higher than those necessary for the job, resulting in ⑤ that economists call underemployment. Another source of inefficiencies is placing employees in jobs beyond their abilities.

*subsidize: 보조금을 주다

8. 다음 글의 밑줄 친 부분 중, 문맥상 낱말의 쓰임이 적절하지 않은 것은? [3점]

The competitive arena is, by its very nature, difficult, unpredictable, and uncontrollable. Despite their best efforts, athletes can never prepare for every eventuality that may occur in competition or ① control everything that may influence their performances. Routines offer a structure within which to prepare for performance and the flexibility to adjust to the ② uncertain nature of competition. Because routines are not inviolate, but rather provide a guide for athletes to follow, they can also be readily altered to ③ fit the demands of a unique or unexpected competitive environment. Unforeseen changes in the competitive setting, such as weather, unexpected opponents, late arrival, insufficient warm-up space, and broken or lost equipment, can have a disturbing and disruptive effect on athletes before a competition. Athletes often perform ④ below expectations because they are unable to respond appropriately to these occurrences or become unsettled mentally (e.g., lose motivation or confidence, get distracted, or experience anxiety). Athletes with well-organized yet ⑤ tight routines will be better able to respond positively to these challenges, keep calm, and maintain a high level of performance.

*eventuality: 만일의 사태 **inviolate: 어길 수 없는

[9~12] 다음 빈칸에 들어갈 말로 가장 적절한 것을 고르시오.

9. What is a pattern? We usually think of it as something that repeats again and again. The math of symmetry can describe what this repetition may look like, as well as why some shapes seem more orderly and organized than others. That's why symmetry is the fundamental scientific "language" of pattern and form. Symmetry describes how things may look unchanged when they are reflected in a mirror, or rotated, or moved. But our intuitions about symmetry can be _____. In general, shape and form in nature arise not from the "building up" of symmetry, but from the breaking of perfect symmetry — that is, from the disintegration of complete, boring uniformity, where everything looks the same, everywhere. The key question is therefore: why isn't everything uniform? How and why does symmetry break?

① precise
② impartial
③ deceptive
④ authoritative
⑤ comprehensive

10. In his book *Man's Search for Meaning* (1946), Viennese psychiatrist Viktor Frankl explains that humans have two psychological strengths that allow us to endure painful and possibly devastating circumstances and to move forward: these are the capacity for decision, and freedom of attitude. Frankl emphasizes that we are not at the mercy of our environment or events, because we dictate how we allow them to shape us. Even suffering can be seen differently, depending on _____. Frankl points to the case of one of his patients who suffered because he missed his dead wife. Frankl asked how it would have been if the patient had died first, and he responded that his wife would have found it very difficult. Frankl suggested that the patient has spared her this grief, but must now suffer the grief himself. In other words, the suffering becomes endurable by giving meaning to it.

① the source and duration
② the time that has passed
③ our interpretation of events
④ the strength of the survivor
⑤ our capacity for understanding

11. The sense of touch is one of the factors which prevent people from being convinced of the truth that the senses of sight, hearing and taste occur within the brain. For example, if you told someone that he sees a book within his brain, he would, if he didn't think carefully, reply "I can't be seeing the book in my brain — look, I'm touching it with my hand." However, there is a fact that such people cannot understand, or perhaps just ignore. The sense of touch also occurs in the brain as much as do all the other senses. That is to say, when you touch a material object, you sense whether it is hard, soft, wet, sticky or silky in the brain. The effects that come from your fingertips are transmitted to the brain as an electrical signal and these signals are perceived in the brain as the sense of touch. For instance, if you touch a rough surface, you can never know whether the surface is, in reality, indeed a rough surface, or how a rough surface actually feels. That is because you can never touch the original of a rough surface. The knowledge that you have about touching a surface is _____. [3점]

① your brain's interpretation of certain stimuli
② your thoughts gained from a learned sense of touch
③ the stimulation of the touch receptors in your fingertips
④ your prediction based on pattern recognition of past events
⑤ selective perception for filtering information about an object

12. Did reading change the way our brains work? Marshall McLuhan believes it did. In *The Gutenberg Galaxy; The Making of Typographic Man* (1962), he argued that reading led to a new "typographic man." According to the book, life prior to widespread literacy was dominated by a cyclical relationship to the environment, the immediate cycle of daylight that determined when you worked and when you slept, and the longer pattern of what you did on a farm in a certain season. After reading became widespread, people were more likely to show an interest in things outside their local community, more likely to investigate patterns of cause and effect, and more likely to see the environment as something they could control, not something to be obeyed. That is, reading led to a more linear way of thinking, more about cause and effect, more freed from _____. [3점]

① the rejection of the grandeur of nature
② the destruction of the natural environment
③ the constraints of our immediate environment
④ the idea of dominating the natural environment
⑤ the conflicts of opinion among members of society

13. 다음 글에서 전체 흐름과 관계 없는 문장은? [3점]

Advocates who believe that animals have rights, sometimes called "rightists," are concerned with animals' quality of life. They make no utilitarian exceptions. ① They argue it's wrong to ever abuse or exploit animals or to cause animals any pain and suffering; animals shouldn't be eaten, held captive in zoos, or used in any (or most) educational or research settings. ② They believe the moral and legal rights of animals include the right to life and the right not to be harmed. ③ As animal cruelty laws pervade as many as 42 states in the USA, laws protecting people from animals should also be established, considering a recent accident where campers were threatened by wild animals. ④ According to Gary Francione, a professor of law at Rutgers University, to say an animal has a "right" to have an interest protected means the animal is entitled to have that interest protected even if it would benefit us to do otherwise. ⑤ Rightists believe humans have an obligation to honor that claim for animals just as they do for nonconsenting humans (like infants, children, and adults with dementia) who can't protect their own interests.

*utilitarian: 실리적인 **nonconsenting: 동의를 표할 수 없는
***dementia: 치매

[14~15] 주어진 글 다음에 이어질 글의 순서로 가장 적절한 것을 고르시오.

14.

One form of energy that appears to have fewer problems than most others is nuclear *fusion* power.

(A) In other words, in attempting to create nuclear fusion, energy is actually lost instead of gained. While humans can make bombs that use fusion power, they are not yet able to control the reaction for use in a power plant.

(B) The fusion process actually releases far more energy than nuclear fission, and it results in much less radioactive waste. So many people are thrilled about the prospect of developing a working hydrogen fusion reactor.

(C) Right now, however, scientists are unable to turn fusion power into a reality. Scientists can produce fusion energy, but right now it requires much more energy to create nuclear fusion than the actual energy that fusion gives us in return. [3점]

*fusion: 융합, 결합; 핵융합 **fission: 분열

① (A) – (C) – (B)   ② (B) – (A) – (C)
③ (B) – (C) – (A)   ④ (C) – (A) – (B)
⑤ (C) – (B) – (A)

15.

For animals with kin nearby, the costs of alarm calling when a predator approaches may be outweighed by the need to protect family. Some chipmunks and squirrels around the forest have youngsters with them, so their squeaks give advanced warning to their offspring.

(A) In doing so they may reap the paradoxical benefit of telling the predator who and where they are. From the predator's perspective, prey that has seen your approach and is poised to flee is likely to be hard to catch.

(B) The predator's time would be better spent looking for unwary prey. Alarm calling can therefore provide a direct benefit to the caller by advertising the unprofitability of an attack and thus buying safety.

(C) But many animals use alarm calls when family are not present, so other benefits must also be in play. Some alarm signals are designed to actively communicate with the predator, drawing attention to the animal in the moment of danger.

*squeak: 찍찍 우는 소리

① (A) – (C) – (B)   ② (B) – (A) – (C)
③ (B) – (C) – (A)   ④ (C) – (A) – (B)
⑤ (C) – (B) – (A)

[16~17] 글의 흐름으로 보아, 주어진 문장이 들어가기에 가장
적절한 곳을 고르시오.

16.

> The strategy works well in Copenhagen, where the city center has buildings between five and six stories high, and there is good visual contact between residences and street space.

Approximately 7,000 residents live in Copenhagen's city center. (①) On an ordinary weekday evening in the winter season a person walking through the city can enjoy the lights from about 7,000 windows. (②) The proximity to housing and residents plays a key role in the feeling of safety. (③) It is common practice for city planners to mix functions and housing as a crime prevention strategy and thus increase the feeling of safety along the most important streets used by pedestrians and bicyclists. (④) However, it does not work as well in Sydney, Australia, despite the 15,000 people living in its heart. (⑤) Here residences are generally from 10 to 50 stories above street level, and no one who lives high up can see what is happening down on the street.

*proximity: 근접, 가까움

17.

> In contrast, ideas that drain resources away from other more valuable uses and turn them into something not as valuable to consumers result in losses, which will provide entrepreneurs with a strong incentive to discontinue such projects.

Before a new idea is tested, it is difficult to tell if it is a good one. (①) From the standpoint of economic growth, it is absolutely essential that entrepreneurs have a strong incentive to pursue new ideas, but it is also important that wasteful projects that reduce the value of resources be brought to a halt. (②) In a market economy, profits and losses satisfy these aims. (③) New ideas that add to the value of resources — by creating enough value to consumers to offset the opportunity cost of production — generate economic profits for the entrepreneurs who discover them. (④) Thus, such market processes promote both the discovery of superior methods for doing things and the termination of projects that reduce the value of resources. (⑤) In this manner, the profit and loss system ensures that resources are directed toward projects that promote economic growth. [3점]

18. 다음 글의 내용을 한 문장으로 요약하고자 한다. 빈칸 (A), (B)에 들어갈 말로 가장 적절한 것은?

One approach to social facilitation that proposes an influence in social presence is based on the idea that people generally try to present the best possible appearance to others and to make a favorable impression. This being the case, observers or coactors may not only motivate individuals to work hard at whatever task is being carried out, but also increase the person's sense of embarrassment when performance leads to failure. Failure is not likely to happen when the task is a simple or familiar one, so that the increased motivation is sufficient to produce improvement. Difficult tasks are often failed, however, at least at the beginning. Embarrassment caused by such failure may cause stress and cognitive interference of sufficient intensity to disrupt performance.

*social presence: 사회적 실재감

↓

> The performance of an individual in the state of being observed can yield _____(A)_____ results depending on the _____(B)_____ level of the task in which the person performs.

	(A)		(B)
①	opposing	……	priority
②	immediate	……	priority
③	opposing	……	complexity
④	immediate	……	complexity
⑤	affirmative	……	intricacy

[19~20] 다음 글을 읽고, 물음에 답하시오.

The priming effect is an interesting cognitive process studied by social psychologists. Priming is the process by which you activate specific (a) associations in memory. Priming taps into clusters of neurons where information is stored. When a cluster is activated, surrounding clusters that store similar information come to the forefront of the conscious mind. New York University students — unaware that they were subjects in a priming study — were asked to make four-word sentences out of a list of five-word sets. The sentences contained words to prime the students for thinking about old age: wrinkle, solitary, forgetful, lonely, and the word old itself. The priming was so effective that students left walking (b) slowly, acting out the external demonstration of their internal priming. These findings underscore how (c) resistant to suggestion we really are.

It makes sense, then, to deliver a (d) positive message. Harold Kelley did a study in 1950 describing a guest lecturer who would be coming to talk to the class. Before the lecturer came, Kelley gave the students a paragraph-size description of him. Half were told, "People who know him consider him to be rather cold, industrious, critical, practical, and determined." The other half were told, "People who know him consider him to be warm, industrious, critical, practical, and determined." All the students then heard the lecture from the guest. What was the priming effect? Fifty-six percent of the students who were told that he was warm were willing participants in the class. Only 32 percent of the students who were told he was cold participated in the discussion. This demonstrates how significant that (e) initial input of information can be.

*priming effect: 점화 효과

19. 윗글의 제목으로 가장 적절한 것은?

① The Effects of Priming on Decision-Making
② The Words Others Prime Change Your Behavior
③ What Is Social Priming and How Does It Occur?
④ Hidden Priming Power of Words: Myths and Facts
⑤ How Physical Actions Can Prime What You Think

20. 밑줄 친 (a) ~ (e) 중에서 문맥상 낱말의 쓰임이 적절하지 않은 것은? [3점]

① (a)   ② (b)   ③ (c)   ④ (d)   ⑤ (e)

1. 다음 글에 드러난 Jacob의 심경 변화로 가장 적절한 것은?

Jacob crawled on his stomach through the passageway in the cave. He gasped as oppressive and utter blackness enveloped him. He was very anxious to see light at the end. Would he ever see his family again? Was he going to make it out alive? He tried to shout "help," but no sound came out. Just then, a noise at the back of the cave started. Jacob strained his eyes to look in the direction of the noise. There was a large box dangling from the cave by a rope. Every time the box hit the side of the cave, it made a large noise. But why was the box swaying? It finally occurred to Jacob that there was a slight breeze. If he followed the direction of the breeze, he could find his way out! Enthusiastically, Jacob worked his way to the entrance of the cave.

① frightened → hopeful
② expectant → disappointed
③ lonely → pleased
④ angry → regretful
⑤ excited → scared

2. 다음 글에서 필자가 주장하는 바로 가장 적절한 것은?

It is important to keep in mind that we perform experiments every single day when we do things as simple as introducing ourselves to someone new or trying a new food. As a result, we get lots of opportunities to practice responding to unexpected results and learning from each one of them. Trained scientists know this well and, therefore, do their best to design experiments that answer an important question, no matter what the specific results. They know that each experiment offers valuable clues on the path to understanding. As the saying goes, "Genius is the ability to make the most mistakes in the shortest period of time." Each of those mistakes provides experimental data and an opportunity to learn something new. Like scientists, we need to stop looking at unexpected results as failures. By changing our vocabulary, by looking at "failures" as "data," we can enhance everyone's willingness to experiment.

① 실수를 빨리 인정하고 대안 마련에 집중하라.
② 인생의 새로운 경험을 두려워 말고 기꺼이 도전하라.
③ 실험을 설계함에 있어 편견이 개입되지 않도록 하라.
④ 긍정적인 사고를 위해 어휘를 선별하는 습관을 갖자.
⑤ 예상치 못한 일을 실패로 보지 말고 배움의 기회로 삼자.

3. 밑줄 친 my share of hammering screws가 다음 글에서 의미하는 바로 가장 적절한 것은? [3점]

A coach helps clients to produce the results they want in their personal and professional lives. I've conducted thousands of successful coaching sessions over the years, but I've done my share of hammering screws as well. My interest in my clients' progress is usually aligned with my desire to be an effective coach. And my interest in achieving closure usually supports both my clients' progress and their independence. But it's important for me to monitor these interests and to gauge their intensity: I should ask myself, "Am I pushing a solution on them, or simply rushing toward closure before they're ready to move on?"

This question has been essential in allowing me to see how my legitimate needs as a person occasionally get in the way of my client's needs and the coaching process.

① negative feedback given during a coaching session
② a slow-paced coaching scheme for a client
③ a one-sided effort on the part of a coach
④ coaching experiences with a sense of urgency
⑤ emotional support rather than professional advice

① importance of stories that are dramatized in a society
② reasons why humans have an innate fondness for stories
③ understanding the relationship of cause and effect in stories
④ storytelling to envision the future by stepping out of the present
⑤ stories functioning to bind society by reinforcing common values

4. 다음 글의 주제로 가장 적절한 것은?

Stories tell us what is laudable and what is contemptible. They subtly and constantly encourage us to be decent instead of decadent. Stories are the grease and glue of society: by encouraging us to behave well, stories reduce social friction while uniting people around common values. Stories homogenize us; they make us one. This is part of what Marshall McLuhan had in mind with his idea of the global village. Technology has saturated widely dispersed people with the same media and made them into citizens of a village that spans the world. Stories — sacred and profane — are perhaps the main cohering force in human life. A society is composed of fractious people with different personalities, goals, and agendas. What connects us beyond our kinship ties? Stories. As John Gardner puts it, fiction "is essentially serious and beneficial, a game played against chaos and death." Stories are the counterforce to social disorder, the tendency of things to fall apart. Stories are the center without which the rest cannot hold.

*homogenize: 균질화하다

5. 다음 글의 제목으로 가장 적절한 것은?

Many tourists purchase wildlife products when they go traveling around the world. Endangered species are often entered into the souvenir trade, and tourists both knowingly and unknowingly buy such endangered items as trip souvenirs. Your tourism dollars make an important contribution to a local community's economy, but you need to spend them wisely so they benefit the local community. Don't be a reckless souvenir hunter. Be ethical by choosing souvenirs that don't exploit or deplete local wildlife or plants. International wildlife legislation and customs restrictions may not allow you to import items such as ivory, tortoiseshell, animal skin accessories, and coral when you return home. Always make positive souvenir choices that support local craftspeople instead of purchasing plastic or "touristy" items that are more than likely imported.

① Souvenirs Hold Symbolic Value Related to Travel Experiences
② Responsible Tourism: Why Should You Purchase Souvenirs?
③ Respect Different Cultures and Customs While Traveling
④ Economics of Souvenir Sales and their Role in Tourism
⑤ Select Your Souvenirs Sensitively and Buy Ethically

6. Star Gazing Tour에 관한 다음 안내문의 내용과 일치하는 것은?

Star Gazing Tour
Come gaze at the stars from Blue Mountain!

Tuesday afternoons Telescopes will be provided. But you are welcome to bring your own.

Tour departs Blue Center at 6 p.m. and returns by 10 p.m.
(+ Star observation time: 7 p.m.-9 p.m.)
$30.00 per person
Entry fee includes packaged meal with drink
Local Astronomical Society volunteers set up telescopes for celestial viewing and provide an introduction to the night sky.

Important Information:
Tour departure is based on "weather permitting."
If cancelled, a refund will be given.
Guests cancelling tour reservations within 24 hours prior to tour departure may be subject to a cancellation fee.

Visit www.ifa.bluem.org/info/vis for more information.

---

① 반드시 자신의 망원경을 가져와야 한다.
② 별 관찰은 6시부터 4시간 동안 진행된다.
③ 별도 신청자에게만 식사와 음료가 제공된다.
④ 기상 상태에 상관없이 진행된다.
⑤ 출발 전 24시간 이내에 예약 취소 시 수수료가 있다.

7. 다음 글의 밑줄 친 부분 중, 어법상 틀린 것은? [3점]

Edison knew, as ① did others, that running electricity through a variety of materials could make those materials glow — a process called *incandescence* — thereby producing a light source that could be used as an alternative to candles and natural gas lamps. The problem was that the glowing material (the *filament*) would degrade after a short while, making its use as a household lighting device ② impractical. Not knowing any of the physical principles by which electricity destroyed the filament, Edison simply tried every material he could ③ see if one would glow brightly, yet resist burning out. After trying 1,600 different materials, including cotton and turtle shell, he happened upon carbonized bamboo, ④ which turned out to be the filament of choice (to the joy of turtles everywhere). When used in an air-evacuated bulb (i.e., a vacuum tube), the carbonized bamboo outshone and lasted much longer than any of the other tested filaments. Edison had his light bulb. Although tungsten soon replaced carbonized bamboo in home light bulbs, illumination by incandescence became the predominant mode of interior lighting for many decades ⑤ to follow.

*incandescence: 고온 발광

8. 다음 글의 밑줄 친 부분 중, 문맥상 낱말의 쓰임이 적절하지 <u>않은</u> 것은? [3점]

Soldiers' wartime exposure to commercially canned foods, though occasional, generated the beginnings of consumer trust. This trust flowed back up the chain of production, ① providing the first faint signs of wider demand that canners needed in order to innovate and expand. Tastes were often ② slow to change when ordinary consumers were given a choice between new products and their go-to standards. But because army men in the American Civil War had little choice when it came to their food supply, they gave new foods a chance and ③ widened their palates to partially accommodate canned foods. After the war, they brought these new preferences home with them. The nature of trust that these battlefield encounters ④ fostered was not yet rooted in scientific certainty, a better understanding of the risks, or knowledge of where the food had come from. Rather, it sprang from exposure and ⑤ unfamiliarity that made a new kind of food seem worth sampling and its convenience and accessibility worth appreciating.

*go-to: 믿을 수 있는 **palate: 미각, 감식력

[9~12] 다음 빈칸에 들어갈 말로 가장 적절한 것을 고르시오.

9. Despite the protection ants offer, aphids are not always content to stick around. When they want to leave, the next generation grows wings so that they can fly to greener pastures. This doesn't escape the notice of their guardians, and the ants end the aphids' dreams of flight by immediately biting off their transparent appendages. And as if that were not enough, the ants also use chemical means to prevent their domesticated herds from escaping. The ants exude compounds that slow the growth of the aphids' wings, and, for good measure, they also slow down the aphids: a research team from Imperial College London discovered that aphids move more slowly when they cross terrain that has previously been walked over by ants. The cause for the slowdown is a chemical message left by the ants that affects the behavior of the aphids and forces them to reduce speed. The beautiful symbiotic relationship between ants and aphids turns out to be not entirely _____, after all. [3점]

*aphid: 진딧물 **appendage: 부속 기관 ***exude: 발산하다, 풍기다

① selfish   ② voluntary
③ temporary   ④ secondary
⑤ compulsory

10. Believe it or not, _____ can be a powerful motivator of human behavior. For example, consider ten-year-old children who were told that their performance on a test was either due to their natural intelligence or their ability to work hard. Both sets were then given a really difficult second task that was well beyond their capability, which no one could complete. However, in a third test, the children who thought their initial successes on the first task were due to their intelligence gave up more easily because they attributed their failure on the second task to their limited natural ability, which made them less likely to persevere on the last task. In contrast, children who thought their performance was all down to hard work not only stuck longer on the third task, but also enjoyed it more. So it's better to tell your kids that they are hard workers rather than simply smart.

① doing for doing's sake
② focusing on knowledge
③ belief about self-control
④ effort for brain development
⑤ optimal conditions for performance

11. In experiments, we are usually interested in overall differences between various conditions. Suppose we find that participants randomly assigned to be alone help a victim more quickly than those assigned to groups of two or four bystanders. Before concluding that the number of bystanders truly influenced the speed of helping, we first must ask whether this difference _____. In other words, because our results are based only on a particular sample of people in each condition, how do we know that similar results would have occurred if we had tested other samples? Perhaps the participants we tested were not truly representative of the populations from which they were selected. Perhaps, despite random assignment, participants assigned to be alone happened to have more highly altruistic personalities than participants in the other conditions, and this is the explanation for the effect we observed.

*population: 모(母)집단

① supports our hypothesis
② was meaningful enough to be studied
③ can be generalized beyond the experiment
④ is in agreement with participants' observations
⑤ was found when comparing every group in the experiment

12. Psychologist and author Jeremy Dean explains in relation to cultivating happiness-boosting habits that 'unfortunately there's rather a large fly in the ointment. That fly is habituation'. Habituation means that we adapt to positive experiences more quickly than negative ones. This means that we lose the pleasure from good habits more quickly than the pain from bad ones. Dean suggests that one way that we can deal with our automatic adaptation to pleasure is by varying our habits rather than repeating them in exactly the same way over and over again. This could mean, for example, making a conscious effort to respond more consciously to the question 'how are you?' (rather than saying 'Fine' every time). _____ can be effective in reducing the effects of habituation. Although Dean explains that this idea stretches the formal definition of a habit which involves the same behavior or thought in the same situation, for 'happy' habits we need an 'automatic initiation of the behavior, but then a continuously mindful way of carrying it out. A new type of hybrid habit: a mindful habit'. [3점]

① Trying our very best to break an old bad habit
② Making sure the new habit is something that we want
③ Introducing conscious variations in some of our habits
④ Starting with simple behavior changes to form a good habit
⑤ Choosing a specific behavior and a specific trigger to form a habit

13. 다음 글에서 전체 흐름과 관계 <u>없는</u> 문장은?

Even in societies that consider religion a central part of their life, temples, churches and mosques seem to have lost their old position in the life of the city, at least as far as their distribution in the city and their size and significance relative to other functions are concerned. ① As urban populations have grown, and movements and functions in cities have become ever more complex and diversified, new modes of working and living have emerged. ② While religious beliefs and practices may rule social norms and public conduct, they do not determine the built form or the spatial structure of the city. ③ As cities have grown, the new urban areas and suburbs have hardly caught up in their numbers of houses of worship with the older central parts. ④ But in cities two of the most pressing problems facing the world today also come together: poverty and environmental degradation. ⑤ The phenomenal growth of urban areas in the twentieth century has primarily been a secular one.

[14~15] 주어진 글 다음에 이어질 글의 순서로 가장 적절한 것을 고르시오.

14.

A company has external economies of scale if it receives preferential treatment from the government or other external sources simply because of its size. For example, most states will lower taxes to attract large companies since they will provide jobs for their residents.

(A) This lowers research expenses for these companies. Small companies just don't have the leverage to take advantage of external economies of scale.
(B) But, they can band together and take advantage of geographic economies of scale by clustering similar businesses in a small area. For example, artist lofts, galleries, and restaurants in a downtown art district benefit from being near each other.
(C) A large real estate developer can often convince a city to build roads and other infrastructure. This saves the developer from paying those costs. Large companies can also take advantage of joint research with universities. [3점]

① (A) – (C) – (B) ② (B) – (A) – (C)
③ (B) – (C) – (A) ④ (C) – (A) – (B)
⑤ (C) – (B) – (A)

15.

Each of us views reality through the thoughts we have accumulated in our individual preserved state of awareness. When you encounter a new thought, you call upon this state to derive meaning, agree, disagree, judge, or remain neutral.

(A) As this happens, consider for a moment where these thoughts came from and why you produced them at this particular moment. Consider their purpose. You did attract them and they do have a purpose. Their purpose is to reinforce your beliefs.
(B) Notice how your mind instantly produces thoughts that validate your point of view. For example, as your friend defends a political candidate who you dislike, notice the rush of opposing thoughts that enter your mind.
(C) Every thought you encounter or conjure up you filter through this state. You can observe this scrutiny as you produce thoughts that stimulate your feelings. Pay attention the next time you disagree with somebody. [3점]

*conjure up: ~을 떠올리다[상기하다]

① (A) – (C) – (B) ② (B) – (A) – (C)
③ (B) – (C) – (A) ④ (C) – (A) – (B)
⑤ (C) – (B) – (A)

[16~17] 글의 흐름으로 보아, 주어진 문장이 들어가기에 가장 적절한 곳을 고르시오.

16.

> This self-defense mechanism — differently from the ability to understand jokes, which is very widespread — does not present itself in every human being.

Laughter resulting from humor shows itself when people find themselves in an unfavorable situation. (①) For that situation, they generally would have felt anger and/or fear, and the detection of incongruent elements allows them to watch it from a different perspective. (②) In this instance, thus, laughter comes from the release of energies generally associated with negative feelings, but that in the specific situation, thanks to the change of perspective, can be expressed as laughter of relief. (③) Humor, in this perspective, represents a defense mechanism that allows people to better handle difficult and stressful life situations. (④) Freud even describes this humor as "the highest of the defense mechanisms." (⑤) Actually, some individuals are able to see the funny and positive side of a certain situation, while others, even in the same circumstances, react showing negative feelings.

*incongruent: 일치하지 않는

17.

> Today we have developed reliable food sources that provide us with a food supply very different from that of our ancestors.

Thanks to millions of years of evolution, we have developed into very intelligent beings. When it comes to managing weight, however, we are influenced by the body's mechanisms designed to get us through times of famine. (①) This means saving excess weight so we have something to use for energy if a time comes when food is scarce. (②) The only problem is that this doesn't happen the same way it did in ancient times. (③) Unfortunately, your brain is still influenced by ancient-brain thinking and may perceive going for periods of time without food (like when you skip meals) as times of famine. (④) As a result of this famine, your brain will slow your metabolism to help you hold on to energy stores for the future. (⑤) Human society has evolved, but the human brain still has some catching up to do. [3점]

18. 다음 글의 내용을 한 문장으로 요약하고자 한다. 빈칸 (A), (B)에 들어갈 말로 가장 적절한 것은? [3점]

Angela Duckworth and her fellow researchers asked a group of University of Pennsylvania undergraduates to list academic goals, such as "study French for an hour every night" or "finish all homework the day before it is due." For a week, some of these students(the first group) were instructed to modify their study spaces to minimize temptation in order to meet their goal. These students set reminders or alarms, installing online apps to block distractions like Facebook, or perhaps reserved study carrels in the library. A second group of students was told to rely solely on willpower and their ability to resist temptation. At the end of the week, students rated on a scale from 1(extremely poorly) to 5(extremely well) how successful they were at meeting their study goal that week. On average, all students were reasonably successful, but the first group of students scored about half a scale point better than the second group of students.

*carrel: (도서관의) 개인 열람석

↓

> Behavior change through _____(A)_____, as University of Pennsylvania students experienced, isn't as successful as behavior change through altering _____(B)_____.

	(A)		(B)
①	goal-setting	⋯⋯	contexts
②	goal-setting	⋯⋯	mindsets
③	self-control	⋯⋯	environments
④	self-control	⋯⋯	mentality
⑤	self-rewards	⋯⋯	attitudes

[19~20] 다음 글을 읽고, 물음에 답하시오.

An insightful study recruited forty-five professional comedy performers from a large comedy festival. Each was given the setup to a comedic scene and four minutes to generate as many endings as they could. The comedians each generated about six funny endings in the four-minute period. All participants then predicted how many more funny endings they would be able to generate if they had four additional minutes. Their conscious selves expected (a) diminishing outputs. The average estimate of new endings was about five, which was fewer than they had produced in the initial four minutes. They were then given an additional four minutes to work. The actual number of new endings they generated was 20 percent higher than they estimated. They didn't give persistence enough (b) credit. With a strong habit of persevering, they would have continued to try to produce ideas, and would have done so successfully, despite their pessimistic predictions.

Like the comedy performers, when college students worked on a task for a few minutes and then estimated their creativity if they continued for a few more, they (c) overestimated the benefits of persistence. Amazingly, when specifically instructed to persist, students generated more solutions than they anticipated. Persistence, put to the test, didn't wear down. It just kept on producing. Our misapprehension is (d) understandable. We know that our executive efforts wear down over time. Our attention ebbs and our motivation wanes. But our habitual selves — where persistence sits — are made of totally (e) different stuff. And it's stuff we can put to work.

19. 윗글의 제목으로 가장 적절한 것은?

① A Habit of Persisting Makes Creativity Flow
② Habits That Help to Unlock Your Creativity
③ How You Can Spark Creativity at Work
④ Being Persistent Motivates You to Try Harder
⑤ Creativity: A Process That Takes Time and Effort

20. 밑줄 친 (a) ~ (e) 중에서 문맥상 낱말의 쓰임이 적절하지 않은 것은? [3점]

① (a)　② (b)　③ (c)　④ (d)　⑤ (e)

○ 답안지의 해당란에 성명과 수험번호를 쓰고, 또 수험번호와 답을 정확히 표시하시오.
○ 문항에 따라 배점이 다르니, 각 물음의 끝에 표시된 배점을 참고하시오. 3점 문항에만 점수가 표시되어 있습니다. 점수 표시가 없는 문항은 모두 2점씩입니다.

1. 다음 글의 목적으로 가장 적절한 것은?

Dear Members of the Parish,

As I write to you I am enjoying a perfect spring day. The sky is a wonderful cerulean blue, the early bulbs are starting to bloom, and I can feel warmth on my face. But I must take you away from this scene and get you to think of autumn and our annual Fall Festival. If you have volunteered in the past, you know that a tremendous amount of work goes into this fundraiser. If you have not already been involved, we hope that you will this year. We need people to chair several committees, ranging from tickets and entertainment to setup and cleanup. We need folks with a lot of enthusiasm to work the booths, and those with a culinary flair to help with the food. The money raised goes to many worthy endeavors. Please call me if you're interested.

Sincerely,
Laura Diamond

*culinary flair: 요리 솜씨

① 자선 축제 행사 내용을 공유하려고
② 가을 축제 준비 상황을 설명하려고
③ 지역민들의 행사 방문을 독려하려고
④ 모금 행사에 자원봉사를 권유하려고
⑤ 축제를 위한 준비 업무를 소개하려고

2. 다음 글에서 필자가 주장하는 바로 가장 적절한 것은?

In pursuing an important objective in the scientific community, you must expect serious competition. Though knowing you are in a race is nerve-racking, the presence of worthy competitors is an assurance that the prize ahead is worth winning. You may feel more than apprehensive, however, if the field is too large. The presence of numerous competitors may also mean that your chance of winning is low since you are unlikely to have a detailed knowledge of their strengths and weaknesses. Nevertheless, avoiding your competitors because you are afraid that you will reveal too much is a dangerous course. Rather, when you stay in close contact with your intellectual competitors, each of you may profit from the other's help. And if it happens that someone else does win outright, better it is someone with whom you are on good terms than some unknown competitor whom you will find it hard not to at least initially detest.

*detest: 몹시 싫어하다

① 지적 경쟁자들과 가깝게 지내며 서로 이익을 얻어라.
② 경쟁자와 멀지도 가깝지도 않게 거리를 두고 경쟁하라.
③ 경쟁자와 협력할 수 있는 사항과 없는 사항을 구분하라.
④ 경쟁자에게 이끌리지 말고 주체적으로 연구를 진행하라.
⑤ 경쟁자와의 친분을 떠나 경쟁에서 객관적인 자세를 유지하라.

3. 밑줄 친 what I have learned from a trial of them all 이 다음 글에서 의미하는 바로 가장 적절한 것은? [3점]

So far as diet is concerned, I belong to no school; I have learned something from each one, and what I have learned from a trial of them all is to be shy of extreme statements and of hard and fast rules. To my vegetarian friends who argue that it is morally wrong to take sentient life, I answer that they cannot go for a walk in the country without committing that offense, for they walk on innumerable bugs and worms. We cannot live without asserting our right; we kill innumerable germs when we swallow a glass of grape juice, or for that matter a glass of plain water. I shall be much surprised if the advance of science does not some day prove to us that there are basic forms of consciousness in all vegetable life; so we shall justify the argument of Mr. Dooley, who said, in reviewing "The Jungle," that he could not see how it was any less a crime to cut off a young tomato in its prime or to murder a whole cradleful of baby peas in the pod!

*sentient: 지각이 있는

① Vegetarianism is not a healthy diet.
② There is a right way to kill an animal.
③ It is inevitable that humans take life for food.
④ Eating both animals and plants is a balanced diet.
⑤ Humans may eat plants but shouldn't eat animals.

4. 다음 글의 주제로 가장 적절한 것은?

For the most part, children are natural, prolific, and happy daydreamers. Too often, however, parents and teachers are quick to label daydreaming as a symptom of ADD (Attention Deficit Disorder) or the sign of a slacker in the making. A new study finds that "positive-constructive" daydreaming, even when heavy in pattern, is not related to psychological disorders as some have previously thought, but rather is a normal activity that reflects the daydreamer's intelligence and imaginative tendencies. There's actually a substantial amount of research connecting daydreaming in children with creativity. A recent New Zealand study has found that imaginary friends benefit children's language skills and may also boost their performance at school. There's also research that says that children who don't get enough down time to daydream or who fill in their down time with too much television produce works that are "tedious and unimaginative." So, if your child is a daydreamer, you may be raising a mini-genius.

*slacker: 게으름뱅이

① usefulness of daydreaming to cope with tedious work
② how to distinguish ADD and children's healthy daydreaming
③ daydreaming as a sign of children's intelligence and creativity
④ differences between daydreaming and psychological disorders
⑤ necessity of controlling daydreaming for children's school performance

5. 다음 도표의 내용과 일치하지 <u>않는</u> 것은?

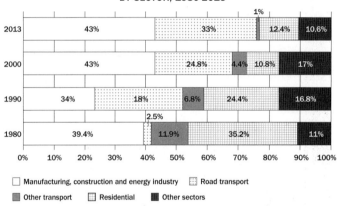

CO₂ EMISSIONS FROM FUEL COMBUSTION IN KOREA BY SECTOR, 1980-2013

The graph above shows CO2 emissions from fuel combustion in Korea by sector in 1980, 1990, 2000, and 2013. ① We can see that over the years emissions from manufacturing, construction, and the energy industry have remained fairly constant, from a minimum of 34% to a maximum of 43%. ② Meanwhile, the share of emissions from the road transport sector has grown drastically from 2.5% in 1980 to 33% in 2013. ③ Over the same time period, the share from other transport dropped by nearly 11 percentage points to just 1 percent of total emissions in 2013. ④ The percentage of emissions from the residential sector decreased continually from 35.2% in 1980 to 12.4% in 2013. ⑤ Finally, we can see that other sectors never accounted for more than 20% or less than 10% of total emissions.

*combustion: 연소

6. Marian Anderson에 관한 다음 글의 내용과 일치하지 <u>않는</u> 것은?

Marian Anderson displayed vocal talent as a child. From the age of six, she began her musical training in a church choir in Philadelphia. Even amid an outstanding church choir, Anderson stood out as a true talent. Her church community helped her pursue formal musical training. Denied a place in the Philadelphia Music Academy because she was African American, she continued to receive musical education wherever she could. Marian Anderson's 1939 concert on the steps of the Lincoln Memorial brought together her history. On January 7, 1955, she became the first African American to perform with the Metropolitan Opera. Anderson continued to deliver powerful performances for decades. Anderson began a farewell tour in October, 1964, which ended in April, 1965 at Carnegie Hall when Anderson was sixty-eight years old.

① Philadelphia 교회 성가대에서 음악 훈련을 시작했다.
② 교회 공동체로부터 음악 교육을 위한 후원을 받았다.
③ 흑인이라서 Philadelphia 음악학교 입학이 거부되었다.
④ 흑인 최초로 Metropolitan Opera와 공연했다.
⑤ 68세의 나이에 고별 순회공연을 시작했다.

7. 다음 글의 밑줄 친 부분 중, 어법상 <u>틀린</u> 것은? [3점]

Jerome Singer, a legendary cognitive psychologist, was the first scientist to suggest that the mental state ① <u>in which</u> the mind is allowed to wander freely is, in fact, our "default" state. Singer further argued in his 1966 book, *Daydreaming*, that daydreaming, imagination, and fantasy ② <u>are</u> essential elements of a healthy mental life. These elements include self-awareness, creative incubation, autobiographical planning, consideration of the meaning of events and interactions, ③ <u>taking</u> another person's perspective, reflecting on your own and others' emotions, and moral reasoning. All of this leads to what we think of as "aha!" moments. The musician, bestselling writer, and neuroscientist Daniel J. Levitin emphasizes that insights are ④ <u>far</u> more likely to come when you are in the mind-wandering mode than in the task-focused mode. It is only when we let our minds wander ⑤ <u>what</u> we make unexpected connections between things that we did not realize were connected. This can help you solve problems that previously seemed to be unsolvable.

*default state: 기본 상태 **incubation: 숙고

8. 다음 글의 밑줄 친 부분 중, 문맥상 낱말의 쓰임이 적절하지 <u>않은</u> 것은? [3점]

Musical judgments are never made in complete isolation. The formation of "taste cultures" has always been ① <u>socially</u> defined. Participation in certain genres of music was historically determined by a person's social position, not by a purely ② <u>independent</u> aesthetic choice. Indeed, from a sociological perspective, taste is always a social category rather than an aesthetic one; it refers to the way we use cultural judgments as social "currency," to mark our social positions. This may be ③ <u>more</u> clear today, since contemporary society is characterized by the fragmentation of older taste cultures and the proliferation of new ones. In this context, cultural transactions take place with increasing rapidity — hence the heating up of the cultural economy and its rapid turnover of new products. Not only are taste cultures themselves shifting, but people now tend to move between them with greater ease. These factors contribute to a sense of the ④ <u>relativity</u> of any single position. Contemporary musical choices are plural as never before, and the effect of that plurality is inevitably to confirm that, in matters of musical judgment, the ⑤ <u>individual</u> can be the only authority.

*proliferation: 확산

[9~12] 다음 빈칸에 들어갈 말로 가장 적절한 것을 고르시오.

9. In 1969, when John was twenty-three, he taught briefly at a Navajo Indian boarding school in Shiprock, New Mexico. His third-grade students were among the poorest children in America, possessing little more than the clothes on their backs. The school had few toys or other sources of entertainment. Yet John never heard the children say they were bored. They were continually making up their own games. They were, at the age of ten, happy and well-adjusted children. That Christmas, John went home to visit his family. He remembers the scene, a floor full of packages under the tree. His own ten-year-old brother opened a dozen or so of them, quickly moving from one to the next. A few days later, John found his brother and a friend watching TV, the Christmas toys tossed aside in his brother's bedroom. Both boys complained to John that they had nothing to do. "We're bored," they proclaimed. For John, it was a clear indication that children's happiness doesn't come from _____.

*proclaim: 단호하게 말하다. 선언하다

① pride
② compliments
③ possessions
④ discipline
⑤ achievement

10. Some scientists compare the brain to a relay station that merely coordinates incoming signals and outgoing responses, whereas others see it as an immense computer that processes information and then arrives at an appropriate response. Francois Jacob, the French molecular biologist and Nobel laureate, suggests that the human mind is far more; it has a built-in need _____ out of the constant flow of information coming from its sensory organs. In other words, the brain creates a narrative, with a beginning, a middle and an end — a temporal sequence that makes sense of events. The brain selects and discards information to be used in the narrative,
constructing connections and relationships that create a web of meaning. In this way, a narrative reveals more than just *what* happened; it explains *why*. When the mind selects and orders incoming information into meaning, it is telling itself a story. [3점]

*molecular: 분자의 **laureate: 수상자 ***temporal: 시간의

① to filter data
② to create order
③ to share stories
④ to mimic others
⑤ to interpret contexts

11. Everyone would like to believe that their wonderful, creative ideas will sell themselves. But as Galileo, Edvard Munch, and millions of others have discovered, they do not. On the contrary, creative ideas as well as those who propose them are often viewed with suspicion and distrust. Because people are attached to their beliefs, it can be incredibly difficult to shake them from their current way of thinking. Thus, children need to learn _____. This is part of the practical aspect of creative thinking. If children create a piece of artwork, they should be prepared to demonstrate why they think it has value. Similarly, teachers may find themselves having to justify their ideas about teaching to their principal. They should prepare their students for the same kind of experience.
[3점]

① what to expect from their elders
② what to give up for their creative ideas
③ how to accept criticism and make use of it
④ how to persuade others of the value of their ideas
⑤ how to make creative innovations and earn a reputation

12. In pluralistic societies, ethnic minorities and indigenous groups sometimes ask the legal system to take their cultural background into account in criminal and civil cases. Most individuals, when first hearing of the cultural defense, immediately reject it for fear that it would lead to anarchy. If each person could demand exemptions from the law, then the law would be powerless to hold society together. Ethnic minorities should change their behavior so it conforms to the law of the land. "When in Rome, do as the Romans do" has been the conventional wisdom for centuries. The official policies of essentially all nation-states mirror these beliefs. Indeed, most governments _____.
This view, which is widely accepted by the public and government elites, has complicated efforts to raise cultural defenses in many instances. [3점]

*pluralistic: 다민족의 **anarchy: 무정부 상태

① pay attention to the positive influence of cultural diversity

② cross cultural boundaries and open doorways to understanding

③ raise the issue of how such cultural alienation can be dissolved

④ favor assimilation over the accommodation of cultural differences

⑤ consider amendment of law to protect minorities from various crimes

13. 다음 글에서 전체 흐름과 관계 <u>없는</u> 문장은? [3점]

Perhaps the most influential in determining authenticity of souvenirs is the meaning that the tourists themselves assign to their merchandise through a process of attribution of meaning. ① For most people, 'buying a souvenir is an act of acquisition of an object perceived as authentic'. ② However, according to a study, the perception of the souvenir vendors was that tourists really do not care if the design is traditional or contrived. ③ The study concludes it is obvious that tourists understand that artificial and non-destination-specific items (e.g. stone chess sets, brass cigarette lighters, etc.) are not part of the craft tradition of local cultures, but rather such items are made specifically for tourists. ④ Therefore, it's crucial for tourists to learn how to tell fake items from real ones. ⑤ Nonetheless, the souvenirs tourists take home are still a sort of trophy, which must reflect their image of the country visited — it must look authentic, traditional, or primitive, because the authenticity of the artifact is a guarantee of the authenticity of one's experience abroad.

*authenticity: 진짜임 **contrived: 억지로 꾸민 듯한

[14~15] 주어진 글 다음에 이어질 글의 순서로 가장 적절한 것을 고르시오.

14.

Did you know that a plant knows when it is being eaten? Well, as recent research reveals, it does, but it doesn't just sit there and accept its fate. It deploys troops to defend itself, in an effort to stop the predator.

(A) Sure enough, the cress responded to the vibrations that mimic a munching caterpillar by upping its production of mildly toxic mustard oils and delivering them to the leaves to deter predators. The plant showed no response to wind or other vibrations.
(B) To find out if the plant was aware of being eaten, the scientists recreated the vibrations that a caterpillar makes as it eats the leaves of the subject. They

also recorded other vibrations that the plant might experience, such as that of wind blowing.

(C) In this case, the research subject was a plant called thale cress(*Arabidopsis thaliana*), a member of the cabbage family. Thale cress was the first plant to have its genome sequenced, so researchers have a better understanding of its inner workings than of most other plants.

> *munch: 우적우적 먹다 **sequence: (유전체의) 배열 순서를 밝히다

① (A) – (C) – (B)　　② (B) – (A) – (C)
③ (B) – (C) – (A)　　④ (C) – (A) – (B)
⑤ (C) – (B) – (A)

15.

> No cucumbers burp, but compounds called cucurbitacins produced in the skin of the fruit can have an adverse effect on the digestive system of those who eat them. Cucurbitacins also taste bitter, ruining the best cucumber sandwich.

(A) But two in five people have an acute sensitivity to cucurbitacins, which makes it understandable if they think the rest of us are crazy for eating cucumbers at all. The standard solution to the problem used to be simply peeling the offending skin. But people are not the only ones affected by cucurbitacins.

(B) Insect pests are attracted to the compounds and focus on cucumber plants that produce them, either naturally or through stress. So when plant breeders developed "burpless" varieties, with little to no cucurbitacin in the skins, everyone was happy but the bugs.

(C) Due to genetic differences, one person in five can't taste cucurbitacins at all, which explains why some people think others are crazy when they complain about bitter-tasting cucumbers. [3점]

> *burp: 트림하다
> **cucurbitacin: 쿠쿠르비타신((오잇과 식물에 포함되어 있는 쓴맛 성분))

① (A) – (B) – (C)　　② (B) – (A) – (C)
③ (B) – (C) – (A)　　④ (C) – (A) – (B)
⑤ (C) – (B) – (A)

[16~17] 글의 흐름으로 보아, 주어진 문장이 들어가기에 가장 적절한 곳을 고르시오.

16.

> Rather, the time-compression technique involves the shortening of pauses between words, and the reduction of the length of vowel sounds.

With reference to the variable of intensity, it is almost stating the obvious to say that bright lights or loud sounds can attract our attention. We have all been exposed to countless examples of commercial advertisements that seem to be based solely upon this premise. (①) One unusual example of the use of intensity in advertising contexts is the practice of time-compressed speech in radio commercials. (②) The experiment conducted by LaBarbera and MacLachlan exposed people to five radio commercials that were either normal or time-compressed on the order of 130%. (③) These time-compressed commercials were not "sped up" by making the tape run faster; that would also increase the frequency of the auditory signal, and make the announcer sound like a high-pitched Mickey Mouse. (④) This results in a message that runs more quickly, without changing the pitch of the announcer's voice. (⑤) These researchers found that the time-compressed advertisements elicited more interest and better recall than the normal ads. [3점]

> *premise: 전제 **elicit: 끌어내다

17.

Because these nutrients are digested more slowly than carbohydrates, meals that are higher in protein and fat tend to keep you satisfied longer than meals that are high in carbohydrates.

When people cut back on carbohydrates (or processed foods or whatever), they usually end up consuming fewer calories — even when they're not trying to restrict their calorie intake. (①) For example, a study found that people who followed a strict low-carb diet but were otherwise allowed to eat as much as they wanted ended up reducing their calorie intake by about the same amount as people who were consciously restricting their calories. (②) There are a couple of things going on here. (③) First, when people have a limited variety of foods to choose from, they tend to eat less than they do when presented with a lot of options. (④) Secondly, when people avoid carbohydrates, they generally increase their intake of protein and fat. (⑤) As a result, people who cut back on carbs often report that they aren't as hungry between meals — and may snack less.

*carbohydrate: 탄수화물 **low–carb diet: 저탄수화물 다이어트

18. 다음 글의 내용을 한 문장으로 요약하고자 한다. 빈칸 (A), (B)에 들어갈 말로 가장 적절한 것은?

For an intriguing field experiment, two Swedish economists visited a regional blood center in Gothenburg and found 153 women who were interested in giving blood. Then researchers divided the women into three groups. Experimenters told those in the first group that they wouldn't receive a payment. The experimenters offered the second group a different arrangement. If these participants gave blood, they'd each receive 50 Swedish kronor (about $7). The third group received a variation on that second offer: a 50-kronor payment with an immediate option to donate the amount to a children's cancer charity. Of the first group, 52 percent of the women decided to donate blood. And the second group? In this group, only 30 percent of the women decided to give blood. Meanwhile, the third group which had the option of donating the fee directly to charity responded much the same as the first group. Fifty-three percent became blood donors. Doing good is what blood donation is all about. It provides a feeling that the American Red Cross brochures say money can't buy. That's why unpaid volunteers invariably increase during natural disasters and other calamities.

↓

Offering people _____(A)_____ rewards when asking for altruistic behavior, such as blood donation, doesn't _____(B)_____ their participation.

	(A)		(B)
①	extrinsic	......	motivate
②	extrinsic	......	inhibit
③	intrinsic	......	promote
④	unexpected	......	motivate
⑤	unexpected	......	inhibit

[19~20] 다음 글을 읽고, 물음에 답하시오.

Every object and person we encounter in the world is unique, but we wouldn't function very well if we perceived them that way. We don't have the time to observe and consider each detail of every item in our environment. Instead, we employ a few (a) prominent traits that we do observe to assign the object to a category, and then we base our assessment of the object on the category rather than the object itself. Categorization helps us to navigate our environment with great speed and efficiency. One of the principal ways we categorize is by maximizing the importance of certain differences while minimizing the relevance of others. But the arrow of our reasoning can also point the other way. If we conclude that a certain set of objects belongs to one group and a second set of objects to another, we may then perceive those within the same group as more similar than they really are — and those in different groups as less similar than they really are. Merely placing objects in groups can (b) affect our judgment of those objects. So while categorization is a natural and crucial shortcut, like our brain's other survival-oriented tricks, it has its (c) drawbacks.

One of the earliest experiments investigating the misinterpretations caused by categorization was a simple study in which subjects were asked to estimate the temperature. In the study, researchers found that if you ask people in a given city to estimate the difference in temperature between June 1 and June 30, they will tend to underestimate it; but if you ask them to estimate the difference in temperature between June 15 and July 15, they will overestimate it. The artificial grouping of days into months (d) distorts our perception. We see two days within a month as being more (e) different to each other than equally distant days that occur in two different months, even though the time interval between them is identical.

19. 윗글의 제목으로 가장 적절한 것은?

① The Principle of Sorting People and Things
② When We Categorize, We Catch Sight of Details
③ Contrast and Comparison in Categorization
④ Categorization: The Double-edged Sword of Perception
⑤ Categorical Perception: The Most Valuable Survival Skill

20. 밑줄 친 (a) ~ (e) 중에서 문맥상 낱말의 쓰임이 적절하지 않은 것은? [3점]

① (a)　　② (b)　　③ (c)　　④ (d)　　⑤ (e)

○ 답안지의 해당란에 성명과 수험번호를 쓰고, 또 수험번호와 답을 정확히 표시하시오.
○ 문항에 따라 배점이 다르니, 각 물음의 끝에 표시된 배점을 참고하시오. 3점 문항에만 점수가 표시되어 있습니다. 점수 표시가 없는 문항은 모두 2점씩입니다.

1. 다음 글에 드러난 'I'의 심경 변화로 가장 적절한 것은?

The wind batters me as I stand in the open door of the plane and face the sky. But I have made a firm decision and will not let anything stop me. "Ready?" calls the team captain. We shout back, "Ready!" and then, "Go!" Suddenly we are out the door of the plane, rolling into the wind of a clear summer sky. Involuntary laughter, a combination of joy and fear, bubbles up in my throat. I face the ground and try to lie flat in the air. One by one the other jumpers join together, grabbing my wrists and ankles, linking with each other until we are a star of eight people speeding toward the earth at 120 miles per hour. Beneath each pair of goggles is a smile. We are jumping together again. Finally at four thousand feet, we break apart and release our parachutes. They swing out and balloon above us, carrying us gently down to the brown field below. I feel as if I were on top of the world.

① regretful → proud
② nervous → terrified
③ frightened → relieved
④ determined → excited
⑤ lonely → content

2. 다음 글에서 필자가 주장하는 바로 가장 적절한 것은?

Parents can help their children succeed by providing productive feedback. Let's consider an example of feedback related to negative behavior: "Mary, I do not like the way you handled not being able to go to the movies. I know that you were disappointed. I would be, too. But when you are disappointed or upset, you cannot kick the door or damage your things. You need to handle your upset feelings differently. What do you think you can do instead to get your angry feelings out?" Notice that this feedback is specific and direct. While the parent gives the child the message that her action is unacceptable, the child herself doesn't feel insulted. This kind of feedback does not usually provoke a defensive response. That is like the old saying, "I love you, but not your behavior."

① 자녀를 꾸짖을 때는 아무도 없는 데서 조용히 해야 한다.
② 자녀 행동의 결과보다는 동기에 대한 피드백을 해야 한다.
③ 사람을 비난하기보다 구체적 행동의 잘못을 지적해야 한다.
④ 자녀를 훈육할 때는 직접적 비난보다 부드러운 충고가 좋다.
⑤ 자녀 행동을 지적할 때에는 객관적이고 냉정하게 해야 한다.

3. 밑줄 친 putting all your self eggs in one basket이 다음 글에서 의미하는 바로 가장 적절한 것은? [3점]

Research suggests that a person's level of self-complexity can have important consequences, particularly when people are confronted with negative events or difficulties in a given life domain. Imagine learning that you did poorly on a midterm exam. If you're someone who is high in self-complexity — that is, you define yourself in terms of many nonoverlapping domains (for example, student, avid skier, committed volunteer, enthusiastic fan of *Glee*) — the negativity that results from your poor exam grade is relatively contained, affecting only how you feel about yourself as a student. But if you're low in self-complexity such that your identity as a student overlaps to a great extent with the few other identities you have — then the negativity associated with your poor exam grade is likely to lower your evaluations of yourself as a student as well as spill over and affect how you evaluate your other, overlapping identities. In short, putting all your self eggs in one basket can be risky in the face of threatening, self-relevant events.

① permitting your few self-aspects to merge together
② evaluating yourself in terms of your personal traits
③ protecting against damage to your mental wellbeing
④ preventing you from thinking positively about yourself
⑤ comparing yourself with others who are doing better than you

4. 다음 글의 요지로 가장 적절한 것은?

When a product features anthropomorphic cues (e.g., a name, gender, voice), it creates an agent that deserves concern for its own well-being. Accordingly, consumers may engage with anthropomorphized products in a more emotionally driven fashion, and show greater care and concern than they would for non-anthropomorphized agents. As an example of this, Chandler and Schwarz found that consumers induced to think of their car in anthropomorphic terms were less willing to replace it, and gave less weight to its quality when making replacement decisions. Instead, they attended more to features usually considered relevant in the interpersonal domain (e.g., those which would determine a good companion, like having a warm personality). This is because anthropomorphic product traits can lead consumers to categorize products as humans, and since product love is a manifestation of interpersonal love, anthropomorphism makes such a relationship with products plausible.

*anthropomorphic: 의인화된

① 제품이 의인화되면 소비자는 제품의 장점을 확대 해석한다.
② 제품을 의인화하는 광고는 구매를 크게 촉진하는 효과가 있다.
③ 의인화된 특성은 신기술에 대한 소비자의 거부감을 완화시킨다.
④ 의인화된 제품은 사용자에게 그 제품에 대한 애착을 갖게 한다.
⑤ 제품을 의인화하면 제품에 관한 불신을 바로잡는 데 도움이 된다.

5. 다음 글의 제목으로 가장 적절한 것은?

In a study, participants first had to perform a series of very lengthy, extremely tedious tasks (like turning pegs in peg holes). Afterwards they were asked to tell the next participant that the tasks they would do were actually really interesting! The idea was to create in each participant the dissonant cognitions that, on the one hand, they had disliked the experiment but, on the other hand, they had told another person that they enjoyed it. In addition, half of the participants were given $20 for compliance with the 'lying' request and the other half a meagre $1. The idea here was that those in the $1 group would experience a higher level of cognitive dissonance than those in the $20 group because they had insufficient justification for the inconsistency between their attitudes (i.e. 'that really was a boring task') and their actual behavior (i.e. lying about the behavior to another person). The $20 group had the justification of a decent money payout and would thus experience less dissonance. It was predicted that the $1 participants, being highly cognitively dissonant, would change their attitude towards enjoying or liking the tasks so as to reestablish consonance; those in the $20 condition would not. This was exactly what happened when attitudes towards the task were measured after the experiment.

*peg: 못 **dissonant: 조화되지 않는 ***meagre: 변변찮은

① Why We Reduce the Cognitive Dissonance We Feel
② Reducing Cognitive Dissonance by Changing Our Attitude
③ Cognitive Dissonance Plays a Big Role in Decision-Making
④ Higher Monetary Rewards Induce Greater Changes in Attitude
⑤ Monetary Rewards Are Not Correlated with Cognitive Dissonance

6. Used Book Sale에 관한 다음 안내문의 내용과 일치하지 <u>않는</u> 것은?

Used Book Sale

The Lakeview Public Library is holding a gigantic used book sale. Stop by and find great books for everyone in your family!

·**When:** June 15 – 18, 2023
·**Where:** The ground floor of the Lakeview Public Library
·**Time:**
- Thursday 12 p.m. – 5 p.m.
- Friday 10 a.m. – 5 p.m.
- Saturday and Sunday 11 a.m. – 6 p.m.

Half-price Sunday:
Beginning Sunday at 3 p.m., all remaining books will be reduced in price by 50%.

Parking:
Due to ongoing construction, the main parking lot of the library is closed on weekdays. However, limited parking for the library is available behind the library. (The parking fee is 5 dollars per hour.)

All profits will go toward the construction of a new children's library.

---

① Lakeview 공립 도서관의 1층에서 열린다.
② 목요일의 판매 시간이 가장 짧다.
③ 일요일 오후 3시부터 반값 할인 행사를 한다.
④ 도서관 사정으로 주차는 불가능하다.
⑤ 수익금은 어린이 도서관 신축에 사용된다.

7. 다음 글의 밑줄 친 부분 중, 어법상 틀린 것은? [3점]

Customer to customer e-commerce (C2C e-commerce) is one ① <u>in which</u> one individual wants to sell an item to another. The items are usually used items, collector's items such as stamps or coins, or antiques. The seller posts the description of the item and the expected price of the item on a web site ② <u>maintained</u> by a company which acts as a broker. An individual who visits this site ③ <u>looking</u> for items may be interested in the item advertised for sale. The buyer and seller then discuss the item and a price. The price is mutually settled between the two parties by exchanging messages by e-mail. The broker then arranges to collect the item from the seller and ④ <u>despatches</u> it to the buyer and collects payment for the item and a fee from the buyer and the seller for services. The primary advantage of this system is that the Internet enables two individuals ⑤ <u>to locate</u> at distant places to come together to buy and sell through an intermediary's web address.

8. 다음 글의 밑줄 친 부분 중, 문맥상 낱말의 쓰임이 적절하지 <u>않은</u> 것은? [3점]

Salovey and Mayer published three articles on the topic of emotion and intelligence. Their thesis was simple: Though frequently conceived as opposites, emotions and intellect typically work in concert, each ① <u>enhancing</u> the other. "Our ability to engage in the deepest levels of thought isn't ② <u>limited</u> to intellectual pursuits such as calculus," Mayer contends. "It also includes reasoning and abstracting about ③ feelings. And that means that some warmhearted or romantic individuals are engaging in very, very ④ sophisticated information processing. This type of reasoning is every bit as formal as that used in solving syllogisms." The exchange also flows in the other direction: Emotions sometimes ⑤ weaken thought. Here the psychologists point to research showing that the experience of strong feeling may help us make better choices and, paradoxically, control our emotions.

*calculus: 미적분학 **syllogism: 삼단논법

[9~12] 다음 빈칸에 들어갈 말로 가장 적절한 것을 고르시오.

9. Gift giving is one of the most mysterious areas of shopping. Irrational behavior is almost the norm in this area of consumer spending and it is tolerated, expected, and even encouraged. Gift giving is less about shopping and more about the emotions of the shopper. This helps to explain the extreme nature of gift shopping and the illogical nature of the whole process. From the consumer's point of view, shopping for gifts is an emotional process that one gets caught up in. It is an area where the laws of supply, demand, and price go out the window as anxious shoppers do their utmost to bring pleasure to another person, and thereby, to themselves. The shopper shopping for gifts is the most susceptible of all shoppers. Smart retailers are ready to take advantage of the defenseless and emotionally vulnerable gift buyer. Meanwhile, the shopper knows he is vulnerable, but he is also _____ to defend himself. Pleasing the recipient and conveying the intended emotional message are often more important than the price.

*susceptible: 쉽게 영향을 받는

① eager   ② content
③ unwilling   ④ prepared
⑤ intolerant

10. Why did evolution decide to ban muscle activity during REM sleep? Because by eliminating muscle activity you are prevented from acting out your dream experience. During REM sleep, there is a nonstop barrage of motor commands swirling around the brain, and they underlie the movement-rich experience of dreams. Wise, then, of Mother Nature to have tailored a physiological straitjacket that forbids these fictional movements from becoming reality, especially considering that you've stopped consciously perceiving your surroundings. You can well imagine the disastrous outcome of falsely enacting a dream fight, or a frantic sprint from an approaching dream foe, while your eyes are closed and you have no comprehension of the world around you. It wouldn't take long before you quickly left the gene pool. The brain paralyzes the body so _____.

[3점]   *barrage: 집중 공세 **straitjacket: 구속복

① the body can take a break
② the mind can dream safely
③ REM sleep affects your dream
④ you can remember your dream
⑤ the dream increases muscle activity

11. Perhaps the most widely used AI technique in games is cheating. For example, in a war simulation game the computer team can have access to all information on its human opponents — the location of their base; the types, number, and location of units, etc. — without having to send out scouts to gather such intelligence the way a human player must. Cheating in this manner is common and helps give the computer an edge against intelligent human players. However, cheating can be bad. If it is obvious to the player that the computer is cheating, the player likely will assume his efforts are useless and lose interest in the game. Also, unbalanced cheating can give computer opponents too much power, making it impossible for the player to beat the computer. Here again, the player is likely to lose interest if he sees his efforts are useless. Cheating must be balanced to create just enough of a challenge _____ _____. [3점]

*scout: 정찰병

① to help the player not to set their goal too high
② to become accustomed to the rules of the game
③ that gives the player optimal control over progression
④ for the player to cooperate while competing with others
⑤ for the player to continually find the game interesting and fun

12. Peripheral vision _____ so that our fovea visits all the interesting and crucial parts of our visual field. Our eyes don't scan our environment randomly. They move so as to focus our fovea on important things, the most important ones (usually) first. The fuzzy cues on the outskirts of our visual field provide the data that helps our brain plan where to move our eyes, and in what order. For example, when we scan a medicine label for a "use by" date, a fuzzy blob in the periphery with the vague form of a date is enough to cause an eye movement that lands the fovea there to allow us to check it. If we are browsing a produce market looking for strawberries, a blurry reddish patch at the edge of our visual field draws our eyes and our attention, even though sometimes it may turn out to be radishes instead of strawberries. If we hear an animal growl nearby, a fuzzy animal-like shape in the corner of our eye will be enough to move our eyes very quickly in that direction, especially if the shape is moving toward us. [3점]

*peripheral vision: 주변시
**forvea: 중심와 ((망막의 중심부에 있는 시각 세포가 밀집된 오목한 부분))
***blob: 윤곽이 뚜렷하지 않은 부분

① enables us to interpret what we are directly looking at
② helps us focus on the size and shapes of objects exactly
③ provides low-resolution cues to lead our eye movements
④ updates our knowledge about the spatial features of an object
⑤ serves as the means of information transmission to the brain

13. 다음 글에서 전체 흐름과 관계 <u>없는</u> 문장은?

We tend to think of myths as silly old stories about the adventures of gods, warriors, and demons, invented by primitive people to explain a world they could not understand in our modern, scientific sense. ① But it is a mistake to dismiss these stories as trivial and old-fashioned, with no more important meaning for humanity. ② Scholars have shown that common themes in myths from many diverse cultures speak to us about the universal concerns of all people and about shared ways of thought. ③ As we move increasingly toward a unified world — a global village, as it has been called — it is important to see how much basic human nature we all share. ④ Also, it is good to acquire greater knowledge and a deeper understanding of the natural world, and the scientific knowledge we have gained through myths informs our lives and colors our views. ⑤ The systematic study of mythology reveals important points about the human psyche, about universal human motivations, fears and thought patterns.

[14~15] 주어진 글 다음에 이어질 글의 순서로 가장 적절한 것을 고르시오.

14.

US researchers suspect that there are definite disadvantages to our powerful brains. They compared the self-destructive programming of human cells with a similar programme that works in great apes, specifically chimpanzees. This programme destroys and dismantles old and defective cells.

(A) But this improvement in intelligence probably comes at a high price, because the chimps' self-cleansing mechanism also gets rid of cancer cells. Whereas chimpanzees hardly ever get cancer, in humans this disease is one of the top causes of death.

(B) Are we paying the price for our intellectual capacities? If our current level of intelligence is not suited to the survival of humankind, it must either be increased or lowered. The latter is probably unacceptable, as we can't reconcile it with our ideas about self-worth.

(C) Their comparison showed that the clean-up mechanism is a lot more effective in chimpanzees than it is in people, and the researchers believe that the reduced rate at which cells are broken down in humans allows for larger brain growth and a higher rate of connections between cells.

*dismantle: 해체하다 **reconcile: 양립하게 하다, 조화시키다

① (A) – (C) – (B) ② (B) – (A) – (C)
③ (B) – (C) – (A) ④ (C) – (A) – (B)
⑤ (C) – (B) – (A)

15.

Unfortunately, there are some social scientists who refuse to admit the limitations of their field of study. They push hard to make social science imitate physical science.

(A) The use of mathematical techniques is not an end in itself but only a means to an end, namely, the discovery of what's true about the material world. The use of numbers is one way to be more precise in our effort to rationally understand causes.

(B) This is usually done by the use of all sorts of numbers, tables, charts, and graphs in order to give the impression of a profound quantification of the subject matter. Now, as a matter of fact, some things can be quantified and some things cannot.

(C) We cannot really quantify prejudice or love, for instance. When all is said and done, such attempted quantification is in vain. What is often forgotten, even in the physical sciences, is that science is not primarily a matter of quantification. [3점]

① (A) – (C) – (B) ② (B) – (A) – (C)
③ (B) – (C) – (A) ④ (C) – (A) – (B)
⑤ (C) – (B) – (A)

[16~17] 글의 흐름으로 보아, 주어진 문장이 들어가기에 가장 적절한 곳을 고르시오.

16.

> Once science has taken off, however, its link to technology becomes much tighter.

From our modern point of view, it is natural to see an important and necessary connection between science and technology. (①) However, technology did not have to await the specific discoveries, concepts, and mathematical equations of the past five hundred years. (②) Indeed, that is precisely why in many respects the China of 1500 seemed more advanced than its European or Middle Eastern counterparts. (③) One can create perfectly functional (even exquisite) clocks, gunpowder, compasses, or medical treatments without convincing scientific theories or well-controlled experiments. (④) It is barely imaginable that we could have nuclear power plants, supersonic airplanes, computers, lasers or a medley of effective medical and surgical interventions in the absence of the sciences of our epoch. (⑤) Those societies that lack science must either remain deprived of technological innovations or simply copy them from societies that have developed them. [3점]

17.

> That is to say, they have accepted the rules of the organization or institution and see the person giving orders as a legitimate representative of a rational authority structure.

Authority is a powerful force. According to sociologist Max Weber, there are several different types of authority. Sometimes we obey an order because of tradition or custom. (①) This is usually what is at work when we willfully follow the orders of our elders. (②) Other times we might follow someone's commands because we are moved by their personal charisma or a belief that they have the power to transform our life. (③) This is typical of individuals who are eager to take direction from a leader of a religious cult. (④) But in modern society, most commands are obeyed because people believe in the legal authority of their superior. (⑤) According to Max Weber, an authority structure in the form of large bureaucracies is the most important defining feature of modern society.

*religious cult: (광신적) 종교 집단 **bureaucracy: 관료제

18. 다음 글의 내용을 한 문장으로 요약하고자 한다. 빈칸 (A), (B)에 들어갈 말로 가장 적절한 것은? [3점]

In a study, Cass Sunstein, a professor at Harvard, and some of his colleagues brought together two groups of people who share the same belief system: liberals from Boulder, Colorado, and conservatives from Colorado Springs. In their respective groups, each was asked to deliberate on three topics: civil partnerships, affirmative action and climate change. But before the discussions began, individual participants recorded their private opinions on each topic. And then the groups were mixed up and encouraged to discuss their views. The group deliberations were consistently respectful, engaged and substantive, but when they were finished, conservatives from Colorado Springs who had been neutral on a climate-change treaty now opposed it. Boulder liberals who had felt somewhat positive about civil partnerships became firmly convinced of their merit.

↓

> According to the study, diversity within like-minded groups _____(A)_____ after being exposed to people of opposing opinions, because they make each other's views more _____(B)_____.

	(A)		(B)
①	increases	……	extreme
②	increases	……	neutral
③	disappears	……	biased
④	disappears	……	extreme
⑤	disappears	……	neutral

[19~20] 다음 글을 읽고, 물음에 답하시오.

Psychologist James Pennebaker has conducted many studies showing that when people write about traumas they've gone through — such as physical abuse or the death of a loved one — they often experience reduced levels of stress hormones, strengthened immune systems, and a decrease in doctor visits. Participants in Pennebaker's studies have seen (a) improvements after only two or three writing sessions of 20 minutes each. In a similar vein, communication scholars have shown that when people are in distress, writing about their positive feelings for a loved one can (b) accelerate their recovery.

In one experiment, for instance, participants were put through a series of (c) stressful tasks, such as mentally solving complicated math problems under time constraints and watching video clips of married couples fighting. These tasks (d) lowered their levels of a hormone called cortisol, which the body produces when people are under stress. The participants were then assigned to one of three conditions. Participants in the first group were instructed to write a letter expressing their positive feelings to someone they loved. The second group merely thought about a loved one but didn't put their feelings into words. Finally, the third group did nothing for 20 minutes. The researchers found that when people wrote about their affectionate feelings, their cortisol levels returned to normal the most quickly. Just thinking about a loved one didn't provide any more benefit than doing nothing. Only those participants who let out their feelings in (e) written form recovered quickly from their elevated stress.

19. 윗글의 제목으로 가장 적절한 것은?

① Get Rid of Your Troubles via Writing
② How Can You Express Yourself More Clearly?
③ How a Writing System Works to Soothe People
④ Connect With Your Loved Ones Through Writing
⑤ The Surprising Link Between Writing and Thinking

20. 밑줄 친 (a) ~ (e) 중에서 문맥상 낱말의 쓰임이 적절하지 <u>않은</u> 것은? [3점]

① (a)　　② (b)　　③ (c)　　④ (d)　　⑤ (e)

○ 답안지의 해당란에 성명과 수험번호를 쓰고, 또 수험번호와 답을 정확히 표시하시오.
○ 문항에 따라 배점이 다르니, 각 물음의 끝에 표시된 배점을 참고하시오. 3점 문항에만 점수가 표시되어 있습니다. 점수 표시가 없는 문항은 모두 2점씩입니다.

---

1. 다음 글의 목적으로 가장 적절한 것은?

Dear Mr. Peeking:

Thank you for your interest in a faculty position at Punxatawney Coalition College. We received many responses from very highly qualified candidates like you. With so many superbly qualified candidates, we looked for someone whose background and qualifications gave us just the right fit for our exact needs this semester. I'm sorry to have to say that the position is being offered to one of the other candidates. This does not mean, however, that we were unimpressed with your credentials. We will keep your résumé in our active file in case a more suitable position opens up. Perhaps in the future we will have another opening that will better fit your qualifications. I wish you well in your pursuit of the right position.

Cordially,
Letitia T. Hall

---

① 교수직 채용 계획을 안내하려고
② 미래에 교수로 채용할 것을 약속하려고
③ 교수직에 채용되지 못했음을 통보하려고
④ 교수 채용 면접 대상자로 선정된 것을 알려 주려고
⑤ 교수 채용에 면접관으로 참여해 달라고 요청하려고

2. 다음 글에서 필자가 주장하는 바로 가장 적절한 것은?

It's amazing how much you can learn about your friends and family, your job, the organization you work in, and yourself when you decide to really listen to others. But not everyone understands this benefit. For example, we heard a story about a tennis pro who was giving a lesson to a new student. After watching the novice take several swings at the tennis ball, the pro stopped him and suggested ways he could improve his stroke. But each time he did, the student interrupted him and gave his opinion of the problem and how it should be solved. After several interruptions, the pro began to nod his head in agreement. When the lesson ended, a woman who had been watching said to the pro, "Why did you go along with that arrogant man's stupid suggestions?" The pro smiled and replied, "I learned a long time ago that it is a waste of time to try to sell real answers to anyone who just wants to buy echoes." Beware of putting yourself into a position where you think you know all the answers. Anytime you do, you'll be putting yourself in danger. It's almost impossible to think of yourself as "the expert" and continue growing and learning at the same time.

① 상대방이 요청하기 전에 먼저 충고하지 말아야 한다.
② 일을 결정하기 전에 먼저 전문가의 말을 들어야 한다.
③ 누구 앞에서나 항상 자신의 의견을 당당히 표현해야 한다.
④ 모든 것을 안다는 태도를 버리고 남의 말을 경청해야 한다.
⑤ 운동에 관한 조언을 할 때는 상대방의 실력을 고려해야 한다.

3. 밑줄 친 embodied the best of both animals가 다음 글에서 의미하는 바로 가장 적절한 것은? [3점]

Taking a cue from an essay by British-American philosopher Isaiah Berlin, Yale professor John Gaddis discusses how great thinkers and leaders can be categorized as either hedgehogs or foxes. This divide may stem from how each animal reacts to its environment. When a fox is hunted, it finds many clever ways to evade predators; when a hedgehog is hunted, it curls up into a spiky ball and lies still. The general gist of the line is this: The former types of people see the details in everything they do and use every means conceivable to achieve their ends, while the latter types are great at having one singular vision and pursue it when other people fall by the wayside. They accomplish things that will resound through history. According to Gaddis, Dante was a hedgehog, but Shakespeare was a fox. He also points out that Abraham Lincoln's leadership <u>embodied the best of both animals</u>.

*fall by the wayside: 도중에 실패하다

① built flexibility regardless of the environmental troubles

② planned in advance and took advantage of small opportunities

③ accepted suggestions from others and found multiple solutions

④ fostered progress through scheming tactics and effective defense

⑤ aimed for the big picture exploiting the complexities of the situation

4. 다음 글의 제목으로 가장 적절한 것은?

While biology influences the way we tend to approach adversity, changing our thinking will change our reactions as well. To do so, we have to understand whether we tend to have either a 'fixed' or a 'growth' mindset. Those with a fixed mindset have less success at overcoming adversity, and are more likely to get stuck at hurt and revenge, because they believe they don't want to take risks. They get discouraged by failure and are likely to give up. They don't like to be challenged at things they are not good at, so they don't learn and grow from their mistakes. Their motto is, "You can't teach an old dog new tricks." Growth mindset individuals, on the other hand, find

more success with overcoming adversity because they are comfortable with uncertainty, and know that with effort, focus, and repeated tries, they will be able to bring about a desired change. Their motto is, "As long as the dog is breathing, he can learn tricks."

① Mindset: The New Psychology of Success
② What Should We Do to Shift Our Mindset?
③ Turn Your Mistake into a Valuable Life Lesson
④ Overcoming Adversity: Conquering Life's Challenges
⑤ Fixed vs. Growth Mindset: Beliefs That Shape Your Life

5. 다음 도표의 내용과 일치하지 <u>않는</u> 것은?

The World's Demand for Meat in 2000 vs. 2030

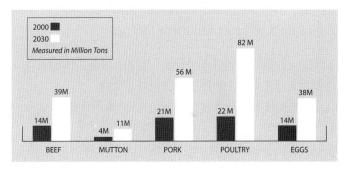

The above graph shows the world's demand for meat in 2000 and 2030. The overall demand for five kinds of meat is expected to rise from 2000 to 2030. ① Beef was tied in third with eggs as the meat most in demand in 2000, although only beef will retain its third position in 2030. ② The smallest increase overall was mutton, which saw an increase in demand by 7 million tons between 2000 and 2030. ③ Expected to grow about 35 million tons in the next 30 years, the demand for pork is the second-largest increase overall. ④ It is the demand for poultry that is forecasted to grow more than any other meat in 2030 when compared to 2000, with more than a four times increase expected. ⑤ The demand for eggs is the same as that for beef in 2000, but the demand for eggs is expected to be less than that for beef by one million ton in 2030.

6. Paulo Freire에 관한 다음 글의 내용과 일치하지 <u>않는</u> 것은?

Paulo Freire was a Brazilian educator and philosopher, known for his methods of using everyday words and ideas to teach the illiterate to read. He was born in 1921 in Recife. Even though Freire studied law as well as philosophy at the University of Recife starting in 1943, he never actually practiced law and instead worked as a teacher. In 1962 the mayor of Recife appointed Freire as head of an adult literacy program for the city. In his first experiment, Freire taught 300 illiterate adults to read and write in just 45 days. As a result, the government approved thousands of similar programs all over Brazil. Unfortunately, after the military coup of 1964 halted the work, he was imprisoned in Brazil for 70 days and spent 15 years in exile. Freire was able to return to Brazil by 1979 and in 1988, Freire was appointed Minister of Education for the City of São Paulo. On May 2, 1997, Paulo Freire died of heart failure at the age of 75.

① 일상 언어를 사용하여 문맹인들에게 읽는 법을 가르쳤다.
② 법학을 공부했지만 법률가 일은 하지 않았다.
③ 문맹인들에게 읽고 쓰는 법을 단 45일 만에 가르쳤다.
④ 군사 쿠데타 이후에도 교육 프로그램을 계속했다.
⑤ 조국에 돌아온 후 시의 교육부 장관으로 임명되었다.

7. 다음 글의 밑줄 친 부분 중, 어법상 틀린 것은? [3점]

Near my old office building, the window of a shoe store advertised the generous offer of a free shoe shine. I walked by this store dozens of times and thought nothing of it. One day, though, with my shoes ① <u>looking</u> a little scuffed and some time on my hands, I decided to avail myself of this small bounty. After my shine, I offered the shoeshine man a tip. He refused. Free was free, he said. I climbed down from the chair feeling distinctly ② <u>indebted</u>. "How could this guy shine my shoes," I thought, "and expect *nothing*?" So

I did what I suspect most people who take the offer ③ <u>done</u> — I looked around for something to buy. I had to even the score, somehow. Since I didn't need shoes, I found myself ④ <u>mindlessly</u> looking at shoe trees, laces, and polish. Finally, I quietly walked out of the store empty-handed and uneasy. Even though I had managed ⑤ <u>to escape</u> from the store, I was sure many others were not so fortunate.

*scuffed: 흠집이 난 **bounty: 선물

8. 다음 글의 밑줄 친 부분 중, 문맥상 낱말의 쓰임이 적절하지 <u>않은</u> 것은? [3점]

Sugar's effects are ironic; that is, it has the opposite effect from the one you intended. You wanted to feel less hungry and nasty, but afterward you feel ① <u>more</u> hungry and nasty. TV has a similar effect, but on happiness as opposed to hungriness. You watch TV because you would like to be entertained, relaxed, involved — you want to feel happy. Unfortunately, although TV can be ② <u>relaxing</u>, it is only intermittently entertaining and hardly ever involving. So, you end up ③ <u>bored</u>, which makes you think you should watch more TV... and you can guess the consequences. Everyone needs a little time to watch TV or just do nothing, just like everyone needs a little sugar now and then. A problem arises when you assume that if a little is good, then more must be ④ <u>worse</u>. I can promise that ⑤ <u>prolonged</u> periods of sitting in front of the TV and eating sugary snacks will not lead to long-term happiness.

[9~12] 다음 빈칸에 들어갈 말로 가장 적절한 것을 고르시오.

9. The pursuit of flavor is one path to a good life, a truth recently discovered by Americans that demands a new account of the meaning of food and its consumption. Any discussion of food and its place in our lives must begin with the role of pleasure. Yet our attitude toward pleasure is _____: "Love People, Not Pleasure," blares the *New York Times*; "There Is More to Life Than Being Happy," proclaims the *Atlantic Monthly*; "pursue pleasure only in moderation," say countless sages throughout history; "it's only transitory," according to the timeless; "it is inimical to spirituality," the bodiless would have us believe; "it will not lead to happiness," the ubiquitous self-help books tell us. We spend much time and many resources pursuing pleasure but then condemn it with a fervor usually reserved for death and taxes.

*blare: 떠들어 대다 **inimical to: ~에 해로운 ***fervor: 열정

① neutral
② coherent
③ conventional
④ ambivalent
⑤ implicit

10. The late political philosopher John Rawls argued that every human being will default to a selfish position — a bias that grows out of survival instincts and, in current evolutionary phrasing, the biasing of genetic kin. To avoid such biases and achieve impartiality, we must imagine a set of principles. If nobody knows who they will be or what social position they will occupy, he argued, there is no opportunity for anyone in an advantaged position to take advantage of that position in order to force a less privileged party to concede to an otherwise unacceptable outcome. If, for example, you're deciding on a healthcare policy, you imagine that you don't know whether you will be wealthy or poor, male or female, black or white, healthy or sick, young or old. You will avoid creating scenarios that you wouldn't want to be in yourself. It is this fact that allows Rawls to claim that principles chosen under _____ are guaranteed to be impartially acceptable to all — and thus, guaranteed not to be unjust. [3점]

*default to: ~을 기본값으로 가지다

① the analysis of data
② the veil of ignorance
③ questions to limit bias
④ open-ended discussions
⑤ detailed qualitative research

11. Manufacturing is undergoing a complex process whereby _____. Manufacturing has become more like a service in which product customization and the 'service' experience of the product are an essential part of the symbiosis that exists between production and consumption. Some manufacturing companies are directly responsible just for the design and marketing of their product; the actual production is subcontracted to a separate manufacturing company. Many products are useless without embedded services. Computers more generally have limited or even no use value without their embedded software as well as content. Another good example is the design and manufacture of elevators; much of the added value in their production does not come from manufacturing but rather from service contracts because, legally, all elevators must be covered by an annual service contract. [3점]

*symbiosis: 공생

① manufacturing companies must consider design as well as technology
② the categories of manufacturing and services are becoming increasingly blurred
③ all manufacturing processes are taken over by robots, increasing unemployment
④ the possibility of newcomers penetrating into the market is barely greater than zero
⑤ extreme competition makes the market environment harsh, leading to the pie shrinking

12. Understanding, for a listener, means mapping the speaker's stories onto the listener's stories. One of the most interesting aspects of the way stories are used in memory is the varied effect they have on understanding. Different people understand the same story differently precisely because the stories they already know are different. When they hear new stories, listeners attempt to construe these stories as old stories they have heard before. They do this because it is actually quite difficult to absorb new information. New ideas ramify through our memories, causing us to revise beliefs, make new generalizations, and perform other effortful cognitive operations. We prefer to avoid all this work. One way to do this is to simply assume that _____. The real problem in understanding, then, is identifying which of all the stories you already know is the one being told to you yet again. [3점]

*construe: 이해[해석]하다 **ramify: 가지를 내다

① we comprehend a small part of what is being said to us
② what we are seeing or hearing is just the same old stuff
③ we process information little by little and recognize patterns
④ what we want to understand relates to what we wish to know
⑤ a listener and a speaker understand each other on the same ground

13. 다음 글에서 전체 흐름과 관계 <u>없는</u> 문장은?

In the broad sweep of human social life, writing is a fairly recent invention: people must have been singing songs and telling tales for many thousands of years before anyone ever devised a means to record their words. ① We are used today to thinking of literature as something an author *writes*, but the earliest written works were usually versions of songs or stories that had been orally composed and transmitted. ② Oral compositions often work differently than purely literary works. ③ Even after poets began to compose with stylus or pen in hand, they often adapted old oral techniques to new uses, and important elements of their work can best be understood as holdovers or creative transformations of oral techniques. ④ Oral literature, then, consists of the songs and stories, and other sayings, that people have heard and listened to, sung and told, without any intervention of writing. ⑤ Epic poems show particularly elaborate uses of oral devices, many of which were developed to aid poets in rapidly composing lines of an ongoing story, and to help illiterate performers remember a long narrative.

*stylus: 철필 ((등사판으로 박을 글씨를 원지에 쓰는 필기도구))
**holdover: 잔존물

[14~15] 주어진 글 다음에 이어질 글의 순서로 가장 적절한 것을 고르시오.

14.

> For millions of years man and his closest ancestors obtained food (and medicinal substances) from nature in a ready form. There was nothing to prevent the whole diversity of biologically active substances from entering his body. Cooking food was an individual domestic affair.

(A) This coincided with the emergence of a second way of deriving material benefits — 'production'. But side by side with production, in the sense of the creation of completely new objects for consumption, goes the process of purification (distillation, refinement, etc.). We have called this process 'anti-gathering'.

(B) 'Gathering' was the first way man received material benefits. The sharp fall in rural populations that accompanied the growth of cities and the development of so-called public catering necessitated the production and storage of enormous quantities of food products.

(C) It has led to finely ground flour products, polished rice and other grain removed from the husk, refined oil, and refined sugar. The choice of vegetables and wild-growing plants has shrunk; pure spirits such as vodka have replaced natural wines.

*husk: (곡물의) 겉껍질 **spirits: 증류주

① (A) – (C) – (B)
② (B) – (A) – (C)
③ (B) – (C) – (A)
④ (C) – (A) – (B)
⑤ (C) – (B) – (A)

15.

> Gas companies add a small amount of an odorous chemical called ethyl mercaptan to the otherwise odorless natural gas in their transmission pipes. If a valve or pipe seam fails, the smelly chemical leaks out with the natural gas, alerting human noses to an explosion hazard.

(A) Because humans have a deep aversion to rotting meat, our noses are extremely sensitive to such a chemical. We can pick out its smell at concentrations two hundred times lower than our limit for ammonia, which is itself strongly odorous.

(B) But vultures also smell the leak and will congregate around cracked pipes, becoming unwitting assistants in the search for pipeline flaws. This gathering of vultures and humans is caused by the scent of death — ethyl mercaptan is given off naturally by corpses.

(C) Gas companies therefore need to add only minuscule amounts of the smelly chemical to their pipes. Unfortunately for vultures, they also can smell these low concentrations and gather in confusion at leaks. [3점]

*vulture: 독수리

① (A) – (C) – (B)
② (B) – (A) – (C)
③ (B) – (C) – (A)
④ (C) – (A) – (B)
⑤ (C) – (B) – (A)

[16~17] 글의 흐름으로 보아, 주어진 문장이 들어가기에 가장 적절한 곳을 고르시오.

16.

In contrast, a zero-sum game where the winner takes all also establishes a proportional relationship, but at any point along the continuum there is only one or the other, black or white, and each retains its full identity.

When opposites blend, they are placed on the far ends of a continuum, and between the two extremes, there is a gradation that mixes the two opposites. (①) For instance, black and white blend into each other through shades of gray. (②) As the amount of white decreases through shades of gray, the amount of black increases. (③) The two opposites are always in a proportional relationship, but at any point along the continuum, there is some amount of each (except at the very extremes). (④) In a blend, pure black and pure white are diluted when combined into gray. (⑤) They both lose their identity; gray is not black and it is not white. [3점]

*continuum: 연속(체) **dilute: 희석하다

17.

Thus, population size was no longer partially controlled by the lack of food resources.

Technological innovation has affected the lives of people in myriad ways. (①) The emergence of a primitive hunting technology involving simple tools was the first great technological advance. (②) This was followed by agricultural developments that led to plant cultivation, which had far-reaching social consequences, since now food could be stored and refilled. (③) Because hunting and gathering societies required physical mobility, it was inefficient to have large numbers of children to take along in the search for food. (④) As a result of the agricultural revolution, however, agriculturists, living in settled communities, found additional children beneficial in helping with chores. (⑤) Moreover, some members of agricultural societies were now free to engage in pursuits other than food gathering, resulting in a more elaborate social structure with a division of labor that allowed for occupational specialization. [3점]

18. 다음 글의 내용을 한 문장으로 요약하고자 한다. 빈칸 (A), (B)에 들어갈 말로 가장 적절한 것은?

Doctor Myriam Horsten and her colleagues at the Karolinska Institute in Stockholm measured the heart rates of 300 healthy women over a 24-hour period. The women were also surveyed about their network of friends and the extent to which they felt angry and depressed. Horsten and her team were interested in "heart-rate variability," a measure of how readily a person's heart rate changes over the course of a normal day. A healthy person destined for a long and happy life will have a wide range of heart-rate variation in a 24-hour period. Heart rates that do not vary greatly have been linked to early death, particularly from heart disease. The findings of the study showed that women who lived alone, with few friends and no-one who could help them with stress-related activities like moving homes, were significantly more likely to have a heart rate with little variation. Quite obviously, living an active, sociable life will necessarily involve the heart in a wide range of rate-swings.

↓

The study suggests that social ____(A)____ can lead you to an early grave because it makes you more susceptible to heart disease by ____(B)____ heart-rate variability.

	(A)	(B)
①	isolation	...... lessening
②	isolation	...... increasing
③	competition	...... measuring
④	competition	...... lessening
⑤	pressure	...... measuring

[19~20] 다음 글을 읽고, 물음에 답하시오.

Beginning chefs don't start cooking when everything is, literally, in place. They're looking, okay, it's flour, it's sugar, probably the first ingredients of the recipe. So they go and get them. Then they start mixing. Then they get down to, 'Oh, I was only supposed to take half the sugar and mix it.' By then, they have to start over. The ingredients and time are (a) wasted. On the other hand, professional chefs prepare the kitchen for cooking so that it's easy to complete the recipe. As a professional chef, Jörin says, "Once I know that I have all the ingredients and all the equipment to make something, then I mentally figure out in which (b) order I need to do it. I have everything logically planned. When I start working, everything is lined up in front of me so that I don't have to think about it."

Culinary school students learn this method of (c) reducing friction in the kitchen on the first day of class. The director of one institute explained, "We do mental repetition. All of the ingredients are within a very short reach. You don't want a lot of extraneous movement. You want to be able to work quickly, comfortably, with the (d) most steps or exertion. A chef wants a flow of movement that becomes natural, comfortable, and almost without thought." Professional chefs remove any barriers that could affect their cooking. They repeatedly and quickly turn out the same quality dishes to keep customers happy. To do this, chefs harness the external forces in their kitchens by creating stable contexts that (e) automatically cue the right response.

19. 윗글의 제목으로 가장 적절한 것은?

① An Organized Space in an Organized Mind
② What Chefs Should Know: Everything in Its Place
③ Advice for Beginning Chefs: Practice Makes Perfect
④ Good Quality Ingredients Make All the Difference
⑤ How Chefs Can Be Taught about Cooking

20. 밑줄 친 (a) ~ (e) 중에서 문맥상 낱말의 쓰임이 적절하지 <u>않은</u> 것은? [3점]

① (a)   ② (b)   ③ (c)   ④ (d)   ⑤ (e)

○ 답안지의 해당란에 성명과 수험번호를 쓰고, 또 수험번호와 답을 정확히 표시하시오.
○ 문항에 따라 배점이 다르니, 각 물음의 끝에 표시된 배점을 참고하시오. 3점 문항에만 점수가 표시되어 있습니다. 점수 표시가 없는 문항은 모두 2점씩입니다.

1. 다음 글에 드러난 'I'의 심경 변화로 가장 적절한 것은?

It was the day before my daughter Annabel's wedding. I was driving down to a tailor shop where I had had my suit pressed. I was on the top of the world, imagining what the wedding would be like. When I turned on the radio, a beautiful song came on. There was something particularly heartfelt in the singer's voice. It was a song about a young man asking for his sweetheart's hand in marriage. The girl's father makes him wait in the living room, where he notices the childhood pictures of father and daughter together. The young man suddenly realizes that he is taking something precious from the father. The song captured something within me: the pain of knowing that I wouldn't always be the most important man in my little daughter Annabel's life. Before the song was over, I was crying so hard that I had to pull off the road.

① excited → sorrowful   ② frightened → relieved
③ pleased → ashamed   ④ hopeful → jealous
⑤ satisfied → furious

2. 밑줄 친 the skin is nearer than the shirt가 다음 글에서 의미하는 바로 가장 적절한 것은? [3점]

In one study, advanced graduate students at the University of Chicago were asked to rate research reports dealing with issues on which they already had an opinion. Unknown to the volunteers, the research reports were all fake. For each issue, half the volunteers saw a report presenting data that supported one side, while the other half saw a report in which the data supported the opposite camp. But it was only the numbers that differed — the research methodology and presentation were identical in both cases. When asked, most subjects denied that their assessment of the research depended on whether the data supported their prior opinion. But they were wrong. The researcher's analysis showed that they had indeed judged the studies that supported their beliefs to be more methodologically sound and clearly presented than the otherwise identical studies that opposed their beliefs — and the effect was stronger for those with strong prior beliefs. When it comes to our perception, as a proverb says, the skin is nearer than the shirt.

① we believe the better theory eventually wins
② we tend to stubbornly cling to our old beliefs
③ we confuse scientific fact and scientific support
④ we often become impartial judges and fact finders
⑤ we change our belief when revolutionary ideas emerge

3. 다음 글의 요지로 가장 적절한 것은?

While quality friendships are the most important for one's happiness, studies have also found that the people we just kind of know — what scientists call "weak ties" — can play an important role in boosting our happiness. One study examined the relationships between students in a classroom and concluded that those who had more daily interactions with other classmates who weren't their close friends were happier and had a greater feeling of belonging than those with a limited social circle. The researchers suggest that we "chat with the coffee barista, work colleague, yoga classmate, and fellow dog owner — these interactions may contribute meaningfully to our happiness, above and beyond the contribution of interactions with our close friends and family." Additionally, while long-lasting friendships aren't always the same as high-quality friendships, researchers have found that friends you know for a long time, even if only casually, make a valuable contribution to your happiness.

① 진정한 우정은 가족 못지않게 행복감을 줄 수 있다.
② 폭넓은 인간관계는 오랜 기간 지속되기 힘든 단점이 있다.
③ 한 번 맺은 인간관계를 지속하려면 많은 노력이 필요하다.
④ 약한 유대 관계가 가까운 관계 이상으로 행복을 증진시킨다.
⑤ 양질의 우정을 쌓는 데 항상 오랜 시간이 필요한 것은 아니다.

4. 다음 글의 주제로 가장 적절한 것은?

In an experiment, psychologist James W. Pennebaker and his colleagues asked 50 college students to write about their own personal experience of anger or what they were going to do after the experiment was over. They wrote for 20 minutes daily for four days. The researchers measured a variety of things, including blood pressure, immune function, and heart rate. The subjects themselves kept daily records of physical symptoms and moods. The researchers also collected information on health visits to the campus infirmary five months before and six weeks after the experiment. During the daily writing sessions, those who dug into their psyches had a more robust immune response, and made significantly fewer visits to the campus infirmary. "People showing the greatest improvements are those who wrote about emotional upheavals that they had actively held back in telling others," Pennebaker said. "The failure to manage anger forces the person to live with it in an unresolved matter."

*infirmary: 병원, 의무실

① anger as the source and cause of stress
② ways of relaxing stress by forgetting anger
③ health effects of expressing anger by writing
④ how to manage anger creatively through writing
⑤ various ways to control and prevent anger

5. 다음 글의 제목으로 가장 적절한 것은?

While we usually think negatively of deviance, it actually can prove functional in a society. Any hostility toward deviants promotes behavioral conformity with social expectations. It strengthens group identity by separating the nonconforming from the well-behaved members centering on an agreement on the norms. We may be familiar with the phrase "the exception makes the rule." Deviance shows us the boundary, or line, that must not be crossed, highlighting not only the importance of the norm but its relative permissible zone for behavior. For example, if there is a rule that "food is not permitted in the classroom," a person with the candy bar or bag of chips might not be admonished by the teacher; yet a person arriving to class with a fast-food meal experiences rebuke and ejection. Others in the class now know where the line is drawn and can adjust their patterns of behavior accordingly.

*deviance: 일탈 (행동) **ejection: 쫓아냄

① Social Functions of Deviation: Good and Evil
② Deviance: An Opportunity to Establish New Rules
③ Deviation from Social Norms: Causes and Solutions
④ Deviance Widens the Range of an Individual's Behavior
⑤ Social Response to Deviation Clarifies Behavioral Norms

6. Rapid Egg Cooker에 관한 다음 안내문의 내용과 일치하는 것은?

Rapid Egg Cooker

Fast & Healthy Breakfast
with the Electric Rapid Egg Cooker
Make Your Life Easy and Simple!

Product Description
• **8-Egg Capacity Steel Egg Cooker**

• **Preset Button for Desired Egg Hardness**
- Preset your desired egg hardness to soft, medium or hard boiled.
- It's more precise and easier to operate than other products which only control egg hardness through water volume.

• **Automatically Turns Off with Buzzer Alert**
- The cooker will turn off automatically when the eggs are cooked.

• **Easy to Clean & Safe**
- All the non-electric parts are dishwasher-safe, 100% BPA-free, FDA approved.

Warranty: The 1-year warranty covers manufacturing defects and is limited to the original purchaser.

Helpful Tips: Always use cold eggs — do not bring them to room temperature before using or the eggs will be slightly overcooked.

---

① 물의 양에 따라 달걀의 익힘 정도가 결정된다.
② 요리가 끝나면 전원을 끄도록 경고음이 울린다.
③ 요리 기구 전체를 식기 세척기에 사용할 수 있다.
④ 원구매자에 한해 1년의 보증 기간이 제공된다.
⑤ 달걀은 실온에 어느 정도 보관 후 조리해야 좋다.

---

7. 다음 글의 밑줄 친 부분 중, 어법상 틀린 것은? [3점]

Social exchange is the general category of social process and involves people in the organization trading resources and attempting to make sure ① that their rewards outweigh their costs. Many of the social interactions occurring in an organization consist of transactions ② in which one person offers resources to the other person and in return receives something from that individual. There are costs involved in the transactions as well as benefits, and the motivation of each party to the exchange is ③ to maximize the positive and minimize the negative. Social exchange theorists propose that all interactions among people constitute social exchanges, even those involving love and marriage. Explaining something as ④ personally as love as an exchange that continues as long as it is profitable may seem cynical. You might protest and say that ⑤ remaining in a loving relationship is not reducible to rewards and costs. Social exchange theorists would counter by stating that an important part of any continuing relationship is achieving a favorable balance sheet in the transactions with the other person.

---

8. 다음 글의 밑줄 친 부분 중, 문맥상 낱말의 쓰임이 적절하지 않은 것은? [3점]

The proportions of the demographic classes ① affect the fitness of the group and, ultimately, of each individual member. A group comprised wholly of infants or aging males will perish — obviously. Another, ② less deviant, group has a higher fitness that can be defined as a higher probability of survival, which can be translated as a longer waiting time to extinction. Either measure has meaning only over periods of time on the order of a generation in length, because a deviant population allowed to reproduce for one to several generations will go far to ③ restore the age distribution of populations normal for the species. Unless the species is highly opportunistic, that is, unless it follows a strategy of colonizing empty habitats and holding on to them only for a relatively short time, the age distribution will tend to approach a ④ steady state. In species with seasonal natality and mortality, which is to say nearly all animal species, the age distribution will undergo annual fluctuation. But even then the age distribution can be said to approach ⑤ instability, in the sense that the fluctuation is periodic and predictable when corrected for season.

*demographic: 개체군 통계학상의 **deviant: 비정상적인 ***natality: 출생률

[9~12] 다음 빈칸에 들어갈 말로 가장 적절한 것을 고르시오.

9. Supple physiology allows lichens to shine with life when most other creatures are locked down for the winter. Lichens burn no fuel in quest of warmth, instead letting the pace of their lives rise and fall with the thermometer. They don't cling to water as plants and animals do. A lichen body swells on damp days, then wrinkles as the air dries. Plants shrink back from the chill, packing up their cells until spring gradually coaxes them out. Lichen cells are light sleepers. When winter eases for a day, lichens float easily back to life. This approach to life has been independently discovered by others. In the fourth century BCE, the Chinese Taoist philosopher Zhuangzi wrote of an old man tossed in the turmoil at the base of a tall waterfall. Terrified onlookers rushed to his aid, but the man emerged unharmed and calm. When asked how he could survive this hardship, he replied, "I accommodate myself to the water, not the water to me." Lichens found this wisdom four hundred million years before the Taoists. The true masters of victory through _____ in Zhuangzi's allegory were the lichens clinging to the rock walls around the waterfall.

*lichen: 지의류 식물, 이끼

① success ② sacrifice
③ optimism ④ vigilance
⑤ submission

10. In contrast to popular belief, integrity isn't an unchanging trait: Someone who has been fair and honest in the past won't necessarily be fair and honest in the future. To understand why, we must first free ourselves of the notion that people wrestle with "good" and "evil" impulses. Except in cases of serious psychopathy, the mind doesn't work that way. Rather, it focuses on two types of gains: _____. And it's the choice between them that typically dictates integrity in any particular situation. Individuals who break a trust — by promising work they won't or can't deliver, for instance — may reap an immediate reward, but they diminish the likelihood of accumulating greater benefits from exchange and cooperation with the same partner (and perhaps others) in the future. It is the weighing of immediate rewards against potential costs further down the road that constitutes the heart of integrity related decisions, and this depends a great deal on the situation and the parties involved. [3점]

① static and dynamic
② spatial and temporal
③ physical and emotional
④ short-term and long-term
⑤ individual and organizational

11. Loyalty to groups in competition, such as sports teams or political parties, encourages us to play out our instinct for dominance vicariously. Jerry Seinfeld once remarked that today's athletes pass through sports teams so rapidly that a fan can no longer support a group of players. He is reduced to rooting for their team logo and uniforms. "You are standing and cheering and yelling for your clothes to beat the clothes from another city." But stand and cheer we do: the mood of a sports fan rises and falls with the fortunes of his team. _____ can literally be observed in the biochemistry lab. Men's testosterone level rises when their team defeats a rival in a game, just as it rises when they personally defeat a rival in a wrestling match or in singles tennis. It also rises or falls when a favored political candidate wins or loses an election. [3점]

*vicariously: 대리로, 간접적으로

① The strength of the communal feelings
② The adaptation to the reality of groups
③ The development of a personal identity
④ The value associated with a particular group of people
⑤ The loss of boundaries between the group and the self

12. The effective use of time is one of the ultimate ways to display authority, even when you don't have it. Whoever controls time controls the situation in most instances. They will always remind anyone who wants to meet with them that their time is valuable. However, there may be situations where you will want to reverse your use of tight time tactics. Let's say you have agreed to meet with one of your peers to discuss a difficult situation that has developed between your two respective departments. You need more help from your peer than she needs from you to get things resolved, even though you've told her your time is limited. When she enters your office at the appointed hour, take your watch off ostentatiously, and place it face down on your desk. Say, "_____ _____." Watch the cooperation level of your peer go up exponentially at the outset of your meeting. You'll be able to get anything you want from her. [3점]

*ostentatiously: 보란 듯이 **exponentially: 기하급수적으로

① It is a pleasure to have your time and assistance
② My time belongs to you for as long as you need it
③ Your time is limited, so don't waste it at the meeting
④ Your time is the most valuable thing I can spend now
⑤ Waiting is the last thing I want to spend my time doing

13. 다음 글에서 전체 흐름과 관계 <u>없는</u> 문장은?

Important decisions take time, commitment, and thought. ① While we usually don't make these types of decisions in haste, many people choose a companion animal based on impulse. ② A cell phone or car can be sold or traded in if it doesn't perform well or is quickly outgrown, but animals shouldn't be thought of as commodities. ③ And unlike switching colleges or majors when we change our minds, it is not reasonable to assume that if a pet doesn't perform well or we outgrow our interest, we can just get rid of it or neglect it. ④ Having an animal to take care of can provide a pet owner with a sense of purpose that may be beneficial to cognitive functions. ⑤ It's a big step to bring an animal into a household, and there are big decisions that should be made before that happens.

*outgrow: 나이가 들면서 ~에 흥미를 잃다

[14~15] 주어진 글 다음에 이어질 글의 순서로 가장 적절한 것을 고르시오.

14.

We have to appreciate that our brains weren't born yesterday. We have mechanisms to warn of threats and guard against instability because they have worked for a very long time.

(A) But we have to know when to override the alarm and take the less comfortable path anyway. Research conducted by a joint American and Italian team of psychologists found that people with less need for "cognitive closure," the human desire to eliminate ambiguity and arrive at definite conclusions (sometimes irrationally), were typically more creative than their counterparts.

(B) Those who are able to work past their brain's appetite for certainty — its need to shut the closure door to preserve stability — are more likely to engage challenges from a broader variety of vantage points. That's the energy that fuels scientific discovery, technological advances, and a range of other human pursuits.

(C) We wouldn't be here without them. In the same way that any sane person feels apprehension about jumping out of an airplane, our brain puts the organism it controls on alert when danger looms. [3점]

*loom: 어렴풋이 나타나다

① (A) – (C) – (B)   ② (B) – (A) – (C)
③ (B) – (C) – (A)   ④ (C) – (A) – (B)
⑤ (C) – (B) – (A)

15.

Diseases may require a minimum limit of population size or density to support their ongoing transmission.

(A) Urban life similarly supports the spread of countless diseases that require higher population densities than found in agricultural settlements. Therefore, throughout history, the breakthroughs in farming that have enabled the growth of urban populations have always been accompanied by deadly bouts of infectious diseases.

(B) Malaria is one such disease that probably developed into its deadly form around five thousand years ago with the establishment of settled farming in Africa. Prior to settled agriculture, hunter-gatherer communities in Africa were too few and far between to support the survival of malaria.

(C) Therefore, an increase in the human population can expose us to a disease that previously could not be sustained by our population. The introduction of agriculture, for example, resulted in the spread of numerous diseases that require greater human densities than existed in hunter-gatherer societies. [3점]

*bout: 한차례, 한고비; 발병 기간, 발작

① (A) – (C) – (B)   ② (B) – (A) – (C)
③ (B) – (C) – (A)   ④ (C) – (A) – (B)
⑤ (C) – (B) – (A)

[16~17] 글의 흐름으로 보아, 주어진 문장이 들어가기에 가장 적절한 곳을 고르시오.

16.

> Against the major principles of reinforcement, some behavioral scientists argue that the more you reinforce a person for doing a certain thing, the faster that person will lose interest in the very thing that they are being rewarded for.

Do children do better at school if reinforced by gold stars, prizes or even monetary rewards? (①) Reinforcement theory says that giving rewards leads to repetition of the behavior rewarded and punishment reduces repetition. (②) Given that most children love candy, reinforcement theory says that if you give candy to a child who has sat quietly in his or her chair for five minutes, that child will quickly learn to sit quietly all the time. (③) That is, getting a reward reduces the fun of the activity. (④) Some studies have shown that if you reward children for sensible behavior, they tend to see the behavior as a "special-occasion" thing rather than something to make a habit of. (⑤) Therefore they are less likely to change in the long term than those not rewarded.

17.

> It describes in fascinating detail the vaporization at the impact point, the earthquakes, the fires, and the debris that caused a worldwide period of intense heat followed by darkness and freezing temperatures.

Trade books can provide the space to bring a subject to life with interesting observations and details, presenting the reader with a richer understanding of the topic. (①) Because textbooks must cover such a large number of topics, they are unable to develop a single idea with any depth. (②) Therefore, textbooks offer a broad and consequently shallower view of subjects that does not allow for the kind of compelling presentation available in trade books. (③) For example, one passage in the textbook simply mentions that asteroids can hit the Earth. (④) The trade book, however, chronicles the event of an asteroid's entry into atmosphere, its collision with the planet, and the blasting of a crater 25 miles deep and 100 miles across. (⑤) It is difficult to provide readers this kind of detail and insight in the limited space allowed by a textbook.

*asteroid: 소행성 **chronicle: 연대순으로 기록하다 ***debris: 잔해, 파편

18. 다음 글의 내용을 한 문장으로 요약하고자 한다. 빈칸 (A), (B)에 들어갈 말로 가장 적절한 것은? [3점]

The limbic brain is vigorously driven by pleasure and pain. At one time, when we were a primitive species, this certainly had some preservation value. But as we evolved and became much more complex and sophisticated, these fundamental drives didn't evolve with us, remaining absolute rather than being attuned to subtleties. If you feel uncomfortable, for instance, then your limbic brain interprets that as a signal that your safety is being seriously threatened, which then triggers a drastic reaction to avert danger and maintain your safety. Your limbic brain by its very nature is not very effective at evaluating different degrees of discomfort and fear. Hence, being at the mercy of these primary drives severely conflicts with the needs of a more complex society and civilization, in which people cannot be constantly acting on their needs for fear. But this is where the survival instinct poses a problem, in that it doesn't easily make distinctions, and tends to view all discomfort and fear as an ultimate threat to our survival.

*limbic brain: 변연계 뇌 ((동기와 정서를 주로 담당한다고 여겨지는 뇌의 부분))

↓

> The limbic brain tends to _____(A)_____ to discomfort or fear, because it has an evolutionary _____(B)_____ with our current environment and lifestyle.

	(A)		(B)		(A)		(B)
①	adapt	…	mismatch	②	adapt	…	connection
③	submit	…	balance	④	overreact	…	mismatch
⑤	overreact	…	connection				

[19~20] 다음 글을 읽고, 물음에 답하시오.

One day psychologist Kip Williams from Purdue University was out in the park walking his dog when he was hit in the back with a Frisbee, a round piece of plastic used as a toy. He threw it back to one of the two guys who were playing with it who then began tossing it back to Kip. This was fun but, after about a minute, they stopped throwing the Frisbee to Kip and returned their attention to each other. Now it became clear that they were not going to (a) include Kip in their game again. The psychology professor was surprised at how upset he was by this exclusion given that he was a complete stranger. He realized that there is a drive, deep inside us, that compels us to be (b) accepted by others.

Kip took his experiences from the park and developed a computer simulation known as 'Cyberball' where adult participants had their brains scanned as they played a game where they had to toss a ball back and forth between two other playmates. Just like the frisbee event, Cyberball was going along fine, until the two others started to only pass the ball back between themselves and (c) ignore the adult in the brain scanner. When this exclusion became obvious, the anterior cingulate cortex (ACC) regions of the brain, which are activated by social cognition, started to light up with activity. The social exclusion of the game had initially caused distress, as it activated areas associated with emotional pain. What is remarkable here is how (d) sensitive we are to being rejected. And this pain had nothing to do with the personality of the players, either. Rather, there is something (e) intentional about it. Kip Williams argues that this reaction must be hardwired and points out that, in many other social species, social exclusion often leads to death.

*anterior cingulate cortex: (뇌의) 전대상 피질

19. 윗글의 제목으로 가장 적절한 것은?

① What Is Our Biggest Fear? Exclusion
② Social Exclusion: A Double-edged Sword
③ Social Exclusion Is a Form of Discrimination
④ Belonging and Body Health's Secret Correlation
⑤ The Need to Belong: A Fundamental Survival Skill

20. 밑줄 친 (a) ~ (e) 중에서 문맥상 낱말의 쓰임이 적절하지 않은 것은? [3점]

① (a)　② (b)　③ (c)　④ (d)　⑤ (e)

○ 답안지의 해당란에 성명과 수험번호를 쓰고, 또 수험번호와 답을 정확히 표시하시오.

○ 문항에 따라 배점이 다르니, 각 물음의 끝에 표시된 배점을 참고하시오. 3점 문항에만 점수가 표시되어 있습니다. 점수 표시가 없는 문항은 모두 2점씩입니다.

---

1. 다음 글의 목적으로 가장 적절한 것은?

Dear Ms. Ervin:

Although we agree with your previous editorials opposing parking meters in downtown Augusta, we are not in agreement with your editorial on October 18. To resurface our streets and make them into malls will irreversibly damage businesses downtown. The city engineers estimate the mall project will disrupt business for a minimum of a full year. Many downtown businesses are now struggling to stay alive, and the mall project would be their death knell. We can see no value in turning the downtown business district into a mall-like area. Additionally, when completed, we would have 50 percent fewer parking places for our customers. Perhaps the downtown area does need cosmetic surgery, but not when it devastates the area's economy. Thank you for your understanding of our opposition. We hope that you will reconsider your position.

Sincerely,
Marvin Quackenbush

*death knell: 종말의 조짐

① 도심 재개발 사업을 촉구하려고
② 쇼핑몰 공사 지연에 대해 문의하려고
③ 도심의 주차난 해소 방안을 건의하려고
④ 쇼핑몰 건립 계획에 대한 찬성 철회를 요청하려고
⑤ 시내의 주차 요금 징수기 설치 방안을 항의하려고

2. 다음 글에서 필자가 주장하는 바로 가장 적절한 것은?

Information from television, Internet, radio and printed materials, collectively termed "mass media," saturates modern society. According to some critics, the media is capable of employing an elaborate and sophisticated array of techniques that allows reporters and media owners to slant news stories in favor of particular groups or interests. Bias is a subtle leaning or point of view which turns the focus of a news story in a certain direction. Many journalists argue that true objectivity is impossible, and that while bias can indeed influence the presentation of facts, biased media is not created with harmful intent. Journalists holding the view that some degree of bias is inevitable aim to limit rather than eliminate bias and to present as balanced a view as possible. The best defense against media bias is getting your information from a wide variety of sources. It's a no-brainer that relying on one media source for information is a slippery slope to being misinformed.

*slant: (정보를) 편향되게 제시하다

① 기자는 편향성을 줄이기 위해 사실에 기반한 뉴스 기사를 써야 한다.
② 독자는 기사의 편향성을 구분할 수 있는 비판적인 시각을 길러야 한다.
③ 독자는 하나의 기사를 여러 관점에서 보려는 열린 마음을 가져야 한다.
④ 기자는 정확한 기사를 위해 다양한 취재원으로부터 정보를 얻어야 한다.
⑤ 독자가 뉴스의 편향성을 극복하려면 여러 출처에서 정보를 얻어야 한다.

3. 밑줄 친 the biggest writing myth가 다음 글에서 의미하는 바로 가장 적절한 것은? [3점]

It seems like there are authors who come out of nowhere, make millions of dollars from the book and ride off into the sunset of legends. It's tempting to think all it takes is an idea and a bit of effort. Very tempting indeed. But writing a book takes time — months, sometimes years — and chances are the first book that you publish won't be the first book you ever write. It takes time to perfect your craft, to learn the ins and outs of writing, to develop your writing style and learn how to write a solid plot and then learn the proper way to market it all when you've finished. J.K. Rowling spent years planning out and writing *Harry Potter* and received dozens of rejections before getting published. Amanda Hocking also spent years building her craft and trying to get published before making it big in the self-publishing world. The list goes on. Don't believe the biggest writing myth.

① There's no single cure for a writer's block.
② All the writer needs to do is publish a book.
③ Writers are influenced by the publishing market.
④ Some writers get overnight success without much effort.
⑤ Before becoming famous, the author spends time writing.

4. 다음 글의 제목으로 가장 적절한 것은? [3점]

In the early industrial era, those who controlled finance capital and the means of production exercised near-total control over the workings of the economy. For a while, during the mid-decades of the past century, they had to share some of that power with labor, whose critical role in production assured it some clout in decisions governing both the ways and means of doing business and the distribution of profits. Now that labor's clout has significantly diminished, knowledge workers have become the more important group in the economic equation. They are the catalysts of the Third Industrial Revolution and the ones responsible for keeping the high-tech economy running. For that reason, top management and investors have had increasingly to share at least some of their power with the creators of intellectual property, the men and women whose knowledge and ideas fuel the high-tech information society. It is no wonder, then, that intellectual-property rights have become even more important than finance in some industries. Having a monopoly over knowledge and ideas ensures competitive success and market position. Financing that success becomes almost secondary.

*clout: 영향력 **catalyst: 촉매제 ***monopoly: 독점(권)

① Intellectual Property Rights vs. Labor's Clout in Industries
② Why Was Labor Getting Important in Industrial Revolution?
③ How Knowledge Is Acquired in the Third Industrial Revolution
④ Roles of Labor in Economic Growth in the Early Industrial Era
⑤ The Power of Knowledge and Ideas in the Third Industrial Revolution

5. 다음 표의 내용과 일치하지 <u>않는</u> 것은?

The Global Top 10 Destination Cities in 2018

2018 Rank (2017)	Destination City	International Overnight Visitors (millions)		2018 Average Spending Per Day (US $)
		2018	Growth from 2017	
1 (1)	Bangkok	22.78	1.69	$184
2 (3) ↑	Paris	19.10	1.68	$296
3 (2) ↓	London	19.09	-0.74	$148
4 (4)	Dubai	15.93	0.14	$553
5 (5)	Singapore	14.67	0.77	$272
6 (7) ↑	Kuala Lumpur	13.79	1.21	$142
7 (6) ↓	New York	13.60	0.47	$152
8 (9) ↑	Istanbul	13.40	2.70	$106
9 (8) ↓	Tokyo	12.93	1.00	$196
10 (11) ↑	Antalya	12.41	2.99	$44

The table above shows the top ten destination cities in the world in 2018 by international overnight visitors and average spending per day. ① Three of the top ten cities' popularity rankings in 2018, Bangkok, Dubai, and Singapore, remained unchanged from 2017. ② In 2018, Bangkok was the top destination, followed by Paris and London, with Dubai and Singapore wrapping up the fourth and fifth spots respectively. ③ Antalya saw the largest growth in the number of visitors from 2017 to 2018 among the top ten cities, whereas London saw a decrease. ④ In terms of average spending per day, Dubai led in the world's top ten cities with US $553, immediately followed by Singapore with US $272. ⑤ On the other hand, among the top ten cities, Antalya was the city where international overnight visitors spent the least money in 2018.

6. Herman Melville에 관한 다음 글의 내용과 일치하지 <u>않는</u> 것은?

Herman Melville was an American author best known for his masterpiece novel named "Moby Dick." He also authored many short stories, poems, and essays during his life. He was born in 1819 in New York City. In 1826, Herman Melville's father died from an unexpected illness, and, that year, he contracted scarlet fever and his eyesight was permanently damaged. From the age of twelve he worked as a clerk and farmhand. In 1841, at the age of twenty-two, Herman Melville set sail aboard the *Acushnet*, a New England whaler heading for the South Seas. His experiences on this and several subsequent voyages served as the basis for a half-dozen sea novels, including "Moby Dick." Herman Melville died in 1891 at the age of 72. His most famous pieces of work did not have a significant impact on literature until after his death.

*scarlet fever: 성홍열

① 소설뿐만 아니라 시와 수필도 저술했다.
② 아버지가 돌아가신 해에 시력이 손상되었다.
③ 12살의 나이로 점원과 농장 인부로 일했다.
④ 선원 생활의 경험이 소설의 기초가 되었다.
⑤ 말년에 미국의 대표 작가로 명성을 떨쳤다.

7. 다음 글의 밑줄 친 부분 중, 어법상 <u>틀린</u> 것은? [3점]

The pedagogical tradition of requiring students to raise their hands in class ① <u>has</u> the obvious instrumental purposes of establishing classroom order, testing student comprehension of content by maintaining a disciplined climate conducive to answering questions, and facilitating group discussion. Morally, however, it regulates turn-taking ② <u>which</u> inevitably involves issues of fairness, respect for others, patience, and self-control. How a teacher ③ <u>navigating</u> in such routine situations is ethically significant. Thoughtlessly ④ <u>done</u>, it may project the image of a teacher who discriminates, favours, or just does not care about students. Thoughtfully carried out, turn-taking may enable the teacher to ensure fair participation as well as ⑤ <u>protect</u> both the less vocal students who may need some gentle and kindly encouragement and the more vocal ones who may become targeted for abuse by other students who grow to resent them.

*pedagogical: 교육적 **conducive: 도움이 되는

8. 다음 글의 밑줄 친 부분 중, 문맥상 낱말의 쓰임이 적절하지 <u>않은</u> 것은? [3점]

Let us now consider the behavior of normal people with low intelligence. We tend to call such people ① <u>stupid</u> — unless, of course, they occupy a higher position than we do! They deserve our attention because of the influence they sometimes exert on the course of vital events, and also because one can only fully recognize and appreciate the most valuable qualities of the mind against a background of its ② <u>deficiencies</u>. Besides, even a man with a high level of general intelligence will sometimes behave in an ③ <u>unintelligent</u> way under the influence of such factors as fatigue or violent emotion. It is also known that the development of various primary abilities, which make up the intelligence, is largely ④ <u>consistent</u>. Thus a person rated as intelligent on account of his eloquence and ingeniousness may not prove to be so clever in dealing with numerical, or perceptual, material, and vice versa. That is why an understanding of typical "unintelligent" behavior may be of real ⑤ <u>importance</u> in education and self-education.

*ingeniousness: 재치가 있음, 독창성

[9~12] 다음 빈칸에 들어갈 말로 가장 적절한 것을 고르시오.

9. Our beliefs about food affect not only the choices we make, but also our _____. Researchers at Yale University gave study participants two shakes: one was labeled a high-fat, 620-calorie "indulgent" shake, the other a low-fat, 130-calorie "sensi-shake." In fact, the two shakes were identical. Yet the participants' belief that one was an indulgence — "heaven in a bottle," the label noted — while the other was a healthier choice had powerful effects on their bodies' response to the shakes. Levels of ghrelin, a hormone that stimulates appetite, rose steeply in anticipation of drinking the "indulgent" shake and then fell sharply afterward, indicating that the drink was satisfying. With the "sensible" shake, ghrelin levels stayed relatively flat or rose only slightly in anticipation, and they did not fall steeply afterward, indicating that the drink was not satisfying. The shake contents were the same, but participants' beliefs changed their appetite-regulation hormones.

*indulgence: 탐닉, 호사

① biology   ② behavior
③ identity   ④ health
⑤ weight

10. A human being is the kind of machine that wears out from *lack* of use. There are physical limits, of course, and we *do* need healthful rest and relaxation, but for the most part we _____.
Often, the best remedy for physical weariness is thirty minutes of aerobic exercise. In the same way, mental and spiritual indifference is often cured by decisive action or the clear intention to act. We learn in high school physics that kinetic energy is measured in terms of motion. The same thing is true of human energy: it comes into existence through use. You can't stockpile it. As Frederich S. Perls, founder of Gestalt therapy, used to say, "I don't want to be saved, I want to be *spent*." It might well be that all of us possess enormous stores of potential energy, more than we could ever hope to use.

① gain energy by using it
② store energy for a rainy day
③ should have regular check-ups
④ gain mental security by resting
⑤ need to have a habit of exercising

11. Almost everyone enjoys hearing some kind of live music. But few of us realize the complex process that goes into designing the acoustics of concert and lecture halls. In the design of any building where audibility of sound is a major consideration, architects have to carefully match the space and materials they use to the intended purpose of the venue. One problem is that the intensity of sound may build too quickly in an enclosed space. Another problem is that only part of the sound we hear in any large room or auditorium comes directly from the source. Much of it reaches us a fraction of a second later after it has been reflected off the walls, ceiling, and floor as reverberated sound (the sound that comes to the listener after it has been reflected off the walls, ceiling and floor). How much each room reverberates depends upon both its size and the ability of its contents to absorb sound. Too little reverberation can make music sound thin and weak; too much can blur the listener's sense of where one note stops and the next begins. Consequently, the most important factor in acoustic design is _____. [3점]

*reverberate: 소리가 울리다

① the planned purpose of a particular room or space
② the amount of the sound that will be produced in the space
③ the time it takes for these reverberations to die down altogether
④ the complete elimination of all audible noise emissions
⑤ how much the reverberated sound interacts with the audience

12. A determinant of developmental differences in the social effects of television is _____ _____. As children mature they are exposed to different people, actions, and norms. This provides a range of choices when they have an opportunity to perform or opine. For example, children who encounter Puerto Ricans only on *Sesame Street* may learn that interactions with them are always cordial and use that as a model for a first encounter with a live Puerto Rican. In contrast, a child who grows up close to a Puerto Rican enclave will understand much more about the variety of ways in which he or she could interact with Puerto Ricans. Hopefully, *Sesame Street* will provide information for this child too, but the information will take its place alongside other relevant information rather than providing the single model for interaction. [3점]

*opine: 의견을 말하다 **enclave: 소수 민족 거주지

① a variety of educational strategies designed to educate children
② the social, cultural and political contexts to which a child belongs
③ the amount of information or experience a child has accumulated
④ goals in a society for which the schools must assume responsibility
⑤ the increase of social media learning at the school and classroom levels

13. 다음 글에서 전체 흐름과 관계 없는 문장은?

Mobile crowd sensing for smart cities can support efficient, safe and green mobility in urban environments. ① Given the ubiquity of mobile devices carried by people worldwide, social mobile crowd sensing through the IoT can allow tourists to know about popular events in a destination, provide interactive feedback with other tourists at different locations, reveal the best places to be at a certain time, local weather forecasts, and expected travel times throughout the day. ② Here crowd sourcing can inform people about whether to seek alternative routes, when best to arrive at attractions or restaurants, how to avoid unpleasant surprises when traveling, where to park, and which public transport solution would be best. ③ Most importantly, connecting a device to the Internet does not mean that its information is universally available and shared. ④ Environmental sensors may also report air or noise pollution levels. ⑤ This enables tourists in unfamiliar places to make even better decisions than well-informed locals might take.

[14~15] 주어진 글 다음에 이어질 글의 순서로 가장 적절한 것을 고르시오.

14.

> When older bees begin collecting nectar and pollen from outside the hive, their brains change, and not really for the better.

(A) Normally, that would mean the larvae from the new queen wouldn't have young nursery workers available to take care of them, and they'd die. In that case, some of the field bees return to the nursery worker job.

(B) Here's where it gets interesting: researchers from Arizona State University discovered that going back to larvae-rearing makes their old brains work again like young brains, restoring their mental agility and ability to learn.

(C) For example, after they memorize the surroundings of the hive, they lose the ability to learn new things. Normally, they stay that way until they die. However, sometimes "normal" gets disrupted; for example, if a hive has to grow a new queen, there can be a month-long gap before any new bees hatch. [3점]

*larva(pl. larvae): 유충 **agility: 민첩성

① (A) – (C) – (B)　　② (B) – (A) – (C)
③ (B) – (C) – (A)　　④ (C) – (A) – (B)
⑤ (C) – (B) – (A)

15.

> When it comes to statistical significance, the size of the groups being compared matters. For instance, a poll of ten athletic friends and ten couch potato friends could give you some insight into whether knee problems were associated with participation in sports.

(A) On the other hand, if 1,000 athletes and 1,000 couch potatoes were randomly selected and polled, and 500 of the athletes and 200 of the nonathletes had knee pain, this would be much stronger evidence that a correlation existed between knee pain and participation in sports.

(B) However, if five of the athletes and two of the couch potatoes complained of knee pain, would this be good evidence that knee pain is related to participation in sports? Not really, because with such small group sizes, the difference easily could have arisen by chance.

(C) With such a large sample size, the 50 percent/20 percent statistic could not be due to a few unusual people throwing off the result, as could have been the case with the smaller group.

① (A) – (C) – (B)　　② (B) – (A) – (C)
③ (B) – (C) – (A)　　④ (C) – (A) – (B)
⑤ (C) – (B) – (A)

[16~17] 글의 흐름으로 보아, 주어진 문장이 들어가기에 가장 적절한 곳을 고르시오.

16.

> This will appear as cold silence or noisy misbehavior during the meeting or as deliberate disregard later for any decisions made.

Meetings are usually excellent ways to resolve conflicts. (①) However, when participants strongly dislike the issue, the process, or the results, and feel as if they have no say in what's going on, then they will put up stubborn resistance. (②) Therefore, be sure to make participants feel listened to in a meeting. (③) Always get in touch with key participants before meetings on controversial issues. (④) Ask for their views, explain your goals, and assure them you are dedicated to a fair outcome. (⑤) Most of all, make sure that you seek a "Both/And" result instead of an "Either/Or" result so that everyone gets what they need.

17.

> Popular legend is that Wagner did this after recognizing that the cards appealed to young boys and encouraged them to smoke.

The most famous and most valuable baseball card in the world is the T206 Honus Wagner card. (①) It was included as a giveaway in packs of cigarettes back in the early 1900s when Wagner was still playing for the Pittsburgh Pirates. (②) Although Wagner was one of the all-time greats of baseball, only a small number of the cards were ever issued because he denied the tobacco companies the right to use his image. (③) The more likely story is that Wagner, who had previously promoted cigars and other tobacco products, was not happy with the compensation he was offered by the company. (④) Whatever the reason, about 40 of the cards are known to exist, and this scarcity, combined with Wagner's elite status as a player, has made the card the holy grail of baseball card collectors. (⑤) So, top condition samples of the card are probably worth $1 million or more today at auction or in private deals. [3점]

*holy grail: 성배(聖杯)

18. 다음 글의 내용을 한 문장으로 요약하고자 한다. 빈칸 (A), (B)에 들어갈 말로 가장 적절한 것은? [3점]

In one experiment, the researchers gave subjects documents regarding the case, which involved an injured motorcyclist who was suing the driver of an automobile that had collided with him. Subjects were told that in the actual case, the judge awarded the plaintiff an amount between $0 and $100,000. They were then assigned randomly to represent one side or the other in mock negotiations. The researchers told the subjects they'd be paid based on their success in those negotiations. But the most interesting part of the study came next: the subjects were also told they could earn a cash bonus if they could guess — within $5,000 — what the judge actually awarded the plaintiff. They'd have the greatest chance at winning the cash bonus if they assessed the payout that would be fair. On average, the subjects assigned to represent the plaintiff's side estimated that the judge would dictate a settlement of nearly $40,000, while the subjects assigned to represent the defendant put that number at only around $20,000. Despite the financial reward they were offered for guessing correctly, the disagreement between them was still significant.

*plaintiff: 원고, 고소인 **defendant: 피고

↓

> According to the experiment, the sense of ____(A)____ of the subjects are likely to make them evaluate information in a(n) ____(B)____ manner.

	(A)		(B)
①	fairness	……	controlled
②	fairness	……	impartial
③	belonging	……	interactive
④	belonging	……	biased
⑤	responsibility	……	simplified

[19~20] 다음 글을 읽고, 물음에 답하시오.

Emotions matter, in countless ways. They alert us to potential opportunities and threats. They allow us to rapidly process vast amounts of data from multiple sources in parallel, without having to rely on the vastly slower process of conscious deliberation. And they (a) enrich the human experience immeasurably: What would it be like to live without joy — or without grief?

The relationship between emotion and consciousness is complex. We certainly have the capacity to reflect on our feelings and take other deliberate actions to influence our emotional state. But emotions are typically generated (b) involuntarily, outside the window of consciousness, and by the time a feeling registers in our conscious mind it can seem thoroughly immersive and all-encompassing. In part this is due to the (c) physiological dimension of emotion, from altering our heart rate and blood pressure to the various expressions we describe as a "pit in the stomach," or a "sinking feeling."

The overpowering nature of our emotional response serves an essential purpose by priming us to take swift, decisive action. But sometimes that's exactly the wrong move, and we're better served by (d) fostering those impulses and considering a broader range of options. This process starts with an awareness that the emotion is a (e) transitory state of mind and body, not an identity. It can feel silly to say "I'm having the experience of anger" rather than "I'm angry!" But we're well-served by heightening our awareness of the distinction between the two. Perhaps "I'm feeling angry" is a reasonable compromise.

19. 윗글의 제목으로 가장 적절한 것은?

① To Stay Focused, Manage Your Emotions
② We Are Not Emotions, We Have Emotions
③ Negative Impacts of Emotion on Consciousness
④ Emotions Affect Our Health More Than Our Mind
⑤ Emotions Can't Be Controlled, But Can Be Nurtured

20. 밑줄 친 (a) ~ (e) 중에서 문맥상 낱말의 쓰임이 적절하지 <u>않은</u> 것은? [3점]

① (a) ② (b) ③ (c) ④ (d) ⑤ (e)

○ 답안지의 해당란에 성명과 수험번호를 쓰고, 또 수험번호와 답을 정확히 표시하시오.
○ 문항에 따라 배점이 다르니, 각 물음의 끝에 표시된 배점을 참고하시오. 3점 문항에만 점수가 표시되어 있습니다. 점수 표시가 없는 문항은 모두 2점씩입니다.

1. 다음 글에 드러난 Laura의 심경 변화로 가장 적절한 것은?

When she heard the news that a storm was coming, Laura looked out the window. The rain was falling in sheets, flooding the ditches, while a fierce wind ripped through the branches of the trees in the backyard, twisting them into bows. Laura had been unable to do anything since her father called after lunch. Her father should have been home two hours ago, she thought with growing concern. Desperate for distraction, she turned on the TV. The newscaster was saying it was the biggest hurricane the state had seen in twenty years. The newscaster's voice floated over scenes of devastation: bridges destroyed, homes reduced to splinters, roads buried beneath the broken trunks and branches of massive trees. Laura turned off the TV, and looked out the window again. Just as she sat down again, the telephone rang. It was her father. He said he was safe and would be home within an hour. She sat down with a sigh on the sofa.

① depressed → regretful   ② excited → bored
③ lonely → calm   ④ worried → relieved
⑤ curious → upset

2. 밑줄 친 what they saw가 다음 글에서 의미하는 바로 가장 적절한 것은? [3점]

Today, *Luddite* is a disparaging term used to refer to a person who is opposed to or cautiously critical of technology. But it's important to remember that the original Luddites were not, in fact, opposed to technology per se. It was not the machines themselves that the Luddites feared and reacted against. Rather, they understood that technology is meant to serve humans, not the other way around. Luddites were not protesting the technology itself; they were objecting to the new economic realities brought about by the machines. In former times, craftsmen had been able to work at their own pace and set their own prices for their goods. But with the dawn of industrialization and mass production, craftsmen fell on hard times and were increasingly forced to work for the hated factories. Suddenly they were answerable not to themselves but to a factory owner; they had to give up autonomy, or starve. They saw what the machines meant to their livelihood, to their lives, to their families, and to their communities. And they didn't like what they saw.

*disparaging: 폄하하는

① Craftsmen couldn't resist factory owners without labor unions.
② Unskilled laborers would be replaced by highly educated workers.
③ Craftsmen were not controlling machines but were controlled by them.
④ The strike of craftsmen brought the opposite result of the one they intended.
⑤ The destruction of the new machinery undermined only the skilled craftsmen.

3. 다음 글의 요지로 가장 적절한 것은?

Scientists hope to someday establish beyond a doubt that aging and all the nefarious things that go with it can be indefinitely postponed simply by reducing the amount of food and calories we consume. Take note that in the prevention of Alzheimer's disease, maintaining an ideal weight may not be enough.

Studies have shown that the risk of Alzheimer's disease is more closely linked to caloric intake than to weight or body mass index (BMI). This means that a junk food junkie who is blessed with a high metabolic rate that keeps her from gaining weight may still be at a higher risk for developing a memory problem. If we consider the logic that explains how caloric restriction exerts its beneficial effects on the body and mind, this makes a lot of sense. The amount of age-accelerating oxygen free radicals generated from our diet is related to the amount of calories we consume, not to our weight. Thus a person with a high metabolic rate who consumes greater calories may actually be producing more harmful forms of oxygen than someone with a slower metabolic rate.

*nefarious: 못된, 사악한 **oxygen free radical: 활성산소

① 지나친 다이어트는 칼로리 부족으로 신체 노화를 가속화시킨다.
② 칼로리 섭취가 많더라도 신진대사율이 높으면 노화가 느리게 온다.
③ 노화를 촉진하는 활성산소의 양은 개인의 신진대사율과 관련이 있다.
④ 칼로리 섭취가 많더라도 정상 체중이면 노화에 영향을 주지 않는다.
⑤ 칼로리 섭취량이 많을수록 노화를 촉진하는 활성산소의 양이 많아진다.

4. 다음 글의 주제로 가장 적절한 것은? [3점]

All of us make the best decision possible given the information we have available. But where do we go from there? The satisfaction you experience from your decisions is based not just on the outcome of those decisions but also on the amount of time you spend considering counterfactual scenarios. We sometimes ask ourselves questions such as "What would have happened if I hadn't taken this job?" or "What if I had pursued a different degree in school?" Because these questions invite you to think about an abstract world in which nothing is certain and every answer can be determined by your imagination, thinking this way can lead to an infinite series of *could-have-beens*. Just the act of spending time on counterfactual questions can undermine the value of the decision you made in the first place. *What-if* questions intrigue us — it can be endlessly fascinating to imagine what might be different — but *what-ifs* do not serve us or help us to reach the best possible outcome for the decisions we have already made.

① key factors that drive successful decisions
② ways to increase satisfaction on decision making
③ difficulty in making decisions on behalf of others
④ reasons why people ask too many what-if questions
⑤ adverse effects of counterfactual thinking on decisions made

5. 다음 글의 제목으로 가장 적절한 것은?

Most people are more likely to do a favor when the request is received in their right ears rather than their left ones, new research suggests. Luca Tommasi and Daniele Marzoli of the University of Gabriele d'Annunzio in Chieti, Italy, have observed ear preference during social interactions in noisy night club environments. The researchers intentionally addressed 176 clubbers in either their right or their left ear when asking for a cigarette. They obtained significantly more cigarettes when they spoke to the clubbers' right ear compared with their left. The result confirms a well-known asymmetry in humans: the right ear dominance for listening to verbal stimuli. The brain's left hemisphere is more involved in language processing, which justifies the preferential use of the right ear for listening in everyday situations.

① Noisy Clubs Deafen Your Ears!
② Bad Effects of Smoking on Hearing
③ Need a Favor? Ask It in the Right Ear!
④ Preference for Listening with the Left Ear
⑤ Different Roles of Each Hemisphere of the Brain

6. What Mom Means To Me Essay Contest에 관한 다음 안내문의 내용과 일치하지 <u>않는</u> 것은?

What Mom Means To Me Essay Contest
Green Life Magazine

Show your love in an essay that tells us what makes your Mom the best. Your essay can be heartfelt or funny!

Details:
- Essays should not exceed 350 words.
- Essays should include text only and not have any attached pictures or drawings.
- Essay Deadline: Friday, April 30.
- Submissions may be sent to: editor@greenlifemagazine.com or mail to: P.O.Box 10, Green City, MI 48035 or bring by: 1007 Avenue K, Green City

* *Green Life* editors will select and publish the winning essay in our June issue.

* The winner, courtesy of some very generous *Green Life* advertisers, will receive a special beauty package: A collagen facial massage (Christine's Spa) & A makeover cut, color, and style (Fiaz Salon) & A $300 gift certificate (Luna Boutique).

---

① 에세이는 최대 350단어를 넘지 않아야 한다.
② 에세이에는 글 외에 사진이나 그림을 첨부할 수 없다.
③ 에세이 제출은 이메일과 우편으로만 가능하다.
④ 에세이 당선작은 6월호 잡지에 실린다.
⑤ 당선자는 광고주가 협찬한 미용 관련 상품을 받는다.

7. 다음 글의 밑줄 친 부분 중, 어법상 <u>틀린</u> 것은? [3점]

Organization survivors have mastered ① <u>what</u> sociologists call the "weak tie": a friendly yet casual social connection. Sociologist Mark Granovetter found that 56 percent of people he talked to ② <u>found</u> their jobs through a personal connection. Nothing ③ <u>surprising</u> here. But of those personal connections, most were described as "weak ties": people who were seen "only occasionally" or "rarely." When it comes to finding new jobs, new information, or new ideas of any sort, weak ties are always more important than strong ties. Your friends, after all, occupy the same world that you do. Your acquaintances, by definition, occupy a much different world and are more likely to know something you ④ <u>aren't</u>. To capture this paradox, Granovetter coined the wonderful term "the strength of the weak tie." Acquaintances represent a source of "social power," expanding your reputation into areas where you might not otherwise ⑤ <u>be known</u>. The more acquaintances you have, the more powerful (and visible) you are.

8. 다음 글의 밑줄 친 부분 중, 문맥상 낱말의 쓰임이 적절하지 <u>않은</u> 것은? [3점]

Focus groups are commonly used in marketing, but in some countries there are very real problems with them. Since it is ① <u>difficult</u> to recruit random people to be in focus groups, research agencies have developed large pools of consumers willing to take part in focus groups at short notice. However, the problem is that many of these consumers are too ② <u>willing</u>. Research has revealed that many consumers enjoy the pay, free food, and experience of being an expert and focus on pleasing the moderator in order to get invited back regularly. Unfortunately, the way to please the very human moderator seems to be to work out what they want to hear, rather than providing them with ③ <u>genuine</u> insights about the brand. This makes much of the data gained from focus-group panels ④ <u>worthwhile</u>. Agencies are aware of this problem and ensure a churn rate within groups to keep them ⑤ <u>fresh</u>, but consumers get around this by using multiple names in order to remain in the pool.

*churn rate: 참가 중단율

[9~12] 다음 빈칸에 들어갈 말로 가장 적절한 것을 고르시오.

9. In their seminal 2002 review of cross-cultural sleep practices, anthropologists Carol Worthman and Melissa Melby found that, in general, sleepers in Westernized, postindustrial countries have routine times for bed and waking to accommodate work or school, while traditional, non-Westernized sleepers have more fluid sleep schedules, moving in and out of sleep in the course of a day. They also discovered that in most cultures around the world (in Asia, Africa, Central and South America, Southern Europe, and parts of Scandinavia), children sleep within arm's reach of other family members, what anthropologists term co-sleeping, despite colonial efforts to encourage indigenous peoples to develop solitary sleep arrangements. They do not necessarily sleep in the same bed, but they are near enough to each other to observe movements and hear sounds, even muffled ones. Only in the societies of Northern mainland Europe and America, and to some extent the places colonized by those powers, has sleep been both reliably compressed into a single stretch of time and become a _____ affair necessitating bedtime rituals.

*indigenous: 토착의 **muffled: (소리를) 낮춘

① formal   ② private
③ foreign   ④ traditional
⑤ predictable

10. The basic hexagonal shape of snowflakes is elaborated in varied ways as the ice crystal grows, with the temperature and humidity of the air determining the final shape. Hexagonal prisms form in very cold, dry air. As temperatures rise, the straightforward hexagonal growth of ice crystals starts to destabilize. In very wet air, arms sprout from the snowflakes' six corners, turning into new hexagonal plates or growing more appendages if the air is warm enough. Other combinations of temperature and humidity cause the growth of hollow prisms, needles, or wrinkled plates. As snowflakes fall, the wind tosses them through the air's innumerable slight variations of temperature and humidity. No two flakes experience exactly the same sequence, and these divergent histories are reflected in the uniqueness of the ice crystals that make up each snowflake. Thus, the chance events of history are layered over the rules of crystal growth, _____ that so pleases our aesthetic sense. [3점]

*hexagonal: 육각형의

① forming patterns that are not unlikely to match
② creating sophisticated and geometrical ensembles
③ producing the tension between order and diversity
④ stabilizing each hexagonal structure easily and quickly
⑤ performing dances triggered by differences in air humidity

11. According to popular wisdom, work is a burden people must endure out of necessity, even as they long for weekends and holidays. Yet when Americans were asked in the early 1980s whether they would retire from work if they could, about 80 percent said they would not. In fact, human beings are programmed twice to be _____: once by the genes and then by the pressure of social expectations. Already in the first year of life, infants display joy in causing events, as when turning on a tap or playing with a ball. Children in a reasonably stimulating and structured environment learn to enjoy concentrated effort. Indeed, our species would not have survived if most of us had not developed a taste for work. And, of course, human communities reinforce this tendency by shaming and turning away from those who do not contribute to the common good.

① curious about the world
② capable of cooperative work
③ aware of the danger of laziness
④ dependent on being productive
⑤ devoted to their social relationships

12. In one of the odder experiments in the field of behavioral economics, Ernst Fehr and his collaborators had people play a Trust game, in which they hand over money to a trustee, who multiplies it and then returns however much he feels like to the participant. Half the participants inhaled a nasal spray containing oxytocin, which can penetrate from the nose to the brain, and the other half inhaled a placebo. The ones who got the oxytocin turned over more of their money to the stranger. Other experiments have shown that sniffing oxytocin makes people more generous in an Ultimatum game (in which they divide a sum while anticipating the response of a recipient, who can veto the deal for both of them), but not in a Dictator game (where the recipient has to take it or leave it, and the proposer needn't take his reaction into account). It seems likely that the oxytocin network is a vital trigger in _____. [3점]

*placebo: 위약

① inducing both pleasant and unpleasant affective states
② the sympathetic response to other people's beliefs and desires
③ understanding the situation an individual is in for self-defence
④ posing affective facial actions, body postures, and vocal expressions
⑤ considering the reaction of the other before expressing his opinion

13. 다음 글에서 전체 흐름과 관계 없는 문장은?

Our relationships with friends are very different from those with parents and siblings. Unlike family relationships, particularly adult-child relationships, peer relationships are based on a degree of equality between the participants. This allows more negotiation of the terms of the relationship. ① Also, unlike family relations, which one cannot pick and choose, peer relationships can be relatively easily established and just as easily destroyed. ② Our parents and siblings are generally stuck with us whether they or we like it or not. ③ But there is always the danger that friends, if we say or do something that hurts or annoys them, will declare, 'I'm not your friend any more.' ④ Relationships with their peers exert such a significant impact on children's character building that parents should always pay close attention to them. ⑤ Children therefore need to make much more of an effort to strengthen and maintain relationships with their peers than with their siblings and parents — or any other adult, for that matter.

[14~15] 주어진 글 다음에 이어질 글의 순서로 가장 적절한 것을 고르시오.

14.

Morality, very much like the legal system, is a public system, containing norms that govern behaviour which, in turn, affects other persons. Unlike law, morality is an informal system.

(A) Taxpayers can comply with the rules but they can also structure their affairs in a manner that minimizes their tax liability. The choices made by these actors may affect, i.e., enhance or undermine, the integrity of the tax system, distributive justice and sustainable societal cooperation.

(B) There are no judges authorized to decide moral conflicts, and there exist no formal decision-making procedures that provide unique and definite answers to all moral questions. Public morality and ethical responsibilities are partially codified in the law, but the legal system will never be able to codify public morality exhaustively.

(C) Moral responsibility begins precisely where actions are not completely determined by the law. That is, freedom of choice entails responsibility, and using, for instance, tax rules is inevitably a matter of exercising that responsibility. [3점]

*liability: 법적 책임 **entail: 수반하다

① (A) – (C) – (B) 　② (B) – (A) – (C)
③ (B) – (C) – (A) 　④ (C) – (A) – (B)
⑤ (C) – (B) – (A)

15.

In the process of selling your property, you may hear the phrases *"real property" and "personal property." Real property* is fixed and attached; *personal property* is usually mobile and unattached. Where this is likely to come up is in regard to items within your property.

(A) Ripping things like banisters, fireplaces, etc. off their moorings and taking them with you is not only boorish behavior, it would most likely be a violation of your sales contract. Even if it is possible to remove them, the buyer is assuming all real property to be his.
(B) Granted, anything is negotiable, but if I were a buyer and I allowed you to do such a thing at all (which I most likely wouldn't), I would demand significant financial consideration off the previously negotiated sales price, so much so that you would most likely say, "Forget it." As the buyer, I don't need you trashing the property as you leave.
(C) Most refrigerators that can roll out, be unplugged, and taken with you, are considered personal property. If a refrigerator is somehow permanently attached to the home (such as a built-in model), it is real property and stays. When selling a property, it is assumed that you are selling all real property. [3점]

*banister: 난간 **moorings: (고정된) 설비 ***boorish: 교양 없는

① (A) – (C) – (B) 　② (B) – (A) – (C)
③ (B) – (C) – (A 　④ (C) – (A) – (B)
⑤ (C) – (B) – (A)

[16~17] 글의 흐름으로 보아, 주어진 문장이 들어가기에 가장 적절한 곳을 고르시오.

16.

> However, if the changes are far-reaching, it may not be within the organism's capacity to move beyond the stressed habitat and death or extinction is likely.

Why did mass extinctions not occur in the plant kingdom? (①) The answer to this question reveals something about the versatility of plants and why they are so successful. (②) Most animal species are very mobile, and if their habitat becomes less suitable for survival, they can simply move to a new region. (③) These major extinction events are all likely to have been global disasters resulting in major changes in the world's climate; therefore, escape would have been impossible. (④) Plants, however, have always had to tolerate the inconvenience of not being able to move; therefore they have evolved to be adaptable to survive local disasters. (⑤) These survival mechanisms appear to have been so effective that even after global disasters plants appear to have bounced back very rapidly. [3점]

*versatility: 가전성 ((다른 것으로 바뀌는 가능성))

17.

> That means friends and family can only provide comments or ask questions about those elements — the ones the teens choose to show.

For some teens, screen use has contributed to an underdeveloped identity. (①) They may be devoting so much time to gaming and staying connected with "friends" that they don't have time or desire to broaden their interests or learn new skills, which would grow and solidify their identity. (②) Also, because technology makes many things easier, they may be lacking the perseverance, diligence, and teachability that are often essential for adding to their skill sets and character development. (③) Posting on social networks can limit identity development because the tendency is for posts to acknowledge only certain aspects of their lives. (④) For example, they may post often about their musical interests and never mention that they volunteer at an animal shelter. (⑤) As time goes by and no friends acknowledge or support the teen's interest in animal rescue, the teen may begin to devalue that interest and let it wane.

*wane: 시들해지다

18. 다음 글의 내용을 한 문장으로 요약하고자 한다. 빈칸 (A), (B)에 들어갈 말로 가장 적절한 것은?

Three Dutch researchers picked an alley in Amsterdam where Netherlanders park their bicycles, and attached an advertising flyer to the handlebars of each one. The commuters had to detach the flyer before they could ride their bikes, but the researchers had removed all the wastebaskets, so they either had to carry the flyer home or toss it on the ground. Above the bicycles was a prominent sign prohibiting graffiti and a wall that the experimenters had either covered in graffiti (the experimental condition) or left clean (the control condition). When the commuters were in the presence of the illegal graffiti, twice as many of them threw the flyer on the ground. In another experiment, passersby were tempted by an addressed envelope protruding from a mailbox with a five-euro bill visible inside it. When the mailbox was covered in graffiti or surrounded by litter, a quarter of the passersby stole it; when the mailbox was clean, half that many did.

↓

> According to the experiments, an _____(A)_____ environment makes people unknowingly _____(B)_____ to the norms that suit the surroundings.

	(A)	(B)		(A)	(B)
①	orderly	object	②	orderly	conform
③	artificial	object	④	artificial	conform
⑤	urban	match			

[19~20] 다음 글을 읽고, 물음에 답하시오.

Long ago, humans began labeling each other. Eventually, lighter-skinned humans became "whites," darker-skinned humans became "blacks," and people with (a) intermediate skin tones became "yellow-," "red-," and "brown-skinned." These labels don't reflect reality faithfully, and if you lined up 1,000 randomly selected people from across the earth, none of them would share exactly the same skin tone. Of course, the continuity of skin tone hasn't stopped humans from assigning each other to (b) discrete categories like "black" and "white" — categories that have no basis in biology but nonetheless go on to determine the social, political, and economic well-being of their members. These racial labels impose boundaries and categories on an infinitely complex social world, but once in place these boundaries are very difficult to dissolve. People are apt to resolve racial ambiguity by resorting to racial labels.

In a Stanford University study, an experimenter showed white students a picture of a young man whose facial features made it (c) difficult to determine whether he was white or black. For half the students, the man was labeled "white," and for the other half he was labeled "black." The students were asked to draw the image in front of them as accurately as they could. To sweeten the deal, the student who created the most accurate drawing was promised a $20 cash prize. The ones who were told that the man was black tended to (d) minimize his "typically black" features, whereas those who were told he was white did the reverse exactly. Although the students were looking at exactly the same photograph, they perceived the image through a lens that was (e) biased with the racial label that the researcher provided earlier in the experiment.

19. 윗글의 제목으로 가장 적절한 것은?

① Ethnic Identity: Formation and Its Effects
② Is Race More Than Just Skin Color Difference?
③ How Skin-color Categories Blur Ethnic Identity
④ Does Our Perception of Race Change Over Time?
⑤ Color Labels Make Ethnic Identity More Important

20. 밑줄 친 (a) ~ (e) 중에서 문맥상 낱말의 쓰임이 적절하지 <u>않은</u> 것은? [3점]

① (a)　　② (b)　　③ (c)　　④ (d)　　⑤ (e)

○ 답안지의 해당란에 성명과 수험번호를 쓰고, 또 수험번호와 답을 정확히 표시하시오.
○ 문항에 따라 배점이 다르니, 각 물음의 끝에 표시된 배점을 참고하시오. 3점 문항에만 점수가 표시되어 있습니다. 점수 표시가 없는 문항은 모두 2점씩입니다.

---

1. 다음 글의 목적으로 가장 적절한 것은?

Dear parents,

I hope you are enjoying the fall weather. Last Friday, as you know, Maple Valley High held another successful Youth Enrichment Day. Students were shown the details of a wide range of professions, and given the opportunity to listen directly to speeches by current working professionals. We know that this was an incredibly valuable opportunity for our students. We also recognize that none of this would have been possible without your help. Volunteers like you distributed lunches, organized events, greeted participants, and even offered your own advice to students. Know that your contributions are sincerely appreciated and that we look forward to seeing you again next year.

Samantha Lord
Vice Principal

① 봉사자들의 참여를 독려하려고
② 직업 탐색의 중요성을 알리려고
③ 다양한 연설 행사를 소개하려고
④ 학교 행사의 세부사항을 안내하려고
⑤ 도움을 준 봉사자들에게 감사하려고

2. 다음 글에서 필자가 주장하는 바로 가장 적절한 것은?

Sometimes, a project that you thought would be almost effortless turns out to be very difficult and draining. There are circumstances that may distract you: relationship problems or illnesses. The worst thing to do is beat yourself up for not getting everything done, for periodically procrastinating, or for slowing down from time to time. The time and energy you spend feeling guilty can extend a less-than-productive morning into a less-than-productive day. Even the most energetic and efficient people occasionally have off days. The thing that makes them good time managers is that they realize these are a part of life. They forgive themselves, make the necessary adjustments to their schedules, and move on. Instead of dwelling on what you haven't achieved, give yourself credit for what you have been able to do.

*procrastinate: 미루다, 질질 끌다

① 현 상태에 안주하지 말고 계속 전진하라.
② 완수하지 못한 일에 대해 자신을 용서하라.
③ 효율적인 시간 관리를 위해 우선순위를 정하라.
④ 생산성을 높이기 위해 정기적으로 휴식을 취하라.
⑤ 마감시한을 잘 맞추려면 일정표를 수시로 점검하라.

3. 밑줄 친 a threshold about to take a momentous step 이 다음 글에서 의미하는 바로 가장 적절한 것은? [3점]

Are there civilizations more advanced than ours? Are there civilizations that have achieved interstellar communication and have established a network of linked societies throughout our galaxy? Such questions were long the exclusive province of theology and speculative fiction. However, these questions have now entered into the realm of experimental science, and scientists are anxiously awaiting encounters with other civilizations. From the knowledge of the processes by which life arose here on the earth, they believe that similar processes must be fairly common throughout the universe. Since intelligence and technology have a high survival value, it seems likely that primitive life forms on the planets of other stars, evolving over many billions of years, would occasionally develop intelligence, civilization, and a high technology. Moreover, all the technology necessary for communicating with other civilizations in the depths of space has been secured. Indeed, we may now be standing on a threshold about to take a momentous step.

① integration of major astronomical data assets
② first contact with an extraterrestrial civilization
③ feasibility of traveling to planets similar to the earth
④ absolute truth to uncover the mystery of the universe
⑤ an advance in human civilization's communication technology

4. 다음 글의 제목으로 가장 적절한 것은?

Worry is where we begin to reflect on and become anxious about possible dangers or unpleasant possibilities that might happen in the future. And this can be accompanied by associated secondary physical responses. Worry is evolution allowing human beings to work out possible consequences of different forms of action in the battle for survival, particularly in earlier times. It is this capacity that distinguishes us from animals, as we can anticipate possible outcomes, which gives us an evolutionary advantage. But with this advantage comes the potential disadvantage that we may end up worrying and anxious about many situations that in practice will never occur. For many, worry can take over their lives, and they can end up not enjoying the present as they are constantly living in a potential future scenario.

① How to Stop Worrying and Start Living
② What Makes Worry Different from Fear
③ It Is No Use Worrying about Bygone Days
④ People with High Anxiety Are More Intelligent
⑤ Two-faced Worry: Our Protector and Our Enemy

5. 다음 도표의 내용과 일치하지 <u>않는</u> 것은?

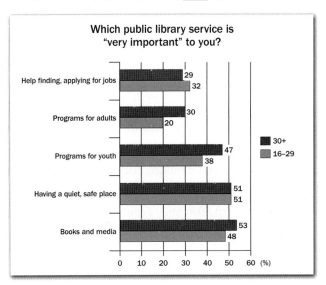

The graph above shows the results of a survey asking people about which public-library services they consider to be "very important." ① For those thirty and over, the greatest percentage of respondents strongly valued the books and media libraries offer. ② This was also popular among those 16 to 29, coming in just 3% behind "having a quiet, safe place," the most chosen response from the younger group. ③ Meanwhile, "help finding and applying for jobs" was very important to 29% of those thirty and over and 32% of those under thirty. ④ Interestingly, programs for adults were ten percentage points more important to the older group, while programs for the youth were nine percentage points more important to the younger group. ⑤ More than half of people aged 30 and over said the services such as "books and media" and "having a quiet, safe place" are very important to them.

6. Stanislavski에 관한 다음 글의 내용과 일치하지 <u>않는</u> 것은?

Stanislavski was a Russian actor and director, as well as the inventor of a famous system for theater training, preparation, and rehearsal. As a child, he was interested in the ballet and the circus. He later became interested in acting and performed and directed as an amateur until the age of 33, when he co-founded the world-famous Moscow Art Theatre company with Vladimir Nemirovich-Danchenko. Its popular productions of *The Seagull* in 1898 and *Hamlet* in 1911 showed Stanislavski's talent to audiences around the world. Unfortunately, Stanislavski suffered a heart attack on-stage during a performance. However, he continued to direct, teach, and write about acting until his death in 1938, at the age of 75. Before his death, he wrote an autobiography, and two English biographies have since been written about his life after his death.

① 어린 시절, 발레와 서커스에 흥미가 있었다.
② 모스크바 예술 극단을 공동 창단했다.
③ 1898년에 'The Seagull'로 연출 능력을 선보였다.
④ 공연 중에 무대에서 심장마비를 일으켰다.
⑤ 사망 전에 두 편의 전기를 집필했다.

7. 다음 글의 밑줄 친 부분 중, 어법상 <u>틀린</u> 것은? [3점]

Strike a bell and the sound it produces will be a note at its "natural frequency." Now attach a sound speaker to the bell and gradually increase the frequency of the sound wave ① <u>played</u> through it. The bell will vibrate in response to the sound, and the amplitude of the vibration will increase, ② <u>reaching</u> a peak when the bell's frequency matches the natural frequency — this is an example of resonance: large-amplitude vibrations caused by relatively small-amplitude inputs. Resonance is the reason why a car with its engine idling can shake ③ <u>violently</u>, experiencing vibrations much larger than when the engine is revving faster. This happens because the engine's idling frequency — the number of revolutions it makes per second — ④ <u>to be</u> close to the natural frequency of the car's body. Engineers try to limit the effects of resonance by limiting the amplitude of resonant vibrations. And so ⑤ <u>do</u> designers in charge of tall buildings in earthquake zones.

*amplitude: 진폭 **engine idling: 엔진 공회전
***rev: (엔진의) 회전 속도가 올라가다

8. 다음 글의 밑줄 친 부분 중, 문맥상 낱말의 쓰임이 적절하지 <u>않은</u> 것은? [3점]

A tight-knit community can minimize the problem of street crime. However, informal social control also poses a threat to the diversity of behavior that exists in a pluralistic society, even though it may ① <u>curb</u> violent crime. Still, street crime would decline if interaction among the residents of a community were more ② <u>frequent</u>, and if social bonds were stronger. A sense of responsibility for other citizens and for the community as a whole would increase individuals' willingness to report crime to the police and the likelihood of their ③ <u>intervention</u> in a crime in progress. Greater willingness of community residents to report crime to the police might also ④ <u>prevent</u> the need for civilian police patrols. More interaction in public places and human traffic on the sidewalks would increase surveillance of the places where people now fear to go. More intense social ties would ⑤ <u>weaken</u> surveillance with a willingness to take action against offenders.

*surveillance: 감시

[9~12] 다음 빈칸에 들어갈 말로 가장 적절한 것을 고르시오.

9. In the fifth century *B.C.E.*, the Greek philosopher Protagoras pronounced, "Man is the measure of all things." In other words, we feel entitled to ask the world, "What good are you?" We assume that we are the world's standard, that all things should be compared to us. Such an assumption makes us _____ a lot. Abilities said to "make us human" — empathy, communication, grief, toolmaking, and so on — all exist to varying degrees among other minds sharing the world with us. Animals with backbones (fishes, amphibians, reptiles, birds, and mammals) all share the same basic skeleton, organs, nervous systems, hormones, and behaviors. Just as different models of automobiles each have an engine, drive train, four wheels, doors, and seats, we differ mainly in terms of our outside contours and a few internal tweaks. But like naive car buyers, most people see only animals' varied exteriors.

*tweak: 변경, 수정

① justify   ② overlook
③ empathize   ④ administer
⑤ investigate

10. Learn to express what you want rather than putting the emphasis on what you don't want when speaking with a child. Children are highly responsive to the messages they receive. If an adult says, "Don't slam the door," the child listening hears the phrase "slam the door," with the word "don't" in front of it. The child must figure out that slamming the door is the undesirable thing to do, which is difficult to comprehend, especially for young children. The chances for a successful response from a child increase dramatically when an adult says, "Please close the door gently." Now the child has a visual image to follow. The words spoken _____, which makes it much easier to understand. [3점]

① have multiple meanings
② can be emphasized slightly
③ have a negative connotation
④ fit together well with the request
⑤ are consistent with nonverbal behaviors

11. Life requires people to estimate uncertain quantities. How long will it take to complete a term paper? How high will mortgage rates be in five years? What is the probability of a soldier dying in a military intervention overseas? There are many ways to try to answer such questions. People tend to use the following judgment strategy. "My last paper took a week to write, but this one is more demanding so maybe two weeks is a good guess." "Mortgage rates are low by historic levels, so perhaps they'll be a couple of points higher in five years." "The fatality rate in the last war was 1.5%, but our enemies are catching up technologically; maybe 4% is a more likely figure in the next conflict." What all these examples share is that individuals gauge numerical size by _____ during the subsequent course of decision-making to arrive at their final judgement. [3점]

① analyzing relevant data first and inferring its exactness

② making a comparison to a known fact based on context

③ starting with an initial anchor value and then adjusting it

④ calculating the number repeatedly until it proves to be correct

⑤ overestimating the ability to foresee the outcome of a particular case

12. History illustrates that there is no simple or enduring connection _____.
At the time of the conquest of the Americas by Columbus, the areas which today include Mexico, Central America, Peru, and Bolivia held the great Aztec and Inca civilizations. These empires were politically centralized and complex, built roads, and provided famine relief. The Aztecs had both money and writing, and the Incas recorded vast amounts of information on knotted ropes. In sharp contrast, at the time of the Aztecs and Incas, the north and south of the area inhabited by the Aztecs and Incas, which today includes the United States, Canada, Argentina, and Chile, were mostly inhabited by Stone Age civilizations lacking these technologies. The tropics in the Americas were thus much richer than the temperate zones. The greater riches in the United States and Canada today represent a stark reversal of fortune relative to what was there when the Europeans arrived. [3점]

① between geopolitical power and openness to trade

② between climate or geography and economic success

③ between race and intelligence in any part of the world

④ between investment in education and economic growth

⑤ between a reserve of natural resources and national wealth

13. 다음 글에서 전체 흐름과 관계 <u>없는</u> 문장은?

Healing, both as a collection of ideas and as a sequence of practices, is surely one of the most ancient and persistent elements of human culture. ① Material remains from prehistoric sites clearly show that our distant ancestors thought that disease had a cause and that someone could use that knowledge to help the sick person. ② Human remains indicate that these people could repair broken bones and even drill a hole into the skull of a living person. ③ Medicine was primitive and people died of injuries and infections that today are considered minor and that we are able to treat effectively with simple antiseptics. ④ The "Ice Man" who died on the high alpine pass of Tisenjoch between Italy and Austria around 2700 BCE had already recovered from several broken ribs long before he set out on his last and fateful journey; he also carried in his travel gear dried birch fungus to treat diseases and wounds. ⑤ Medicine, if not as old as the hills, is at least as old as the human ambition to climb over hills.

*antiseptic: 살균제 **alpine: 알프스 고산지대의
***birch fungus: 자작나무 버섯

[14~15] 주어진 글 다음에 이어질 글의 순서로 가장 적절한 것을 고르시오.

14.

What makes a story effective? Any Hollywood writer will tell you that attention is a scarce resource. Scientists liken attention to a spotlight.

(A) This is why you can drive on the freeway and talk on the phone or listen to music at the same time. Your attentional spotlight is dim, so you can absorb multiple informational streams.

(B) We are only able to shine it on a narrow area. If that area seems less interesting than some other area, our attention wanders. In fact, using one's attentional spotlight is metabolically costly, so we use it sparingly.

(C) You can do this until the car in front of you jams on its brakes and your attentional spotlight illuminates fully to help you avoid an accident. From a story-telling perspective, the way to keep an audience's attention is to continually increase the tension in the story. [3점]

*jam on the brake: 급하게 브레이크를 밟다

① (A) – (C) – (B)　　② (B) – (A) – (C)
③ (B) – (C) – (A)　　④ (C) – (A) – (B)
⑤ (C) – (B) – (A)

15.

We are often surprised at the purposefulness and precision of some animals' behavior when directed to the preservation of themselves and their species.

(A) A closer study of this phenomenon, however, has revealed its rigid and innate nature: although they are useful and show purpose, such actions are not accompanied by insight on the part of the animal, and are performed in an automatic manner.

(B) This kind of behavior came to be called instinctive. Instinct enables the animal to adjust to a given type of environment with great precision. Owing to the inflexible and stereotyped nature of instinctive behavior, any unexpected change in the environment may make such behavior ineffective.

(C) Nest construction, food storage for winter, the long journeys accomplished by some species of fish and bird, and the placing of eggs by insects to ensure for them adequate nutrition, are examples of the type of behavior which has always led man to ascribe some kind of reason or wisdom to these animals. [3점]

*ascribe ~ to …: ~을 …에게 속한 것으로 생각하다

① (A) – (C) – (B)　　② (B) – (A) – (C)
③ (B) – (C) – (A)　　④ (C) – (A) – (B)
⑤ (C) – (B) – (A)

[16~17] 글의 흐름으로 보아, 주어진 문장이 들어가기에 가장 적절한 곳을 고르시오.

16.

> Though few schools took it to that extreme, the movement left a mark on educational practice.

As A. S. Neill wrote in his influential book *Summerhill*, "A child is innately wise and realistic. (①) If left to himself without adult guidance of any kind, he will develop as far as he is able to develop." (②) Neill and his colleagues of the 1960s and 1970s believed that schools should abandon examinations, grades, curricula, and even books. (③) For example, in the method of reading instruction known as Whole Language, children are not taught which letter corresponds to which sound but are immersed in a book-rich environment where reading skills are expected to blossom spontaneously. (④) In the philosophy of mathematics instruction known as constructivism, children are not drilled with arithmetic tables but are enjoined to rediscover mathematical truths on their own by working out problems in groups. (⑤) Both methods fare badly when students' learning is measured objectively, but advocates of such methods tend to disdain standardized testing. [3점]

*fare badly: 잘못되어 가다

17.

> Furthermore, once you make it to the door, that long line ahead of you now means that the museum is overly crowded, and therefore, a lot less appealing.

Consumer behavior is broken down into purchase, use, and disposal activities. (①) Categorizing consumer behavior by type of activity is useful because consumers' responses to stimuli may differ depending on whether they are purchasing, using, or disposing of a single product or service. (②) For example, when leading up to purchase, a long line outside a museum is a positive factor in evaluating that museum. (③) Long lines imply that everyone wants to go there, and that the museum is probably very good. (④) But, after you have purchased your ticket, that long line is no longer a desirable factor, as you impatiently wait to get in. (⑤) So, from this example, categorizing activities by whether they occur prior to purchase versus during use shows how consumer responses can change significantly within a situation.

18. 다음 글의 내용을 한 문장으로 요약하고자 한다. 빈칸 (A), (B)에 들어갈 말로 가장 적절한 것은?

Duke University professor Dan Ariely describes a clever experiment. A group of people are given an intelligence test, but half of them are "accidentally" shown a response sheet, allowing them to look up correct answers before recording their own. Needless to say, they score above the rest. Next, everybody is asked to predict their grades on the next IQ test, in which there will be absolutely no cheat sheets — and those who predict correctly will get paid. Surprisingly, the half of the group that scored higher with cheat sheets predicted higher results for the next test. The cheaters wanted to believe they were very smart, even though their incorrect predictions of success would cost them money.

↓

> Even when accurate prediction brought them economic _____(A)_____, those who scored higher with cheating tended to give a(n) _____(B)_____ prediction about their ability.

	(A)		(B)
①	benefit	······	deflated
②	benefit	······	inflated
③	stability	······	gloomy
④	loss	······	arbitrary
⑤	loss	······	consistent

[19~20] 다음 글을 읽고, 물음에 답하시오.

Plants are acutely aware of the world around them. They are aware of their (a) visual environment; they differentiate between red, blue, and UV lights and respond accordingly. They are aware of aromas surrounding them and respond to minute quantities of volatile compounds wafting in the air. Plants know when they are being touched and can distinguish different (b) tactile senses. They are aware of gravity: they can change their shapes to ensure that shoots grow up and roots grow down. And plants are aware of their past: they remember past infections and the conditions they've weathered and then modify their current physiology based on these memories.

If a plant is aware, what does this mean for us regarding our own interactions with the green world? A plant is aware of its environment, and people are part of this environment. But it's not aware of the myriad gardeners and plant biologists who develop what they consider to be personal relationships with their plants. While these relationships may be meaningful to the caretaker, they are not dissimilar to the relationship between a child and her imaginary friend; the flow of meaning is (c) two-way. I've heard world-famous scientists and undergraduate research students alike use anthropomorphic language with abandon as they describe their plants as "not looking too happy" when mildew has taken over their leaves or as "satisfied" after they've been watered. These terms represent our own (d) subjective assessment of a plant's decidedly unemotional physiological status. For all the rich sensory input that plants and people perceive, only humans render this input as an (e) emotional landscape.

*anthropomorphic: 의인화된 **mildew: 흰곰팡이

19. 윗글의 제목으로 가장 적절한 것은?

① Plants Have Evolved for Two Billion Years
② What Plants Perceive Is Not What We Perceive
③ Mysterious Plant Thinking: A Philosophy of Vegetal Life
④ Plants Are Self-Conscious Without Eyes, Ears or Mouths
⑤ What a Plant Knows: Plant Sensing and Communication

20. 밑줄 친 (a) ~ (e) 중에서 문맥상 낱말의 쓰임이 적절하지 <u>않은</u> 것은? [3점]

① (a)　　② (b)　　③ (c)　　④ (d)　　⑤ (e)

ANSWERS

제1회																				
	1 ②	2 ①	3 ④	4 ①	5 ③		6 ③	7 ④	8 ⑤	9 ④	10 ⑤
	11 ③	12 ③	13 ④	14 ⑤	15 ②		16 ⑤	17 ⑤	18 ①	19 ①	20 ③

제2회																				
	1 ①	2 ⑤	3 ③	4 ③	5 ②		6 ③	7 ⑤	8 ③	9 ①	10 ⑤
	11 ①	12 ①	13 ④	14 ②	15 ⑤		16 ⑤	17 ②	18 ②	19 ⑤	20 ④

제3회																				
	1 ②	2 ①	3 ②	4 ③	5 ④		6 ⑤	7 ⑤	8 ④	9 ③	10 ③
	11 ⑤	12 ②	13 ④	14 ⑤	15 ③		16 ②	17 ④	18 ②	19 ④	20 ②

제4회																				
	1 ④	2 ⑤	3 ④	4 ④	5 ⑤		6 ③	7 ③	8 ④	9 ④	10 ④
	11 ②	12 ②	13 ③	14 ③	15 ④		16 ③	17 ⑤	18 ④	19 ②	20 ④

제5회																				
	1 ⑤	2 ②	3 ⑤	4 ③	5 ⑤		6 ③	7 ③	8 ④	9 ①	10 ②
	11 ②	12 ④	13 ③	14 ③	15 ②		16 ①	17 ④	18 ③	19 ②	20 ④

제6회																				
	1 ②	2 ②	3 ③	4 ①	5 ④		6 ⑤	7 ③	8 ④	9 ⑤	10 ①
	11 ⑤	12 ⑤	13 ③	14 ④	15 ③		16 ③	17 ⑤	18 ④	19 ④	20 ⑤

제7회																				
	1 ④	2 ④	3 ④	4 ③	5 ⑤		6 ④	7 ⑤	8 ②	9 ⑤	10 ⑤
	11 ①	12 ③	13 ④	14 ③	15 ②		16 ②	17 ②	18 ①	19 ②	20 ④

제8회																				
	1 ⑤	2 ③	3 ⑤	4 ②	5 ②		6 ③	7 ④	8 ③	9 ⑤	10 ④
	11 ⑤	12 ⑤	13 ④	14 ④	15 ⑤		16 ⑤	17 ④	18 ⑤	19 ⑤	20 ⑤

제9회																				
	1 ③	2 ①	3 ③	4 ④	5 ④		6 ④	7 ④	8 ③	9 ①	10 ⑤
	11 ③	12 ②	13 ③	14 ②	15 ④		16 ④	17 ③	18 ③	19 ④	20 ④

제10회																				
	1 ④	2 ②	3 ③	4 ④	5 ③		6 ④	7 ④	8 ⑤	9 ①	10 ④
	11 ③	12 ②	13 ④	14 ②	15 ④		16 ③	17 ④	18 ⑤	19 ②	20 ④

제11회	1 ⑤	2 ②	3 ④	4 ③	5 ②	6 ⑤	7 ⑤	8 ④	9 ⑤	10 ⑤
	11 ④	12 ④	13 ③	14 ②	15 ⑤	16 ③	17 ④	18 ②	19 ②	20 ⑤

제12회	1 ①	2 ②	3 ②	4 ③	5 ③	6 ③	7 ⑤	8 ④	9 ④	10 ④
	11 ①	12 ①	13 ④	14 ④	15 ②	16 ⑤	17 ③	18 ④	19 ④	20 ③

제13회	1 ⑤	2 ②	3 ⑤	4 ③	5 ④	6 ⑤	7 ⑤	8 ③	9 ②	10 ④
	11 ③	12 ③	13 ④	14 ②	15 ④	16 ④	17 ②	18 ③	19 ④	20 ⑤

제14회	1 ②	2 ③	3 ④	4 ⑤	5 ③	6 ⑤	7 ④	8 ④	9 ④	10 ③
	11 ④	12 ⑤	13 ④	14 ⑤	15 ②	16 ②	17 ③	18 ①	19 ⑤	20 ③

제15회	1 ①	2 ⑤	3 ⑤	4 ②	5 ④	6 ⑤	7 ⑤	8 ③	9 ①	10 ③
	11 ④	12 ④	13 ④	14 ②	15 ⑤	16 ③	17 ⑤	18 ④	19 ⑤	20 ④

제16회	1 ⑤	2 ①	3 ④	4 ①	5 ②	6 ⑤	7 ③	8 ⑤	9 ③	10 ③
	11 ④	12 ⑤	13 ④	14 ③	15 ②	16 ④	17 ③	18 ④	19 ②	20 ⑤

제17회	1 ⑤	2 ②	3 ⑤	4 ②	5 ③	6 ③	7 ⑤	8 ⑤	9 ③	10 ③
	11 ①	12 ③	13 ③	14 ③	15 ④	16 ④	17 ④	18 ③	19 ②	20 ③

제18회	1 ①	2 ⑤	3 ③	4 ⑤	5 ⑤	6 ⑤	7 ③	8 ⑤	9 ②	10 ③
	11 ③	12 ③	13 ④	14 ④	15 ⑤	16 ⑤	17 ③	18 ③	19 ①	20 ③

제19회	1 ④	2 ①	3 ③	4 ③	5 ④	6 ⑤	7 ⑤	8 ③	9 ③	10 ②
	11 ④	12 ④	13 ④	14 ⑤	15 ④	16 ④	17 ⑤	18 ①	19 ④	20 ⑤

제20회	1 ④	2 ③	3 ①	4 ④	5 ②	6 ④	7 ⑤	8 ⑤	9 ③	10 ②
	11 ⑤	12 ③	13 ④	14 ④	15 ③	16 ④	17 ⑤	18 ④	19 ①	20 ④

제21회	1 ③	2 ④	3 ⑤	4 ⑤	5 ④		6 ④	7 ③	8 ④	9 ④	10 ②
	11 ②	12 ②	13 ④	14 ②	15 ②		16 ④	17 ③	18 ①	19 ②	20 ④

제22회	1 ①	2 ②	3 ④	4 ③	5 ⑤		6 ④	7 ④	8 ⑤	9 ⑤	10 ④
	11 ⑤	12 ②	13 ④	14 ④	15 ⑤		16 ③	17 ⑤	18 ④	19 ①	20 ⑤

제23회	1 ④	2 ⑤	3 ④	4 ⑤	5 ④		6 ⑤	7 ③	8 ④	9 ①	10 ①
	11 ③	12 ③	13 ③	14 ④	15 ③		16 ②	17 ③	18 ④	19 ②	20 ④

제24회	1 ④	2 ③	3 ⑤	4 ⑤	5 ③		6 ③	7 ④	8 ④	9 ②	10 ③
	11 ④	12 ②	13 ④	14 ③	15 ④		16 ③	17 ④	18 ②	19 ②	20 ④

제25회	1 ⑤	2 ②	3 ②	4 ⑤	5 ④		6 ⑤	7 ④	8 ⑤	9 ②	10 ④
	11 ③	12 ②	13 ③	14 ②	15 ④		16 ③	17 ⑤	18 ②	19 ②	20 ③

MEMO

1 구문

판매 1위 '천일문' 콘텐츠를 활용하여 정확하고 다양한 구문 학습

(끊어읽기) (해석하기) (문장 구조 분석) (해설·해석 제공) (단어 스크램블링) (영작하기)

2 문법·서술형

쎄듀의 모든 문법 문항을 활용하여 내신까지 해결하는 정교한 문법 유형 제공

(객관식과 주관식의 결합) (문법 포인트별 학습) (보기를 활용한 집합 문항) (내신대비 서술형) (어법+서술형 문제)

3 어휘

초·중·고·공무원까지 방대한 어휘량을 제공하며 오프라인 TEST 인쇄도 가능

(영단어 카드 학습) (단어 ↔ 뜻 유형) (예문 활용 유형) (단어 매칭 게임)

4 선생님 보유 문항 이용

(Online Test) (OMR Test)

수능실감

쎄듀

독해
최우수
문항

정답 및 해설

25회 × 20문항

500

제

독해
최우수
문항

500제

정답 및 해설

1	②	2	①	3	④	4	①	5	③	6	③	7	④	8	⑤	9	④	10	⑤
11	③	12	③	13	④	14	⑤	15	②	16	⑤	17	⑤	18	①	19	①	20	③

1 글의 목적　　　　　　　　　　　②

해설 마을의 부모 및 조부모님들이 협동조합을 만들어서 서로의 아이를 돌봐주고, 돌본 시간은 계좌에 적립하여 이후에 자신의 아이를 돌봐줄 사람이 필요할 때 사용하자는 제안을 하는 내용이므로 글의 목적으로 가장 적절한 것은 ②이다.

- -

해석 Cindy에게

방금 마을에서 어린이 돌봄 협동조합을 만든 부모님 모임에 대한 멋진 이야기를 보고, 이곳 Fairview에도 멋진 부가물이 될 거라고 생각했습니다. 그것이 작동하는 방법이 여기 있습니다. 몇몇 돌봄 서비스 제공자들(어머니, 아버지, 한부모, 조부모)이 함께 모여서 서로의 아이를 돌봐주는 일을 할 수 있다고 약속하는 겁니다. 모임의 다른 회원을 위하여 베이비시터로 일한 시간당 회원의 계좌에 한 시간이 입금되는 겁니다. 회원들은 그러면 그들이 자신의 아이들을 위해 돌봄 서비스를 받을 필요가 있을 때 그들 계좌에 예치된 시간을 이용할 수 있습니다. 당신도 알다시피, 이곳 주변에서 믿을 수 있는 베이비시터를 찾는 것은 매우 어렵고, 좋은 베이비시터들은 수요가 너무 높아서 그들의 일정을 잡는 것이 거의 불가능합니다. 협동조합을 세우는 것이 우리 아이들에게 고급의 돌봄 서비스를 제공해줄 수 있다고 생각합니다. 당신의 답장을 고대합니다.

진심을 담아,

Karen Diamond 드림

- -

구문 [13행~16행] As you know, finding a reliable ***babysitter*** around here is very difficult, // and **the good *ones*** are in **such** *demand* **that** it is almost impossible to schedule them.

앞 절에서 finding ~ here이 주어이고 동사는 is이다. the good ones에서 ones는 babysitters를 지칭한다. 「such ... that ~」은 '너무 …하여 ~하다'의 뜻인데 such 다음에는 명사가 나온다.

- -

어휘 cooperative 협동조합　pledge 약속하다　credit 예금하다　draw upon ~을 이용하다, ~에 의지하다　bank 예금하다　reliable 믿을 수 있는　look forward to A A를 고대하다

2 필자 주장　　　　　　　　　　　①

해설 자신과 다른 사람들을 비교하지 않고, 자신의 현재 상태를 즐기면 깊은 만족감을 얻을 수 있다는 글이므로 필자의 주장으로는 ①이 가장 적절하다.

- -

해석 기쁨과 행복을 추구하는 것은 보편적인 욕망이다. 하지만, 사람들이 너무나 자주 그 추구가 완벽한 직업을 찾거나, 새로운 도구를 얻거나, 체중을 감량하거나, 또는 어떤 이미지를 유지함으로써 완전히 성취될 것이라고 믿는 것은 불행한 일이다. 행복의 원천을 찾기 위해 외부로 눈길을 돌리는 것에 내재되어 있는 문제는 당신이 가지지 못한 것이나 당신답지 않은 것에 초점을 맞추는 것이 필연적으로 불행을 초래한다는 것이다. '남의 떡이 더 커 보인다'는 말이 있다. 당신 자신과 당신의 자산을 다른 사람들과 비교하는 것을 중단할 때, 다른 사람들에게는 당신이 더욱 축복받은 쪽이라는 것을 깨달을 수 있을 것이다. 현재를 사는 법을 배우고 당신 자신의 운명을 즐기는 것이 깊은 만족감의 원천이 될 수 있다.

- -

구문 [2행~5행] **It** is unfortunate, however, // **that** people so often believe / that the search will be entirely fulfilled / by underline{finding} the perfect job, underline{acquiring} some new gadget, underline{losing} weight, or underline{maintaining} an image.

It은 뒤에 나오는 that ~ an image를 대신하여 쓰인 가주어이다. 「by v-ing」는 'v함으로써'의 의미이며, 네 개의 v-ing가 전치사 by의 목적어로 병렬구조를 이룬다.

[5행~8행] The problem (inherent in looking outward / for sources of happiness) is // that focusing on underline{what you do not have} or underline{what you are not} inevitably **leads to** unhappiness.

( )는 앞의 The problem을 수식하는 형용사구이다. 접속사 that이 이끄는 보어절 안의 주어는 focusing on ~ what you are not이며, 동사는 leads to이다. 보어절에서 전치사 on의 목적어인 what ~ have와 what ~ not이 or로 병렬 연결되었다.

- -

어휘 quest 추구, 탐색, 탐구　universal 보편적인; 일반적인　entirely 완전히, 전적으로　fulfill 성취하다, 완수하다　acquire 얻다, 습득하다; 획득하다　gadget 도구, 기구, 장치　maintain 유지하다, 지키다　inherent 내재적인, 타고난　inevitably 필연적으로, 반드시　asset 자산, 재산　lot 운명, 운　profound 깊은, 엄청난; 심오한　contentment 만족[자족](감)

3 밑줄 함의　　　　　　　　　　　④

해설 '쌍방이 이익이다'라는 밑줄 친 문장에서 쌍방은 삽입 광고 기고자와 소식지 출판인을 가리키며, 이 문장은 구체적으로 기고자는 자신의 메시지를 고객들에게 전할 수 있고 출판인은 발송비와 콘텐츠 확보에서 이익을 얻을 수 있다는 뜻이므로, 이를 가장 잘 반영한 뜻풀이는 ④ '삽입 광고를 제공하는 것은 소식지 출판인과 기고가 양쪽 모두에 이득이다.'이다.

① 소식지 출판인들과 광고주들은 성공적인 마케팅 도구를 공유한다.
② 다른 사람들의 소식지에 기고하는 것은 값도 싸고 효과적이다.
③ 출판인들은 기고가와 메일링 시스템 양쪽 모두로부터 도움을 받는다.
⑤ 소식지에 기고하는 것은 기고가들에게 소식지에 대한 접근을 제공한다.

- -

해석 다른 사람들의 소식지에 기사나 삽입 광고로 기고하는 것은 새로운 시장에 도달하고 다른 사업체에 점유된 고객들에게 다가가는 비싸지 않고 훌륭한 방법이다. 대부분의 소식지 출판인들은 소식지를 위한 콘텐츠를 찾는 것이 계속되는 도전이기 때문에 다른 사람들로부터 온 투고문을 환영한다. 당신이 그들에게 경쟁적이지 않은 정보를 제공한다면, 당신은 다른 회사의 소식지에 쉽게 접근할 수 있다. 예를 들어 마사지 치료사는 척추 지압 요법사의 소식지에 투고할 수 있을 것이다. (그들의) 서비스는 같은 독자들에게 호소할 수 있을 정도로 충분히 비슷하지만, 별개의 서비스를 제공할 수 있을 정도로 충분히 다르다. 당신은 이야기를 투고하거나, 소식지 출판인에게 삽입 광고를 제공할 수 있다. 후자의 경우에 그것은 합동 발송과 매우 흡사하게 작동한다. 당신은 당신의 삽입 광고가 함께 나가게 하는 대가로 소식지의 발송 비용을 부담하는 데 도움을 줄 수 있다. 쌍방이 이익이다.

- -

구문 [6행~9행] If you **provide** them **with** non-competing information, // you can easily **gain access to** another company's newsletter.

「provide A with B」는 'A에게 B를 제공하다'의 의미이다. 「gain access to」는 '~에 접근하다'의 뜻이다.

[10행~12행] The services are **similar enough to** appeal to the same audience, but different enough to offer distinct services.

「형용사 + enough to-v」는 '~할 정도로 충분히 …하다'의 뜻이다.

어휘 contribute to A A에 기고[기여]하다　**newsletter** 소식지　**tap into** ~에게 다가가다　**capture** 점유하다, 차지하다　**submission** 제출　**ongoing** 계속 진행 중인 **massage therapist** 마사지 치료사　**appeal** 호소하다　**distinct** 별개의　**joint** 합동의　**in exchange for** ~와 교환하여　**both parties** 쌍방

4 글의 주제 ①

해설 노벨상 수상자들과 기업가, 발명가들과 같은 창의적인 사람들이 예술에 몰두하는 경향이 있다는 것은 결국 예술이 그들의 창의성에 영향을 미친다는 내용이므로, 주제로 가장 적절한 것은 ① '창의적인 통찰력의 원천으로서 예술의 중요성'이다.
② 혁신가들이 예술가들과 협업하기 위한 필요조건들
③ 평범한 사람들과 비범한 사람들 간의 차이점들
④ 독창적인 사고를 위해 호기심을 장려해야 하는 이유들
⑤ 위대한 생각을 행동으로 옮기기 위한 전문 지식의 필요성

해석 1901년부터 2005년까지 노벨상을 수상한 모든 과학자와 동시대의 전형적인 과학자들을 비교한 한 최근의 연구에서, 두 집단은 모두 자신들 각자의 연구 분야에서 깊이 있는 전문 지식을 이루었다. 하지만 노벨상 수상자들은 덜 뛰어난 과학자들보다 예술에 몰두할 가능성이 훨씬 더 높았다. 수천 명의 미국인들에 대한 한 대표 연구는 기업가들과 발명가들과 같은 창의적인 사람들에게 있어 (위의 연구와) 비슷한 결과를 보여주었다. 창업을 하고 특허 출원에 기여한 사람들은 자신들의 동료보다 소묘, 그림, 건축, 조각, 그리고 문학을 포함하는 여가 시간 취미를 가질 가능성이 더 높았다. 기업가들, 발명가들, 그리고 저명한 과학자들 사이에 예술에 대한 관심은 분명히 그들의 호기심과 적성을 반영한다. 과학과 사업을 바라보는 새로운 방식에 열려있는 사람들은 또한 이미지, 소리, 그리고 단어들을 통해 아이디어와 감정을 표현하는 것에 매료되는 경향이 있다.

구문 [1행~4행] In *a recent study* (comparing every Nobel Prize-winning scientist / from 1901 to 2005 / with typical scientists of the same era), / both groups attained deep expertise in their respective fields of study.
( )는 현재분사 comparing이 이끄는 형용사구로 앞에 있는 a recent study를 수식하며 최근 연구에 대한 구체적인 설명을 더하고 있다.
[9행~13행] *People* [who started businesses and contributed to patent applications] were more likely (than their peers) to have *leisure time hobbies* [that involved drawing, painting, architecture, sculpture, and literature].
주격 관계대명사가 이끄는 두 개의 [ ]는 앞에 있는 명사 People과 leisure time hobbies를 각각 수식한다. 비교 대상을 나타내는 ( ) 부분이 동사구 사이에 삽입되었다.

어휘 **typical** 전형적인; 일반적인　**era** 시대　**attain** 이루다, 획득하다; (나이, 수준 등이) 이르다　**expertise** 전문 지식[기술], 전문성　**respective** 각자의, 각각의 **accomplished** 뛰어난; 성취한　**representative** 대표하는　**entrepreneur** 기업가, 사업가　**patent application** 특허 출원　**peer** 동료, 또래; 유심히 보다　**eminent** 저명한; 탁월한　**aptitude** 적성, 소질　**fascinate** 매료하다; 마음을 사로잡다　[**선택지 어휘**] **insight** 통찰력; 이해, 간파　**innovator** 혁신가　**ordinary** 평범한; 보통의, 일상적인 **inventive** 독창적인; 창의적인

5 도표 이해 ③

해설 원그래프는 캐나다의 여러 에너지 소스들의 비율을 나타낸 것이다. 풍력은 4%에서 9%로 두 배 이상 증가할 것으로 예측되는 것은 맞지만, 모든 에너지원 중 가장 큰 퍼센트 포인트 증가는 천연가스(15% → 22%)에서 나타나므로 the biggest

---

를 the second biggest로 고쳐야 한다.

해석 캐나다의 다양한 에너지 원천별 비율
위의 원그래프는 2012년 다양한 원천으로 얻은 캐나다의 에너지와 2035년의 그것들의 예측되는 지분의 비율을 보여준다. ① 수력, 풍력, 조력 에너지원이 5퍼센트 포인트 축소되지만 우세한 에너지원으로 남을 것임을 볼 수 있다. ② 석탄과 코크스는 7퍼센트 포인트 줄어들 것으로 예측되는 반면 천연가스는 같은 양으로 증가할 것으로 예측된다. ③ 풍력은 4%에서 9%로 두 배 이상 증가할 것으로 예측되는데, 이는 모든 에너지원 중 가장 큰 퍼센트 포인트의 증가이다. ④ 한편, CCS 처리 된 석탄은 2012년에 쓰이지 않았지만, 2035년에는 캐나다의 에너지의 2%를 차지할 것으로 예측된다. ⑤ 우라늄과 석유는 시간이 흐르며 줄어들 것으로 예측되는 두 개의 에너지원인데, 전자는 3퍼센트 포인트 정도 감소하며 후자는 2퍼센트 포인트 감소할 것이다.

구문 [13행~16행] Uranium and Oil are two sources (predicted to shrink over time), **with** *the former* **dropping** by three percentage points ⌐and⌐ **the latter by two**.
the former는 Uranium을, the latter는 Oil을 각각 지칭한다. 「with O v-ing」는 'O가 v한 채로'의 뜻이다. the latter by two는 with the latter dropping by two percentage points를 간단히 쓴 것이다.

어휘 **share** 몫, 할당, 지분　**hydro** 수력 전기[발전소]　**tidal** 조수의　**shrink** 줄어들다, 줄어들게 하다　**dominant** 주된, 지배적인　**account for** 차지하다　**uranium** 우라늄

6 내용 불일치 ③

해설 Ole Gunnar Solskjaer는 Manchester United로 이적하여 Blackburn Rovers와의 경기에서 교체선수로 데뷔했다고 했으므로 정답은 ③이다.

해석 Ole Gunnar Solskjaer는 1973년에 노르웨이의 Kristiansund에서 태어났다. 1994년에서 1996년 사이에 Solskjaer는 Molde FK팀에서 활동했고, 그 기간 동안 38경기에서 31골을 득점하여 Hamburger SV와 Cagliari의 주목을 끌었다. 그러나 1996년 7월에 이 축구선수는 Manchester United로 이적을 완료했다. 그는 Blackburn Rovers와의 경기에서 교체선수로 데뷔했고 첫 시즌에 18골로 팀이 우승하는 데 도움이 되었다. Solskjaer가 Manchester United에 합류한 뒤 몇 시즌 동안 그는 비록 교체선수로 필드에 출전했지만 탁월한 스트라이커로 스스로를 입증했다. 2001/02 시즌에 그는 선발 선수 11명에 정식 자리를 얻었다. 그는 노르웨이를 대표하는 선수로서 67 차례의 대표선수 자리를 획득했다. 그는 1998 FIFA World Cup과 Euro 2000 국가 대표팀으로 소집되었다.

구문 [2행~5행] Between 1994 and 1996 Solskjaer played for Molde FK, // **during which** he netted 31 goals in 38 matches ⌐and⌐ attracted the attention of Hamburger SV and Cagliari.
during which는 'and during that period'의 뜻으로 쓰였다. during which 절에서 동사 netted와 attracted가 병렬구조를 이룬다.

어휘 **net** (공을 차거나 쳐서) 득점하다　**debut** 데뷔, 첫 출전　**substitute** 교체 선수 **win a title** 타이틀을 획득하다, 우승하다　**call up** (특히 국가 간 경기에) ~을 출전시키다 **national squad** 국가 대표팀

7 밑줄 어법 ④

해설 ④ 주어 the willpower에 상응하는 동사가 나와야 하므로 to match를 matches로 바꿔 써야 한다.

① the Sirens 뒤에 이를 수식하는 관계대명사절이 나와야 하는데, '사이렌의' 목소리가 선원들을 꾀어내는 것이므로 소유격 관계대명사 whose를 적절히 사용했다.

② 오디세우스가 자기 자신을 묶은 것이므로 재귀대명사 himself를 적절히 사용했다.

③ more prepared는 '좀 더 준비된 상태로'라는 뜻으로 주어 Odysseus를 보충 설명하는 표현이다. 오디세우스가 준비시키는 상황이 아니라 준비가 된 상황이므로 과거분사 형태를 적절히 사용했다.

⑤ that we have a lot of willpower는 The belief에 대한 동격절이므로 동격을 나타내는 접속사 that을 적절히 사용했다.

해석 기원전 800년쯤의 호메로스의 고전 작품인 〈오디세이〉에서 주인공 오디세우스는 트로이 전쟁으로부터의 귀향길에 많은 위험과 시련에 직면한다. 어느 한 곳에서 그의 배는 그 잊을 수 없는 목소리가 선원들을 해안 근처의 암초에 부딪혀 죽도록 꾀어내는 사이렌들을 지나야 한다. 오디세우스는 사이렌들의 목소리를 듣고 싶어서 부하들의 귀에 밀랍을 넣고 자신은 미치지 않고 사이렌의 노래를 안전하게 들을 수 있도록 배의 돛대에 자신을 묶었다. 그는 의지력 하나만으로는 사이렌의 유혹을 극복하기에 충분하지 않다는 것을 알고 있었다. 그리하여 오디세우스는 죽지 않고 집으로의 여정을 완수할 준비가 더 잘 된 상태로 사이렌의 반대편에 나타났다. 그러나 오디세우스와는 달리, 직면하게 될 난제를 예견하는 사람은 우리들 중에 거의 없다. 결과적으로 우리가 목표를 세울 때 가정하는 의지력은 그 목표를 달성할 때 우리가 발휘하는 의지력에 좀처럼 미치지 못한다. 무언가가 항상 우리의 배를 가라앉히려고 나타난다. 우리가 의지력을 많이 가지고 있다는 믿음이 과도한 자신감을 촉발한다.

구문 [6행~9행] Odysseus wanted to hear the Sirens, // so he put wax in his men's ears [and] tied himself to the ship's mast // **in order that** he could safely hear the Sirens' singing / without going mad.

so절에서 밑줄 친 두 개의 동사구가 and로 연결되어 병렬구조를 이룬다. 「in order that ~은 '~하기 위하여'라는 뜻으로 that 다음에 절이 나온다.

[13행~14행] Unlike Odysseus, however, few of us foresee *the challenges* [(which[that]) we will face].

[ ]는 앞에 목적격 관계대명사 which[that]가 생략되어 the challenges를 수식한다.

어휘 peril 위험   haunting 잊을 수 없는 *cf.* haunt 뇌리에서 떠나지 않다; 귀신[유령]이 나타나다   lure 꾀다, 유혹하다   wax 밀랍   willpower 의지력   temptation 유혹   perish 죽다   foresee 예견하다   trigger 촉발하다

8 밑줄 어휘   ⑤

해설 '음악은 보편적인 언어'라는 통념과는 달리 한 사람이 실제로 듣는 것은 자신의 문화에 영향을 받는다는 내용이다. 마지막 문장의 경우 not always라는 부분 부정의 표현과 함께 서로 다른 문화 간에 음악에 대한 이해는 '항상 가능한 것은 아니다'의 의미가 되어야 하므로, ⑤의 impossible을 ensured로 고쳐야 한다.

해석 우리는 종종 '음악은 보편적인 언어다.'라는 표현을 듣는다. 이것은 비록 두 사람이 서로의 언어로 이야기하지 않더라도, 최소한 그들은 ① 함께 음악을 감상할 수 있다는 것을 의미한다. 그러나 널리 알려진 매우 많은 격언들처럼, 이것은 단지 ② 부분적으로만 사실이다. 비록 모든 사람들이 청각에 대한 같은 생리적 구조를 정말로 가지고 있기는 하지만, 한 사람이 실제로 듣는 것은 그 사람의 문화에 의해 영향을 받는다. 서양인들은 자바섬과 스리랑카 음악의 풍부함을 듣도록 ③ 길들여지지 않았기 때문에 그것의 많은 부분을 놓치는 경향이 있다. 우리가 비서양 음악 한 곡을 우연히 접할 때마다, 우리는 음계, 멜로디, 음의 높이, 화음, 그리고 리듬을 포함한 우리 자신의 ④ 문화적으로 영향을 받은 일련의 음악적 범주의 측면에서 그것을 듣는다(처리한다). 그리고 그 범주들이 문화마다 다르게 정의되기 때문에, 서로 다른 문화 사이에서 음악에 대한 올바른 이해가 항상 ⑤ 불가능한(→ 보장되는) 것은 아니다.

구문 [7행~8행] ~, **what** a person actually hears is influenced by his or her culture.

what은 관계대명사로 문장의 주어 역할을 하는 명사절을 이끈다.

어휘 universal 보편적인; 전 세계적인   appreciate 감상하다; 진가를 알아보다; 이해하다; 감사하다 *cf.* appreciation (올바른) 이해, 평가; 감상; 감사   saying 격언, 속담   partially 부분적으로, 불완전하게   mechanism 구조, 기제; 기계 장치   influence 영향을 미치다[주다]; 영향력   tend to-v v하는 경향이 있다   condition 길들이다, 훈련시키다; 조건; 상황   encounter (우연히) 접하다, 맞닥뜨리다   category 범주, 카테고리   scale 음계; 규모, 범위   pitch 음의 높이; 정점, 최고조   harmony 화음; 조화, 화합   define (단어·구의 뜻을) 정의하다; (입장 등을) 밝히다

9 빈칸 추론   ④

해설 빈칸 문장으로 보아 영화가 개봉될 당시에 '어떠한' 배경을 제공했는지 찾아야 한다. 원작의 배경은 19세기 말의 아프리카 콩고이지만, 〈Apocalypse Now〉 영화에서는 그 당시 현대의 상황으로 새롭게 되었다고 했으므로 빈칸에는 ④ '동시대의'가 들어가는 것이 가장 적절하다.
① 지나치게 단순화한 ② 서구화된 ③ 정교한 ⑤ 관습에 얽매이지 않는

해석 Francis Ford Coppola가 제작하고 감독한 영화 〈Apocalypse Now〉는 인기를 얻었는데, 그것엔 충분한 이유가 있었다. 그 영화는 J. Conrad의 소설 〈Heart of Darkness〉를 각색한 것인데, 그 소설은 19세기 말 아프리카의 콩고를 배경으로 하고 있다. 원작 소설과는 달리 〈Apocalypse Now〉는 베트남 전쟁 때의 베트남과 캄보디아를 배경으로 하고 있다. 배경, 시기, 대화, 그리고 다른 부수적 세부 사항은 그 당시 현대로 새롭게 되었지만 〈Apocalypse Now〉의 기본적인 줄거리와 주제는 〈Heart of Darkness〉의 그것들과 똑같다. 둘 다 문명의 최악의 측면을 나타내는 비정상적인 Kurtz라는 인물을 대면하기 위해 강을 따라 내려가는, 주인공의 정신적 그리고 영적인 여행을 나타내는, 물리적 여행을 묘사한다. 〈Apocalypse Now〉에 그것이 개봉될 당시에 동시대의 배경을 제공함으로써, 관객들은 영화가 소설을 원문에 충실하게 각색한 것이었다면 그랬을 것보다 더 쉽게 그것의 주제를 경험하고 동질감을 느낄 수 있었다.

구문 [7행~11행] The setting, time period, dialogue, and other incidental details / are updated to the then present day, // [but] the fundamental story line and themes of *Apocalypse Now* / are the same as those of *Heart of Darkness*.

밑줄 친 those는 the fundamental story line and themes를 의미한다.

[15행~20행] By giving *Apocalypse Now a setting* [that was contemporary at the time of its release], / audiences were able to experience and identify with its themes more easily // than they **would have** / if the film **had been** a literal adaptation of the novel.

주격 관계대명사 that이 이끄는 [ ] 부분이 앞의 a setting을 수식한다. they ~ novel은 「If + S′ + had p.p., S + 조동사 과거형 + have p.p.」 형태의 가정법 과거완료 구문으로 if절과 주절의 위치가 뒤바뀐 형태이다. they would have 뒤에는 been able to experience and identify with its themes가 생략되었다.

어휘 popularity 인기; 대중성   adaptation 각색; 적응   set (연극·소설·영화의) 배경[무대]을 설정하다   incidental 부수적인, 부차적인   fundamental 기본적인, 기본의; 근본[본질]적인   story line 줄거리   describe 묘사하다; 서술하다; 말하다   reflect 나타내다; 비추다; 반사하다   confront 대면하다; 맞서다   release 개봉, 발표; 풀어주다   identify with ~와 동질감을 느끼다; ~와 동일시하다   literal (번역·해석 등이) 원문에 충실한; 글자 그대로의

10 빈칸 추론 ⑤

해설 우리 생활은 스트레스성 사건으로 가득 차있고 이때마다 스트레스를 겪는 것은 필연적인 일이므로, 스트레스는 제거하려 하지 말고 잘 다스려야 한다는 내용이다. 그러므로, 스트레스를 다루는 것은 ⑤ '과정이지 결과가 아니다'라고 할 수 있다.
① 사실이지 이론이 아니다
② 이론이지 사실이 아니다
③ 능력이지 연습이 아니다
④ 결과이지 과정이 아니다

해석 스트레스는 오늘날 미국 문화에서 관심의 초점이 되는 주제이다. 그것에 대한 많은 관심은 이러한 상태를 이해하고자 하는 욕구, 즉 '정상적'이고 행복한 삶을 살기 위해 스트레스를 충분히 효과적으로 다루고자 하는 욕구에서 비롯된다. 그러나 스트레스를 다루는 것은 과정이지 결과가 아니다. 많은 사람들의 태도는, 성급한 생활 방식과 즉각적인 충족에 대한 기대감에 영향을 받아서, 스트레스에 대한 그들의 인식을 다스리거나, 줄이거나, 조절하기보다는, 스트레스를 없애려는 욕구를 반영하고 있다. 그 결과, 스트레스는 결코 사라지지 않고, 새로운 얼굴로 다시 나타날 뿐이다. 조금만 생각해보면 이것을 피할 수 없다는 것이 보일 것이다. 전공을 선택하거나 직업을 바꾸는 것에서부터 아이를 갖거나 가족을 잃는 것에 이르기까지 스트레스성 생활 사건은 어떤 만족스런 삶을 통해서든 계속해서 일어날 것이다. 그것을 피하거나 무시하지 않고 그것을 다루는 것이 유일한 해결책이다. 연구 결과는 이러한 충고를 거절하는 사람들에게 심장병이나 암의 형태로 된 실제 신체적 손상이 일어날 수 있는 결과임을 보여준다.

구문 [6행~9행] Many people's attitudes, / influenced by their rushed lifestyles and expectations of immediate satisfaction, / reflect the need (to eliminate stress **rather than** to manage, reduce, or control their perceptions of it).
주어는 Many people's attitudes이고 동사는 reflect이며, influenced ~ satisfaction은 수동의 의미의 분사구문이다. ( )는 the need를 수식하며, 「A rather than B」는 'B보다는 오히려 A'의 뜻이다.

어휘 stem from ~에서 비롯되다　get a handle on ~을 처리하다, 다루다　effectively 효과적으로　perception 인식, 지각　inevitable 불가피한, 필연적인　fulfilling 성취감을 주는, 만족감을 주는

11 빈칸 추론 ③

해설 Gombrich의 주장에서 어떠한 미술도 '무엇'하지 않는지를 찾아야 한다. Gombrich는 화가들이 자신이 그리는 것을 본다는 관점을 고수하며, 선입견(preconceptions, stereotypes, categories)에 따라 세상을 표현한다고 했다. 또한, 빈칸 문장의 주어인 'No art(어떠한 미술도 ~하지 않다)'로 보아 빈칸에는 Gombrich의 주장과 반대되는 내용인 ③ '사실에 대한 정확한 표현을 제공한다'가 들어가야 함을 알 수 있다.
① 그 자체를 위해 추구되어서는 (안 된다)
② 모방의 영역을 벗어날 수 (없다)
④ 화가의 자연에 대한 자의적 해석을 포함하지 (않는다)
⑤ 화가들이 세상을 상상하는 다양한 방법들에 대해 이야기하지 (않는다)

해석 Kant와 Wittgenstein에게 영향을 받았음에도 불구하고, 자신의 유명한 〈Art and Illusion〉에서 Ernst Gombrich는 "화가는 자신이 보는 것을 그리는가? 아니면 자신이 그리는 것을 보는가?"라는 질문을 했다. 후자의 관점을 강하게 고수하는 Gombrich는 심지어 미술의 명백한 목적이 모방인 때 조차도, 묘사나 표현의 과정은 항상 화가의 선입견에 달려 있다고 주장한다. 일련의 고정관념이나 범주들이 없으면, 시각 예술가는 결코 자신이 직면한 신기루와 같은 느낌들을 분류하는 데 성공할 수 없을 것이고, 자신의 인식을 질서 정연하고, 체계적이고, 인식 가능한 경험으로 조직화할 수 없을 것이다. 미술사는 일련의 계속해서 변화하는 스타일과 고정관념들을 보여준다. Gombrich에 따르면 어떠한 미술도

사실에 대한 정확한 표현을 제공하지 않는다.

구문 [1행~4행] In his famous *Art and Illusion*, Ernst Gombrich, <u>influenced as</u>
(= though he is influenced)
he is by Kant and Wittgenstein, asks, "Does a painter paint what he sees? Or does he see what he paints?"
접속사 as가 '양보(비록 ~일지라도)'의 의미로 쓰일 때에는 문어체적인 표현으로 「형용사[부사, 명사] + as + S′ + V′」 형태를 취할 수 있다.
[8행~12행] Without a set of stereotypes or categories, / the visual artist **would never succeed** / in classifying *the mirage of impressions* [(which[that]) he is confronted with] / and (would never) organize his perception / into *an experience* [that is orderly, structured,and recognizable].
Without ~ categories가 '조건'의 뜻을 함축하고 있는 가정법 문장이다. If he didn't have a set of ~ categories로 바꿔 쓸 수 있다. 목적격 관계대명사 which 또는 that이 생략된 첫 번째 [ ]는 앞의 the mirage of impressions를 수식한다. 두 번째 [ ]는 주격 관계대명사 that이 이끄는 형용사절로 앞의 an experience를 수식한다.

어휘 adhere to A A를 고수하다　explicit 명백한, 분명한; 솔직한　imitation 모방; 모조품　depiction 묘사, 서술　representation 표현, 묘사　preconception 선입견, 편견; 예상　a set of 일련의　stereotype 고정관념　classify 분류[구분]하다　impression 느낌, 인상; 감명　confront 직면하다; 맞서다　perception 인식, 지각; 통찰력　orderly 질서 정연한　a succession of 일련의　[선택지 어휘] seek for ~을 추구하다　for one's sake ~을 위해　depart from ~에서 벗어나다[출발하다]　arbitrary 자의적인, 임의의, 제멋대로인　interpretation 해석; 설명　envision 상상[구상]하다, 마음에 그리다

12 빈칸 추론 ③

해설 빈칸 문장으로 보아 글에서 직업적으로 사람들은 어떠한지를 찾아야 한다. 사람들이 직장 밖에서는 다른 사람들의 이익을 위해 행동하는 베푸는 사람(the giver)으로 행동하는 것이 흔하지만 직장에서는 다른 사람을 도울 때 상호 이익을 추구하고 공정함의 원리에 따라 움직이고 호의의 동등한 교환을 추구한다는 내용이다. 그러므로 빈칸에 들어가기에 가장 적절한 것은 ③ '주는 것과 얻는 것의 동등한 균형을 유지하려고 애쓴다'이다.
① 자신들의 타고난 이기심을 집단의 이익으로 옮긴다
② 자신들의 이익을 집단의 이익과 행복으로 나눈다
④ 이타적이기 보다는 이기적이어서 자신들의 이익을 추구하는 경향이 있다
⑤ 자신들의 손해를 협동으로부터 기대되는 이익과 비교한다

해석 '베푸는 사람'이라는 명칭은 테레사 수녀, 마하트마 간디와 같은 전설적인 영웅들을 위해 남겨두고 싶은 유혹이 들지만, 베푸는 사람이 되는 것이 희생이라는 대단한 행위를 요구하는 것은 아니다. 그것은 다만 도움을 주는 것, 멘토링을 제공하는 것, 공적을 나누는 것 또는 다른 사람을 위해서 연결을 해주는 것 등을 함으로써 타인의 이익을 위한 행위에 초점을 맞추는 것을 포함한다. 직장 밖에서는 이런 형태의 행동은 대단히 흔하다. Yale 대학교의 심리학자 Margaret Clark이 주도한 연구에 따르면, 대부분의 사람들은 가까운 관계에서 베푸는 사람처럼 행동을 한다. 결혼 생활과 교우 관계에서 우리는 이익을 얻지 않아도 할 수 있을 때마다 기여를 한다. 하지만 직장에서는 주고받는 것이 좀 더 복잡해진다. 직업적으로, 사람들은 <u>주는 것과 얻는 것의 동등한 균형을 유지하려고 애쓴다</u>. 그들이 다른 사람을 도울 때, 그들은 상호 이익을 추구함으로써 자신들을 보호한다. 그들은 공정함의 원리에 따라 움직이며, 그들의 관계는 호의의 동등한 교환에 의해서 좌우된다.

구문 [1행~3행] It's tempting <u>to reserve the "giver" label for larger-than-life heroes such as Mother Teresa or Mahatma Gandhi</u>, ~
여기에서 It은 뒤에 나오는 to reserve ~ Mahatma Gandhi를 대신 받는 가주어이다.

[4행~7행] It just involves a focus on acting in the interests of others, / such as by <u>giving</u> help, <u>providing</u> mentoring, <u>sharing</u> credit, or <u>making</u> connections for others.

네 개의 동명사 giving, providing, sharing, making이 콤마(,)와 접속사 or로 연결되어 병렬 구조를 이루고 있다.

어휘 tempting 유혹적인; 매력적인 reserve 남겨두다, 비축하다; 예약하다 larger-than-life 전설[영웅]적인; 실제보다 큰[과장된] extraordinary 대단한, 비범한 credit 공적, 인정; 신용(도) contribute 기여하다; 기부하다 keep score 이익[점수]을 얻다 fairness 공정(함), 공평 govern 좌우하다, 통제하다 even 동등한, 균등한 **[선택지 어휘]** inborn 타고난, 선천적인 selfishness 이기심, 이기주의 collective 집단[단체]의; 공동의 strive to-v v하려고 애쓰다[노력하다] preserve 유지[보존]하다; 지키다, 보호하다 anticipate 기대[고대]하다; 예상하다

---

13 흐름 무관 문장 ④

해설 수은을 축적한 생선은 동등한 양의 셀레늄을 축적하여 수은의 독성 효과를 없앨 수 있다는 내용의 글이므로, 수은에 노출되는 것을 우려하는 사람들이 해산물 섭취를 줄여야 한다는 ④는 글의 흐름과 무관하다.

해석 특히 유기적 형태에 있어서, 수은의 축적은 생선 섭취량이 많은 식단을 가진 인구 집단에게 잘 인식되고 있는 문제들이다. ① 그러나 수은을 축적하고 있는 생선은 또한 동등한 양의 셀레늄을 축적한다는 증거가 존재하고, 셀레늄이 동시에 존재하는 것은 수은의 독성효과를 없앨 수 있다고 믿어진다. ② 매일 수산물 섭취량이 생선 200g과 바다표범 고기 180g으로 구성된 East Greenland의 Inuit 바다 표범잡이 인구 집단에 대한 연구는 혈액 수은 수준이 임상 메틸수은 중독에서 관찰되는 가장 낮은 농도라고 여겨지는 수준인, 200μg/l을 자주 초과했음을 보여 주었다. ③ 이런 높은 수준의 수은에도 불구하고, 독성의 조짐은 없었다. ④ 그러나 수은에 노출되는 것을 우려하는 사람들은 그들의 해산물 음식의 섭취. 특별히 상어나 백참치 같은 먹이 사슬에서 높은 곳에 있는 물고기의 섭취를 제한할 필요가 있다. ⑤ 이것은 바다 표범잡이들과 그들의 가족이 섭취한 생선과 바다표범 고기 내의 높은 수준의 셀레늄의 존재 덕분이다.

구문 **[8행~13행]** A study of *a population of Inuit sealers in East Greenland* [whose daily intake of marine foods was made up of 200g of fish and 180g of seal meat], found // **that** blood mercury levels often exceeded 200 μg/l, a level regarded as the lowest concentrations observed in clinical methyl mercury intoxication.

[ ]는 소유격 관계대명사 whose가 이끄는 절로 a population of Inuit sealers in East Greenland를 수식하고 있고, that 이하는 동사 found의 목적어절이다.

어휘 accumulation 축적 organic form 유기적 형태 well-recognized 잘 인식된 population 인구 (집단); (특정 범주에 속하는) 동물들 intake 섭취(량) equivalent 동등한 simultaneous 동시에 counteract ~의 효과를 줄이다[없애다], 중화하다 toxic 독성의 *cf.* toxicity (유)독성 sealer 바다 표범잡이 marine food 수산물 exceed 초과하다 concentration 농도 clinical 임상의 intoxication 중독 exposure 노출 be attributed to A A 덕분이라고 생각되다, A 탓으로 돌려지다

---

14 글의 순서 ⑤

해설 생태계에 관한 많은 것들이 야생 생물을 연구하는 것으로부터 나왔다는 주어진 글 다음에는 예시로 점박이 올빼미(spotted owls)가 처음 언급된 (C)가 나와야 적절하다. 그 다음으로 점박이 올빼미가 노숙림의 부족에 가장 먼저 영향을 받고 있다고 설명하는 (B)가 나와야 하며, 점박이 올빼미의 개체수와 노숙림을 보고 다른

종들의 상태를 추론할 수 있다고 언급한 (A)가 마지막으로 나와야 한다.

해석 야생 생물의 과학적 가치는 그것이 과학의 발전에 기여하는 역할에서 나온다. 우리가 생태계와 행동에 대해 알고 있는 것의 많은 부분은 야생 생물을 연구하는 것으로부터 나왔다.
(C) 어떤 유형의 야생 생물은 보초병 종으로서 역할을 하여 환경의 건강 상태를 추적 관찰하는 데 이용된다. 예를 들어 점박이 올빼미는 우리가 미국의 태평양 연안 북서부에 충분한 노숙림을 보존해 왔는지를 추적 관찰하기 위해 환경보호 운동가들에 의해 이용된다.
(B) 점박이 올빼미는 넓은 행동 범위를 가지고 있기 때문에 그것들은 노숙림이 부족해질 때 가장 먼저 영향을 받는 종들 중 하나이다.
(A) 그러므로 우리는 만약 점박이 올빼미의 건강한 개체수를 지탱해 줄 충분한 노숙림이 있다면, 그때는 다른 종들이 필요로 하는 것들을 충족해 줄 충분한 양의 숲이 있을 것이라고 추론한다.

구문 **[1행~2행]** The scientific value of <u>wildlife</u> results from *the role* [(which[that] **it** serves] in the advancement of science.
[ ]는 목적격 관계대명사 which[that]가 생략된 관계사절로 선행사 the role을 수식하며, it은 wildlife를 대신한다.

어휘 wildlife 야생 생물 advancement 발전, 진보 ecology 생태계 spotted owl 점박이 올빼미 sufficient 충분한 meet the needs of ~의 필요에 응하다 home range 활동 범위 scarce 부족한, 드문 monitor 추적 관찰하다, 감시하다 environmentalist 환경보호 운동가

---

15 글의 순서 ②

해설 주어진 글에서 저작권에서의 모든 독점권의 이동인 '양도(assignment)'라는 개념에 대한 언급이 나오고 (B)에서 첫 문장의 It은 주어진 글의 assignment를 가리키며, 양도가 어떻게 성립되는지에 대한 내용이 이어진다. (A)에서 첫 문장의 This는 (B)의 두 번째 문장의 양도된 권리를 받은 사람이 법적인 권리를 부여받는다는 내용을 가리키고, 이 내용을 구체적으로 부연설명하고 있으며, 이에 대한 구체적인 예를 드는 (C)가 마지막에 오는 것이 자연스럽다.

해석 저작권 소유자는 저작권 전체나 그것의 어느 부분이든 다른 사람에게 넘길 수 있거나 다른 사람들에게 그 저작물을 복제할 제한적인 허가를 부여할 수 있다. 저작권에서의 모든 독점적인 권리의 이동은 일반적으로 '양도'라고 알려져 있다.
(B) 그것은 서면으로 행해지고 저작권 소유자 또는 소유자의 대리인에 의해 서명이 되어야 한다. 일단 권리들이 양도되고 나면, 그 양도를 받은 당사자는 법규에 의해 저작권 소유자에게 주어진 보호와 처리 방안 모두의 권리를 부여 받는다.
(A) 이것은 양수인이 다른 사람들에게 그 저작을 복제할 허가를 주고 (저작권) 침해에 맞선 (법률상의) 집행을 할 수 있다는 것을 의미한다. 저작권을 양도한 당사자는 그것의 권리들을 모두 양도한다.
(C) 예를 들어, 기사에 대한 모든 권리를 잡지사에 양도한 작가는 더 이상 다른 사람들에게 그 텍스트를 이용할 허가를 부여할 수 없거나 자신의 허가 없이 그 저작을 복제한 당사자들을 고소할 수 없다.

구문 **[11행~14행]** Once the rights are assigned, / *the party* [who receives the assignment] / is entitled to *all of the protection and remedies* (accorded to the copyright owner by the statute).
[ ]는 주격 관계대명사가 이끄는 관계사절로 the party를 수식한다. ( )는 과거분사인 accorded가 이끄는 형용사구로서 앞의 all of the protection and remedies를 수식한다.
[15행~18행] For example, *a writer* [who assigns all rights to an article to a magazine] / can no longer grant permission to others to use the text / or sue *parties* [who reproduce the work without his or her permission].

두 개의 [ ]는 모두 주격 관계대명사가 이끄는 관계사절로 각각 a writer와 parties를 수식한다.

어휘 copyright 저작권, 판권   entire 전체의; 완전한   grant 부여하다, 주다   permission 허가, 승인   exclusive 독점적인   assignment 양도; 과제; 임무; 배정; 배치 cf. assign 양도하다; 배정하다; 배치하다 cf. assignee 양수인   enforce 집행[시행]하다; 강요하다   infringement 침해[위반] (행위)   agent 대리인; 중개상   party (계약) 당사자; (정치) 정당; 일행, 단체   entitle 권리[자격]를 주다   remedy 처리 방안; 해결책; 치료(약); 바로잡다, 개선하다   accord 주다, 부여하다; 부합(하다), 일치(하다); 합의   sue 고소하다, 소송을 제기하다   reproduce 복제하다; 재생[재현]하다; 번식하다

16 문장 넣기   ⑤

해설 주어진 문장의 this는 문맥상 제조업의 (임금이 더 낮은 국가로의) 해외 이전이라 볼 수 있으므로, 해외 이전 문제가 제시된 이후인 ⑤에 문장이 위치해야 한다.

해석 실업의 세 가지 주된 원인은 산업과 경제의 변화, 임금의 변화와 정부 정책의 변화이다. 산업의 변화는 경제에 심대한 영향을 미쳐 왔다. 제조업, 즉 블루칼라 일자리는 자동화의 도래와 더불어 많은 일자리가 상실되었기 때문에 감소해왔다. 블루칼라 노동자가 다시 고용 가능해질 때까지, 그들은 새로운 일자리를 위해 다시 연수를 받아야 한다. 한편, 대개 노동조합 덕분에 유럽, 북미와 일본의 임금은 다른 국가들의 임금과 비교할 때 꽤 높다. 이것이 초래하는 문제는 많은 회사들이 제조업 일자리를 임금이 훨씬 더 낮은 멕시코 같은 국가들로 옮겼다는 것이다. 비록 이것이 많은 기업들에게 도움이 되었지만, 일부 노동자들은 제조업 장소의 변화 때문에 이 국가에서 그들의 일자리를 잃었다. 종종 연방 정부는 경제가 변화에 적응하도록 돕는 것을 목표로 하는 새로운 정책을 도입하겠지만, 몇몇 경제학자들은 실업 수당과 복지와 같은 정책들이 실업을 촉진시키거나 연장하는 데 기여할 뿐이라고 주장한다.

구문 [13행~14행] ~ wages in Europe, North America, and Japan are quite high / when (they(= wages) are) compared with wages of other countries.
when과 compared 사이에 they(= wages) are가 생략된 것으로 볼 수 있다.
[15행~17행] *The problem* [(which[that]) this creates] is // that many companies have moved manufacturing jobs to *countries*, (such as Mexico), / **where** wages are much lower.
[ ]는 앞에 목적격 관계대명사 which[that]가 생략되어 The problem을 수식한다. where 이하는 countries에 대한 설명을 제시한다.

어휘 wage 임금   profound 심오한   advent 도래   automation 자동화   employable 고용할 만한   meanwhile 그동안에   organized labor 노동조합, 조직 노동자   federal 연방의   institute 도입하다   adjust to ~에 적응하다   unemployment compensation 실업 수당   welfare 복지   serve 도움이 되다; 복무하다   prolong 연장하다

17 문장 넣기   ⑤

해설 knowledge of the head(머리의 지식)와 knowledge of the hand(손의 지식)가 대조되는 내용의 글에서 주어진 문장은 손의 지식이 머리의 지식보다 우선적이고 더 근원적이라고 말하고 있다. 그러므로 머리의 지식에서 손의 지식으로 내용이 However로 반전된 ④ 문장 다음, 즉 ⑤에 주어진 문장이 들어가는 것이 적절하다.

해석 지식을 논할 때, 우리는 흔히 이론적인 '머리의 지식'에 초점을 두고 실질적인 '손의 지식'은 간과한다. 정말로, 후자에 대해 약간의 편견이 있는 것 같다. 예를 들어, 과학자의 추상적인 지식은 일반적으로 자동차 정비공이나 장인의 실질적인 지식보다 더 높은

존경을 받고 있다. 이런 편견은 이성을 사용하는 우리의 능력이 우리를 동물 세계의 나머지와 구별해 주는 것이라는 널리 퍼진 가정에서 생기는 수도 있다. 하지만, 사물을 조작할 수 있는 우리의 능력은 매우 독특하고, 마주 볼 수 있는 엄지손가락을 지닌 손은 불룩 나온 두개골을 지닌 머리만큼 인간 지능의 좋은 상징이라고 주장할 수 있을 것이다. 실제로 어떤 의미에서는 실질적인 지식은 이론적인 지식보다 앞서며 더 근본적이다. 결국, 우리는 어떤 종류의 지식이라도 습득할 수 있기 전에, 말하는 능력과 사물을 조작하는 능력과 같은 기본적인 기술을 필요로 한다.

구문 [10행~13행] This prejudice may derive from the widespread assumption // **that** our capacity for reason is **what** distinguishes us from the rest of the animal kingdom.
that 이하는 동격의 명사절로 the widespread assumption을 부연설명하고, what은 동사 is의 보어절을 이끌고 있다.

어휘 there is a sense in which 어떤 의미에서는 ~이다   know-how 실제적[전문적] 지식   prior to ~에 앞선, ~보다 중요한   fundamental 근본적인   theoretical 이론적인   overlook 간과하다   practical 실질적인   prejudice 편견, 선입관   abstract 추상적인   esteem 존중, 평가   craftsman 장인   derive from ~에서 나오다[유래하다]   widespread 널리 퍼진   assumption 가정, 추정   distinguish 구별하다, 분별하다   manipulate 조작하다, 능숙하게 다루다   opposable thumb 마주 볼 수 있는 엄지손가락

18 요약문 완성   ①

해설 주입된 새로운 정보가 잘못된 것이어도 이미 이전에 저장되었던 정보를 대체한다는 것을 실험을 통해 설명한 글이므로, 이것을 요약하여 완성하면 '사후의 정보는 원래의 기억을 바꾸고(altering), 진짜처럼 보이는 왜곡된(distorted) 기억을 만들 가능성이 매우 크다.'가 된다.
② 강화하는 것 – 왜곡된   ③ 강화하는 것 – 자세한
④ 재개하는 것 – 자세한   ⑤ 바꾸는 것 – 자세한

해석 대체 이론은 기억 속에 들어오는 새로운 정보가 이미 저장된 이전의 정보를 대체한다고 주장한다. 이 이론을 지지하는 연구는 잘못된 정보가 사람들의 원래 기억을 대체한다는 것을 보여 준다. 예를 들어, 한 연구는 두 그룹의 사람들에게 자동차 사고에 대한 사진을 보여 주었다. 한 그룹에서는 사진이 실제로는 정지 표지를 보여 주었을 때, 연구원들은 사람들이 양보 표지를 보았다고 생각하도록 만들기 위해서 유도 질문을 했다. 다른 그룹에 있는 사람들은 유도 질문을 받지 않았고, 따라서 정지 표지를 본 것을 기억했다. 두 그룹이 나중에 함께 모였을 때, 그들은 그 실험에 숨겨진 목적을 듣고 자신이 속게 된 그룹 일부였다고 생각하는지를 추측해 보라고 요청받았다. 속게 된 그룹의 거의 모든 사람은 자기들은 진짜로 양보 표지를 보았고 속지 않았다고 주장했다. 이것은 연구원들이 주입된 기억이 실제 기억을 대체한다고 결론을 내리게 하였다.

↓

> 한 심리학 연구에 따르면, 사후의 정보는 원래의 기억을 (A) 바꾸고, 진짜처럼 보이는 (B) 왜곡된 기억을 만들 가능성이 매우 크다.

구문 [1행~3행] The replacement theory holds // that *new information* (entering the memory) replaces *old information* (already stored).
that 이하는 holds의 목적어 역할을 하며 that은 접속사이다. ( )는 각각 앞에 위치한 new information과 old information을 수식한다.

어휘 replacement 대체   hold 주장하다   mislead 속이다   leading question 유도 질문   yield 양보(하다)   claim 주장하다   deceive 속이다   conclude 결론을 내리다   implant 주입하다   post-event 사후의   genuine 진짜의   **[선택지 어휘]** alter 바꾸다   distorted 왜곡된   reinforce 강화하다   renew 재개하다

해설 19. 긍정적 자기진술이 자존감이 높은 사람에게는 기분과 자기평가를 더 좋게 해주지만 자존감이 낮은 사람에 대해서는 오히려 기분과 자기평가를 더욱 악화시키는 결과를 가져올 수 있다는 내용의 글이므로 제목으로 가장 적절한 것은 ① '긍정적 단언: 친구인가 적인가?'이다.

② 긍정적인 단언은 전염성이 있다!
③ 감정의 양면: 긍정성과 부정성
④ 긍정적인 사고는 잊고, 단지 좀 더 현실적으로 되어라
⑤ 긍정적 자기 진술은 기분과 자아존중감을 신장시킨다

20. (c)의 뒷부분의 내용을 보면 "나는 마음이 넓은 사람이야."나 "나는 나 자신을 전적으로 인정해"와 같은 일반적인(general) 진술보다 "나는 사람들에게 좋은 선물을 골라주지."와 같은 구체적(specific) 진술이 논박과 상세한 고려가 의미 없으므로 더욱 효과적일 수 있다고 했으므로, general을 specific으로 바꿔 써야 한다.

해석 캐나다의 심리학자 Joanne V. Wood와 동료들은 '긍정적인 자기진술'의 효과를 검증해보기로 결정했다. 연구자들은 자존감이 낮다고 보고된 사람들에게 다음의 단언을 암송하도록 요청했다. "나는 사랑받을 만한 사람이다." 그들은 그러고 나서 이 사람들의 기분과 그들의 자기 자신에 대한 감정을 측정했다. 전반적으로 낮은 자존감 집단은 긍정적 단언을 암송하도록 지시받은 후 기분이 더 나빠졌다. 반면에 자존감이 높다고 보고된 사람들은 기분이 더 나아졌다. 심리학자들은 그 후 참가자들에게 자기 자신에 대한 부정적인 그리고 긍정적인 생각을 나열해보라고 요청했다. 발견된 것은 자존감이 낮은 사람들이 자기 자신에 대한 부정적인 생각을 갖는 것을 허용 받았을 때 더 나은 기분 상태가 되었다는 것이다. 사실 피실험자들은 긍정적인 단언에 집중하도록 요청 받았을 때보다 부정적인 생각을 하면서 더 기분 좋은 상태에 있었다. 연구자들은 "나는 사랑받을 만한 사람이다"와 같은 긍정적인 칭찬과 단언이 자존감이 낮은 사람들의 사고방식과 (a) 맞지 않았다고 말한다. 이것은 갈등의 감정과 단지 기분 나쁜 것으로 이어졌고, 이는 그러고 나서 자

기 자신에 대한 더욱 (b) 부정적인 생각들로 이어졌다.
긍정적인 생각은 그러면 무가치한가? Wood는 그렇게 생각하지 않는다. 그녀는 사람들이 논쟁을 벌이거나 지나치게 상세하게 고려하는 것이 불가능한 매우 (c) 일반적인(→ 구체적인) 진술들을 하는 상황에서, 혹은 위태로운 주된 문제가 전혀 없을 때 그것이 효과를 발휘할 수 있을 것이라고 말한다. 예를 들어 사람들은 "나는 마음이 넓은 사람이야."보다는 "나는 사람들에게 좋은 선물을 골라주지."를 말하면 더 잘될지도 모른다. 그러나 그녀가 말하는 것처럼, "나는 나 자신을 전적으로 인정해"와 같은 (d) 불합리하게 긍정적인 자기진술이 자기계발서에 의해 종종 장려된다. 우리의 결과는 그러한 자기진술이 목표로 하여 고안된 바로 그 사람들, 즉 자존감이 낮은 사람들에게 (e) 해를 끼칠지도 모른다는 점을 암시한다."

구문 [8행~9행] ~ the group with low-esteem felt worse / after **being made to recite** the positive affirmation.
사역동사 「make O 원형부정사」는 수동태로 쓰이면 「be made to-v」로 동사원형이 to-v로 바뀌게 된다.

[16행~18행] In fact, the subjects were in a better mood thinking negative thoughts / than they <u>were</u> / **when** asked to focus on positive affirmations.
were는 대동사로 were in a mood를 나타낸다. when 다음에는 they(the subjects) were가 생략되어 있다.

[35행~37행] Our results suggest that such self-statements may harm *the very people* [(that) they are designed for] ~
[ ]는 앞에 목적격 관계대명사 that이 생략되어 the very people을 수식한다.

어휘 colleague 동료   statement 진술   self-esteem 자아존중감   recite 암송하다   affirmation 확언, 단언   across the board 전반적으로   list 목록을 나열하다   subject 피실험자   mindset 사고방식   at stake 위태로운   better off 형편이 더 나은   self-help book 자기계발서

제 2 회

본문 p.12

| 1 ① | 2 ⑤ | 3 ③ | 4 ③ | 5 ② | | 6 ③ | 7 ⑤ | 8 ③ | 9 ① | 10 ⑤ |
| 11 ① | 12 ① | 13 ④ | 14 ② | 15 ⑤ | | 16 ⑤ | 17 ② | 18 ② | 19 ⑤ | 20 ④ |

1 심경 변화   ①

해설 Jeff는 다이빙대가 자신이 생각했던 것보다 훨씬 높아 손에 땀이 나고 속이 메스꺼웠지만, 뛰어내리고 나선 활짝 웃는 얼굴로 힘차게 수영을 하며 물 위로 돌아오는 상황이므로 Jeff의 심경 변화는 ① '초조한 → 자신감 있는'이다.

② 창피한 → 놀란   ③ 질투하는 → 평화로운
④ 짜증 난 → 안도한   ⑤ 불안해하는 → 무서운

해석 오늘은 Jeff의 수영 수업에서 중요한 날이었다. 모든 학생들은 높은 다이빙대에서 수영장의 수심 깊은 곳으로 뛸 예정이었다. Jeff가 다이빙대로 걸어갔을 때, 그는 이상한 느낌이 들기 시작했다. 그것은 그가 생각했던 것보다 훨씬 높았고, 그의 손은 땀이 나기 시작했다. 다이빙대에 올라선 후, 그는 주변을 둘러보았고 포기하는 것에 대해 생각했다. 그 높이는 그의 속을 메스껍게 만들었다. 그때 그는 자신의 형이 수영장 가에 앉아 미소를 짓고 있는 것을 보았다. 이것이 Jeff가 필요로 한 동기였다. 마음이 바뀌기 전에, 그는 침을 삼키고 뛰기로 결심했다. 그것은 순식간에 끝났다. 곧, Jeff는 활짝 웃는 얼굴로 수영장 가장자리 쪽으로 힘차게 수영을 하며 물 위로 돌아왔다. 그는 세상에서 어떤 것도 할 수 있을 것 같은 느낌이 들었다.

구문 [8행] The height **made** *his stomach* **turn**.
여기에서 made는 사역동사이며, 「make+O+C」 구문으로 목적격보어로 원형부정사가 쓰였다. 'O로 하여금 C하게 만들다'의 뜻이다.

어휘 deep end (수영장 등의) 수심이 깊은 곳[쪽]   sweaty 땀에 젖은, 땀이 나서 축축한   back down 포기하다; 후퇴하다, 퇴각하다   make one's stomach turn ~의 속을 메스껍게 만들다[뒤집어 놓다], ~의 기분을 나쁘게 하다   swallow hard 침을 삼키다   in an instant 순식간에; 곧, 당장, 즉시   edge 가장자리; 모서리; (칼 등의) 날   grin (소리 없이) 활짝[크게]웃다

2 밑줄 함의   ⑤

해설 기억이 비디오카메라처럼 작동하여 불변하고 신뢰할 수 있다고 믿는 일반 대중의 믿음이 잘못된 것임을 지적하는 글이다. 첫 문장에서 경험은 시간이 지나며 분해되고 다른 경험들과 통합되어 경험이 발생한 방식과 다르게 인간이 기억할 수 있으므로 인간의 기억은 퇴비 더미처럼 부패하고 변질되기 마련이라는 추론을 할 수

있다. 따라서 ⑤ '우리의 기억은 시간이 흐르며 쉽게 혼합되고 왜곡될 수 있다'가 가장 적절하다.
① 우리의 기억은 기록된 순서로 차례차례 배열된다
② 우리의 기억 오류는 우리의 환경 변화로 인해 발생한다
③ 우리의 기억은 점차 사라지지만, 그중 일부는 두드러진다
④ 우리의 경험은 우리의 신경계에서 종종 잘못 이해된다

해석 우리의 경험은 많은 세부사항과 구조를 여전히 보유하면서도 가장 최근의 것으로 축적되지만, 시간이 흐르며 그것들은(경험은) 결국 부서지고 우리의 나머지 경험들과 통합된다. 그것이 우리가 종종 경험이 실제로 발생한 방식과 다르게 그것을 기억하는 이유이다. 심리학자 Dan Simons와 Chris Chabris는 최근에 1,500명의 미국의 성인들을 조사하여 일반 대중이 견지하는 근본적인 오해를 발견했다. 약 3분의 2(63퍼센트)의 성인들은 기억이 나중에 다시 재생될 수 있는 경험을 기록하는 비디오카메라처럼 작동한다고 생각했다. 응답자 중 절반은 일단 기억이 형성되면 그것은 불변하고 신뢰할 수 있다고 믿었다. 이러한 오해는 영구적인 저장고라는 어떤 개념을 불러일으키는 정보 저장의 다른 방식들과의 비교로 이어졌다. 일반적인 은유는 인간의 기억을 막대한 정보를 저장하고 있는 거대한 도서관과 비유하는 것인데, 이는 옳지 않다. 오히려 인간의 기억은 퇴비 더미와 같다.

구문 [6행~9행] Psychologists Dan Simons and Chris Chabris recently surveyed 1,500 US adults [and] discovered *fundamental misunderstandings* (held by the general public).
밑줄 친 두 개의 동사구가 and로 연결되어 병렬구조를 이룬다. ( )는 과거분사 held가 이끄는 분사구로 fundamental misunderstandings를 수식한다.
[9행~12행] About two out of three adults (63 percent) thought that memory works like *a video camera*, **recording** experiences [that can be played back later].
recording 이하는 a video camera를 수식하는 분사구이다. [ ]는 관계대명사절로 선행사 experiences를 수식한다.

어휘 lay down ~을 모아서 축적하다[쌓다]; ~을 내려놓다; 그만두다[포기하다] retain (계속) 보유[유지]하다; 간직하다 integrate 통합시키다[되다] fundamental 근본[본질]적인; 핵심[필수]적인 misunderstanding 오해 general public 일반 대중 reliable 신뢰할[믿을] 수 있는 misconception 오해, 그릇된 생각 evoke 불러일으키다; 환기시키다 permanent 영구적인; 불변의 metaphor 은유; 비유 liken A to B A를 B에 비유하다 compost heap 퇴비 더미; 불필요한 물건[서류]을 쌓아두는 곳 [선택지 어휘] stand out 두드러지다[눈에 띄다]; 견디다 distort 왜곡하다; 비틀다

---

3 글의 요지 ③

해설 각각의 명작은 독특한 면을 지니고 있지만, 공통적으로 사람들을 매료시키는 특성을 지니고, 모든 시대의 인류에게 공통적인 경험을 표현하고 있다는 내용의 글이다. 따라서 이 글의 요지로 가장 적절한 것은 ③이다.

해석 "아름다움은 보는 사람의 눈에 있다." 이 진술이 사실일지도 모르나, 어떤 예술 작품들은 많은 '보는 사람들'의 눈에 아름답게 보인다. 비록 그런 명작들은 독특하지만, 그것들은 어떤 특성들을 공통적으로 가지고 있다. 파블로 피카소의 '세 명의 음악가'는 그의 스타일의 이해를 통해서만 해석될 수 있다. 경험이 풍부한 미술 애호가조차 자신이 보고 있는 것에 관해서는 확신을 갖지 못할 수도 있다. 하지만 그것을 이해하건 이해 못 하건간에, 그는 그 작품에 강한 흥미를 느낄 것이다. 수련으로 가득 찬 연못 위의 일본식 다리를 그린 모네의 그림도 마찬가지로 매력적이다. 짧은 순간 동안 흘깃 보는 것조차 작품을 찬미하는 사람에게 자신이 보고 있는 것에 대해 의심의 여지를 남기지 않는다. 하지만 각각의 작품들은 명작들이다. 각 작품은 언제까지나 보는 사람의 바로 그 영혼을 끌어당겨서 그들을 매료시킨다. 각각은 그저 특정한 시대가 아닌 모든 시대의 인류에게 공통적인 경험을 표현한다.

구문 [9행~11행] Equally appealing is **Claude Monet's painting of a Japanese bridge over a pond full of water lilies**.
「C+V+S」 형태의 도치구문으로, 주어의 길이가 상당히 긴데 상대적으로 보어의 길이가 짧으면 이해를 쉽게 하기 위해 종종 보어를 앞으로 보내고 도치시킨다. Claude Monet's painting과 a Japanese ~ water lilies는 동격 관계이다.
[13행~14행] Each indefinitely attracts the viewer, **drawing his very soul to them**.
drawing ~ them은 주절의 주어 Each를 의미상 주어로 하는 능동 분사구문이다.

어휘 beholder 보는 사람, 구경꾼 statement 진술, 서술; 성명 have A in common A를 공통적으로 가지고 있다 interpret 해석[이해]하다; 통역하다 experienced 경험이 풍부한; 능숙한 as to A A에 관해서는 comprehend 이해하다 intrigue 강한 흥미[호기심]를 불러일으키다 appealing 매력적인; 호소하는 (듯한) water lily ((식물)) 수련 glance 흘깃 봄; 휙[흘깃] 보다 admirer 찬미하는 사람, 팬 indefinitely 무기한으로; 막연히 very 바로 그[이]; 매우, 아주 mankind 인류; (모든) 인간, 사람들 era 시대

---

4 글의 주제 ③

해설 나쁜 행동을 하는 어린이가 왜 그러한 행동을 하는지를 살펴보면, 감정적 연결과 긍정적인 관심을 기반으로 한 사회적 연결에 대한 기본적 필요가 충족되지 않은 것이 근원임을 알 수 있다. 따라서 이 글의 주제로 가장 적절한 것은 ③ '어린이의 나쁜 행실을 연결에 대한 욕구로 이해하기'가 된다.
① 어린이들의 사회적 기술을 향상시키는 데 있어서 부모의 역할
② 훈육을 통해 나쁜 행동을 하는 어린이에 대처하는 방법
④ 양육 방식과 어린이의 나쁜 행실 간의 관계
⑤ 다양한 사회적 연결이 어린이에게 좋은 이유

해석 어린이들이 나쁜 행동을 할 때, 행동이란 외부와 단절된 상태에서 발생하는 것이 아니므로 좌절감, 화 혹은 심지어 분노의 감정으로 반응하기가 대단히 쉽다. 우리의 감정에 기반을 두고 반응하기보다는 이 순간에 우리 아이의 진정한 필요를 숙고해보기 위해 잠시 멈출 수 있다. 왜 아이들이 진짜로 나쁜 행동을 하는가? 그 질문에 답하기 위하여 우리는 먼저 그러한 짜증스럽고 좌절감을 주고 사람을 미치게 하는 행동의 근원을 파악해야 한다. 우리 아이들이 정말로 짜증스럽고 비이성적인 것 같은 방식으로 나쁜 행동을 하고 있을 때, 그것은 흔히 심리적 필요, 즉 사회적 연결의 결과이다. 우리 아이들의 가장 깊숙한 욕망은 우리와 그들 주변에 있는 다른 사람들과 관계를 맺는 것이다. 그것은 단지 우리가 타고난 방식이다. 소속은 우리가 서로에게 필요로 하는 감정적 연결과 긍정적인 관심을 나타낸다. 이러한 선천적인 필요 둘 다가 충족되지 않는다면 아이들은 나쁜 행동을 할 것이다. 일단 연결이 이루어지면, 어린이들은 예의 바른 교정에 마음을 열게 된다.

구문 [1행~3행] When children misbehave // it can be very easy to react with frustration, resentment or even anger // because behavior doesn't happen in a vacuum.
it이 가주어, to react ~ even anger가 진주어이다.
[14행~16행] Belonging refers to *the emotional connection and positive attention* [(which[that]) we need with one another].
[ ]는 목적격 관계대명사 which[that]이 생략된 관계사절로 the emotional connection and positive attention을 수식한다.

어휘 misbehave 나쁜 행동[못된 짓]을 하다 *cf.* misbehavior 나쁜 행실; 부정행위; 비행(非行) frustration 좌절감, 불만(스러운 점) *cf.* frustrating 좌절감을 주는, 불만스러운 resentment 분노, 억울함, 분개 in a vacuum 외부와 단절된 상태에서 maddening 미치게[격노하게] 하는 irritating 짜증나게[화나게] 하는; 거슬리는 irrational 비이성

[비논리]적인　hardwired 타고난; 하드웨어에 내장된　belong 소속하다; 소속감을 느끼다　refer to A A를 나타내다; A와 관련 있다　innate 선천적인, 타고난　meet 충족시키다
[선택지 어휘] parent 부모; 양육하다; 어버이의　enhance 향상시키다; 높이다　cope with 대처하다, 다루다　discipline 훈육; 지식 분야

5 글의 제목　　

해설 팀의 명칭을 '창의적 마케팅'으로 바꾼 후, 실제로 팀 구성원이 놀라울 정도로 상상력을 발휘하여 창의적으로 되었다는 한 회사의 예를 통해 명칭을 어떻게 부르느냐가 실제 수행에 영향을 미친다는 것을 보여주는 내용이므로 제목으로 가장 적절한 것은 ② '당신은 당신 자신을 부르는 대로 된다'이다.
① 때로는 사소한 일에 목숨을 걸라
③ 창의적인 어휘가 창의적인 사람을 만든다
④ 소비자를 위해 변화하는 것을 두려워 마라
⑤ 회사에서 당신의 역할을 상상력으로 재정의하라

해석 Facebook에서, Randi Zuckerberg는 팀원들에게 팀의 명칭을 '소비자 마케팅'에서 '창의적 마케팅'으로 바꾸겠다고 말했다. 그것이 작은 변화인 것처럼 보인다는 사실에도 불구하고, 그것은 그 집단에 즉각적인 영향을 미쳤다. 비록 회사의 다른 사람들은 아무도 그 명칭의 변화에 대해서 알지 못했지만, 즉시 팀 구성원들은 스스로를 회사의 창의력이 있는 중추로 재정의했다. 며칠 안에 그 팀은 공간을 재구성하였는데, 가구와 물품들을 새로 들여오고 자신들의 창의적 성과물을 전시하기 위해 미디어 벽도 고안해 만들었다. 그들은 더 많은 혁신적인 아이디어를 내놓기 시작했고 회사 내에서 새롭게 정의된 그들의 역할을 반영한 새로운 계획안을 제안했다. 그 팀이 엄청나게 창의적이었지만 새로운 아이디어를 만들어 내는 것이 자신들의 주요 역할이라는 것을 이전에는 생각하지 못했었다는 것이 아주 분명해졌다. 명칭의 변화가 그들이 상상력을 발휘할 수 있도록 명백한 허가를 그들에게 제공해 주었다.

구문 [4행~5행] Despite the fact that it seemed like a small change, it had an instant impact on the group.
접속사 that이 이끄는 that ~ change와 앞선 명사 the fact는 동격 관계이다.
[8행~11행] Within a few days, the team reorganized the space, **bringing in new furniture and supplies and designing a media wall to showcase their creative accomplishments**.
bringing ~ accomplishments는 동시상황을 나타내는 분사구문이다.

어휘 impact 영향(력)　redefine 재정의하다　hub 중추, 중심(지)　firm 회사; 단단한; 확고한　showcase 전시[진열]하다; 진열(장)　accomplishment 성과, 업적; 성취　innovative 혁신적인, 획기적인　reflect 반영하다; 반사하다　abundantly 아주, 풍부하게　incredibly 엄청나게, 믿을 수 없을 만큼　primary 주요한, 주된; 초기[최초]의　generate 만들어 내다, 생산하다　explicit 명백한, 뚜렷한　permission 허가, 허락
[선택지 어휘] sweat the small stuff ((속담)) 사소한 일에 목숨 걸다

6 안내문 일치　　③

해설 ③ 비회원은 강의료가 300달러인데 회원은 20% 할인받는다고 했으므로 60달러 할인이 맞다.
① 대상 연령은 17세 이상의 연령이라고 했다.
② 일주일에 개설되는 2개의 강좌 중 하나만 선택하면 된다고 했다.
④ 심폐소생(CPR) 마스크를 포함한 모든 강의 자료가 강의료에 포함되었다고 했다.
⑤ 등록은 온라인, 전화와 직접 등록으로 적어도 일주일 전까지 하라고 했다.

해석　YMCA 구조원 강좌
우리 프로그램은 여러분에게 구조의 기초 분야에서 자격증을 줄 뿐만 아니라 여러분이 응급 처치와 심폐소생술을 하도록 준비시킬 것입니다. 이것은 신나고 보람 있는 직업으로 가는 첫 단계입니다!
연령: 강좌에 등록하려면 학생들은 반드시 17세 이상이어야 합니다.
언제: 7월 11일 – 8월 21일
• 아래 두 강좌 중 하나를 선택할 수 있습니다.
– 월요일, 오후 4시 – 오후 7시 30분
– 토요일, 오전 10시 – 오후 2시
연락처: 이메일: ccdavies@bulkmail.net
　　　　　전화: 447-349-0010
비용: 비회원은 300달러, YMCA 회원은 20% 할인을 받습니다.
(이것은 정보를 제공하는 소책자와 심폐소생술 마스크를 포함한 모든 강좌 자료를 포함합니다.)
등록: 온라인은 www.lifeguardcert.org로, 전화는 447-349-0010으로, 혹은 직접 하려면 시내 YMCA로, 적어도 일주일 전에 등록하십시오. 강좌가 빨리 차니 미루지 마십시오!

어휘 lifeguard 구조원, 감시원; 구조원으로 일하다　first aid 응급 처치　certify in ~에 대한 자격증[면허증]을 주다　rewarding 보람 있는　informational 정보의, 정보를 제공하는　booklet 소책자, 팸플릿　in person 직접　fill up 가득 차다

7 밑줄 어법　　

해설 ⑤ those는 the participants를 지칭하고, who 다음의 대동사는 앞의 does not win or place라는 일반동사를 대신하므로 are를 do로 바꿔 써야 한다. 여기서 do는 win or place를 지칭한다.
① timely는 '시기적절한'이라는 뜻의 형용사로, 명사 feedback을 수식한다.
② whether ~ or prizewinner는 about의 목적어 역할을 하는 명사절이며, 「whether A or B」는 'A인지 B인지'의 뜻이다.
③ 「shift O to v-ing」는 'O를 v하는 것으로 전환하다'의 뜻이다. to가 전치사이므로 동명사 demonstrating은 적절하다.
④ requires와 같은 '요구'의 뜻을 가지는 동사는 「require + that + S′ + (should +) 동사원형」의 형태로 사용되면 'S′가 V할 것을 요구하다'의 뜻으로 쓰인다. go 앞에 should가 생략되어 동사원형 형태가 온 것은 적절하다.

해석 경쟁 활동은 최고는 인정받고 나머지는 무시되는, 단지 수행 기량을 보여 주는 공개 행사 그 이상이 될 수 있다. 참가자에게 수행 기량에 대한 시기적절하고 건설적인 피드백을 제공하는 것은 일부 대회와 경연이 제공하는 자산이다. 어떤 의미에서는 모든 대회가 피드백을 제공한다. 많은 경우에 이것은 참가자가 수상자인지에 관한 정보로 제한된다. 그러한 유형의 피드백을 제공하는 것은 반드시 탁월함이 아니라 우월한 수행 기량을 보여 주는 것으로 강조점을 이동하는 것으로 해석될 수 있다. 최고의 대회는 단순히 승리하는 것이나 다른 사람을 '패배시키는 것'이 아니라, 탁월함을 장려한다. 우월성에 대한 강조는 우리가 일반적으로 경쟁의 해로운 영향을 조장하는 것이라고 간주하는 것이다. 수행 기량에 대한 피드백은 프로그램이 '이기거나, 입상하거나, 보여 주는' 수준의 피드백을 넘어설 것을 요구한다. 수행 기량에 관한 정보는 이기지 못하거나 입상하지 못하는 참가자뿐만 아니라 이기거나 입상하는 참가자에게도 매우 도움이 될 수 있다.

구문 [13행~15행] The emphasis on superiority is **what** we typically see as fostering a detrimental effect of competition.
관계대명사 what이 이끄는 명사절이 문장의 보어 역할을 하고, 이때 what은 관계사절 내 see의 목적어로 볼 수 있다.
[17행~19행] Information about performance can be very helpful, **not only** to *the participant* [who does not win or place] **but also** to *those* [who **do**].
「not only A but also B」는 'A뿐만 아니라 B도'의 뜻이다. A와 B 자리에 모두 to로 시작하는 전명구가 위치해 있다. 첫 번째 [ ]는 the participants를, 두 번째 [ ]는

those를 수식하며 those는 the participants를 나타낸다.

어휘 showcase 공개 행사; 진열장　overlook 무시하다, 간과하다　provision 제공
timely 시기적절한　constructive 건설적인; 구조상의　asset 자산　restrict 제한
하다　superior (~보다 더) 우월한[우수한]　*cf.* superiority 우월[우수]성　foster 조성
하다　detrimental 해로운　place 입상하다; 놓다[두다]

8 밑줄 어휘 　③

해설 ③ 앞 문장에 있는 a positive one in the presentation of fact를 통해 텔레비
전은 '실제의' 세상에 대해서 가르치는 강력한 도구가 될 수 있다는 것을 알 수 있으
므로, imaginary는 real로 바꾸어야 한다.

해석 아이들은 책을 텔레비전보다 더 빠르게 허구로 인식한다. 분명히, 인쇄물이 그것이
상징하는 사물과 사건들을 물리적으로 닮지 않았다는 사실은 그 내용을 현실 세계와 분
리하는 것을 ① 더 쉽게 해준다. 따라서, 많은 사람들이 두려워해 왔듯이, 텔레비전은 실
제 행동을 보여주면서, 공상을 현실로 바꾸는 데 있어 보다 더 ② 유혹적인 매체이다. 하
지만 허구를 보여주는 데 있어서 부정적 영향인 것이 사실을 보여주는 데 있어서는 긍정
적인 것이 될 수 있다. 텔레비전은 ③ 가상의(→ 실제의) 세상에 관해 아이들을 가르치기
위한 대단히 강력한 매체가 될 수 있다. 스칸디나비아에서 만약 열한 살짜리가 똑같은 뉴
스 사건에 대해 텔레비전, 부모, 교사, 그리고 신문을 통해 배운다면, ④ 다수는 주로 텔레
비전에 의존할 것이라는 것이 밝혀졌다. 그들은 텔레비전을 ⑤ 최고의 정보 매체로 간주
하고, 텔레비전에서는 '당신은 스스로 무슨 일이 일어나는지를 볼 수 있다'고 말한다.

구문 [2행~5행] Apparently, / the fact that print does not physically resemble
the things and events [(which[that]) it symbolizes] / makes *it* easier **to separate
its content from the real world**.

the fact와 that ~ symbolizes는 동격 관계이다. [ ]는 목적격 관계대명사 which 또
는 that이 생략된 관계사절로 the things and events를 수식한다. makes 다음의 it
은 가목적어이고, to separate ~ real world가 진목적어이다.

[12행~15행] In Scandinavia / it was found // that if eleven-year-olds learn of
the same news event / from television, parents, teachers, and the newspaper,
/ the majority will rely primarily on television.

it은 가주어, that if ~ on television이 진주어이다.

어휘 recognize 인식하다; 인정하다　fiction 허구, 꾸며낸 이야기; 소설　apparently
분명히, 명백하게　resemble 닮다, 유사하다　symbolize 상징하다　separate 분리
[구분]하다; 분리된　tempting 유혹적인　medium 매체, 수단; 중간의　transform
바꾸다; 변형시키다　extremely 대단히; 극도로　compelling 강력한; 설득력 있는
imaginary 가상의, 상상의　majority 다수　primarily 주로; 처음에는

9 빈칸 추론 　①

해설 빈칸 문장으로 보아 '어떠한' 행동이 앞 문장에 나왔고, 동물 세계 전반에서
나타나는지 찾아야 한다. 빈칸 앞부분의 다른 등산객이 뱀을 보고 움찔하는 것을 보
고 당신도 놀란다는 내용과 한 마리의 새가 날아오르면 다른 새들도 함께 날아오른
다는 뒷부분의 내용을 통해 빈칸에는 ① '모방하는'이 들어가는 것이 가장 적절하다.
② 감정적인 ③ 계산된 ④ 위협하는 ⑤ 비생산적인

해석 타인의 자세에서 위험을 감지하는 능력은 신경 과학자 Beatrice Gelder에 의해 연
구되어 왔다. 그녀의 연구는 관찰자의 뇌가 심지어 두려워하는 얼굴 표정보다 두려움을
나타내는 자세를 취하는 사람의 신체 언어에 더 강하게 반응한다는 것을 보여주었다. 두
려워하는 표정은 두려움에 근거한 우리 자신의 강력한 반응을 마비시키거나, 혹은 적어도

생기게 할 수는 있다. 하지만, 얼굴 표정이 위험을 전달함에 있어서 강력하다 하더라도, 한
사람의 긴장한 자세와 수상한 움직임이 우리를 훨씬 더 불편하게 만든다. 당신도 몸을 휘
감고 있는 뱀의 쉿쉿 하는 소리를 듣기 아주 짧은 시간 '전'에 당신 앞에 있는 등산객이 갑
자기 움찔하는 것에 당신도 깜짝 놀라지 않겠는가? 이러한 종류의 모방 행동은 동물 세계
전반에서 나타난다. 예를 들어, 만약 땅 위에 있는 새 떼 중 한 마리가 갑자기 날아오르면,
모든 다른 새들은 그 후 즉시 따라갈 것이다. 그들은 그 이유를 알 필요도 없다.

구문 [3행~6행] Her research has demonstrated // that *the brain* (of an
observer) reacts [more] powerfully / to the body language of a person in *a
posture* (indicating fear) // [than] **it does** even to a fearful facial expression.
( )는 a posture를 수식하는 분사구이다. than 뒤의 it은 the brain을, does는 reacts
를 각각 받는다.

[8행~11행] Yet, **as powerful as** facial expressions are in conveying danger,
// a person's uptight posture and furtive movements / make us even more
uncomfortable.

「as+원급+as」가 문두에 나오면 양보의 부사절을 이끌며, (al)though facial
expressions are powerful in conveying danger의 의미와 같다.

어휘 detect 감지하다; 발견하다　posture 자세; 태도　neuroscientist 신경 과학자
demonstrate (증거, 실례를 통해) 보여주다, 설명하다; 시위하다　indicate 나타내다. 가리
키다　look 표정; 보기; 보다, 바라보다　paralyze 마비시키다; 무력하게 하다　evoke
(감정 등을) 생기게 하다, (불러)일으키다　potent 강력한; 효과적인　uptight 긴장한, 불안
한　startle 깜짝 놀라게 하다　split second 아주 짧은 시간, 순식간　coil 휘감다, 돌
돌 말다; 고리　flock (특히 새의) 떼, 무리; (많은 수가) 모이다

10 빈칸 추론 　⑤

해설 구체적인 심리적인 몰입(a specific psychological commitment)을 하려고
자신의 과업을 글로 적어본 것이 과업을 달성하는 효과적인 행동 계기가 되었다는
내용이므로 빈칸에는 ⑤ '작은 정신적 투자'가 들어가야 적절하다.
① 쓰기 기술　　② 널널한 마감시간
③ 무의식적 행동　④ 예기치 않은 전략

해석 Peter Gollwitzer와 그의 동료 Veronika Brandstatter는 행동 계기를 이용하는 것이
행동에 동기를 부여하기 위한 매우 효과적인 방법이라는 것을 발견했다. 그들의 연구는
구체적인 심리적 몰입이 강력한 행동 계기로서 작용할 수 있다는 것을 보여주었다. 한 연
구에서 그들은 크리스마스이브를 어떻게 보냈는가에 대한 보고서를 써서 제출함으로써
수업에서 추가 학점을 얻을 수 있는 선택권을 가졌던 대학생들을 추적했다. 그러나 함정
이 하나 있었다. 그들은 학점을 따기 위해서는 반드시 12월 26일까지 보고서를 제출해야
만 했다. 많은 학생들이 보고서를 쓸 의사는 충분히 있었지만 그들 중 단지 33퍼센트만이
시간을 내서 글을 써서 제출했다. 그 연구의 다른 학생들은 행동 계기를 설정하도록 요구
받았다. 다시 말해 미리 정확히 언제, 어디에서 그들이 보고서를 쓸 생각인지를 적어 보도
록 (예를 들면, "모든 사람들이 일어나기 전인 크리스마스 아침에 거실에서 이 보고서를
쓰겠다.") 요구 받았다. 그 학생들의 75퍼센트라는 인상적인 비율이 보고서를 썼다. 그것
은 그런 작은 정신적 투자였다는 점을 고려해 볼 때 아주 놀라운 결과이다.

구문 [12행~15행] Other students in the study were required to set action
triggers — **to note**, in advance, exactly when and where they intended to
write the report ~.

to note 이하는 앞에 나온 내용을 부연 설명하는 것으로 to 앞에 they(= other
students in the study) were required가 생략된 것으로 보면 이해하기가 쉽다.

어휘 specific 구체적인　psychological 심리적　commitment 몰입, 전념
function 작용하다　trigger 계기, 유발　track 추적하다　credit 학점　catch 함정
intention 의사, 의도　impressive 인상적인, 감명 깊은

11 빈칸 추론 ①

해설 문자 소통이 시각적이고 청각적 연결이 없으므로 갖는 한계점을 설명한 글이다. 빈칸 문장에서 의사소통에 물리적인 것이 없으면 '어떠한지'를 묻고 있고, 이어지는 내용에서 타이핑된 문자는 딱딱하고 냉정하며 상대방의 신원을 확인할 수 없다고 했다. 따라서 빈칸 문장은 ① '친밀함과 신뢰의 감각을 감소시킬(지도 모른다)'가 적절하다.
② 흥미롭고 신비로운 감정을 증가시킬
③ 표현의 자유와 신체 언어를 허용할
④ 새로운 형식의 문자 소통을 탄생시킬
⑤ 이해의 결여와 관련되어 있지 않을

해석 문자 소통은 그것에 능숙한 사람들에게조차 분명 문제를 일으킨다. 듣는 것과 보는 것이 없으므로 그것은 풍부한 감각상의 만남이 아니다. 여러분은 다른 사람들의 얼굴을 보거나 그들이 말하는 것을 들을 수 없다. 목소리, 신체 언어, 신체적 외형에 의해 제공되는, 대인 관계의 모든 중요한 단서가 사라지는데, 이는 사람들이 서로를 이해하는 방식을 극적으로 바꿔버릴 수 있다. 그런 단서가 없으면 상대방을 오해하기가 더 쉽다. 여러분의 온라인 친구는 여러분이 모르는 사이에 아프거나 취해 있거나 우울할지 모른다. 일부 사람들에게, 목소리와 외형의 단서가 만들어내는 물리적 존재가 없는 것은 <u>친밀함과 신뢰의 감각을 감소시킬지도 모른다</u>. 타이핑된 문자는 딱딱하고, 거리감 있고, 냉정하고, 지지와 공감의 어조가 없는 것으로 느껴진다. 사실 시각적이고 청각적인 연결 없이 여러분은 상대방의 신원에 대해 결코 완전히 확신할 수는 없다. 이러한 대면을 통한 단서의 부재는, 약간의 익명성을 보태는데, 일부 사람들이 부적절하게 행동하도록 부추긴다.

구문 [4행~7행] *All the important interpersonal cues* (provided by voice, body language, and physical appearance) disappear, // **which** can dramatically alter how people relate to each other.
( )는 All the important interpersonal cues를 수식한다. which는 앞 절 전체를 선행사로 하는 관계대명사이다.

어휘 sensory 감각[지각]상의 encounter 만남 interpersonal 대인 관계의 cue 단서 alter 바꾸다 relate to A A를 이해하다 companion 친구, 동료 presence 존재, 실재 unemotional 냉정한 supportive 지지가 되는 auditory 청각의 absence 부재, 없음 [선택지 어휘] intimacy 친밀함 novel 새로운

12 빈칸 추론 ①

해설 빈칸 문장으로 보아 반려동물이 농업에 대한 부담을 증가시키는 이유가 '무엇'인지를 찾아야 한다. 과거에 반려동물의 먹이는 인간이 먹는 음식을 만드는 중에 버려지는 것(human food manufacturing waste)이었는데, 지금은 인간들이 먹는 수준의 재료로 만들어지고 있기 때문에 농업에 부담이 되는 것으로, 빈칸에는 ① '그들이 더 이상 '먹다 남은 것으로 만든' 제품을 먹고 있지 않기'가 들어가는 것이 가장 적절하다.
② 현재 반려동물 먹이의 안전성에 대한 기준이 없기
③ 반려동물 먹이를 공급하는 사람들 사이의 경쟁이 치열하기
④ 농부들이 '예측 불가능함'에 의해 제한되는 경향이 있기
⑤ 그들의 먹이는 '일상품'으로 변한 '사치품'이기

해석 반려동물 먹이는 과거에는 동네 사료 가게나 식료품 가게에 있는 모든 것들 중에서 작은 봉지, 중간 봉지, 또는 큰 봉지를 선택하는 것에 관한 것이었다. 오늘날에는, 170억 달러 규모의 미국 시장에 있는 수백 가지의 다양한 먹이 가운데 반려동물 먹이를 고르는 것은 복잡한 일이 될 수 있다. 소고기, 오리고기, 야채, 그리고 연어가 오늘날 반려동물 식단의 일부이다. 한 때 인간의 식품 제조 중에 버려지는 것에서 이득을 얻기 위해 만들어졌지만, 반려동물 먹이 산업은 이제 사람이 먹는 수준의 재료로 잘 팔리는 제품을 만드는데, 그 이유는 사람들이 자신이 아끼는 반려동물을 위해 더 좋은 것을 원하기 때문이다. 인간이 먹는 수준의 재료로 만든 반려동물 먹이를 구매하는 사람들의 수는 계속 증가하고 있다. 그 결과, 반려동물은 정말로 농업에 대한 부담을 증가시키고 있는데, 그 이유는 <u>그들이 더 이상 '먹다 남은 것으로 만든' 제품을 먹고 있지 않기</u> 때문이다.

구문 [7행~11행] Once created to profit from human food manufacturing waste, / the pet food industry now makes *products (with human-grade ingredients)* [that sell well] // because people want something better / for their beloved animal companions.
( )는 전명구로 앞의 products를 수식하며, [ ]는 관계사절로 products with human-grade ingredients를 수식한다.

어휘 medium (치수·양·길이·온도 등이) 중간의; 매체, 수단 feed 사료, 먹이; 사료[먹이]를 주다 stock (물품을) 가지고 있다; 비축하다; 재고(품), 저장품 variety 종류; 다양성 salmon 연어 profit from ~에서 이득[이익]을 얻다 food manufacturing 식품 제조 ingredient 재료, 성분 companion 반려, 친구; 상대 burden 부담[짐](을 지우다) agriculture 농업, 농사 [선택지 어휘] leftover 먹다 남은; 남은 음식 standard 기준, 수준; 일반적인 fierce 치열한; 격렬한; 사나운 restrict 제한[한정]하다 unpredictability 예측 불가능

13 흐름 무관 문장 ④

해설 이 글은 기상 상태와 기후에 따라 온실의 여러 형태와 기능이 결정된다는 주제를 뒷받침하는 여러 예시들이 제시되고 있는 흐름이다. 그런데 ④는 지붕이 안전 규정을 만족하고 있는지 확인하기 위해서 전문가에게 연락할 것을 권하는 내용이므로 글의 흐름과 무관하다.

해석 계절에 따라 다른 기상 상태는 언제나 온실 채소 재배자들의 관심사이다. ① 기후는 온실이 언제 어떻게 이용될 것인지를 결정할 뿐만 아니라 애초에 구조물을 어떤 유형으로 지어야 할지를 결정한다. ② 예를 들어 폭설을 빈번하게 경험하는 추운 날씨의 기후에서는, 경사가 큰 지붕이 이상적일 수 있는데, 왜냐하면 그것이 얼음과 눈이 미끄러져 내리는 것을 효율적으로 도와줌으로써 그것들이 쌓이는 것을 막을 수 있기 때문이다. ③ 더 적은 강설량을 보이지만 차갑고 강한 바람이 부는 지역에서는, 구조물 대부분이 땅 아래 들어간 온실인, 태양열 지하온실이 가장 최선의 선택일 수 있는데, 왜냐하면 그것이 자연적으로 단열처리가 되어 가동하는 데 열을 덜 필요로 하기 때문이다. ④ <u>이런 이유로 여러분의 지붕이 안전 규정을 만족하고 있는지 확인하기 위해서 전문가에게 연락을 하는 것은 좋은 생각이다.</u> ⑤ 기후가 더 온화한 지역에서는 이와 똑같은 종류의 구조물이 실용적이지 못할 수도 있다.

구문 [13행~15행] For this reason, / it's a good idea <u>to contact a professional / in order to *ensure*</u> // (that) your roof satisfies safety regulations.
it은 가주어이고, 진주어는 to contact 이하이다. ensure 다음에는 목적어절을 이끄는 접속사 that이 생략되었다.

어휘 seasonal 계절에 따라 다른 snowfall 강설량 high-pitched 경사가 큰 ideal 이상적인 build-up 증가, 축적 efficiently 효과적으로, 능률적으로 slide 미끄러져 내리다 structure 구조물 house 보관[수용]하다; 살 곳을 주다 safety regulations 안정 규정 temperate (기후가) 온화한

14 글의 순서 ②

해설 피고인 측이 피고의 긍정적인 성격을 증언해줄 증인을 내세울 수 있다는 주어진 글 뒤에 이러한 종류의 증언(this kind of testimony)이 역설적으로 피고인의 유

죄 선고 가능성을 증가시킬 수 있다는 (B)가 이어지고, 이러한 역설적인 결과(This ironic outcome)가 생기는 이유는 증인이 판단이 잘못되었다는 것을 보여주는 검사의 반대 심문이 있을 수 있기 때문이라는 (A)가 이어진다. 다음으로 그러한 반대 심문의 구체적인 예(For example)가 나오는 (C)가 이어지는 것이 자연스럽다.

해석 어떤 상황에서, 피고인 측은 피고가 특정 범죄를 저질렀을 것 같지 않게 만들 수 있는 그의 긍정적인 성격을 묘사해줄 증인을 소개할 수 있다.
(B) 비록 이런 종류의 증언이 피고를 도울 것이라고 예상할지도 모르지만, 연구는 긍정적인 성격 증거가 배심원들의 유죄 선고나 유죄 판결의 가능성에 거의 영향을 미치지 않는다는 것을 보여준다. 역설적이게도, 성격 증거의 사용은 사실은 피고가 유죄를 선고받을 가능성을 증가시킬지도 모른다.
(A) 이 역설적인 결과는 성격 증거의 증인들이 피고인의 성격을 잘 판단하지 못한다는 것을 보여주려 하기 위해 검찰 측이 그들에게 반대 심문을 할 수 있기 때문에 생겨난다. 반대 심문을 하는 동안, 검사는 증인에게 그녀의 증언과 모순되는 피고가 행한 이전 행동에 대해 알고 있는지를 물을 수 있다.
(C) 예를 들어, 검사는 "당신은 피고가 친절하고 유순하다고 말했습니다. 그가 주먹 싸움에서 다른 학생을 다치게 한 후 고등학교에서 퇴학당했던 것을 알고 있습니까?"라고 말할 수 있다. 배심원들은 오직 성격 증거 증인의 신뢰성을 평가하기 위해서만 이 정보를 사용하기로 되어있을지라도, 그것은 피고에 대한 그들의 인상에도 역시 영향을 미칠지도 모른다.

구문 [1행~4행] ~, the defense can introduce witnesses to describe *positive characteristics* (of a defendant) [that would make *it* unlikely <u>that he committed a particular crime</u>].
전명구 ( )와 관계대명사절 [ ]가 각각 positive characteristics을 수식한다. [ ]에서 it은 가목적어이고, that ~ crime이 진목적어이다.
[8행~11행] During cross-examination, prosecutors might **ask** *a witness* **whether she knows about *previous behaviors by the defendant* [that contradict her testimony]**.
a witness는 ask의 간접목적어이고, whether ~ her testimony가 직접목적어이다. [ ]는 주격 관계대명사가 이끄는 관계사절로 앞에 있는 previous behaviors by the defendant를 수식한다.

어휘 circumstance 상황, 환경, 정황 the defense 피고(인) 측 *cf.* defendant 피고(인) witness 증인; 목격자; 목격하다 commit (범죄를) 저지르다; 약속하다; 헌신하다 ironic 역설적인, 아이러니한 outcome 결과 cross-examine 반대 심문하다 contradict 모순되다; 부정[부인]하다, 반박하다 testimony 증언; 증명, 증거 juror 배심원 guilt 유죄(임); 죄책감 likelihood 가능성, 가망 conviction 유죄 판결 [선고]; 신념, 의견 *cf.* convict 유죄를 선고하다[입증하다] paradoxically 역설적이게도, 역설적으로 injure 상처를 입히다[입다]; 해치다 fistfight 주먹 싸움, 주먹다짐 evaluate 평가하다, 감정하다 credibility 신뢰성

15 글의 순서 ⑤

해설 주어진 글의 내용은 환경 파괴 없이 지속될 수 있으려면 고려해야 할 요인이 많다는 것이므로 어떤 요인들이 있는지 구체적인 예를 들어 서술을 시작하는 (C)가 뒤따르는 것이 자연스럽다. (B)는 (C)에서 언급된 친환경적인 건물의 부정적인 면을 however로 연결하고 있고 (A)는 (B)를 뒷받침하는 내용이므로 (C) – (B) – (A)의 순서가 되어야 한다.

해석 환경 파괴 없이 지속될 수 있는 것에는 다양한 측면이 있으며, 비록 당신이 그 측면들에 대해 모두 다루기를 원한다고 결심할지라도, 문제는 건물이 다양한 요소의 복잡한 집합체라는 것이다. 균형을 이루어야 할 많은 다른 요소가 항상 있을 것이다.
(C) 예를 들어, 당신이 멀리 외떨어진 곳에 있는 아름다운 공원 옆에 건물을 위치시킨다면, 태양을 이용하도록 그 건물을 완벽하게 일직선으로 만들고 소음이 거의 없을 것이기

에 열리는 창문을 설치하는 것이 가능할 것이다.
(B) 그러나 그 건물을 이용하는 대부분의 사람들이 그곳에 대중교통이나 도보 또는 자전거로 도달하는 것은 가능하지 않을 것이다. 거의 모든 사람들이 운전을 해야 할 것이다.
(A) 연구에 의하면, 그러한 장소에 있는 대단히 친환경적인 건물의 전반적인 탄소 발자국은, 대중교통이 잘 연결된 도심에 있는 이상에 못 미치는 건물의 그것(탄소 발자국)보다 더 클 것이다.

구문 [6행~9행] ~ *the overall carbon footprint* of a super-green building (in such a location) / **will be** larger than ***that*** of a less-than-ideal building in *a city center* (well connected to public transport).
the overall carbon footprint가 주어이고 will be가 동사이다. than 뒤의 that은 the overall carbon footprint를 지칭한다.
[10행~12행] **It** will not, however, be possible / for *most users* of the building / to reach it by public transport / or to walk or cycle there.
It은 가주어이고 밑줄 친 두 개의 to-v구가 진주어이며, most users는 to-v의 의미상의 주어이다.

어휘 address (문제를) 다루다, 고심하다 element 요소 overall 전반적인 in the middle of nowhere 멀리 외떨어진 곳에 있는 align 나란히 하다 take advantage of ~을 이용하다

16 문장 넣기 ⑤

해설 전통적으로 인간이 환경에 맞춰 미기후를 만들어 냄으로써 생존 방법을 개발했지만, 화석 연료의 발견 이후 건물을 기후 환경에 맞출 필요성이 적어지게 되었다는 내용이 역접을 이룬다. 주어진 문장은 건물의 실내를 항상 온도 면에서 편안하게 하는 중앙 냉난방 시스템을 갖추게 되었다는 내용으로 화석 연료의 발견 이후인 현대의 방법을 설명하므로 ⑤에 들어가야 적절하다.

해석 인간은 두드러지게 기략이 풍부하여 우리의 조상들은 지구상의 모든 환경에서 아주 잘 생존할 방법을 개발할 수 있었다. 사막, 툰드라, 또는 정글에서 살기 원하는가? 문제 없다. 사람들은 자신들의 환경의 한계와 제약 안에서 일할 수 있는 방법을 찾았다. 한 해의 일부 기간 정말 더웠더라도, 그들에게는 중앙 냉방 장치를 설치할 선택권이 없었다. 대신에, 그들은 온도 면에서 편안한 미기후(微氣候)를 만들어 냄으로써 시원하게 지내는 방법을 찾아냈다. 하지만 화석 연료를 발견한 이후에, 건물을 지역 기후 환경에 맞출 필요성이 덜 중요해졌다. 건물은 실내가 냉난방이 되고, 따라서 항상 온도 면에서 편안하게 하는 중앙 냉난방 시스템을 갖추어 세워질 수 있었다. 결과적으로, 편안함을 유지하는 전통적인 방법 중 많은 것들이 사라지거나 잊혔다.

구문 [1행~4행] Buildings could be constructed with *a central heating and air-conditioning system* [**that** allowed the interior to be <u>climate controlled</u> <u>and</u> thus <u>thermally comfortable</u> at all times].
[ ]는 관계대명사 that이 이끄는 형용사절로 a central ~ system을 수식한다. 두 개의 밑줄 친 형용사구는 and로 병렬 연결된다.
[14행~16행] However, after the discovery of fossil fuels, / *the need* (to fit a building into the local climatic environment) became less important.
( )는 형용사적 용법으로 쓰인 to부정사로 the need를 수식한다.

어휘 air-conditioning 냉방; 공기 조절 interior 실내; 내부 climate controlled 냉난방이 되는 remarkably 두드러지게, 눈에 띄게 resourceful 기략이 풍부한, 수단이 좋은 tundra 툰드라, 동토대 constraint 제약; 강제 option 선택(권) install 설치하다 central air 중앙 냉방 장치 figure out 찾아내다; 알아내다 fossil fuel 화석 연료 fit A into B A를 B에 맞추다

17 문장 넣기 ②

해설 이 글은 효과적인 설득법에 관한 내용이다. 글의 초반에서 육군신병 훈련을 받던 시절을 회상하며, 효과적인 설득 전략을 사용했던 한 부사관에 관한 이야기를 하고 있다. ② 이후부터 군대에서 직장에서의 상황으로 흐름이 전환되고, 상사가 '왜 이 일이 자네와 우리 조직에 중요한지'에 관하여 이야기하는 것이 주어진 문장에서 말한 '바라는 일을 하게 시키는 것'에 해당한다. 따라서 주어진 문장은 ②에 위치하는 것이 자연스럽다.

해석 내가 육군 신병 훈련을 받던 시절 한 부사관이 지뢰에 대한 교육을 시행하고 있는 동안 내가 동료에게 이야기하고 있을 때 설득의 한 전형적인 사례가 발생했다. 그는 우리 대화를 갑자기 중단시켰고 "이봐, 내가 너희에게 말하는 것을 잘 듣는 게 나을 거야. 그게 너희들의 목숨을 구할 수 있을 거니까."라고 말했다. 내 목숨이라는 관심을 끄는 것으로 그가 나를 설득했기에, 그때부터 나는 열심히 귀를 기울였다. 사업의 세계에서는 사람들이 이해 주었으면 하고 여러분이 바라는 일을 그들이 하도록 끊임없이 시켜야 한다. 여러분이 직장 상사라면 여러분의 부하 직원에게 "여기 당신이 해 줬으면 하는 일이 있습니다. 어떤 질문도 하지 마십시오. 그냥 하세요."라고 말하며, (남을) 조종하는 전략을 사용할 수 있다. 아니면 "여기 당신이 해 줬으면 하는 일이 있습니다. 시작하기 전에, 왜 이 일이 당신과 우리 조직에 중요한지를 먼저 의논해봅시다."와 같이 설득력이 있는 전략을 사용할 수 있다. 지도자는 관심을 끄는 것으로 설득한다. 바보들은 힘으로 조종한다.

구문 [7행~8행] You'**d better listen** to what I'm telling you, boy, // because it could save your life.

「had better v」는 'v하는 것이 낫다'의 뜻이다.

[14행~16행] Before you get started, // let's first **discuss** [**why** it's important to you and our organization].

[ ]는 관계부사 why가 이끄는 관계절이며, 동사 discuss의 목적어 역할을 한다.

어휘 be challenged to-v v해야 한다, v하도록 요구받다   persuasion 설득(력) *cf.* persuasive 설득력이 있는   conduct 실시하다   land mine 지뢰   abruptly 갑자기   interrupt 중단시키다   be all ears 열심히 귀를 기울이다   hook 관심을 끄는 것   manipulative 조종하는 *cf.* manipulate 조종하다   tactic 전략   subordinate 부하 직원   idiot 바보

18 요약문 완성 ②

해설 작곡가가 아무리 문서상으로 꼼꼼히 연주 방식을 기입한다 해도 공연자가 그 표시를 철저히 존중하지 않고 '재해석(reinterpretation)'할 여지가 있으며, 공연자 능력의 한계상 작곡가의 의도를 재현할 수 없을지도 모르므로 작곡가는 자신의 음악을 '통제할(control)' 수 없다.

① 통제하다 - 단련   ③ 비판하다 - 단련
④ 비판하다 - 재해석   ⑤ 모방하다 - 재능

해석 노래는 공연자가 그것을 문서화된 페이지에서 가져와야 비로소 생명을 얻는다. 좋건 나쁘건, 작곡자는 개인들이 그의 작품을 해석할 방식을 알지 못한다. 작곡가들은 노래에 대한 자신의 의도를 가수와 피아니스트에게 전달하기 위해 문서화된 페이지에 많은 표시를 하겠지만 그러한 의도가 항상 존중받는 것은 아니다. 명확한 조 및 박자표, 박자와 다른 표시면 충분할 것 같지만, 가수들과 피아니스트들이 항상 엄격하게 표시를 고수하는 것은 아니다. 진정한 노래 공연은 또한 곡의 난이도와 공연자의 능력과 한계에 달려 있다. 예를 들어, 한 젊은 가수가 고인이 된 드뷔시의 노래를 공연하려고 애쓰고 있는데 프랑스어로 노래해본 적이 없다면, 언어에 대한 도전은 그녀가 작품의 뉘앙스를 통달하지 못하게 막을 수 있을 것이다. 음성적 부족함은 주의를 음악에서 끌어내어 가수 자신에게 향하게 할 수 있다. 이러한 이유로, 가수들이 자신의 연령과 능력에 적합한 음악을 공연하는 것이 결정적으로 중요하며 동일한 것이 피아니스트에게도 해당한다.

↓
> 작곡가들이 음악을 작곡한 후에는 자신들의 음악을 많이 (A) 통제할 수 없는데 각각의 공연이 공연자의 곡에 대한 (B) 재해석 및 그의 능력에 달려 있기 때문이다.

구문 [1행~2행] A song does **not** come to life **until** performers take it off the written page.

「not A until B」는 'B하고 나서야 비로소 A하다'의 뜻이다.

[14행~16행] ~ the challenges of the language could **prevent** her **from mastering** the nuances of the piece.

「prevent O from v-ing」는 'O가 v하지 못하게 막다'의 뜻이다.

어휘 for better or for worse 좋건 나쁘건   marking 표시   intention 의도   honor 존중하다   adhere to A A를 고수하다   authentic 진짜인   late 고인이 된, 이미 사망한   nuance 미묘한 차이, 뉘앙스   deficiency 결점, 결함

19~20 장문 19 ⑤ 20 ④

해설 19. 영국 사이클 팀의 코치로 새로 부임한 Brailsford가 자전거 안장 새로 디자인하기, 타이어에 알코올 바르기, 트럭 내부 흰색으로 칠하기 등과 같은 사소한 개선을 통해서 거의 100년간 뚜렷한 성과를 내지 못했던 영국 사이클 팀을 올림픽에서 우승하도록 이끌었다는 내용이므로 정답은 ⑤ '사소한 개선: 영국 사이클 운명의 게임 체인저'이다.
① 목표는 잊고, 대신에 시스템에 집중하라
② 완벽한 장비가 여러분을 완벽한 사이클리스트로 만든다
③ 영국 사이클의 절정이 그저 잊히게 놔두지 마라
④ 무적의 사이클 선수는 어떻게 실패의 상징이 되었는가

20. 트럭 내부를 흰색으로 칠해서 사이클 선수들이 정교하게 튜닝된 자전거의 성능을 저하시킬 수도 있는 먼지를 발견해서 제거할 수 있도록 도와주었다고 했으므로 (d)의 upgrade를 '저하시키다'라는 뜻의 degrade로 바꾸어 써야 한다.

해석 영국의 프로 사이클링의 관리 기관이었던 British Cycling은 최근 Dave Brailsford를 새로운 감독으로 고용했다. 당시 British Cycling은 뛰어난 성적을 거둔 영국 사이클 선수 없이 거의 100년 동안 (a) 미미한 시기를 견뎌 냈다. Brailsford는 British Cycling을 새로운 궤도에 올려놓기 위해 고용되었다. Brailsford를 이전의 코치들과 다르게 만든 것은 자신이 (b) 작은 개선의 집합이라고 불렀던 전략에 대한 끊임없는 헌신이었다. Brailsford는 여러분이 프로 사이클 팀에서 기대할 수 없을지도 모르는 약간의 조정을 함으로써 시작했다. 자전거 안장이 더 편안하게 느껴지도록 다시 디자인되었고, 더 나은 접지력을 위해 타이어에 알코올이 문질러졌다. 사이클 선수들은 경기력을 (c) 향상시키기 위해 이상적인 근육 온도를 유지시키는 전기로 가열되는 사이클복을 입도록 요구받았고, 선수들이 특정한 운동에 어떻게 반응하는지 관찰하기 위해 바이오피드백 센서가 이용되었다. 하지만 그는 거기서 멈추지 않았다. 사이클 팀의 트럭 내부는 흰색으로 칠해졌는데, 이것은 일반적으로 눈에 띄지 않은 채로 지나치겠지만 정교하게 튜닝된 자전거의 성능을 (d) 향상시킬(→ 저하시킬) 수 있는 작은 먼지들을 사이클 선수들이 발견해서 제거하는 데 도움을 주었다. 감기에 걸릴 가능성을 줄이도록 손을 씻는 가장 좋은 방법을 가르치기 위해 의사가 고용되기까지 했다. 수백 개의 다른 아주 작은 개선들이 축적됨에 따라서, 그 결과는 그 누가 상상했던 것보다 더 빨리 찾아왔다. Brailsford가 취임한 지 5년 후, 2008년 베이징 올림픽에서 British Cycling 팀은 사이클 종목을 (e) 지배했는데, 그곳에서 그들은 수여되는 금메달 중에서 무려 60%를 획득했다.

구문 [3행~6행] At the time, British Cycling had endured nearly one hundred years of insignificance / **with** *no British cyclist* **achieving** outstanding results.

「with + O + v-ing/p.p.」는 동시동작을 나타낸다. 목적어 British cyclist가 '(목표를) 성취하다'라는 능동의 의미이므로, 현재분사 achieving이 쓰였다.

[8행~10행] What made him different from previous coaches **was** his relentless commitment to a *strategy* [that he **referred to as** the aggregation of small gains].

명사절 주어(What ~ coaches)가 왔으므로 단수동사 was가 쓰였다. [ ]는 선행사 a strategy를 수식하는 관계대명사절이다. 「refer to A as B」는 'A를 B라고 부르다'의 뜻이다.

[20행~24행] The inside of the team truck was painted white, // which helped cyclists spot and remove *little bits of dust* [that would normally slip by unnoticed

[but] could degrade the performance of the finely tuned bikes].

which 이하는 앞 절(This inside ~ white) 전체를 선행사로 하는 계속적 용법의 관계대명사절이다. [ ]는 little bits of dust를 수식하는 관계대명사절이다.

어휘 governing body 관리부, 이사회 endure 견디다, 참다 relentless 끊임없는, 집요한 commitment 헌신 aggregation 집합 adjustment 조정, 수정 jersey 사이클복 spot 발견하다 finely 정교하게, 섬세하게 accumulate 축적되다, 쌓이다 dominate 지배하다 astounding 놀라운, 놀랄만한

1 ②	**2** ①	**3** ②	**4** ③	**5** ④		**6** ⑤	**7** ⑤	**8** ④	**9** ③	**10** ③
11 ⑤	**12** ②	**13** ④	**14** ⑤	**15** ③		**16** ②	**17** ④	**18** ②	**19** ④	**20** ②

1 글의 목적   ②

해설 편지의 내용으로 보아 수신 단체가 굶주린 사람들에게 먹을 것을 주는 일을 한다고 했으므로 무료 급식 단체에게 쓰는 글임을 알 수 있다. 편지 중반에 유감스럽게(Regretfully)로 시작하는 문장에서 자기들이 최대 기부 한도에 도달해서 현재로서는 기부를 할 수 없다고 했으므로 글의 목적으로 가장 적절한 것은 ②이다.

해석 Victoria Food Bank께:

귀하의 자선 단체인 Victoria Food Bank의 업무와 그것의 지속적인 지원 필요성에 관한 귀하의 최근 서신에 대해 Michigan Islanders 단체를 대표해서 감사드립니다. 귀하의 편지에 근거하면 귀하의 단체가 바로 여기 우리 지역에서 굶주린 사람들에게 먹을 것을 주어 돕고 우리 지역의 삶의 질을 향상시키는 데 중요한 역할을 하고 있음이 분명합니다. 우리는 귀하가 우리의 관심을 끌기 위해 시간을 들여 애써주신 것에 깊이 감사드립니다. 유감스럽게도 우리가 매일 받는 엄청난 수의 요청을 고려해볼 때, Michigan Islanders는 우리의 최대 기부 한도에 도달했기 때문에 현재로서는 귀하의 우수한 단체에 기부를 제공해 드릴 수 없습니다. 그러나 귀하를 앞으로 나아갈 수 있게 해줄 추가 자원을 모색할 때 귀하가 저희 기관에 접촉했던 것에 대해 우리는 감동했고 영광스럽게 생각합니다. 다시 한번, Michigan Islanders의 모든 사람을 대표해서 귀하의 편지에 감사드리며 성공적인 행사를 기원합니다.

Mark Foster 올림

구문 **[5행~9행]** Based on your letter, / **it** is clear **that** your organization is playing an important role *in* helping feed the hungry right here in our area [and] enhancing our region's quality of life.

it은 가주어, that 이하가 진주어이다. 전치사 in의 목적어로 밑줄 친 두 개의 동명사구가 and로 연결되어 병렬 구조를 이룬다.

[15행~18행] We are touched and honored, however, that you reached out to our organization // as you seek *the additional resources* [that will enable you to move forward].

[ ]는 주격 관계대명사 that이 이끄는 관계사절로 the additional resources를 수식한다. [ ] 내에서 「enable+O+to-v(O가 v할 수 있게 하다)」 구문이 사용되었다.

어휘 on behalf of ~을 대표[대신]하여; ~ 때문에 correspondence 서신, 편지; 일치; 대응 ongoing (계속) 진행 중인 enhance 향상시키다, 높이다 regretfully 유감스럽게도 enormous 엄청난, 거대한 outstanding 우수한, 뛰어난; 두드러진 contribution 기부(금), 성금; 기여

2 필자 주장   ①

해설 제 역할을 다하기 위해 전문화가 필요하긴 하지만 새로운 생각, 즉 창의적인 생각을 하는 경우엔 오히려 방해가 될 수 있고, 다양한 출처를 가질수록 더욱 독창적이게 될 수 있다는 것이 주제이므로, 필자의 주장으로 가장 적절한 것은 ①이다.

해석 전문화는 피할 수 없는 인생의 현실이다. 세상에서 제 역할을 하기 위해, 당신은 자신의 초점을 좁히고 자신의 시야를 한정시켜야 한다. 그러나 당신이 새로운 생각을 만들어 내려고 노력할 때, 정보를 다루는 그런 태도는 당신을 제한할 수 있다. 그러한 태도는 당신이 자신의 문제를 너무 좁게 제한하도록 강요할 뿐만 아니라 당신이 아이디어를 위해 바깥 영역을 바라보는 것 또한 막을지도 모른다. 사실, 당신의 출처가 다양하면 다양할수록, 당신이 창조해내는 아이디어들이 더 독창적일 가능성이 크다. 다른 사람들이 성공적으로 사용했던 새롭고 흥미로운 아이디어들을 세심히 살피는 것을 습관으로 삼아라. 당신의 아이디어는 당신이 애쓰고 있는 문제에 적용하는 데 있어서만 독창적이면 된다.

구문 **[8행~9행]** Indeed, **the more** divergent your sources (are), **the more** original *the idea* [(which[that]) you create] is likely to be.

「the 비교급 ~, the 비교급 ...」은 '~하면 할수록, 더 ...하다'의 의미이다. [ ]는 목적격 관계대명사 which 또는 that이 생략된 관계사절로 선행사 the idea를 수식한다.

어휘 specialization 전문[특수]화; (의미의) 한정 a fact of life 피할 수 없는 인생의 현실 function (제대로) 역할을 하다; 기능[작용]하다 narrow 좁히다; 좁은; 편협한 *cf.* narrowly 좁게; 가까스로; 면밀히 generate 만들어 내다; 발생시키다 handle 다루다, 처리하다 attitude 태도, 자세 restrict 제한[한정]하다 divergent 다양한, 일치하지 않는; 갈라지는 source 출처; 원천, 근원 original 독창적인; 원래[본래]의 make it a rule to-v v하는 것을 습관[규칙]으로 삼다 be on the lookout 세심히 살피다[지켜보다] adaptation 적용 work on A A에 애쓰다

3 밑줄 함의   ②

해설 '나쁜' 학과장은 교수와 자원을 배정할 때 형편없는 결정을 내리며 비생산적인 회의를 여느라 교수들의 시간을 낭비한다. 비생산적인 회의에서 중요한 존재인 '음료를 휘젓는 빨대'는 이러한 '나쁜' 학과장과 반대되는 '리더십과 효율성을 갖춘 학과장'일 것이다. 따라서 밑줄 친 부분이 의미하는 바는 ② '학과는 리더십과 효율성을 갖춘 학과장을 필요로 한다.'이다.

① 학과장의 부담은 경감되어야 한다.
③ 어떤 교수들은 학과장이 되는 것이 그들의 연구에 방해된다고 생각한다.
④ 학과장의 역할은 학부의 운영을 검사하는 것이다.
⑤ 학과장은 의사결정에 참여할 책임이 있다.

해석 최고 대학의 대부분의 교수들은 연구로부터 시간을 앗아가는 의무를 등한시한다. 그들은 행정 업무를 지루한 일이라고 생각하고, 모두가 다른 사람이 학과장이 되기를 바란다. 책임을 무시한 결과 대부분의 학과는 마땅한 상태보다 덜 흥미로운 장소가 된다. 나쁜 학과장들은 중요한 강좌 수업과 귀중한 학과 공간과 시설 사용을 배정할 때 어리석은 선택을 내린다. 부적절한 교수들이 학과 세미나를 처리하고 도서관이 계속해서 아무도 읽지 않는 학술지를 구매하게 한다. 학과 회의는 회의실에 산소가 없어질 때까지 중요한 문제를 다루는 것 없이 너무 오래 계속된다. 음료를 휘젓는 빨대는 아주 중요하다. 학과장이 되는 것이 똑똑한 교수의 시간 중 10퍼센트가 넘는 시간을 소비하는 것이 될 필요는 없는데, 이는 아마 그가 다른 사람들이 내린 형편없는 결정에 대해 불평하느라 낭비할지도 모르는 것보다 적을 것이다.

구문 [2행~4행] They **see** administration **as** a bore, // and everyone **wants** *someone else* **to be** the department chairman.
「see A as B」는 'A를 B로 보다'의 뜻이다. 두 번째 절의 「want+O+C(to-v)」 구문은 'O가 v하기를 원하다'로 해석한다.
[15행~18행] Being chairman **need** not consume / more than 10 percent of an intelligent professor's time, / possibly less than he or she might **waste griping about** *bad decisions* (made by others).
Being chairman이 동명사 주어이며 need는 조동사여서 뒤에 동사원형 consume이 나왔다. 「waste (시간) v-ing」는 'v하는 데 (시간을) 낭비하다'의 뜻이다. ( )는 bad decisions를 수식하는 과거분사구이다.

어휘 disregard 등한시[무시]하다(= neglect)　administration 행정 (업무)
department chairman 학과장　academic department 학과　assign 배정하다
faculty member 교수진　journal 학술지　address (문제를) 다루다　stir 휘젓다
count for a lot 아주 중요하다　possibly 아마

4 글의 주제　　　　　　　　③

해설 우리는 나이를 먹어감에 따라 뇌세포의 기능과 조직이 점진적으로 저하된다고 생각하지만, 노화된 뇌에서 새로운 세포의 생성, 운동으로 인한 신경조직 형성의 향상, 노화된 신경 세포의 성장 등이 과학적으로 발견되고 줄기세포 연구가 계속 진행됨에 따라 손상 부분을 재생시킬 가능성이 높아졌다는 것이 글의 요지이다. 그러므로 ③ '과학적 발견을 통해 젊음을 되찾을 가능성'이 글의 주제로 가장 적절하다.
① 노화를 긍정적인 성장 경험으로 재정의하는 것
② 기대 수명의 증가에 영향을 미치는 요인들의 발견
④ 늙은 동물들의 신경 세포 악화의 자연적인 결과
⑤ 건강한 노화의 가장 중요한 요소로서의 줄기세포 연구

해석 우리는 나이를 먹어감에 따라 뇌세포의 조직과 기능이 점진적으로 악화된다고 생각하곤 했다. 하지만 널리 퍼진 그 가정은 틀렸다는 것이 밝혀졌다. 나이 먹은 동물들의 뇌에서 새로운 신경 세포가 생성되는 것이 발견됐으며 노화된 뇌의 이처럼 놀라운 속성이 어떻게 조절될 수 있는지를 우리는 점점 더 알아가고 있다. 예를 들어 가벼운 수준의 정기적인 운동은 기억을 다루는 뇌 조직인 해마에서 신경조직의 형성을 엄청나게 향상시킨다는 사실이 발견됐다. 더욱이 최근 우리 연구소의 연구는 늙은 쥐의 눈에 있는 특정 신경 세포들은 새로운 (신경 전달) 과정을 성장시킬 수 있다는 것을 보여주었다. 우리는 또한 노인들의 눈에 있는 신경 세포들도 그런 식으로 성장한다는 것을 발견했다. 그리고 아직 초창기에 있지만, 손상되었거나 제대로 기능을 하지 않는 인체 장기의 교체를 위한 줄기세포 연구의 엄청난 가망성이 있다. 우리는 살면서 닳아서 없어졌거나 손상을 입은 뇌의 일부를 재생시킬 수 있을 것이며 현재는 노인으로 여겨지는 사람들에게 새로워진 능

력을 제공할 것이다.

[5행~7행] ~ we're learning more and more *how this amazing property of the aged brain* can be manipulated.
밑줄 친 부분은 동사 are learning의 목적어로 「의문사(how)+주어(this ~ brain)+동사(can ~ manipulated)」의 어순인 간접의문문이 쓰였다.
[14행~16행] Then there is the tremendous promise of *stem-cell research*, **which is still in its infancy**, for replacing damaged or dysfunctional body organs.
계속적 용법으로 쓰인 관계대명사 which가 이끄는 which is still in its infancy는 stem-cell research를 부연 설명한다.
[17행~20행] We will be able to regenerate *parts of the brain* [that have worn out or been damaged in the course of a lifetime], **providing** renewed capabilities to *those* [who are currently considered old folks].
첫 번째 [ ]는 관계사절로 parts of the brain을 수식한다. providing 이하는 동시동작을 나타내는 분사구문이다. 두 번째 [ ] 역시 관계사절로 바로 앞의 명사 those를 수식한다.

어휘 progressive 점진적인; 진보[혁신]적인　deterioration 악화, 저하; 퇴보
widespread 널리 퍼진, 광범위한　assumption 가정; 수락　nerve 신경; 긴장, 불안
property 속성; 재산; 부동산　manipulate 조절하다, 다루다; 조종하다　hippocampus (대뇌 측두엽의) 해마　deal with 다루다; 처리하다　tremendous 엄청난, 대단한
promise 가망성, 전망; 약속(하다)　stem-cell 줄기세포　infancy (발달의) 초창기 [초기]; 유아기　dysfunctional 제대로 기능을 하지 않는, 고장 난　organ 장기; 기관
regenerate 재생시키다; 혁신하다　wear out (닳아서) 없어지다　old folks 노인들
[선택지 어휘] redefine 재정의[재정립]하다　life expectancy 기대 수명
consequence 결과

5 도표 이해　　　　　　　　④

해설 드론 배송을 싫어하는 여성은 41%로 5분의 2가 넘는 것은 맞지만, 드론 배송을 싫어하는 남성의 비율인 27%보다 14퍼센트 포인트 더 높다. 그러므로 ④는 도표의 내용과 일치하지 않는다.

해석 드론 배송이라는 아이디어를 얼마나 좋아하거나 싫어하는가?
위 그래프는 2018년 드론 배송이라는 아이디어를 좋아하거나 싫어하는 미국 남성과 여성의 백분율을 보여준다. ① 27%로 드론 배송이라는 아이디어를 매우 좋아하는 남성의 백분율은 그것을 매우 좋아하는 여성의 그것(백분율)의 두 배 미만이었는데, 이는(여성의 백분율) 15%이다. ② 남성 넷 중 하나는 드론 배송이라는 아이디어를 다소 좋아하는데, 이는 그 아이디어를 다소 좋아한다고 응답했던 여성 다섯 중 하나보다 크다. ③ 드론 배송에 관하여 중립적인 입장을 가지고 있는 남성들의 백분율은 여성들의 그것보다 3퍼센트 포인트 더 낮다. ④ 5분의 2가 넘는 여성들이 드론 배송이라는 개념을 싫어하는데, 이는 그것을 싫어하는 남성보다 15퍼센트 포인트 더 높은 것이다. ⑤ 그 아이디어를 대단히 싫어하는 여성과 남성의 백분율 차이는 6퍼센트 포인트이다.

구문 [3행~6행] At 27%, the percentage of *men* [who like the idea of drone delivery very much] is *less than* twice as much as **that of *women*** [who like it very much], **which is** 15%.
관계대명사 who가 이끄는 두 개의 [ ]는 각각 선행사 men과 women을 수식한다. 밑줄 친 부분은 「배수사 as 원급 as ~」의 구조로 '~보다 두 배 …한'의 의미로 쓰였다. 관계대명사 which 이하는 that of women을 보충 설명하며 이때 that은 the percentage를 나타내는 대명사이다.
[6행~9행] *One in four men* like the idea of drone delivery somewhat, // *which is* **greater than** *the one in five women* [who replied that they like the idea

somewhat].
관계대명사 which가 이끄는 절은 One in four men을 보충 설명한다. 관계사절 내에 「비교급＋than」의 구조가 쓰였고 [ ]는 관계사절로 앞에 있는 the one in five women을 수식한다.

어휘 somewhat 다소, 어느 정도 neutral 중립의 stance 입장[태도]; 자세

6 내용 불일치 ⑤

해설 마지막 문장을 보면 Lysippos의 모든 작품이 청동으로 제작되었다고 했으므로 ⑤의 재료를 다양하게 사용했다는 내용은 일치하지 않는다.

해석 Lysippos는 4세기의 세 명의 위대한 그리스 조각가들 중 한 명으로 여겨졌다. 그는 청년 시절에 스스로 독학하면서 조각하는 일을 시작했다. 후에, 그는 Argos and Sicyon 예술학교의 교장이 되었다. 불행히도, Lysippos의 스타일을 모방하기 위해 적극적으로 노력한 많은 수의 학생들이 있었기 때문에, 오늘날 학자들은 그를 연구하는 데 어려움에 직면한다. 결과적으로, 그의 작품의 모방들이 많아서, 진품을 식별하기 어려울 수 있다. 미술사가들은 Lysippos의 (조각된) 인물들의 더 작은 머리와 세부적인 것에 큰 주의를 기울인 것을 주목하면서 그의 우아함과 정밀함에 대해 그를 찬양해 왔다. 당대의 전형적인 그리스 조각품들과는 대조적으로, Lysippos에 의해 만들어진 작품들은 정밀한 눈꺼풀과 발톱을 가진 놀라울 정도로 사실적인 인간의 모습을 묘사한다. 그는 1,500작이 넘는 작품을 제작했다고 전해지는데, 그것들 모두 청동으로 제작되었다.

구문 [11행~14행] In contrast to the typical Greek sculptures of the time, / *the works* (created by Lysippos) / **portray** incredibly realistic human forms with detailed eyelids and toenails.
( )는 created가 이끄는 과거분사구로 주어 the works를 수식하고, 동사는 portray이다.
[14행~16행] **It** is said **that he produced more than 1,500 works**, // [and] all of them were (produced) in bronze.
It은 가주어, that이 이끄는 절이 진주어이고, 두 번째 절에선 produced가 생략되어 있다.

어휘 sculptor 조각가 *cf.* sculpt 조각하다; 형태를 만들다 *cf.* sculpture 조각(품) teach oneself 독학[자습]하다 scholar 학자; 장학생 face 직면[직시]하다; 향하다. 마주보다 identify 식별[감정]하다; 찾다, 발견하다; 확인하다 praise 찬양하다; 칭찬하다 grace 우아함; 품위 elegance (과학적인) 정밀[정확]함, 고상함, 우아함 note 주목[주의]하다 figure (중요한) 인물; 모습, 형상; 숫자 portray 묘사하다; 그리다 eyelid 눈꺼풀 toenail 발톱 bronze 청동(빛의)

7 밑줄 어법 ⑤

해설 ⑤ 접속사 If가 ~ and a fox까지 이끌며, 그 다음에 주절의 주어가 나와야 하므로 which가 아니라 명사절을 이끄는 관계대명사 what을 사용해야 한다. what they see가 주절의 주어로 적절하다.
① must understand의 목적어절로서 앞의 that you don't see the same thing a butterfly sees와 and로 연결된 것이므로 적절하다.
② 형용사인 visible을 수식하므로 부사 completely를 잘 사용하였다.
③ happen은 자동사이므로 올바른 태를 사용하였으며 현재진행시제도 적절하다.
④ the light of the sun과 filter는 수동관계이므로 filtered가 적절하다.

해석 꽃을 볼 때 당신은 나비가 보는 것과 같은 것을 보고 있지 않다는 것과, 당신이 눈을 곤충의 눈으로 바꾼다면 꽃의 세계가 광기의 폭발로 전환될 것이라는 것을 이해해야 한다. 밤 시간엔 불가능한(볼 수 없는) 거실이 고양이에게는 완벽히 잘 보이는 놀이터이며,

레이저 포인터를 아기고양이 옆에 비춰본 적이 있다면, 당신의 머릿속에서는 일어나지 않는 무언가가 그것의 작은 고양이 머릿속에서 일어나고 있다는 것을 확실히 깨달았을 것이다. 당신은 세계가 겉으로 드러나는 모습과 같지 않다는 것을 알고 있으며, 그것을 증명하는 데에 필요한 것이라고는 하나의 거대한 시각적 환상이 전부다. 다른 식으로 믿는 것은 너무 단순하다. 별은 항상 하늘에 있지만 대기를 통해 여과된 태양의 빛은 그것들을 낮에 보기 불가능하게 만든다. 당신이 돌을 연못에 던지고 그 물방울이 개구리와 여우의 머리를 돌린다면, 그들이 보는 것은 당신이 보는 것이 아니다. 각 생물의 현실 형태는 그 생물의 신경계로만 볼 수 있다.

구문 [1행~2행] When you look at a flower, // you must understand / that you don't see *the same thing* [(that) a butterfly sees]. ~
[ ]는 목적격 관계대명사 that이 생략되어 the same thing을 수식한다.
[10행~11행] You know the world is not **as** it appears, // and all it takes / is one great optical illusion to prove it.
접속사 as는 '~하는 대로'의 뜻이다. and 이하 절에서 all it takes가 주어이며 is가 동사이다. all it takes는 '필요한 것이라고는'의 뜻이다.
[13행~14행] ~, but the light of the sun (filtered through the atmosphere) makes *them* impossible to see in the day.
them은 the stars를 지칭하며, 진목적어(to see them)의 목적어가 가목적어 자리를 대신 차지하여 쓰인 형태이다. makes them impossible to see in the day를 가목적어를 사용하여 표현하면 makes it impossible to see them(= the stars) in the day이다.

어휘 switch 전환하다, 바꾸다 floral 꽃의 turn into ~로 전환되다 explosion 폭발 kitten 아기고양이 optical 시각적인 otherwise 다른 방법으로 filter 여과하다, 거르다 toss 던지다 splash (물)방울 version 판, 형태

8 밑줄 어휘

해설 이 글은 조종하기 쉬운 비행기가 조종하기 더 어려운 항공기에게 길을 비켜줘야 한다는 항공법에 관해 설명하고 있다. 조종하기 어려운 항공기가 정상적으로 운행되고 있는 항공기보다 더 높은 우선 통행권을 가지고 있으므로, ④ 'lesser'은 'greater(더 높은)'로 바꿔야 한다.

해석 국제 해양법은 조종하기가 더 어려운 선박에게 조종하기가 더 쉬운 선박이 길을 비켜 주어야 한다고 명시한다. 동력으로 움직이는 배와 같은 조종하기가 더 쉬운 선박의 선장은 범선, 낚시 하고 있는 배, 통제되지 않는 선박과 같은 조종하기가 더 어려운 선박을 피하는 것에 대한 ① 책임이 있다. 동력선이 범선과 충돌하는 것을 피하는 것이 그 반대의 경우보다 더 쉽다. 항공법도 이와 동일한 원칙에 기초를 두고 있다. 하늘에서의 우선 통행권은 ② 조종되기 쉬운 순서로 항공기의 순위를 매긴다. 가장 쉽게 조종되는 정상적으로 운행되고 있는 비행기는 우선 통행권에 있어서 ③ 가장 낮은 우선 순위를 갖는다. 조종하기가 덜 용이한, 다른 항공기에 연료를 재급유하는 비행기는 정상적으로 운행되는 비행기보다 ④ 더 낮은(→ 더 높은) 우선 통행권을 갖는다. 다른 항공기에 연료를 재급유하는 비행기보다 훨씬 더 조종하기가 어려운 열기구 풍선은 ⑤ 더 높은 우선 통행권을 갖는다. 마지막으로 조난 사고를 당한 항공기는 통제하기가 매우 어렵거나 불가능하기 때문에, 조난 사고를 당한 항공기는 모든 것들 중 가장 높은 우선 통행권을 갖는다.

구문 [7행~9행] It is **easier** *for powerboats* to avoid hitting sailing ships **than** vice versa.
「비교급 ~ than ....」의 비교 구문이 쓰였고, 이때 for powerboats는 to avoid의 의미상의 주어이다.
[19행~22행] Finally, aircraft in distress have the highest priority right of way of all, // **since** an aircraft in distress is very difficult or impossible to control.
since 이하는 '~하기 때문에'라는 의미로 이유를 나타내는 부사절이다.

어휘 specify (구체적으로) 명시하다   vessel 선박, 배   steerable 조종 가능한 command 지휘, 통솔   vice versa 반대로   aviation code 항공법   principle 원칙   the right of way 우선 통행권   maneuver 조종하다; 연습시키다   priority 우선권

9 빈칸 추론   ③

해설 빈칸 문장으로 보아 사고 능력이 이미 다른 일에 몰두해 있을 때 사고에 대한 더 이상의 필요를 '무엇하기' 위해 사람들이 지름길(빠르고 쉬운 방법)을 택하는지를 찾아야 한다. 우리의 예상과는 달리 인간은 많은 사고를 하길 꺼리는데 그 이유는 인간의 사고하는 능력이 제한되어 있어서 사고를 아껴야 할 필요가 있기 때문이라는 내용이므로 빈칸에는 추가적인 사고를 하지 않으려 한다는 말이 나와야 한다. 그러므로 빈칸에 들어가기에 가장 적절한 것은 ③ '줄이기'이다.
① 성취하기 ② 만들기 ④ 확인하기 ⑤ 인지하기

해석 여러분은 인간이 사고하는 데 필요한 능력을 잘 갖추고 있으므로, 사고하는 것을 좋아하고, 모든 자유 시간을 사고를 하며 보낼 거라고 예상할지도 모른다. 이것은 확실히 사실은 그렇지 않다. (모든 사고가 재미있다면, 사람들은 아마도 자신의 자유 시간의 많은 시간을 수학 문제를 풀면서 보내겠지만, 그들은 그러지 않는다.) 연구자들은 사람들이 흔히 사고하는 데 게으르거나 무관심해 보인다는 것을 알아냈다. 사회심리학자들은 사람이 추가로 많은 사고를 하는 것을 내키지 않아 한다는 것을 서술하기 위해 '인지적 구두쇠'라는 용어를 사용한다. 구두쇠가 돈을 지출하는 것을 피하려고 하는 것처럼, 인지적 구두쇠도 너무 열심히 혹은 너무 많이 사고하는 것을 피하려고 노력한다. 물론, 이것이 전적으로 게으름의 문제만은 아니다. 사람들의 사고하는 능력은 제한되어 있어서 사람들은 자신들의 사고를 아껴 써야 한다. 자신들의 사고 능력이 이미 (다른 일에) 몰두해 있을 때, 사고에 대한 더 이상의 필요를 <u>줄이기</u> 위해 사람들은 훨씬 더 많은 지름길을 택한다는 많은 증거가 있다.

구문 [4행~6행] If all thinking **were** fun, / people **would** probably **spend** much of their free time doing math problems, // ⌐but⌐ they **don't** (spend much of their free time doing math problems).
「If+S'+동사의 과거형, S+조동사 과거형+동사원형」의 형태의 가정법 과거 표현으로 '만약 ~하면 …할 텐데'의 뜻이다. but 이후에 don't는 직설법으로 ( ) 부분이 생략되어 실제 그들은 자유 시간의 많은 시간을 수학 문제를 풀면서 보내지 않는다는 의미이다.
[10행~12행] **Just as** a miser tries to **avoid spending** money, // the cognitive miser tries to **avoid thinking** too hard or too much.
Just as ~는 '~한 것과 꼭 마찬가지로'의 뜻이고, avoid는 동명사를 목적어로 취하므로 목적어로 spending과 thinking이 사용되었다.
[14행~17행] There is much <u>evidence</u> // <u>that when people's capacity for</u> <u>thinking is already preoccupied, / they take even more shortcuts **to reduce**</u> <u>further need for thought.</u>
접속사 that이 이끄는 절은 evidence와 동격 관계를 이룬다. to reduce는 부사적 용법으로 쓰여 목적(~하기 위해)을 나타낸다.

어휘 equip (능력·지식 등을) 갖추게 하다, 갖추다   term 용어; 기간; 조건   cognitive 인지적인, 인식의   reluctance 내키지 않음, 꺼림   entirely 전적으로, 완전히   capacity 능력; 용량   conserve 아껴 쓰다, 보존하다   evidence 증거(물)   preoccupied 몰두한, 마음을 빼앗긴   shortcut 지름길   further 더 이상의, 추가의

10 빈칸 추론   ③

해설 글의 요지는 경쟁에서 비롯된 스트레스로 인해 수행과 성취에 방해가 된다는

것이다. 어린 학생이 선생님의 질문에 답하는 경쟁을 벌이면서 무조건 손을 들고 주목을 끌어 답할 기회를 받게 되더라도 정작 질문의 핵심은 놓쳐버리는 상황을 예로 들고 있으므로, 어린 학생이 질문 자체보다는 ③ '자신의 급우들을 이기는 데 집중했다'는 내용이 적절하다.
① 질문하는 데
② 선생님의 주의를 딴 데로 돌리는 데
④ 시험을 잘 보는 데
⑤ 자신의 불안감을 억누르는 데

해석 경쟁은 주로 스트레스를 많이 주기 때문에 일의 성취를 방해하는 것처럼 보인다. 질 가능성에서 생기는 불안은 (일의) 수행을 방해한다. 이런 불안을 억누를 수 있을지라도, 두 가지 일, 즉 잘하려고 노력하는 것과 남을 이기려 노력하는 것을 동시에 하는 것은 어렵다. 경쟁은 당면한 일에서 주의를 쉽게 돌릴 수 있다. 한 교사가 자신의 제자들에게 질문을 던지고 있다고 생각해 보라. 한 어린 소년이 그녀의 관심을 끌기 위해 손을 마구 흔들며, "제발요! 제발요! 저요!"라고 외친다. 마침내 그가 (교사에게) 인지되었지만, 그는 답을 잊고 만다. 그래서 그는 머리를 긁적이며, "질문이 뭐였죠?"라고 묻는다. 문제는 그가 주제(질문에 답하는 것)가 아닌 <u>자신의 급우들을 이기는 데</u> 집중했다는 것이다.

구문 [10행~11행] **Finally recognized**, he has forgotten the answer.
Finally recognized는 분사구문으로 Although he has finally been recognized로 바꾸어 쓸 수 있다.

어휘 interfere with ~을 방해하다   primarily 주로   arise from ~에서 발생하다   suppress 억누르다   distract (주의를) 딴 데로 돌리다; 기분전환하다   at hand 당면한; 가까운   pupil 학생

11 빈칸 추론   ⑤

해설 빈칸 문장으로 보아 어떤 단어들은 '어떠한' 방법으로 좀 더 정교한 개념이나 새로운 제품을 위해 어휘를 풍성하게 해왔는지 찾아야 한다. '독일어에서는 고유의 어근들이 결합되어 고전적 방식의 복합어와 똑같은 의미를 가진 새로운 복합어를 형성한다'와 같은 내용이면서, 대조가 되는 영어에 대한 설명인 '다른 언어의 어근을 첨가하고 재활용했다'는 것과 반대 개념이 빈칸에 들어가야 하므로, 빈칸에는 ⑤ '그 언어 자체의 자원에 의존해'가 가장 적절하다.
① 비유적인 의미 채택을 고려해
② 복합어를 분리한 것을 사용해
③ 단어의 원래의 의미를 확장해
④ 다양한 차용어를 발전시켜

해석 영어에서 관찰되는 사용 빈도와 어원 사이의 상관관계가 반드시 모든 언어에 적용되는 것은 아니다. 어떤 언어들은, 독일어가 적절한 사례인데, 좀 더 정교한 개념이나 새로운 제품을 위한 단어들로 어휘를 풍부하게 하기 위해 전통적으로 <u>그 언어 자체의 자원에 의존해</u> 왔다. 예를 들어, 'Übersetzung'은 영어 단어 'translation(번역)'과 같은 것이지만, 글자 그대로는 'setting over(양도하는 것)'를 의미한다. 'Fernsehen'은 'television(텔레비전)'과 같은 것이지만, 글자 그대로는 'far-seeing(먼 곳을 보는 것)'을 의미한다. 'Lautlehre'는 'phonology(음운론)'과 같은 뜻이지만, 글자 뜻대로는 'sound study(소리 연구)'를 의미한다. 다시 말해서, 독일어에서는 고유의 어근들이 결합되어 고전적 방식의 복합어와 똑같은 의미를 가진 새로운 복합어를 형성한다. 어휘를 풍부하게 하는 이런 방법은 영어에서도 또한 익숙한데, 'doorbell(초인종)', 'horseshoe(편자)', 'lighthouse(등대)', 'shorthand(속기)', 'stronghold(요새)'는 모두 고유의 요소들만을 담고 있는 복합어이다. 하지만 독일어에 비해, 영어는 고유의 어근에서 새로운 단어를 만드는 데 있어서 덜 창의적이었다. 대신에, 영어는 다른 언어들의 어근을 (영어에) 첨가하고 창의적으로 재활용해 왔다.

구문 [3행~7행] Some languages — German is a case in point — have traditionally depended on the resources of the language itself / for enriching

the vocabulary / with words for more sophisticated notions or new products.
주어는 Some languages, 동사는 have depended on이며 중간에 두 개의 대시 사이에 절이 삽입되었다.

어휘 correlation 상관관계, 연관성　frequency 빈도; 빈발, 잦음　be true of ~에 적용되다　in point 적절한　enrich 풍부[풍성]하게 하다　*cf.* enrichment 풍부, 풍성　sophisticated 정교한, 복잡한　notion 개념, 관념　equivalent 같은, 동등한　literally 글자[말] 그대로　set over ~을 양도하다[지배하다]　phonology 음운론; 음운체계　root 어근; 뿌리; 근원　combine 결합하다　compound 복합어; 화합물; 복합[합성]의　method 방법; 체계성　element (구성) 요소; 원소　**[선택지 어휘]** look to-v v를 고려해[생각해]보다　adopt 채택하다　figurative 비유적인

12 빈칸 추론 ②

해설 아이들이 이름에 대해 갖는 생각에 대한 예시를 종합하면, 사물에 어떤 내적인 속성이 있을 경우이다. 단추는 언제나 누를 수 있는 속성이 있는 것으로, 폭력적인 친구는 남을 아프게 하는 천성을 가진 사람으로, 당근을 먹는 사람이라는 말을 듣고는 당근을 먹는 내적인 속성을 가지고 있다고 보았다. 그러므로 빈칸에는 ② '깊이 숨어 있는 속성을 공유하는 사물들'이라는 말이 들어가야 가장 적절하다.
① 의도를 가지고 만들어진 사물들
③ 같은 지리적 위치를 점유하는 사물들
④ 유사점과 차이점을 모두 가진 사물들
⑤ 부모에 의해 유용성이 강조되는 사물들

해설 성인과 마찬가지로 유아도 이름은 깊이 숨어 있는 속성을 공유하는 사물들을 가리킨다고 생각한다. Susan Gelman은 13개월 된 아들에게 그녀 셔츠의 단추를 보여주면서 '단추'라고 말했다. 그러자 아들은 단추를 누르기 시작했는데 전자 장난감에 달린 단추와 생김새는 다르지만 그것이 어떤 범주에 속한 것인지를 이해했고, 그게 바로 버튼으로 하는 일이기 때문이었다. 조금 큰 아이는 여러분이 성인에게서 발견하는 것과 거의 같은 명사의 위력을 이해하는 듯하다. 네 살 된 아동은 폭력적인 놀이 친구에 관해 이렇게 말한다. "Gabriel이 저만 아프게 한 것이 아니에요! 다른 애들도 아프게 했어요. 걔는 남을 아프게 하는 아이예요! 맞죠, 엄마. 걔는 남을 아프게 하는 아이예요!" 이 아이는 아마도 폭력적인 행동이 Gabriel의 본성에서 심오한 일면을 반영한다고 강조하고 있는 것이다. 그리고 Gelman은 한 실험에서 다섯 살 된 아이들에게 당근을 자주 먹는 Rose라는 이름의 아이에 대해 말하고 아이들 절반에게는 'Rose는 당근 먹는 아이'라고 추가로 설명해 주었다. 이름의 효과가 곧바로 드러났다. 그것은 아이들이 Rose를 영원히 당근을 먹는 사람으로 생각하게 했다. 그녀는 가족들이 말려도 미래에도 당근을 먹을 것이라고 생각했다. 당근을 먹는 것이 Rose의 본성이라고 생각했다.

구문 [4행~7행] He then started to press it, // because, though it didn't look much like a button on his electronic toys, / he knew what category it belonged to, and that's what you do with a button.
접속사 because가 이끄는 부사절 내에 접속사 though가 이끄는 부사절이 포함되어 있는 구조이다.

어휘 electronic 전자의　category 범주　subtle 포착하기 힘든, 미묘한　presumably 아마, 짐작건대　reflect 반영하다　discourage 억제하다

13 흐름 무관 문장 ④

해설 기술의 진보가 식품 보존에 영향을 끼쳐 식료품의 저장 수명과 편리성, 다양성을 증대시켰다는 내용의 글인데, ④는 식품의 가격과 선택에 영향을 끼치는 정치적 결정에 관한 문장이므로 글의 전체 흐름과 관계가 없다.

해석 기술의 진보는 부패와 오염의 위험을 줄이는 한편, 식료품이 한 대륙에서 또 다른 대륙으로 유통될 수 있도록 함으로써 새로운 식품 선택에 대한 직접 체험을 증가시켰다. ① 19세기 이전에 육류를 보존하기 위해 이용 가능한 방법은 단지 건조, 염장, 그리고 훈제뿐이었지만, 대량의 식품이 가공되거나 아주 오랫동안 보존될 수 없었기 때문에 그것들 중 어느 것도 완전히 실용적이지는 않았다. ② 통조림 가공은 1809년에 개발되었고 나폴레옹 전쟁의 산물이었다. 그 가공은 가열 살균 처리된 식품이 상하지 않고 더 오랫동안 저장될 수 있게 해 주었다. ③ 20세기의 더 발전된 가공법은 탈수, 냉동, 그리고 초고온 처리를 포함하였는데, 이들은 식료품의 저장 수명, 편리성, 그리고 다양성을 증대시켰다. ④ 식품의 유통이 전 세계적으로 계속 확장됨에 따라, 식품 시스템과 관련된 정치적 결정이 결국 식품의 가격과 식품 선택에 영향을 끼칠 것이다. ⑤ 게다가 냉장, 진공 포장, 급속 냉동 등은 경제적으로 발달된 사회에서 특정 계절에 나오는 품목들을 연중 내내 이용할 수 있게 보장해 주었다.

구문 [1행~4행] Technological advances have increased exposure to new food choices / by **allowing** *food products* **to be distributed** from one continent to another / while reducing the risk of spoilage and contamination.
allowing ~ another는 전치사 by의 목적어 역할을 하는 동명사구이다. 여기서 「allow A to-v」는 'A를 v하게 하다'라는 뜻으로, 목적어인 food products가 사물이므로 to 다음에 수동태인 be distributed가 쓰였다. while 이하는 접속사가 생략되지 않은 분사구문으로 주절의 주어인 Technological advances가 의미상의 주어이다.
[5행~9행] Before the nineteenth century, the only methods available for preserving meat / were *drying*, *salting*, *and smoking*, // none of **which** were entirely practical / **since** large quantities of food could not be processed or preserved for very long.
관계사 which는 drying, salting, and smoking을 선행사로 하여 보충 설명한다. since가 이끄는 절은 이유를 나타낸다.

어휘 exposure 직접 체험; 노출　distribute 유통하다　continent 대륙　spoilage (음식물의) 부패　contamination 오염　preserve 보존하다　dehydrate 탈수시키다　ultrahigh temperature 초고온　shelf life 저장 수명　ultimately 결국　refrigeration 냉장　vacuum packing 진공 포장　ensure 보장하다　year-round 연중 내내

14 글의 순서 ⑤

해설 온혈 동물이 추울 때 몸을 움츠리고 서로서로 모여 있다는 주어진 문장 다음에는 이에 대한 구체적인 이유가 나오는 (C)가 와야 한다. 그리고 반대되는 상황, 즉 더울 때 이루어지는 같은 유형의 자세 조정에 대해 설명한 (B)가 이어져야 한다. (A)는 (B)의 마지막 상황과는 반대로 주변 온도가 체온보다 따뜻할 때를 설명하고 있기 때문에 마지막에 나오는 것이 적절하다.

해석 온혈 동물을 포함한 많은 동물들이 내부 온도를 조절하는 데 도움이 되기 위해 신체 위치나 자세를 바꾼다. 이것은 또한 동물들이 열을 보존하려고 몸을 웅크리고 강아지와 고양이 새끼 같은 동물 집단이 추위로부터의 보호를 얻기 위해 함께 옹기종기 모일 때 추위 속에서 나타나는 익숙한 행동이다.
(C) 움츠린 자세는 열을 교환하는 데 이용할 수 있는 표면적을 감소시킴으로써 환경에 빼앗기는 열 손실을 줄인다. 그것은 주변 온도가 체온보다 훨씬 더 낮을 때 지지된다.
(B) 같은 유형의 자세 조정이 열기 속에서도 관찰된다. 확장된 자세는 환경에 노출된 신체 표면적을 증가시킴으로써 열 손실을 증가시킨다. 그것은 환경이 덥지만 여전히 체온보다 낮을 때 열을 소멸시키는 데 유용하다.
(A) 그러나 주변 온도가 체온보다 따뜻할 때는 열이 축적되는 속도가 더 빠르기 때문에 신체 확장은 효과가 없다. 따라서 땀 흘리기 같은 생리학적 전략이 동원되어야 한다.

구문 [3행~6행] This, too, is a familiar behavior in the cold // when animals curl up to conserve heat ⌐and⌐ groups of animals, such as puppies and kittens, huddle together for protection from the cold.

when절에서 밑줄 친 두 절이 병렬구조를 이룬다.

[13행~15행] Extended postures increase heat loss / by increasing *the surface area of the body* (exposed to the environment).

( )는 the surface area of the body를 수동의 의미로 수식한다. exposed to는 '~에 노출된'의 뜻이다.

어휘 warm-blooded 온혈의   posture 자세 *cf.* postural 자세의   regulate 조절하다   familiar 익숙한, 잘 아는   curl up 몸을 웅크리다   conserve 보존하다   huddle 옹송그리며 모이다   extension 연장, 확장   accumulate 쌓이다   physiological 생리학적인   sweat 땀을 흘리다   call ~ into play ~을 이용[동원]하다   adjustment 조정   lessen 줄이다   surface area 표면적   favor 호의를 보이다, 지지하다

15 글의 순서   ③

해설 미학이 주로 예술이나 자연의 아름다움을 다룬다는 주어진 글의 내용 다음에는 그것이 너무 의미가 좁으며 예술가들은 당혹, 충격, 심지어 혐오감을 불러일으킬 수도 있다고 말하는 내용인 (B)가 나와야 한다. 그 다음에는 게르니카의 예를 든 (C)가 나와야 한다. 이 작품을 설명하고 폭넓은 미학의 정의를 내리는 (A)가 맨 나중에 오는 것이 자연스럽다.

해석 한 전통적 정의에 의하면, '미학'은 아름다움, 특히 예술의 아름다움을 다루는 철학의 분야이다. 예를 들어, '모나리자'나 꼭대기가 눈에 덮인 산의 유쾌한 특징들을 살펴보는 것이 미학의 범위에 해당될 것이다.
(B) 하지만, 예술 작품들과 자연의 물체가 아름답다는 것 외에 다른 특징을 가지고 우리의 관심을 끌 수 있기 때문에 그러한 정의는 너무 좁아 보인다. 아름다움에 대한 경탄을 불러일으키는 대신에, 예술가들은 당혹, 충격, 심지어 혐오감을 불러일으킬 수도 있다.
(C) 스페인 내란 동안에 독일과 이탈리아의 전투기들에 의한 스페인 민간인 대량 학살에 대응하여 피카소가 그린 검은색, 흰색, 회색으로 이루어진 거대한(11피트×25.6피트) 그림인 피카소의 '게르니카'에 대해 생각해보라. 죽어가는 군인들과 비명을 지르는 사람들의 이미지가 캔버스를 지배한다.
(A) 이 작품은 널리 칭송되고 있으나 아름답기 때문이 아니다. 그러므로 미학에 대한 더 나은 정의는, 미학이란 사물이 경험되면서 사람들을 즐겁게 하는 방식을 연구하는 철학의 분야라는 것이 될 것이다.

구문 [11행~13행] That definition seems too narrow, / however, // **since** works of art and natural objects may attract us with features **other than** their beauty.

여기서 since는 이유를 표시하는 부사절을 이끄는 접속사이다. other than에서 than은 '~밖에는, ~와 다른'의 뜻이다.

어휘 aesthetics 미학   snow-capped 꼭대기가 눈에 덮인   evoke 불러일으키다   puzzlement 당혹   disgust 혐오감   in response to A A에 응하여   civilian (군인이 아니라는 의미로) 민간인   dominate 지배하다

16 문장 넣기   ②

해설 ②를 전후로 '프랜차이즈 대기업이 지역의 소규모 업체의 수입을 가져간다'는 문장과 '이는 지역 업체가 지역 사회와 상호의존적 경제망을 형성하기 때문이다'라는 문장은 논리적으로 이어지지 않는다. '지역 업체에서 구매하면 지역 사회에 도움이 된다'는 주어진 문장이 ②에 위치하면, ② 바로 뒤의 This가 '지역 업체에서 구매하여 지역 사회에도 도움을 주기'를 지칭함을 알 수 있고, 그 이유를 제시한 바로 뒤

의 문장과도 논리적으로 잘 연결된다.

해석 대기업으로부터 물건을 살 때, 여러분은 소수의 수중에 있는 부와 권력을 더욱 공고히 하는 것을 지원하는 것이다. 프랜차이즈 기업은 흔히 수입의 손실을 감당할 수 없는 더 작은 규모의 지역 업체로부터 그 돈을 직접 가져간다. 지역 업체에서 구매함으로써, 여러분은 그 부를 더 많은 지역 사람들에게 퍼뜨리고 여러분의 지역 사회의 생활 수준을 증대시킨다. 이것은 지역 업체가 지역의 공급업체와 서비스 제공업체에 더 많이 의존하고, 일자리와 번영하는 지역 사회를 만들어 내는 일종의 상호 의존적인 지역 경제망을 형성하기 때문이다. 그러므로 여러분이 지역 업체에서 쓰는 모든 돈은 풍족한 생활을 탐색하는 이웃들을 지원하는 동시에 지역 사회가 그것의 개성, 독특함, 다양성을 유지하도록 돕는다. 지역 업체는 많은 경우 신용 카드 회사가 모든 거래마다 각각 부과하는 과중한 수수료를 감당할 능력이 가장 없는 이들이기 때문에 신용카드보다는 현금으로 지불하는 것 또한 지역 업체에 도움이 될 수 있다. 전화번호부에서 대형 프랜차이즈 기업을 대신할 지역의 대안을 찾아보라.

구문 [9행~12행] This is because local businesses rely more on local suppliers and service providers, **forming** a kind of local economic web of interdependence [that creates jobs and a thriving community].

forming 이하는 local businesses를 의미상 주어로 하여 '결과'를 나타내는 분사구문이다. [ ]은 주격 관계대명사 that이 이끄는 관계사절로 a kind of local economic web of interdependence를 수식한다.

[13행~16행] Therefore, every dollar [(that) you spend at a local business] **helps** your community *maintain* its individual character, uniqueness, and diversity while supporting your neighbors in their quest for the good life.

[ ]은 목적격 관계대명사 that이 생략된 관계사절로 every dollar를 수식한다. 「동사(help)+목적어(your community)+목적격보어(maintain~)」의 SVOC 구조이다.

[17행~20행] Paying in cash, **rather than** by credit card, can also help local businesses as they are often *the ones* (least able to afford *the hefty fees*) [(which[that]) the credit card companies charge them for each and every transaction].

'A rather than B'는 'B라기보다는 차라리 A'의 뜻이다. ( )은 the ones를 수식하며 the ones는 the local businesses를 지칭한다. [ ]는 목적격 관계대명사 which[that]가 생략된 관계사절로 the hefty fees를 수식한다. charge는 여기서 'charge 사람 사물(…에게 ~의 비용을 청구하다)'의 형태의 SVOO 구조로 사용되었다.

어휘 corporation 기업 *cf.* corporate 기업의   chain business 프랜차이즈 기업   interdependence 상호 의존   thriving 번영하는   individual character 개성   quest 탐색   transaction 거래

17 문장 넣기   ④

해설 주어진 글이 녹색 혁명의 부작용에 대한 구체적인 내용이므로 녹색 혁명의 기여도를 언급한 후 사회적 환경적 부작용이 논란이 되었다는 내용과 이와는 다른 의심이 추가적으로 표명된 내용 사이에 오는 것이 적절하다.

해석 1960년대에 시작된, 화학 비료와 다수확 종자 품종의 개발도상국으로의 도입은 오늘날 '녹색 혁명'으로 알려져 있다. 이 혁명은 장기적인 영향을 미치는 결과를 가져왔다. 인구의 급격한 증가를 촉발했을 뿐만 아니라 그것은 수억 명의 사람들을 가난에서 벗어나도록 도왔고 아시아 경제의 역사적인 부활과 중국과 인도의 급속한 산업화를 뒷받침했는데, 이것은 지정학을 변형시키는 발달이다. 하지만 녹색 혁명의 다른 많은 사회적, 환경적 부작용은 그것(녹색 혁명)을 극도로 논란의 여지가 있는 것으로 만들었다. 그것의 비판자들은 그것이 심각한 환경 피해를 초래했고, 전통적인 농업 관행을 파괴했고 불평등을 증가시켰으며, 서구 회사들이 제공하는 값비싼 종자와 화학제품에 농부들이 의지하게 두었다고 주장한다. 화학적으로 집약적인 농업의 장기적인 지속 가능성에 대해서도 의혹이 표명되었다. 하지만 좋든 나쁘든, 녹색 혁명이 20세기 후반에 세계의 식량 공급을 단지 바꾸

는 것보다는 더 많은 것을 했다는 것에는 이의가 없다. 그것은 세상을 바꿔었다.

구문 [1행~5행] Its critics argue // that it <u>has resulted</u> in massive environmental damage, <u>destroyed</u> traditional farming practices, <u>increased</u> inequality, [and] left farmers reliant on expensive *seeds and chemicals* (provided by Western companies).

argue의 목적어절인 that절의 동사는 모두 시제가 현재완료로 destroyed, increased, left 앞에 has가 생략되어 있다. ( )는 과거분사구로 seeds and chemicals을 수식한다.

어휘 practice 관행, 관습 inequality 불평등, 불공평 reliant 의지하는 fertilizer 비료, 거름 high-yield 다수확의 variety 종류, 다양성 developing world 개발 도상국 far-reaching 광범위한, 멀리까지 미치는 consequence 결과 trigger 일으키다, 유발하다 boom 급격한 증가 lift out of ~에서 들어 올리다 rebirth 재생, 부활 transform 바꾸다, 변형하다 controversial 논쟁의, 논쟁의 여지가 있는 intensive farming 집약농업 for better or worse 좋든 나쁘든

18 요약문 완성 ②

해설 실험에서 피실험자들은 자신이 선택한 것이 다른 선택지로 몰래 바뀌치기 당했을 때, 바뀐 선택지(선택했던 사진의 반대 이미지)를 옹호하며 생각지도 못하게 스스로의 행동을 수정하는(change) 모습을 보였는데, 이는 자신이 주체적이고 의도를 갖고(deliberately) 결정을 내린 거라고 스스로의 행동을 정당화하고 싶어 하기 때문이다.

① 바꾸다 – 우연히 ③ 간과하다 – 상징적으로
④ 유지하다 – 우연히 ⑤ 유지하다 – 의도적으로

해석 한 실험에서 100명이 넘는 지원자들에게 두 장의 사진을 보여주었는데, 각각에 여성의 얼굴이 있었다. 두 사진을 몇 초 동안 본 후에, 그들은 자신들에게 가장 매력적으로 보인 사진 하나를 선택해야 했다. 세 번의 그러한 선택 직후, 피실험자들에게 그들이 방금 선택한 얼굴을 다시 보여주고, 자신의 선택에 대해 설명해보라고 요청했다. 그들은 순순히 따랐다. 세 번의 다른 실험에서, 실험자는 날랜 손재주를 써서 선택된 여성의 사진을 반대의 이미지로 바꿨다. 즉, 여성 A가 더 매력적이라고 결정한 직후에, 두 개의 카드 책략을 사용해서 피실험자들에게 여성 B의 사진을 들이대었고, 피실험자들은 자신이 왜 그녀를 선택했는지 설명해야 했다 (사진에 묘사된 두 여성들은 꽤 달랐다). 놀랍게도, 대부분의 경우 피실험자들은 속았다. 단지 25%보다 적은 실험에서만 참가자들이 자신의 원래 선택이 존중되지 않았고, 그들이 속았다는 것을 알았다. 대부분의 경우, 그들은 원래의 의식적인 결정과 자신이 결정했다고 들은 것 사이의 불일치를 무시했다. 그리고 훨씬 더 놀랍게도, 그들은 그것이 몇 초 전에 자신이 실제로 했던 것과 모순됨에도 불구하고 이 선택을 정당화함에 이르렀다.

↓

우리는 내내 (B) 의도적으로 결정을 내려왔던 것처럼 보이게 하기 위해 생각지도 못하게 우리의 행동을 (A) 바꾸는 경향이 있다.

구문 [16행~19행] Only in fewer than 25% of trials **were** <u>participants</u> aware that their original choice was not honored, that they had been fooled.
Only가 이끄는 부사구가 문두에 나가 주어(participants)와 동사(were)가 도치되었다.

[19행~21행] Most of the time, they ignored **the discrepancy between** <u>their original conscious decision</u> **and** <u>what (they were told) they had decided</u>.
'the discrepancy between A and B'는 'A와 B 사이의 차이[불일치]'의 뜻이다. A와 B 자리에 각각 명사구와 what으로 시작되는 명사절이 위치하여 병렬구조를 이룬다. what they were told they had decided에서 they were told는 삽입되었다.

어휘 readily 쉽게 comply 따르다 trial 실험, 시험 experimentalist 실험자 ploy 책략 confront (증거를) 들이대다; 직면하게 만들다, 맞서다 depict 묘사하다 distinct 구별되는 remarkably 놀랍게도, 신기하게도 honor 존중하다 discrepancy 불일치 proceed to ~에 이르다, ~이 되다; ~로 나아가다 justify 정당화하다 contradict 반박하다, 모순되다 unknowingly 모르고 all along 내내

19~20 장문 19 ④ 20 ②

해설 19. 잉카 사람들이 안데스 고원에서 감자를 재배하면서 단일 재배와 정반대되는 농법을 개발했고 그 감자는 극적으로 변하는 기후를 잘 견디며 가치를 증명했다. 또한 그것은 야생종과 교배하면서 유전적 다양성을 가진 감자로 진화했으므로 글의 제목으로는 ④ '잉카 감자의 진화는 다양성을 초래했다'가 적절하다.
① 감자 재배의 역사
② 감자가 잉카 사람들에게 중요했던 이유
③ 우리는 잉카 사람들이 먹던 똑같은 감자를 먹는다
⑤ 감자: 전 세계적 재배를 위한 안데스의 선물

20. 잉카 사람들이 만든 작은 구획이 일관성이 없고, 질서 정연한 풍경이 주는 만족감을 주지 못한다고 했으므로 (b) organized(정리된)는 chaotic(무질서한)으로 고쳐야 문맥상 적절하다.

해석 우리가 심은 감자는 안데스 고원에서 자라던 야생 원종 선조의 후손이다. 잉카 사람들은 가장 잘될 것 같지 않은 경작 조건에서도 놀라운 감자 수확량을 산출하는 법을 알아냈고, 오늘날에도 안데스 산맥 일부 지역에서 여전히 사용되고 있는 접근법을 개발했다. 고도가 바뀔 때마다 혹은 태양과 바람의 방위에 따라 미기후가 극적으로 변하기 때문에 다소 수직적인 서식지는 식물(감자)과 그것을 재배하는 사람 둘 다에게 특별한 (a) 도전을 제공한다. 그런 환경에서는 어떤 단일 재배도 성공할 수 없기에 잉카 사람들은 단일 재배와 정반대되는 농법을 개발했다. 단일 식물 변종에 농장을 거는 대신, 안데스 농부는 지금처럼 모든 생태적 적소마다 적어도 하나씩 아주 많은 내기를 걸었다. 그 결과 만들어진 밭은 서구인의 눈에는 (b) 정리된(→ 무질서한) 것 같았는데, 작은 구획은 일관성이 없어서 명확하게 질서 정연한 풍경이 주는 친숙한 만족감을 전혀 제공하지 않았다. 그러나 안데스의 감자밭은 이를테면 1999년의 베르사유나 1845년의 아일랜드와는 달리, 자연이 그것에 던지기 쉬운 사실상 모든 것을 견딜 수 있는 복잡한 자연의 질서를 상징했다. 안데스 밭의 가장자리와 주변 환경은 야생 감자가 살고 있었기 때문에 농부가 재배하는 품종은 자연스레 주기적으로 그것들의 야생 동족들과 교배해 왔는데, 그것은 유전자 풀을 (c) 새롭게 하고 새로운 잡종을 만들어냈다. 이런 새로운 감자들 중 하나가 가령 가뭄이나 폭풍에서 살아남거나 저녁 식탁에서 찬사를 받으면서 그 가치를 (d) 증명할 때마다, 그것은 가장자리에서 경작지로, 때로는 이웃 경작지로도 승격된다. 그래서 인위적인 선택은 지속적인 국지 과정이며, 각각의 새로운 감자는 토지와 그 경작자 사이에 끊임없이 진행되는 주고받기의 산물인데, 모든 가능한 감자의 영역, 즉 그 종의 유전체에 의해 매개된다. 잉카 사람들과 그 후손이 재배한 유전적 (e) 다양성은 놀라운 재배상의 업적이며 전 세계 사람들에게는 헤아릴 수 없는 가치를 가진 선물이다.

구문 [2행~6행] The Incas *figured out* **how to grow** impressive yields of potatoes / under the most unlikely conditions, / **developing** *an approach* [that is still in use in parts of the Andes today].
동사 figured out의 목적어로 「의문사+to-v」가 쓰였고 developing 이하는 부대상황을 나타내는 분사구문이다. 관계대명사 that이 이끄는 형용사절이 선행사 an approach를 수식한다.

[20행~23행] Yet the Andean potato farm represented *an intricate ordering of nature* [that, (unlike Versailles in 1999, say, or Ireland in 1845,) can withstand virtually *anything* [(that) nature is apt to throw at it]].
첫 번째 [ ]는 선행사 an intricate ordering of nature를 수식하는 관계사절이다. 관계대명사 that 다음에 ( )는 전명구로 that과 can withstand 사이에 삽입되었다. nature ~ throw at it은 목적격 관계대명사 that이 생략된 형용사절로 선행사 anything을 수식한다.

[28행~33행] **Whenever** one of these new potatoes proves its worth — surviving a drought or storm, say, or winning praise at the dinner table — // it is promoted **from** *the margins* to *the fields* and, in time, **to** *the neighbors' fields as well.*

whenever는 복합관계부사로 부사절을 이끌며 양쪽 — 사이의 분사구는 부사절의 예시를 나타낸다. 「from A to B」는 'A부터 B까지'의 의미이다.

어휘 descend ~에서 유리하다; 내려가다 plateau 고원; 정체기 yield 수확[산출]량; 생산력 vertical 수직의; 직립한 cultivator 경작[재배]자 microclimate 미기후,

좁은 지역 내의 기후 dramatically 극적으로; 급격하게 orientation 방향성; 지향; 경향 monoculture 단일재배 plot 작은 지면[터]; 줄거리; 계략 discontinuous 일관성 없는; 두절된 explicitly 명백하게; 솔직하게 landscape 풍경, 경관 intricate 복잡한; 얽힌 withstand 견디다, 이겨내다 be apt to-v v하기 쉽다; v하는 경향이 있다 margin 가장자리; 여백; 여유 populate 살다; 거주시키다 variety 품종; 종류; 변화 cross 교배하다; 잡종이 되다 relative 동족; 친척(의) gene pool 유전자 풀; 유전자 공급원 hybrid 잡종; 혼합물 mediate 중재[조정]하다 cultural 재배의; 문화의 incalculable 막대한; 무수한; 변덕스러운

제 4 회

| 1 ④ | 2 ⑤ | 3 ④ | 4 ④ | 5 ⑤ | 6 ③ | 7 ③ | 8 ④ | 9 ④ | 10 ④ |
| 11 ② | 12 ② | 13 ③ | 14 ③ | 15 ④ | 16 ③ | 17 ⑤ | 18 ④ | 19 ② | 20 ④ |

1 심경 변화 ④

해설 '나'는 물건을 옮기는 일에 자원하여 우쭐하고 신나는(excited) 기분이었지만, 실수로 어항을 놓쳐 깨뜨리게 되어서 충격을 받았다(shocked). 그러므로 심경 변화로는 ④ '신나는 → 충격을 받은'이 가장 적절하다.
① 좌절한 → 기쁜　　　② 지루한 → 당황한
③ 침착한 → 짜증이 난　　④ 외로운 → 무서워 하는

해석 4학년 때 나는 토론토에 있는 우리 초등학교에서 우리 교실에서 근처에 있는 교실로 몇몇 물품을 옮기도록 모집된 소수의 아이들 중 하나였다. 나는 내 자신이 그러한 책임을 부여받은 사람들에 속한다는 것을 알고 우쭐한 기분이었다. 나의 학급 친구들은 그 일을 맡은 것에 대해 나를 부러워했다. 품목 중에는 홀로 있는 금붕어를 담고 있는 유리 어항이 있었다. 그 용기는 4분의 3이 물로 채워져 있었으며 꽤 무거웠다. 물고기가 나보다 마음을 덜 쓸지도 모르는 누군가의 손에 놓이는 것이 걱정되어, 나는 목적지인 인접한 교실의 싱크대 옆에 있는 테이블로 어항을 옮기는 일을 자원했다. 얼마나 아이러니한지. 나는 내 어린아이의 손으로 어항을 굳게 잡고 차근차근 문밖으로 나가 복도를 따라 새 교실로 걸어갔다. 조심조심 테이블로 접근했을 때, 어항이 꽉 잡고 있던 내 손길에서 미끄러져 단단한 바닥에 부딪혔다. 그것은 느린 동작으로 재생된 공포의 순간이었다. 유리 조각들이 깨졌고 물은 바닥 여기저기에 튀었다. 나는 망연자실하여 그곳에 서 있었다. 그것은 나쁜 꿈같았다.

구문 [6행~7행] Among the items was a glass fishbowl (containing a lone goldfish).

(C: Among the items, V: was, S: a glass fishbowl)

전명구(Among the items)가 문두에 나와 주어와 동사가 도치되었다. ( )는 a glass fishbowl을 수식하는 분사구이다.

[8행~12행] Concerned that the fish would be placed in the hands of *someone* [who might care less than I did], / I volunteered to transport the bowl to *its destination, a table* (next to the sink in the adjoining room).

Concerned that ~ than I did는 수동의 의미의 분사구문이다. 밑줄 친 its destination과 a table ~ the adjoining room은 동격관계이고, ( )는 a table을 수식하는 형용사구이다.

어휘 flattered 우쭐해 하는, 어깨가 으쓱한 endow A with B A에게 B를 부여하다[주다]; A가 B를 지니고 있다고 믿다[생각하다] vessel 용기, 그릇; 배 adjoining 인접한; 부

근의 methodically 차근차근, 체계적으로 gingerly 조심조심, 신중히 grasp 꽉 쥠; 꽉 잡다; 이해[파악](하다) smash 부딪히다; 박살나다 splinter 깨지다; 조각 splash 튀다; 끼얹다 stun 망연자실하게 만들다; 기절시키다

2 밑줄 함의 ⑤

해설 핀 공장에서 열 개의 작업 과정을 한 명의 노동자가 수행해서 한 개의 완전한 핀을 만드는 경우보다, 노동자 한 명이 한 가지 작업에만 집중하는 경우에 훨씬 더 많은 핀이 생산될 수 있다고 하면서 노동의 분화를 강조했으므로 밑줄 친 부분의 의미로 가장 적절한 것은 ⑤ '노동의 분화가 확립되었을 때 잘 기능한다'이다.
① 개인의 차이를 인정함으로써 만들어지다
② 제품의 질을 향상시키는 데 집중하다
③ 필요한 노동력의 고갈을 이겨내고 생존할 수 있다
④ 합의된 목표를 달성하지 못하면 위기에 처하다

해석 Adam Smith는 자신의 책 《국부론》에서 핀 공장의 사례를 이용해서 현대 사회에 대한 자신의 생각을 설명하고 발전시켰다. 10명의 사람들이 핀을 만드는 일을 맡았다고 상상해보자. 만약 한 사람이 한 개의 완전한 핀을 만들어야 한다면, 아마도 각각의 사람은 하루에 열 개의 핀을 만들 것이다. 한 개의 완전한 핀을 만드는 것은 여러 다른 과정을 포함한다. 그것이 열 가지 다른 작업을 포함한다고 가정해보자. 만약 한 사람이 이 모든 작업을 수행해야 한다면, 그 사람이 한 작업에서 다른 작업으로 옮겨가면서 낭비되는 시간이 있을 것이다. 게다가 이 모든 다양한 작업에 능숙해지는 것은 어려울 것이고, 그것은 많은 훈련과 노력이 필요할 것이다. 하지만 그렇게 하지 않고 이 공장에서 각각의 사람이 열 가지 작업 중에서 단지 한 가지 작업에 집중한다면 어떻게 될까? 무수히 많은 방식으로 시간이 절약될 것이고, 공장은 훨씬 더 많은 핀을 생산할 수 있을 것이다. 누구도 혼자서 완전한 핀을 만들지는 않겠지만 말이다. 결과적으로, 이 공장은 아마 하루에 총 10,000개의 핀을 생산할 것인데, 분업화 없이 단지 100개만 생산했을 것이다. 현대 사회는 더 큰 규모로 핀을 만드는 이 공장과 같다.

구문 [10행~12행] Furthermore, **it** would be hard **to become skilled at all these different tasks** — **that** would require lots of training and effort.

it은 가주어, to become ~ tasks가 진주어이다. that은 바로 앞에 언급된 to become ~ tasks를 가리키는 지시대명사로, 주어 역할을 한다.

어휘 involve 포함하다; 관계가 있다 distinct 다른, 별개의 skilled 능숙한 a myriad of 무수한 specialization 분업화 **[선택지 어휘]** depletion 고갈, 감소 consensus goal 합의된 목표 *cf.* consensus 합의, 일치 division 분화, 분배

3 글의 요지 ④

해설 긍정적인 감정은 빨리 사라져버리기 마련이지만 감사함을 갖게 되면 긍정적인 것들을 더 많이 발견하고 인생에 더욱 적극적으로 참여하는 혜택이 있다는 내용이므로, 글의 요지로 가장 적절한 것은 ④이다.

해석 감정에 관한 연구는 긍정적인 감정들이 빨리 사라진다는 것을 보여준다. 우리의 감정 체계는 새로움을 좋아한다. 그것들은 변화를 좋아한다. 우리는 긍정적인 생활 환경에 적응해서 곧 새 차, 새 배우자, 새집들이 더 이상은 그다지 새롭고 흥미롭게 느껴지지 않는다. 하지만 감사함은 우리가 무언가의 가치를 인정하게 만들고, 우리가 그렇게 인정할 때, 우리는 그것에서 더 많은 혜택을 얻는데, 즉 그것을 당연시 여길 가능성이 줄어든다. 사실상, 감사함은 우리가 인생에 더 많이 참여하게 만든다. 우리는 긍정적인 것들을 더 많이 발견하고, 그것이 인생에서 얻는 즐거움을 더 크게 만든다. 좋은 것에 적응하는 것 대신에, 우리는 좋은 것을 기념한다. 우리는 너무 많은 시간을 영화, 컴퓨터 화면, 스포츠와 같은 것들을 보면서 보내지만, 감사함이 있으면 우리는 관중이 아니라 우리 삶에 더 큰 참여자가 된다.

구문 [6행~8행] But gratitude **makes** *us* **appreciate** *the value* (of something), // and when we do so, / we extract more benefits from it; ~.
「make+O+C」는 'O를 C하게 만들다'의 뜻이다. ( )는 the value를 수식하는 전명구이다.
[13행~16행] We **spend** *so much time* **watching things** — movies, computer screens, sports — // but with gratitude we become greater participants in our lives / as opposed to spectators.
「spend+시간+v-ing」는 'v하면서 시간을 보내다[쓰다]'의 뜻이다. 대시(—) 사이의 movies, computer screens, sports는 things를 부연 설명한다.

어휘 wear off 사라지다, 없어지다 adapt to A A에 적응하다 circumstance 환경; 상황, 사정 spouse 배우자 gratitude 감사, 고마움 appreciate (진가를) 인정하다[알아보다]; 고마워하다; 감상하다; 이해하다 extract 얻다, 뽑아내다; 추출하다 take A for granted A를 당연시하다 in effect 사실상, 실제로는 participate in ~에 참여[참가]하다 *cf.* participant 참여자; 참여하는 magnify 확대하다; 과장하다 as opposed to A A가 아니라; A와는 대조적으로 spectator 관중

4 글의 주제 ④

해설 네 번째 문장의 But을 기점으로, 앞부분은 환자가 직접 온라인상에서 건강 정보를 찾아보는 것이 의료 종사자들의 노력을 덜어주는 등 장점(advantages)이 있다고 제시하지만, 뒷부분에서는 웹상에서 단편적이고 왜곡된 정보가 제시될 수 있고, 정보 검색자가 선입견에 따라 자신의 입맛에 맞는 정보만을 선별적으로 취득한다는 문제점(disadvantages)도 있다고 말하고 있으므로 글의 주제로 가장 적절한 것은 ④ '온라인에서 건강 정보를 찾는 것의 이점과 약점'이다.
① 건강 정보를 온라인에서 발전시킬 때 고려할 점
② 온라인에서 건강 정보를 찾는 행동의 패턴
③ 온라인에서 가치 있는 건강 정보를 검색하는 것의 어려움
⑤ 사람들이 온라인의 건강 정보가 잘못되었다고 믿는 경향

해석 일반적으로 건강 정보를 온라인에서 검색하는 것은 타당하고, 놀랍고, 교육적이고, 심지어는 유용할 수도 있다. 많은 의사들이 환자로부터 "조사를 해 봤어요."라는 말을 들

을 때 눈알을 굴리지만(못마땅해하지만), 때때로 그 조사가 괜찮을 수 있다. 환자가 희귀병을 앓고 있는데 이에 관한 논문을 제시해 주면, 우리 중 많은 이들은 추가적인 일을 면제받은 것에 대해 고마워할 것이다. 그러나 의견, 개인적인 일화, 과장 그리고 허위 주장으로 왜곡된 사이트들이 정보 검색자가 게시된 것을 믿도록 조종할 때 웹은 뒤얽히게 된다. 사람들은 또한 사전에 형성된 개념에 의거하여 온라인에서 정보를 찾을 때 곤경에 처한다. 여기에서 원래의 믿음의 저주가 나타난다. 여러분이 비타민 C의 대량 투여가 감기를 예방해줄 거라고 믿으면, 이러한 생각을 촉진하는 사이트를 찾아 나설 (그리고 쉽게 발견할) 것이다. 해독 주스가 더 나은 건강과 웰빙을 위한 방법이라고 생각한다면, 이를 뒷받침해 주는 웹사이트를 찾기가 쉽다. 백신을 늦추는 것이 기호에 맞는 일이라면, 온라인 정보 출처는 넘쳐난다. 여러분이 유기농 음식만 먹어야 할지에 대해 토론하고 있다면, 이용 가능한 많은 정보가 이를 뒷받침해 줄 것이다.

구문 [6행~7행] ~ many of us will be grateful that we **were saved** some extra work.
'save 사람 사물'은 '…에게 ~을 면하게 해 주다'의 뜻인데, 이를 수동태로 바꾸면 '사람 be saved 사물'의 형태로 쓰이고 '…가 ~을 면제받다'의 뜻이 된다.
[7행~11행] But the Web becomes entangled // when *sites* (angled with opinions, personal anecdotes, exaggeration, and false claims) **manipulate** the navigator to believe *what is posted*.
접속사 when이 이끄는 절 내에서 ( ) 부분은 sites를 수식하는 과거분사구이고, 동사는 manipulate이다. to believe의 목적어로 what이 이끄는 관계사절이 쓰였다.
[16행~18행] If you think that juice cleanses are the way to better health and well-being, **it**'s easy to find *websites* (supporting this).
it은 가주어, to find 이하가 진주어고, ( )은 websites를 수식하는 현재분사구이다.

어휘 valid 타당한, 유효한 eye-opening 놀랄 만한, 눈이 휘둥그레질 만한 sound 괜찮은 rare 희귀한 anecdote 일화 exaggeration 과장 manipulate 조종하다 preconceived 사전에 형성된 megadose 대량 투여하다 cup of tea 기호에 맞는 것 abound 풍부하다

5 글의 제목 ⑤

해설 수학을 가르칠 때 정답풀이식의 교수법을 이용하지 말고 역사와 발전사를 가르쳐서 수학을 재미있게 하고 인간성을 부여하자는 내용의 글이므로 제목으로 가장 적절한 것은 ⑤ '역사적 맥락 안에서 수학의 발전을 가르쳐라'이다.
① 학생들이 수학을 배우는 것을 포기하지 않도록 동기를 부여하라
② 수학을 가르치는 데 표준화된 방법은 없다
③ 수학을 위한 다양한 교수법의 적용
④ 수학 교육이 학생들의 성공에 영향을 미치는 방법들

해석 학교에서 교육되는 수학은 대부분의 중등학교 학생들에게 역사가 결여된 과목으로 인식된다. 교사는 수학 과목에서 학습되어야 할 모든 것의 원천이 되고, 그의 임무는 그 지식을 학생에게 전달하는 것이다. 보통 교육 과정에서, 수학적 창출 과정과 아주 오래된 수학 문제 해결을 위한 노력에 대한 이해는 완전히 상실된다. 대부분의 학생들에게 수학은 정답이 맞는지 틀린지를 결정하는 교사의 머리에 위치한 폐쇄된 과목이다. 이러한 상황은 대부분의 다른 과학에서의 가르침보다 수학의 가르침에 특히 해롭다. 수학은 본래 누적되는 과목이라서, 수천 년 전에 만들어진 것의 대부분은 내용과 과정 둘 다 오늘날에도 여전히 유효하다. 학생들을 이러한 발전의 일부에 노출시키는 것은 그 과목을 재미있게 만들고 학생들을 위해 그것에 인간성을 부여할 잠재성을 가진다.

구문 [1행~3행] Mathematics **as** (it is) **taught** in school *is perceived* / by most secondary school students / *as a subject* (lacking history).
as와 taught 사이에 it(mathematics) is가 생략된 것으로 볼 수 있으며, 접속사 as의 뜻은 '~처럼, ~대로'이다. be perceived as는 '~로 인식되다'의 뜻이다. ( )는 능동의 의미로 a subject를 수식한다.

[16행~18행] **Exposing** *students* **to** *some of this development* / *has the* potential (to make the subject fun and to humanize *it* for ***them***).
Exposing ~ development는 주어이며 「expose A to B」는 'A를 B에 노출시키다'의 뜻이다. ( )는 두 개의 to-v구가 병렬구조를 이루며 the potential을 수식한다. to humanize 뒤의 it은 the subject를, them은 students를 지칭한다.

어휘 perceive 인식하다   secondary school 중등학교   instructional 교육 (상)의   age-old 아주 오래된   by nature 천성적으로   accumulative 누적되는   millennium 천 년 *pl.* millennia   valid 유효한, 타당한   humanize 인간성을 부여하다

6 안내문 불일치 ③

해설 발표는 독일어로 제공된다고 했으므로 ③이 일치하지 않는다.

해석 두려움을 극복하기 Greg Milson의 워크숍
Greg Milson은 25년 동안 등반가이자 두 권의 책의 저자입니다. 2007년에, 그는 Matterhorn에서의 등반 사고에서 두 팔을 모두 잃었습니다. 이번 90분의 워크숍에서 그는 신체의 장애를 극복한 것에 대해 이야기할 것입니다.

장소 & 일시: Zermatt 시에 있는 Shanty Hall에서 7월 28일 금요일, 오후 7시 30분
발표: 발표 연설은 독일어로 제공되지만, 영어를 비롯하여 4개 국어로 동시통역이 이용 가능할 것입니다.

예약은 7월 27일까지 www.shantyhall.com에서 온라인으로 하셔야 합니다.
(입장료는 18달러이고, 좌석은 200석으로 제한됩니다.)
좌석은 선착순으로 배정됩니다.
발표장 안에서는 식음료가 허용되지 않습니다.

어휘 conquer (다루기 힘든 것) 극복[정복]하다   climbing accident 등반 사고   overcome 극복하다; 이기다   disability (신체적·정신적) 장애   simultaneous 동시의, 동시에 일어나는   admission 입장(료), 가입   first-come basis 선착순

7 밑줄 어법 ③

해설 ③ 모든 동사는 반드시 주어가 있어야 하므로 동사 sends의 주어가 필요하다. 따라서 동사 Make를 주어 역할을 할 수 있는 동명사 Making이나 to부정사 To make로 고쳐야 어법상 적절하다.
① do damage to A의 표현으로 'A에게 해를 끼치다'라는 의미이다. 동사 do의 목적어로 명사 damage가 쓰였으므로 어법상 적절하다.
② 앞에 나온 something을 수식하는 형용사 sad는 어법상 적절하다. -thing, -body, -one으로 끝난 부정대명사는 형용사가 뒤에서 수식한다.
④ 비교급 better과 함께 비교표현을 만드는 than은 어법상 적절하다.
⑤ 앞에 나온 복수 명사인 The ~ snapshots를 가리키므로 복수형의 지시대명사 those는 어법상 적절하다.

해석 여러분이 무엇을 하든지, 제발 얼굴에 가짜 미소를 붙이지(띠지) 마라. 진실하지 못한 미소는 영혼에 피해를 입힌다. 우리는 모두 슬픈 어떤 것에 대해 말하면서 바보 같은 웃음을 지었던 사람들을 알고 지내왔다. 여러분이 그렇게 하고 싶지 않을 때조차 미소를 짓는 이러한 경향은 어린 시절에 생겼는데, 그때 우리의 부모님은 비록 우리가 미소 짓고 싶지 않더라도, 카메라 또는 다른 사람들을 향해 미소를 짓도록 설득했다. 아이들이 미소를 지을 수 없을 때 미소를 짓게 만드는 것은 진정한 것이 괜찮지 않다는 메시지를 전달한다. 카메라 앞에서조차 거짓된 응시보다는 진실한 짜증 난 얼굴을 포착하는 것이 더 낫다. 가장 매력적인 스냅 사진은 진실한 것, 즉 사람들이 진실한 모습을 포착한 사진이다. 거짓된 사람들은 오히려 울고 싶을 때 억지 미소를 띠거나, 화나거나 슬플 때 미소를

짓는다. 그들은 천천히 자신의 영혼과 접촉이 끊어진다.

구문 [4행~8행] This tendency to smile even when you don't feel like it developed in *childhood*, // **when** our parents persuaded us into smiling for the camera or for other people / even though we didn't feel like it.
This tendency와 to smile ~ like it은 동격 관계이다. 여기에서 when은 계속적 용법의 관계부사로 when이 이끄는 절은 childhood를 보충 설명한다.
[8행~10행] **Making kids smile** *when they aren't up to it* **sends** a message that it's not OK to be authentic.
동명사 주어 Making kids smile과 동사 sends 사이에 부사절이 끼어있는 구조이다. 접속사 that이 이끄는 절은 a message와 동격 관계를 이룬다.

어휘 paste (풀로) 붙이다; 풀; 반죽   fake 가짜의, 거짓된   plastic 진실하지 못한; 인조 같은; 플라스틱(의)   grin (소리 없이) 활짝 웃음   tendency 경향; 추세, 동향   be up to A A를 할 수 있다; A에 달려 있다   authentic 진정한, 진짜인; 진품인   genuine 진실한, 진심의; 진짜[진품]의   irritable 짜증 난, 화가 난   stare 응시; 빤히 쳐다보다   fascinating 매력적인, 흥미로운   snapshot 스냅 사진   plaster on smiles ((비유적)) 억지 미소를 띠다   lose touch with ~와 접촉[연락]이 끊어지다

8 밑줄 어휘 ④

해설 같은 범주에 있는 것들을 통해 어떤 실체를 유추하는 것이 불확실성을 줄이는 한 가지 근원이라는 것을 자동차, 바비큐 갈비의 예를 들어 설명하고 있다. 따라서 어떤 실체의 범주를 알면 그것과 연관된 불확실성을 줄여준다는 문맥이 자연스러우므로 ④ 'increase'는 reduce(줄이다)로 고쳐야 한다.

해석 불확실성은 삶의 기본적인 사실이다. 불확실성에도 불구하고, 사람들은 세상에 대한 ① 예측을 해야 한다. 여러분이 사는 것을 고려하고 있는 자동차가 믿을 만할 것인가? 여러분은 자신이 주문하는 음식을 좋아할 것인가? 여러분이 숲에서 동물을 보면, 무엇을 해야 하는가? 불확실성을 줄이는 한 가지 근원(근거)은 범주의 일원이라는 것이다. 비록 모든 Xpress Sportscar들이 정확히 똑같지는 않더라도, 그것들은 너무 ② 유사해서 여러분이 (구매를) 고려하고 있는 새로운 Sportscar가 믿을 만할 것이라고 어느 정도 확신을 가지고 예측할 수 있다. Kansas City 방식의 바비큐 갈비들이 ③ 동일하지는 않지만, 그것들은 구운 닭 요리나 두부 요리보다는 서로 더 비슷한 맛이 난다. 따라서 어떤 실체의 범주를 아는 것은 여러분이 하고 싶어 하는 예측에 관하여 범주에 속하는 것들이 균일하다는 정도까지 그것과 연관된 불확실성을 ④ 높여 준다(→ 줄여준다). 이 '범주에 기반을 둔 귀납법'은 범주들이 일상생활에서 우리에게 ⑤ 유용한 주된 방식 중의 하나이다.

구문 [7행~10행] Although all Xpress Sportscars are not exactly the same, // they are **so** *similar* **that** you can predict with some confidence / that the new Sportscar [(which[that]) you are considering] will be reliable.
'너무 ~해서 …한'이라는 뜻의 「so ~ that ...」 구문이 사용되었다. that ~ reliable은 predict의 목적어 역할을 하는 that절이고 with some confidence는 삽입구문이다. [ ]는 목적격 관계대명사 which[that]가 생략되어 the new Sportscar를 수식하는 관계사절이다.
[13행~17행] **Knowing** the category of an entity / therefore / serves to reduce *the uncertainty* (associated with it) / to the degree that the category members are uniform with respect to *the prediction* [(which[that]) you want to make].
Knowing the category of an entity는 문장의 주어 역할을 하는 동명사구이다. ( )는 수동의 의미로 the uncertainty를 수식한다. [ ]는 목적격 관계대명사가 생략되어 the prediction을 수식하는 관계사절이다.

어휘 uncertainty 불확실성   reliable 믿을[신뢰할] 수 있는   category 범주, 카테고리   rib (고기의) 갈비   identical 동일한, 똑같은   tofu 두부   entity 실체   serve to (~하는) 역할을 하다   to the degree that ~ 하는 정도까지   with respect to A A에 관하여   induction 귀납법

9 빈칸 추론 ④

해설 빈칸 문장으로 보아 인간이 건강할 가능성이 그 생태계의 건강 기능에 '어떠한지'를 파악해야 한다. 이 글은 질병의 원인이 환경적인 것에 있다는, 즉 인간의 건강 가능성이 생태계의 건강 기능에 영향을 받는다는 생태계 건강(ecosystem health)이라는 개념에 관한 내용이므로, 빈칸에 들어가기에 가장 적절한 것은 ④ '비례하는'이다.
① 열등한 ② 선호되는 ③ 부차적인 ⑤ 기여하는

해석 의학적 관점에서, 건강은 개인의 속성으로 여겨진다. 의학과 공중위생 분야는 전통적으로 질병의 환경적 원인들을 인정해 왔고 특정한 노출에 대해 위험성을 부여해 왔다. 지난 10년간, 생물학자들, 생태학자들, 그리고 의사들은 생태계 건강이라는 개념 또한 발전시켜 왔다. 이 생각은 인간이 복잡한 생태계의 참여자이고 인간이 건강할 가능성이 그들 생태계의 건강 기능에 비례하는 것을 인정한다. 생태계에 기반을 둔 건강 관점은 자연환경이 제공하는 건강과 관련된 서비스(예를 들어, 흙 생산, 수분, 그리고 물 정화)를 고려하고, 건강한 환경과 인간의 건강 사이의 근본적인 연관성을 인정한다. 생태계 건강론의 입장은 생물학 과학자들이 점점 더 많이 공유하는 인간 중심적이 아닌 전체론적인 세계관이다.

구문 [11행~16행] An ecosystem-based health perspective takes into account *the health-related services* [that the natural environment provides] (e.g., soil production, pollination, and water cleansing) / and acknowledges the fundamental connection (between a healthy environment and human health). and가 밑줄 친 두 개의 동사(구) takes into account와 acknowledges를 병렬 연결한다. [ ]는 목적격 관계대명사 that이 이끄는 절로 the health-related services를 수식한다.

어휘 standpoint 관점, 견해   attribute 속성, 자질; ~탓[덕]으로 보다   acknowledge 인정하다; 감사를 표하다   assign 부여하다, 할당하다; 배치하다   exposure 노출; 폭로   decade 10년   biologist 생물학자   *cf.* biological 생물학(상)의   ecologist 생태학자   recognize 인정하다; 알아보다, 분간하다   complex 복잡한; 복합건물   potential 가능성(이 있는); 잠재력   function 기능(하다); 작동하다   perspective 관점, 시각; 균형감   take into account ~을 고려하다   fundamental 근본적인, 기본적인; 핵심[필수]적인   stance 입장, 태도; 자세   holistic 전체론적인, 전체론의

10 빈칸 추론 ④

해설 화자의 의도는 비언어적 신호로 드러나며 빈정거림의 본질이 의도와 메시지 간의 모순을 의미한다고 했으므로, 화자가 빈정대고 있다는 결론을 내리려면 ④ '언어적 메시지와 비언어적 메시지'가 서로 상충되는지 비교하여야 한다.
① 화자의 기분과 비언어적 메시지
② 빈정대는 메시지와 속이는 메시지
③ 언어적 단서와 그들 자신의 감정
⑤ 언어적 단서와 글

해석 연구자들은 빈정거림의 다양한 비언어적 특성들을 보고했다. 대부분의 연구자들은 비언어적 신호가 빈정거림 혹은 그것을 유발하는 감정을 인지하는 데 필수적인 것인지에 대해서는 의견이 다르다. 그렇다하더라도 연구는 특히 언어적 신호와 비언어적 신호가 상충될 때는 비언어적 신호가 언어적 신호보다 더 믿을 만하다는 연구 결과를 확증해 준다. 또한, 비언어적 신호는 화자의 의도를 보여주는 더 좋은 지표이다. 빈정거림의 본질이 의

도와 메시지 사이의 모순을 시사하므로, 속임수를 쓸 때에 그러는 것처럼 비언어적 신호가 말하는 사람의 진정한 기분 상태를 '새어나오게 하며' 폭로할지도 모른다. 일반적으로 빈정대는 사람은 받아들이는 사람이 그 빈정대는 의도를 알아차리기를 의도하지만, 반면에 속임수를 쓸 때에는 일반적으로 화자가 그 속이려는 의도를 듣는 사람이 알아차리지 못하도록 의도한다는 점에서, 표면상으로 빈정거림은 속임과 반대되는 것이다. 그러므로 의사전달자들이 어떤 화자가 빈정대는 것인지 판단하려고 할 때에, 언어적 메시지와 비언어적 메시지를 비교하여 그 둘이 서로 반대이면 화자가 빈정대고 있다는 결론을 내릴 수도 있다.

구문 [2행~4행] Most disagree *as to* **whether** nonverbal cues are essential to the perception of sarcasm or the emotion [that prompts it]. '~에 관하여'라는 뜻의 구 as to의 목적어로 whether ~ 가 쓰였다. the perception of의 목적어로 sarcasm과 the emotion that prompts it이 병렬을 이루고 있다.

어휘 nonverbal 비언어적인, 말을 쓰지 않는   cue 신호, 단서   perception 인지, 지각   prompt 유발하다, 자극하다; 즉각적인, 지체 없는   confirm 확증하다, 확인해 주다   credible 믿을 수 있는, 확실한   conflict 상충되다, 모순되다   indicator 보여주는 것, 지표   intent 의도   imply 시사하다   contradiction 모순   leak 새게 하다, 누설하다   deception 속임, 사기   in that ~라는 점에서

11 빈칸 추론 ②

해설 동물에게 어떤 행동을 보상 기법을 써서 훈련시키려 했지만 이것이 본능적 행동을 이길 수 없어서 실패한 사례를 반영하여 빈칸을 완성하면 ② '생물학적으로 프로그램된 행동의 중요성'이 된다.
① 야생 동물 길들이기의 어려움
③ 훈련을 통한 본능 억제 가능성
④ 강화에 의해 압도된 본능적 행동
⑤ 긍정적 강화와 부정적 강화 간의 균형

해석 서커스, TV와 영화 스턴트를 위해 동물을 훈련시키기 위한 조작적 조건 형성을 사용했을 때의 그들의 경험에 의존하여, Kellar Breland와 Marian Breland는 동물의 행동을 조건화시키려는 그들의 시도가 동물의 내재된 본능과 정면으로 부딪혔던 수많은 상황을 설명했다. 예를 들어 조작적 조건 형성 이론에서, 행동을 보상하는 것은 그 행동의 빈도를 증가시켜야 마땅했다. 그러나 Breland 부부가 두 개의 동전을 돼지 저금통에 떨어뜨리는 반응을 먹을 것으로 보상함으로써 이 행동을 하도록 너구리를 훈련시키려 시도했을 때, 너구리는 협조하지 않았다. 너구리가 두 개의 동전을 돼지 저금통에 넣는 것에 대해 먹을 것으로 보상받은 후에, 그것은 그 다음 동전 두 개를 가져다가 새로 잡힌 가재의 껍데기를 제거하기 위해 자신들이 그러는 것처럼, 그것들을 함께 문지르기 시작했다. 결국 동전 문지르기 반응은 동전 떨어뜨리기 반응을 압도했고 Breland 부부는 너구리를 훈련시키려는 시도를 포기해야 했다. Breland 부부는 생물학적으로 프로그램된 행동의 중요성을 강조하기 위해 이것과 다른 예들을 사용했다.

구문 [3행~6행] ~, Kellar Breland and Marian Breland described *a number of situations* [in which their attempts to condition an animal's behavior **ran** head-on into the animal's built-in instincts].
[ ]는 a number of situations를 수식하는 관계사절이며 여기에서 밑줄 친 부분이 주어이고 ran이 동사이다.
[13행~15행] ~ it took the next two coins and began rubbing them together, // **just as** *they do* to remove the shells of newly caught crayfish.
동사 took과 began이 병렬구조를 이룬다. just as는 '꼭 ~처럼'의 뜻이다. just as 다음의 they는 racoons를, do는 동사 rub를 지칭한다.

어휘 draw on ~에 의존하다   condition 길들이다, 훈련시키다   run into ~을 들이받다, 충돌하다   head-on 정면으로 부딪친   built-in 타고난, 고유의, 내장된   instinct

본능 reward 보상을 주다 frequency 빈도 raccoon 미국너구리 piggy bank 돼지 저금통 rub 문지르다 shell 껍데기 overpower 압도하다

12 빈칸 추론 ②

해설 빈칸 문장으로 보아 할 수 있는 유일한 것이 '무엇'인지 찾아야 한다. 좋지 않은 아이디어를 만들지 않고는 좋은 아이디어를 만들 수 없다는 본문의 내용을 통해서, 좋은 아이디어를 만들어 내기 위해서는 먼저 실패를 많이 해야 한다는 것을 알 수 있으므로, ② '다음 아이디어로 이동할 수 있도록 더 빨리 실패하는'이 적절하다.
① 당신을 독특하게 만들기 위해 관습에 얽매이지 않는 아이디어를 사용하는
③ 시행착오를 피하기 위해서 다른 사람들로부터 빌려오는
④ 좋은 아이디어의 본질적인 장점과 특성을 인식하는
⑤ 너무 많은 것이 충분하지 않은 것보다는 낫다는 느낌을 극복하는

해석 창의성에 관해 입 밖에 내지 않는 하나의 진실은, 그것이 아주 특이한 재능에 관한 것이라기보다는 생산성에 관한 것이라는 점이다. 효과가 있는 몇 개의 아이디어를 발견하기 위해서는 당신은 그렇지 않은(효과가 없는) 많은 것들을 시도할 필요가 있다. 그것은 순전히 숫자 게임이다. 천재들이 반드시 다른 창조자들보다 더 높은 성공률을 나타내는 것은 아니다. 그들은 단순히 더 많이 하며, 그리고 여러 가지 다양한 것들을 한다. 그들은 더 많은 성공과 더 많은 실패를 한다. 그것은 팀과 회사에도 해당된다. 많은 좋지 않은 아이디어를 만들어 내지 않으면서도 많은 좋은 아이디어를 만들어 내는 것은 불가능하다. 창의성에 관한 것은, 처음에 당신은 어떤 아이디어가 성공하고 어떤 것이 실패할 것인지를 알 수 없다는 것이다. 그래서 당신이 할 수 있는 유일한 것은 <u>다음 아이디어로 이동할 수 있도록 더 빨리 실패하는</u> 것이다.

구문 [4행~6행] Geniuses **don't necessarily** have a **higher** success rate / **than** other creators; ~.
부분부정을 나타내는 not necessarily가 쓰였으며, '반드시 ~한 것은 아니다'로 해석한다. 「비교급 ~ than ....」 형태의 비교급 구문이 사용되었다.
[8~10행] It's impossible / **to generate a lot of good ideas** / **without also generating a lot of bad ideas**.
It은 to generate ~ bad ideas를 대신하는 가주어이다.

어휘 unspoken 입 밖에 내지 않는, 무언의 not A so much as B A라기보다는 B productivity 생산성 pure 순전한; 순수한; 깨끗한 go for A A에 해당되다; A를 선택(선호)하다; A를 얻으려 애쓰다 generate 만들어 내다; (감정 등을) 일으키다 [선택지 어휘] unconventional 관습에 얽매이지 않는; 색다른; 자유로운 trial and error 시행착오 essential 본질적인; 필수적인

13 흐름 무관 문장 ③

해설 사람들이 본능에 따라 다양한 것에 욕망을 가지게 되고, 욕망을 가질수록 그것을 잃는 것을 더 두려워한다는 내용의 글이다. ③은 '필수품을 확보한 사람만이 소유 본능을 절제할 수 있다'는 내용이므로 글의 전체 흐름과 관계없는 문장이다.

해석 두려움은 욕망과 직접 연결되어 있다. 우리가 어떤 것을 더 강하게 바랄수록, 우리는 그것을 잃는 것을 더 심하게 두려워한다. 다양한 본능에 의해 충동을 받아 우리는 유형의 것과 무형의 것 모두를 강력히 원하고, 바라며, 그리고 필요로 한다. ① 이것들의 범위는 삶 그 자체와 사랑하는 사람의 존재에서부터 명성, 재산, 권력, 명망, 사랑, 예술, 스포츠 등의 것들을 원하는 것에 이른다. ② 이것들은 각기 우리에게 서로 다른 종류의 즐거움과 만족감을 줘서 삶이 더 풍요롭고 매우 바람직한 것이 되고, 그래서 이 대상들을 잃는다는 생각은 우리의 마음속에 두려움을 불어넣는다. ③ <u>오직 기본적인 필수품들을 확보하는 데 성공한 사람들만이 소유 본능을 다스릴 절제력을 얻을 수 있다.</u> ④ 어떤 것을 가장

소중히 여기는가에 따라 우리는 그것을 잃는 것을 가장 심하게 두려워한다. ⑤ 특히, 죽음은 이 애착의 대상물들과 그것들과 관련된 즐거움을 끝내서, 사람들은 보통은 죽음을 가장 두려워한다.

구문 [1행~3행] **The stronger** we desire something, **the more** intensely we fear losing it.
「The 비교급 ~, the 비교급 ....」 구문으로 '~하면 할수록 더 …하다'의 뜻이다.
[3행~4행] **Urged** by various instincts, / we strongly want, desire, and need both material and immaterial things.
Urged ~ instincts는 분사구문으로 주절의 주어 we가 의미상의 주어로 충동을 겪는 대상이므로 과거분사 Urged를 사용했다.
[13행~15행] Depending on which we cherish the most, / we fear losing **that** (the most intensely).
that은 '우리가 가장 소중히 여기는 것'을 의미한다. ( )는 '가장 심하게'의 의미로 바로 앞 내용을 수식한다.

어휘 desire 욕망 intensely 강하게 urge 충동을 주다, 자극하다 instinct 본능 material 유형의(↔ immaterial 무형의) presence 존재 fame 명성 desirable 바람직한 discipline 절제력; 훈육 possessive 소유욕이 강한 cherish 소중히 여기다 put an end to ~을 끝내다 attachment 애착

14 글의 순서 ③

해설 주어진 문장에서는 첫째 아이가 두 가지 장점을 누리며, 그 중 첫 번째는 인생 초반에 부모의 관심을 온전히 누린다는 내용이 나온다. (B)에 나오는 중단과 간섭 없는 사랑이 이러한 첫째가 누리는 독점적 사랑이므로 주어진 문장 다음에는 (B)가 나와야 한다. (C)에는 둘째가 태어난 새로운 상황이 제시되고, (A)에는 그러한 상황에서 오히려 나눔을 배우고 자아를 굳건히 견지할 수 있는 첫째가 누리는 두 번째 장점이 제시된다. (C)의 then은 첫째가 외동아이로서 독점적 사랑을 누리는 (B)의 시점을 가리킨다. (A)의 This는 (C) 마지막의 '첫째는 둘째가 태어나도 자아 존중감을 잃지 않는 것'을 나타낸다.

해석 남동생이나 여동생이 있는 첫째 아이는 다른 아기들보다 이중의 이점을 얻는다. 인생의 첫 해나 두 해 동안 그는 자신의 새로이 부모가 된 엄마 아빠의 완전한 관심을 향유하게 되며 외동아이로서 아주 훌륭하게 대접받는다.
(B) 그는 어떠한 중단이나 개입 없이 자신이 얼마나 사랑받는지를 알게 된다. 그의 자기 존중이 피어나고, 그는 자신을 '사랑 받을 가치가 있는' 존재로 평가한다.
(C) 그러나 그 때, 그가 자만심이 강해질 기회를 갖기 전에, 두 번째 아기가 나오고 그는 부모의 거의 모든 관심이 이제 이 작은 신참자에게 쏠려 있음을 갑자기 깨닫게 된다. 그는 이것을 받아들이려고 애써야 하지만, 이렇게 할 때 그는 자신의 자아 존중감을 잃지 않는다.
(A) 이는 그가 이제 토대 삼아 사회적 공유의 제한 인자를 쌓아올릴 수 있는 '자아'의 확고한 기반을 갖췄음을 의미한다. 그 결과는 다른 사람들과 진정으로 섞여 들어갈 수 있는 자신감 있는 성격이다.

구문 [6행~8행] ~ he has a *solid foundation of "self"* [**on which** he can now build the limiting factors of social sharing].
[ ]는 a solid foundation of "self"를 수식하며, on which는 on the solid foundation of "self"를 나타낸다.
[14행] ~ along *comes* baby number two ~
부사 along이 문두로 나와 강조되고 있으며, 동사 comes 다음에 주어 baby number two가 나온 도치구문이다.

어휘 royally 아주 훌륭하게 self-assured 자신감 있는 genuine 진짜의 interruption 방해, 중단 interference 간섭, 개입 self-respect 자기 존중

blossom 꽃을 피우다   rate A as B A를 B로 평가하다   self-important 자만심이 강한   come to terms with 받아들이는 법을 배우다, 받아들이려고 애쓰다   self-worth 자아 존중감

15 글의 순서   ④

해설 (C)의 At the time은 주어진 문장의 11세기 중반을 가리킨다. 생선의 수요는 증가했지만 공급은 급락한 사태를 내용으로 한 (C) 다음에는 서식지가 없어지고 수질이 오염된 예를 들어 공급 급락을 더 자세히 서술한 (A)가 나온다. (A)를 이어서 제분소와 댐 건설이라는 추가적인 공급 급락의 원인이 제시된 (B)는 (A) 다음에 나와야 한다.

해석 11세기 중반 경의 몇 십 년의 기간 내에 생선 공급원이 80%의 민물고기에서 80%의 대구, 해덕과 청어 같은 해수어로 극적으로 변했다.
(C) 그 당시에 수요는 인구 증가와 도시화의 결합 덕분에 가파르게 증가하고 있었다. 민물고기 공급은 강, 호수와 포구에서 인간이 유발한 서식지 변화의 결과 수직 낙하 상태였다. (A) 농업의 확산과 더불어 숲은 베어 없어졌고 땅은 작물을 위해 깊숙이 쟁기질되었다. 토양 침식은 곧 빠르게 흐르는 시원하고 맑은 물을 느릿느릿한 따뜻하고 탁한 물로 바꾸어 놓았는데, 이를 연어와 같은 종들은 반기지 않았다.
(B) 연어와 알을 낳기 위해 바다에서 강으로 이동한 다른 물고기들도 또한 옥수수 제분소와 다른 산업체에 전력을 공급하려고 유럽의 강을 가로질러 있는 수천 개의 댐의 건설로부터 이익을 얻지도 못했다. 이동 경로가 막히자 민물고기 어장의 생산은 붕괴됐다.

구문 [11행~13행] Nor *did* **salmon, and** *other fish* **[that migrated from sea to rivers to spawn]**, *benefit* from the construction of thousands of dams ~
「Nor+조동사+주어+동사원형」은 '~도 또한 그렇지 않다'의 뜻인 도치구문이다. did 다음의 salmon ~ to spawn이 주어이고 benefit이 동사원형이다.
[14행~16행] **With** *their migration routes* **blocked,** / freshwater fisheries' production collapsed.
「with O p.p.」는 'O가 ~된 채로, O가 ~된 상태에서'의 뜻을 가지는 분사구문이다.

어휘 freshwater 담수   saltwater 해수의   cod 대구   haddock 해덕   herring 청어   fell 베어 넘어뜨리다   plough 쟁기질하다   erosion 침식   sluggish 느릿느릿한   salmon 연어   migrate 이동하다   mill 방앗간, 제분소   fishery 어장   collapse 붕괴하다   urbanization 도시화   freefall 자유 낙하, (가치의) 급락

16 문장 넣기   ③

해설 ③의 이전 부분에서는 포괄적인 원격 의료에 대해 논하고 ③ 이후의 세 문장에서는 고해 성사를 언급하고 있다. '정신 의학 분야에서 원격 의료에 장점이 있다'는 내용의 주어진 문장이 ③에 위치하면, '원격 의료가 성공적으로 시행되고 있다 → 정신 의학 분야에서 원격 의료가 장점을 보인다 → 이 성공의 원리는 고해 성사의 원리와 비슷하다'는 논리적 구조가 완성된다. 따라서 주어진 문장은 ③에 들어가야 한다.

해석 논리를 따르면 우리가 전자 통신에 점점 더 많이 의존하는 것은 사회적 고립을 증가시킬지도 모른다. 실제로, 어떤 연구는 이메일에 무제한적으로 접근할 수 있는 것이 실제로 사람들의 외로움과 고립감을 증가시킨다고 말한다. 그러나 원격 의료라는 새로운 매체에서 종사하며 전자 통신이 사람들이 교류하는 것을 더 쉽게 만들어줄 수도 있다는 것을 발견한 다른 사람들도 있다. 규모가 너무 작아서 상근 의료 서비스 제공자를 쓸 여유가 없는 고립된 사회에서, 원격 의료, 즉 화상 회의 기술의 도움을 활용하는 진단과 치료는 성공적으로 시험되고 있다. 원격 정신 의학 진료를 도입해온 어떤 사람들은 환자들이 이러한 소통 방식으로 인해 어색해하기보다는, 실제로 정신 의학과 의사와 대면하여 말할

때보다 거리낌을 덜 느낀다는 점에 주목했다. 이것은 우리가 훌륭한 분이지만 개인적인 감정을 섞지 않는 고해 신부에게 우리의 가장 깊숙한 짐을 전할 때 느끼는 편안함과 같은 현상의 일부일 수 있다. 그것은 가톨릭의 고해 성사실에 가려져 있는 사제에게 죄를 고백하는 행위의 이면에 숨어있는 성공적인 원리의 일부일 수 있다. 그러나 이 새로운 시대에 우리가 마음을 털어놓는 사람은 오크 나무 벽면과 벨벳 커튼 뒤가 아니라 빛을 내는 보호용 컴퓨터 스크린 뒤에 감춰져 있다.

구문 [10행~13행] But there are *others* (working in the new medium of telemedicine) [who have found // that electronic communications may **make it** *easier for people* **to interact**].
( )와 [ ] 모두 others를 수식한다. [ ]절에서 make 다음의 it은 가목적어, to interact가 진목적어이며 for people은 to interact에 대한 의미상 주어이다. 「make+it+형용사+for A+to-v」는 'A가 v하는 것을 형용사하게 만들다'의 뜻이다.
[23행~26행] However, / in this new age, / **the person** [to whom we bare our hearts] **is not** hidden behind oak walls and velvet curtains **but** behind a glowing, protective computer screen.
[ ]는 '전치사+관계대명사'로 시작되는 형용사절로서 주어 the person을 수식하며, the person에 상응하는 동사는 is이다. is 이하에서는 「not A but B (A가 아니라 B다)」 구문이 사용되었다.

어휘 institute 도입하다, 개시하다; 기관   telepsychiatric 원격 정신 의학의   session 진료; 시간, 회기   inhibited 어색해하는, 거리끼는   telemedicine 원격 의료   diagnosis 진단   videoconferencing 화상 회의 시스템   impersonal 개인의 감정을 섞지 않는   confessor 고해 신부   priest 사제   bare one's heart 마음을 털어놓다

17 문장 넣기   ⑤

해설 주어진 문장에 나온 these connections는 ⑤ 앞 문장에 있는 how they are connected를 지칭한다. 또한 주어진 문장에 나온 the basic, "general" laws는 ⑤ 뒤 문장에서 To be sure, "general" laws apply to everything으로 재언급되고 있으므로, 주어진 문장은 이 두 문장 사이인 ⑤에 위치해야 한다.

해석 많은 과학자들은 화학과 물리학을 심리학이 어떤 것이어야 하는지에 대한 이상적인 모델로 여긴다. 어쨌든, 뇌 속에 있는 원자들은 모든 다른 형태의 물질을 지배하는 동일한 포괄적인 물리 법칙의 지배를 받는다. 그렇다면 우리는 또한 완전히 그러한 동일한 기본 법칙의 관점에서 우리의 뇌가 실제로 하는 일을 설명할 수 있는가? 수십억 개의 뇌세포가 각각 개별적으로 작용하는 방식을 우리가 이해한다고 해서 이것이 우리에게 뇌가 하나의 작용 주체로서 작용하는 방식을 알려 주지는 못할 것이기 때문에 대답은 아니오이다. '생각의 법칙'은 그러한 뇌세포의 속성에 의존할 뿐만 아니라 그것들이 연결되어 있는 방식에도 의존한다. 그리고 이러한 연결을 확립하는 것은 기본적인, '일반적' 물리 법칙이라기보다는 오히려 우리가 물려받은 유전자 속에 있는 수백만 정보의 특정한 배열이다. 물론, '일반적' 법칙은 모든 것에 적용되지만, 바로 그러한 이유로, 그것들은(일반적 법칙들은) 특정한 어떤 것은 거의 설명할 수가 없는 것이다.

구문 [15행~17행] The "laws of thought" depend **not only** upon the properties of those brain cells **but also** on how they are connected.
「not only A but also B」는 'A뿐만 아니라 B도'의 뜻이다. A와 B에 해당하는 부분이 각각 upon과 on으로 시작하고 있는데, 이 두 구문은 depend 뒤에 이어지며, depend on[upon]은 '~에 달려있다'의 뜻이다.

어휘 arrangement 배열   inherit 물려받다   gene 유전자   look on A as B A를 B로 간주하다   ideal 이상적인   after all 결국   atom 원자   subject to A A의 영향을 받는   all-inclusive 모두를 포함한   govern 지배하다   in terms of ~의 측면에서   separately 따로따로, 별도로   agency 작용, 힘   property 특성   apply to A A에 적용되다

18 요약문 완성 ④

해설 아시아인들은 개인의 잘못이 자신이 속한 집단의 평판을 해친다고 생각하기 때문에 잘못된 행동을 했을 때 수치심을 느낀다. 그러므로 아시아에서 개인은 '명예롭게(honorably)' 행동하도록 강조된다. 반면에 서양인들은 외부의 기준이 아닌 양심과 내적 감각, 즉 '내적(internal)' 규준으로 스스로의 행동을 평가하므로 죄책감의 지배를 받는다.

① 안전하게 – 내적인
② 안전하게 – 외적인
③ 책임감 있게 – 객관적인
⑤ 명예롭게 – 외적인

해석 많은 '아시아' 사회에서 사람들은 '수치심'과 '다른 사람들이 뭐라고 할까'와 통제의 외적 중심지에 의해 지배받는다. 집단, 예컨대 가족, 팀 혹은 조직의 평판을 유지하라는 집단의 압력이 존재한다. 개인이 선을 넘으면, 그는 다른 사람들이 뭐라고 할지에 대해 걱정하게 된다. 개인과 그가 속한 집단에 대한 수치 혹은 '체면 손실'의 감정이 존재할지도 모른다. '죄책감'에 의해 지배되는 '서구' 사회에서는 사람들이 잘못된 일을 했을 때 다른 사람들이 뭐라고 할지에 대해서는 그다지 걱정하지 않는다. 개인들은 자기 자신의 양심과 옳고 그름에 대한 내적 감각에 더 응답하도록 양육된다. 과연 유대교–가톨릭교 사회에서 어린이들은 매우 강력한 죄책감과 함께 양육된다.

↓

집단 내에서 (A) 명예롭게 행동하는 것을 강조하는 아시아인들은 수치심에 지배받는 반면 (B) 내적 규준을 따르는 서양인들은 죄책감에 의해 지배받는다.

구문 [7행~9행] There may be feelings of shame or 'loss of face' / **for** the individuals [and] *the group* [to which he/she belongs].
[ ]는 '전치사+관계대명사'로 이어지는 절로서 앞의 the group을 수식한다. the individuals와 the group은 and로 연결되어 병렬구조를 이루며 전치사 for의 목적어 역할을 하고 있다.

어휘 govern 지배하다 reputation 명성, 평판 concerned 걱정하는 conscience 양심 rear 기르다, 양육하다

19~20 장문 19 ② 20 ④

해설 19. 인간과 동물은 자기 자신의 신경계만을 가지고 살아가는 것이 아니라 다른 구성원들의 신경계도 광범위하게 활용하여, 개체로서 놓친 경고 신호도 놓치지 않고 받을 수 있게 되며 이러한 생존 전략을 최상으로 활용하기 위하여 군집 생활을 한다는 내용의 글이므로, 제목으로 가장 적절한 것은 ② '생존을 위한 다른 이들의 신경계 이용'이다.

① 생존을 위한 신체적 힘의 중요성
③ 모여 살기 위한 도움으로서의 소리
④ 의사소통을 증진시키는 인지 원리
⑤ 언어와 생존, 즉 우리는 어떻게 서로를 모방하는가

20. 문맥상 군거성은 신경계를 분리시키는 것이 아니라 결합시키는 것, 즉 타인의 신경계도 자신의 생존에 유리하게 활용하는 것의 필요성으로 인해 인간과 동물이 갖추어야 할 특성이므로 ④ 'separating'을 'uniting' 등으로 고쳐 써야 한다.

해석 어떤 사람이 당신에게 "조심해!"라고 외쳐서 당신이 딱 제때에 자동차에 치이는 것을 피하도록 점프할 때, 당신은 소리를 수단으로 하는 의사소통 덕분에 부상으로부터 탈출한다. 당신은 차가 오는 것을 보지 못했는데, 그럼에도 불구하고 누군가는 봤고, 그는 자신의 경고를 당신에게 전달하기 위해 특정한 소리를 내었다. 다시 말해서, 비록 당신의 신경계가 위험을 기록하지 못했어도, 당신은 다른 신경계가 기록했기에 (a) 해를 입지 않았다. 당신은 잠시 당신 자신의 신경계뿐만 아니라 다른 누군가의 신경계의 이점을 누렸다. 정말로, 우리가 사람들이 만드는 소리를 듣거나 그러한 소리를 상징하는 종이 위의 검은 표시를 보고 있는 대부분의 시기에, 우리는 우리 자신이 (b) 놓쳤던 것을 보상하기 위하여 다른 사람들에 경험에 의존하고 있는 것이다. 확실히 개인이 자기 자신의 신경계를 (c) 보충하기 위하여 타인의 신경계를 더 많이 사용할 수 있으면 있을수록, 그가 생존하는 것이 더 쉬워진다. 그리고 물론, 집단 속의 개인들이 서로에게 도움이 되는 소리를 더 많이 내면 낼수록, 사회 조직을 위하는 집단의 재능 있는 사람들의 한계 내에서, 당연히 그것은 모두를 위해 더 좋다. 새와 동물은 그들 자신들의 부류와 함께 모여 있으며 식량을 발견하거나 경고를 받으면 소리를 낸다. 사실 생존과 자기방어의 보조 도구로서의 군거성은 신체적 힘을 결합시키는 것의 필요성에 의해서보다 훨씬 더 신경계를 (d) 분리시키는것(→ 결합시키는 것)의 필요성에 의해 인간에게뿐만 아니라 동물들에게도 강요된다. 사회는 동물과 인간 둘 다 거의 거대한 (e) 협동 신경계로 간주될 수도 있다.

구문 [7행~9행] ~ although your nervous system did not record the danger, // you were unharmed because another nervous system **did**.
did는 recorded the danger를 나타내는 대동사이다.

[16행~19행] Obviously **the more** an individual can make use of the nervous systems of others to supplement his own, / **the easier** it is *for him* to survive.
「The 비교급 ..., the 비교급 ~」은 '…하면 할수록 더 ~하다'의 뜻이다. his own 다음에는 nervous system이 생략되어 있다. the easier 다음의 it은 가주어, to survive가 진주어이며 for him은 to-v의 의미상 주어이다.

[25행~27행] In fact, gregariousness as an aid to survival and self-defense / is forced upon animals **as well as** upon man ~
「A as well as B」는 'B뿐만 아니라 A도'의 뜻이다.

어휘 look out 조심해라 by means of ~을 써서 for the time being 당분간 stand for 상징하다 draw upon ~에 의지하다 make up for 보상하다 make use of ~을 이용하다 supplement 보충하다 congregate 모이다

제 5 회   본문 p.36

| 1 ⑤ | 2 ② | 3 ⑤ | 4 ③ | 5 ⑤ | | 6 ③ | 7 ③ | 8 ④ | 9 ① | 10 ② |
| 11 ② | 12 ④ | 13 ③ | 14 ③ | 15 ② | | 16 ① | 17 ④ | 18 ③ | 19 ② | 20 ④ |

1 글의 목적 ⑤

해설 필자는 세입자인데 얼마 전에 해고를 당해서 집주인에게 봉사를 대가로 집세를 감면해줄 수 있을지 문의하고 있다. 따라서 글의 목적으로 가장 적절한 것은

⑤이다.

해석 Hagen 씨께,
아시다시피, 저는 지난 2년간 당신이 Broad 가(街)에 소유하고 계신 집의 세입자였습니다. 저는 제 아파트에 꽤 만족했고, 집세를 안 낸 일도 결코 없었습니다. 제가 다른 모든 면으로

도 모범적인 세입자였다고 믿습니다. 저는 여기서 계속 살고 싶습니다. 불행히도, 저는 이제 막 직장에서 해고되었습니다. 저는 이 지역에서 다른 직장을 찾고 있고, 다가오는 몇 달 내에 새로운 일자리를 찾을 거라고 예상합니다. 그때까지 저는 집에서 당신을 위해 봉사함으로써 제 월세의 일부 혹은 전부를 줄일 수 있는 방법이 있는지 알아보고 싶습니다. 저는 유능한 정원사이자 페인트공이며, 당신이 요청하실 집 이곳저곳의 어떤 일이라도 기꺼이 할 것입니다. 곧 답장을 주시면 감사하겠습니다.

감사합니다.

Steven Abbott 드림

구문 [10행~13행] Until then, I would like to see // if there is *a way* [I could reduce some or all of my monthly rent / by performing services for you at the house].

if 이하는 see에 대한 목적어 역할을 하는 명사절이며 if는 '~인지'의 뜻이다. [ ]는 '방법'의 관계부사절로서 a way를 수식한다.

[13행~15행] I am a capable landscaper and painter, // and I would be happy to do / whatever jobs around the house you would ask.

밑줄 친 부분은 복합관계형용사 whatever가 이끄는 명사절로 동사 do의 목적어 역할을 한다. 이때 whatever는 '어떤 ~이든지, 어떤 ~일지라도'의 뜻이다.

어휘 tenant 세입자, 임차인 rent 집세 model 모범적인; 모범, 본보기 lay off ~을 해고하다 employment 직장 capable 유능한 landscaper 정원사, 조경사

2 필자 주장   ②

해설 이 글은 '식량 위기'를 소재로 하고 있으며, 현재의 식량 위기로 인해 소수 기업의 종자 및 농약 시장 지배가 더욱 심화되는 문제가 있으므로, 소규모 농업과 현지 생산 부분에 우선적으로 투자해야 한다는 주장을 담고 있다.

해석 현재의 식량 위기는 취약한 사람들에게서 그들의 식량에 대한 권리를 박탈할 뿐만 아니라, 먹이 사슬을 독점하는 거대 국제 기업들에게 혜택을 주고 있다. 단 열 개의 기업들이 230억 미 달러의 상업적 종자 시장의 3분의 1뿐만 아니라 280억 미 달러의 전 세계 농약 시장의 80퍼센트를 장악하고 있다. 지역 농부들의 상황을 변화시키기 위하여, 우리는 농업 정책 결정을 위한 전 세계 패러다임을 바꾸고, 관개, 기반 시설, 종자, 농약 등을 포함하여 개개 가정에 식량을 제공하는 소규모 텃밭 농업과 현지 생산 투자에 절대적 우선순위를 부여할 필요가 있다. 소작농과 소규모 농업은 너무나 오랫동안 무시되어 왔다. 소작농을 개발 과정에서 배제하고 그들의 권리를 무시하는 문제는 즉각 처리되어야 한다. 국가 정부와 국제기구는 소규모 농업과 현지 생산에 대한 투자에 절대적인 우선순위를 부여해야 한다.

구문 [1행~4행] The current food crisis **not only** deprives vulnerable people of their right to food, // **but** it **also** benefits *huge international corporations* [that monopolize the food chain].

「not only A but also B」는 'A뿐만 아니라 B도'의 뜻이다. [ ]는 huge international corporations를 수식한다.

[14행~16행] *The issue* (of the exclusion of peasants from the development process and the neglect of their rights) / **should be** immediately **addressed**.

주어는 The issue이고 동사는 should be addressed이다.

어휘 deprive A of B A에게서 B를 박탈하다 monopolize 독점하다 irrigation 관개 infrastructure 사회 기반 시설 and so on 기타 등등 peasant 소작농

3 밑줄 함의   ⑤

해설 기존의 잘못된 체계에 이의를 제기하지 않고 그것들을 받아들이면서 자신의

분야에서 성공하는 어른이 되는 신동들에 관한 글이다. 밑줄 친 '그들은 우리를 계속해서 트레드밀 위를 달리게 한다'는 신동들이 사회 체계에 변화를 가져오지 않아 발전 없는 상태가 유지된다는 뜻이므로 ⑤ '대부분의 신동들은 사회 체계를 변화시키려 애쓰지 않는다'가 적절하다.

① 천재들은 사회에서 제대로 기능하기 위한 실용적인 기술들을 갖고 있지 않다.
② 신동들의 비범한 능력은 나이가 들면서 줄어든다.
③ 신동들은 쉽지만 지루한 업무를 평범한 사람들에게 맡긴다.
④ 신동들은 규칙을 만들어내는 관행을 따르지 않는 사람들이 된다

해석 어른이 되면 많은 신동들이 자신의 분야의 전문가나 자신의 조직의 지도자가 된다. 하지만 "영재들 중에 아주 극소수만이 궁극적으로 획기적인 성인 창조자가 된다."고 심리학자 Ellen Winner는 한탄한다. '그렇게 하는 사람들은' '확립된 영역 안에서 빠르고 쉽게 배우는' 아이로부터 '궁극적으로 하나의 영역을 만드는' 어른으로의 '고통스런 변화를 해야만 한다.' 대부분의 신동들은 그러한 도약을 결코 하지 않는다. 그들은 자신들의 뛰어난 능력을 평범한 방식으로 적용해서, 기본적인 것들에 이의를 제기하지도 풍파를 일으키지도 않고 자신들의 일에 숙달한다. 그들이 들어가는 모든 영역에서, 그들은 성공으로 가는 관습적인 길을 따라감으로써 안전책을 강구한다. 그들은 애초에 많은 환자들이 의료비를 감당할 수 없게 만드는 엉망인 (의료) 체계를 고치기 위해 싸우지 않고 환자들을 치료하는 의사들이 된다. 그들은 스스로 법을 바꾸려고 노력하지 않고 시대에 뒤처진 법을 위반한 의뢰인을 변호하는 변호사가 된다. 비록 우리가 이 세상이 계속해서 부드럽게 돌아가게 하기 위해 그들에게 의존해야 하지만, <u>그들은 우리를 계속해서 트레드밀 위를 달리게 한다.</u>

구문 [9행~11행] They apply their extraordinary abilities in ordinary ways, / **mastering** their jobs / without questioning defaults and without making waves.

mastering 이하는 분사구문으로 and they master their jobs ~로 바꿔 쓸 수 있다.

어휘 prodigy 신동, 천재 expert 전문가(의) fraction 부분; 파편 revolutionary 획기[혁명]적인 lament 한탄하다, 슬퍼하다 transition 변화, 이행 established 확립[입증]된 domain 영역; 영토 leap 도약; (높이) 뛰다 default 기본 값 make waves 풍파를 일으키다 conventional 관습적인 afford ~할 수 있다, ~할 여유 [형편]가 되다 outdated 시대에 뒤처진, 낡은 transform 바꾸다, 변형하다 [선택지 어휘] practical 실용적인; 현실적인 function 기능(하다) tedious 지루한 non-conformist 관행을 따르지 않는 (사람)

4 글의 제목   ③

해설 예전에는 하류층의 상징이었던 미국의 통나무집이 60년대 유행 변화의 흐름에 맞추어 미국의 상징으로 거듭났다는 내용의 글이므로 제목으로 가장 적절한 것은 ③ '통나무집: 오두막에서 미국의 상징으로'이다.
① 미국인들이 통나무집을 개선해온 방식
② 미국 통나무집의 기원
④ 통나무집: 명망 높은 친환경적이고 건강한 집
⑤ 통나무집의 현대 디자인의 기반과 현재의 지위

해석 유행과 사회적 압력은 바뀐다. 20세기의 처음의 거의 4분의 3 시기 전반에 걸쳐, 미국의 통나무집들은 노르웨이에서와 마찬가지로 대충 지어지고 원시적인 하류층의 주택으로 여겨졌다. 그 결과 비막이 판자가 이전의 통나무 건축물을 가리기 위해 널리 사용되었다. 그러나 많은 사람들이 현 상태에 대한 도전을 추구하고 있었던 번영의 1960년대에 유행은 바뀌었고 사회적 압력은 느슨해졌다. 이런 변화들은 변화하는 유행으로 성공을 구가하기를 바라던 사람들이 숨겨져 있던 통나무 건물을 찾아내어, 외장용 자재를 제거하고, 사회가 자신의 유산을 재발견하는 것을 자신들이 시각적으로 확인하는 만족감을 누리도록 장려했다. 말할 필요도 없이, 이것은 널리 추구된 혁신은 아니었지만, 충분한 수의 부유한 사람들이 사회 지도자로서의 자신의 지위 유지를 추구하여 정말로 그렇게 했

다. 그 결과 통나무집은 그것을 원래 지었던 사람들의 민족적 배경에 상관없이 미국의 상징으로서의 위치를 다시 분명히 했다.

구문 [9행~14행] These changes **encouraged** *persons* [who wished to ride the crest of changing fashion], {to seek out hidden log buildings}, {to remove the siding}, and {to enjoy the glow of their visual confirmation of society's rediscovery of its heritage}.

「encourage+O+to-v (O가 v하도록 장려하다)」 구문으로 목적어인 persons를 [ ]가 수식하고, 세 부분이 목적격보어로서 콤마(,)와 and로 연결되어 병렬구조를 이룬다.

어휘 log 통나무   rough 대충한; 거친   primitive 원시적인   housing 주택   weatherboard 비막이 판자   prosperous 번영한   siding 외장용 자재   glow (만족의) 감정   confirmation 확인   heritage 유산   needless to say 말할 필요도 없이   affluent 부유한   reassert 다시 분명히 하다   regardless of ~에 관계없이   ethnic 민족[인종]의   hut 오두막   prestigious 명망 높은, 일류의   status 지위

5 도표 이해   ⑤

해설 남성과 여성 간의 가장 큰 백분율 차이는 발의 감각 손실에서 발견되고, 그 차이는 13.7퍼센트 포인트이며 그 뒤를 청각 손실이 13.2퍼센트 포인트 차이로 따른다. 그러므로 ⑤의 진술에서 청각 장애를 발의 감각 손실로, 발의 감각 손실을 청각 장애로 고쳐야 한다.

해석 70세 이상의 남성과 여성 간의 감각 장애의 발병률, 미국, 1999~2006
위 그래프는 미국에서 1999년부터 2006년까지 70세 이상의 남성과 여성 간의 감각 장애의 발병률을 보여준다. ① 가장 적게 발병하는 손상은 시각 장애인데, 남성과 여성 간의 차이는 단지 0.6퍼센트 포인트이다. ② 거의 남성 셋 중 한 명이 손상된 청력을 가지고 있으며 여성의 거의 5분의 1은 손상된 청력을 갖는데, 이는 남성과 여성 둘 다에서 세 번째로 가장 흔한 것이다. ③ 여성들이 남성들보다 균형 장애를 가질 가능성이 더 높은 것으로 밝혀졌고, 두 집단 간의 차이는 정확히 7퍼센트 포인트이다. ④ 남성이 여성보다 발의 감각 손실을 가지는 것이 더 흔한데, 대략 14퍼센트 포인트의 차이이다. ⑤ 두 집단 간의 가장 큰 백분율 차이는 청각 장애에서 발견되고, 발의 감각 손실이 그 뒤를 따른다.

구문 [13행~15행] It is more common *for men* **to have** loss of feeling in the feet than women, with a difference of roughly 14 percentage points.
밑줄 친 it은 가주어, to have 이하가 진주어이며 의미상 주어가 'for+명사'의 형태로 to부정사 앞에 쓰였다.

어휘 sensory 감각(상)의   impairment 장애; 결함; 손상   no more than 단지   impair 손상시키다; 약화시키다   gap 차이; 간격

6 내용 불일치   ③

해설 아홉 권의 시집은 그녀가 죽고 난 후 기원전 3세기에 알렉산드리아의 도서관에서 정리한 시집이다. 그러므로 ③은 내용과 일치하지 않는다.

해석 Sappho는 고대 그리스의 유명한 서정 시인이었다. 그녀는 기원전 630년에서 612년 사이 어느 때에 Lesbos라는 그리스의 섬에서 태어났다. 그녀는 Lesbos에 불안정한 정부가 있던 시기를 살았다. 그녀는 기원전 604년과 594년 사이에 알려지지 않은 이유로 시칠리아로 일시 추방되었다. Sappho는 기원전 570년에 그리스 Lesbos에서 사망했다. 일생동안 그녀는 사랑을 표현하는 시를 썼다. 기원전 3세기에 알렉산드리아 도서관은 Sappho의 시를 아홉 권의 책으로 정리했지만 남은 부분은 아주 적은데, 단 하나의 완전

한 형태로 된 시 "아프로디테 찬가"를 포함하고 있다. 그녀는 좀 어려운 아이올리스 지방의 방언으로 글을 썼는데 그것이 그녀의 작품이 시간이 지나면서 점점 더 적게 필사된 이유이다. 그러나 그녀의 시는 언어의 명료성과 사고의 단순성으로 칭송받는다.

구문 [10행~12행] ~ but the surviving portion is very small, **containing** only one poem in complete form, the "Hymn to Aphrodite."

containing은 앞의 내용을 부연 설명하는 분사 구문을 이끌며, and it contains ~로 바꾸어 쓸 수 있다. only one poem과 the "Hymn to Aphrodite"은 동격구문이다.

어휘 lyric 서정시   unstable 불안정한   temporarily 일시적으로, 임시로   exile 추방하다   lifetime 일생, 생애   hymn 찬가   dialect 방언   clarity 명료, 명확   simplicity 수수함, 단순

7 밑줄 어법

해설 ③ 여기에서 produce는 '농작물'이라는 뜻으로 명사이다. 선행사 local farmers와 관계사 뒤의 produce가 소유 관계이므로 소유격 관계대명사 whose로 바꿔 써야 한다.
① 문맥상 the best practice in tourism이 주어이므로 동사 is와 and로 연결되어 병렬을 이루는 동사 extends의 쓰임은 적절하다.
② '전치사+관계대명사' 형태의 in which가 이끄는 절 내에 주어(both local farmers and tourists)와 자동사(benefit)로 이루어진 완전한 문장이므로 적절하다. 또한 and both local ~ benefit in an initiative로 바꿔 쓸 수 있다.
④ 'have helped+O+to-v'의 능동태를 수동태로 바꾼 것으로 능동태 문장에서 목적격 보어였던 to supply가 그대로 쓰인 것은 적절하다.
⑤ see의 목적어 역할을 하는 how가 이끄는 의문사절 내 동사 자리에 능동 진행형으로 쓰인 is working은 쓰임이 적절하다. 이때 work는 '작동하다'라는 뜻의 자동사이다.

해석 지속 가능한 관광업을 위한 연례 시상식의 2008년 수상자들은 모두 관광업에서의 모범 사례는 광범위하며, 주로 그저 비행기, 호텔 및 해변이었던 한때 관광업을 구성하는 것으로 이해되었던 것을 넘어서서 확장된다는 것을 보여 준다. 한 예로 빈곤 감축 상의 수상자는 현지 농부와 관광객 둘 다가 득을 보는 활동 계획이었다. 이 상을 받은 나라의 호텔 경영자들은 전통적으로 그들의 식품 대부분을 수입해 오면서 현지 농부들을 무시하여 그들의 농작물은 쓸모없게 되고 있었다. 지금은 대부분이 여성인 1,000명의 농부들이 현지 호텔에 납품하도록 도움을 받고 있다. 동시에, 자금 지원 단체 중 하나인, 그 나라의 여행 재단과 그 활동 계획은 모범 사례를 증명하고 진가를 발휘해 관광 명소가 되기 위해 그들 자신의 농장을 개시했다. 예를 들어, 관광객을 그 농장에 데리고 가는 것은 그들(관광객)이 지속 가능성에 대한 자신들의 기여가 어떻게 작동하는지를 알 수 있는 하나의 방법이다.

구문 [8행~11행] The hoteliers (in this award-winning nation) have traditionally imported much of their food while ignoring *local farmers* [**whose** produce was going to waste].
( ) 부분은 전명구로 The hoteliers를 수식하고 [ ] 부분은 소유격 관계대명사 whose가 이끄는 관계사절로 선행사 local farmers를 수식한다.
[17행~19행] Taking tourists to the farmyard, for example, is *one way* [**in which** they can see **how their contribution to sustainability is working**].
[ ] 부분은 '전치사+관계대명사' 형태의 in which가 이끄는 관계사절로 앞에 있는 one way를 수식하고, 관계사절 내에서 동사 see의 목적어로 how가 이끄는 명사절이 간접의문문(how ~ is working)의 어순으로 쓰였다.

어휘 sustainable 지속 가능한   *cf.* sustainability 지속 가능성   demonstrate 보여 주다, 증명하다   far-reaching 광범위한   extend 확장[확대]되다; 뻗다   constitute 구성[조직]하다   reduction 감축; 감소   initiative 활동 계획; 솔선; 발의   produce

농작물: 생산하다   go to waste 쓸모없게 되다: 낭비되다   foundation 재단; 토대
funding 자금 지원   launch 착수[시작]하다   tourist attraction 관광 명소   on
one's own merits 진가를 발휘하여; 공적에 따라   contribution 기여, 공헌; 기부(금)

8 밑줄 어휘   ④

해설 새로운 매체 환경에 수반된 위협은 사람들이 자신의 견해를 강화하는 미디어
만 선택하며 자신과 같은 생각을 하는 사람들과만 교류하고, 다른 견해를 가진 사람
들과 만나서 생각을 나눌 기회는 차단한다는 것이다. 여기서 경고하는 '배울 게 없
는' 세계는 잘 모르는 것으로부터 건설된 새로운 세계가 아니라 기존부터 잘 알고
있고 자신의 울타리 내의 생각만 곱씹는 세계를 지칭할 것이므로 ④의 unfamiliar를
familiar 등으로 바꿔 써야 한다.

해석 하버드대 정치학자 Robert Putnam, 존경받는 법학자이자 오바마 행정부의 전 고
위 관료 Cass Sunstein, 그리고 MoveOn.Org의 임원인 Eli Pariser는 케이블과 웹 기반 미
디어가 일련의 정체성의 고립 집단을 만들며 강화시키고 있다고 경고하는 사람들에 속한
다. 그들의 주장은 오래된 '선별적 노출' 논지의 변형이다. 우리는 이미 가지고 있는 견해
를 ① 강화시키는 미디어에만 노출되기로 선택한다는 것 말이다. 그들의 우려는 사람들이
자기 자신의 안락한 고립된 미디어 장소에 모이면서 다른 견해를 가진 사람들과 만나서
생각을 교류할 기회는 ② 사라지고 있다는 것이다. 정치 활동가들, 하키 팬들, 그리고 상상
할 수 있는 모든 쇼, 게임, 뮤직비디오, 혹은 유명인사의 추종자들은 모두 거대한 공적 장
소가 아닌 자기 자신의 집단으로 이루어진 제한되고 보호 받는 영역에 ③ 끌린다. Pariser
가 주장하는 것처럼 "정의상, ④ 모르는(→ 아는) 것으로부터 건설된 세계는 배울 게 없
는 세계이다." Pariser에게 있어서 위험은 "당신이 ⑤ 정적이고, 계속 좁아지기만 하는 자
신의 버전, 즉 끝없는 당신 (자신)의 고리 속에서 꼼짝 못하게 될 수 있다"는 것이다. 결국
"사용자가 콘텐츠가 되었다."

구문 [9행~13행] Their concern is // **that** as people congregate in their own
comfortable media enclaves, // **the opportunity** (to meet and exchange
ideas **with** *those* [who have different views]) **is vanishing**.
that은 문장의 보어로 쓰인 명사절을 이끈다. that절속 주절의 주어는 the opportunity
이고 동사는 is vanishing이다. ( )는 the opportunity를 수식하는 형용사구이며 [ ]는
those를 수식하는 관계사절이다. those는 동사 meet과 전치사 with의 공통 목적어
이다.
[13행~17행] Political activists, hockey fans, and followers of every imaginable
show, game, music video, or celebrity all *gravitate* **not** to great public spaces,
but to the limited and protected confines of their own groups.
Political ~ celebrity가 주어이고 gravitate가 동사이다. 「not A but B (A가 아니라 B)」
구문이 쓰였으며, A, B 자리에 모두 to로 시작되는 전치사구가 위치해있다.

어휘 political scientist 정치학자   senior official 고위 관료   administration
행정부   reinforce 강화시키다   variant 변형, 이형   thesis 논지   congregate
모이다   vanish 사라지다   gravitate 인력에 끌리다   confine 영역; 경계; 한정[제한]
하다; 가두다   static 정적인   loop 고리

9 빈칸 추론   ①

해설 다트판에 아이의 사진을 고정시켰을 때 사람들은 그것이 사진에 불과함을 알
고 있음에도 불구하고 맞추지 못했다고 했으므로 기억력이나 신체적, 정신적 능력
외에 논리적 사고에 기여하는 것은 '감정'임을 알 수 있다.

해석 지금까지 우리는 (일반적으로 기억력과 신체적, 정신적인 수행 능력뿐만 아니라) 논
리적 사고에 아주 중요한 기여자를 간과해왔다. 그것은 바로 감정이다. 분명히 그것은 신

체의 수행에 엄청난 역할을 한다. 이것을 알아보려면, 혼자서 다트 게임을 몇 판 해보라.
(이때) 당신의 수행 능력에 주목하라. 이제 당신 아이 중 한 명이나 당신이 알고 있는 아이
의 사진을 다트 판 중앙에 고정하고 다시 시작해보라. 다소 불쾌한 이런 상황을 실험하는
최초의 연구에서, 대부분의 사람이 아이의 사진을 맞히는 것을 힘들어했는데, 특히 그것이
자신의 아이의 사진일 때 그러했다. 그것은 단지 사진일 뿐이라는 인식에도 말이다. 다시
말해, 실체와 이미지의 차이를 완전히 머리로만 인식하는 것은 예리한 도구를 아이의 사
진에 던지는 것에 대한 거리낌을 상쇄시키기에 부족했다. 대부분의 사람들이 마찬가지로
사랑하는 사람의 이름이 적혀 있는 종잇조각을 찢어버리는 것을 주저한다.

구문 [6행~8행] Now position *a picture* [of one of your children or *a child*
[known to you]] / on the bull's-eye of the board // **and** start again.
두 개의 절이 and로 병렬 연결된 구조.
[8행~12행] In *the original study* [**testing** this rather grim situation], most people
were hard-pressed to hit the child's photo — especially if it was of their own
child — despite their recognition that it was only a picture.
testing이 이끄는 현재분사구가 the original study를 수식. their recognition은 that
~ a picture와 동격.
[12행~16행] In other words, *full intellectual recognition* [of the distinction
[between reality and image]] / wasn't sufficient to offset *the reluctance* [to
throw a sharp instrument at an image of their child].

어휘 logical thinking 논리적 사고   play a round (경기를) 한 판하다   solitary
혼자 하는; 혼자서 잘 지내는   grim 엄숙한; 음산한   be hard-pressed to-v v하는 것
을 힘들어하다   recognition 알아봄, 인식   offset 상쇄[벌충]하다   reluctance 마지
못해 함, 꺼림   *cf.* reluctant to-v v하기를 주저하는, 마지못해 v하는

10 빈칸 추론   ②

해설 빈칸 이후에 제시된 혁신적인 직무 환경을 가진 기업의 예를 보면, 사업부 구
성원 중에 경영학 석사 학위를 가진 사람은 거의 없고 역사, 문화, 정치, 환경, 외교
등 다양한 배경의 지식과 경험을 가진 구성원들이 많았다고 했기 때문에, 이러한 기
업이 추구하는 가치가 ② '특별한 종류의 다양성'임을 알 수 있다.
① 진정성의 느낌
③ 다양한 인종적 배경
④ 해외 경험이 있는 사람들
⑤ 팀워크를 향상시키기 위한 획기적인 방법

해석 최고의 사람들을 끌어들이고 기업으로 성공하기 위해, 신뢰할 만한 미래의 조직은
창의성과 혁신이 귀중하고, 직원들이 참여하고 헌신하고 있다고 느끼며, 리더십 파이프라
인이 미래의 성공을 위해 신중하게 구축된 환경을 조성할 필요가 있을 것이다. 우리의 연
구에서 그런 특성들을 가진 직장은 특별한 종류의 다양성을 찾아 피상적인 것 이상의 차
이를 이유로 사람을 고용한다. 특히 사고 과정, 준거 틀, 기량에서의 차이 말이다. 좋은 예
가 있다. 1980년대로 돌아가, 미국의 한 출판사의 사업부는 가장 폭넓게 다양한 직원 집
단 중 하나를 갖추고 있었다. 한 수석 편집자는 워싱턴 두뇌 집단의 일원이자 아시아 문화
전문가였다. 또 다른 사람은 미국사 박사 학위를 가지고 있었다. 또 다른 사람은 미국 대
통령의 연설 원고 작성자로 일한 적이 있었으며 환경 운동가였다. 잡지 'New Yorker'에서
인턴으로 근무했던 부편집자도 있었고, 외교 문제 관련 경험이 있는 사람도 있었다. 이 편
집자 중 2명만이 경영학 석사 학위를 가지고 있었고 이것이 사업부였다!

구문 [2행~6행] ~ the authentic organization of the future will need to foster
environments [where creativity and innovation are at a premium, employees
feel engaged and committed, **and** leadership pipelines are carefully cultivated
for future success].
관계부사 where가 이끄는 [ ]은 environments를 수식한다. [ ]에서 밑줄 친 세 절
이 콤마(,)와 and로 연결되어 병렬구조를 이룬다.

[6행~9행] In our research, *workplaces* (with those qualities) look for an unusual kind of diversity, **hiring** people for *differences* [that are more than skin deep].
( )은 workplaces를 수식하는 전명구이다. hiring 이하는 분사구문으로 관계사절 [ ]이 differences를 수식한다.

─────────────────────────

어휘 authentic 믿을 만한; 진짜의 *cf.* authenticity 진정성; 진짜임 foster 조성하다; 양육하다 at a premium 가치 있는; 구하기 힘든 committed 헌신적인, 전념하는 leadership pipeline 리더십 파이프라인 ((조직 내에서 구성원이 성장함에 따라 리더로서 계속해서 성장할 수 있는 체계)) cultivate 구축하다, 함양하다 frame of reference 준거 틀 among other things 특히, 그중에서도 case in point 좋은 예 workforce 직원; 노동력 think tank 두뇌 집단 speechwriter 연설 원고 작성자 associate editor 부편집자 foreign affairs 외교 문제, 외무 ethnic 인종[민족]의

11 빈칸 추론

해설 명명 오류의 한 측면에 대한 내용으로 '이론', '법', '힘'을 예로 들어 그것이 과학자에게 주는 의미와 일반적 담론에서 갖는 의미가 다르고 심지어 완전히 반대인 경우도 있어서 심각한 오해가 생길 수 있음을 설명하고 있다. 그러므로 빈칸에 들어갈 말로는 ② '그것에 과학적 의미를 부여하는'이 적절하다.
① 그것들을 위한 새로운 맥락을 찾는
③ 사전의 과학 지식을 활용하는
④ 명백한 이해의 부족을 나타내는
⑤ 그것들을 적절한 비유에 응용하는

─────────────────────────

해석 호칭이 설명 정보를 가지고 있다고 믿는 오류인 명명 오류의 한 측면은 일반적인 단어를 사용해 그것에 과학적 의미를 부여하는 위험이다. 이것은 흔히 부주의한 대중을 오해의 길로 이끄는 처참한 결과를 가져온다. 일반적인 담화에서 '이론', '법', '힘'과 같은 단어들은 그것들이 과학자에게 의미하는 바를 의미하지는 않는다. Darwin의 진화론에서의 '성공'은 Dale Carnegie가 가르친 것과 같은 '성공'과 동일하지 않다. 물리학자에게 있어서 '힘'이란 정치 담론에서 사용되는 것과는 상당히 다른 의미를 가지고 있다. 하지만 이것들 중 가장 최악의 것은 '이론'과 '법'이 될 수 있는데, 그것들은 거의 완전히 반대인 것들로, 이론은 과학에서 강력한 개념인 반면에 일반적 담화에서는 모호하고, 법은 과학적 개념이라기보다는 훨씬 더 강력한 사회적 개념이다. 이러한 차이점은 과학자와 그들의 연구를 지지하는 일반 대중 사이에 때로 심한 오해를 불러온다.

─────────────────────────

구문 **[1행~4행]** One facet of **the nominal fallacy, the error of believing that the label carries explanatory information**, is the danger *of* using common words and giving them a scientific meaning.
the nominal fallacy와 the error ~ explanatory information은 동격 관계이다. 전치사 of의 목적어로 using common words와 giving them a scientific meaning이 and로 연결되어 병렬 구조를 이룬다.
[6행~8행] Words like "theory," "law," "force" do not **mean** (in common discourse) *what they mean to a scientist.*
( ) 부분이 문장의 동사 mean과 목적어절(what ~ a scientist) 사이에 삽입되었다.

─────────────────────────

어휘 facet (측)면, 양상 nominal 이름의, 명칭상의; 명목상의 fallacy 오류; 틀린 생각 explanatory 설명의 misunderstanding 오해; 언쟁 polar opposite 완전히 반대인 것 vague 모호한; 불확실한 context 맥락; 배경, 상황 utilize 활용[이용]하다 analogy 비유; 유사점

12 빈칸 추론 ④

해설 지문의 초반부에 단일 종에만 의존하는 꽃가루받이 매개는 위험한 전략이라고 했고, 다양한 꽃가루받이 생물을 통해 뛰어난 품질과 많은 양의 매개를 이룰 수

있다고 했으므로 정답은 ④ '꽃가루받이 생물의 다양성이 보호받거나 강화되어야 한다'이다.
① 양봉은 더 엄격한 규제하에 이뤄져야 한다
② 유해한 외래종의 수입 규제가 시행되어야 한다
③ 희귀종은 그들만의 생존 전략을 가져야 한다
⑤ 두 가지 이상의 농작물을 함께 재배하는 것이 안정적일 수 있다

─────────────────────────

해석 꽃가루받이 매개를 유럽산 꿀벌에만 단독으로 의존하는 것은 단일 종의 생물이 하는 수행에 의존하는 것이므로 위험 부담이 큰 전략이다. 캘리포니아의 아몬드 꽃가루받이는 유럽산 꿀벌에 의존하며 동남아시아의 기름야자나무 꽃가루받이는 수입된 아프리카산 딱정벌레 단일 종에 의존한다. 최근의 연구들은 벌의 충분한 공급에 있어 비동시적인 연간 변수로부터 꽃가루받이를 지킴으로써 이러한 약점을 보완할 필요성을 강조한다. 서로 다른 꽃가루받이 종들은 또한 풍부하고 다양한 공급자의 수집만이 높은 품질과 많은 양의 (꽃가루받이) 매개로 이어지게 할 서로 다른 공간적, 시간적, 조건적 틈새를 차지한다. 이러한 사실들이 시사하는 것은 다양한 상황에서 그리고 (다양한) 공간과 시간에 걸쳐서 꽃가루받이 매개를 보장하기 위해 농업 지역에서 꽃가루받이 생물의 다양성이 보호받거나 강화되어야 한다는 것이다.

─────────────────────────

구문 **[9행~13행]** Different pollinating species / also occupy *different spatial, temporal, and conditional niches* [**in which** only an abundant and varied collection of providers / will lead to a high quality and quantity of services].
[ ]는 선행사 different ~ niches를 수식하는 관계사절이다. in which는 관계부사 where로 바꿔 쓸 수 있다.

─────────────────────────

어휘 pollination 수분((꽃식물의 암꽃술에 수꽃술의 꽃가루를 붙여 주는 일)) *cf.* pollinate ~에 수분하다 pollinator 꽃가루 매개자 compensate for ~을 보상하다, 보충하다 variation 변화(량); 변종 abundant 풍부한 *cf.* abundance 풍부, 충만 spatial 공간의, 공간적인 temporal 시간의; 일시적인; 속세의, 세속적인 **[선택지 어휘]** regulation 규정; 규제 alien species 외래종 enforce (법을) 집행[시행]하다; 강요하다 conceive (~을) 마음속으로 하다, 상상하다 multiplicity 다수(多數); 다양성

13 흐름 무관 문장

해설 팬, 부모, 미디어는 선수의 플레이를 보고 사후적으로 전략을 평가할 수 있지만 코치는 선수의 플레이를 보기 전에 미리 전략을 세운다는 내용의 글인데, ③번 문장은 선수가 기술을 습득하기 위해 막대한 반복적 수행을 해야 한다는 내용이므로 전략 평가나 전략 수립과는 무관하다.

─────────────────────────

해석 코치들은 전략 결정을 내릴 때, 플레이가 성공적이었는지 성공적이지 못했는지에 근거를 두는 것이 아니라 결정이 이루어진 그 시점에서 선수의 능력, 상황, 그리고 백분율에 근거를 두어서 그것이 좋은 결정 아니면 나쁜 결정이라고 이해해야 한다! ① 코치들은 자신들이 이용 가능한 모든 요인에 근거를 두어 결정을 내리고, 그런 후에 선수들은 코치가 요구한 플레이를 수행해야 한다. ② 특정한 플레이에서 선수들이 자신들의 기술을 수행하는 방식은 코치가 내린 결정이 타당한가와는 아무런 관계가 없다. ③ 높은 수준의 기술에 도달하기 위하여 선수들은 기술을 연습하고 수행할 다수의 기회를 갖도록 하나의 기술 혹은 경기 상황을 수천 번 수행할 필요가 있을지도 모른다. ④ 코치는 선수들이 어떻게 수행할지를 알기 전에 (최초의 추측이라고 알려져 있는) 결정을 내려야 하지만, 팬과 부모, 미디어는 플레이가 끝날 때까지 기다렸다가, 그 후에 그 결정이 좋은 것이었는지 나쁜 것이었는지 (두 번째 추측이라고 알려져 있는) 결정을 할 호사를 누린다. ⑤ 팬, 부모, 미디어는 따라서 전략 결정에서 결코 틀리지 않는다!

─────────────────────────

구문 **[2행~5행]** ~ it is a good or bad decision at *the time* [(when) it is made] based on the players' abilities, the situation, and the percentages, not (based) *on* {**whether** the play was successful **or** unsuccessful}!
[ ] 부분은 앞에 관계부사 when이 생략되어 있으며 the time을 수식한다. not과 on

사이에는 based가 생략되어 있다. { } 부분은 on의 목적어 역할을 하는 명사절이다. 'whether A or B'는 'A인지 B인지'의 의미이다.

[15행~18행] ~ but the fans, parents, and media have the luxury of [**waiting** until a play is over] and then [**determining** *if* the decision was a good or bad one] ~

두 [ ] 부분은 동명사구로 전치사 of의 목적어 역할을 하며 병렬구조를 이룬다. determining 다음의 전치사 if는 '~인지'의 뜻이다.

어휘 based on ~에 근거하여   execute 수행하다   have nothing to do with ~와 전혀 관계없다   wisdom 타당성; 지혜

14 글의 순서   ③

해설 문화에 따라 청취 행동이 다르다는 주어진 글 다음에 (C)는 나올 수 없는데 People in such cultures에서 such cultures가 아직 명시되지 않았기 때문이다. 그러므로 주어진 문장 다음에는 우선 개인주의 문화에서의 청취 양상에 대해 설명한 (B)가 와야 한다. 그 다음에 (A)와 (C) 중에서 '능률을 중시하고 간접적 화법을 싫어하는 문화'에 대해 설명한 (C)가 개인주의 문화에 대해 이어지는 설명이므로 (B) 다음에 나와야 하고, In contrast(대조적으로)라는 연결어와 함께 집단주의 문화에 대해 제시한 (A)가 마지막으로 나와야 한다.

해석 문화적 메시지는 많은 의사소통 행동을 형성하는데, 청취도 예외는 아니다. 특히, 청취 행동은 특정한 문화에 있는 사람들이 시간의 중요성에 대해 어떻게 생각하는지에 의해 영향을 받는 것처럼 보인다.
(B) 개인주의적인 문화에서 사람들은 자주 시간을 자원으로 여긴다. 예를 들어, 미국인들은 보통 "시간은 돈이다"라고 말하며, 그들은 시간을 절약하고, 쓰고, 그리고 허비할 수 있는 상품으로 여긴다.
(C) 그런 문화에 있는 사람들은 일반적으로 효율성을 중요시하고, 다른 사람들도 똑같이 하기를 기대한다. 그들은 직접적이고 솔직한 의사소통을 중시하고, 이야기를 듣는 사람은 '요점을 언급하지' 않는 화자를 견디지 못한다.
(A) 그에 반해서 한국처럼 집단주의적인 문화는 효율성보다는 사회적 화합을 강조한다. 이런 문화의 사람들은 자신들의 청취 행동의 일부로서 화자의 메시지의 의미를 알아내기 위해 자주 비언어적인 행동과 문맥상의 단서에 세심한 주의를 기울인다.

구문 [2행~5행] In particular, / listening behavior appears to be affected / by **how people** in a given culture **think** about the importance of time.
how 이하는 by의 목적어인 간접의문문이며, 「의문사(how)+주어(people)+동사(think)」의 어순으로 쓴다.

어휘 shape 형성하다, 모양 짓다   exception 예외, 제외   given 특정한, 주어진   efficiency 능률, 효율   nonverbal 비언어적, 말에 의하지 않는   contextual 문맥상의, 전후 관계의   cue 단서   individualistic 개인[이기]주의적인   resource 자원   commodity 상품, 물품   straightforward 솔직한   get to the point 본론으로 들어가다, 요점을 언급하다

15 글의 순서   ②

해설 과거의 병원은 부검을 제법 실시했지만 이러한 관행이 중단되었다는 주어진 글 뒤에 관행이 중단된 현황을 제시한 (B)가 나온다. 부검을 실시하지 않는 몇 가지 요인들이 있다는 (B) 다음에는 그 중 첫 번째 요인부터 제시한 (A)가 나온다. 세 가지 요인을 제시한 (A) 다음에는 가장 중요한 요인이 제시된 (C)가 마지막으로 나오는 것이 적절하다.

해석 병원은 품질 관리 조치로 그들의 기관에서의 특정 비율의 사망(자)에 대한 부검을 실행할 것을 요구받곤 했다. 그러나 그러한 요구는 오래 전에 중단되었다.
(B) 몇몇 새로운 병원들은 심지어 부검 시설을 갖고 있지도 않다. 오늘날 부검은 보통 범죄나 변사에서만 실행된다. 부검은 '자연스러운' 죽음의 경우 희귀하다. 이러한 종류의 부검을 실행하는 데 또한 몇 가지 저해 요인들이 있다.
(A) 한 가지는 비용이다. 부검 당 대략 2천에서 3천 달러이다. 보험은 보통 이 절차를 보장해주지 않는다. 의사들 또한 그것이 생전에 그들이 놓친 무언가를 나타나게 할지도 모르기 때문에 부검을 장려할 것 같지 않으며, 가족들은 종종 부검을 그들이 사랑하는 사람에게 무례한 것으로 본다.
(C) 그러나 부검의 가장 큰 저해 요인은 의학적 기술에 대한 우리의 끝없는 믿음이다. 검사가 죽음의 원인을 이미 확인해주었다면 왜 부검을 하는가? 그 밖의 어떤 것이 관여되었을 수도 있다는 생각은 거의 하지 않는다.

구문 [7행~10행] Doctors also are not likely to encourage an autopsy because it might turn up *something* [(that) they missed in life], and families often **see** *autopsies* **as** *disrespectful of their loved one.*
[ ] 부분은 목적격 관계대명사 that이 생략된 형용사절로 something을 수식한다. and 이후에 나오는 'see A as B'는 'A를 B로 보다[간주하다]'의 의미이다.
[19행~20행] There is little thought that anything else could have been involved.
밑줄 친 thought와 that절은 서로 동격 관계이다.

어휘 perform 실시[시행]하다; 공연하다   institution (공공) 기관, 시설   quality control 품질 관리   measure 조치; 수단   requirement 요구 (사항)   drop 중단하다, 그만두다   insurance 보험; 보증   cover 보장하다   procedure 절차, 순서   turn up ~을 나타나게 하다[찾아내다]   disrespectful 무례한, 불경스러운   facility 시설   unusual death 변사(變死)   disincentive 저해하는[의욕을 꺾는] 요인

16 문장 넣기

해설 주어진 문장은 아기들이 물건이 사라지면 찾으려 하지 않는 것을 뜻하므로 이에 대한 구체적인 예가 등장하는 For example 앞에 와야 한다.

해석 물건이 시야에서 사라진 후에도 존재한다는 것을 깨닫는 것은 아기들이 생애 첫해에 해내는 주요 성취물이다. 이를 깨닫기 전에 아기의 좌우명은 "안 보이면 마음에서도 사라진다."인 것 같다. 예를 들어, 세 달 된 아기는 사물을 매우 흥미롭게 바라보지만 당신이 그것을 종이 뒤에 감춘다면 아기는 그것을 찾으려고 노력하지 않을 것이다. 여섯 달쯤 되면 유아는 감춰진 사물이 사실 여전히 여기 어딘가에 있다는 것을 이해하기 시작한다. 이 연령대의 아기는 탁자에서 장난감을 떨어뜨리면 그것을 찾을 것이고, 일부가 가려진 장난감을 찾아 천 밑에도 살펴볼 것이다. 한 살이 될 때까지 대부분의 아기는 사물의 영속성에 대한 인식을 키운다. 이때가 아기들이 숨어 있다가 '까꿍'하며 놀래주는 장난을 좋아하는 나이이다.

구문 [3행~5행] **Realizing** *that a thing exists even after it disappears from sight* / is a major accomplishment ~ of life.
주어는 Realizing ~ sight, 동사는 is. that ~ sight는 Realizing의 목적어절.

어휘 prior to A A에 앞서   realization 이해, 자각; 실현, 달성   partially 부분적으로; 불공평하게   awareness 인식, 자각   permanence 영속(성), 영구

----

17 문장 넣기 ④

해설 ④ 앞에서는 유전자 서열을 완성하려는 민간 기업과 공적 연구소가 있음을 소개했는데 뒤에서는 공공 연구소는 '그러한 사업상의 이해관계(such business interest)'를 가지고 있지 않다고 하여 비약이 있다. 민간 회사의 유전자 서열 특허 취득에 대한 논쟁이 소개된 주어진 문장이 ④에 위치하면, 공공 연구소가 가지고 있지 않다고 주장하는 '그러한 사업상의 이해관계'가 '유전자 서열 특허 취득'으로 발생할 이득임을 알 수 있으므로 주어진 문장은 ④에 위치해야 한다.

해석 과학 연구는 매우 빈번하게 국방을 위해 혹은 그 연구 결과의 적용으로부터 이익을 얻기를 바라는 민간 기업의 후원하에 수행되기 때문에, 공유권과 공개라는 규범은 종종 유보된다. 그런 상황은 과학계에서 무수한 갈등으로 이어졌다. 한 가지 두드러진 사례는 인간 게놈의 완전한 지도와 목록을 공개하기 위한 경쟁인데, 그것(게놈)은 우리의 유전자를 구성하는 인간 DNA의 모든 서열이다. 2001년에 두 라이벌 집단은 그 연구를 최초로 완수하기 위해 경쟁했는데, 한 집단은 J. Craig Venter가 이끈 민간 부문인 Celera Genomics 회사였고, 다른 하나는 Francis Collins가 이끈 정부가 자금을 지원한 연구였다. 민간 회사가 인간 유전자 서열에 대한 특허를 확보하려 하는지, 즉 공개 규범의 위반인지에 대해 논쟁이 맹렬하게 계속되었다. 공공 연구소는 그런 사업상의 이해관계를 전혀 가지고 있지 않았거나, 가지고 있지 않다고 주장했다. 결국 경쟁 팀들은 타협했고 그 지도에 대한 공개물을 공동으로 발행했지만, 유전 물질에 대한 특허를 발급하는 것에 대한 논란과 법적 공방은 계속되었다.

구문 [1행~4행] An argument raged **over** *whether* the private corporation was trying to establish patents on human genetic sequences, a violation of the norm of openness.
whether가 이끄는 밑줄 친 명사절이 전치사 over의 목적어 역할을 하고, 두 개의 밑줄 친 부분은 서로 동격 관계이다.

[5행~8행] Because scientific research is so often **conducted** in the interests of national defense or under the sponsorship of *private firms* [that hope to profit from applications of the findings], ~
두 개의 밑줄 친 전명구가 or로 연결되어 병렬구조를 이룬다. [ ]은 private firms를 수식한다.

어휘 rage 맹렬하게 계속되다 patent 특허 genetic 유전자의 sequence 순서, 서열 violation 위반 norm 규범 openness 공개: 개방성 in the interests of ~을 위하여 sponsorship 후원 common ownership 공유권 publication 발표, 공개 suspend 유보[유예]하다 inventory 물품 목록 constitute 구성하다 sector 부문 laboratory 연구실, 실험실 controversy 논란

18 요약문 완성 ③

해설 후판단 편파에 대한 내용으로서 일어난 일에 대해 자신이 이미 예측하고 있었다고 믿는 경향에 대해 설명하고 있다. 그러므로 요약문의 빈칸에는 predictable이 적절하다. 후판단 편파를 조심해야 할 이유로 발전 범위를 제한한다고 본문에서 언급했으므로 두 번째 빈칸에는 limits가 적절하다.
① 필연적인 - 과대평가하다 ② 예측할 수 있는 - 제한하다
④ 의심스러운 - 제한하다 ⑤ 필연적인 - 통제하다

해석 교사로서 나는 학생들이 채점된 시험지를 받은 후에 "42번 답이 (b)인줄 알고 있었어!"라고 스스로를 나무라는 소리를 종종 듣는다. 내가 하는 전형적인 반응은, 시험문제에 고의적으로 틀리게 답하는 학생은 결코 없었다는 것이고 그래서 그들이 답이 (b)임을 알았다면 왜 (a)에 동그라미를 쳤느냐는 것이다. 이로 말미암아 그들은 인간의 추론에 있어 흔히 나타나는 결함을 조용히 떠올리게 된다. 그것은 '후 판단 편파'라 불리는 것으로서 우리의 예측이 실제로 그랬던 것보다 더 정확했다고 믿는 경향이다. 그러한 경향은 냉전 후

많은 사람들이 러시아의 붕괴가 필연적이었음을 알고 있었다고 주장했을 때와 마찬가지로, 2014년 월드컵 이후에 스포츠 분석가들이 독일이 브라질을 충격적인 7대 1로 이긴 결승전을 예측했었다고 주장했을 때 볼 수 있다. 비록 표면적으로는 해가 없지만 우리는 후 판단 편파를 조심해야만 한다. 이런 편파의 위험은 그것이 우리가 실제 우리보다 더 낫다고 믿게 만드는 것이다. 그것은 과거의 실수로부터 우리가 배우는 것을 방해하고 그래서 우리가 발전할 수 있는 범위를 저지한다.

↓

> 사람들은 이미 일어난 사건을 실제보다 더 (A) 예측할 수 있던 것으로 보는 경향이 있는데 그것은 발전할 능력을 (B) 제한한다.

구문 [10행~14행] It could be seen / after the 2014 World Cup / when sports analysts claimed / **to have predicted** the shocking 7-to-1 final victory of Germany over Brazil, / as well as after the Cold War / when many claimed / **to have seen** that the collapse of Russia had been inevitable.
「to have p.p.」는 완료 부정사로서 주절의 시제보다 이전에 일어난 일임을 나타낸다. 즉, 스포츠 분석가들은 경기 이전에 그 경기 스코어를 예측했었다고 주장한 것과, 많은 사람들은 벌써 이전에 구소련의 붕괴를 알고 있었다고 주장했음을 뜻한다.

어휘 scold 꾸짖다, 나무라다 typical 전형적인, 일반적인 intentionally 계획적으로, 고의로 incorrectly 틀리게, 부정확하게 circle 동그라미를 그리다 flaw 결점 reasoning 추론 hindsight bias ((실험 심리학)) 후 판단 편파 forecast 예상, 예측 collapse 붕괴, 와해 inevitable 피할 수 없는, 당연한 on the surface 외견상으로 hinder 방해하다 hence 그러므로 hold back 저지하다, 방해하다 extent 정도, 범위

19~20 장문 19 ② 20 ④

해설 19. 글에서 제시된 실험에 의하면 우리가 피로함을 느낄 때 융통성 사고력과 창의성은 오히려 증진될 수 있다고 했으므로 제목으로 가장 적절한 것은 ② '피로가 정신을 해방시키는 데 도움이 될 수 있다'이다.
① 창의적 피로를 피하는 방법
③ 어떻게 집중력을 향상시킬 수 있는가
④ 왜 기민할 때 창의성이 높아지는가
⑤ 우리는 가장 피곤할 때 업무를 거의 하지 못한다

20. (d) renewed가 있는 문장의 다음 문장에서는 우리가 '극도로 피로하다고' 느낄 때 우리의 융통성 사고력이 최상이 될지도 모른다고 했으므로, 피실험자의 운영 기능 수용력이 재개되었을(renewed) 때가 아니라 고갈되었을(depleted) 때 실험 과업을 더 잘 수행했을 것이다. 그러므로 renewed는 depleted로 고쳐야 적절하다.

해석 2015년에 프랑스의 연구자 집단이 그들의 피실험자들을 Simon 과업이라는 이름의 (a) 반복적인 연습을 수행하도록 함으로써 그들의 운영하는 뇌를 피로하게 했다. 거기에서 참가자들은 컴퓨터 스크린 상으로 일련의 왼쪽을 가리키는 화살표와 오른쪽을 가리키는 화살표들을 보게 되는데, 그중 하나는 항상 스크린의 중앙에 위치한다. 피실험자들은 그 중앙의 화살표가 가리키는 방향에 따라 키보드의 왼쪽 혹은 오른쪽 화살표 키를 누르라는 지시를 받는다. 이 실험의 핵심은 중앙의 화살표에 집중하기 위하여 피실험자들이 다른 화살표들의 영향을 억제해야 한다는 것이었다. 피실험자들은 40분 동안 휴식 없이 계속 반복하여 과업을 수행했다. Simon 과업이 피실험자들의 운영 능력을 (b) 무디게 한 후에 연구자들은 그들에게 융통성 사고 테스트를 제시했다. 피실험자들은 양동이, 신문, 벽돌 같은 여러 가지 가정의 물체들에 대해 할 수 있는 만큼 많은 쓰임새를 상상해 보도록 몇 분을 부여받았다. 그들의 답변은 피실험자가 상상할 수 있는 쓰임새의 총수와 (그 쓰임새를 또한 생각했던 다른 피실험자들의 수로 판단하는 것과 같은) 각각의 아이디어의 (c) 독창성과 같은 기준에 따라 점수가 매겨졌다. 그러고 나서 그 점수는 처음에 Simon 과업에 참여하지 않았던 통제집단의 점수와 비교되었다. 피실험자의 운영 기능 수용력이 (d) 재개되었을(→ 고갈되었을) 때 상상해본 쓰임새들의 총수와 창의성 둘 다 유의미하게 더 높았음을 연구자들은 발견했다. 우리가 '극도로 피로하다고'느낄 때 우리의 융통성 사고

력이 최상일지도 모른다는 것이 교훈이다. 그것은 당신의 과제 계획을 세울 때 알면 좋은 것이다. 당신의 집중력을 혹사시키는 (e) 지루하고 집중적인 노력의 기간을 포함하는 허드렛일을 수행한 후에 그러한 종류의 사고(상상력이 풍부한 아이디어 생성하기)를 한다면 당신은 상상이 풍부한 아이디어를 생성하는 일에 더 능숙해질 수 있다.

구문 [4행~6행] In it, participants are shown *a set of left and right pointing arrows on a computer screen*, one of **which** is always positioned at the screen's center.

which는 a set of left and right pointing arrows on a computer screen을 지칭한다.

[20행~23행] Their answers were scored according to criteria **such as** the total number of *uses* [(which[that]) the subject was able to imagine] and the originality of each idea ~.

두 밑줄 친 부분이 such as의 목적어로 병렬구조를 이룬다. [ ]은 앞에 목적격 관계대명사 which[that]가 생략된 관계사절로 uses를 수식한다.

[25행~27행] The scores were then compared with those of *a control group* [who had not first engaged in the Simon task].

those는 the scores를 지칭하고, [ ]은 a control group을 수식하는 관계사절이다.

어휘 fatigue 피곤하게 하다; 피로, 피곤   executive 운영[경영]의; 집행의   put through (곤경 · 불쾌한 일 등을) 겪게 하다   suppress 억누르다   over and over 계속하여, 반복하여   dull 무디게 하다; 무딘   faculty 능력; 교수   elastic 융통성 있는   criterion(pl. criteria) 규준   originality 독창성; 진품   engage in ~에 참여하다   chore 허드렛일   tedious 지루한   strain 혹사하다

---

1 ②	**2** ②	**3** ③	**4** ①	**5** ④	**6** ⑤	**7** ③	**8** ④	**9** ⑤	**10** ①
11 ⑤	**12** ⑤	**13** ③	**14** ④	**15** ③	**16** ③	**17** ⑤	**18** ④	**19** ④	**20** ⑤

1 심경 변화   ②

해설 Jean은 처음에는 어머니의 가혹한 관리하에 피아노를 연습하여 우울했지만, 어머니가 엄격한 스케줄을 그만두고 자신의 의지대로 피아노를 연습하게 되자 큰 기쁨을 느끼게 되었으므로 Jean의 심경의 변화로 가장 적절한 것은 'depressed → delighted (우울한 → 기쁜)'이다.

해석 Jean의 어머니는 딸의 연습 기간을 무자비하게 지배했다. 그녀는 Jean에게 일절 여유를 주지 않았다. Jean에 대한 그녀의 규칙은 일주일에 7일 1시간씩의 연습이었다. Jean은 연습 시간의 가혹한 스케줄을 더 이상 견딜 수 없었다. 연습 시간이 되면 그녀가 깊은 한숨을 쉴 때 우울함이 그녀의 얼굴을 뒤덮었다. Jean에게 이것이 얼마나 힘든지를 깨달은 후 Jean의 피아노 선생님은 그녀의 어머니에게 빡빡한 스케줄을 끝내라고 설득했다. 어머니는 그 충고를 기꺼이 받아들였다. 자신의 생각대로 피아노를 칠 수 있게 되자마자 그녀는 수업을 고대했고 연주에서 대단한 기쁨을 발견했다. 그녀는 피아노를 연주하는 것을 정말로 즐긴다고, 너무나 즐거워서 피아노를 칠 때 시간이 얼마나 빨리 흐르는지를 깨닫지조차 못한다고 선생님에게 말했다.

구문 [6행~9행] After **realizing** [how difficult **it** was for Jean], Jean's piano teacher *persuaded* her mother *to do* away with the tight schedule.

[ ] 부분은 realizing의 목적어이다. it은 혹독한 스케줄로 피아노를 연습해야 하는 앞의 상황을 나타낸다. 'persuade O to-v'는 '…에게 v하도록 설득하다'의 뜻이다.

[12행~15행] She told her teacher that she really enjoyed playing the piano, **so much so that** she didn't even **realize** [how quickly time passed when she was playing the piano].

'so much so that ~'은 '~할 정도까지(to the extent that ~)'의 뜻이다. [ ] 부분은 realize의 목적어이다.

어휘 session 시간, 기간   iron fist 냉혹함, 무자비   cut (someone) no slack (어떤 사람에게) 전혀 여유를 주지 않다   rigorous 엄격한   gloom 우울   sigh 한숨 쉬다   persuade 설득하다   do away with 없애다, 끝내다   willingly 기꺼이   on one's own terms 자기 생각대로, 자기 방식으로   look forward to 고대하다

2 밑줄 함의   ②

해설 우리는 기계에 익숙해져 기계 없이 살 수 있다는 생각조차 못한다는 내용이므로 밑줄 친 '대안은 상상조차 되지 않는다'는 말은 ② '우리는 기계를 사용하지 않고 살 수 있다고 생각하지 않는다'를 뜻한다.

① 우리는 새로운 삶을 찾기 위해 기계를 계속 연구한다.
③ 우리는 생소한 기계를 사용하는 것을 망설인다.
④ 기계를 사용할 수 없을 경우를 대비해서 다른 계획을 세워야 한다.
⑤ 우리는 기계가 우리의 일상을 통제하고 있다고 믿지 않는다.

해석 우리 자신을 기계에 적응시키려는 우리의 노력이 가져온 축적된 좌절과 분노에도 불구하고, 기계에 대한 진정한 저항은 비교적 드물다. 새로운 것을 선호하도록 우리가 사전 조건화된 것은 우리를 기계에 계속 매료되게 한다. 일반적으로 사람들은 자신을 적응시키기 위해 용감하게, 심지어 열정적으로 노력한다. 그들은 왜 그들이 그 결과로 불행한지 잘 모른다. 그들은 기계를 비난하지 않는데, 왜냐하면 기계의 놀라운 특성과 그것에 대한 우리의 큰 필요에 대해 우리 스스로가 납득했거나 아니면 광고와 홍보를 통해 납득되었기 때문이다. 내연 기관이나 휴대폰 없이도 우리가 수십만 년 동안 하나의 종(種)으로서 생존하고 번성했다는 사실을 잊고, 우리는 아무런 의존도 없었던 곳에 의존증을 만들어냈다. 이제는 우리 중 너무 많은 사람이 불이 꺼지면 어찌할 바를 모르고 무력하고 무섭다고 느낀다. 우리는 결국 우리의 기계를 사랑하는데, 그것은 우리가 지속되는 나쁜 결혼 생활에서 배우자를 사랑하는 것과 같이, 그 배우자의 결함이 아주 익숙하고, 그 배우자의 짜증 나는 목소리가 너무나 배경의 일부가 되어 그것이 거기에 없다는 것은 생각할 수 없는 것과 같다. 대안은 상상조차 되지 않는다.

구문 [11행~15행] We have created dependency where none existed, / **forgetting** // that we survived and thrived as a species for hundreds of thousands of years / without the internal combustion engine or the cell phone.

forgetting 이하는 동시상황을 나타내는 분사구문이며, that ~ cell phone은 명사절로 forgetting의 목적어로 쓰였고, 명사절에서 두 개의 동사 survived와 thrived가 병렬구조를 이루고 있다.

어휘 accumulated 축적된, 누적된 rage 분노 bring about ~을 가져오다, ~을 초래하다 precondition 미리 조건화하다 novelty 새로운 것 *cf.* novel 새로운, 참신한; 소설 enthusiastically 열정적으로 accommodate 적응시키다; 수용하다 consequently 그 결과로서 convince A of B A에게 B를 납득시키다 marvelous 놀라운 dependency 의존증 thrive 번성하다 species 종(種) inadequate 무력한; 불충분한, 부적당한 spouse 배우자 enduring 지속되는 flaw 결함 irritating 짜증나는 conceive 생각하다, 상상하다 alternative 대안(적인)

3 글의 요지 ③

해설 두 번째 문장에서 감정은 그 감정이 경험된 상황에 대한 지식을 토대로 새로이 재구성되는 것이라고 했고, 그 이하의 기술도 이를 뒷받침하고 있다. 즉 사람들은 감정을 상기하라는 요청을 받았을 때 자신이 과거의 상황에서 어떻게 느꼈을지를 추측하여 감정을 재기술하고, 나아가 현재 상황에서 감정을 새롭게 경험하기도 한다. 따라서 글의 요지로 가장 적절한 것은 ③이다.

해석 감정이 그 자체로 기억 속에 저장되는지에 대한 오래도록 계속되고 있는 논쟁이 심리학 안에 있다. 일부 연구자들은 감정은 기억 속에 저장될 수 있는 것이 아니라, 그 감정이 경험된 상황에 관한 지식을 토대로 재구성되는 것이 틀림없다고 주장한다. 이 견해에 따르면, 감정을 상기하라는 요청을 받을 때, 사람들은 순간적인 감정적 경험이 아니라 그 사건에 관한 관련 세부 사항에 대한 기억에 기초하거나 자신이 어떻게 느꼈을 것 같은지에 대한 믿음에 기초해 그것을 재기술한 것을 생각해 낸다. 감정이 경험된 상황을 상기하는 것은 또한 사람들이 비슷하지만 새로운 감정을 현재에 경험하게 할 수도 있는데, 그때 전해지는 것은 바로 이 새로운 감정이다. William James가 말한 대로, "기억 속에서 감정이 되살아날 가능성은, 하등 감각의 모든 느낌이 되살아날 가능성과 마찬가지로 매우 낮다…. 우리는 옛 슬픔이나 환희의 직접적인 원인에 대한 선명한 생각을 소환함으로써 옛 슬픔이나 환희의 상기가 아니라 새로운 슬픔과 환희를 만들어 낼 수 있다."

구문 [3행~6행] Some investigators argue that emotion **cannot** be stored in memory **but** must be reconstructed based on knowledge concerning *the circumstances* [in which the emotion was experienced].
'not A but B'는 'A가 아니라 B다'의 뜻이고, 밑줄 친 두 부분이 각각 A, B에 해당한다. '전치사+관계대명사'형태의 in which가 이끄는 [ ]은 the circumstances를 수식한다.
[6행~11행] According to this view, when (they are) asked to remember emotions, people retrieve **not** the fleeting emotional experience **but** a redescription of it / {based on memory for relevant details concerning the event} or {based on beliefs about how one is likely to have felt}.
when과 asked 사이에 they(people) are가 생략되어 있다. 'not A but B'는 'A가 아니라 B다'의 뜻이다. based on(~에 기반을 두어)으로 시작되는 두 { }은 분사구문으로 병렬구조를 이룬다.

어휘 long-standing 오래도록 계속되고 있는 reconstruct 재구성하다; 재건[복원]하다 concerning ~에 관하여 retrieve 회수하다; 생각해 내다 fleeting 순식간의; 덧없는 redescription 재기술 relevant 관련 있는 revivability 소생 가능성 remembrance 기억, 추억 summon up 불러일으키다 lively 선명한, 활기찬 exciting (원인 등이) 직접적인; 흥미진진한

4 글의 주제 ①

해설 곤충들은 내적인 삶이 부족하지 않고 인간이 이해할 수 있는 표현으로 곤충의 의식을 인간에게 전달할 수 있는 방법이 없다고 하면서, 곤충에게서 의식과 같은 현상이 실제로 발생하는 많은 징후가 보인다고 했으므로 이 글의 주제로 가장 적절

한 것은 ① '의식을 소유하는 곤충 두뇌의 가능성'이다.
② 동물의 지능에 관해 밝히는 것에 대한 어려움
③ 인간과 곤충 사이의 인지 체계의 차이
④ 의사소통에서 인간의 두뇌보다 못한 곤충 두뇌의 열등함
⑤ 곤충이 의식을 갖는지의 비밀을 드러내는 방법

해석 많은 사람들은 여전히 벌과 개미를 세상의 내부적 표현이나 심지어 가까운 미래조차도 예측하는 능력이 부족한, '반사 기계'에 지나지 않는 것으로 보는 것을 타당하다고 생각한다. 곤충들은 '철학적 좀비'에 가까운데, 즉 아무런 의식도 없이 루틴과 반사작용에 전적으로 의존하는 가상의 존재들이다. 그러나 아마도 문제는 곤충들이 내적인 삶이 부족하다는 것이 아니라 그것들이 우리가 이해할 수 있는 표현으로 그것을 전달할 수 있는 방법이 없다는 것이다. 그래서 아마도 우리는 동물의 뇌를 기계와 같은 특성을 가지고 있는 것으로 오진하는데 왜냐하면 단순히 우리가 기계가 어떻게 작동하는가를 이해하기 때문이다. 반면에 오늘날까지 우리는 심지어 가장 단순한 두뇌가 어떻게 정보를 처리하고 저장하고 검색하는지에 대하여 오로지 단편적이고 불완전한 통찰력을 가지고 있다. 그러나 이제 의식과 같은 현상들이 인간과 심지어 유인원 사이에서만 존재하는 것이 아니라 곤충들 또한 그것들을 지니고 있을지도 모른다는 많은 징후가 있다. 만약에 동일한 행동 및 인지 기준이 훨씬 더 큰 두뇌를 지닌 척추동물에게처럼 적용된다면, 일부 곤충들은 의식이 있는 행위자로서 자격을 부여받을 것이다.

구문 [1행~4행] Many still find **it** plausible **to look** at bees and ants / as little more than 'reflex machines', / **lacking** an internal representation of the world, / or an ability to foresee even the immediate future.
it은 가목적어이고 to look at ~ machines가 진목적어이다. lacking 이하는 'reflex machines'를 보충 설명하는 분사구이다.
[7행~9행] But perhaps the problem is **not** that insects lack an inner life, **but** that they don't have a way to communicate it / in terms we can understand.
'A가 아니라 B'라는 뜻의 「not A but B」 구문으로 보어 역할을 하는 밑줄 친 두 개의 명사절이 병렬구조를 이루고 있다.

어휘 plausible 타당한, 그럴듯한 reflex 반사의 foresee 예측하다 hypothetical 가상의, 가설의 misdiagnose 오진하다 property 특성 fragmentary 단편적인 retrieve (정보를) 검색하다; 회수하다 cognitive 인지의 criteria ((criterion의 복수형)) 기준 qualify 자격을 부여하다 agent 행위자 inferiority 열등함

5 글의 제목 ④

해설 걸작을 만들 수 있는 가능성을 극대화하기 위한 방법이 다수의 아이디어, 즉 다수의 작품을 만드는 것이라고 말하고 이를 고전 음악가와 화가를 예로 들어 설명하고 있으므로, 제목으로 가장 적절한 것은 ④ '보다 많을수록, 걸작의 가능성이 높아진다.'이다.
① 위대한 예술가는 타고 나는가 만들어지는가?
② 세 명의 가장 사랑받는 작곡가들
③ 질에 집중하는 것이 걸작을 가져온다
⑤ 노력보다는 영감이 더 중요하다

해석 사람들은 걸작을 만들 가능성을 어떻게 극대화하는가? 그들은 다수의 아이디어를 생각해낸다. 평균적으로, 창의적인 천재들은 자신들의 분야에서 동료들보다 질적으로 더 뛰어나지는 않았다. 그들은 단지 더 많은 작품을 만들어냈고, 그것은 그들에게 더 많은 다양성과 독창성에 대한 더 높은 가능성을 주었다. 런던 필하모니 오케스트라가 가장 위대한 클래식 음악 50곡을 선정했을 때, 그 목록에는 모차르트 작품 6곡, 베토벤 작품 5곡, 그리고 바흐 작품 3곡이 있었다. 소수의 걸작을 만들어 내기 위해, 모차르트는 서른다섯의 나이로 죽기 전까지 600곡 넘게 작곡했고, 베토벤은 평생 650곡을 작곡했으며, 바흐는 1000곡 넘게 작곡했다. 이것은 또한 피카소에게도 적용된다. 그의 작품 목록은 인쇄물, 깔개, 태피스트리는 말할 것도 없고, 1,800점이 넘는 그림과 1,200개의 조각품, 2,800개의

도자기, 12,000개의 소묘를 포함하는데, 그중 극소수만이 찬사를 받아왔다.

구문 [10행~14행] To generate a handful of masterworks, <u>Mozart composed more than 600 pieces before his death at thirty-five</u>, <u>Beethoven produced 650 in his lifetime</u>, 〔and〕 <u>Bach wrote over a thousand.</u>
밑줄 친 세 개의 절이 콤마(,)와 and로 병렬 연결되었다.

[14행~18행] *His list of works includes more than 1,800 paintings, 1,200 sculptures, 2,800 ceramics, and 12,000 drawings, not to mention prints, rugs, and tapestries* — **only a fraction of which have received acclaim.**
only ~ acclaim에서 which는 관계대명사로 앞의 more than ~ tapestries를 선행사로 한다.

어휘 odds 가능성; 역경, 곤란   masterpiece 걸작, 명작; 일품(= masterwork)   come up with ~을 생각해내다; 제시[제안]하다   qualitatively 질적으로   peer 동료   variation 다양성; 변화, 차이; 변형   originality 독창성   a handful of 소수(량)의   compose 작곡하다; 구성하다   *cf.* composer 작곡가   ceramic 도자기   not to mention ~은 말할 것도 없고, 물론이고   fraction 극소수; 일부, 부분; 분수   acclaim 찬사, 칭찬; 칭송하다   [선택지 어휘] beloved 사랑받는; 인기 많은   perspiration 노력; 땀   outweigh ~보다 더 중요[중대]하다; ~보다 무겁다

6 안내문 일치 ⑤

해설 ① 참가자들의 연령을 기준으로 반이 편성된다.
② 종일 캠프는 반일 캠프보다 참가비가 1.5배 더 비싸다.
③ 참가비는 캠프가 시작하는 날의 전날까지 전액 납부해야 한다.
④ 배트와 글러브는 무료 대여가 가능하다.

해석 Longbeach 여름 야구 캠프
모든 어린이들을 환영합니다!
Longbeach 여름 야구 캠프에서 즐거움을 함께 해요! 이 야구 캠프는 소년소녀들에게 많은 공을 치고 던지고, 능력을 향상시키고, 오래도록 지속되는 우정을 개발할 수 있는 흥미진진하고 건강한 환경을 제공합니다.
7-13세의 소년소녀들에게 전일 혹은 반일 캠프를 제공합니다. 캠프 참가자들은 연령 기준으로 분류됩니다.
기간: 5월 3일 월요일 – 5월 14일 금요일 (2주)
장소: Longbeach 고등학교 테니스 코트
캠프 선택
전일 캠프: 오전 9:30 – 오후 3:00 (450달러)
반일 캠프: 오전 9:30 – 오후 12:30 (300달러)
• 전일 캠프에 등록하기 위하여 어린이들은 10세 이상이어야 합니다.
• 5월 2일까지 지불 금액을 내 주세요. (이 가격에는 식사와 훈련복이 포함되어 있습니다.)
– 아침은 연습, 훈련과 코트 외부 놀이로 구성됩니다. 오후는 재미있는 경쟁 게임에 집중합니다.
– 아이들은 자신의 배트와 글러브를 가져와도 되고 또는 캠프에서 무료 대여할 수 있습니다.
– 캠프 자리는 한정되어 있으니 등록은 선착순 기준임을 주의하세요.

구문 [5행~8행] This baseball camp **provides** boys and girls **with** *an exciting, healthy environment* [where they can <u>hit and throw</u> lots of balls, <u>improve</u> their abilities, 〔and〕 <u>develop</u> lasting friendships].
「provide A with B」는 'A에게 B를 제공하다'의 뜻이다. [ ]는 an exciting ~ environment를 수식한다. [ ]에서 조동사 can 뒤의 동사원형 hit and throw, improve, develop이 병렬구조를 이룬다.

어휘 lasting 지속적인   drilling 훈련, 연습   conditioning 훈련   note 주목하다, 주의하다   registration 등록

7 밑줄 어법

해설 ③ knowing that 이하를 보면 「it is ~ that ... (…한 것은 바로 ~이다)」 강조 구문이 쓰였다. (knowing) that절에서 only the elderly bees within a colony, the foragers가 실질적 주어이고 여기에 대응되는 동사가 get이다. 따라서 they라는 주어를 한 번 더 쓰면 안 되고 they를 that으로 바꿔 써야 한다.
① those는 basic questions를 지칭하며 related to behavior의 수식을 받는다. 수식을 받는 대명사는 them이 아닌 those를 사용하므로 옳게 쓰였다.
② Whether ~ in animal cognition, behavioral genetics, or social behavior 절은 「Whether A, B, or C」의 형태이며 'A이든 B이든 C이든'이라는 의미를 가지는 양보의 부사절이다.
④ 문장 구조가 「If S′ had p.p., S might have p.p. (…했다면 ~했을지도 모른다)」인 가정법 과거완료이므로 have failed가 적절히 쓰였다.
⑤ their는 honey bees를 지칭하므로 3인칭 복수 형태를 잘 사용했다.

해석 자연계에서 꿀벌이 어떻게 사는지를 아는 것은 광범위한 과학 연구에 중요하다. 이것은 Apis mellifera가 생물학의 기본적인 질문들, 특히 행동과 관계된 것들을 조사하는 데 모델계 중의 하나가 되어왔기 때문이다. 어떤 미스터리를 풀려고 이 벌들을 연구하고 있는 것이 동물 인지에서이든 행동 유전학에서이든 혹은 사회적 행동에서이든지 간에, 실험 연구를 고안하기 전에 그들의 자연적 생태를 잘 알게 되는 것은 결정적으로 중요하다. 예를 들어, 수면 연구자는 수면의 기능을 탐구하기 위해 꿀벌을 사용했을 때, 대부분의 수면을 밤에, 비교적 긴 시간 동안 취하는 것은 바로 군집 내에서 오직 나이 든 벌들, 즉 먹이 조달자들뿐이라는 것을 아는 데서 그들은 큰 이익을 얻었다. 이 연구자들이 해질녘이 되었을 때 어떤 벌들이 군집에서 잠을 가장 깊게 자는 벌들인지를 알지 못했다면, 그들은 진정으로 유의미한 수면 부족 실험을 설계하지 못했을지도 모른다. 모든 유기체들과 마찬가지로 꿀벌을 데리고 하는 좋은 실험은 그들의 자연스러운 생활 방식을 활용한다.

구문 [1행~2행] Knowing // how the honey bee lives in its natural world / **is** important for **a broad range of** scientific studies.
Knowing ~ world는 동명사 주어이며 이것에 상응하는 동사는 is이다. a broad range of는 '광범위한'의 뜻이다.

[6행~10행] Whether one is studying these bees / to solve some mystery in animal cognition, behavioral genetics, or social behavior, // **it** is critically important **to become** familiar with their natural biology / **before designing** one's experimental investigations.
it은 가주어이고 to become 이하가 진주어이다. become familiar with는 '~을 잘 알게 되다'의 뜻이다. before 이하는 분사구문인데 의미를 확실하게 하기 위해 before와 같은 접속사를 생략하지 않기도 한다.

어휘 model system 모델계   cognition 인지   genetics 유전학   critically 결정적으로   colony 군집   comparatively 비교적으로   sound (잠이) 깊은   nightfall 해질녘   sleep-deprivation 수면 부족(의)

8 밑줄 어휘

해설 ④번이 있는 문장에서 실수를 저지른 후 오랜 시간이 지난 뒤에 발생하는 결과는 원인과 결과의 연관을 '모호하지' 않게 하는 것이 아니라 '명확하지' 않게 할 것이므로 obscure를 obvious로 바꿔 써야 한다.

해석 정신 의학은 인간 본성에 대한 막대한 지식을 요구하는 분야야다. 정신의학 의사는 가능한 한 빠르고 정확하게 정신적 장애가 있는 환자의 정신 속을 들여다보는 통찰력을 ① 획득해야 한다. 이 의학 분야에서 의사는 환자의 마음속에서 무슨 일이 벌어지고 있는지를 제법 확신할 때에만 효과적으로 진단, 치료, 그리고 처방을 할 수 있다. ② 피상성은 여기에 있을 곳이 없다. 진단상의 잘못은 곧 분명해지는 반면 장애에 대한 ③ 올바른

이해는 성공적인 치료로 이어진다. 다시 말해서, 인간 본성에 대한 우리의 지식은 엄격하게 검증된다. 일상생활에서 우리가 다른 인간을 판단할 때 하는 실수가 반드시 극적인 결과와 연결되는 것은 아닌데, 왜냐하면 이러한 결과들은 실수를 저지른 후 너무나 오랜 시간이 지난 뒤에 발생할지도 몰라서 원인과 결과의 연관이 ④ 모호하지(→ 분명하지) 않기 때문이다. 다른 사람에 대해 ⑤ 오해한 후 여러 해가 지나 끔찍한 불운이 발생할 때 우리는 자주 놀라움을 느낀다. 이러한 불행한 사건은 인간 본성에 대한 실용적 지식을 획득하는 것이 모든 인간의 의무임을 우리에게 가르쳐준다.

구문 [2행~4행] The psychiatrist must **gain insight into** the mind of the disturbed patient *as* quickly and accurately *as possible*.
'gain insight into'는 '~을 간파하다, 통찰하다'의 뜻이다. 'as ~ as possible'은 '가능한 한 ~하게'의 뜻인데, 부사 quickly와 accurately가 병렬구조를 이루며 as와 as 사이에 위치해 있다.

[11행~16행] In everyday life [errors in our judgement of another human being] **are** *not necessarily* linked with dramatic consequences, for these consequences may occur **so** long after the mistake has been made **that** the connection between cause and effect is not obvious.
[ ]가 주어이며 are가 동사이다. 'not necessarily'는 '반드시 ~한 건 아니다'라는 뜻의 부분부정 표현이다. 접속사 for는 '이유(~이므로)'의 뜻이다. for 절에서 'so … that ~ (너무 …해서 ~하다)' 구문이 사용되었다. 'the connection between A and B'는 'A와 B 사이의 연관'이라는 뜻이다.

어휘 tremendous 거대한   psychiatrist 정신의학 의사   insight 통찰력   disturbed 정신적 장애가 있는, 매우 불안해하는   practitioner 의사   diagnose 진단하다   prescribe 처방하다   superficiality 천박, 피상   apparent 분명한   rigorously 엄격히, 엄밀히   astonished 깜짝 놀란   working knowledge 실용적 지식

9 빈칸 추론 ⑤

해설 집단에서 배척당한 개인은 타인의 의견에 더 순응하고 타인에 대한 정보에 더욱 민감해지며 사회적으로 관련 있는 정보를 기억할 가능성이 더 높다는 연구 결과에 의하면, 사회에 다시 속하고자 하는 ⑤ '귀속(belongingness)' 욕구가 정보 처리 및 보유 방식에 영향을 미침을 알 수 있다.
① 혁신 ② 리더십 ③ 자아실현 ④ 보안

해석 몇몇 연구는 다른 사람들에 의해 배척, 배제 또는 거부당한 개인들이 자신의 포함 지위(즉 집단에 포함되거나 배제되는 것)를 증대시킬 방식으로 행동한다는 것을 보여 주었다. 이러한 행동의 범위는 집단 환경에서 더 열심히 일하는 것에서부터 집단 인식에 순응하는 것, 또는 다른 사람들에 대한 정보에 더 민감해지는 것까지 아우른다. 예를 들어 Williams와 Sommer는 여성들이 이어지는 집단 과업에 더 많은 노력을 쏟음으로써 배척에 대응한다는 것을 발견했다. 마찬가지로 Williams, Cheung, Choi는 배척당한 개인들이 다른 사람들보다 타인의 의견에 순응할 가능성이 더 높다는 것을 발견했다. 따라서 이러한 연구들은 사회적 거부에 대응하여 사람들이 자신들을 사회 세계와 다시 연결하기를 추구한다는 것을 보여 준다. 게다가 Gardner, Pickett, Brewer는 사회적 거부를 경험한 개인이 사회적으로 관련 있는 정보를 기억할 가능성이 더 높다는 것을 발견했다. 따라서 귀속 욕구는 사람의 동기와 일치하는 정보의 처리와 보유를 유도하는 것으로 보인다.

구문 [1행~4행] Several studies have shown that *individuals* [who are ostracized, excluded, or rejected by others] behave in *ways* [that will increase their inclusion status (i.e., being included or excluded in a group)].
첫 번째 [ ]은 관계대명사 who가 이끄는 관계사절로 individuals를 수식하며 관계사절 내에서 과거분사 ostracized, excluded, rejected가 병렬구조를 이룬다. 두 번째 [ ]는 ways를 수식하는 관계사절이다.

어휘 exclude 배제하다: 무시하다   inclusion 포함   status 지위   range from A to B 범위가 A부터 B까지이다   conform to ~에 순응하다; ~에 적합하다   subsequent 이어지는, 차후의   relevant 관련 있는   consistent 일치하는   motive 동기   self-actualization 자아실현

10 빈칸 추론 ①

해설 유전학에서는 조상을 추적할 때 윗대로 올라갈수록 조상의 수가 점점 더 많아지지만, 언어학에서는 언어의 조상을 추적할 때 각 단계의 조상 언어가 하나씩만 있어서, 즉 유전학보다 ① '더 적은 가능성을 허락하기' 때문에 예컨대 옛 인류의 이주 경로 연구에 유전학보다 유용하게 쓰인다.
② 역사 유물의 흔적을 가진다   ③ 지역에 따라 변형될 수 있다
④ 구전으로 전해진다   ⑤ 불변의 원형을 가진다

해석 역사언어학자들은 오늘날 사용되는 언어들을 연구하여 그것들로부터 그 언어들이 유래한 조상어에 관해 추정한다. 가능한 상황에서라면, 언어학자들은 또한 옛날의 언어에 관한 기록된 자료로부터 연구하기도 한다. 언어학의 경우(유전학의 경우와 마찬가지로), 우리는 현재의 자료가 우리에게 옛날 공동체 사회의 자취를 제공한다고 여긴다. 그러나 '옛날 공동체'의 정의는 각각의 경우에 다르다. 언어의 경우, 각각의 언어는 하나의 조상을 가진다고 여겨진다. 하나의 언어는 각 단계에서 하나의 조상만을 가지는 반면, 유전학의 경우에 한 사람은 더 이전 세대로 올라갈수록 점점 더 많은 조상들을 가진다. 언어의 '가계도 모형'은 조상으로부터 유래된 언어들의 범위를 제시해 주고, 동일한 조상으로부터 유래된 다른 언어들과의 관계를 보여 준다. 언어학적 '가계도 모형'의 단일 조상이라는 특성 때문에, 언어는 유전학보다 옛 인류의 이주 경로에 관해 더 많은 증거를 제공해 주는데, 이는 그것이 더 적은 가능성을 허락하기 때문이다.

구문 [1행~3행] Historical linguists study *the languages* (spoken today), and from them make estimates about *the ancestral languages* [from which they descended].
동사 study와 make가 병렬구조를 이룬다. ( )은 the languages를 수식하고 [ ]은 the ancestral languages를 수식하며, 밑줄 친 they는 the languages spoken today를 지칭한다.

[13행~16행] The "tree model" of languages presents the range of *languages* (descended from an ancestor), and indicates relationships with *other languages* (descended from the same ancestor).
동사 presents와 indicates가 병렬구조를 이룬다. 두 개의 ( )은 각각 바로 앞의 languages, other languages를 수동의 의미로 수식하는 분사구이다.

어휘 linguist 언어학자 *cf.* linguistics 언어학   make estimates 추정하다; 견적 내다   ancestral 조상(대대로)의   descend (언어 등이) 유래하다 ((from)); 내려가다[오다]   genetics 유전학   assume (당연하다고) 여기다; 추정하다   migration 이주   relic 유물, 유적   be handed down 전해지다

11 빈칸 추론 ⑤

해설 빈칸 문장의 this issue는 앞 내용에 나온 신뢰가 형성되어야 상담 치료가 가능함을 말하고 그것이 중요하기 때문에 우리는 어떻게 할 필요가 있는지를 추론해야 한다. 빈칸 문장 뒤는, 아이들은 자신의 이야기를 할 때까지 준비할 시간이 필요하며 따라서 아이들을 대상으로 하는 상담 교사는 치료 과정을 서두르지 말아야 한다는 내용이므로 빈칸에는 ⑤가 적절하다.
① 자기 자신의 정보를 자진해서 말할   ② 자신의 행동에 일관성을 보일
③ 아이들을 동등한 존재로 여길   ④ 재밌는 활동으로 아이들을 즐겁게 할

해석 신뢰는 아이들을 대상으로 하는 상담 교사들에게 핵심적인 요소이다. 적절한 수준의 신뢰가 없다면, 치료 관계가 방해받을 것이다. 때로는 이러한 문제의 중요성 때문에 우리는 처음에 아주 천천히 진행할 필요가 있다. 초기에는 아이가 자유로이 놀 시간을 허용할 수 있을 것이다. 만일 상담 교사가 아이의 문제에 대한 이야기로 시작한다면, 아이는 스트레스를 받고 말하길 거부할지도 모른다. 대신, 아이들은 (상담을) 준비할 시간이 필요하며 그래서 아이들을 대상으로 하는 상담 교사는 인내심이 필요하다. 아이들 스스로 마음을 터놓을 준비가 되어야만 아이에게 자신의 이야기를 하도록 요청할 수 있을 것이다. 아이에게 요청할 때 상담 교사는 치료 과정을 서두르려 하는 게 아니라, 아이에게 자신을 표현하고 자신을 애먹일지 모르는 감정들과 문제들을 찾을 기회를 준다. 상담 교사는 추궁하는 것이 아니라, 그 대신 아이가 자신이 바라는 것을 털어놓기를 청한다.

구문 [11행~12행] **Only when** they are ready to open themselves up / **can children be invited** to tell their story.
　　S　　V
(조동사)

Only when이 이끄는 절이 문두로 나가면서 주어가 조동사 뒤에 위치한 도치구문이다. 조동사가 있을 경우 도치구문은 「조동사+주어+본동사」의 구조. only는 준부정어로 hardly, little 등의 부정어와 같이 도치구문으로 잘 쓰인다.

[12행~16행] **When inviting the child**, / the counselor does**n't** *try to hurry the therapeutic process* **but** *allows* *the child opportunities* / to express themselves and to explore *feelings and issues* [**which** may be troubling for them].

의미를 분명히 하기 위해 접속사(When)를 남긴 분사구문이다. 「not A but B」(A가 아니라 B) 구문이 사용되었다. allow는 뒤에 간접목적어+직접목적어를 취하여 '~에게 …을 주다'의 의미로도 쓰인다.

어휘 therapeutic 치료상의, 치료법의; 긴장을 푸는 데 도움이 되는　hinder 방해하다. 못하게 하다　issue 쟁점, 주제; 발행(물); 발행하다; 발표하다　initial 처음의, 초기의; 머리글자　open oneself up (to A) (A에게) 마음을 터놓다　[선택지 어휘] consistency 일관성

12 빈칸 추론 ⑤

해설 빈칸 문장은 역접의 접속사인 However로 시작하고 있으므로 퓨전 음식의 발전이 '어떠할' 수 있다는 빈칸의 내용은 앞에서 서술된 내용과 대조적인 것이며 이는 빈칸 문장 뒤에서 상술될 것임을 추론할 수 있다. 뒷내용에서, 퓨전 음식은 '뿌리 없는', '진짜가 아닌' 요리로 표현되었으며, 그것은 '전통적인', '진짜' 음식, 즉 토속 음식과 구별되고 있다. 그러한 퓨전 음식이 발달하면 상대적으로 토속 요리를 경험하기는 힘들어질 것이므로 정답은 ⑤ '토속 요리에 대한 경험이 발전하는 것을 방해할'이다.
① 해외 관광의 발달을 가속화할
② 음식 문화의 발전에 기여할
③ 여행객들보다 현지인들의 입맛을 더 만족시킬
④ 영양상 더 균형 잡힌 식단을 제공할

해석 관광업은 퓨전 요리의 발전에서 중요한 매개인데, 그것은 음식을 만들거나 먹으려고 여행하는 사람들에 의해 여러 요리 전통이 섞이는 일이 자주 활성화되기 때문이다. 여러 나라를 연결하는 역사적인 음식 교역 발전의 분석에서 드러났듯이, 이동하면서 음식을 음미하는 이러한 과정은 수 세기 동안 진행되어 오고 있다. 그러나 퓨전 음식의 발전은 토속 요리에 대한 경험이 발전하는 것을 방해할 수 있다. 관광객들이 '전통적인' 혹은 '진짜' 음식을 요구하는 일은 매우 빈번하지만, 새롭고 익숙하지 않은 음식을 시도해 보기를 꺼리는 관광객들도 많다. 아시아에서 퓨전 요리의 발전을 자극한 한 가지는 외국인 방문객들에게 더 익숙해서 입맛이 도는 음식을 만들어 내고자 하는 바람 때문이었다. 하지만 한편으로 '뿌리 없는' 요리는 또한 독특한 원래대로의 음식을 경험하기를 추구하는 외국인 관광객들에 의해 '진짜가 아닌' 것으로 보일지도 모른다.

구문 [4행~8행] This process of mobile food appreciation has been going on for centuries, // **as** has been shown in *the analysis* (of the development of *the*

historical food trade [that linked different countries]).

접속사 as 뒤에 앞문장 전체를 받아주는 주어 it을 생략한 구조이다.

어휘 mediator 중재인; 매개자, 매개체　fusion 용해; 융합, 결합　cuisine 요리법; (보통 비싼 식당의) 요리　culinary 요리[음식]의　authentic 진본[진품]인; 진짜인, 정확한(↔ inauthentic 진품이 아닌)　averse to ~을 싫어하는　impulse (사람·행동이) 충동적인; 충동; 자극　appetizing 구미를 동하게 하는　[선택지 어휘] nutritionally 영양상으로, 영양 면에서　*cf.* nutritional 영양상의　hinder 방해하다

13 흐름 무관 문장 ③

해설 에너지 절감을 위해 더 효율적인 기술을 사용하지만, 반발 효과로 인해 새로운 기술의 에너지 효율성을 인식해 전등을 덜 절약하여 결과적으로 예상 절감 목표에 도달하지 못한다는 것이 글의 요지이므로 작은 자동차를 사려는 경향이 연료 효율성을 향상시킨다는 내용의 ③은 글의 흐름과 무관하다.

해석 가계 소비 영역 내에서 연구는 특히 가정의 에너지 가전제품과 차량의 연료 효율성에 대한 소비자의 직접적인 '반발 효과'에 대개 초점을 맞춘다. ① 예를 들어, 소비자들이 전통적인 백열전구를 보다 효율적인 소형 형광등으로 바꿀 때 흔히 많은 에너지가 절감될 것으로 예상된다. ② 그러나 연구가 보여 주듯이, 많은 소비자들이 전등을 작동하는 데 비용이 덜 든다는 것을 인식하여 전등을 끄는 것에 덜 철저한 것처럼 보이고, 이는 더 오랜 시간의 사용, 즉 더 많은 에너지 소비라는 결과로 이어지기 때문에, 이러한 절감은 좀처럼 예상 목표에 도달하지 못한다. ③ 같은 방식으로, 자동차의 연료 효율성이 상당히 높아졌는데 소비자들이 더 작은 차를 사려는 경향이 연료 효율에서의 향상을 높였기 때문이다. ④ 마찬가지로, 연구 결과에 따르면, 예를 들어, 더 효율적인 공간 난방 장치 또는 증가한 단열 수준과 같은 효율성 향상을 통해 얻은 에너지 절감(량)은 그다음에는 종종 높아진 난방 기준에 맞춰 사용된다. ⑤ 여기서 소비자는 동일하거나 더 낮은 비용으로 이전보다 더 따뜻한 집을 가동함으로써 이득을 얻을 수 있다.

구문 [8행~12행] However, these savings rarely reach their predicted targets as research indicates that *many consumers*, **recognizing that the light costs less to operate**, appear less thorough about switching it off, / **resulting in more hours of use, i.e. higher energy consumption**.

recognizing이 이끄는 분사구는 앞에 있는 명사 many consumers를 보충 설명한다. resulting in ~ energy consumption은 결과를 나타내는 분사구문이다.

[16행~20행] Similarly, studies *have indicated* **that** energy savings (from *efficiency improvements*), for example, a more efficient space heating unit [or] increased levels of insulation, are often then spent on increased heating standards].

have indicated의 목적어로 that이 이끄는 명사절이 쓰였다. or가 연결하는 밑줄 친 두 개의 명사구는 efficiency improvements에 대한 예시를 나타낸다.

어휘 arena 영역; 무대; 경기장　household consumption 가계 소비　predominantly 대개, 주로　rebound 반발; 반향　appliances 가전제품　compact 소형의; 간편한　operate 가동[작동]하다, 운영하다　thorough 철저한; 완전한　insulation 단열 (처리)

14 글의 순서 ④

해설 주어진 글에서 "one-size-fits-all" approach를 언급했는데 (C)의 this approach가 이를 지칭하므로 주어진 글 다음에는 (C)가 나온다. (C) 마지막 부분에서 이러한 접근법은 '자료가 자신의 생각에 맞춰지도록 한다'고 했는데, 이러한 잘못된 접근법은 (A)에서 피드백 고리를 지식에서 현실이라는 잘못된 방향으로 움직이

는 것이라고 표현되어 있다. (A)의 마지막 부분에서는 이러한 잘못된 접근법은 조정이 가능한 핵심 가치(core values)와는 다르다고 했는데, (B)의 those values가 core values를 지칭하므로 (A) 다음에는 (B)가 나온다.

해석 우리는 각 상황의 중요한 세부 요소들은 고려하지 않고 많은 다른 정황에 한정된 일련의 설명을 적용한다. 이것은 문제 해결에 대한 '두루 적용되는' 접근법이다.
(C) 이러한 접근법을 택하는 사람들에게는 맹점, 즉 상황에 관한 중요한 것들을 놓치는 영역이 있다. 그들의 해결책은 자주 실패할 뿐만 아니라 그들은 그러한 실패들을 인식조차 하지 못할 수도 있는데, 이것은 그들이 배우지 못하게 한다. 대신에, 그들은 자료가 자신의 선입견에 맞춰지도록 하는 경향이 있다.
(A) 이것은 피드백 고리에서 잘못된 방향, 바로 지식에서 현실로 이동하는 것이다. 그것은 우리가 이미 믿고 있는 것에서 출발하여 현실이 그것(= 이미 믿고 있는 것)에 맞춰야 한다고 주장하는 것이다. 이것은 핵심 가치를 가지는 것과 같지 않은데, 그것(= 핵심 가치)은 언제나 조정될 수 있기 때문이다.
(B) 그 가치가 너무 엄격해서 더 이상 잘 작동되지 않고 주의 깊게 생각하지 않고 제멋대로 적용될 때 문제가 나타난다. 이것은 우리가 어려운 질문을 스스로에게 던지지 않고 관련 있는 피드백이 무시될 때 발생한다.

구문 [10행~12행] The problem comes // when those values become **so** *rigid* // **that** they no longer work well / and are applied arbitrarily without careful consideration.
when절에서 동사 become과 are applied가 병렬구조를 이룬다. become 다음에는 「so ~ that ... (너무 ~해서 …하다)」 구문이 쓰였다.
[17행~19행] **Not only do their solutions** often **fail**, // they may not even recognize those failures, / **preventing** *them* **from learning**.
Not only라는 부정어 표현이 문두에 나오면서 「조동사(do) + 주어(their solutions) + 동사(fail)」로 어순이 도치되었다. preventing 이하는 분사구문이며 「prevent + O + from v-ing (O가 v하지 못하게 하다)」 구문이 쓰였다.

어휘 finite 한정된, 유한한   subtlety 중요한 세부 요소들; 미묘함   one-size-fits-all 두루 적용되는   adapt 조정하다   rigid 엄격한   arbitrarily 제멋대로; 독단적으로   relevant 관련 있는   blind spot 맹점   preconceived 선입견의; 사전에 형성된

15 글의 순서   ③

해설 이끼를 대기 오염의 지표로 활용할 수 있다는 주어진 글 다음에는 고도로 오염된 지역과 중간 정도로 오염된 지역의 이끼 생태를 소개한 (B)가 나온다. In contrast로 연결되는 (C)에는 오염 지역과 대조되는 청정 지역의 이끼 생태를 논한다. 특정 화학 물질에 민감한 이끼를 소개한 (C) 다음에는 이 이끼 종을 이용하여 대기오염원을 밝힌 사례가 제시된 (A)가 나와야 한다.

해석 '이끼'는 보통 상호 의존적인 관계에서 함께 살아가는 균류와 조류로 구성된 생물이다. 이 강인한 종은 대기 오염의 좋은 생물학적 지표인데 왜냐하면 그것들은 자양분의 원천으로 계속 공기를 흡수하기 때문이다.
(B) 산업 공장 주변의 매우 오염된 지역은 단지 회녹색의 껍질이 딱딱한 이끼들만 있거나 아니면 이끼가 아예 없을 수 있다. 중간 정도로 공기가 오염된 지역은 오렌지 빛깔의 껍질이 딱딱한 이끼들만 살게 할 수 있다.
(C) 대조적으로, 공기가 깨끗한 지역은 더 다양한 이끼들을 살게 할 수 있다. 어떤 이끼 종들은 공기를 오염시키는 특정한 화학 물질에 민감하다. 예를 들어 old man's beard(소나무겨우살이과의 이끼)와 노란 Evernia 이끼는 과도한 이산화황이 존재하면 그 오염 물질이 아주 멀리서 발생한 경우라도 병들고 죽을 수 있다.
(A) 이런 이유로 과학자들은 Superior 호에 있는 Michigan 주의 Isle Royale에서, 즉 어떠한 자동차나 높은 공장 굴뚝도 존재한 적이 없는 섬에서 이산화황 오염을 발견했다. 그들은 북서쪽에 있는 Ontario 주의 Thunder Bay라는 캐나다 도시 안과 주변에 있는 석탄을 태우는 시설에 책임을 묻기 위해 Evernia 이끼를 이용했다.

구문 [1행~3행] A *lichen* is an *organism* (**consisting** of *a fungus and an alga* (**living together**, usually in an interdependent relationship)).
consisting ~ relationship은 an organism을 수식하고 그 안의 living together ~ relationship은 a fungus and an alga를 수식한다.
[6행~9행] For this reason, scientists discovered SO₂ pollution on Isle Royale, Michigan, in Lake Superior, *an island* [where no car or tall factory chimney has ever existed].
밑줄 친 두 부분은 동격 관계이고, 관계부사 where가 이끄는 [ ]이 an island를 수식한다.

어휘 fungus 곰팡이, 균류   interdependent 상호 의존적인   hardy 강인한   indicator 지표   absorb 흡수하다   nourishment 자양분, 영양, 음식물   point the finger 비난하다   moderate 중간 정도의, 온건한   crusty 딱딱한 껍질이 있는   pollutant 오염 물질, 오염원   originate 발생하다

16 문장 넣기   ③

해설 ③의 앞 문장에서는 리더들이 조화롭고 갈등이 없는 팀을 선호한다고 했고 ③의 다음 문장에서는 '사람들이 이러한 종류의 토론(this kind of debate)'을 즐긴다고 했으므로 두 문장 간에 논리적인 균열이 있다. '아이러니한 점은 팀원들은 서로에게 도전할 기회를 '원한다'는 것이다'라는 주어진 문장이 ③에 들어가면, '리더들은 조화로운 팀을 선호한다 → 그런데 아이러니하게도 팀원들은 도전할 기회를 원한다 → 정중하고 평등한 한 팀원들은 이러한 종류의 토론을 즐긴다'라는 구조가 성립되므로 주어진 문장이 들어가기에 가장 적절한 곳은 ③이다.

해석 가장 유능하고 혁신적인 팀은 주기적인 치열한 토론을 벌이는데, 이것은 우리가 관찰하기에 재미있었다. 기분 나쁘게 하지 않으면서 동의하지 않는 능력은 팀 내에서의 왕성한 의사소통과 문제 해결에 필수적이다. 그러나 리더 집단에게 거의 항상 조화로운 팀과 갈등과 논쟁이 있는 팀 중 어느 것이 더 나은지를 질문할 때, 압도적인 다수가 불협화음이 없는 팀에 표를 던진다. 아이러니한 점은 팀원들은 서로에게 도전할 기회를 '원한다'는 것이다. 토의가 정중하고 모든 사람들이 동등하게 기여할 기회를 갖는 한, 대부분의 사람들은 이러한 종류의 토론을 즐기며, 그것이 지적으로 자극을 줄 뿐만 아니라 문제의 경로에 당도하여 최적의 해결책을 도출해내는 데 중요하다고 생각한다. 팀들은 도전적인 토의에 정기적으로 참여할 때, 구성원들이 서로의 아이디어와 관점에 반박하도록 장려받을 때, 유대감과 유능함을 더 많이 느낀다. 이것은 토론이 약간 과열되더라도 또한 마찬가지이다.

구문 [12행~17행] **As long as** discussions are respectful / and everyone gets the chance to contribute equally, // most people thrive on this kind of debate — / finding **it not only** intellectually stimulating **but** important **to** getting to the route of problems and working out optimal solutions.
As long as ~ contribute equally 절에서 접속사 As long as는 '~하는 한'의 뜻이다. As long as 다음에 이어지는 밑줄 친 두 개의 절이 병렬구조를 이룬다. finding 다음의 it은 this kind of debate를 지칭하며 목적어 it을 설명하는 보어 자리에 「not only A but (also) B (A뿐만 아니라 B도)」 구문이 쓰였다. A, B에 해당하는 두 밑줄 부분은 형용사(각각 stimulating과 important)로 이루어진 구로서 병렬구조를 이루어 「find + O + 형용사 (O가 (형용사)하다는 것을 알게 되다)」 구문을 완성한다. important 다음에 to는 전치사로 뒤에 두 개의 동명사구가 목적어로 왔다.

어휘 intense 치열한   pose (문제를) 제기하다   respectful 정중한, 공손한   thrive on ~을 즐기다. 잘 하다 *cf.* thrive 번창하다; 잘 자라다   stimulating 자극이 되는, 고무적인   work out ~을 도출하다, 해결하다   engage in ~에 참여하다   argue with ~을 반박하다

17 문장 넣기   ⑤

해설 주어진 문장이 That is으로 시작하는데, 이는 앞에 나온 내용을 다른 말로 풀어서 다시 말한 것이다. 주어진 문장의 내용, 즉 작은 지름의 전선이 더 큰 지름의 전선보다 저항이 더 크다는 것은 ⑤ 앞에 나온 '전선의 지름이 커질수록 전선의 저항이 작아진다'는 내용과 일맥상통하고 ⑤ 뒤의 내용은 전선의 '길이'와 저항 간의 관계를 설명한 것이므로, 주어진 문장은 ⑤에 들어가는 것이 적절하다.

- -

해석 (옴으로 측정되는) 전기 저항은 전류가 어떤 물질을 얼마나 쉽게 통과하는지를 나타낸다. 여러 금속과 같은 일부 물질들은 저항이 낮아서 전류가 그것들을 쉽게 통과한다. 그와 대조적으로 유리와 고무 같은 물질들은 저항이 높아서, 그것들은 약한 전기 전도체이다. 어떤 물질이 전기 회로에 놓였을 때 그 물질의 실제 저항은 그것의 물리적 특성, 예를 들어, 전선의 경우에는 지름과 길이에 의해 결정된다. 전선의 지름이 커질수록 전선의 저항은 작아진다. 즉, 다른 모든 것이 동일하다면, 지름이 작은 전선이 지름이 더 큰 전선보다 더 저항이 크다. 게다가 어떤 물질의 저항은 그것의 길이가 커지면서 증가한다. 즉 2피트 길이의 전선은 같은 전선 1피트보다 저항이 두 배이다.

- -

구문 [1행~3행] That is, **all other things (being) equal**, _a wire_ (of small diameter) is more resistant than _one_ (of larger diameter).
all other things (being) equal은 주어가 포함된 분사구문으로 if all other things are equal로 바꾸어 쓸 수가 있다. one of larger diameter의 one은 앞에 나온 명사 a wire를 대신하는 대명사이다.

- -

어휘 diameter 지름, 직경   resistant 저항력 있는, ~에 잘 견디는; 저항하는   electrical resistance 전기 저항   ohm 옴((전기 저항의 단위))   refer to ~을 나타내다, ~와 관련 있다   electrical current 전류   substance 물질   electrical conductor 전기 전도체   electrical circuit 전기 회로   property (사물의) 속성, 특성; 재산, 소유물; 부동산

18 요약문 완성   ④

해설 같은 정도의 가치일 때 무언가를 얻는 것보다 잃는 것에 대한 거부감이 더 큰 것이 부정행위를 저지르는 동기라는 내용의 글이므로, 이를 요약하면 '비슷한 가치의 이득을 포기하는 것과 비교했을 때, 잠재적 실패를 맞이하는 것에 대한 더 큰 거리낌(unwillingness)은 부정행위를 끌어낼(elicit) 수 있다'가 된다.

- -

해석 사람들은 같은 가치를 지닌 무언가를 얻는 것보다 잃는 것을 더욱 싫어한다. 인간의 마음에 관한 이러한 거의 보편적인 진리를 고려해 볼 때, 현실 세계에서 부정직과 부정행위의 여러 행동이 우리가 가치 있게 여기는 무언가를 잃는 것에 대한 두려움으로부터 생긴다는 것은 놀랍지 않을 수 있다. 수업에서 'F 학점'을 받는 것을 피하려는 압박감은, 'A 학점'을 받을 가능성이 그러는 것보다 많은 학생이 시험에 부정행위용 쪽지를 들고 들어오도록 더 많이 유도한다. 시장 점유율을 잃는 것을 피하려는 압박감은, 새로운 판매 기록을 세우는 것이 그러는 것보다 사업하는 사람들이 더 자주 법을 어기도록 유혹한다. 정부에게 추가의 돈을 빚지려 하지 않는 것은 더 큰 환급을 받는 것보다 탈세하는 것에 대한 더 큰 동기 요인이 된다. 물론, 이 모든 경우에서 더 큰 매출액이나 더 큰 환급 같은 이득은 사람들이 부정행위를 하도록 자극할 수 있으나, 요지는 그것이 결코 같은 양의 손실을 피하는 것만큼 자극하지 못하리라는 것이다.

↓

> 비슷한 가치의 이득을 포기하는 것과 비교했을 때, 잠재적 실패를 맞이하는 것에 대한 더 큰 (A) 거리낌은 부정행위를 (B) 끌어낼 수 있다.

- -

구문 [2행~6행] Given this near-universal truth about the human psyche, **it** may not be surprising **that** many acts of dishonesty and cheating in the real world / are born / from fear of losing _something_ [(that[which]) we value].
it이 가주어이며 that 이하는 진주어이다. [ ] 부분은 선행사 something을 수식하는 관계절로 목적격 관계대명사 that 혹은 which가 생략되어있다.

- -

어휘 given ~을 고려해 볼 때   universal 보편적인   dishonesty 부정직   cheating 부정행위   _cf._ cheat sheet 부정행위용 쪽지   pressure 압박감   market share 시장 점유율   tempt 유혹하다   owe 빚지다   additional 추가의   motivator 동기   _cf._ motivate 자극하다, 동기를 주다   refund 환불   potential 잠재적인   wrongdoing 부정행위   [선택지 어휘] willingness 의욕(→ unwillingness 거리낌)   urge 충동   trigger 촉발시키다, 유발하다   elicit (정보·반응 등을) 끌어내다

19~20 장문   19 ④ 20 ⑤

해설 **19.** 이 글은 손글씨를 쓰는 것과 전자적인 방식으로 쓰는 것을 비교, 대조하면서 손글씨를 쓰는 것의 장점을 언급하며 더 낫다는 것을 강조하고 있으므로 ④ '왜 펜은 키보드보다 더 강력한가?'가 제목으로 가장 적절하다.
① 우리는 필기를 어떻게 보존할 수 있는가?
② 필기의 밝은 면과 어두운 면
③ 필기 대 타이핑 : 어느 것이 더 빠른가?
⑤ 펜은 키보드보다 세부사항을 더 잘 기억한다
20. 이모티콘이 문자 메시지에 약간의 감정을 되찾게 하기 위해 발명되었다는 것으로 보아 손으로 쓸 때 춤추는 요소, 즉 메시지에 선율은 글 쓰는 사람의 개성적인 면을 더하는 것으로 볼 수 있다. 그러므로 (e) '비개성적인(impersonal)'은 '개성적인(personal)'으로 바꾸어 써야 적절하다.

- -

해석 우리가 글을 읽을 때, 우리 중 거의 아무도 그 글이 손으로 쓰였는지 워드프로세서로 쓰였는지 궁금해하지 않는다. 그러나 글쓰기 전문가들은 그렇지 않다. 펜과 키보드는 매우 다른 (a) 인지 과정을 작동시킨다. 손으로 쓰는 것은 펜과 종이를 느끼고, 필기도구들을 움직이고, 생각으로 움직임을 지시하는 등 다양한 기술을 필요로 하는 복잡한 작업이다. 아이들은 이 정밀한 (b) 근육의 운동을 숙달하는 데 몇 년이 걸린다. 각 글자를 서로 다르게 표시를 남기는 방식으로 필기도구를 움직이면서 그 도구를 단단히 잡아야 한다. 키보드를 조작하는 것은 전혀 동일하지 않다. 여러분이 해야 할 일은 맞는 키를 누르는 것이다. 그것은 아이들이 매우 빨리 배울 수 있을 정도로 쉽지만, 무엇보다도 어떤 문자이건 그 모든 움직임은 정확히 (c) 동일하다. 그것은 큰 변화이다. 타자를 치는 것은 몸의 단일한 움직임의 결과인데, 손으로 쓰는 것은 그렇지 않다.
게다가, 전자 텍스트는 손으로 쓴 대응물과 같은 표시를 남기지 않는다. 화면에서 글의 초안을 작성할 때 여러분은 원하는 만큼 그것을 바꿀 수 있지만 여러분의 편집 기록은 전혀 없다. 소프트웨어는 어딘가에 변화를 기록은 하지만, 사용자들은 그것에 접근할 수 없다. 하지만 펜과 종이만 있으면, 모든 것이 거기에 있다. 줄을 그어 지워지거나 고쳐진 단어들, 여백에 휘갈겨 쓴 글 조각, 그리고 나중에 추가되는 것들은 영원히 그곳에 있어서, 여러분의 작품과 그것의 창작 단계에 대한 시각적 기록을 남긴다. 일부 필적 옹호자들은 이러한 (d) 장식 효과가 사라진 것을 한탄한다. 이것은 단순히 문자를 쓰는 것에 대한 문제일 뿐 아니라 그것은 또한 조화감과 균형감을 얻으면서 둥근 형태로 그리는 것을 포함한다. 우리가 글을 쓸 때는 춤추는 요소, 즉 메시지에 선율이 있는데, 그것은 (e) 비개성적인(→ 개성적인) 측면을 텍스트에 더한다. 결국, 그런 이유로 이모티콘이 발명되었다. 문자 메시지에 약간의 감정을 되찾게 하기 위해서 말이다.

- -

구문 [8행~12행] Children **take** _several years_ **to master** this precise muscular exercise: you need to hold the scripting tool firmly while moving it in such a way as to leave a different mark for each letter.
'take+시간+to-v'의 형태로 'v하는 데 시간이 걸리다'라는 의미이다. 밑줄 친 부분은 'v하는 (그런) 식으로'라는 의미이다.
[25행~28행] _Words_ (crossed out or corrected), _bits_ (scribbled in the margin) |and| later additions are there for good, **leaving** a visual record of your work and its creative stages.

밑줄 친 세 개의 명사구가 콤마(,)와 and로 연결되어 주어 역할을 한다. ( ) 부분은 각각 바로 앞의 명사 Words, bits를 수식하는 분사구이다. leaving 이하는 결과를 나타내는 분사구문이다.

[33행~35행] There is *an element of dancing* when we write, *a melody in the message*, **which** adds the personal aspect to the text.
두 개의 밑줄 친 명사구는 동격 관계를 이룬다. 계속적 용법의 관계대명사 which가 이끄는 절은 앞에 있는 명사 an element of dancing에 대해 부연 설명한다.

어휘 bring into play …을 작동[활동]시키다; …을 도입[이용]하다 cognitive 인지 [인식]의 implement 도구, 기구; 시행하다 master 숙달하다, 완전히 익히다; 주인 muscular 근육의; 박력 있는 firmly 단단히; 확고히; 단호히 counterpart 대응 관계에 있는 것[사람]; 상대 draft 초안을 작성하다; 초안 keep track of ~을 기록하다 scribble 갈겨쓰다; 휘갈기다 margin 여백; 차이 for good 영원히 advocate 옹호자, 지지자 regret 유감스럽게 생각하다; 후회하다 ornamental 장식용의 restore 되찾게 하다; 회복하다 preserve 보존하다; 보호하다 mighty 강력한; 훌륭한

| 1 | ④ | 2 | ④ | 3 | ④ | 4 | ③ | 5 | ⑤ | | 6 | ④ | 7 | ⑤ | 8 | ② | 9 | ⑤ | 10 | ⑤ |
| 11 | ① | 12 | ③ | 13 | ④ | 14 | ③ | 15 | ② | | 16 | ② | 17 | ② | 18 | ① | 19 | ② | 20 | ④ |

1 글의 목적

해설 편지를 쓴 사람은 아트 캠프의 활동 책임자로 루미나리아 제작 전문가에게 지역사회의 젊은이들을 위해 루미나리아 제작 예술 기법 프로그램을 맡아줄 수 있는지 요청하고 있으므로 글의 목적으로 가장 적절한 것은 ④이다.

해석 Nelson 씨께.
저는 아트 캠프의 Patrick White Adventures의 활동 책임자입니다. 저는 또한 중심가에 있는 당신의 Jacksonville 루미나리아 상점을 정말 좋아해서 이미 당신의 아름답게 디자인된 루미나리아를 몇 개 가지고 있습니다. 축제 장식이 요즘 가장 인기 있는 복고 열풍 중 하나이기에 지역의 많은 소년 소녀들이 당신의 상점을 자주 방문한다는 것을 알고 있습니다. 저는 지금 다음 역년을 위한 우리 프로그램을 계획 중입니다. 당신의 루미나리아 제작 예술 기법을 저희 젊은이들과 나누시기 위해 11월 셋째 주에 한 시간 정도 시간을 내주실 수 있을지 궁금합니다. 당신이 가장 편리할 시간에 방문하시도록 제가 주선할 수 있습니다. 가능하실 때 johnlee@whiteadven.com으로 메일을 보내주시거나 555-1234로 전화주시겠습니까? 이 아이디어를 고려해주셔서 감사합니다.
진심을 담아,
John Lee 드림.

구문 [10행~12행] I am wondering <u>if you have an hour or so during the third week of November</u> / **to share** your luminary-making artistry **with** our young people.
접속사 if가 이끄는 밑줄 친 부분은 am wondering의 목적어 역할을 하는 명사절이다. to share 이하는 '목적(~하기 위해)'을 나타내는 to부정사구이다.

어휘 retro 복고(풍)의 rage (일시적) 대유행; 격노 calendar year 역년 ((1월 1일부터 12월 31일까지의 기간)) share A with B B와 A를 나누다[공유하다] artistry 예술적 기교 arrange 주선[마련]하다; 배열하다; 정리하다

2 밑줄 함의 ④

해설 집단의 의견은 하나로 결집되는 방향으로 흐르기 때문에 반대되는 의견을 제시하는 구성원은 배척되거나 조롱당할 수 있어서 집단 구성원들이 집단에 반대되는 목소리를 내기를 꺼린다는 태도가 'are careful not to rock the boat(평지풍파를 일으키지 않으려고 주의한다)'라는 말로 표현된다. 이 어구의 의미를 가장 잘 나타낸

것은 ④ '집단의 사고에 반하는 의견을 피력하는 데 주저한다'이다.
① 집단 내의 반대 의견을 장려하는 데 중요한 역할을 한다
② 집단 구성원 간의 갈등을 해결하기 위해 노력한다
③ 집단의 의사결정 과정상의 문제를 지적한다
⑤ 집단 구성원을 불리한 정보로부터 보호하기 위해 노력한다

해석 예일대의 심리학자 Irving Janis는 거의 모든 집단이 상황에 대한 하나의 합의된 관점, 다시 말해 합의 현실인 'PC' 즉 정치적으로 올바른 관점을 발전시킨다는 것을 보여주었다. 반대되는 어떠한 증거도 심사숙고 없이 자동적으로 거부되고 흔히 조롱당하며 정치적으로 올바르지 못한 자료를 제시하는 사람에 대한 배척으로 이어질 수 있다. 그러므로 집단 구성원들은 평지풍파를 일으키지 않으려고 주의한다. Janis는 그의 대표적인 책 〈Groupthink〉에서 전문가 집단이 어떻게 엄청난 실수를 저지르는지 설명했다. 전문가 집단의 사람들은 자신들의 개인적인 적합성과 능력에 대해 걱정하며, 만약 합의에서 너무 멀리 벗어난다면, 자기들이 진지하게 받아들여지지 않을 것으로 느낀다고 그는 말했다. 사람들은 위상을 얻기 위해 경쟁하고, 의견은 흔히 그 뒤를 따를 뿐이다. 집단 순승 사고는 집단이 자기들의 행동 방침에 갇히고 대안을 탐색할 수 없게 하는데, 그 이유는 아무도 확실히 자리 잡은 방침에 의문을 제기하지 않기 때문이다. 집단이 더 단결될수록, 어떠한 불화라도 일으키기를 회피하려는 집단 구성원들의 욕구는 더 커진다.

구문 [4행~7행] Any evidence to the contrary <u>is</u> automatically <u>rejected</u> without consideration, ***often ridiculed***, [and] <u>may lead</u> to exclusion of *the person* (presenting the un-PC data).
동사 is rejected와 may lead가 병렬구조를 이룬다. often ridiculed는 수동의 의미를 가지는 분사구문이다. ( )은 능동의 의미를 나타내는 분사구로 the person을 수식한다.

[17행~19행] **The more cohesive** the group (is), **the greater** *the urge of the group members* (to avoid creating any discord) (is).
「The+비교급 ~, the+비교급 …(~하면 할수록 더 …하다)」 구문이 사용되었고, 각각의 동사 is가 생략되어 있다. 'to avoid creating any discord'는 the urge of the group members를 수식하는 to부정사구이다.

어휘 consensus 합의, 의견 일치 ridicule 조롱(하다), 비웃다 exclusion 배척, 제외 rock the boat 평지풍파를 일으키다 classic 대표적인, 최고 수준의 panel 전문가 집단 relevance 적절함, 타당성; 관련(성) deviate 벗어나다 tag along 따라가다 established 확실히 자리 잡은, 인정받는; 저명한 cohesive 단결된 urge 욕구, 충동 discord 불화 dissent 반대 (의견); 반대하다 resolve 해결하다; (굳게) 다짐하다 reluctant 주저하는, 꺼리는 adverse 불리한, 부정적인

3 글의 요지 ④

해설 운동 코치의 주관적인 관찰이나 평가가 부정확할 수밖에 없는 이유에 대해 설명한 글로, 운동 코치들은 인간 인지의 한계와 자신의 감정 및 개인적 편향 등으로 인해 경기에 대해 왜곡되고 불완전한 인식을 가질 수밖에 없다는 내용이다. 그러므로, 요지로 가장 적절한 것은 ④이다.

해석 다른 모든 인간 활동과 마찬가지로, 스포츠는 인간이 정보를 처리하는 방식에 의해 영향받는다. 자료를 기억하고 나서 나중에 그것을 되찾는 것은 많은 간섭 기회가 있는 복잡한 과정이다. 경기의 특징적인 부분(즉 논란이 많은 결정, 비범한 기술적 수행, 경기 중단 다음에 나온 행동 등)은 종종 코치와 관중들이 똑같이 쉽게 기억하는 반면 중요하지 않은 사건들은 더 잊히기 쉽다. 이러한 형태의 강조는 코치의 감정과 개인적 편향과 결합될 때 전체적으로 경기에 대한 왜곡된 인식을 유발할지도 모른다. 게다가 우리의 처리 체계에는 경기장 내에서 일어나는 모든 행동을 보고 완전히 이해하고 저장하는 것을 거의 불가능하게 하는 한계가 있다. 이러한 한계로 인해 주변적인 행동은 대개 무시되며 코치는 경기의 특정 영역(보통 가장 중요한 영역이라고 여겨지는 것)에만 주의를 집중시키게 된다.

구문 [13행~16행] Furthermore, our processing system has *limitations* [that make *it* near impossible **to view**, **assimilate** and **store** *all actions* [that take place within the playing area]].
첫 번째 [ ]는 limitations를 수식하는 관계사절이다. [ ]절 내의 it은 가목적어이고 밑줄 친 부분이 진목적어이다. to 다음의 동사원형 view, assimilate, store는 병렬구조를 이루며 all actions를 공통의 목적어로 가진다. 두 번째 [ ]는 all actions를 수식한다.
[16행~19행] These limitations result in *the coach* **focusing** attention on a specific area of play ~ **with** *the peripheral action largely* **ignored**.
result in의 목적어는 동명사구 focusing 이하이며 the coach는 focusing의 의미상 주어이다. 「with O p.p.」는 'O가 ~된 채로'의 뜻이다.

어휘 commit ~ to memory ~을 기억하다, 암기하다 **retrieve** 되찾다, 회수하다 **interference** 간섭, 개입 **distinctive** 특유의, 특징적인 **controversial** 논란이 많은 **exceptional** 예외적인, 비범한 **stoppage** (경기) 중단 **spectator** 관중 **highlighting** 강조하기 **bias** 편견, 편향 **assimilate** 완전히 이해하다

4 글의 주제 ③

해설 시를 읽으면 복잡하고 미묘한 요소로부터 의미를 적극적으로 도출해내는 능력을 함양할 수 있는데, 이것은 사업을 하며 복잡한 문제에 마주쳤을 때 효과적인 해결책을 도출하고자 할 때 적용될 수 있다는 내용의 글이므로 주제로 가장 적절한 것은 ③ '사업상 문제 해결 기술을 증진시키는 도구로서의 시 읽기'이다.
① 사업상의 리더십의 귀중한 구성 요소로서의 엄격한 태도
② 정신적 고통을 완화하기 위한 방법으로서의 단순화된 시적 접근
④ 시적 사고와 사업적 사고 간의 대조와 비교
⑤ 기업가들이 자신의 사고 능력을 향상시키는 데 도움을 주는 시의 유형

해석 시를 읽을 때, 당신은 의도적인 애매성과 비의도적인 애매성 둘 모두로 가득한 단어들로부터 의미를 전개하고 이야기를 해석한다. 즉, 당신은 시의 내용, 맥락과 시적 장치의 사용에 의지하여 그러한 의미를 추출한다. 경영상의 (혹은 다른 어떤 사업적인 기능의) 입장에서 복잡한 질문들에 직면할 때, 미지의 것들에 균형을 잡고 미묘한 추론으로부터 해결책을 산출하는 이러한 능력을 갖고 있는 것은 더욱 상상력이 풍부하고 효과적인 해결책들을 가능하게 한다. 오로지 과학적 기법의 엄격함에만 의존하는 것은 거의 모든 복잡한 문제에 대한 결함 있는 접근법이 될 것이다. 시는 당신에게 복잡성을 붙들고 씨름하며 단순화하는 법을 가르쳐준다. 모든 사업은 복잡한 문제에 마주치며, 복잡한 질문은 복잡한 해법을 요구한다. 정기적으로 시를 읽는 사람은 시를 읽을 때 이루어지는 것처럼 모호하고

역동적인 논쟁으로부터 의미를 끌어낼 수 있기 때문에 그러한 해결책에 당도할 가능성이 더 높다.

구문 [1행~3행] In reading a poem, / you underline{develop} meaning 「and」 underline{interpret} a story / from *words* (filled with **both** intentional **and** unintentional ambiguities); ~.
동사 develop과 interpret이 병렬구조를 이룬다. ( )는 수동의 의미로 words를 수식한다. 여기서 「both A and B (A와 B 둘 다)」 구문이 쓰였으며, A, B 자리에 모두 형용사가 왔다.
[5행~9행] When facing complicated questions from a managerial (or any other business function's) stance, / **having** this ability (to balance unknowns 「and」 generate solutions from nuanced reasonings) / **allows for** more imaginative and effective solutions.
When ~ stance는 분사구문인데 의미를 확실하게 하기 위하여 접속사(When)를 생략하지 않았다. having ~ reasonings가 동명사 주어이고 allows for가 동사이다. to balance ~ reasonings는 this ability를 수식한다.

어휘 **interpret** 해석하다 **ambiguity** 애매성 **extract** 추출하다 **draw upon** ~에 의지하다 **managerial** 경영상의 **stance** 입장 **nuance** ~에 미묘한 차이를 주다 **reasoning** 추론 **allow for** ~을 가능하게 하다 **exclusively** 배타적으로, 오로지 **rigidity** 엄격; 엄밀; 단단함 **flawed** 결함이 있는 **wrestle with** (힘든 문제를 해결하기 위해) 씨름하다 **derive A from B** A를 B에서 끌어내다 **vague** 모호한 **dynamic** 역동적인

5 도표 이해 ⑤

해설 연평균 변화율에서 공은 수입액에서는 소폭 증가(0.3퍼센트)했고 수출액에서 유일하게 감소(−0.1퍼센트)했다. 그러므로 ⑤는 도표와 일치하지 않는다.

해석 2014년과 2019년 유럽연합(EU)과 유럽 연합 외 국가들(Extra-EU) 간에 종류별 스포츠용품 교역
위 표는 2014년과 2019년에 유럽연합(EU)과 유럽 연합 외 국가들(Extra-EU) 간에 종류별 스포츠 용품의 수출, 수입, 그리고 연평균 변화율의 금전적 가치를 보여준다. ① 보트의 수출액은 2014년과 2019년에 모두 가장 높았던 반면, 가장 높은 수입액은 2014년의 스포츠 신발 수입액 때문에 동일한 추세를 따르지 않았다. ② 2019년에 스키 수출액은 보트 수출액의 10분의 1에도 미치지 못했다. ③ 수입 부문에서는, 4개의 스포츠 용품 부문이 2019년에 10억 유로 이상을 기록했다. ④ 스포츠 신발은 2014년부터 2019년까지 가장 큰 연평균 수출액 변화율을 보여준 반면, 스포츠 엽총의 변화율은 수출액이 0.8퍼센트로 가장 조금 증가한 것으로 나타났다. ⑤ 공의 연평균 변화율은 수입액에서 유일하게 감소했다.

구문 [5행~8행] The export value of Boats was the highest **both in 2014 and in 2019**, // **while** the highest import value didn't follow the same trend / because of the import value of sports footwear in 2014.
「both A and B (A와 B 둘 다)」 구문이 쓰였으며, A, B 자리 모두 전치사구가 위치해 있다. while은 접속사로서 '반면에'의 의미를 지닌다.

어휘 **monetary** 금전의; 화폐[통화]의 **sector** 부문 **indicate** 나타내다; 가리키다

6 내용 불일치 ④

해설 말년에 그의 생산성은 양적인 면과 창의적인 생각면에서 줄어들지 않았다고 했으므로 ④가 본문의 내용과 일치하지 않는다.

해석 Titian으로도 알려진 Tiziano Vecellio는 베니스의 가장 위대한 화가이자 이탈리아의 르네상스 시대 최후의 거장이었다. 그의 그림은 풍부한 색채와 삶의 기쁨을 나타냈고, 그는 인체의 찬란한 아름다움뿐만 아니라 영적 기운도 묘사하려고 했다. Vecellio는 1477년 베네치아 알프스의 가난한 소작농 가정에서 태어났다. 9살에 그는 베니스로 보내져 그곳에서 처음으로 미술을 공부하기 시작했다. Vecellio는 Charles 5세, 스페인의 Philip 2세와 같은 황제들과 교황 Paul 3세의 초상화를 그렸다. 말년에, 양적인 면과 창의적인 생각 면에서 그의 생산성은 줄어들지 않았다. 이 위대한 거장은 1576년 전염병으로 사망했다. 그는 Santa Maria dei Frari의 교회에 안치되었는데, 그곳에서 그의 가장 유명한 두 개의 작품을 여전히 볼 수 있다.

구문 [6행~7행] Vecellio **was** born to a family of poor peasants in the Venetian Alps **in 1477**.
과거를 나타내는 in 14777이 있으므로 과거동사 was가 사용되었다.

어휘 represent 나타내다　seek to-v v하려고 하다　depict 묘사하다　glory 찬란한 아름다움; 영광　aura 기운　spirituality 영적인 것; 정신성　peasant 소작농　portrait 초상화　undiminished 줄어들지 않은　plague 전염병　bury 매장하다. 묻다

7 밑줄 어법　　　⑤

해설 ⑤ 앞의 spend와 and로 연결되는 병렬구조이므로 repeat이 되어야 한다.
① 「let+목적어+목적보어」 구조에서 목적보어로는 원형부정사가 되어야 하므로 적절히 사용되었다.
② 주어가 동명사구(drawing a deep breath)이므로 단수동사가 적절하다.
③ charge와 oxygen은 수동 관계이므로 charged가 맞다.
④ which의 선행사는 복수명사인 alpha waves이므로 복수동사로 받아야 한다.

해석 여러분의 창의력이 서서히 멈추었는가? 좌절감에 지지 말고, 의자에 깊숙이 앉아 몇 번 심호흡해보라. 심호흡이 산소 내의 음이온을 증가시킴으로써 여러분의 창의력에 활력을 불어넣는다는 것을 알고 있었는가? 음전하를 띤 산소는 뇌의 곳곳을 순환하면서 신경 세포에 생기를 준다. 이 음이온이 창의적 사고와 연관된 더 큰 진폭의 알파파를 뇌 속에 촉진하기 때문에 돌연 여러분의 창의력이 북돋아진다. 그러므로 다음에 여러분의 창의적 기운이 부담을 느낄 때에는, 5초마다 숨을 들이쉬고 내쉬면서 2분 동안 심호흡을 하고, 적어도 12번 그 과정을 반복하라.

구문 [10행~14행] So, ~, spend two minutes **taking** deep breaths, *breathing* in and out every five seconds, and repeat the cycle at least 12 times.
「spend+시간+v-ing」는 'v하는 데 시간을 보내다'란 의미이고 breathing은 부대상황의 분사구문을 이끈다. spend와 repeat은 and로 연결된 병렬관계이다.

어휘 grind to a stop 서서히 멈추다 (땅을 끌면서 서서히 멈추는 것)　get the better of 이기다. 능가하다　charge 청구하다; 기소하다; 충전하다　circulate 순환하다. 순환시키다

8 밑줄 어휘　　　②

해설 선사 시대 사람들의 춤추는 행위가 그들에게는 매우 중요한 삶의 일부였는데 우리가 이러한 의식을 하찮게 폄하하는 것은 적절하지 않다는 내용이므로 ② 'justified'는 unjustified(정당하지 않은)로 바꿔야 한다.

해석 분명히, 춤을 추는 의식은 선사 시대의 사람들에게는 에너지의 ① 낭비로 보이지 않았다. 그들은 가면과 의상을 만드는 것에 시간을 들였고, 춤을 추는 데에 즐겁게 칼로리를 소모하였으며, 이 장면들을 기록하는 것을 다른 어떤 단체 활동보다 더 선호했다. 따라서 인류학자 Victor Turner가 춤을 추는 의식을, 가끔 일어나거나, 지엽적이거나, 혹은 초기 단계의 지위로 귀속시킨 것은 특히 선사 시대의 경우에는 ② 정당한(→ 정당하지 않은) 것 같고, 선사 시대의 우선 사항보다는 오늘날 우리가 사는 산업 시대의 생산 지향적인 사고방식의 전형성을 보여주는 것 같다. 확실히 이 사람들은 역경을 알고 있었으며, 식량 부족, 질병, 야생 동물에 의해 자주 ③ 위협받았다. 그러나 춤으로 이루어지며 어쩌면 황홀 상태의 특징을 가진 의식은 그들의 삶에 ④ 중요했다. 아마도 단지 여러 면에서 훨씬 더 수월한 우리 자신의 삶이, 일해야 하는 현대의 의무에 의해서 또한 매우 ⑤ 제약을 받기 때문에, 우리는 '왜 그런지'를 궁금해해야 한다.

구문 [6행~11행] Thus *anthropologist Victor Turner's attribution* (of danced ritual to an occasional, marginal, or liminal status) **seems** especially unjustified in the prehistoric case — and (seems) more representative of the production-oriented mentality of our own industrial age than of prehistoric priorities.
( )의 수식을 받는 anthropologist Victor Turner's attribution이 주어이고 동사는 seems이다. especially ~ case와 more ~ priorities가 동사 seems의 보어로 쓰였으며, more 앞의 seems가 중복되어 생략되었다. 또한, 비교급 구문 「more A than B」에서 'of+명사' 형태가 앞의 representative에 연결되어 쓰였다.

어휘 ritual 의식　prehistoric 선사 시대의　fashion 만들다; 유행　execution 실행. 수행　anthropologist 인류학자　attribution 귀결; 귀인　occasional 이따금의. 때때로의　marginal 여백의; 여분의; 지엽적인　representative 전형적인. 대표하는; 대표자　mentality 사고방식　constrain 제한하다　imperative 의무; 명령

9 빈칸 추론　　　⑤

해설 예술가와 관람객 사이의 소통이 어려운 이유는 아무리 간단한 그림을 감상하더라도 관람객은 예술가의 생각을 알 수 없으며 관람객마다 그림을 해석하는 방식이 너무나 많기 때문인데, 이를 한 개념으로 표현하면 예술의 '주관성(Subjectivity)'이 된다.
① 일관성 ② 신비 ③ 정교함 ④ 보편성

해설 주관성은 모든 예술의 필수적인 부분이고 때로는 전혀 그럴 것 같지 않은 곳에서조차 우리는 예술가와 관람객 사이의 포괄적인 소통이 매우 어렵다고 생각한다. 예를 들어 추상화에서뿐만 아니라 가장 간단한 그림에서도 말이다. Leonardo da Vinci가 그린 '모나리자'라는 가장 잘 알려진 그림 중 하나를 예로 들어보자. 누구도 이 그림이 한 여성의 초상화라는 것을 오해하지 않는다. 그 정도는 우리도 안다. 그러나 이 그림에서 호기심을 자아내는 미소는 이 미소가 어떤 마음 상태를 묘사하는지의 측면에서 너무나 많은 다른 방식으로 해석된다. 따라서 관람객은 예술가가 정확히 무엇을 생각하고 있었는지를 결코 확신할 수 없다. 이것은 모든 수준에서 유효하며, 따라서 대부분의 예술가와 그들의 관람객들 사이에서 예술품만을 통해 완벽한 소통은 일어날 수 없다.

구문 [2행~4행] ~ one **finds** a comprehensive communication between the artist and the audience *very difficult*.
밑줄 친 부분은 finds의 목적어이고 very difficult는 목적격보어이다.
[4행~6행] For example, **not just** in abstract painting, **but** in the most straightforward painting.
'not just A but B'는 'A뿐만 아니라 B도'의 뜻이다.

어휘 integral 필수적인; 완전한　likely ~할 것 같은; 가능한　comprehensive 포괄적인. 종합적인　abstract painting 추상화　portrait 초상화　interpret 해석하다; 통역하다　depict 묘사하다　hold true 유효하다. 진실이다

10 빈칸 추론 ⑤

해설 빈칸 문장이 So로 시작하고 있으므로 앞 내용의 '결과'에 해당한다는 것과 빈칸 문장 뒤에 이어지고 있는 Yellow candy는 빈칸 문장을 상술하는 구체적인 예시임을 판단할 수 있다. 빈칸 문장으로 보아, 다른 감각들로부터 수신된 메시지들이 어떤 경우 무시되는지를 알아내야 하는데 앞에서는 인간의 시각이 다른 감각보다 고도로 발달했다는 내용이 등장하고, 뒤에서는 시각과 미각이 서로 다른 정보를 전달하면 시각의 정보를 옳은 것으로 간주하는 예가 서술되기 때문에 정답은 ⑤ '보이는 것(시각)과 충돌하면'이다.
① 다른 감각이 특별히 발달하지 않았으면
② 우리가 이미 알고 있는 것과 일치하면
③ 겉모습이 압도적으로 훌륭하면
④ 메시지가 신뢰할 수 없다고 판명되면

해석 겉모습은 고객이 음식에 대해 가지는 첫인상을 만들어내고 있으며, 첫인상은 중요하다. 아무리 끌리는 맛일지라도, 좋지 않은 겉모습은 못 본 척하기 어렵다. 인간으로서, 우리는 시각이 다른 감각들보다 더욱 고도로 발달했기 때문에 정말로 '눈으로 먹는다.' 이는 많은 동물에게 해당하는 경우는 아니다. 예를 들어, 개는 세상을 살펴보기 위해 주로 후각에 의존한다. 하지만 인간은 고도로 발달한 시각을 가지고 있다. 그러므로 다른 감각들로부터 수신된 메시지들은 <u>보이는 것(시각)과 충돌할 경우</u> 종종 무시되곤 한다. 노란 사탕은 레몬 맛이 날 것으로 기대되는데, 포도 맛이 나면 많은 사람이 그 맛을 정확하게 식별할 수 없다. 빨간 식용 색소가 가미된 딸기 아이스크림은 심지어 실질적인 차이가 없을 때도 식용 색소를 첨가하지 않은 아이스크림보다 더 진한 딸기 맛을 가진 것처럼 보인다.

구문 [14행~16행] A strawberry ice cream (tinted with red food coloring) seems to have a stronger strawberry flavor than **one** [that has no added food coloring], ~.
one은 a strawberry ice cream과 반복을 피하기 위한 것이며, [ ]는 one을 한정하는 주격 관계대명사절이다.

어휘 tint 엷은 색; 색조; ~에 색깔을 넣다   food coloring 식용 색소   **[선택지 어휘]** exceptionally 특별히; 예외적인 경우에만   unreliable 신뢰할 수 없는   correspond with ~와 일치하다   conflict with ~와 상충[상반]되다

11 빈칸 추론 ①

해설 시각적 지각에 대하여 과거에는 '감지하는 것'과 '이해하는 것'을 이질적인 현상이라고 생각했지만, 기술의 발달로 인해 현대에서 지각은 '보는 것'과 '이해하는 것'이 동시에 수반되는 과정임이 밝혀졌다. 따라서 시각 정보의 통합은 ① '시각적 세계에 대한 감각적 지각과 인식 둘 다를 구성한다'.
② 청각 지각의 정확성을 향상시키기 위해 중요한 역할을 한다
③ 어수선해지고 어리둥절하게 만들 수 있어, 어떠한 유의미한 통찰도 제시하지 못한다
④ 텍스트에 있는 핵심 아이디어를 연결시키고 복잡한 주제를 설명하는 데 유용하다
⑤ 보는 사람의 지식 기반에 따라 여러 가지 복잡한 의미를 가진다

모든 영장류와 마찬가지로 인간의 제1의 지각 능력은 '시각'이다. 따라서 지각 과정에 대한 향상된 이해의 많은 부분이 시각적 지각에 대한 신경생물학에서 비롯되었다. 이 분야의 주요한 연구원인 Semir Zeki가 말했듯이, 시각에 대한 연구는 '완전히 철학적인 일'인데, 왜냐하면 그것은 '뇌가 어떻게 외부 세계에 대한 지식을 습득하는가(이는 결코 간단한 문제가 아니다)'에 대한 연구가 되기 때문이다. Zeki는 1970년대까지 지각에 대한 신경학적 모델들은 현실을 '감지하는 것'과 그것을 '이해하는(파악하는) 것'이 근본적으로 이질적 현상이라는, 아마도 Kant에 기인하는, 잘못된 철학적 관점에 의해 깊이 영향을 받았다고 지적한다. 그러나 이제는 정상적인 피실험자와 다양한 뇌 기능 장애를 겪는 환자

을 연구하기 위한 정교한 기술들을 통해, 정상적인 지각은 '보는 것'과 '이해하는 것'을 동시에 수반한다는 것을 우리는 알고 있다. 뇌의 특정 영역은 색, 형태, 움직임과 같은 가시적 속성을 감지할 뿐만 아니라 그것들을 '식별하여' 통일되고 일관성 있는 '그림'으로 통합한다. 결과적으로 발생하는 시각 정보의 통합은 <u>시각적 세계에 대한 감각적 지각과 인식 둘 다를 구성한다</u>.

구문 [10행~14행] ~ neurological models of perception were heavily influenced by **the mistaken philosophic view**, probably traceable to Kant, that {"sensing" reality} and {"understanding" (grasping) it} **are** fundamentally disparate phenomena.
that 이하는 the mistaken philosophic view에 대한 동격절이다. that절에서 두 { } 부분은 동명사 주어이고 are가 동사이다.
[15행~17행] ~ through sophisticated techniques for studying [both] normal subjects [and] patients [who have suffered various impairments of brain function], ~
'both A and B'는 'A와 B 둘 다'의 뜻이다. [ ]은 patients를 수식하는 관계사절이다.
[19행~22행] Specialized areas of the brain [not only] detect visible attributes (such as color, form, and motion) [but also] "identify" and integrate **them** into a unified, coherent "picture."
'not only A but also B'는 'A뿐만 아니라 B도'의 뜻이다. A 자리의 ( )은 visible attributes를 수식하고, B 자리의 them은 'visible attributes such as color, form, and motion'을 지칭하며 identify와 integrate의 공통 목적어이다.

어휘 primary 제1의, 주요한   perceptual 지각의   faculty 능력   primate 영장류   derive from ~로부터 나오다   neurobiology 신경생물학   observe 말하다   profoundly 완전히; 심오하게   enterprise 사업; 기업; 진취성   constitute 구성하다; ~이 되다   inquiry 연구   traceable to ~에 기인[유래]하는   grasp 파악하다   sophisticated 정교한   impairment 장애, 손상   entail 수반하다   simultaneous 동시의   attribute 속성   integrate A into B A를 B로 통합시키다   cf. integration 통합   unify 통일하다   coherent 일관성 있는   cluttered 어수선한   disorienting 어리둥절하게 하는

12 빈칸 추론 ③

해설 고대 유목민 사회에서 수렵-채집인들의 삶이 힘들지 않았던 이유는 수렵, 채집, 요리, 운송 및 방어를 위한 단순한 기술 때문이었다. 현대의 수렵-채집인들도 외진 곳에 살게 되어 나머지 우리와 달리 광범위하고 복잡한 기술 시스템에 의존하지 않고 단순한 기술로 살고 있다는 내용이므로 빈칸에는 ③ '기술적으로 더 집약적인 삶의 방식으로의 전환을 피하는'이 들어가야 가장 적절하다.
① 빈곤을 줄이기 위한 신기술 개발하는
② 데이터 수집 분야의 지역적 협력을 강화하는
④ 자연재해와 같은 외부 환경의 급격한 변화에 적응하는
⑤ 기술이 중요한 역할을 수행하는 정보 기반 사회를 만드는

해석 오늘날의 수렵-채집인과 마찬가지로, 고대 유목민 사회는 그들 자신이 가지고 다닐 수 있는 물건만으로 심한 제약을 받았다. 그래서 그들은 사냥, 채집, 요리, 운송, 방어를 위해 간단한 휴대 가능한 기술을 개발하는 경향이 있었다. 아마도 놀랍겠지만, 수렵-채집인들에게 살아가는 것은 특별히 힘들지 않았던 것 같다. 그들의 성공 비결은 식량 공급량을 넘지 않는 인구, 단순하고 제한된 물질적 필요, 그리고 그 지역의 식량 공급이 소진되었을 때 다른 지역으로 이주할 수 있는 능력이었던 것 같다. 유목 수렵-채집인들의 사회는 20세기까지 아프리카 사막, 열대 우림, 북극 툰드라와 같은 다양한 환경에서 지속되어 왔다. 멀리 떨어져 있다는 것은 기술적으로 더 집약적인 삶의 방식으로의 전환을 피하는 비결일지도 모른다. 나머지 우리들에게는 삶이 이제 광범위하고 복잡한 기술 시스템에 깊이 의존하고 있다.

구문 [6행~7행] Perhaps surprisingly, life *does not seem* **to have been** especially hard for hunter-gatherers.
완료부정사 'to have p.p.'는 does not seem보다 먼저 일어난 사실을 나타낸다.

[7행~11행] The secrets of their success seem to have been *populations* [that did not exceed the food supply], simple and limited material needs, and the *ability* (**to move** to another area) when the local food supply ran out.
문장의 보어인 세 개의 밑줄 친 명사구를 콤마와 and가 병렬 연결한다. [ ] 부분은 관계대명사 that이 이끄는 형용사절로 populations를 수식한다. ( ) 안의 to move to another area는 형용사적 용법의 부정사구로 the ability를 수식한다.

어휘 hunter-gatherer 수렵 채집인 nomadic 유목민의, 유목 생활을 하는 portable 휴대할 수 있는, 휴대용의 exceed 초과하다; 능가하다 run out 소진되다, 고갈되다 persist 지속[존속]하다; 고집하다 diverse 다양한 tropical rain forest 열대 우림 remoteness 멀리 떨어져 있음, 외진 곳에 있음 poverty 빈곤, 가난 conversion 전환, 변환 intensive 집약적인, 집중적인 drastic 급격한; 철저한; 맹렬한 external 외부의 condition 환경; 상태; 상황

13 흐름 무관 문장 ④

해설 글을 길게 쓰는 것보다 짧게 쓰는 것이 더 어렵고 많은 노력을 요한다는 내용의 글인데, ④는 칸트가 글을 쓰기 전에 생각하기 위해 바라보던 석탑이 자라나는 나무 때문에 안 보이게 되자 나무를 잘라버렸다는 내용으로, '글을 짧게 쓰는 것의 어려움'이라는 전체적 글의 흐름과 무관하다.

해석 의심할 바 없이, 요약하기는 모든 분야의 사람들에게 도전적인 일이다. ① 많은 유명한 소설들, 즉 예를 들어 마크 트웨인과 어니스트 헤밍웨이는 편집자들에게 자신들의 원고의 극단적인 길이를 후회한다고 썼다. 자신들에게 시간이 더 있었다면, 작품은 상당히 더 짧았으리라는 것이다. ② 윈스턴 처칠은 5분 전에 공지가 있으면 하루 종일 말할 수 있지만, 그가 말할 수 있는 시간이 겨우 5분밖에 없다면 준비하는 데 하루가 필요하다고 말했다고 한다. ③ 시인 Edwin Arlington Robinson은 나이가 들어감에 따라 짧은 운문에서 긴 작품을 쓰는 것으로 이행했으며, "내가 이제 60이 넘어서 짧은 시가 너무나 힘듭니다."라고 말했다. ④ 철학자 Immanuel Kant는 글을 쓰기 전에 생각하기 위해 창밖의 석탑을 응시하곤 했는데, 나무가 자라서 그의 시야를 막을 위협이 되자 그것들을 잘라버렸다. ⑤ 이들은 글쓰기의 본질이 단어를 페이지 위에 놓는 것이 아니라 불필요한 단어들을 알아보고 없애는 것을 아는 것이라고 주장한다.

구문 [5행~7행] ~ if they **had had** more time, the work **would have been** significantly shorter.
「if S′ had p.p., S would have p.p.」는 가정법 과거완료로서 '…했다면 ~했을 것이다'의 뜻이다.

[17행~20행] The essence of writing, *these individuals claim*, is **not** putting word on the page **but** learning to recognize and eliminate the unnecessary **ones**.
these individuals claim은 삽입된 구이다. 「not A but B」는 'A가 아니라 B'의 뜻이며, A와 B 자리에 각각 쓰인 동명사구가 병렬구조를 이루고 있다. the unnecessary ones에서 ones는 words를 지칭한다.

어휘 abstract 요약하다 challenging 도전적인 discipline 지식 분야; 규율; 훈련 editor 편집자 manuscript 원고 significantly 상당히 notice 통지, 예고 transition 이행[변천]하다 verse 운문 lengthy 긴 remark 말하다, 언급하다 chop ~ down ~을 베어 넘기다 essence 본질, 정수

14 글의 순서 ③

해설 경기 위기에 소비가 중요하다는 주어진 글 다음에 구체적으로 9/11 사건과 같은 경기 침체기에 소비를 장려한 정부 지도자의 예를 제시한 (B)가 나와야 한다. (B) 마지막에 소비가 멈추면 경제가 멈춘다고 했고, (C)는 'In contrast(대조적으로)'로 연결되어 소비가 활성화되면 소비 주체와 생산 주체 모두에게 상황이 개선된다고 했으므로 (B) 다음에 바로 (C)가 연결되어야 자연스럽다. (A)는 연결어 'Meanwhile(그러는 동안)' 뒤에 (C)에 나온 상황에서 정부에도 이익이 되는 점들을 언급하였고, 이 모든 것의 중심에는 소비자가 있다는 결론으로 마무리했으므로 마지막으로 나와야 한다.

해석 세계 경제에서 소매업 부문의 중요성은 위기의 시기 동안에 특히 명백하다. 세계의 지도자들은 심각한 경기 침체에 직면하여 소비자가 도움을 주리라고 기대한다.
(B) 9/11사태 이후 부시 미국 대통령은 미국인들에게 일상생활을 계속 이어나갈 것, 자신감을 잃지 말 것, 그리고 계속 돈을 소비할 것을 부탁했다. 최근의 세계적 경기 불황에 대응하여 지도자들은 비슷한 요청을 했는데, 왜냐하면 소비자들이 구매를 멈추면 경제가 서서히 멈추기 때문이다.
(C) 이와 반대로, 소비자들이 자신감이 있고 자유롭게 돈을 쓰면, 돈은 소매점을 통해 흐르고, 공급망을 타고 올라가서, 제조업자, 농부, 그리고 다른 생산자들까지 거슬러 올라가며, 그렇게 가는 도중에 변호사, 은행가, 그리고 다른 서비스 회사들에 들른다.
(A) 그러는 동안 정부는 법인세, 토지세, 소득세와 소비세를 통해 자기 몫을 챙긴다. 소비자들은 이 모든 경제 활동의 중심에 있다.

구문 [15행~20행] In contrast, when consumers are confident and spending freely, // money flows through retail stores, up the supply chain, and all the way back to the manufacturers, farmers, and other producers, / making stops along the way with lawyers, bankers, and other service firms.
접속사 when이 이끄는 부사절 뒤에 이어지는 주절에서 money가 주어 flows가 동사이며 전치사구와 분사구문(making 이하)이 연결된 구조이다.

어휘 retail 소매의 sector 부문 downturn 침체, 하강 look to ~ for … …가 …을 주리라고 기대하다 supply chain 공급망 manufacturer 제조업자 carry on with ~을 계속하다 in response to ~에 대응하여 corporate 법인의, 기업의 consumption tax 소비세

15 글의 순서 ②

해설 약초는 복용량 조절이 어렵다고 회의적으로 말하는 의사들이 있다는 주어진 글 다음에는 복용량 조절의 의미를 소개하는 (B)가 나온다. 회의론자들의 말에도 일리가 있다고 한 (B) 다음에는 그 이유(제약 제품은 복용량을 정확히 맞출 수 있지만 약초는 여러 가지 요인으로 인해 그렇지 못함)를 제시한 (A)가 나온다. (A)는 이러한 논거에 숨겨져 있는 더 큰 진실(a larger truth)이 있다고 말하는데 그 내용은 (C)에서 '사실 약초의 과다 복용 위험은 대단히 낮다'로 풀이된다.

해석 약초에 대해 논할 때, 뉴스 매체는 약초를 가지고 장난을 치면 불장난을 하는 것과 같다고 경고하는 회의적인 의사들의 말을 종종 인용한다. 약초로는 적절한 복용량 조절을 보장하는 것이 불가능하다고 그들은 말한다.
(B) 복용량 조절은 유효 성분, 즉 치유 효과를 내는 화학 물질을 1회 복용량 당 정확히 얼마나 먹는 건지를 알고 있는 것을 의미한다. 어느 정도는 저 회의론자들이 옳다.
(A) 약은 보통 밀리그램으로 측정되어 정확한 양의 화학 물질을 제공한다. 약초의 경우 개별 식물의 건강 상태, 제품이 저장 상태로 얼마나 오랫동안 있었는지, 그리고 다른 요인들로 인해 약효가 달라질 수 있다. 그러나 복용량 조절에 관한 경고는 더 큰 진실을 가린다.
(C) 훌륭한 한의사들이 추천해주는 대로 사용되면, 약초는 제약계의 대응물보다 거의 항상 덜 효능이 있다. 그러므로 대부분의 약초 치료에서 과다 복용의 위험은 아주 작다. 사

실 최근 연구에 따르면 그것은 거의 존재하지 않는다.

구문 [1행~3행] When **discussing** medicinal herbs, / the news media often quote *skeptical doctors* [who warn // that if you fool around with herbs, // you're playing with fire].

discussing으로 시작되는 분사구문 앞에 접속사 When이 생략되지 않고 남아있다. [ ]는 skeptical doctors를 수식하는 주격 관계사절이다. that ~ fire는 warn에 대한 목적어절이다.

[12행~14행] Dose control means / knowing exactly // how much of the active ingredient — the chemical [that exerts the healing effect] — you're getting per dose.

how ~ dose는 knowing에 대한 목적어 역할을 하는 간접의문문으로, 「의문사(how much) + 주어(you) + 동사(are getting)」의 어순으로 쓴다. the active ingredient 와 the chemical은 동격 관계이며, [ ]는 the chemical을 수식하는 주격 관계대명사절이다.

어휘 medicinal herb 약초   quote 인용하다   skeptical 회의적인 *cf.* skeptic 회의론자   fool around 장난치다   dose (약의) 복용량, 1회분(량) *cf.* overdose 과다 복용   obscure 가리다, 숨기다; 모호하게 하다   active ingredient 유효 성분   exert 내다, 발휘하다   to a certain extent 어느 정도까지, 얼마간   reputable 훌륭한, 평판이 좋은   potent 효능이 있는; 강력한   pharmaceutical 제약의   counterpart 대응물; 상대방   virtually 거의, 사실상   nonexistent 존재하지 않는

16 문장 넣기 ②

해설 주어진 문장이 but으로 시작하므로 앞에는 주어진 문장과 대조적인 내용이 와야 한다. 즉 주어진 문장에서 사리 추구를 '공리주의적'이라고 했으므로, 앞에서는 사리 추구를 그와 대조적으로 '이기주의적'으로 보는 입장이 서술되는 것이 자연스럽다. 또한, ② 뒤 문장의 such a view는 개인적 이윤을 추구하면 사회의 이익에도 도움이 된다는 Adam Smith의 관점이자, 주어진 문장의 견해 뒤에 자연스럽게 이어진다. 따라서 정답은 ②이다.

해석 사리(私利)와 공리(公利)는 모두 조직의 결정에 중요한 역할을 하고, 기업가들은 이 두 가지 이론을 조합한다. 각각의 기업이 자신들의 이윤을 추구하고 각각의 기업가가 개인적 성공을 최대화하려고 노력할 경우, 기업은 이기주의적이다. 하지만 기업은 또한 사리를 추구하는 것이 전체 이익을 최대화하는 것으로 생각된다는 것과 경쟁적 게임의 정해진 규칙에 따라 경기를 하는 것은 사회의 이익을 증진하는 것으로 보인다는 점에서 공리주의적이다. 경제학자 Adam Smith는 그러한 견해를 가지고 있었다. 그는 만약 기업이 사리를 추구하게 내버려둔다면, 사회의 이익에도 도움이 될 것이라고 주장하였다. 확실히 Smith는 단지 이기적 추구를 통해서만 가장 큰 경제적 이익이 나올 것이라고 믿었다. Smith 사상의 핵심은 《국부론》에서 볼 수 있는데, 그 책에서 Smith는 사리와 사회의 이익 간의 상호 작용을 강조한다.

구문 [1행~4행]
But business is also utilitarian **in that**
┌ *pursuing* self-interest is thought to maximize the total good,
├ and
└ *playing* by the established rules of the competitive game is seen as advancing the good of society.
in that은 '~이므로, ~라는 점에서'라는 뜻. 동명사구가 주어인 명사절이 and로 대등하게 연결되어 있다.

어휘 utilitarian 공리적인; 실용의; 공리주의의 *cf.* utility 공익사업; 유용(성); 공리(성)   pursue 추구하다, 밀고 나가다; 추적하다 *cf.* pursuit 추적; 추구; 취미   self-interest

사리사욕, 사리 추구   maximize 극대화하다; 최대한 활용하다 (↔ minimize 최소화하다)   established 기존의, 확립된; 인정받는   organizational 조직(상)의; 유기적 구조의; 관리 기관의   to the extent that ~인 정도까지; ~인 경우에; ~이므로   egotistical 자기중심[본위]의, 이기적인   essence 본질, 정수(精髓); 진액, 에센스   underscore ~에 밑줄을 긋다; 강조하다, 분명히 보여주다 (= underline)   interplay 상호 작용

17 문장 넣기 ②

해설 주어진 문장의 '애초에 쓰레기 증가의 원인이 된 소비의 증가를 이 과정(This process)은 간과하게 한다'라고 했는데, 글의 주제가 '재활용 과정만 강조하면 소비 감축의 필요성을 간과하게 된다'이므로 This process는 '(소비 감축은 신경 쓰지 않고) 재활용만 강조하는 과정'임을 추론할 수 있다. ② 이전 부분에서는 지금 지배적인 재활용 모델이 재활용 재료 시장에만 의존(즉 재활용 재료로 물건을 만들고 소비하는 것)한다는 비판이 나왔는데, 이것이 This process를 지칭한다. 소비 감축이 진정한 논점이라는 주어진 문장 다음에는 '소비 감축'을 논해야 하는데, ② 이후로는 '재활용을 많이 해도 소비를 감축하지 않으면 소용없다'는 논지가 전개되므로 주어진 문장은 ②에 위치해야 한다.

해석 재활용이 지속 가능한 공동체에 기여할 수 있는 잠재 가능성에는 의문이 제기되어 왔다. 비판하는 사람들은 지배적인 재활용 모델이 재활용 가능한 재료의 시장에 의존한다는 점을 지적한다. 수익성을 가지려면 신제품들은 재활용된 물질을 사용하여 제조되고 소비되어야 한다. 이 과정은 소비를 감축할 필요성에 대한 강조를 거둬들이는데, 애초에 그것(= 소비)의 증가가 쓰레기 증가의 주요 요인이다. 심지어 재활용 비율이 상승해도 소비 감축이 없다면, 쓰레기 매립지와 소각로로 보내지는 쓰레기의 양과 소비되는 원료의 양은 계속해서 증가할 것이다. 재활용 프로그램의 존재는 때때로 소비를 줄일 필요에 대항하는 방어로 나타난다. 예를 들어, 생수 산업은 다수의 환경적 근거를 토대로 비판받아왔는데, 플라스틱 병의 재활용을 장려한다고 말한다. 그러나 대부분의 재활용된 플라스틱 음료수병은 다른 제품으로 제조되고, 새로운 플라스틱 병은 원재료로 만들어진다.

구문 [1행~3행] This process takes emphasis off the need to reduce *consumption*, // **the increase in which is** a major factor in the waste increase in the first place.
the increase in which가 is에 대응하는 주어이다. 여기서 which는 consumption을 지칭한다.
[4행~5행] *The potential* (*for recycling* to contribute to sustainable communities) **has been questioned**.
주어는 The potential이고 동사는 has been questioned이며, ( )는 The potential을 수식한다. for recycling은 to-v에 대한 의미상 주어이다.

어휘 sustainable 지속 가능한   prevailing 지배적인, 우세한; 널리 행해지는   profitable 수익성 있는   landfill 쓰레기 매립지   raw material 원료   beverage 음료   virgin 원래 그대로의

18 요약문 완성 ①

해설 경구는 흔히 두 개의 양립할 수 없는 모순된 내용을 지니고 있어서 우리가 결정을 내려야 하는 특정한 상황에서는 그야말로 거의 아무런 지침도 주지 못한다는 것이 글의 요지이다. 그러므로 (A)에는 '모순되는'이 적절하고, (B)에는 '특정한'이라는 말이 들어가야 적절하다.

해석 상식적인 지식이 장점을 지닐 수 있겠지만, 그것은 또한 단점도 지니는데, 그중에서 중요한 것은 그것이 종종 모순된다는 것이다. 가령, 우리는 비슷한 사람들이 서로 좋아

하기 마련이라는 말('같은 깃털의 새가 함께 모인다')을 듣지만, 닮지 않은 사람들이 서로 좋아하기 마련이라는 말('반대되는 사람들이 서로에게 끌린다') 또한 듣는다. 우리는 집단이 개인보다 더 지혜롭고 더 똑똑하다는 말('두 사람의 머리가 한 사람의 머리보다 낫다')을 듣지만, 집단적인 작업이 필연적으로 형편없는 결과를 만든다는 말('요리사가 너무 많으면 국을 망친다')도 듣는다. 이런 모순되는 진술들 각각은 특정한 상황에서는 사실일 수 있지만, 그것들이 언제 적용되는지와 언제 적용되지 않는지에 관한 명확한 진술이 없다면 경구는 사람들 사이의 관계에 대한 통찰력을 거의 제공하지 않는다. 그것들은 우리가 결정을 내려야 하는 상황에서는 그야말로 거의 아무런 지침도 주지 못한다. 예를 들어, 위험을 수반하는 선택에 직면할 때, '모험하지 않으면 아무것도 얻을 수 없다' 또는 '후회하는 것보다 안전한 것이 낫다' 중에 우리는 어느 지침을 사용해야 하는가?

↓

> 경구는 (A) 모순되는 의미를 가지고 있어서, (B) 특정한 상황에서 지침을 찾기 위해 경구를 사용하는 것은 어렵다고 판명될 것이다.

구문 [1행~3행] Although commonsense knowledge may have merit, it also has *drawbacks*, **not the least of which** is that it often contradicts itself.
계속적 용법으로 쓰인 which의 선행사는 drawbacks이고 이를 not the least of which가 이끄는 관계사절이 보충 설명한다. 일반적으로 'not the least of which'는 복수명사를 선행사로 하여 '~ 중에서 중요한 것은'이라는 의미이다.
[15행~16행] They provide even less guidance in *situations* [**where** we must make decisions].
[ ] 부분은 관계부사 where가 이끄는 형용사절로 선행사 situations를 수식한다.

어휘 commonsense 상식적인 merit 장점: 우수함 drawback 결점 contradict 모순되다: 단호히 부정하다 flock 모이다. 떼 짓다: 무리 dissimilar 닮지 않은, 다른 inevitably 필연적으로, 불가피하게 broth 국: 수프 contradictory 모순된 statement 진술 hold true 진실이다: 유효하다 insight 통찰 guidance 지침. 지도, 안내 entail 수반하다. 일으키다 venture 모험(하다) conflicting 모순되는: 상충하는 practical 실용적인: 실제의 abstract 추상적인

19~20 장문   19 ② 20 ④

해설 19. 첫 번째 단락은 '인간의 기억'이라는 핵심어에 대한 도입에 해당하고, 두 번째 단락이 주된 본문에 해당한다. 즉, 기억의 재생이 현재를 고양시켜주는 감정 때문에 일어난다는 것이 주된 내용이므로 제목으로 가장 적절한 것은 ② '인간은 왜 과거의 경험을 재생하는가?'이다.
① 기억 왜곡과 방지
③ 새로운 경험은 오래된 기억을 강화할 수 있다
④ 기억을 향상하기 위해 기호와 상징을 사용하는 방법
⑤ 감정이 학습과 기억에 미치는 영향
20. (a)는 signs and symbols와 대비되는 것이므로 physical이 적절하고, (b)는 a stone을 설명하는 것이지만 짐승과 인간의 차이를 표시하는 signs and symbols

에 해당해야 하므로 monument가 적절하다. (c)는 앞선 내용에서 우리를 흥미롭게 하는 것을 기억한다고 했고, 이어지는 내용에서 야만인은 오늘의 지루함에서 탈출하기 위해 어제 일을 기억한다고 했으므로 emotional이 적절하다. (d)의 forgetting은 야만인들이 어제 있었던 동물과의 투쟁을 기억하여 오늘의 지루함을 탈출한다는 것이므로 '되찾는'의 뜻을 가진 regaining으로 바꾸어 써야 적절하다. (e)는 기억은 전투의 위험과 걱정 없이 모든 흥분을 가지고 있는 것이고 기억을 재생하여 그 속에서 즐긴다고 했으므로, 과거와는 다른 의미로 현재의 순간을 enhance하는 것이라 할 수 있다.

해석 인간은 들판의 짐승처럼 단지 (a) 물리적인 것들로 이루어진 세상에서 사는 것이 아니라 기호와 상징의 세상에서 산다. 돌은 단지 단단한, 부딪치는 물체가 아니라 죽은 조상의 (b) 기념비이다. 그리고 짐승과 인간의 차이를 표시하는 이것은 전적으로 인간이 자신의 경험을 보존하고 기록하면서 기억하기 때문이다.
그러나 기억의 재생은 좀처럼 문자 그대로가 아니다. 우리는 당연히 우리를 흥미롭게 하기 때문에 우리를 흥미롭게 하는 것을 기억한다. 과거는 그 자체 때문이 아니라 그것이 현재에 더해주는 것 때문에 기억된다. 따라서 기억의 주된 생명은 실용적이라기보다는 (c) 감정적이다. 야만인은 과학적인 방식으로 동물의 품질을 연구하기 위해서나 내일 어떻게 더 잘 싸울 것인지를 계산하기 위해서가 아니라, 어제의 사건을 (d) 잊음으로써(→ 되찾음으로써) 오늘의 지루함에서 탈출하기 위하여 어제 있었던 동물과의 투쟁을 상기했다. 기억은 전투의 위험과 걱정 없이 그것의 모든 흥분을 가지고 있다. 그것을 재생하고 그 속에서 즐기는 것은 새로운 의미로, 실제로 그것 혹은 과거에 속해 있는 것과는 다른 의미로 현재의 순간을 (e) 고양시키는 것이다. 기억은 그 속에 그것의 긴장과 곤경 없이 실제 경험의 모든 감정적 가치가 있는 간접적 경험이다. 전투의 승리는 승리의 순간에서보다 추모 전승 기념 춤에서 훨씬 더 선명하게 느껴진다. 실제적인 경험의 순간에 인간은 그 순간의 임무에 정신이 팔려 매 순간 존재한다. 그가 생각 속에서 모든 순간을 재조사할 때, 시작과 중간과 성취 혹은 패배의 클라이맥스로 향하는 움직임이 있는 드라마가 나타난다.

구문 [14행~19행] Savage man recalled yesterday's struggle with an animal **not** in order to study in a scientific way the qualities of the animal [or] for the sake of calculating how better to fight tomorrow, **but** to escape from the dullness of today by regaining the event of yesterday.
'not A but B' 구문은 'A가 아니라 B'의 뜻이다. in order to ~ the animal과 for the sake of ~ tomorrow는 or로 연결되어 병렬구조를 이룬다.
[21행~24행] [To revive it and revel in it] is to enhance the present moment with a new meaning, a meaning different from *that* {which actually belongs **either** to it **or** to the past}.
[ ] 부분은 주어이며 to enhance 이하는 보어이다. a new meaning과 a meaning ~ the past는 동격 관계이다. { } 부분은 that을 수식한다. 'either A or B'는 'A나 B 둘 중 하나'의 뜻이다.

어휘 merely 단지 bump 부딪치다 monument 기념물 deceased 사망한 preserve 보존하다 revival 재생 rarely 좀처럼 ~않다 savage 야만적인 for the sake of ~을 위하여 dullness 지루함 revel 한껏 즐기다 strain 긴장 vividly 생생하게, 선명하게 preoccupied with ~에 정신이 팔린 emerge 나타나다 defeat 패배

1 ⑤	2 ③	3 ⑤	4 ②	5 ②		6 ③	7 ④	8 ③	9 ⑤	10 ④
11 ⑤	12 ⑤	13 ④	14 ④	15 ⑤		16 ⑤	17 ④	18 ⑤	19 ⑤	20 ⑤

1 심경 변화 ⑤

해설 숲속에서 반딧불을 볼 때는 황홀함에 행복했지만, 집으로 돌아가는 길에 독사에 물릴까 봐 걱정하는 내용이다. 그러므로 심경 변화로 가장 적절한 것은 ⑤ '즐거운 → 겁나는'이다.
① 기쁜 → 외로운　　　　② 지루한 → 초조한
③ 침착한 → 짜증이 나는　④ 안도하는 → 우울한

해석 늦은 오후에, 나는 농가를 떠나 숲속으로 들어왔다. 반딧불이를 찾으려 신이 나서 뛰어다녔던 어린 시절이 생생하게 기억났다. 해가 지자 많은 반딧불이의 섬광이 나를 맞이했다. 그 초록빛은 몇 인치 올라가더니, 숲을 가로질러 급강하했다. 나는 황홀하여 그 광경을 응시하고 있었다. 마치 어린 시절로 돌아간 것 같은 기분이었다. 시간은 굉장히 빨리 흘러갔고, 내 위에 있는 하늘에서는 밤의 어둠이 칠흑 같았다. 그러나 멋진 숲을 떠나려고 서 있을 때, 나는 칠흑 같은 어둠 속을 걸어 농가로 가야 한다는 것을 깨달았다. '갈고리 이빨 트위스터'라고 불리는 황갈색 독사가 나를 가장 걱정하게 했다. 이 뱀들은 무더운 여름 밤에 특히 활동적이었다. 나는 희미한 빛 속 곳곳에 잎사귀로 위장하고 있을 독사를 살피며 천천히 움직였다. 안개 낀 공기를 헤치며 걸어가는 길에서 내 몸은 긴장되어 있었다.

구문 [7행] I felt // as if I had gone back to my childhood.
as if 가정법 과거완료 구문으로 주절보다 앞선 때의 일을 가정하므로 as if가 이끄는 절의 동사로 had p.p.(had gone)가 쓰였다.

[14행~16행] I moved slowly, / seeing the copperhead's leafy camouflage everywhere in the failing light.
seeing 이하는 동시동작을 나타내는 분사구문이다.

어휘 vividly 생생하게　firefly 반딧불이　swoop 급강하하다　gaze at ~을 응시하다　in rapture 황홀해하는, 크게 기뻐하는　copperhead (황갈색) 독사　hooked 갈고리 모양의; (약물에) 중독된　muggy 무더운, 후텁지근한　leafy 잎이 무성한　camouflage 위장(하다), 속임수　tense 긴장된; 긴박한　misty 안개 낀; 희미한

2 필자 주장 ③

해설 본문은 자녀들이 부모의 지시를 무시하는 이유 중 하나는 부모가 지시나 규칙 이행에 일관성이 없는 것이기에, 부모가 일관성 있게 지시와 규칙을 이행할수록 자녀들이 더 말을 잘 들을 것이라는 내용이다. 그러므로 필자의 주장으로는 ③이 적절하다.

해석 우리 자녀들이 우리의 지시를 무시할지도 모르는 한 가지 이유는, 만약 우리가 지시와 규칙을 '이행하는 것'에 대해 지금까지 일관되지 않았다면, 우리 자녀들이 우리가 이번에는 정말로 그것을 의도한다고 생각하지 않을 것이기 때문이다. 그래서 그들은 무슨 일이 일어나는지 기다려 보기만 할 것이고, 그렇게 해서 자신들이 하고 싶은 것을 할 더 많은 시간을 얻는다. 부모의 반응의 예측 불가능함은 미묘하게 시험해 보고 노골적으로 나쁜 행실을 할 많은 여지를 남겨둔다. 대체로 협력적인 자녀들조차도 부모의 초기 반응으로부터 부모가 (지시와 규칙을) '이행하는 것'에 대해 불편해한다는 것을 감지하는 상황에서는 시험을 할 것이다. 그들은 규칙을 완전히 위반하지는 않으면서 '규칙을 변칙 적용하려'고 할 수도 있다. 이것은 공공장소에서 자주 일어나는데, 그곳에서 자녀들은 부모가

당황해서 (지시와 규칙을) '이행하지' 못한다는 것을 알 수 있다. 때때로 우리가 규칙에 대해 유연하다고 여기는 것이 자녀에게는 마치 우리가 굴복하는 것처럼 보인다. 우리가 더 일관성 있게 (지시와 규칙을) '이행할수록' 우리 자녀들은 더 많이 우리의 말을 잘 들을 것이고, 우리의 지시를 진지하게 받아들이고 협력할 것이다.

구문 [9행~12행] Even children [who are usually cooperative] will test in situations [where they sense, from their parents' initial reaction, that parents are uncomfortable about following through].
첫 번째 [ ]은 주격 관계대명사 who가 이끄는 관계사절로 children을 수식하고, 두 번째 [ ]은 관계부사 where가 이끄는 관계사절로 situations를 수식한다.

[18행~20행] The more consistently we follow through, the more our children will listen to us, take our instructions seriously, and cooperate.
'더 ~ 할수록, 더욱 …하다'는 의미의 'the 비교급 ~, the 비교급 …' 구문이 쓰였다. 밑줄 친 세 개의 동사(구)는 콤마(,)와 and로 병렬 연결된다.

어휘 instruction 지시 (사항); 훈련; 교육　consistent 일관된; 일치하는　follow through 이행[완수]하다　in the past (완료형과 함께) 지금까지　assume 당연하다고 생각하다[보다]; 추정하다; (역할 등을) 맡다　unpredictability 예측 불가능　room 여지　subtle 미묘한; 희박한　outright 노골적인, 완전한, 전면적인　misbehavior 나쁜 행실; 무례; 비행　bend the rules 규칙을 변칙 적용하다　embarrassment 당황, 곤혹; 낭패　give in 굴복[항복]하다　take A seriously A를 진지[심각]하게 받아들이다

3 밑줄 함의 ⑤

해설 두 사람이 직접적 교류를 할 때 그들은 무의식적으로 비언어적 동작을 일치시키며 의식적 수준과는 비교할 수 없을 정도로 빠르게 비언어적 정보를 처리한다는 글의 맥락을 반영하여 밑줄 친 '우리 자신의 생각은 그 춤의 복잡성을 도저히 추적할 수 없다'는 말은 우리의 의식적 생각이 ⑤ '대화 속 비언어적 단서를 따라잡을' 수 없다는 것을 의미함을 추론할 수 있다.
① 개인적 접촉을 계속 반복할
② 언어적 요인과 비언어적 요인 둘 다에 영향을 줄
③ 상대측이 말하고자 의도하는 바를 이해할
④ 언어적 요소 간의 동시성을 탐지할

해석 개인적 접촉의 장점으로 우리가 의식적으로 알아채지 못하는 경험이 포함된다. 공유 공간에서, 사람들은 심리학자 Daniel Goleman이 '신경의 와이파이', 즉 '신체 간의 피부와 두개골로 된 장벽을 넘어서는 피드백 회로'라 칭한 것으로 접촉하게 된다. 과학자들이 대화를 녹화하여 프레임 단위로 관찰하기 위해 속도를 늦추면, 그들은 비언어적 요소 간의 동시성, 즉 재즈에서 즉흥 연주를 이끄는 박자와 매우 흡사한 공유된 리듬을 탐지한다. 움직임 그 자체는 1초의 몇 분의 1 내로 조정되는데, 우리의 두뇌는 대략 천분의, 혹은 백만분의 몇 초 데이터를 받아들이고 있다. 그러나 의식적인 정보 처리는 비교적 느릿한 초 단위로 일어난다. 두 사람이 서로에게 말할 때, '우리 자신의 생각은 도저히 그 춤의 복잡성을 추적할 수 없다.'고 Goleman은 적는다.

구문 [1행~2행] The advantages of personal contact include experiences [(which[that]) we can't consciously register].

[ ] 부분은 앞에 목적격 관계대명사 which[that]가 생략되어 experiences를 수식한다.

[6행~10행] When scientists videotape conversations **and** slow them down to watch frame by frame, they detect synchronies between nonverbal elements — *a shared rhythm* [very much like *the beat* {that guides an improvisation in jazz}].

밑줄 친 두 부분은 When절의 두 동사구로 병렬구조를 이룬다. [ ] 부분은 a shared rhythm을 수식하고 { } 부분은 the beat를 수식한다.

어휘 register 알아채다 plug into ~에 연결되다 feedback loop 피드백 회로 barrier 장벽 detect 탐지하다 nonverbal 비언어적인 beat 박자 coordinate 조직화하다, 조정하다 a fraction of a second 1초의 몇 분의 1 동안에, 순식간에 on the order of ~와 비슷한, 대략 ~ millisecond 천분의 1초 microsecond 백만분의 1초 process 처리하다 comparatively 비교적 scale 규모, 척도 cannot possibly 도저히 할 수 없다 track 추적하다

4 글의 주제 ②

해설 소규모 상점은 목표로 하는 고객에게 지리적으로 더 가까이 위치할 입지 결정이 중요하고 큰 규모의 상점은 뚜렷이 다른 여러 고객군의 마음에 호소하는 다양하고 광범위한 상품을 취급하면서 많은 수의 고객을 끌어들여야 한다고 했으므로 글의 주제는 ② '매장 규모에 따른 고객 유치 전략의 변화'가 적절하다.
① 고객 유치를 관리하기 위한 다양한 서로 관련된 과업
③ 상점에 고객을 유치하기 위한 제품 차별화 방법
④ 고객 유치를 위한 기존 시장 분석의 필요성
⑤ 상점 크기를 기반으로 한 세분화 전략의 시행

해석 근본적으로, 소매상이 더 큰 상점을 지으려고 결정할 때는, 그 추가되는 면적과 확대된 상품 목록을 이용해서 투자에 대해 만족스러운 수익을 산출하는 데 필요한 더 많은 손님을 끌어모을 수 있다고 확신하는 것이다. 대조적으로, 소매점의 면적이 감소함에 따라, 소매상이 취급할 수 있는 상품의 수도 감소한다. 게다가, 더 작은 상점은 상권도 더 작고 고객도 더 적은 경향이 있다. 결과적으로, 그들(더 작은 점포)이 취급하는 상품이 자신들이 끌어들이는 고객과 잘 맞도록 확실히 해야 한다. 제한된 공간에서, 다수의 세분 시장에 동시에 호소하는 것은 어렵다. 그러므로 입지 결정이 특히 중요하며, 그 때문에 소규모 소매상은 지리적 세분화를 강조해야 한다. 즉, 상점이 작아질수록 목표로 하는 고객군에게 대체로 더 가까이 위치할 필요가 있다. 반면에, 더 큰 형태의 상점은 뚜렷이 다른 고객군의 마음에 호소하는 더 다양하고 더 광범위한 상품을 취급할 수 있지만, 그 확장된 공간의 추가된 비용을 정당화할 만큼 충분한 고객을 각 고객군으로부터 끌어들여야 한다.

구문 **[1행~5행]** In essence, when *a retailer* decides to build a larger store, // it bets that it can use that extra square footage and expanded inventory / to attract *the higher volume of customers* [(whom[that]) it needs / to generate an acceptable return on investment].

밑줄 친 it은 a retailer를 가리킨다. [ ]는 생략된 목적격 관계대명사 whom 또는 that이 이끄는 형용사절로 앞에 있는 명사구 the higher ~ customers를 수식한다.

[5행~7행] In contrast, as retail square footage decreases, **so too does** *the number of products* [(which[that]) a retailer can carry].

「so+V+S」는 'S도 역시 그렇다'라는 의미로 주어와 조동사의 도치가 일어난 형태이고 이는 the number of products a retailer can carry decreases, too로 바꿔 쓸 수 있다. [ ]는 목적격 관계대명사가 생략된 형용사절로 the number of products를 수식한다.

어휘 retailer 소매상(인) bet ~이라고 확신[단언]하다 square footage 피트 단위의 길이[부피] inventory 상품 목록; 재고품 volume of 다수의[다량의] return 수익, 수입; 귀환 simultaneously 동시에 appeal to ~에 호소하

다; 간청하다; 상소하다 segment 부문; 영역 geographic 지리적인 distinct 별개의; 독특한 justify 정당화하다 **[선택지 어휘]** tactic 전략, 전술 implementation 시행

5 글의 제목 ②

해설 bristlecone 소나무는 보호된 환경보다 혹독한 환경에서 살 때 다섯 배 정도 더 오래 살 수 있다는 내용이므로, 이 글의 가장 적절한 제목은 ② '혹독한 환경에서의 더 오랜 삶'이다.
① 현대의 나무들이 단명하는 이유
③ bristlecone 소나무의 나이를 알아보는 방법
④ 나무가 인간 불멸의 비밀을 쥐고 있다
⑤ 특별한 나무를 위해 보호 받는 장소를 세워라

해석 bristlecone 소나무는 5천 년이 넘는 최대 수명이 기록되어 있으며, 세상에서 가장 장수하는 유기체 중 하나이다. 그러나 그러한 장수는 오직 캘리포니아의 White 산맥의 혹독하고 강한 바람에 노출되어 있는 봉우리에 살고 있는 나무들만이 획득할 수 있다. 좀 더 보호된 환경에서 사는 같은 종의 개체들은 대략 천 년이라는 상당히 더 짧은 삶을 산다. 이러한 수명은 어떠한 기준으로 보더라도 여전히 엄청나게 긴 것이지만, 80%의 수명 감소는 현저하다. 혹독한 환경은 연장된 장수에 이상적인데, 왜냐하면 그것으로 인해 (그 나무에) 기생하는 생물이 더 적어지고, 우연한 죽음으로 이어지는 인화성 덤불의 양도 더 적어지기 때문이다. 비록 많은 증거로 보건대 이러한 장수하는 나무가 계속적 세포 분열에 대해 겉보기에 무제한적인, 혹은 적어도 굉장히 큰 수용력을 가지고 있지만, 생장 시즌이 짧다는 것 또한 역할을 하는 것 같다.

구문 **[12행~14행]** ~ it results *in* **fewer parasites** **and** **smaller amounts of flammable underbrush**, which leads to accidental death.

fewer parasites와 smaller amounts of flammable underbrush가 병렬구조를 이루며 in의 목적어 역할을 하고 있다. which는 앞에 나온 flammable underbrush를 가리킨다.

어휘 documented 문서로 기록된 lifespan 수명 longevity 장수 organism 유기체, 생물체 harsh (날씨 등이) 혹독한; 가혹한 windswept 강한 바람에 노출되어 있는 peak (산의) 봉우리, 꼭대기; 정점 significantly 상당히 on the order of 대략 ~; ~의 명에 따라; ~와 비슷한 extended 길어진, 늘어난 parasite 기생 동물[식물] flammable 가연성의, 인화성의 underbrush 덤불 capacity 용량; 수용력; 능력

6 안내문 불일치 ③

해설 안내문의 어린이용 자동차는 실외와 실내에서 모두 운행할 수 있지만 평평한 지면에서 타는 것이 적합하다. 따라서 ③은 내용과 일치하지 않는다.

해석 어린이들을 위한 ABC 배터리 전력 공급 자동차

여러분의 자녀들이 자기 자신의 자동차를 운전할 수 있습니다!
어린이들의 전기 자동차는 진짜 자동차의 미니어처 버전이며, 재충전되는 배터리로 달리는 모터가 달려있습니다.

제품 정보
- 진짜 경적과 엔진 소리가 있어서 이 화려한 자동차는 차에 대한 가장 진짜 같은 느낌을 제공합니다.
- 이것은 야외에서뿐만 아니라 실내에서, 다만 평평한 지면에서만 타기에 적합한 12볼트 배터리 전력 공급 모터와 함께 나옵니다.
- 운행 시간 1~2시간

– LED 조명과 MP3 입력 (단자)와 함께 나옴

– 3~6세 어린이에게 적합함

안전 정보

– 안전모와 무릎 및 팔꿈치 보호대와 같은 적절한 보호 장비를 항상 착용해야 합니다.

– 어린이들은 차량을 이용할 때 어른에 의해 항시 감독되어야 합니다.

구문 [9행~11행] It comes with *a 12v battery-powered motor* [that **is suitable for** riding indoors **as well as** outdoors but only on flat surfaces].

[ ]는 a 12v battery-powered motor를 수식하는 관계사절이다. 'be suitable for'는 '~에 적합하다, 알맞다'의 뜻이다. 「A as well as B (B뿐만 아니라 A도)」 구문이 쓰였으며, A, B 자리 모두 부사가 위치해 있다.

어휘 rechargeable 재충전되는 horn 경적 glossy 화려한; 윤[광]이 나는 vehicle 차량, 탈 것 authentic 진짜인; 진품인 suitable 적합한, 알맞은 surface 지면; 표면 input 입력(하다); 투입 appropriate 적절한 supervise 감독하다

---

7 밑줄 어법 ④

해설 ④ recommend와 같이 '주장, 제안, 요구, 명령, 추천' 등의 의미를 가지는 동사 다음에 나오는 that절은 당위의 의미를 가질 때 「that + S′ + (should) 동사원형」의 형태로 쓰므로 are를 '(should) be'로 바꿔 써야 한다.

① which는 cases of escapes, contamination, and spread of disease를 지칭하며, all of which는 이하 절에서 주어로 쓰였다. 따라서 사물을 나타내는 주격 관계대명사 which를 올바르게 사용했다.

② 앞에 있는 분사 resulting과 and로 연결된 병렬구조로 altering을 적절히 사용했다. resulting in 이하는 분사구문으로 resulting은 which results로 바꿔 쓸 수 있으며, resulting의 의미상 주어는 앞 문장의 that절이다. 분사구문은 앞 절의 내용을 의미상 주어로 할 수 있다.

③ Shrimp production이 주어이므로 이에 대응되는 단수형 형태의 동사 has를 올바르게 사용했다.

⑤ where 이후로 완전한 문장이 이어지며 where절은 앞의 terrestrial, man-made tanks라는 '장소'를 수식하므로 장소를 나타내는 관계부사 where를 알맞게 사용했다.

해석 양식은 통제된 환경에서 발생하지만, 탈출과 오염과 질병 확산의 사례들이 기록되어왔는데, 이는 모두 주변 지역의 자연 생태계에 해를 끼칠 수 있다. 예를 들어 칠레의 연구는 탈출한 연어과 어류가 자신의 새로운, 토착지가 아닌 환경에서 대량 서식할 수 있고, 이는 자원 경쟁을 낳아서 잠재적으로 지역 생태계 과정을 바꿀 수 있음을 보여주었다. 아시아와 세계 다른 지역에서의 새우 생산은 새우 양식장으로 쓸 공간을 만들기 위해 맹그로브와 습지의 파괴를 일으켰다. 육식성 어류의 사육은 어류 사료로 사용되는 굵은 가루로 전환되는 야생 어류의 추출물에 달려있다. 세계의 몇몇 지역에서는 이것이 지역 어부들에게 어족이 고갈됨을 의미해왔는데, 그들은 식단의 보충이나 수입을 위해 이러한 종들에 여전히 의존하고 있다. 전문가들은 최근 이러한 잠재적 문제 중 일부를 피하기 위하여 외래 육식종보다는 토종 초식종 혹은 여과 섭식 동물을 양식해야 한다고 권고해왔다. 제안된 또 다른 해결책으로는 폐기물 처리를 포함한 생산의 모든 단계가 관리될 수 있는 육상의 인공 탱크에서만 양식하는 것이 있다.

구문 [14행~17행] In some parts of the world, / this has meant depleted stocks for *local fishermen*, // **who** still depend on these species for a supplement to their diet or for income.

who는 local fishermen을 지칭하며 who 이하는 local fishermen에 대한 추가적인 설명을 제시한다. for로 시작하는 두 개의 전치사구가 or로 연결되어 병렬구조를 이룬다.

어휘 aquaculture 양식(업), 수산 재배 contamination 오염 colonize 대량 서식하다 nonnative 토종이 아닌 deforestation 삼림 벌채[파괴] wetland 습지 carnivorous 육식 동물의 (↔ herbivorous 초식 동물의) extraction 추출(물) fin-fish (지느러미가 있는) 물고기 be converted to ~로 전환되다 meal 굵은 가루, (사료용) 으깬 곡물 deplete 고갈시키다 stock 종족, 군집[군체] supplement 보충(물) exclusively 오로지, 오직 ~뿐 terrestrial 육지의, 육상의 man-made 인공적인 disposal 처리, 처분

---

8 밑줄 어휘 ③

해설 ③ 아래의 뜨거운 공기 분자들은 차가운 공기로 더 많은 운동 에너지를 가져오고, 차가운 공기 분자들은 에너지 결손을 가져온다는 말로 세워졌던 열 경계선은 무너지게 되는 것을 유추할 수 있다. 그러므로 '세우다'라는 뜻의 establish는 '넘다'라는 뜻의 cross 등으로 바꾸어 써야 적절하다.

① 햇빛은 지면을 데우지만 지상 몇 센티미터 이내에서 일어날 뿐이라는 말로 보아 공기는 '형편없는(poor)' 열전도체라는 말은 적절하다.

② 열 경계선이 존재하게 된다는 말은 뜨거운 지표면 공기와 그 위의 차가운 공기를 분리되는 것을 뜻하므로 '분리하는(separating)'이라는 말의 쓰임이 적절하다.

④ 바람이 없는 날에는 열 교환이 더디어서 상당한 온도 '차이(difference)'가 생긴다는 말은 문맥에 맞다.

⑤ 맑고 바람이 없는 여름날 오후에 발과 허리에서 온도 차를 경험하게 된다는 내용은 문맥에 맞기에 '경험하다'는 뜻의 experience는 적절하다.

해석 해가 아침에 떠오를 때, 햇빛은 지면을 데우고, 지면은 전도에 의해 그것(지면)과 접촉하는 공기를 따뜻하게 한다. 하지만 공기는 매우 ① 불량한 열전도체라서 이 과정은 지상 몇 센티미터 이내에서 일어날 뿐이다. 해가 하늘로 더 높이 떠오를수록, 지면과 접촉하는 공기는 훨씬 더 따뜻해지고, 뜨거운 지표면 공기와 그 위의 약간 더 차가운 공기를 ② 분리하는 열 경계선이 존재하게 된다. 일부 공기 분자들의 일정치 않은 움직임을 고려해 보면, 그것들은 이 경계선을 ③ 세울(→ 넘어갈) 것인데, 아래의 '뜨거운' 분자들은 더 차가운 공기로 더 많은 운동 에너지를 가져오고, 위의 '차가운' 분자들은 뜨거운 지표면 공기로 에너지 결손을 가져온다. 그러나 바람이 불지 않는 날에는 이런 형태의 열 교환이 느려서, 지면 바로 위에는 대개 상당한 온도 ④ 차이가 생긴다. 이것은 맑고 바람이 없는 여름날 오후에 달리는 사람들이 양발에서는 섭씨 50도(화씨 122도)를 초과하는 기온을 ⑤ 경험하고, 허리에서는 불과 섭씨 32도(화씨 90도)의 기온을 경험할 수도 있는 이유를 설명한다.

구문 [5행~9행] **As** the sun rises higher in the sky, *the air* (in contact with the ground) becomes even warmer, and there exists *a thermal boundary* (separating the hot surface air from the slightly cooler air above).

As는 시간을 나타내는 접속사로 부사절을 이끈다. 첫 번째 ( )은 the air를 수식하는 전명구이고, 두 번째 ( )은 a thermal boundary를 수식하는 분사구이다.

어휘 in contact with ~와 접촉하는 conduction (전기나 열의) 전도 heat conductor 열전도체 boundary 경계(선) surface (지)표면 given ~을 고려해 보면 random 일정치 않은; 임의의 molecule 분자 deficit 결손, 부족(량) substantial 상당한 temperature 온도, 기온

---

9 빈칸 추론 ⑤

해설 사교적인 성격의 투자 클럽은 구성원들이 사교적 관계를 해치지 않으려고 반대 의견을 내지 않으며 이는 저성과로 이어진다는 내용의 글이므로, 낮은 수입을 산출하는 것은 결국 반대 의견을 말하지 못하는 ⑤ '순응'임을 추론할 수 있다.

① 탐욕 ② 자부심 ③ 조급함 ④ 과신

해석 투자 클럽은 주식 시장에 돈을 모으고 합동 결정을 내리는 사람들의 소집단이다. 어떤 클럽이 고수익을 올리고, 어떤 클럽이 저수익을 내는가? 최저 성과 클럽은 주로 사교적 클럽임이 드러났다. 그 구성원은 서로 알고 있고, 함께 식사하고, 애정의 유대로 연결되어 있다. 대조적으로, 최고 성과 클럽은 제한된 사교적 관계만을 제공하며 수익을 증가시키는 데 초점이 맞춰져 있다. 반대 의견은 고성과 클럽에서 훨씬 더 빈번하다. 저성과자들은 보통 만장일치의 투표를 하며, 공개 토론은 거의 하지 않는다. 저성과 그룹은 높은 경제적 수익을 확실히 하기보다는 사교적 관계를 쌓는 데 더 투신한다. 간단히 말해서, 순응은 상당히 더 낮은 수입을 산출한다.

구문 [12행~14행] The votes in low-performing groups are cast <u>to build social connections</u> **rather than** <u>to ensure high economic returns.</u>
「A rather than B」는 'B라기보다는 오히려 A'의 뜻으로, A와 B에 해당하는 자리에 각각 to부정사구가 위치해 있다.

어휘 pool (자금을) 모으다 　 joint 공동의, 합동의 　 stock market 주식 시장 primarily 주로 　 bond 유대 　 affection 애정 　 dissent 반대 (의견) 　 unanimous 만장일치 　 cast 던지다 　 significantly 상당히

10 빈칸 추론 　 ④

해설 빈칸 문장 뒤에 예시가 이어지고 있다. 점원은 두세 개밖에 안 되는 물건의 가격조차도 그것을 기억해서 암산하기보다는 기계에 입력하여 계산한다고 하므로 기억력이 감소할 것이며, 수업 내용을 꼼꼼히 기록하는 학생이 그렇지 않은 학생보다 기억을 잘 못한다고 했다. 즉 정보를 외우지 않고 어딘가에 기록하는 것은 기억력을 감소시킴을 알 수 있다.
① 업무와 우선순위를 정리해준다
② 일시적인 기억력 저하를 막는다
③ 정보에 대한 접근을 높인다
⑤ 빈틈없다는 인상을 준다

해석 현대 사회에서 사람들이 알고 있어야 하는 정보의 양을 고려하면, 일정량의 필기를 하거나 책에 정보를 담아 두는 일은 피할 수 없다. 그러나 기억하는 일에서 멀어지는 (기억력에 덜 의존하는) 경향이 눈에 띨 정도를 넘어서 커지고 있다. 뭔가를 적는 것이 우리의 기억력을 감소시킨다는 사실은 스스로 쉽게 그리고 가장 잘 알 수 있지만, 몇 가지 일상적인 사례가 이 점을 설명하는 데 도움이 될지도 모른다. 그러한 한 가지 예가 상점에서 일어난다. 오늘날 점원은 두세 가지 물품의 단순 합산을 암산으로 하는 일이 좀처럼 없을 것이며, 그보다는 기기에 숫자를 입력할 것이다. 학교가 또 다른 예를 제공한다. 교사들은 강의의 한 마디 한 마디를 부지런히 기록하는 학생들이 종종, 자신의 이해력을 신뢰하고 그리하여 최소한 핵심적인 내용을 제시할 수 있는 학생들만큼 잘 기억해 내지 못한다는 것을 알 수 있다.

구문 [13행~17행] Teachers can observe <u>that</u> *the students* [who diligently record every word of the lecture] often do not perform **as** *well* at recall **as** *those* [who trusted their capacity to understand and, hence, can produce at least the essentials].
that 이하가 문장의 목적어 역할을 한다. 원급 비교 형태인 「as ... as ~」(~만큼 …하다) 구문이 쓰였다. those는 앞의 the students와 반복을 피하기 위한 것이다.

어휘 volume (두꺼운) 서적; (전집 따위의) 권; 양, 부피; (TV 등의) 음량 　 contemporary 동시대의; 현대의 　 keep track of 기록하다; ~에 대해 계속 알고 있다 　 recall 기억해 내다 　 sensible 분별력 있는; 눈에 띨 정도의; 의식하고 있는 　 proportion 부분; 비율; 균형 　 observe 보다; 관찰하다; (법을) 준수하다 　 illustrate 삽화를 넣다; (실례 등을 넣어) 설명하다 　 diminish 줄어들다, 약해지다; 줄이다, 약화시키다 　 thorough 빈틈없는, 철두철미한

11 빈칸 추론 　 ⑤

해설 빈칸 문장은 그 윗부분에서 서술된 내용을 뒷받침하는 맥락이므로, 많은 결정을 해야 하는 선수들은 인지 처리 속도가 떨어지면 안 되므로 화가 나면 안 된다는 내용이 되어야 한다. 그러므로 정답은 ⑤ '그렇지 않은 선수들에 비해 더 낮은 수준의 화를'이다.
① 논리적, 합리적인 과업에 대한 선호를
② 팀 동료보다 더 큰 화를
③ 다른 선수들보다 고통에 대해 더 큰 인내를
④ 그들을 둘러싼 사람들에 대해 우월한 태도를

해석 연구로 밝혀진 바에 의하면 화가 심해지면 인지 처리 속도가 떨어지고 미세한 운동 협응과 고통에 대한 민감도가 줄어들며 근육의 힘은 흔히 증가한다. 그러므로 어떤 과업을 하는 일부 선수들에게 화는 이로울 수 있다. 예를 들어 태클하려는 블로커를 지나 전진해야 하는 수비 라인맨은 어느 정도의 화를 가지고 있으면 이득을 볼지도 모른다. 다른 과업들에서는 화가 방해가 될 것이다. 어느 리시버에게 (공을) 던져야 할지를 결정하기 전에 수비를 읽어야 하는 쿼터백은 화가 나 있지 않다면 수행을 더 잘할 것이다. 실제로, 몇몇 연구는 이런 논리를 뒷받침한다. 많은 결정이 요구되는 축구 포지션에 있는 선수들은 그렇지 않은 선수들에 비해 더 낮은 수준의 화를 보여주는 경향이 있다.

구문 [6행~8행] ~, the defensive lineman [who must make his way past *a blocker* (to make a tackle)] / **might benefit** from having some level of anger.
[ ]이 주어인 the defensive lineman을 수식하는 구조로서 동사는 might benefit 이다.
[9행~11행] The quarterback [who needs to read the defense / before deciding **which receiver to throw to**] / would likely perform better // if he were not angry.
which receiver to throw to는 동명사인 deciding의 목적어이다. 여기서 which는 의문형용사로 receiver를 수식한다.

어휘 cognitive 인식[인지]의 　 fine 질 높은; 미세한; 고운 　 motor coordination 운동 협응 　 sensitivity 감성; 민감함 　 lineman ((미식축구)) 라인맨[전위] 　 make one's way 나아가다; 출세하다 　 blocker ((미식축구)) 블로커(몸을 부딪혀 상대를 방해하는 선수) 　 hindrance 방해, 장애물 　 quarterback ((미식축구)) 쿼터백(라인맨과 하프백의 중간 위치에서 뛰면서 공격을 지휘하는 선수) 　 thesis 논지; 학위 논문 　 demonstrate 입증하다; (행동으로) 보여주다

12 빈칸 추론 　 ⑤

해설 컨설턴트를 고용한 고객은 자신이 그 문제를 처리할 수 없다는 무능을 인정함으로써 다른 사람들의 눈에 자신의 평가가 낮아질 것이라는 불안감을 갖고 있으므로, 컨설턴트는 이러한 마음을 헤아려 겸손하게 자신을 낮추는 자세로 처신해야 한다는 내용이므로, 노련한 고문이라면 취할 행동은 ⑤ '저자세를 유지하려 노력하고 공적으로 공을 차지하는 일은 피한다'이다.
① 객관적이고 중립적인 입장을 취하는 경향이 있다
② 자신이 판단하는 것이면 무엇이든지 기꺼이 예의 바르게 표현한다
③ 현지인들의 호의를 얻기 위해 그들과 잘 어울리는 방법을 알고 있다
④ 부정적인 면보다는 긍정적인 면을 강조한다

해석 조언을 구할 때, 고객은 문제를 처리하지 못한다는 것을 인정하는 것이다. 어떤 개인들에게 고문을 고용하는 것은 따라서 지위나 위신의 상실을 나타내는데, 왜냐하면 그들은 다른 사람들이 자신을 처음 가정했던 것보다 덜 유능하거나 박식하다고 판단할 거라고 두려워하기 때문이다. 숙련된 관리자들은 많은 경우 이러한 이유로 경영 컨설턴트를 고용하라는 제안에 저항한다. "컨설턴트가 내가 아직 알지 못하는 뭔가를 내게 말해줄 수 있

겠습니까?"가 그들의 흔한 반응이다. 개도국 정부 또한 때때로 외국의 컨설턴트에게 공적으로 의존한다고 인정하기를 꺼리는데 그렇게 하는 것이 지역 주민들의 눈에서 정부의 지위를 축소시킬지도 모르기 때문이다. 그 결과, 노련한 고문은 고객의 행동과 결정에 대하여 저자세를 유지하려 노력하고 공적으로 공을 차지하는 일은 피한다. 경험이 부족한 컨설턴트는 때때로 자신의 지식과 영향력을 뽐내지 않고는 못 배길 때가 있고, 그 결과 때때로 고객을 잃는다. 서아프리카의 한 나라에서 세제 개혁 작업을 하고 있던 한 미국인 고문은 많은 현지 공무원들과 기업 임원들에게 자신이 '그 나라의 새로운 세금 정책을 결정하는 일'에 책임을 지고 있다고 말했다. 이 대화에 대한 보고가 재무부 장관에게 도달했을 때, 그는 그 미국인 고문을 해고했다.

구문 [6행~8행] Experienced managers often resist <u>suggestions</u> that they hire management consultants for this reason.

that ~ reason은 suggestions에 대한 동격절이다. suggestions가 '제안'의 의미이므로 (동사 suggest 다음의 that절과 마찬가지로) that절에서 주어 they 다음에 should가 생략된 동사원형 hire를 썼다. 따라서 they hire는 '그들은 고용해야 한다'의 '당위'의 의미를 가진다.

어휘 acknowledge 인정하다 engage 고용하다: 약속하다: 사로잡다 prestige 위신, 명망 knowledgeable 박식한 be reluctant to-v v하기를 꺼리다 reliance 의존 diminish 축소[약화]시키다 inexperienced 경험이 부족한 show off 뽐내다, 자랑하다 occasionally 때때로 reform 개혁[개선](하다) official 공무원 executive 임원 minister of finance 재무부 장관

13 흐름 무관 문장 ④

해설 자선은 처음에는 지원을 베푼다는 개념이었으나 점점 의미가 확장되어 가난한 사람들이 자립하고 지속적으로 스스로를 구제할 수 있게끔 교육 등을 제공해 주는 것으로 그 개념이 변화되어 왔다는 내용의 글이다. ④는 회사에서 직원들에게 교육을 제공하는 것이 회사와 직원 양쪽 모두에게 이익이라는 내용으로 '자선의 개념 변화'라는 글의 중심 내용과는 무관하다.

해석 자선은 가난한 사람들에게 베푸는 데에 초점을 맞추며 시작되었다. 그러고 나서 15세기에, 그것(자선)은 가난한 사람들이 사는 환경 문제를 다루는 것으로 확대되었다. ① 19세기에는 기업가들과 이상주의자들의 영향으로, 그 초점이 가난한 사람들이 스스로를 구제하도록 돕는 데에 있었다. ② 자선 사업에서 이러한 사고와 방법의 진전은 하나의 결론, 즉 친절하다는 것은 단지 친절을 보여주는 것 이상을 의미한다는 것으로 이어졌다. ③ 예를 들어, 어떤 사회봉사 단체가 실업자의 금전적 지원 요청은 거절하고 대신 교육을 제안할 수 있다. ④ 조직들은 그들이 얼마나 그들의 직원들을 가치 있게 여기는지를 보여주기 위한 수단으로 교육에 의지하는데, 이는 회사와 직원 모두에게 이익이다. ⑤ 이러한 행동이 빈곤한 사람에게는 잔인해 보일 수 있지만, 그 사람의 경제권과 장기적 지속 가능성이 단 한 번의 지원보다 더 가치 있다는 것이 반론이다.

구문 [11행~14행] Organizations rely on training / as a way to demonstrate **how much they value their employees**, // which is a benefit to both the company and the employee.

demonstrate의 목적어로 의문사 how가 이끄는 간접의문문 형태의 명사절이 왔다.

어휘 address 다루다: 주소 progression 진행, 진전: 연속 charity work 자선 사업 counter-argument 반론, 반박 sustainability 지속 가능성·

14 글의 순서 ④

해설 고고학이 수많은 곳에 적용이 된다는 주어진 내용에 이어, 고고학적 기록을 밝히는 것이 원주민들이 자신의 땅과 자원에 접근함을 가능하게 해 준다는 부연

설명으로 (C)가 이어지고, (C)에서 고고학이 기록을 남기지 않은 집단의 역사 이해에 기초가 될 수 있다는 내용이 (A)에서 예시로 이어진다. (A) 마지막에서 고고학의 또 다른 적용으로 때때로 현대 세계의 기술적 적용을 도출해냈다는 설명 후, 이에 대한 예시인 (B)가 이어지는 것이 적절하다.

해석 고고학은 수많은 곳에 적용된다.
(C) 고고학적 기록을 밝히는 것은 종종 원주민들이 역사적으로 자신들에게 속했던 땅과 자원에 다시 접근하는 것을 가능하게 해주었다. 고고학에서의 작업은 기록을 거의 남기지 않은 집단의 역사를 이해하는 데 종종 기초가 된다.
(A) 뉴욕 시의 African Burial Ground에서 행해진 것과 같은 발굴은 우리에게 글로 된 기록에서 잘 묘사되지 않은 집단의 생활 상태에 대한 통찰력을 준다. 그러한 지식은 흔히 문화적 정체성의 기초가 된다. 이것 이외에도 고고학은 때때로 현대 세계와 관련 있는 기술적인 적용을 도출해냈다.
(B) 예를 들어, 이스라엘의 네게브 사막, 페루, 그리고 다른 장소에서 고대 민족들에 대한 고고학적 연구는 현대인들이 환경을 더 효과적으로 사용하고 농업 산출량을 끌어올리게 해준 관개 시설 설계와 주변보다 높게 만든 경작지 시스템에 대한 정보를 만들어내었다.

구문 [15행~17행] <u>Establishing the archaeological record</u> **has** often **enabled** *native peoples* **to regain** access to *land and resources* [that historically belonged to them].

밑줄 친 동명사구가 주어이며 '(사물이 사람에게) ~ 할 수 있게 하다'는 뜻의 「enable O to-v」 구문이 쓰였다. [ ]는 관계사절로 land and resources를 수식한다.

어휘 archaeology 고고학 numerous (수)많은 application 적용, 응용 insight 통찰력: 이해 represent 묘사하다 fundamental 기초가 되는 relevant 관련된 current 현대의, 지금의 yield 산출량: 산출하다 irrigation 관개 raised-field 주변보다 높게 만든 경작지 agricultural 농업의 establish 밝히다: 설립하다

15 글의 순서 ⑤

해설 친환경 접착제의 출현에 대해 말한 주어진 문장 다음에는 green adhesives를 지칭하는 these가 나오는 (C)가 이어진다. 여러 국가에서 접착제의 화학물질 방출에 관한 규제를 도입했다는 (C) 다음에는 이 규제가 접착제에도 적용되어 접착제의 해로운 화합물의 양을 제한하는 조치로 이어졌다는 (B)가 나오는데, (B)의 These는 (C) 마지막의 'regulations'를 지칭한다. 접착제 규제가 에너지 절약 및 쓰레기양 감소에도 관련된다는 (B) 다음에는 그 예로 '핫멜트 접착제'를 소개하는 (A)가 나오는 것이 적절하다.

해석 상업적 용도를 위해 천연의 그리고 더 지속 가능한 접착제를 개발하려는 노력 외에도, 최근 몇 년 동안 매우 다양한 '친환경 접착제'가 출현했다.
(C) 이러한 제품을 생산하여 시장에 내놓으려는 노력은 더 지속 가능한 원료의 사용뿐만 아니라, 접착제의 환경적 영향을 최소화하는 것과도 관계가 있었는데, 특히 접착제에 함유된 유해 화합물과 용제를 줄이는 것과 관련하여 그렇다. 많은 국가에서 접착제를 사용할 때 발생하는 화학물질 배출에 대한 규제를 도입했다.
(B) 이는 접착제에 함유된 휘발성 유기 화합물의 양을 제한하고자 하였는데, 이런 화합물이 건강과 환경 모두에 위험을 유발하는 위험한 대기 오염 물질을 배출한다고 여겨지기 때문이다. 다른 제품들은 에너지를 절약하고 쓰레기를 줄이도록 고안된다.
(A) 예를 들어, 저온 핫멜트 접착제는 녹여서 도포하는 데 더 적은 에너지를 필요로 하며, 플라스틱 튜브로 된 도포용 도구로부터 생기는 매립 폐기물을 줄이기 위해 새로운 마분지와 포일을 기본으로 한 포장재 또한 개발되었다.

구문 [10행~14행] These have attempted to place limits on the amount of *volatile organic compounds* (contained in adhesive products), as these compounds are thought to release *hazardous air pollutants* (posing both health and environmental risks).

두 개의 ( )은 모두 분사구로 각각 바로 앞의 명사구 volatile organic compounds 와 hazardous air pollutants를 수식한다.

[16행~19행] *Efforts* (to produce and market these) have been associated not only with the use of more sustainable raw materials but also with minimizing the environmental impacts of adhesives, ~.

( )은 형용사적 용법으로 쓰인 to부정사구로 Efforts를 수식한다. 「not only A but also B(A뿐만 아니라 B도)」 구문이 쓰였고 밑줄 친 두 개의 전명구가 A와 B에 해당된다.

어휘 sustainable 지속 가능한　emergence 출현　melt 녹(이)다　apply 바르다, 도포하다　cardboard 마분지, 판지　landfill 쓰레기 매립지　applicator 도포용 도구　place a limit on ~에 한계를 두다　compound 합성물　hazardous 위험한　pollutant 오염 물질　pose (위협 등을) 제기하다　raw material 원료　with regard to ~에 관하여　regulation 규제　emission 방출, 배출

16 문장 넣기　⑤

해설 ⑤의 앞 문장에서 엽록소에는 '녹색 공백'이 있어서 이 녹색 파장의 빛을 이용할 수 없다고 했는데, As a result로 시작되는 주어진 문장을 ⑤에 위치시키면 '그 결과로(그러한 이유로) 녹색 빛은 쓰이지 못하고 튕겨져 나간다'는 내용과 자연스럽게 연결된다. 또한 주어진 문장 뒤에 나오는 마지막 문장의 all the other wavelengths of light는 녹색 빛의 파장을 제외한 나머지 빛을 말한다는 것을 알 수 있으므로 주어진 문장은 ⑤에 들어가야 한다.

해석 숲의 대부분은 어두운데, 태양빛의 오직 3퍼센트만 숲의 우거진 윗부분을 관통하기 때문이다. 이것은 나무 아래에 있는 식물들에게 그것은(= 숲을) 칠흑같이 어둡게 만든다. 당신이 숲을 걸어갈 때는 그런 생각이 안 들지도 모르겠지만, 이것은 당신이 그곳에서 발견하는 녹색의 색조와 관련이 있다. 나무들은 빛과 물과 이산화탄소를 당으로 전환시키기 위해 잎의 엽록소를 이용한다. 그러나 엽록소에는 '녹색 공백'이 있는데, 이는 그것이(= 엽록소) 이 빛의 파장을 이용할 수 없다는 것을 의미한다. 그 결과 녹색 빛은 반사되고, 이것은 숲이 식물들에게 보이는 것보다 인간 방문객들에게 더 밝게 보이게 하는데, 식물들은 이 색을 '볼' 수 없기 때문이다. 97퍼센트의 다른 모든 빛의 파장은 숲의 우거진 윗부분에서 이미 흡수되고 처리되었으므로, 숲의 바닥에 있는 녹색 식물들이 있는 곳에서 보면 사물은 말 그대로 어두워 보인다.

구문 [1행~4행] As a result, / green light is reflected, // and this **makes** *the forest* **seem brighter** to human visitors / than **it does to plants**, // because plants cannot "see" this colour.

사역동사 「make + O + 동사원형」 구문은 'O가 v하게 하다'의 뜻이다. than 다음의 it does to plants는 this makes the forest seem (bright) to plants를 나타낸다.

[8행~10행] You might not think so // when you walk through the forest, // but this has to do with *the green shade* [(which[that]) you find there].

[ ]는 앞에 목적격 관계대명사 which[that]가 생략되어 the green shade를 수식한다.

어휘 penetrate 관통하다, 뚫고 들어가다　pitch-black 칠흑같이 어두운　have to do with ~와 관계가 있다　convert A into B A를 B로 전환[변환]시키다　make use of ~을 이용하다　wavelength 파장, 주파수　gloomy 어둑어둑한

17 문장 넣기　④

해설 ④ 앞부분에는 망치와 같이 비효율적이고 위험한 도구가 예시로 나온다. However로 시작되는 주어진 문장은 그것의(its) 불편함에도 불구하고 사람들이 그

것(it)에 익숙해져서 계속 사용하는 상황이 나오고 ④ 뒤의 문장은 그 사람들이 망치를 혁신적으로 바꿔볼 생각도 하지 않는 상황이 제시되므로 주어진 문장의 'it'은 망치를 가리킴을 알 수 있다. ④ 뒤의 문장에 있는 The people은 주어진 문장에 있던 '불편한 망치를 잘 사용하는 사람들'을 나타낸다. 따라서 답은 ④이다.

해석 혁신이 사회 집단의 요구를 충족시키는 것과 연관된다는 생각은 혁신적인 사람들이 해결하고자 추구하는 문제가 적어도 부분적으로 사회적으로 결정된다는 것이다. 문제가 존재한다는 사회적 인식이 없는 곳에서는 해결책을 만들어내려는 동인도 없을 것이며 따라서 혁신도 없을 것이다. 한 가지 간단한 예는 예컨대 도구와 같은 일상적인 물체의 디자인 영역이다. 도구는 사용하기에 어색하고 비효율적이거나, 아마 심지어 위험할 수도 있다. 망치가 좋은 예다. 그러나 그것이 너무나 많은 사람들에게 그토록 익숙하여 그들이 그것의 불리한 점에 익숙해졌고, 불리함과 불편함에도 불구하고 그것을 매우 효과적으로 사용할 수 있을지도 모른다. 그 사람들은 심지어 망치가 달라질 수 있다는 상상을 못할지도 모른다. 이러한 경우에는 효과적인 새로운 것을 도입하려는 사회적 압박이 없으며, 어떤 의미에서 사회가 문제가 없다고 결정했으므로 디자인이 얼마나 형편없든 문제도 존재하지 않는다.

구문 [6행~9행] The idea that innovation is linked with meeting the needs of social groups *means* that *the problems* [(which[that]) innovative people seek to solve] are at least partly socially determined.

밑줄 친 The idea와 that innovation ~ social groups는 동격 관계이고, 동사는 means이다. [ ] 부분은 목적격 관계대명사 which 또는 that이 생략된 관계사절로 the problems를 수식한다.

[17행~21행] In this case, there is *no social pressure* (to introduce effective novelty) and, in a sense, no problem, **no matter how bad the design may be**, because society has decided there is no problem.

( ) 부분은 형용사적 용법으로 쓰인 to부정사구로 no social pressure를 수식한다. no matter how ~ may be는 양보의 부사절로 however the design may be bad로 바꿔 쓸 수 있다.

어휘 become accustomed to ~에 익숙[친숙]해지다　disadvantage 불리함, 단점　inconvenience 불편함　be linked with ~와 연관[관련]이 있다　awareness 인식　awkward 어색한, 불편한　inefficient 비효율적인　hammer 망치　incapable of ~할 수 없는　pressure 압박, 압력　novelty 새로운 것; 참신함

18 요약문 완성　⑤

해설 본문은 사람들이 다른 사람들의 존재[시선]에 자극을 받아 친사회적인 행동을 하게 된다고 하며, 본문의 실험에서 피실험자들은 기부해달라는 요청을 받았을 때 자신이 관찰하고 있다고 느낄 경우에 그렇지 않은 경우보다 7배 더 많은 기부를 했다. 이를 반영하여 요약문을 완성하면 '사람들은 (A) 관찰되는 상황에서 그렇지 않은 상황에서보다 더 (B) 관대하게 행동하는 경향이 있다.'가 된다.

해석 어떤 사람이 다른 사람들이 지켜보고 있기 때문에 더 예의 바르게 행동하는 경우와 같이, 많은 친사회적 행동은 다른 사람들에 의해 자극받는다. 개들은 주인이 있을 때에는 가구와 쓰레기로부터 멀리 떨어져 있겠지만, 혼자 있을 때 그것들은 아무 생각 없이 그러한 규칙들을 어긴다. 인간은 더 많은 양심을 지니고 있을지 모르겠지만, 그들도 또한 여전히 다른 사람들의 존재나 부재에 반응한다. 공개적인 상황은 일반적으로 친사회적 행동을 촉진한다. Kay L. Satow의 한 연구에서 참가자들은 방에 혼자 앉아 테이프에 녹음된 지시를 따랐다. 절반은 자신들이 한쪽 방향에서만 볼 수 있는 거울을 통해 관찰되고 있다고(공적 조건) 믿었고, 반면에 다른 사람들은 아무도 보고 있지 않다고(사적 조건) 믿었다. 연구의 마지막에서 테이프에 녹음된 지시로 참가자에게 테이블 위에 놓인 단지에 약간의 잔돈을 남겨 놓음으로써 기부를 해달라고 요청했다. 사적 조건에서보다 공적 조건에서 기부금액이 7배 더 많았다는 것을 결과가 보여주었다. 보아하니 너그러운 도움을 베푸는 한 가지 중요한 이유는 지켜보고 있는 사람들에게 좋은 인상을 주기 위한 (혹은 유지하기 위한) 것처럼 보인다.

↓

사람들은 (A) 관찰되는 상황에서 그렇지 않은 상황에서보다 더 (B) 관대하게 행동하는 경향이 있다.

구문 [13행~16행] At the end of the study, the tape-recorded instructions **invited** *the participant* **to make** a donation by leaving some change in the jar on the table.

「invite+O+to-v」는 'O에게 v 해달라고 요청하다'의 뜻이다.

[18행~21행] Apparently, one important reason for generous helping *is* **to make** (or sustain) a good impression on *the people* [who are watching].

to make 이하는 동사 is의 보어 역할을 하는 명사적 용법의 to부정사구이다. [ ]은 관계사절로 the people을 수식한다.

어휘 stimulate 자극하다　casually 아무 생각 없이, 무심코　conscience 양심
instruction 지시　impulsively 충동적으로　perplexed 당황한

19~20 장문　　　　　　　　　　　19 ⑤ 20 ⑤

해설 19. 이 글은 예술적 기교의 발휘에 외적 보상을 주는 것은 창조성을 방해한다는 내용이다. 그러므로 ⑤ '외적인 보상이 예술의 창작 동기를 손상시킨다'가 제목으로 가장 적절하다.
① 예술 작품에 대한 보상으로서의 행복
② 금전적 보상이 작가의 영감을 향상시킨다
③ 예술에서 보상하기: 혁신을 향한 길
④ 예술 활동을 증가시키는 효과적 방법은 무엇인가?
20. 최근 사회심리학 연구는 예술 창작에서 외적 보상을 부정적으로 생각하므로, 그런 주장이 외적 보상을 긍정적으로 보는 전통적 심리학의 개념을 '확증한다(confirms)'라는 (e)는 그 개념과 '상반된다(contradicts)' 등으로 바꾸어야 문맥상 적절하다.

해석 Pat Darcy가 말하듯이, 우리 뇌는 우리가 예술에 관여할 때 우리를 행복하게 해주기 위해서 진화했다. 예술적 기교의 발휘는 우리 종의 기원보다도 먼저 일어났다. 아이디어의 생산, 유형 인식, 확산적 사고, 상상력 같은 탄력적인 사고 기술을 사용하는 것이 본질적으로 보람이 된다는 것은 사람들이 (대부분) 물질적 보상이 (a) 적어도 언제나 예술에 에너지를 쏟아 온 이유이다. 사실 물질적인 보상은 그런 활동을 했을 때 우리가 느끼는 (b) 기쁨에 방해가 되기도 한다. 예를 들어 러시아 출판업자가 소설을 써달라고 꽤 많은

선금을 지불했을 때 위대한 러시아 작가인 Fyodor Dostoyevsky가 어떻게 반응했는지를 생각해 보자. 무엇을 쓸 것인지와 관련해서 그가 엄격한 지침을 받지 않았다는 점에 주목해야 한다. 그는 단순히 돈을 받는 대가와 관련되는 무엇인가를 써달라는 요청을 받았을 뿐이었다. 그럼에도 Dostoyevsky는 친구에게 보낸 편지에 '자네는 주문을 받고 장황하게 글을 쓴 적이 결코 없었고 그러한 지옥 같은 고문을 겪은 적이 없다고 믿네.'라고 썼다. 그가 언급한 지옥 같은 고문은 이 위대한 소설가가 유난스럽기 때문만은 아니었다. 자신의 작품에 대해서 돈을 받는 벌이 될 듯한 것이 Dostoyevsky에게는 창작의 (c) 걸림돌로 작용한 것이다.

이것은 Dostoyevsky만의 사례는 아니었다. 사회심리학에서 많은 최근의 연구는 본질적으로 즐거운 행동에 대해 외적인 보상을 제공하는 것이 역효과를 줄 수 있다고 말하면서 창조적 산물을 금전적으로 평가하는 것이 혁신에 이르는 과정을 (d) 방해할 수 있다고 주장한다. 그런 주장은 심지어 사람의 행동을 부추기거나 조절하기도 하는 보상의 중요성을 조사하는 논문으로 가득한 전통적인 심리학의 개념(e)을 확증한다(→ 과 상반된다). 독창적 사고는 '잘못된 이유에서 시도할 때는' 나오기 어렵다고 심리학자인 Teresa Amabile은 말한다.

구문 [4행~9행] That the exercise of *elastic thinking skills* (such as idea generation, pattern recognition, divergent thinking, and imagination) is inherently rewarding **is** *the reason* [(why) people have always put energy into the arts, despite the lack of material reward (for most)].

명사절 접속사 That이 이끄는 밑줄 친 절이 문장의 주어이고, 동사는 is이다. such as ~ and imagination은 전명구로 elastic thinking skills를 수식하고, [ ] 부분은 관계부사 why가 생략된 관계사절로 선행사 the reason을 수식한다.

[24행~29행] Many recent studies in social psychology suggest that monetizing creative output can disrupt *the processes* [**that** lead to innovation], ***saying*** that offering an extrinsic reward for an intrinsically enjoyable behavior can be counterproductive.

[ ] 부분은 관계사 that이 이끄는 형용사절로 the processes를 수식한다. saying 이하는 부대상황을 나타내는 분사구문이다.

어휘 engage in ~에 관여[참여]하다; ~에 종사하다　predate ~보다 먼저[앞서] 오다
elastic 탄력적인; 융통성 있는　divergent thinking 확산적 사고　inherently 본질적으로; 선천적으로　rewarding 보람 있는; 돈을 많이 버는　recompense 보상[배상](하다)　get in the way of 방해되다　advance 선금, 선불; 다가가다; 진전을 보이다　by the yard 장황하게　hellish 지옥과 같은, 끔찍한　torture 심한 고통; 고문　drama queen 유난스러운[호들갑을 떠는] 사람　prospect 벌이가 될 듯한 것; 가망　isolated 단 하나[한 번]의; 외딴; 고립된　monetize 화폐화하다　disrupt 방해하다, 지장을 주다　extrinsic 외적인, 외부의　intrinsically 본질적으로　counterproductive 역효과를 낳는; 비생산적인　undermine 약화시키다

1 ③	2 ①	3 ③	4 ④	5 ④		6 ④	7 ④	8 ③	9 ①	10 ⑤
11 ③	12 ②	13 ③	14 ②	15 ④		16 ④	17 ③	18 ③	19 ④	20 ④

1 글의 목적　　　　　　　　　　　③

해설 퇴원한 어머니를 집에서 돌봐야 하는 연로한 아버지를 위해 도우미를 보내주기를 관계 기관에 요청하는 글이므로 글의 목적은 ③이다.

해석 책임자께
저희 어머니 Emma Miller는 현재 Beacon 종합병원의 환자입니다. 어머니께서는 심장병에서 회복하는 중이고 곧 퇴원하게 될 겁니다. 어머니를 주로 돌봐주시는 분은 저희 아버지이십니다. 두 분 다 80대이십니다. 어머니께서 건강을 회복하시는 일정 기간 동안, 아버지께서 잔심부름과 물건 구매를 하시는 동안 교대할 수 있도록 재택 케어를 필요로 하십니다. 노인 관할청이 바로 이러한 종류의 상황에 있는 노인들에게 도우미 분을 집으로 보내주는 프로그램을 운영한다는 것을 알고 있습니다. 저희는 한 번에 2시간 동안 일주일에

두세 번 도우미께서 저희 어머니와 함께 해주시도록 준비하고 싶습니다. 날짜와 시간을 조정하기 위해 저희 아버지 Ron Miller에게 목록에 나와 있는 번호로 직접 연락해 주세요. 진심을 담아.

Laura Hall

구문 [5행~6행] Both are **in their eighties**.
'in their eighties'는 '(그들이) 80대에'의 뜻이다.
[12행~14행] We would like to arrange *for an aide* **to be** with my mother two or three times a week for a period of two hours at a time.
for an aide는 to be의 의미상 주어이다.

어휘 presently 현재 shortly 곧 primary 제1의, 주요한 in-home 집에서의 relieve 교대하다, 완화하다 run errands 심부름을 하다 administrate 운영하다, 관리하다 aide 조력자 arrange 조정하다, 마련하다

2 필자 주장 ①

해설 선거를 통해 선출되고 국민의 요구에 부응하는 입법부와 행정부와는 달리, 법원은 시류에 휩쓸리지 말고 타당한 법률 추론을 고수하기 위해 최선을 다해야 한다고 했으므로 필자의 주장으로 가장 적절한 것은 ①이다.

해석 민의(民意)를 반영하는 법원이 우리를 하나의 국가로 나아가게 하는 것 같지만, 우리가 법적 판결을 내리는 것에 대한 명분으로 변화하는 시대에 의존한다면 위험한 상황에 들어서게 된다. 변화하는 시대에 발맞추는 일은 대개 입법부와 행정부, 즉 정식으로 선출된 국민의 대표들이 할 일이다. 그들은 국민들이 요구할 때 정책을 제정하거나 바꾸는 일을 담당해야 한다. 2년 혹은 4년마다 있는 선거 그리고 유권자들과의 진중한 참여가 있어서, 정부의 저 두 부문이 사회와 늘 접촉하는 데 최적이다. 반면에 법원에는 대중에 대한 그만한 노출이 없다. 법원이 국민을 따르려고 노력하는 일에 발을 담그면, 그것은 위험한 미래를 야기할 것이다. 법원은 무엇이 합법이고 무엇이 불법인지 대신에 무엇이 옳고 무엇이 그른지를 결정하기 시작할 수 있다. 법원은 판결을 내릴 때 타당한 법률 추론을 고수하기 위해 항상 최선을 다해야 한다.

구문 [1행~4행] While **it seems that** *the Court* (reflecting the will of the people) takes us forward as a nation, // we get into a dangerous situation // if we rely on changing times as justification / for making legal decisions.
접속사 While은 '~이지만, ~인 반면에'의 뜻으로 쓰였다. While 절에서 it seems that ~은 '~인 것 같다'의 뜻이다. ( )는 the Court를 수식하는 형용사구이다.

어휘 the will of the people 민의, 국민의 의사 justification 명분; 타당한 이유, 정당화 keep up with ~에 뒤지지 않다 be up to ~가 할 일이다, ~에 달려 있다 legislature 입법부 administration 행정부 be in charge of ~을 담당하고[책임지고] 있다 enact 제정하다 constituent 유권자; 구성 (성분) keep in touch with ~와 접촉을 유지하다 stick to ~을 고수하다 sound 타당한; 건전한, 건강한 reasoning 추론

3 밑줄 함의 ③

해설 우리는 외계 지적 생명체의 신호를 포착해본 적이 없고, 생명체의 항성 간 여행은 그 막대한 거리로 인해 불가능에 가까운 일이므로 '우리는 우리가 사는 행성을 다루는 선에서 그치게 될 것이다'라는 말은 우리가 외계 생명체를 접촉할 가능성이 거의 없고 지구에만 국한된 연구를 하게 될 것이라는 의미가 된다. 이를 반영하여 밑줄이 의미하는 바를 고르면 ③ '외계 지적 생명체 탐색은 다소 무의미하다'가 된다.
① 우리는 지구 연구보다는 SETI에 집중할 필요가 있다

② 외계 생명체의 존재에 대한 명백한 증거가 있다
④ 우리는 외계 지적 생명체와 접촉할 준비가 되어 있지 않다
⑤ 외계인과 접촉할 가능성이 높다

해석 지구와 비슷할 가능성이 있는 수십억 개의 행성을 두고, 많은 사람들은 우리 것과 비슷한 문명이 분명 우리 은하계에 흔할 것이라고 주장해 왔다. 하지만 우리가 더 많이 알수록, 그게 그렇지 않은 것 같다. 외계 지적 생명체 탐사 프로그램 SETI는 40년이 넘는 기간에 걸쳐 무선 신호를 찾아 창공을 살펴 오고 있지만, 그들은 단 하나의 일관된 메시지도 수신하지 못했다. 더 근본적으로, 복잡한 생물학적 존재는 항성 간의 광활한 공간을 통과하도록 진화하지 못했다. 만약 항성 간 이동하는 존재가 있다면, 그것은 수천 년 넘게 '잠을 잘 수 있는 로봇'일 것이다. 항성은 '광년'으로 측정되는 거리로 떨어져 있으며, '단 1초 만에' 186,000마일(300,000km)을 가는 광속에서는 생명체에 의한 항성 간의 이동은 여전히 환상으로 남아있다는 것을 기억하라. ('대상 없는 과학'인) 우주생물학을 논외로 하면 <u>우리는 우리가 사는 행성을 다루는 선에서 그치게 될 것이다</u>.

구문 [3행~4행] However, **the more** we learn, **the more** unlikely that appears.
'…하면 할수록 더 ~하다'를 의미하는 「the 비교급 …, the 비교급 ~」 구문이 사용되었다.
[16행~18행] Setting astrobiology ("the science without a subject") aside we'll confine ourselves to *the planet* [on which we live].
'Setting ~ aside'는 '~을 고려하지 않으면'이라는 의미로 쓰인 분사구문이다. '전치사+관계대명사'형태의 on which가 이끄는 [ ]은 the planet을 수식한다.

어휘 civilization 문명 (사회) extraterrestrial 외계의; 외계인 scan 살피다, 조사하다 intercept (방송을) 수신하다; 가로채다 coherent 일관성 있는 vastness 광대함 interstellar 행성 간의 set A aside A를 한쪽으로 치워놓다[고려하지 않다] astrobiology 우주생물학 confine 국한시키다, 가두다 definite 명백한; 확고한 likelihood 가능성

4 글의 제목 ④

해설 실험 참가자들이 시간을 낭비하거나 자신을 위해 시간을 쓸 때보다 다른 사람들에게 도움을 줄 때 시간이 더 풍족하다고 느꼈다는 실험을 소개하고 있으므로 제목으로 가장 적절한 것은 ④ '시간에 쫓기는가? 당신 시간의 일부를 나눠줘라'이다.
① 다른 사람들을 도와주는 것은 왜 자신을 돕는 것보다 더 쉬운가
② 행복의 비결: 자선을 더 베풀기
③ 시간 관리: 당신의 목표를 깨닫는 능력
⑤ 도움이 필요한 다른 사람들을 돕는 진짜 방법

해석 일련의 연구에서 와튼의 Cassie Mogilner는 몇몇 피실험자들을 예를 들어 아픈 어린이에게 쪽지를 적어줌으로써, 혹은 어떤 학생의 에세이를 편집함으로써 다른 사람을 도와주도록 배정했다. 또 다른 피실험자 집단은 다른 일을 하도록 지시받았다. 한 연구에서 그들은 라틴어로 된 글에서 문자 'e'를 세면서 시간을 낭비했고, 두 번째 연구에서는 자신을 위한 일을 했으며 세 번째 연구에서는 그냥 대학 연구실을 일찍 나갔다. 각각의 실험에서 다른 사람들에게 도움을 준 사람들은 그렇지 않은 사람보다 마치 시간이 더 많은 것처럼 느꼈다. 다른 사람들에게 베푸는 것은 남는 시간을 낭비하거나 자신에게 쓰기로 선택하는 경우보다 당신이 더욱 '시간이 풍족하다'고 느끼고 시간 제약은 덜 느끼게 만들 수 있다고 연구는 보여준다. 다음에 당신이 바쁜 하루에서 휴식을 필요로 한다면, 웹서핑처럼 생각 없는 일은 하지 마라. 대신에 다른 누군가를 돕는 활동을 골라라. 동료에게 커피 한 잔을 가져다주거나 딸의 학교 에세이를 편집해줘라.

구문 [9행~11행] In each experiment *the people* [who lent a hand to others] **felt** // **as if** they **had** more time / than *the people* [who did not].
첫 번째 [ ]는 주어 the people을 수식하며 동사는 felt이다. 「as if + S' + 과거동사」

는 '마치 ~하는 것처럼'이라는 뜻의 가정법 과거이다. 두 번째 [ ]는 앞의 the people를 수식하며, did not 다음에는 lend a hand to others가 생략되어 있다.

[11행~14행] Research shows // that <u>giving to others</u> can **make** you **feel** <u>more "time affluent"</u> and <u>less time-constrained</u> / than if <u>you choose to waste your extra time or spend it on yourself.</u>

비교급 문장이며 A, B에 해당하는 이중 밑줄 친 두 부분이 비교 대상이다. 사역동사 make가 「make + O(you) + 동사원형(feel) (O가 v하게 하다)」 구문으로 쓰였다. feel 다음의 보어 more "time affluent"와 less time-constrained가 and로 연결되어 병렬구조를 이룬다.

어휘 a battery of 일련의 *cf.* battery 일련의 것; 배터리 **assign** 배정하다 **lend a hand** 도움을 주다 **affluent** 풍족[풍부]한 **constrain** 제약[제한]하다 **mindless** 아무 생각이 없는

5 도표 이해 ④

해설 오일 섭취가 부족한 사람은 72%이고 충분한 사람은 28%여서 오일 섭취가 부족한 사람들의 백분율이 충분한 사람들의 백분율보다 낮지 않다. 그러므로 ④는 도표의 내용과 일치하지 않는다.

해석 **권장 수준과 비교한 식이 섭취 (미국, 2015-2020)**
위 그래프는 2015년부터 2020년까지 다양한 식품군에서 권장되는 수준과 비교한 미국 인구의 음식물 섭취 백분율을 보여준다. ① 채소와 유제품이 권장 기준을 충족시키지 못한 사람들에서 가장 높은 비율과 두 번째로 높은 비율을 보여주었다. ② 단백질 식품은 58%로, 권장되는 섭취 수준보다 더 많이 섭취한 사람들에서 최고의 백분율을 보였다. ③ 미국 인구의 절반이 넘는 사람들이 총 곡식과 단백질 식품 권장(량)을 초과했다. ④ 오일의 경우, 권장되는 섭취 수준보다 덜 먹은 사람들의 백분율이 그렇게 하지 않았던(덜 먹지 않았던) 사람들보다 더 낮았다. ⑤ 미국 인구의 4분의 3은 과일을 권장 수준보다 덜 먹었는데, 이는 권장 수준 이상을 섭취한 사람들의 백분율보다 세 배 더 높았다.

구문 **[11행~13행]** For Oils, the percentage of *people* [who ate less than the recommended intake level] was lower than **those** [who **did not**].
첫 번째 [ ]는 바로 앞의 people을, 두 번째 [ ]는 바로 앞의 those를 각각 수식한다. those는 people을 지칭하고 who did not 다음에는 eat less than the recommended intake level이 생략되어 있다.

[13행~16행] *Three-quarters of the U.S. population* ate less Fruit than the recommended amount, // **which** was three times higher than the percentage of *people* [who consumed the recommended amount or more].
굵게 표시된 which는 계속적 용법으로 쓰인 관계대명사로 which가 이끄는 절이 Three-quarters of the U.S. population을 보충 설명한다. [ ]는 people을 수식하는 관계사절이다.

어휘 **dietary** 음식물의; 식이 요법의 **intake** 섭취(량) **exceed** 초과하다

6 내용 불일치 ④

해설 예이츠는 노벨상 수여 이후에 가장 위대한 작품을 집필했다.

해석 윌리엄 버틀러 예이츠는 아일랜드의 더블린에서 태어났다. 그의 아버지는 변호사이자 저명한 초상화 화가였다. 예이츠는 런던에서 아버지에게 교육받았는데, 그곳에서 그의 아버지는 미술을 공부하는 중이었다. 그러나 그(윌리엄 버틀러 예이츠)는 또한 자주 아일랜드로 돌아왔다. 그의 첫 번째 운문 책은 1887년에 나왔지만, 초창기에는 그의 극작품이 양적으로나 중요도로 보나 그의 시를 능가했다. 그는 'Irish Theatre'를 설립했고 극장의 주

책임 극작가로 일했다. 그의 희곡은 보통 아일랜드 전설을 다루고, 그것들은 또한 그가 신비주의와 강신론에 매혹된 점을 반영한다. 비록 투철한 애국자였지만, 예이츠는 민족주의 운동의 증오를 개탄했으며, 그의 시는 그에 반대하는 감동적인 항의로 가득하다. 예이츠는 (자신의) 가장 위대한 작품이 노벨상 수여 이후에 집필된 소수의 작가들 중 하나이다. 주로 희곡 작품들로 그 상을 받았지만, 오늘날 그의 중요성은 그의 서정시의 성취에 있다.

구문 **[11행~12행]** Although (Yeats was) a convinced patriot, Yeats deplored the hatred of the Nationalist movement ~.
접속사가 생략되지 않은 분사구문으로, 본래 접속사가 이끄는 문장의 주어와 동사(Yeats was)가 생략된 형태이다.

어휘 **volume** 책; (책의) 권; 용량; 양 **verse** 운문, 시 **dramatic** 희곡의; 극적인; 인상적인 **outweigh** 더 중요하다, 능가하다 **bulk** 양, 규모 **import** 중요성; 수입(품) **playwright** 극작가 **fascination** 매혹[매료]됨; (아주 강한) 매력 **mysticism** 신비주의 **spiritualism** 강신론, 심령론 **convinced** 투철한, 신념이 있는 **patriot** 애국자 **deplore** 개탄하다 **hatred** 증오, 혐오 **lyric** 서정시(의)

7 밑줄 어법 ④

해설 ④ 밑줄 their를 전후로, 앞부분에 완전한 절이 있고 뒤에도 trading preferences와 run을 주어, 동사로 하는 절이 전개된다. 두 절을 연결하는 역할도 해야 하므로 단순 대명사가 아닌 관계대명사로 바꿔 써야 하며, 소유격 their를 대체하므로 소유격 관계대명사 whose로 바꿔 써야 한다.
① 'played by ~ and sales'는 수동의 의미로 앞의 명사 the strong role을 수식한다. 'play a role'은 '역할을 하다'의 뜻이다.
② result in 다음에 이어지는 목적어 부분이 'being subject ~ unattractive' 부분으로서, 목적어 역할을 해야 하므로 동명사 being은 적절하다. organic produce는 being에 대한 의미상 주어이다.
③ 'likely to-v'는 'v할 것 같은, v하기 쉬운'의 뜻이다.
⑤ be동사 are의 보어 자리에 형용사 likely(가능성 있는)는 적절하다.

해석 유기농 제품을 세계 시장에 내놓는 것은 많은 영향을 미친다. 세계 시장의 특징은 운송, 출하, 유통, 마케팅 그리고 판매에서 기업이 강력한 역할을 한다는 것이다. 재래식 농산물과 동일한 시장에 진입하는 것은 유기농 농산물을 재래식 농업을 형성하고 지속 가능한 관행들을 매력이 없는 것으로 만들었던 것과 똑같은 경제적 상황에 처하게 하는 결과를 가져올 가능성이 있다. 기존 세계 시장에서 경쟁하는 유기농 생산자들은 유기 농업의 원칙을 무너뜨릴 가능성이 있는 경제적 인센티브에 직면하게 될 것이다. 잠재적으로 큰 우려가 될 수 있는 새로 떠오르는 문제는 (국가의) 무역 편애가 세계무역기구와 같은 단체에 역행하는 국가들에 제기되는 어려움이다. 세계 시장 진출은 재래식 농업에 대한 국가 보조금에 이의를 제기할 근거를 제공할 수도 있지만, 유기 농업에 대한 보복성 도전이 나타날 가능성도 있다. 추가적인 우려는 세계 시장이 불확실하고 자주 불안정하다는 것인데, 이는 농업 기업의 안정성을 감소시키는 결과를 낳고 더 큰 규모의 기업에 대한 경제적 인센티브에 추가될 수 있다.

구문 **[16행~18행]** Entry into global markets may offer *grounds* [on which to challenge national subsidies for conventional agriculture], ~
[ ]는 '전치사+관계대명사+to부정사' 구조로서 앞의 명사 grounds를 수식한다.

[20행~24행] A further concern is *that global markets are uncertain and often volatile*, **which has** the effect of reducing the security of farming enterprises and **can be added** to the economic incentives for larger-scale enterprises.
which는 앞의 밑줄 친 부분을 가리키며, which 이하가 밑줄 친 부분에 대한 보충 설명을 한다. which 다음의 동사 has와 can be added가 병렬구조를 이룬다.

어휘 **implication** 영향; 함축, 암시 **handling** 출하 **distribution** 유통 **conventional** 관습적인, 재래식의 **be subject to** ~의 영향을 받다[받기 쉽다]

sustainable 지속 가능한 existing 기존의 erode 침식하다, 무너뜨리다 emerging 최근 생겨난 run counter to ~을 위반하다[거스르다] subsidy 보조금

8 밑줄 어휘 ③

해설 뒤에 예시로 제시된 허리케인이나 경쟁사의 파산은 통제할 수 없는 외부 요인이다. 그러므로 ③ 'Controllable'을 Uncontrollable(통제 할 수 없는)로 고쳐야 한다.

해석 조직에서 경영 기법을 도입하는 것과 향상된 사업 실적을 얻는 것 사이에는 어떤 단순한 인과 관계도 없다. 이것은 단순한 인과 관계가 정말로 작용하는 것처럼 보이는 다른 활동 영역들과 ① 대조를 이룬다. 망치로 못을 치면, 못은 나무 안으로 들어간다. 개에게 음식을 보여 주면, 개는 침을 흘린다. 이런 종류의 단순한 인과 관계 논리가 조직이라는 복잡한 세상에 적용되면, 그것은 ② 오해를 일으킬 수 있는데, 거기서는 단 한 가지 결과를 단 한 가지 원인으로 추적하기 어렵다. ③ 통제할 수 있는(→ 통제할 수 없는) 외부 요인이 훌륭하게 계획된 팀을 망칠 수 있다(허리케인이 모든 재고품을 막 바다로 휩쓸어 갔다). 혹은 계획이 너무 볼품없어서 실패가 ④ 확실해 보인 팀을 구할 수도 있다(계약을 놓고 경쟁하던 회사가 막 파산했다). 조직에서는 ⑤ 다양한 원인들이 동시에 작용하고 있으며 오랜 시간에 걸쳐 서로 상호작용하고 있다.

구문 [7행~10행] This kind of simple cause-and-effect logic can be misleading / **if** applied to *the complex world of organizations*, // where **it** is difficult **to trace** single effects to single causes.
if 이하는 접속사 if가 명시된 분사구문이다. where 이하는 the complex world of organizations를 부연 설명하는 관계절이다. 이때 it은 가주어이고 to trace 이하가 진주어이다.
[13행~16행] Or they can rescue *one* [whose design was **so** bad **that** failure seemed assured] (the firm that was competing for the contract just went belly-up).
[ ]는 one을 수식하는 관계절이다. 이때 '너무 ~해서 …하다'라는 의미의 「so ~ that …」 구문이 사용되었다.

어휘 cause-and-effect relationship 인과 관계 management (사업체·조직의) 경영 contrast with ~와 (뚜렷한) 대조[차이]를 보이다 sphere 영역 causal 인과 관계의 operate 작동[가동]되다 misleading 오해를 일으키는 inventory 재고(품) assured 자신감 있는, 확실한 extended 장기간에 걸친, 광범위한

9 빈칸 추론 ①

해설 침 자절은 자신을 희생시키는 행동이기 때문에 자신의 적응도를 후대에 남길 수 없으므로 언뜻 보면 다윈의 자연선택설에 위배되는 것 같지만, 넓게 보면 자신과 가까운 친족을 도와 자신의 혈통이 후대에 전달되게 하는 행위이므로 자연선택설에 부합하는 행동이다. 이를 정리하여 빈칸을 완성하면 혈통을 친척을 통해 전달되게 한 것은 ① '이타적인 희생'이 된다.
② 과격한 복수 ③ 수동적인 방어 ④ 생존 본능 ⑤ 이기적인 동기

해석 생명의 경제는 놀라운 결과를 산출한다. 이 중에는 침 자절이 있는데, 이는 침을 쏘는 곤충이 자기 몸의 일부를 떼어서 자신의 침을 목표물의 살에 끼워 넣은 채로 두는 무시무시한 과정이다. 이 자살 행동은 찰스 다윈이 자신의 자연선택설을 만들어 낼 때 그를 괴롭혔다. 그는 자살이 후손을 통하여 후대에 적응도를 전해주는 것을 어떻게 촉진시킬 수 있는지를 숙고했다. 곤충이 자기 몸의 일부를 떼어 내는 것은 그의 이론에 반하는 강력한 증거를 제공할 수 있었다. 놀랍게도 DNA에 대한 현대의 개념은 말할 것도 없고 그레고어 멘델의 유전학을 다윈은 알지 못했지만 그는 본질적으로 올바른 답을 생각해 냈다. 당신과 가까운 친척들, 주로 둥지의 동료들의 번식을 용이하게 함으로써 당신의 혈통은 당신의

이타적인 희생으로 인해 친척들을 통해 전달될 것이다. 침 자절은 침으로 인한 고통과 해를 극대화하고 그렇게 함으로써 큰 포식자들에 맞서서 군집을 방어하는 데 도움을 준다.

구문 [2행~4행] Among these **is sting autotomy**, *the horrible process* [in which a stinging insect self-eviscerates, / **leaving** its stinger **embedded** in the target's flesh].
is가 동사이고 주어는 sting autotomy인 도치구문이다. sting autotomy와 the horrible process는 동격 관계이며 [ ]는 the horrible process를 수식한다. leaving 이하는 분사구문이며 「leave + O + p.p.」(O가 ~된 상태로 두다)」의 뜻이다.
[6행~8행] He pondered // how killing oneself could promote passing fitness / via descendants to future generations.
how ~ generations는 pondered에 대한 목적어 역할을 하는 간접의문문으로 「의문사(how) + 주어(killing oneself) + 동사(could promote)」의 어순으로 쓴다.

어휘 stinger 침 embed 끼워 넣다, 박다: 깊이 새겨 두다 flesh 살 formulate 만들어 내다 ponder 숙고하다 fitness 적응도, 적합성 via ~을 통하여 descendant 자손, 후손 genetics 유전학 much less 하물며 ~은 아니다 come up with 생각해내다 facilitate 용이[수월]하게 하다 reproduction 번식 lineage 혈통 thereby 그렇게 함으로써

10 빈칸 추론 ⑤

해설 지구 온난화 등 지구의 여러 환경적 문제는 인간들이 공짜나 다름없는 지구의 자원을 무분별하게 사용하기 때문에 발생하는데, 이는 시장 체계에서처럼 인간의 소비를 조절하는 가격 신호가 없기 때문으로, 즉 세계 경제가 ⑤ '자연에 적절한 가격을 매기지' 못하고 있기 때문이다.
① 위기로부터 회복하지
② 장기간 성장하지
③ 지속 가능 에너지를 생산하지
④ 생산량을 충분히 높이지

해석 종의 멸종, 토양 유실, 그리고 지구가 그곳에 사는 인류를 지속시키는 데 어려움을 겪고 있다는 다른 모든 신호와 마찬가지로, 지구 온난화는 세계 경제가 자연에 적절한 가격을 매기지 못함을 강조한다. 시장 체계에서 가격은 자원을 효율적으로 할당하도록 의도된다. 수요가 공급을 초과할 때, 가격은 상승하여 더 많은 생산자를 시장으로 이끌고 가격을 의식하는 소비자들을 밀어 치우면서 균형을 재빠르게 약간 조정할 것으로 기대된다. 그러나 자연 환경에 관한 한 이런 일이 발생하지 않는다. 우리는 아무리 많이 소비한다 해도 그것을 종종 '공짜로' 얻는다. 다른 공짜 물건들에도 흔한 일이지만, 우리의 소비를 조절하는 가격 신호의 결여는 우리가 가까운 장래에 자원을 고갈시킬 때까지 너무 많이 소비하는 결과를 낳을 것이다.

구문 [13행~16행] **As is the case with** other free things, / *the lack of a price signal* (to regulate our consumption) results in *us* consuming too much, // until we exhaust the resource at hand.
As is the case with은 '~에게 흔히 있는 경우지만, ~에게 흔히 있듯이'의 뜻이다. 주어는 the lack of a price signal이고 ( )는 주어를 수식한다. us는 consuming의 의미상 주어이다.

어휘 sustain 지속시키다 cf. sustainable (환경 파괴 없이) 지속 가능한 humanity 인류, 인간 underscore 강조하다; 밑줄을 긋다 allocate 할당하다, 배분하다 readjust 다시 적응하다 when it comes to ~에 관한 한 no matter how 아무리 ~하더라도 as is the case with ~에게 흔히 있는 경우지만, ~에게 흔히 있듯이 at hand 가까이에, 가까운 장래에 [선택지 어휘] bounce back (병, 곤경에서) 다시 회복되다

11 빈칸 추론 ③

해설 본문의 어부는 기름 유출 사고를 일으킨 회사가 제시한 보상금을 거부하고 사건을 법정으로 가져가기를 원했는데, 이는 경제적으로는 손해인 비합리적인 행위이지만 정의가 구현되기를 바라는 마음에서 한 행동이므로 ③ '법의 힘은 모든 사람들에게 동등하게 적용되어야 한다'는 요구라고 볼 수 있다.

① 법은 자유 시장이 잘 작동하게 해야 한다
② 모든 사람들은 공정하고 공적인 재판의 권리를 부여받는다
④ 인권은 기본적인 권리이자 자유이다
⑤ 법은 쉽게 알 수 있기도 하고 이용할 수 있는 것이어야 한다

해석 사람들이 자신이 잘 살게 되는 것보다 과도하게 특권을 누리는 권력층에게 정의의 심판이 내려지는 것에 신경을 더 많이 쓰는 때가 필연적으로 있다. 2010년 멕시코 만에서의 British Petroleum(BP) 기름 유출 이후로 BP는 총 합이 수십억 달러에 이르는 법정 밖에서의 합의로 현지 어부들에게 보상하는 일에 착수했다. 그러나 루이지애나 주의 Grand Isle의 한 새우 생산업자에게 이것은 그가 원하던 것이 아니었다. "저는 법정에서 저의 의견을 말할 기회를 원합니다."라고 그는 말했다. "그들이 돈만 내고 떠날 수 있다면, 그래요, 그들이 돈이 많으니까요, 그들은 정말로 교훈을 배우지 못하겠지요." 몰인정하게 보면 이것은 복수를 요구하는 것이다. 더 동정적으로 보면, 그것은 정의와 공정한 처벌의 원칙이 다른 어느 곳에서만큼 경제계 내에서도 유효하며, 돈만 사용해서는 상쇄될 수 없다는 것을 보여준다. 어느 방식이든, 이 어부는 경제학의 합리주의자 관점으로는 이해할 수 없는 것을 표현하고 있었다. 그것은 영국의 정치 철학자 Thomas Hobbes라면 이해했을 요구, 즉 법의 힘은 모든 사람들에게 동등하게 적용되어야 한다는 것으로, 그러나 이것은 점점 더 테크노크라시가 되어가는 지배 계층은 흔히 이해할 수 없는 요구이다.

구문 [1행~4행] There are inevitably *times* [when people care **more** about *justice* being visited upon **the overprivileged and powerful than** about becoming better off themselves].

[ ]는 times를 수식하는 관계부사절이다. [ ]절은 비교급 문장으로, about으로 시작되는 두 전치사구가 동등한 비교 대상이다. about justice being visited에서 전치사 about의 목적어는 동명사 being visited이며 justice는 동명사의 의미상 주어이다. the overprivileged and powerful은 「the + 형용사 (~한 사람들)」의 형태와 의미로 쓰였다.

[13행~16행] More sympathetically, / it shows // that principles of justice and fair punishment **are as** *valid* within the economy **as** anywhere else, / and **cannot be balanced** / using money alone.

「as 형용사 as」의 비교 구문이 쓰였으며 within the economy와 anywhere else가 비교 대상이다. that절에서 동사 are와 cannot be balanced가 병렬구조를 이룬다.

어휘 inevitably 필연적으로, 불가피하게　overprivileged 과도하게 특권을 받은　better off 잘 사는, 부유한　set about ~을 시작하다　compensate 보상하다　out-of-court 법정 밖의　settlement 합의; 해결; 정착　get off 떠나다　valid 유효한; 타당한　incomprehensible 이해할 수 없는　rationalist 합리[이성]주의자

12 빈칸 추론 ②

해설 최면에서 행복함을 느끼도록 유도되었던 참가자들은 최면에서 벗어난 후 그들이 읽은 구절에서 긍정적 유인가를 갖는 사건들에 대해 더 많은 부분을 떠올렸으므로, 정보가 접수될 때 사람들이 경험하고 있는 감정이 기억에 영향을 준다는 것을 추론할 수 있다. 그러므로 빈칸에는 ② '사람들이 우연히 경험하는 감정적 반응'이 가장 적절하다.

① 상황에 따라 변하는 감정의 전환
③ 한 문화에서 널리 통용되는 감정 표현 방식
④ 효과적인 의사소통에 방해가 되는 열정적인 반응
⑤ 사람의 감정 상태와 관계없는 예기치 못한 행동

해석 사람들이 정보를 처리하는 목적이 그들이 다루는 정보에 대해 편견을 품지 않을 때, 목표와 관련 없는 요소들이 영향을 미칠 수도 있다. 그러한 요소 중 하나는 정보가 받아들여지는 시점에 사람들이 우연히 경험하는 감정적 반응일 수 있다. Bower, Gilligan, 그리고 Monteiro에 의한 연구가 실례가 된다. 최면 상태의 참가자들은 그들을 행복하거나 슬프게 만드는 과거의 경험을 떠올린 다음 최면 상태에서 벗어나게 된 후에도 이러한 감정들을 유지하도록 지시를 받았다. 그리고 나서 그들은 본인에게 일어난 행복한 사건과 불행한 사건 둘 다를 묘사하는 두 사람에 관한 한 구절을 읽었다. 마지막으로 그들은 자신들이 읽었던 정보를 떠올렸다. 행복함을 느끼도록 유도되었던 참가자들은 슬픔을 느끼도록 유도되었던 참가자들보다 긍정적 유인가를 갖는 사건들에 대해 더 많은 부분을, 그리고 부정적 유인가를 갖는 사건들에 대해 더 적은 부분을 기억해냈다.

구문 [6행~10행] Participants under hypnosis were instructed to recall *a past experience* [that made them feel either happy or sad] and then to maintain these feelings after they were brought out of their hypnotic state.

to recall과 to maintain이 and로 병렬 연결된다. [ ] 부분은 주격 관계대명사 that 이 이끄는 관계사절로 a past experience를 수식한다.

[13행~17행] *Participants* [who had been induced to feel happy] recalled a greater proportion of positively-valenced events, and a lower proportion of negatively-valenced events, **than did *participants* [who were induced to feel sad]**.

두 개의 [ ] 부분은 각각 바로 앞의 participants를 수식한다. 굵게 표시된 than 뒤에는 주어(participants ~ feel sad)와 동사(did)가 도치되었다.

어휘 objective 목적, 목표; 객관적인　bias ~에 대해 편견을 품다, 편향되게 하다　attend to ~을 다루다[처리하다]　goal-irrelevant 목표와 무관한　illustrative 실례가 되는, 설명의　induce 유도하다, 설득하다　proportion 부분, 비율　conversion 전환, 변환　affective 감정[정서]적인　expression 표현 (방식); 표정　passionate 열정적인; 강렬한　get in the way of 방해되다[방해하다]

13 흐름 무관 문장 ③

해설 시민의식은 학교 교육뿐만 아니라 다양한 환경에서 일생에 걸쳐 복잡한 과정을 이루며 습득된다는 것이 글의 요지이다. 학교 외에 예시로 든 가족, 대중매체, 지역사회 협회 등 다양한 환경이 시민의식 가치와 정치적 역량의 발전을 위한 강력한 사회화 기관이라는 문장 다음에 학교 교육 과정에서 특정 과목인 지리와 역사가 시민의식 교육에 중요한 역할을 한다는 ③의 내용은 글의 흐름과 무관한 문장이다.

해석 시민의식 교육은 보통 교육 기관과 관련되어 있는데, 그곳에서 시민의식은 흔히 교과 내용으로 시행되지만, 때때로 범교과 교육과정의 방식으로, 교과 외 수업 혹은 대부분의 활동을 형성하는 더 넓은 기관의 프로젝트로서 시행된다. ① 학교는 시민의식 학습에 중요한 장소임에도 불구하고 시민의식 지식, 능력, 태도 및 가치의 습득(그리고 성찰)은 일생에 걸쳐 이어지는 복잡한 과정을 이루며 다양한 범위의 환경을 포함한다. ② 예를 들어 가족, 대중매체, 지역사회 협회, 직장과 사회 운동은 시민의식 가치와 정치적 역량을 발전시키기 위한 강력한 사회화 기관이다. ③ <u>그럼에도 불구하고 학교 교육 과정의 다양한 과목 영역, 특히 지리학과 역사는 시민의식 교육에서 결정적인 역할을 수행할 수 있다.</u> ④ '요람에서 무덤까지'라는 비유는 시간적인 연속을 나타낼 수 있지만, 평생의 시민의식 학습이 연속적이고, 중단이 없으며, 학습 경험의 순차적인 축적인 경우는 거의 없다. ⑤ 그것은 서로 보완하고 모순되는 학습 경험들의 산란한 복합체이며, 우리가 이전에 가정했던 것들 중 일부에 이의를 제기하고 우리의 의식에 상당한 긴장을 만든다.

구문 [1행~6행] Citizenship education is usually associated with *educational institutions*, **where** it is often implemented as a subject matter, but sometimes as cross-curricular approaches, as extracurricular programs or as *a broader* *institutional project* [that shapes most activities].

where는 계속적 용법으로 쓰인 관계부사로 where가 이끄는 절이 선행사 educational institutions를 보충 설명한다. 밑줄 친 세 개의 전명구가 병렬구조를 이루고 [ ] 부분은 관계사절로 a broader institutional project를 수식한다.

[21행~24행] It is *a messy complex of learning experiences* [that complement and contradict each other], **challenging** some of our prior assumptions **and** creating significant tensions in our consciousness.

[ ]은 선행사 a messy complex of learning experiences를 수식하는 관계사절이다. challenging ~ our consciousness는 분사구문으로 현재분사 challenging과 creating이 and로 연결되었다.

어휘 citizenship 시민의식 educational institution 교육 기관 implement 시행[실행]하다 cross-curricular 범교과의, 학교 교육과정 전반에 관련된 extracurricular 정식 교과 외의 institutional 기관의[시설]; 제도상의 acquisition 습득 reflection 성찰, 사색 constitute ~을 이루다 span ~에 걸쳐 이어지다 from cradle to grave 일생 동안, 요람에서 무덤까지 socialization 사회화 competency 역량, 능력 curriculum 교육[교과] 과정 geography 지리학 metaphor 비유, 은유 chronological 시간 순으로 일어나는, 연대순의 sequence 연속 uninterrupted 중단이 없는, 방해받지 않는 linear 순차적인, 선형의 accumulation 축적(물), 누적 messy 산란한, 어질러진; 지저분한 complement 보완하다 contradict 모순되다, 반박하다 assumption 가정; 수락 tension 긴장 consciousness 의식, 정신

14 글의 순서 ②

해설 본문은 곤충의 수면에 관한 글이다. 주어진 문장의 '곤충도 잠을 잔다'는 내용이 (A)에서 예시로 제시되고 있고, (A)에서 언급한 '눈꺼풀이 없어서 눈을 보고서는 자고 있는지를 알 수 없다.'는 내용이 (C)의 '하지만, 더듬이를 통하여 자고 있다는 것을 알 수 있다'로 이어진다. (C)에서 이를 관찰할 수 있는 병 안의 벌 실험이 소개된 후, '그 병(the jar)'을 언급하며 실험에 대한 설명이 (B)에서 이어지고 있다.

해석 곤충에게서 휴식이라기보다는 수면, 그래서 '무의식(의 상태)'(이 용어가 사용될 수 있는 때)이 확실히 발견될 수 있다.
(A) 예를 들어, 야간에 벌은 약 6시간에서 8시간가량 잠을 자는데 그때 흔히 그것은 더듬이를 '축 늘어뜨리고', 자신에게 충돌하는 다른 벌들에 대해 거의 반응을 보이지 않는다. 대부분 곤충이 시력이 아주 좋지만, 눈꺼풀이 없어서 눈을 보고서는 그것들이 자고 있는지를 분간할 수 없다.
(C) 하지만, 더듬이가 눈만큼이나, 그리고 아마도 눈보다 더 중요하기 때문에, 축 늘어진 더듬이는 그 동물이 현실과 접촉한 상태가 아니고 단지 쉬고 있는 것이 아니라는 것을 확실히 보여준다. 예를 들어 벌은 끊임없이 움직이는 병에 그것들을 가둬두어 그 곤충들이 내내 날아다녀야 하게 만듦으로써 쉽게 잠을 빼앗기게 될 수 있다.
(B) 병이 움직임을 멈출 때, 그것들은 편안히 자리를 잡고 병의 추가적인 부드러운 흔들림에 대해 보통 때보다 훨씬 덜 반응을 한다. 그것은 마치 그것들의 수면 상태가 손실에 대한 보상으로 더 깊어진 것 같다.

구문 [4행~6행] For example, at night the bee sleeps for about *6-8 hours*, [**when** it will often have 'droopy' antennae, and be fairly unresponsive to other bees bumping into it].
[ ] 부분은 관계부사 when이 이끄는 관계절이며, 선행사는 6-8 hours이다. 관계부사절 속에서 동사 have와 be가 and로 연결되어 병렬구조를 이루고 있다.
[12행~13행] It is **as if** their sleep has become deeper in compensation for its loss.
'as if'는 '마치 ~인 것처럼'의 뜻이다.

어휘 unconsciousness 무의식 term 용어 antenna 더듬이(pl. antennae) unresponsive 반응이 늦은; 무반응의 *cf.* responsive 반응하는 bump 충돌하다

---

eyelid 눈꺼풀 compensation 보상 in contact with ~와 접촉하는 deprived of ~을 빼앗긴

15 글의 순서 ④

해설 '델파이'라는 조사 기법을 소개한 주어진 글 다음에는 이 기법의 첫 단계(응답자에게 질문지를 주고 의견과 이유를 작성한 답변서를 받는 것)에 대해 논한 (C)가 나온다. 이 각각의 답변서를 취합하여 보고서를 작성한 후, 이를 응답자들에게 배부하고 그들의 원래 의견을 수정할 기회를 준다는 (A)가 이어지고 이 의견 수정에 대해 구체적으로 소개하며 이 기법이 합의에 도달하는 좋은 방법임을 마무리로 제시한 (B)가 마지막에 나오는 것이 적절하다.

해석 그리스 신화에 따르면 전쟁을 수행하는 것의 위험성을 판단하기 위해 델포이 신전에서 신탁을 구했다. 현대에 들어서 '델파이'라는 용어는 집단 공동의 판단을 개발하기 위해 여러 사람들의 의견을 합치는 집단 조사 기법을 가리킨다.
(C) 그 기법은 일련의 구조화된 질문과 피드백 보고로 구성된다. 각각의 응답자는 일련의 질문을 받는데 (예를 들면, 이 프로젝트에서 다섯 개의 가장 중요한 위험 요소는 무엇인가?) 그에 대해 응답자는 자기 의견과 이유를 쓴다.
(A) 조사를 받는 모든 사람들의 의견은 보고서로 요약되어 응답자들에게 되돌려 보내지는데, 그들은 그런 다음 자신의 의견을 수정할 기회를 가진다. 글로 쓴 응답은 익명으로 유지되기 때문에 아무도 다른 어떤 사람의 의견에 따라야 한다는 압박을 느끼지 않는다.
(B) 만일 사람들이 자신의 의견을 바꾸면 그들은 그 이유를 설명해야 하는데, 그렇지 않는다고(의견을 바꾸지 않는다고) 해도 이유를 역시 설명해야 한다. 그 과정은 집단이 공동의 의견에 도달할 때까지 계속된다. 여러 연구들은 그 기법이 의견 일치에 도달하는 효율적인 방법임을 입증했다.

구문 [6행~9행] The opinions of *everyone* **surveyed** are summarized in a report and returned to *the respondents*, **who** then have *the opportunity* (to modify their opinions).
surveyed는 앞의 everyone을 수식한다. 과거분사로 시작되는 두 밑줄 친 부분은 are에 연결되어 병렬구조를 이룬다. 계속적 용법으로 쓰인 관계대명사 who가 이끄는 절은 the respondents를 보충 설명하고 ( )은 the opportunity를 수식하는 to부정사구이다.
[18행~21행] Each respondent is given *a series of questions* (e.g., what are the five most significant risks in this project?), **to which** he writes his opinions and reasons.
to which 이하는 a series of questions를 보충 설명하는 관계사절이다.

어휘 mythology 신화 gauge 판단[평가]하다; 측정하다 wage (전쟁을) 수행하다 collective 집단의, 공동의 summarize 요약하다 respondent 응답자 modify 수정하다, 변경하다 anonymous 익명의 conform to ~에 따르다; ~을 지키다 consensus (의견의) 일치, 합의 comprise ~로 구성되다

16 문장 넣기 ④

해설 주어진 문장의 '이것이(this) 신체에 수명을 통제하는 내장 시계가 있다는 것을 의미한다'라는 내용에서 this는 ④ 앞의 '말단소체가 분열할 때마다 짧아지고 다 닳으면 세포는 분열을 멈추고 악화된다(즉 수명이 제한된다)'라는 내용을 가리킨다. However로 시작되는 ④ 뒤 문장에는 일반 통념에 반하는 과학자들의 의견이 제시되어 있으므로 일반 의견을 내용으로 한 주어진 문장은 ④에 위치해야 한다.

해석 세포가 분열하는 횟수를 조절하는 것은 무엇인가? 그 답은 우리 염색체 끝에 있는 보호용 끝부분(신발 끈의 끝에 있는 보호용 끝부분과 약간 비슷하다)인 말단소체에 있을

것이다. 이 끝부분들은 세포가 분열할 때마다 더 짧아진다. 결국 말단소체가 거의 사라졌을 때, 세포들은 분열을 멈추어서 세포가 늙고 악화되게 한다. 당신은 이것이 신체에 세포 복제를 제한하여 수명을 통제하는 내장 시계가 있다고 의미한다고 생각하고 싶어 할 수도 있다. 그러나 과학자들은 이러한 과정을 이런 식으로 보지 않고 오히려 인생 초반기에 종양의 생장을 예방하기 위해 진화를 통해 발달해왔을지 모르는 메커니즘으로 본다. 이러한 메커니즘은 인간의 기대 수명이 짧았을 때는 이로웠을 것이나, 보충될 수 없는 세포들이 시간이 경과함에 따라 노화되며 결함을 갖게 될 것이므로 기대 수명이 늘어남에 따라 큰 대가를 치르게 되었다.

구문 [1행~3행] You might be inclined to think this *means* **that** the body has *a built-in clock* [**that** controls the length of life by limiting cell reproduction].
[ ] 부분은 주격 관계대명사 that이 이끄는 관계사절로 a built-in clock을 수식한다. 동사 means의 목적어로 밑줄 친 that이 이끄는 명사절이 쓰였다.
[9행~11행] Eventually, when the telomeres have nearly disappeared, the cells stop dividing, **causing the cells to age and deteriorate**.
causing 이하는 결과를 나타내는 분사구문이다.

어휘 inclined to-v v하고 싶어 하는   built-in 내장된; 내재한   reproduction 복제; 번식; 재생, 재현   divide 분열하다, 나누다   tip 끝부분   shoestring 신발 끈   deteriorate 악화하다, 쇠약해지다   mechanism 메커니즘, 기제   life expectancy 기대 수명   costly 대가가 큰   replenish 보충하다   defective 결함[결점]이 있는

17 문장 넣기   ③

해설 주어진 문장에 however가 있고 주어진 문장의 내용이 '때로는 신기술을 상상해낼 때 과학적 이해에 변혁이 필요하다'라는 것이므로 과학적 이해에 대한 다른 관점이 설명되기 시작하는 부분을 찾는다. ③을 기점으로, 그 앞은 신기술에 과학적 이해가 꼭 필요하지 않다는 내용이고, 그 뒤에 이어지는 아인슈타인의 증명은 과학적 이해(물질과 에너지는 서로 교체될 수 있다)가 신기술(원자력 에너지)을 가능하게 하였다는 내용이므로, 주어진 문장은 ③에 위치해야 한다.

해석 과학과 기술은 긴밀히 연결되지만, 그것들은 같지 않다. 작동하는 기술을 개발하기 위하여 어떤 것에 대한 정확한 과학적 이해를 갖는 것이 필수적이지는 않다. 결과는 알지만 그 결과를 만들어내는 과정은 이해되지 않는 블랙박스처럼 사물을 취급하는 시행착오라면 여러 가지 형태의 기술을 개발하는 데 충분하다. 그러나 때때로 신기술을 상상하는 데 과학적 이해에 있어서의 변혁이 필요하다. 그러한 것이 아인슈타인이 물질과 에너지가 서로 교체될 수 있다는 것을 증명했을 때 그가 물리학에 가져온 전환이었는데, 이는 원자력 에너지에 대한 가능성을 열어주었다. 유사한 혁명이 생물학에서 발생하였는데, 생물이 DNA에 암호화되어 있는, 네 개의 동일한 구성 요소로 만들어진 유전자의 발현을 통해 성장하고 발달한다는 이해와 함께였다. 이러한 이해는 우리가 살아있는 유기체를 재편하는 방법을 상상하게 해주며 유전공학과 함께 복제와 유전체학 같은 현대 생명공학의 다른 측면들이 나타나게 해준다.

구문 [14행~18행] A similar revolution has occurred in biology, / with <u>the understanding that living organisms grow and develop through the expression of **genes**, encoded in DNA</u>, // **which** are built from the same four building blocks.
that living organisms ~ DNA는 동격절로 앞의 the understanding을 구체적으로 설명해준다. 관계대명사 which는 앞의 genes를 지칭한다.

어휘 conceive of ~을 상상하다   trial and error 시행착오   interchangeable 교체할 수 있는   encode 암호화하다   re-engineer 재설계하다   give rise to ~이 생기게 하다   genetic engineering 유전공학   biotechnology 생명공학   genomics 유전체학

18 요약문 완성   ③

해설 신입을 선발하려는 확실한 목적과 필요(need)를 가지고 상대방을 대할 때 더 주의 깊고 계획된 자세로 접근하게 되며 나중에 기억에 남는(remember) 것도 더 많다는 내용의 글이다.
① 필요 – 전달하다   ② 기회 – 기억하다
④ 기회 – 전달하다   ⑤ 능력 – 분석하다

해석 회사가 당신을 새 프로젝트의 책임자로 앉히기로 결정한다고 가정해보자. 첫째, 당신은 팀을 모을 필요가 있다. 그래서 당신은 같은 회사의 다른 부서에서 온 새로운 구성원이 될지도 모르는 Kevin과 저녁 식사를 하고자 자리를 마련한다. 이 상황에서 당신은 그가 어떤 종류의 사람인지를 정확히 알아내야 하는 것이 필수여서 그에 대한 정확한 그림을 그려보려고 최선을 다한다. 당신은 그의 진정한 성격을 이끌어내고자 특정한 질문을 하고 그가 새 프로젝트에 딱 맞는 자질을 갖추었는지 검증해본다. 이제 다른 시나리오를 상상해 보도록 잠시 시간을 내 보자. 당신이 Kevin을 우연히 마주쳤고 함께 저녁식사를 하기로 결정한다고 말해보자. 당신은 아마 그가 어떤 종류의 사람인지 혹은 그가 직원으로서 어떤 자질을 전달할 것인지를 알아내기 위해 애쓰지 않을 것이다. 대신에 당신은 가벼운 대화로 당신들의 시간을 즐기려고 단순히 노력할 것이다. 당신이 논하는 것에 관계없이, 당신은 아마 이 두 번째 즉흥적인 식사로부터 기억하는 것이 더 적을 것이다.

↓

> 다른 사람에 대한 인상을 형성하려는 (A) 필요는 당신이 그 사람에 대한 정보에 더 면밀한 주의를 기울이고 정보를 더 잘 (B) 기억하게 만들 것이다.

구문 [8행~10행] You ask specific questions to draw out his true personality and test **if** he has *the qualities* [that fit the bill for the new project].
접속사 if는 '~인지 (아닌지)'란 의미로 test의 목적어가 되는 명사절을 이끈다. [ ]는 the qualities를 수식한다.

어휘 in charge of ~을 책임지는   put together (모아서) 만들다   arrange 마련하다, 조정하다   recruit 신입 사원, 새로운 구성원   imperative 반드시 해야 하는, 필수의   fit the bill 만족시키다; 딱 필요한 것을 공급하다   run into ~을 우연히 마주치다   by accident 우연히   regardless of ~와 관계없이   impromptu 즉흥적으로 한

19~20 장문   19 ④   20 ④

해설 19. 전문가의 지식은 직업 수행에 도움이 되지만 새로운 요소와 마주쳤을 때는 눈을 가려버리는 방해 요소로 작용할 수 있다는 내용의 글이므로 제목으로 가장 적절한 것은 ④ '왜 얼어붙은 사고는 전문가에게 위험한가'이다.
① 얼어붙은 사고: 이를 어떻게 다룰 수 있을까?
② 허약한 비판적 사상가들과 관련된 위험들
③ 끊임없이 변하는 세계에서의 유연한 사고
⑤ 의학에서 전문가 기술의 가치
20. 노련한 의사들은 처음 분석과 '일치하지 않는' 문제의 새로운 측면이 튀어나올 때 이를 놓치기 쉽다는 내용이 되어야 하므로 ④ consistent는 inconsistent로 바꾸어야 적절하다.
① 전문가의 지식은 늘 하던 대로 하는 관습적(conventional) 지혜에 함몰될 때 독이 될 수 있다.
② 얼어붙은 사고는 과학자들의 경력에 재앙이 되었으며 많은 기업의 건강을 망쳤다(ruined).
③ 사람들은 보통 노련한 의사에게 치료받기를 원하지만, 연구 결과에 따르면 일부 경우에는 상대적으로 초보자(novices)에게 치료받는 것이 더 결과가 좋았다.
⑤ 경험이 덜한 수련의들은 새롭고 특이한 케이스, 더 미세하고 더 감지하기 힘든

(subtler) 증상도 열린 눈으로 볼 수 있다.

해석 당신이 전문가일 때, 당신의 심층 지식은 확실히 당신의 직업에서 일상적인 도전에 직면할 때 대단히 중요하지만, 저 거대한 (a) 관습적 지혜 속에 함몰되면 이는 새로운 아이디어들을 만들거나 받아들이는 것을 지연시킬 수 있고, 새로움과 변화에 맞닥뜨릴 때 당신에게 방해가 될 수 있다. 그러한 얼어붙은 사고는 과학자들의 경력에 재앙이 되었으며 많은 기업의 건강을 (b) 망쳤다. 예를 들어 당신이 병원에 도착하면, 직원 중에서 가장 노련한 의사에게 치료받고 싶은 게 당연하다. 그러나 2014년의 연구에 따르면, 상대적으로 (c) 초보자에게 치료받으면 더 나을 것이다. 그 연구는 명망 있는 미국의학협회 학술지(JAMA)에 실렸다. 그것은 수 만 건의 병원 입원을 포함한 10년의 자료를 조사했고 고위험급성 치료 환자 중 30일 동안의 사망률이 최고의 의사들이 시외로 나갔을 때(예를 들어 그들이 학회로 출타 중이었을 때) 3분의 1 더 낮아진다는 것을 발견했다. JAMA 연구는 감소된 사망률의 이유를 정확히 집어내지는 않았지만, 저자들은 의사들이 한 대부분의 실수가 이전 경험에 근거를 두어 의견을 빠르게 형성하려는 경향과 연관된다고 설명했다. 일상이 아닌 경우에는 그것에 오해의 소지가 있는데, 왜냐하면 전문가 의사들이 그들의 처음의 분석과 (d) 일치하는(→ 일치하지 않는) 문제의 중요한 측면들을 놓칠 수 있기 때문이다. 결과적으로 비록 수련들이 더 느리고 지극히 평범한 케이스를 다루는 데에 자신감이 덜할 수 있어도, 그들은 특이한 케이스를 처리하거나 (e) 더 감지하기 힘든 증상을 가진 환자들을 치료할 때 더욱 열린 마음으로 임할 수 있다. 노련한 골프 선수가 자신의 운동 피질에 암호화되어 있는 많이 연습한 타격법을 바꾸는 데 어려움을 겪을 수 있는 것과 꼭 마찬가지로, 전문적 사상가는 자신의 전두엽 피질에 박혀 있는 낡은 사고방식에서 벗어나는 데 어려움을 느낀다.

구문 [1행~3행] When you are an expert, your deep knowledge is obviously **of great value** in facing the usual challenges of your profession, ~.

「of+명사」는 형용사와 같은 기능을 수행하여 of great value를 very valuable로 바꿔볼 수 있다.

[25행~28행] In *cases* [that are not routine], that can be misleading, because the expert doctors may miss *important aspects of the problem* [that are inconsistent with their initial analysis].

두 개의 [ ]은 모두 관계사절로 선행사 cases와 important aspects of the problem을 각각 수식한다.

[32행~37행] **Just as** an experienced golfer can have difficulty altering *the much-rehearsed stroke* [that is encoded in his motor cortex], **so** too may a professional thinker **have** difficulty shedding *the old ways of thinking* (lodged in her prefrontal cortex).

「Just as ..., so ~ (…한 것과 꼭 마찬가지로 ~하다)」 구문이 사용되었고, so 뒤에 조동사(may)와 주어(a professional thinker)가 도치된 형태이다. [ ]은 선행사 the much-rehearsed stroke를 수식하는 관계사절이고, 과거분사 lodged가 이끄는 ( )은 the old ways of thinking을 수식한다.

어휘 immersion 몰두, 몰입 conventional 관습적인, 전통적인 impede 지연시키다, 방해하다 hamper 방해하다 be confronted with ~에 직면하다 novelty 새로움 plague 괴롭히다 physician 의사 novice 초보자 prestigious 명망 있는 admission 입원; 입장 mortality rate 사망률 acute 급성의 pinpoint 정확히 집어내다 misleading 호도하는, 오해의 소지가 있는 junior doctor 수련의 run-of-the-mill 지극히 평범한 subtle 미묘한, 감지하기 힘든 stroke 타격(법), 치기 encode 암호화하다 shed 떨구다, 벗다 lodge ~에 박대[꽂다] flexible 유연한

| 1 ④ | 2 ② | 3 ③ | 4 ④ | 5 ③ | 6 ④ | 7 ④ | 8 ⑤ | 9 ① | 10 ④ |
| 11 ③ | 12 ② | 13 ④ | 14 ② | 15 ④ | 16 ③ | 17 ④ | 18 ⑤ | 19 ② | 20 ④ |

1 심경 변화 ④

해설 앞부분에서 'I'는 생명이 없는 모래 언덕의 단조로운 풍경을 보면서 라디오에서 느린 옛날 노래를 듣다가 마침내 졸음이 와서 여러 차례 하품을 하고 있으므로 이때 심경은 'bored'이다. 산의 동쪽 비탈을 향하면서 산들바람에 향기가 실려 오고 어린 시절의 고향을 떠올리며 집에 있는 것 같다고 했으므로 'I'의 심경의 변화는 ④ '지루해하는 → 기쁜[만족스러운]'임을 알 수 있다.

① 실망한 → 만족한 ② 놀란 → 편안한
③ 후회하는 → 궁금한 ⑤ 우울한 → 공감하는

해석 나는 고지대 사막을 가로질러 부모님 댁으로 차를 몰기 시작했다. 차창 밖으로 내다보이는 풍경은 끝없이 펼쳐진 사람이 살지 않는 모래 언덕인, 똑같은 모양의 생명이 없는 풍경이었다. 풍경의 단조로움은 가끔 신기루에 의해 깨진다. 라디오를 켰지만 느린 옛날 노래가 흘러나왔다. 나는 졸음이 와서 여러 차례 하품을 했다. 라디오를 껐다. 그러나 Timpanogos산의 동쪽 비탈을 향해 차를 몰자 풍경이 극적으로 바뀌었다. 이끼와 매발톱꽃의 향기를 머금은 부드러운 산들바람이 바위투성이의 산기슭을 휩쓸었다. 희미한 향기를 맡는 것이 갑자기 내 기분을 바꾸어 놓았다. 이 향기는 의식적인 기억에서 사라진 지 오래된 소년 시절의 친구들과 행동들에 대한 수많은 기억을 불러일으켰다. 그 연상이 너무 강해서 나는 즉시 내 고향의 몇몇 장면을 떠올렸다. 그 부드러운 공기와 아늑한 햇살과 선명한 이슬을 머금은 꽃과 아버지와 함께한 행복한 낚시 여행을! 나는 마치 집에 있는 것 같았다.

구문 [2행~4행] The view out of the car window was the same lifeless landscape, an endless reach of uninhabited sand dunes.

두 개의 밑줄 친 부분은 콤마(,)가 나타내는 동격 관계이다.

[14행~18행] The association was **so** *strong* **that** I immediately recalled some scenes of my hometown — its gentle airs, its balmy sunshine, its bright and dewy flowers and happy fishing expeditions with my father!

'너무 ~해서 …하다'의 뜻인 「so ~ that ...」 구문이 사용되었다.

어휘 uninhabited 사람이 살지 않는 monotony 단조로움, 지루함 mirage 신기루; 망상 drowsy 졸리는; 활기 없는 breeze 산들바람, 미풍 bear 지니다; 가지고 오다 fragrance 향기 moss 이끼 columbine 매발톱꽃; 비둘기의 base 기슭; 토대 subtle 희미한; 미묘한 scent 향기 alter 바꾸다, 변하다 odor 향기, 냄새 evoke 불러일으키다, 일깨우다 deed 행동; 업적 vanish 사라지다 association 연상, 연관(성); 협회 balmy 아늑한; 온화한; 향기로운 dewy 이슬에 젖은, 이슬 맺힌 expedition 여행; 원정(대), 탐험(대)

2 밑줄 함의 ②

해설 비상 차선에서의 삶을 사는 사람들은 모든 것을 비상사태처럼 중대하게 여기기 때문에 항상 허둥지둥하고 전전긍긍한다는 내용이므로 밑줄 친 부분은 ② '일을 너무 심각하게 생각하다'의 의미임을 알 수 있다.
① 모두를 영원히 떠나다
③ 과거 결정을 후회하다
④ 생각없이 다른 사람들을 따르다
⑤ 의미있는 모든 것들을 놓치다

해석 인생은 삶의 여정으로 택할 수 있는 수많은 길이 있다는 점에서 고속도로와 좀 비슷하다. 대부분의 경우, 우리는 우리가 어느 길에 있는 지를 알지 못한 채 그저 계속 간다. 그러나 피하기 위해 의식적인 노력을 할 필요가 있는 차선이 있다. 당신이 비상 차선에서의 삶을 산다면, 이는 당신에게 많은 절망을 가져올 것이다. 비상 차선에 있는 사람은 언제나 서두르며 어딘가 다른 곳에 이르기를 항상 간절히 바란다. 모든 의사 결정이 중요해 보이고, 모든 실수가 잠재적 재앙인 것처럼 보인다. 모든 일이 마치 뉴스 1면에 나오는 일인 것 같다. 그렇게 많은 시간 동안 그토록 속상해한다는 것이 얼마나 어리석고 무의미한지를 잠시 생각해 보라. 내가 생각하기에 이것에서 벗어나는 최선의 방법은 나쁜 일은 일어나기 마련이라는 사실을 인식하는 것이다. 우리는 운전 중일 때 끼어들기를 당할 것이고, 물건을 잃어버리고 실수를 저지를 것이며, 우리의 계획은 엉망진창이 될 것이다. 그러나 그것이 인생이다. 인생이 언제나 잘되지는 않을 거라는 사실을 받아들이는 것은 중요하다.

구문 [11행~12행] **Consider** for a moment just how silly and pointless it is / to be so upset / so much of the time.
동사 consider의 목적어로 의문사절 「how + 형용사 + S + V」가 쓰인 명령문이다.
[12행~14행] I think // (that) the best way out of this / is **to appreciate** the fact that bad things happen.
동사 think 뒤에는 목적어절을 이끄는 접속사 that이 생략되었다. that절에서 주어는 the best way out of this이고 동사는 is이다. to appreciate 이하는 문장의 보어로 쓰인 명사적 용법의 to-v이다. the fact와 that ~ happen은 동격 관계이다.

어휘 lane 차선; 좁은 길 **conscious** 의식적인 **emergency** 비상(상황) frustration 절망, 좌절 **anxious** 열망하는, 간절히 바라는; 불안해하는 **critical** 매우 중요한; 비판적인 **potential** 잠재적인, 가능성이 있는; 잠재력, 가능성 **pointless** 무의미한 **appreciate** (제대로) 인식하다; 감상하다; 감사하다 **cut off in traffic** ~의 길을 막다, 끼어들기하다 **mess up** ~을 엉망으로 만들다

3 글의 요지 ③

해설 오늘날 민주주의 국가에서는, 정당들이 선거에서 이기기 위해 자신들의 지지자들뿐만 아니라 부동층과 상대 정당 지지자까지 붙잡아야 하다 보니 정책적 대안의 차이가 없게 되고, 같은 전문가들이 내놓는 유사한 경제 분석도 차이가 없는 정책의 원인이 된다는 내용이다. 그러므로 글의 요지로는 ③이 적절하다.

해석 대안에 의한 변화는 어느 민주주의 국가에서든 효과가 있는 방법으로 여겨진다. 야당은 여당에 정책 대안을 제안하고, 유권자들이 그 대안을 선호하면 그들은 다음 선거 기회에서는 야당에 투표한다. 그러나 다양한 이유로, 그것이 완전히 그런 방식으로 작용하지는 않는다. 어느 야당이나 다시 정권을 잡으려면 자기들의 지지자를 안고 있어야 할 뿐만 아니라 부동층 유권자나 다른 당에 투표하는 사람들의 일부도 붙잡아야 한다는 것을 알고 있다. 그래서 대안은 점점 더 차이가 없게 되고 결국 아무런 진정한 대안도 제시되지 않는다. 더군다나 복잡한 세계에서는 같은 전문가들이 경제 분석을 하고 그래서 제안된 정책들이 결국 아주 비슷하게 된다. 오늘날 대부분의 민주주의 국가에서 야당에 의해 제시되는 정책에서 진짜 차이점을 찾기는 매우 어렵다. 이전 정부가 추진하던 정책을 취

소할 가능성이 더욱 적어지면서 유사성은 아마 더 커질 것이다. 정당들이 역사적 계급 기반을 가진 영국과 같은 나라들에서만 정책의 차이가 존재할 수 있다.

구문 [7행~10행] Any party in opposition knows // **that** *to get back into power* it must **not only** hold its own supporters / **but also** capture some of the floating voters or other party voters.
that이 이끄는 명사절은 knows의 목적어 역할을 하고 접속사 that과 명사절 내 주어 it 사이에 부사적 용법의 to부정사구가 쓰였다. 상관접속사 「not only A but also B」는 must에 이어져 hold와 capture를 병렬 연결한다.
[14행~17행] In most democratic countries today / it is quite hard **to see** the real differences in *the policies* (offered by the opposing parties).
밑줄 친 it은 가주어이고, 명사적 용법의 to see 이하가 진주어이다. ( )는 과거분사구로 the policies를 수식한다.
[19행~21행] **It is** only in *countries like the UK* [where the parties have a historical class base] **that** differences of policy can exist.
「It is ~ that ...」 강조구문이 쓰여 밑줄 친 전명구를 강조한다. 관계부사 where가 이끄는 [ ]는 countries like the UK를 수식한다.

어휘 alternative 대안(의); 대체 가능한 opposition party 야당 put forward 제안하다[내다]; 앞당기다 governing party 여당 electoral 선거의 capture 붙잡다; 포착하다 floating voter 부동층 유권자 undo 취소하다, 무효로 만들다; 풀다, 열다 be set in motion 추진하다; 시행되다

4 글의 주제 ④

해설 이 글은 수자원 절약에 대한 것으로서 수자원 절약을 논할 때 사람들은 통상적으로 가정에서 쓰는 수자원에 대해 생각하는 경향이 있으나 의외로 소고기 생산에 막대한 양의 물이 사용된다는 내용의 글이므로 주제로 가장 적절한 것은 ④ '소고기 생산의 물 집약적 속성'이다.
① 소에게 풀을 먹이로 주는 것에 있어서의 문제
② 소를 위해 깨끗한 물을 사용할 필요성
③ 곡물로 소를 기르는 것의 몇 가지 장점
⑤ 최소한의 자원을 사용한 육류 생산 방법

해석 대부분의 사람들이 수자원의 주요 소비자들에 대해 생각할 때, 그들은 샤워와 잔디밭 스프링클러처럼 자기들이 볼 수 있는 것들에 집중하는 경향이 있다. 그러나 소고기에는 특별히 그리고 용인할 수 없을 정도로 물이 많이 사용된다는 것을 우리가 최근에 인식하게 되었는데, 소를 기르는 데 필요한 풀과 곡물을 설명할 때 특히 그렇다. 가정용수 사용은 빙산의 일각에 불과하며, 소고기를 위해 소비되는 물의 대부분은 가려져서 쉽게 보이지 않는다. 그러한 이유 때문에 엄격한 채식주의자와 환경 단체들에 대한 옹호 자료가 소고기를 반대하는 기소 목록에 물 사용을 맨 위에 둔다. 가장 흔히 인용되는 (또한 주류 언론에서 자주 사용되는) 수치는 소고기 1파운드를 생산하는 데 2,500갤런의 물이 필요하다는 (1kg당 약 20,820리터와 동일한) 것이다.

구문 [5행~7행] ~, especially **when accounting for** *the grass and grain* (required to raise cattle).
when accounting for는 when we account for로 바꿀 수 있다. ( )는 수동의 의미로 앞의 the grass and grain를 수식한다.
[12행~15행] *The figure* (most commonly cited (also often used in the mainstream press)) / is that **it takes** *2,500 gallons of water* / **to produce** a single pound of beef ~
( )는 과거분사 cited(그리고 used)가 수동의 의미로 The figure를 수식하고 있다. 보어로 쓰인 that절에서 「it takes A to-v(v하는 데 A가 들다)」 구문이 사용되었다.

어휘 unacceptably 받아들이기 어려울 정도로 　 -intensive ~이 많이 사용되는 account for 설명하다 　 grain 곡물 　 cattle 소 　 the tip of the iceberg 빙산의 일각 　 plain 분명한; 소박한; 쉬운; 못생긴 　 advocacy 지지, 옹호 　 vegan 엄격한 채식주의자 　 usage 용법, 사용 　 cite 인용하다 　 mainstream 주류, 대세

5 글의 제목　③

해설 거울 뉴런은 다른 사람들의 행동을 관찰하기만 해도 마치 자신이 그 행동을 하는 것처럼 두뇌의 동일한 운동 영역에서 활성화되며, Rizzolatti에 따르면 다른 사람들을 이해하는 것은 개념적 추론보다는 거울 뉴런을 통한 시뮬레이션에 가깝다고 했으므로 제목으로 가장 적절한 것은 ③ '거울 뉴런: 우리의 타고난 독심술사'이다.
① 무엇이 거울 뉴런을 촉발시키는가?
② 거울 뉴런의 장단점
④ 다른 사람들을 모방하는 것은 사회생활에 왜 중요한가?
⑤ 우리는 거울 뉴런 없이는 다른 사람들을 관찰할 수 없다

해석 파르마 대학의 Giacomo Rizzolatti는 원숭이 뇌에서 움직임의 계획을 맡은 영역에서 거울 뉴런을 발견했다. 이 신경 세포는 원숭이가 (땅콩을 집는 것과 같은) 행동을 수행할 때와 다른 누군가가 같은 행동을 하는 것을 볼 때 모두 점화된다. 오래지 않아 비슷한 체계들이 인간의 뇌에서도 발견되었다. 놀라운 결론은 우리가 누군가가 무슨 일을 하는 것을 볼 때, 마치 우리 자신이 그 일을 하고 있는 것처럼 우리 뇌의 동일한 영역이 활성화된다는 것일 수 있다. 우리는 다른 사람들이 하고 있는 일을 우리 자신의 뇌에 있는 동일한 운동 영역 내부에서 시뮬레이션 해봄으로써 그들이 의도하고 느끼는 바를 알 수도 있다. Rizzolatti가 말하듯 "우리가 다른 사람들의 정신을 직접 이해하게 해주는 근본적인 메커니즘은 개념적 추론이 아니라 거울 메커니즘을 통해 관찰된 사건을 직접 시뮬레이션 하는 것이다."

구문 [3행~6행] These nerve cells fire **both** when a monkey performs an action (like picking up a peanut) **and** when the monkey **sees** *someone else* **do** the same thing.
「both A and B」는 'A와 B 둘 다'의 뜻이다. A, B 자리 모두 when절이 왔다. 두 번째 when절에서 지각동사 see가 「see+O+동사원형」 구문으로 쓰여 'O가 v하는 것을 보다'를 의미한다.
[13행~17행] As Rizzolatti puts it, // *The fundamental mechanism* [that **allows** us a direct grasp of the mind of others] is **not** conceptual reasoning **but** direct simulation of the observed events / through the mirror mechanism."
[ ]는 주어 The fundamental mechanism을 수식하며 동사는 is이다. [ ]에서 「allow+IO+DO (…에게 ~을 허락해주다)」 구문이 쓰였다. is 이하에서는 「not A but B (A가 아니라 B)」 구문이 쓰였다.

어휘 neuron 뉴런, 신경 세포 (= nerve cell) 　 fire 점화되다; 사격하다; 해고하다 　 before long 오래지 않아 　 activate 활성화시키다 　 simulate 시뮬레이션 하다, 모의 실험하다 　 motor 운동의, 운동 신경의 　 grasp 이해, 파악 　 conceptual 개념의 　 reasoning 추론 　 trigger 촉발시키다

6 안내문 일치　④

해설 ① 이틀간 한 시간 반씩 진행된다.
② 행사 옷차림은 정장이다.
③ 홀 내부에서 다과가 제공된다.
⑤ 어머니와 아들은 이번 행사에 참가할 수 없다.

해석 부녀 댄스와 함께 하는 밸런타인데이

날짜: 2월 8일 금요일과 2월 9일 토요일 오후 6:30–8:00
당신의 딸을 '아빠와 딸 댄스'에 데려가서 밸런타인데이를 기념하세요. Floral Hall에서 시에서 주관하는 행사입니다.
정장이 요구됩니다.
가벼운 다과가 댄스홀에서 제공될 것이며 모든 참가자들의 사진을 찍을 것입니다.
비용은 아버지/딸 두 사람당 29달러이고, 딸이 한 명씩 추가될 때마다 6달러가 더해집니다.
모든 참가자들은 저희 웹사이트를 통해 사전에 등록하고 지불해야 함을 주목하세요.
엄마들과 아들들에게는 유감이지만 이 행사는 아버지와 딸만 됩니다. 하지만 핼러윈 시즌쯤 시의 어머니와 아들 댄스에 계속해서 주목해 주세요.

구문 [9행~10행] Light refreshments will be served at the dance hall [and] all participants will **have** *their photo* **taken**.
밑줄 친 부분은 「사역동사 have+O+p.p.」의 구조로 목적어인 their photo가 찍히는 수동 관계이므로 p.p.가 쓰였다.

어휘 arrange 정하다; 미리 준비하다 　 refreshment 다과, 간식 　 duo 2인조 　 attendee 참가자, 출석자 　 stay tuned 계속해서 주목하다

7 밑줄 어법　④

해설 ④ 주절(few parents ~ their children's eating habits)에 동사가 없으므로 밑줄 친 부분은 동사 자리이다. 따라서 using을 use로 고치는 것이 적절하다.
① 동사 is의 주격 보어로 나온 to부정사는 명사적 용법으로 쓰여 어법상 적절하다.
② 'how some people grow to like black coffee'는 방법을 나타내는 관계부사절로 문장의 보어 역할을 한다. 관계부사 how는 선행사 the way와 함께 쓰이지 못한다.
③ '증대된 선호'라는 수동의 의미이므로 과거분사 increased가 preference를 수식한다.
⑤ 'in that ~'은 '~라는 점에서'라는 의미의 접속사이다.

해석 (음식) 훈련 과정이 때때로 음식을 싫게 만들 수 있는 것과 꼭 마찬가지로, 그러한 과정은 또한 음식에 더욱 식욕이 당기게 만들 수도 있다. 예를 들어 싫어하는 음식에 대한 선호를 증대시키는 강력한 방법은 그 음식을 우리가 강력하게 선호하는 어떤 식품이나 감미료와 섞는 것이다. 이것이 일부 사람들이 블랙커피를 좋아하게 된 방식일지도 모른다. 그들은 처음에 그것을 크림과 설탕을 넣어 마신 후 커피 그 자체의 맛이 즐길 만하게 되어감에 따라 추가적인 재료를 점차 제거한다. 마찬가지로, 한 연구에서 대학생들은 브로콜리나 콜리플라워를 설탕을 곁들여 몇 번 먹어본 후 그것에 대한 선호를 더욱 증가시켰다. 불행히도 자녀의 식습관을 향상시키기 위해 그러한 방법을 사용하는 부모는 거의 없는데, 이는 아마 그들이 설탕은 건강하지 않다고 인식하고 나중에 설탕을 빼낼 수 있음을 깨닫지 못하기 때문일 것이다. 대신에 부모들은 종종 디저트를 보상으로 제공하여 자녀가 싫어하는 음식을 먹도록 유도하려 애쓴다. 이는 싫은 음식과 차후의 디저트 사이의 대조가 전자(싫은 음식)가 훨씬 더 싫어지게 되는 결과를 낳을 수도 있다는 점에서 쉽게 역효과를 일으키는 전략이다.

구문 [3행~5행] For example, *a powerful way* (to increase our preference for a disliked food) is to mix it with *some food item or sweetener* [**that** we strongly prefer].
( ) 부분은 형용사적 용법의 to부정사구로 a powerful way를 수식한다. 목적격 관계대명사 that이 이끄는 [ ] 부분은 some food item or sweetener를 수식한다.
[16행~21행] Instead, parents often try to entice their children to eat a disliked food by offering dessert as a reward — *a strategy* [**that** easily backfires **in that** the contrast (**between** the disliked food **and** the subsequent dessert) might result in the former becoming even more disliked].
[ ] 부분은 a strategy를 수식하는 관계절이다. in that은 '~라는 점에서'라는 의미의 부사절을 이끄는 접속사이고, 부사절 내에서 'between A and B'는 밑줄 친 두

개의 명사를 병렬 연결한다.

어휘 condition 훈련시키다, 길들이다; 상태   appetitive 식욕을 증진시키는; 욕구의   eliminate 제거하다, 없애다   ingredient 재료   cauliflower 콜리플라워, 꽃양배추   withdraw 빼내다; 회수하다   entice 유도[유인]하다; 유혹하다   backfire 역효과를 일으키다   contrast 차이, 대조   subsequent 차후의, 그 이후의

---

8 밑줄 어휘   ⑤

해설 구전 문화의 구성원들은 놀라운 기억의 재주를 보여주었다는 내용 다음에는 〈일리아드〉가 구전으로 전승되었음에도 불구하고 충실하게 '파괴된' 것이 아니라 충실하게 '보존되었다'고 표현해야 문맥상 자연스럽다. 따라서 ⑤의 destroyed를 preserved 등으로 바꿔 써야 한다.

해석 구전 문화에서 지식은 집단의 집합적 기억에 국한된다. 이것은 알 수 있는 양을 심각하게 제한하고 그러한 지식을 매우 ① 취약하게 만든다. 부족의 지혜가 기억되지 않으면 다음 세대에 전해질 수 없으며 영구적으로 상실될 것이다. 이 점을 고려해볼 때, 구전 사회는 그들의 지식을 각운, 속담, 상투적 문구와 같은 정형화된 패턴으로 ② 표현하는 경향이 있는데, 이것들은 암기하기 쉽다. 그것은 또한 인지적으로 ③ 보수적인 경향이 있다. 어떠한 실험이나 확립된 사고방식에서의 일탈도 수 세대에 걸쳐 축적돼온 지혜를 위험에 빠뜨리기 때문이다. 긍정적인 측면에서 보면, 구전 문화의 구성원들은 때때로 놀라운 기억의 재주를 ④ 부릴 수 있다. 몇몇 학자들은 호머의 〈일리아드〉가 원래는 구전 텍스트로서, 한 이야기꾼으로부터 다음 이야기꾼으로 구전으로 전해지고 있었음에도 불구하고 놀랍도록 충실하게 ⑤ 파괴(→ 보존)되었다고 추측한다. 실제로, 이야기 그 자체는 처음으로 기록되기 수 세기 전에 구성되었을 것이다.

구문 [15행~19행] Some scholars speculate // that Homer's *Iliad* was originally *an oral text* [**which**, / despite being passed on by word of mouth from one storyteller to the next, / **was preserved** with remarkable fidelity].
[ ]는 an oral text를 수식한다. [ ] 절에서 despite로 시작되는 전치사구가 삽입되어 있는데, despite는 전치사이므로 뒤에 동명사(being passed on)가 목적어로 나왔다. 주격 관계대명사 which와 상응하는 동사는 was preserved이다.
[19행~21행] Indeed, the story itself **may have been composed** centuries // before it was first written down.
「may have been p.p.」는 과거 일에 대한 추측을 나타내는 수동 표현으로 '~되었을지도 모른다, ~되었을 것이다'의 뜻이다.

어휘 oral 구전의   fragile 약한   tribe 부족   be committed to memory ~을 기억하다, 마음에 새기다   given ~을 고려할 때   encode 표현하다, 글을 쓰다; 부호화하다   formulaic 정형화된   rhyme 운, 압운, 각운   cognitively 인지적으로   conservative 보수적인   experimentation 실험   divergence 일탈; 차이; 발산   put A at risk A를 위험에 처하게 하다   accumulate 축적하다, 쌓다   on the plus side 긍정적으로, 호의적인 관점에서 보면   feat 위업, 재주, 솜씨   speculate 추측하다   remarkable 놀라운, 주목할 만한

---

9 빈칸 추론   ①

해설 혁신가들에게 중요한 특성을 찾아야 한다. 이어지는 내용을 간추려보면, 그들은 주위 사람들의 동의를 구하지 않으며, 친화적이라면 그 아이디어로 어떤 것도 할 수 없다고 했으므로, ① '친화적이지 않아야'가 빈칸에 들어갈 말로 적절하다.
② 배려해야 ③ 설득력 있어야 ④ 호기심이 많아야 ⑤ 이기심이 없어야

해석 혁신가들은 친화적이지 않아야 하는 것이 매우 중요하다. 이는 쉬운 일이 아니다. 인간으로서 우리는 주위 사람들의 동의를 추구하도록 되어있다. 그러나 급진적이면서 변화시키는 힘이 있는 생각은 관습에 기꺼이 저항하려는 마음이 없다면 아무런 성과도 낳지 못할 것이다. Peterson은 이렇게 말한다. "만약 당신이 새로운 아이디어가 있는데, 그것이 파괴적인데. 당신이 친화적이라면 그 아이디어로 무엇을 하겠습니까? 사람들의 감정을 상하게 하고 사회구조를 뒤엎는 것을 걱정한다면 당신의 아이디어를 내놓지 못할 것입니다." 극작가인 George Bernard Shaw가 언젠가 말했듯이, "합리적인 사람은 자신을 세상에 맞춘다. 비합리적인 사람은 집요하게 세상을 자신에게 맞추려고 노력한다. 따라서 모든 진보는 비합리적인 사람에게 달려 있다."

어휘 innovator 개혁자, 혁신자   program 계획하다, 프로그램을 짜다   radical 급진적인, 과격한   transformative 변화시키는 힘이 있는   go nowhere 아무 성과를 못보다   convention 관습; (대규모) 대회; (국가 간의) 협약   persist ~을 집요하게 계속하다

---

10 빈칸 추론   ④

해설 사람들은 근래에 소셜 미디어상에서 끊임없이 관심을 갈구하고 있는데, 이러한 관심은 현실 세계에서 물리적으로 기술을 갈고 닦아야 겨우 힘들게 얻을 수 있는 인정에 비하면 제대로 된 대체물이 되어주지 못하므로, 진정한 자아 존중감의 달성은 비록 어렵고 힘들지라도 '기술(craft)'을 통해서만 가능하다는 내용의 글이다. 이를 반영하면 자아 존중감의 진정한 발산 수단이 되는 것은 ④ '명료한 기술 실연'이라고 정리할 수 있다.
① 수작업과 관련된 반복적 과정
② 다른 사람들로부터 얻는 존경과 인정
③ 누적되는 문화적 성취
⑤ 그들의 능력의 향상에 대한 인식

해석 철학자 정비공인 Matthew Crawford는 스크린이 기술을 대체하는 문화에서 사람들은 명료한 기술 실연을 통해 확립되는 자아 존중감의 발산 수단을 상실한다고 주장한다. 최근 몇 년간의 소셜 미디어 플랫폼의 폭발적인 인기를 이해하는 한 가지 방법은 그것이 지위 확대의 대체 원천을 제공해준다는 것이다. 손으로 가리킬 잘 만들어진 나무 벤치나 음악 공연에서의 갈채가 없을 때에 당신은 대신 '좋아요'를 바라면서 멋진 레스토랑에 최근에 방문한 사진을 올리거나, 기발하고 재치 있는 말로 된 리트윗을 필사적으로 확인할 수 있다. 그러나 Crawford가 넌지시 말하듯이, 이러한 관심을 갈구하는 디지털의 외침은 많은 경우 손끝의 숙련으로 생성되는 인정에 대한 형편없는 대체재인데, 그것이 물리적 실제의 '틀림없는 판단'을 다스리기 위해 요구되는 힘들게 획득한 기술에 의해 뒷받침되지 않으며, 대신 '소년의 자랑'이라는 인상을 주기 때문이다. 기술은 이러한 천박함으로부터 벗어나게 해주고 대신 더 깊은 자부심의 원천을 제공한다.

구문 [4행~7행] *One way* (to understand the exploding popularity of social media platforms in recent years) **is** // that they offer a substitute source of aggrandizement.
주어는 One way이고 동사는 is이며 ( )는 to-v의 형용사적 용법으로서 One way를 수식한다. that 이하는 문장의 보어 역할을 하는 명사절이다.
[9행~12행] ~, / you can instead **post** a photo of your latest visit to a hip restaurant, **hoping for likes**, / or desperately check for retweets of a clever quip.
can 다음의 동사원형 post와 check가 or로 연결되어 병렬구조를 이룬다. hoping for likes는 분사구문으로 문장 사이에 삽입되었다.

어휘 craft 기술, 기교; 공예   mechanic 정비공   outlet 발산[배출] 수단   self-worth 자아 존중감, 자부심   substitute 대체물; 대체하다   in the absence of ~이 없을 때에   applause 박수 (갈채)   hip 멋진; 유행에 밝은   imply 넌지시 밝히다. 암시하다   handicraft 손끝의 숙련; 수공예   tame 다스리다, 길들이다   infallible 틀림없는   come across as ~라는 인상을 주다   boast 자랑, 뽐냄   shallowness 천박함; 얕음

11 빈칸 추론 ③

해설 인간은 형상보다 색을 먼저 인식하게끔 되어 있는데, 화가, 건축가, 디자이너는 사람들이 자신의 작품을 감상할 때 색과 형상을 함께 볼 수 있게끔 구성하고, 이는 보는 사람에게 미적 즐거움을 제공하고 메시지를 즉시 전달하는 효과를 거둔다. 따라서 화가, 건축가, 디자이너가 관심을 두는 것은 ③ '색과 형상을 동시에 인식시키는 것'이다.
① 자신의 작품을 가능한 한 현실적으로 만드는 것
② 완벽한 형태를 포착하기보다는 빛과 색채
④ 사람들이 물체와 환경에 반응하는 방식
⑤ 생각을 시각화하는 기술을 가능하게 해주는 표시를 하는 것

해석 색은 우리의 세계와 우리의 감정을 뚜렷이 밝혀 준다. 그것은 보통 형상보다 먼저 보인다. 우리 눈은 물체의 모양과 선에 의해 전해지는 세부 사항보다 먼저 물체의 색이 인식될 정도로 색에 끌린다. 처음 흘긋 볼 때 우리는 여름 삼림 지대에 있는 서로 다른 종의 나무는 보지 못하고, 오히려 초록색만 압도적으로 많이 본다. 그러나 화가, 건축가, 그리고 디자이너는 일반적으로 색과 형상을 동시에 인식시키는 데 관심이 있다. 방에 들어서자마자, 우리는 실내 디자인에 사용된 색이나 색들을 먼저 본 다음에 그 공간에 들어 있는 가구와 공예품을 파악한다. 미술 작품은, 순수 미술이건 상업 미술이건 간에, 그것의 색채 사용이 보는 사람으로 하여금 작품의 내용(색과 형상 모두)을 함께 볼 수 있게 해 줄 때 보는 사람에게 미적 즐거움을 준다. 이것이 달성되면, 보는 사람 측에서 '재차 보지' 않아도 작품의 메시지가 즉시 전달된다.

구문 [5행~7행] At first glance, we do **not** see *the different species of trees* (present in a summer woodland), **but** rather see the preponderance of green.
「not A but B」는 'A가 아니라 B다'의 뜻이고 밑줄 친 두 부분이 A, B에 해당한다. ( )은 the different species of trees를 수식하는 형용사구이다.
[12행~16행] An artwork, be it fine or commercial, is aesthetically pleasing to the viewer **when** its color usage *allows* the viewer *to see* the content of the piece (both color and imagery) together.
「be it A or B」는 'A이든 B이든'의 뜻으로, 밑줄 친 부분은 'whether it is fine or commercial'로 바꿔 쓸 수 있다. 시간의 접속사 when이 이끄는 부사절은 「allows+목적어(the viewer)+목적격보어(to see)」의 SVOC 구조이다.

어휘 imagery 상. 형상   woodland 삼림 지대   be concerned with ~에 관심이 있다; ~와 관련이 있다   discern 파악하다   artifact 공예품   realistic 현실적인; 사실주의의   simultaneously 동시에; 일제히   visualize 시각화하다

12 빈칸 추론 ②

해설 자발적인 운동과는 달리 강제적 운동은 불안을 유발하고, 불안은 장 염증을 악화시키는 박테리아를 증가시키므로 강제적이지 않고 불안을 유발하지 않을 정도의 운동을 해야 한다. 따라서 빈칸에 들어갈 말은 ② '당신이 편안함을 느끼는 만큼의 운동만을 해야 한다'이다.
① 적당한 불안을 가지고 격렬한 정기적 운동을 해야 한다
③ 당신의 면역체계를 증진시키기 위해 매일 운동해야 한다
④ 아픈 근육은 당신이 더 강해지고 있다는 표시임을 알아야 한다
⑤ 당신의 연령과 신체적 능력에 따라 항상 운동해야 한다

해석 우리는 당신이 임신을 했든 아니든, 당신의 운동 수준이 당신의 장내 미생물에 영향을 미칠 것인지를 아직 알지 못한다. 그러나 쥐를 이용한 연구들이 한 가지 흥미로운 사실을 보여주었다. 자발적인 운동과 반대로 강제적 운동은 쥐의 미생물 군집에, 특히 장 염증 정도에 관해 다르게 영향을 미친다. 어떻게 이 모든 것이 작용하는지를 아직 이해하지 못하지만, 강제적 운동이 불안으로 이어질 수 있다는 것이 가능한데, 이는 장 염증을 유발

하거나 장 염증 예방을 그르치는 박테리아의 증가로 이어질 수 있다. 이것이 추정이긴 하지만, 임신 기간 동안 운동에 대한 당신의 의사나 조산사의 충고를 따르면서도 당신이 편안함을 느끼는 만큼의 운동만을 해야 한다는 점을 정말로 시사한다. 그러나 전반적으로 약간의 운동이 당신의 미생물 군집을 변화시키고 염증을 줄이는 데 도움이 될 것이며, 이는 무조건 환영할 일이다. 그리고 당신이 외출할 수 있다면 그로 인해 아마 기분이 더 나아질 것이다.

구문 [7행~11행] While we don't yet understand how this all works, it's possible **that** forced exercise could lead to *anxiety*, **which** could lead to an elevation of *bacteria* [that induce or fail to prevent gut inflammation].
밑줄 친 it은 가주어, 접속사 that이 이끄는 명사절이 진주어이다. 계속적 용법으로 쓰인 관계대명사 which가 이끄는 절은 앞에 나온 anxiety를 부연 설명한다. [ ] 부분은 관계대명사 that이 이끄는 형용사절로 선행사 bacteria를 수식한다.
[14행~16행] But on the whole *a little exercise may help change your microbiome* and *reduce inflammation*, **which** is all to the good.
help에 이어진 change와 reduce는 and로 연결되어 병렬 구조를 이룬다. 계속적 용법의 관계대명사 which가 이끄는 절은 앞 문장 전체(a little exercise ~ inflammation)를 부연 설명한다.

어휘 gut 장(腸); 용기, 배짱   microbe 미생물; 병원균   with regard to ~에 관해서   elevation (정도·양의) 증가; 높이   induce 유발하다; 유도하다   supposition 추정, 가설   midwife 조산사   all to the good (예상과는 다르지만) 무조건 환영할 일인   intensive 격렬한; 집중적인   moderate 적당한; 온건한   boost 끌어올리다; 늘리다   immune system 면역체계   sore 아픈, 쓰린; 감정을 해치는

13 흐름 무관 문장 ④

해설 이 글은 검증되지 않은 사실이 언론에 의해서 미리 보도되는 문제점에 관한 내용인데, ④는 '언론이 보도한 귀리의 혈중 콜레스테롤을 낮춘다는 사실이 과학적인 조사에 의해서 확립이 되었다'를 논하고 있으므로 글의 흐름과 관계가 없다.

해석 뉴스 미디어는 새로운 발견에 목말라 있고, 기자들은 종종 아이디어가 충분히 검증되기도 전에 과학 실험실에서 그것을 입수한다. ① 또한, 과학에 대한 확실한 이해가 부족한 기자는 복잡한 과학 원리를 잘못 이해하거나 틀리게 보도할 수도 있다. ② 사실 때로는 과학자들도 자신의 발견에 대해 흥분해서 자신들의 동료들에 의한 철저한 검토를 마치기 전에 언론에 그것들을 누설한다. ③ 그 결과 대중들은 연구 결과가 완전히 확인되기 전에 속보로 들어온 영양에 관한 뉴스 기사를 흔히 접한다. ④ 예를 들어, 미디어는 귀리 제품이 혈중 콜레스테롤을 낮춘다는 것을 보도해왔는데, 이것은 과학적 조사에 의해 확립된다. ⑤ 그 후 검증받고 있는 가설이 이후의 이의제기를 견디지 못하면, 소비자들은 단순히 작동 중인 과학의 일상적인 과정인 것에 의해 배신감을 느낀다.

구문 [6행~9행] To tell the truth, sometimes scientists **get excited about their findings, too**, and **leak them to the press** {before they have been through a thorough review by the scientists' peers}.
밑줄 친 두 부분이 and로 병렬연결 되었다. { }로 표시된 부분은 접속사 before가 이끄는 절이다.
[12행~14행] For example, the media **have reported** [that *oat products lower blood cholesterol*], **which is well-established by scientific research.**
[ ] 부분은 동사 have reported의 목적어 역할을 하는 명사절이다. which 이하는 oat products ~ cholesterol를 선행사로 하는 관계절이다.
[14행~17행] Then, when *the hypothesis* (being tested) / fails to hold up to a later challenge, consumers feel betrayed / by {what is simply the normal course of science at work}.
the hypothesis를 being tested가 수식하고 있으며, '테스트가 되고 있는 중인'의 의미이므로 수동태의 진행형이 쓰였다. { } 부분은 전치사 by의 목적어로 what으

로 시작하는 명사절이다.

어휘 finding (조사·연구 등의) 결과　leak (비밀을) 누설하다, 유출하다　peer 동료　late-breaking (뉴스가) 속보의　nutrition 영양　confirm 확인하다　well-established 확립된, 안정된　hypothesis 가설　hold up 견디다　feel betrayed by ~에 배신감을 느끼다

14 글의 순서　②

해설 주어진 글에서는 관광산업이 환경에 미치는 영향에 대해 주민들이 엇갈리는 반응을 보인다고 제시한다. 우선 관광산업에 대해 우호적인 입장이 제시된 (B)가 나오고 나서, '그 대신에(Alternatively)'로 시작하며 관광산업에 대해 부정적인 견해를 가진 주민들의 의견인 (A)가 나오는 것이 자연스럽다. (C)에 언급된 '이러한 분열(this divide)'은 (B)와 (A)를 종합하여 지칭하는 표현이므로 (C)는 마지막으로 와야 한다.

해석 관광산업이 환경에 미치는 영향은 과학자들에게는 명확하지만, 모든 주민들이 환경 훼손을 관광산업의 탓으로 돌리지는 않는다. 주민들은 대개 관광산업이 삶의 질에 미치는 경제적인 그리고 몇 가지 사회문화적인 영향에 대해 긍정적인 견해를 가지고 있지만 환경적 영향에 대한 그들의 반응은 엇갈린다.
(B) 몇몇 주민들은 관광산업이 더 많은 공원과 휴양지를 제공하고, 도로와 공공시설의 질을 개선하며, 생태계 쇠퇴의 원인이 되지는 않는다고 생각한다. 많은 이들이 교통 문제, 초만원인 야외 오락 활동이나 공원의 평화로움과 고요함을 방해하는 것에 대해 관광산업을 탓하지는 않는다.
(A) 그 대신에 몇몇 주민들은 관광객들이 현지의 낚시터, 사냥터 및 기타 휴양지에 지나치게 몰리거나 교통과 보행자 혼잡을 초래할지도 모른다는 우려를 표한다.
(C) 몇 가지 연구들은 환경 훼손과 관광산업의 관계에 대해 주민들이 가지는 생각의 이러한 분열이 관광산업의 유형, 주민들이 자연환경이 보호될 필요가 있다고 생각하는 정도, 그리고 주민들이 관광 명소에서 떨어져 사는 거리와 연관이 있음을 보여준다.

구문 [1행~3행] The impacts of tourism on the environment / are evident to scientists, // but not all residents attribute environmental damage to tourism.
주어 The impacts ~ environment에서 'the impact of A on B'는 'A가 B에 미치는 영향'이라는 뜻이다. 「not all ~」은 '전부 ~한 건 아니다'라는 뜻의 부분부정 표현이다. 「attribute A to B」는 'A를 B의 탓으로 돌리다'의 뜻이다.

어휘 evident 명백한　sociocultural 사회 문화적인　alternatively 그 대신에　overcrowd 혼잡하게 하다　pedestrian 보행자　congestion 혼잡　decline 쇠퇴, 감소(하다)　disturbance 방해　tourist attraction 관광 명소

15 글의 순서　④

해설 웹사이트 방문 고객은 머무를지 떠날지를 10초 안에 결정한다는 주어진 글 다음에는 '달리 말하면(In other words) 고객들은 웹사이트에서 순식간에 판단을 내린다'는 (C)가 나온다. 그러므로 웹사이트의 외관, 느낌 순향성에 신경을 써야 한다는 (C) 다음에는 '안타깝게도(Unfortunately) 이것은(this) 많은 경우 사실이 아니다'로 시작되는 (A)가 나온다. 여기서 this는 '웹사이트 주인들이 방문객이 웹사이트에 반하도록 할 수 있는 모든 것을 하고 있는 것'을 지칭한다. 많은 기업가들이 웹사이트의 중요성을 간과하고 있다는 (A) 다음에는 그러므로 웹사이트에 돈을 아끼지 말라는 충고인 (B)가 이어진다.

해석 온라인 소비자 조사 연구는 방문객들이 웹사이트에 올 때, 처음 10초 이내에 '머무름' 혹은 '떠남'의 순간을 경험한다고 확인해준다. 그것은(= 웹사이트) 비전문적이거나 사

용하기 힘들어 보이면, 그들은 떠나고 보통은 돌아오지 않을 것이다.
(C) 달리 말하면 당신의 표적이 되는 관중은 당신, 당신의 제품과 서비스, 그리고 당신의 회사를 순식간에 판단할 것이다. 그리고 당신이 그들에게 인상을 남길 기회는 오직 한 번뿐인 것 같다. 이 점을 고려할 때, 모든 웹사이트 주인들은 온라인 방문객들이 웹사이트의 외관, 느낌, 순향성에 확실히 반하게 하기 위해 할 수 있는 모든 것을 하고 있어야 한다.
(A) 안타깝게도, 이것은 많은 경우 사실이 아니다. 상당수의 근시안적인 기업가들이 형편없이 작성된 카피, 아마추어적인 디자인과 대단히 복잡한 항행이 주는 부정적인 영향을 과소평가한다.
(B) 이것이 소탐대실이 이득이 되지 않는 분야 중 하나임을 명심하라. 그러기엔 너무 중요하다. 당신 사촌의 친구의 고모의 옆집 이웃의 형이 당신의 웹사이트를 저렴하게 디자인해주겠다고 자청했다고 해서 장래의 고객들을 짜증나게 하거나 (더 나쁜 것은) 멀어지게 만들지 마라.

구문 [10행~12행] Remember // that this is one of *those areas* [where it doesn't pay **to be penny wise and pound foolish**] — it's just too important.
[ ]는 those areas를 수식하는 관계부사절이다. [ ]에서 it은 가주어이고 to be penny ~ foolish가 진주어이며, 자동사 pays는 '이득이 되다'의 뜻이다.
[19행~22행] **Given** this, / all website owners should be doing *everything* [(that) they can] / to ensure // that their online visitors are blown away / by their website's look, feel, and navigability.
Given은 '~을 고려할 때'의 뜻이다. [ ]는 앞에 목적격 관계대명사 that이 생략되어 everything을 수식한다. their website's 다음의 look, feel, navigability는 콤마(,)와 and로 연결되어 병렬구조를 이룬다.

어휘 quite a few 상당수의　shortsighted 근시안적인　entrepreneur 기업가　navigation 항행, 항해 *cf.* navigability 순향성, 항행할 수 있음　penny wise and pound foolish 소탐대실(한푼 아끼려다 열냥 잃는다))　alienate 멀어지게 만들다　prospective 장래의, 유망한　on the cheap 저렴하게　in a snap 순식간에, 즉시　blow A away A를 반하게 하다; 감동시키다

16 문장 넣기　③

해설 주어진 문장은 피실험자의 생각을 건드리지 않고 그들의 생각을 추출하는 심리학 연구의 어려움을 기술했는데, 관찰되고 있음을 알기만 해도 피관찰자가 다르게 행동한다는 ③ 바로 뒤의 문장과, 자신의 감정을 사회적으로 더 용인 가능하도록 다듬는다는 ④ 바로 뒤의 문장은 바로 이 주어진 문장의 두 가지 예시라 할 수 있으므로 주어진 문장이 들어갈 곳은 ③이다. ③의 앞부분은 심리학 실험 설계에서 피실험자의 생각에 영향을 미친다는 어려움이 아니라, 더 쉬운 실험환경과 접근성이 더 높은 피실험자를 선정한다는 다른 종류의 어려움을 기술하고 있으므로 ①, ②는 답이 될 수 없다.

해석 심리학 연구자들은 인간 행동을 설명하는 데 도움이 되며 예측할 수도 있는 연구를 수행할 과학적 방법을 따른다. 이것은 달팽이나 음파를 연구하는 것보다 훨씬 도전적인 일이다. 그것은 종종 자연스런 환경보다는 실험실 내에서 행동 검증하기와, 모집단의 진정한 단면에서 추출된 자료를 수집하기보다는 (심리학 개론 수업의 학생들 같은) 쉽게 쓸 수 있는 사람들에게 참여해 달라고 부탁하기와 같은 타협을 요구한다. 사람들의 생각을 바꾸지 (이를 반응성이라 한다) 않고 그들이 생각하는 바에 다가가는 방안을 상상해내는 것은 종종 대단한 영리함을 요구한다. 그들이 관찰되고 있다는 것을 단지 알고 있는 것만으로도 사람들은 다르게 행동하게 (예를 들어 더 예의 바르게 행동한다든지!) 될 수 있다. 사람들은 그들의 진정한 감정보다 사회적으로 더 바람직하다고 느끼는 답을 내놓을지도 모른다. 그러나 심리학의 이러한 어려움에도 불구하고, 과학적 기법의 대가는 연구 결과가 반복 가능하다는 것이다. 즉, 같은 절차를 따라서 동일한 실험을 다시 작동시켜 보면, 같은 결과를 얻을 가능성이 매우 클 것이다.

구문 [8행~13행] It often requires compromises, such as [testing behavior within laboratories **rather than** natural settings], and (asking those readily available (such as introduction to psychology students) to participate **rather than** collecting data from a true cross-section of the population}.

[ ]와 { }은 and로 연결되어 병렬구조를 이룬다. 'A rather than B (B라기보다는 차라리 A)' 구문이 [ ]와 { }에 사용되었다.

[15행~17행] People may give *answers* [that **(they feel)** are more socially desirable than their true feelings].

[ ] 부분이 answers를 수식하며, ( ) 부분은 삽입구문이다.

어휘 cleverness 영리함   conceive 생각을 품다, 상상하다   measures 방안, 조치   tap into ~에 다가가다   alter 바꾸다, 변경하다   reactivity 반응성   compromise 타협   setting 환경   readily 쉽게   cross-section 단면   population 모집단   desirable 바람직한   for all ~에도 불구하고   payoff 대가   procedure 절차

17 문장 넣기   ④

해설 '파일 공유' 도구가 발명되자 엔터테인먼트 업계가 유통의 권익을 상실할까 봐 두려워하게 됐다는 주어진 문장은 '블로그' 도구가 발명되고 출간이 쉬워지자 많은 사람들이 자기표현을 하게 됐다는 내용과 병치되므로 블로그에 대한 내용 다음인 ④에 위치해야 한다. ④ 다음 문장에서는 '그들(they)'이 디지털 저작권 관리 소프트웨어의 발명으로 음악이나 영화의 공유에 대항했다고 했는데, 이는 블로그보다는 파일 공유와 관련 있는 내용이므로 주어진 문장은 역시 ④에 들어가야 한다.

해석 우리는 소프트웨어로 만들어진 세상에 살고 있으므로, 프로그래머는 건축가이다. 그들이 내리는 결정은 우리의 행동을 안내한다. 그들이 어떤 일을 새로 하기 쉽게 만들 때, 우리는 그것을 훨씬 더 많이 한다. 그들이 무언가를 하는 것을 힘들거나 불가능하게 만들면, 우리는 그것을 덜 한다. 프로그래머들이 90년대 후반과 2000년대 초반에 최초의 블로그 도구를 만들었을 때, 그것은 폭발적인 자기표현을 산출했다. 무언가를 발표하는 것이 갑자기 쉬울 때 수백만의 더 많은 사람들이 그것을 한다. 그리고 프로그래머들이 같은 시기 무렵에 '파일 공유' 도구를 발명했을 때, 엔터테인먼트 업계가 유통에 걸어 놓은 잠금장치가 갑자기 사라지는 모습을 지켜보면서 업계에 전율이 흘렀다. 사실 그들은 '디지털 저작권 관리' 소프트웨어를 발명하기 위해 자신들의 프로그래머를 고용하여 반격했고, 그것을 음악과 영화 출시작들에 넣었으며, 일반인들이 그 상품들을 복제해서 친구들에게 나눠주는 것을 더 까다롭게 했다. 그들은 인위적인 희소성을 일으키려고 노력했던 것이다. 부유한 이익단체들은 어떤 코드가 하고 있는 일이 맘에 들지 않으면, 반대 방향으로 싸워줄 소프트웨어를 만들기 위해 돈을 지불할 것이다.

구문 **[8행~10행]** If they make **it** hard or impossible **to do something**, // we do less of it.

it은 가목적어이고 to do something이 진목적어이다. 「make + it + 형용사 + to-v」는 'v하는 것을 (형용사)하게 만들다'의 뜻이다.

[13행~18행] In fact, / they fought back / by hiring their own programmers / to invent "digital rights management" software, / putting it in music and film releases, / **making *those wares* trickier** *for everyday folks* **to copy and hand out** to their friends; ~.

동사는 fought back이며 putting ~ releases와 making ~ friends는 분사구문이 연이어 나온 것이다. making ~ friends에서 those wares는 원래 to copy and hand out to their friends에서 copy와 hand out의 공통 목적어였는데, 가목적어 it의 자리를 대체하며 채우고 있다. making 구를 'making it trickier for everyday folks to copy and hand out those wares to their friends'로 바꿔 쓸 수 있다. for everyday folks는 to-v에 대한 의미상 주어이다.

어휘 distribution 유통: 분배   evaporate 사라지다, 증발하다   coder 프로그래머   publish 발표하다: 출판하다   ware 상품   tricky 까다로운, 힘든   hand out 나누어 주다   scarcity 품귀, 희귀함: 부족   interest 이익단체

18 요약문 완성   ⑤

해설 정부가 외국 회사를 차별적으로 대하기도 하지만, 외국과 국내 회사의 구분이 점점 모호해지고 있으며 국제적 회사들이 거시 경제 정책에 끼치는 긍정적인 영향 때문에 정부는 다국적 기업에 우호적인 정책을 선호하게 된다고 흐름이 바뀌는 글이다. 따라서 이를 요약하면 '모든 경우에 국내 산업을 선호하는(preferring) 대신, 정부의 대다수는 이제 외국으로부터의 생산 회사들을 환영하는(welcome) 경향이 있다.'가 된다.

① 제한하는 – 용인하다   ② 옹호하는 – 무시하다
③ 선호하는 – 처벌하다   ④ 제한하는 – 지원하다

해석 때때로 정부는 국내 회사에 이익이 되도록 외국 회사를 노골적으로 차별한다. 예를 들어 2005년 아르헨티나 정부는 Shell사가 기름값을 올린 후, 그 회사에서 구매하는 것을 거부하도록 소비자들을 (성공적으로) 자극했다. 많은 나라에서 자국의 회사로부터 나온 상품의 소비가 '외국' 상품보다 선호되는 좀 더 교묘한 '국내 상품을 사라' 캠페인이 여전히 시행되고 있다. 그러나 국내 상품 속에 증가하는 외국산 내용물과 점점 더 모호해지는 선도적인 회사들의 소유권 구조 때문에, '외국'과 '국내'의 구분이 점점 더 어려워졌다. 게다가 중앙 및 지방의 자국 정부는 외국의 대형 다국적 기업을 유치할 (또는 계속 보유할) 타당한 이유가 있다. 국제적 회사들은 특히 그들의 무역과 투자 흐름, 경쟁, 기술 이전, 과세 소득이 끼치는 (잠재적인) 긍정적 영향을 통해서 각 나라의 거시 경제 정책에 영향을 끼친다. 결과적으로 정부는 다국적 기업에 대한 정책에서 제재보다는 장려책을, 차별적 관행보다는 무차별 원칙을 사용하기를 선호한다.

↓

산업 자체 내에서의 변화 때문에 모든 경우에 국내 산업을 (A) <u>선호하는</u> 대신에, 정부의 대다수는 이제 외국으로부터의 생산 회사들을 (B) <u>환영하는</u> 경향이 있다.

구문 **[20행~23행]** In consequence, governments prefer to **use** incentives **rather than** sanctions, [and] non-discrimination principles **rather than** discriminatory practices ~.

두 밑줄 친 부분은 use의 목적어이며, 접속사 and로 병렬구조를 이루고 있다. 「A rather than B」는 'B라기보다는 오히려 A'의 뜻이다.

어휘 explicitly 노골적으로   discriminate against ~에 대해 차별하다   *cf.* discriminatory 차별적인   in favor of ~에게 이익이 되도록   domestic 국내의   boycott 구매를 거부하다   subtle 교묘한   implement 시행하다   ambiguous 모호한   retain (계속) 보유하다   multinational 다국적의   enterprise 기업   macro-economic 거시 경제의   tax income 과세 소득   incentive 장려책   sanction 제재   manufacturer 생산회사, 제조사

19~20 장문   19 ②   20 ④

해설 19. 게임과 스포츠를 볼 때 사람들은 소속감을 느끼고, 더욱 용감하게 자신의 감정을 표출할 수 있으며, 현대 사회에서 가능해진 막대한 여가 시간을 채울 수 있다는 내용의 글이므로, 제목으로 가장 적절한 것은 ② '사람들은 왜 게임과 스포츠를 보는가'이다.

① 스포츠 관람: 지금과 예전
③ 게임을 하는 것의 매력은 무엇인가?
④ 의식, 정체성과 대안적 라이프스타일
⑤ 경기 관람은 당신이 스스로를 자랑스러워하게 만든다

20. 사람들은 게임이나 스포츠를 관람할 때 평소에는 소심하여 말하지 못했던 의견을, 비록 그것이 편견이나 혐오일지라도 마음껏 표출하는 경향이 있으므로, 정제된 (refined) 감정이 아닌 날것의(raw) 감정을 드러낸다고 볼 수 있다.

① 관람을 전제로 한 현대 스포츠는 경기 수행 그 자체라기보다는 극이나 의식에 더

가깝다고 볼 수 있어서 조직화된(organized) 연극과 같다고 할 수 있다.
② 텔레비전으로 경기를 관람할 때 사람들은 자신이 군중의 일부(part)가 되었다고 느낀다.
③ 사람들은 스포츠를 관람하는 동안 평소에는 소심하여(timid) 말하지 못하던 의견을 과감하게 표현한다.
⑤ 현대 스포츠와 게임은 사람들의 여가를 채워주어 막대한 돈과 감정과 활동이 생성되는(generated) 매체이다.

해석 의심할 여지 없이 텔레비전과 스포츠가 상품 판매의 주요 방법인 방식에 의해 깊은 영향을 받은 관중 스포츠의 대단한 성장이 우리 세계의 특징 중 하나이다. 기술 역사학자인 Lewis Mumford는 현대 스포츠가 '관중이 선수보다 더 중요한 (a) 조직화된 연극의 형식'으로 정의될 수 있다고 말한다. 그것은 장관이며, 여러 가지 면에서 경기 수행보다 극이나 의식에 더 가깝다. 군중은 합창단의 부분이 되어, 감정적으로도 심리적으로도 함께 섞이고, 잠시 동안 자신의 일상적인 삶과 걱정거리에서 벗어나게 된다. 심지어 사적인 집안의 상황에서조차 사람들은 자신의 팀 색깔로 옷을 차려입고, 텔레비전을 볼 때 자신이 군중의 (b) 부분인 체한다. 군중 속에 있다는 것이 우리를 용감하게 만든다. 우리는 보통 의 경우우라면 너무 (c) 소심해서 표현할 수 없을 것들을 외치고 말할 수 있다. 그것은 많은 경우 단독의 개인으로서는 불가능하다고 여기는 방식으로 우리의 국가에 대해서든, 우리의 정치적 의견에 대해서든, 혹은 우리의 혐오에 대해서든 우리의 편견과 열정을 알릴 수 있는 때이다. 게임과 스포츠를 볼 때 사람들이 그토록 (d) 정제된(→ 날것의) 감정을 드러내는 것이 놀랍지 않다.

대중 스포츠와 개인적인 경기 시청은 눈에 잘 띄는 소비 형태이다. 많은 현대 사회에는 막대한 여가가 존재하며, 사람들은 경기 시청을 통해 자신의 여가 시간을 채운다(그리고 많은 경우 새롭게 발견한 풍요로움을 보여준다). 종종 그들은 이것을 컴퓨터 게임과 인터넷상의 경쟁의 세상 속에서 사적으로 행한다. 많은 경우 기계가 만들어준 점점 증가하는 여가 시간은 채워져야 한다. 그래서 어떤 것이 세상의 새로운 '종교'라 한다면, 그것은 게임이나 스포츠이다. 더 많은 돈과 감정과 활동이 이제 전쟁만 제외한 지구상의 그 어떤 다른 것보다 스포츠와 게임에 의해 (e) 생성된다.

구문 [1행~4행] *The extraordinary growth of spectator sports*, **undoubtedly deeply influenced by television** and **by** *the way* [in which sports are the main way of selling goods], **is** one of the marks of our world.
The extraordinary ~ spectator sports가 주어이고 동사는 is이다. undoubtedly ~ goods는 수동의 의미를 가지는 분사구문이고, 분사구문 내에서 두 밑줄 부분이 and로 연결되어 병렬구조를 이룬다. in which가 이끄는 관계사절 [ ]은 the way 를 수식한다.

[10행~13행] *The crowd* becomes part of a chorus, emotionally and psychologically blending together, **taken** for a moment out of their ordinary lives and worries.
밑줄 친 부분은 The crowd를 의미상 주어로 하여 능동(blend는 '섞이다'라는 뜻의 자동사로 사용되었다)의 의미를 가지는 분사구문이고 taken 이하는 수동의 의미를 가지는 분사구문이다.

[18행~22행] It is often *the time* [when we can **make** our prejudices and *passions* **known**, whether for our country, our political opinions, or our hatreds], in *a way* [that as single individuals we find impossible].
It은 시간 상황을 나타낼 때 사용하는 주어로 특별한 의미나 지칭하는 바는 없다. 첫 번째 [ ]은 시간을 나타내는 관계부사절로 the time을 수식한다. 'make O p.p.' 는 'O가 ~되게 하다'의 뜻이다. 세 밑줄 부분은 콤마(,)와 or로 연결되어 병렬구조를 이루고, 두 번째 [ ]는 관계대명사 that이 이끄는 관계사절로 a way를 수식한다.

어휘 extraordinary 대단한 spectator 관중 undoubtedly 의심할 여지없이 spectacle 장관 ritual 의식 chorus 합창곡, 합창단 blend 섞이다 timid 소심한 refined 정제된; 세련된 conspicuous 눈에 잘 띄는 spare 남는, 여분의 affluence 풍요 rivalry 경쟁 fascination 매력

| 1 ⑤ | 2 ② | 3 ④ | 4 ③ | 5 ② | | 6 ⑤ | 7 ⑤ | 8 ④ | 9 ⑤ | 10 ⑤ |
| 11 ④ | 12 ④ | 13 ③ | 14 ② | 15 ⑤ | | 16 ③ | 17 ④ | 18 ② | 19 ② | 20 ⑤ |

1 글의 목적   ⑤

해설 글을 전체적으로 보고 글쓴이의 진짜 의도를 파악해야 한다. 글의 앞부분에서 대회의 특징을 소개한 뒤 Unfortunately(안타깝게도)부터 애로 사항을 말하면서 수상자 발표를 한 주 늦춘다는 것으로 보아, 이 글의 목적으로는 ⑤ '수상자 발표가 지연된 것을 알리려고'가 가장 적절하다.

해석 매년, 전국의 대학생들은 콩코드 영화제의 포스터 디자인 대회에서 자신의 예술적 기교를 시험하도록 초대받습니다. 수천 명의 학생들이 우승을 다투고, 수상자는 전문 심사위원단에 의해 선정됩니다. 지난 수년간 창의력과 재능이 놀랍게 드러났고, 올해의 경쟁도 예외가 아니었습니다. 안타깝게도, 올해 엄청난 수의 출품작으로 인해, 저희 심사위원들이 단 세 개의 뛰어난 포스터를 선택하는 것은 매우 어려웠습니다. 결과적으로, 저희는 원래 예정된 것보다 한 주 늦게 수상자를 발표하기로 결정했습니다. 그러나 상과 다른 세부 사항은 그대로 유지될 것이므로 걱정하실 필요는 없습니다. 수상자들은 여전히 표창과 상금을 받을 것이고, 그들의 작품은 여전히 공표될 것입니다. 이 훌륭한 행사를 지원해 주신 것에 대해 모든 분께 감사드립니다.

구문 [8행~10행] Unfortunately, due to the great number of entries this year, **it** has been very difficult **for our judges to choose only three outstanding posters**.
여기에서 it은 뒤에 나오는 to choose ~ posters를 대신하는 가주어이고, for our judges는 의미상의 주어이다.

어휘 artistic 예술[미술]적인; 예술[미술]의 compete 다투다, 경쟁하다, 겨루다 panel (전문가) 집단[패널]; 틀; 판 professional 전문적인; 직업[직종]의 see ((때를 나타내는 명사를 주어로 써서 그때가 어떤 일이 있는 때임을 나타냄)) 보다, 알다 exception 예외; 제외 entry 출품[응모/참가]작; 입장, 등장 outstanding 뛰어난, 눈에 띄는 announce 발표하다, 알리다; 선언하다 recognition 표창, 인정, 인지, 인식, 승인, 허가 publish 공표[발표]하다; 출판하다 support 지원하다; 후원하다

2 밑줄 함의 ②

해설 실험에서 사람들이 자신의 트라우마를 신체 움직임 같은 비언어적 형태만을 통해서 표현하는 것보다는 글쓰기를 통해 표현하는 인지적 과정이 포함될 경우 신체와 정신 건강이 향상되었다는 내용이므로 밑줄 친 '인지과정'은 ② '충격적인 경험을 글쓰기로 표현하는 정신적인 과정'을 의미한다.
① 무엇이 트라우마를 야기했는지 입증하는 체계적인 과정
③ 충격적인 경험을 비언어적으로 표현하는 자연스러운 과정
④ 부정적인 감정을 긍정적인 감정으로 바꾸는 동적인 과정
⑤ 언어적 추론을 통해 트라우마를 분석하는 논리적 과정

해석 글쓰기의 가치에 대한 한 가지 가능한 설명은 그것이 사람들로 하여금 스스로를 표현할 수 있게 해 준다는 것이다. 만약 추진하는 과정이 자기표현이라면, 언어적 표현 형태와 비언어적 표현 형태 모두 동등한 이점을 줄 것이라고 주장할 수 있다. 그러나 감정의 분출에 대한 전통적인 연구는 인지적 처리가 없으면 감정 표현의 임상적 가치를 뒷받침하지 못했다는 것에 유의해야 한다. Anne Krantz와 James W. Pennebaker의 최근 실험은 춤이나 신체 움직임을 통하여 트라우마를 드러내는 것이 글쓰기와 동등한 방식으로 건강 증진을 유발하는지를 알아보고자 했다. 이 연구에서, 학생들은 신체 움직임을 이용하여 충격적인 경험을 표현하거나, 움직임을 이용하여 경험을 표현하고 그 뒤에 그것에 대해 글을 쓰거나, 또는 하루에 10분씩 3일간 정해진 방법대로 운동을 하도록 요구받았다. 움직임으로 표현하는 두 집단은 연구 후 몇 달 동안 더 행복감을 느꼈고 정신적으로 더 건강하다고 느꼈다고 보고했지만, 움직임에다가 글쓰기를 덧붙인 집단만이 신체 건강과 평균 평점에서 의미 있는 향상을 보였다.

구문 [1행~2행] A possible explanation for the value of writing is // that *it* **allows** people **to express** themselves.
that 이하는 접속사 that이 이끄는 명사절로 문장의 보어 역할을 한다. 대명사 it은 앞에 나온 writing을 가리키며 「allow + O + to-v (O가 v하게 하다)」 구문이 쓰였다.

어휘 driving 추진하는 verbal 언어적인 (↔ nonverbal 비언어적인) comparable 동등한, 비슷한 benefit 이점 clinical 임상적인 absence 없음, 부재 cognitive 인지적인 processing 처리; 가공 seek to ~하고자 하다 disclosure 드러냄, 폭로 trauma 트라우마, 충격적 경험 bring about ~을 유발하다, ~을 가져오다 prescribed (미리) 정해진 evidence (증거로) 보이다, 입증하다; 증거 significant 의미 있는, 상당한

3 글의 요지 ④

해설 인쇄기의 발명까지 '그 이상의' 발명품의 도움이 필요했고, 에너지를 동력화하기 위해서 여러 기술적 발명이 필요했음을 설명하고 있다. 'Such necessary combination of technologies is characteristic of scientific advance.(기술들의 그러한 필연적 결합이 과학적 진보의 특성이다.)'라는 말에서 알 수 있듯이, 글의 요지로는 ④가 가장 적절하다.

해석 알파벳을 읽고 쓰는 능력이 방법의 한계를 극복하고 최대한의 잠재력을 달성하기 위해서는 인쇄기의 발명을 기다려야 했다. 최초의 성인인 그리스 알파벳은 추상적인 분석을 적용하여 경험적인 문제를 해결했다. 그러나 결과를 최대화하기 위한 물질적 수단은 그 이상의 발명품의 도움이 필요했고 그것을 위해 오랜 시간을 기다려야만 했다. 기술들의 그러한 필연적 결합이 과학적 진보의 특성이다. 물이 증기로 변환될 때 이용 가능한 에너지가 존재한다는 것을 인식하는 것과, 그 에너지를 성공적으로 동력화하는 것은 완전 별개였다. 그런데 후자는 피스톤이 실린더에 딱 들어맞도록 미세한 허용 오차를 만들어 낼 수 있는 기계 도구의 병행 시공, 접합부를 밀폐할 수 있는 윤활유의 제조, 증기 압력의 시기를 조정하기 위한 미끄럼 막대 장치 및 추진력을 회전으로 전환시키는 크랭크와 연결봉의 병행 발명을 필요로 했다. 마찬가지로 알파벳의 에너지가 완전히 방출되기 위해서는 유럽

의 과학 발전의 여명기가 제공하는 도움을 기다려야 했다.

구문 [11행~18행] To harness the energy successfully was another, **requiring** the parallel construction of *machine tools* (capable of producing fine tolerances to fit piston to cylinder), the manufacture of *lubricants* (capable of sealing the fit), the parallel invention of *slide-rod mechanisms* (to control the periods of steam pressure), and of *crank and connecting rod* (to convert the thrust into rotation).
requiring 이하는 분사구문이다. 네 개의 ( ) 부분은 각각 바로 앞에 있는 명사(구)를 수식한다.
[19행~21행] The energy of the alphabet likewise had to await *the assistance* (provided by the dawning age of scientific advance in Europe) in order to be fully released.
( ) 부분은 과거분사 provided가 이끄는 분사구로 the assistance를 수식한다.

어휘 literacy 글을 읽고 쓸 줄 아는 능력 await 기다리다 printing press 인쇄기 empirical 경험상의 apply 적용[응용]하다; 바르다; 지원하다 abstract 추상적인 analysis 분석 means 수단, 방법 combination 결합 be characteristic of ~의 특성[특질/특색]이다 convert 전환하다 harness 동력화하다; 이용하다 parallel 병행하는, 평행한 fine 미세한, 정교한 slide-rod 미끄럼 막대 crank (기계의) 크랭크 connecting rod (내연 기관의) 연접봉, 연결봉 thrust 추진력 rotation 회전; 순환 dawning age 여명기

4 글의 주제 ③

해설 이제까지의 학교 개혁은 뇌의 기능과 아동의 발달을 고려하지 않고 지역과 국가가 아동에게 갖출 것을 요구하는 지식을 하달하는 방향으로 설정되었기 때문에 실패했다는 내용의 글이므로 주제로 가장 적절한 것은 ③ '전통적인 학교 개혁이 실패해 온 이유'이다.
① 학교 개혁이 교사와 학생에게 미치는 영향
② 학생들의 교육을 지원함에 있어 교사의 역할
④ 학교에서 학생의 수행을 향상시키기 위한 전략
⑤ 학교의 질적 수준과 학생 성취에 영향을 미치는 요소

해석 20년이 넘는 기간 동안, 학교 개혁은 뇌의 기능이나 아동의 건강한 발달에 대해 우리가 현재 알고 있는 것에 대한 심지어 가장 기본적인 연구가 제공한 지식도 얻지 못한 것처럼 보이는 의제에 의해 추진되어 왔다. 교육 지도자들과 정책 입안자들은 "건강한 두뇌 발달을 위해서 아동에게 무엇이 필요한가?" "그들은 어떻게 하면 가장 잘 배울까?" 또는 "아동에게 책을 읽거나 대수학을 공부하는 것을 가르칠 최적의 시기는 언제인가?"라고 묻고 있지 않다. 오히려 그들은 "우리 학교의, 지역의, 또는 국가의 기준을 충족하기 위해 우리는 이 아동에게 무엇을 할 수 있어야 한다고 요구하는가?"라고 묻고 있는 것 같다. 대부분의 개혁은 아동의 두뇌를 발달시키기보다는, 그들의 머리에 무엇을 밀어 넣어야 하는지에 (그리고 그들을 지겹도록 테스트하여 무엇이 (기억에) 머물러 있는지를 알아보는 것에) 초점이 맞춰져 왔다. 이것이 의미하는 것은 우리가 더 많이 하지만 성취는 더 적다는 것이다. 교육 개혁은 학생, 교사, 그리고 행정가의 통제력을 똑같이 떨어뜨려, 예상대로 스트레스를 더 크게 하고, 학생 참여를 더 낮게 하고, 교사의 불만과 기력 쇠진을 더욱더 많이 초래하는 정책에 의존하기 때문에 실패한다.

구문 [16행~21행] Educational reforms fail because they hinge on *policies* [that lower the sense of control of students, teachers, and administrators alike], **predictably leading** to greater stress, lower student engagement, and ever more teacher dissatisfaction and burnout.
[ ]은 policies를 수식하는 관계사절이다. predictably leading 이하는 분사구문으로 세 밑줄 부분이 콤마(,)와 and로 연결되어 병렬구조를 이룬다.

어휘 reform 개혁(하다)　agenda 의제, 안건　uninformed 정보를 받지 않은, 지식이 없는　optimal 최적의　algebra 대수학　cram 밀어[쑤셔] 넣다　stick 머무르다. 지속하다　administrator 행정가　predictably 예상대로　engagement 참여　burnout 기력 쇠진; 연료 소진　conventional 전통적인; 관습적인

5 도표 이해　　　　　　　　　　②

해설 키위 가지의 당분의 양이 전분의 양보다 많은 달은 12월, 1월, 2월이므로, 1월이 당분의 양이 전분의 양을 초과하는 유일한 달이라고 진술한 ②는 그래프와 맞지 않다.

- -

해석　키위 가지의 당분과 전분 함량의 계절적 변화
위의 그래프는 키위 가지의 1그램 당 당분과 전분 질량의 계절적 변화를 보여준다. ① 키위 가지에 들어 있는 전분은 11월에 가장 높은 수치를 보이고 5월에 가장 수치가 낮다. ② 키위 가지에 들어 있는 당분은 1월에 가장 수치가 높고, 그때가 키위 가지에 들어 있는 당분의 양이 전분의 양을 초과하는 유일한 달이다. ③ 일 년 내내, 전분의 양이 당분의 양보다 많은 기간이 당분이 전분을 초과하는 기간보다 길다. ④ 5월과 8월 사이에는 전분과 당분의 양에 있어서 거의 차이가 없다. ⑤ 전분과 당분을 결합한 총 양은 11월에 가장 높고 5월에 가장 낮은데, 그것은 전분 단독의 경우와 같다.

- -

구문 [5행~8행] Sugars in kiwifruit branches are at their highest level in *January*, **which** is *the only month* [(when) the amount of sugars in kiwifruit branches exceeds that of starch].
관계대명사 which는 앞의 January를 지칭한다. the only month 뒤에는 시간을 나타내는 관계부사 when이 생략되어 있다.

- -

어휘 seasonal 계절적인. 계절에 따라 다른　mass 질량　kiwifruit ((과일)) 키위. 참다래　exceed 초과하다　combine 결합하다　identical to A A와 동일한

6 내용 불일치　　　　　　　　　　⑤

해설 비단뱀은 멸종 위기가 아니라 멸종 위협에 가까이 처한 동물 목록에 올라 있다.

- -

해석 비단뱀은 어떤 다른 뱀과보다 보아 뱀과 더 밀접하게 관련되어 있다. 그러나 차이점에 관해서라면, 비단뱀은 머리에 뼈를 하나 더 가지고 있으며 보아 뱀보다 더 많은 이빨을 가지고 있다. 비단뱀의 길이는 종에 따라 4피트에서 29피트까지 이른다. 큰 비단뱀은 집고양이나 다 자란 사슴만큼 큰 동물을 먹이로 삼을 수 있다. 아프리카에는 가젤을 먹는 비단뱀도 있다. 그 크기에도 불구하고 비단뱀은 인간에게 좀처럼 위험하지 않다. 비단뱀은 30년까지 살 수 있다. 번식기는 60일에서 70일 사이이다. 비단뱀의 가죽은 조끼, 벨트, 부츠, 신발 같은 의류나 아니면 핸드백 같은 패션 액세서리를 만드는 데 사용된다. 비단뱀은 멸종 위기는 아니지만 멸종 위협에 가까이 처한 동물로 등재되어 있는데, 그것들은 비단뱀 가죽 판매를 위해 사냥되기 때문이다. 캘리포니아 주에서 비단뱀 가죽이나 부위의 판매는 1970년 이래로 불법화되었다.

- -

구문 [11행] Python skin **is used to make** clothing ~
「be used to-v」는 '~하기 위하여 사용되다'의 뜻이다.
[15행~16행] In California, the sale of python skin or parts **has been outlawed** / since 1970.
since(~ 이래로)는 현재완료 시제와 사용한다. 「have been p.p.」는 '~되어 왔다'의 뜻이다.

- -

어휘 family (동식물 분류상의) 과　as far as ~ go ~에 관한 한　range from A to B 범위가 A부터 B까지이다　prey on ~을 먹이로 하다　rarely 좀처럼 ~ 않다　breeding 번식　vest 조끼　endangered 멸종 위기에 처한　outlaw 불법화하다

7 밑줄 어법　　　　　　　　　　⑤

해설 ⑤ 문장의 동사는 do not know이므로 help는 동사 형태로 사용할 수 없어서 준동사로 바꿔 써야 한다. 문맥상 all the teaching tips and pedagogical knowledge를 수식하는 to-v가 가장 적절하므로 help를 to help로 바꿔 써야 한다.
① 동명사구 주어인 Being ~ outside of school은 단수로 취급되므로 단수형 동사 is를 적절하게 사용했다.
② whose parents are English-language learners 절은 앞의 students를 수식하는 관계사절이며 문맥상 '학생들의 부모'가 되므로 소유격 관계대명사 whose를 적절히 사용했다.
③ them은 these students를 지칭하므로 3인칭 복수형의 대명사인 them을 잘 사용했다.
④ Given은 '~을 고려해볼 때'라는 뜻의 전치사로 쓰였다.

- -

해석 학교 밖에서 학생들이 어떤 자원을 갖고 있는지를 이해하는 데 세심하게 마음을 쓰는 것은 학생들의 학습을 지원하려고 노력할 때 극히 도움이 된다. 내 아들과 함께 초등 교육 수준의 언어 과목 숙제를 해봤기 때문에 나는 영어를 배우고 있는 부모를 둔 학생들이 연습 문제지를 완성할 때 어떤 식으로 심각하게 불리한 상황에 처하는지를 알 수 있다. 그들이 지시를 이해하지 못하거나 읽을 수 없다면, 혹은 학생들의 숙제를 도와줄 문화적 지식을 갖고 있지 않다면, 이 학생들은 학습에서 그들을 도와줄 이러한 자원을 갖지 못한 것이다. 뿐만 아니라 맞벌이 부모 혹은 한부모는 학생들에게 시간이나 에너지라는 자원을 갖고 있지 못하거나 베풀지 못할 수 있으므로 이러한 특수한 상황은 이 학생들을 매일의 숙제와 더 광범위한 프로젝트 둘 다에서 불리한 입장에 처하게 할 수 있다. 이러한 딜레마를 고려해볼 때, 교사들이 부모에게 학생들을 도울 수 있는 방법에 대한 실용적인 제안을 제시할 수 있을 때 이는 대단히 감사한 일이다. 많은 경우에 부모들이 그저 자녀가 학업 기량을 향상시키는 데 도움을 줄 온갖 교수 비법과 교육학적 지식을 갖고 있는 것은 아니다.

- -

구문 [4행~8행] **Having worked** with my own sons / on their language arts homework / at the primary level, / I can see // how **students** [whose parents are English-language learners] **are** at a severe disadvantage / **when completing** worksheets.
'Having p.p. ~'의 형태로 시작되는 분사구문은 주절의 동사(여기서는 can see)보다 앞선 시제를 나타낼 때 쓰는 표현이다. 아들들과 언어 과목 숙제를 한 것이 영어를 배우고 있는 부모를 둔 학생들이 겪는 어려움을 이해한 것보다 이전 상황이므로 Having worked의 형태를 사용했다. how절에서 주어 students를 [ ]가 수식하고 있으며, students에 상응하는 동사는 are이다. when과 completing 사이에는 'they (= students) are'가 생략된 것으로 볼 수 있다.

- -

어휘 language arts 언어 과목　primary 초등 교육의　severe 심한　worksheet 연습 문제지　extend 베풀다. 주다; 연장하다　given ~을 고려해볼 때; 주어진, 정해진　practical 실용적인

8 밑줄 어휘　　　　　　　　　　④

해설 이 글은 이타주의와 생물의 진화에 관하여 설명하고 있다. 이타적 유전자를 가진 동물들은 동료들을 위해 자신을 희생하는 반면, 이기적 유전자를 가진 동물들은 계속해서 살아남는다는 문맥이므로 ④ 'die'는 survive(살아남다)로 바꿔야 한다.

- -

해석 다른 개체의 행복에 대한 욕심 없는 관심인 이타주의는 사회생물학과 진화론 전반에 아주 정말로 ① 어려움을 준다. Edward Wilson과 같은 작가에게 종과 개체들의 행동 유형은 생물학적인 설명이 완전히 가능한데, 어떤 동물들은 다른 것들의 안녕을 위해 자신을 ② 희생하도록 하는 유전자에 영향을 받기 때문에 이타적이라는 것이다. 예를 들어, 작은 새는 포식자가 다가올 때 경고의 울음소리를 낼 것이고, 동료를 보호하기 위해 자신의 생명을 위태롭게 할 것이다. Wilson의 말에 의하면, 문제는 '죽은 영웅은 자식을 가질

수 없다.'는 것이다. 이타주의가 유전자 속에 뿌리를 내리고 있다면 그 유전자를 지닌 개체들은 ③ 사라질 것이다. 이기적인 유전자를 가진 개체들만이 ④ 죽을(→ 살아남을) 것이다. 그러나, 이타주의는 여전히 존재하는데, 진화론이 이것을 어떻게 설명할 수 있을까? Wilson은 ⑤ 계속된 이타주의는 종의 유전자 풀을 방어하고 보호하려는 유전자의 진화적 동기에서 기인한다는 의견을 제시한다.

구문 [16행~18행] Wilson **suggests** // that continued altruism is due to *the evolutionary motivation of genes* (to defend and (to) protect the species gene pool).
that 이하는 동사 suggest의 목적어이며, ( )는 the evolutionary motivation of genes를 수식하는 to부정사구이다. 이때 and로 연결된 병렬 구조에서 뒤에 오는 to부정사의 to가 생략되었다.

어휘 altruism 이타주의 *cf.* altruistic 이타적인 welfare 안녕[행복]; 복지 sociobiology 사회생물학 evolutionary 진화의 gene 유전자 predator 포식자 approach 접근 risk (~을) 위태롭게 하다 safeguard 보호하다 fellow 동료 root 뿌리를 내리다 gene pool 유전자 풀[공급원]

9 빈칸 추론 ⑤

해설 불안과 두려움은 옛날부터 우리의 생존을 위협했던 수많은 요소들로부터 스스로를 보호하기 위해 우리가 오랫동안 품고 있던 심리적 방어물이 현재까지 ⑤ '남아있는 것'이라 할 수 있다.
① 피해 ② 스트레스 유발 인자 ③ 애매함 ④ 소통

해석 불안에 대해 이해해야 할 첫 번째는 그것이 우리의 생물학적 유산의 일부라는 것이다. 어떤 것이든 기록된 인간의 역사가 있기 오래전에, 우리의 선조들은 포식자, 기아, 독초, 적대적인 이웃들, 높은 곳, 질병, 익사와 같은 생명을 위협하는 위험들로 가득 찬 세상에서 살았다. 인간의 정신이 진화를 했던 것은 바로 이러한 위험들에 직면해서였다. 위험을 피하는 데 필수적인 특성들은 진화가 인간으로서 우리에게 심어 준 특성들이었다. 그러한 특성들 중 다수는 결국 단순히 각기 다른 형태의 조심성이 되었다. 두려움이 (인간을) 보호해주었는데, 왜냐하면 살아남기 위해서 많은 것들에 대해 조심해야 했기 때문이다. 이러한 조심스러움은 우리의 가장 깊은 증오와 두려움의 일부라는 형태로 우리의 현재 심리적 구조 안에서 계속된다. 이러한 두려움의 남은 부분으로, 우리는 그들의 존재에 많은 것을 빚지고 있다.

구문 [6행~7행] **It was** *in the face of these dangers* **that** the human mind evolved.
「It is … that ~」 강조구문으로서 '~한 것은 바로 …이다'의 뜻이며, 이 문장에서는 전치사구인 in the face of these dangers가 강조되고 있다.

어휘 heritage 유산 predator 포식자 toxic 독성이 있는 drowning 익사 evolve 진화하다 breed A into B B의 마음속에 A를 심어주다 amount to 결과적으로 ~이 되다, ~에 해당[상당]하다 cautious 조심스러운 persist (없어지지 않고) 계속[지속]되다 makeup 구성 owe A to B A를 B에 빚지다

10 빈칸 추론 ⑤

해설 빈칸의 이전 내용에서 수학, 물리학, 화학은 역사적이지 않은 학과목이며 시간을 초월한 논리 구조 혹은 우주의 특성을 다루고, 다른 사람들이 다른 시대, 다른 장소에서 실험을 반복해도 똑같은 결과가 도출될 것이라고 했으므로 물리학자들과 화학자들이 도달한 결론은 ⑤ '시간과 공간에서 독립되어 있다'고 표현할 수 있다.
① 새로운 연구 결과에 근거하여 바뀌기 쉽다

② 나이에 대한 정확한 추정치를 내놓는다
③ 사학자들의 일에 기여한다
④ 우주에 있는 모든 것을 다룬다

해석 자연과학을 구성하는 학과목은 두 부류로 나뉠 수 있다. 역사적인 분야와 그렇지 않은 분야로 말이다. 우주론, 지질학, 생물학과 같은 과목에서 역사는 극히 중요하다. 이러한 학과목의 많은 활동 목표는 우주, 지구, 그리고 그 속에서 살아온 생명체들의 역사를 각각 재구성하는 것이다. 반면에 수학자, 물리학자 혹은 화학자에게 역사는 중요하지 않다. 수학자들이 탐구하는 논리적 구조는 시간을 초월하며, 물리학과 화학은 둘 다 이제까지 혹은 앞으로와 마찬가지로 오늘도 같다고 믿을 이유가 다분한 우주의 특성들을 다룬다. 따라서 원칙적으로 물리학과 화학에서 모든 미결 문제는 올바른 실험이 행해진다면 오늘 오후에라도 답변될 수 있을 것이다. 게다가 그 실험들이 다른 사람들에 의해, 다른 때에, 혹은 다른 장소에서 행해진다면 그 결과가 조금이라도 다를 것이라고 생각할 이유가 없다. 물리학자들과 화학자들이 도달한 결론이 시간과 공간에서 독립되어 있다는 가정은 지질학자들, 생물학자들과 우주론자들이 그것을 사용하는 방식에 필수적이다.

구문 [10행~14행] *The logical structures* [(which[that]) mathematicians explore] are timeless, / and **both** physics **and** chemistry deal with *properties of the universe* [that we have every reason to believe / are the same today / as they ever have been, / or ever will be].
첫 번째 [ ]는 앞에 목적격 관계대명사 which[that]가 생략되어 The logical structures를 수식한다. 「both A and B」는 'A와 B 둘 다'의 뜻이다. 두 번째 [ ]는 앞의 properties of the universe를 수식하며, 여기서 that은 believe와 are 사이의 주어를 생략하고 쓴 주격 관계대명사이다.
[14행~17행] Thus, in principle, / all the open questions in physics and chemistry / **could be answered** this afternoon // **if** the right experiments **were done.**
「If + S' + 과거동사, S + could 동사원형(…한다면 ~할 것이다)」의 가정법 과거 표현으로 현재 사실에 대한 반대의 가정을 나타낸다.

어휘 discipline 학과목; 지식 분야; 규율 geology 지질학 utmost 극도의 reconstruct 재구성하다; 재건하다 inhabit 살다 respectively 각각 physicist 물리학자 timeless 시간을 초월한 property 특성 open question 미결 문제 fundamental 필수적인

11 빈칸 추론 ④

해설 우리가 세상을 인지하는 방식에 영향을 미치는 것이 무엇인지 찾아야 한다. 빈칸이 첫 문장에 있으므로 첫 문장이 주제문이며 부연 설명이 이어질 것이다. 이후를 보면 청각, 시각, 후각과 같은 감각이 제 기능을 다하지 못할 때 세상을 인지하는 방식에 영향이 미치는 것을 알 수 있다. 마지막 문장에서, 이와 반대로 지나치게 민감해도 환경과의 상호 작용에 영향을 받는다는 설명을 볼 때, ④ '자극에 대해 민감한 정도'가 세상을 보는 방식에 영향을 미친다는 것을 알 수 있다.
① 마음속에 품고 있는 선입관
② 구체적인 사항들을 수용하고 처리하는 방법
③ 담화를 이해하는 능력
⑤ 취약한 환경 요소

해석 각양각색의 자극에 대한 민감성이라는 측면에서 우리 각자가 경험하는 타고난 차이는 우리가 세상을 인지하는 방식에 크게 영향을 미친다. 당신이 다른 사람들이 말할 때 듣는 데 문제가 있다면, 당신은 대화의 이런저런 소소한 것들만을 듣고 아주 적은 정보를 토대로 결정과 판단을 내릴 것이다. 당신의 시력이 안 좋다면 어떨까? 그러면 당신은 더 적은 세부 사항들에 주력할 것이고 당신의 세상과의 상호 작용은 영향을 받을 것이다. 당신의 후각에 결함이 있다면, 당신은 안전한 환경과 건강에 미치는 위험을 구별하지 못할 수도 있어, 이는 당신을 더 취약하게 만든다. 정반대의 극단적인 경우로, 당신이 자극에 지나치게 민감하다면, 당신은 환경과 상호 작용하는 것을 피하고 삶의 소박한 즐거움을

놓칠지도 모른다.

구문 [1행~3행] *The innate differences* [(that) we each experience / in terms **of** how sensitive we are to different types of stimulation] contribute greatly **to** how we perceive the world.

[ ]는 목적격 관계대명사가 생략된 관계사절로 The innate differences를 수식한다. how로 시작하는 두 개의 의문사 절이 각각 전치사 of와 to의 목적어 역할을 하고 있다.

[9행~12행] *If your sense of smell is deficient, you may not be able to discriminate between a safe environment and a health hazard, // **which** would render you more vulnerable.*

계속적 용법으로 쓰인 관계대명사 which는 앞 내용 전체를 선행사로 한다.

어휘 innate 타고난, 선천적인 in terms of ~ 면에서, ~에 관하여 contribute to ~에 기여[공헌]하다; ~의 원인이 되다; ~에 기부하다 perceive 지각하다, 인지하다 bits and pieces 이런저런 소소한 것들 deficient (필수적인 것이) 부족한, 결핍된; 결함이 있는 discriminate between A and B A와 B를 구별하다 hazard 위험(요소) render ~이 되게 하다; 제공하다; 표현하다 vulnerable (~에) 취약한, 연약한 stimulation 자극, 고무, 격려 miss out on ~을 놓치다 [선택지 어휘] preconception 예상; 선입관, 편견

---

12 빈칸 추론 ④

해설 쇠퇴하고 오래된 도시는 오락과 여가를 찾아온 관광객들에게 소비될 수 있는 관광특구를 개발하여 문제 해결의 돌파구로 삼는데, 낡은 도시 속에 개발된 반짝이는 세트(관광특구)를 ④ '쇠퇴의 바다에 있는 재생의 섬'으로 비유할 수 있다.
① 매우 금처럼 보이는 돌   ② 누구도 아직 걷지 않은 길
③ 작은 정원에서 자라는 장미   ⑤ 광대한 바다에 있는 빙산의 일각

해석 도심의 사무실 단지처럼, 관광업은 흔히 쇠퇴의 바다에 있는 재생의 섬으로 발전해 왔다. 오락과 여가의 중산층 소비자를 위해 경계가 뚜렷하게 설정되고 방어되는 구역을 개척하는 전략은 범죄, 빈곤 및 물리적인 방치의 문제에 직면한 더 오래된 도시에는 자연스러운 일이었다. '관광객을 위한 특별한 장소'를 만드는 것은 개발 공간을 확보할 뿐만 아니라 부족한 자원을 효율적으로 활용하는 것을 달성하는 방법으로도 솔깃한(어떤 사람은 꼭 필요하다고 말할 수 있는) 일이었다. 적대적인 환경에서는 경계 설정 구역이 겉으로 보기에 해결할 수 없어 보이는 이미지와 사회적 통제 문제를 해결할 수 있다. 개조된 도시를 방문하는 관광객들은 공항에서 오는 길 외에는 쇠퇴의 도시를 볼 가능성이 전혀 없다. 관광객을 위해, 도시는 그 도시 전체를 표현하는 독립된 세트인 복제품으로 변형될 수 있다. 그러므로 Harbor Place나 the Renaissance Center와 Greektown으로 변형된 볼티모어와 디트로이트 모두 우리가 놀기에 빛나는 새로운 장소로 제시될 수 있다.

구문 [3행~7행] *The strategy* (of carving out sharply demarcated and defended zones for middle-class consumers of entertainment and leisure) **came** naturally to *older cities* (confronted with problems of crime, poverty, and physical neglect).

주어는 The strategy이고 동사는 came으로, 둘 사이에 있는 전명구 ( )가 주어를 수식한다. 두 번째 ( )은 수동의 의미를 나타내는 과거분사구로 older cities를 수식하며 그 안에서 crime, poverty, physical neglect는 병렬구조를 이룬다.

[7행~11행] Creating a "tourist bubble" was tempting — some might say necessary — as a way not only of securing a space for development, but for achieving an efficient application of scarce resources.

「not only A but (also) B」는 'A뿐만 아니라 B도'의 뜻이며, A와 B 자리 각각에 way에 이어지는 밑줄 친 전명구가 위치해 있다.

어휘 complex 단지 carve out 개척하다 be confronted with ~에 직면하다

---

poverty 빈곤 neglect 방치 tempting 솔깃한 scarce 부족한; 희귀한 hostile 적대적인 seemingly 겉으로 보기에 convert 개조하다; 변환시키다 reduce A to B A를 B로 바꾸다[축소하다] entirety 전체 gleaming 빛나는 tread(-trod-trod[trodden]) 걷다, 지나다; 짓밟다 decay 쇠퇴(하다); 부식[부패](하다)

---

13 흐름 무관 문장 ③

해설 기후 변화의 영향을 받아 서식지가 이동될 때, 생존은 그 종의 이동 가능성과 새로운 지역으로 가는 경로의 이용 가능성에 달려 있다는 내용의 글이므로 지구 온난화를 막기 위한 노력을 언급한 ③은 글의 흐름과 무관하다.

해석 기후 변화가 동물과 식물에 미치는 영향은 서식지 상실 및 단편화와 상호 작용을 한다. 이것은 기후 변화의 주된 영향이 어느 한 종이 성공적으로 살 수 있는 지역을 바꾸는 것이기 때문이다. ① 온난화되고 있는 세상에서, 이러한 서식할 수 있는 공간이 전 지역에서 북극이나 남극의 극지로, 또는 높은 지역으로 이동되면서, 종들은 과거 그 어느 때보다도 더 높은 산에 산다. ② 이러한 현상은 예를 들어, 평균 기온이 섭씨 15도인 지역은 지구 온난화하에서 이 방향(= 더 높은 쪽)으로 이동하기 때문에 발생한다. ③ 지구 온난화의 영향을 제한하기 위해서, 여러 나라들은 지구를 위협하는 더 많은 기온의 상승을 막는 데 노력하도록 촉구된다. ④ 그러면 생존은 특정한 종이 이동할 수 있는지, 그리고 만약 그렇다면 그 이동이 일어나는 적합한 통로가 있는지에 달려 있다. ⑤ 이 두 가지 중 어느 것도 당연시될 수 없는데, 서식지가 너무 단편화되는 곳에서는 유기체가 다른 지역으로 이동하기에 적합한 통로는 현실적인 가능성이 더 낮아진다.

구문 [2행~4행] This is // because the main effect of climate change is / **to shift** the area **of** where any one species can live successfully.

to shift 이하는 because절의 주격 보어 역할을 한다. where ~ successfully는 전치사 of의 목적어로 쓰인 명사절이다.

어휘 interact with ~와 상호 작용하다 polewards 극지역으로 elevation 높은 지역; 고도 mean 평균의 make a commitment 노력하다, 헌신하다 *cf.* commitment 헌신; 약속; 책임 threaten 위협하다 assume 당연한 일로 생각하다; 가정하다; (책임을) 떠맡다 suitable 적합한, 적당한 pathway 통로

---

14 글의 순서 ②

해설 일반 쓰레기의 처리 방법을 언급하는 주어진 글 다음에는 쓰레기를 처분하는 최선의 방법으로 퇴비로 바뀌는 봉투를 떠올릴 것이라는 (B)가 나온다. 그러나 그 봉투도 사용하지 않아야 하는데, 그 이유로 쓰레기 매립지가 분해를 장려하는 곳이 아님을 언급한다. (A)의 They는 건조한 무산소성의 공간으로 분해가 일어나기 힘든 (B)의 landfills를 가리키며 보충 설명하므로 (A)가 (B)에 이어진다. 또한 (C)의 이 물질(this material)은 문맥상 (A)의 메탄(methane)을 지칭하며 기후 변화의 원인이 되므로 쓰레기를 최소화하라고 결론짓는다.

해석 어떤 방식으로 재활용되거나 다른 용도로 사용될 수 없는 당신의 쓰레기는 일반 쓰레기로 들어갈 필요가 있으며 아마 결국 쓰레기 매립지에 당도할 것이다. 이러한 쓰레기는 보통 완전히 건조되어 작은 봉투에 들어가거나, 당신이 사는 지역에서 가능하다면 봉투를 전혀 쓰지 않고 곧장 쓰레기통으로 들어가야 한다.
(B) 당신은 퇴비로 바뀔 수 있는 쓰레기봉투가 이러한 쓰레기를 처분하는 최선의 방법이 될 것으로 생각할지도 모르지만, 최선은 가능하면 정말 봉투를 전혀 사용하지 않는 것이다. 그 이유는 쓰레기 매립지가 분해를 장려하도록 의도된 것이 아니기 때문이다.
(A) 그것들은 플라스틱을 포함하여 그 속에 든 어떤 것도 본질적으로 '미라로 만드는' 건조하고 무산소성의 공간이다. 쓰레기 매립지가 꽉 차서 폐쇄될 때까지 그 속에서 정말로 발생하는 어떠한 분해도 이산화탄소보다 대략 30배 강력한, 열을 붙잡아두는 온실가스인 바람직하지 않은 메탄을 만들어낸다.

(C) 공개된 쓰레기 매립지에서 나오는 이 물질의 배출은 지구온난화, 따라서 기후 변화의 원인이 된다. 물론 최선은 어떤 것도 쓰레기 매립지로 보내지 않도록 당신의 쓰레기를 최소화하는 것이다.

구문 [7행~9행] They are *dry and anaerobic spaces* [**that** essentially "*mummify*" *anything* (contained in them), including plastic].
[ ] 부분은 주격 관계대명사 that이 이끄는 관계사절로 선행사 dry and anaerobic spaces를 수식한다. ( ) 부분은 과거분사구로 anything을 수식한다.
[9행~12행] Until it is full and closed, *any decomposition* [**that** does occur in a landfill] creates <u>undesirable methane</u>, *a heat-trapping greenhouse gas* [**that** is roughly thirty times stronger than carbon dioxide].
두 개의 [ ] 부분은 관계대명사 that이 이끄는 관계사절로 각각 선행사 any decomposition과 a heat-trapping greenhouse gas를 수식한다. 밑줄 친 undesirable methane과 a heat-trapping greenhouse gas는 동격 관계이다.

어휘 repurpose 다른 용도에 맞게 만들다 landfill 쓰레기 매립지 mummify 미라로 만들다; 바싹 말리다 undesirable 바람직하지 않은, 불쾌한 heat-trapping 열을 가두는 dispose of ~을 처리하다 rubbish 쓰레기 release 방출(하다); 석방(하다) contribute to ~의 원인이 되다; ~에 기여하다

15 글의 순서 ⑤

해설 새로운 과학적 발견이 기존 지식을 단지 늘리는 것이라는 생각에 대한 내용 다음에는 그뿐만 아니라 기존 지식을 근본적으로 바꾸어 버리며 진보한다는 (C)가 오는 것이 적절하다. 그 다음에는 대체되는 이유를 언급하는 (B)가 오고 마지막으로 결론적인 내용인 (A)가 오는 게 적절하다.

해석 새로운 과학적 발견이 기존의 지식을 기반으로 하여 우리가 가진 지식을 단지 늘린다고 생각할 수 있다.
(C) 하지만 흔히 새로운 과학적 결과는 우리가 알고 있는 것을 늘릴 뿐만 아니라 우리가 알고 있는 것(혹은 우리가 알고 있다고 생각했던 것을) 근본적으로 바꾸어 버린다. 우리가 맞다고 믿었던 것이 틀린 것이 되고 새로운 지식이 그 자리를 대신한다. 흔히 과학은 단지 기존의 지식을 늘리는 것에 의해서가 아니라 과거의 지식을 새로운 지식으로 대체하는 것에 의해서 진보한다.
(B) 오래된 지식이 대체되는 이유는 자연이 논리적인 규칙을 따른다는 사실과 관련이 있다. 자연의 이치는 일관적이고 '잘 들어맞아야' 한다. 하나의 새로운 과학적 사실이 기존의 논리적 구조 전체가 틀렸다고 증명할 수 있다.
(A) 올바른 새로운 이해를 만들어 내기 위해서 오래된 구조는 해체되어야 하고 새로운 구조가 그 자리에 만들어져야 한다. 새로운 지식이 이전에 알려진 것과 논리적으로 모순된다면 기존의 지식을 그저 늘릴 수는 없다.

구문 [4행~6행] ~ the old structure *has to be* dismantled and a new one (has to be) created in its place.
a new one과 created 사이에는 반복을 피하기 위해 has to be가 생략되었다.

어휘 contradict 모순되다 fundamentally 근본적으로 false 틀린, 그릇된 existing 기존의 have to do with ~와 관련이 있다 consistent 일치하는, 시종일관한 hang together 잘 들어맞다, 일치하다

16 문장 넣기 ③

해설 ③ 앞 문장은 눈과 두뇌와 사지 간의 공동 작용이 도구 사용에 기여했다는 내용이고, As a result로 시작되는 ③ 뒤 문장은 걸으면서 동시에 손으로 더 많은 업무를 수행하게 된 상황이 나오는데, 이것의 원인이 앞에 나와야 함을 알 수 있다. also

를 포함하는 주어진 문장은 '직립은 팔과 손이 더 광범위한 용도로 사용되게 하여 직립 또한 도구 사용에 기여했다'라는 ③ 앞 문장에 대한 추가적인 내용이므로 주어진 문장은 ③에 들어가야 자연스럽다.

해석 인간의 두뇌 성장은 도구 사용을 증가시킨 것과 관련 있었을지도 모른다. 인간이 도구를 사용한 유일한 동물은 아니지만, 우리 종은 다른 어떤 동물보다 훨씬 더 큰 정도로 이러한 기술을 발달시켜왔다. 도구 사용의 출현은 입체적으로 보는 눈과 두뇌와 사지 간의 전례 없는 공동 작용의 결과였는데, 이는 우리의 인류 조상이 여전히 숲에서 거주하던 종이었던 동안 처음으로 나타났다. 직립 상태의 걸음 또한 매우 유용했는데, 그것이(나무들 속을 여기저기 매달리는 것은 더 힘들어졌지만) 팔과 손이 훨씬 더 광범위한 용도로 사용되게 해주었기 때문이었다. 결과적으로 인간들은 심지어 걸으면서 손을 가지고 훨씬 더 많은 일을 수행하는 법을 학습했다. 대조적으로 오늘날에는 유인원들은 이를 하지 못한다. 그들은 그러한 일을 수행하기 위해 가만히 앉아야 한다. 이러한 발달의 결과 초기 인류는 다른 더 큰 동물들에 대하여 서서히 더욱 강해졌다.

구문 [6행~9행] Although humans are not *the only animals* [who use tools], // our species has developed this skill / to a *far* **greater** extent **than** any other animal.
[ ]는 관계사절로 앞에 있는 the only animals를 수식한다. 「비교급 + than」의 구문이 쓰였고 far는 비교급을 강조하는 부사이다.
[9행~13행] The emergence of tool use was the result of *an unprecedented coordination between stereoscopic eyes, brains and limbs,* // **which** had first emerged / while our human ancestors were still a forest-dwelling species.
관계대명사 which는 계속적 용법으로 쓰여 which가 이끄는 절은 an unprecedented ~ and limbs를 부연 설명한다.

어휘 upright 직립의; 똑바른; 정직한 stride 큰 걸음; 발전; 성큼성큼 걷다 swing 매달리다; 흔들리다 extent 정도; 범위 emergence 출현 unprecedented 전례 없는, 새로운 coordination 공동 작용, 협동 limb 사지(四肢), 팔다리 dwell 거주하다, 살다 great ape 유인원 still 가만히 있는; 여전히 execute 수행[실행]하다 with respect to ~에 대하여[관한]

17 문장 넣기 ④

해설 ④ 뒤의 문장은 '이것이 특화를 가져왔다'는 진술인데 ④ 앞의 문장은 '사람들이 1만 년 전에 기후가 안정화됨에 따라 정착했다'는 내용이어서 인과관계가 성립하지 않는다. '특화를 가져온 것'의 원인이 되는 것은 주어진 문장의 내용(지역마다 사정이 달라서 잘 되는 작물이 달랐다)에 있으므로 주어진 문장은 ④에 위치해야 한다.

해석 인간은 20만 년 동안 지구상에 존재해왔다. 이 기간의 처음 99% 기간 동안, 우리는 번식하고 생존하는 것 외에는 그다지 한 일이 없다. 이것은 주로 가혹한 지구 기후 환경 때문이었는데, 기후는 1만 년 정도 전의 어느 시기에 안정되었다. 사람들은 그 이후로 곧 농경과 관개를 발전시켰고 안정적인 작물을 경작하고 기르기 위해 방랑하는 생활 방식을 포기했다. <u>그러나 모든 농지가 동일하지는 않다. 햇빛, 토양, 그리고 다른 상황들의 지역적 차이는 어떤 농부가 특별히 좋은 사과를 기르는 동안 다른 농부는 특별히 좋은 양파를 기를지도 모른다는 것을 의미했다.</u> 이것이 결국 특화를 가져왔다. 자신의 가족을 위해 모든 작물을 기르는 대신, 농부는 자신이 가장 잘 하는 것만을 길러서 그 일부를 자신이 재배하지 않은 것들로 교환할 수 있다. 각각의 농부가 오직 하나의 작물을, 자신이 필요한 것보다 더 많이 생산하고 있었기 때문에, 시장과 교역이 생기고 성장했으며, 뒤따라 도시가 설립되었다.

구문 [14행~16행] ~ a farmer <u>might grow</u> only **what he was best at** and trade some of it for things [he wasn't growing].
동사 might grow와 (might) trade가 병렬구조를 이루고 있다. 선행사를 포함한 관계대명사 what이 이끄는 절은 might grow의 목적어 역할을 하고 있다.

어휘 plot 작은 땅 조각　regional 지역의　variation 차이　but ~을 제외하고　reproduce 번식하다　harsh 거친, 가혹한　stabilize 안정되다　thereafter 그 후에　irrigation 관개, (논 등에) 물을 끌어들임　nomadic 유목의, 방랑의　cultivate 경작하다　tend 돌보다　specialization 특수화, 전문화　marketplace 시장　emerge 출현하다

18 요약문 완성   ②

해설　자신을 실험하는 것은 윤리적인(moral) 문제를 피할 수 있는 장점이 있지만, 여전히 위험성을 갖고 제한된 데이터라서 전체 집단을 대표하지(represent) 못하는 한계점을 가지고 있다는 내용의 글이다.

① 도덕적인 – 선택하다 　　③ 법적인 – 선택하다
④ 법적인 – 설명하다 　　⑤ 정치적인 – 대표하다

해석　인간 피험자에 관한 과학 실험을 다루는 규정은 엄격하다. 피험자는 충분한 설명에 입각한 서면으로 된 동의를 해야 하고, 실험자는 자신들의 계획된 실험을 제출해 감독 기관에 의한 철저한 정밀 조사를 받아야 한다. 자신을 실험하는 과학자들은 다른 사람을 실험하는 것과 관련된 규제를 피할 수 있다. 그들은 관련된 윤리적인 문제를 대부분 피할 수 있다. 실험을 고안한 과학자보다 그것의 잠재적인 위험을 더 잘 알고 있는 사람은 아마 없을 것이다. 그럼에도 불구하고, 자신을 실험하는 것은 여전히 문제가 심각하다. 한 가지 명백한 문제점은 (실험에) 수반되는 위험이다. 위험이 존재한다는 것을 안다고 해서 위험이 줄어드는 것은 결코 아니다. 덜 명백한 문제점은 실험이 만들어 낼 수 있는 데이터의 제한된 범위이다. 인체의 해부학적 구조와 생리 기능은 성별, 나이, 생활 방식, 그리고 기타 요인에 따라 사소하지만 의미 있는 방식으로 각기 다르다. 따라서, 단 한 명의 피험자로부터 얻어진 실험 결과는 가치가 제한적이며, 피험자의 반응이 집단으로서의 인간 반응의 전형적인 것인지 이례적인 것인지 알 방법이 없다.

↓

> 과학자의 자기 실험은 그 실험과 관련된 (A) 도덕적 문제를 피하는 이점을 가지고 있지만 또한 그 실험에 관련된 위험과, 그 결과가 다양한 모집단을 (B) 대표하지 못하는 한계가 있다.

구문　[5행~7행] Scientists [who experiment on themselves] can avoid *the restrictions* (associated with experimenting on other people).
[ ]은 관계사절로 Scientists를 수식하고 분사구인 ( )은 the restrictions를 수식한다.
[12행~14행] One obvious drawback is *the danger* **involved**; knowing {that it exists} does nothing to reduce it.
밑줄 친 부분에서 '관련된'의 뜻을 가진 형용사 involved가 앞에 나온 명사 the danger를 수식한다. { } 부분은 동명사 knowing의 목적어 역할을 하는 명사절로 knowing이 이끄는 동명사구가 문장의 주어이다.

어휘　regulation 규정, 규제　subject 피험자, 대상　informed consent 충분한 설명에 입각한 동의　rigorous 철저한, 엄격한　oversee 감독하다　restriction 규제, 제한　associated with ~와 관련된　sidestep 피하다　ethical 윤리적인　involved 수반되는　presumably 아마, 짐작건대　hazard 위험　devise 고안하다, 생각해 내다　drawback 문제점, 결점　physiology 생리, 생리 기능　derive 얻다, 끌어내다　typical 전형적인, 대표적인(→ atypical 이례적인)

19~20 장문   19 ② 20 ⑤

해설　19. 소비자가 물건을 살 때 양자택일의 경우 결정이 어려우면 둘 다 사지 않을 수 있지만 덜 매력적인 제3의 제품을 추가한다면 나머지 것에 더 호감이 가게 하

면서 구매로 이어진다고 했다. 이 매력이 덜한 제품은 미끼의 역할을 하면서 구매를 유도한다고 했으므로 글의 제목으로는 ② '마케팅 전략으로 미끼 효과를 사용하라'가 적절하다.
① 소비자들은 왜 비교로 고생하는가?
③ 미끼 효과: 합리적 선택을 하는 방법
④ 마케팅 전술: 고객의 선호를 바꿔라
⑤ 선택의 역설: 더 매력적인 것이 덜 선호된다
20. 선택을 더 쉽게 만드는 제3의 선택물을 포함한 세 가지 선택물을 고려할 때 부정적인 감정과 관련된 뇌의 활동은 감소해야 하므로 (e)는 'decrease' 등으로 바꿔 써야 한다.

해석　만약 여러분의 고객이 재킷과 스웨터 중에 어느 것을 살지를 결정하려는데, 그 사람이 마음을 결정하지 못하면 둘 중 어느 하나도 사지 않을 수도 있다. 여러분은 어떻게 그 고객이 정말로 원하는 것을 결정하도록 도울 수 있을까? 최근 연구는 고객이 덜 매력적인 제3의 선택을 고려하면 의사결정이 쉽게 된다는 것을 보여준다. 마케팅 교수인 Akshay Rao는 위와 같은 상황에서 덜 매력적인 스웨터가 고려될 때, 쇼핑객은 더 매력적인 스웨터를 선택해서 그의 어려운 문제를 (a) 해결할 수 있다는 것을 보여주는 연구를 수행했다. Akshay Rao는 "덜 매력적인 스웨터는 다른 스웨터를 전보다 더 (b) 만족스러워 보이게 만드는 미끼의 역할을 한다. 어찌 보면 그것은 아주 간단하다. 소비자가 선택에 직면할 때 상대적으로 매력이 덜한 선택물의 존재는 가장 유사하고 더 좋은 품목의 선택의 몫을 (c) 늘린다."고 말한다.
실제로 실험 대상자들이 선택을 하는 동안 그들의 뇌를 정밀 검사했는데, 추가 가능성의 존재는 보다 나은 선택물에 대한 선호도를 조직적으로 증가시켰다. 뇌의 촬영 결과는 실험 대상자들이 똑같이 마음에 드는 제품 두 개 사이에서 선택할 때 선택 과정의 (d) 어려움으로 초조함을 보여주는 경향이 있음을 보여주었다. 제3의 선택물의 존재가 선택과정을 더 쉽게 만들었다. 물건을 사는 사람들은 세 가지 선택물을 고려할 때에, 부정적인 감정과 관련된 뇌의 부위인 편도체의 활동에서 (e) 증가(→ 감소)를 보여주었다. 이러한 연구는 몇 가지 중요한 함의를 갖고 있다. 양자택일은 인터넷 기반 여행 시장과 휴대전화 약정을 포함한 다양한 배경에서 일상적으로 마주친다. 이런 시장에서 부적절한 선택물의 추가는 부정적 감정을 감소시키는 전략이다.

구문　[7행~11행] Akshay Rao, a marketing professor, conducted *research* [that shows **that**, when a less desirable sweater is considered in the situation above, the shopper could solve her conundrum by choosing the more attractive sweater].
[ ]은 관계사절로 선행사 research를 수식한다. [ ] 내에서 shows의 목적어로 that이 이끄는 명사절이 쓰였다.
[19행~22행] In fact, subjects **had** *their brains* **scanned** while they made their choices, and the presence of the extra possibility systematically increased preference for the better options.
「사역동사(had)+목적어(their brains)+p.p.(scanned)」의 구조이다.
[27행~30행] When considering three options, buyers displayed a decrease in activation of the amygdala, *an area of the brain* (associated with negative emotions).
밑줄 친 두 명사구는 서로 동격 관계이다. ( ) 부분은 과거분사가 이끄는 형용사구로 an area of the brain을 수식한다.

어휘　make up one's mind 결정[결심]하다　simplify 쉽게[간단하게] 하다; 단순화하다　conduct 수행[시행]하다　desirable 매력 있는; 바람직한　conundrum 어려운 문제, 수수께끼　straightforward 간단한; 정직한; 똑바른　scan 정밀 검사[촬영]하다; 훑어보다　systematically 조직적으로, 질서 정연하게　irritation 초조함; 짜증; 자극(상태)　activation 활동; 활성화　implication 함의; 암시; 영향; 결과　alternative 양자택일, 대안, 선택 가능한 것　routinely 일상적으로, 관례대로　comparison 비교, 대조　rational 합리적인; 이성적인　tactic 전술, 전략　paradox 역설

| 1 | ① | 2 | ② | 3 | ② | 4 | ③ | 5 | ③ | | 6 | ③ | 7 | ⑤ | 8 | ④ | 9 | ④ | 10 | ④ |
| 11 | ① | 12 | ① | 13 | ④ | 14 | ④ | 15 | ② | | 16 | ⑤ | 17 | ③ | 18 | ④ | 19 | ④ | 20 | ③ |

1 심경 변화   ①

해설 돈이 필요해서 야구 카드를 벼룩시장에 내놓은 노인은 물건을 보러 온 사람이 가격을 듣고 구매를 거절하자 가슴이 철렁했지만, 그가 카드의 진가를 알려주며 골동품 중개인에게 가보라고 조언해주었을 때 그의 정직함에 고마워했다. 따라서 노인의 심경 변화로 가장 적절한 것은 ① '절박한 → 고마워하는'이다.

② 무관심한 → 신이 난   ③ 걱정하는 → 확신에 찬
④ 후회하는 → 안도한   ⑤ 기대하는 → 슬픈

해석 벼룩시장 판매가 시작되었고 대부분의 물품들은 빨리 나갔다. 한 노인이 오래된 야구 카드 한 장을 테이블에 놔두었다. Mark는 회색의 이미지를 뚫어지게 보다가 카드를 뒤집었다. "저건 제가 가장 좋아하는 것 중 하나네요." 그 남자는 말했다. "얼마... 얼마죠?" Mark는 물었다. "50달러예요." 그는 말했다. Mark가 고개를 젓고 카드를 돌려주었을 때, 그 남자는 심장이 가라앉았다. "저는 지금 당장 돈이 몹시 필요해요. 20달러는 어떤가요?" 그 노인이 간청했다. "저기요." Mark는 말했다. "제가 야구 카드에 대해서는 많이 압니다. 이건 골동품 중개인에게 가져가셔야 해요. 저 카드는 적어도 1,500달러의 가치가 있어요." 갑자기 그 남자의 눈이 커졌다. 그는 눈에 눈물이 고인 채로 말했다. "당신의 정직함을 결코 잊지 않겠소." 그러고 나서 그는 그 카드를 가슴팍에 움켜쥐고 걸어갔다.

구문 [2행~3행] An elderly man **had** *one old baseball card* **left** on his table. 「have + O + p.p.」 구문은 'O가 ~되게 하다'를 뜻한다. '카드'가 '남겨진' 것이므로 목적어와 보어는 수동 관계이다. 따라서 보어 자리에 과거분사 left가 왔다.

어휘 flea market 벼룩시장   turn A over A를 뒤집다   plead 간청하다, 애원하다   antique 골동품   dealer 중개인   clutch 움켜잡다

2 필자 주장   ②

해설 역사가들은 사실만을 다루므로 미래에 대해 논하지 않아서 정책 결정 과정에 참여하지 않지만, 그들이 정책 결정에 참여한다면 정교하고 적응성 있는 정책을 내놓을 수 있으며 역사 연구 또한 정당한 가치를 인정받을 수 있다는 내용의 글이므로 필자의 주장으로 가장 적절한 것은 ②이다.

해석 모든 역사가들은 미래에 대해 결코 말해서는 안 된다는 것을 알고 있다. 그들의 규율이 요구하는 바는 사실을 다루어야 한다는 것인데, 미래는 아직 어떠한 것(= 사실)도 갖고 있지 않다. 역사에 대한 견고한 이론이 미래를 아우를 수 있을지 모르겠으나, 그러한 이론들은 모두 신용되지 않아 왔다. 따라서 역사가들은 공공 정책을 형성하는 데 참여할 것을 제안하지도 않고 좀처럼 요청받지도 않는다. 그들은 그 일을 경제학자들에게 남겨둔다. 그러나 공공 정책 입안자들에게 역사가들을 고용할 의무가 있고, 역사가들에게는 돕기 위해 노력해야 하는 의무가 있다면 어떻게 될까? 올바르게 행해지면 역사는 의사 결정과 정책을 훨씬 더 정교하고 적응성 있게 만들 수 있을 것이며, 이는 역사 연구에 역사학이 받아 마땅한 수준의 중요성을 부여할 수 있을 것이다. 우리는 역사로부터 배워야 하며, Santayana의 경고에는 여전히 힘이 있다. 그것은 바로 역사에서 배우지 못하는 사람들은 그것을 되풀이할 신세에 처한다는 것이다.

구문 [10행~14행] Done right, / history could **make** *decision making and*

policy **far more sophisticated and adaptive**, // and this could invest the study of history / with *the level of consequence* [(which[that]) it deserves]. Done right은 수동의 의미를 가지는 분사구문이다. 「make + O + C (O가 C하도록 만들다)」 구문이 쓰였다. [ ]는 앞에 목적격 관계대명사 which[that]가 생략되어 the level of consequence를 수식하는 관계사절이며 여기서 it은 the study of history를 가리킨다.

[14행~17행] We should learn from history, // and Santayana's warning continues in force: that *those* [who fail to learn from history] are condemned to repeat **it**.

that ~ repeat it은 Santayana's warning에 대한 동격절이다. [ ]는 those를 수식하는 주격 관계사절이다. to repeat it에서 it은 history를 지칭한다.

어휘 discipline 규율; 훈련, 수양   deal in 다루다, 취급하다   embrace 아우르다, 포괄하다; 수용하다   discredit 신용하지 않다, 의심하다; 신빙성을 없애다   obligation 의무   engage 고용하다   sophisticated 정교한   adaptive 적응할 수 있는   consequence 중요함; 결과   deserve ~을 받을 만하다   be condemned to (상황에) 처하게 되다 *cf.* condemn 처하게 만들다; 비난하다; 선고를 내리다

3 밑줄 함의   ②

해설 우리의 소비와 폐기물 생성의 환경적 영향이 우리와 멀리 떨어져 있고 직접 경험하지 않다 보니, 우리는 그 부정적 영향으로부터 공간적으로 또한 인지적으로도 멀리 떨어져 있다는 내용이다. 그러므로 밑줄 친 부분은 ② '우리는 우리와 직접적인 관계가 없는 환경 문제에 관심을 갖지 않는다.'의 의미임을 알 수 있다.

① 우리는 각 나라의 환경 문제를 해결하는 방법에 관심이 없다.
③ 우리는 가난한 나라에 의해 야기된 환경적 문제점에 관해 전혀 생각하지 않는다.
④ 우리는 원인을 알기 전까지 환경 문제의 해결책을 생각할 수 없다.
⑤ 환경 문제를 자세히 보면 우리는 그것들에 대해 더 잘 이해할 수 있다.

해석 사람들과 환경적 특징 사이의 상호 작용에는 자주 간과되는 공간적 측면이 있다. 산림, 어류 자원, 그리고 우리가 소비하는 물건을 만드는 데 사용되는 다양한 광물 및 금속과 같은 자원 물자에 미치는 우리의 영향은 특정한 장소에서 일어난다. 종종 우리의 소비와 폐기물 생성의 환경적 영향은 우리와 멀리 떨어져 있고, 우리는 그것들을 직접 경험하지 않는다. 북미, 유럽, 그리고 일본에서 사랑의 상징으로서의 다이아몬드에 대한 수요는 다이아몬드를 생산하는 서아프리카의 이전의 유럽 식민지에서의 부정적이고 폭력적인 영향과 관련이 있다. 마찬가지로, 비록 우리가 조금도 줄지 않는 온실 가스 배출에 대해 중국을 비난할지 모르지만, 낮은 환경 기준에 의해 부분적으로 가능하게 된 그곳의 산업 생산성은 전 세계 소비자들에게 저렴한 제품을 제공한다. 세계의 더 부유한 지역의 소비는 그것이 하이브리드 자동차의 배터리를 위한 원료를 채굴하는 것이든 수입원을 간절히 원하는 가난한 나라에 유독성 전자 폐기물을 쏟아버리는 것이든 간에, 자주 그것의 부정적인 영향으로부터 공간적으로 그리고 인지적으로 모두 멀리 떨어져 있다. 우리 눈에 보이지 않으면, 우리는 그것에 대해 생각하지 않는다.

구문 [3행~6행] Our impact on resource supplies, such as forests, fish stocks, and *the various minerals and metals* (used to make *the things* [**that** we consume]), happens in particular places.

( ) 부분은 과거분사구로 the various minerals and metals를 수식한다. 분사구 안

에 [ ] 부분은 목적격 관계대명사 that이 이끄는 관계사절로 선행사 the things를 수식한다.

어휘 spatial 공간적인, 공간의　dimension 측면, 관점; 차원; 치수　overlook 간과하다; 못 본 체하다　mineral 광물, 무기질　generation 생성, 생산; 세대　distance ∼을 멀리에 두다; 먼 곳; 거리　colony 식민지; 군집　fault 비난하다, 나무라다; 흠, 잘못　emission 배출(물)　spatially 공간적으로; 우주적으로　cognitively 인지적으로　mining 채굴　dumping 쏟아버림, 투기, 폐기　toxic 유독성의　desperate 간절히 필요로 하는; 필사적인　income 수입, 소득

4 글의 요지 ③

해설 이야기가 과거에는 인간을 사회와 문화의 공동체로 결속시키는 순기능을 수행했으나, 각종 매체를 통하여 이야기가 범람하는 현대 사회에서 이야기에 탐닉하는 것은 정신적 과식과 해로운 영향을 유발할 수 있다는 내용의 글이다. 따라서 글의 요지로 가장 적절한 것은 ③이다.

해석 인간은 이야기를 갈망하도록 진화했다. 이러한 갈망은 대체로 우리에게 좋은 것이었다. 이야기는 우리에게 즐거움과 교훈을 준다. 그것(이야기)은 우리가 이 세계에서 더 잘 살 수 있도록 세계들을 모방해서 만들어진다. 그것은 우리를 공동체로 결속시키고 문화로 정의하는 데 도움이 된다. 이야기는 우리 종에게 대단히 요긴한 것이었다. 그러나 그것이 약점이 되어가고 있는가? 이야기에 대한 우리의 갈망과 음식에 대한 우리의 갈망 간에 이루어져야 할 비유가 있다. 과식하는 경향은 식량 부족이 삶의 너무 뻔한 부분이었을 때 우리 조상들에게 대단히 도움이 되었다. 그러나 우리 현대 사무직들에게는 싸구려 기름과 콘 시럽이 넘쳐나고 있으므로, 과식이 우리를 살찌우고 요절하게 할 가능성이 더욱더 높다. 마찬가지로 이야기에 대한 강렬한 탐욕이 우리 조상들에게는 건강한 것이었으나, 책과 TV와 인터넷이 이야기를 어디에나 존재하게 만드는 세상에서는 몇몇 해로운 결과를 일으킬 수도 있다. 문학자 Brian Boyd가 쓰레기 이야기로 가득한 세상에서 과소비가 '정신적 당뇨 전염병'과 같은 것으로 이어질 수 있는지를 궁금해 하는 것이 옳다고 생각한다.

구문 [11행∼13행] But **now that** we modern desk jockeys are awash in cheap grease and corn syrup, // overeating is more likely to fatten us up and (to) kill us young.
now that(∼이므로, ∼이기 때문에)은 부사절을 이끄는 접속사이다. to fatten과 kill이 병렬구조를 이루고 반복되는 to는 생략되었다.
[13행∼17행] Likewise, **it** could be **that** an intense greed for stories was healthy for our ancestors but has some harmful consequences in a world [where books, TVs, and the Internet **make** stories **omnipresent**].
it은 가주어 that 이하가 진주어이다. [ ]는 a world를 수식하는 관계부사절로 관계부사절 내에 「사역동사 make+목적어(stories)+목적격보어(omnipresent)」의 구문이 사용되었다.

어휘 crave 갈망[열망]하다 *cf.* craving 갈망, 열망　on the whole 대체로, 전반적으로　instruction 교훈, 가르침; 교육　simulate ∼을 모방해서 만들어지다; ∼한 척[체]하다　bind 결속시키다; 감다　analogy 비유; 유사점　desk jockey 사무직원　grease 기름(을 바르다); 윤활유　fatten 살찌우다; 비옥하게 하다　intense 강렬한, 극심한　greed 탐욕, 욕심　consequence 결과; 영향(력)　omnipresent 어디에나 있는　diabetes 당뇨병　epidemic (유행성) 전염병; 급속한 확산

5 글의 제목 ③

해설 식당 예약을 받을 때 의문문으로 묻고, '네' 혹은 '아니오'라고 고객이 직접 발화하게 하는 것이 노쇼 비율을 줄였다는 내용의 글이므로 제목으로 가장 적절한 것

은 ③ '한 레스토랑의 노쇼 해법: 고객이 '네'라고 말하게 하라'이다.
① 식당의 노쇼 문제를 다루는 여러 전략들
② 나타나지 않는 손님에게 식당이 요금을 부과해야 하는가?
④ 명확한 예약 정책이 노쇼의 비용을 줄이는 데 도움이 된다
⑤ 처음의 작은 요청이 고객을 더욱 편안하게 한다

해석 한 시카고의 식당 주인이 '노쇼'로 곤경을 겪고 있었다. 사람들은 저녁 식사 예약을 하고서도 식사에 나타나지 못하곤 했다. 게다가 그들은 예약을 취소하기 위해 전화를 하지도 않곤 했다. 이 식당에서는 접수 담당자가 전화로 예약을 받고 '계획이 변경되면 전화해주세요.'라고 말하는 것이 보통이었다. 몇 달 동안 이 식당의 노쇼 비율은 대략 30%였다. 행동 과학 연구의 일부로 연구자들은 한 실험을 수행했는데, 그에 따라 그들은 접수 담당자에게 '계획이 변경되면 전화주세요.'라고 말하기를 그만두고 '계획이 변경되면 전화 주시겠습니까?'라고 말하기 시작하라고 지시했다. 뿐만 아니라 접수 담당자는 의도적으로 잠시 멈추고 전화 건 사람이 대답할 것을 기다리라는 지시도 받았다. 단지 대본에 두 단어를 추가하고 물음표로 끝맺음으로써 무슨 일이 일어났다고 생각하는가? 놀랍게도 이러한 단순하고 거의 힘이 안 드는 변화를 줌으로써, 즉 전화 건 사람이 네 혹은 아니오 둘 중 하나로 약속을 하게 하여, 이 식당의 노쇼 비율은 30%에서 10%로, 20퍼센트 포인트라는 엄청난 수치가 감소했다.

구문 [4행∼7행] At this restaurant, / **it** was common *for the receptionist* **to take** the reservation by phone and then **say**, "Please call if you change your plans."
it은 가주어, to take 이하가 진주어이며 for the receptionist는 to-v의 의미상 주어이다. to 다음의 동사원형 take와 say가 and로 연결되어 병렬구조를 이룬다.
[15행∼17행] **What** do you think **happened** / by simply *adding* two words to the script and *ending* with a question mark?
what happened가 think의 목적어 역할을 하는 간접의문문이다. do you think[believe/suppose] 등으로 시작하는 문장에서 동사의 목적어로 간접의문문이 나올 때는 「의문사+do you think+주어+동사」의 어순을 쓴다. 이 문장에서는 what이 의문사이기도 하고 주어이기도 하다. by 다음에 동명사 adding과 ending이 and로 연결되어 병렬구조를 이룬다.

어휘 additionally 게다가　receptionist 접수 담당자　approximately 대략　whereby 그에 따라　intentionally 고의로　script 대본　effortless 힘이 들지 않는　commitment 약속

6 안내문 불일치 ③

해설 공공 보건 규정에 의해 가정에서 만든 식품은 받을 수 없다고 하였다.

해석 연례 명절 음식 자선 행사
12월 10일 ∼ 14일
이제 그 어느 때보다 우리는 우리 사회를 변화시키기 위해 당신의 도움이 필요합니다. 12월 10일이 속한 주간 동안, 상하지 않는 식품을 모을 것입니다. 모든 기부는 도움을 필요로 하는 Arlington 거주 가족들에게 바로 갈 것입니다. 연례 명절 음식 자선 행사에 함께 해주세요!

필요한 품목들:
시리얼, 박스 포장된 파스타, 파스타 소스, 통조림 고기, 통조림 과일과 야채, 땅콩버터, 쌀, 조리용 기름 (유통기한을 확인해주세요.)
공공 보건 규정에 의해 저희는 가정에서 만들었거나 이미 개봉되었거나, 혹은 상표가 없는 식품은 받을 수 없습니다.

장소:
2100 Central가에 있는 Arlington 시민회관에 (음식을) 전달해주세요.
월요일 오전 10시 ∼ 오후 9시, 화–금 오전 10시 ∼ 오후 6시
* 이후 시간에는 상하지 않는 식품을 정문 옆에 위치한 저희 수거함에 두실 수 있습니다.

더 많은 정보가 필요하시면 ArlingtonCivicCenter.org를 방문해주세요.

구문 [13행~14행] Public health rules **prevent *us* from accepting** any homemade, already opened, **or** unlabeled *food*.
'prevent O from v-ing'는 '…가 ~ 못하게 막다'의 뜻이다. homemade, already opened, unlabeled는 or로 연결되어 병렬구조를 이루는 과거분사이며, 공통적으로 food를 수식한다.

어휘 non-perishable 잘 부패하지 않는 canned 통조림으로 된 expiration date 유통기한 unlabeled 상표가 없는 drop off (어떤 장소에 물건을) 전달하다 civic center 시민회관

7 밑줄 어법 ⑤

해설 'Whether ~ the natural world'는 부사절이고 your local park가 문장의 주어이다. 이 다음에 동사가 와야 하므로 having을 has로 고쳐 써야 한다.
① 동사 are becoming을 수식하므로 부사가 적절하다.
② 앞의 maintaining과 병렬 구조를 이루므로 적절하게 쓰였다.
③ '목적'을 의미하는 to부정사이므로 적절하다.
④ '~에 따라'의 의미인 접속사 as 뒤의 동사 자리이므로 적절하다.

해석 도시의 더 높은 밀도 생활은 자신만의 정원 공간을 가진 사람이 더 적으며 요즘 가정의 정원은 끊임없이 더 작아지고 있음을 의미한다. 이것은 공공 정원을 유지하고 정원 공간을 새로운 개발에 통합시키는 중요성에 대한 한 가지 이유이다. 정원이 제공하는 혜택 중 많은 것은 모든 사람들이 공공 정원과 공원에서 즐길 수 있도록 이용 가능하며, 이러한 장소는 종종 결혼식, 파티, 그리고 모든 종류의 가족 모임 현장이 된다. 공공 정원은 우리에게 오락, 사색, 교육과 영감을 주는 기회를 제공한다. 그것이 지역사회와 환경에 갖는 중요성은 아무리 말해도 과장이라 할 수 없으며 더 높아진 인구밀도 생활이 더 많은 사람들에게서 사적 정원 공간을 박탈함에 따라 (중요성은) 오직 증가하기만 할 것이다. 그것이 친구들과 교제하는 장소든 스포츠를 하는 장소든 요가를 행하는 장소든 명상하는 장소든 소풍 가는 장소든 탐험하는 장소든 노는 장소든 자연 세계에 대해 배우는 장소든, 당신이 정말로 당신만의 정원을 갖고 있다 하더라도 당신의 지역 공원은 제공해 줄 많은 것을 가지고 있다.

구문 [4행~6행] This is one reason for the importance **of** [maintaining public gardens] and [integrating *garden spaces* into *new developments*].
두 [ ] 부분은 공통적으로 of 뒤에 연결되며 병렬구조를 이룬다. 'integrate A into B'는 'A를 B 속에 통합하다'의 의미이다.
[12행~15행] [Their importance to the community and to the environment] **cannot** be overstated and will only grow **as** higher density living **deprives *more people* of *private garden spaces***.
주어는 [ ]이고 동사는 cannot be overstated와 will only grow가 병렬구조를 이룬다. cannot이 too 혹은 'over-'와 함께 쓰이면 '아무리 ~해도 지나치지 않다'의 뜻이 된다. as 절에서 'deprive A of B'는 'A에게서 B를 박탈하다'의 의미이다.

어휘 density 밀도 integrate 통합하다 get-together 모임 contemplation 사색, 명상 inspiration 영감 overstate 과장하다 deprive A of B A에게서 B를 박탈하다 socialize with ~와 교제하다

8 밑줄 어휘 ④

해설 지난 2세기 동안 미국에서 습지가 많이 사라지게 된 원인들과 그로 인한 부정적인 결과들에 관한 글이다. 2005년 허리케인 Katrina로 인한 멕시코 만 해안의 범

람은 습지를 잃어버린 것의 결과여야 하므로 ④의 conserved를 lost로 고쳐야 한다.

해석 대략 2세기 동안, 미국인들은 자국의 늪과 습지를 경작하거나 그 위를 덮어왔다. 비옥한 습지의 토양은 작물을 대량으로 생산하는 농지를 만들고, 큰 강 또는 해안 근처에 있는 장소는 개발하기에 ① 바람직한 장소이다. 이러한 신비한 생태계는 또한 악어와 모기와 같이 많은 사람들이 바람직하지 않다고 생각하는 생물의 서식지인데, 이는 그것들을 ② 제거해야 하는 또 다른 이유를 제공한다. 캘리포니아가 90%가 넘는 습지를 잃었다. 이제, 그 주의 토착 물고기들 중 거의 3분의 2가 멸종되거나, 멸종 위기에 이르거나, (멸종을) 위협받거나, 감소하는 중이다. 미시시피 강 주변 숲이 울창한 강가의 습지는 한때 60일 정도의 하천 ③ 유출량을 저장할 수용력이 있었지만 이제는 단지 12일 정도의 양만 저장할 수 있다. 연구자들은 그 지역이 지난 한 세기 동안 습지를 그만큼 많이 ④ 보존하지 (→ 잃지) 않았더라면 2005년의 허리케인 Katrina로 인한 멕시코 만 해안의 범람은 훨씬 규모가 덜했을 것이라고 말한다. 습지가 없다면, 오염 물질이 개울과 호수 그리고 바다로 더 ⑤ 손쉽게 나아간다.

구문 [16행~20행] Researchers say // that the flooding (of the Gulf of Mexico coast from Hurricane Katrina in 2005) would have been much less extensive / **had the region not lost so much of its wetlands in the past century**.
had ~ century는 if가 생략된 가정법 과거완료의 조건절로 if the region had not lost ~ century의 의미이다. if를 포함하는 가정법 문장에서 if가 생략되면 '주어-(조)동사'가 도치된다.
[20행~22행] **Without wetlands**, / pollutants make their way more readily to streams, lakes, and the oceans.
Without wetlands는 '조건'의 뜻을 함축하고 있는 가정법 문장이며, If an area doesn't have wetlands로 바꿔 쓸 수 있다.

어휘 plow 경작(하다); 쟁기 pave (땅을 포장하여) 덮다; 포장하다 wetland 습지(대) desirable 바람직한, 호감 가는(↔ undesirable 바람직하지 않은, 원하지 않는) ecosystem 생태계 eliminate 제거[삭제]하다, 없애다 extinct 멸종된; 사라진 capacity 수용(력); 능력 discharge 유출량; 방출하다; 석방하다; 해고하다 extensive 대규모의, 아주 넓은[많은] region 지역, 지방 conserve 보존[보호]하다; 아끼다 pollutant 오염 물질 make one's way to A A로 나아가다 readily 손쉽게, 순조롭게; 기꺼이

9 빈칸 추론 ④

해설 아기들이 부모와 양육자들에게 반복적으로 요청해서 받는 것이 무엇인지를 찾아야 한다. 뒤에 이어지는 예시에서, 엄마에게 눈이 안전한 것이라는 말과 신호를 받은 뒤 위험한 것이 아니라는 결론을 내린다고 했으므로 빈칸에는 안심시키는 말[행동]을 뜻하는 ④ '안도'가 들어가야 한다.
① 경고 ② 목적 ③ 한계 ⑤ 혼동

해석 아기들은 성장해 가면서, 비언어적인 신호들을 읽는 것을 통해, 그리고 결국에는 말로 된 언어를 이해하는 것을 통해 스스로 안도감을 얻는 방법을 배울 뿐만 아니라 무엇이 위험한지를 계속해서 이해한다. 그들은 부모와 다른 양육자들에게 반복적으로 안도(안심시키는 말이나 행동)를 요청해서 받는다. 처음으로 눈을 보는 유아는 아마도 불안한 마음으로 눈과 엄마를 번갈아 보고 손가락으로 가리키며 곤경을 나타내면서 "엄마!"라고 말할지도 모른다. 그녀의 엄마는 "아가, 그건 그저 눈일 뿐이란다."라고 웃으면서 아이를 안심시킨다. 그 유아는 '눈'이 무엇을 의미하는지 혹은 그것이 위험한지 어떤지를 전혀 모르기 때문에 오랜 시간 동안 이해하도록 배운 엄마의 얼굴 표정과 안심시키는 어조로부터 엄마가 두려워하고 있지 않다는 것을 인식하게 되고 눈은 위험하지 않다는 결론을 내린다.

구문 [6행~9행] A toddler (seeing snow for the first time) / might say "Mamma!" with alarm, / **alternating** looking at the snow **with** looking at her mother, pointing, and showing distress.

( )는 능동의 뜻으로 A toddler를 수식한다. alternating 이하는 분사구문이며 alternating과 pointing과 showing이 콤마와 and로 연결되어 병렬구조를 이룬다. 「alternate A with B」는 'A와 B를 번갈아 나오게 만들다'의 뜻이다.

---

10 빈칸 추론 ④

해설 우리는 공기, 물, 흙에 대해서 관심을 쏟을 수 있음에도 불구하고 그것이 너무 오염되어 이용할 수 없을 때가 되어야만 관심을 기울이고, 자신의 생산 수단[자원]으로 당장 이용하는 경우가 아니라면 대개 무시해버린다. 그러므로 빈칸에 들어갈 말로는 ④ '고의적인 무시'가 가장 적절하다.
① 감정의 분출　② 빠른 내면화
③ 무해한 저항　⑤ 계속되는 걱정

해석 우리가 숨 쉬는 공기, 우리가 마시는 물, 혹은 우리의 농업 복합 기업이 우리의 채소를 심는 토양에 대해 우리는 얼마나 자주 생각하는가? 충분히 자주는 아니다. 천연자원에 대한 일반적인 태도는 종종 고의적인 무시이다. 자동차의 연료통을 채우기 위해 몇 시간 동안 줄을 서서 기다려야 할 때만 휘발유가 관심사가 된다. 사람들이 자신이 숨 쉬는 공기를 눈으로 볼 수 있고 냄새 맡을 수 있으며, 숨을 들이쉬면 기침이 나올 때만 공기가 눈에 보이는 자원이 된다. 보편적인 용매인 물은 부족 현상이 발생할 때까지 또는 너무 더러워서 어떤 것도 안에서 살 수 없거나 마실 수 없게 될 때까지는 전혀 관심을 (그리고 거의 아무런 생각을) 일으키지 않는다. 물이 부족하거나 수질이 나쁠 때만 우리는 물을 '걱정해야 할' 자원으로 생각한다. 토양은 자원인가, 아니면 '먼지'인가? 여러분이 농사를 짓거나 정원에 나무를 심지 않으면, 토양은 단지 '먼지'일 뿐이다. 여러분이 토양/먼지의 논쟁에 어떠한 주의라도 기울이는지 아닌지는 여러분이 토양을 무슨 목적으로 사용하는지 그리고 얼마나 여러분이 갈망하는지에 달려있다.

구문 [1행~3행] How often do we think about *the air* [(which[that]) we breathe], *the water* [(which[that]) we drink], or *the soil* [(which[that]) our agribusiness conglomerates plant our vegetables in]?
세 개의 밑줄 친 부분은 모두 관계사절로 각각 앞에 있는 the air, the water, the soil을 수식하고 모두 목적격 관계대명사 which[that]가 생략된 형태이다.
[5행~7행] Only when someone must wait in line for hours to fill the car gas tank **does** *gasoline* **become** a concern.
Only로 시작되는 부사절이 문두에 위치하여 「조동사(does)+주어(gasoline)+동사원형(become)」 어순으로 도치되었다.

---

11 빈칸 추론 ①

해설 좋은 좋은 시는 단어의 사용을 최대한 절약해야 한다는 내용이므로 빈칸에는
① "적을수록 더 많다'는 개념이 적용된다'가 들어가는 것이 가장 적절하다.
② 단어의 의미가 다소 비유적이다
③ 그것의 형태가 군살이 없고 경제적이어서는 안 된다
④ '불합리성'이 대체로 포용될 수밖에 없다

⑤ 마음대로 쓸 수 있는 단어의 대부분이 자격을 얻지 못한다

해석 정확성의 언어인 시는 가장 풍부한 형태임에도 불구하고 가장 응축된 형태로 생각과 감정을 표현해야 할 필요가 있다. 그러므로, 본질적으로 좋은 시는 내용과 의미를 훼손하지 않고 가차 없이 단어 사용을 절약해야 한다. 당신이 물에 흠뻑 젖은 천 조각을 가지고 있는데 이러저러한 이유에서 가능한 한 물기가 없게 그리고 가능한 한 빨리해야 한다고 가정해보라. 이 천 조각을 당신이 열심히 비틀어 짤수록, 그 천이 찢어지지 않는 한, 그것으로부터 그만큼 더 많은 물을 짜내고, 더 많이 마르게 된다. 어떤 면에서, 시도 그것과 마찬가지이다. 당신이 의도했던 의미의 완전성은 여전히 보존하면서 글자, 단어, 형용사, 동사, 명사 등을 더 많이 짜낼수록, 그 시는 더욱 좋아진다. 그러므로, 시에는, '적을수록 더 많다'는 개념이 적용된다.

구문 [11행~14행] **The more** you squeeze letters, words, adjectives, verbs, nouns, and so on / **while still preserving** *the integrity* (of the intended meaning), // **the better** the poetry becomes.
「the 비교급 ~, the 비교급 ...」은 '~하면 할수록, 더 ...하다'의 의미이다. while ~ meaning은 접속사가 생략되지 않은 분사구문이며, 전명구인 ( )는 the integrity를 수식한다.

---

12 빈칸 추론 ①

해설 밑줄 이하의 예시에서 보면 에디슨은 자신이 발명한 축음기가 통신 매체가 될 거라고 생각했고 벨은 자신이 발명한 전화가 음악의 매체가 될 거라고 생각했지만, 결국 축음기가 음악 매체, 전화가 통신 매체가 된 것으로 결론이 났다. 따라서 음향 기술의 발명가는 ① '그 도구가 결국 어떻게 쓰일지를 상상하는 데 어려움을 겪는다'고 할 수 있다.
② 발명품에 대한 대중의 반응을 추적하여 그것을 개선하는 일에 실패한다
③ 사람들에게 자신의 발명품이 사람들의 생활을 어떻게 향상시켜주었는지를 보여주고 싶어한다
④ 도구를 사용하는 여러 방법들을 제안하여 대중에게 인상을 남긴다
⑤ 장애인들이 다른 사람들과 소통하는 데 도움이 되는 장치를 개발하려고 노력한다

해석 어떤 이유로 음향 기술은 그것의 가장 앞선 선구자들에게 이상한 종류의 귀먹음을 유발하는 것 같다. 어떤 새로운 도구가 새로운 방식으로 소리를 공유하거나 전달하려고 나타나고, 되풀이하여 그것의 발명가는 그 도구가 결국 어떻게 쓰일지를 상상하는 데 어려움을 겪는다. 토마스 에디슨이 1877년에 축음기를 발명했을 때, 그는 그것이 우편제도를 통해 오디오 편지를 보내는 수단으로서 정기적으로 사용될 거라고 상상했다. 개인들은 자신의 편지를 축음기의 밀랍 두루마리 편지에 녹음하고, 며칠 후에 재생되도록 그것을 우편물에 탁 넣어 두리라. 벨은 전화를 발명할 때 실질적으로 거울상의(= (좌우가) 반대로 된) 계산 착오를 범했다. 그는 전화의 주된 용도 중 하나는 라이브 음악을 공유하는 매체로서가 될 거라고 상상했다. 오케스트라나 가수는 전화선의 한 쪽 끝에 앉고, 청중들은 편안히 앉아서 다른 쪽 끝의 전화 스피커를 통해 나오는 음을 즐기리라. 그리하여 이 두 전설적인 발명가들은 그것을 정확히 반대로 했다. 사람들은 결국 음악을 들으려고 축음기를 사용하게 되었고 친구와 소통하려고 전화를 사용하게 되었다.

구문 [18행~21행] So, the two legendary inventors **had** *it* exactly **reversed**: // people **ended up using** the phonograph to listen to music / and **using** the

telephone to communicate with friends.
사역동사 have가 「have + O + p.p. (O가 ~되게 하다)」의 형태로 쓰였다. 「end up v-ing」는 '결국 V하게 되다'의 뜻이며 end up 다음에 이어지는 두 using이 and로 연결되어 병렬구조를 이룬다.

어휘 induce 유발하다, 유도하다   pioneer 선구자   come along 나타나다
transmit 전달하다   again and again 되풀이하여   means 수단   postal system
우편제도   wax 밀랍   scroll 두루마리   pop A into B A를 B 속에 탁 넣다
effectively 실질적으로, 사실상   miscalculation 계산 착오   envision 상상하다
sit back 편안히 앉다   reverse 반대(로 하다); 뒤집다

13 흐름 무관 문장 ④

해설 뛰어난 오락은 관객의 정서를 건드리고 추천의 의견이나 박수, 웃음 같은 물리적 반응을 일으킨다는 내용의 글인데, ④번 문장은 훌륭한 농담과 희극인에게는 비극적 요소가 있다는 내용이므로 글의 전반적인 흐름과 맞지 않다.

해석 오락의 질은 관객에 의해 그것이 관객들 간에 감정적 반응을 불러일으키는 정도로 종종 측정되는데, 이것이 의견으로 이어진다. ① 우리가 정서적으로 오락에 의해 영향을 받는 정도는 일반적으로 그것이 얼마나 좋다고 혹은 나쁘다고 우리가 생각하는지에 대한 우리의 의견에 영향을 미친다. ② 혼자 공연하는 코미디언을 본 후 관객 중 한 명이 '정말 재밌었어요'라고 말했다면, 그것은 그 코미디언이 좋았다고 그 사람이 생각했음을 암시할 것이며, 이는 추천의 암시를 포함한다. ③ 코미디라고 '꼬리표가 붙은' 쇼를 봄으로써 이 사람은 행복과 즐거움, 그리고 기쁨을 포함한 긍정적인 감정을 느낄 것을 예상했다. ④ 비극적 반전을 삽입하지 않고 농담을 만들 수 없으며, 단시간조차 관객들에게 약간의 우울감을 갖지 않고는 코미디언이 될 수 없다. ⑤ 이러한 감정들은 그러고 나면 관객들에 의해 웃음과 갈채의 형태로 물리적으로 변형되는데, 웃음과 갈채를 유발하는 관객들 간의 정서적 반응을 일으키지 못하는 코미디언은 보통 '재미없다' 따라서 '형편없는' 코미디언이라고, 혹은 그 관객의 의견에서 저급한 오락이라고 여겨진다.

구문 [4행~6행] *The degree* [to which we are emotionally affected by entertainment] typically **influences** our opinion of {how good or bad (we think) it is}.
주어는 The degree이고 동사는 influences이며 [ ]은 주어를 수식한다. { }은 of의 목적어 역할을 하는 간접의문문이다. we think는 삽입절이다.
[18행~21행] ~ *a comedian* [that doesn't invoke *an emotional response* among the audience] {that results in laughter and applause} **is** usually **considered as** being 'not funny' ~.
주어는 a comedian이고 동사는 is이다. [ ]은 a comedian을, { }은 an emotional response를 각각 수식한다. 'be considered as'는 '~로 여겨지다'의 뜻이다.

어휘 invoke (느낌을) 불러일으키다   suggestion 제안, 시사, 암시   label 꼬리표를 붙이다   insert 삽입하다   twist (예상 밖의) 전환, 전개   melancholy 우울감   transform 변형하다   applause 박수, 갈채

14 글의 순서 ④

해설 전통 경제학이 자원을 효율적으로 할당하는 장점이 있다는 주어진 글 다음에는, however로 연결되며 전통 경제학의 이러한 자원 할당이 근시안적이라고 단점을 언급한 (C)가 나온다. 환경 제품은 전통 경제학에서와는 대조적으로 장기적인 자원 할당이 중요하다는 내용의 (A)가 그 다음에 나온다. 화석 연료를 소비한다는 결정이 장기적인 영향을 미칠 수 있다는 (A)의 예시 다음에는, Similarly로 이어지며 이와 비슷한 예시(오늘 새우를 다 잡아버리면 미래에는 새우가 없다)가 나오는 (B)가

그 다음에 나와야 한다.

해석 환경 경제학에서 자주 결정적이고 규정적인 역할을 하는 것은 바로 시간이다. 전통 경제학은 상품과 서비스를 생산하기 위한 자원을 할당하는 효율적인 방법들을 결정할 수 있다. (C) 그러나 그러한 할당은 오늘 상품을 한 단위 추가 생산하는 것이 내일 한 단위 생산하는 것을 막지 않는다는 근본적인 가정과 함께 단순화되고 단일 기간으로만 제한된다. (A) 많은 환경 제품의 경우 장기간에 걸친 자원의 할당이 중요하다. 예를 들어 오늘 화석 연료를 태우고 환경을 오염시키는 동안 우리는 미래 세대에게 수년간 혹은 영원히 문제를 만들어주고 있는지도 모른다. (B) 마찬가지로, 오늘 새우를 몽땅 수확하면, 공급은 영원히 사라질 것이다. 어떤 환경 제품에 대한 우리의 소비 결정은 '비가역적'일 수 있으며 미래 세대의 행복에 심대한 영향을 미칠 수 있다.

구문 [1행~2행] **It is** time **that** often **plays a crucial and defining role** / in environmental economics.
「It is ~ that ...」 강조구문으로 '…한 것은 바로 ~이다'의 뜻이다. play a role은 '역할을 하다'의 뜻이다.
[15행~19행] The allocation is, however, simplified and confined / to a single period of time / with the underlying presumption that the production of an additional unit of a commodity today / does not prevent producing one tomorrow.
that ~ tomorrow는 the underlying presumption에 대한 동격절이다.

어휘 defining (본질적인 의미를) 규정하는   allocate 할당[배분]하다 *cf.* allocation 할당, 배분   irreversible 비가역적인, 되돌릴 수 없는   confine 제한[한정]하다   underlying 근본적인   presumption 가정, 추정   unit 단위   commodity 상품

15 글의 순서 ②

해설 (B)의 첫 문장에서는 상담에서 내담자에게 침묵이 가지는 의미와 중요성을 구체적으로 제시하고 있기 때문에 침묵이 초보 상담가에게는 힘들지만, 내담자에게는 중요하다는 주어진 글 다음에 (B)가 이어진다. 내담자에게는 침묵이 상담가에게 느껴지는 만큼 길게 느껴지지 않는다는 (B) 다음에는 침묵을 깨는 것이 내담자에게 침해가 될 수 있다는 (A)가 나오고, 상담가가 침묵에 편해져야 한다는 (A)의 마지막 부분 다음에는 상담가가 또한 침묵을 신뢰해야 한다고 추가 제안한 (C)가 이어지는 것이 적절하다.

해석 우리 중 많은 이들이 사회적 상황에서 그러는 것처럼, 능동적인 듣기 기법을 배우고 있는 초보 상담가는 침묵이 어렵다고 자주 생각한다. 하지만 능동적인 듣기 상황에서 여러분의 내담자는 매우 힘든 몇몇 감정을 처리하고 알맞은 단어를 찾으려고 애쓰고 있을 수도 있다는 것을 기억하라. (B) 여러분의 내담자는 멈추고 생각하고 느낄 여유가 필요할지도 모른다. 여러분이 초심자이면 짧은 침묵이 매우 길게 느껴진다. 내담자에게는 그것이 여러분에게 느껴지는 만큼 길게 느껴질 것 같지 않다. (A) 여러분은 보통 질문으로 불쑥 끼어들고 싶은 유혹을 느낄지도 모르는데, 그것은 내담자에게는 자기 생각에 대한 침해처럼 느껴질 수 있다. 여러분은 침묵에 편안해지는 것을 배울 필요가 있을 것이다. (C) 그리고 여러분은 도움을 주는 관계에서의 이러한 공백에 대해 스스로를 신뢰하는 법을 배울 필요가 있을 것이다. 만약 결국 여러분이 침묵을 깰 필요가 있다면 아마도 어떤 종류의 반영하기로 이것(침묵 깨기)을 하는 것이 질문하는 것보다 더 나을 것이다.

구문 [13행~14행] It is unlikely to feel **as** long to the client **as** it **does** to you.
밑줄 친 두 개의 It과 it은 모두 앞 문장의 a short silence를 지칭한다. 「as+원급+as ~(~만큼 …하다)」 쓰였고, it 다음의 대동사 does는 feels (long)를 의미한다.

어휘 novice 초보자 setting 환경 struggle 애쓰다, 투쟁하다 jump in (대화에) 불쑥 끼어들다 be unlikely to-v v할 것 같지 않다 reflection 반영 ((상담에서 내담자의 감정을 상담자의 말로 되돌려 주는 것))

16 문장 넣기 ⑤

해설 주어진 문장은 식품 회사가 광고를 시작하게 되었다는 내용이다. 그러므로 식품 제조업자들이 광고를 시작하게 된 이유인 브랜드 제품의 우수성을 소비자에게 납득시킬 필요가 있었다는 내용 다음에 오는 것이 적절하다. 또한 결과적으로 식품 광고가 미국인들에게 어떤 영향을 주었는지에 대한 내용이 주어진 문장 다음에 이어지는 것 역시 문맥상 자연스러우므로 ⑤가 정답이다.

해석 19세기 내내, 많은 미국인들은 농장이나 정원에서 그들 자신이 먹을 식량의 상당한 부분을 재배했다. 소규모 잡화점들은 소규모 지역 사회에 살고 있거나, 현지에서 구할 수 없는 사치품을 원하는 사람들의 요구를 채워주었다. 식품은 주로 표시가 없는 통, 자루, 단지에서 분량을 재서 꺼낸 상표가 붙지 않은 제품으로 판매되었다. 이것은 식품 생산이 산업화되면서 바뀌었다. 필라델피아 100주년 박람회 이후에, 잉여 농산물이 시장에 넘쳐나고 기술이 생산 비용을 낮추면서 식품 가공업자와 제조업자가 번창했다. 그 결과는 대형 식품 제조업자들의 부상이었는데, 그들은 상표가 붙지 않은 제품보다 브랜드가 있는 제품의 우수성을 소비자에게 납득시킬 필요가 있었다. 이것을 성취하려고 식품회사들은 지역과 전국적으로는 신문, 잡지를 통해서, 그리고 국지적으로는 광고 전단과 광고판, 그리고 매장 내 판촉을 통해 자기들의 제품을 광고하기 시작했다. 식품 광고는 무엇을, 언제, 그리고 어떻게 먹어야 하는지에 관한 미국인들의 의견과 행동의 주요한 근원이 되었다.

구문 [16행~19행] The result was the rise of *large food manufacturers*, **who** needed to persuade consumers of the superiority of branded products over generic groceries.
계속적 용법의 관계대명사 who가 이끄는 절은 앞에 있는 명사 large food manufacturers에 대한 부연 설명을 한다.

어휘 regionally 지역적으로 locally 국지[지방]적으로; 현지에서 circular 광고 전단; 안내장; 순환적인 billboard 광고판, 게시판; 빌보드 promotion 판매 촉진; 승격 luxury 사치품 measure out ~을 재서 덜어[떼어]내다 barrel (맥주) 통 jar 단지, 병 centennial 100주년의, 100년마다의 exposition 박람회; 설명[해설] processor (농산물) 가공업자 prosper 번창하다, 번영하다 surplus 잉여(품) superiority 우수성

17 문장 넣기 ③

해설 ③ 뒷문장의 these efforts에 해당하는 내용이 주어진 문장 속에 들어있고, ③의 앞 문장은 아이의 첫 반응이고 주어진 문장은 그 뒤의 반응이기 때문에 주어진 문장은 ③에 위치해야 한다.

해석 다른 사람들의 감정을 이해하는 유아의 능력을 지지해주는 증거 하나를 Edward Tronick이 개발한 '정지한 얼굴' 실험이 제공한다. 이 실험에서 어머니는 아이와 정상적인 놀이 교류를 일정 기간 하고 난 후에 무표정한 얼굴(정지한 얼굴)을 만듦으로써 그녀의 아기에 대한 정서적인 피드백을 왜곡하라는 지시를 받는다. 아이는 처음에는 어머니의 감정 없는 표정을 보고 불쾌하게 놀란다. 아이는 그러고 나서 그녀의 감정적으로 텅 빈 얼굴에 정서를 복구하려는 노력으로 그녀의 관심을 얻기 위해 노력한다. 이러한 노력들이 실패하면, 아이는 매우 불편하고 고통스러우며 불안해진다. 마지막으로, 어머니의 얼굴이 변하지 않으면 아이는 무관심하고 고립되며 지루해지게 된다. 대부분의 유아들은 또한 어머니의 정지한 얼굴에 심박동수가 증가하며 생리적으로 반응하는데, Edward Tronick은 이를 유아의 타인과 관계하고 싶은 욕구의 붕괴에 기인하는 것으로 보았다.

구문 [3행~5행] *A piece of evidence* [that supports the infant's capacity to understand other people's emotions] / **is provided** by *the "still-face" test* (developed by Edward Tronick).
주어는 A piece of evidence이고 동사는 is provided이다.
[15행~19행] Most infants also react physiologically to the mother's still face with an increased heart rate, // which Edward Tronick **attributed to** disruption of the infant's desire to relate to others.
which는 앞문장 전체를 가리키며, 「attribute A to B」는 'A를 B의 탓으로 돌리다'의 뜻이다. A에 해당하는 부분이 관계대명사 which이다.

어휘 restore 복원[복구]하다 affect 정서 still 가만히 있는, 정지한 distort 왜곡하다 affective 정서적인 expressionless 표정이 없는 distressed 고통스러워하는 detached 무심한, 고립된 physiologically 생리적으로 heart rate 심박동수 disruption 붕괴, 분열, 중단

18 요약문 완성 ④

해설 본문의 인용문 중에 젊은이들이 시간과 공간에 대해 느슨(loose)해졌으며 지각이 더 이상 금기시되는 것(taboo)이 아니라는 언급이 있다. 시간과 공간에 대해 느슨해진 것은 휴대 전화로 인해 계속 연락이 닿아 시공간 개념이 확장된(expanded) 것이고 지각이 더 이상 금기가 아니라는 것은 지각이 용납할 수 없는(unacceptable) 것으로 여겨지지 않게, 즉 용납할 수 있게 된 것이다.

해석 Showa 여자 대학교의 대학원생인 Kawamura는 술집에서 파티를 준비하고 있는 30명으로 이루어진 집단에 의해 교류되는 의사소통을 기록했다. "날짜가 다가옴에 따라 메시지의 빈도는 증가했습니다. 그러나 겨우 네 사람만 합의된 장소에 제시간에 나왔습니다."라고 Kawamura는 말했다. 그러나 수십 명의 다른 사람들은 드문드문 오는 동안 음성 메시지와 문자 메시지를 통해 계속 연락이 닿는 상태에 있었다. "아이들이 시간과 공간에 대해 느슨해졌습니다. 전화를 가지고 있으면 지각을 할 수 있는 거죠."라고 Kawamura는 첨언했다. 다른 대학원생인 Kamide는 지각이 더 이상 금기시되는 것이 아님에 동의했다. "오늘날의 금기시되는 것은 휴대전화를 깜빡하거나 배터리가 방전되게 놔두는 것입니다." 라고 Kamide는 추정했다. 나중에 이러한 '시간의 유연화'가 노르웨이의 동일한 연령 집단에서도 나타났음이 발견됐다. "즉석에서 결정을 내릴 수 있는 기회는 젊은이들이 더 나이 든 세대들이 하는 데 익숙한 것처럼 자신의 삶을 시간대로 나누는 것을 주저하게 만들었습니다."라고 한 노르웨이 연구자가 동의했다.

↓

휴대폰이 젊은이들의 시공간 개념을 (A) 확장함에 따라, 지각은 (B) 용납할 수 없는 것으로 여겨지지 않는다.

구문 [1행~4행] Kawamura, a graduate student at Showa Women's University, documented *communications* (exchanged by *a group of thirty* [**who** were organizing a party at a bar]).
( ) 부분은 과거분사구로 communications를 수식한다. [ ] 부분은 관계대명사 who가 이끄는 관계사절로 a group of thirty를 수식한다.
[14행~16행] Later it was discovered **that** this "softening of time" was noted for the same age group in Norway.
밑줄 친 it은 가주어이고, 접속사 that이 이끄는 명사절이 진주어이다.

어휘 document (상세한 내용을) 기록하다; 서류로 입증하다 frequency 빈도; 주파수 loose 느슨한; 자유로운; 절제 없는 taboo 금기시되는 것, 터부 presume 추정하다; 전제로 하다 reluctant 주저하는, 꺼리는 time slot 시간대 contract 수축시키다 agreeable 받아들일 수 있는; 승낙하는 offensive 불쾌한; 모욕적인

19~20 장문　　　　　　　　　　　　　　　19 ④ 20 ③

해설 19. 사람들은 손쉽게 얻을 수 있는 편안함에만 게으르게 만족하는 것 같지만, 새로움이 없는 환경이나 콘텐츠에 둘러싸여 있으면 결국 지루함을 느끼고 새로움과 변화를 적극적으로 찾아 나서는 성향이 있으며, 이것이 문화적 창의성이 극대화된 미래를 낙관적으로 전망할 수 있게 한다는 내용의 글이므로 제목으로 가장 적절한 것은 ④ '인간의 본성은 편안한 영역을 넘어서는 새로움을 추구한다'이다.

① 왜 우리는 복잡함보다 단순함을 선호하는가
② 우리의 뇌는 새로움과 변화를 어떻게 처리하는가
③ 좋은 욕망은 증진시키고 나쁜 욕망은 억제하라
⑤ 우리는 기본 욕구가 충족된 후에야 변화한다

20. 사람들은 게으른 제작자들이 내놓는 '요구하는 바가 많고 까다로운(demanding)' 콘텐츠가 아니라 '별다른 노력이 필요치 않은(undemanding)' 콘텐츠를 멀리하며 결국 영리하고 즐거운 프로그램을 추구할 것이다.

- -

해석 John Stuart Mill은 우리 각자가 차라리 만족한 돼지가 될 것인지 불만족한 소크라테스가 될 것인지에 의문을 품었는데, 때로는 마치 많은 사람들이 전자를 선택한 것처럼 보일 수도 있다. 그러나 그것은 단지 단기적 관점에서만 그렇다. 장기적으로 보면 우리는 일이 끊임없고 변함없을 때 (a) 불만족을 느낄 수밖에 없다. 식욕의 물림, 같은 생각과 감정의 끝없는 반복은 결국 우리가 머릿속에서 다음으로 넘어가고 (b) 신선한 투입을 찾게끔 한다. 처음에는 사람들이 편안함을 얻기 위해 자신의 자유를 쉽사리 희생할 수도 있지만, 변화의 부재, 환경과 일상의 단조로움은 점점 더 극심한 불편과 새로운 것에 대한 탐색으로 이어질 것이다. 그러한 이유로 나는 똑같은 생각, 똑같은 음식, 혹은 똑같은 TV 프로그램으로 된 불변의 식단을 받아먹는 사람들이 결국엔 다르게 생각하게 될 것임을 낙관한다. 시간은 걸릴지 모르지만, 변화와 넘어가기는 불가피할 것이다. 사람들은 점점 더

게으른 텔레비전 업계 중역들과 영화 제작자들이 제공하는 익숙하고 (c) 요구하는 게 많은(→ 별다른 노력이 필요치 않은) 쇼와 영화를 끄며 멀리하고 있다. 대신에 영리하고 즐거운 프로그램을 향한, 그리고 독립영화 제작을 향한 공간은 활짝 열렸다. 대중적 성공이 발견될 곳은 바로 여기, 문화의 창의적 극한 영역이다. 기업계에서는 이미 교훈을 학습하고 있는데, 그곳에서 독점 회사들은 자신의 서비스 범위를 (d) 다각화함으로써 대처하려고 노력한다. 점점 더 세계화되는 시장은 흥미로운 지역 시장에 대한 더욱 견고한 이해로 이어져 왔다. 그리고 나는 사람들이 (e) 지루함, 그리고 새로운 것에 대한 필요를 통해 더 나쁜 경험이 아니라 더 좋은 경험을 찾아 나설 것임을 낙관한다.

- -

구문 [15행~18행] That is why I am optimistic **that** *people* [who are fed a constant diet of the same ideas, the same foods, [or] the same TV programs] **will eventually come** to think differently.

'That is why ~'는 '그것이 ~한 이유이다'의 뜻이다. that 이하는 optimistic이라는 감정에 대한 이유를 제시한다. [ ]은 people을 꾸미는 관계사절이며, people에 상응하는 동사는 will eventually come이다. [ ]에서 세 밑줄 부분은 콤마(,)와 or로 연결되어 병렬구조를 이룬다.

[25행~27행] It is here, at the creative end of the culture **that** popular success is to be found.

「It is … that ~」 강조구문은 '~한 것은 바로 …이다'라는 뜻으로, It is와 that 사이에 강조하고 싶은 표현이 위치한다.

- -

어휘 have no choice but to-v v하지 않을 수 없다　 discontented 불만족한　 satiety 물림, 포만　 appetite 식욕　 readily 쉽게　 monotony 단조로움　 acute 극심한　 inevitable 불가피한, 필연적인　 monopoly 독점 (기업); 독점적 상품[서비스]　 cope 대처하다　 novelty 새로움

제13회　　　　　　　　　　　　　　　　　　　　　　　본문 p.100

| 1 ⑤ | 2 ② | 3 ⑤ | 4 ③ | 5 ④ | | 6 ⑤ | 7 ⑤ | 8 ③ | 9 ② | 10 ④ |
| 11 ③ | 12 ③ | 13 ④ | 14 ② | 15 ④ | | 16 ④ | 17 ② | 18 ③ | 19 ④ | 20 ⑤ |

---

1 글의 목적　　　　　　　　　　　　　　　　⑤

해설 'Would you consider ~ that focuses on health, obedience, and grooming?' 문장에서 볼 수 있듯이, 반려견 관련 서적의 편집자에게 자신이 저술하고자 하는 책의 출판 계획을 제시하고 검토해 달라고 하고 있으므로 정답은 ⑤이다.

- -

해석 Jones 씨께
우리 중 많은 사람들에게, 반려동물은 가족의 일부입니다. 그것들은 적어도 받는 만큼 줍니다. 하지만 이러한 기쁨에는 책임이 따릅니다. 반려동물의 주인들은 그들의 개, 고양이, 새와 다른 동물 공동 주민들을 위해 목소리를 내야 하고, 그들이 가능한 최고의 돌봄을 받는 것을 보장해야 합니다. 12년 동안 저는 강아지 예절 학교의 소유주였으며, 반려동물 주인들에게 이러한 주제에 대해 많은 귀중하고 초보적인 조언을 제공할 수 있는 책을 출판하기 위해 준비했습니다. 저는 당신이 '재미와 유익을 위해 반려견을 기르는 방법'의 편집자임에 주목했습니다. 반려견 주인을 겨냥한, 건강, 복종과 털 손질에 집중한 논픽션 DIY(do-it-yourself) 책을 위한 저의 출판 계획을 살펴봐 주실 것을 고려하실 수 있으신지요? 고려해주신다면 대단히 감사할 것입니다. 당신의 답장에 사용하실 반환 주소와 우표가 있는 봉투를 동봉합니다.
Kevin Smithers 드림

- -

구문 [4행~7행] ~ pet owners must **speak for** their dogs, cats, birds, [and]

other animal coresidents, [and] **ensure** that they receive the best possible care.

밑줄 친 네 개의 명사(구)를 콤마와 첫 번째 and가 병렬 연결한다. 두 번째 and는 문장의 동사 speak for와 ensure를 병렬 연결한다.

[12행~15행] Would you consider looking at my publishing plan for *a nonfiction, do-it-yourself book*, **aimed at pet dog owners**, [that focuses on health, obedience, and grooming]?

aimed ~ owners는 a nonfiction, do-it-yourself book을 수식하는 분사구이다. [ ] 부분은 주격 관계대명사 that이 이끄는 관계사절로 역시 a nonfiction, do-it-yourself book을 수식한다.

- -

어휘 charm school 예의범절을 가르치는 곳　 obedience 복종, 순종　 groom 깔끔하게 다듬다; 손질하다　 envelope 봉투; 싸는 것　 enclose 동봉하다; 에워싸다

2 밑줄 함의　　　　　　　　　　　　　　　　②

해설 'fail to act accordingly(그에 따라 행동하는 것을 실패하다)'는 바로 앞부분을 반영하면 '게임에서 실패해도 된다고들 말하지만, 실제로는 그런 식으로 행동

하지 못한다'는 뜻이며, 좀 더 구체적으로 말하면 '말로는 게임에서 져도 괜찮다고 하면서도 막상 지면 속상해하고 화를 낸다'는 의미가 된다. 이에 따라 fail to act accordingly가 글에서 의미하는 바를 고르면 ② '게임에서 실패할 때 속상하고 화가 난다'가 된다.

① 게임에서 승리하기 위한 우리의 계획을 바꾸려고 노력한다
③ 우리가 혼자일 때 좌절감을 표출한다
④ 우리가 만족할 때 게임을 그만둔다
⑤ 우리의 실패로부터 배우는 것을 잊는 경향이 있다

해석　우리는 일상의 노력하는 일에 실패하는 것을 싫어하지만, 게임은 완전히 다른 것으로, 실패해도 괜찮고 고통스럽지도 않고 조금도 불쾌하지도 않은 안전한 공간이다. '단지 게임일 뿐이야'라는 문구는 이것이 사실일 것이라는 암시를 준다. 그리고 우리는 종종 게임에서 일어나는 것이 게임 밖에 있는 것과는 다른 의미가 있다고 정말로 생각한다. 다른 사람들이 그들 자신의 목표를 이루는 것을 방해하는 것은 보통 우정을 끝낼 수도 있는 적대적인 행동이지만, 우리는 친선 게임을 할 때 다른 선수들이 그들의 목표를 달성하는 것을 보통 방해한다. 이런 관점에서 게임은 보통의 세상과는 다른 어떤 것으로, (게임 속에서의) 실패가 전혀 괴롭지 않은 구조이다. 하지만 이것이 분명하게 온전히 진실인 것은 아니다. 우리는 게임을 하는 동안 실패할 때 자주 속상하고, 실패를 피하고자 상당한 노력을 쏟고, 심지어 우리의 기발한 게임 속 계획을 저지하는 사람들에 대해 분노를 보이기도 할 것이다. 즉, 우리는 게임 속 실패가 무해하고 중립적인 것이라고 종종 주장하지만, 우리는 반복적으로 그에 따라 행동하는 것을 실패한다.

구문　[1행~4행] While we dislike failing in our regular endeavors, games are an entirely different thing, *a safe space* [in which failure is okay], neither painful nor the least unpleasant.
두 밑줄 부분은 동격 관계이고, '전치사+관계대명사'가 이끄는 [ ]은 a safe place를 수식한다. 「neither A nor B」는 'A도 B도 아니다'의 뜻이다.
[11행~13행] Games, in this view, are *something* (different from the regular world), *a frame* [in which failure is not the least distressing].
밑줄 친 두 부분은 동격 관계로 형용사구 ( )은 something을, 관계사절 [ ]은 a frame을 각각 수식한다.

어휘　endeavor 노력(하다)　phrase 어구　the case 사실, 실정　hostile 적대적인　not the least 조금도 ~ 않다　distressing 괴로운　neutral 중립적인　frustration 좌절(감)

3 글의 요지 ⑤

해설　어린이는 '왜'로 시작되는 질문을 많이 하며, 질문은 인류에게 너무 중요해서 모든 언어에는 질문을 위한 보편적인 억양이 있을 정도이고, 사회의 많은 분야에서 적절한 질문은 가치 있게 평가받고 침팬지는 기본적인 의사소통을 학습해도 결코 질문하지 않는다는 내용의 글이므로 요지로 가장 적절한 것은 ⑤이다.

해석　어린 자녀가 있는 사람은 누구라도 '왜'로 시작되는 질문을 향한 그들의 사랑을 알고 있다. 1920년대에 심리학자 Frank Lorimer는 나흘에 걸쳐 네 살 된 소년을 관찰했고 그 아이가 그동안 했던 모든 '왜'들을 기록했다. 그것은 40개였는데, '왜 물뿌리개는 손잡이가 두 개예요?', '왜 우리한테 눈썹이 있어요?'와 같은 질문들이었다. 질문의 행위는 우리 종에게 너무나도 중요해서 우리는 그것에 대한 보편적인 지표를 가지고 있다. 그것은 모든 언어가 성조 언어이든 비성조 언어이든 질문에 대해 유사한 상승 억양을 사용하는 것이다. 어떤 종교 전통은 질문을 가장 높은 형태의 이해로 간주하며, 과학과 산업에서도 올바른 질문을 하는 능력은 절대적으로 필수적이다. 반면에 침팬지들은 트레이너들과 소통하기 위해 가장 기본적인 수화를 사용하는 법을, 그리고 심지어 질문에 대답하는 법을 배울 수 있지만 결코 질문을 던지지는 않는다. 그들은 육체적으로 강하지만 생각하는 존재는 아니다.

구문　[2행~5행] In the 1920s, psychologist Frank Lorimer observed a four-year-old boy over four days and recorded all the "whys" [(that) the child asked during that time].
동사 observed와 recorded가 and로 연결되어 병렬구조를 이룬다. [ ]는 앞에 목적격 관계대명사 that이 생략되어 all the "whys"를 수식한다.
[7행~10행] The act of questioning is **so** important to our species // **that** we have a universal indicator for it: // all languages, **whether** tonal **or** nontonal, employ a similar rising intonation / for questions.
「so ~ that ....」 구문은 '너무 ~해서 …하다'의 뜻이다. 삽입된 구인 「whether A or B」는 'A이든 B이든'의 뜻이다.

어휘　watering pot 물뿌리개　universal 보편적인　indicator 지표　tonal 음색의 *cf.* tonal language 성조 언어　employ 사용하다　intonation 억양　apprehension 이해; 우려　rudimentary 가장 기본적인, 근본의　signing 수화

4 글의 주제 ③

해설　같은 양의 단백질을 먹더라도 매 끼니마다 균등하게 먹었을 때 근육 단백질 합성이 더 잘 된다는 장점이 있다는 내용의 글이므로 주제로 가장 적절한 것은 ③ '단백질 섭취를 고르게 분산시킬 필요성'이다.

① 너무 많은 단백질이 건강에 나쁜 이유
② 단백질의 필요성을 상승시킬 수 있는 신체적 조건들
④ 식단에서 단백질의 양을 증가시키는 쉬운 방법들
⑤ 체중 감량을 위한 고단백 식품 섭취의 중요성

해석　최근 연구에서 연구자들은 주로 기름기가 적은 소고기의 형태로 매일 90그램의 단백질을 섭취한 자원자 두 집단을 비교했다. 한 집단은 각각의 식사에서 30그램의 단백질을 먹었고, 반면에 나머지 한 집단은 아침에 10그램, 점심 때 15그램, 그리고 저녁 때 65그램을 먹었다. 고르게 배분된 단백질 식사를 섭취한 자원자들은 편향된 단백질 분포 패턴에 따라 식사한 피실험자들보다 25% 더 높은 24시간 근육 단백질 합성을 보였다. 더 나은 근육 합성은 칼로리의 더 효율적인 활용, 그리고 더 적은 단백질이 산화되어 결국 포도당이나 지방이 됨을 의미한다. 그러므로 당신의 단백질 섭취를 하루 종일 균형 있게 만드는 것이 핵심이다. 아침에 30그램의 단백질에 더 가까이 가기 위하여 계란 하나, 혼합 야채 주스 한 잔, 그릭 요거트나 견과류 한 줌을 더하라. 30그램에 도달하기 위해 점심 식사로 비슷한 것을 하고 나서 저녁 식사로 30그램의 단백질만 섭취하라. 내 환자들 중 많은 사람들이 단지 그들이 지방을 없애고 근육을 키우고 더 젊어 보이는 데 도움이 되는 균형을 다시 도입함으로써 50이 넘은 후에도 그들 인생에서 최상의 상태에 있다.

구문　[10행~13행] Better muscle synthesis **means** a more efficient utilization of calories, and *less protein* **being oxidized** and **ending** up as glucose or fat.
두 밑줄 친 부분이 병렬구조를 이루어 means의 목적어 역할을 하고 있다. less protein은 동명사 being oxidized와 ending의 의미상 주어이다.
[19행~22행] Many of my patients are in the best shape of their lives after fifty by simply bringing back *the balance* [that **helps** *them* **shed** the fat, **build** muscle, and **look** younger].
[ ]은 the balance를 수식하는 관계사절이다. 「help O v(O가 v하는 것을 돕다)」 구문이 사용되었으며, 동사원형으로 시작되는 세 밑줄 친 부분이 help 다음의 목적격 보어로서 and로 연결되어 병렬구조를 이루고 있다.

어휘　primarily 주로　lean (고기가) 기름기가 없는[적은]　evenly 고르게　distribute 분배하다, 배부하다　synthesis 종합, 합성　subject 피실험자　utilization 이용, 활용　oxidize 산화시키다　intake 섭취　a handful of 한줌의　midday 한낮의　shape 상태　bring back ~을 다시 도입하다　shed (원하지 않는 것을) 없애다, 버리다

5 도표 이해 ④

해설 보건비용, 교육, 가난하고 도움이 필요한 사람들의 문제가 모두 2020년보다 2019년에 주요 우선순위로 더 높은 비율을 차지한 쟁점들이었지만 환경 문제는 2019년(56%)보다 2020년(64%)에 더 높은 비율이었다. 그러므로 ④는 표와 일치하지 않는다.

해석 위의 표는 2012년 1월부터 2020년 1월까지 8년에 걸쳐 어떤 쟁점을 대통령과 의회가 우선으로 여겨야 하는지에 대한 미국 대중의 생각을 보여준다. ① 대테러 방어를 최고의 우선순위로 생각한 대중의 비율은 2012년에는 세 번째로 높았지만, 2020년에는 최고 순위였다. ② 2012년에 압도적인 지분의 사람들(86%)이 경제 강화를 주요 우선순위로 언급했고, 4년 뒤에는 75%가 그렇게 했지만, 그 수치는 2020년에 67%로 떨어졌다. ③ 2016년에 47%의 미국인들이 환경 보호를 최고의 우선순위로 평가했으나 2020년에는 10명 중 6명이 넘는 사람들이 그렇게 했다. ④ 보건비용, 교육, 환경 그리고 가난하고 도움이 필요한 사람들의 문제가 모두 2020년보다 2019년에 주요 우선순위로 더 높은 비율을 차지한 쟁점들이었다. ⑤ 일자리 상황을 개선하는 것이 최고의 우선순위라고 말하는 미국인들의 지분이 2012년에서 2020년까지의 정책 우선순위 중에서, 33퍼센트 포인트 차이로 가장 급격히 감소했다.

구문 [1행~4행] The above table shows the U.S. public's thoughts on <u>which issues the president and Congress should prioritize</u> over eight years, from January 2012 to January 2020.
밑줄 친 부분은 간접의문문으로 전치사 on의 목적어로 쓰였다. 이때 which는 의문형용사로 '어떤'이라고 해석한다.
[12행~15행] Health care costs, education, the environment, and problems of the poor and needy were *all issues* [that had a **higher** percentage as a top priority in 2019 **than** in 2020].
[ ] 부분은 주격 관계대명사 that이 이끄는 관계사절로 선행사 all issues를 수식하며, 관계사절 내에 「비교급+than」 구문이 쓰였다.

어휘 Congress (미국 등의) 의회[국회] prioritize 우선순위를 매기다 *cf.* priority 우선순위 overwhelming 압도적인 share 지분, 몫 cite 언급하다; 인용하다

6 내용 불일치 ⑤

해설 Samuel Clemens는 세계 투어를 통해 강연을 하며 빚을 갚고 재정적 어려움을 극복했다.

해석 Mark Twain이라는 필명으로 알려진 Samuel Clemens는 미국의 작가이자 해학가이자 강연자였다. 그는 미시시피 강의 마을인 미주리 주의 해니벌에서 자랐다. 그의 이야기 중 많은 것이 그곳에서의 경험에서 영감을 받았다. 그는 인쇄공의 견습생으로 일하고 나서 식자공으로 일하며, 그의 형인 Orion Clemens의 신문사에 기사를 기고했다. 그의 첫 번째 이야기 'The Celebrated Jumping Frog of Calaveras County'는 1865년에 출간되었다. 그 단편 소설은 국제적 주목을 불러왔고 심지어 불어로 번역되었다. '톰 소여의 모험(1876년)'과 그것의 속편 '허클베리 핀의 모험(1884년)'은 미시시피 강에서 일어난 두 소년의 모험을 이야기해 준다. Twain은 자신의 글로 대단히 많은 돈을 벌었지만, 벤처 사업에 투자하여 그 대부분을 잃었다. 그는 빚을 갚기 위해 세계를 돌아다니며 강연을 하기 시작했고, 결국 재정적 난관을 극복했다. 그는 1910년에 74세의 나이로 심장마비로 사망했다.

구문 [5행~8행] He served an apprenticeship with a printer and then worked as a typesetter, **contributing** articles to the newspaper of his older brother Orion Clemens.
contributing 이하는 부대 상황을 나타내는 분사구문이다.

어휘 pen name 필명 humorist 해학적인 사람; 유머 작개[배우] apprenticeship 견습[수습]직; 수습 기간 typesetter 식자공; 식자기 contribute 기고하다; 기여[기부]하다 sequel 속편, 후편 venture 벤처 (사업); 모험 pay off ~을 청산하다[다 갚다]

7 밑줄 어법 ⑤

해설 ⑤번의 문장에서 some organisms must starve in nature라는 완전한 절이 나오므로 앞에 관계대명사가 아닌 접속사를 써야 한다. 따라서 What을 That으로 바꿔 써야 한다.

해석 모든 유기체가 생존하기에 충분한 식량을 발견할 수 있는 건 아니어서 굶주림은 자연에서 종종 발견되는 일종의 반(反)가치이다. 그것은 또한 생물학적 진화가 기능하는 선택 과정의 일부이기도 하다. 굶주림은 생존에 덜 적합한 자들, 자기 자신과 자신의 새끼를 위해 식량을 발견하는 데 수완이 덜 뛰어난 자들을 걸러내는 데 도움이 된다. 어떤 상황에서 그것은 유전적 변종이 종의 개체 수를 장악하여 궁극적으로 오래된 종을 대신하는 새로운 종의 출현을 허용하는 길을 닦아줄지도 모른다. 따라서 굶주림은 더 큰 다양성이라는 선(善)을 가능하게 해 주는 데 도움이 될 수 있는 반가치이다. 굶주림은 심지어 그것이 본질적인 반가치일 때조차도 실용적 혹은 도구적으로 가치 있을 수 있다. 몇몇 유기체가 자연에서 굶주려야 하는 것은 대단히 유감스럽고 슬픈 일이다. 비록 굶주림이 또한 때때로 선한 목적에 공헌할지라도, 그 말은 확고하게 사실로 남아 있다.

구문 [7행~10행] In some circumstances, it may pave the way <u>for genetic variants</u> **to** <u>take</u> hold in the population of a species [and] eventually <u>allow</u> the emergence of a new *species* in place of the old *one*.
for genetic variants는 to부정사의 의미상 주어이다. to 다음의 동사원형 take와 allow가 병렬구조를 이룬다. the old one의 one은 species를 지칭한다.
[10행~12행] Thus starvation is a disvalue that can **help make** *possible* **the good of greater diversity**.
help 다음에는 to부정사 혹은 동사원형(make)이 나온다. make 다음의 possible은 목적격 보어이고, the good of greater diversity가 목적어이다. 여기서 of는 '동격'의 의미를 가진다.

어휘 organism 유기체 sufficient 충분한 starvation 굶주림 function 기능하다 filter out 걸러내다 fit 적합한 resourceful 수완이 있는 young (동물의) 새끼 pave the way for ~을 위한 길을 닦다, 상황을 조성하다 genetic 유전의 variant 변종, 이형 take hold 장악하다 emergence 출현 in place of ~을 대신해서 instrumental 도구적인 intrinsic 본질적인, 고유한 regrettable 유감스러운

8 밑줄 어휘 ③

해설 창의력의 핵심적인 의의는 소위 천재라는 사람이 예전에 아무도 가져본 적이 없는 생각을 발전시키는 것이라고 했으므로 천재성은 모방 정신과 동일한 것이 아니라 반대의 것으로 간주될 것이다. 따라서 ③의 same을 opposite 등으로 고쳐야 한다.

해석 'genius'라는 용어의 기원은 라틴어 단어인 'ingenium(천부적 재능)'으로 거슬러 올라갈 수 있다. 이 재능의 핵심은 ① 독창적인 생산성이라고 여겨지는데, 이는 창의성이라는 새로운 영역에 접근하기 위해 대담한 직관을 사용한다. genius(천재성), 즉 뛰어난 창의력을 가진 사람 또한 genius(천재)로 알려져 있다. 르네상스에 이르러서야 사람들은 예술적인 창의적 잠재력 또는 ② 영감의 원천을 천재성이라고 묘사하기 시작했다. 창의력의 핵심적인 의의는 소위 천재라는 사람이 예전에 아무도 가져본 적이 없는 생각을 발전시키는 것이며, Immanuel Kant의 말에 따르면, 'genius는 모방 정신의 ③ 동일한 것(→ 정반

대)으로 간주되어야 한다'는 것이다. 게다가 천재성은 그것의 산물을 어떻게 끌어내는지를 과학적으로 보여 줄 수 있는 게 아니라, 오히려 규칙을 ④ 본질로 제시한다. 그러므로 작가가 자신의 천재성 덕분에 산물을 만들어낸 경우, 그는 어떻게 그 발상을 품게 되었는지 스스로 알지 못하고, 또한 임의로든 체계적으로든 그와 비슷한 것을 만들어내는 것은 그의 능력으로 할 수 없는 일이기도 하며, 다른 사람들이 ⑤ 비슷한 산물을 만들어내는 위치에 놓을 수 있게 하는 지침 하에서도 그들에게 동일한 것을 전달하지 못한다고 Kant는 확정했다.

구문 [6행~9행] **It was not until** the Renaissance **that** people began to describe an artistic creative potential or the source of inspiration as genius.

'It is not until ... that ~'은 '…가 되어서야 비로소 ~하다'의 뜻이다.

[9행~13행] The key significance for invention is that the so-called genius develops *ideas* [that no one has had previously] and, in the words of Immanuel Kant, that 'genius must be considered the very opposite of a spirit of imitation'.

동사 is의 보어 역할을 하는 두 개의 밑줄 친 부분이 and로 연결되어 병렬구조를 이룬다. [ ]은 ideas를 수식하는 관계사절이다.

[16행~21행] Hence, where an author owes a product to his genius, he does not himself *know* **how he conceived the ideas**, nor is it in his power **to invent** the like at pleasure, or methodically, and (to) **communicate** the same to others in such precepts as would put them in a position to produce similar products.

굵게 표시된 how가 이끄는 명사절은 동사 know의 목적어 역할을 한다. 부정어구 nor가 문두로 나가 주어(it)와 동사(is)가 도치되었는데, 이때 it은 가주어, to invent 이하가 진주어이다. to invent 이하와 (to) communicate는 and로 연결되어 병렬구조를 이룬다.

어휘 trace back to ~의 기원[유래]이 …까지 거슬러 올라가다   essence 핵심, 정수   employ 사용하다; 고용하다   intuition 직관   bring about 야기하다, 초래하다   owe A to B A를 B에 빚지다   conceive (생각을) 품다; 상상하다   at pleasure 임의로   methodically 체계적으로

9 빈칸 추론   ②

해설 스포츠가 마케팅의 도구로서 전통적인 광고나 홍보와 차별화되는 지점은 결과를 예측할 수 없어서 팬들의 충성심 깊은 애정과 자발적인 신뢰를 쌓을 수 있다는 것인데 스포츠에 '대본이 있다면(scripted)' 스포츠는 이러한 장점을 상실할 것이다.
① 금지된 ③ 광고된 ④ 자본화된 ⑤ 경쟁적인

해석 계획된 광고나 홍보와 같은 전통적인 마케팅 활동과는 달리, 스포츠 경기는 본질적으로 예측할 수 없다. 팬, 운동선수, 팀, 회사는 결과를 모른다. 심지어 가장 어마어마한 성공 실적이 있어도 과거의 스포츠 성과가 계속될지 아니면 기대가 거꾸로 뒤집힐지 확실하게 알 수 없다. 바로 이러한 예측 불가능성이 스포츠를 거의 모든 다른 기업 마케팅 활동과 구분 짓는다. 실제로 많은 업체의 관리자들이 이러한 불확실성에 대한 전망을 명백히 불편하다고 느끼고 결과적으로 스포츠를 마케팅 플랫폼으로 사용하기를 피한다. 그러나 스포츠팬들은 부분적으로 결과가 보장되지 않기 때문에 스포츠를 추종한다. 팬들은 (대개) 최근의 경기 성과와 상관없이 자신이 좋아하는 팀과 선수들에 대해 감정적인 애착을 갖고 있다. 만약 스포츠에 대본이 있다면, 그러면 신뢰를 잃을 것이고, 자발성은 사라질 것이며, 그것들은 전통적인 회사 주도의 광고 캠페인과 다를 바가 없을 것이다.

구문 [5행~8행] **Despite** even the most formidable track records of success, one cannot **know** for certain whether past sport performances will continue or whether expectations will be turned upside down.

despite는 전치사로 뒤에 명사(구)가 나온다. 주절의 동사 know의 목적어로 밑줄 친 두 개의 명사절이 병렬 구조를 이룬다.

[10행~13행] Indeed, many business managers **find** this prospect of uncertainty *distinctly uncomfortable* and consequently **shy away** from using sports as a marketing platform.

동사 find와 shy away가 and로 연결되어 병렬구조를 이루고, find 이하는 「find+목적어(this prospect of uncertainty)+목적격보어(distinctly uncomfortable)」로 '목적어가 ~하다는 것을 깨닫다'의 의미이다.

[17행~20행] If sports **were** scripted, then they **would lose** credibility, spontaneity **would be** lost, and they **would be** no different than a conventional company-directed ad campaign.

「If+S+과거동사 ~, S+would+동사원형…」의 가정법 과거 구문으로 '~하면 …할 것이다'의 의미(현재의 사실을 반대로 가정)이고, 밑줄 친 세 개의 절이 병렬 구조를 이룬다.

어휘 conventional 전통적인; 관습적인; 형식적인   inherently 본질적으로   formidable 어마어마한; 무서운   track record (개인·기관의 모든) 실적   upside down 거꾸로   corporate 기업[회사]의; 법인의   prospect 전망   distinctly 명백하게, 뚜렷하게   consequently 그 결과, 따라서   shy away from ~을 피하다   attachment 애착   irrespective of ~와 관계[상관]없이   credibility 신뢰성   spontaneity 자발적임   ban 금(지)하다   capitalize 자본화하다; 대문자로 쓰다

10 빈칸 추론   ④

해설 유년기 공상은 권력을 위한 분투가 두드러진 역할을 한다고 하였으므로 어린이들의 공상은 거의 항상 ④ '어린이가 권력을 발휘하는 상황을 포함한다'가 된다.
① 지역사회를 도울 그들의 계획을 반영한다
② 정체성을 형성하는 특정한 흥미를 반영한다
③ 그들의 성공 경험과 관련이 있다
⑤ 그들의 현실과 공상을 식별하는 능력의 부족을 드러낸다

해석 어린이들과 어른들의 공상은, 때때로 몽상이라 불리며, 항상 미래와 관련돼 있다. 이러한 '공기 중의 성'은 그들의 활동 목표이며, 실제 활동을 위한 모델로서 허구적 형식으로 구축된다. 유년기 공상에 대한 연구는 권력을 위한 분투가 두드러진 역할을 한다는 것을 보여준다. 어린이들은 그들의 몽상 속에서 그들의 야망을 표현한다. 대부분의 그들의 공상은 '내가 크면' 등의 말로 시작된다. 자신들 역시 아직 다 자라지 않은 것처럼 사는 많은 어른들이 있다. 권력을 위한 분투에 대한 명확한 강조는 특정 목표가 설정되었을 때에만 정신이 발달할 수 있음을 다시 한 번 나타낸다. 우리의 문명에서, 이러한 목표는 사회적 인정과 중요성을 포함한다. 개인은 어떠한 중립적 목표를 가지고는 결코 오래 가지 못하는데, 인류의 공동생활이 우월성에 대한 욕망과 경쟁에서의 성공이라는 희망을 낳으며 끊임없는 자기평가가 수반되기 때문이다. 어린이들의 공상은 거의 항상 어린이가 권력을 발휘하는 상황을 포함한다.

구문 [10행~11행] There are *many adults* [who live **as though** they too were not yet grown up].

[ ]은 many adults를 수식한다. 'as though'는 '마치 ~인 것처럼'의 뜻으로, 이 절에서 가정법 과거 표현이 쓰여 동사 were를 사용하였다.

[15행~19행] An individual never stays long with any neutral goal, **for** the communal life of humankind is accompanied by *constant self-evaluation* [giving rise to the desire for superiority and the hope of success in competition].

접속사 for는 '~이므로'의 뜻이다. [ ]은 능동의 의미로 constant self-evaluation을 수식한다. [ ]에서 the desire for superiority와 the hope of success in competition 이 병렬구조를 이룬다.

어휘 grown-up 성인   daydream 백일몽, 몽상   be concerned with ~와 관계있다   strive 분투하다   play a role 역할을 하다   predominant 두드러진

ambition 야망   as though 마치 ~인 것처럼   emphasis 강조   indicate 나타내다   psyche 마음, 정신   civilization 문명   recognition 인정   significance 중요성   neutral 중립적인   humankind 인류   accompany 동반하다   give rise to 낳다, 일으키다   superiority 우월성

11 빈칸 추론   ③

해설   음악의 보편성에는 이론의 여지가 없고 우리 생활의 거의 모든 곳을 음악이 채우고 있다는 내용의 글이며, John Blacking은 사회는 말로는 제한된 수의 사람만이 음악성을 갖고 있다고 주장하지만, 모두가 음악성을 갖고 있는 것처럼 행동한다는 모순을 지적하고 있다. 따라서 그가 지지한 생각은 ③ '비음악적인 인간 같은 것은 없다'이다.
① 음악과 인간의 문화는 항상 협업한다
② 청중은 음악 산업의 성공의 핵심이다
④ 청중은 최고의 음악가들과 시시한 음악가들을 구별한다
⑤ 음악적 재능은 음악에 반복 노출되는 데에서 나온다

해석   음악의 보편성은 아마 언어의 보편성보다도 더 이론의 여지가 있을 것인데, 왜냐하면 많은 개인들은 자신이 음악적 소양이 없다고 선언하며, 우리는 듣기보다 생산에 더 역점을 두기 때문이다. 이 점에서 자신이 성장했던 중산층 서구 사회에서의 이론과 실제 사이의 모순에 대해 John Blacking이 1970년대에 했던 말은 오늘날에도 여전히 적절하다. 음악은 우리 주위의 도처에 존재했고 계속 남아있다. 우리는 레스토랑, 공항 라운지에서 먹을 때와 대화하려고 할 때 그것을 듣는다. 그것은 라디오에서 하루 종일 재생된다. 사실 누군가가 잠재적 침묵의 순간을 음악으로 채우려고 노력하지 않는 때는 거의 없다. Blacking은 '사회는 오직 제한된 수의 사람들만이 음악성이 있다고 주장하지만, 그것(= 사회)은 이 능력이 없으면 어떤 음악적 전통도 존재할 수 없는 기본 능력, 즉 듣고 소리의 패턴을 구별하는 능력을 모두가 소유한 듯이 행동한다.'고 말했다. 그는 비음악적인 인간 같은 것은 없다는 생각을 지지했고, 바흐나 베토벤 같은 사람의 존재는 오직 안목 있는 청중의 존재로 인해 가능했다고 언급했다.

구문   [1행~5행] The universality of music is, perhaps, / more contentious than **that** of language // because we place greater emphasis on production than listening, / **with** *many individuals* **declaring** themselves to be unmusical.
that은 the universality를 지칭한다. 「with + O + v-ing」 분사구문은 'O가 v하면서, v한 채로'의 뜻이다.
[5행~8행] In this regard, / **John Blacking's comments,** / made in the 1970s, / on **the contradiction between** theory **and** practice in *the middle-class, Western society* [in which he grew up], / **remain** relevant today.
주어는 John Blacking's comments이고 동사는 remain이다. made in the 1970s는 분사구문이다. 「the contradiction between A and B」는 'A와 B 사이의 모순'을 뜻한다. [ ]는 the middle-class, Western society를 수식하는 관계부사절이다.

어휘   universality 보편성   declare 선언하다   in this regard 이 점에서   contradiction 모순   relevant 적절한; 관련 있는   occasion 경우, 때   favo(u)r 지지하다; 찬성하다; 호의를 보이다   discriminating 안목 있는; 구별할 수 있는   *cf.* discriminate 구별[식별]하다; 차별하다

12 빈칸 추론   ③

해설   발이 걸렸을 때 바닥에 넘어지지 않고 몸이 허공으로 떠오르는 상황은 중력 법칙이 위배된 것이 아니라 법칙이 적용되지 않는 다른 환경 혹은 중력 외에 더 큰 다른 힘이 작용하고 있는 상황이다. 즉 몸이 허공으로 떠오른 것은 중력 법칙 하나

로만 설명될 수 없고 환경과 다른 힘을 고려해야 충분히 설명이 가능하다. 따라서 '법칙'은 '위배될' 수 없으며 다만 ③ '일어나고 있는 일에 대한 완전한 설명을 내놓기에 불충분하다'고 판명될 수 있을 뿐이다.
① 설명이 근거가 되는 증거를 담고 있다면 유효성을 가진다고
② 물리적 세계에서 반복되는 관찰을 바탕으로 옳거나 그르다고
④ 인간의 해석에 관계없이 별개의 확실한 증거를 갖고 있다고
⑤ 상황에 따라 다르게 적용될 정도로 충분히 융통성 있다고

해석   확립된 과학 이론은 보통 '자연 법칙' 혹은 '물리학 법칙'으로 불리는데, 그러나 이 경우 '법칙'이 의미하는 바를 정확히 인식하는 것이 중요하다. 이것은 따라야 하는 종류의 법칙이 아니다. 과학 법칙은 사물이 어떠해야 하는지 명령할 수 없다. 그것은 단지 그것들(사물)을 표현할 뿐이다. 중력 법칙은 발을 헛디뎠을 때 내가 인도에서 엎드린 자세를 취해야 한다고 요구하지 않는다. 그것은 단지 발을 헛디뎠을 때 내가 넘어진다는 현상을 표현할 뿐이다. 따라서 내가 발이 걸려 몸이 위로 둥실 뜨면, 나는 법칙에 불복종하는 게 아니라, 이는 단지 내가 '중력 법칙'으로 표현되는 현상이 적용되지 않는 환경(즉 궤도상)에 있다는 것을, 혹은 중력의 영향을 내가 위로 떠 오를 수 있게 해주는 다른 힘들이 거스른다는 것을 의미할 뿐이다. '법칙'은 이러한 상황에서 '위배될' 수 없으며 다만 일어나고 있는 일에 대한 완전한 설명을 내놓기에 불충분하다고 판명될 수 있을 뿐이다.

구문   [1행~4행] Confirmed scientific theories are often referred to as 'laws of nature' or 'laws of physics', but **it** is important **to recognize** exactly what is meant by 'law' in this case.
it은 가주어, to recognize 이하가 진주어이다.
[10행~15행] Hence, if I trip and float upwards, I am not disobeying a law, it simply *means* that I am in *an environment* (e.g. in orbit) [**in which** *the phenomenon* (described by 'the law of gravity') does not apply], or that the effect of gravity is countered by *other forces* [that enable me to float upwards].
동사 means의 목적어로 밑줄 친 두 개의 명사절이 or로 연결되어 병렬구조를 이룬다. 첫 번째 [ ] 부분은 '전치사+관계대명사' 형태의 in which가 이끄는 관계사절로 선행사 an environment를 수식한다. 그 안의 ( ) 부분은 the phenomenon을 수식하는 과거분사구이다. 두 번째 [ ] 부분은 other forces를 수식하는 관계사절이다.

어휘   confirmed 확립[확증]된   be referred to as ~라고 불리다   obey 따르다   dictate 명령하다, 지시하다   gravity 중력   trip 발 헛디디다; 넘어뜨리다   adopt 취하다, 채택하다   prone (배를 바닥에 대고) 엎어져 있는; ~하기 쉬운   pavement (포장한) 인도; 포장 도로   phenomenon (*pl.* phenomena) 현상   float 뜨다, 떠오르다   disobey 불복종[거역]하다   orbit 궤도(를 돌다)   counter 거스르다, 반대하다; 계산대; 반대의   validity 유효성; 타당성   contain 담고 있다   inadequate 불충분한; 부적절한   discrete 별개의, 분리된   definite 확실한, 뚜렷한; 한정된

13 흐름 무관 문장   ④

해설   인간이 토양을 망가뜨리는 많은 방식에 대해 설명하는 글로 국제 사회가 토양 자원의 지속 가능한 사용을 지지한다는 ④는 전체 흐름과 무관하다.

해석   생태계에 부정적인 영향을 끼치고 토양에도 해를 끼치는 가뭄이나 곤충의 피해, 혹은 질병의 발생과 같은 불운한 사건의 자연적 순환이 있다. 하지만 인간들이 이 중요한 자원(토양)을 방치하거나 남용하는 보다 많은 방식이 있다. ① 한 가지 해로운 관행은 토양을 제자리에 붙잡아 두는 역할을 하는 식물을 제거하는 것이다. ② 때로 같은 곳 위에서 걷거나 자전거를 타는 것만으로도 거기에서 정상적으로 자라는 풀을 죽일 것이다. ③ 다른 때에는 토지가 다른 용도로 쓰일 공간을 마련하기 위해 의도적으로 개간된다. ④ 토양 자원은 식품 안전의 기저 역할을 하기 때문에, 국제 사회는 그것의 지속 가능한 사용을 지지한다. ⑤ 토양에 너무 많은 소금이 축적되거나 오염 물질이 땅으로 들어가게 되어 있다면, 토양이 또한 오염될 수 있다.

구문 [13행~15행] Soils can also be contaminated // if too much salt accumulates in the soil or if pollutants are allowed to enter the ground.
if로 시작되는 부사절이 or로 연결되어 병렬구조를 이루고 있다.

어휘 drought 가뭄 insect plague 곤충의 피해 outbreak (전쟁·질병 등의) 발생, 발발 neglect 무시; 소홀히 하다; 방치하다 abuse 남용(하다) vegetation 초목, 식물 in place 제자리에 deliberately 고의로, 계획적으로; 신중히 clear 개간하다, 개척하다; 분명한; 치우다 advocate 지지[옹호]하다; 지지자, 옹호자 sustainable (환경 파괴 없이) 지속 가능한 contaminate 오염시키다 accumulate 모으다, 축적하다; 쌓이다

14 글의 순서 ②

해설 주어진 문장은 과일이나 채소가 건강에 좋다는 연구결과가 나오면 사람들은 그 이익이 그 식품의 오직 한 가지 구성요소에서 나왔다고 생각한다는 것으로 이에 대한 구체적인 연구를 설명하는 (B)가 이어져야 한다. (A)는 (B)에 언급된 연구의 결과를 설명하는 것이므로 (B)에 이어지는 것이 적절하다. (C)는 과일과 채소의 구성요소가 훨씬 더 많으므로, 좋다는 하나의 성분을 먹는다는 것과 전체를 먹는 것이 같을 수 없다는 내용으로서 (B), (A)와 상반되므로 맨 마지막에 나오는 것이 적절하다.

해석 우리가 아는 한, 식물의 이익을 거두는 가장 좋은 방법은 그것들을 천연 형태로 섭취함에 의해서이다. 새로운 연구가 특정 과일과 채소를 먹는 이익을 밝힐 때, 많은 사람들은 재빨리 그 이익을 한 가지 특정 성분 탓으로 돌린다.
(B) 예를 들어, 연구에 의하면 카로티노이드가 풍부한 과일과 채소를 먹는 것은 몇 가지 암을 발달시킬 위험을 줄인다는 것이 발견되었다.
(A) 이러한 연구결과는 베타카로틴(비타민 A)에 대한 많은 관심을 불러일으켰고 많은 사람들이 암 위험을 줄이기 위해 비타민 A 보충제를 복용하기 시작하도록 유도했다.
(C) 그러나 과일과 채소는 종종 베타카로틴보다 더 높은 수준으로서 적어도 40개의 각기 다른 카로티노이드를 포함하고 있다. 우리는 단지 하나의 성분이 식물과 같은 복잡한 꾸러미의 일부일 때 그러할 것과 같은 결과를 분리 상태에서 생산해낼 것이라고 가정할 수 없다. 그것은 단지 요소 하나를 따로 떼어서 대량으로 알약 하나에 꾸려 넣는 문제인 것만은 아니다.

구문 [4행~6행] ~ many people are quick to **attribute** that benefit **to** one particular ingredient.
A(결과) ... B(원인)
「attribute A to B」는 'A를 B의 탓으로 돌리다'의 뜻으로, A 자리에는 결과가, B 자리에는 원인이 위치한다.

[16행~18행] We cannot just assume that *one ingredient* will produce **the same** result in isolation **as *it will*** when *it*(= one ingredient) is part of a complex package like a plant.
「the same ... as ~」는 '~와 같은 …'의 뜻이고 as it will은 as it will produce a result의 뜻이다. when절의 it은 앞서 언급된 one ingredient를 지칭한다.

어휘 reap 거두다, 수확하다 attribute A to B A를 B의 탓으로 돌리다 ingredient 성분 stir up 불러일으키다 supplement 보충물, 보충제; (책의) 부록 in isolation 별개로 component (구성) 요소 dose 복용량

15 글의 순서 ④

해설 주어진 문장은 피실험자들이 프라이버시를 보호받기를 원한다는 내용이다. (C)는 대부분의 연구에서 자료는 개인과 연결되지 않아 익명성이 보장됨을 보여준다. However로 연결되는 (A)에서는 불가피하게 자료와 개인이 연결될 수밖에 없는 연구도 있지만 여전히 피실험자의 비밀과 프라이버시를 지키기 위해 노력해야 한다

고 말한다. In other words로 연결되는 (B)에서는 프라이버시를 지키기 위한 구체적인 노력으로 암호화 시스템이 소개되어 있다.

해석 연구의 피실험자들은 프라이버시가 위태로워지면 위험해질 수 있다. 그래서 피실험자들은 연구자들이 그들의 프라이버시를 보호해주고 그들의 연구 참여와 연구에서 나온 결과를 비밀로 지켜줄 것을 기대한다.
(C) 대부분의 조사 연구에서는 자료를 개인과 결부시킬 필요가 없을 것이다. 따라서 많은 경우 참가자들은 익명성을 갖기 때문에 프라이버시와 비밀은 쟁점이 아니다.
(A) 그러나 자료를 개인과 결부시켜야만 하는 상황(예를 들어, 동일한 피실험자들로부터 여러 다양한 상황에서의 자료가 수집될 때)에서는, 자료를 안전하게 지키고 참가자들의 신원으로부터 분리시켜 놓기 위해 모든 예방 조치가 취해져야 한다.
(B) 다시 말해서, 연구자가 개인을 확인하게 해 주는 암호화 시스템이 사용되어야 하지만, 그들의 신원확인 정보는 누군가 자료를 보았을 때 어느 특정 개인과 연관될 수 없도록 실제 자료와 분리된 상태로 보관되어야 한다.

구문 [2행~5행] Therefore, subjects **expect** // **that** researchers will protect their privacy / and keep their participation **in**, and results **from**, the study confidential.
that 이하는 expect의 목적어이다. that절의 동사 protect와 keep은 and로 연결되어 병렬구조를 이룬다. the study는 앞의 전치사 in과 from의 공통 목적어이다. confidential은 앞의 목적어 their participation ~ the study를 설명해 주는 보어이다.

어휘 compromise 위태롭게 하다; 타협(안); 타협하다 confidential 비밀의 cf. confidentiality 비밀 occasion 때, 경우; 행사 precaution 예방책, 예방 조치 employ (방법 등을) 이용하다; 고용하다 anonymity 익명성

16 문장 넣기 ④

해설 주어진 문장은 Further로 시작하며 '서로에게 긍정적인 평가를 내리는 것이 가져오는 이점(즉 관계 형성 촉진)'에 관한 것으로, 앞 내용에는 '서로에게 긍정적인 평가를 내리는 것'의 다른 이점이 제시되어야 한다. ④의 앞 문장에 그것이 '상대방의 자아상을 확인해주는 보상'으로 제시되어 있으므로 주어진 문장은 ④에 들어가야 한다. ④ 다음 문장에 나온 '서로에게 좋은 말(nice things)을 해주면 우정을 형성할 수 있다는 주장(this assertion)'은 주어진 문장에 제시된 '긍정적인 평가를 해주면 관계 형성이 촉진된다'는 내용을 가리킴을 알 수 있다.

해석 많은 사람들은 자신을 어떻게 평가해야 할지에 대해 확신을 갖지 못한다. 그들은 자신의 능력, 자신의 사회적 자극 값, 혹은 자신의 가치에 대해 확신하지 못한다. 이러한 사람들에게 그들의 자기 평가는 그들이 관심을 갖고 있으며 사회적 지지를 필요로 하는 의견이 된다. 따라서 우리는 서로에 대해 두 개인이 각자의 자기 평가와 유사한 의견을 가지고 있을 때 대인 관계의 형성이 촉진되는 것을 발견하리라 기대할 것이다. 이것은 각자가 상대 자아상의 정확성을 입증해줄 의견을 표현함으로써 각자가 상대에게 보상할 수 있는 상황을 만든다. 게다가 사람들이 일반적으로 자신에 대해 대개 긍정적인 태도를 가지고 있다는 점을 가정하면, 그들이 서로에 대해 긍정적인 평가를 가짐으로써 관계 형성은 촉진될 것이다. 일상적인 용어로 표현하면, 이러한 주장은 두 사람이 서로에 대해 좋은 말을 솔직하게 할 수 있다면 우정이 더 일어날 것 같다는 것이다. '친구를 얻고 사람들에게 영향을 미치는' 방법의 전략에서 이것은 칭찬과 감언의 중요성을 암시한다.

구문 [1행~4행] Further, **assuming** // that people generally have predominantly positive attitudes about themselves, / relationship formation would be facilitated / by *their* **having** positive evaluations of each other.
assuming ~ themselves는 '가정'의 의미를 나타내는 분사구문이다. by 뒤의 소유격 their는 동명사 having의 의미상 주어이다.
[7행~10행] For these persons, / their self-evaluations constitute *opinions*

[**about which** they are <u>concerned</u> [and] in need of social support].
[ ]는 '전치사 + 관계대명사'로 시작되는 관계사절로 앞의 opinions를 수식한다. [ ]절에서 두 밑줄 부분이 병렬구조를 이룬다.

어휘 predominantly 대개, 대부분   facilitate 촉진하다, 용이하게 하다   regard 평가하다, 여기다   constitute ~이 되다, ~을 구성하다   interpersonal 대인 관계의   validate 입증하다   assertion 주장   flattery 감언, 듣기 좋은 말

17 문장 넣기   ②

해설 주어진 문장은 사용자가 많으면 제품이나 서비스의 가격이 낮아진다는 내용이므로 가격 하락의 사례를 설명하는 내용이 시작되는 문장 앞인 ②에 들어가야 적절하다. ①과 ③ 내용의 흐름이 단절된다는 것에서 힌트를 찾을 수 있다.

해석 과학기술이 널리 퍼지게 하려면, 더 약한 구매 동기를 가진 사용자들에게 호소해야 한다. 신기술을 처음으로 이용하는 사람들을 넘어 훨씬 더 큰 대중에게까지 확대함으로써만이, 과학기술은 개발자들이 초기 투자 금액을 되찾게 하는 규모에 대한 수익을 달성할 수 있다. <u>결과적으로 더 큰 사용자 집단에 도달한다는 것은 그 제품이나 서비스의 가격이 하락할 수 있다는 것을 뜻한다.</u> 예를 들어 이전의 휴대 전화 사용자들은 흔히 자신이 사는 도시 내의 서비스에 대해 매달 1,000달러의 청구서를 받았다. 오늘날, 그런 서비스는 고작 매달 25달러만큼의 비용이 들 것이다. 광범위한 채택은 또한 새로운 수준의 성능, 신뢰성, 사용의 용이성, 그리고 지원을 필요로 한다. 이들 중 일부는 개발자들이 기술에 대해 배우고 제조 과정이 더 효율적으로 되면서 자연스럽게 발생한다.

구문 [5행~9행] **Only** (by expanding beyond *the first people* [who make use of the new technology] to the much larger communities) **can it achieve** *the returns to scale* [that **allow** the developers **to recover** their initial investments].
only가 문장 첫머리에 위치하면 「Only+조동사+주어+동사」의 어순으로 도치된다. 여기서는 Only와 조동사 can 사이에 부사구 (   )가 삽입되었다. that 이하는 앞의 the returns to scale을 수식하며, 관계사절 내의 동사 allow는 「allow O to-v(O가 v할 수 있게 하다)」의 구조로 쓰였다.

어휘 in turn 결국, 결과적으로; 차례차례   reliability 신뢰할 수 있음, 믿음직함

18 요약문 완성   ③

해설 글에 나온 동물은 세 마리의 집단이 있을 경우 자신보다 순위가 높은지(ranking), 자신과 가까운 관계인지를 따져서 다른 두 마리 중 누구와 동맹을 맺고 누구를 편들지를 결정하는 갈등(conflicts) 대처 행동 방침을 보인다.
① 집단화 – 갈등   ② 집단화 – 의사소통
④ 서열 – 의사소통   ⑤ 관계망 – 상호작용

해석 어떤 종은 마음 이론뿐만 아니라 명백하게 관계 이론도 발달시켜 왔다. 이는 진화상으로 유리한데, 왜냐하면 다른 개체 간의 관계를 인식하는 것이 그들의 사회적 행동을 예측하는 데 도움이 되기 때문이다. 그러한 지식의 가장 기본적인 유형은 한 동물이 다른 두 동물과 관련된 자신의 순위뿐만 아니라 그 두 동물의 상대적 우위 순위를 알고 있을 때이다. 이 중요한 능력은 널리 퍼져 있어서, 하이에나, 사자, 말, 돌고래, 그리고 물론 영장류에서뿐만 아니라 물고기와 새에서도 보인다. 싸움 중인 꼬리감는원숭이는 상대보다 순위가 더 높은 것으로 알고 있는 동맹자를 우선적으로 찾으며, 또한 상대보다 자기와 더 가까운 관계를 맺고 있다고 알고 있는 동맹자를 찾기도 한다. 만약 침팬지 두 마리가 싸우고 구경하던 침팬지가 패자에게 위로를 건넨다면, 이것은 그 싸우는 두 침팬지를 화해시킬수 있지만, 구경하던 침팬지가 공격한 침팬지와 친분이 있는 경우에만 그렇다. 세 동물 모두 그들 중에서 둘이 특별한 유대감을 갖고 있다는 것이 무엇을 의미하는지를 알고 있다.

↓

어떤 동물이 자신의 사회적 관계, 즉 (A) 서열과 그들 간의 사회적 유대를 이해하는 능력을 갖추고 있는데, 이는 그들의 (B) 갈등을 다루는 데에서 역할을 한다.

구문 [11행~15행] Capuchin monkeys in a fight preferentially seek out *allies* [that they know to be higher ranked than their opponents], and they also seek out *allies* [that (they know) have closer relationships with them than with their opponents].
두 개의 관계사절 [ ]은 각각 바로 앞에 있는 allies를 수식하며, 두 번째 관계사절 내에서 they know가 삽입되었다.

[18행~20행] All three animals understand **what it** means *for two of them* **to have** a special bond.
what 이하는 understand의 목적어 역할을 하는 간접의문문이다. what절 내에서 it은 가주어이고 to have 이하가 진주어이며, for two of them은 to have에 대한 의미상 주어이다.

어휘 distinctly 명백하게, 뚜렷하게   dominance 우위, 우월   with respect to ~에 관하여   preferentially 우선적으로   ally 동맹자, 협력자   opponent 상대, 반대자   bystander 구경꾼   aggressor 공격자   bond 유대

19~20 장문   19 ④ 20 ⑤

해설 19. 의식은 우리가 의미를 만들어 부과하는 것이며 반복과 정해진 순서를 특징으로 한다는 점, 그리고 반복 그 자체가 통제감 등을 부여하여 보상의 기능이 있다는 내용의 글이므로 제목으로 가장 적절한 것은 ④ '의식의 수행: 그것의 의의와 기능들'이다.
① 의식에 뿌리내린 미신적 믿음
② 의식, 형식적인 수행과 문화
③ 의식에서 전통을 보존하는 것이 필요한가?
⑤ 의식은 목적을 위한 수단이지, 목적 그 자체가 아니다
20. 프로 선수들이 경기 전에 미신적인 의식을 수행하는 것은 압박이 크고 얻을 수 있는 것도 많지만 자칫하면 잃을 것도 많은 프로의 세계에서, 즉 대단히 '예측 불가능한' 환경에서 통제감을 얻기 위함이다. 따라서 (e)의 predictable을 unpredictable로 바꿔 써야 한다.

해석 모든 의식은 반복과 엄격하게 고정된 행동의 순서들에 근거를 둔다. 그러나 그것은 한 가지 중요한 방식에서 습관과는 다르다. 의식에는 직접적이고 즉각적인 보상이 결여돼 있다. 대신에 우리는 의미를 만들고 그것(= 의미)을 그것들(= 의식들)에 부과해야 한다. 우리는 건배하기 위해 잔을 들어올리고, 생일 케이크의 초를 불어 끄고, 졸업식에서 모자와 가운을 착용한다. 노래를 위해 조용히 서 있는 행위, 초가 타는 동안 노래하는 행위, 혹은 의식용 의상을 입는 행위는 피드백 역할을 하며, (a) 유의미한 일, 즉 조국에 대한 존경, 또 다른 한 해의 기념, 혹은 교육적 성취의 행위가 일어나고 있다는 우리의 믿음을 강화시킨다.
뿐만 아니라 의식은 (b) 보편적인 인간의 충동이다. 아메리카 원주민들은 특히 서남부 지역에서 기우제를 지냈다. 일본인들은 다도의 예술을 가지고 있다. 아즈텍인들은 그들의 피라미드 꼭대기에서 인신 공양을 했다. 객관적인 눈으로 볼 때 이러한 의식들은 특별히 (c) 이성적이지도 않고 확실히 전부 바람직한 것은 아니다. 그러나 연구자들은 특히 불확실과 불안의 시대에서 그것들 이면에 있는 논리를 발견하고 있다. 반복은 그 자체로 보상이다. 엘리트 선수들의 고부담, 고압력의 세계를 생각해보자. 그들이 경쟁할 때마다 많은 돈과 명성과 재능이 위태로워진다. 승리는 많은 자신감과 어느 정도의 운을 요구한다. 선수들이 받는 압력을 고려하면, 프로 중 80퍼센트가 경기 전에 미신적인 의식을 (d) 수행하는 것이 놀랍지 않은데, 이것의 범위는 항상 네 개의 팬케이크를 먹는 것부터 적어도 한 번은 숫자 13을 보는 것까지 이른다. 선수들은 이 대단히 (e) 예측 가능한(→ 예측 불가능한) 환경에서 통제감을 얻기 위해 그것을 이용한다.

구문 [7행~11행] The act **of** standing silently for a song, singing while candles burn, or wearing a ceremonial costume **acts** as feedback, / **reinforcing** our belief that something meaningful is taking place ~.

주어는 The act이고 동사는 acts이다. 밑줄 친 세 동명사구는 전치사 of의 목적어로 콤마(,)와 or로 연결되어 병렬구조를 이룬다. reinforcing 이하는 분사구문이다. that ~ place는 out belief에 대한 동격절이다.

[27행~31행] **Given** *the pressures* [that athletes are under], / **it** is no surprise (that) **eighty percent of pros perform** *superstitious rituals* before **playing,** // **which range from** always eating four pancakes **to** seeing the number 13 at least once.

Given은 '~을 고려하면'의 뜻이다. [ ]는 the pressures를 수식하는 관계대명사절이다. it은 가주어이고 eighty percent ~ playing이 진주어이다. eighty percent 앞에 that이 생략되어있다. which절은 superstitious rituals를 부연 설명한다. 「range from A to B」는 '범위가 A에서 B까지 이르다'의 뜻이며, A와 B 자리 모두 동명사구가 위치해 있다.

어휘 ritual 의식 be grounded in ~에 근거를 두다 rigidly 엄격히 sequence 순서; 연속 impose A on B A를 B에 부과하다 toast 건배하다 blow out (불어서) 끄다 take place 일어나다 universal 보편적인 impulse 충동 tea ceremony 다도 human sacrifice 인신 공양 desirable 바람직한 high-stakes 판돈이 큰. 이판사판의 on the line 위태로운 given ~을 고려하면 superstitious 미신의

제14회
본문 p.108

| 1 ② | 2 ③ | 3 ④ | 4 ⑤ | 5 ③ | | 6 ⑤ | 7 ④ | 8 ④ | 9 ④ | 10 ③ |
| 11 ④ | 12 ⑤ | 13 ④ | 14 ⑤ | 15 ② | | 16 ② | 17 ③ | 18 ① | 19 ⑤ | 20 ③ |

1 심경 변화　　　　②

해설 함께 뮤지컬을 보러 가자는 Ethan의 제안을 거절하고 캠핑장에 간 Archer가 시원한 바람. 상쾌한 나무 냄새 등으로 캠핑장에 온 것에 대해 만족스러워했지만, 갑자기 비가 와서 모든 것이 엉망이 되자 Ethan의 제안을 따랐어야 했다고 후회한 상황이므로 Archer의 심경 변화로 가장 적절한 것은 ② '만족한 → 후회하는'이다.
① 안도하는 → 겁에 질린　　　③ 기쁜 → 시샘하는
④ 우울한 → 기뻐하는　　　⑤ 스트레스를 받는 → 자신감 있는

해석 아름다운 어느 여름날의 끝자락이었고, 하늘은 서서히 붉게 물들고 있었다. 해변에서 강아지들과 뛰노는 아이들을 보면서, Archer는 함께 뮤지컬을 보러 가자는 Ethan의 제안을 거절한 것은 잘 한 결정이었다고 생각했다. 시원한 산들바람이 그의 얼굴을 스쳤고, 오크나무 잎의 상쾌한 내음이 그의 콧구멍을 간지럽혔으며, 지저귀는 새 소리가 그의 귀를 가득 채웠다. 그는 Bondi 해변 캠핑장의 모든 것이 완벽하다고 혼잣말을 하고는 옅게 미소 지었다. 바로 그때 하늘에서 무언가가 떨어져서 그의 손에 닿았다. 빗방울이었다! 비는 점점 더 세게 내렸다. 캠핑장에 있던 모든 사람들이 텐트를 걷기 시작했고, Archer도 그들 중 한 사람이었다. 저녁 전부가 이제 엉망진창이라고 Archer가 깨달았을 때 Ethan의 제안이 다시 한번 갑자기 생각났다. 이미 너무 늦었다 할지라도, Archer는 Ethan을 따라 뮤지컬 극장으로 갔어야 했다는 생각을 멈출 수가 없었다.

구문 [9행~11행] **It was** *just then* **that** something fell from the sky and touched his hand.

부사구 just then을 강조하는 「it is[was] ~ that ...」 강조구문이 쓰였다. that절에서 동사 fell과 touched가 and로 연결되어 병렬구조를 이룬다.

어휘 turn down 거절하다 breeze 산들바람 brush 스치다, 스치고 지나가다 oak leave 오크나무 잎사귀 tickle 간지럽히다 chirp 지저귀다 take down 치우다, 분해하다 pop into one's head 갑자기 생각나다 should have p.p. ~했어야 했다

2 필자 주장　　　　③

해설 과학의 모든 분야가 서로 연관되어 있다고 하며 학생을 위해 통합된 방식으로 과학의 다양한 분야를 다루는 게 가치 있다고 말하고 있다. 그러므로 필자의 주장으로는 ③이 적절하다.

해석 생명 과학, 식물학, 동물학, 생리학, 물리학, 화학, 농학, 그리고 지질학 등과 같은 모든 과학 분야는 서로 연관되어 있고 상호 관계되어 있다. 예를 들어, 만약 우리가 지구의 암석과 광물에 관한 지질학 단원을 공부하고 있다면, 그러면 우리는 분명히 이런 암석과 광물의 화학적 구성 요소와 구조와 특성을 공부하고 있을 것이다. 마찬가지로, 농학 공부에 있어서 암석과 화학물질에 관한 지식이 관련되어 있다. 암석과 토양을 공부하는 것은 서로 다른 농작물에 대해 서로 다른 토양을 선택하는 데 도움이 된다. 화학에 관한 지식은 우리가 각기 다른 종류의 비료를 결정하는 데 도움을 준다. 그러므로 학생들을 위해 통합된 방식으로 과학의 각기 다른 분야들을 다루는 것은 항상 가치가 있다. 과학 교육을 더욱 의미 있고 효과적으로 만들기 위해 과학의 한 분야와 다른 분야의 상관관계를 끌어내는 것이 필요하다.

구문 [15행~18행] It is necessary **to bring out** correlation of one branch of science with another branch / **to make** *science education* **more meaningful and effective**.

밑줄 친 It은 가주어, to bring out 이하가 진주어이다. to make 이하는 부사적 용법의 '목적'을 나타내는 to부정사구로 'make+목적어+목적격보어'의 5문형 구조이다.

어휘 branch 분야; 파생물; 나뭇가지 botany 식물학 geology 지질학 correlate 연관성이 있다 interrelate 상호 관계를 갖게 하다 composition 구성 요소들; 작품; 작곡 property 특성; 재산; 부동산 unified 통합된, 통일된 for the benefit of ~을 위해 correlation 상관관계; 연관성

3 밑줄 함의　　　　④

해설 칼로리론에서는 섭취된 열량과 소비된 열량이라는 두 가지 변수를 가지고 열량을 계산하는 단순화된 공식을 제시하지만 건강을 생각한다면 그것은 목표 달성에 도움이 되지 않는다는 내용이다. 그러므로 밑줄 친, 총체적인 모델이 필요하다는 말은 칼로리론이 아닌 새롭고, 종합적인 체중 감량 이론을 개발할 필요가 있다는 뜻으로 정답은 ④ '새롭고, 종합적인 체중 감량 이론을 개발해야 한다'이다.
① 체중 감량을 위한 역할 모델을 가져야 한다
② 다이어트에 대한 장기적 관점을 가질 필요가 있다
③ 우리의 마음과 몸을 최상의 상태로 유지해야 한다

⑤ 성공적인 식습관과 체중 감량을 위해 전통적인 방법을 시도해야 한다

해석 칼로리론은 몸무게, 연령, 그리고 다른 몇 가지 변수에 근거하여 우리는 각자 하루에 특정한 수의 열량이 필요하다고 주장한다. 이 모델에서 체중을 줄이거나 늘리거나 혹은 유지하기 위해서는 여러분에게 두 가지 변수, 즉 섭취된 열량과 소비된 열량이 있다. 이 이론에 따르면, 체중을 줄이기 위해서 우리는 단순하게 덜 먹고 더 많이 움직인다. 체중을 늘리기 위해서는 우리는 덜 움직이고 더 많이 먹는다. 만약 우리가 이런 단순화된 공식을 따른다면, 우리는 온종일 트윙키를 먹고 러닝머신 위를 달려서 그 열량을 뺄 수 있다. 그러나 일반 상식은 우리에게 이것이 건강이 아니라고 알려 준다. 확실히 열량을 계산하는 것은 가장 나쁜 다이어트 방해꾼을 제거함으로써 일부 사람들을 올바른 방향으로 움직이도록 도울 수 있지만, 건강을 진지하게 생각하는 사람들에게는 단순히 열량을 계산하는 것은 목표를 달성하는 게 아니다. 열량을 계산하는 것은 식욕을 관리하거나 (음식에 대한) 갈망을 제거하는 데 도움이 되지 않으며, 이런 것들은 체중 감량에 심각한 방해가 될 수 있다. 그것은 또한 질병을 관리하거나 되돌리는 데(질병이 악화되는 것을 막는 데) 도움이 되지 않는다. 우리는 더 총체적인 모델이 필요하다.

구문 [1행~3행] The calorie argument *claims* **that**, (based on weight, age, and several other variables,) we each need a specific number of calories per day.

that 이하는 문장의 동사 claims의 목적어 역할을 하는 명사절이다. 접속사 that과 명사절 내 주어인 we 사이에 based on ~ variables가 삽입되었고 그 안에서 콤마와 and가 세 개의 밑줄 친 명사(구)를 병렬 연결한다.

[8행~10행] **If** we *followed* this simplified formula, we **could eat** Twinkies all day and run those calories off on a treadmill.

'If+S'+동사의 과거형 ~, S+조동사 과거형+동사원형'의 형태로 가정법 과거 표현이 쓰였다.

어휘 argument 논(論); 논쟁; 논거   variable 변수; 가변적인   expend 소비하다
formula 공식; 방식   Twinkie 트윙키 ((케이크의 한 종류))   treadmill 러닝머신
common sense 상식   eliminate 제거[삭제]하다   offender 방해꾼; 범죄자; 위반자
make the cut (특정) 목표를 달성하다; 본선에 진출하다   craving 갈망; 열망
reverse 되돌리다; 반대   holistic 전체적인; 전체론의   perspective 관점; 조망
comprehensive 종합적인; 포괄적인

---

4 글의 주제 ⑤

해설 소멸 위기에 처한 언어들은 세계화와 의사소통 기술의 혁명으로 더욱더 어려운 상황에 몰렸으나, 최근의 디지털 혁명으로 인해 탄생한 도구들은 언어 보존에 구명줄 역할을 하며 유용하게 사용될 수 있다는 내용의 글이므로 주제로 가장 적절한 것은 ⑤ '기술과 디지털 도구를 통해 소멸 위기 언어 구하기'이다.
① 소멸 위기의 언어를 보존하고 되살리는 것의 어려움
② 디지털 시대에 소멸 위기의 언어를 공부하는 것의 필요성
③ 소멸 위기의 언어 보존의 주요 목표
④ 디지털 세계에서 언어적 다양성을 보존하는 것의 중요성

해석 죽어가는 언어를 되살리려는 노력은 존경스럽지만 그 소멸 과정을 역전시키려는 사람들이 직면해 있는 난제들은 위협적이다. 미국 역사 대부분에 걸쳐 미국 인디언들의 경우에서처럼 소멸이 모두 지배적인 정부의 적대와 억압의 직접적인 결과는 아니다. 그러나 잔인한 억압이 토착 언어와 문화를 소멸시키지 못한 곳에서, 1980년대 이후의 극심한 세계화는 더 성공을 거두어 왔다. 의사소통 기술에 있어서의 최근의 혁명은 (방송 전파와 사이버 공간을 통해) 주류 서양 문화와 언어의 전파를 위한 강력한 도구를 제공해 왔다. 그러나 몇몇 소멸 위기에 처한 언어들에서, 디지털 혁명을 통해 흐름이 바뀌고 있다. Rosenberg가 지적하듯이, 디지털 기술, 토론 집단, 소프트웨어 회사, 그리고 앱들은 소수 집단을 위한 언어 보존과 소멸 위기에 처한 언어 의사소통의 필요에 대한 구명줄이다. 한때 기술은 일부 언어 사용자들이 자신의 공동체나 국가의 지배적인 언어를 채택하도록 강

요했다. 이제, 새로운 도구는 언어에 새로운 활력을 부여하고 소멸 위기에 처한 언어 사용자들을 유지할 가능성을 만들고 있다.

구문 [1행~3행] Although *the efforts* (to revive dying languages) are admirable, *the challenges* (**facing** *those* [who would reverse the extinction process]) are intimidating.

to revive dying languages는 형용사적 용법으로 쓰인 to부정사구로 the efforts를 수식한다. 현재분사 facing이 이끄는 (   )은 the challenges를 수식하고 그 안의 [   ]은 those를 수식하는 관계사절이다.

[3행~7행] **Not all** of the extinctions are the direct result of hostility and repression from a dominant government, **as** *was* the case with American Indians throughout most of U.S. history.

not all은 '모두 ~한 것은 아니다'라는 뜻의 부분부정 표현이다. 접속사 as 뒤에 대동사 was와 밑줄 친 주어 부분이 도치되어 있고 이때 as는 '~처럼'의 의미이다.

어휘 revive 되살리다   admirable 존경스러운   reverse 역전시키다; 반대로 하다
hostility 적의, 적대감   dominant 지배적인, 우세한   brutal 잔혹한   airwave
방송 전파   mainstream 주류(의)   endangered 멸종 위기에 처한   tide 조수, 흐름
lifeline 생명줄, 구명선   preservation 보존   revitalize 새로운 활력을 주다   retain
보유하다, 유지하다   primary 주요한; 최초의

---

5 글의 제목 ③

해설 인류는 문화를 통해 유전자의 한계를 극복하고 시간과 공간의 거리를 뛰어넘을 수 있게 되었다는 것이 글의 요지이므로, ③ '문화는 유전자를 초월할 수 있는 인간의 능력'이 글의 제목으로 가장 적절하다.
① 사회적 진화란 유전자에서 문화로 가는 것이다
② 유전자가 문화에 영향을 주고, 문화는 유전자에 영향을 준다
④ 문화 적응력과 지식의 축적
⑤ 언어와 문화의 관계는 무엇인가?

해석 무엇이 우리가 그렇게 잘 적응할 수 있게 하는가? 한마디로 말해서, 다른 사람들로부터 배울 수 있는, 즉 따라하고, 모방하며, 공유하고, 향상할 수 있는 능력인 문화이다. 인간이 구어(口語), 그리고 나중에는 문어(文語)를 이용해 의사소통하는 법을 배웠을 때, 낚시 바늘을 만들고, 배를 건조하고, 창을 만들고, 노래를 부르며, 혹은 신의 모습을 조각하는 방법과 같은 관념과 지식, 그리고 관습은 유전자처럼 복제하고 결합할 수 있었다. 하지만 유전자와는 달리, 그것들은 한 사람에게서 다른 사람에게로 시간과 공간의 거리를 가로질러 뛰어넘어갈 수 있었다. 문화는 생명 활동의 한계로부터 인간을 자유롭게 했는데, 진화생물학자인 Mark Pagel에 따르면, 문화를 발견했을 때, 인간은 '유전자와 정신 사이의' 힘의 균형에서 중대한 변화를 이루었다. 인간은 단지 자신의 유전자로부터가 아니라 조상들이 축적한 지식으로부터 사는 방법에 관한 안내를 습득한 유일한 종이 되었다.

구문 [3행~7행] When humans learned to communicate using oral and, later, written language, // ideas, knowledge, and practices — how to make a fishhook, build a boat, fashion a spear, sing a song, carve a god — could replicate and combine like genes.

문장의 주어는 ideas ~ god이고 could와 이어지는 두 개의 동사 replicate와 combine이 병렬구조를 이루고 있다.

[14행~17행] Humans became the only species to acquire guidance on how **to live** from the accumulated knowledge of their ancestors, rather than just from their DNA.

두 밑줄 친 부분은 rather than을 사이에 두고 병렬구조로 부정사 to live와 연결되어 있다.

---

6 안내문 일치   ⑤

해설 ① 지역 단체 두 곳을 후원하기 위한 걷기 행사이다.
② 기부금은 지역 노인들을 위한 것이다.
③ 등록은 오전 9시, 걷기가 오전 10시에 시작된다.
④ 참가자들은 정오까지 주차장을 무료로 이용할 수 있다.

- -

해석 2020년 10월 4일 일요일 Warwick Castle 가족 걷기 행사에서 여러분의 지역 자선 단체들을 도와주세요.
지역 노인들을 위한 봉사와 지원을 제공하는 이들 중요한 지역 자선단체인 Age UK Coventry와 Age UK Warwickshire를 후원해주세요.
• Warwick Castle 사적지에서 3km 걷기
• 오전 9시부터 등록, 걷기는 10시 정각에 시작
• 한 사람 당 6파운드, 12세 미만 어린이는 3파운드
• 정오 12시까지 참가자들을 위한 Castle 입장료와 무료 주차 포함
• 25파운드의 기부금을 모금하면 무료입장
예약 및 자리 등록을 위해
info@ageukwarks.org.uk로 이메일 하거나 01725 497400로 전화주세요

- -

어휘 charity 자선 단체   historic ground 사적   registration 등록   sharp 꼭, 정각   admission 입장료   donation 기부, 기증

7 밑줄 어법   ④

해설 ④ while이 이끄는 절에서 believing in ~ one does가 주어이고 is가 동사이다. 전치사 in 다음에는 목적어가 나와야 하는데 that one does에서 that을 관계대명사로 볼 경우 선행사가 없으므로 선행사를 포함하는 관계대명사인 what으로 고쳐 써야 한다.
① working과 feeling이 or로 연결되어 병렬 구조를 이룬다.
② to structure their own time은 앞의 more time을 수식하는 to부정사의 형용사적 용법이다.
③ 'required ~ economic returns'는 앞의 the time and money를 수동의 의미로 수식하는 과거분사구이다.
⑤ 「the 비교급 ~, the 비교급 ....」은 '~하면 할수록 더 …하다'의 뜻으로 「the+형용사 비교급(more likely)+S(it)+V(is) ~」의 형태는 알맞다.

- -

해석 학문은 그 본질상 결코 완수되지 않는다. 시간에 대한 융통성이 우리 일의 특권 중 하나지만, 그것은 항상 일하거나 그래야(일해야) 한다고 느끼는 것으로 쉽게 옮겨질 수 있다. Mary Morris Heiberger와 Julia Miller Vick은 다음의 역설에 주목한다. "과중한 작업량에도 불구하고, 교수들은 경제생활 속에서 다른 누구보다 사실상 자신의 시간을 구성할 수 있는 더 많은 자유를 누린다. 어떤 사람들에게, 이것은 진로의 대단한 이점이다. 다른 사람들에게, 그것은 스트레스의 근원이다." 게다가 박사 학위와 그것이 가져다주는 불확실한 경제적 이익을 얻는 데 요구되는 시간과 돈을 고려하면, 우리들 대부분이 실용적이라기보다는 이상적인 이유로 학문적 진로를 추구한다는 점이 확실하다. 자신이 하는 일을 믿는 것이 직업 만족의 핵심적 측면이지만, 이상주의는 또한 과로로 이어질 수 있다. 아이러니한 점은 우리가 직업에 더 많이 헌신할수록, 시간 스트레스와 극도의 피로를 경험할 가능성이 더 크다는 것이다.

- -

구문 [10행~13행] Furthermore, given *the time and money* (required to get a PhD and its uncertain economic returns), **it** is clear **that** most of us pursue an

academic career for idealistic, rather than pragmatic, reasons.
( ) 부분은 과거분사구로 the time and money를 수식한다. 굵게 표시된 it은 가주어, that이 이끄는 절이 진주어이다.
[16행~18행] The irony is that **the more committed** we are to our vocation, **the more likely** it is that we will experience time stress and burnout.
「the 비교급 ~, the 비교급 ....」 구문으로 '~하면 할수록, 더 …하다'의 의미이다.

- -

어휘 academic 학문의, 학자의; (대학) 교수   by nature 본질[선천]적으로; 본래   flexibility 융통성; 유연성   privilege 특권; 특전   translate 옮기다; 바꾸다; 번역하다   note 주목하다; 언급하다   paradox 역설   workload 작업량   structure 구성하다, 조직화하다   practically 사실상, 거의   career path 진로   return 수익   pursue 추구하다   idealistic 이상(주의)적인   aspect (측)면   idealism 이상주의   overwork 과로   committed 헌신[전념]하는   vocation 직업, 천직   burnout 극도의 피로; 연료 소진

8 밑줄 어휘   ④

해설 하이데거는 의식 있는 관찰자로부터 분리된 외부 세계를 인정하지 않았고, 세계는 존재가 일부로서 속할 때만 가능한 개념이며 존재는 세상과 차단될 수 없다고 했으므로, 하이데거가 생각한 의식과 환경의 분리는 '불가능하지' 않은 것이 아니라 '가능하지' 않은 것이라고, 즉 의식과 환경은 분리될 수 없다고 정리할 수 있다. 따라서 ④의 impossible을 possible로 바꿔 써야 한다.

- -

해석 하이데거는 실존하는 존재에 대해 'Dasein', 즉 '거기에 있음'이라는 용어를 사용했다. 그는 의식 있는 관찰자로부터 ① 분리된 외부 세계가 있다는 생각을 거부했다. 대신에 그는 '현상학적' 견해를 발달시켰는데, 여기에서 사물에 대한 우리의 이해는 항상 ② 우리 자신과 관련이 있다. 예를 들어 당신이 스웨터를 입는다면, 그것은 그 스웨터가 당신을 따뜻하게 유지해주거나 당신에게 그것이 잘 어울릴 거라고 당신이 생각하기 때문이다. 그 스웨터가 꼬인 실로 만들어졌고 두께가 몇 밀리미터이기 때문이 아니다. 이것은 지식에도 적용된다. 우리는 흥미를 불러일으키기 때문에, 혹은 정치를 이해하는 것이 우리가 보기에 주변에서 일어나는 것을 이해하는 데 도움이 되기 때문에 정치에 관한 책을 읽는 것일지도 모른다. 우리는 ③ 도구, 즉 필요 충족의 측면에서 그것을 본다. 하이데거는 'Dasein'(주로 인간 '존재')을 그것을 정의하는 세계에 깊이 빠져있는 것으로 그리고 그 세계의 일부가 된 것으로 보았다. 의식과 환경 간의 어떠한 분리도 ④ 불가능하지(→ 가능하지) 않다. '거기에 있다는 것'은 '거기(우리의 환경)'가 '존재'의 규정적 측면이라는 것을 뜻한다. 우리는 ⑤ 바깥세상과 접촉이 거의 없는 정신(이를 하이데거는 '의식의 캐비닛'이라고 불렀다) 속에 놓여 세상으로부터 차단되어 있지 않다.

- -

구문 [2행~4행] He rejected the idea that there is *an external world* (separate from a conscious observer).
that ~ observer는 the idea에 대한 동격절이다. 형용사 separate(분리된)로 시작되는 ( )는 an external world를 수식한다.
[14행~17행] Heidegger **saw** the Dasein (principally the human "being") **as** completely immersed **in** and part **of** *the world* [that defines it].
「see A as B」는 'A를 B로 보다'의 뜻이다. B 자리에서 completely immersed in과 part of가 병렬구조를 이루며, the world that defines it은 전치사 in과 of의 공통 목적어이다. [ ]는 the world를 수식한다.

- -

어휘 jumper 스웨터   make sense of 이해하다   in terms of ~의 측면에서   principally 주로   immersed in ~에 깊이 빠진   shut off from ~에서 차단하다   enclosed 바깥세상과 접촉이 거의 없는

9 빈칸 추론 ④

해설 망고로 인한 질병의 원인을 조사해보니, 농장에서 벌레를 없애는 데 발암 물질이 있는 살충제를 쓰지 않으려고 열탕 처리를 했는데, 이로 인해 세균이 과일 안으로 침투했으므로 벌레를 없애려고 취한 조치가 세균 감염이라는 더 나쁜 결과를 초래한 역설적인 상황으로 볼 수 있다. 따라서 빈칸에 들어갈 말로 가장 적절한 것은 ④ '역설적인'이다.

① 다양한 ② 임의적인
③ 불가사의한 ⑤ 실험적인

해석 수입 망고와 관련된 질병 발생의 최초로 알려진 사례에서 감염 경로는 특히 역설적이다. 1999년에 미국의 13개 주의 78명의 사람들이 '살모넬라 엔테리카'의 흔한 균주로 병에 걸려, 15명의 환자들이 입원했고 2명은 사망했다. 조사관들은 망고의 출처를 브라질의 한 농장으로 밝혀냈다. 놀랍게도 그들은 동일 농장에서 나온 망고를 먹은 유럽인들은 누구도 병에 걸리지 않았음을 발견했다. 조사관들은 미국행 망고는 아마 과실파리를 물리치기 위해 사용된 열탕 처리의 결과로 인해 세균을 흡수했을 거라고 추론했다. 이 처리는 지중해 과실파리를 가져오는 농산물을 막는 미국 기준을 충족시키기 위해 요구되었는데, 이는 유럽인들은 부과하지 않았던 기준이었다. 농부는 과실파리를 물리치려고 암을 유발하는 살충제를 사용하는 것을 피하기 위해 열수 처리를 채택했다. 그러나 조사관들은 망고를 열탕에 담근 후 포장하기 전에 찬물에 잠기게 한 것이 과일 안의 공기가 수축하여 오염된 물을 빨아들인 과정을 개시했다는 것을 발견했다. 그래서 농부들이 발암 물질을 사용하지 않고 망고에서 벌레를 없애기 위해 취했던 조치가 결국 병원균을 위한 입장 허가를 제공했던 것이다.

구문 [13행~15행] The treatment was required / to meet *US standards* (barring *produce* (carrying the Mediterranean fruit fly)) — *standards* [(which[that]) the Europeans did not impose].
barring ~ fly는 앞의 US standards를 능동의 의미로 수식한다. carrying ~ fly는 앞의 produce를 능동의 의미로 수식한다. [ ]는 앞에 목적격 관계대명사 which[that]가 생략되어 standards를 수식한다.
[18행~22행] But investigators discovered // **that** dipping the mangoes in hot water, then submerging them in cool water before packing / initiated *a process* [in which gases inside the fruit contracted, / drawing in contaminated water].
that절에서 dipping ~ packing이 동명사 주어이고 initiated가 동사이다. [ ]는 a process를 수식하는 관계사절이다.

어휘 contamination 오염 pathway 경로 outbreak (질병의) 발생 strain 균주 hospitalize 입원시키다 investigator 조사관 trace ~ back to ... ~의 출처를 …까지 밝혀내다 affect 병이 나게 하다 destined for ~행인 bar 막다, 금지하다 produce 농산물 impose 부과하다 employ 사용하다 submerge 물속에 잠그다 initiate 개시하다 contract 수축하다 draw in 빨아들이다 take steps 조치를 취하다 clear A of B A에게서 B를 치우다 entree 입장 (허가); 앙트레((주요리 혹은 주요리 전에 나오는 요리))

---

10 빈칸 추론 ③

해설 현대의 전자 장비 생활 방식으로 인해 외부 사회와 마찬가지로 대학에서 현재 문제가 되고 있는 상황은, 빠른 활동이 선호되고 깊이 있는 사고를 할 시간과 여유가 감소했다는 것이므로 빈칸에 들어갈 알맞은 말은 ③ '사고할 시간의 감소'이다.
① 현대의 편리함에 대한 거부
② 빠른 활동에 대한 경멸
④ 사회적 고립 문제
⑤ 단순한 지혜에 대한 과소평가

해석 〈순간의 횡포〉의 저자인 Oslo 대학의 Thomas Eriksen에 따르면, 현대의 전자 장비 생활방식은 (이메일, 휴대폰 통화 등의) 즉각적이고 긴급한 반응을 요구하는 빠른 활동에 체계적으로 호의를 보인다. 그러한 자극들은 사색, 놀이와 장기적 연인관계와 같은 느린 활동을 몰아내는 경향이 있다. 이러한 역학은 학계에 특히 유감스러운 영향을 미치고 있는데, 학계란 학생들과 학자들이 좀 더 넓게 장기적인 관점을 가지고서 사고할 수 있도록 더 큰 사회로부터 다소 격리되어야 마땅한 곳이기 때문이다. 그러나 사실상 대학은 나머지 사회를 반영하며, 사고할 시간의 감소는 그 어느 곳 못지않게 학교 내에서도 문제가 된다. 도구적이며 단기적인 응용 목표가 중심 자리를 차지하게 되자, 우리 사회는 심층적이며 성찰적인 사고가 제공해줄 수 있는 지혜와 복잡함에는 덜 미치게 되었다. 이것은 중대한 손실이다.

구문 [12행~14행] But in fact, universities mirror the rest of society, // and the dwindling time to think is **as much an issue** within the academy / **as** anywhere else.
as 뒤의 어순은 「as+형용사+a(n)+명사」이며, within the academy와 anywhere else를 비교하고 있다.

어휘 urgent 긴급한 crowd out ~을 몰아내다 reflection 반사; 반영; 심사숙고, 사색 dynamic 역학 academia 학계 somewhat 다소 insulate ~을 보호[격리]하다; ~에 단열 처리를 하다 long range 장거리를 가는; 장기적인 perspective 관점; 원근법; 전망 instrumental 수단[도구]이 되는 [선택지 어휘] contempt 경멸 dwindling 줄어드는

---

11 빈칸 추론 ④

해설 자연보호와 보존에는 비용이 매우 많이 들기 때문에 가난하고 생계 보장이 안 되는 지역에서는 보존이 더 어렵고 오히려 자연을 착취할 가능성이 있으므로, 오늘날의 많은 환경보호 프로그램들은 시골 주민들을 위해 '④ 경제적 기회를 제공할 필요를 이해하고 있다'고 볼 수 있다.

① 그것들의 강점을 최대화하는 데 노력을 집중시킨다
② 적극적으로 매우 다양한 조력자들과 안내인들을 주선한다
③ 고품질의 무료 교육 기회를 제공한다
⑤ 환경에 관한 문헌 작성에 참여한다

해석 몇몇 경우에서 개발은 천연 자원의 보호와 보존 모두 혹은 어느 한쪽에 필요할지도 모른다. 예를 들어 시골 지역에서 보존 지역권을 확립하는 것은 일반적으로 재정적 자원을 요구한다. 보호 프로그램은 비용이 매우 많이 들 수 있고 이러한 비용의 많은 부분이 지역사회에 강요될지도 모른다. 그러므로 매우 가난한 지역은 그것의 자연 경관을 보존하는 것이 더 어려울지도 모른다. 가난한 사람들이 그들의 생계를 향상시킬 다른 기회가 없으면 그들의 자연 환경을 착취할 가능성이 있음을 암시하는 대량의 문헌이 있다. 따라서 오늘날의 많은 보호 프로그램들은 성공적인 보존 프로그램을 만들기 위하여 시골 주민들을 위해 경제적 기회를 제공할 필요를 이해하고 있다. 이러한 예에서 환경과 일자리 간의 상호적 관계가 있다.

구문 [7행~8행] Thus, **it** may be more difficult *for a very poor area* **to conserve** its natural amenities.
it은 가주어, to conserve 이하가 진주어이고 for a very poor area는 to conserve의 의미상 주어이다.
[8행~11행] There is *a large body of* literature [suggesting that the poor are likely to exploit their natural environment if there are no other opportunities to improve their livelihoods].
[ ]은 능동의 의미로 a large body of literature를 수식한다. 'a large body of'는 '~의 많은 양, 모음'의 뜻이다.

어휘 conservation 보호, 보존 preservation 보존, 유지 natural resource

천연 자원 rural 시골의 costly 값비싼 amenity 주택(지)의 가치를 높이는 것(건물 양식·위생적 환경·주위의 경치 따위) literature 문헌 exploit 착취하다 livelihood 생계 resident 주민 mutual 상호 간의

12 빈칸 추론 ⑤

해설 수가 인간의 존재 이전에 자연에 이미 존재했다고 말할 수 있지만 자연에 있는 문어 다리나 음력 주기의 날들은 규칙적으로 일어나는 '양'이고 인간의 정신적 경험과는 별개다. 인간은 수라는 개념을 만들어 양을 구별한다고 했으므로 빈칸에는 ⑤ '일반적으로 수 없이는 인간의 정신에 접근하기 어렵다'가 적절하다.
① 인간이 자연적으로 존재하는 양을 시각화하도록 허용한다
② 유형의 것과 추상적인 것 사이의 차이를 희미하게 한다
③ 인간의 정신을 숫자로 나타낸 이론적 개념에 적응시키다
④ 그 양의 가치에 대한 측정 기준이다

해석 수가 인간의 발명이라고 말하는 것은 이상해 보일지도 모른다. 어쨌든 어떤 사람들은 인간이 존재했는지 아닌지에 상관없이 8(문어 다리)이든, 4(계절)이든, 29(음력 주기의 날들)이든 기타 등등, 자연에는 여전히 예측 가능한 수가 있을 것이라고 말할 수도 있을 것이다. 그러나 엄밀히 말하면, 이것들은 단지 규칙적으로 일어나는 '양'이다. 양과 여러 개의 양 사이의 일치는 인간의 정신적 경험과는 별개로 존재한다고 말할 수 있을 것이다. 문어 다리는 비록 우리가 그 규칙성을 인지할 수 없더라도 규칙적인 집단으로 존재할 것이다. 하지만 '수'는 우리가 양을 구별하려고 사용하는 단어이자 다른 상징적 표현이다. 색채 용어가 가시광선 스펙트럼의 인접한 부분을 따라 여러 색 사이의 더 명확한 정신적 경계를 만드는 것처럼, 수는 여러 양 사이의 개념상 경계를 만든다. 그러한 경계들은 물리적 세계에서 여러 양 사이의 실제적인 구분을 반영할 수도 있지만, 이러한 구분들은 일반적으로 수 없이는 인간의 정신에 접근하기 어렵다.

구문 [10행~11행] Octopus legs *would occur* in regular groups **even if** we *were* unable to perceive that regularity.
even if 뒤에 현재 사실의 반대 내용이 이어지고 있으므로 가정법 과거의 형태로 '주어+조동사 과거 ..., even if+주어+were'가 쓰였다.
[12행~13행] *Numbers*, though, are *the words and other symbolic representations* [(which[that]) we use to differentiate quantities].
[ ] 부분은 목적격 관계대명사 which 또는 that이 생략된 관계사절로 선행사 the words and other symbolic representations를 수식한다.

어휘 odd 이상한; 홀수의 lunar cycle 음력 주기 quantity 양 correspondence 일치; 부합; 유사 representation 표현; 설명 differentiate 구별하다 term 용어; 기간 boundary 경계; 한계; 영역 adjacent 인접한, 근방의 visible light 가시광선 conceptual 개념상의 inaccessible 접근할 수 없는; 이용할 수 없는 blur 흐리게 하다; 더럽히다 tangible 유형의; 닿을 수 있는; 명백한 orient (어떤 방위·대상물에) 적응시키다; 맞추다 numerical 숫자로 나타낸; 수의

13 흐름 무관 문장 ④

해설 건축학은 학문으로서의 정체성이 모호하여 인문학, 과학, 기술, 예술, 미학, 철학 등 다양한 학문 분야와 공유하는 성격을 갖고 있으며, 스스로를 규정하기 위해 끊임없이 다른 학문 분야와의 관계를 탐색한다는 점을 특징으로 한다. ④에서는 건축학이 예술 분야임을 단정적으로 진술하고 있기 때문에 글의 전체 흐름과는 맞지 않는다.

해석 학문 분야로서의 건축학은 인문학의 밖에 '존재하고', 그래서 그러한 점에서 그것이 인문학 중 하나가 아니라는 것에는 의문의 여지가 없다. 얼마간의 가족 유사성이 있다

하더라도, 적어도 제도적으로는 아니다. ① 건축학과 학생들은 인문학 내의 학생들과 전적으로 같은 방식으로 사고하고, 읽고, 쓰는 것에 적응되어 있지 않다. ② 건축학에 있어 흥미로운 것은 건축학은 학문 분야로서 그 자체와 그 자체의 정체성을 어디에 두어야 하는지에 대해 항상 확신이 없었다는 것이다. 그것이 과학인지, 기술의 학문 분야인지, 아니면 예술이나 미학적 제작의 한 양식인지에 대해 자체 내부적으로 분열되어 있다. ③ 그 자체의 정체성에 관한 이러한 불확실성은, 그것이 예를 들어 공학이나 의학 같은 다른 학문 분야에서는 상상할 수 없는 방식으로 철학적이고 비판적인 이론에 상당히 개방된 상태가 되도록 이끌었다. ④ 중요한 것은 우리가 건축학을 순수 과학이 아니라 예술적 실천으로 인정하는 것이다. ⑤ 내가 외부인으로서 분명히 말할 수 있는 것은, 건축학은 자기 인식을 추구하는 학문 분야이며, 그 자기 인식을 위해 그것은 다른 학문 분야가 그것에 대해 뭐라고 말하는지 알기 위해 자신의 밖을 내다본다는 것이다.

구문 [5행~7행] Architecture students aren't oriented **to** thinking, reading, and writing in quite **the same** way **as** are students within the humanities.
전치사 to의 목적어로 밑줄 친 thinking, reading, writing이 콤마와 and로 연결되어 병렬구조를 이룬다. 'the same A as B'는 'A와 같은 B'라는 의미이다. as 다음에는 「동사(are)+주어(students)」 어순으로 도치가 일어났으며, 대동사 are는 앞의 aren't oriented와 상응하여 'are oriented to thinking, reading, and writing'을 함축한다.
[10행~12행] ~ it is itself internally divided *about* **whether** it is a science, a technological discipline, **or** a mode of art or aesthetic production.
명사절을 이끄는 접속사 whether로 시작되는 절이 전치사 about의 목적어 역할을 하고 있으며, 'whether A, B, or C(A인지, B인지, C인지)'의 구조로 사용되었다.

어휘 discipline (학문의) 분야; 훈련 architecture 건축학 humanities 인문학 institutionally 제도적으로 resemblance 유사(성), 닮음 be oriented to v-ing v에 적응되어 있다 as to ~에 관하여 regarding ~에 관하여 acknowledge 인정하다 self-definition 자기 인식

14 글의 순서 ⑤

해설 (C)의 If절의 they는 주어진 문장에 나온 '우리가 첫인상에 따라 사람들에게 붙이는 꼬리표들'을 언급하므로 주어진 문장 다음에는 (C)가 나와야 한다. (C)에서 언급된, 잘못된 꼬리표를 붙였을 때의 문제에 대한 예시가 for instance로 시작되는 (B)에서 제시된다. (A)에 언급된 the neighbor는 (B)의 your new neighbor를 지칭하므로 (B) 다음에 (A)가 나와야 한다.

해석 우리가 느낀 첫인상에 따라 사람들에게 꼬리표를 붙이는 것은 인지 과정의 불가피한 부분이다. 이러한 꼬리표는 해석을 하는 한 방법이다. '그녀는 명랑한 것 같아.' '그는 진실해 보여.' '그들은 끔찍할 정도로 자만심이 강해.'
(C) 그것들이 정확하다면, 이러한 인상은 미래의 사람들에게 가장 잘 대응하는 방법을 결정하는 유용한 방법일 수 있다. 그러나 우리가 붙이는 꼬리표가 부정확할 때 문제가 발생하는데, 왜냐하면 우리가 누군가에 대한 의견을 형성한 후, 우리는 그것을 고집하고 어떠한 상충하는 정보도 우리의 이미지에 들어맞게 만드는 경향이 있기 때문이다.
(B) 예를 들어 당신이 친구에게 당신의 새로운 이웃의 이름을 언급한다고 가정해 보자. "아, 나 그 사람 알아." 당신의 친구가 대답한다. "그는 처음엔 친절한 것 같지만 그건 전부 연기였어." 아마 이러한 평가는 완전히 틀릴지도 모른다.
(A) 그 판단이 정확하든 그렇지 않든, 당신 친구의 평가를 받아들이고 나면, 그것은 십중팔구 당신이 그 이웃에게 대응하는 방식에 영향을 줄 것이다. 당신은 당신이 들었던 위선의 예를 찾아볼 것이며 십중팔구 그것을 찾아낼 것이다.

구문 [6행~8행] **Whether** the judgment is accurate **or not**, // after you accept your friend's evaluation, / it will probably influence *the way* [you respond to the neighbor].
여기서 「Whether A or not」은 'A이든 아니든'이라는 뜻의 양보의 부사절이다. it은 your friend's evaluation을 지칭한다. [ ]는 the way를 수식한다.

[19행~20행] ~ we tend to hang on to it and **make** *any conflicting information* **fit** *our image*.

두 밑줄 친 부분은 tend to 다음에 공통으로 연결된다. 두 번째 밑줄 부분에서 「make+O+v」 구조가 사용되었다.

어휘 label 꼬리표를 붙이다　inevitable 불가피한　perception 인지, 인식　interpretation 해석　cheerful 발랄한, 쾌활한　conceited 자만하는　insincerity 불성실, 위선　appraisal 평가　off-base 완전히 틀린　hang on to ~을 꽉 잡다, 고집하다　conflicting 모순되는, 상충되는

15 글의 순서　 ②

해설 인간의 문화는 환경을 지배하는 데 성공을 거둘 수 있지만 개미나 흰개미는 그렇지 못하다는 주어진 글 다음에는 '굴 짓기, 냄새 자취 설정, 혹은 혼인 비행' 수행과 같은 개미의 행동을 나열한 (B)가 나온다. 개미의 환경 대응 실패가 멸종으로 이어질 수 있다는 (B) 다음에는 육식 동물과 유인원도 마찬가지라는 내용의 (A)가 나온다. 동물은 환경적 제약에서 자유재량을 가질 수 없다는 내용의 (A) 다음에는 인간은 동물과는 달리 이러한 제약을 덜 받는다는 내용의 (C)가 나온다.

해석 지난 만 년 혹은 그 이상의 기간 동안 인간은 전체적으로 자신의 환경을 지배하는 데 너무나 성공적이어서 거의 어떤 종류의 문화도 보통 정도의 내적 일관성을 갖추며 번식을 완전히 정지시키지 않는 한, 한동안은 성공을 거둘 수 있다. 개미나 흰개미 중 어떠한 종도 이러한 자유를 누리지 못한다.
(B) 굴 짓기, 냄새 자취 설정, 혹은 혼인 비행 수행에서 아주 약간의 비효율은 다른 사회적 곤충들로부터의 포식과 경쟁으로 종의 빠른 멸종을 초래할 수도 있다.
(A) 그보다 거의 덜하지 않은 정도로, 사회적 육식 동물과 영장류도 마찬가지이다. 간단히 말해서 동물 종은 실험이나 놀이의 여지가 거의 없이 생태계 내에 빽빽하게 채워져 있는 경향이 있다.
(C) 인간은 일시적으로 종간(種間)의 경쟁이 주는 제약에서 탈출했다. 비록 문화들은 서로를 교체하지만, 그 과정은 변동을 줄임에 있어 종간 경쟁보다 훨씬 덜 효과적이다.

구문 [1행~6행] During the past ten thousand years or longer, / man as a whole has been **so** successful / in dominating his environment // **that** almost any kind of culture can succeed for a while, // **so long as** it has a modest degree of internal consistency / and does not shut off reproduction altogether.
주절에서 「so ~ that ... (너무 ~해서 …하다)」 구문이 사용되었다. so long as(~하는 한) 절에서 동사 has와 does not shut off가 병렬구조를 이룬다.
[12행~16행] **The slightest inefficiency** in constructing nests, in establishing odor trails, or in conducting nuptial flights / **could result in** the quick extinction of the species / by predation and competition / from other social insects.
The slightest inefficiency가 주어이고 동사는 could result in이다. 전치사 in으로 시작하는 세 전치사구가 콤마(,)와 or로 연결되어 병렬구조를 이룬다.

어휘 as a whole 전체로서　modest 보통의; 겸손한　a degree of 어느 정도의　consistency 일관성　shut off 정지시키다　reproduction 번식; 재생　altogether 완전히, 전적으로　scarcely 거의 ~ 않다　lesser (중요성이) 덜한　to an extent 어느 정도로　primate 영장류　room 여지; 공간　trail 자취　predation 포식; 약탈　constraint 제약　variance 변동[변화](량)

16 문장 넣기　 ②

해설 주어진 문장이 어떤 예가 시사하는 바를 언급하고 그것이 다른 관찰과 일치하지 않는다는 내용이므로 본문 중 두 개의 예 사이에 오는 것이 적절할 것이다. 그 다음 내용을 이어보면 앞의 예는 주술의 사용이 위험 여부인 것이고 뒤의 예는 통제 가능 여부의 예로 연결이 자연스러우므로 답은 ②이다.

해석 인류학자 Bronislaw Malinowski가 남태평양의 Trobriand 제도에 사는 원주민들의 일상생활을 관찰했을 때, 그는 그 섬사람들이 주술 의식을 많이 사용하기 했지만, 특정한 활동들을 위해서만 그것들을 아껴두었던 것에 주목했다. 예를 들면 그들은 보호받고 있는 (환초로 둘러싸인) 초호의 많은 물고기를 잡으러 갈 때는 주술을 사용하지 않았지만, 넓은 바다에서 물고기를 잡을 때는 그렇게 했다(주술을 사용했다). 그것이 그들이 주술을 사용하는지 안 하는지를 결정하는 것은 위험의 존재라는 것을 시사했을지도 모르지만, 그 설명은 다른 관찰에는 맞지 않았다. 예를 들어 그 섬사람들은 곤충들이 그들의 농작물을 망치지 못하게 하기 위해서는 주술을 사용했지만, 정원 가꾸기에서는 일반적으로 그렇게 하지 않았다. Malinowski는 그 차이를 만들어낸 것이 통제력이라는 것을 깨달았다. 그 섬사람들은 자신의 노력과 기술이 성공이나 실패를 결정할 것이라고 생각할 때는 주술에 의지하지 않았다. 결과가 운이나 그들이 통제할 수 없는 다른 요소들을 포함할 때는 그렇게 했다(주술에 의지했다).

구문 [1행~4행] **That** might have suggested // (that) *it was the presence of danger* / **that** determined whether they used magic or not, // but **that** explanation didn't match with other observations.
모두 네 개의 that이 등장한다. 첫 번째 That은 앞 내용을 받는 대명사이고, suggested 다음에는 목적어절을 이끄는 접속사 that이 생략되었다. 그 뒤의 that은 「it was ~ that ...」 강조용법에 쓰인 것으로 the presence of danger를 강조하고 있다. 마지막 that은 explanation을 수식하는 지시형용사이다.

어휘 presence 존재　match 어울리다, 일치하다　anthropologist 인류학자　islander 섬사람　ritual 의식　abundantly 풍부하게, 많이　sheltered 보호받고 있는　open sea 망망대해, 넓은 바다　turn to ~에 의지하다

17 문장 넣기　 ③

해설 Rather(오히려)로 시작되는 주어진 문장은 '정서적 경험은 도덕적 판단의 중요한 요소이다'라고 진술했으므로, 이 문장의 앞에는 도덕적 판단에서 정서적 문제를 배제하는 태도가 나와야 한다. 그것이 ③ 앞의 내용인데, 도덕적 판단에서 감정과 추론을 별개로 다루는 것은 잘못된 이분법이라고 하여, 이 문장 바로 다음에 주어진 문장의 '오히려, 정서적 경험은 도덕적 판단의 중요한 요소이다'라는 진술이 나오면 글의 흐름이 자연스럽다.

해석 사회적 영역 이론은 감정과 도덕적 판단을 떼어질 수 없는 상호적인 과정으로 여긴다. 이 견해는 도덕성에 대한 정의주의적 또는 직관론적 접근법과는 다른데, 그것들(접근법들)은 주로 성인에게 하는 연구에 기초하고 있으며, 대체로 사후(事後) 합리화로서의 추론을 피하면서 감정적, 암묵적 과정에 우선순위를 부여한다. 사회적 영역 관점에서 보면, 이렇게 감정과 추론을 별개의, 대립되는 영향력으로 다루는 것은 잘못된 이분법에 해당한다. 오히려, 정서적인 경험은 도덕적 판단의 중요한 요소이며 후자는 사고, 감정, 그리고 경험의 복합적인 통합을 수반한다고 가정된다. 칸트의 유명한 말을 빌리자면, 감정이 없는 도덕적 추론은 공허하고, 추론이 없는 감정은 맹목적이다. 어린이들의 정서적인 경험은 도덕적 위반에 대한 그들의 이해, 부호화, 그리고 기억에 영향을 미치며, 복합적인 평가 과정의 일부분이다. 도덕적 상황에 대한 과거의 또는 즉각적인 감정적 반응뿐만 아니라 행동이 타인에게 미치는 정서적인 영향을 관찰하는 데서 얻어지는 정보도 도덕적 이해가 구축되는 토대를 구성할 수 있다.

구문 [5행~7행] Social domain theory **views** emotions and moral judgments **as** *reciprocal processes* [that cannot be disentangled].

「view A as B」는 'A를 B로 보다'의 뜻이다. 밑줄 친 두 부분이 각각 A, B에 해당하며, [ ]은 reciprocal processes를 수식하는 관계사절이다.

[20행~24행] *Information* (obtained from observing the affective consequences of acts for others), as well as past or immediate emotional responses to moral situations, may constitute *the foundation* [on which moral understanding is constructed].

문장의 동사는 may constitute이며 주어에서 「A as well as B (B뿐만 아니라 A도)」 구조가 사용되었다. ( )은 수동의 의미로 Information을 수식하는 분사구이다. [ ]은 '전치사+관계대명사'로 시작되는 관계사절로 the foundation을 수식한다.

어휘 assumption 가정; 인수 affective 정서적인 component 구성요소 the latter (둘 중에서) 후자 integration 통합 domain 영역 reciprocal 상호 간의 emotivist 정의주의자 intuitionist 직관론자 implicit 암시된 represent ~에 해당하다; 대표하다; 표현[상징]하다 encoding 부호화 constitute 구성하다

18 요약문 완성　　　　　　　　　　①

해설 요리나 운동의 설명이 읽기 어려운 서체로 인쇄되어있을 때, 피실험자들은 과제가 더 어렵고 앞으로 수행할 가능성도 낮게 평가했으므로 서체와 같은 형식(form)이 정보에 대한 판단(judgments)에 영향을 미쳤음을 알 수 있다.

② 수준 – 태도　　　　③ 원천 – 믿음
④ 의미 – 인식　　　　⑤ 외양 – 집중

해석 현대 세계에서 우리는 막대한 양의 새로운 정보를 끊임없이 처리하고 있지만, 우리의 정보 수용이 그것(= 정보)이 이해하기 쉬운 정도에 따라 어떤 식으로 영향을 받는지는 많은 경우 깨닫지 못한다. 정보 처리의 능숙함의 수준에 관한 한 연구에서, 참가자들은 일식 점심을 만들기 위한 조리법을 읽고 나서 그 조리법이 필요로 하리라 생각되는 노력과 기술의 양 그리고 집에서 그 요리를 준비할 가능성이 얼마나 될지를 평가해달라는 요청을 받았다. 읽기 어려운 서체로 된 조리법을 제시받은 피실험자들은 조리법을 더 어렵다고 평가했고 요리를 해볼 시도를 할 가능성이 더 낮다고 말했다. 연구자들은 실험을 반복하여, 다른 피실험자들에게 조리법 대신에 한 페이지로 된 운동 일정 설명을 보여주었고, 비슷한 결과를 발견했다. 피실험자들은 지시가 읽기 힘든 서체로 인쇄되어있을 때, 운동을 더 어렵다고 평가했고 그것을 시도할 가능성이 더 낮다고 말했다.

↓

정보의 (A) 형식이 이해하기 어려우면, 그것은 그 정보의 내용에 대한 우리의 (B) 판단에 영향을 미친다.

구문 [4행~9행] In *a study* (concerning the level of fluency in processing information), / participants **were asked** / to read a recipe for creating a Japanese lunch dish, / then to rate the amount of *effort and skill* [(which[that]) they thought // the recipe would require] and how likely they were to prepare the dish at home.

( )는 a study를 수식하는 전명구이다. 「be asked to-v (v해달라는 요청을 받다)」 구문에서 to read와 to rate가 나란히 were asked 다음에 이어진다. 두 이중 밑줄 친 부분은 to rate에 대한 목적어로 and로 연결되어 병렬구조를 이룬다. [ ]는 앞에 목적격 관계대명사 which[that]가 생략되어 effort and skill을 수식한다.

어휘 intake 수용; 섭취; 흡입 comprehend 이해하다 concerning ~에 관하여 fluency 능숙함; 유창성 font 서체 substance 내용; 실체, 본질; 핵심

19~20 장문　　　　　　19 ⑤ 20 ③

해설 19. 학업에 임할 때 맹목적인 노력만으로는 완전한 효과를 거두기 어렵고, 공부에 대해 스스로 전략을 짜고 가용 자원을 점검하는 과정이 차이를 만들어낸다는 내용의 글이므로 제목으로 가장 적절한 것은 ⑤ '스스로 관리하는 학습이 향상된 시험 점수로 이어진다'이다.
① 더 적은 학습 자원이 더 높은 시험 점수를 만든다
② 왜 스트레스가 우리의 시험 결과에 부정적으로 영향을 미치는가?
③ 불규칙적인 공부 습관이 학생 성적을 향상시키도록 돕는다
④ '15'가 학업 성공을 위한 마법의 숫자인 이유
20. (c) 학생들에게 학업 전략을 점검하도록 유도한 것은 학생들로 하여금 학습 방식에 대해 생각이 없게 한 것이 아니라 더욱 유념하게 하는 계기가 되었으므로 mindless를 mindful 등으로 바꿔 써야 한다.

해석 스탠퍼드 대학의 연구자인 Patricia Chen이 수행한 최근의 실험에 의하면 학생들은 공부와 가용 자원에 접근하는 방법에 대해 (a) 자기반성을 해야 한다고 한다. 그 실험에서 학급 절반으로 구성된 통제 집단이 일주일 후에 있을 통계학 시험에 대해 단지 주기적인 환기를 받았다. 개입 집단은 환기와 함께 학생들이 시험에 무엇이 나올 거라고 예상하는지, 어떤 학점을 받을 것 같은지, 준비를 위해 어떤 자원이 가장 잘 쓰일 수 있는지, 그리고 그것들을 어떻게 사용할 것인지에 대해 생각하게 하는 15분짜리 온라인 설문조사를 받았다. 특히 그들은 연습 문제, 교재에서 뽑은 읽기 자료, 강의 노트 혹은 동료 토론과 같은 15가지 가용 수업 자원에서 선택하라는 요청을 받았다. 그 연구에서, 공부하기 전에 자신의 자원 사용에 대한 전략을 짠 학생들이 통제 집단의 비슷한 학급 친구들보다 (b) 더 높은 성취를 보였다. 그들은 전략을 짜지 않은 학생들보다 평균 3.45% 더 높은 점수를 받았다. 개입이 왜 이렇게 효과적이었을까? 연구자들은 잠깐의 개입 연습이 학생들로 하여금 학습에 접근하는 방식에 대해 더욱 (c) 생각이 없도록(→ 유념하도록) 했음을 발견했다. 이는 단지 공부를 위해 더 많은 자원을 사용하는 것에 관한 문제가 아니다. 여기서 중점은 자원을 더욱 효과적으로 사용하는 것이다. "(d) 맹목적인 노력만으로는, 효과적인 방식으로 그 노력의 방향을 잡아주지 않고서는, 당신이 가고자 하는 곳으로 당신을 항상 데려가지 못합니다."라고 Chen은 말했다. 연구자들은 전략적 사고에 추가적인 (e) 심리적 이점이 있음을 발견했는데, 학생들이 자신의 교육에 대해 더 큰 자율권이 있다고 느끼는 데 도움이 된다는 것이다. 개입 집단의 학생들은 또한 다가오는 시험에 대해 스트레스도 덜 받았다.

구문 [8행~13행] The intervention group got the reminder and *a 15-minute online survey* [that made students **think about** what (they expected) would be on the exam, what grade they might get, what resources would be best used for preparation and how they would use them].

[ ]은 a 15-minute online survey를 수식하는 관계사절로, 관계사절 내에서 think about의 목적어로 밑줄 친 네 개의 간접의문문이 병렬구조를 이룬다. they expected는 삽입절이다.

어휘 conduct 수행하다 self-reflect 자기반성하다 control group 통제 집단 ((동일한 시험에서 실험 요건을 가하지 않는 그룹)) reminder 상기시켜주는 메모 등 statistics 통계학 intervention 개입 strategize 전략을 짜다 outperform 능가하다 comparable 비슷한, 비교할 만한 mindless 아무 생각이 없는; 어리석은 empower 권한[자율권]을 주다

1 ①	2 ⑤	3 ⑤	4 ②	5 ④	6 ⑤	7 ⑤	8 ③	9 ①	10 ③
11 ④	12 ④	13 ④	14 ②	15 ⑤	16 ③	17 ⑤	18 ④	19 ⑤	20 ④

1 글의 목적   ①

해설 교통사고 현장에서 피해자들에게 무례하게 굴며 취재를 한 기자의 취재 태도에 대해 항의하려고 해당 언론사의 편집인에게 보내는 편지이므로 글의 목적으로 가장 적절한 것은 ①이다.

해석 편집자께,
저희 아들이 지난주 Crosstown 쇼핑센터 근처에서 심각한 다중 차량 사고에 휘말렸습니다. 그는 상대적으로 사소한 부상만 당했지만, 불행히도 다른 사람들은 그렇게 운이 좋지 않았습니다. 기자가 그곳에 와서 사건을 취재할 권리를 가진다는 점은 전적으로 이해합니다. 하지만 현장에 있던 당신 회사의 기자인 John Stevens는 부상당한 사람들에게 극도로 무신경하더군요. 제 남편과 저는 우리 아들에게 가기 위해 당신 측의 기자를 지나서 밀치고 나아가야 했습니다. Stevens 씨는 계속하여 질문하며 우리의 프라이버시를 침해했습니다. 우리는 그에게 우리를 내버려둬 달라고 부탁했지만 그는 집요하게 굴었죠. 저는 대학 수준의 정치학을 가르치며 언론의 자유를 전적으로 지지하지만, 무례한 행동은 어떠한 상황에서도 용인되어서는 안 됩니다. 아마 Stevens 씨는 정중함이 다뤄지는 날의 수업에 결석했나 봅니다.
Laura Pottenger 드림

구문 [5행~7행] I fully appreciate the fact that a reporter had *the right* (to be there [and] cover the incident).
the fact와 that ~ incident는 동격 관계이다. ( )는 the right를 수식하며, 동사원형 be와 cover는 병렬구조이다.

어휘 be involved in ~에 관계되다   sustain (피해를) 당하다   cover 취재하다
incident 사건   insensitive 둔감한   push one's way 밀치고 나아가다   invade 침입하다   persist 끈질기게 계속하다   political science 정치학   tolerate 용인하다
circumstance 상황   courtesy 정중함, 공손함

2 밑줄 함의   ⑤

해설 가볍고 개방적이던 이탈리아의 건축이 이탈리아의 입지가 악화되면서 육중하게 되었다고 하였다. 마찬가지로 히틀러가 연합군과 전쟁을 하면서 공적인 건축물이 육중한 양식이 되고 가벼운 건축이 금지되었다. 이와는 반대로 안정감 있던 스칸디나비아의 건축물은 매우 허약하게 보인다. 이를 통해 내릴 수 있는 결론인 '정부 건축물은 정부 자체의 거울이다'라는 표현은 ⑤ '정부의 안정성은 그 건물의 무게에서 명백히 나타난다.'를 뜻한다고 볼 수 있다.
① 위대한 건물은 강력한 정부에서 나온다.
② 지방 정부가 건물 규정을 통제해야 한다.
③ 건축이 항상 정치 문화를 나타내는 것은 아니다.
④ 정부 건물은 정치가 말 그대로 형성되는 공간이다.

해석 내가 30대에 유럽에서 건축학 학생이었을 때, 나는 다양한 국가들의 정부 건물의 외관이 굉장히 다르다는 관찰에 깊은 인상을 받았다. 무솔리니 정권 초기, 비교적 차분한 시기의 이탈리아에서 건축된 건물들은 상대적으로 가볍고 개방적이었지만, 유럽의 상황이 악화됨에 따라 이탈리아의 입지도 악화되어 새로운 건물들은 더 두꺼운 벽, 더 무거운 세세한 것들과 일반적으로 더 육중한 외관을 얻게 되었다. 마찬가지로, 히틀러가 독일에서 권력을 잡은 뒤, 그의 만연한 지배를 유지하기 위해 연합군을 상대로 싸우게 되자, 공식적인 건축물은 극히 육중한 무게를 가졌고, 구조와 외관 상 매우 가벼운 현대적인 건축은 금지되었다. 반면에, 왕과 다른 지배층 인사들이 시내 전차에 탑승한 모습이 목격되는 것이 금시초문이 아닐 정도로 안정감 있던 스칸디나비아 반도에서는, 정부 건축물이 명백한 허약함이라는 유례없는 단계에 도달했다. 많은 생각 후 나는 마침내 정부 건축물은 정부 자체의 거울이다라는 결론에 이르렀다.

구문 [2행~4행] ~ I was struck by *the observation* [that the appearance of government buildings in various countries differed greatly].
[ ]은 the observation에 대한 동격절이다.
[17행] ~ **it** was not unheard of {for them} [to be seen on street cars], ~
it은 가주어, [ ]이 진주어이며, { }은 to be seen에 대한 의미상 주어이다.

어휘 strike 인상을 주다   differ 다르다   regime 정권   massive 크고 육중한
personage 저명인사, 명사   unheard 들어 보지 않은   street car 시내 전차
unprecedented 유례없는   apparent 명백한   fragility 허약

3 글의 요지   ⑤

해설 전기 작가들의 목표는 작가의 주관과 해석이 개입되지 않은 객관적인 사실의 연대기적 진술이지만, 실제로 전기를 쓸 때 작가의 주관과 해석이 영향을 미치는 것은 불가피하다는 내용의 글이므로 요지로 가장 적절한 것은 ⑤이다.

해석 평판이 좋은 학구적인 전기의 목표는 단순히 연대순으로 사실을 제공하는 것이다. 이러한 방식으로 독자는 전기 작가의 주의를 흩뜨리는 정보 투입 없이, 그리고 잠재적으로 위험한 주관성의 영향 없이 그 대상의 삶에 대해 배울 수 있다. 이것은 전기 쓰기의 정점, 그리고 대상의 삶을 과학으로서 명시하는 정점을 나타낸다. 이러한 과학적 기법은 주관성이 제거될 수 있으며 제거되어야 함을 암시하지만, 이것이 가능한 일이기는 할까 아니면 단지 오류일까? 작가는, 마치 그 문제에 대해 이미 어떻게든 투자를 받지 않은 것처럼 그 대상과 완전히 분리되어 공정한 상태로 있을 수 없고, 그렇지 않다면 그들은 아마 그러한 작업에 착수하기 시작하지 않았을 것이다. 전기 작가는 불가피하게 자기 자신의 해석과 사전에 형성된 관념을 가지고 이 과정을 시작할 것이며, 비록 그들이 객관적인 전기를 만드는 것을 목표로 한다 할지라도, 이러한 관념은 그들의 글에 불가피하게 영향을 줄 것이다.

구문 [10행~13행] An author cannot remain fully detached and impartial to the subject, // **as if** they **were** not already somehow invested in the matter, / [or] they probably **wouldn't have begun** to undertake such a task.
fully detached and impartial to the subject는 과거분사(detached)와 형용사(impartial)로 이루어진 보어이다. as if는 '마치 ~인 것처럼'의 뜻이며, as if 이하는 가정법 과거로 be동사를 were로 사용하였다. 「wouldn't have p.p.」는 '~하지 않았을 것이다'의 뜻이다.

어휘 reputable 평판이 좋은   scholarly 학구적인   biography 전기
chronological 연대순의   subject 대상   distract 주의를 흩뜨리다   subjectivity
주관성   pinnacle 정점   manifestation 명시   imply 암시하다   eliminate

제거하다 **fallacy** 오류 **detach** 분리하다, 떼다 **impartial** 공정한 **somehow** 어떻게든 **undertake** 착수하다 **inevitably** 불가피하게 **interpretation** 해석 **preconceived** 사전에 형성된

4 글의 주제   ②

해설 과학은 너무나 빠르게 발전하고 상업적, 정치적 영향을 강하게 받으며 윤리와 규제에서 벗어나 적용될 것이라는 냉소적이고 자포자기하는 태도는 위험하다는 내용의 글이므로 주제로 가장 적절한 것은 ② '과학은 통제 불가능하다고 믿는 것의 위험'이다.
① 과학 통제의 난제와 어려움
③ 과학의 막대한 잠재성과 처참한 부정적인 면
④ 과학을 규제하려는 시도가 해로운 이유
⑤ 과학이 어떻게 적용되는지에 대한 윤리적 선택의 중요성

해석 거의 어떠한 과학적 발견에도 선뿐만 아니라 악의 잠재성이 있다. 그것의 적용은 우리의 개인적, 정치적 선택에 따라 어떤 방향으로든 틀어질 수 있다. 그러나 최고의 정책을 위해 힘차게 캠페인을 하기보다는, 우리가 운명론, 즉 과학은 너무 빠르게 발전하고 있으며 상업적, 정치적 압박의 영향을 너무 강하게 받고 있어서 우리가 하는 어떤 것도 조금의 차이도 만들어낼 수 없다는 믿음으로 인해 무대책에 빠질 진짜 위험이 존재한다. 냉소적인 사람들은 한술 더 떠서 과학적, 기술적으로 가능한 것이면 무엇이라도 윤리적이고 신중한 반대에도 불구하고 규제 제도가 무엇이든, 어딘가에서 언젠가는 수행될 것이라고 말한다. 이 생각은 참이든 거짓이든 극도로 위험한 것인데, 왜냐하면 그것은 체념하는 비관주의를 낳고 더 안전하고 더 공정한 세상을 지키려는 노력에 대한 의욕을 꺾기 때문이다.

구문 [4행~9행] But there's a real danger <u>that</u> rather than campaigning energetically for optimum policies, // we will be lulled into inaction by fatalism — **by a belief** that science is advancing **so** fast and is **so** strongly influenced / by commercial and political pressures // **that** nothing [(that) we do] will make any difference.
that rather ~ by fatalism은 a real danger에 대한 동격절이다. by fatalism과 by a belief는 동격 관계이다. that science ~ difference는 a belief에 대한 동격절이며 여기서 「so ~ that ... (너무 ~해서 …하다)」 구문이 쓰였다. [ ]는 앞에 목적격 관계대명사 that이 생략되어 nothing을 수식한다.

어휘 channel ~에 돌리다, 쏟다; 보내다 optimum 최고의, 최적의 inaction 무대책; 활동 부족 fatalism 운명론, 숙명론; 체념 *cf.* fate 운명 cynic 냉소적인 사람 prudential 신중한 objection 반대 regulatory 규제하는 regime 제도, 체제 exceedingly 극도로, 대단히 engender ~을 낳다 despair 체념[절망]하다 pessimism 비관주의 demotivate 의욕을 꺾다, 동기를 잃게 하다 secure 안전하게 지키다; 획득[확보]하다 detrimental 해로운

5 도표 이해   ④

해설 '현대 재생 가능 에너지' 소비 점유율에서는, '생물자원/태양열/지열' 소비가 4.2퍼센트이고 '수력전기'와 '수송용 바이오연료'의 점유율 합계는 4.4퍼센트이므로 전자가 더 크다는 ④의 진술은 일치하지 않는다.

해석 2017년 세계 최종 에너지 소비에서 재생 가능 에너지
위 도표는 2017년 세계 최종 에너지 소비에서 재생 가능 에너지의 점유율을 보여 준다. ① 2017년에, 세계 최종 에너지 소비에서 '화석 연료' 소비의 점유율은 거의 80퍼센트를 차지했던 반면 '현대 재생 가능 에너지' 소비의 점유율은 약 10퍼센트였다. ② 세계 최종 에너

지 소비에서 '핵에너지' 소비의 비율은 2퍼센트를 약간 초과했다. ③ '전통 생물자원'의 소비는 7.5퍼센트를 이뤘는데, 이것은 '수력 전기' 소비보다 2배 넘게 높았다. ④ '현대 재생 가능 에너지' 소비의 점유율에서는, '생물자원/태양열/지열' 소비가 4.2퍼센트로 가장 큰 점유율을 차지했는데, 이는 '수력 전기'와 '수송용 바이오연료'의 점유율의 합계보다 더 컸다. ⑤ '풍력/태양열/생물자원/지열/해양 동력'의 소비는 2.0퍼센트로 이는 '수송용 바이오연료'의 소비보다 두 배 넘게 높았다.

구문 [9행~11행] *The consumption of "Traditional Biomass"* made up 7.5 percent, **which** was more than ***twice* as** high **as** the consumption of *"Hydropower."*
계속적 용법의 관계대명사 which가 이끄는 절이 The consumption of "Traditional Biomass"를 보충 설명한다. 「배수사+as 원급 as ~」의 비교 표현은 '~보다 몇 배 …한'의 의미이다.

어휘 share 점유율; 몫 renewable energy 재생 가능 에너지 fossil fuel 화석 연료 account for (부분·비율을) 차지하다; 설명하다 ratio 비율 nuclear energy 핵에너지, 원자력 exceed 초과하다; ~보다 낫다 make up ~을 이루다; 구성하다 hydropower 수력 전기 renewables 재생 가능 에너지 sum 합계 biofuel 바이오연료

6 내용 불일치   ⑤

해설 Northern Pike는 뛰어난 위장술로 조용히 숨어있을 수 있는 능력 덕분에 완벽한 포식자가 되는 것이지, 포식자를 피하는 것은 아니다. 따라서 ⑤는 본문의 내용과 일치하지 않는다.

해석 Northern Pike(강창꼬치속(屬)의 물고기)는 중세에 사용되던 창(pike)이라고 알려진 막대처럼 생긴 무기와의 유사성에서 그 이름을 얻는다. Northern Pike는 북반구 전역의 담수에서 발견된다. 그들은 여러 수역에서 포식자 어류로서 중요한 역할을 한다. 그들은 대식가이며 꽤 쉽게 미끼를 덥석 무는 경향이 있어서 어부들 사이에서 인기가 최고다. 그들의 이빨이 드러난 턱은 개구리, 가재와 심지어 오리 새끼를 포함한 미끈거리는 먹이를 쉽게 잡아채서 붙든다. Northern Pike는 큰 사이즈와 육중한 무게에도 불구하고 헤엄을 매우 잘 친다. 그들은 평균적으로 시속 8에서 10마일 사이의 속도로 헤엄친다. Pike는 덮인 영역에서 위장을 잘 한다. 그들의 위장 기질은 장기간에 걸쳐 완벽하게 정지한 상태로 있을 수 있는 능력과 더불어 Northern Pike를 완벽한 포식자가 되게 한다.

구문 [6행~8행] They are large eaters <u>and</u> <u>tend</u> to snap at bait quite readily, / **making** them a favorite among fishermen.
동사 are와 tend가 병렬구조를 이룬다. making 이하는 능동의 의미를 갖는 분사 구문이다.

어휘 resemblance 유사함, 닮음 pike 창 the Northern Hemisphere 북반구 body of water 수역 snap at ~을 덥석 물다 bait 미끼 readily 쉽게 fisherman 어부 toothy 이를 드러낸 slippery 미끄러운, 미끈거리는 crayfish 가재 duckling 오리 새끼 camouflage 위장(하다) tendency 기질, 성향 still 정지한, 고요한

7 밑줄 어법   ⑤

해설 ⑤ that절에서 주어는 these images이고 동사 exploit, play, contribute가 병렬 관계를 이루고 있다. 따라서 복수동사 contribute가 적절하다.
① used는 과거분사로 Animals를 수식하며 '사용[이용]되는'의 의미로 쓰였다.
② with which에서 which는 앞의 선행사 an animal image를 의미한다. 이때 선

행사를 관계절 내에 위치시켜보면 전치사의 목적어로 쓰여야 자연스러우므로(we are all familiar with an animal image) 전치사 with가 관계대명사와 함께 쓰였다.

③ 선행사 the wildness and independence를 수식하고 관계절 내에서 주어 역할을 하므로 주격 관계대명사 that이 적절히 쓰였다.

④ 'view+목적어+as+명사[형용사]' 구문에서 형용사 harmless가 적절히 쓰였다.

해석 광고에서 동물의 이미지를 사용하는 것의 효과와 영향은 미묘하다. 아이들을 대상으로 하는 상품과 서비스를 판매하는 데 사용되는 동물들은 대개 어리석거나 '귀엽게' 보인다. 'Tony the Tiger'는 우리 모두에게 익숙하고, 아이들에게 판매되는 특정 식품과 밀접하게 관련이 있게 된 동물 이미지의 단지 하나의 예이다. 호랑이는 본래 타고난 야생성과 독립성이 존중되어야 하며, 아침 식사용 시리얼의 친근한 제공자로 묘사되어서는 안 된다고 많은 사람이 주장할 것이다. 대부분의 사람들이 동물 이미지 사용을 해가 없는 것으로 볼 것이다. 하지만, 많은 동물 권리 옹호자들은 이러한 이미지가 동물을 착취하고, 동물을 하찮아 보이게 만드는 관점을 영속화하는 역할을 하며, 궁극적으로 다른 종의 구성원에 대한 존중 결여의 원인이 된다고 주장한다.

구문 [2행~4행] *Animals* (used to sell *products and services* [that are aimed at children]) are usually shown as silly or "cute."
( ) 부분은 Animals를 수식하는 과거분사구이며 [ ] 부분은 products and services를 수식하는 관계절이다.

어휘 implication 영향[결과]; 함축, 암시   subtle 미묘한; 교묘한, 영리한   be associated with ~와 관련[연관]되다   value 가치 있게 여기다   inherent 타고난, 선천적인   advocate 옹호자, 지지자   exploit (부당하게) 이용하다, 착취하다   trivialize 하찮아 보이게 만들다

8 밑줄 어휘 ③

해설 환경이 변하면 유전적으로 준비된 일부 종은 그 변화를 이용하지만 그 외의 종들은 그렇지 않은데, 한 동물이 기회를 이용하기 위해 변했을 때 다른 동물도 같은 방식으로 바뀌는 것은 아니라고 했으므로 ③의 transformed를 unchanged로 바꿔야 한다.

해석 환경 변화는 몇몇 종에게 새로운 기회를 열어줄 수 있다. 이런 기회가 나타날 때마다, 자연은 그것에 맞서는 현존 개체들의 특성에서의 변화를 ① 시험한다. 현존하는 종들의 일부는 유전적으로 그러한 새로운 기회들을 이용할 준비가 될 것이다. 각각의 종이 식량원과 경쟁자, 개체들 사이의 변종, 그리고 화학적 오차 측면에서 ② 독특하기 때문에, 한 종에게 기회가 되는 것이 모든 종에게 기회가 되는 것은 아닐 것이다. 그 기회를 이용하지 못하는 종들은 ③ 변형될(→ 변하지 않을) 것이다. 한 동물이 새로운 기회를 이용하기 위해 변한 방식에 대한 구체적인 예가 주어졌을 때, 그것이 모든 유형의 동물이 또한 그와 같은 방식으로 바뀌리라는 것을 뜻하지는 않는다. 만약 그런 일이 발생한다면 모든 동물들이 곧 ④ 동일해지고 멸종할 것이다. 기회가 주어질 때 일부의 종만이 ⑤ 적응한다는 것이 항상 사실이다.

구문 [15행~17행] If that **took place** // then all animals **would** soon **become** identical — and extinct.
「If + 주어 + 과거동사 ~, 주어 + 조동사 과거형 + 동사원형 .....」의 가정법 과거로, '만약 ~라면 …일[할] 텐데'라는 뜻이다. 현재 사실에 반대되거나 현재나 미래에 실현 가능성이 희박한 상황을 가정하여 말한다.

어휘 variation 변화, 차이   trait 특질, 특성   portion 부분   genetically 유전적으로   equip (~에게) 준비를 갖춰 주다   take advantage of ~을 이용하다   competitor 경쟁자   identical 동일한   extinct 멸종한

9 빈칸 추론 ①

해설 정직함이 보편적인 미덕이긴 하지만, 사이버 공간에서는 상대방을 신뢰하기 위해 필요한 정보가 누락되어 있는 경우가 많기 때문에 '익명으로(anonymous)' 남는 것이 부정직한 것이 아니라 신중한 태도가 될 수 있다.

② 공손한 ③ 회의적인 ④ 헌신적인 ⑤ 변하지 않는

해석 솔직함과 정직함은 우리 사회가 높이 평가하는 자질이다. 우리는 사람들이 자기가 누구인지 자기 입으로 말하는 그 모습이기를 기대하고, 우리에게 자기 자신에 대한 진실을 말해 주기를 기대한다. 컴퓨터의 출현 이전에는, 가명을 사용하는 사람은 누구나 불명예스러운 무언가를 숨기고 있는 것으로 생각되었다. 경험이 부족한 컴퓨터 사용자들은 온라인 연결에 대해서도 계속해서 이렇게 느낄 수도 있다. 우리가 사람들을 평가하기 위해 사용하는 단서들 중 너무나 많은 것들이 사이버 공간에서는 없기 때문에, 컴퓨터 사용자들은 가상의 만남 장소가 대면 접촉과 다르다는 것을 이해할 필요가 있다. 우리가 인스턴트 메시지 팝업이나 채팅방 화면 뒤에 있는 사람들을 알고 믿을 만한 충분한 이유가 있을 때까지는, 우리는 익명으로 남아야 하며 그렇게 하는 것이 정직하지 않은 것이 아니다.

구문 [2행~3행] We **expect** *people* **to be** who (they say) they are ⬚and⬚ **tell** us the truth about themselves.
「expect+O+to-v (O가 v할 것을 기대하다)」 구문인데 to 다음의 동사원형 be와 tell이 병렬구조를 이룬다. be동사 다음의 보어 역할을 하는 간접의문문 'who they say they are'에서 they say는 삽입절이다.

어휘 directness 솔직함; 똑바름   advent 출현, 도래   assumed name 가명   disreputable 불명예스러운, 평판이 좋지 않은   cue 단서, 실마리   virtual 가상의; 사실상의   courteous 공손한; 친절한   committed 헌신적인   anonymous 익명의

10 빈칸 추론 ③

해설 과거의 병원들이 환자를 위하기보다 최신 장비를 더 우선시했다는 내용이다. 환자는 치료의 '목표'이고 기계 설비는 환자들을 치료하기 위한 '수단'에 해당하므로 이러한 상황에 대하여 기술 철학자가 할 수 있는 말은 ③ '수단이 목적을 지배한다'가 적절하다.

① 비전(미래상)이 현실에 선행한다
② 행동은 발전을 추진시킨다
④ 막대한 양에서 질이 나온다
⑤ 지식은 문명의 어머니이다

해석 20세기 말 무렵 최신식 병원들은 일반적으로 최신식 장비를 둘러 설계되었다. 병원이 스캐너와 엑스레이 기계를 더 많이 가지고 있으면 있을수록, 그리고 그것의 생화학적 혈액 및 소변 검사가 더 정교할수록, 병원의 치료가 더 선진적이라고 여겨졌다. 종종 병원의 물리적 공간이 환자를 돌보는 것보다 장비를 돌보는 것을 우선시하는 것처럼 보였다. 1970년대 초반, 민감한 장비는 여름의 열기를 견딜 수 없기 때문에 냉방 장치가 되어 있는 유일한 과거 영상의학과인 병원이 여전히 있었다. 의학 기술에 대한 의존과 경탄이 20세기 중반에 증가함에 따라, 환자들의 편안함은 왠지 제쳐두게 되었고 그들의 환경은 종종 무시되었다. 병원 계획 설계자들은 기술이 환자의 요구에 적응하기보다는 환자들이 기술의 요구에 적응할 수 있을 거라고 추정했다. 기술 철학자 Jacques Ellul이 현대 병원에 대하여 말한 대로, "수단이 목적을 지배한다."

구문 [3행~6행] **The more** scanners and X-ray machines a hospital had, / and **the more** sophisticated its biochemical blood and urine tests, // **the more** advanced its care was thought to be.
「The 비교급 ~, the 비교급 ....」 구문은 '~하면 할수록, 더 …하다'의 뜻이다. 앞의 두 절이 '~하면 할수록'의 뜻이고 //의 뒤가 '더 …하다'인 구조이다.

[9행~11행] ~ one could still find *hospitals* [**where** *the only department* [that was air-conditioned] / was the Radiology Department], // because ~.

[ ]는 hospitals를 수식하고 [ ] 내의 that was air-conditioned는 앞의 the only department를 수식하는 구조이다.

어휘 state-of-the-art 최신식의 sophisticated 세련된, 정교한 biochemical 생화학의 urine 소변 advanced 진보한, 선진의, 고급의 prioritize 우선순위를 매기다 tolerate 참다, 견디다 admiration 존경, 감탄, 경탄 somehow 왠지, 알 수 없는 이유로 the other way around 반대로 **[선택지 어휘]** precede 앞서다

11 빈칸 추론 ④

해설 본문은 세계 경제의 심화하는 상호 의존성에 관하여 다루고 있다. 빈칸 문장 앞에서 국가들의 연쇄적인 재정적 붕괴와 이런 국가들의 경제 불안정화가 아시아 경제 위기를 재촉했고, 세계적 불황을 촉발했다는 내용이 나온다. 또한, 빈칸 뒷부분에는 효과적인 국제 규제 기관이 긴급하게 필요하게 되었다는 내용이 나오므로 각 국가들의 독립적 기관들에 대해 빈칸에 들어갈 말로 가장 적절한 것은 ④ '최근 생겨난 경제적 문제를 처리할 수 없으며'이다.
① 아시아에서 사업하는 것을 선호하고 있으며
② 다른 기관들의 재정적 결정을 무시하며
③ 작은 나라들에 투자하는 것을 거부하고 있으며
⑤ 경제적 불평등 촉진에 대한 비난을 받으며

해석 제2차 세계대전 이전에 민족국가들은 경제와 재정 문제를 주로 국내 문제로 규제했다. 그러나 전후 시대에 우리는 경제적 상호 의존의 거대한 확장과 심화를 목격해 왔다. 그 결과 세계 경제는 단일 민족국가의 재정적·정치적 제도의 기능 불량에 의한 붕괴에 극도로 취약한데, 심각한 기능 불량은 흔히 '도미노 효과'라고 알려진 연쇄 반응을 유발할 수 있다. 그러한 붕괴적인 사건은 1997년에 발생했는데, 비교적 국가 경제 규모가 작았던 태국은 인접한 말레이시아, 인도네시아 그리고 한국으로부터 자신들의 자금을 빼낼 정도로 충분한 불확실성을 투자자들 사이에 촉발한 재정적인 붕괴를 겪었다. 이러한 국가 경제의 결과로 초래된 불안정화는 '아시아의 경제 위기'를 재촉했고 세계적인 불황을 촉발했다. 점점 더 국가 기관들은 최근 생겨난 경제적 문제를 처리할 수 없으며, 이것은 효과적인 국제적 규제 기관의 긴급한 필요를 유발해왔다.

구문 **[10행~15행]** Such a disruptive event occurred in *1997* [when Thailand, with a relatively small national economy, suffered *a financial collapse* {which touched off **sufficient** uncertainty among investors **that** they pulled their money out of neighbouring Malaysia, Indonesia, and South Korea}].

[ ] 부분은 when이 이끄는 관계절로서 1997을 수식하며, { } 부분은 a financial collapse를 수식하는 관계절이다. 'sufficient ~ that ...'은 '…할 정도로 충분한 ~'이라는 의미이다.

어휘 prior to ~ 이전에 nation-state 민족국가, 국민국가 regulate 규제하다, 통제하다 domestic 국내의 post-war era 전후 시대 witness 목격하다 expansion 확대, 확장 intensification 심화, 격화 interdependence 상호 의존 acutely 대단히, 몹시 vulnerable 취약한, 영향을 받기 쉬운 disruption 붕괴, 파멸 malfunction 기능 불량 trigger 유발하다 chain reaction 연쇄 반응 collapse 붕괴 touch off ~을 촉발하다 hasten 재촉하다 spark 촉발하다 recession 불황, 침체 prompt 유발하다, 자극하다 **[선택지 어휘]** emerging 최근 생겨난 inequality 불평등

12 빈칸 추론 ④

해설 이 글에서는 인간이 동물계의 일부이기 때문에 동물의 전쟁을 연구하면 많은 것을 얻을 수 있지만, 인간의 전쟁에는 그 외에도 목적, 의도 등의 추상적 개념이 들어간다고 하였다. 그러므로 빈칸을 완성하면 ④ '동물로부터 배울 수 있는 모든 것이 인간의 행동에 적용된다'는 것을 암시하지는 않는다가 된다.
① 동물의 전쟁 전략은 물리적 활동에만 국한된다
② 영장류는 인간의 사회 구조와 비슷한 사회 구조를 형성한다
③ 인간과 동물 간에 유사성은 없다
⑤ 인간은 동물의 전쟁 전략으로부터 영향을 받아왔다

해석 인간은 또한 동물이기 때문에, 거의 틀림없이 동물의 전쟁의 속성에 대해, 특히 지배와 활동의 역할에 대해 배움으로써 많은 것을 얻을 수 있다. 많은 연구가 인류의 가장 가까운 친척인 영장류에 대한 면밀한 관찰을 따랐지만, 그것이 동물로부터 배울 수 있는 모든 것이 인간의 행동에 적용된다는 것을 암시하지는 않는다. 유사와 비유는 특히 동물들이 발달시켰고 인간이 모방하고자 노력하는 추적, 기만, 위장, 포위 등의 전쟁의 전술 기법에 적용될 수 있다. 그럼에도 불구하고 인간의 두뇌는 또한 동물계에는 알려져 있지 않은 (예를 들어 자살 폭탄범) 목적, 의도, 개념, 그리고 명료한 이해를 생성한다. 이것은 인간의 군대 전략에서의 시행착오 과정이 자연계에 진화해온 전략에 수렴하거나 이를 모방한다 하더라도 여전히 사실이다.

구문 **[7행~11행]** Similarities and analogies can be applied, / especially in *the tactical methods of warfare* ~ [that animals have evolved] and [which humans try to mimic].

두 개의 관계사절 [ ]가 이중으로 the tactical methods of warfare를 수식한다.
[14행~17행] ~ even if trial-and-error processes in man's military strategy converge on 또는 mimic *strategies* [that have evolved in the natural kingdom].

strategies는 converge on과 mimic의 공통 목적어이며, 관계사절 [ ]의 수식을 받는다.

어휘 arguably 주장하건대, 거의 틀림없이 warfare 전쟁, 전투 dominance 우월, 지배 humanity 인류, 인간; 인간성 imply 암시하다 analogy 비유, 유추 tactical 작전[전술]의 deception 기만 camouflage 위장 encirclement 포위 mimic 흉내를 내다 explicit 분명한 trial-and-error 시행착오 converge on ~에 모여들다 **[선택지 어휘]** correspondence between A and B A와 B 사이의 관련성[유사함]

13 흐름 무관 문장 ④

해설 예전의 디지털 혁명(새로운 기계, 똑같은 이전의 과학)이 오늘날의 전산 혁명(똑같은 기계, 새로운 과학)으로 전환되었으며 컴퓨터 분야에서 새로운 과학이 발전되고 있다는 내용의 글인데, ④는 공적 관리와 사적 관리의 갈등을 진술하고 있으므로 글의 전체적인 흐름과 맞지 않다.

해석 20년에서 30년은 정보기술의 역사에 있어서 긴 시간이며, 어제와 오늘의 전산 도구의 내부적인 작동 방식 사이의 근본적인 간극을 우리가 알아차리게 해줄 만큼 충분히 길다. ① 초창기인 1990년대에는 우리가 알고 있던 이전의 과학을 이행하기 위해 우리의 최신식 디지털 기계를 사용했는데, 어떤 의미에서 우리는 우리가 갖고 있던 모든 과학을 그 당시 막 발견하고 있던 새로운 전산 플랫폼으로 옮겼다. ② 이제는 반대로, 우리는 컴퓨터가 어떠한 다른, 인간에 의한 것이 아닌, 포스트 과학적인 방법을 따르도록 할 때 더 잘, 그리고 더 빠르게 작동할 수 있다는 것을 알아가고 있고, 우리가 컴퓨터가 무엇을 하는지 또는 그것을 어떻게 하는지를 이해하지 못할 때도 '그것 나름의 방식'으로 문제를 해결하도록 하는 것이 더 쉽다고 점점 더 깨닫게 된다. ③ 은유적인 의미에서, 컴퓨터는 이제 그것만의 과학, 즉 새로운 종류의 과학을 발전시키고 있다. ④ 지능 있는 도구 보급의

증가하는 확산으로 인해 이미 플랫폼의 공적 관리와 사적 관리 사이의 긴장이 드러났다. ⑤ 따라서 1990년대의 디지털 혁명(새로운 기계, 똑같은 이전의 과학)이 새로운 제작 방식을 낳았듯이, 오늘날의 전산 혁명(똑같은 기계, 그러나 완전히 새로운 과학)은 새로운 사고방식을 낳고 있다.

구문 [7행~9행] ~ in a sense, we **carried** *all the science* [(which[that]) we had] **over to** *the new computational platforms* [(which[that]) we were then just discovering].

'carry A over to B'는 'A를 B로 넘기다'의 뜻이다. 두 개의 [ ]는 앞에 목적격 관계대명사 which[that]가 생략되어 각각 all the science, the new computational platforms를 수식한다.

[12행~14행] ~ and we increasingly find **it** easier **to let** *computers* solve problems *in their own way*]

it은 가목적어이고 to let 이하가 진목적어이다. 「find it C to-v」는 'v하는 것이 C하다는 것을 깨닫다'의 뜻이고, 사역동사 let은 「let+O+동사원형(…가 ~하게 하다)」의 형태로 쓰였다.

어휘 discern 알아차리다, 식별하다   implement 실행하다   metaphorical 은유적인   diffusion 확산, 보급   governance 통치, 관리

14 글의 순서   ②

해설 로마인들이 그릇 내부를 코팅하는 데 납을 사용했다는 주어진 글 다음에는 그 납을 산성이 강한 로마 음식이 녹여버렸다는 내용의 (B)가 나온다. 이로 인해 로마인들이 만성적인 납 중독에 시달렸다는 (B) 다음에는 납 중독의 증상을 제시한 (A)가 나온다. 납 중독의 증상으로 인해 미각이 나빠진 로마인들이 이를 상쇄하고자 풍미가 강한 음식을 선호하게 됐다는 (A) 다음에는, 그 결과로 병원균 수치를 줄일 수 있게 되었다는 내용의 (C)가 나온다.

해석 로마인들은 풍미가 강한 허브와 향신료를 많이 사용했으며, 음식에 매우 복합적이고 강한 맛이 나는 것을 좋아했던 것으로 보인다. 이에 대한 이유 중 하나는 음식 안전 문제와 관련이 있을지 모르겠으나, 이를 극복했던 건 아니었다. 로마인들은 많은 요리 및 저장 용기의 안벽을 붙이는 데 납을 사용했다.
(B) 그들의 많은 음식은 제법 산성이 강해서 납을 녹여버렸다. 로마인들의 뼈에 대한 연구에서 보면 그들의 체내 축적 유해 물질로 납 수치가 높았다는 점은 분명하며, 정말로 많은 로마인들이 만성적인 납 중독에 시달리고 있었음에 틀림없다.
(A) 납 중독의 증상 중 하나는 바뀐 미각이며, 많은 경우 입 안에 금속성의 맛이 나게 된다. 아마 그들은 강한 허브와 향신료로 그 금속성의 맛을 위장하려고 노력했거나, 혹은 아마 그들의 미각이 납 중독으로 인해 너무 나빠져서 무엇이라도 맛볼 수 있는 유일한 방법이 그것을 믿을 수 없을 정도로 풍미가 매우 강하게 만드는 것이었을 것이다.
(C) 이유가 무엇이든 향신료가 많이 첨가된 음식에 대한 그들의 욕구는 좋은 연쇄적 효과가 있었다. 많은 허브와 향신료는 항균성 화학물질을 포함하고 있어서 로마 음식에 그것들이 고농도로 포함된 것은 병원균 수치를 아마도 감소시켰을 것이다.

구문 [8행~13행] Perhaps they tried to disguise the metallic taste / with strong herbs and spices, // or perhaps their sense of taste was / **so** poor due to lead poisoning // **that** *the only way* [that they could taste anything] / was to make it incredibly highly flavoured.

「so ~ that ...(너무 ~해서 …하다) 구문이 사용되었다. [ ]는 the only way를 수식하는 관계부사절이다.

[15행~18행] **It** is clear from *studies* (on Roman bones) **that** they had a high body burden of lead, // and indeed many of them **must have been suffering** from chronic lead poisoning.

It은 가주어이고 that ~ lead가 진주어이다. ( )는 studies를 수식한다. 「must have

----

been v-ing」는 'v해오고 있었음에 틀림없다'의 뜻이다.

어휘 lead 납   vessel 용기, 그릇; 선박   alter 바꾸다   dissolve 녹이다; 해소하다   body burden 체내 축적 유해 물질 *cf.* burden 부담, 짐   chronic 만성적인   knock-on 연쇄적인, 연쇄 반응을 일으키는   antibacterial 항균성의   concentration 농도; (정신) 집중

15 글의 순서   ⑤

해설 종의 변화가 생태계에 영향을 줄 수 있다는 주어진 문장 다음에는 이러한 영향이 커져서 생태계 전반을 뒤흔들 수 있다는 심화된 내용의 (C)가 나온다. 그러나 모든 종의 변화가 생태계 붕괴의 조짐이 되는 것은 아니라는 (C) 마지막 문장 다음에는 대부분 종의 출현과 퇴장은 거시적으로 볼 때 생태계에 큰 영향을 주지 않는다는 내용의 (B)가 이어진다. 생태계에는 경미한 영향만을 미칠지라도 인간에게는 다양한 생명체가 있는 혼합체가 중요한 문제일 수 있다는 (B) 다음에는 생태계를 위한 목적 외에도 국립공원과 관광 산업 등을 위해 생태계를 잘 유지하려는 인간의 노력이 (A)에 제시된다.

해석 생태계에서 종의 변화는 공동체 안에서 유기체 간의 관계를 붕괴시킬 수 있을 뿐만 아니라 몇 세기 동안 생태계에 반향을 불러일으킬 수 있는 부수적 혹은 간접적인 영향을 발동시킬 수 있다.
(C) 결국 이렇게 넓어지는 교란의 순환이 공동체의 구조나 안정성에 영향을 미치고 더 큰 생태계 과정을 방해할지도 모른다. 그러나 모든 종의 손실, 혹은 토종이 아닌 생물에 의한 모든 침략이 생태계 전반의 붕괴 조짐이 된다고 주장하는 것은 오해의 소지가 있다.
(B) 종들은 대개 토양 비옥도, 식물 생산성, 혹은 물의 순환과 같은 대규모의 과정에 영향을 미치지 않고 나타났다 사라질 수 있다. 물론 인간의 관점에서 보면 종의 정확한 혼합체는 매우 중요할지 모른다.
(A) 전 세계의 많은 국립공원 같은 장소에서 사회의 목표는 중요한 생태 과정의 유지를 위한 것뿐만 아니라 그것이 지탱하는 오락 산업과 관광 산업을 위해서도 다양하고 스스로 재생되는 자연의 공동체를 영속시키는 것이다.

구문 [1행~5행] A change in species in an ecosystem can **not only** disrupt relationships among the organisms in a community, **but** can **also** set in motion *secondary or indirect effects* [that can reverberate through a system for centuries].

'not only A but also B(A뿐만 아니라 B도)'의 상관접속사가 두 개의 밑줄 친 동사구를 병렬 연결한다. [ ] 부분은 관계사절로 선행사 secondary or indirect effects를 수식한다.

[18행~21행] But **it** would be misleading **to claim** *that* every species loss — or every invasion by a non-native creature — threatens systemwide disruptions.
밑줄 친 it은 가주어, 명사적 용법으로 쓰인 to claim이 이끄는 to부정사구가 진주어이다. to claim의 목적어로 접속사 that이 이끄는 명사절이 쓰였다.

어휘 ecosystem 생태계   disrupt 붕괴시키다; 방해하다, 지장을 주다   organism 유기체; 생물   set in motion ~에 시동을 걸다   secondary 부수적인; 부차적인   reverberate 반향[파문]을 불러일으키다; 울리다   perpetuate 영속시키다, 영구화하다   renew 재생하다; 갱신하다   maintenance 유지[지속]   vital 극히 중대한; 생명의   recreational 오락의   scale 규모, 범위   fertility 비옥함; 생식력   perspective 관점   precise 정확한; 정밀한   matter 중요하다; 문제되다   disturbance 교란, 방해; (마음의) 동요   interfere with 방해하다   misleading 오해의 소지가 있는, 오도하는   claim 주장하다; 청구하다   invasion 침략[침입]   threaten 조짐을 보이다; 위협하다   systemwide 전 조직[체계]에 미치는[걸치는]   disruption 붕괴; 분열

16 문장 넣기   ③

해설 ③의 앞부분은 Ray Anderson의 카펫 회사가 환경오염을 많이 일으켰다는 내용이고 뒷부분은 Anderson이 손해를 감수하고서도 환경오염을 일으키지 않는 회사로 탈바꿈시키려는 노력이 나온다. 주어진 문장은 '후손들에게 많은 부를 남겨주어도 지구가 살 수 없는 곳이 되면 무슨 소용이겠는가'라는, 친환경적 기업을 만들겠다고 Anderson이 결심한 계기에 관한 것이므로 Anderson의 결심과 변화의 노력이 소개된 내용의 바로 앞인 ③에 위치해야 한다.

해석 약 20년 전에, 지금은 고인이 된 엄청나게 성공한 카펫 제조업체 Interface의 CEO인 Ray Anderson은 그가 깨달음이라고 묘사한 것을 얻었다. 그는 자신이나 자신의 후계자들이 어떻게 써야 할지 알 만한 수준보다 더 많은 돈을 가지고 있었는데, 그 때 그의 회사가 환경을 유독 물질로 오염시키고 있다는 것을 깨달았다. 카펫 제조는 석유 집약 산업이(었)고 그의 회사의 환경 발자국(= 자원 사용이나 오염물 배출로 인한 환경적 영향)은 거대했다. Anderson은 많은 부를 축적한 대가가 지구가 사람이 살 수 없는 곳이 되는 거라면, 손주들에게 그 부를 물려주는 것이 무슨 이로움이 있을지 의아했다. 그래서 Anderson은 그의 회사의 작업의 모든 측면을 바꾸기로 결심했고, 2020년까지 제로 발자국의 목표를 달성하려고 움직였다. 그는 새로운 생산 과정의 개발과 오염 통제에 대한 책무에는 돈이 그것도 아주 많은 돈이 들 거라고 추정했다. 그러나 그는 공익을 달성하기 위해 이익을 기꺼이 희생하려 했다.

구문 [1행~4행] Anderson wondered // what good **it** would do **to leave his grandchildren great wealth** // if the price of accumulating that wealth was an uninhabitable planet.
what ~ planet은 wondered의 목적어이다. 여기에서 it은 가주어이고 to leave ~ wealth가 진주어이다.

[15행~18행] He assumed // that the development of new production processes and a commitment to pollution control **would cost** money — a lot of it.
that절에서 두 밑줄 부분은 주어로 and로 연결되어 병렬구조를 이루며, 동사는 would cost이다.

어휘 do good 이롭다, 도움이 되다   accumulate 축적시키다, 쌓다   uninhabitable 사람이 살 수 없는   immensely 엄청나게   heir 후계자, 상속인   poison (유독 물질로) 오염시키다   petroleum 석유   intensive 집약[집중]적인   resolve 결심하다   transform 바꾸다; 변형시키다   operation 작업, 운영   commitment 책무; 공약   social good 공익 (= common good)

17 문장 넣기   ⑤

해설 주어진 문장이 이집트인들이 유용한 절기의 달력을 제공할 수 있다는 것을 알아냈다는 내용이고 But으로 시작되는 것으로 보아 앞 내용에는 달력에 결함이 있었다는 내용이 나와야 한다. 그러므로 초기 이집트 달력의 기준이 된 '나일강의 수위계'가 달의 위상과 맞지 않았다는 내용 다음인 ⑤에 주어진 문장이 들어가야 적절하다. ⑤ 뒤 문장의 This는 주어진 문장의 이집트인들이 알아낸 유용한 달력을 가리킨다.

해석 나일 강의 리듬은 이집트인 생활의 리듬이었다. 나일 강의 강물이 매년 불어나는 것으로 인해 범람, 재배, 그리고 추수라는 그것의 세 절기에 따라 씨 뿌리기와 수확의 일정이 결정되었다. 6월 말부터 10월 하순까지의 나일 강의 범람은 비옥한 토사를 유입시켰는데, 그 토사에 10월 하순부터 2월 하순까지 농작물이 심어져 자랐고, 2월 하순부터 6월 말까지 수확되었다. 태양이 뜨는 것만큼 정기적이고 삶에 필수적이었던 나일 강의 물이 불어나는 것은 나일 역년의 특징을 이루었다. 당연히 초기의 이집트 달력은 범람의 수위가 매년 표시된 단순한 수직 모양의 척도였던 '나일 강의 수위계'였다. 나일 역년을 몇 년만 계산해 보더라도 그것이 달의 위상과 맞지 않는다는 것이 드러났다. 그러나 아주 일찍

이 이집트인들은 각각 30일로 된 12개월이, 끝에 또 5일이 더해져서 365일로 된 1년을 만들면 유용한 절기의 달력을 제공할 수 있다는 것을 알아냈다. 이것이 이집트인들이 일찍이 기원전 4241년에 사용하기 시작한 '상용하는' 역년, 즉 '나일 역년'이었다.

구문 [1행~4행] But very early the Egyptians *found* that twelve months of thirty days each **could** provide a useful calendar of the seasons **if another five days were added at the end, to make a year of 365 days**.
if가 이끄는 부사절은 조건절을 나타낸다. found 이후의 that절 내 could는 조동사의 과거형으로 과거의 능력을 나타낸다.

[8행~12행] The flooding of the Nile from the end of June till late October brought down *rich silt*, **in which** crops were planted and grew from late October to late February, **to be harvested from late February till the end of June**.
'전치사+관계대명사' 형태의 in which가 이끄는 관계사절은 rich silt를 보충 설명한다. to be harvested ~ of June은 to부정사의 결과적 용법으로 '(결국) ~하게 되다'의 의미이다.

어휘 rhythm (규칙적으로 반복되는) 리듬, 변화   set 결정하다; 세우다   sow 씨를 뿌리다   reap 수확하다, 거두어들이다   harvest 추수[수확](하다)   flood 범람하다; 쇄도하다   mark 특징[성격] 짓다; 표시하다   primitive 초기의, 원시적인 단계의   nilometer (특히 홍수 때의) 나일 강의 수위계   vertical 수직의, 세로의   scale 척도, 기준; 규모   reckon 계산하다; 추정하다   keep in step with 보조를 맞추다   phase (주기적으로 형태가 변하는 달의) 상[모습]; 국면   civil 상용하는, 보통의; 일반인의, 시민의

18 요약문 완성   ④

해설 정보와 지식의 차이에 대해 논하고 있는 글로, 정보는 즉시 접할 수 있는 컴퓨터상의, 혹은 출간된 자료, 즉 다양한 출처에서 얻은 처리된(processed) 자료이다. 반면, 지식은 독자의 정신 속에서 구축되어야 하며 쌓아 올리는 데 많은 시간이 걸린다. 즉 지식은 무언가를 아는 정신의 상태(state)이며, 특정 기간에 걸쳐 축적된다.

① 개인적인 – 상태   ② 개인적인 – 패턴
③ 연구 – 방식   ⑤ 처리된 – 패턴

해석 정보화 시대에는 지식과 정보의 차이를 이해하는 것이 매우 중요하다. 컴퓨터로 접할 수 있는 것, 그리고 실로 학술지에 출간된 것은 정보이다. 지식은 전문가 독자의 정신 속에 구성되어야 하는 것이다. 이것이 바로 학식이 관여하는 영역이다. 오늘날 정보는 즉시 접할 수 있지만, 지식은 여전히 얻으려면 수년간의 헌신적인 연구가 필요하다. 어떤 주제에 관한 분야 전체의 전문가들이 모두 학술회의에 참석하는 동안 매우 이상한 사고로 인해 몰살되었다고 상상해 보라. 또다시 연구가 진척될 수 있도록 그 분야의 전문 지식을 복원하는 데 얼마나 오랜 시간이 걸릴까? 그들의 연구가 모두 출간되어 있다는 사실에도 불구하고 아마도 여러 해가 걸릴 것이다. 또 다른 예를 들자면, 텔레비전 프로그램용 과학 다큐멘터리의 프로듀서들은 자신들의 주제를 조사하고 있을 때 무엇을 하는가? 그들은 학술지를 읽으려 하기보다는 전문가들과 이야기를 나눈다. 매우 당연한 일인데, 그곳, 즉 학자들의 머릿속이 지식이 발견될 수 있는 유일한 곳이기 때문이다.

↓

> 정보는 다양한 출처에서 얻은 (A) 처리된 자료인 반면, 지식은 무언가를 아는 (B) 상태이며, 그것은 한 사람의 연구들에 근거를 두어 특정 기간에 걸쳐 축적된다.

구문 [11행~13행] How long would **it take to reconstruct** expertise in the field *so that* research could once again progress?
「it takes 시간 to-v」는 'v하는 데 (시간)이 걸리다'의 뜻이다. so that은 '~하기 위하여'를 의미하는 목적의 접속사이다.

[13행~15행] It would probably take many years, despite the fact that their research was all published.

밑줄 친 두 부분은 서로 동격 관계이다.

어휘 accessible 접근 가능한   scholarship 학문, 학식   dedicated 헌신적인 wipe out ~을 완전히 없애버리다   expertise 전문적 지식[기술]   journal 학술지 rightly 당연히, 마땅히   accumulate 축적하다, (서서히) 모으다

19~20 장문   19 ⑤ 20 ④

해설 19. 인간은 자신이 선택한 물건과 거부한 물건에 대해 재평가해볼 때, 자신이 선택한 물건의 가치는 부풀리고 거부한 물건에 대한 가치는 폄하하는 경향이 있다는 실험이 소개되었는데, 이 실험의 결론을 반영한 적절한 제목은 '⑤ 당신이 선택한 물건이 그렇지 않은 것보다 왜 더 가치가 큰가'가 된다.
① 결정 내리기는 자기성장에 중요하다
② 우리가 비싼 물건을 선호하는 이유에 대한 심리
③ 당신은 무엇을 가치 있게 여기는가?: 빠른 결정을 내리는 기술
④ 사람들은 물건을 소유하기를 원하기에 그것에 가치를 둔다

20. 두 개의 근접한 선택지 중에 고를 때, 미래에 다시 선택할 때 그것이 더 쉬워지려면, 당신의 선택은 선택지들 간의 차이를 더 '커' 보이게 만드는 것일 것이다. 그러므로 (d)의 smaller를 bigger로 바꿔 써야 한다.

해석 사회 심리학자 Jack Brehm은 주부들에게 커피 메이커와 토스터 같은 일련의 가정 품목들을 얼마나 좋아하는지 평가해달라고 요청했다. 각각의 여성들에게 그는 그 여성이 동등하게 매력적이라고 순위를 매긴 품목들을 가져다가, 그것들 중 하나를 집으로 가져갈 수 있다고 말했고, 그녀가 고를 수 있게 허용해주었다. 선택 이후에 각 여성은 품목들을 재평가해달라는 요청을 받았고, Brehm은 선택된 품목의 순위가 오르고 다른 것들의 순위가 (a) 떨어졌음을 발견했다.

술집에서 해볼 수 있는 종류로 이러한 경향의 간단한 증명이 있다. 컵 받침과 같은 세 개의 동일한 물건을 가져다가 그 중 두 개를 당신의 피실험자 앞에 두어라. 그에게 그것들 중 하나를 고르라고 요청해라. 일단 그가 선택하면, 선택된 물건을 넘겨주고 나서 세 번째 것을 꺼내고 이제 그에게 거부된 물건과 새 물건 간에 선택하라고 요청해라. 당신이 발견하는 경향이 있는 것은 거부된 물건의 가치가 하락했다는 것이다. 그것은 첫 번째 시기에

서 선택되지 않았던 것으로 오명을 얻었으므로 여기서의 경향은 (b) 새 물건을 선택하는 것이다. 왜 이런 일이 생기는지 정말로 아는 사람은 없다. 아마 그것은 (c) 자아 증진과 관련 있을 것이다. 우리는 우리 자신에 대하여 좋은 감정을 갖고 싶어 하므로 우리의 선택의 가치를 부풀리고 선택하지 않은 길은 폄하한다. 혹은 아마 그것은 반복되는 힘든 결정을 더 쉽게 만들기 위해 진화한 정신적 속임수일지도 모른다. 당신이 일단 두 개의 근접한 선택지 중에서 고르면, 당신의 선택은 선택지들 간의 차이를 (d) 더 작아(→ 더 커) 보이게 만들며, 그것을 미래의 더 쉬운 선택으로 만들 것이다. 세 번째 제안은 자아 인식 이론이다. 우리는 우리 자신의 선택이 다른 사람에 의하여 행해진 것처럼 평가하여, 내 자신이 B 말고 A를 선택하는 모습을 관찰할 때, 나는 누군가 다른 사람이 이러한 선택, 즉 A가 십중팔구 B보다 낫다는 선택을 한다면 내리게 될 것과 (e) 같은 결론을 내린다.

구문 [18행~19행] it is tainted by **not having been chosen** the first time around, ~
'not having been p.p.'는 주절의 시제보다 한 시제 앞서 부정의 의미와 수동의 의미를 복합적으로 가지는 동명사 형태이며 '~되지 못했던 것'의 뜻이 된다.
[31행~35행] We assess our own choices **as if** they *were done* by another person, and so when I **observe *myself* choosing** A over B, I draw *the same conclusion* [that I would (draw) if someone else made this choice — A is probably better than B].
as if는 '마치 ~인 것처럼'의 뜻의 접속사이며, 이 절에서 가정법 과거시제로 동사 were done을 사용하였다. I observe myself choosing A over B에서 주어와 주어의 행위의 대상인 목적어의 존재가 일치하므로 재귀대명사 myself를 사용하였다. 'observe O v-ing'는 '…가 ~하는 모습을 관찰하다'의 뜻이다. [ ]은 the same conclusion을 수식하며, would 다음에 draw가 생략된 것으로 볼 수 있다. [ ]절 속에는 가정법 과거인 'if S 과거동사, S would 동사원형 (…한다면 ~할 것이다) 표현이 쓰였다.

어휘 household 가정의   demonstration 증명   identical 동일한   coaster 컵 받침   subject 피실험자   hand over 넘겨주다   taint 오염시키다, 오명을 남기다 have to do with ~와 관계있다   self-enhancement 자기 고양, 자아 증진   pump up 인상하다, 증가시키다   denigrate 폄하하다   proposal 제안   self-perception 자아 인식

| 1 ⑤ | 2 ① | 3 ④ | 4 ① | 5 ② | | 6 ⑤ | 7 ③ | 8 ⑤ | 9 ③ | 10 ③ |
| 11 ④ | 12 ⑤ | 13 ④ | 14 ③ | 15 ② | | 16 ④ | 17 ③ | 18 ④ | 19 ② | 20 ⑤ |

1 심경 변화   ⑤

해설 밴드에서 원하는 자리를 얻기 위해 오디션에 참가하여 경쟁자를 이겼음을 확신했지만, 뜻하는 바를 이루지 못했다는 것을 알게 되었으므로 'I'의 심경 변화로 가장 적절한 것은 ⑤ '희망찬 → 실망한'이다.
① 차분한 → 분노한
② 우울한 → 기쁜
③ 겁에 질린 → 안도한
④ 만족한 → 후회하는

해석 7학년 때 한 번은 내가 밴드에서 세 번째 자리여서 수석 연주자 지위를 차지하고 있던 Jim에게 도전하기로 결심했다. 나는 한 곡을 계속하여 연습했고, 내가 더 높은 자리

를 차지할 가능성이 꽤 높다고 생각했다. 오디션 날에 나는 긴장했지만 내가 아는 모든 여자아이들이 나에게 행운을 빌어주고 있었고 '아, 네가 이길 거야!'라고 말해주어서 자신감이 있었다. 밴드실에 도착했을 때쯤 나는 스스로에 대해 제법 확신을 느꼈다. 나는 곡을 연주했고 몇 번 실수했지만 꽤 잘했다고 생각했다. 내가 나갈 때 Jim이 밴드실로 들어왔고, 나는 문 밖으로 그가 연주하는 소리를 들을 수 있었다. 곧 그는 실수했고 연주를 멈추었다. 이때쯤 나는 내가 '해냈다'고 확신했다. 선생님께서 마침내 방에서 나오셨을 때, 나는 선생님이 미소 지으며 나를 축하해주기를 기다렸다. 대신에 선생님께서는 말씀하셨다. "유감이구나, Lee Ann, 우린 동일한 자리 배열을 유지하기로 했다." 나는 그의 말에 어쩔 줄을 몰랐다. 나는 멍하니 클라리넷을 치우고 잠시 창밖을 바라보았다.

구문 [14행~15행] ~ I waited *for him* to smile and congratulate me.
for him은 to smile and congratulate me의 의미상 주어이다. to 다음의 동사원형 smile과 congratulate가 병렬구조를 이룬다.

어휘 over and over 계속하여, 반복하여   confident 자신감 있는, 확신하는
congratulate 축하하다   arrangement 배열   at a loss 당황하여, 어쩔 줄을 몰라
numbly 멍하게   stare 응시하다

2 필자 주장 ①

해설 회사는 과도한 업무 수행을 통하여 성과를 낸 직원들에게 어떠한 형식으로든 감사의 마음을 표해야 한다는 내용의 글이므로 필자의 주장으로 가장 적절한 것은 ①이다.

해석 사람들에 대해 인도적으로 생각할 필요는 개인뿐만 아니라 집단에도 적용된다. 나는 고객이 문제를 해결하는 것을 돕기 위해 고객의 회사에 불려갔다. 그의 회사는 팀이 두 달 동안 일주일에 7일, 하루에 거의 24시간 일할 것을 요구했던 단기 집중 개발 프로젝트를 이제 막 마친 참이었다. 그것은 대성공이었다. 그러나 한 달 뒤에 팀 구성원 중 두 명이 경쟁사에서 일하기 위해 그들의 일터를 떠났다. 왜 그런가? 내 고객은 알고 싶어 했다. 나는 그에게 출시를 기념하기 위해 회사가 무엇을 했는지 물어보았다. 그는 어리둥절하여 나를 바라보았다. 아무것도 하지 않았다고 그는 말했다. 그의 팀은 단지 그들의 보통의 근무 시간을 다시 시작했을 뿐이었다. 그토록 정신 나간 근무시간이 팀 구성원들과 그들의 가족들에게 어떤 영향을 미쳤는지 인정하기보다는, 회사는 인간적인 영향을 저버렸다. 회사는 감사와 고마움을 표현하기 위해 팀에게 휴식이나 보너스, 또는 한 달간 일주일에 하루 재택근무를 할 기회, 즉 뭐라도 정말 제공할 수도 있었을 것이다. 아무런 감사도 오지 않았을 때, 몇몇 팀 구성원들이 달아나기로 결심한 것은 놀랄 것이 없다.

구문 [1행~2행] **The need** to think about people humanely **applies** *not only* **to** individuals *but* **to** groups *as well*.
주어는 The need이고 동사는 applies이다. 'not only A but B as well'은 'A뿐만 아니라 B도'의 뜻이다. A와 B에 해당하는 자리에 applied 뒤에 이어지는 전치사 to로 시작되는 어구가 배치되어 있다.
[16행~18행] It **could have offered** the team [time off], or [a bonus], or [the chance to work at home one day a week for a month] ~
'could have p.p.'는 '~할 수 있었을 것이다'의 의미이다. 세 [ ]는 or로 연결되어 병렬구조를 이루며 offered의 직접목적어이다.

어휘 humanely 인도적으로   firm 회사   launch 개시, 출시   puzzled 어리둥절한
resume 다시 시작하다   acknowledge 인정하다   insane 미친, 정신 이상의   turn one's back on ~에게 등을 돌리다, 저버리다, 무시하다   time off 한가한 시간, 휴식
gratitude 고마움   forthcoming 다가오는

3 밑줄 함의 ④

해설 링컨은 평소 건강할 때는 많은 탄원인들로부터의 다양한 요구에 시달렸는데, 전염병에 걸리고 모든 사람들에게 일괄적으로 줄 수 있는 것(전염병)을 갖게 되자 정작 탄원인이 전염병을 두려워해 도망가게 된 상황이 아이러니하다고 할 수 있으므로 밑줄 친 부분이 의미하는 바를 상술하면 ④ '아이러니하게도 사람들은 이제 감염이 두려워 저와 접촉하지 않으려 할 겁니다.'가 된다.
① 저는 제가 지금 향유하는 특권을 다른 사람들과 공유하고 싶습니다.
② 저는 제 병이 다른 사람들에게 쉽게 옮길까 봐 걱정입니다.
③ 다행히도 저에게 오는 모든 사람들이 제게 부탁할 수 있습니다.
⑤ 제 병 때문에 사람들이 제게 부탁하러 오지 않는 일은 없을 겁니다.

해석 링컨은 알선이나 호의를 구하는 사람들에게 대단히 시달렸다. 그는 어느 날 몸이 좋지 않아서 그런 요구를 경청할 마음이 아니었다. 그러나 한 탄원인이 용케 그의 집무실로 들어왔다. 그 사람이 긴 면담을 하려고 자리를 잡고 있을 때 링컨의 의사가 들어왔다.

양손을 그에게 내밀며 링컨은 손의 반점이 무엇인지 물었다. 의사는 즉시 천연두의 가벼운 형태인 가두(경증 천연두)라는 진단을 내렸다. "제 생각에는 전염성이지요?" 링컨은 물었다. "전염성이 높죠."가 대답이었다. 방문객은 이 시점에 자리에서 일어났다. "저, 제가 지금 지체할 수가 없군요, 링컨 선생님. 전 단지 안부를 여쭈러 찾아뵌 거였습니다." 그가 말했다. "아, 서두르지 마세요." 링컨이 친절하게 말했다. "감사합니다, 선생님. 다시 찾아 뵙겠습니다." 재빨리 문으로 향하며 방문객이 말했다. 문이 뒤에서 닫히자, 링컨은 자신의 의사에게 말했다. "이 일에 대한 좋은 점은 이제 제가 모두에게 줄 수 있는 무언가를 갖게 됐다는 거네요."

구문 [6행~7행] **Holding out his hands to him**, Lincoln asked what the blotches on them were.
Holding out ~ to him은 동시상황을 나타내는 분사구문이다. 문장의 동사 asked의 목적어로 밑줄 친 간접의문문(의문사+주어+동사)이 쓰였다.
[15행~17행] As it closed behind him, Lincoln said to his physician, "A good thing about this is that I now have *something* [**that** I can give to everybody]."
[ ]는 목적격 관계대명사 that이 이끄는 관계사절로 something을 수식한다.

어휘 unwell 몸이 편치 않은; 기분이 좋지 않은   feel inclined to-v v하고 싶다
petitioner 탄원[청원]자; 원고(原告)   settle down 편안히 앉다[눕다]; 진정되다
lengthy 긴; 장황한   physician 의사   diagnose 진단하다   varioloid 가두(假痘),
경증성 천연두   contagious 전염성의   get to one's feet 일어서다   privilege 특
권; 특전   infection 감염, 전염

4 글의 주제 ①

해설 그림책은 세상을 배우려고 노력하는 아이들에게 아주 유용한 매체이며, 이미지가 범람하고 기술이 발전해 양질의 그림책을 저가로 생산할 수 있게 된 현대 사회에서 그림책은 더욱 발전된 모습으로 나오게 되었다는 내용의 글이므로 주제로 가장 적절한 것은 ① '그림책의 가치와 현저한 진보'이다.
② 그림책의 증가하는 가격에 대한 문제점
③ 책이 기술적 도구보다 우위로 갖는 장점들
④ 그림책이 어린이의 상상력을 제한하는 이유들
⑤ 어린이들이 그림책을 읽도록 돕는 것의 필요성

해석 태어날 때부터, 어린이들은 주변 세상에 대해 배우려고 노력한다. 어린 시절부터 책은 이 과업을 돕는다. 어린이가 책장의 단어를 해독하기 오래 전에 시각적 독해력이 나오기 때문에 그림이 있는 책은 자연스러운 시작점이다. 어린이가 읽을 수 있게 되기 한참 전에 그들은 그림을 따라 질문과 답변을 하고 이야기를 이해하기 위하여 필요한 정보를 종합할 수 있다. 어린 독자들에게 그림은 글에 대한 도움이 되는 단서를 계속해서 제공한다. 어른에게도 그림 하나가 천 마디 말의 가치가 있다는 말이 있다. 오늘날의 스크린과 이미지의 세상에서, 어린이들은 그림을 통해 그들의 세상을 배울 것으로 예상한다. 그리고 지난 40년에 걸친 레이저 스캐닝 기술 진보와 서적 제작의 다른 변화는 모든 페이지에 놀라운 이미지를 실은 상대적으로 비싸지 않은 책을 생산하는 것을 가능하게 했다. 많은 매력적이고 재미있는 그림책이 그 결과이다.

구문 [6행~8행] ~ they can follow the pictures / and put together *the information* [(which[that]) they need **to ask and answer** questions and **to grasp** a story].
조동사 can 뒤에 동사원형 follow와 put together가 병렬구조를 이루고 있다. [ ]는 the information을 수식하며, need의 목적어에 해당하는 목적격 관계대명사 which[that]가 생략되어 있다. [ ]절 속에서 두 to-v 부분은 '목적'의 의미를 가지는 to-v로서 병렬구조를 이룬다.
[12행~16행] And advances ~ and other changes ~ / have made **it** possible / to produce relatively inexpensive books with astonishing images on every page.

주어는 advances와 other changes가 병렬구조를 이루고 있다. made 다음의 it은 가목적어이며 밑줄 친 to-v 이하가 진목적어이다.

어휘 strive 노력하다 literacy 읽고 쓸 줄 아는 능력 decode 해독하다 put together (모아서) 만들다, 조립하다 grasp 이해하다 cue 단서, 실마리 a wealth of 수많은, 풍부한 [**선택지 어휘**] gadget (작고 유용한) 도구, 장치

5 글의 제목 ②

해설 과학 소통과 스토리텔링은 배타적이라기보다는 인간의 노력을 강조하고 투명성을 증진시켜주는 동맹적인 관계가 될 수 있다는 내용의 글이므로 제목으로 가장 적절한 것은 ② '스토리텔링: 과학 정보 전달을 위한 강력한 도구'이다.
① 과학의 이야기는 설득이 아니라 정보를 주려 한다
③ 개별 이야기가 데이터 모음보다 더 설득력 있다
④ 스토리텔링은 과학 연구의 객관성을 위태롭게 한다
⑤ 효과적인 과학 발표: 강연자가 아닌 스토리텔러가 되어라

해석 이야기는 과학을 잘못 표현하는 데 사용될 수 있다. '과학적 결과의 스토리텔링에 반대한다'는 제목의 기사에서 Yarden Katz는 이야기의 어떤 결정적인 특징들이 과학 연구의 핵심적인 이상 및 관행과 상반된다고 설명한다. 그러나 신뢰할 수 있는 과학 소통과 스토리텔링이 상호 배타적인 것은 아니다. 그것들은 훌륭한 동맹이 될 수 있다. 실험 결과의 직선적인 소통과는 대조적으로, 개별 연구 이야기를 들려주는 것은 과학을 인간이 주도하는 노력으로 묘사하며, (그것은) 성공, 불확실성, 실수와 실패로 가득하므로 이는 결과적으로 투명성을 증진시킨다. 진정으로 중요한 것은 무슨 이야기가 들려지고 있고 누가 하고 있느냐이다. 예를 들어 기후 변화에 관한 정부 간 협의체(IPCC)는 그것의 연구 결과들로 광범위한 이해 당사자들의 관심을 사로잡으려고 스토리텔링을 이용한다. IPCC는 이야기식의 접근법과 최신 과학으로 정책 입안에 중립적으로 영향을 미쳐야 하는 자신의 임무 간에 어떠한 갈등도 인지하지 못한다.

구문 [7행~12행] In contrast with straight communication of experimental results, / **telling individual research stories portrays** science **as** a human-driven endeavour, / full of successes, uncertainties, missteps and failures, // **which** in turn promotes transparency.
telling ~ stories가 동명사 주어이고 portrays가 동사이다. 「portray A as B」는 'A를 B로 묘사하다'의 뜻이다. full of ~ failures는 앞에 being이 생략된 분사구문이다. which는 앞 문장 전체를 가리킨다.
[16행~19행] The IPCC perceives no conflict / **between** a narrative approach **and** its mandate (to neutrally inform policymaking with the latest science).
「between A and B (A와 B 사이에)」 구문이 쓰였다. ( )는 its mandate를 수식한다.

어휘 misrepresent 잘못 표현하다 narrative 이야기[식의], 서술 antithetical 정반대의, 상반되는 mutually 상호간에, 서로 exclusive 배타적인 ally 동맹자, 동맹국 portray 묘사하다, 그리다 endeavo(u)r 노력 misstep 실수 transparency 투명도 engage (관심을) 사로잡다, (주목을) 끌다 stakeholder 이해 당사자 mandate 임무; 권한; 명령 neutrally 중립적으로 inform 영향을 미치다; 알리다 policymaking 정책 입안

6 안내문 불일치 ⑤

해설 타이머를 작동하면 1시간 후 5번의 삐 소리가 나고 다시 1시간 후 삐 소리가 1번 나면서 자동으로 꺼진다고 했으므로 2시간 후 자동으로 꺼지는 것이다. 그러므로 ⑤가 내용과 일치하지 않는다.

해석 LED 탁상 램프
시작하기
– 금속 받침을 테이블 윗면에 놓고 제어판 박스를 금속 받침 홈(투입구)에 삽입하십시오.
– 전원 플러그를 올바르게 전선이 연결된 콘센트에 삽입하십시오.

제어판 버튼 작동하기
• 전원 터치 버튼
– 녹색 LED 버튼이 켜지면서 램프가 꺼집니다.
– 안전 및 에너지 절약을 위해 10시간 사용 후에는 램프가 자동으로 꺼집니다.

• 밝기 터치 버튼
– 제어판의 LED 장치에 표시된 대로 5단계로 밝기가 있습니다.
– 다음번에 탁상 램프를 켜면 마지막으로 사용한 밝기 수준으로 사용됩니다.

• 타이머 터치 버튼(타이머 기능이 켜지면 파란색 LED 버튼이 켜짐)
– 한 시간이 지나면 5번의 삐 소리를 냅니다. 또 한 시간이 지나면 삐 소리가 한 번 나면서 탁상 램프가 자동으로 꺼집니다.

구문 [3행~5행] **Place** the metal base on the surface of the table and then **insert** the control panel box into the metal-based slot.
동사 원형으로 시작하는 명령문으로 두 개의 동사 Place와 insert가 병렬구조를 이루고 있다.
[17행~18행] *The next time* [(when[that]) the desk lamp is switched to ON], the last-used brightness level is used.
생략된 관계부사 when[that]이 이끄는 [ ]가 The next time을 수식한다.

어휘 start up 시작하다, 시작되다 insert 삽입하다, 끼워 넣다 control panel 제어반(盤), 조작반 slot (무엇을 집어넣도록 만든 가느다란) 구멍[홈] wire 전선을 연결하다, 배선하다 electrical outlet 콘센트 indicate 가리키다 beep 삐 소리를 내다

7 밑줄 어법 ③

해설 ③ to prove의 목적어절에서 주어는 people이고 whose land disappeared가 명사 people을 수식하기 때문에 동사가 필요하고, 문장의 시제가 과거이므로 complaining은 과거 동사 complained로 바꾸어 써야 적절하다.
① whose 뒤에 완전한 문장이 나오고, 의미상 '자신의 땅'이라는 소유관계이므로 소유격 관계대명사 whose의 쓰임이 적절하다.
② 앞에 나온 내용을 보충하는 분사구이다.
④ 과거분사로 앞에 나온 명사 the land를 수식한다.
⑤ that 이하절이 완전한 문장이고, warning에 대한 부연 설명이 이어지므로 동격의 접속사 that의 쓰임은 적절하다.

해석 1900년대 초반에 영국에서 자신의 땅이 파도 작용으로 침식되고 있는 토지 소유자들이 정부에게 예방 조처를 하라고 아우성쳤다. 그들의 섬이 바다 밑으로 사라지고 있었다! 그들이 너무나도 시끄럽게 주장해서 왕립위원회가 그 문제를 조사하도록 임명되었다. 주의 깊은 조사 후, 그 위원회는 35년 동안 잉글랜드와 웨일스에서 4,692에이커가 사라지고 35,444에이커가 생겨서 1년에 거의 900에이커의 순증가가 발생했다고 보고했다. 이 조사 결과는 땅이 사라진 사람들이 땅이 증가하고 있는 사람들보다 더 큰 소리로 불평했다는 점을 입증하는 것처럼 보였다. 그러나 잃어버린 땅은 아마도 극적으로 사라진 탁 트인 해변의 멋진 절벽 부지였던 반면 얻은 땅은 저지대의 모래땅이며 별로 가치가 없었다는 점이 인정되어야 한다. 지질학자가 아닌 사람들은 그 변화가 매우 천천히 일어나는 듯해도 절벽의 존재 자체가 침식작용이 일어나고 있다는 경고라는 것을 보통 인식하지 못한다.

구문 [5행~6행] They argued **so** loudly **that** a Royal Commission was appointed to study the matter.

'너무 …해서 ~하다'를 의미하는 「so ... that ~」 구문이 사용되었다.

[13행~17행] It must be admitted, however, **that** the land lost probably was *good cliffland on the open coast* [which disappeared in a spectacular way], whereas the land gained was low, sandy and not particularly valuable].

It은 가주어이고 that 이하가 진주어이다. [ ] 부분은 주격 관계대명사가 이끄는 관계사절로 앞에 나온 good cliffland on the open coast를 수식한다.

어휘 property 토지, 부동산   preventive 예방의   Royal Commission 왕립위원회 ((영국에서 특정 법률의 검토·개정·도입을 논의하기 위한 정부 자문 위원회))   appoint 임명[지명]하다   prove 입증하다   cliffland 절벽인 땅   open (사방이) 탁 트인; 막혀[둘러싸여] 있다   geologist 지질학자   erosional 침식의; 부식의

8 밑줄 어휘   ⑤

해설 근원암을 떠나 주위 암석을 통과해 이동하던 석유와 가스가 침투할 수 없는 암석을 만나 더 이상 이동하지 못하고 상대적으로 가벼운 가스가 석유 위에, 그리고 암석 아래에 있는 상황이다. 그 암석은 밀폐 부분을 구성하므로 추가적인 이동을 가속화한다는 것은 문맥상 적절하지 않으므로 ⑤의 accelerates는 prevents 등이 되어야 적절하다.

해석 일단 형성되고 나면, 석유와 천연가스는 반드시 그것들의 원천인 근원암(根源巖)에 갇힌 채로 있는 것은 아니다. 대신 그것들은 주위 암석의 압력 차이에 반응하여 ① 이동할 수 있다. 그러기 위해서, 근원암에는 석유와 가스가 이동할 수 있는 경로를 만드는 미세한 작은 구멍이 있어야 한다. 만약 근원암의 ② 결이 너무 고우면, 그러면 석유 물질은 근원암 내부에 갇힌 채로 남는다. 종종 석유 근원암 위의 암석은 물에 흠뻑 젖는데, 이 경우에 가스와 석유는 둘 다 물보다 가벼워서 ③ 위로 올라간다. 그 결과, 일반적인 이동 경로는 위쪽 또는 옆쪽이며, 그것은 석유와 가스가 침투할 수 없는 암석 형태의 장벽, 즉 더 멀리 이동하기 위해 필요한 작은 구멍과 통로를 포함하기에 너무 ④ 밀도가 높은 암석과 마주칠 때까지 계속된다. 가스는 석유보다 가볍기 때문에, 그것은 석유층 위에, 그리고 밀폐 부분을 구성하여 추가적인 이동을 ⑤ 가속화하는(→ 막는) 침투할 수 없는 암석 바로 아래에 축적된다.

구문 [1행~2행] **Once formed**, oil and natural gas do not necessarily stay trapped in the source rocks of their origin.

Once formed는 분사구문의 뜻을 분명히 하기 위해 분사 앞에 접속사 Once를 그대로 둔 경우이다.

[4행~6행] To do so, the source rock must have *tiny pores* [that create *pathways* (**for the oil and gas** to travel)].

[ ] 부분은 관계사절로 선행사 tiny pores를 수식하고, ( ) 부분은 앞에 있는 명사 pathways를 수식하는 형용사구로 to부정사의 의미상 주어는 'for+명사'로 쓴다.

어휘 trap 가두다; 함정   source rock 근원암   differential 차이, 격차   pathway 경로, 진로   fine-grained 결이 고운   petroleum 석유   ascend (위로) 올라가다   barrier 장벽; 장애물   impermeable (액체·기체를) 통과시키지 않는   dense 조밀한, 빽빽한   accumulate 축적되다, 늘어나다   constitute 구성하다; 설립하다   seal 밀폐[밀봉] 부분

9 빈칸 추론   ③

해설 빈칸은 모든 종류의 과학에 꼭 필요한 것을 묻고 있다. 의사가 자신의 전반적 지식을 적용할지라도 같은 종류의 모든 가능한 경우들에 공통이 되는 것을 알아야 한다고 했고, 한 명의 환자에 대해서만 연구를 할 경우 다른 환자가 생겼을 때 속수무책인 상태가 된다는 의사의 예를 통해서 빈칸에는 ③ '보편성'이 가장 적절하다.

------

① 인과 관계 ② 증거 ④ 상상 ⑤ 실용성

해석 보편성이 없으면 어떤 종류의 과학도 결코 있을 수 없다. 개체는 그 자체일 뿐이고 어떤 다른 것도 설명할 수 없다. 그것은 심지어 자신을 설명할 수조차 없다! 비록 한 의사가 자신의 전반적인 지식을 특정 환자에게 적용한다 할지라도, 그녀는 같은 종류의 모든 가능한 경우들에 공통이 되는 것을 알아야만 한다. 그녀가 의과 대학에서 한 명의, 그것도 오직 유일한 한 명의 환자만을 연구하면서 4년을 보낸다고 상상해 보라. 그녀는 자신이 치료해야 할 유일한 환자가 그 한 가지 경우라면 괜찮을 것이다. 하지만 다른 환자가 진료실로 걸어 들어오자마자 무슨 일이 일어날지를 상상해 보라. 그녀는 새로운 신체를 다루는 데 있어서 완전히 속수무책일 것이고 자신의 업무를 포기하거나 다른 사례들에 관하여 배우기 위해 의과 대학으로 되돌아가야 할 것이다.

구문 [8행~10행] She **would be** fine // **if** *the only patient* [she ever had to treat] **were** that one case.

가정법 과거 문장으로, if절 내에서 [ ]가 the only patient를 수식하며 주절의 동사는 would be, if절의 동사는 were가 쓰였다.

어휘 individual 개인, 개체   apply 적용하다   case 사례, 환자   helpless 속수무책인, 무력한   practice (의사 등 전문직 종사자의) 업무

10 빈칸 추론   ③

해설 Marc Bloch는 지형학이 사회적, 경제적, 정치적 구조와 같은 다양한 현상에 대한 통찰력을 제공하고 농지 형태를 공부하는 것은 그 농지를 만든 사회에 대한 통찰력을 제공한다고 했다. 또한 그가 학생들을 농촌 지역으로 현장 학습을 데려갔을 때 그 관련성을 입증했다는 말로 보아, 빈칸에는 ③ '인간과 토양의 활기찬 상호 작용'이 들어가야 가장 적절하다.

① 시간이 흐르며 점진적인 지리적 변화
② 농지 보전을 위한 노력
④ 토양 보전과 개발의 딜레마
⑤ 생산적인 농업 시스템을 위한 노력

해석 1936년 파리의 Sorbonne 대학교로 옮겨 가기 전인, 1920년대와 1930년대에 Strasbourg 대학교의 중세사 교수로서 Marc Bloch는 학생들에게 풍경을 역사적 기록으로 여기라고 장려했다. 작성된 글이 의식적인 역사 과정에 대한 하나의 관점을 제공한다면, 지형학은 사회적, 경제적, 그리고 정치적 구조와 같은 무의식적이고 눈에 보이지 않는 현상에 대한 가치 있는 통찰력을 제공한다고 그는 말했다. Bloch는 농촌 역사를 인간과 토양의 활기찬 상호 작용으로 묘사했다. 그는 비행기에서 목격된 농지 형태를 공부하는 것은 그것들을 만든 사회에 대한 통찰력을 제공한다고 주장했다. Bloch는 자신이 북유럽 전체의 특징으로 여겼던 Alsace의 길게 늘어진 농지를 볼 수 있도록 학생들을 Strasbourg 근처의 농촌 지역으로 현장 학습을 데려갔을 때 이 관련성을 입증했다. Bloch에 따르면, 역사학과 학생들은 여전히 매우 생생하게 살아 있는 역사 과정을 바라봄으로써 역사 과정을 가장 잘 이해할 수 있었다.

구문 [5행~9행] If written texts provided a view into conscious historical processes, **topography**, (he suggested), **provided** valuable insight into *phenomena* [**that** were unconscious and invisible, such as social, economic, and political structure].

주절의 주어 topography와 동사 provided 사이에 he suggested가 삽입되었다. [ ] 부분은 관계대명사 that이 이끄는 형용사절로 phenomena를 수식한다.

[11행~13행] Studying the form of agricultural fields as seen from an airplane, (he contended), provided insight into *the society* [that had produced them].

Studying the form ~ airplane은 문장의 주어 역할을 하는 동명사구이다. ( ) 부분은 주어 동사 사이에 삽입된 절이다. [ ] 부분은 관계사절로 the society를 수식하며 밑줄 친 them은 agricultural fields를 가리키는 대명사이다.

어휘 medieval 중세의 view 관점, 견해; 조망 insight 통찰력 phenomenon(*pl.* phenomena) 현상 rural 농촌의; 시골의 vibrant 활기찬; 선명한 contend (강력히) 주장하다 demonstrate 입증[증명]하다 characteristic 특징 gradual 점진적인, 단계적인 exploitation 개발, 개척; 착취 struggle 노력

11 빈칸 추론 ④

해설 실험 참가자들은 더 긴 숫자를 암기해야 했을 때 다이어트 중이었음에도 불구하고 샐러드보다 초콜릿 케이크를 선택하는 경우가 증가했는데, 이는 두뇌를 활발하게 쓰고 있을 때는 이성적이고 신중한 결정을 내리기가 어려워진다는 점을 암시한다. 따라서 연구자들이 내린 결론은 지력을 더 많이 사용하는 사람들은 ④ '품목을 신중하게 고려할 가용 지력을 덜 가지고 있었다'로 정리할 수 있다.
① 그들의 절대적인 한계를 넘어서 정신력을 북돋웠다
② 건강에 좋지 않은 음식을 먹으려는 충동에 잠재의식적으로 저항했다
③ 내재적 보상을 얻는 데 완전히 전념했다
⑤ 더 많은 식사를 하고자 하는 충동에 맞서 싸우도록 격려를 받았다

해석 심리학자 Baba Shiv와 Alexander Fedorikhin은 사람들이 생각할 것이 적은 때와 비교하여 사람들의 인지 체계가 점유되어있을 때 내리는 결정의 종류를 보는 실험을 개발했다. 이 연구에서 다이어트 중인 165명의 참가자들은 두 자리 수 혹은 일곱 자리 수를 암기하라는 요청을 받았다. 잠깐 숫자를 보게 된 후에 그들은 그것을 암기한 다음 간식을 고르라는 요청을 받았는데, 그것(= 간식)은 실험에 참가한 데 대한 보상으로 되어있었다. 참가자들은 초콜릿 케이크 한 조각이나 샐러드 중 하나를 골라야 했다. 두 자리 숫자를 암기해야 했던 다이어터들 중 41퍼센트는 초콜릿 케이크를 고른 반면에 일곱 자리 숫자를 암기한 사람들 중 63퍼센트가 초콜릿 케이크를 골랐는데, 이는 22퍼센트 포인트 증가한 것이다. 일곱 자리 숫자를 암기해야 했던 사람들은 자신의 결정이 자신의 이성적이고 신중한 면보다 감정적이고 충동적인 면의 영향을 더 많이 받았다고 말했다. 연구자들은 더 긴 숫자를 암기한 집단에게는 품목을 신중하게 고려할 가용 지력을 덜 가지고 있었다는 결론을 내렸다.

구문 [1행~5행] Psychologists Baba Shiv and Alexander Fedorikhin / developed *an experiment* [that looked at the kind of *decisions* [(which[that]) people make // when their cognitive systems are occupied, / compared to when they have less to think about]].
that looked ~ about은 an experiment를 수식한다. people ~ about은 앞에 목적격 관계대명사 which[that]가 생략되어 decisions를 수식한다.

어휘 cognitive 인식[인지]의 occupy 점유하다, 차지하다; 전념하다 digit (0에서 9까지의) 숫자 impulsive 충동적인 rational 이성적인 prudent 신중한 subconsciously 잠재의식적으로, 반 무의식적으로 be committed to ~에 전념하다 intrinsic 내재적인; 고유한 impulse 충동

12 빈칸 추론 ⑤

해설 언어는 시대 특정적이며, 현대 언어의 틀에서 과거의 단어를 해석하면 의미에 오염이 될 수 있으므로 단어는 그 시대적 맥락에 맞추어 의미를 고민해봐야 한다는 내용의 글이다. 그러므로 역사가들이 언어로부터 효과적으로 의미를 추출하기 위해 그들(역사가들)이 ⑤ '이러한 단어들이 그 시대적 맥락에서 기능하던 방식에 대한 명확한 생각을 가지는 것이 필수적이다'가 된다.
① 언어가 역사적 맥락에서 문법을 발달시키는 방식
② 자신들이 단어의 현재 의미를 이해하는 방식
③ 인간들이 언어 기반 문화를 발전시켜온 방식
④ 과거가 역사가의 정신 속에서 재창조되는 방식

해석 언어는 종종 시대 특정적이며 역사가들은 과거 시대에 현대의 정의를 부여함으로써 의미를 오염시키지 않도록 극도로 조심해야 한다. 단어들은 과거에 현대 용법과 매우 다른 특정 의미나 용법을 갖고 있었을지도 모른다. 게다가 현대 영어에도 그 자체의 특수 용어와 관용어구가 있는 것과 꼭 마찬가지로, 그것들은 과거에도 존재했다. 예를 들어 아이콘이라는 단어의 역사적인 사용은 종교적 함의를 가지겠지만, 반면에 21세기에 그 단어는 종종 컴퓨터 바탕화면에 나와 있는 클릭할 수 있는 이미지와 연관될 것이다. 옥스퍼드 영어 사전이나 다른 어원사전을 참조용으로 가까이 두는 것은 연구자들이 이러한 형태의 잠재적 오역을 피하도록 도와줄 것이다. 이것은 단어들이 전달할지도 모르는 불안정성과 때로는 정해지지 않은 의미 때문에 특히 중요하다. 역사가들이 언어로부터 효과적으로 정확한 의미를 추출하기 위하여, 그들이 이러한 단어들이 그 시대적 맥락 내에서 기능하던 방식에 대한 명확한 생각을 가지는 것이 필수적이다.

구문 [6행~8행] Further, **just as** modern English has its own *jargon and idioms, they* were also present in the past.
'just as'는 '~한 것과 꼭 마찬가지로'의 뜻이다. they는 jargon and idioms를 지칭한다.
[12행~15행] [Having the *Oxford English Dictionary* or another etymological dictionary close at hand for reference] **will help *researchers* avoid** this form of potential misinterpretation.
[ ]가 동명사 주어이며 동사는 will help이다. 'help O 동사원형 (…가 ~하는 것을 돕다)' 구문이 사용되었다.
[17행~19행] In order *for historians* **to extract** precise meaning **from** language effectively, ~.
for historians는 to extract의 의미상 주어이다. 'extract A from B'는 'A를 B로부터 추출하다'의 뜻이다.

어휘 cautious 조심스러운 read ... into ~ (지나치게) ~에 …의 의미를 부여하다 corrupt 부패하게 만들다; 오염시키다 usage 용법 idiom 관용구 icon 성상, (컴퓨터 화면의) 아이콘 connotation 함축, 내포 close at hand 가까운 곳에 reference 참고, 참조 misinterpretation 오해, 오역 instability 불안정성 open-ended 제약을 두지 않은 extract 추출하다

13 흐름 무관 문장 ④

해설 우리가 개인적 행복의 설정값을 바꾸기 쉽지 않은 이유가 유전자에 의해 강하게 영향을 받기 때문이라는 내용인 것에 반해, ④는 유전 과학과 기술의 발달로 인해 가능해진 것을 서술하고 있으므로 글의 흐름과 무관하다.

해석 우리들 각자는 특정한 장기적 기질에 그대로 머물러있는 경향이 있다. 즉, 우리는 바꾸기 쉽지 않은 개인적 행복의 설정값을 가지고 있는 것 같다. ① 사실, 개인적인 행복은 다른 성격의 특성들처럼 우리의 유전자에 강하게 영향을 받는 것처럼 보인다. ② 연구들은 일란성 쌍둥이들이 이란성 쌍둥이나 다른 형제자매들보다 똑같은 수준의 행복을 보일 가능성이 현저하게 더 많다는 것을 보여 준다. ③ 행동 유전학자들은 유전자가 얼마나 많이 중요한지 가늠하기 위하여 이 연구들을 사용해 왔고, 그들의 최적의 추측은 장기적인 행복의 50%가 사람의 유전적 설정값에 좌우된다는 것이다. ④ 오늘날, 유전 과학과 기술의 발달은 우리가 우리 신체 내에서의 유전자 활동에 대해 분석할 수 있도록 해주었다. ⑤ 물론 우리가 삶에서 경험하는 것은 일정 기간 동안 우리의 기분을 바꿀 수 있겠지만, 대부분의 경우 이러한 변화들은 일시적이다.

구문 [5행~8행] Studies demonstrate // that identical twins are significantly more likely to exhibit the same level of happiness / than **are fraternal twins or other siblings**.
than 이하 절은 도치된 형태로 주어는 fraternal twins or other siblings이고 동사는 are이다.

----

14 글의 순서   ③

해설 주어진 글에서 산업용 로봇은 꽉 짜인 공연을 수행하는 눈 먼 배우와 같다고 했는데, (B)의 '정확한 타이밍과 위치 선정(precise timing and positioning)'이 꽉 짜인 공연이 비유하는 바이므로 주어진 글 다음에는 (B)가 나온다. 로봇이 2차원의 시각 능력만 갖고 있다는 내용의 (B) 다음에는 이를 상술하여 로봇에게는 깊이를 인지하는 능력이 없다는 내용의 (C)가 나온다. 그리하여 로봇에게 모든 일을 맡길 수 없고 인간에게 일이 남겨진다는 (C) 다음에는 인간이 기계간의 틈을 메꾸는 일을 맡는다는 내용의 (A)가 나온다. (A)의 these are jobs에서의 these는 (C) 끝부분의 '인간을 위해 남겨진 일(routine factory jobs have been left for people)'을 지칭한다.

해석 산업용 로봇은 속도, 정밀성과 완력의 무적의 조합을 제공하지만, 대개는 꽉 짜인 공연의 눈 먼 배우들이다.
(B) 그들은 정확한 타이밍과 위치 선정에 주로 의존한다. 로봇들이 기계 시야 능력을 갖고 있는 소수의 경우에 그들은 단지 2차원으로만 그리고 통제된 조명 환경에서만 일반적으로 볼 수 있다.
(C) 예를 들어, 그들은 평평한 표면에서는 부품을 고를 수 있을지 모르지만, 그들의 시야에서 깊이를 인지하는 능력은 없어서 이로 인해 어떠한 유의미한 정도로도 예측 불가능한 환경에 대해서는 허용 범위가 낮아진다. 그 결과 많은 틀에 박힌 공장 일이 인간들에게 남겨졌다.
(A) 많은 경우에 이것은 기계간의 틈을 메꾸는 것과 관련된 일이고, 혹은 생산 과정의 끝 지점에 위치하게 된다. 사례로는 통에서 부품을 고른 후 그것을 다음 기계에 투입하는 일, 혹은 제품을 공장으로 보내고 공장에서 받아오는 트럭에 짐을 싣고 내리는 일을 들 수 있다.

구문 [12행~15행] In the minority of *cases* [where robots have machine vision capability], / they can typically see in just two dimensions [and] only in controlled lighting conditions.
[ ]는 cases를 수식하는 관계부사절이다. 두 밑줄 부분은 모두 전치사 in이 있는 전치사구이며 and로 연결되어 병렬구조를 이룬다.
[16행~20행] They might, for example, be able to select parts from a flat surface, / but *an inability* (to perceive depth in their field of view) **results in** a low tolerance for *environments* [that are **to any meaningful degree** unpredictable].
but 다음의 an inability ~ view가 주어이고 동사는 results in이며 그 뒤에 결과가 제시된다. [ ]는 environments를 수식하는 관계사절이다. to a degree는 '어느 정도로'의 의미이며 to any meaningful degree는 '어떤 유의미한 정도로'의 뜻이다.

어휘 unrivaled 무적의   precision 정밀(성)   brute strength 완력   for the most part 대개, 보통   part 부품   bin 통   load 싣다   unload (짐을) 내리다   two dimensions 이차원   lighting 조명   field of view 시야

15 글의 순서   ②

해설 주어진 글에는 영장류가 텃세를 강하게 주장할 거라는 통념이 있었지만, 실제로 영장류를 관찰하면 그렇지 않다는 내용이 나온다. 이로 인해 갈등이 존재하지만, 대부분은 갈등을 최소화한다는 내용의 (B)가 이어지고 그렇다 해도 갈등은 존재한다는 내용의 (A)가 그다음에 나온다. 다만 이러한 갈등이 부상 혹은 죽음을 초래할 정도로 심각해지는 경우는 거의 없고 나름의 갈등 해결 전략이 통용된다는 내용의

(C)가 마지막으로 나온다. (A)의 This는 '영장류가 같은 시간 같은 장소에 함께 있는 것을 피하여 갈등을 최소화한다'는 (B)의 내용을 지칭하고, (C)의 These conflicts는 (A)에 나온 울부짖고 소리치고 싸우는 행위를 지칭한다.

해석 대부분의 초기 영장류 연구들은 영장류가 고도로 텃세를 부리는 습성을 가졌고 영장류 집단은 그들의 영역을 지키기 위해 싸울 것이라고 가정했다. 우리는 이제 대부분의 영장류들이 이른바 '텃세를 부리는 습성이 있는' 것이 아니라는 것을 아는데, 왜냐하면 영장류들이 사용하는 영역이 같은 종의 다른 집단들이 사용하는 영역과 겹치기 때문이다.
(B) 공간에 대한 갈등은 존재하며, (항상 그렇지는 않지만) 대부분의 경우 같은 종의 집단들은 같은 시간에 같은 장소에 있는 것을 피하는 경향이 있다. 연구자들은 이것이 집단 간 갈등의 위험을 최소화하기 위한 방법이라고 주장해 왔다.
(A) 이것이 만약 어떤 사람이 영장류를 관찰하는 데 충분한 시간을 가진다면, 그 사람이 두 집단이 경쟁적인 영역에 함께 와서 서로에게 크게 과시하는 것, 즉 엄청나게 울부짖고 큰 소리를 내며, 아마 심지어 싸우기도 하는 것을 볼 수 없다는 이야기는 아니다.
(C) 이러한 충돌은 심각한 부상이나 죽음을 초래할 수 있지만, 그런 일은 거의 없다. 집단 내에서 그렇듯, 집단 간 갈등도 협상이나 회피 등을 통해 흔히 해결된다. 혹은 그저 달아나는 것을 통해서도 해결된다. 집단 간의 심한 폭력과 공격은 드물며 죽음을 초래하는 경우는 좀처럼 일어나지 않는다.

구문 [7행~10행] This is not to say that if one **spends** *enough time* **watching** primates // she won't **see** *two groups* **coming together over a contested area** and **putting on a big show for each other** ~.
「spend (시간) v-ing」는 'v하는 데 (시간)을 쓰다'의 뜻이다. 지각동사 see가 「see O v-ing (O가 v하고 있는 것을 보다)」의 형태로 사용되었으며, 목적격보어로 'coming ~ area'와 'putting ~ each other'가 병렬구조를 이룬다.
[17행~18행] These conflicts can result in serious injury or death but **rarely do**.
do는 대동사로, rarely do는 'rarely result in serious injury or death'를 함축한다.

어휘 primate 영장류   territorial 텃세권을 주장하는; 영토의   *cf.* territory 영역, 세력권; 영토   overlap 겹치다   put on a show 치장하다, 가장하다   resolve 해결하다   via ~을 통하여   negotiation 협상   avoidance 회피, 도피   aggression 공격(성)

16 문장 넣기   ④

해설 주어진 문장의 '이러한 종류의 업계에 있는 사람들'은 앞서 언급된 회계사와 간호사를 지칭하므로 주어진 문장은 두 직업이 언급된 ③ 이후에 와야 한다. ③ 바로 뒤 문장에서 기술된 '더 높은 수준의 사고력'을 상술한 것이 주어진 문장에 기술된 능력(아는 지식을 새로운 상황에 적용하는 능력)이며, ④ 다음의 문장은 In addition으로 시작되어 고급 수준의 사고력의 두 번째 특징(판단과 결정의 기준이 되어 줌)이 기술되어 있으므로, 주어진 문장은 이 두 문장의 사이인 ④에 위치해야 한다.

해석 매년 전국 대학 고용주 협회는 고용주들에게 대학 졸업생들이 어떤 능력을 갖고 있기를 바라는지 묻는다. 매년 그 목록의 맨 위 혹은 그 근처에는 일종의 비판적 사고력인 '분석적 추론'이 있다. 그러나 회계학 전공자들은 물을지도 모른다. "수학적 기술과 사업 기술이 회계사로서의 경력에 더욱 중요하지 않습니까?" 마찬가지로, 간호학 전공자들은 의학 지식이 그들에게 더 중요하다고 말할지도 모른다. 회계사와 간호사는 이러한 기술들을 분명히 필요로 하지만, 그들은 또한 더 높은 수준의 사고력을 완전히 전부 갖추고 있어야 한다. 이러한 종류의 업계에 있는 사람들은 그들의 지식을 새로운 상황에 적용해 봄으로써 어려운 문제를 해결할 준비가 되어 있어야 한다. 게다가 그들은 새로운 생각 중 어떤 것은 받아들이고 어떤 것은 거부할지 결정할 수 있어야 하며 그들의 결정을 정당화할 수 있어야 한다. 어떤 특정한 날에 이 직종의, 그리고 여러분이 대학 졸업 후 고려할 수도 있는 대부분의 직종들에 있는 사람들은 비판적 사고력을 효과적으로 사용할 수 있어야 한다.

구문 [6행~8행] At or near the top of that list each year **is "*analytical reasoning,*"** a kind of critical thinking skill.

동사는 is이고 주어는 "analytical reasoning"인 도치구문이다. "analytical reasoning"과 a kind of critical thinking skill은 동격 관계이다.

[18행~21행] On any given day, / **people** in these careers, and *most of the careers* [(which[that]) you may be considering after college], / **must be able to** effectively use critical thinking skills.

주어는 people이고 동사는 must be able to이다. [ ]는 앞에 목적격 관계대명사 which[that]가 생략되어 most of the careers를 수식한다.

어휘 apply A to B A를 B에 적용하다 **analytical** 분석적인 **reasoning** 추론 **accounting** 회계학 **accountant** 회계사 **nursing** 간호학 **complement** 보충(하다) **high-order** 높은 수준의 **given** 특정한

17 문장 넣기 ③

해설 인간이 인지, 기억, 감정을 통제하는 데에는 한계가 있지만 인지, 기억, 감정에 기반을 둔 행동을 통제할 수 있는 재량권은 그보다 훨씬 폭넓다는 주제의 글이다. ③의 앞부분에서는 인지, 기억, 감정 통제의 어려움을 서술하고 ③ 이후로는 행동 통제의 가능성을 논하고 있으므로, However로 시작하며 행동에 가하는 통제력은 엄청나게 더 크다는 내용의 주어진 문장은 ③에 위치해야 한다.

해석 우리가 인지하고 기억하고 감정을 여과 없이 드러내는 능력을 통제하는 데에는 어떤 구체적인 한계가 있고, 그것은 그 자체로 이러한 능력이 통제를 행하는 과정과 근본적으로 분리되어있음의 표시이다. 예를 들어 색맹인 사람은 절대로 색을 올바르게 보기 시작하기로 결정할 수 없다. 기억력이 나쁜 나이 든 사람은 절대로 기억하기 시작하려고 결정할 수 없다. 자신이 해친 사람들에게 공감을 느끼지 못하는 소시오패스는 절대로 공감을 느끼기 시작하려고 결정할 수 없다. 그러나 우리가 우리의 인지, 기억, 감정에 기반을 두고 하는 행동에 가하는 통제는 엄청나게 더 크다. 일단 색맹인 사람이 자신이 빨간색과 녹색을 둘 다 녹색으로 본다는 것을 알게 되면, 그는 자신의 행동이 자신이나 다른 사람들을 위험에 빠뜨리지 않는 것을 확실히 하기 위해 조치를 취할 수 있다. 예를 들어 빨간 신호등과 녹색 신호등이 그에게 동일하게 보일지라도, 그는 사고를 일으키지 않는 것을 확실히 하기 위해 신호등의 위치(빨간색은 위, 녹색은 아래)를 암기할 수 있다. 그는 지각 결손을 교정하기 위해 집행적 과정을 이용할 수 있다.

구문 [1행~3행] However, our control over *the actions* [(which[that]) we take / on the basis of <u>our perceptions, memories,</u> and emotions] **is** vastly greater.

our control ~ emotions가 주어이고 is가 동사이다. [ ]는 앞에 목적격 관계대명사 which[that]가 생략되어 the actions를 수식한다. 전치사 of의 목적어로 쓰인 our perceptions, memories, emotions는 병렬구조를 이룬다.

[13행~16행] **Once** the color-blind person knows // **that** he <u>sees</u> **both** red **and** green <u>as</u> green, // he can take steps to ensure // **that** his actions do not endanger himself or others.

접속사 Once는 '일단 ~하면'의 뜻이다. 두 개의 that절이 각각 동사 knows와 ensure의 목적어로 쓰였다. knows 다음의 that절에서 「see A as B (A를 B로 보다)」와 「both A and B (A와 B 둘 다)」 구문이 쓰였다.

어휘 on the basis of ~을 기반으로 **concrete** 구체적인 **empathy** 공감 **take steps** 조치를 취하다 **executive** 집행의 *cf.* executive processing 집행적 과정((인지와 관련된 집행 과정을 통제하는 능력)) **deficit** 결손, 장애

18 요약문 완성 ④

해설 돈을 책상 구석에 둔 채로 실험에 참여한 학생들은 어려운 과제를 수행할 때 도움을 청한 비율이 현저히 낮았던 것으로 보아, 남에게 의지하지 않고 독립적으로

(independence) 과제를 수행하려는 자세를 보였다. 또한 돈을 염두에 둔 이들은 연필을 떨어뜨린 사람을 덜 적극적인 자세로 도왔으므로 이기심(selfishness)이 더 높아진 것으로 나타났다.

해석 한 연구에서 학생들은 열두 개의 모양을 조작해서 큰 정사각형 하나를 만들 것을 요구하는 어려운 지적 과제를 완수했다. 과제를 설명한 실험자는 그들이 어려움에 맞닥뜨리면 도와주겠다고 제안한 후, 학생들이 방해받지 않고 문제를 해결하기 위해 노력할 수 있도록 방을 나갔다. 일부 학생들의 경우 모노폴리 보드게임에서 가져온 적은 돈 무더기가 그들의 책상 구석에 놓여 있었는데, 이는 돈에 대한 끊임없는 미묘한 환기 작용을 했다. 4분이 흘렀을 때쯤 돈을 떠올리지 않았던 학생들 중 거의 75퍼센트가 도움을 요청했다. 대조적으로, 모노폴리 돈을 응시하며 앉아 있던 학생들 중 단 35퍼센트만이 4분 후에 도움을 요청했다. 1분 후에, 마침 실험실을 가로질러 걸어가게 된 한 학생이 우연히 사소한 불행에 맞닥뜨렸는데, 그때 그녀는 27자루의 연필을 바닥에 떨어뜨렸다. 무심결에 마음속으로 돈을 생각한 참가자들은 돈의 개념이 주입되지 않은 학생들보다 더 적은 연필을 주었다.

위 연구에 따르면 돈은 학생들에게 그들의 (A) <u>독립심</u>을 상기시켰을 뿐만 아니라 또한 그들을 (B) <u>이기심</u>의 방향으로 몰고 갔다.

구문 [1행~3행] In one study, students completed *a difficult intellectual task* [**that** required them to manipulate twelve shapes to form a large square].

[ ] 부분은 관계대명사 that이 이끄는 관계사절로 선행사 a difficult intellectual task를 수식한다.

[17행~19행] *The participants* (with money unconsciously on their mind) picked up fewer pencils **than *did*** *the students* [**who** weren't primed with the concept of money].

( ) 부분은 전명구로 주어 The participants를 수식한다. [ ] 부분은 관계사절로 앞에 있는 the students를 수식한다. than 이후에 주어(the students ~ of money)와 대동사(did)가 도치되었고 이때 did는 picked up pencils를 대신 받는다.

어휘 **manipulate** 조작[조종]하다, 솜씨 있게 처리하다 **encounter** 맞닥뜨리다; 마주치다 **uninterrupted** 방해받지 않는; 중단[차단]되지 않는; 연속된 **Monopoly** 모노폴리 ((주사위를 사용해서 하는 부동산 취득 게임)) **subtle** 미묘한; 절묘한 **reminder** 생각나게 하는[상기시키는] 것 **elapse** (시간이) 흐르다[지나다] **peer at** ~을 응시하다 **run into** ~와 우연히 만나다[마주치다] **unconsciously** 무심결에; 무의식적으로 **prime** 주입하다, 가득 채우다; 대비시키다 **adaptability** 적응[순응]성; 융통성 **selfishness** 이기심 **generosity** 너그러움, 관대 **perseverance** 인내(심) **competitiveness** 경쟁력 **independence** 독립(심)

19~20 장문 19 ② 20 ⑤

해설 19. 마지막 문장에서 명확히 드러난 이 글의 주제는 '자유롭고 독립적인 개인들이 교류할 때 필요한 효과적인 의사소통 전략'이다. 글 전반적으로 친구들 간의 의사소통은 간접적이고 암시적인 특성을 띠며 침묵이 최상의 의사소통 형태가 될 수 있음을 기술하고 있다. 이를 반영하면 제목으로 가장 적절한 것은 ② '어떻게 친구들이 효과적으로 의사소통할 수 있을까?'이다.
① 의사소통 능력을 향상시키는 방법
③ 더 나은 우정을 위하여, 말을 더 잘 들어주는 사람이 되어라
④ 의사소통 능력이 당신을 유능한 사람으로 만들어준다
⑤ 우정의 유형은 의사소통으로 규정된다
20. 가까운 친구들 간의 의사소통은 명확성과 직접성이 아니라 간접성과 암시성을 특징으로 한다. 따라서 '발신자와 수신자 간의 거리가 가까운 것이 아니라 멀수록 명확성과 직접성에 대한 필요는 더 커진다고 할 수 있다. 따라서 (e)의 shorter를 greater로 바꿔 써야 한다.

(a) 군대의 명령처럼 메시지가 더 노골적이고 명확할수록 메시지를 받아들일 때 식별력을 작용시키는 것, 즉 자유의지를 발휘하는 것은 더 (a) 어려워진다.

(b) 군대의 명령과는 반대로 우정의 의사소통은 (b) 간접적이고 암시적이다.

(c) 우정의 간접적이고 조심스러운 의사소통은 상대방의 진실성을 침해하는 일을 (c) 피할 수 있게 해준다.

(d) 우정의 의사소통에서 침묵이 최상의 형태라 할 수 있으며 진정한 우정은 정보가 말의 (d) 부재[없음]로 전달되는 것을 가능하게 한다.

해석 모든 연설은 화자와 청자가 존재하므로 권력의 작용이다. 그래서 메시지가 더 노골적이고 명확할수록 메시지를 받아들일 때 식별력을 작용시키는 것(자유의지)이 더 (a) 어려워진다. 군대에서처럼 명백한 명령이 최악이다. 그것은 단호히 강압적이고 구속적이며 복종을 요구한다. 반면에 우정의 독특한 특징인 (b) 간접적이고 암시적인 종류의 의사소통은 생각이 흐르고 감정이 멈추지 않게 해준다. 친구인 사람이 결론을 내릴 기회를 제시받는다. "아마 네가 이걸 고려해준다면 좋겠는데…"이러한 접근법에는 몇 가지 이점이 있다. 그것은 상대방의 진실성을 침해하지 (c) 않는다. 이성적인 개인들의 계약처럼 행동은 명백히 자유의지를 가지고 시작된다. 따라서 우리는 친구에게 부탁할 때 "너 이거 해야 해"라고 말하지 않고 "네가 혹시 해줄 수 있을지 모르겠는데…"라고 말한다.

많은 경우 친구와 하는 의사소통의 최상의 형태는 놀랍게도 침묵이다. 우정은 우리가 실제로 하는 말에 관한 것일 뿐만 아니라 훨씬 더 중요한 것은 우리가 말하지 않는 것에 관한 것이라는 점이다. 진정한 우정은 '정보'가 말의 (d) 부재로 전달될 때 생긴다. 노력할 점은 가능한 한 많은 것을 간접적으로, '행간에' 전달하는 것이다. 그러한 '음'의 의사소통이 중요한 이유는 그것이 양의 의사소통보다 더 큰 밀접함을 요하기 때문이다. 발신자와

수신자 간의 거리가 (e) 가까울수록(→ 멀수록) 명확성과 직접성에 대한 필요는 더 커진다. 둘 이상의 사람들이 막대한 양을 대화로 주고받을 때만 훨씬 더 경제적인 음의 의사소통이 일어날 수 있다. 이러한 전략은 자유롭고 독립적인 개인들이 교류할 때 필요하다.

구문 [2행~5행] So **the more blatant and explicit** the message, **the more difficult it** is **to exercise** discrimination — that is free will — in receiving the message.

「The 비교급 …, the 비교급 ~」은 '…하면 할수록 더 ~하다'의 뜻이다. difficult 다음의 it은 가주어이고 to exercise 이하가 진주어이다.

[31행~34행] Only when two or more people converse an enormous amount *can* **the much more economical negative communication** *take place*.

Only가 이끄는 절이 문두에 나와 주절의 어순이 「조동사+주어+동사원형」으로 도치되었다.

어휘 blatant 노골적인　explicit 명백한　*cf.* explicitness 명백함; 솔직함　exercise 발휘하다, 작용시키다　discrimination 식별(력); 차별　free will 자유 의지　flatly 단호히; 단조롭게; 평평히　coercive 강압적인　binding 구속[속박]하는　obedience 복종　allusive 암시적인　peculiar 독특한, 고유한; 이상한　bruise 멍이 생기게 하다　infringe 침해하다, 위반하다　integrity 진실성, 정직　enter into 시작하다　ask for a favor 부탁하다　strive 노력하다; 분투하다

| 1 ⑤ | 2 ② | 3 ⑤ | 4 ② | 5 ③ | 6 ③ | 7 ⑤ | 8 ⑤ | 9 ③ | 10 ③ |
| 11 ① | 12 ③ | 13 ③ | 14 ③ | 15 ④ | 16 ④ | 17 ④ | 18 ③ | 19 ② | 20 ③ |

---

1 글의 목적　　　　　　　　　　⑤

해설 죽은 아들의 이름으로 재산을 대학 장학금으로 기부하고자 하는 뜻을 가지고 그 방법을 논하고자 편지를 작성했으므로 글의 목적으로 가장 적절한 것은 ⑤ '재산을 장학금으로 기부하는 방법을 의논하려고'이다.

해석 *Black씨께*
귀하가 재산 계획을 전문으로 하는 분이라고 추천 받았습니다. 제 아내와 저는 둘 다 80대입니다. 저희는 최근에 집을 팔았고 Willow Grove에 있는 은퇴자 커뮤니티로 이주했습니다. 저희는 둘 다 나이에 비해 건강이 좋지만 제 아내는 휠체어에 매인 몸입니다. 저희 인생의 이 시점에서 저는 저희가 가진 돈이 적절히 처리되고 있음을 알고 싶습니다. 제 아내와 제가 제공하고 싶은 금일봉이 하나 있습니다. 저희 아들 Donald는 Willow Grove 고등학교의 학생이었을 때인 거의 30년 전에 사망했습니다. 저는 그 아이의 이름으로 대학 장학금을 기부하고 싶지만, 제 재산으로 그것을 하는 방법에 대해서는 확신이 없습니다. 귀하의 말씀을 곧 들을 수 있기를 고대합니다. 귀하가 저희 아파트에서 저희와 만나주실 수 있다면 감사하겠습니다.
Ron Miller 올림

구문 [7행~9행] At this point in our lives, I would like to see that *the money* [we have] **is being handled** properly.

[ ]은 앞에 목적격 관계대명사 which[that]가 생략되어 the money를 수식한다. 'be being p.p.'는 '~되고 있다'의 뜻이다.

[9행~11행] There is *one gift of money* [my wife and I would like to make].

[ ]은 앞에 목적격 관계대명사 which[that]가 생략되어 one gift of money를 수식한다.

어휘 specialize in ~을 전문으로 하다　estate 재산　retirement 은퇴　confine (휠체어 등에) 얽매이다　gift of money 금일봉　endow 기부하다　scholarship 장학금　look forward to 고대하다

2 밑줄 함의　　　　　　　　　　②

해설 모호함은 책임을 회피하고자 하는 사람에게 의사소통의 한 책략으로 이용될 수 있으며, 이것의 한 예로 술집에 들러서 약속에 늦은 사람이 술집에 들른 사실은 모호하게 숨기고 그저 일이 있어서 늦었다고 변명하는 상황이 제시되어 있다. 이 예에서 '진실에 경제성을 발휘했다'는 것은 진실을 모호하게 생략한 행위, 즉 ② '관련된 정보를 생략하여 진실을 숨긴'것을 의미한다.
① 말이나 시간을 낭비하지 않고 깔끔하게 표현하여
③ 주제를 바꿔서 사건의 세부사항을 강조하여
④ 사실의 쟁점에서 감정적 쟁점으로 주의를 돌려
⑤ 이야기해야 할 중요한 요점들에 대해 질문하여

해석 모호함은 효율적인 의사소통에 장애가 되는 것이다. 때때로 특정한 행동 방침에 대해 약속하기를 피하고자 하는 사람들은 모호함을 책략으로 이용한다. 예를 들어 공공 부문에서 정확히 어떻게 돈을 절약하려 하는지에 대해 질문 받은 정치인은 향상되는 효율

성의 필요성에 대하여 모호한 일반화를 할지도 모르는데, 그것은 사실이긴 하지만, 이것을 달성하는 그 어떤 특정 방법에 대해서도 그에게 책무를 지우지는 않는다. 그렇다면 훌륭한 기자는 그가 이 모호함의 베일 뒤에서 나올 것을 강요하며, 이 효율성이 정확히 어떻게 달성될지에 관한 추가적 정보를 얻기 위해 압박을 가할 것이다. 혹은 약속에 늦었지만 이것이 오는 길에 술 한잔하러 들렀기 때문이라는 것을 인정하기 싫은 사람이 지연의 원인을 고의로 모호한 상태로 남겨두고, 진실에 특정한 종류의 경제성을 발휘하여 "늦어서 미안해. 여기 오는 길에 해야 할 일이 있었는데 예상했던 것보다 조금 더 오래 걸렸어."라고 말할지도 모른다.

구문 [4행~9행] For instance, *a politician* (asked *how precisely he intends to save money in the public sector*) **might make** *vague generalisations* about the need for improved efficiency, **which**, while (they are) true, don't commit him to any particular way of achieving this.

주어는 a politician이고 동사는 might make이다. 과거분사구인 ( ) 부분이 a politician을 수식하며, 분사구 내의 how가 이끄는 명사절이 asked의 목적어이다. 관계대명사 which가 이끄는 절은 vague generalisations를 보충 설명하고, 관계사절 내에 삽입된 while과 true 사이에는 they(vague generalisations) are가 생략되어 있다.

[9행~12행] A good journalist would then press for further information about precisely how this efficiency **was to be achieved**, *forcing* him to come out from behind this veil of vagueness.

밑줄 친 부분은 간접의문문의 어순으로 쓰인 명사절로 전치사 about의 목적어 역할을 한다. was to be achieved는 be to-v 용법으로 'v할 예정이다'를 의미한다. forcing 이하는 동시동작을 나타내는 분사구문이다.

[12행~19행] Or *someone* [who was late for an appointment but didn't want to admit that this was because he'd stopped for a drink on the way] **might say** 'Sorry I'm late, I had something I needed to do on the way here and it took slightly longer than I expected', deliberately leaving the cause of the delay vague, and exercising a particular kind of economy with the truth.

주격 관계대명사가 이끄는 관계사절 [ ]이 주어 someone을 수식하고, 동사는 might say이다. 밑줄 친 두 부분은 병렬 연결되어 주절의 내용을 보충 설명하는 분사구문이다.

어휘 vagueness 모호함 *cf.* vague 모호한 obstacle 장애 commit oneself to ~을 약속하다[구속하다] sector 부문 deliberately 고의로 exercise 행사[발휘]하다 neatly 깔끔하게; 교묘하게 omit 생략하다 divert (주의 등을) 돌리다

3 글의 요지 ⑤

해설 시냅스 연결을 많이 사용하면 할수록 연결이 강력해지는 원리는 자제력에도 적용되므로, 늦었다고 생각하지 말고 꾸준히 연마하면 자제력이 향상될 수 있다는 내용의 글이므로 요지로 가장 적절한 것은 ⑤이다.

해석 신경가소성은 시냅스 연결을 끊임없이 형성하고 재조직하는 뇌의 능력인데, 이것(= 시냅스 연결)은 개별 뉴런 간의 연결이다. 특정 연결이 더 많이 사용되면 될수록 그것은 더 강해지며 사람이 미래에 이 경로를 활성화시키기가 더 쉬워진다. 훈련을 책임지는 시냅스 연결도 마찬가지이다. 유전의 복권이 당신에게 이상적인 수준보다 못한 전두엽 피질을 부여했을지라도, 당신은 주어진 것을 '늘이고' 자신의 자제력을 향상시키는 방식으로 당신의 환경을 조직할 수 있다. 언어가 어려울 때 학습하기 더 쉽다고 판명된 것처럼 당신이 더 어렸을 때 이 기술들을 배우는 것이 확실히 더 쉬웠겠지만, 성인기에 자제력으로 고군분투하고 있다면 낙담해선 안 된다. 자제력은 어떤 나이 때라도, 시간에 걸쳐 지속 가능한 향상을 달성하기 위해 꾸준히 훈련될 수 있다. 어떠한 기술과 마찬가지로, 스스로가 단련되는 연습을 더 많이 하면 할수록 그 일에 더 능숙해진다.

구문 [3행~6행] **The more** a particular connection is used, / **the stronger it** becomes / and the easier **it** is *for the person* **to activate** this pathway in the future.

「The 비교급, the 비교급」 구문은 '~하면 할수록 더 …하다'의 뜻이다. the stronger 다음의 it은 a particular connection을 지칭한다. the easier 다음의 it은 가주어이고 to activate 이하가 진주어이며 for the person은 to-v에 대한 의미상 주어이다.

[11행~16행] It certainly **would have been** easier **to learn** the skills / when you were younger, // **just as** languages have been proven to be easier to learn / when young, // but you shouldn't feel discouraged // if you struggle with self-discipline in your adulthood.

It은 가주어이고 to learn ~ younger가 진주어이다. would have been은 가정법 과거완료 표현으로 '~였을 것이다'의 뜻이다. just as는 '~한 것과 꼭 마찬가지로'의 뜻이다.

어휘 neuroplasticity 신경가소성 synaptic 시냅스의 linkage 연결 activate 활성화시키다 pathway 경로 discipline 훈련; 절제력; 규율 *cf.* self-discipline 자제(력) genetic 유전의 lottery 복권 structure 조직하다, 구조화하다 consistently 일관성 있게 exercise 행사하다 sustainable 지속 가능한

4 글의 제목

해설 생물학적 진화 속도는 환경 변화의 속도와 비할 수 없이 느려서 우리 몸은 환경에 제대로 적응하지 못하며, 비만, 고혈압, 충치, 천식 등은 이러한 부조화의 예라는 글이므로 제목으로 가장 적절한 것은 ② '진화적 부조화는 현대 질병의 근원'이다.
① 생물학적 진화는 문화적 변화에 뒤처진다
③ 우리가 아프게 되는 이유는 예기치 않은 환경 변화
④ 우리의 적응으로 야기된 현대 질병의 유형들
⑤ 진화적 부조화와 그것에 대해 우리가 할 수 있는 일

해석 일반적으로 환경은 생명 작용보다 훨씬 더 빠르게 변한다. 농업은 12,000년 전에 발명되었고 포테이토칩은 200년이 안 되는 과거에 발명되었다. 대조적으로, 우리의 음식 섭취와 소화를 조절하는 생물학적 시스템은 여전히 우리의 영장류 조상들의 그것과 매우 흡사하다. 한때는 이로웠던 우리의 진화된 특성이 환경의 변화로 인해 부적응적인 것이 되었다. 비만, 관상 동맥 질환, 고혈압, 그리고 심지어 충치의 빠르게 증가하는 비율은 이러한 부조화로 설명될 수 있다. 또 다른 부조화의 예는 위생 가설인데, 이는 현대의 공중위생 관행이 인간과 공진화한 중요한 박테리아를 제거했기 때문에 몇몇 질병들이 발달했음을 암시한다. 예를 들어, 도시에서 양육된 어린이들은 농장에서 길러진 아이들보다 천식이 발달할 가능성이 더 높다. 우리의 천식에 대한 취약성은 따라서 우리의 현재의 박테리아에 대한 노출과 우리의 수렵 채집 시절의 과거의 그러한 노출의 역학 간의 부조화의 결과이다.

구문 [2행~3행] ~ agriculture *was invented* 12,000 years ago and potato chips (was invented) less than 200 years ago.

potato chips 다음에 was invented가 생략되어 있다.

[3행~6행] In contrast, *biological systems* [that regulate our consumption and digestion of food] are still very similar to **those** of our primate ancestors.

[ ]는 biological systems를 수식하며, those는 biological systems를 지칭한다.

어휘 biology 생명 작용; 생물학 agriculture 농업 regulate 조절하다 digestion 소화 primate 영장류 advantageous 이로운 maladaptive 부적응의 obesity 비만 cavity 충치의 구멍 mismatch 부조화 hygiene 위생 hypothesis 가설 sanitation 공중위생 co-evolve 공진화하다 asthma 천식 vulnerability 취약성 dynamics 역학 (관계)

5 도표 이해 ③

해설 2017년에 PC 게임과 콘솔 게임을 합한 비율은 54퍼센트(각각 27퍼센트)로서 모바일 게임의 비율인 46퍼센트보다 높다. 그러므로 ③은 도표와 일치하지 않는다.

해석 2014~2020 세계 게임 시장
연평균 성장률을 포함한 부문별 수익
위 그래프는 2014년부터 2020년까지의 부문별 세계 게임 시장의 수익을 보여준다. 시장 내 위치는 이리저리 변동이 있었지만, 의심할 여지없이 전반적으로 시장은 규모 면에서 빠르게 성장을 계속했다. ① 세계 게임 시장의 총 수익은 2014년에 848억 달러에서 2020년에 1,659억 달러로 꾸준히 증가했다. ② 이 기간 동안 모바일 게임의 비율이 거의 2배 가까이 늘어난 반면, PC와 콘솔 게임은 3분의 1 수준으로 꾸준히 줄었다. ③ PC게임과 콘솔 게임을 합한 비율은 2017년에 모바일 게임의 비율보다 낮았다. ④ PC게임은 2015년에 콘솔 게임보다 더욱 인기가 있었지만, 이 부문은 그 후 2016년과 2017년에 2년 연속 동률을 이뤘다. ⑤ 콘솔 게임은 2020년에 PC 게임보다 더 큰 시장 점유율을 차지했다.

구문 [2행~5행] **While** positions in the market shuffled, // there is no <u>doubt</u> that the market as a whole continued to grow rapidly in size.
while은 부사절 접속사로서 '반면에'를 의미하며 두 개의 절을 연결한다. 밑줄 친 that절은 doubt와 동격 관계이다.

어휘 revenue 수익 shuffle 이리저리 바꾸다 segment 부문 proportion 비율 combine 합치다, 결합하다 account for 차지하다; 설명하다 consecutive 연속적인 take up 차지하다 share 점유율

6 내용 불일치 ③

해설 생후 4주가 되면 어미는 먹이를 찾기 위해 매일 밤 캠프에 새끼를 남겨두기 시작한다고 했으므로 생후 1개월이 됐을 때 직접 먹이를 구하는 것은 아니다. 따라서 ③은 본문의 내용과 일치하지 않는다.

해석 black flying fox(검정날여우박쥐)는 세계에서 가장 큰 박쥐에 속하며 1미터가 넘는 날개폭을 가지고 있다. 그것은 호주, 파푸아뉴기니와 인도네시아의 토착 동물이다. 그들은 캠프라고 알려진, 보통 열대우림과 유칼립투스의 탁 트인 숲에 있는 거대 군집에 모인다. black flying fox는 1년에 한 번 새끼를 낳는다. 생의 첫 4주 동안 갓 태어난 박쥐는 어미에게 완전히 의존한다. 이 기간 후에는 암컷은 먹이를 찾기 위해 매일 밤 캠프에 새끼를 남겨두기 시작한다. black flying fox의 전체 개체군은 현재 멸종 위기에 처해 있지 않지만, 이 동물들은 정말로 심각한 위험에 직면해있다. 예를 들어 그들의 서식 범위 중 많은 지역에서 이 박쥐들은 식용으로 사냥된다. 뿐만 아니라 기후 변화는 기온 상승으로 이어지는데, 이것은 이 종의 개체 수에 부정적인 영향을 미친다.

구문 [10행~13행] Although **the population** of black flying foxes as a whole / **is** not currently endangered, // these animals **do** face some serious threats.
Although 절에서 주어는 the population이고 동사는 is이다. 주절에서 do는 강조용법으로 쓰였으며 '정말로'의 뜻이다.
[14행~16행] Additionally, climate change leads to rising temperatures, // **which** negatively impact the population of this species.
which는 rising temperatures를 지칭하며 which 절은 rising temperatures에 대한 추가 설명을 제시한다.

어휘 wingspan 날개폭, 날개 길이 native 토착의 colony 군집 breed 새끼를 낳다 range 서식 범위; 구역

7 밑줄 어법 ⑤

해설 ⑤ result in ((결과적으로) ~을 낳다, 야기하다)의 전치사 in 다음에는 명사절이 나와야 하므로, 선행사를 포함하는 관계대명사로서 명사절을 이끄는 what이 나와야 한다.

해석 비록 실업은 수입원이 없는 사람들에게 고통스럽지만, 실업을 줄이는 것은 공짜가 아니다. 단기적으로, 실업 감소는 특히 경제가 완전한 수용력에 근접하여 자원이 거의 모두 사용되는 경우, 높은 비율의 인플레이션이라는 대가를 지불하여 일어날지도 모른다. 더구나, 피고용인들을 일자리와 맞춰주려 애쓰는 것은 노동자의 기술 수준과 일자리를 위해 요구되는 기술 수준 간의 부조화로 인해 상당한 비효율로 빠르게 이어질 수 있다. 예를 들어 생화학 박사 학위를 가진 사람들이 택시를 몰거나 바에서 손님의 시중을 들고 있다면 경제는 교육에 보조금을 지급하는 데 자원을 낭비하고 있는 것일 것이다. 다시 말해서, 피고용인의 기술은 일자리에 필요한 기술보다 더 높을 것이므로, 경제학자들이 저고용이라 일컫는 것을 초래할 것이다. 또 다른 비효율의 원천은 피고용인들을 그들의 능력을 넘어서는 일자리에 배치하는 것이다.

구문 [10행~13행] For example, the economy **would be** *wasting* resources subsidizing education **if** people with PhDs in biochemistry **were** driving taxis or tending bars.
가정법 과거 문장으로 'if S 과거동사, S would 동사원형'의 형태로 '…하면 ~할 것이다'의 의미를 가진다. 'waste (자원) v-ing'는 '~하는 데 (자원)을 낭비하다'의 뜻이다.
[13행~15행] That is, the skills of the employee may be higher than **those** (necessary for the job) ~
those는 the skills를 나타낸다. ( )은 those를 수식한다.

어휘 costless 비용이 들지 않는 in the short run 단기적으로 at the expense of ~을 잃어가며, ~의 비용으로 employ 사용하다 match 맞추다, 연결시키다 mismatch 부조화 PhD 박사학위 biochemistry 생화학 tend (바에서 손님의) 시중을 들다 underemployment 저고용

8 밑줄 어휘 ⑤

해설 선수들이 경쟁 상황에서 발생할 모든 만일의 사태에 대비하는 것은 불가능하므로 예상치 못한 상황에 따라 쉽게 변경될 수 있으면서도 시합의 온갖 불확실성에 선수들이 대비할 수 있도록 도움을 주는 '루틴'이 필요하다. 루틴은 이와 같이 유연성을 특징으로 갖고 있으므로 ⑤의 tight(꽉 짜인, 촘촘한)를 flexible(유연한) 등으로 바꿔 써야 한다.

해석 경쟁이 일어나는 경기장은 바로 그 본질상 어렵고 예측 불가능하며 통제할 수 없다. 최선을 다 한 노력에도 불구하고 운동선수들은 결코 시합에서 발생할 수 있는 모든 만일의 사태에 대비하거나 그들의 수행에 영향을 미칠 수 있는 모든 것을 ① 통제할 수 없다. 루틴(규칙적으로 하는 운동의 통상적인 순서와 방법)은 그 속에서 수행을 대비할 수 있는 구조와 시합의 ② 불확실한 성질에 적응할 수 있는 유연성을 제공한다. 루틴은 어길 수 없는 것이 아니라 오히려 운동선수들이 따를 지침을 제공하므로, 그것은 독특하거나 예상치 못한 경쟁 환경의 요구에 ③ 맞추기 위해 쉽게 변경될 수도 있다. 날씨, 예상치 못한 적수, 늦은 도착, 불충분한 준비 운동 공간, 고장 나거나 분실된 장비와 같은 경쟁 환경에서의 예측 못한 변화들은 시합 전에 운동선수들에게 불안감을 일으키는 파괴적인 영향을 미칠 수 있다. 운동선수들은 이러한 사건에 적절히 반응할 수 없거나 정신적으로 불안정(예를 들어 동기나 자신감을 상실함, 주의가 산만해짐, 혹은 불안을 경험함)해지기 때문에 많은 경우 기대보다 ④ 낮게 수행을 한다. 잘 조직되어 있으면서도 ⑤ 꽉 짜인(→ 유연한) 루틴을 가진 운동선수들은 이러한 도전들에 긍정적으로 반응하고, 차분한 상태를 유지하며, 높은 수준의 수행을 유지하는 일을 더 잘 할 수 있을 것이다.

구문 [6행~8행] Routines offer *a structure* [**within which to prepare** for performance] and *the flexibility* (to adjust to the uncertain nature of competition).

동사 offer 다음에 목적어 a structure와 the flexibility가 and로 연결되어 병렬구조를 이룬다. [ ]는 「전치사＋관계대명사＋to-v」의 형태로 a structure를 수식한다. within which to prepare는 within which they(= the athletes) can prepare와 같이 바꿔 쓸 수 있는데, 주어가 특정 가능하고 동사가 「조동사＋동사원형」일 경우에는 주어와 조동사를 생략하고 동사만 to-v로 간략히 쓸 수 있다. ( )는 the flexibility를 수식하는 형용사구이다.

[8행~12행] Because routines are **not** inviolate, **but** rather provide *a guide* (for athletes to follow), // they can also be readily altered / to fit the demands of a unique or unexpected competitive environment.

Because 절에서 「not A but B (A가 아니라 B)」 구문이 쓰였으며 A, B 자리 모두 현재동사가 위치해있다. for athletes는 to follow에 대한 의미상 주어이다. ( )는 a guide를 수식한다.

어휘 adjust to ~에 적응하다 readily 쉽게 alter 변경하다, 바꾸다 unforeseen 예상하지 못한, 뜻밖의 disturbing 불안감을 주는, 충격적인 disruptive 파괴적인; 지장을 주는 unsettled 불안정한 distract 산만하게 하다, (주의를) 흐트러뜨리다

9 빈칸 추론 ③

해설 대칭이 패턴과 형태에 대한 근본적인 과학 언어이고, 물체가 거울에 반사되거나 회전되거나 움직일 때 어떻게 변함없이 보일 수 있는지를 기술하는 것으로 여겨지지만 자연 속의 모양과 형태는 대칭으로부터 생기는 것이 아니고, 대칭을 깨는 것으로부터 생겨난다. 즉, 대칭에 관한 우리의 직관은 자연 속에서 대칭이 활용되는 방식에 반하므로 빈칸에는 ③ '기만적인'이라는 말이 들어가야 가장 적절하다.
① 정확한 ② 공정한 ④ 권위 있는 ⑤ 포괄적인

해석 패턴이란 무엇인가? 우리는 보통 그것을 계속 반복되는 어떤 것으로 생각한다. 대칭에 대한 수학은 이러한 반복이 어떻게 보일 수 있는지를 묘사할 수 있고, 게다가 왜 어떤 모양이 다른 것들에 비해 더 규칙적이고 더 잘 조직된 것처럼 보이는지도 묘사할 수 있다. 그것이 대칭이 패턴과 형태에 대한 근본적인 과학 '언어'인 이유이다. 대칭은 물체가 거울에 반사되거나 회전되거나 움직일 때 어떻게 변함없이 보일 수 있는지를 기술한다. 하지만 대칭에 대한 우리의 직관은 기만적일 수 있다. 일반적으로 자연 속의 모양과 형태는 대칭을 '창조하는 것'으로부터 생겨나는 것이 아니라, 완벽한 대칭을 깨뜨리는 것, 다시 말해 모든 것이 어디에서나 똑같이 보이는 완벽하고 지루한 획일성의 해체로부터 생겨난다. 그러므로 핵심 질문은 '왜 모든 것이 똑같지는 않은가? 어떻게 그리고 왜 대칭이 깨지는가?'이다.

구문 [1행~2행] We usually **think of** it **as** *something* [that repeats again and again].

'think of A as B'는 'A를 B로 생각하다[간주하다]'의 의미이다. [ ] 부분은 관계사절로 something을 수식한다.

[10행~15행] In general, shape and form in nature arise not from the "building up" of symmetry, but from the breaking of perfect symmetry — that is, from the disintegration of *complete, boring uniformity*, **where** everything looks the same, everywhere.

밑줄 친 두 부분을 상관접속사 「not A but B(A가 아니고 B)」가 병렬 연결한다. 계속적 용법으로 쓰인 관계부사인 where가 이끄는 절이 complete, boring uniformity를 부연 설명한다.

어휘 symmetry 대칭 repetition 반복, 되풀이 orderly 규칙적인, 정연한 fundamental 근본적인, 주요한; 기초[기본]의 rotate 회전시키다 intuition 직관

----

in general 일반적으로 arise from ~에서 생기다[나타나다] disintegration 해체, 붕괴 uniformity 획일, 균일; 한결같음 impartial 공정한, 편견 없는 deceptive 기만적인, 현혹하는 authoritative 권위 있는, 믿을 만한; 권위적인 comprehensive 포괄[종합]적인

10 빈칸 추론 ③

해설 빈칸 문장으로 보아, 무엇에 따라 고통이 다르게 보일 수 있는지를 찾아야 한다. 빈칸 문장 뒤에 이어지는 예시에서, 환자의 고통에 의미를 부여함, 즉 고통을 준 사건을 다르게 해석함으로써 고통의 정도를 다르게 느끼도록 한 것이므로, 빈칸에는 ③ '우리의 사건 해석'이 오는 것이 적절하다.
① (고통의) 원천과 지속성 ② 흘러간 시간
④ 생존자의 힘 ⑤ 우리의 이해 능력

해석 빈의 정신과 의사 Viktor Frankl은 그의 책 〈Man's Search for Meaning(1946)〉에서, 인간이 고통스럽고 아마도 충격적인 상황을 견디며 앞으로 나아갈 수 있는 정신적 힘 두 가지를 가지고 있는데, 그것은 결정 능력과 태도의 자유라고 설명한다. Frankl은 우리는 환경이나 사건에 휘둘리지 않는데, 왜냐하면 우리가 그것들이 우리를 형성하는 방식을 지휘하기 때문이라고 강조한다. 심지어 고통도 우리의 사건 해석에 따라 다르게 보일 수 있다. Frankl은 죽은 아내가 그리워 괴로워하던 환자의 경우를 지적한다. 만약 환자 자신이 먼저 죽었다면 어떠했겠느냐고 Frankl이 묻자, 환자는 아내가 무척 힘들어했을 것이라고 대답했다. Frankl은 환자 덕분에 아내가 그 고통을 면하게 됐지만 이제 환자가 고통을 직접 겪어야 함을 말해주었다. 즉, 고통에 의미를 부여하면 고통은 참을만해 진다는 것이다.

구문 [13행~16행] Frankl asked / how it **would have been** / if the patient **had died** first, // and he responded / that his wife **would have found** it very difficult.

Frankl과 환자가 묻고 대답한 내용이 if 가정법 과거완료 구문으로 제시되었다. if 가정법 과거완료는 「if＋주어＋had p.p. ~, 주어＋조동사 과거형＋have p.p. ....」의 형태로, 과거의 일을 반대로 가정하여 '만약 (그때) ~했다면 …했을 텐데'를 의미한다.

어휘 psychiatrist 정신과 의사 psychological 심리적인 devastating 대단히 파괴적인; 엄청나게 충격적인 capacity 용량; 수용력 at the mercy of ~에 휘둘리는 dictate 받아쓰게 하다; 지시[명령]하다 [선택지 어휘] interpretation 해석, 이해

11 빈칸 추론 ①

해설 사람들은 촉각에 대해서만 유독 물체를 실제로 만지고 느낀다는 감각을 갖지만, 사실 촉각도 시각, 청각, 미각만큼이나 뇌 속에서 일어나는 감각이며, 어떤 물건을 만졌을 때 감각을 느끼는 것은 손이 아니라 뇌이다. 이는 감각이 물체의 촉감 원형에는 결코 도달할 수 없기 때문이고 그러므로 표면을 만지는 것에 대한 우리의 지식은 ① '특정한 자극에 대한 뇌의 해석'이라 할 수 있다.
② 학습된 촉각으로부터 얻은 여러분의 생각
③ 여러분 손끝에 있는 감각 수용기의 자극
④ 과거 사건의 패턴 인식에 기반을 둔 여러분의 예측
⑤ 물체에 대한 정보를 걸러내기 위한 선별적인 인지

해석 촉각은 시각, 청각, 미각이 뇌 안에서 일어난다는 진실을 사람들이 확신하지 못하게 하는 요인 중 하나이다. 예를 들어 만약 당신이 누군가에게 그가 그의 뇌 안에서 책을 본다고 말한다면, 그는 신중하게 생각하지 않는다면 "내가 내 뇌에서 그 책을 보고 있을리 없어. 봐, 내 손으로 그것을 만지고 있잖아."라고 대답할 것이다. 그러나 그런 사람들이 이해할 수 없거나, 어쩌면 단지 무시하는 사실이 있다. 촉각도 다른 모든 감각이 그런 것만

큰 뇌에서 일어난다. 다시 말해서, 물질로 된 사물을 만질 때 여러분이 그것이 단단한지, 부드러운지, 축축한지, 끈적이는지 혹은 비단 같은지를 뇌 안에서 감지하게 된다. 손 끝에서 나오는 느낌은 뇌에 전기 신호로 전송되며, 이러한 신호가 뇌에서 촉각으로 인식된다. 예를 들어 여러분이 거친 표면을 만진다 해도, 그 표면이 실제로 정말 거친 표면인지 혹은 거친 표면이 실제로 어떻게 느껴지는지 여러분은 결코 알 수 없다. 그것은 여러분이 거친 표면의 원형을 결코 만질 수 없기 때문이다. 여러분이 표면을 만지는 것에 대해 가지고 있는 지식은 특정한 자극에 대한 여러분의 뇌의 해석이다.

구문 [1행~4행] The sense of touch is one of *the factors* [which **prevent** people **from** being convinced of the truth that the senses of sight, hearing and taste occur within the brain].
[ ]은 the factors를 수식하는 관계사절이다. 'prevent O from v-ing'는 'O가 v 못하게 막다'의 뜻이고 밑줄 친 두 부분은 서로 동격 관계이다.

[4행~6행] For example, if you **told** *someone* that he sees a book within his brain, he **would**, if he **didn't think** carefully, reply ~
「If+S+과거동사 ~, S+would+동사원형(reply)...」의 가정법 과거 구문으로 '~하면 …할 것이다'의 의미(현재의 사실을 반대로 가정)이다. told의 간접목적어는 someone, 밑줄 친 명사절이 직접목적어이다.

[9행~11행] The sense of touch also **occurs** in the brain as much as *do* all the other senses.
원급을 나타내는 접속사 as 뒤에 대동사 do와 주어 all the other senses가 도치되었고, 이때 do는 occurs를 나타낸다.

어휘 be convinced of ~을 확신하다 sticky 끈적거리는 transmit 전송하다 rough 거친; 울퉁불퉁한 stimulus(*pl.* stimuli) 자극 *cf.* stimulation 자극 receptor 수용기, 감각 기관

12 빈칸 추론 ③

해설 읽기가 두뇌의 작동방식을 바꾸었다고 했으므로, 읽기 이전의 인간의 사고방식이 환경의 순환에 지배받는 것이었다면, 읽기의 보급 이후 인간은 선형적 사고방식을 가지고 인과관계를 논하며, ③ '우리의 근접한 환경의 속박'에서 좀 더 해방될 수 있게 되었을 것이다.
① 자연의 장엄함에 대한 거부
② 자연환경의 파괴
④ 자연환경을 지배하려는 생각
⑤ 사회 구성원 사이에서의 의견 충돌

해석 읽기는 우리의 두뇌가 작동하는 방식을 바꾸었는가? Marshall McLuhan은 그렇게 했다고 믿었다. 〈구텐베르크의 은하: 인쇄술 적 인간의 형성(1962)〉에서 그는 읽기가 우리를 새로운 '인쇄술적 인간'으로 만들었다고 주장했다. 그 책에 따르면, 읽고 쓰는 능력이 널리 보급되기 전의 생활은 환경에 대한 순환적 관계, 언제 일하고 언제 잠잘지를 결정하는 낮의 햇빛의 즉각적인 순환, 그리고 특정 계절에 농장에서 하던 일의 더 장기적인 패턴의 지배를 받았다. 읽기가 널리 퍼진 후, 사람들은 그들의 지역사회 바깥의 일들에 관심을 보이고, 인과관계의 패턴을 살피고, 환경을 복종 당하는 것이 아니라 지배할 수 있는 것으로 여기는 가능성이 더욱 커졌다. 즉, 읽기는 좀 더 선형적인 사고방식과 인과관계로 인도했고, 우리의 근접한 환경의 속박에서 좀 더 해방되게 했다.

구문 [5행~10행] According to the book, life prior to widespread literacy was dominated by a cyclical relationship to the environment, *the immediate cycle of daylight* [that determined when you worked and when you slept], and the longer pattern of what you did on a farm in a certain season.
전치사 by의 목적어로 밑줄 친 세 개의 명사구가 병렬구조를 이룬다.

어휘 typographic 인쇄상의; 인쇄술의 literacy 글을 읽고 쓸 줄 아는 능력 cyclical 순환하는, 주기적인 linear 선의 [선택지 어휘] grandeur 장엄함; 위엄 constraints 속박, 제한

13 흐름 무관 문장 ③

해설 동물들의 윤리적 법적 권리에 생명권과 해를 입지 않을 권리가 포함되어 있다고 믿고 그것을 보호해줘야 한다고 말하는 동물권 옹호자들의 주장에 대한 글이다. 그러므로 동물로부터 사람들을 보호하는 법안에 관한 언급인 ③은 글의 전체 흐름과 관계가 없다.

해석 동물들에게 권리가 있다고 믿는 옹호자들은, 때로 '(동물) 권리 옹호자'라고 불리는데 동물의 삶의 질에 관심을 갖는다. 그들은 실리적인 예외를 두지 않는다. ① 그들은 어쨌든 동물들을 학대하거나 착취하는 것 또는 동물에게 어떠한 아픔이나 고통을 일으키는 일은 잘못됐다고 주장하는데, 동물들은 잡아먹히거나, 동물원에 갇혀 있거나, 어떤 (또는 대부분의) 교육이나 연구 환경에서도 이용되어서는 안 된다. ② 그들은 동물들의 윤리적 및 법적 권리에는 생명권과 해를 입지 않을 권리가 포함된다고 믿는다. ③ 동물 학대 법이 미국에서 무려 42개 주에서 널리 퍼진 것처럼, 야영객들이 야생동물에 의해 위협을 받은 최근의 사고를 고려하면 동물로부터 사람들을 보호하는 법안 또한 확립되어야 한다. ④ Rutgers 대학교의 법학 교수인 Gary Francione에 따르면, 동물에게 어떤 권익을 보호받을 '권리'가 있다고 말하는 것은 비록 다르게 하는 것이(동물의 권익을 보호해 주지 않는 것이) 우리에게 이익이 될지라도 그 동물이 그 권익을 보호받을 자격이 있다는 것을 의미한다. ⑤ (동물) 권리 옹호자들은, 자기 자신의 권익을 보호할 수 없는 (유아, 아이들, 그리고 치매에 걸린 어른들과 같은) 동의를 표할 수 없는 사람들을 위해서 사람들이 한 것과 똑같이 동물을 위해서도 그런 주장을 존중해야 할 의무가 사람들에게 있다고 믿는다.

구문 [4행~8행] They argue **it**'s wrong **to ever abuse or exploit animals** or **to cause animals any pain and suffering**; animals shouldn't be eaten, held captive in zoos, or used in any (or most) educational or research settings.
it은 가주어, to ever abuse ~ suffering이 진주어이다. 굵게 표시된 두 개의 to부정사구가 진주어로서 or로 연결된다. 밑줄 친 세 개의 과거분사(구)는 콤마(,)와 or로 병렬 연결된다.

[14행~18행] According to Gary Francione, a professor of law at Rutgers University, **to say an animal has a "right" (to have an interest protected)** *means* (that) the animal is entitled to have *that interest* protected even if it would benefit us to do otherwise.
to say ~ an interest protected는 to부정사의 명사적 용법으로 쓰여 문장의 주어 역할을 한다. 동사 means의 목적어절을 이끄는 접속사 that이 생략되었다. 밑줄 친 부분은 '사역동사(have)+목적어(that interest)+p.p.(protected)'의 형태이다.

어휘 advocate 옹호자, 지지자 make an exception 예외를 두다 abuse 학대하다; 남용[오용]하다 exploit 착취하다 suffering 고통 captive 감금된, 포로가 된 moral 윤리적인, 도덕적인 animal cruelty 동물 학대 pervade ~에 널리 퍼지다 establish 확립[수립]하다 interest 권익, 이익 be entitled to ~할 자격이 있다 obligation 의무 honor 존중하다, 이행하다 claim 주장(하다)

14 글의 순서 ③

해설 주어진 글부터 순서를 보면 '핵융합은 문제가 적은 것으로 보이는 에너지 형태이다 → (B) 기존 방식보다 에너지 산출량은 많고 폐기물 양은 더 적다 → (C) 그러나 현재는 보상으로 얻게 될 에너지보다 그 에너지를 만드는 데 드는 에너지가 더 크다 → (A) 다시 말해 얻는 것보다 잃는 게 많아서 아직 발전소에서 사용될 수 없

다'의 흐름이 자연스럽다.

해석 대부분의 다른 에너지 형태보다 문제가 적은 것으로 보이는 에너지 형태가 핵'융합' 발전이다.
(B) 융합 과정은 실제로 핵분열보다 훨씬 더 많은 에너지를 방출하며, 그 결과 훨씬 더 적은 방사성폐기물을 배출한다. 그래서 많은 사람들은 작동하는 수소 핵융합로 개발 전망에 대해 흥분하고 있다.
(C) 그러나 지금 당장은 과학자들이 융합 발전을 실현시킬 수 없다. 과학자들은 융합 에너지를 생산할 수 있지만, 지금 당장은 융합의 결과로 우리에게 제공되는 실제 에너지보다 핵융합을 만들어내는 데 훨씬 더 많은 에너지가 필요하다.
(A) 다시 말해서, 핵융합을 만들기 위해 시도할 때, 에너지를 얻는 대신 실제로는 잃게 된다. 인간들이 융합 발전을 사용하는 폭탄을 만들 수는 있을지라도 아직 발전소에서 사용하기 위해 반응을 통제할 수는 없다.

어휘 nuclear fusion power 핵융합 발전   radioactive waste 방사성 폐기물
fusion reactor 핵융합로   in return (~에 대한) 보답으로, 답례로

15 글의 순서   ④

해설 동물들의 경보 발령이 동족 보호의 효과가 있다는 주어진 글 다음에는 지킬 가족이 없는 경우에도 경보를 발령하는 반례를 제시한 (C)가 나온다. 경보를 발령하면 그 동물에게 포식자의 주의가 집중된다는 (C) 다음에는 이것이 역설적인 이익이 될 수 있다는 내용의 (A)가 나온다. (A)의 In doing so는 동물이 경보를 발령하여 포식자가 자신에게 주목하도록 하는 행동을 가리키고, (A)에 나온 경보 발령의 '역설적 이익'에 대해 상술하는 (B)가 마지막으로 오는 것이 적절하다.

해석 근처에 동족이 있는 동물들에게, 포식자가 접근할 시 경보 발령의 대가는 가족을 보호할 필요보다 덜 중대할지 모른다. 숲 여기저기에 사는 몇몇 얼룩다람쥐와 다람쥐는 새끼를 함께 데리고 있어서, 그들의 찍찍 우는 소리는 그들의 새끼에게 상급 경고를 제공한다.
(C) 그러나 많은 동물들이 가족이 있지 않을 때 경보 발령을 사용하므로, 다른 혜택이 또한 작용하고 있음이 분명하다. 몇몇 경보 신호는 포식자와 적극적으로 소통하도록 고안되어, 위험의 순간에 그 동물에게 관심을 집중시킨다.
(A) 그렇게 하면서 그들은 포식자에게 그들이 누구이며 어디에 있는지를 말해주는 역설적인 이익을 거둘지도 모른다. 포식자의 관점에서 보면 자신이 접근하는 것을 보았고 달아날 태세를 취하는 먹잇감은 잡기 힘들 가능성이 높다.
(B) 포식자의 시간은 경계를 게을리하는 먹잇감을 찾는 데 더 잘 쓰일 것이다. 경보 발령은 따라서 공격의 무익함을 알려 안전을 획득함으로써 발령자에게 직접적인 이익을 제공할 수 있다.

구문 [8행~11행] From the predator's perspective, *prey* [**that** has seen your approach and is poised to flee] is likely to be hard to catch.
[ ] 부분은 주격 관계대명사 that이 이끄는 절로 prey를 수식한다.
[13행~15행] Alarm calling can therefore provide a direct benefit to the caller **by** advertising the unprofitability of an attack [and] thus buying safety.
전치사 by의 목적어로 밑줄 친 두 개의 동명사구가 and로 병렬 연결된다.

어휘 kin 동족; 친척   alarm call[calling] 경보 발령[호출]   predator 포식자
outweigh ~보다 중대하다[뛰어나다]   chipmunk 얼룩 다람쥐   youngster 어린 동물; 젊은이   offspring 새끼, 자손   reap 거두다; 수확하다   paradoxical 역설적인
perspective 관점; 전망   prey 먹이; 희생자   be poised to-v v할 만반의 태세를 갖추다   flee 달아나다   unwary 주의를 게을리 하는; 속기 쉬운   advertise 알리다, 광고하다   unprofitability 무익함; 이익이 없음   draw attention 관심을 끌다

16 문장 넣기   ④

해설 주어진 문장에서 '그 전략은 코펜하겐에서 효과가 좋았다'라고 나와 있으므로 이 문장 앞에는 그 전략이 언급되어야 한다. 그러므로 a crime prevention strategy가 있는 문장의 뒷부분인 ④가 가장 적절하다. 이후로는 그 전략이 효과가 없었던 호주 시드니에 대한 내용이 However, ~에 이어지고 있으므로 흐름이 자연스럽다.

해석 대략 7천 명의 거주자가 코펜하겐의 도시 중심에 산다. 겨울철의 평범한 주중 저녁에 시내를 걸어 다니는 사람은 약 7천 개의 창문에서 나오는 불빛을 즐길 수 있다. 주택과 거주자들의 가까움은 안전감에 주요 역할을 한다. 도시 계획 입안자들이 범죄 예방 전략으로서 기능과 주택을 혼합하여 보행자와 자전거를 타는 사람들이 이용하는 가장 주요한 거리들을 따라 안전감을 증대시키는 것은 흔한 관행이다. 그 전략은 코펜하겐에서 효과가 좋았는데, 그 도시 중심에는 5층에서 6층 사이 높이의 건물들이 있어서 거주지와 도로 공간 사이에 충분한 시각적 접촉이 있다. 그러나 호주 시드니는 중심부에 만 5천 명이 살고 있는데도 그것이(= 전략이) 그만큼 효과가 좋지 않다. 호주의 거주지는 일반적으로 지상 위로 10층에서 50층에 있어서 높은 곳에 사는 사람 누구도 아래쪽 거리에서 무슨 일이 일어나고 있는지 볼 수가 없다.

구문 [10행~14행] **It** is common practice *for city planners* **to mix** functions and housing as a crime prevention strategy / [and] thus **increase** the feeling of safety along *the most important streets* (used by pedestrians and bicyclists). It은 가주어이고 to mix 이하가 진주어이다. for city planners는 to-v의 의미상의 주어이다. to 뒤의 동사원형 mix와 increase가 병렬구조를 이룬다. ( )는 수동의 의미로 앞의 the most important streets를 수식한다.

어휘 strategy 전략, 작전   residence 거주지, 주택   *cf.* resident 거주자, 주민
approximately 대략, 대강   ordinary 흔한, 보통의   housing 주택   practice
관행, 실시   planner 계획[입안]자   pedestrian 보행자

17 문장 넣기   ④

해설 주어진 문장이 In contrast로 시작하고 있으므로 그 앞의 내용과는 대조를 이루어야 한다. 주어진 문장이 손실을 초래하는 아이디어에 대한 것이므로 경제적 이익을 발생시키는 아이디어에 대한 언급 뒤인 ④에 들어가는 것이 적절하다.

해석 하나의 새로운 아이디어가 검증되기 전에 그것이 좋은 것인지 알기는 것은 어렵다. 경제 성장이라는 관점에서, 새로운 아이디어들을 얻기 위해 기업가들이 강력한 장려책을 갖는 것은 무척 중요하지만, 자원의 가치를 축소하는 낭비적인 계획들을 중단시키는 것 역시 중요하다. 시장경제에서는 이윤과 손실이 이러한 목표들을 달성시킨다. 소비자들에게 생산의 기회비용을 상쇄할 충분한 가치를 만들어주므로, 자원의 가치를 더해주는 새로운 아이디어들은 그것들을 발견한 기업가들에게는 경제적 이익을 발생시킨다. 대조적으로, 다른 더 가치 있는 이용으로부터 자원을 빼내고, 그것들을 소비자들에게는 가치 없는 것으로 바꿔놓는 아이디어는 손실을 초래할 것이고, 기업가에게는 그러한 계획들을 중단시키려는 강력한 동기를 제공할 것이다. 그러므로 그러한 시장의 절차는 일을 하는 더 나은 방식의 발견과 자원의 가치를 축소하는 계획의 종료 모두를 촉진시킨다. 이런 방식으로 이익과 손실의 체계는 자원이 경제 성장을 촉진하는 계획으로 향하는 것을 보장할 것이다.

구문 [9행~11행] ~ but it is also **important** // that *wasteful projects* [that reduce the value of resources] **be brought** to a halt.
it은 가주어이고 that 이하 절이 진주어이다. 동사가 be brought로 동사원형이 나온 것은 당연, 필요 등을 나타내는 형용사(important, necessary 등) 뒤에 오는 that절에는 「(should+)동사원형」이 와야 하기 때문이다.

어휘 in contrast 그에 반해서 drain 빼내다, 유출시키다 entrepreneur 기업가 incentive 장려[우대]책 standpoint 관점 bring to a halt 정지[중단]시키다 offset 상쇄하다, 벌충하다 generate 일으키다, 발생시키다 termination 종료

18 요약문 완성 ③

해설 다른 사람들에게 좋은 모습을 보이고 싶어 하는 마음은 단순하거나 익숙한 과업을 할 때는 동기 향상을 가져오지만, 어려운 과업에서 실패하는 경우 더 큰 당혹감을 초래하고 수행 능력을 떨어뜨려 과업의 복잡성(complexity)의 정도에 따라 서로 다른(opposing) 결과를 산출한다.
① 서로 다른 – 우선순위   ② 즉각적인 – 우선순위
④ 즉각적인 – 복잡성   ⑤ 긍정하는 – 복잡성

해석 사회적 실재감의 영향(이라는 생각)을 제시하는 사회적 촉진에 대한 한 가지 접근법은 사람들이 일반적으로 다른 사람들에게 가능한 한 가장 좋은 모습을 제시하고 호의적인 인상을 주려고 노력한다는 생각에 근거를 둔다. 이것이 사실인 경우, 관찰자나 협력자는 수행되고 있는 과업이 무엇이든 개인이 열심히 일하도록 동기를 부여할 수 있을 뿐만 아니라, 수행이 실패로 이어질 때 그 사람의 당혹감을 증가시킬 수 있다. 실패는 과업이 단순하거나 익숙한 것일 때는 일어나기 쉽지 않아서 증가된 동기부여가 개선을 만들어 내기에 충분하다. 하지만 어려운 과업은 적어도 초기 단계에서는 자주 실패한다. 그러한 실패로 야기된 당혹감은 충분한 강도의 스트레스와 인지적 간섭이 과업 수행에 지장을 주게 할 수도 있다.

↓

관찰되는 상태에 있는 개인의 수행은 그 사람이 수행하는 과제의 (B) 복잡성의 정도에 따라 (A) 서로 다른 결과를 산출할 수 있다.

구문 [1행~5행] **One approach** to *social facilitation* [that proposes an influence in social presence] **is** based on the idea that people generally try to present the best possible appearance to others and to make a favorable impression].
문장의 주어는 One approach이고 동사는 is이다. [ ]은 social facilitation을 수식하는 관계사절이다. the idea와 밑줄 친 that절은 동격 관계이고, that절 내에서 to present ~ to others와 to make ~ impression은 병렬구조를 이룬다.
[5행~9행] **This being the case**, observers or coactors may not only motivate individuals to work hard at *whatever task is being carried out*, but also increase the person's sense of embarrassment when performance leads to failure.
This being the case는 의미상 주어가 This이고 접속사가 생략된 분사구문이다. 「not only A but also B」는 'A뿐만 아니라 B도'의 뜻이다. whatever가 이끄는 명사절이 at의 목적어 자리에 쓰였다.

어휘 facilitation 촉진, 조장 appearance (겉)모습, 외모 favorable 호의적인 coactor 협력자 sufficient 충분한 cognitive 인지적인 interference 간섭, 방해 disrupt 방해하다, 지장을 주다 affirmative 긍정[동의]하는; 확언적인 intricacy 복잡(함)

19~20 장문   19 ② 20 ③

해설 19. 첫 번째 단락의 실험에서 피실험자들은 실험자들이 제시한 노년과 관련된 단어들이 일으킨 점화 효과로 인해 실험실을 천천히 걸어 나가는 행동을 보였다. 두 번째 단락에서 처음 만나는 강사를 설명해주는 단어에 따라 학생들의 수업 참여도에 유의미한 차이를 보였다. 두 단락은 공통적으로 점화 효과가 행동(천천히 걷기,

---

수업 참여도)의 변화를 일으킨 사례를 제시하므로 이를 반영한 제목으로 가장 적절한 것은 ② '다른 사람들이 점화시키는 단어가 당신의 행동을 바꾼다'이다.
① 점화가 의사 결정에 미치는 영향들
③ 사회적 점화란 무엇이며 어떻게 발생하는가?
④ 말의 숨겨진 점화의 힘: 통념과 사실
⑤ 신체적 행동이 당신이 생각하는 것을 점화할 수 있는 방식
20. 피실험자들은 노년에 관련된 단어로 작문을 한 것만으로도 걸음이 느려지는 행동 변화를 보였는데, 이는 점화된 단어의 암시에 영향을 받는 것이므로 우리가 암시에 저항력이 있는(resistant) 것이 아니라 개방되어 있음을(open) 의미한다.

해설 점화 효과는 사회심리학자들이 연구하는 흥미로운 인지 과정이다. 점화는 당신이 기억 속의 특정한 (a) 연상을 활성화하는 과정이다. 점화는 정보가 저장된 뉴런의 무리들을 활용한다. 한 무리가 활성화될 때, 비슷한 정보를 저장하고 있는 주변의 무리들이 의식적 정신의 전면에 대두한다. New York 대학교 학생들은 (그들이 점화 연구의 피실험자임을 알지 못하고) 다섯 단어로 구성된 세트 목록으로부터 네 단어로 이루어진 문장들을 만들라는 요청을 받았다. 문장들은 노년에 대해 생각하는 방향으로 학생들을 점화시킬 단어들(주름, 쓸쓸한, 잘 잊는, 외로운 그리고 '나이 든'이라는 단어 그 자체)을 포함했다. 점화가 너무나 효과적이어서 학생들은 그들의 내적인 점화를 외적으로 드러내는 것을 행동에 나타내며 (b) 천천히 걸어서 떠났다. 이러한 연구 결과는 우리가 과연 암시에 얼마나 (c) 저항력이 있는지(→ 개방되어 있는지)를 강조한다.
그러면 (d) 긍정적인 메시지를 전달하는 것이 이치에 맞다. Harold Kelley는 1950년에 학급에 강연하러 올 초청 연사를 설명하는 연구를 수행했다. 강연자가 오기 전에 Kelley는 학생들에게 그에 관한 한 단락 길이의 설명을 제공했다. 절반(의 학생들)은 "그를 아는 사람들은 그가 다소 냉정하고, 근면하고, 비판적이고, 현실적이며 단호하다고 생각한다."라고 들었다. 나머지 절반은 "그를 아는 사람들은 그가 따뜻하고, 근면하고, 비판적이고, 현실적이며 단호하다고 생각한다."라고 들었다. 모든 학생들은 그리고 나서 초청 연사로부터 강연을 들었다. 점화 효과는 무엇이었는가? 그가 따뜻하다는 말을 들었던 학생 중 56퍼센트가 수업에 기꺼이 참여했다. 그가 냉정하다고 들었던 학생 중 오직 32퍼센트만이 토론에 참여했다. 이것은 그러한 (e) 최초의 정보 투입이 얼마나 중요할 수 있는지를 입증한다.

구문 [6행~8행] When a cluster is activated, *surrounding clusters* [**that** store similar information] come to the forefront of the conscious mind.
현재분사 surrounding이 clusters를 수식하고, 관계대명사 that이 이끄는 형용사절이 선행사 surrounding clusters를 수식한다.
[14행~17행] The priming was **so** *effective* **that** students left walking slowly, **acting out** the external demonstration of their internal priming.
「so+형용사+that …」 구문이 쓰여 '너무 ~해서 …하다'의 의미를 나타낸다. acting out 이하는 분사구문으로 의미상 주어는 students이다.
[30행~32행] Fifty-six percent of *the students* [**who were told** that he was *warm*] were willing participants in the class.
관계대명사 who가 이끄는 형용사절은 앞에 있는 the students를 수식한다. 4문형이던 문장이 수동태로 전환되며 본래 직접목적어였던 that절이 동사 뒤에 그대로 쓰였다.

어휘 cognitive 인지[인식]의 activate 활성화시키다 association 연상, 연관; 협회 tap into ~을 활용[이용]하다; ~에 다가가다 cluster 무리; 송이; 모이다 forefront 맨앞, 선두; 중심 conscious 의식하는, 자각하는 solitary 쓸쓸한; 혼자의 act out (무의식적으로) 행동에 나타내다 demonstration 드러냄, 표출; 증명 underscore 강조하다; 밑줄을 긋다 description 설명, 기술 industrious 근면한, 부지런한 practical 현실적인; 실용적인 determined 단호한 significant 중요한; 상당한 input 투입; 입력 prime 점화시키다; 준비시키다; 최고의; 주된

| 1 | ① | 2 | ⑤ | 3 | ③ | 4 | ⑤ | 5 | ⑤ | | 6 | ⑤ | 7 | ③ | 8 | ⑤ | 9 | ② | 10 | ③ |
| 11 | ③ | 12 | ③ | 13 | ④ | 14 | ④ | 15 | ⑤ | | 16 | ⑤ | 17 | ③ | 18 | ③ | 19 | ① | 20 | ③ |

1 심경 변화   ①

해설 어두운 동굴에 고립되어 살아 나갈 수 있을지 확실하지 않은 상황에서 동굴 출구를 발견할 실마리를 얻어 출구를 찾아나서는 것으로 글이 마무리되므로, Jacob의 심경 변화로 가장 적절한 것은 ① '겁을 먹은(frightened) → 희망찬(hopeful)'이다.

해석 Jacob은 동굴의 통로를 통과하여 엎드려 기어갔다. 그는 공격적이고 완전한 어둠이 그를 감쌀 때 숨이 막혔다. 그는 끝에서 빛을 보기를 간절히 원했다. 다시 가족을 보게 될까? 살아서 밖으로 나가게 될 것인가? 그는 '도와줘'라고 외치려 애썼지만 어떤 소리도 나오지 않았다. 바로 그 때, 동굴 뒤에서 소리가 시작됐다. Jacob은 소리의 방향을 보려고 눈에 힘을 주었다. 동굴에서 밧줄로 매달린 큰 상자가 있었다. 상자가 동굴 옆면을 칠 때마다, 그것은 큰 소리를 내었다. 그러나 상자가 왜 흔들리는 걸까? 약간의 산들바람이 있다는 생각이 마침내 Jacob에게 떠올랐다. 바람의 방향을 따라간다면, 그는 밖으로 나가는 길을 찾을 수 있을 것이다! 신이 나서 Jacob은 동굴 입구로 가는 길을 찾아 나섰다.

구문 [9행~10행] **Every time** the box hit the side of the cave, it made a large noise.
접속사 Every time은 '~할 때마다'의 뜻이다.
[11행~12행] **It** finally *occurred* to Jacob [that there was a slight breeze].
It은 가주어이고 [ ]가 진주어이다. 'occur to+(사람)'은 '(생각이) ~에게 떠오르다'의 뜻이다.

어휘 crawl 기다   passageway 통로   gasp 숨이 턱 막히다   oppressive 공격적인   utter 완전한   envelop 감싸다, 뒤덮다   anxious 열망하는   strain 안간힘을 쓰다   dangle 매달리다   sway 흔들리다   occur to (생각이) ~에게 떠오르다   slight 약간의   breeze 산들바람   enthusiastically 열광적으로

2 필자 주장   ⑤

해설 숙달된 과학자들이 결과와 상관없이 실험을 설계하고, 그로부터 나오는 결과를 실패가 아니라 새로운 무언가를 배울 수 있는 데이터로 여기듯이, 우리도 매일 매일의 경험을 실험처럼 여기고 실수를 실패로 여기지 말고 배움의 기회로 삼자는 내용이다. 그러므로 필자의 주장으로 가장 적절한 것은 ⑤이다.

해석 우리 자신을 새로운 누군가에게 소개하거나 새로운 음식을 맛보는 것과 같은 단순한 일을 할 때, 우리는 매일 매일 실험을 수행한다는 것을 명심하는 것이 중요하다. 그 결과, 우리는 예상치 못한 결과들에 대응하는 것과 그것들 각각으로부터 배우는 것을 연습할 많은 기회들을 얻는다. 숙달된 과학자들은 이것을 잘 알기 때문에, 특정한 결과가 무엇이든 중요한 질문에 해답을 주는 실험들을 설계하기 위해 최선을 다한다. 그들은 각 실험이 이해를 향한 값진 단서들을 제공한다는 것을 안다. 속담에서 말하듯이, '천재성은 가장 단기간에 가장 많은 실수를 하는 능력이다.' 그러한 각각의 실수가 실험적인 데이터와 새로운 무언가를 배울 수 있는 기회를 제공한다. 과학자들처럼, 우리는 예상치 못한 결과들을 실패라고 보는 것을 중단할 필요가 있다. 어휘를 변화시킴으로써, 즉 '실패'를 '데이터'로 봄으로써, 우리는 기꺼이 실험을 하고자 하는 모든 사람들의 의향을 높일 수 있다.

구문 [1행~4행] It is important to keep in mind // that we perform experiments every single day when we do things as simple as introducing ourselves to

someone new or trying a new food.
It은 가주어이고 to keep ~ new food가 진주어이며, that we ~ a new food는 to-v의 목적어이다.
[4행~6행] As a result, we get lots of opportunities to practice **responding** to unexpected results and **learning** from each one of them.
두 밑줄 친 부분은 동격 관계이며, to practice의 목적어로 responding과 learning이 and로 연결되어 병렬구조를 이룬다.

어휘 keep in mind ~을 명심하다[기억하다]   perform 수행[실시]하다; 공연하다   experiment 실험(하다) *cf.* experimental 실험적인; (과학) 실험의   opportunity 기회   trained 숙달된, 훈련받은   specific 특정한; 구체적인, 명확한   clue 단서; 실마리   enhance 높이다, 향상시키다   willingness 기꺼이 하는 의향[마음]; 쾌히[자진하여] 하기

3 밑줄 함의   ③

해설 나사(screw)는 드라이버로 돌려서 사용해야 하며, 망치질(hammering)에 상응하는 것은 screw가 아니라 nail(못)이다. 따라서 '나사에 망치질을 하는 것'은 '적합한 방법을 쓰지 않고 일방적으로 밀어붙이는 행동'을 비유적으로 표현한다. 이 글에서 코치인 필자가 고민하는 것은 코칭을 진행할 때 고객과 나란히 가고 있는지, 혹시 자신이 제시한 해결책을 고객에게 밀어붙이고 종결을 강요하는 것은 아닐지에 관한 것이므로, 이를 정리하면 '나사에 망치질을 한 데에는 내 몫을 했다'는 말은 ③ '코치 측의 일방적인 노력'을 의미한다고 할 수 있다.
① 코칭 활동 동안 주어지는 부정적인 피드백
② 고객을 위한 느린 속도의 코칭 계획
④ 긴박감이 있는 코칭 경험
⑤ 전문적인 충고보다는 정서적인 지지

해석 코치는 고객들이 그들의 개인적 삶과 직업적 삶에서 원하는 결과를 생산하도록 돕는다. 나는 수 년 간에 걸쳐서 수천 번의 성공적인 코칭 활동을 수행했지만, 나사에 망치질을 한 것의 내 몫도 했다. 나의 고객들의 진전에 대한 나의 관심은 보통 유능한 코치가 되고자 하는 나의 욕망과 나란히 있다. 그리고 종결을 달성하는 데 대한 나의 관심은 보통 나의 고객들의 진전과 그들의 독립 둘 다를 지지한다. 그러나 내가 이러한 관심들을 감시하고 그것의 강도를 측정하는 것이 중요하다. 나는 자문해야 한다. "내가 그들에게 해결책을 밀어붙이고 있는 걸까, 아니면 그들이 넘어갈 준비가 되기 전에 종결을 향해 그저 달려가고 있는 걸까?" 이 질문이 개인으로서의 나의 정당한 요구가 때때로 나의 고객의 필요와 코칭 과정에 어떻게 방해가 되는지를 내가 알아보게 해주는 데 필수적인 것이었다.

구문 [9행~10행] But it's important *for me* to monitor these interests and to gauge their intensity:
it은 가주어이고 두 밑줄 친 부분이 진주어이며, for me는 두 to-v구에 대한 의미상 주어이다.
[13행~16행] This question has been essential / in **allowing** me **to see** // how my legitimate needs as a person occasionally get in the way of my client's needs and the coaching process.
in 이하에 「allow + O + to-v (O가 v하는 것을 허용하다)」 구문이 쓰였다. how ~ process는 to see의 목적어 역할을 하는 간접의문문이며, 「의문사(how) + 주어(my legitimate needs as a person) + 동사(get)」의 어순으로 쓰였다.

어휘 session 활동; 시간 align 나란히 만들다; 조정하다 gauge 측정하다; 판단하다 intensity 강도 legitimate 정당한; 합법적인 occasionally 때때로 get in the way 방해되다 scheme 계획; 책략 urgency 긴급; 위급

4 글의 주제 ⑤

해설 이야기는 올바른 공동의 가치를 전파함으로써 사회의 마찰을 줄이는 윤활유 역할을 한다. 또한 이야기는 혈연관계를 넘어서 인간들을 공동체로 묶어주는 접착제 역할을 한다. 이러한 이야기의 기능을 반영하는 주제로 가장 적절한 것은 ⑤ '공동의 가치를 강화함으로써 사회를 결속시키는 기능을 하는 이야기'이다.
① 사회에서 극적으로 표현되는 이야기의 중요성
② 인간이 이야기에 선천적인 애정을 갖고 있는 이유들
③ 이야기 속의 인과관계 이해하기
④ 현재에서 벗어남으로써 미래를 상상하도록 하는 스토리텔링

해석 이야기는 무엇이 칭찬할 만하고 무엇이 경멸을 살 만한지를 우리에게 말해준다. 그것은 우리가 타락한 대신 품위 있는 사람이 되도록 미묘하고도 끊임없이 장려한다. 이야기는 사회의 윤활유이자 접착제이다. 우리가 품행을 올바르게 하도록 장려함으로써, 이야기는 사람들을 공동의 가치 주변으로 결집시키면서 사회적 마찰을 감소시킨다. 이야기는 우리를 균질화한다. 즉, 그것은 우리를 하나로 만든다. 이것이 Marshall McLuhan이 지구촌이라는 자신의 아이디어와 함께 마음에 품고 있던 것의 일부이다. 기술은 널리 흩어진 사람들을 동일한 매체로 포화시켰고 그들을 세계를 아우르는 마을의 시민으로 만들었다. 이야기가 (신성한 것과 불경한 것 모두) 아마 인간의 삶에서 주된 응집력일 것이다. 사회는 다른 성격, 목표와 의제를 가진 까다로운 사람들로 구성되어 있다. 무엇이 우리의 친족 유대관계를 넘어서서 우리를 연결해주는가? 바로 이야기이다. John Gardner가 표현했듯이, 지어낸 이야기는 '본질적으로 진지하고 이로운, 혼란과 죽음에 대항하여 이루어지는 게임이다.' 이야기는 사회의 무질서, 즉 무너지려는 것들의 경향에 대한 반대 세력이다. 이야기는 그것이 없으면 나머지가 지속될 수 없는 중심이다.

구문 [8행~11행] Technology **has saturated** widely dispersed people with the same media and (**has**) **made** them into citizens of *a village* [that spans the world].
동사 has saturated와 (has) made가 병렬구조를 이룬다. [ ] 부분은 관계사절로 앞의 a village를 수식한다.
[15행~17행] As John Gardner puts it, fiction "is essentially serious and beneficial, *a game* (**played** against chaos and death)."
( ) 부분은 과거분사 played가 이끄는 분사구로 a game을 수식한다.

어휘 laudable 칭찬[감탄]할 만한 contemptible 경멸받을 만한 decent 품위 있는, 예의 바른; 괜찮은; 적절한 decadent 타락한, 퇴폐적인 grease 윤활유; 기름(을 바르다) glue 접착제; (접착제로) 붙이다 friction 마찰; 불화 unite 결속[통합]시키다; 연합하다 common value 공동의 가치 saturate 포화시키다; 흠뻑 적시다 dispersed 흩어진, 분산된 span 걸치다; 기간[시간] sacred 신성한, 성스러운 profane 불경한; 세속적인 cohere 응집[결합]하다; 일관성 있다 fractious 까다로운, 짜증을 잘 내는 personality 성격; 인간(성) agenda 의제[안건] (목록) kinship 친족(임); 연대감 tie (강한) 유대[관계] chaos 혼란 counterforce 반대[대항] 세력 disorder 무질서; 장애 fall apart 무너지다; 결딴나다 dramatize 극적으로 표현하다; 각색하다 fondness 애정; 좋아함 envision 상상하다, 구상하다 bind 결속시키다; 감다

5 글의 제목 ⑤

해설 관광지에서 관광 기념품을 구매할 때 야생 생물들에게 해가 되지 않고 지역 사회를 이롭게 할 수 있는 윤리적인 구매를 하라는 내용의 글이므로 제목으로 가장

적절한 것은 ⑤ '기념품을 세심하게 선택하고 윤리적으로 구매하라'이다.
① 기념품은 여행 경험과 관련된 상징적 가치를 지닌다
② 책임 있는 관광: 왜 기념품을 구매해야 하는가?
③ 여행하는 동안 다른 문화와 관습을 존중하라
④ 기념품 판매의 경제학과 관광에서의 역할

해석 많은 관광객들은 전 세계를 여행하러 다닐 때 야생 생물 제품을 구매한다. 멸종 위기에 처한 종들이 종종 기념품 거래에 들어서고, 관광객들은 알면서도 모르면서도 그러한 멸종 위기에 처한 품목들을 여행 기념품으로 산다. 당신의 관광 달러는 지역 사회 경제에 중대한 기여를 하지만, 당신은 그것(달러)이 지역 사회를 이롭게 하도록 그것을 현명하게 쓸 필요가 있다. 무모한 기념품 사냥꾼이 되지 마라. 지역 야생 생물이나 식물을 착취하거나 격감시키지 않는 기념품을 고름으로써 윤리적인 사람이 되어라. 국제 야생 생물 법률 제정과 세관 제한은 당신이 집으로 돌아갈 때 상아, 거북딱지, 동물 가죽 액세서리와 산호와 같은 품목을 수입하는 것을 허용하지 않을지도 모른다. 수입될 확률이 높은 플라스틱이나 '관광객에게 인기 있는' 품목을 구입하는 대신, 지역의 장인들을 돕는 긍정적인 기념품 선택을 항상 하라.

구문 [7행~8행] ~ but you need to spend them wisely // **so (that)** they benefit the local community.
so 다음에는 that이 생략되어 있으며 so that은 '~하도록, ~하기 위하여'의 뜻이다.

어휘 endangered 멸종 위기에 처한 reckless 무모한 exploit 착취하다 deplete 고갈시키다, 격감시키다 legislation 법률 제정 customs 세관 restriction 제한, 규제 tortoiseshell 거북딱지 coral 산호 craftspeople 장인 touristy 관광객에게 인기 있는

6 안내문 일치 ⑤

해설 투어 출발 전 24시간 이내의 예약 취소는 취소 수수료가 부과된다고 했으므로 ⑤가 안내문의 내용과 일치한다.
① 망원경이 제공되지만 자신의 것도 가져와도 된다고 했다.
② 투어는 오후 6시부터 10시까지이지만 별 관측은 오후 7시부터 9시까지이다.
③ 입장료에 포장된 식사와 음료가 포함된다고 했으므로 별도 신청자에게만 제공되는 것은 아니다.
④ weather permitting(날씨가 좋으면)이라고 했으므로 기상의 영향을 받는다.

해석 별 관측 투어
블루마운틴에 오셔서 별을 관측하세요!

매주 화요일 오후 망원경이 제공될 것입니다. 그러나 여러분의 망원경을 가져오셔도 좋습니다.
투어는 오후 6시 Blue Center에서 출발하여 오후 10시까지 돌아옵니다.
(+ 별 관찰 시간: 오후 7시~오후 9시)
인당 30달러
입장료에는 음료와 포장된 식사가 포함됩니다.
지역 천문학 협회 자원봉사자들이 천체 관측을 위한 망원경을 설치하고 밤하늘에 대한 소개를 해 줍니다.

중요한 정보:
투어는 '날씨가 좋으면' 출발합니다. 취소 시 환불이 제공될 것입니다.
투어 출발 전 24시간 내에 취소하는 손님들은 취소 수수료가 부과될 것입니다.

더 많은 정보를 위해서는 www.ifa.bluem.org/info/vis를 방문하세요.

구문 [16행~18행] *Guests* (cancelling tour reservations / within 24 hours prior to tour departure) may be subject to a cancellation fee.

어휘 gaze 응시하다, 바라보다 telescope 망원경; 단축하다 entry 입장; 출입; 가입 astronomical 천문학의, 천문학적인 celestial 천체의, 하늘의 be subject to ~의 대상이다 cancellation fee 취소 수수료

7 밑줄 어법 ③

해설 ③ Edison simply tried every material he could에서 he could는 앞에 목적 격 관계대명사 which[that]가 생략되어 있고 could 다음에는 try가 생략되어 every material을 수식하며, 여기까지 봤을 때 이 문형은 「S(he) + V(could try) + O(which = every material)」로 이루어진 완전한 문장이다. 따라서 see와 같은 동사를 또 사 용하면 안 되므로 동사 see를 준동사로 바꿔 써야 하는데, 문맥상 '~하기 위하여'라 는 '목적'의 의미를 가지는 to see로 바꿔 쓰는 것이 가장 자연스럽다.

① did는 앞의 동사 knew를 지칭하는 대동사인데, 일반 동사의 과거형을 대신하는 대동사이므로 did를 적절히 사용했다.

② 「make + O(its use as a household lighting device) + C(impractical)」 구문으로 보아 자리에 형용사를 적절히 사용했다.

④ which는 carbonized bamboo를 지칭하며 which 이하는 carbonized bamboo 에 대한 추가적인 설명을 제시한다. which는 사물을 지칭하며 주어 역할을 하는 주 격 관계대명사로서 적절히 사용되었다.

⑤ to follow는 형용사적 용법으로 앞의 many decades를 수식한다.

해석 다른 사람들과 마찬가지로 에디슨은 다양한 물질들에 전기를 흐르게 하는 것이 그 물질들을 빛나게('고온 발광'이라 불리는 과정) 해서 양초와 천연 가스 램프의 대체재로 사 용될 수 있는 광원을 생성할 수 있다는 것을 알고 있었다. 문제는 발광 물질(필라멘트)의 질이 조금 후에 저하되어, 그것을 가정용 조명 장치로 사용하는 것을 실용적이지 못하게 만들 거라는 점이었다. 전기가 필라멘트를 파괴하는 물리적 원리 중 어떤 것도 알지 못했 기 때문에 에디슨은 그저 어떤 물질이 밝게 빛나도 다 타버리는 것을 견뎌내는지를 알아 보기 위해 할 수 있는 모든 물질들을 시도해봤다. 면화와 거북이 등껍질을 포함한 1,600 개의 다른 물질들을 시도해 본 후, 그는 탄화된 대나무를 우연히 발견했는데, 이는 (도처 의 거북이들에게는 기쁘게도) 선택할 수 있는 필라멘트인 것으로 판명되었다. 공기가 빠 진 전구(즉 진공관)에서 사용될 때, 탄화된 대나무는 다른 어떤 실험된 필라멘트보다 더 밝게 빛났고 훨씬 더 오랫동안 지속되었다. 에디슨은 자신의 전구를 얻었다. 가정용 전구 에서 텅스텐이 곧 탄화 대나무를 대체했지만, 고온 발광에 의한 조명은 향후 수십 년 간 실내 조명의 지배적인 방식이 되었다.

구문 [1행~5행] Edison knew, // as did others, // that running electricity through a variety of materials **could make** those materials **glow** — a process called incandescence — / thereby producing a light source [that could be used as an alternative to candles and natural gas lamps].

running ~ materials는 that절의 동명사 주어이며 이에 상응하는 동사는 could make이다. make those materials glow는 「make + O + 동사원형(O가 v하게 하 다)」 구문이다. thereby producing 이하는 분사구문이며 [ ]는 a light source를 수 식하는 관계사절이다.

[9행~11행] **Not knowing** any of the physical principles [by which electricity destroyed the filament], / Edison simply tried every material he could ~

Now knowing ~ filament는 '이유'의 의미를 가지는 분사구문이다. [ ]는 '전치 사 + 관계대명사'로 시작되는 관계대명사절로서 앞의 the physical principles를 수 식한다.

어휘 glow 빛나다; 타다 thereby 그렇게 함으로써 light source 광원 degrade 저 하시키다; 비하하다 lighting 조명 happen upon ~을 우연히 발견하다 carbonize 탄화시키다; 숯으로 만들다 evacuate 비우다; 대피시키다 outshine ~보다 더 빛나다

---

illumination 조명 cf. illuminate 밝게 하다; 명백히 하다 predominant 지배적인, 우세한 interior 내부의

8 밑줄 어휘 ⑤

해설 보통 신뢰하는 제품이 있는 상황에서 신제품이 나오면 수용하는 데 시간이 오래 걸리는데, 남북 전쟁 시에는 참전 군인들이 다른 선택권이 거의 없이 군용식 량으로 통조림 식품을 체험하게 되면서 신뢰를 형성했다고 한다. 이런 신뢰는 과 학적인 확신이나 지식에 근거한 것이 아니고 체험에서 비롯된 것이므로 ⑤ '생소함 (unfamiliarity)'은 '친숙함(familiarity)' 등으로 바뀌어야 문맥상 적절하다.

해석 비록 가끔이긴 하지만 군인들이 전시에 상업적인 통조림 식품을 체험한 것이 소비 자 신뢰의 시작을 낳았다. 이런 신뢰가 일련의 생산으로 다시 흘러들어, 혁신하고 확장하 기 위해 통조림 제조업자들이 필요로 하는 더 광범위한 수요에 대한 최초의 희미한 징조 를 ① 제공했다. 보통의 소비자들에게 신제품과 그들이 믿을 수 있는 기준이 되는 제품 간 의 선택권이 주어질 때 미각은 종종 ② 느리게 바뀌었다. 그러나 미국 남북 전쟁에 참전한 군인들은 자신들의 식량 보급에 관한 한 선택권이 거의 없었기 때문에, 새 식품에 기회를 주었고, 자신들의 미각을 ③ 넓혀 통조림 식품을 부분적으로 수용했다. 전쟁 후에 그들은 이런 새로운 기호를 고향으로 가져갔다. 이런 전장에서의 우연한 만남이 ④ 조성한 신뢰 의 본질은 과학적 확신이나 그 위험성에 대한 더 나은 이해, 혹은 그 식품이 어디에서 왔 는지에 대한 지식에 근거한 것은 아직 아니었다. 오히려, 그것은 새로운 종류의 식품을 시 식할 만한 가치가 있어 보이게 하고 그것의 편리함과 접근성의 진가를 인정할 만한 가치 가 있어 보이게 한 체험과 ⑤ 생소함(→ 친숙함)에서 비롯되었다.

구문 [3행~6행] This trust flowed back up the chain of production, **providing** the first faint signs of wider demand [**that** canners needed in order to innovate and expand].

providing 이하는 분사구문으로 동시 상황을 나타낸다. [ ] 부분은 목적격 관계대명 사 that이 이끄는 관계사절로 선행사 wider demand를 수식한다.

[17행~20행] Rather, it sprang from exposure and familiarity [that **made** a new kind of food seem worth sampling and its convenience and accessibility (seem) worth appreciating].

[ ] 부분은 exposure and familiarity를 수식하는 관계사절이고, 관계사절 내에서 동사 made 이후 두 개의 밑줄 친 부분이 and로 병렬 연결되었다. 첫 번째 밑줄 친 부분에서 a new kind of food는 목적어, seem worth sampling이 목적격보어이고, 두 번째 밑줄 친 부분에서는 its convenience and accessibility가 목적어, (seem) worth appreciating이 목적격보어로 반복되는 seem이 생략되었다.

어휘 commercially 상업적으로 generate (결과 · 상태 등을) 낳다[초래하다] faint 희미한; 아주 적은 canner 통조림 제조업자 expand 확장[확대]하다; 발전[성장]하다 accommodate 수용하다; 받아들이다 encounter (우연한) 만남 foster 조성[육성] 하다 sample 시식[시음]하다; 견본품

9 빈칸 추론 ②

해설 개미는 진딧물을 보호해주며 두 종이 공생관계를 이루는 것 같지만, 진딧물이 탈출하려고 날개를 성장시키면 개미가 화학 작용을 통해 이를 막는 것으로 보아 두 종의 공생관계는 전적으로 ② '자발적인' 것은 아님을 알 수 있다.

① 이기적인 ③ 일시적인 ④ 부차적인 ⑤ 강제적인

해석 개미가 제공해주는 보호에도 불구하고, 진딧물이 머무르는 것에 항상 만족하는 것 은 아니다. 그들이 떠나고 싶을 때, 다음 세대는 더 나은 환경으로 날아갈 수 있도록 날개 를 기른다. 이것은 그들의 수호자들의 주목을 벗어나지 못하며, 개미는 진딧물의 투명한 부속 기관을 즉각 물어뜯음으로써 비행하고자 하는 그들의 꿈을 끝장낸다. 그리고 마치

그것만으로는 충분하지 않다는 듯이, 개미는 자기들의 길들인 무리가 탈출하는 것을 막기 위해 화학적 수단도 사용한다. 개미는 진딧물의 날개의 성장을 늦추는 화합물을 발산하고, 추가로 진딧물도 느려지게 한다. Imperial College London의 한 연구 팀은 진딧물이 개미가 이전에 걸었던 영역을 건널 때 더 느리게 이동한다는 것을 발견했다. 지체의 원인은 진딧물의 행동에 영향을 미치고 그들이 감속하게 만드는 개미들이 남겨놓은 화학적 메시지이다. 개미와 진딧물 간의 아름다운 공생관계는 결국 전적으로 자발적인 것은 아닌 것으로 판명된다.

구문 [1행~2행] Despite *the protection* [(which[that]) ants offer], / aphids are **not always** content to stick around.

Despite는 '~에도 불구하고'라는 전치사이며 목적어는 the protection이다. [ ]는 앞에 목적격 관계대명사 which[that]가 생략되어 the protection을 수식한다. not always는 '항상 ~인 건 아니다'라는 뜻의 부분부정 표현이다.

[7행~9행] And **as if** that **were** not enough, // the ants also use chemical means / to **prevent** *their domesticated herds* **from escaping**.

「as if + S' + 과거동사」는 가정법 과거 표현으로 '마치 ~인 것처럼'의 뜻이다. 「prevent + O + from v-ing」는 'O가 v하는 것을 막다'의 뜻이다.

[14행~17행] The cause for the slowdown is *a chemical message* (left by the ants) [that affects the behavior of the aphids and **forces** them **to reduce** speed].

( )는 수동의 의미로 a chemical message를 수식한다. [ ]도 a chemical message 를 수식하며, [ ]에서 동사 affects와 forces는 병렬구조를 이루고 「force + O + to-v (O가 v하도록 강요하다)」 구문이 쓰였다.

어휘 stick around 머무르다 greener pastures ((비유적)) 더 나은 환경 guardian 수호자; 보호자 transparent 투명한 means 수단, 방법 domesticate 길들이다 herd 무리, 떼 compound 화합물 for good measure 추가로 terrain 영역, 지형 symbiotic 공생의

10 빈칸 추론 ③

해설 과업에서 성공하는 것이 지능 때문이라고 믿는 어린이들은 어려운 과업을 수행하는 것을 끈기 있게 노력하지 못하고 쉽게 포기한 반면에, 성공이 노력하는 능력에 있다고, 즉 노력을 통해 자기가 성공할 수 있는 가능성을 통제할 수 있다고 믿는 어린이들은 어려운 과제에 더 오래 매달렸다. 그러므로 빈칸에는 ③ '자기 통제에 대한 믿음'이 들어가야 가장 적절하다.
① 행동 자체를 위해 행동하는 것
② 지식에 초점을 맞추는 것
④ 두뇌 발전을 위한 노력
⑤ 수행을 위한 최적의 환경

해석 여러분이 안 믿을지도 모르겠지만, 자기 통제에 대한 믿음은 인간행동의 강력한 동기 부여 요소가 될 수 있다. 예를 들어, 시험의 성과가 타고난 지능 때문이라고 듣거나 아니면 열심히 노력하는 능력 때문이라는 말을 들은 10살짜리 어린이들을 생각해보자. 그다음에 두 집단 모두가 그들 능력을 훨씬 넘어서는 정말 어려운 두 번째 과제를 받았는데, 그것을 아무도 끝낼 수 없었다. 그러나 세 번째 시험에서는 첫 번째 과업에서의 처음 성공이 자신의 지능 때문이라고 여겼던 아이들은 더 쉽게 포기했는데 왜냐하면 그들은 두 번째 과업에서의 실패를 자기들의 제한된 타고난 능력 탓으로 돌렸고, 그것이 그들이 마지막 과업을 덜 끈기 있게 노력하도록 만들었기 때문이다. 대조적으로 자신들의 성적이 열심히 노력했기 때문이라고 생각한 아이들은 세 번째 과제에 더 오래 참았을 뿐 아니라 또한 그것을 더 즐겼다. 그러므로 여러분의 자녀들에게 단순히 그들이 똑똑하다고 말하기보다는 노력가라고 이야기해주는 편이 더 낫다.

구문 [6행~8행] Both sets were then given *a really difficult second task* [that **was** well beyond their capability], **which** no one could complete.

관계대명사 that이 이끄는 형용사절은 선행사 a really difficult second task를 수식한다. 계속적 용법의 관계대명사 which는 a really ~ their capability를 부연 설명한다.

[8행~13행] However, in a third test, *the children* [**who** thought (that) their initial successes on the first task were due to their intelligence] gave up more easily because they attributed their failure on the second task to their limited natural ability, **which** made them less likely to persevere on the last task.

관계대명사 who가 이끄는 [ ] 부분은 형용사절로 the children을 수식한다. [ ] 내에 thought의 목적어로 접속사 that이 이끄는 명사절이 쓰였다. 계속적 용법의 관계대명사 which가 이끄는 절은 because 이하의 부사절 전체에 대해 보충 설명한다.

어휘 motivator 동기 부여 하는 것[사람] due to ~때문에 natural 타고난, 천성의 capability 능력; 적성 initial 처음의; 초기의 give up 포기하다 attribute A to B A를 B의 탓으로 돌리다 persevere 끈기 있게 노력하다; 견디어내다 be down to ~ 때문에 생기다 stick 찌르다; 찌르다 for one's sake ~를 위해서 optimal 최적의, 최상의

11 빈칸 추론 ③

해설 빈칸 문장의 this difference는 빈칸 문장 앞에서 나온 실험의 결과, 즉 혼자 배정된 사람과 집단으로 배정된 사람들 간에 나타난 차이를 뜻한다. 빈칸 문장은 그 차이가 '어떠하다'는 것을 물어야 한다는 것인데, In other words로 환언되어 이어지는 뒷문장에서 그 차이가 사람들을 바꿔서 시험해도 항상 같은 차이를 보이는 일반화될 수 있는 결과인지 혹은 실험 내에서만 적용되는 것인지를 따져봐야 한다고 했으므로, 빈칸에 가장 적절한 것은 ③ '실험 밖에서도 일반화될 수 있는지'이다.
① 우리의 가설을 지지하는지
② 연구할 만큼 충분히 의미 있었는지
④ 참가자들의 관찰과 일치하는지
⑤ 실험에 참가한 모든 집단을 비교해볼 때 발견되었는지

해석 실험에서, 우리는 보통 다양한 조건 간의 전반적인 차이에 관심이 있다. 무작위로 혼자 배정된 참가자가 두 명 내지 네 명의 방관자 집단으로 배정된 참가자들보다 더 신속하게 피해자를 돕는다는 것을 알게 된다고 가정해보라. 방관자의 수가 돕는 속도에 정말로 영향을 미쳤다고 결론을 내리기 전에, 우리는 먼저 이 차이가 실험 밖에서도 일반화될 수 있는지 물어야 한다. 다시 말해서, 우리의 결과는 각 조건에서 사람들의 특정한 표준집단에만 근거하고 있기 때문에, 다른 표준집단을 측정했을 때도 유사한 결과가 나왔을 것이라고 어떻게 알겠는가? 어쩌면, 우리가 시험한 참가자들은 자신들이 선발된 모(母)집단을 충실히 대표하지 않았을지도 모른다. 어쩌면, 무작위 배정에도 불구하고, 혼자 배정된 참가자가 다른 조건의 참가자보다 공교롭게도 더 이타적인 성품을 가졌을 수도 있고, 이것이 우리가 관찰한 결과에 대한 설명일지도 모른다.

구문 [2행~5행] Suppose // we find / that *participants* (randomly assigned to be alone) help a victim more quickly than *those* (assigned to groups of two or four bystanders).

Suppose 뒤에 접속사 that이 생략되었으며 절 내의 participants와 those는 각각 과거분사구의 수식을 받고 있다.

어휘 randomly 무작위로, 임의로 *cf.* random 무작위의, 임의의 assign (사람을) 배치하다; (일 등을) 할당하다 conclude (~라고) 결론을 내리다; 끝나다 bystander 구경꾼, 행인 representative 대표(자); 대표하는 altruistic 이타적인 [선택지 어휘] generalize 일반화하다 observation 관찰, 관측; 감시; 주시 *cf.* observance (법률 · 규칙 등의) 준수

12 빈칸 추론 ③

해설 좋은 습관을 계발하는 데 지장을 초래하는 것은 인간이 좋은 습관이 가져다주는 쾌락에 빠르게 적응하여 이를 상실한다는 점이다. 이를 극복하기 위해서는 '똑같은 행동을 몇 번이고 무의식적으로 반복하는 것'이라는 습관에 대한 기존 정의에서 탈피하여, 습관에 대해 생각해보고(mindful) 다양화해보는 시도가 해법이 될 수 있다. 이를 반영하여 빈칸을 완성하면, 습관화의 부정적인 영향을 줄일 방법은 ③ '우리의 습관 일부에 의식적인 변화를 도입하는 것'이다.
① 오래되고 나쁜 습관을 없애기 위해 최선에 최선을 다하는 것
② 새로운 습관이 우리가 원하는 것임을 확실히 하는 것
④ 좋은 습관을 형성하기 위해 간단한 행동 변화를 시작하는 것
⑤ 습관을 형성하기 위해 특정한 행동과 특정한 계기를 선택하는 것

해석 심리학자이자 작가인 Jeremy Dean은 행복을 신장시키는 습관을 계발하는 것과 관련하여, '불행하게도 상당히 큰 허점이 있다. 그 허점은 습관화이다.'라고 설명한다. 습관화는 우리가 부정적인 경험보다 긍정적인 경험에 더 빠르게 적응한다는 것을 의미한다. 이것은 우리가 나쁜 습관에서 오는 고통보다 좋은 습관에서 오는 즐거움을 더 빠르게 잃는다는 것을 의미한다. Dean은 우리가 즐거움에 자동적으로 적응하는 것에 대처할 수 있는 한 가지 방법은 계속해서 정확히 똑같은 방식으로 우리의 습관을 반복하기보다는 습관을 다양화하는 것이라고 말한다. 예를 들어, 이것은 '잘 지내니?'라는 질문에 (매번 '잘 지내'라고 말하기보다는) 더 의식적으로 대답하려고 의식적으로 노력을 기울이는 것을 의미할 수 있다. 우리의 습관 일부에 의식적인 변화를 도입하는 것은 습관화의 영향을 줄이는 데 효과적일 수 있다. Dean은 이러한 생각이 같은 상황에서의 같은 행동이나 사고를 수반하는 습관의 정식 정의를 확대 해석하고 있다고 설명하지만, '행복한' 습관을 위해 우리는 '행동의 자동적인 시작이 필요하지만, 그 후에는 그것을 수행함에 있어 계속해서 유념하는 방식 또한 필요하다. 새로운 형태의 혼성 습관인, 유념하는 습관'이 필요하다.

구문 [8행~11행] Dean suggests **that** *one way* [that we can deal with our automatic adaptation to pleasure] **is** by varying our habits **rather than** repeating them in exactly the same way over and over again.
suggests의 목적어절을 이끄는 that절의 주어는 one way이고 동사는 is이며 관계부사절 [ ]이 주어 one way를 수식한다. 'A rather than B'는 'B라기보다는 차라리 A'라는 뜻인데, 밑줄 친 A와 B 자리에 전치사의 목적어로 동명사구가 위치한다.

어휘 cultivate 기르다, 계발하다 boost 신장시키다 a fly in the ointment 옥에 티, 허점 habituation 습관화 adaptation 적응; 각색 vary 다양화하다, 변화를 주다 over and over again 계속해서, 반복해서 conscious 의식적인 *cf.* consciously 의식적으로 stretch 확대 해석하다, 왜곡하다 initiation 시작, 개시 mindful 유념하는 carry A out A를 수행하다 hybrid 혼성(물); 잡종

13 흐름 무관 문장 ④

해설 옛 도시에서는 중심적 위치를 차지하던 종교 건물들이 현대의 급격한 도시화의 속도에 맞추지 못하여 숫자나 규모 등의 면에서 상대적으로 그 위치를 잃게 되었다는 내용으로서, 이를 뒷받침하는 설명으로 도시의 변화와 종교 기관들의 침체 원인을 서술하는 글인데, ④는 도시의 빈곤과 환경 문제를 말하고 있으므로 글의 전체적 흐름과 맞지 않다.

해석 종교를 그들 삶의 중심적 부분으로 생각하는 사회들에서조차도 절, 교회, 그리고 회교 사원은 적어도 다른 기능들과 비교하여 그것들의 도시 속 분포와 규모, 그리고 중요성에 관한 한, 도시의 삶에서 그 오래된 자리를 상실한 것처럼 보인다. ① 도시 인구가 증가하고 도시의 이동과 기능이 훨씬 더 복잡하고 다양해짐에 따라, 일과 생활의 새로운 방식이 나타났다. ② 종교적 믿음과 실천이 사회적 규범과 대중의 행위를 지배할지도 모르지만, 그것들은 도시의 건설된 형태 혹은 공간적 구조를 결정하지 않는다. ③ 도시들이 성

장했을 때, 새로운 도시 지역과 교외는 예배당의 숫자 면에서 옛 중심지를 거의 따라잡지 못했다. ④ 그러나 도시에서 오늘날의 세계와 직면한 두 가지 가장 압박적인 문제가 또한 함께 나온다. 가난과 환경 악화가 그것이다. ⑤ 20세기 도시 지역의 경이로운 성장은 주로 세속적인 성장이었다.

구문 [3행~6행] ~ at least **as far as** their distribution in the city and their size and significance [relative to other functions] **are concerned**.
'as far as ~ is concerned'는 '~에 관한 한'의 뜻이다. [ ]은 앞의 밑줄 부분을 수식한다.
[12행~15행] As cities have grown, the new urban areas and suburbs have hardly **caught up** [in their numbers of houses of worship] **with** the older central parts.
'catch up with'는 '~을 따라잡다'의 뜻이다. up과 with 사이에 전치사구 [ ] 부분이 삽입되어 있다.

어휘 temple 사원, 절 mosque 모스크, 회교 사원 as far as ~ is concerned ~에 관한 한 distribution 분포 urban 도시의 diversify 다양화하다 emerge 나타나다 conduct 행동 spatial 공간의 suburb 교외 catch up with ~을 따라잡다 house of worship 예배당 poverty 가난 degradation 저하, 악화 phenomenal 경이적인 secular 세속적인

14 글의 순서 ④

해설 규모 때문에 정부 혹은 다른 기관으로부터 특혜적 대우를 받는 외적 규모의 경제를 가지는 것의 예시로 끝나는 주어진 문장 다음에는 또 다른 예시로 대규모 개발업자에 혜택에 대한 내용인 다른 예시가 언급된 (C)가 나오는 것이 적절하다. 이것이 연구비용을 낮춘다는 (A)의 말은 (C)의 세 번째 문장의 내용을 가리키는 것이므로 (A)가 나와야 하고, (A)의 소규모 기업들에 대한 언급과 이어질 내용으로는 소규모 기업의 지리적 경제 이용 방법이 언급된 (B)가 마지막으로 나와야 적절하다.

해석 회사는 만약 그것이 단순히 그 규모 때문에 정부 혹은 다른 외부 원천으로부터 특혜적 대우를 받는다면 외적 규모의 경제를 가지고 있는 것이다. 예를 들어, 대기업이 그 거주민들에게 일자리를 제공해줄 것이므로 대부분의 주들은 그 기업을 끌어들이기 위해 세금을 낮춰줄 것이다.
(C) 흔히 대규모 부동산 개발업자는 도로와 다른 기반시설을 설치해 주도록 시를 설득할 수 있다. 이것은 그 개발업자들이 그러한 비용을 쓰는 것을 절약시켜 준다. 대기업들은 또한 대학들과의 합동 연구를 이용할 수 있다.
(A) 이것은 이런 회사들의 연구비용을 낮추어 준다. 소기업들은 그저 외적 규모의 경제를 이용할 영향력을 가지고 있지 않다.
(B) 그러나 그들은 함께 모여 작은 지역에서 유사한 기업들을 모음으로써 지리적 경제를 이용할 수 있다. 예를 들어, 시내 예술 구역의 화가 작업 구역, 화랑, 그리고 식당은 서로 가까이 있음으로써 혜택을 얻는다.

구문 [16행~17행] This **saves** the developer **from paying** those costs.
「save A from v-ing」는 'A가 v하는 것을 막아주다[구해주다]'의 뜻이다.

어휘 economies of scale 규모의 경제((생산 요소 투입량의 증대에 따른 생산비 절약 또는 수익 향상)) preferential 특혜를 주는 leverage 영향력 geographic 지리적인 cluster 모이게 하다, 모여들다 loft 로프트((예전의 공장 등을 개조한 아파트)) gallery 미술관, 화랑 district 지역, 지구 real estate 부동산 convince 확신시키다, 납득시키다 infrastructure 사회 기반 시설 take advantage of ~을 이용하다

15 글의 순서 ⑤

해설 우리가 세계를 인식할 때 '인식 상태'가 준거가 된다는 주어진 글 다음에는 이 상태가 새로운 생각을 대할 때 여과 장치 역할을 한다는 (C)가 나온다. (C)의 this state는 주어진 글의 our individual preserved state of awareness를 지칭한다. 인식 상태의 작동 원리를 보려면 타인과 의견이 일치하지 않을 때를 살펴보라는 (C)의 마지막 부분 다음에는 그 예시가 제시된 (B)가 나오고 친구에게 반박하는 생각이 밀려드는 (B)의 상황 다음에는 그 이유를 설명하는 (A)가 나온다. (A)의 As this happen의 this는 친구에게 반박하는 생각이 쇄도하는 (B)의 상황이고, where these thought came from에서 these thoughts는 친구에게 반박하는 생각을 지칭한다.

해석 우리들 각자는 보존된 개별적 인식 상태에 축적해 온 생각을 통해 현실을 본다. 새로운 생각에 마주칠 때 당신은 의미를 끌어내거나, 동의하거나, 동의하지 않거나, 판단하거나, 중립을 지킬 것을 이 상태에 요구한다.
(C) 당신은 자신이 마주치거나 떠올리는 모든 생각을 이 상태를 통해 여과한다. 감정을 자극하는 생각을 만들 때 당신은 이 정밀 조사를 관찰할 수 있다. 다음에 누군가와 의견이 일치하지 않을 때 주의를 기울여라.
(B) 정신이 어떻게 즉각적으로 당신의 관점을 입증하는 생각을 만들어 내는지에 주목하라. 예를 들어, 친구가 당신이 싫어하는 정치 후보자를 옹호할 때, 당신의 마음에 들어오는 반대되는 생각의 쇄도에 주목하라.
(A) 이런 일이 생길 때, 이러한 생각들이 어디에서 왔는지, 그리고 왜 이 특정한 순간에 그 생각들을 하게 되었는지를 잠시 생각하라. 그것들의 목적을 생각하라. 당신이 정말로 그것들을 끌어들였고 그것들에게는 정말로 목적이 있다. 그것들의 목적은 당신의 믿음을 강화하는 것이다.

구문 [6행~8행] As this happens, **consider** for a moment where these thoughts came from 〔and〕 why you produced them at this particular moment.
밑줄 친 두 부분은 동사 consider의 목적어 역할을 하는 간접의문문절로, and로 연결되어 병렬구조를 이룬다.
[16행~17행] *Every thought* [(which[that]) you encounter or conjure up] **you filter** through this state.
주어는 굵게 표시된 you, 동사는 filter이고 밑줄 친 부분이 목적어인데 강조를 위하여 문두로 나왔다. [ ]는 앞에 목적격 관계대명사 which[that]가 생략된 관계사절로 Every thought를 수식한다.

어휘 accumulate 축적하다 preserve 보존하다 call upon 요구하다, 청하다 derive 끌어내다 neutral 중립적인 reinforce 강화하다 validate 입증하다, 인정하다 candidate 후보자, 지원자 rush 쇄도, (감정의) 북받침 filter 여과하다 scrutiny 정밀 조사 stimulate 자극하다

16 문장 넣기 ⑤

해설 유머로부터 나오는 웃음은 관점의 변화를 통해 안도의 웃음이 될 수 있는 방어기제이지만 모든 인간에게 보편적으로 나타나는 것은 아니라는 내용의 글이다. 주어진 문장의 This self-defense mechanism을 통해 self-defense mechanism에 관한 언급이 주어진 문장 앞에 나와 있어야 하고 주어진 문장의 '모든 인간에게서 이 기제가 나타나는 것은 아니다'라는 것에 대해 ⑤ 이후 문장에서 구체적으로 설명을 하고 있으므로 주어진 문장이 ⑤에 들어가는 것이 가장 적절하다.

해석 유머로 인해 나오는 웃음은 사람들이 자신이 불리한 상황에 있음을 발견할 때 나온다. 그 상황에 대해, 그들은 보통 분노 그리고/또는 두려움을 느꼈을 것이고, 그 일치하지 않는 요소를 감지하는 것이 그들로 하여금 그것을 다른 관점에서 보도록 한다. 그러므로 이러한 경우, 웃음은 일반적으로 부정적인 감정과 연관된 에너지의 방출로부터 나오는 것이지만, 그 특정 상황에서 그것은 관점의 변화 덕으로 안도의 웃음으로 표현될 수 있다. 이러한 관점에서 유머는 사람들로 하여금 어렵고 스트레스를 주는 생활환경을 더 잘 다스리도록 해 주는 방어기제를 나타낸다. Freud는 심지어 이러한 유머를 '최고의 방어기제'라고 말한다. 이러한 자기방어기제는, 매우 널리 퍼져 있는 농담을 이해하는 능력과는 다르게, 모든 인간에게서 나타나는 것은 아니다. 실제로, 어떤 사람들은 특정 상황에서 재미있고 긍정적인 측면을 볼 수 있는 반면, 다른 사람들은 심지어 똑같은 상황에서도 부정적인 감정을 나타내는 반응을 보인다.

구문 [10행~14행] In this instance, / thus, laughter comes from the release of *energies* (generally associated with negative feelings), // 〔but〕 *that* (in the specific situation), (thanks to the change of perspective), **can be expressed** as laughter of relief.
과거분사 associated가 이끄는 ( )는 앞에 있는 명사 energies를 수식한다. but 뒤의 주어 that과 동사 can be expressed 사이에 두 개의 전명구 ( ) 부분이 삽입되었다.
[14행~16행] Humor, in this perspective, represents *a defense mechanism* [that **allows** *people* **to better handle** difficult and stressful life situations].
[ ]는 주격 관계대명사 that이 이끄는 관계사절로 앞의 명사 a defense mechanism을 수식하고, 관계사절 내에 「allow + O + to-v(O가 v하는 것을 허락하다)」가 사용되었다.

어휘 defense mechanism 방어기제 result from ~에서 나오다[기인하다] unfavorable 불리한, 좋지 않은 detection 감지, 간파, 발견 perspective 관점, 시각; 전망 instance 경우, 사례 release 방출(하다); 석방(하다); 발매(하다) associated 연관된, 관련된 relief 안도, 안심; (고통 등의) 경감 handle 다스리다, 처리하다 circumstance 상황, 사정; 환경

17 문장 넣기 ③

해설 ③번의 뒤 문장은 Unfortunately로 시작되며 두뇌가 변화를 따르지 못하는 좋지 않은 상황이 전개된다. 따라서 이 문장의 앞 문장에는 긍정적인 상황이 나와야 되는데 The only problem으로 시작되는 이 문장에는 부정적 상황이 진술되어 있어 두 문장이 잘 연결되지 않는다. 따라서 안정적 식량 공급원을 확보한 현대의 상황이 진술된 주어진 문장은 ③에 위치해야 한다.

해석 수백만 년의 진화 덕분에 우리는 매우 지능 있는 존재로 발전했다. 그러나 체중 관리에 관해서는 우리는 우리를 기근의 시기를 견디게 해 주도록 고안된 신체 메커니즘의 영향을 받는다. 이것은 식량이 부족한 시기가 온다면 에너지를 위해 사용할 것을 갖고 있도록 초과 체중을 비축하는 것을 의미한다. 유일한 문제는 이것이 고대 시대에 발생했던 것과 동일한 방식으로 발생하지 않는다는 것이다. 오늘날 우리는 우리에게 우리 조상들의 식량 공급과는 매우 다른 식량 공급을 제공해주는 믿을 수 있는 식량원을 개발했다. 불행히도 당신의 두뇌는 여전히 고대 두뇌의 사고의 영향을 받고 (식사를 건너뛸 때처럼) 식량 없는 시기를 지내는 것을 기아의 시기로 인지할지도 모른다. 이러한 기근의 결과 당신의 두뇌는 당신이 미래를 위해 에너지 저장을 붙들어놓는 것을 돕도록 당신의 신진대사를 늦출 것이다. 인간 사회는 진화했지만 인간의 두뇌는 여전히 해야 할 따라잡기가 좀 있다.

구문 [1행~3행] Today we have developed *reliable food sources* [that **provide** us **with** *a food supply* {very different from **that** of our ancestors}].
[ ]은 reliable food sources를 수식한다. 'provide A with B'는 'A에게 B를 제공하다'의 뜻이다. { }은 a food supply를 수식하며 { } 속의 that은 a food supply를 지칭한다.
[8행~10행] This means saving excess weight **so** we have something to use for energy if *a time* comes [when food is scarce].
접속사 so는 so that에서 that이 생략된 형태로, '~하기 위하여'의 뜻이다. [ ]은 a

time을 수식한다.

어휘 reliable 믿을 수 있는　when it comes to ~에 관한 한　mechanism 방법, 기제　famine 기근　scarce 부족한　metabolism 신진대사　hold on to 지키다, 계속 보유하다　catch up 따라잡다

---

18 요약문 완성　③

해설 목표를 설정하여 달성하는 실험에서 주의를 산만하게 하는 것이 없도록 환경을 바꾼 집단이 오로지 의지력만 사용한 집단보다 좋은 결과를 얻었으므로 '자제력(self-control)을 통한 행동 변화는 환경(environments) 변화를 통한 행동 변화만큼 성공적이지 않다'고 요약할 수 있다.
① 목표 설정 – 정황　　② 목표 설정 – 사고방식
④ 자제력 – 정신력　　⑤ 자기 보상 – 태도

해석 Angela Duckworth와 그녀의 동료 연구자들은 펜실베이니아 대학 학부생 한 집단에게 '매일 밤 한 시간씩 불어 공부하기' 혹은 '마감 전날에 모든 숙제 마치기'와 같은 학업 목표 목록을 작성해달라고 요청했다. 일주일 동안 이 학생들 중 일부(첫 번째 집단)는 목표를 달성하기 위해 유혹을 최소화하도록 공부 공간을 조정하라는 지시를 받았다. 이 학생들은 페이스북 같이 주의를 산만하게 하는 것들을 막기 위해 온라인 앱을 설치하며 리마인더(알림)나 알람을 설정했거나, 아마 도서관에서 공부용 개인 열람석을 잡아두었던 것 같다. 학생들의 두 번째 집단은 오로지 의지력과 유혹에 저항하는 자신의 능력에만 의존하라는 말을 들었다. 그 주가 끝날 때 학생들은 1(극히 못 함)에서 5(극히 잘 함)의 등급으로 그 주에 공부 목표를 얼마나 성공적으로 충족시키고 있었는지를 평가했다. 평균적으로 모든 학생들이 상당히 성공했으나, 첫 번째 집단의 학생들이 두 번째 집단의 학생들보다 등급에서 약 0.5점 더 득점했다.

↓

> 펜실베이니아 대학 학생들이 경험했던 것처럼, (A) 자제력을 통한 행동 변화는 (B) 환경 변화를 통한 행동 변화만큼 성공적이지 않다.

구문 [1행~5행] Angela Duckworth and her fellow researchers **asked** *a group of University of Pennsylvania undergraduates* **to list academic goals**, / such as "study French for an hour every night" or "finish all homework the day before it is due."
「ask + O + to-v (O에게 v해달라고 요청하다)」 구문이 쓰였다.

[8행~10행] These students set reminders or alarms, / **installing** online apps to block distractions like Facebook, / or perhaps reserved study carrels in the library.
과거동사 set과 reserved가 or로 연결되어 병렬구조를 이룬다. installing ~ Facebook은 분사구문이 삽입된 것이다.

어휘 undergraduate 대학생, 학부생　due 만기가 된, 지급 기일이 된　modify 조정(수정)하다　reminder 리마인더, 상기시키는 것　distraction 주의 산만　reserve (자리 등을) 따로 잡아두다　solely 오로지　scale 등급, 척도　reasonably 상당히, 꽤

19~20 장문　19 ① 20 ③

해설 19. 창의력이 필요한 일을 수행할 때, 해낼 수 없을 것 같다고 생각되는 일도 끈기를 갖고 계속 하다 보면 예상을 뛰어넘는 성과를 낼 수 있다는 내용의 글이므로 제목으로 가장 적절한 것은 ① '끈질기게 계속하는 습관은 창의력이 샘솟게 한다'이다.
② 당신의 창의력을 여는 데 도움을 주는 습관들
③ 업무에서 창의력을 어떻게 점화시킬 수 있는가
④ 끈기가 있다는 것은 당신이 더 열심히 노력하도록 동기를 부여한다
⑤ 창의력: 시간과 노력이 드는 과정

20. 대학생들은 전 단락의 코미디 공연자들과 마찬가지의 추정을 했다고 했으므로, 코미디언들이 추가 시간에 생성할 수 있는 아이디어의 개수에 대해 과소평가했듯이, 자신의 창의성을 추정해봤을 때 끈기가 주는 이로움을 과소평가했을 것이다. 따라서 (c)의 overestimated를 underestimated로 고쳐 써야 한다.

해석 한 통찰력 있는 연구에서 대규모 코미디 페스티벌에서 45명의 프로 코미디 공연자들을 모집했다. 각각의 사람들은 코미디 장면의 설정과 가능한 한 많은 결말을 만들어내도록 4분의 시간을 부여받았다. 코미디언들은 각자 4분의 시간 동안 약 6개의 재밌는 결말을 만들어냈다. 모든 참가자들은 그런 다음 4분이 추가로 주어지면 재밌는 결말을 몇 개 더 만들어낼 수 있을지를 예측했다. 그들의 의식적인 자아는 (a) 감소하는 산출을 예상했다. 새로운 결말들에 대한 평균적 추정은 약 5개였는데, 이것은 그들이 처음 4분 동안 만들었던 것보다 더 적었다. 그들은 그런 후 작업하도록 추가 4분을 받았다. 그들이 만들어낸 새로운 결말의 실제 수는 그들이 추정했던 것보다 20퍼센트 더 높았다. 그들은 끈기의 (b) 공을 충분히 인정해주지 않았다. 인내하는 강한 습관이 있었으면, 그들은 비관적인 예측에도 불구하고 아이디어를 생산하기 위해 계속 노력했을 것이며 그 일을 성공적으로 해냈을 것이다.

코미디 공연자들과 마찬가지로, 대학생들이 몇 분 동안 임무를 수행한 후 몇 분 더 계속하는 경우의 자신의 창의성을 추정했을 때, 그들은 끈기의 이로움을 (c) 과대평가했다(→ 과소평가했다). 놀랍게도 끈질기게 계속 하라고 구체적으로 지시받았을 때, 학생들은 그들이 예상했던 것보다 더 많은 해결책을 만들어 냈다. 끈기는 시험받았을 때 마모되지 않았다. 단지 계속 생성할 뿐이었다. 우리의 오해는 (d) 이해할만하다. 우리는 우리의 수행 노력이 시간이 지나며 마모된다는 것을 알고 있다. 우리의 주의는 사그라지고 우리의 동기는 약해진다. 그러나 우리의 습관적인 자아, 즉, 끈기가 있는 곳은 완전히 (e) 다른 물질로 만들어져 있다. 그리고 그것은 우리가 일을 시킬 수 있는 물질이다.

구문 [7행~9행] All participants then predicted // how many more funny endings they **would be** able to generate // if they **had** four additional minutes.
how ~ minutes는 predicted의 목적어인 간접의문문이다. 여기에 「if + S' + 과거동사, S + would 동사원형 (…한다면 ~할 것이다)」의 가정법 과거가 쓰였다.

[17행~20행] With a strong habit of persevering, / they would have continued to try to produce ideas, / and would have done so successfully, / **despite** their pessimistic predictions.
동사 would have continued와 would have done은 병렬구조를 이루며, 「would have p.p.」는 '~했을 것이다'라는 의미의 가정법 과거완료 표현이다. despite는 '~에도 불구하고'라는 뜻의 전치사로 뒤에 목적어로 명사구(their pessimistic predictions)를 이끈다.

어휘 insightful 통찰력 있는　recruit 모집하다　setup 설정; 구성　persistence 끈기, 버팀 *cf.* persist 끈질기게 계속하다　credit 공, 인정; 칭찬; 신용 (거래); 학점　persevere 끈기 있게 노력하다; 인내하다　pessimistic 비관적인　anticipate 예상하다　put ~ to the test ~을 실험해보다　wear down 마모되다　misapprehension 오해　executive 실행[수행]의　ebb 서서히 사그라지다　wane 약해지다　put ~ to work ~에게 일을 시키다

1 ④	**2** ①	**3** ③	**4** ③	**5** ④		**6** ⑤	**7** ⑤	**8** ③	**9** ③	**10** ②
11 ④	**12** ④	**13** ④	**14** ⑤	**15** ④		**16** ④	**17** ⑤	**18** ①	**19** ④	**20** ⑤

1 글의 목적   ④

해설 올해 가을 축제의 모금 행사에서 자원봉사를 해 줄 것을 부탁하는 내용의 편지이다.

해석 교구민들께,
여러분께 편지를 쓸 때 저는 완벽한 봄날을 즐기고 있습니다. 하늘은 놀랍도록 짙푸른 색이고, 이른 구근이 꽃피우기 시작하며, 저는 얼굴에 온기를 느낄 수 있습니다. 하지만 저는 여러분을 이 장면에서 벗어나게 해서 가을과 우리의 연례 가을 축제에 대해 생각하게 해야 합니다. 과거에 자원봉사를 하셨다면, 이 모금 행사에 막대한 양의 노동이 투입된다는 점을 알고 계시겠지요. 아직 참여해본 적이 없으시면, 올해에는 해주시기를 희망합니다. 매표와 오락에서 설치와 청소에 이르는 몇몇 위원회에서 직책을 맡아주실 분들이 필요합니다. 많은 열정을 가진 분들은 부스에서 일해주시고, 요리 솜씨를 지닌 분들은 음식 일을 도와주실 것을 요합니다. 모금된 돈은 많은 가치 있는 노력에 투입됩니다. 관심 있으시면 전화 주세요.
Laura Diamond 드림

구문 [9행~10행] If you have not already been involved, // we hope that you will (be involved) this year.
you will 다음에 be involved가 생략되어 있다.
[10행~12행] We need people to chair several committees, / **ranging from** tickets and entertainment **to** setup and cleanup.
ranging 이하는 분사구문이다. 「range from A to B」는 '범위가 A에서 B까지이다'의 의미이다.

어휘 parish (교회·성당의) 교구   cerulean 하늘색의, 짙은 청색의   bulb ((식물)) 구근, 알뿌리   bloom 꽃을 피우다   annual 해마다의   tremendous 엄청난   fundraiser 모금행사   involve 참여시키다   chair 조직·위원회의 책임자가 되다, 의장을 맡다   committee 위원회   setup 장치, 설치   folk 사람들   enthusiasm 열광   endeavor 노력, 시도

2 필자 주장   ①

해설 과학계는 경쟁이 심한 곳이지만, 경쟁을 회피하지 말고 그들과 가까운 관계를 유지해야 서로 도움을 주고받을 수 있다는 내용의 글이므로 필자의 주장으로 가장 적절한 것은 ①이다.

해석 과학계에서 중요한 목표를 추구할 때, 당신은 심한 경쟁을 예상해야 한다. 당신이 경주에 참여하고 있다는 것을 아는 것은 안절부절못하게 만들겠지만, 가치 있는 경쟁자들의 존재는 앞에 놓인 상이 획득할 가치가 있는 것이라는 보증이 된다. 그러나 분야가 너무 넓으면 걱정 이상의 마음이 들 수도 있다. 수많은 경쟁자들의 존재는 당신이 그들의 강점과 약점에 대해 세세히 알고 있을 가능성이 없으므로 당신이 이길 가능성이 낮다는 점을 또한 의미한다. 그럼에도 불구하고 당신이 너무 많이 드러낼까봐 두려워서 경쟁자들을 피하는 것은 위험한 길이다. 오히려 당신의 지적 경쟁자들과 밀접한 관계를 유지할 때, 여러분 각자는 상대방의 도움으로 이득을 얻을 수 있다. 그리고 공교롭게도 다른 누군가가 정말로 완전히 승리한다면, 그가 싫어하지 않기가 적어도 처음에는 어렵다고 생각될 어떤 모르는 경쟁자인 것 보다는 사이좋은 관계를 맺고 있는 사람인 편이 더 낫다.

구문 [3행~5행] Though knowing you are in a race is nerve-racking, // the presence of worthy competitors is an assurance that the prize ahead is worth winning.
Though 절에서 knowing ~ race가 동명사 주어이고 is가 동사이다. 주절에서 that ~ winning은 an assurance에 대한 동격절이다.
[15행~18행] And if **it happens that** someone else does win outright, // better it is *someone* [with whom you are on good terms] than *some unknown competitor* [whom you will **find it** *hard* **not to at least initially detest**].
it happens that~은 '공교롭게도[우연히] ~하다'의 뜻이다. whom ~ detest에서 it은 가목적어이고 not to ~ detest가 진주어이다. 「find + it + C + to-v」는 'v하는 것이 C하다는 것을 알게 되다'의 뜻이다.

어휘 nerve-racking 안절부절못하게 하는   assurance 보증; 확언   apprehensive 걱정되는   outright 완전히, 드러내 놓고   be on good terms with ~와 좋은 사이이다

3 밑줄 함의   ③

해설 가령 채식주의를 추구하며 식량으로 삼기 위해 다른 생명체를 죽이지 않는 것을 목표로 한 사람이 있다 하더라도 그는 산책을 하거나 맹물만 마셔도 실제로 수많은 생명체를 불가피하게 줄일 수밖에 없다. 그러므로 식단 문제에 있어서 극단적인 목표를 세우는 것은 바람직하지 않다는 것이 필자가 배운 바이다. 이를 정리하면 필자가 배운 것은 ③ '인간이 식량을 얻기 위해 생명을 빼앗는 것은 불가피하다.'이다.
① 채식주의는 건강한 식이요법이 아니다.
② 동물을 죽이는 정당한 방법이 있다.
④ 동식물을 둘 다 먹는 것이 균형 잡힌 식단이다.
⑤ 인간은 식물을 먹을 순 있지만 동물을 먹어서는 안 된다.

해석 음식에 관한 한 나는 아무 유파에도 속해 있지 않다. 나는 각각의 것으로부터 무언가를 배웠으며, 그것들을 모두 시도해 보는 것으로부터 내가 배운 것은 극단적인 진술과 어떤 경우에도 변치 않는 규칙을 멀리하는 것이다. 지각이 있는 생명을 빼앗는 것이 도덕적으로 잘못된 것이라고 주장하는 나의 채식주의자 친구들에게, 나는 그들이 수없이 많은 작은 곤충들과 벌레들을 밟고 걸으므로, 시골에 산책하러 나가면 반드시 그 위법행위를 저지르게 돼 있다고 대답한다. 우리는 우리의 권리를 주장하지 않고서는 살 수가 없다. 우리는 포도 주스 한 컵을 마실 때 수없이 많은 세균을 죽이며, 그 점에 있어서는 맹물 한 컵을 마실 때에도 마찬가지이다. 나는 언젠가 과학의 진보가 모든 식물에 기본적인 형태의 의식이 있다는 것을 우리에게 증명해주지 못한다면 크게 놀랄 것이고, 그래서 우리는 Mr. Dooley의 주장을 정당화할 것인데, 그는 'The Jungle'을 논평하며, 한창때인 어린 토마토를 잘라내거나 꼬투리 안의 요람에 가득한 아기 완두콩들을 죽이는 것이 어떻게 조금이라도 덜 범죄가 될 수 있는지 이해할 수 없다고 말했다!

구문 [4행~8행] To *my vegetarian friends* [who argue that **it** is morally wrong **to take sentient life**], I answer that they **cannot** go for a walk in the country *without committing* that offense, **for** they walk on innumerable bugs and worms.

[ ]은 my vegetarian friends를 수식하는 관계사절이고, 그 안에서 it은 가주어, to take sentient life가 진주어이다. 「cannot ... without v-ing」는 'v하지 않고는 …할 수 없다', 즉 '…하면 반드시 v하게 되다'라는 뜻의 이중부정 표현이고, 밑줄 친 for는 이유를 나타내는 접속사로 쓰였다.

[16행~18행] ~ he could not see how **it** was any less a crime <u>to cut off a young tomato in its prime</u> or <u>to murder a whole cradleful of baby peas in the pod</u>!
it은 가주어, 밑줄 친 두 개의 to부정사구가 진주어이고, 두 개의 to부정사구는 접속사 or로 병렬연결된다.

어휘 so far as ~ is concerned ~에 관한 한   school 파(派), 유파   trial 시도; 공판   hard and fast 어떤 경우에도 변치 않는   commit offense 위법행위를 저지르다   innumerable 셀 수 없이 많은   assert 주장하다, (권리 등을) 확고히 하다   vegetable life 식물   in one's prime 한창때에   cradleful 요람에 가득 담긴   pea 완두(콩)   pod 꼬투리   inevitable 불가피한

4 글의 주제 ③

해설 주변 어른들은 어린이들의 공상을 심리적 장애로 인식할 수 있으나 사실 공상은 언어 발달과 학교에서의 성과에 이로우며 창의성과 연관된다는 내용의 글이므로 주제로 가장 적절한 것은 ③ '어린이의 지능과 창의성의 징후로서의 공상'이다.
① 지루한 일에 대처하기 위한 공상의 유용성
② ADD와 어린이의 건강한 공상을 구별하는 방법
④ 공상과 심리적 장애 간의 차이점들
⑤ 어린이의 학업 성과를 위하여 공상을 통제하는 것의 필요성

해석 대개 어린이들은 자연스럽고 상상력이 풍부하며 행복한 공상가들이다. 그러나 너무나 빈번히 부모님들과 선생님들은 공상을 ADD(주의력 결핍 장애)의 표시로 혹은 형성 중인 게으름뱅이의 징후로 규정하는 데 주저함이 없다. 새로운 연구에 의하면 '긍정적이고 건설적인' 공상은, 패턴에 있어 과도할 때조차도, 일부 사람들이 이전에 생각하던 것처럼 심리적 장애와 연관되지 않으며, 오히려 공상가의 지능과 상상력이 풍부한 경향을 반영하는 정상적인 활동이라고 한다. 실제로 어린이의 공상을 창의성과 연관시키는 상당한 양의 연구가 있다. 최근의 뉴질랜드의 연구는 가상의 친구가 어린이들의 언어 발달에 이로우며 또한 그들의 학교에서의 성과를 신장시켜줄 수도 있다는 점을 발견했다. 또한 공상할 수 있는 한가한 시간을 충분히 받지 못한 어린이들 혹은 그들 자신의 시간을 텔레비전으로 너무 많이 채우는 어린이들은 '지루하고 상상력이 부족한' 작품을 생산한다고 말하는 연구도 있다. 그러므로 당신의 아이가 공상가라면, 당신은 작은 천재를 키우고 있는 것일지도 모른다.

구문 **[6행~10행]** ~ "positive-constructive" daydreaming, even **when (it is) heavy** in pattern, is **not** related to psychological disorders as some have previously thought, **but** rather is *a normal activity* [that reflects the daydreamer's intelligence and imaginative tendencies].
when과 heavy 사이에는 'it("positive-constructive" daydreaming) is'가 생략되어 있다. 'not A but B'는 'A가 아니라 B이다'의 뜻이다. [ ]은 a normal activity 를 수식한다.

[16행~19행] ~ *children* [who don't get enough down time to daydream] or [who fill in their down time with too much television] **produce** *works* {that are "tedious and unimaginative."}
두 [ ]는 주어 children을 수식하며 동사는 produce이다. { }은 works를 수식한다.

어휘 for the most part 대부분, 대개   prolific 다작의, (상상력이) 풍부한   daydreamer 공상가   label 꼬리표를 붙이다   deficit 결핍   sign 징후, 조짐   in the making 형성되고 있는   constructive 건설적인   imaginative 상상력이

풍부한   substantial 상당한   imaginary 가상의   boost 신장시키다, 북돋우다   down time 한가한 시간   tedious 지루한

5 도표 이해 ④

해설 주거 부문에서의 배출량 비율이 1980년부터 2013년까지 계속해서 감소하지 않고 2000년에서 2013년까지의 배출량 비율은 오히려 10.8%에서 12.4%로 증가했으므로 ④가 일치하지 않는다.

해석 한국의 부문별 연료 연소에서 나온 이산화탄소 배출량 (1980~2013)
위 그래프는 1980, 1990, 2000, 2013년에 한국의 부문별 연료 연소에서 비롯되는 이산화탄소 배출량을 보여 준다. ① 우리는 여러 해 동안 제조, 건설, 그리고 에너지 산업에서 나온 배출량이 최저 34%에서 최고 43%로 꽤 일정하게 유지되어 온 것을 볼 수 있다. ② 한편, 도로 운송 부문에서 나온 배출량의 비율은 1980년에 2.5%에서 2013년에 33%로 급격하게 증가해 왔다. ③ 같은 기간 동안, 다른 운송으로부터 나온 비율은 2013년에 전체 배출량의 단지 1%로 거의 11퍼센트포인트까지 떨어졌다. ④ 주거 부문에서의 배출량 비율은 1980년에 35.2%에서 2013년에 12.4%로 계속해서 감소했다. ⑤ 마지막으로, 우리는 기타 부문이 전체 배출량의 20%를 초과하거나 10% 미만을 차지한 적이 없다는 것을 볼 수 있다.

구문 **[3행~6행]** We can see // **that** over the years *emissions* (from manufacturing, construction, and the energy industry) / have remained fairly constant, / from a minimum of 34% to a maximum of 43%.
that over the years ~ 43%는 명사절 접속사 that이 이끄는 명사절로서 동사 can see의 목적어 역할을 한다. ( )는 전명구로서 앞에 나온 명사 emissions를 수식한다. from 뒤의 세 개의 명사들이 콤마(,)와 and로 연결되어 병렬구조를 이룬다.

어휘 emission 배출(물); (빛, 열등의) 발산   sector 부문, 분야, 영역   manufacturing 제조(업)   fairly 꽤, 상당히   constant 변함없는; 끊임없는   meanwhile 한편; (다른 일이 일어나고 있는) 그동안에   share 비율, 몫; 나누다; 공유하다   drastically 급격하게; 과감하게   residential 주거의; 거주하기 좋은   account for (비율을) 차지하다; 설명하다

6 내용 불일치 ⑤

해설 Marian Anderson은 1964년에 고별 투어를 시작했고 68세가 된 1965년에 그 투어를 마쳤으므로 ⑤는 본문의 내용과 일치하지 않는다.

해석 Marian Anderson은 어렸을 때 성악 재능을 보였다. 6살 때부터 그녀는 필라델피아의 교회 성가대에서 음악 훈련을 시작했다. 뛰어난 교회 성가대의 한가운데에서도 Anderson은 진정한 재능으로 두드러졌다. 그녀의 교회 공동체는 그녀가 정규 음악 훈련을 추구하는 것을 도와주었다. 아프리카계 미국인이어서 필라델피아 음악원 자리를 거부당하고 그녀는 (받을) 수 있는 어느 곳에서든 음악 교육을 계속해서 받았다. Marian Anderson이 링컨 기념관 계단에서 했던 1939년 콘서트는 그녀의 역사를 한 데 모은 것이었다. 1955년 1월 7일에 그녀는 메트로폴리탄 오페라단과 공연한 최초의 아프리카계 미국인이 되었다. Anderson은 수십 년 동안 계속해서 강렬한 공연을 펼쳤다. Anderson은 1964년 10월에 고별 투어를 시작했는데, 이것은 Anderson이 68세가 된 때인 1965년 4월에 카네기홀에서 막을 내렸다.

구문 **[6행~9행]** **Denied** a place in the Philadelphia Music Academy // because she was African American, // she continued to receive musical education // **wherever** she could.
Denied ~ African American은 수동의 의미를 가지는 분사구문이다. wherever는 '~하는 곳은 어디든'의 의미이다.

----

7 밑줄 어법 ⑤

해설 ⑤ what 이후에 완전한 문장이 오므로 관계대명사 what이 올 수 없다. 어법상 부사절 only when we let our minds wander를 강조하는 「It ~ that ...」 강조 구문이므로 what은 that으로 고쳐 써야 한다.

① in which 뒤에 완전한 문장(the mind ~ wander freely)이 이어지므로 '전치사+관계대명사' 형태의 in which는 적절하다. in which가 이끄는 절이 the mental state를 수식한다.

② that절의 주어가 daydreaming, imagination, and fantasy이므로 복수 동사 are는 쓰임이 적절하다.

③ 동사 include의 목적어 중의 하나로 콤마와 접속사로 연결되어 앞에 있는 명사(구)와 병렬을 이루는 동명사 taking의 쓰임이 적절하다.

④ 비교급(more likely)을 강조하는 부사로 far는 적절하다.

- -

해석 아주 유명한 인지 심리학자인 Jerome Singer는 생각이 자유롭게 다른 데로 흘러갈 수 있게 허용되는 정신 상태가 사실은 우리의 '기본' 상태라고 말한 첫 번째 과학자였다. Singer는 더 나아가 1966년에 나온 자신의 저서 '백일몽'에서 백일몽과 상상, 공상이 건강한 정신생활에 근본적인 요소라고 주장했다. 이 요소들은 자기 인식, 창의적인 숙고, 자전적 계획, 사건과 상호 작용의 의미에 대한 고찰, 다른 사람의 관점을 취하는 것, 여러분 자신과 다른 사람의 감정에 대해 심사숙고하는 것, 그리고 도덕적 추론을 포함한다. 이 모든 것이 우리가 '아하!'하는 깨달음의 순간이라 생각하는 것으로 이끈다. 음악가이자 베스트셀러 작가이며 신경 과학자인 Daniel J. Levitin은 과업에 집중하는 모드에 있을 때보다 생각이 이리저리 돌아다니는 모드에 있을 때 통찰이 올 가능성이 훨씬 더 크다는 것을 강조한다. 우리가 관련되어 있다고 생각하지 못했던 것들 사이에서 뜻밖의 연관성을 찾는 것은 바로 우리가 이런저런 생각을 할 때뿐이다. 이것은 여러분이 이전에 풀 수 없는 것으로 보였던 문제를 해결하는 데 도움을 줄 수 있다.

- -

구문 [1행~4행] Jerome Singer, a legendary cognitive psychologist, was *the first scientist* (to **suggest** that *the mental state* [**in which** the mind is allowed to wander freely] is, in fact, our "default" state).

( ) 부분은 형용사적 용법으로 쓰인 to부정사구로 the first scientist를 수식한다. suggest의 목적어로 쓰인 that절 내에서 in which가 이끄는 [ ]이 the mental state를 수식한다.

[17행~19행] It is only when we let our minds wander **that** we make unexpected connections between *things* [that (we did not realize) **were** connected].

「It is ~ that ...」 강조구문이 쓰여 밑줄 친 부사절을 강조한다. [ ] 부분은 things를 수식하는 관계사절로 주격 관계대명사 that과 동사 were 사이에 ( ) 부분이 삽입되었다.

- -

어휘 **legendary** 아주 유명한, 전설적인; 전설 속의 **cognitive psychologist** 인지심리학자 **mental state** 정신 상태 **wander** (생각 등이) 다른 데로 흐르다[팔리다]; (이리저리) 돌아다니다 **daydreaming** 백일몽 **essential** 근본[필수]적인; 가장 중요한 **element** 요소 **self-awareness** 자기 인식, 자각 **autobiographical** 자(서)전적인 **consideration** 고찰; 숙고 **perspective** 관점; 원근(법) **reflect on** ~에 대해 심사숙고하다[깊이 생각하다] **moral** 도덕적인 **reasoning** 추론, 추리 **aha moment** 아하 하는 깨달음의 순간 **neuroscientist** 신경 과학자 **emphasize** 강조[역설]하다 **insight** 통찰, 통찰력 **unexpected** 뜻밖의, 예기치 않은 **previously** 이전에, 사전에 **unsolvable** 풀 수 없는, 해결 불가능한

8 밑줄 어휘 ③

해설 ③ 현대 사회에서는 취향 문화 자체가 급변하고 사람들이 취향을 굉장히 쉽게 전환하고 있으므로, 취향이 자신의 사회적 위치를 나타내는 일이 과거에 비해 '덜' 분명해졌다. 따라서 more를 less 등으로 바꿔 써야 한다.

- -

해석 음악적 판단은 절대로 완전한 고립 상태에서 이뤄지지 않는다. '취향 문화'의 형성은 항상 ① 사회적으로 정의되어 왔다. 특정 장르의 음악에 참여하는 것은 역사적으로 순전히 ② 독립된 미적 선택에 의해서가 아니라, 개인의 사회적 위치에 의해 결정되었다. 실제로 사회학적 관점에서 취향은 미적인 범주라기보다는 항상 사회적 범주이다. 그것은 우리가 우리의 사회적 위치를 나타내기 위해 문화적 판단을 사회적 '통화'로 사용하는 방식을 지칭한다. 이것은 오늘날 ③ 더(→ 덜) 분명할 수도 있는데, 현대 사회의 특징이 더 오래된 취향 문화의 해체와 새로운 취향 문화의 확산이기 때문이다. 이런 상황에서 문화 거래는 점점 빠르게 일어나고, 따라서 문화 경제의 가열과 그것의 빠른 신제품 회전율이 나타나게 됐다. 취향 문화 자체가 변화하고 있을 뿐만 아니라, 사람들은 이제 그것들 사이에서 매우 더 쉽게 이동하는 경향도 있다. 이 요인들은 모든 개개의 위치가 ④ 상대적이라는 느낌을 일으킨다. 현대의 음악적 선택은 전에 없이 다양하며, 그 다양성의 효과는 필연적으로 음악적 판단의 문제에서 ⑤ 개인이 유일한 권위자일 수 있다는 것을 확인하는 것이다.

- -

구문 [8행~10행] ~ it refers to *the way* [we use cultural judgments as social "currency,"] to mark our social positions.

[ ]은 the way를 수식하는 관계사절이다.

[16행~18행] [Not only] *are* taste cultures themselves shifting, [but] people now tend to move between them with greater ease.

'not only A but (also) B'는 'A뿐만 아니라 B도'의 뜻이다. 부정어 Not only가 문두로 나가면서 '동사(are)+주어(taste cultures themselves)'의 어순으로 도치되었다.

- -

어휘 **aesthetic** 미적인 **currency** 통화 **contemporary** 현대의 **fragmentation** 분열, 파쇄 **transaction** 거래 **hence** 이 사실에서 …이 유래하다 **turnover** 회전율 **plural** 복수의; 다원적인 *cf.* **plurality** 복수, 다수; 과반수

9 빈칸 추론 ③

해설 나바호 인디언 학교의 가난한 아이들은 장난감이 없어도 스스로 게임을 만들며 지루할 틈이 없이 지내는 반면 풍족한 가정의 아이들은 크리스마스 선물을 잔뜩 받고도 곧 싫증을 내며 할 일이 없다고 불평하는 상황에서, 아이들의 행복은 ③ '가지고 있는 것들'에서 나오는 게 아님을 알 수 있다.

① 자존심 ② 칭찬 ④ 규율 ⑤ 성취

- -

해석 1969년, John이 23살이었을 때, 그는 New Mexico 주의 Shiprock에 있는 나바호 인디언 기숙학교에서 잠시 가르쳤다. 그의 3학년 학생들은 미국에서 가장 가난한 아이들에 속했고, 등에 걸친 옷 외에는 가진 것이 거의 없었다. 그 학교는 장난감이나 다른 오락거리가 거의 없었다. 하지만 John은 아이들이 지루하다고 말하는 것을 전혀 듣지 못했다. 그들은 끊임없이 그들 자신의 게임을 만들어 내고 있었다. 10살의 나이에 그들은 행복했고 정서적으로 안정된 아이들이었다. 그 해 성탄절에 John은 가족을 방문하러 집으로 돌아갔다. 그는 트리 아래에 상자로 가득한 바닥의 광경을 기억한다. 그의 10살 난 동생은 한 상자에서 다른 상자로 재빨리 옮겨가며 상자를 십여 개 열어보았다. 며칠 후에, John은 성탄절 장난감이 동생의 침실에서 내던져져 있는 채로 자기 동생과 친구가 TV를 보고 있는 것을 발견했다. 두 소년 모두가 John에게 할 게 없다고 불평했다. "우리는 지루해요."라고 그들은 선언했다. John에게 그것은 아이들의 행복이 소유물에서 나오지 않는다는 것을 분명히 보여주는 것이었다.

- -

구문 [14행~16행] A few days later, John **found** *his brother and a friend* **watching TV**, / *the Christmas toys* (being) tossed aside in his brother's bedroom.

「find O v-ing」는 'O가 v하고 있는 것을 알게 되다[발견하다]'의 뜻이다. John이 주어, found가 동사이며, tossed 이하는 수동의 의미를 가지는 분사구문이고 the Christmas toys는 tossed의 의미상 주어이다.

어휘 briefly 잠시 boarding school 기숙학교 scene 장면 entertainment 놀이, 오락 continually 끊임없이 well-adjusted 잘 적응한 toss (가볍게) 던지다 indication 보여주는 것, 지적, 암시

10 빈칸 추론 ②

해설 뇌는 정보를 조건 없이 받아들이지 않고 시간 순서에 따른 이야기의 구조에 들어맞고 연관성을 가질 수 있도록 능동적으로 재구성하므로 정보의 흐름으로부터 ② '질서를 만들어 내려는' 필요를 가지고 있다고 표현할 수 있다.
① 자료를 걸러내려는   ③ 이야기를 공유하려는
④ 다른 사람들을 모방하려는   ⑤ 맥락을 해석하려는

해석 몇몇 과학자들은 뇌를 단지 들어오는 신호와 나가는 반응을 조정하는 중계국에 비유하는 반면, 다른 과학자들은 그것을 정보를 처리하고 나서 적절한 반응에 도달하는 엄청난 컴퓨터로 본다. 프랑스의 분자 생물학자이자 노벨상 수상자인 Francois Jacob은 인간의 정신은 훨씬 더 이상의 것이라고 말한다. 그것은 그것의 감각 기관으로부터 오는 끊임없는 정보의 흐름으로부터 질서를 만들어 내려는 내장된 필요를 가지고 있다는 것이다. 다시 말해, 뇌는 사건을 이해하는 시간 순서인 시작과 중간과 끝이 있는 이야기를 만든다. 뇌는 의미망을 만들어 내는 연관성과 관계성을 구성하며 이야기에 사용될 정보를 선별하고 버린다. 이러한 방식으로, 이야기는 단순히 '무엇'이 일어났는지보다 더 많은 것을 밝혀낸다. 그것은 '왜'를 설명한다. 정신이 들어오는 정보를 선택하고 정리하여 의미로 엮어낼 때, 그것은 그 자신에게 이야기를 하는 것이다.

구문 [1행~5행] Some scientists compare the brain to *a relay station* [that merely coordinates incoming signals and outgoing responses], whereas others see it as *an immense computer* [that **processes** information and then **arrives** at an appropriate response].
첫 번째 [ ]은 주격관계대명사 that이 이끄는 관계사절로 a relay station을 수식하고, 두 번째 [ ]은 an immense computer를 수식한다. 두 번째 관계사절 내에서 동사 processes와 arrives는 병렬구조를 이룬다.
[12행~15행] The brain selects and discards *information* (to be used in the narrative), **constructing** *connections and relationships* [that create a web of meaning].
( )은 to부정사의 형용사적 용법으로 information을 수식한다. constructing 이하는 분사구문으로 관계사절 [ ]이 connections and relationships를 수식한다.

어휘 compare A to B A를 B에 비유하다 relay station (통신) 중계국 coordinate 조정하다 see A as B A를 B로 보다[간주하다] immense 엄청난, 굉장한 built-in 내장된; 타고난, 고유의 sensory 감각(기관)의 organ 기관, 장기 temporal 시간의; 일시적인 sequence 순서, 차례 make sense of 이해하다 discard 버리다 mimic 모방하다

11 빈칸 추론 ④

해설 빈칸 문장이 Thus로 시작하고 있으므로 앞서 서술된 것은 '원인', 빈칸 문장은 '결과', 그리고 이어지는 내용은 그 결과에 대한 상술의 구조일 것으로 짐작할 수 있다. 빈칸 문장의 앞은 창의적인 아이디어가 다른 사람들에게 잘 받아들여지지 않는 현상에 대해 서술하고 있고 빈칸 문장은 그래서 아이들이 '무엇을' 배워야 하는가이다. 이어지는 내용은 자기 생각의 타당함을 다른 이들에게 납득시켜야 하는 예

시 상황들이므로 빈칸에는 ④ '어떻게 자기 생각의 가치를 다른 사람들에게 설득시킬지'가 가장 적절하다.
① 어른들로부터 무엇을 기대해야 할지
② 창의적인 아이디어를 위해 무엇을 포기할지
③ 어떻게 비판을 받아들이고 활용할지
⑤ 어떻게 창의적인 혁신을 만들고 명성을 얻을지

해석 모든 사람은 자신의 훌륭하고 창의적인 아이디어가 저절로 선전될 것이라고 믿고 싶어 한다. 그러나 갈릴레오, 에드바르 뭉크 그리고 수백만의 다른 사람들이 발견해냈듯이, 그것들은 그렇게 되지 않는다. 반대로, 창의적 아이디어를 낸 이들뿐만 아니라 그 아이디어들도 종종 의심과 불신으로 바라보아진다. 사람들은 자신들의 신념을 굳게 믿고 있기 때문에 현재 사고방식으로부터 그들을 떼어내기란 믿을 수 없을 정도로 어려울 수 있다. 그러므로 아이들은 어떻게 자기 생각의 가치를 다른 사람들에게 설득시킬지 배울 필요가 있다. 이는 창의적 사고의 실제적 측면의 일부이다. 아이들이 예술 작품을 한 점 만든다면, 그들은 왜 그 작품이 가치 있는지 입증할 준비가 되어 있어야 한다. 마찬가지로, 교사들은 교장에게 자신들의 교수 방안이 옳음을 보여주어야 하는 자신들을 발견할지도 모른다. 그들은 학생들을 똑같은 종류의 경험에 대해 준비시켜야 한다.

구문 [13행~15행] Similarly, teachers may **find** *themselves* **having** to justify their ideas about teaching to their principal.
'(경험으로) 알다, 알게되다'는 의미의 동사 find가 쓰인 SVOC 구조로 「find + O + C」는 'O가 ~하다는 것을 알게 되다[발견하다]'로 해석한다.

어휘 sell oneself 자기를 선전하다 suspicion 의심, 불신(= distrust); 혐의 be attached to ~에 애착[애정]을 가지다; ~에 소속하다 incredibly 믿을 수 없을 정도로, 엄청나게 aspect 측면; 모양 demonstrate (실례를 들어) 입증하다; 설명하다; 시위에 참여하다 justify 옳음을 보여주다; ~을 정당화하다, 해명하다 **[선택지 어휘]** criticism 비판, 비난; 비평, 평론 innovation 혁신; 획기적인 것 reputation 평판, 명성

12 빈칸 추론 ④

해설 소수 집단이 사법 체계에게 그들의 문화적 배경을 고려해달라고 요청하는 '문화적 항변'은 사회를 유지하는 법의 힘을 무력화시킬 것이므로 국가의 공식 정책상 거부된다. 따라서 대부분의 정부들은 ④ '문화적 차이의 수용보다는 동화를 지지한다'고 표현할 수 있다.
① 문화적 다양성의 긍정적인 영향에 주의를 기울인다
② 문화적 경계를 넘어 이해의 출입구를 연다
③ 그러한 문화적 소외가 어떻게 해소될 수 있는지의 문제를 제기한다
⑤ 소수 집단을 다양한 범죄로부터 보호하기 위해 법 개정을 고려한다

해석 다민족 사회에서 소수 민족과 토착 집단은 때때로 형사와 민사 사건에서 법률 제도에 자신들의 문화적 배경을 고려해달라고 요청한다. 대부분의 개인들은 문화적 항변에 대해 처음 들을 때, 그것이 무정부 상태로 이어질 것을 우려하여 그것을 즉각 거부한다. 각각의 사람이 법으로부터의 면제를 요구할 수 있다면, 법은 사회를 유지되게 하는 데 무력해질 것이다. 소수 민족은 그 나라의 법에 따르도록 자신들의 행동을 바꾸어야 한다. "로마에서는 로마법을 따르라"는 수 세기 동안 일반적인 통념이었다. 본질적으로 모든 민족 국가들의 공식적인 정책은 이러한 믿음을 반영한다. 정말로 대부분의 정부들은 문화적 차이의 수용보다는 동화를 지지한다. 이러한 견해는 대중과 정부 엘리트들에게 널리 수용되며, 많은 사례에서 문화적 항변을 제기하자 하는 노력을 곤란하게 해왔다.

구문 [6행~8행] **If** each person **could demand** exemptions from the law, // then the law **would be** powerless to hold society together.
「If + S' + could 동사원형, S + would 동사원형 (S'가 …할 수 있다면, S는 ~할 것이다)」은 '현재 사실의 반대'를 가정하는 가정법 과거 표현이다.
[9행~10행] Ethnic minorities should change their behavior // **so** (that) it

conforms to the law of the land.
접속사 so는 so that에서 that이 생략된 형태이며 의미는 '~하도록, ~하기 위하여'이다.

어휘 ethnic 민족의   indigenous 토착의   legal system 법률 제도   take ~ into account ~을 고려하다   criminal case 형사 사건   civil case 민사 사건   cultural defense 문화적 항변   for fear that ~ would[should] ~을 우려하여   exemption 면제   hold ~ together ~을 유지되게 하다; 단결시키다   conform to ~을 따르다   conventional wisdom 일반적[사회적] 통념   nation-state 민족 국가   mirror 반영하다   complicate 곤란하게 하다; 복잡하게 만들다

13 흐름 무관 문장   ④

해설 글 전체의 내용은 여행지에서 구입하는 기념품이 실제로 그 지역 문화의 전통을 나타내지 않고, 관광객들을 위해 만들어졌다는 것을 알면서도 관광객 스스로가 부여하는 의미 때문에 진품처럼 느낀다는 것이다. 그러므로 ④의 일부 어구(tell fake items from real ones)는 주제와 관련이 있지만, 기념품에 대해 여행자들이 가짜와 진짜를 구별할 능력을 배우는 것이 중요하다는 내용은 글의 전체 흐름과 관계가 없다.

해석 아마도 기념품이 진짜임을 결정하는 데 가장 큰 영향력 있는 것은 의미 부여의 과정을 통해 여행자 스스로가 상품에 부여하는 의미일 것이다. ① 대부분의 사람들에게, '기념품을 산다는 것은 진짜라고 인식되는 상품을 획득하는 행위이다.' ② 그러나 한 연구에 따르면 기념품 판매자의 인식은 여행자들이 (기념품의) 디자인이 전통적인지 혹은 억지로 꾸며낸 것인지를 실제로 신경 쓰지 않는다는 것이었다. ③ 그 연구는 관광객이 인공적이고 목적지 특유의 물품이 아닌 것들은 (예를 들어, 돌로 만든 체스 세트, 놋쇠로 된 담배 라이터 등) 지역 문화의 공예 전통의 일부가 아니며, 오히려 그러한 물품은 여행자들을 위해 특별하게 만들어진다는 것을 알고 있는 것이 확실하다고 결론짓는다. ④ 그러므로 여행자들은 가짜 물품과 진짜 물품을 구별하는 법을 배우는 것이 매우 중요하다. ⑤ 그럼에도 불구하고, 여행자들이 집으로 가져가는 기념품은 여전히 일종의 전리품이어서, 그것은 방문한 나라에 대한 이미지를 분명히 반영할 것이다. 즉, 그 공예품이 진짜임이 그 사람의 해외 경험이 진짜임을 보증하므로, 그것은 분명히 진짜거나 전통적이거나 원시적으로 보일 것이다.

구문 [1행~4행] Perhaps the most influential in determining authenticity of souvenirs is *the meaning* [that the tourists **themselves** assign to their **merchandise** / through a process of attribution of meaning].
목적격 관계대명사 that이 이끄는 절이 the meaning을 수식한다. 또한, [ ] 안의 주어 the tourists 뒤에 재귀대명사 themselves가 쓰여 주어를 강조한다.
[9행~14행] The study concludes **(that)** it is obvious that tourists understand that artificial and non-destination-specific items (e.g. stone chess sets, brass cigarette lighters, etc.) are not part of the craft tradition of local cultures, but rather such items are made specifically for tourists.
concludes의 목적어절을 이끄는 명사절 접속사 that이 생략되었고, 이 that절 안에서 it은 가주어, that tourists ~ for tourists가 진주어이다.

어휘 influential 영향력 있는, 영향력이 큰   determine 결정하다; 결심하다   souvenir 기념품, 선물   assign 부여하다; 배정[배치]하다   merchandise 상품, 물품   process 과정, 절차   attribution (의미의) 부여; 귀속, 귀인   acquisition 획득, 취득; 습득   perceive 인식[감지]하다; 여기다   cf. perception 인식; 자각; 통찰력   authentic 진짜[진품]인; 정확한   vendor 판매인, 행상인   obvious 확실한, 분명한   artificial 인공[인위]적인   non-destination-specific 목적지 특유의 것이 아닌   brass 놋쇠, 황동   craft (수)공예(품); 선박; 비행기   specifically 특별하게; 명확히   crucial 중대한, 결정적인   tell 구별하다; 알다   nonetheless 그럼에도 불구하고, 그렇더라도   trophy

전리품; 트로피   reflect 반영하다; 반사하다; 심사숙고하다   primitive 원시적인; 원시[초기]의   artifact 공예품, 인공물   guarantee 보증(하다); 보증서, 담보(물)

14 글의 순서   ⑤

해설 식물이 포식자를 멈추려고 군대를 배치한다는 주어진 글 다음에는 이를 실험하기 위한 연구 대상으로 애기장대라고 불리는 식물이 처음 언급되는 (C)가 나와야 한다. 그다음에는 식물이 먹히고 있다는 것을 인지하는지를 알아내기 위해 그 연구 대상(애기장대)이 먹히고 있을 때의 진동을 재현하는 (B)가 나오고, 그에 대한 결과로 진동에 반응하는 애기장대를 언급하는 (A)가 마지막으로 나오는 것이 적절하다.

해석 식물이 자신이 먹히고 있을 때를 알고 있다는 것을 여러분은 알았는가? 음, 최근의 연구가 나타내는 것처럼 그것은 그렇지만(알고 있지만), 그저 그곳에 앉아서 자신의 운명을 받아들이는 것은 아니다. 그것은 그 포식자를 막기 위한 노력으로 자신을 방어하기 위하여 군대를 배치한다.
(C) 이러한 경우에, 그 연구 대상은 양배추과에 속하는 애기장대(Arabidopsis thaliana)라고 일컫는 식물이었다. 애기장대는 그것의 게놈 배열 순서가 밝혀진 최초의 식물이었고, 그래서 연구자들은 그것의 내부 활동을 대부분의 다른 식물보다 더 잘 이해하고 있다.
(B) 그 식물이 먹히고 있다는 것을 인식하고 있는지를 밝히기 위해서, 그 과학자들은 애벌레가 그 연구 대상의 잎을 먹을 때 만드는 진동을 재현했다. 그들은 또한 바람이 부는 진동과 같은 그 식물이 경험했을 다른 진동도 기록했다.
(A) 예상대로 애기장대는 포식자들을 저지하기 위해서 다소 독성이 있는 겨자기름의 생산을 증가시켜 그것을 잎으로 전달하여 우적우적 먹는 애벌레를 흉내 내는 진동에 반응했다. 이 식물은 바람이나 다른 진동에는 반응을 보이지 않았다.

구문 [5행~8행] Sure enough, the cress responded to *the vibrations* [**that** mimic a munching caterpillar] **by** upping its production of mildly toxic mustard oils **and** delivering them to the leaves to deter predators.
[ ] 부분은 주격 관계대명사 that이 이끄는 관계사절로 the vibrations를 수식한다. 수단을 나타내는 전치사 by의 목적어로 두 개의 밑줄 친 동명사구가 and로 병렬 연결된다.
[10행~12행] To find out **if the plant was aware of being eaten**, the scientists recreated *the vibrations* [**that** a caterpillar makes **as** it eats the leaves of the subject].
To find out의 목적어로 if(~인지 아닌지)가 이끄는 명사절이 나온다. [ ] 부분은 목적격 관계대명사 that이 이끄는 관계사절로 the vibrations를 수식하며 [ ] 내에 접속사 as가 이끄는 부사절이 쓰였다.

어휘 fate 운명; 죽음   deploy 배치하다; 알맞게 사용하다   troop 군대; 떼, 무리   predator 포식자   vibration 진동   mimic 흉내 내다   mildly 다소, 약간; 부드럽게   toxic 독성이 있는   deter 저지하다; 방해하다   recreate 재현하다, 되살리다   subject 연구[실험] 대상   thale cress 애기장대   cabbage 양배추   genome 게놈 ((세포나 생명체의 유전자 총체))

15 글의 순서   ④

해설 오이 껍질에 있는 쿠쿠르비타신이라는 화합물은 소화에 안 좋고 쓴 맛이 난다는 주어진 글 다음에는, 사람들 중 5분의 1은 이 화합물의 맛을 느낄 수 없다는 내용의 (C)가 나온다. But으로 시작되며 반대로 이 화합물의 맛에 민감한 5분의 2의 사람들에 대해 논하는 (A)가 그 다음에 나온다. 쿠쿠르비타신의 영향을 받는 것은 인간만은 아니라고 끝나는 (A) 다음에는 이 화합물에게 끌리는 해충에 대해 논한 (B)가 나온다.

해석 어떤 오이도 트림하지 않지만, 이 열매의 껍질에서 만들어지는 쿠쿠르비타신이라는 화합물은 그것을 먹는 사람들의 소화계에 역효과를 미칠 수 있다. 쿠쿠르비타신은 또한 쓴 맛이 나서 최고의 오이 샌드위치조차 망쳐버린다.
(C) 유전적 차이로 인해 다섯 중 한 명은 쿠쿠르비타신을 전혀 맛볼 수 없는데, 이것이 왜 어떤 사람들은 다른 사람들이 쓴 맛이 나는 오이에 대해 불평할 때 그들이 정상이 아니라고 생각하는지를 설명해준다.
(A) 그러나 다섯 중 두 명은 쿠쿠르비타신에 극심한 민감성을 갖고 있고, 이것은 오이를 조금이라도 먹는다는 이유로 그들이 나머지 우리들을 정상이 아니라고 생각하더라도 이해할 수 있게 한다. 이 문제에 대한 표준 해법은 불쾌함을 주는 껍질을 그저 벗겨내는 것이었다. 그러나 인간이 쿠쿠르비타신의 영향을 받는 유일한 존재는 아니다.
(B) 해충은 이 화합물에 끌리며, 본성적으로 혹은 스트레스로 그것을 만드는 오이 식물에 집중한다. 그래서 식물 품종 개량가들이 껍질에 쿠쿠르비타신이 거의 없는 '트림이 안 나는' 품종을 개발했을 때, 곤충을 제외한 모두가 기뻐했다.

구문 [1행~4행] No cucumbers burp, // but **compounds** (called *cucurbitacins* (produced in the skin of the fruit)) **can have an adverse effect on** the digestive system / of *those* [who eat them].
첫 번째 ( )는 수동의 뜻으로 compounds를 수식하고 두 번째 ( )는 cucurbitacins를 수식한다. but 이후의 주어는 compounds이고 동사는 can have이다. have an adverse effect on은 '~에 부정적인[불리한] 영향을 미치다'의 뜻이다. [ ]는 those를 수식하는 주격 관계사절이다.
[6행~9행] But two in five people have an acute sensitivity to cucurbitacins, // **which** makes **it** understandable // **if** they think // (that) the rest of us are crazy for eating cucumbers at all.
which는 앞 문장 전체의 내용을 가리킨다. makes 다음의 it은 가목적어이고 if 이하가 진목적어이다. the rest 앞에서 접속사 that이 생략되어 있다.

어휘 compound 화합물   adverse 반대의; 부정적인, 불리한   acute 극심한 offending 불쾌하게 하는   insect pest 해충   breeder 품종 개량가, 재배자 *cf.* breed (품종을) 개량하다; (새끼를) 낳다; 기르다   variety 품종; 다양성   little to no ~가 거의 없는

16 문장 넣기 ④

해설 ④ 앞 문장은 광고 테이프를 빨리 돌려 속도를 높이면 음이 높아진다는 단점이 있다고 하는데, ④ 다음의 문장은 '이것이 음높이를 변화시키지 않는다'라고 하여 두 문장 간에 논리적 균열이 있다. 테이프를 빠르게 돌리지 않고 휴지기를 짧게 하고 모음의 길이를 줄이는 시간 압축 기법을 소개한 주어진 문장이 ④에 들어가면, 음이 높아지지 않는 것이 주어진 문장에서 언급된 시간 압축 기법의 장점임을 알 수 있다.

해석 강도의 변수와 관련하여, 밝은 빛이나 시끄러운 소리가 우리의 주의를 끌 수 있다고 말하는 것은 당연한 말을 하는 것과 거의 같다. 우리 모두는 오로지 이러한 전제에 기초한 것처럼 보이는 무수한 상업광고의 예들을 접해 왔다. 광고 상황에서 강도를 이용하는 흔치 않은 한 가지 사례는 라디오 광고에서 시간 압축된 말을 실황하는 것이다. LaBarbera와 MacLachlan에 의해 수행된 실험은 사람들을 일반 속도 또는 대략 130% 정도 시간 압축된 다섯 개의 라디오 광고에 노출시켰다. 이런 시간 압축된 광고들은 테이프를 빠르게 돌려서 '속도가 높여진' 것이 아니었는데, 그렇게 하는 것은 또한 청각 신호의 주파수를 증가시켜 아나운서의 말이 높은음의 미키마우스처럼 들리게 할 것이기 때문이었다. 오히려 시간 압축 기법은 단어 사이의 휴지를 줄이고 모음 소리의 길이를 줄이는 것과 관련이 있다. 이것은 아나운서 목소리의 음높이를 변화시키지 않으면서 더 빠르게 재생되는 메시지를 만든다. 이 연구자들은 시간 압축된 광고가 보통 광고보다 더 많은 흥미와 더 나은 기억을 끌어낸다는 것을 발견했다.

구문 [4행~6행] With reference to the variable of intensity, **it** is almost *stating*

the obvious **to say** that bright lights or loud sounds can attract our attention.
it은 가주어이고 to say 이하가 진주어이다. state the obvious는 '당연한 것을 말하다'라는 뜻의 표현이다.
[12행~15행] The experiment (conducted by LaBarbera and MacLachlan) **exposed** people **to** *five radio commercials* [that were either normal or timecompressed on the order of 130%].
( )은 수동 의미의 분사구로 주어 The experiment를 수식하며 문장의 동사는 exposed이다. 'expose A to B'는 'A를 B에 노출시키다'의 뜻이다. [ ]은 five radio commercials를 수식하는 관계사절이고 「either A or B」는 'A나 B 둘 중 하나'의 뜻이다.

어휘 compression 압축   vowel 모음   with reference to ~에 관하여 variable 변수; 변하기 쉬운   intensity 강도   state the obvious 당연한 말을 하다 countless 무수한, 셀 수 없이 많은   commercial 상업의; 광고   solely 오로지, 단지 on the order of 대략   frequency 주파수   auditory 청각의   high-pitched 고음의   pitch 음의 높이   recall 기억(력); 생각해내다

17 문장 넣기 ⑤

해설 주어진 문장에서 '이러한' 영양소들이 탄수화물보다 더 천천히 소화되기 때문에 단백질과 지방이 풍부한 식사는 포만감을 오래 지속되게 해준다고 되어 있으므로 '이러한 영양소들'은 단백질과 지방임을 알 수 있다. 그러므로 주어진 문장은 바로 앞 문장에서 단백질과 지방이 등장하는 ⑤에 위치해야 한다. 이는 주어진 문장의 결과에 해당하는, ⑤ 뒤의 문장과도 잘 연결된다.

해석 사람들이 탄수화물(혹은 가공식품이든 뭐든)을 줄이면, 그들이 칼로리 섭취량을 제한하려고 애쓰고 있지 않을 때에도 보통은 결국 더 적은 칼로리를 섭취하게 된다. 예를 들어, 엄격한 저탄수화물 다이어트를 했으나 그것만 빼고는 원하는 만큼 먹도록 허용되었던 사람들은 의식적으로 칼로리를 제한하고 있었던 사람들이 줄인 것과 대략 같은 양만큼 자신들의 칼로리 섭취량을 결국 줄였다는 것이 한 연구에서 밝혀졌다. 여기에는 몇 가지 일이 일어나고 있다. 첫째로, 고를 수 있는 음식의 다양성이 제한되어 있을 때, 사람들은 많은 선택사항을 제공받을 때보다 덜 먹는 경향이 있다. 두 번째로, 사람들이 탄수화물을 피할 때, 그들은 일반적으로 단백질과 지방의 섭취량을 늘린다. 이 영양소들이 탄수화물보다 더 천천히 소화되기 때문에 단백질과 지방이 더 풍부한 식사는 탄수화물이 풍부한 식사보다 더 오랫동안 포만감이 지속되게 만드는 경향이 있다. 그 결과, 탄수화물을 줄인 사람들은 식간에 전만큼 배가 고프지 않다고 흔히 말하는데, 아마 간식도 덜 먹을지 모른다.

구문 [9행~13행] ~ people [who followed a strict low-carb diet but were otherwise allowed to eat as much as they wanted] / **ended up** reducing their calorie intake / by about **the same** amount / **as** people [who were consciously restricting their calories].
두 개의 [ ]는 각각 앞의 people을 수식한다. 첫 번째 [ ] 절 속에서 동사 followed와 were allowed는 병렬구조를 이룬다. 주어는 앞의 people이고 동사는 ended up 이며, 「the same A as B」는 'B와 같은 A'의 뜻이다.
[16행~17행] ~ they tend to eat less than they **do** / when (they are) presented with a lot of options.
they do에서 do는 대동사로 eat을 지칭한다. when 다음에는 they are가 생략되었다.

어휘 nutrient 영양소   digest 소화하다   protein 단백질   cut back on ~을 줄이다   processed food 가공식품   consume 섭취하다; 소비하다   restrict 제한하다 intake 섭취(량)   strict 엄격한   otherwise 그 밖에는   consciously 의식적으로 present 제공하다, 주다   snack 간식을 먹다

18 요약문 완성 ①

해설 혈액 기증이라는 선행은 현금이라는 외적인 보상이 주어졌을 때 오히려 줄어들었다는 실험의 결과와 자연재해나 여타 재난 사태가 벌어질 때마다 돈을 받지 않는 자원봉사자들이 항상 증가한다는 말로 보아 빈칸 (A)는 '외적인' 빈칸 (B)에는 '동기를 주다'라는 의미의 ①이 적절하다.

해석 흥미 있는 현장 실험을 위해서 두 명의 스웨덴 경제학자들이 Gothenburg에 있는 지역 헌혈의 집을 방문해서 헌혈에 관심이 있는 여성 153명을 찾았다. 그런 다음 연구원들은 그 여인들을 세 그룹으로 나누었다. 실험자들은 첫 번째 그룹의 사람들에게 보상이 없을 것이라고 말했다. 실험자들은 두 번째 그룹에게 다른 방식을 제시했다. 이 참가자들이 혈액을 제공하면, 그들은 각각 50스웨덴 크로나(약 7달러)를 받게 될 것이다. 세 번째 그룹은 50스웨덴 크로나의 보상을 받지만 그 액수를 소아암 자선기금에 기부할지를 즉시 선택하는 두 번째 제안의 변형을 제안받았다. 첫 번째 그룹에서 52퍼센트의 여성들이 혈액을 기증하기로 결정했다. 두 번째 그룹은 어떠했을까? 이 그룹에서 단지 30퍼센트의 여성들이 혈액을 기증하기로 결정했다. 한편 자선단체에 즉시 비용을 기부할 선택권을 가진 세 번째 그룹은 첫 번째 그룹과 거의 동일하게 응답했다. 53퍼센트가 혈액 기증자가 되었다. 혈액 기증에서 중요한 것은 선행이다. 그것은 미국 적십자 안내 책자가 말하는 돈으로는 살 수 없는 감정을 제공한다. 그것이 자연재해나 다른 재난 동안에 돈을 받지 않는 자원봉사자들이 언제나 증가하는 이유이다.

↓

혈액 기증 같은 이타적 행동을 요청할 때 (A) 외적인 보상을 사람들에게 제공하는 것은 사람들의 참여에 (B) 동기를 부여하지 못한다.

구문 [16행~18행] Meanwhile, *the third group* [**which** had the option of donating the fee directly to charity] responded much the same as the first group.
[ ] 부분은 주격 관계대명사 which가 이끄는 관계사절로 the third group을 수식한다.

[20행~22행] It provides *a feeling* [that (the American Red Cross brochures say) money can't buy].
[ ] 부분은 a feeling을 수식하는 관계사절이고, 관계사절 내에서 the American Red Cross brochures say가 삽입되었다.

어휘 intriguing 아주 흥미로운 field experiment 현장 실험 regional 지역[지방]의 blood center 헌혈의 집, 혈액원 give blood 헌혈하다(= donate blood) arrangement (처리) 방식; 합의; 준비; 배치 krona 크로나 ((스웨덴과 아이슬란드의 화폐 단위)) variation 변형; 변화, 차이 immediate 즉각적인; 직접적인; 당면한 donate 기증[기부]하다 blood donor 혈액 기증자, 헌혈인 Red Cross 적십자 brochure (안내·광고용) 책자 invariably 언제나, 변함없이 calamity 재난, 재앙 altruistic 이타적인 extrinsic 외적인, 외부의 inhibit 저해하다; 못하게 하다 intrinsic reward 내적 보상

19~20 장문   19 ④ 20 ⑤

해설 19. 범주화하여 인식하는 것은 사람이 살아나가는 데 필수적이지만 사물을 왜곡해서 볼 수 있는 단점도 있다는 것이 글의 요지이므로 제목으로 ④ '범주화는 인식의 양날의 검'이 가장 적절하다.
① 사람과 사물을 분류하는 원리
② 우리는 범주화 할 때 세부사항을 본다
③ 범주화에서의 대조와 비교
⑤ 범주적 인식: 가장 귀중한 생존 기술

20. 6월 1일과 6월 30일의 기온 차이는 과소평가하는 경향이 있었으나 6월 15일과 7월 15일의 기온 차이는 과대평가하는 경향이 있었다는 내용으로 보아, 같은 달의 두 날은 다른 달의 두 날보다 더 유사하다고 여겨진다. 그러므로 (e) 'different'는 similar로 바꾸어 써야 적절하다.

해석 세상에서 우리가 만나는 모든 사물과 사람은 독특하지만, 만약 우리가 그들을 그렇게 인식한다면 우리는 그다지 잘 기능하지 못할 것이다. 우리는 우리 환경의 모든 항목에 대해 각각의 세부사항을 관찰하고 고려할 시간이 없다. 대신, 그 사물을 하나의 범주로 할당하기 위해서 우리가 관찰한 소수의 (a) 주요한 특징을 사용하고, 그러고 나서 사물에 대한 평가를 그 사물 자체가 아닌 그 범주에 기반을 둔다. 범주화는 우리의 환경을 매우 빠르고 효율적으로 헤쳐 나가는데 도움이 된다. 우리가 범주화하는 주요한 방법 중의 하나는 특정 차이점들의 중요성은 최대화하되 다른 차이점들의 관련성은 최소화하는 것이다. 그러나 우리 추론의 화살표는 또한 반대 방향을 가리킬 수도 있다. 일단 어떤 사물들을 한 집단으로 분류하고 다른 사물들을 다른 집단으로 분류하면 이후에는 같은 집단의 사물들을 실제보다 더 비슷하다고 인식하고 다른 집단의 사물들은 실제보다 덜 비슷하다고 인식하게 되는 것이다. 단지 사물을 집단에 위치시키는 것만으로 그 사물에 대한 우리의 판단에 (b) 영향을 줄 수 있는 것이다. 따라서 범주화가 자연스럽고 필수적인 지름길이긴 해도, 우리 뇌의 여느 생존 지향적 기교와 마찬가지로 그것은 그것의 (c) 결함이 있다.
범주화가 초래하는 오해를 조사한 초기 실험들 중의 하나는 피실험자들에게 온도를 추정하라고 요청하는 간단한 연구였다. 그 연구에서 연구원들은 어느 도시의 시민들에게 6월 1일과 6월 30일 사이의 기온 차이를 짐작해보라고 했을 때는 차이를 과소평가하는 경향이 있었으나 6월 15일과 7월 15일 사이의 기온 차이를 추정해보라고 했을 때는 그 차이를 과대평가했다는 것을 알아냈다. 날짜를 달로 묶는 인위적 범주 때문에 인식이 (d) 왜곡된 것이다. 우리는 설령 날짜 사이의 간격이 같더라도 같은 달의 두 날은 다른 달의 두 날보다 더 (e) 다르다고 (→ 비슷하다고) 생각한다.

구문 [5행~9행] Instead, we employ *a few prominent traits* [that we do observe] to assign the object to a category, and then we **base** our assessment of the object **on** {the category} rather than {the object itself}.
[ ] 부분은 관계절로 a few prominent traits를 수식한다. then 이하 절은 '~을 …에 기반을 두다'의 뜻을 가진 'base ~ on ...' 구문으로 { }으로 표시된 두 개의 명사구가 병렬구조를 이루고 있다.

[25행~28행] One of the earliest experiments **investigating** the misinterpretations **caused** by categorization was *a simple study* [in which subjects were asked to estimate the temperature].
분사 investigating은 앞에 나온 명사 the earliest experiments를 수식하고, 과거분사 caused는 앞에 나온 명사 the misinterpretations를 수식한다. [ ] 부분은 관계절로 앞에 나온 a simple study를 수식한다.

어휘 function 기능을 하다, 구실을 다하다 prominent 중요한; 두드러진 trait 특징 assign 할당하다, 부여하다 assessment 평가 navigate 헤쳐나가다, 통과하다 relevance 관련성, 타당성 crucial 중대한 shortcut 지름길, 손쉬운 방법 -oriented ~ 지향적인, ~ 경향의 drawback 결점, 약점 misinterpretations 오해; (사실의) 곡해 identical 동일한

1	④	2	③	3	①	4	④	5	②	6	④	7	⑤	8	⑤	9	③	10	②
11	⑤	12	③	13	④	14	④	15	③	16	④	17	⑤	18	④	19	①	20	④

1 심경 변화   ④

해설 두 번째 문장 'But I have made a firm decision ~'에서 스카이다이빙에 대한 두려움보다는 단호히 결심한 결연한(determined) 태도를 알 수 있으며, 뛰어내린 뒤에 고공에서 미소를 지은 것과 마지막 문장 'I feel as if I were on top of the world.'을 통해 흥분한(excited) 마음을 알 수 있다.
① 후회하는 → 자랑스러운   ② 긴장한 → 겁에 질린
③ 무서운 → 안도한   ④ 외로운 → 만족한

해석 내가 비행기의 열린 문에 서서 하늘을 마주할 때 바람이 나를 때린다. 그러나 나는 굳게 결심했고 어떤 것도 나를 멈추게 하지 않을 작정이다. "준비 됐습니까?" 팀장이 부른다. 우리는 "준비 됐습니다!" 그 다음에 "간다!"라고 대답하며 외친다. 갑자기 우리는 비행기 문 밖에 나와, 맑은 여름 하늘 바람 속으로 굴러간다. 기쁨과 두려움의 조합인 부지불식간의 웃음이 내 목에 끓어오른다. 나는 땅을 마주하고 공중에서 납작하게 누우려고 노력한다. 뛰어내린 다른 사람들이 하나씩 하나씩 함께 모여, 내 손목과 발목을 움켜잡고, 우리가 시속 120마일로 땅을 향해 질주하는 여덟 명의 사람들로 이루어진 별이 될 때까지 서로를 연결한다. 고글 밑에서 미소가 보인다. 우리는 다시 함께 점프하고 있다. 마침내 4천 피트에서 우리는 분리되어 낙하산을 펼친다. 그것들은 밖으로 흔들리며 우리 위에서 부풀어 오르고, 우리를 아래의 갈색 들판으로 부드럽게 내려 보낸다. 나는 마치 내가 세상의 꼭대기에 있는 느낌이다.

구문 [12행~13행] Beneath each pair of goggles *is* **a smile**.
a smile이 주어인 도치구문이며 '장소부사구+동사+주어'의 어순이다.
[17행] I feel **as if** I <u>were</u> on top of the world.
'as if'는 '마치 ~인 것처럼'의 뜻이며, 가정법 과거시제를 사용하여 be동사의 형태가 were이다.

어휘 batter 두드리다, 때리다   firm 굳은   roll 구르다   involuntary 자기도 모르게 하는   bubble up 끓어오르다   wrist 손목   parachute 낙하산   swing 흔들리다   balloon 부풀어 오르다

2 필자 주장   ③

해설 자녀의 잘못된 행동에 대해 교육할 때 행동에 관한 구체적이고 직접적인 피드백을 제공하는 것이 효과도 좋고 자녀가 모욕을 느끼게 하지 않는다는 내용의 글이므로 필자의 주장으로 가장 적절한 것은 ③이다.

해석 부모는 생산적인 피드백을 제공함으로써 자녀들이 성공하도록 도울 수 있다. 부정적인 행동과 관련된 피드백의 한 예를 생각해보자. "Mary, 난 네가 영화 보러 갈 수 없는 상황을 처리하는 방식이 맘에 들지 않는구나. 네가 실망했다는 거 알아. 나도 그랬을 거야. 하지만 네가 실망하거나 기분이 상했을 때, 문을 차거나 네 물건을 손상시키면 안 돼. 넌 너의 상한 감정을 다른 방식으로 처리할 필요가 있어. 너의 화난 감정을 배출하려면 대신 뭘 할 수 있다고 생각하니?" 이러한 피드백이 구체적이며 직접적임을 주목하라. 부모가 아이에게 그 아이의 행동이 용납될 수 없다는 메시지를 주지만, 아이 자신은 모욕받았다고 느끼지 않는다. 이러한 종류의 피드백은 보통 방어적 반응을 유발하지 않는다. 그것은 "나는 널 사랑하는 거지, 네 행동을 사랑하는 건 아니다."라는 옛 속담과 같다.

구문 [8행~9행] What do you think you can do instead ~?
간접의문문이며, 「의문사 + (do you think) + S + V」의 어순이다.
[11행~12행] While the parent gives the child <u>the message</u> <u>that her action is unacceptable</u>, ~
두 밑줄 친 부분은 동격 관계이다.

어휘 productive 생산적인   unacceptable 용납할 수 없는   insult 모욕하다   provoke 유발하다   defensive 방어적인

3 밑줄 함의   ①

해설 자아 복잡성이 낮은 사람은 부정적인 사건이나 어려움에 직면했을 때 부정적인 영향력이 다른 정체성까지 미칠 수 있다는 내용으로 밑줄 친 부분에서 'self eggs'는 여러 자아 정체성을 의미하고 이를 하나의 바구니에 담는다는 것은 여러 정체성이 겹치게 되는 것을 나타내므로 밑줄 친 부분의 뜻은 ① '자신의 소수의 자아상이 합쳐지도록 허용하는 것'이 가장 적절하다.
② 개인적 특성의 관점에서 자신을 평가하는 것
③ (자신을) 정신적 행복의 손상으로부터 보호하는 것
④ 자신에 대해 긍정적으로 생각하는 것을 막는 것
⑤ 자신보다 더 잘하고 있는 다른 사람과 자신을 비교하는 것

해석 연구에 따르면, 한 개인의 자아 복잡성의 정도는 중요한 결과를 가져올 수 있는데, 특히 사람들이 주어진 삶의 영역에서 부정적인 사건이나 어려움에 직면했을 때 그렇다. 여러분이 중간고사를 잘 못 봤다는 것을 알게 된다고 상상해 보라. 여러분이 자아 복잡성이 높은 사람이라면, 다시 말해서 겹치지 않는 많은 영역의 관점에서 스스로를 정의한다면(예를 들어, 학생, 열렬한 스키어, 헌신적인 자원봉사자, 'Glee(미국의 인기 뮤지컬 코미디 드라마)'에 열광하는 팬), 형편없는 시험 성적으로부터 비롯되는 부정적임은 상대적으로 억제되어, 학생으로서의 자신에 대해 느끼는 방식에만 영향을 끼친다. 그러나 학생으로서의 정체성이 여러분이 갖고 있는 소수의 다른 정체성과 크게 겹칠 정도로 자아 복잡성이 낮다면, 그렇다면 여러분의 좋지 않은 시험 성적과 관련된 부정적임이 번져 여러분이 여러분의 다른, 겹치는 정체성을 평가하는 방식에 영향을 끼칠 뿐만 아니라 학생으로서의 스스로에 대한 평가를 낮출 가능성도 있다. 요컨대, <u>자신의 자아 달걀을 모두 하나의 바구니에 담는 것</u>은, 위협적인 자아 관련 사건에 직면할 때 위험할 수 있다.

구문 [6행~12행] If you're *someone* [who is high in self-complexity] ~ *the negativity* [that results from your poor exam grade] is relatively contained, / **affecting** only how you feel about yourself as a student.
두 개의 [ ] 부분은 모두 관계대명사가 이끄는 형용사절로 각각 선행사 someone과 the negativity를 수식한다. affecting 이후는 부대상황을 나타내는 분사구문이다.
[12행~18행] But if you're low in self-complexity **such that** your identity as a student overlaps to a great extent with *the few other identities* [**(which[that])** you have] — then *the negativity* (associated with your poor exam grade) is likely <u>to lower your evaluations of yourself as a student</u> **as well as** (to) <u>spill over and affect how you evaluate your other, overlapping identities</u>.
such that은 '~할 정도로'라는 의미를 가진 부사절 접속사이다. [ ] 부분은 목적격 관계대명사 which 또는 that이 생략된 관계사절로 선행사 the few other identities를 수식한다. associated ~ exam grade는 과거분사구로 앞에 있는 the negativity

를 수식한다. 상관접속사 as well as는 밑줄 친 두 개의 to부정사구를 병렬 연결하며 반복되는 to는 생략되었다.

어휘 self-complexity 자아 복잡성 confront 직면하다 domain 영역, 분야; 영토 in terms of ~의 관점에서 nonoverlapping 겹치지 않는 *cf.* overlap 겹치다 avid 열렬한, 열심인 committed 헌신적인 contain 억제하다, 억누르다 spill over 번지다; 넘치다 trait 특성; 특징 merge 합치다; 융합되다

4 글의 요지 ④

해설 제품이 의인화된 특징을 가질 때 인간은 그 제품과 정서적인 관계를 맺고 배려와 관심을 쏟게 되며, 제품을 품질과 물질적인 측면에서 평가하지 않고 제품을 인간처럼 대하며 사랑할 수 있게 된다는 내용의 글이므로 요지로는 ④가 가장 적절하다.

해석 제품이 의인화된 신호(예컨대 이름, 성별, 목소리)를 특징으로 할 때, 그것은 그 자신의 안녕을 위하여 관심을 받을 만한 주체를 창조한다. 따라서 소비자들은 더욱 정서적으로 끌리는 방식으로 의인화된 제품과 관계를 맺으며 그들이 비의인화된 주체에게 그러할 것보다 더 큰 배려와 관심을 보여줄 수도 있다. 이것의 한 예로서 Chandler와 Schwarz는 자신의 차를 의인화된 방식으로 생각하도록 유도된 소비자들은 그것을 기꺼이 교체하려는 마음이 덜했으며, 교체 결정을 내릴 때 그것의 품질을 덜 중시했음을 발견했다. 대신에 그들은 대인 영역과 관련 있다고 보통 여겨지는 특징들(예컨대 따뜻한 성격을 지닌 것과 같이 좋은 동반자를 결정해줄 특징들)에 더 많이 주의를 기울였다. 이것은 의인화된 제품 특성이 소비자들로 하여금 제품을 인간으로 범주화하도록 유도할 수 있기 때문이며, 제품에 대한 사랑이 대인 간의 사랑의 표명이므로, 의인화는 제품과 맺는 그러한 관계를 있을법하게 만든다.

구문 [3행~7행] Accordingly, consumers may **engage with** anthropomorphized products in a more emotionally driven fashion, and **show** *greater* care and concern *than* they *would* (show care and concern) for non-anthropomorphized agents.
조동사 뒤에 오는 동사원형 engage with와 show가 and로 연결되어 병렬구조를 이룬다. 「비교급(greater) ~ than ...」 형태의 비교급 구문이 사용되었고, would 뒤에는 반복되는 show care and concern이 생략되었다.
[7행~12행] As an example of this, Chandler and Schwarz found that *consumers* (**induced** to think of their car in anthropomorphic terms) **were** less willing to replace it, and **gave** less weight to its quality *when* **making** replacement decisions.
( )은 과거분사 induced가 이끄는 분사구로 consumers를 수식한다. that절 내의 동사 were와 gave가 and로 병렬 연결된다. making 이하는 consumers를 의미상의 주어로 하는 분사구문으로 분사구문의 뜻을 분명히 하기 위하여 분사 앞에 접속사 when을 그대로 둔 경우이다.

어휘 feature 특징으로 하다; 특징 cue 신호, 암시 agent 주체; 동인; 대리인; 물질 deserve ~을 받을 만하다; ~을 (당)해야 마땅하다 accordingly 그에 따라; 그래서 engage with ~와 관계를 맺다[맞물리게 하다] anthropomorphize 의인화하다 induce 유도[설득]하다; 유발하다 be willing to-v 기꺼이 v하다 give weight to ~을 중요시하다 attend 주의를 기울이다; 참석하다 interpersonal 사람과 사람 사이의 domain 영역 companion 동반자, 친구 personality 성격; 개성 trait 특성 categorize 범주화하다; 분류하다 manifestation 표명, 징후; 나타남 anthropomorphism 의인화, 인격화 plausible 있을법한, 그럴듯한

5 글의 제목 ②

해설 보상을 받고 거짓말을 하도록 지시받은 피실험자 중에서 보잘것없는 보상을 받았던 사람들은 과제가 지루하다고 느낀 자신의 '태도'와 과제가 흥미롭다고 거짓말해야 하는 자신의 '행동' 간에 존재하는 부조화의 간극을 보상으로 메꿀 수가 없어서 차라리 지루한 과제를 즐기는 쪽으로 자신의 태도를 변화시켰다고 했으므로 글의 제목으로 가장 적절한 것은 ② '우리의 태도를 변화시켜서 인지 부조화 감소시키기'이다.
① 우리는 왜 우리가 느끼는 인지 부조화를 줄이는가
③ 인지 부조화는 의사 결정에 큰 역할을 한다
④ 더 많은 금전적 보상이 더 큰 태도 변화를 유도한다
⑤ 금전적 보상은 인지 부조화와 상관관계가 없다

해석 한 연구에서 참가자들은 먼저 (못을 못 구멍에 넣고 돌리기와 같은) 일련의 매우 길고 극도로 지루한 과업을 수행해야 했다. 그 후에 그들은 다음 참가자에게 그들이 할 과업이 실제로 정말 흥미롭다고 말하라는 요청을 받았다! 그 의도는 각각의 참가자들에게 그들이 한편으로는 실험을 싫어했지만, 다른 한편으로는 다른 사람에게 그들이 그것을 즐겼다고 말한 조화되지 않는 인지를 만들어 내는 것이었다. 게다가 참가자의 절반은 '거짓말하기' 요청을 따른 것에 대해 20달러를 받았고, 나머지 절반은 변변찮은 1달러를 받았다. 여기서의 생각은 1달러 그룹에 속한 사람들이 그들의 태도(즉, '그것은 정말 지루한 과제였어')와 그들의 실제 행동(즉, 다른 사람에게 그 행위에 대해 거짓말을 하는 것) 사이의 불일치에 대한 정당한 이유가 불충분했기 때문에 20달러 그룹에 속한 사람들보다 더 높은 수준의 인지 부조화를 경험하리라는 것이었다. 20달러 그룹은 적당한 액수의 돈을 지급받았다는 정당한 이유가 있었고 따라서 부조화를 덜 경험할 것이었다. 1달러 그룹의 참가자들은 인지적으로 매우 부조화하기 때문에, 조화를 회복하기 위해 그 과업을 즐기거나 좋아하는 방향으로 자신들의 태도를 바꾸겠지만, 20달러 조건의 참가자들은 그렇지 않을 것으로 예상되었다. 이것이 실험이 끝난 후 그 과업에 대한 태도를 측정했을 때 정확하게 일어난 일이었다.

구문 [3행~5행] Afterwards they were asked to **tell** *the next participant* that *the tasks* [(which[that]) they would do] were actually really interesting!
to부정사구는 「tell+간접목적어(the next participant)+직접목적어(that ~ interesting)」의 구조이다. 직접목적어를 이루는 that절 내에서 목적격 관계대명사 which[that]가 생략된 [ ]이 the tasks를 수식한다.
[20행~23행] It was predicted **that** *the $1 participants*, being highly cognitively dissonant, would change their attitude towards enjoying or liking the tasks so as to re-establish consonance; ~.
It은 가주어이고 that 이하가 진주어이다. 밑줄 친 부분은 the $1 participants를 의미상 주어로 하는 능동 분사구문이다.

어휘 lengthy 긴; 장황한 tedious 지루한, 싫증 나는 cognition 인지, 인식 compliance 준수, 따름 justification 정당한 이유 inconsistency 불일치 decent 괜찮은, 제대로 된 re-establish 회복[복구]하다 consonance 일치, 조화 induce 유도하다

6 안내문 불일치 ④

해설 '주차'에서 도서관 뒤쪽의 한정된 주차 공간은 이용 가능하다고 했으므로 일치하지 않는 것은 ④이다.

해석 중고 책 판매
Lakeview 공립 도서관은 대규모의 중고 책 판매를 개최할 예정입니다. 잠시 들르셔서 여러분의 가족 모두를 위해 좋은 책들을 찾아보세요!
• 언제: 2023년 6월 15일~18일

• 어디에서: Lakeview 공립 도서관 1층

• 시간:

– 목요일 오후 12시~5시

– 금요일 오전 10시~오후 5시

– 토요일과 일요일 오전 11시~오후 6시

반값 일요일:

일요일 오후 3시부터, 모든 남아있는 책들은 50%까지 가격이 할인될 것입니다.

주차:

진행 중인 공사로 인해, 도서관의 메인 주차장은 평일에 폐쇄됩니다. 그러나, 도서관 뒤 쪽의 한정된 주차 공간은 이용 가능합니다. (주차 요금은 시간당 5달러입니다.)

모든 수익금은 어린이 도서관 신축에 사용될 것입니다.

어휘 hold 개최[주최]하다; 잡고 있다; 견디다 **gigantic** 대규모의; 거대한 **stop by** (~에) 잠시 들르다 **ground floor** 1층 **remaining** 남아있는, 남은 **parking** 주차; 주차 공간[지역] *cf.* parking lot 주차장 *cf.* parking fee 주차 요금 **due to A** A 때문에 **ongoing** (계속) 진행 중인 **construction** 공사; 건축, 건설 **available** 이용할[구할] 수 있는 **profit** 수익(금), 이익, 이윤

7 밑줄 어법 ⑤

해설 「enable+목적어+to-v」의 to locate가 아니고, 앞의 명사 individuals를 수식하는 과거분사 located가 되어야 적절하므로 ⑤가 정답이 된다. 「enable+목적어+to-v」의 to-v에 해당하는 것은 to come이다.

① in which 뒤의 구조가 완전하므로 관계부사 where로 바꿔 쓸 수 있는 in which가 나오는 것이 적절하다.

② a web site가 중개인 같은 역할을 하는 회사에 의해 '유지되는' 것이므로 과거분사 maintained가 적절하다.

③ 분사구의 수식을 받는 명사는 this site가 아니라 그 앞의 명사 An individual이다. who가 이끄는 관계대명사절과 함께 한 명사를 동시에 수식하고 있음에 유의한다. An individual과의 관계가 능동이므로 현재분사 looking이 적절하다.

④ arranges와 and로 연결된 병렬구조이므로 despatches가 적절하다.

해석 고객과 고객 간의 전자 상거래 (C2C 전자 상거래)는 한 개인이 하나의 물품을 다른 사람에게 팔기를 원하는 상거래이다. 물품들은 보통 중고품, 우표나 동전이나 골동품 같은 수집가의 물품이다. 판매자는 중개인 같은 역할을 하는 회사에 의해 유지되는 웹사이트에 물품에 대한 설명과 물품의 예상 가격을 게시한다. 물품을 찾는 사이트를 방문하는 개인이 판매하려고 광고된 물품에 관심을 가질 수도 있다. 그러면 구매자와 판매자는 물품과 가격에 대해 논의한다. 가격은 이메일을 통해 메시지를 주고받음으로써 두 당사자 사이에서 상호 간에 결정된다. 그러면 중개인이 판매자로부터 물품을 받아 준비하고 그것을 구매자에게 발송하고 물품의 지급 금액과 판매자와 구매자로부터 서비스에 대한 수수료를 수금한다. 이런 시스템의 주요한 이점은 인터넷이 멀리 떨어진 장소에 위치한 두 개인이 중간의 웹 주소를 사용해 사고팔기 위해 함께 하는 것을 가능하게 한다는 것이다.

어휘 e-commerce 전자 상거래 **antique** 골동품 **post** 게시하다. 붙이다 **description** 서술, 기술; 설명서; 기재 사항 **maintain** 유지하다 **broker** 중개인 **mutually** 서로, 공동으로 **settle** 결정하다 **party** 당사자, 관계자 **despatch** 보내다, 발송하다 (= dispatch) **payment** 지급 금액 **intermediary** 중간의, 매개의

8 밑줄 어휘 ⑤

해설 맨 마지막 문장에서 감정의 경험이 더 나은 선택을 하게 한다고 하였으므로 감정은 우리의 사고를 약화시키기보다는 강화하거나 풍요롭게 할 것이다. 따라서 ⑤ weaken은 enrich 등으로 바꿔야 한다.

해석 Salovey와 Mayer는 감정과 지성을 주제로 한 세 건의 논문을 발표했다. 그들의 논지는 간단했다. 비록 정반대의 것으로 이해되는 일이 빈번하지만, 감정과 지성은 보통 협력하여 작용하며 서로를 ① 향상시킨다는 것이다. "가장 심오한 수준의 사고에 관여하는 우리의 능력은 미적분학 같은 지적인 일에 ② 제한된 것이 아니다."라고 Mayer는 주장한다. "그것은 또한 ③ 감정에 대해 추론하고 끌어내는 것을 포함한다. 그것은 친절하거나 낭만적인 어떤 사람들도 정말로 매우 ④ 정교한 정보 처리를 하고 있다는 것을 의미한다. 이런 유형의 추론은 삼단논법을 푸는 데에 사용되는 것만큼 틀림없이 형식을 갖춘 추론이다." 이러한 교류는 또한 반대로 가기도 한다. 감정은 때때로 사고를 ⑤ 약화시킨다(→ 풍성하게 한다). 이에 관해 심리학자들은 강한 감정의 경험이 우리가 더 나은 선택을 하게하고 역설적으로 우리의 감정을 조절할 수 있다는 것을 보여주는 연구를 거론한다.

구문 [3행~5행] Though (they are) frequently conceived as opposites, // emotions and intellect typically work in concert, / *each enhancing the other*. Though 다음에는 they(=emotions and intellect) are가 생략되어 있는데, 부사절을 이끄는 접속사 다음에 오는 「주어+be동사」는 주절의 주어와 같을 경우 생략 가능하다. each enhancing the other는 분사구문으로, each는 분사구문의 의미상 주어이다.

어휘 thesis 학위 논문; 논지 **conceive** 상상하다, 마음속에 그리다 **in concert** 협력하여; 소리를 맞추어 **engage in** ~에 참여하다 **pursuit** 추구; *pl.* 일, 활동; 취미 **contend** 주장하다; 싸우다 **reasoning** 추론 **abstract** 추상적인; 추상화; 추출하다, 끌어내다 **sophisticated** 세련된, 교양 있는; 정교한, 복잡한 **paradoxically** 역설적으로

9 빈칸 추론 ③

해설 빈칸 문장으로 보아 쇼핑객이 자신이 취약하다는 것을 알면서도 스스로 방어하는 것에 '어떠한' 반응을 보이는지를 찾아야 한다. 선물을 사는 쇼핑은 선물을 받는 사람과 선물을 주는 사람 모두의 기쁨을 위한 감정적인 행동으로, 공급, 수요, 가격의 법칙을 쓸모없이 만드는 비이성적인 행동이어서 영리한 소매상들이 이러한 쇼핑객의 심리를 이용하는 것을 알면서도 쇼핑객들은 가격보다 감정을 더 중요하게 여긴다는 내용이므로 빈칸에 들어가기에 가장 적절한 것은 ③ '꺼리는'이다.

① 갈망하는 ② 만족해하는 ④ 준비가 된 ⑤ 과민한

해석 선물을 주는 것은 쇼핑의 가장 설명할 수 없는 영역 중의 하나이다. 비이성적인 행동은 이러한 소비자 지출의 영역에서 거의 표준이고, 그것은 용인되고, 예상되며, 심지어 장려된다. 선물을 주는 것은 쇼핑보다 쇼핑하는 사람의 감정에 관한 것이다. 이것은 선물 쇼핑의 극단적인 본질과 전체 과정의 비논리적인 본질을 설명하는 것을 돕는다. 소비자의 관점에서, 선물을 위한 쇼핑은 사람이 휘말릴 수 있는 감정적인 과정이다. 그것은 갈망하는 쇼핑객이 다른 사람에게 즐거움을 선사하기 위해, 그리고 그렇게 함으로써 자신에게도 기쁨을 주려고 최선을 다하기 때문에 공급, 수요, 그리고 가격의 법칙이 쓸모없게 되는 영역이다. 선물을 위해 쇼핑하는 쇼핑객은 모든 쇼핑객 중에서 가장 쉽게 영향을 받는다. 영리한 소매업자는 무방비하고 감정적으로 취약한 선물 구매자를 이용할 준비가 되어 있다. 한편, 쇼핑객은 자신이 취약하다는 것을 알지만, 또한 스스로를 방어하길 꺼린다. 받는 사람을 즐겁게 하고 의도된 감정적 메시지를 전달하는 것이 종종 가격보다 더 중요하다.

구문 [8행~10행] From the consumer's point of view, // shopping for gifts is *an emotional process* **[that one gets caught up in]**.

[ ] 부분은 목적격 관계대명사 that이 이끄는 관계사절로 앞의 명사 an emotional process를 수식한다.

[10행~13행] It is *an area* **[where the laws of supply, demand, and price go out the window]** // **as** anxious shoppers do their utmost / to bring pleasure to another person, and thereby, to themselves.

[ ] 부분은 관계부사 where가 이끄는 절로 an area를 수식하고, 종속절을 이끄는 접속사 as는 이유를 나타낸다.

[18행~20행] Pleasing the recipient [and] conveying the intended

emotional message are often more important than the price.
밑줄 친 두 개의 동명사구가 주어를 구성하고 있고, 동사는 are이다.

어휘 irrational 비이성적인, 비논리적인 norm 표준, 일반적인 것 tolerate 용인하다, 참다 emotion 감정 *cf.* emotional 감정적인; 감정을 자극하는 extreme 극단적인, 지나친 nature 본질; 특성 illogical 비논리적인 point of view 관점, 입장; 견해 get caught up in A A에 휘말리다 go out the window 쓸모없게 되다 do one's utmost 최선을 다하다 pleasure 즐거움, 기쁨 *cf.* please 즐겁게[기쁘게]하다; 부디, 제발 thereby 그렇게 함으로써 retailer 소매업자 take advantage of ~을 이용하다 defenseless 무방비의 vulnerable 취약한, 연약한; ~하기[받기] 쉬운 meanwhile 한편; 그동안에 recipient 받는 사람, 수령인 convey 전달하다; 운반하다 intended 의도된; 계획된

10 빈칸 추론   ②

해설 렘수면 상태에서는 근육 활동이 극도로 억제되는데 그 이유는 꿈속에서 벌어지는 싸움이나 전력 질주와 같은 활동이 현실 세계에서 그대로 행동으로 표출된다면 그 사람의 안전에 위협이 되기 때문이다. 따라서 빈칸을 완성하면 뇌가 몸을 마비시키는 이유는 ② '정신이 안전하게 꿈꿀 수 있게' 하기 위해서이다.
① 몸이 쉴 수 있다
③ 렘수면이 여러분의 꿈에 영향을 미친다
④ 당신이 당신의 꿈을 기억할 수 있다
⑤ 꿈이 근육 활동을 증가시킨다

해석 왜 진화는 렘수면 중에 근육 활동을 금지하기로 결정했을까? 근육 활동을 제거함으로써 여러분이 꿈의 경험을 실연하지 못하게 되기 때문이다. 렘수면 중에는 뇌 여기저기서 소용돌이치는 운동 명령의 쉴 새 없는 집중 공세가 있고, 그것들은 꿈에서 일어나는 움직임이 풍부한 경험의 밑바탕이 된다. 그러면 대자연이 이러한 허구적 움직임이 현실이 되는 것을 금지하는 생리적 구속복을 제작한 것은 현명한 일인데, 특히 여러분이 주위 환경을 의식적으로 인식하기를 멈춘 것을 고려하면 그러하다. 여러분은 눈을 감고 여러분 주변 세계를 전혀 이해하지 못하는 동안에 그릇되게 꿈속의 싸움이나 다가오는 꿈속의 적으로부터 미친 듯한 전력 질주를 상연하는 것의 처참한 결과를 잘 상상할 수 있다. 오래지 않아서 여러분은 곧 유전자 풀을 떠나게 될 것이다. 뇌는 <u>정신이 안전하게 꿈을 꿀 수 있도록 몸을 마비시킨다.</u>

구문 [7행~11행] Wise, then, *of Mother Nature* **to have tailored** a *physiological straitjacket* [that forbids these fictional movements from becoming reality], especially considering that you've stopped consciously perceiving your surroundings.
of Mother Nature는 to have tailored의 의미상 주어이다. wise와 같이 성격을 나타내는 형용사가 나오면 의미상의 주어를 「of+목적격」으로 나타낸다. 'to have p.p.'는 주절의 동사(이 문장에서는 생략되어 있다)보다 더 이전의 상황을 기술할 때 쓰는 to부정사의 형태이다. [ ]은 a physiological straitjacket을 수식하는 관계사절이다.

어휘 act out 실연하다 motor 운동의, 운동 신경의 swirl 소용돌이치다 underlie 기저를 이루다 tailor 맞추다, 조정하다 physiological 생리(학)적인 enact 상연하다, 연기하다; (법을) 제정하다 frantic 미친 듯한 sprint 단거리 경기, 전력 질주 foe 적 comprehension 이해 paralyze 마비시키다

11 빈칸 추론   ⑤

해설 플레이어가 컴퓨터에 대항하여 게임을 할 때 컴퓨터는 인간 플레이어에 대한 모든 정보를 이미 알고 있다는 우위를 점하는데, 그 정도가 심하면 인간 플레이어는

게임에 대한 흥미를 잃고 포기할 것이므로 게임에서의 컴퓨터 부정행위는 ⑤ '플레이어가 그 게임이 흥미롭고 재미있다고 계속 생각하게 할' 정도의 난이도에 맞춰지도록 균형이 잡혀야 한다.
① 플레이어가 자신의 목표를 너무 높게 설정하지 않도록 돕다
② 게임의 규칙에 익숙해지다
③ 플레이어에게 진행에 대한 최적의 통제력을 주다
④ 플레이어가 다른 사람들과 경쟁하면서 협력하다

해석 아마도 게임에서 가장 널리 사용되는 AI 기법은 부정행위일 것이다. 예를 들어 전쟁 시뮬레이션 게임에서 컴퓨터 팀은 자기의 인간 적수에 대한 모든 정보, 즉 그들의 기지 위치, 부대의 종류, 수와 위치 등에 접근할 수 있으며, 인간 플레이어가 그런 정보를 수집하기 위해 정찰대를 파견해야 하는 방식으로 해야 할 필요는 없다. 이러한 방식의 부정행위는 일반적이며 컴퓨터에게 똑똑한 인간 플레이어들에 대항하는 우위를 부여하는 데 도움이 된다. 그러나 부정행위는 나쁠 수 있다. 컴퓨터가 부정행위를 하고 있다는 점이 인간 플레이어에게 확실해지면, 플레이어는 아마 자신의 노력이 소용없다고 생각하고 게임에 대한 흥미를 잃을 것이다. 또한 불균형한 부정행위는 컴퓨터 적수에게 너무 많은 힘을 부여할 수 있고, 이는 플레이어가 컴퓨터를 이기는 것을 불가능하게 만든다. 여기서 다시 플레이어는 자신의 노력이 소용없다는 점을 알면 흥미를 잃을 가능성이 있다. 부정행위는 플레이어가 그 게임이 흥미롭고 재미있다고 계속 생각하게 할 정도로만 해 볼 만한 도전을 만들도록 균형이 잡혀야 한다.

구문 [10행~13행] If **it** is obvious to the player **that the computer is cheating**, // the player likely will <u>assume</u> // (that) his efforts are useless / and lose interest in the game.
If절에서 it은 가주어이고 that ~ cheating이 진주어이다. 주절에서는 will 다음의 동사 assume과 lose가 병렬구조를 이룬다. assume 뒤에는 목적어절을 이끄는 접속사 that이 생략되었다.
[13행~15행] Also, unbalanced cheating can give computer opponents too much power, / making **it** impossible *for the player* **to beat the computer**.
making 이하는 분사구문이다. it은 가목적어이고 to beat the computer가 진목적어이며 for the player는 to-v의 의미상 주어이다. 「make + it + 형용사 + for A + to-v」는 'A가 v하는 것을 (형용사)하게 만들다'의 뜻이다.

어휘 opponent 적수, 상대 base (군사) 기지; 기초, 기반 unit 부대 intelligence 정보, 기밀; 지능 edge 우위 beat 이기다

12 빈칸 추론   ③

해설 우리의 눈은 무작위로 보는 것이 아니라 시야의 주변에 있는 어렴풋한 신호들이 눈을 어디로, 어떤 순서로 움직일지를 계획하는 데 도움을 준다고 설명한다. 그러므로 우리의 중심와가 흥미롭고 중요한 부분을 방문하기 위해서는 주변시가 ③ '우리의 눈의 움직임을 유도하기 위해 저해상의 신호를 제공한다'는 것이 적절하다.
① 우리가 직접 보고 있는 것을 해석할 수 있게 한다
② 우리가 물체의 크기와 형태에 정확하게 집중하도록 돕다
④ 물체의 공간적 특징에 관한 우리의 지식을 갱신해준다
⑤ 두뇌로 가는 정보 전달의 수단으로서 역할을 한다

해석 주변시는 중심와가 시야의 모든 흥미롭고 매우 중요한 부분들을 방문하도록 <u>우리의 눈의 움직임을 유도하기 위해 저해상의 신호를 제공한다.</u> 눈은 무작위로 환경을 자세히 살피는 것이 아니다. 눈은 중심와의 초점을 중요한 것들에, (보통은) 가장 중요한 것들에 우선 맞추기 위해 움직인다. 시야의 변두리에 있는 흐릿한 신호들은 두뇌가 눈을 어디로, 어떤 순서로 움직일지를 계획하는 데 도움이 되는 자료를 제공한다. 예를 들어 '소비 기한' 날짜를 찾아서 약의 라벨을 훑어볼 때, 날짜의 희미한 형태를 갖춘 주변부의 어렴풋하고 뚜렷하지 않은 부분이 우리로 하여금 그것을 검토할 수 있게 해주기 위해 중심와를 그곳에 안착시키는 눈의 움직임을 유발하기에 충분하다. 우리가 딸기를 찾아서 농산물 시

장을 둘러보고 있다면, 시야 가장자리에 있는 흐릿한 불그스름한 부분이, 비록 때로는 그것이 딸기 대신에 무로 판명될지 모르지만, 우리의 눈과 주목을 끈다. 우리가 동물이 근처에서 으르렁거리는 것을 듣는다면, 눈의 구석에 있는 어렴풋한 동물 같은 형태는, 특히 그 형태가 우리를 향해 이동하고 있다면, 눈을 그 방향으로 매우 빠르게 이동시키기에 충분할 것이다.

구문 [1행~3행] Peripheral vision provides low-resolution cues *to lead our eye movements* **so that** our fovea visits all the interesting and crucial parts of our visual field.
to lead ~ eye movements는 부사적 용법으로 쓰인 to부정사구로 목적을 나타낸다. so that은 목적을 나타내는 부사절 접속사로 '~하기 위해'라는 의미이다.
[9행~13행] For example, when we scan a medicine label for a "use by" date, a fuzzy blob in the periphery with the vague form of a date is *enough* (to cause *an eye movement* [**that** lands the fovea there]) to allow us to check it.
( ) 부분은 앞에 있는 형용사 enough를 수식한다. [ ] 부분은 관계대명사 that이 이끄는 관계사절로 an eye movement를 수식한다.

어휘 crucial 매우 중요한; 결정적인 visual field 시야, 시계 scan …을 자세히[꼼꼼히] 살피다 fuzzy 흐릿한, 명확하지 않은 cue 신호, 단서 on the outskirts of ~의 변두리에, 외곽에 use by date 소비 기한, 유효일 periphery 주변부; 표면 vague 희미한; 불명확한 browse 둘러보다, 훑어보다 produce 농산물 blurry 흐릿한 reddish 불그스름한 patch 부분, 조각 edge 가장자리 radish 무 growl 으르렁거리다; 투덜거리다 low-resolution 저해상도의 spatial 공간적인; 공간의 transmission 전달; 전송

13 흐름 무관 문장 ④

해설 신화 이야기가 인간의 보편적 사고에 대해 알려줄 수 있다는 글의 내용에 반해 ④는 신화를 통해 얻는 과학적 지식에 관한 내용이므로 글의 전체적인 흐름과 맞지 않는다.

해석 우리는 신화를 원시 사람들이 우리의 현대적이고 과학적인 의미로 이해하지 못했던 세상을 설명하기 위해 만들어 낸, 신, 전사와 악마의 모험에 대한 어리석은 옛날이야기로 여기는 경향이 있다. ① 하지만 이러한 이야기들을 더 이상 인류에게 중요한 의미가 없는 사소하고 구식인 것으로 묵살하는 것은 잘못이다. ② 학자들은 많은 다양한 문화의 신화들의 공통적인 주제가 모든 인간들의 보편적인 관심과 공유된 사고방식에 관해 우리에게 말해 준다는 것을 보여 주었다. ③ 우리가 하나의 통일된 세계, 즉 사람들에게 지구촌으로 일컬어지는 것으로 점점 나아감에 따라 우리 모두가 얼마나 많은 기본적인 인간 본성을 공유하고 있는지 아는 것은 중요하다. ④ 또한 자연 세계에 대한 더 큰 지식과 더 깊은 이해를 얻는 것은 유익하고, 우리가 신화를 통해 얻은 과학적인 지식은 우리의 삶에 영향을 주고, 우리의 관점에 영향을 준다. ⑤ 신화에 관한 체계적인 연구는 인간의 정신, 즉 보편적인 인간의 동기, 두려움, 그리고 생각의 패턴에 관한 중요한 점들을 드러낸다.

구문 [10행~13행] As we move increasingly toward a unified world — a global village, as *it* has been called — **it** is important **to see how much basic human nature we all share**.
삽입절 a global ~ called 부분에서 대명사 it은 앞에 나온 a unified world를 가리킨다. to see ~ share는 진주어로 가주어 it을 대신하고 있다.

어휘 warrior 전사, 무인 demon 악마 primitive 원시적인, 원시 사회의 dismiss (고려할 가치가 없다고) 묵살하다; 해산시키다 trivial 사소한, 하찮은 universal 보편적인 unified 통일된 inform 영향을 미치다 psyche 정신

14 글의 순서 ④

해설 연구자들이 인간과 침팬지의 세포 파괴 프로그래밍을 비교했다는 주어진 글 다음에는, Their comparison으로 시작하며 이러한 비교의 결과를 제시한 (C)가 나온다. (C)에 제시된 '뇌의 더 큰 생장과 세포 간의 더 높은 연결 비율'을 (A)의 주어인 'this improvement in intelligence'가 지칭하므로 (C) 다음에는 (A)가 나와야 한다. 인간은 높은 지능을 얻었지만 그 대가로 암세포를 잘 처리하지 못한다는 (A) 다음에는 '우리가 지적 능력에 대한 대가를 치르고 있는 것인지도 모르겠다'는 내용의 문장으로 시작되는 (B)가 자연스럽게 연결된다.

해석 미국의 연구자들은 우리의 강력한 두뇌에는 명백한 단점이 있다고 의심한다. 그들은 인간 세포의 자기 파괴 프로그래밍을 유인원, 구체적으로 침팬지에게서 작용하는 비슷한 프로그램과 비교했다. 이 프로그램은 오래되고 결함이 있는 세포를 파괴하고 해체시킨다.
(C) 그들의 비교는 그 청소 메커니즘이 사람에게서 보다 침팬지에게서 훨씬 더 효과적이라는 점을 보여줬고 연구자들은 인간에게서 세포가 분해되는 속도의 감소가 뇌의 더 큰 생장과 세포 간의 더 높은 연결 비율을 가능하게 해준다고 믿는다.
(A) 그러나 이러한 지능 향상은 아마도 많은 대가를 치르고 나오는 것일지도 모르는데, 왜냐하면 침팬지의 자정 메커니즘은 암세포도 제거해주기 때문이다. 침팬지가 거의 결코 암에 걸리지 않는 반면, 인간에게서 이 질병은 최고의 사망 원인 중 하나이다.
(B) 우리는 우리의 지적 능력에 대한 대가를 지불하고 있는 걸까? 우리의 현재의 지능 수준이 인류의 생존에 적합하지 않다면, 그것은 상승되거나 하락돼야 한다. 후자(= 하락)는 우리의 자아 존중감에 관한 관념과 양립할 수 없으므로 아마 받아들일 수 없을 것이다.

구문 [14행~16행] If our current level of intelligence is not suited to the survival of humankind, // it must **either** be increased **or** lowered.
「either A or B」는 'A나 B 둘 중 하나'의 뜻이다.
[19행~24행] Their comparison showed // that the clean-up mechanism is a lot more effective in chimpanzees / than **it** is in people, // and the researchers believe // that *the reduced rate* [at which cells are broken down in humans] allows for larger brain growth and a higher rate of connections between cells.
than 다음의 it은 바로 앞의 주어인 the clean-up mechanism을 지칭한다. [ ]는 '전치사 + 관계대명사'로 시작되는 관계사절로서 앞의 the reduced rate를 수식하며, the reduced rate에 대응되는 동사는 allows for이다. allows for 다음의 밑줄 친 두 개의 명사구가 and로 연결되어 병렬구조를 이룬다.

어휘 great ape 유인원 defective 결함이 있는 at a high price 상당한 대가를 치르고 suited 적합한 the latter 후자 *cf.* the former 전자 self-worth 자아 존중감, 자부심 break down 분해시키다 allow for ~을 가능하게 해주다; 참작[감안]하다

15 글의 순서 ③

해설 (B)의 숫자와 그래프 등의 수량화를 수단으로 이루어지는 This는 주어진 문장의 '사회 과학이 자연 과학을 모방하려 함'을 지칭한다. 수량화될 수 없는 것도 있다는 (B) 다음에는 그것의 예(편견, 사랑)를 제시한 (C)가 이어지며, (C)의 for instance는 (B)의 마지막 부분과 조응한다. 과학이 전적으로 수량화의 문제만은 아님을 논한 (C) 다음에는 수량화는 단지 탐구의 한 방법[수단]일 뿐이라는 (A)가 나오는 것이 적절하다.

해석 불행히도 자신의 연구 분야의 한계를 인정하기를 거부하는 일부 사회 과학자들이 있다. 그들은 사회 과학이 자연 과학을 모방하게 하려고 힘껏 밀어붙인다.
(B) 이것은 주제를 심도 있게 수량화했다는 인상을 주기 위해 일반적으로 모든 종류의 숫자와 표, 차트, 그리고 그래프를 사용하여 이루어진다. 자, 사실 어떤 것들은 수량화될 수 있고, 어떤 것들은 그럴 수 없다.
(C) 예를 들어 우리는 편견이나 사랑을 정말로 수량화할 수 없다. 모든 것을 고려해 보면,

그렇게 시도된 수량화는 헛되다. 심지어 자연 과학에서조차도 자주 망각되는 것은 과학이 주로 수량화의 문제는 아니라는 것이다.

(A) 수학적 기법의 사용은 그 자체로 목적이 아니라 목적, 즉 물질세계에 관한 진리의 발견에 대한 수단일 뿐이다. 숫자의 사용은 우리가 합리적으로 원인을 이해하려고 노력함에 있어 더 정확해지기 위한 한 가지 방법이다.

구문 [5행~7행] The use of mathematical techniques is not an end in itself but only a means to *an end*, **namely**, *the discovery of what's true about the material world*.

상관 접속사 「not A but B(A가 아니라 B)」가 밑줄 친 두 부분을 연결한다. namely (즉)는 an end와 the discovery ~ world가 동격 관계임을 나타낸다.

[17행~19행] What is often forgotten, even in the physical sciences, **is** that science is not primarily a matter of quantification.

관계사 What이 이끄는 명사절이 문장의 주어 역할을 하고, 동사는 is, 접속사 that이 이끄는 절이 보어이다.

어휘 in itself 그 자체로   means 수단   namely 즉   rationally 이성적으로   profound 심오한   quantification 수량화   *cf.* quantify 수량화하다   subject matter 주제   as a matter of fact 사실   prejudice 편견, 선입견   when all is said and done 모든 것을 고려할 때   in vain 헛된, 소용없는   primarily 주로

16 문장 넣기   ④

해설 주어진 문장은 일단 과학이 급격히 발전하면, 기술과의 연계가 강해진다는 내용인데 역접의 접속사인 however가 포함되어 있으므로 앞에는 과학과 기술의 연계를 거의 느끼지 못했다는 내용이 나올 것을 짐작할 수 있다. 따라서 과학의 도움 없이도 기술이 발전했다는 내용과, 과학의 발전으로 이룬 기술의 발전에 대한 내용 사이에 위치하는 것이 적절하다.

해석 현대의 관점에서 보면, 과학과 기술 사이의 중요하고도 필수적인 연관성에 대해 이해하는 것은 당연하다. 그러나 지난 500년 동안, 기술은 특정한 발견, 개념, 수학방정식을 기다릴 필요가 없었다. 실은 그것이 바로 1500년의 중국이 많은 측면에서 유럽이나 중동 국가들보다 더 선진적인 것처럼 보였던 이유이다. 설득력 있는 과학 이론이나 잘 통제된 실험이 없이도 완벽하게 작동하는 (심지어 정교하기까지 한) 시계, 화약, 나침반 혹은 의학적 치료를 탄생시킬 수 있다. 하지만 일단 과학이 급격히 발전하면, 그것(과학)과 기술의 연계는 훨씬 더 강해진다. 우리 시대의 과학이 없이도 핵발전소나 초음속 항공기, 컴퓨터, 레이저 또는 여러 가지의 효과적인 의학적, 외과적 중재를 얻을 수 있을 것이라고는 거의 상상할 수 없다. 과학이 없는 그런 사회는 기술 혁신이 박탈당한 채로 남아있거나 기술 혁신을 이룬 사회로부터 그것을 단지 모방할 것임이 틀림없다.

구문 [14행~18행] **It** is barely imaginable / **that** we could have nuclear power
　　　　　　　　　　가주어　　　　　　　　　진주어
plants, ~ medical and surgical interventions in the absence of the sciences of our epoch.

가주어 It이 진주어 that절 전체(문장 끝까지)를 대신한다.

[19행~21행] *Those societies* [**that** lack science] must **either** remain deprived
　　　　　　　　　　　　　　　　　　　　　　　　　　　　　　　A
of technological innovations **or** simply copy ***them*** from *societies* [**that** have
　　　　　　　　　　　　　　　　　　　　　　　　　　　B
developed ***them***].

「either A or B」는 'A와 B 둘 중의 하나'라는 뜻으로 A와 B는 문법적으로 성격이 대등해야 한다. 두 개의 them은 모두 technological innovations를 뜻한다.

어휘 take off (항공기 등이) 이륙하다; 급격히 인기를 얻다[유행하다]   equation ((수학)) 방정식, 등식   in many respects 많은 점에서   counterpart 상대, 대응 관계에 있는 사람[것]   functional 실용적인; 기능적인   exquisite 매우 아름다운; 정교한

convincing 설득력 있는; (승리 등이) 확실한   supersonic 초음속의   medley 메들리; 여러 가지 뒤섞인 것   intervention 조정, 중재; 간섭   in the absence of ~이 없을 때에, ~이 없어서   epoch 시대 (= era)   remain[be] deprived of 빼앗기다   innovation 혁신

17 문장 넣기   ⑤

해설 막스 베버의 권위를 세 종류로 나눠볼 수 있는데, 첫째는 관습에서 생기는 권위이고 둘째는 특정 개인의 카리스마에서 발생하는 권위, 셋째는 법적 권위이다. 주어진 문장은 '규칙을 인정하고 명령자를 권위 구조의 합법적인 대표자로' 보는데, 여기에 해당하는 권위는 법적 권위이다. 법적 권위에 대해 논하고 있는 부분은 But in modern society, 이하이므로 주어진 문장은 ⑤에 와야 한다. (④에 위치하면 뒤에 나오는 역접의 접속사 But 때문에 논리적이지 않은 흐름이 된다.)

해석 권위는 강력한 힘이다. 사회학자 막스 베버에 따르면 몇 가지 다른 종류의 권위가 있다. 때때로 우리는 전통이나 관습 때문에 명령에 복종한다. 이것은 보통 우리가 연장자들의 명령에 의도적으로 따를 때 작용하는 것이다. 다른 때에 우리는 누군가의 개인적인 카리스마 혹은 그들이 우리 삶을 바꾸어줄 힘을 가지고 있다는 믿음에 마음이 움직여서 그의 명령을 따를지도 모른다. 이것은 광신적 종교 집단의 지도자가 내리는 지시를 받고 싶어 하는 개인들에게 전형적이다. 그러나 현대 사회에서 대부분의 명령은 사람들이 상급자의 법적 권위를 믿기 때문에 지켜지는 것이다. 즉 그들은 조직이나 기관의 규칙을 받아들였고 명령을 내리는 사람을 합리적인 권위 구조의 적법한 대표자로 본다. 막스 베버에 따르면, 거대 관료제의 형태를 한 권위 구조는 현대 사회의 가장 중요한 결정적인 특징이다.

구문 [1행~4행] That is to say, / they have accepted the rules of the organization or institution / and **see** *the person* (giving orders) **as** a legitimate representative of a rational authority structure.

동사 have accepted와 see가 병렬구조를 이룬다. 「see A as B」는 'A를 B로 보다'의 뜻이다. ( )는 the person을 수식하는 형용사구이다.

[10행~12행] Other times / we might follow someone's commands // because we are moved **by their personal charisma** / or a belief that they have the power to transform our life.

by 다음의 목적어는 their personal charisma와 a belief이며 이 둘은 or로 연결되어 병렬구조를 이룬다. that they ~ life는 a belief에 대한 동격절이다.

어휘 institution 기관; 제도   legitimate 적법한, 합법적인   representative 대표(자)   willfully 의도적으로, 고의로   transform 변형시키다   be eager to-v v하고 싶어 하다   superior 상급자, 상관   defining 결정적인, 본질적인 의미를 규정하는

18 요약문 완성

해설 실험에서 진보주의자 집단과 보수주의자 집단 내부의 개인들은 논쟁적인 사회 현안에 대하여 개별적으로 다양한 의견을 가질 수 있지만, 토론을 통해 반대 측의 주장을 접하면 중립 의견자들은 반대쪽으로 생각이 바뀌고, 긍정 의견을 가진 사람들은 더 긍정하게 되는, 즉 더 극단으로(extreme) 치우친 생각을 갖게 되므로 개인들의 다양성은 사라진다(disappears).

해석 한 연구에서 Harvard 대학의 교수인 Cass Sunstein과 몇몇의 그의 동료들은 동일한 신념 체계를 공유하는 사람들의 두 집단을 보았다. Colorado의 Boulder 출신의 진보주의자들과 Colorado Springs 출신의 보수주의자들이었다. 그들 각각의 집단에서, 각각의 사람들은 세 가지 주제인 시민 동반자법, 차별 철폐 조치와 기후 변화에 대해 숙고해보도록 요청받았다. 그러나 토론이 시작되기 전에, 개별 참가자들은 각각의 주제에 대한 그들

의 사적인 의견을 기록했다. 그러고 나서 집단은 서로 섞였고 그들의 견해를 논하도록 독려 받았다. 집단 숙의는 일관성 있게 공손하고 열심이었으며 실질적이었으나, 그것이 끝났을 때 기후 변화 조약에 중립적이었던 Colorado Springs 출신의 보수주의자들은 이제 그것을 반대했다. 시민 동반자법에 대해 다소 긍정적이었던 Boulder의 진보주의자들은 그것의 장점을 확고하게 확신하게 되었다.

↓

연구에 따르면, 같은 생각을 가진 집단 내부의 다양성은 반대되는 의견을 가진 사람들에게 노출된 후에 (A) 사라지는데, 그것이 서로의 견해를 더욱 (B) 극단적으로 만들기 때문이다.

구문 [9행~11행] And then the groups were **mixed** up and **encouraged** to discuss their views.

were 다음의 과거분사 mixed와 encouraged가 and로 연결되어 병렬구조를 이룬다.

[13행~15행] ~ *conservatives* from Colorado Springs [who had been neutral on a climate-change treaty] now opposed it.

주어는 conservatives이고 동사는 opposed이며 [ ]은 conservatives를 수식한다. 보수주의자들이 기후 변화 협정에 대해 중립적이었던 것은 이에 반대하기(opposed) 이전의 일이므로 had been과 같은 대과거 시제를 사용하였다.

어휘 colleague 동료 liberal 진보주의자 conservative 보수주의자 respective 각각의 deliberate 숙고하다 civil partnership 시민 동반자법 affirmative action 차별 철폐 조처 consistently 일관성 있게 respectful 공손한 engaged 바쁜, 열심인 substantive 실질적인 neutral 중립의 treaty 조약 somewhat 다소 convince 확신시키다

19~20 장문　　　　　　　　　19 ① 20 ④

해설 19. James Pennebaker의 연구와 의사소통학자들이 시행한 연구에서 나타나 있듯이 단지 글을 쓰거나 긍정적인 감정을 글로 표현하는 것이 걱정과 스트레스를 덜어준다는 내용이므로 ① '글을 써서 근심을 없애라'가 제목으로 가장 적절하다.
② 어떻게 자신을 더 명확하게 표현할 수 있는가?
③ 문자 체계가 사람들을 진정시키기 위해 작용하는 방식
④ 글쓰기를 통해 당신의 사랑하는 사람과 연결하라
⑤ 글쓰기와 사고의 놀라운 관련성

20. 스트레스를 받을 때 나오는 호르몬의 수치는 스트레스를 받는 일을 겪게 되면 높아져야 하므로 (d)의 lowered는 elevated 등으로 바꿔 써야 한다.

해석 심리학자 James Pennebaker는 사람들이 신체적 학대나 사랑하는 사람의 죽음과 같이 자신이 겪은 트라우마에 대해 글을 쓸 때, 종종 스트레스 호르몬의 수치가 감소하고, 면역 체계가 강화되고, 병원 방문의 감소를 경험한다는 것을 보여주는 많은 연구를 수행했다. Pennebaker의 연구에 참여한 사람들은 각각 20분씩 불과 두세 번의 글쓰기 기간 후에 (a) 개선되는 것을 겪었다. 이와 비슷한 맥락에서 의사소통학자들은 사람들이 고통 속에 있을 때 사랑하는 사람에 대한 긍정적인 감정에 대해 글을 쓰는 것이 그들의 회복을 (b) 가속화시킬 수 있다는 것을 보여주었다.

예를 들어, 한 실험에서 참가자들은 시간이 제한된 상태에서 복잡한 수학 문제를 머릿속에서 풀고 결혼한 부부들이 싸우는 비디오 클립을 보는 것과 같은 일련의 (c) 스트레스를 받는 일을 겪게 되었다. 이러한 과제는 사람들이 스트레스를 받을 때 신체가 만들어 내는 코르티솔이라는 호르몬의 수치를 (d) 낮췄다(→ 높였다). 그러고 나서 참가자들은 세 가지 조건 중 하나에 배정되었다. 첫 번째 그룹의 참가자들은 사랑하는 사람에게 자신의 긍정적인 감정을 표현하는 편지를 쓰도록 지시받았다. 두 번째 그룹은 단지 사랑하는 사람에 대해 생각했을 뿐 그들의 감정을 단어로 표현하지는 않았다. 마지막으로, 세 번째 그룹은 20분 동안 아무것도 하지 않았다. 연구원들은 사람들이 그들의 애정 어린 감정에 대해 썼을 때, 그들의 코르티솔 수치가 가장 빨리 정상으로 돌아왔다는 것을 발견했다. 사랑하는 사람을 단지 생각하는 것만으로는 아무것도 하지 않는 것보다 더 큰 혜택을 주지는 않았다. 단지 그들의 감정을 (e) 글로 쓴 형태로 표출한 참가자들만이 그들의 높아진 스트레스로부터 빨리 회복했다.

구문 [9행~13행] In a similar vein, communication scholars *have shown* **that** when people are in distress, **writing about their positive feelings for a loved one** can accelerate their recovery.

문장의 동사 have shown의 목적어로 that이 이끄는 명사절이 쓰였다. that절 내에서 동명사구인 writing ~ loved one이 주어 역할을 한다.

[18행~20행] These tasks elevated their levels of *a hormone (called cortisol)*, **which** the body produces when people are under stress.

( ) 부분은 분사구로 a hormone을 수식한다. 계속적 용법의 관계대명사 which는 앞에 있는 명사 a hormone called cortisol을 보충 설명한다.

어휘 conduct 수행하다; 행동하다 trauma 트라우마, 정신적 충격 go through 겪다; 살펴보다 abuse 학대(하다); 남용하다 immune system 면역 체계 improvement 개선, 향상 session 기간; 수업 vein 맥락; 정맥 distress 고통, 괴로움 accelerate 가속화하다 recovery 회복; 되찾기 put through 달성하다, 실행하다 a series of 일련의 mentally 마음속으로; 정신적으로 complicated 복잡한; 뒤얽힌 constraint 제약; 억제 cortisol 코르티솔 ((부신 피질에서 생기는 호르몬의 일종)) assign 배정하다; 할당하다 condition 조건; 환경 instruct 지시하다 merely 단지, 오직 affectionate 애정 어린 let out ~을 나가게 하다, 내다 recover 회복하다 get rid of 없애다, 제거하다 via 통하여; 경유하여 soothe 진정시키다, 달래다 link 관련성; 유대

제21회　　　　　　　　　　　　　　　　본문 p.164

	1 ③	2 ④	3 ⑤	4 ⑤	5 ④		6 ④	7 ③	8 ④	9 ④	10 ②
	11 ②	12 ②	13 ④	14 ②	15 ②		16 ④	17 ③	18 ①	19 ②	20 ④

1 글의 목적　　　　　　　　　③

해설 네 번째 문장 'I'm sorry ~ to one of the other candidates.'에서 단적으로 드러나듯이, 교수직 지원자에게 다른 지원자가 선정되어서 교수직에 채용되지 못했

음을 말하고 있으므로 글의 목적으로 가장 적절한 것은 ③이다.

해석 Peeking 씨께
Punxatawney Coalition 대학의 교수직에 보여주신 귀하의 관심에 감사드립니다. 저희는 귀하와 같이 충분한 자격을 갖춘 지원자들로부터 많은 회신을 받았습니다. 훌륭한 자격을

갖춘 많은 지원자들이 계신 상황에서, 저희는 (지원자의) 배경과 자격이 이번 학기에 저희가 정확히 필요로 하는 것에 바로 부합하는 것을 저희에게 제공해주는 분을 찾고 있었습니다. 이 자리가 다른 지원자 중 한 분께 제공됨을 말씀드리게 되어 유감입니다. 하지만 이것이 저희가 귀하의 자격에 인상을 받지 못했다는 뜻은 아닙니다. 저희는 더 적합한 자리가 날 경우에 대비하여 귀하의 이력서를 저희의 유효 파일에 보관할 것입니다. 아마 향후 귀하의 자격에 더욱 적합할 다른 자리가 나올 것입니다. 귀하의 적합한 자리를 찾으시는 일이 잘되기를 기원합니다.
진심을 담아,
Letitia T. Hall 드림

구문 [6행~8행] ~ we looked for *someone* [whose background and qualifications gave us just the right fit for our exact needs this semester].
소유격 관계대명사 whose가 이끄는 [ ] 부분이 someone을 수식한다.

어휘 faculty 교수진 superbly 최고로, 아주 훌륭하게 qualified 자격을 갖춘; 적당한 *cf.* qualification 자격 credential 자격(증을 수여하다); 신임장 cordially 진심으로, 다정하게; 몹시

2 필자 주장 ④

해설 다른 사람의 말을 경청할 때 많이 배울 수 있다고 전제하면서, 전문가의 말을 듣지 않는 테니스 초보자의 일화가 이어진다. 마지막에 자신을 전문가로 생각하면서 동시에 성장하고 배우는 것은 거의 불가능하다고 말하고 있으므로 필자의 주장으로는 ④가 적절하다.

해석 여러분이 다른 사람들의 말을 진짜로 경청하기로 할 때 여러분의 친구와 가족, 직업, 여러분이 일하는 조직, 그리고 여러분 자신에 대해 얼마나 많이 배울 수 있는지는 놀랍다. 그러나 모든 사람이 이 이로움을 이해하는 것은 아니다. 예를 들어, 우리는 새로 온 학생에게 강습을 하고 있는 테니스 프로에 대한 이야기를 들었다. 그 초보자가 테니스공을 향해 몇 번 스윙하는 것을 지켜본 후, 프로는 그를 멈추게 하고 그의 타법을 개선할 수 있는 방법을 제안했다. 그러나 매번 그가 그렇게 할 때마다, 그 학생은 그의 말을 가로막았고, 문제와 그것이 어떻게 해결되어야 하는지에 대한 자신의 의견을 냈다. 몇 번의 중단 후, 프로는 동의하며 고개를 끄덕이기 시작했다. 강습이 끝났을 때 지켜보고 있었던 한 여자가 프로에게 "왜 그 오만한 남자의 어리석은 의견에 동의했습니까?"라고 말했다. 프로는 미소를 지으면서 "나는 누구든 단지 공감만을 사고 싶은 사람에게 진정한 답을 납득시키려 애쓰는 것은 시간 낭비라는 것을 오래전에 배웠습니다."라고 대답했다. 여러분이 모든 답을 알고 있다고 생각하는 입장을 취하는 것을 경계하라. 여러분이 그럴 때마다, 여러분은 자신을 위험에 빠뜨릴 것이다. 자신을 '전문가'로 생각하면서 동시에 성장하고 배우는 것을 계속하기란 거의 불가능하다.

구문 [1행~4행] It's amazing how much you can learn about your friends and family, your job, *the organization* [(which[that]) you work in], and yourself // when you decide to really listen to others.
It은 가주어, 의문사 how가 이끄는 명사절이 진주어이다. [ ]는 목적격 관계대명사 which 또는 that이 생략된 관계사절로 선행사 the organization을 수식한다.
[6행~9행] After **watching** *the novice* **take** several swings at the tennis ball, // the pro stopped him [and] suggested ways [he could improve his stroke].
「지각동사(watch) + 목적어(the novice) + 원형부정사(take)」의 형태로 '목적어가 v하는 것을 보다'로 해석된다. [ ]는 ways를 수식하는 관계부사절이다. 관계부사 how와 선행사 ways는 함께 쓰일 수 없으므로 관계부사절 내에 how가 쓰이지 않았다.

어휘 novice 초보[초심]자 swing 스윙, 휘두르기; 휘두르다 stroke (테니스 등의) 타법, 치기 interrupt 가로막다; 방해하다 *cf.* interruption 중단; 가로막음, 방해 nod

----

끄덕이다 go along with ~에 동조하다, 찬성하다 arrogant 오만한 sell 납득시키다, 팔다 echo 공감; 메아리 beware 경계[조심]하다

3 밑줄 함의 ⑤

해설 고슴도치 유형은 하나의 비전(one singular vision)을 견지하고 끝까지 추구하고 여우 유형은 모든 세부사항(details)을 살피고 가능한 모든 수단을 사용해 목표를 이루는데, 링컨은 이 두 유형의 최선을 구현한 지도자라고 했으므로 ⑤ '상황의 복잡성(≒ details)을 활용하면서 큰 그림(≒ one singular vision)을 목표로 삼았다'는 것을 의미한다.
① 환경적 어려움에 관계없이 융통성을 길렀다
② 미리 계획하고 작은 기회들을 이용했다
③ 다른 사람들의 제안을 수용하고 다수의 해결책을 발견했다
④ 전술과 효과적인 방어를 계획해서 진보를 촉진했다

해석 영국계 미국인 철학자 Isaiah Berlin의 에세이에서 암시를 받아서, 예일대 교수 John Gaddis는 위대한 사상가들과 지도자들이 어떻게 고슴도치 혹은 여우 둘 중 하나로 분류될 수 있는지를 논한다. 이러한 구분은 각 동물이 자신의 환경에 반응하는 방식에서 나올 수 있다. 여우는 사냥당할 때, 포식자를 피하는 많은 영리한 방법들을 찾아낸다. 고슴도치는 사냥당할 때, 삐죽삐죽한 공 모양으로 몸을 말고 가만히 누워있다. 이 말의 일반적인 요지는 다음과 같다. 전자 유형의 사람들은 자신이 하는 모든 일에서 세부사항을 보고 그들의 목적을 달성하기 위해 생각해낼 수 있는 모든 수단을 사용하며, 반면에 후자 유형의 사람들은 단 하나의 비전을 가지는 데 능하고 다른 사람들이 도중에 실패할 때에도 그것을 추구한다. 그들은 역사를 관통해 널리 알려질 일을 달성한다. Gaddis에 따르면 단테는 고슴도치였지만 셰익스피어는 여우였다. 그는 또한 에이브러햄 링컨의 리더십은 두 동물의 최선을 구현했다고 지적한다.

구문 [1행~4행] **Taking** a cue from an essay by British-American philosopher Isaiah Berlin, / Yale professor John Gaddis discusses // how great thinkers and leaders can be categorized as **either** hedgehogs **or** foxes.
Taking ~ Isaiah Berlin은 원인을 나타내는 분사구문이다. how 이하는 discusses의 목적어로 쓰인 간접의문문이며 「의문사 + 주어 + 동사」의 어순을 따른다. 「either A or B」는 'A나 B 둘 중 하나'의 뜻이다.
[9행~13행] The former types of people see the details in *everything* [(that) they do] / [and] use every means conceivable to achieve their ends, // while the latter types are great at having one singular vision / [and] pursue it // when other people fall by the wayside.
주절에서 동사 see와 use가 병렬구조를 이룬다. [ ]는 앞에 목적격 관계대명사 that이 생략되어 everything을 수식하는 관계사절이다. while이 이끄는 부사절에서 동사 are와 pursue가 병렬구조를 이룬다.

어휘 cue 암시; 단서; 신호 categorize 분류하다, ~을 범주에 넣다 hedgehog 고슴도치 divide 구분; 분할 stem from ~로부터 나오다 evade 피하다 curl up 동그랗게 말다 spiky 삐죽삐죽한 still 가만히 있는, 정지한 gist 요지 the former 전자(↔ the latter 후자) means 수단 conceivable 생각할 수 있는 resound 널리 알려지다, 떨치다; 울려 퍼지다 embody 구현하다; 포함하다 scheme 계획(하다); 책략(을 꾸미다)

4 글의 제목 ⑤

해설 고정된 사고방식을 가진 사람들은 역경을 극복하는 데 성공하지 못하고 도전하지 않으므로 배우고 성장할 기회를 갖지 못하는 반면, 성장식 사고방식을 가진 사람들은 변화를 믿고 역경을 더욱 잘 극복한다는 내용의 글이므로 제목으로 가장 적

절한 것은 ⑤ '고정식 vs. 성장식 사고방식: 당신의 인생을 형성하는 믿음'이다.
① 사고방식: 성공의 새로운 심리학
② 우리의 사고방식을 전환시키기 위해 우리는 무엇을 해야 하는가?
③ 당신의 실수를 귀중한 삶의 교훈으로 바꿔라
④ 역경 극복하기: 삶의 도전을 정복하기

해석 생활사가 우리가 역경에 접근하는 경향을 보이는 방식에 영향을 주지만, 우리의 사고를 바꾸는 것 또한 우리의 반응을 바꿀 것이다. 그렇게 하기 위하여 우리가 '고정된' 사고방식을 갖는 경향이 있는지 아니면 '성장' 사고방식을 갖는 경향이 있는지를 이해해야 한다. 고정된 사고방식을 가진 사람들은 역경을 극복하는 일에 성공하는 일이 더 적으며, 위험을 감수하고 싶지 않다고 믿기 때문에 상처와 복수에 계속 머물러있게 될 가능성이 더 크다. 그들은 실패로 낙담하고 포기할 가능성이 있다. 그들은 잘 하지 못하는 일에 도전받기를 좋아하지 않으므로, 자신의 실수로부터 배우고 성장하지 않는다. 그들의 좌우명은 '늙은 개에게 새로운 재주를 가르칠 순 없어'이다. 반면에 성장식 사고방식을 가진 개인들은 불확실성에 편안한 마음을 가지므로 역경을 극복하는 데에 더 많이 성공하고, 노력과 집중과 반복되는 시도로 바라는 변화를 가져올 수 있을 것을 알고 있다. 그들의 좌우명은 '개가 숨을 쉬는 한 재주를 배울 수 있어'이다.

구문 [3행~5행] To do so, / we have to understand / *whether* we tend to have **either** a 'fixed' **or** a 'growth' mindset.
whether 이하는 to understand에 대한 목적어이다. whether는 '~인지 아닌지'의 뜻이고 「either A or B」는 'A나 B 둘 중 하나'의 뜻이다.
[9행~11행] They don't like to be challenged at *things* [(that) they **are** not **good at**], // so they don't learn and grow from their mistakes.
[ ]는 앞에 목적격 관계대명사 that이 생략되어 things를 수식한다. 'be good at'은 '~을 잘 하다, 능숙하다'의 뜻이다.

어휘 biology 생활사; 생명 작용; 생물학 tend 경향을 보이다; 경향이 있다 adversity 역경 mindset 사고방식 revenge 복수 bring about ~을 가져오다, ~을 초래하다

5 도표 이해 ④

해설 2000년 대비 2030년의 가금류 수요 증가가 나머지 육류보다 큰 것은 맞지만, 2천 2백만 톤에서 8천 2백만 톤으로 4배를 넘지는 않는다. 그러므로 ④는 도표의 내용과 일치하지 않는다.

해석 2000년 대비 2030년의 세계 고기 수요
위 그래프는 2000년과 2030년 세계의 고기 수요를 보여준다. 다섯 종류의 고기의 전반적인 수요는 2000년에서 2030년까지 상승할 것으로 예상된다. ① 비록 쇠고기만이 2030년에 3위 자리에 남아 있겠지만, 2000년에는 계란과 함께 가장 수요가 많은 육류로 공동 3위에 올랐다. ② 전반적으로 가장 적은 증가는 양고기였는데, 이는 2000년과 2030년 사이에 7백만 톤 정도의 수요에서 상승을 보였다. ③ 다음 30년 후에 약 3천 5백만 톤이 증가할 것으로 예상되어, 돼지고기의 수요는 전체적으로 두 번째로 큰 증가이다. ④ 2000년과 비교할 때 2030년에 어떤 다른 육류보다 더욱 성장할 것으로 예측되는 것은 바로 가금류 수요로, 4배를 넘는 증가가 예상된다. ⑤ 계란 수요는 2000년에는 쇠고기의 수요와 동일했으나, 계란 수요는 2030년 쇠고기 수요보다 1백만 톤 정도 더 적어질 것으로 예상된다.

구문 [10행~13행] It is *the demand for poultry* **that** is forecasted to grow more than any other meat in 2030 / when compared to 2000, / **with** *more than a four times increase* **expected**.
「it is[was] ~ that ...」 강조 구문이 쓰여 the demand for poultry를 강조한다. 밑줄 친 부분은 각각 접속사를 포함한 분사구문과 「with + O + p.p.」 형태의 분사구문을 나타낸다.

어휘 overall 전반적인 tie 동점을 이루다. 비기다; 묶다 retain 유지하다 mutton 양고기 poultry 가금류의 고기; 가금((닭·오리·거위 따위)) forecast 예측[예보]하다

6 내용 불일치 ④

해설 Paulo Freire의 교육 프로그램은 1964년의 군사 쿠데타로 인해 중단되었다.

해석 Paulo Freire는 브라질의 교육학자이자 철학자이며, 문맹인들에게 읽는 법을 가르치기 위해 일상 언어와 아이디어를 사용하는 기법으로 유명하다. 그는 1921년에 Recife에서 태어났다. 비록 Freire가 1943년부터 Recife 대학에서 철학뿐만 아니라 법학도 공부했지만, 그는 실제로 법을 업으로 삼은 적은 없고 대신에 교사로 일했다. 1962년에 Recife의 시장은 Freire를 시의 성인 문자 해득 프로그램의 책임자로 임명했다. 자신의 첫 번째 실험에서 Freire는 300명의 문맹 성인들에게 읽고 쓰는 법을 단 45일 만에 가르쳤다. 결과적으로 정부는 브라질 전역에서 수천 개의 비슷한 프로그램을 승인했다. 불행히도 1964년의 군사 쿠데타로 인해 작업이 중단된 후에, 그는 70일 동안 브라질에 투옥되었고 15년을 망명 상태로 지냈다. Freire는 1979년경에 브라질로 돌아올 수 있었고, 1988년에 Freire는 상파울루 시의 교육부 장관으로 임명되었다. 1997년 5월 2일 Paulo Freire는 75세의 나이에 심부전으로 사망했다.

구문 [1행~3행] Paulo Freire was a Brazilian educator and philosopher, / known for his methods of using everyday words and ideas to **teach** *the illiterate* **to read**.
known for 이하는 분사구문이다. 밑줄 친 부분은 부사적 용법으로 쓰인 to부정사구로 '목적'을 나타내며 「teach + O + to-v」는 'O가 v하도록 가르치다'를 의미한다.
[12행~15행] Unfortunately, after the military coup of 1964 halted the work, // he was imprisoned in Brazil for 70 days and spent 15 years in exile.
밑줄 친 동사 was와 spent가 and로 연결되어 병렬구조를 이룬다.

어휘 illiterate 문맹의; 문맹자 practice (법률 등을) 업으로 하다; 연습하다; 실행[실천]하다 mayor 시장 appoint 임명[지명]하다 literacy 글을 읽고 쓸 줄 아는 능력 approve 승인[허가]하다; 시인하다 military coup 군사 쿠데타 halt 중단시키다; 멈추다 imprison 투옥[감금]하다 exile 망명(자); 추방 minister 장관; 성직자 heart failure 심부전

7 밑줄 어법 ③

해설 what I suspect most people who take the offer ③ done에서 I suspect는 삽입구이다. what 다음의 주어는 most people이고 who take the offer는 most people을 수식하며, 그다음에는 주어 most people에 상응하는 동사 do가 나와야 한다.
① 「with O v-ing」는 'O가 v한 채로'의 뜻이다. 신발이 흠집이 나 보이는(look) 상황인데 look은 자동사이므로 현재분사 형태로 쓴다.
② 2문형 자동사 feel 다음에 보어 자리에 형용사 indebted를 적절히 사용했다.
④ 「find O v-ing」는 'O가 v하고 있는 것을 알게 되다'의 뜻이며, mindlessly는 부사로서 분사 looking을 수식한다.
⑤ 'manage to-v'는 '용케 v해내다'의 뜻이다.

해석 내 오래된 사무실 건물 근처에서 한 구두 가게의 창문에 무료로 구두를 닦아 주겠다는 후한 제안을 하는 광고가 붙었다. 나는 수십 번 이 가게 옆을 지나갔고 이에 대해 아무 생각도 없었다. 그러나 어느 날 내 구두가 약간 흠집이 난 것처럼 보였고 시간도 좀 있어서 나는 이 작은 선물을 이용하기로 결심했다. 내 구두 닦기가 끝난 후에 나는 구두 닦는 사람에게 팁을 드렸다. 그는 거절했다. 공짜면 공짜죠, 그는 말했다. 나는 참으로 신세를 졌다고 느끼면서 의자에서 내려왔다. '어떻게 이 사람은 내 구두를 닦아주고는 '아무것

도' 기대하지 않을 수 있지?'라고 나는 생각했다. 그래서 나는 그 제안을 받아들이는 대부분의 사람들이 할 듯 싶은 것을 했다. 살 만한 무언가가 있는지 주위를 둘러보는 것 말이다. 나는 어떻게든 갚아주어야 했다. 구두는 필요하지 않아서, 나는 어쩌다 보니 무심결에 구두 골, 구두끈, 그리고 광택제를 바라보고 있었다. 마침내 나는 빈손인 채 불편한 마음으로 가게 밖으로 조용히 걸어 나왔다. 비록 나는 가게에서 겨우 빠져나왔지만, 많은 다른 사람들은 그렇게 운이 좋지 않았을(가게에서 빠져나오지 못했을) 것이라고 확신했다.

구문 [10행~12행] So I *did* what *(I suspect) most people* [who take the offer] do — I looked around for *something* (to buy).

동사 did의 목적어 역할을 하는 what절 내에 I suspect가 삽입되었고, [ ]은 what절의 주어 most people을 수식한다. to buy는 something을 수식하는 to부정사구이다.

어휘 avail oneself of ~을 이용하다 distinctly 참으로, 뚜렷하게 indebted 신세를 진; 부채가 있는 even the score 응징하다. 동점이 되다 somehow 어떻게든. 왠지 mindlessly 아무 생각 없이 shoe tree 구두 골 lace 구두끈 polish 광택제

8 밑줄 어휘 ④

해설 TV 시청이 간헐적인 재미를 주기 때문에 더 많이 봐야 한다는 생각을 들게 하고, 이는 약간이 좋다면 더 많은 건 더 좋다는 가정하에 나올 수 있는 생각이므로 ④ worse는 better로 바뀌어야 적절하다.

해석 설탕의 효과는 역설적이다. 즉, 설탕은 당신이 의도했던 것과 반대의 영향을 미친다. 당신은 덜 배고프고 덜 불쾌해지고 싶었겠지만, 후에 ① 더 배고프고 더 불쾌하게 느낀다. TV도 비슷한 영향을 미치는데, 배고픔이 아닌 행복에 영향을 주고 있다. 당신은 즐겁고, 긴장을 풀고, 참여하고 싶어서, 즉 행복을 느끼고 싶어서 TV를 본다. 불행히도, 비록 TV가 ② 긴장은 풀어줄 수 있지만, 그것은 오직 간헐적으로만 재미를 주고 당신을 참여시키는 일은 거의 없다. 그래서 당신은 결국 ③ 따분해지는데, 이것은 당신에게 TV를 더 많이 봐야겠다는 생각이 들게 하고… 당신은 그 결과를 추측할 수 있다. 모든 사람이 때때로 약간의 설탕이 필요한 것과 같이, TV를 보거나 그냥 아무 일도 하지 않는 약간의 시간이 필요하다. 약간이 좋다면 더 많은 게 ④ 더 나쁠(→ 더 좋을) 것임이 틀림없다고 가정할 때 문제가 발생한다. ⑤ 연장된 기간 동안 TV 앞에 앉아있는 것과 설탕이 든 간식을 먹는 것이 오래 지속되는 행복으로 이어지지 않을 것임을 장담할 수 있다.

구문 [9행~11행] So, you end up bored, // which makes you think / (that) you should watch more TV... and you can guess the consequences.

which는 앞 문장 전체를 가리킨다. 사역동사 make는 「make O 동사원형(…가 ~하게 하다)」의 구문으로 쓴다. you think와 you should watch 사이에는 접속사 that이 생략되어 있다.

어휘 nasty 불쾌한; 역겨운 intermittently 간헐적으로 end up 결국 ~하게 되다 now and then 때때로 prolong 연장하다 sugary 설탕이 든, 매우 단; 아첨하는 lead to ~로 이어지다

9 빈칸 추론 ④

해설 맛을 추구하는 것은 좋은 삶의 구성 요건이지만 수많은 매체들이 쾌락을 부정적으로 기술해 와서 쾌락에 대한 우리의 태도는 ④ '양면적'이라 할 수 있다. 이러한 양면적 태도는 특히 마지막 문장에 잘 드러나 있다.
① 중립적인 ② 일관성 있는 ③ 관습적인 ⑤ 암시된

해석 맛을 추구하는 것은 좋은 삶으로 가는 하나의 길인데, 이는 미국인들이 최근에 발견한, 음식과 그것의 소비의 의미에 대해 새로운 설명을 요구하는 사실이다. 우리의 삶에

서 음식과 그 음식이 차지하는 위치에 대한 어떤 논의든 쾌락의 역할과 함께 시작해야 한다. 하지만 쾌락에 대한 우리의 태도는 양면적이다. "쾌락이 아니라 사람을 사랑하라"고 'New York Times'는 떠들어 댄다. "인생에는 행복 말고도 더 많은 것이 있다"고 'Atlantic Monthly'는 선언하고, "오직 절제하며 쾌락을 추구하라"고 역사를 통틀어 수많은 현자들은 말한다. 시대를 초월한 말에 따르면 "그것(쾌락)은 일시적일 뿐이다." 무형의 것들은 우리가 "쾌락은 영성에 해롭다"고 믿게 하곤 했다. 도처에 널린 자기계발서들은 우리에게 "쾌락이 행복으로 이어지지는 않을 것이다"라고 말해 준다. 우리는 많은 시간과 자원을 쾌락을 추구하는 데 소비하지만 그런 다음 보통 죽음이나 세금을 위해 아껴 둔 열정으로 그것을 비난한다.

구문 [12행~13행] "it is inimical to spirituality," the bodiless would **have** us believe;

사역동사 have가 'have O 동사원형(O가 ~하게 하다)'의 형태로 사용되었다. "it is inimical to spirituality,"는 believe의 목적어이다.

[14행~17행] We **spend** much time and many resources **pursuing** pleasure but then **condemn** it with *a fervor* (usually reserved for death and taxes).

동사 spend와 condemn이 병렬구조를 이룬다. 'spend 시간[자원] v-ing'는 'v하는 데 시간[자원]을 쓰다'의 뜻이다. ( )은 a fervor를 수동의 의미로 수식하는 분사구이다.

어휘 pursuit 추구; 추격 *cf.* pursue 추구[추격]하다 account 설명(하다). 이야기 proclaim 선언하다 moderation 절제, 중용 sage 현자 transitory 일시적인, 덧없는 timeless 영원한. 시대를 초월한 spirituality 영성. 정신성 ubiquitous 어디에나 있는 condemn 비난하다 reserve 따로 남겨두다. 유보하다 neutral 중립적인 coherent 일관성 있는 conventional 관습적인 ambivalent 양면적인 implicit 암시적인; 내재하는

10 빈칸 추론 ②

해설 인간은 기본적으로 이기적이어서 이기적인 결정을 내릴 수밖에 없지만, 자신이 어떠한 사회적 지위를 차지하게 될지 모르는 상태라고 가정하여 결정을 내리면, 특정 집단에게 극도로 불리한 결정을 내리지 않고 적어도 사회 구성원 모두가 납득할 만한 결정을 내릴 수 있다는 내용이다. 즉 ② '무지의 장막' 뒤에서 결정을 내리면 그 장막이 걷혔을 때 자신이 어느 집단에 속하게 될지를 알 수 없으므로 공정한 결정을 내릴 수 있다.
① 자료 분석 ③ 편향을 제한하기 위한 질문
④ 열린 결말의 토론 ⑤ 세세한 질적 조사

해석 정치 철학자인 고 John Rawls는 모든 인간이 이기적인 입장, 즉 생존 본능과 현대 진화론의 표현에 의하면 유전적 친족에 대한 편향으로부터 자라나는 편견을 기본값으로 가질 거라고 주장했다. 그러한 편향을 피하고 공명정대를 성취하기 위하여, 우리는 일련의 원칙을 생각해야 한다. 자신이 누가 될지 혹은 어떤 사회적 지위를 차지하게 될지 아는 사람이 아무도 없다면, 유리한 지위에 있는 누군가가 특권이 덜 있는 당사자로 하여금 다른 경우면 용납 불가능할 결과를 인정하도록 강요하기 위하여 그 지위를 이용할 기회가 없다고 그는 주장했다. 예를 들어 당신이 보건 정책을 결정하고 있다면, 자신이 부자가 될지 가난하게 될지, 남성이 될지 여성이 될지, 흑인이 될지 백인이 될지, 건강하게 될지 아프게 될지, 젊은 사람이 될지 나이 든 사람이 될지를 알지 못한다고 상상하게 된다. 당신은 자신이 처하고 싶지 않을 시나리오를 만드는 것을 피할 것이다. <u>무지의 장막의 조건에서 선택된 원칙들은 모두에게 공정하게 용납될 만할 것임이 보장되고, 따라서 부당하지 않을 것임이 보장된다고 Rawls가 주장하게 한 것은 바로 이러한 사실이다.</u>

구문 [6행~11행] If nobody *knows* who they will be or what social position they will occupy, he argued, there is *no opportunity* **for anyone in an advantaged position** (to take advantage of that position in order to force a less privileged party to concede to an otherwise unacceptable outcome).

동사 knows의 목적어로 두 개의 밑줄 친 의문사절이 병렬 구조를 이룬다. 형용사적 용법으로 쓰인 to부정사구 ( )가 no opportunity를 수식한다. for anyone in an advantaged position은 to부정사구의 의미상 주어이다.

[16행~20행] It is *this fact* **that** allows Rawls to claim that *principles* (**chosen** under the veil of ignorance) are guaranteed to be impartially acceptable to all — and thus, guaranteed not to be unjust.

「it is ~ that …」 강조구문이 쓰여 this fact를 강조한다. ( ) 부분은 과거분사 chosen이 이끄는 분사구로 principles를 수식한다.

어휘 bias 편견(을 갖게 하다), 편향 instinct 본능: 직관 evolutionary 진화(론)적인, 발달[발전]의 phrasing 표현, 말 genetic 유전적인; 유전(학)의 kin 친족, 친척 impartiality 공명정대: 공정, 공평 take advantage of ~을 이용하다 privileged 특권이 있는 concede 인정하다; 허락하다 impartially 공정하게, 편견 없이: 공명정대하게 unjust 부당한, 불공평한 veil 장막: 면사포 open-ended 열린 결말의; 제약[제한]을 두지 않은 qualitative 질적인

11 빈칸 추론

해설 오늘날의 많은 제품들이 서비스 없이는 쓸모없거나, 제품 판매보다는 서비스로 부가가치를 창출하는 경우가 많아진 것에서 알 수 있듯이 제조와 서비스는 떼려야 뗄 수 없는 관계가 되었다고 말하고 있다. 따라서 빈칸을 완성하면 제조는 '제조와 서비스의 범주가 점점 더 흐려지고 있는 복잡한 과정을 겪고 있다.'가 된다.
① 제조사는 기술뿐만 아니라 디자인도 고려해야 하는
③ 모든 제조 과정을 로봇이 넘겨받아서, 실업을 증가시키는
④ 신생 기업이 시장에 침투할 가능성이 가까스로 0보다 큰
⑤ 극심한 경쟁이 시장 환경을 가혹하게 만들어 파이가 줄어드는 결과가 나오는

해석 제조는 제조와 서비스의 범주가 점점 더 흐려지고 있는 복잡한 과정을 겪고 있다. 제조는 제품 주문 제작과 제품에 대한 '서비스' 경험이 생산과 소비 간에 존재하는 공생의 필수적 부분인 서비스와 좀 더 비슷해졌다. 어떤 제조사는 단지 그들의 제품의 디자인과 마케팅에만 직접적으로 책임이 있다. 실제 생산은 별개의 제조사에 하청으로 맡겨진다. 많은 제품들은 채워진 서비스가 없다면 쓸모없다. 컴퓨터는 그것들에 채워진 콘텐츠뿐만 아니라 소프트웨어가 없으면 일반적으로 제한된 사용 가치만을 가지며 심지어 사용 가치를 전혀 갖지 못한다. 또 다른 좋은 예는 엘리베이터의 디자인과 제조이다. 합법적으로 모든 엘리베이터는 연간 서비스 계약에 포함되어야 하기 때문에, 그것의 생산에서의 부가가치 중 많은 것이 제조에서 오는 것이 아니라 오히려 서비스 계약에서 온다.

구문 [11행~13행] Computers more generally have **limited** or **even no** use value without their embedded software as well as content.

limited와 even no는 공통적으로 use value를 수식한다. 'A as well as B'는 'B뿐만 아니라 A도'의 뜻이다.

[15행~17행] ~ much of the added value in their production does **not** come from manufacturing **but** rather from service contracts ~.

'not A but B' 구문은 'A가 아니라 B'의 뜻이다. A와 B에 해당하는 위치에 공통적으로 from으로 시작되는 전치사구가 위치하여 병렬구조를 이루고 있다.

어휘 undergo 겪다 whereby (그것에 의하여) ~하는 customization 주문에 따라 만듦 subcontract 하도급을 주다 embed 끼워 넣다, 채워놓다 added value 부가 가치

12 빈칸 추론

해설 새로운 정보를 받아들이는 데는 많은 인지적 노력이 들기 때문에 우리는 이

러한 노력을 회피하고자 한다. 그 방법은 ② '우리가 보거나 듣고 있는 것은 그저 변함없는 예전의 것일 뿐이다'라고 생각하는 것이다. 빈칸이 있는 문장의 다음 문장에서 '이때 문제는 이미 알고 있는 이야기 중 어떤 이야기를 내가 지금 다시 듣고 있는 것인가를 확인하는 것이다'라고 진술되어 있으므로, 빈칸에는 '내가 지금 새로 듣고 있는 이야기를 내가 이미 알고 있는 이야기로 치부해버린다'는 내용이 오는 것이 적절하다.
① 우리는 (누군가가) 우리에게 하고 있는 말의 작은 일부만 이해한다
③ 우리는 정보를 조금씩 처리하고 패턴을 인식한다
④ 우리가 이해하기 원하는 것은 우리가 알고 싶은 것과 관계있다
⑤ 청자와 화자는 같은 입장에서 서로를 이해한다

해석 듣는 사람에게 있어서, 이해란 말하는 사람의 이야기를 듣는 사람의 이야기에 연관시키는 것을 의미한다. 이야기가 기억 속에서 이용되는 방식의 가장 흥미로운 양상 중 하나는 이야기가 이해에 미치는 다양한 영향이다. 각양각색의 사람들이 같은 이야기를 다르게 이해하는데, 정확한 이유는 그들이 이미 알고 있는 이야기가 서로 다르기 때문이다. 새로운 이야기를 들을 때 듣는 사람은 이 이야기를 자신들이 전에 들었던 이야기로서 이해하려고 시도한다. 그들이 그렇게 하는 이유는 사실상 새로운 정보를 받아들이는 것이 꽤 어렵기 때문이다. 새로운 생각은 우리의 기억을 통해 가지를 내며 우리가 믿음을 수정하고, 새롭게 일반화하고, 다른 수고스러운 인지 작용을 수행하게 한다. 우리는 이 모든 일을 피하는 것을 더 좋아한다. 이렇게 하는 한 가지 방법은 단지 우리가 보거나 듣고 있는 것을 동일한 예전 것이라고 추정해버리는 것이다. 그러면 이해에 있어서 진정한 문제는 이미 알고 있는 모든 이야기 가운데 어느 것이 또 다시 여러분이 듣고 있는 이야기인지 확인하는 것이다.

구문 [2행~5행] **One** of the most interesting aspects of *the way* [stories are used in memory] / **is** *the varied effect* [(which[that]) they have on understanding].

주어는 One이며 동사는 is이다. 첫 번째 [ ]는 앞의 the way를 수식하는 관계부사절이다. 두 번째 [ ]는 앞에 목적격 관계대명사 which[that]가 생략된 관계대명사절로 앞의 the varied effect를 수식한다.

[11행~13행] New ideas ramify through our memories, / **causing** *us* **to revise** beliefs, **make** new generalizations, [and] **perform** other effortful cognitive operations.

causing 이하는 분사구문이며 「cause O to-v (O가 v하도록 유발하다)」의 구조가 쓰였다. to부정사에서 to 다음의 동사원형 revise, make, perform이 병렬구조를 이루고 있다.

어휘 map A onto B A를 B와 연관[연결]시키다 aspect 측면 precisely 바로, 정확히 absorb 받아들이다. 흡수하다 revise 수정[개정]하다 make a generalization 일반화하다 effortful 수고스러운 cognitive 인지의, 인식의 assume 추정하다; (책임을) 맡다; ~인 척하다 identify 확인하다. 식별하다

13 흐름 무관 문장

해설 초기 문학에서 널리 사용된 구술 작문에 관해 언급한 글로, 문학가들은 글을 사용해 작품 활동을 시작했을 때조차도 구술 기법을 지속적으로 사용해 그것이 초기 문학 작품의 형성 및 활용에 중요한 역할을 해 왔다는 내용이다. 따라서 구술 문학이 글쓰기의 개입 없이 구성되었다는 ④의 내용은 글의 흐름과 무관하다. ⑤의 서사시는 ③에서 언급된 구술 기법의 잔존물이나 창의적 변형의 예이다.

해석 인간 사회생활의 폭넓은 범위에서, 글쓰기는 꽤 최근의 발명품이다. 즉, 사람들은 누군가가 그들의 말을 기록하는 수단을 고안하기 전까지 수천 년간 노래를 부르고 이야기를 전했음이 틀림없다. ① 우리는 오늘날 문학을 작가가 '쓰는' 어떤 것으로 여기는 데 익숙하지만, 가장 초기에 쓰인 작품들은 주로 구두로 구성되어 전해진 노래나 이야기의 형태였다. ② 구술 작품은 종종 순수 문학 작품과 다르게 작용한다. ③ 심지어 시인들이 손

에 철필 또는 펜을 들고 시를 쓰기 시작한 이후에도, 그들은 종종 오랜 구술 기법을 새로운 용도에 맞추었고, 그들 작품의 중요한 요소는 구술 기법의 잔존물이나 창의적 변형으로서 가장 잘 이해될 수 있다. ④ 그러므로 구술 문학은 글쓰기의 개입 없이 사람들이 듣고, 경청하고, 노래 부르고, 말하는 노래, 이야기, 그 밖의 속담들로 이루어져 있다. ⑤ 서사시는 특히 구술 기법의 정교한 사용을 보여 주는데, 그중 많은 것들은 시인이 진행되는 이야기의 시구를 빠르게 쓰는 것을 돕기 위해, 그리고 글을 모르는 공연자가 긴 이야기를 기억하는 것을 돕기 위해 개발되었다.

구문 [5행~8행] We **are used** today **to thinking of** literature as *something* [(that) an author *writes*], but the earliest written works were usually versions of *songs or stories* [that had been orally composed and transmitted].

'be used to v-ing'는 '~하는 데 익숙하다'라는 의미이다. 첫 번째 [ ] 부분은 생략된 목적격 관계대명사 that이 이끄는 절로 something을 수식한다. 두 번째 [ ] 부분은 주격 관계대명사가 이끄는 관계사절로 songs or stories를 수식한다.

[18행~21행] Epic poems show particularly elaborate uses of *oral devices*, **many of which** were developed to aid poets in rapidly composing lines of an ongoing story, and to help illiterate performers remember a long narrative.

「대명사+of+목적격 관계대명사」 형태의 many of which가 이끄는 절이 oral devices를 부연 설명한다. 밑줄 친 두 개의 to부정사구는 모두 '목적'을 나타내며 and로 병렬 연결된다.

어휘 sweep 범위 devise 고안하다 means 수단, 방법 literature 문학 orally 구두로 compose 구성하다; 쓰다; 작곡하다 transmit 전(도)하다; 보내다 composition 작품; 구성 (요소들) in hand 수중에[쓸 수] 있는; 현재 다루고 있는 adapt 맞추다; 적응시키다 transformation 변형 intervention 개입; 중재; 간섭 epic poem 서사시 elaborate 정교한 ongoing (계속) 진행 중인 illiterate 글을 모르는, 문맹의 narrative 이야기, 대사

14 글의 순서 ②

해설 인간이 식량을 얻는 방법을 3단계로 설명한 글이다. 첫째, 인간은 '채집'을 통해 자연에서 직접 식량을 얻었다. (B)에서 '채집'에 대해 설명하고 있으므로 주어진 글 다음에는 (B)가 온다. 둘째, 식품의 대량 생산과 저장이 필요해짐에 따라 '생산' 방법이 출현했는데 그 내용이 (B)의 후반부와 (A)의 전반부에 걸쳐 기술된다. (A)의 This는 (B)의 '식품의 대량 생산과 저장이 필요해진 상황'을 지칭한다. 셋째, 자연물과 완전히 동떨어진 식품을 생산하는 '반채집'이라 불리는 '정제' 방법이 나타났다. 그 내용이 (A)의 후반부와 (C)에 기술되어 있으며, (C)에 제시된 밀가루, 백미, 정제 기름과 당, 증류주는 '정제' 방식의 예들이다. (C)의 It은 (A)의 '반채집'을 지칭한다.

해석 수백만 년 동안 인간과 인간의 가장 가까운 조상은 자연으로부터 즉시 먹을 수 있는 형태로 식품을 (그리고 약재를) 얻었다. 대단히 다양한 생물학적 활성 물질이 인간의 몸으로 들어오는 것을 막을 수 있는 것은 아무것도 없었다. 음식을 요리하는 것은 개인적인 집안의 일이었다.
(B) '채집'은 인간이 물질적 혜택을 받은 첫 번째 방법이었다. 도시의 성장에 수반된 농촌 인구의 급격한 감소와 소위 공공 음식 공급업의 발전은 엄청난 양의 식품의 생산과 저장을 필요로 했다.
(A) 이것은 물질적 혜택을 얻는 두 번째 방법인 '생산'의 출현과 동시에 일어났다. 그러나 완전히 새로운 소비 물품을 창조한다는 의미에서, 생산과 나란히 (증류, 정련 등) 정제 과정이 진행된다. 우리는 이 과정을 '반(反)채집'이라고 불러왔다.
(C) 이것은 곱게 빻은 밀가루 제품, 겉껍질이 제거된 백미와 다른 곡물, 정제된 기름, 그리고 정제된 설탕을 만들어 냈다. 야채와 야생 식물을 선택하는 일은 줄어들었다. 보드카와 같은 순수한 증류주가 천연 포도주를 대체했다.

구문 [3행~5행] There was *nothing* (to **prevent** the whole diversity of biologically active substances **from** entering his body).

'prevent O from v-ing'는 'O가 v하지 못하게 막다'의 뜻이다. ( )은 nothing을 수식한다.

[9행~12행] But side by side with production, in the sense of the creation of completely new objects for consumption, **goes** the process of purification (distillation, refinement, etc.).

동사는 goes이고 밑줄 부분이 주어인 도치구문이다.

어휘 medicinal substances 약재, 약물 active substances 활성 물질, 작용물질 domestic 가정의 affair 일 coincide with ~와 동시에 일어나다[일치하다] emergence 출현 derive 도출하다 purification 정제, 정화 distillation 증류(물) refinement 정련, 정제 *cf.* refine 정제하다 rural 시골의 so-called 소위 catering 음식 공급(업) necessitate ~을 필요하게 만들다 finely 곱게, 잘게 polished rice 백미, 도정미 shrink(-shrank[shrunk]-shrunk[shrunken]) 줄어 들다

15 글의 순서 ②

해설 가스 유출이 있으면 인간은 에틸메르캅탄의 냄새를 알아채고 경고를 받을 수 있다는 주어진 문장 다음에는 독수리 또한 이 냄새를 감지하여 모여든다는 (B)가 나온다. 인간과 독수리가 에틸메르캅탄에 반응하는 이유로 이것이 시체에서 나오는 기체이기 때문이라는 (B) 다음에는 인간이 시체에서 나오는 기체에 반응하는 이유를 보충 설명한 (A)가 제시된다. 인간이 그 물질의 냄새에 극도로 민감하다는 (A) 다음에는 그로 인해 가스 회사들이 천연가스에 에틸메르캅탄을 아주 미량으로만 주입해도 효과를 거둘 수 있다는 내용의 (C)가 마지막으로 오는 것이 적절하다.

해석 가스 회사들은 다른 경우라면 냄새가 없는 송기관 속 천연가스에 에틸메르캅탄이라 불리는 소량의 냄새가 나는 화학물질을 첨가한다. 밸브나 파이프 이음매가 제구실을 못하면, 그 냄새 나는 화학물질이 천연가스와 함께 밖으로 유출되어 인간의 코에 폭발 위험을 경고한다.
(B) 그러나 독수리들도 유출의 냄새를 맡고 금이 간 파이프 주위에 모일 것인데, 이는 송기관의 흠을 찾는 데 뜻밖에 도움이 된다. 독수리와 인간의 이러한 모임은 죽음의 냄새에 의해 생겨난다. 에틸메르캅탄은 자연적으로 시체에 의해 방출되기 때문이다.
(A) 인간이 부패하는 고기에 뿌리 깊은 혐오를 가지고 있기 때문에, 우리의 코는 그러한 화학물질에 극도로 민감하다. 우리는 그 자체로 냄새가 강한 암모니아에 대한 한계점보다 200배 더 낮은 농도에서 그것의 냄새를 가려낼 수 있다.
(C) 가스 회사들은 따라서 그들의 파이프에 오직 미량의 냄새 나는 화학물질만을 첨가하면 된다. 독수리에게는 불행하게도, 그들 또한 이러한 저농도의 냄새를 맡고 혼란을 느끼며 유출이 일어난 장소에 모일 수 있다.

구문 [3행~6행] If a valve or pipe seam fails, the smelly chemical leaks out with the natural gas, **alerting** human noses to an explosion hazard.

alerting 이하는 결과를 나타내는 분사구문이다.

[9행~11행] We can pick out its smell at *concentrations* (two hundred times lower than our limit for *ammonia*), **which is itself strongly odorous**.

( ) 부분은 형용사구로 concentration을 수식하고, 계속적 용법으로 쓰인 관계대명사 which가 이끄는 절은 ammonia를 부연 설명한다.

어휘 odorous 냄새가 나는 odorless 냄새가 없는, 무취의 transmission 전달, 전송; 전염 seam 이음매, 접합선; 경계선 leak out 유출[누설]되다 alert (위험 등을) 경고하다, 알리다; 기민한 explosion 폭발(적인 증가); 폭파 hazard 위험 (요소) aversion 혐오감, 아주 싫어함 rot 부패[부식]하다, 썩다 pick out 가려내다; 분간하다; 선택하다 concentration 농도; 집중 congregate 모이다 cracked 금이 간, 갈라진 unwitting 자신도 모르는 give off (냄새 등을) 풍기다[내다] corpse 시체, 송장 minuscule 극소의

16 문장 넣기 ④

해설 주어진 문장의 'In contrast'에 유의한다. 제로섬 게임이 비례관계가 있지만 연속체의 어느 지점이든 검은색이나 흰색이 완전한 정체성을 유지하고 있다는 것이 주어진 문장의 내용이므로 색들이 연속체의 어느 지점에서든 각각이 어느 정도의 양을 갖고 있다는 주어진 문장과 대조되는 내용 다음에 와야 적절하다. 그러므로 정답은 ④이다.

해석 정반대의 것들이 뒤섞일 때, 그것들은 연속체의 가장 끝부분에 놓이고 양극단 사이에는 두 개의 정반대의 것들을 섞는 단계적인 변화가 있다. 예를 들어, 검은색과 흰색은 회색의 색조를 통해서 서로 뒤섞인다. 여러 색조의 회색을 통하면서 흰색의 양이 줄어들면서 검은색의 양은 증가한다. 두 개의 정반대인 색들은 항상 비례 관계에 있지만 연속체의 어느 지점에서든 (아주 양극단을 제외하고는) 각각이 어느 정도의 양을 갖고 있다. 그에 반해서 승자가 모든 것을 취하는 제로섬 게임은 역시 비례 관계를 확립하지만, 연속체의 어느 지점에서든 단지 하나의 것 또는 다른 하나의 것, 즉 검은색 아니면 흰색이 있으며, 각각은 자신의 완전한 정체성을 유지한다. 혼색에서는 순수한 검은색과 순백색이 회색으로 화합될 때 희석된다. 그 색들은 둘 다 자기 정체성을 잃는데 회색은 검은색도 아니고 흰색도 아니다.

구문 [1행~5행] In contrast, *a zero-sum game* [where the winner takes all] also establishes a proportional relationship, but at any point along the continuum there is only one or the other, black or white, and each retains its full identity.
[ ]은 관계절로 주어 a zero-sum game을 수식한다. 밑줄 친 두 부분은 동격 관계로 one or the other의 대상은 black or white를 가리킨다.

어휘 zero-sum game 제로섬 게임 ((게임 이론에서 참가자 각각의 이득과 손실의 합이 제로가 되는 게임)) proportional 비례의 retain 유지하다 identity 정체성 opposite 정반대(의 것) extreme 극단 gradation 단계적 변화 blend 혼합하다, 섞다; 혼합, 혼색 shade 색조; 그늘 combine into ~로 결합하다, 화합하다

17 문장 넣기 ③

해설 ③ 앞부분에 농업으로 식량 저장이 가능해졌다고 제시됐고, '따라서 인구 규모는 더 이상 식량 자원 부족으로 통제되지 않게 됐다'는 주어진 문장과 인과관계가 성립하므로 주어진 문장은 ③에 위치해야 한다.

해석 기술적 혁신은 무수한 방식으로 사람들의 삶에 영향을 끼쳤다. 간단한 도구를 포함하는 원시 사냥 기술의 출현은 최초의 위대한 기술적 진보였다. 이것 다음에 식물 경작의 결과를 가져온 농업 발달이 이어졌고, 이는 바야흐로 식량이 저장되고 다시 채워질 수 있었으므로 광범위한 사회적 결과를 가져왔다. 따라서 인구 규모는 더 이상 식량 자원의 부족에 의해 부분적으로 통제되지 않게 되었다. 수렵 채집 사회는 물리적 이동을 필요로 했기 때문에 식량을 찾으러 갈 때 데리고 다녀야 하는 아이들이 많은 것은 비효율적이었다. 그러나 농업 혁명의 결과로 농경인들은 정착 사회에서 생활하면서 늘어난 아이들이 허드렛일을 돕는 데 유익하다는 것을 알게 되었다. 게다가 농경 사회의 일부 구성원들은 이제 식량 채집이 아닌 일에 자유롭게 종사할 수 있게 되어, 결과적으로 직업의 전문화를 감안한 분업이 이루어진 더 정교한 사회 구조를 가져왔다.

구문 [7행~9행] This **was followed by** *agricultural developments* [that **led to** plant cultivation], // which had far-reaching social consequences, ~
「A is followed by B」는 'A 다음에 B가 나온다'의 뜻이다. [ ]는 agricultural developments를 수식하며 led to 다음에는 '결과'가 제시된다.
[11행~13행] ~ it was inefficient / to have large numbers of *children* (to take along in the search for food).
it은 가주어이고 to have 이하가 진주어이며, ( )는 children을 수식한다.

어휘 partially 부분적으로 technological 기술의; 기술상의 innovation 혁신 myriad 무수한 emergence 출현 primitive 원시적인 agricultural 농경의, 농업의 *cf.* agriculturist 농경인 cultivation 경작, 재배 far-reaching 광범위한 consequence 결과 mobility 이동 chore 허드렛일 engage in ~에 종사하다 pursuit 일, 활동 elaborate 정교한 division of labor 분업 allow for ~을 감안하다, 참작하다 occupational 직업적인 specialization 전문화

18 요약문 완성 ①

해설 요약문과 선택지를 먼저 읽고 지문을 읽으며 요점을 파악한다. 요약문을 보면, 사교적인 '무엇'이 당신을 일찍 죽게 만들 수 있고, 그 '무엇'이 심장박동 변동을 '어떻게' 함으로써 심장 질환에 더 걸리기 쉽게 만드는지를 찾아야 한다. 여성들의 '교우 관계'와 '심장박동 변동' 간의 상관관계에 대한 연구에서 사교적일수록 심장박동 변동이 크고 반대로 사교적이지 않고 고립된 삶을 살수록 심장박동 변동이 적어서 특히 심장 질환으로 인한 조기 사망의 결과가 생겨날 수 있다는 내용의 글이므로 빈칸 (A)에는 isolation(고립), 빈칸 (B)에는 lessening(줄임)이 가장 적절하다.

해석 스톡홀름의 Karolinska 연구소의 Myriam Horsten 박사와 그녀의 동료들은 24시간 동안 300명의 건강한 여성의 심장박동 수를 측정했다. 그 여성들은 또한 교우 관계와 그들이 분노하거나 우울한 정도에 대한 설문조사를 받았다. Horsten과 그녀의 팀은 '심장박동 변동', 즉 평범한 하루를 보내는 동안 한 사람의 심장박동 수가 얼마나 쉽게 변화하는가를 측정하는 것에 관심이 있었다. 장수하고 행복한 삶을 살 운명인 건강한 사람은 24시간 동안 광범위한 심장박동 변동을 겪을 것이다. 크게 다양하지 않은(광범위한 변화를 겪지 않은) 심장박동 수는 조기 사망, 특히나 심장 질환으로 인한 사망과 관련이 있어 왔다. 연구의 결과는 혼자 살고, 친구가 거의 없고 이사를 하는 것과 같은 스트레스와 관련된 활동들을 도와줄 사람이 아무도 없는 여성들이 변동이 거의 없는 심장박동 수를 가질 가능성이 훨씬 높다는 것을 보여주었다. 아주 분명히, 활동적이고 사교적인 삶을 사는 것은 광범위한 심장박동의 변동 속에 있는 심장을 필연적으로 수반할 것이다.

↓

> 연구에 따르면 사교적인 (A) 고립은 당신을 일찍 죽게 만들 수 있는데, 그것이 심장박동 변동을 (B) 줄임으로써 심장 질환에 더 걸리기 쉽게 만들기 때문이다.

구문 [4행~6행] The women were also surveyed about their network of friends and *the extent* [to which they felt angry and depressed].
'전치사+관계대명사' 형태인 to which가 이끄는 절은 앞에 있는 the extent를 수식한다.
[9행~11행] *A healthy person* [destined for a long and happy life] will have a wide range of heart-rate variation in a 24-hour period.
과거분사구 [ ] 부분이 앞에 있는 A healthy person을 수식한다.
[13행~17행] The findings of the study showed **that** *women* [who lived alone, with few friends and *no-one* [who could help them with stress-related activities like moving homes]], **were** significantly more likely to have a heart rate with little variation.
[who lived ~ moving homes]가 that절의 주어인 women을 수식하고, women의 동사는 were이다. [who could ~ moving homes]는 앞의 no-one을 수식하는 관계사절이다.

어휘 institute 연구소; 기관, 협회 measure 측정(하다); 척도; 평가[판단]하다; 조치 heart rate 심장박동 수 survey 설문조사하다 extent 정도, 규모 variability 변동성, 가변성; 변하기 쉬움 *cf.* variation 변동, 변화, 차이 *cf.* vary 다양하게 하다, 다르게 하다 readily 쉽사리; 선뜻 destined ~할 운명인 a wide range of 광범위한 link 관련되다; 관련(성) sociable 사교적인, 붙임성 있는 necessarily 필연적으로, 반드시 involve 수반하다; 연루[관련]시키다 swing 변동; 흔들리다 susceptible 걸리기[영향 받기] 쉬운, 취약한; 민감한 [선택지 어휘] isolation 고립, 격리; 분리 lessen 줄이다, 줄다 competition 경쟁; 대회, 시합 pressure 압력(을 가하다), 압박(감)

19~20 장문

19 ② 20 ④

본문 p.172

해설 19. 숙련된 요리사들은 요리를 위해 필요한 모든 것을 제자리에 놓고 모든 준비를 마치고 나서야 요리에 돌입한다. 업무상의 마찰을 줄이고 최소한의 노력으로 빠르고 편안하게 요리 그 자체에만 집중할 수 있기 때문이다. 이를 반영하면 제목으로 가장 적절한 것은 ② '요리사들이 알아야 하는 것: 모든 것을 제자리에'가 된다.
① 정리된 정신에 정리된 공간
③ 초보 요리사들을 위한 충고: 연습이 완벽을 만든다
④ 양질의 재료가 온갖 차이를 만들어낸다
⑤ 요리사들은 요리에 대해 어떻게 배울 수 있는가

20. 요리사들은 쓸데없는 동작을 최소화하기 위해 모든 재료와 도구를 손닿는 범위 내에 두고 빠르고 편안하게 일하기를 원한다. 그러므로 최대한의 단계가 아니라 최소한의 단계만 밟기를 원할 것이다. 따라서 (d)의 most를 least로 고쳐 써야 한다.

해석 초보 요리사들은 모든 것이 문자 그대로 제자리에 있을 때 요리를 시작하지 않는다. 그들은 둘러보며 말한다. 좋아, 밀가루와 설탕이로군, 조리법에 나오는 처음 재료들이지, 아마. 그래서 그들은 가서 그것들을 가져온다. 그러고 나서 그들은 섞기 시작한다. 그러고 나서 그들은 '아, 설탕은 반만 가져다가 섞여야 했던 거구나.'에 관심을 기울이기 시작한다. 그때쯤이면 그들은 다시 시작해야 한다. 재료와 시간은 (a) 낭비된다. 반면에 프로 요리사들은 조리법을 완성하는 일이 용이하도록 주방을 조리를 위해 준비해놓는다. 프로 요리사로서 Jörin은 말한다. "일단 무언가를 만들기 위해 모든 재료와 모든 장비를 갖췄다는 것을 알면, 그 후에 전 마음속으로 그 일을 어떤 (b) 순서로 해야 하는지 파악합니다. 저는 모든 것을 논리적으로 계획해놓습니다. 일을 시작할 때는 그것에 대해 생각할 필요가 없도록 모든 것이 제 앞에 배열돼 있죠."
요리 학교 학생들은 수업 첫 날에 부엌에서의 마찰을 (c) 줄이는 이러한 기법을 배운다. 한 기관의 장이 설명했다. "저희는 정신적 반복을 수행합니다. 모든 재료들은 매우 가까운 손닿는 위치 내에 있습니다. 많은 관련 없는 동작을 원치 않으시죠. (d) 최대한의(→ 최소한의) 단계 혹은 노력으로 빠르게, 편안하게 일할 수 있기를 바라실 겁니다. 요리는 자연스럽고 편안하며 거의 생각이 없어지는 움직임의 흐름을 원합니다." 전문 요리사들은 그들의 조리에 영향을 미칠 수 있는 어떠한 장애물이라도 치워버린다. 그들은 고객들을 계속 행복하게 해주기 위해 반복적으로 빠르게 동일한 품질의 요리를 내놓는다. 이렇게 하기 위해 요리사들은 올바른 반응에 (e) 자동적으로 신호를 주는 안정적인 상황을 만듦으로써 자신의 주방에서 외부의 힘을 이용한다.

구문 [8행~10행] On the other hand, professional chefs prepare the kitchen for cooking // **so that it**'s easy **to complete the recipe**.
so that은 '~하도록, ~하기 위하여'의 뜻이다. so that 절에서 it은 가주어이고 to complete the recipe가 진주어이다.
[14행] I **have** everything logically **planned**.
「have + O + p.p.」는 'O가 ~되게 하다'의 의미로 여기서 have는 사역동사이다.

어휘 in place 제자리에 ingredient (요리) 재료 get down to ~에 관심을 기울이기 시작하다; ~을 시작하다 culinary 요리의 friction 마찰 extraneous 관련 없는 exertion 노력; (영향력의) 행사 turn out 만들어 내다; 나타나다 harness 이용[활용]하다 cue 신호를 주다

제22회

본문 p.172

| 1 ① | 2 ② | 3 ④ | 4 ③ | 5 ⑤ | 6 ④ | 7 ④ | 8 ⑤ | 9 ⑤ | 10 ④ |
| 11 ⑤ | 12 ② | 13 ④ | 14 ④ | 15 ⑤ | 16 ③ | 17 ⑤ | 18 ④ | 19 ① | 20 ⑤ |

---

1 심경 변화

①

해설 'I'는 딸의 결혼식 전날에 들뜬 마음으로 양복을 찾으러 가던 중 라디오에서 청혼하는 젊은이에 대한 노래를 듣고 자신이 딸에게 있어서 더 이상 가장 중요한 사람이 아닐 것임을 깨닫고 슬퍼한다. 따라서 'I'의 심경 변화로 가장 적절한 것은 ① '들뜬 → 슬픈'이다.
② 무서워하는 → 안도하는 ③ 기쁜 → 부끄러운
④ 기대하는 → 질투하는 ⑤ 만족스러운 → 화가 난

해석 내 딸 Annabel의 결혼식 전날이었다. 나는 내 정장을 다려준 양복점으로 운전해 가고 있었다. 결혼식이 어떨지를 상상하면서 세상의 정점에 올라선 기분이었다. 라디오를 켰을 때, 아름다운 노래가 흘러나왔다. 가수의 목소리에 특히 진심 어린 뭔가가 있었다. 그것은 연인에게 청혼하는 한 젊은이에 관한 노래였다. 여자의 아버지는 그를 거실에서 기다리게 하는데, 그곳에서 그는 아버지와 딸이 함께 찍은 어린 시절의 사진들을 알아본다. 젊은이는 자신이 그 아버지로부터 소중한 것을 가져가고 있다는 것을 갑자기 깨닫는다. 그 노래는 내 안의 어떤 것을 사로잡았다. 내가 내 어린 딸 Annabel의 삶에서 언제나 가장 중요한 사람이 되지는 않으리라는 것을 알게 된 고통 말이다. 그 노래가 끝나기도 전에 나는 너무 심하게 울어서 도로를 빠져나가야만 했다.

구문 [2행~3행] I was driving down to a tailor shop [where I **had had** my suit pressed].
[ ]는 '장소'의 관계부사절로서 a tailor shop을 수식한다. 관계부사절에는 「have + O + C」 구문이 쓰여 'O가 C하게 하다'를 나타낸다. '정장'이 '다려지는' 것이므로 목적어와 보어는 수동 관계이다. 따라서 보어 자리에 과거분사 pressed가 왔다. 정장이 다려지도록 맡긴 것은 양복점에 그것을 찾으러 가기 전의 일이므로 과거완료(had p.p.)를 사용했다.
[15행~17행] Before the song was over, // I was crying **so hard that** I had to pull off the road.
「so ~ that ...」 구문은 '너무 ~해서 …하다'의 뜻이다.

어휘 tailor shop 양복점 heartfelt 진심 어린 ask for one's hand in marriage 청혼하다 sweetheart 연인 capture (마음을) 사로잡다; 붙잡다 pull off (정차하기 위해 도로를) 빠져나가다

---

2 밑줄 함의

②

해설 동일한 방법론과 제시 방식으로 쓰인 가짜 보고서를 평가하는 연구에서 피험자는 자신의 신념을 지지하는 보고서를 반대 신념을 지지하는 보고서보다 더 좋게 평가를 했다는 내용의 글이다. 그러므로 밑줄 친 부분의 내용 '팔은 안으로 굽는다'는 말의 함축 의미는 ② '우리는 우리의 오래된 믿음에 고집스럽게 집착하는 경향이 있다'는 뜻에 가장 가깝다.
① 우리는 더 나은 이론이 결국 승리한다고 믿는다
③ 우리는 과학적 사실과 과학적 지지를 혼동한다

---

④ 우리는 종종 공정한 심판이자 사실의 발견자가 된다
⑤ 우리는 혁명적인 아이디어가 나타날 때 믿음을 바꾼다

해석 한 연구에서 시카고 대학의 상급 대학원생들은 자신이 이미 어떤 의견을 가지고 있는 문제들을 다루는 연구 보고서를 평가하라고 요청받았다. 피험자들은 몰랐지만 연구 보고서는 전부 가짜였다. 각각의 문제에 대해서 피험자 절반은 한쪽 의견을 지지하는 데이터가 제시된 보고서를 보았고, 나머지 절반은 데이터가 반대 측 의견을 지지하는 보고서를 보았다. 하지만 양쪽의 차이는 숫자뿐이었고 연구 방법론과 제시 방식은 같았다. 질문을 받았을 때, 대부분의 피험자들은 연구에 대한 자신들의 평가가 그 데이터가 자신의 이전 의견을 지지하는지 아닌지에 의존했다는 것을 부인했다. 그러나 그들의 생각은 틀렸다. 그 연구자들의 분석은 피험자들이 자신의 신념과 반대되는 다른 면에서는 동일한 연구보다는 자신의 신념을 지지하는 연구가 방법론적으로 더 타당하고 더 명료하게 제시된다고 실제로 평가했다는 것을 보여주었다. 그 효과는 기존의 신념이 강한 학생일수록 더 강하게 나타났다. 우리의 인식에 관하여 말하자면, 속담이 말하는 것처럼 셔츠보다는 피부가 더 가깝다(팔은 안으로 굽는다.).

구문 [1행~4행] In one study, advanced graduate students at the University of Chicago were asked to rate *research reports* (dealing with *issues* [**on which** they already had an opinion]).
( ) 부분은 research reports를 수식하는 분사구이다. [ ] 부분은 '전치사+관계대명사' 형태의 on which가 이끄는 관계사절로 issues를 수식한다.
[13행~19행] The researcher's analysis showed that they had indeed judged *the studies* [that supported their beliefs] to be **more** methodologically sound and clearly presented **than** *the otherwise identical studies* [that opposed their beliefs] — and the effect was stronger for *those* (with strong prior beliefs).
첫 번째 [ ] 부분은 관계사절로 the studies를 수식한다. 「비교급 ~ than ...」 형태의 비교급 구문이 사용되어 밑줄 친 두 부분을 비교한다. 두 번째 [ ] 부분 역시 관계사절로 the otherwise identical studies를 수식하고, 전명구인 ( )은 바로 앞의 those를 수식한다.

어휘 advanced 상급의; 진보적인 graduate student 대학원생 rate 평가하다; 비율; 요금 camp (경쟁 세력들 중 한) 측[진영); 캠프 methodology 방법론 deny 부인[부정]하다 assessment 평가 (의견) analysis 분석 (연구) methodologically 방법론(적)으로 sound 타당한, 건실한; 철저한; 손상되지 않은 perception 인식, 인지 stubbornly 고집스럽게, 완고[완강]하게 cling to ~에 집착하다[매달리다]; ~을 고수하다 impartial 공정한 revolutionary 혁명적인; 혁명의 emerge 나타나다; 드러나다

3 글의 요지 ④

해설 깊은 우정은 아닐지라도 매일 교류할 수 있는 사람들과 맺는 인간관계가 가까운 친구와 가족과의 관계보다 더 우리에게 행복을 가져다준다는 연구를 인용한 글이므로 요지로 가장 적절한 것은 ④이다.

해석 양질의 우정은 사람의 행복에 가장 중요하지만, 연구는 또한 우리가 단지 약간 아는 사람들(과학자들이 '약한 유대'라고 일컫는 것)이 우리의 행복을 신장시키는 데 중요한 역할을 할 수 있다는 것을 발견했다. 한 연구에서 교실의 학생들 간의 관계를 조사했고 가까운 친구가 아닌 다른 급우들과 더 많이 매일 교류했던 학생들이 제한된 사회 집단을 가진 학생들보다 더 행복하고 소속감도 더 컸다는 결론을 내렸다. 연구자들은 우리가 "커피 바리스타, 직장 동료, 요가 수업 친구, 동지 견주들과 대화하는데, 이러한 교류는 우리의 가까운 친구들과 가족과의 교류가 주는 기여를 넘어서서 우리의 행복에 의미 있게 기여할 수 있다"고 말한다. 뿐만 아니라 오래 지속되는 우정이 양질의 우정과 항상 동일한 것은 아니지만, 연구자들은 당신이 오랫동안 알고 있는 친구들이 단지 가볍게만 아는 사이일지라도, 당신의 행복에 귀중한 기여를 한다는 것을 발견했다.

구문 [5행~10행] One study examined the relationships / between students in

a classroom and concluded // that *those* [who had more daily interactions / with *other classmates* [who weren't their close friends]] were happier and had a greater feeling of belonging / than *those* (with a limited social circle).
One study를 주어로 하는 동사 examined와 concluded가 병렬구조를 이룬다. [ ]는 각각 앞의 those와 other classmates를 수식하는 관계대명사절이다. concluded의 목적어인 that절에서 동사 were와 had가 병렬구조를 이룬다. 두 번 나오는 those는 둘 다 students in a classroom을 지칭한다. ( )는 앞의 those를 수식한다.

어휘 kind of 약간, 어느 정도 boost 신장시키다, 북돋우다 colleague 동료 (= fellow) above and beyond (기대 · 요구 등을) 넘어서서 long-lasting 오래 가는

4 글의 주제 ③

해설 매일 분노의 경험에 대해 적어본 피실험자들은 건강이 호전되고 학교 의무실을 찾는 빈도가 줄었음을 입증한 실험에 관한 글이므로 주제로 가장 적절한 것은 '③ 글쓰기로 분노를 표출하는 것의 건강 효과'이다.
① 스트레스의 원천이자 원인으로서의 분노
② 분노를 잊음으로써 스트레스를 푸는 방법들
④ 글쓰기를 통해 창의적으로 분노를 관리하는 방법
⑤ 분노를 통제하고 예방하는 다양한 방법들

해석 한 실험에서 심리학자 James W. Pennebaker와 그의 동료들은 50명의 대학생들에게 그들 자신의 분노의 경험 혹은 실험이 끝난 후 그들이 무엇을 할 예정인지에 대해서 써 보라고 요청했다. 그들은 나흘 동안 매일 20분 간 썼다. 연구자들은 혈압, 면역 기능과 심박동수를 포함한 다양한 것들을 측정했다. 피실험자들 자신은 신체적 증상과 기분에 대해 매일 기록했다. 연구자들은 또한 실험 5일 전과 6주 후에 건강상의 이유로 인한 캠퍼스 의무실 방문에 대한 정보를 수집했다. 매일의 글쓰기 기간 동안 그들의 정신을 파고들어간 사람들은 더욱 튼튼한 면역 반응을 보였으며, 캠퍼스 의무실에 현저히 더 적게 방문했다. "가장 큰 개선을 보여준 사람들은 그들이 다른 사람들에게 이야기하는 것을 적극적으로 저지했던 감정적 격변에 대해 쓴 사람들이었습니다." Pennebaker는 말했다. "분노 조절의 실패는 그 사람으로 하여금 해결되지 못한 문제에서 그것(분노)을 감수하도록 강요합니다."

구문 [1행~5행] ~ psychologist ~ **asked** *50 college students* **to write about** [their own personal experience of anger] or [what they were going to do after the experiment was over].
'ask O to-v'는 '…에게 ~해달라고 부탁[요청]하다'의 뜻이다. 두 [ ]부분은 병렬구조를 이루며 write about의 목적어로 쓰였다.
[15행~18행] *People* (showing the greatest improvements) **are** *those* {who wrote about *emotional upheavals*} [that they had actively held back in telling others] ~
( )은 능동의 의미로 주어 People을 수식하며 동사는 are이다. { }은 those를 수식하며 [ ]은 emotional upheavals를 수식한다.

어휘 colleague 동료 immune 면역의 subject 피실험자 keep a record of 기록에 남기다 mood 기분 session 시간, 시기, 기간 dig into 파헤치다 psyche 정신 robust 원기 왕성한, 튼튼한 significantly 상당히 upheaval 격변 hold back ~을 저지하다 live with 감수하다 unresolved 미해결의

5 글의 제목 ⑤

해설 일탈이 규범의 중요성과 허용 가능한 범위를 강조하는 사회적 기능을 한다는 내용의 글이다. 음식이 금지된 교실에 간식을 가져온 학생은 별다른 훈계를 듣지 않

는 반면 패스트푸드 음식을 가져온 학생은 질책을 받고 쫓겨나는 것을 보면서 학생들이 그 경계를 알게 된다고 했으므로 글의 제목으로는 ⑤ '일탈에 대한 사회적 반응이 행동 규범을 명확하게 한다'가 적절하다.
① 일탈의 사회적 기능: 선과 악
② 일탈: 새로운 규칙을 확립할 기회
③ 사회적 규범으로부터의 일탈: 원인과 해결책
④ 일탈은 개인행동의 범위를 넓힌다

해석 비록 우리는 보통 일탈에 대해 부정적으로 생각하지만, 그것이 실제로는 사회에서 기능을 하는 것으로 판명될 수도 있다. 어떠한 일탈을 하는 사람에 대한 반감이라도 사회의 기대에 맞추는 행동상의 순응을 촉진한다. 그것은 규범에 대한 동의에 초점을 맞추어 순응하지 않는 구성원과 품행이 좋은 구성원을 구별함으로써 집단 정체성을 강화한다. 우리는 '예외가 규칙을 만든다.'라는 관용구에 익숙할지도 모른다. 일탈은 우리에게 넘어서는 안 되는 경계, 혹은 선을 보여 주어, 규범의 중요성뿐만 아니라 행동에 대한 그것의 상대적으로 허용되는 범위 또한 강조한다. 예를 들어 '교실 안에서 음식이 허용되지 않는다.'라는 규칙이 있다면, 초코바나 포테이토칩 봉지를 지닌 사람은 교사에게 꾸짖음을 받지 않을 수 있지만, 패스트푸드 음식을 들고 수업에 오는 사람은 꾸지람과 쫓아냄을 경험한다. 교실에 있는 다른 사람들은 이제 선이 어디에 그어져 있는지 알고 그에 맞게 자신의 행동 양식을 조정할 수 있다.

구문 [4행~6행] It strengthens group identity / by separating the nonconforming from the well-behaved members / **centering** on an agreement on the norms.
centering 이하는 분사구문으로 separating ~ the well-behaved members와 동시에 일어나는 상황을 나타낸다.
[8행~11행] Deviance shows us *the boundary*, or *line*, [that must not be crossed], / **highlighting** not only the importance of the norm but its relative permissible zone for behavior.
관계대명사 that이 이끄는 형용사절이 선행사 the boundary를 수식하며 이와 동격 관계인 line이 콤마 or로 연결되었다. highlighting 이하는 부대 상황을 나타내는 분사구문이며 「not only A but also B」는 상관접속사로 밑줄 친 두 개의 명사구를 병렬 연결한다.

어휘 hostility 반감, 적의 deviant 일탈 행위자; (정상에서) 벗어난 conformity 순응; 일치 nonconforming 따르지 않는 center on ~에 초점을 맞추다 norm 규범; 표준; 기준 boundary 경계(선); 한계 highlight 강조하다, 돋보이게 하다 permissible 허용되는 admonish 꾸짖다; 충고하다 rebuke 꾸지람, 비난; 질책하다 accordingly 그것에 맞게, (그것에) 따라서 deviation 일탈; 편차

---

6 안내문 일치 ④

해설 물의 양에 의해 달걀의 굳기 정도가 결정되는 것은 다른 달걀 조리기이고 요리가 끝나면 자동으로 전원이 꺼진다고 했다. 또한 비전자 부속품만 식기 세척기 사용이 가능하다고 했고 차가운 달걀을 사용하라고 했으므로 안내문과 일치하는 것은 ④이다.

해석 Rapid 달걀 조리기
전기 Rapid 달걀 조리기로 하는 빠르고 건강한 아침 식사가 여러분의 생활을 쉽고 간편하게 해줍니다!

제품 설명
• 8개 용량의 강철 달걀 조리기

• 원하는 달걀 굳기를 위한 미리 설정하는 버튼
– 원하는 달걀의 굳기를 반숙, 중간 혹은 완숙으로 미리 설정하세요.
– 물의 양으로만 달걀의 굳기를 조절하는 다른 제품보다 더 정확하고 작동하기가 더 쉽습니다.

• 버저 경보와 함께 자동으로 꺼짐
– 달걀이 조리되면 조리기는 자동으로 꺼집니다.

• 세척하기 쉽고 안전함
– 모든 비전자 부속품은 식기 세척기에 안전하고, BPA가 100% 없으며 FDA 승인을 받음

보증: 원구매자에 한해 제조상 결함에 대해 1년의 보증 기간이 있음.

유용한 팁: 항상 차가운 달걀을 사용하십시오 — 달걀을 사용하기 전에 실온으로 가져지 마십시오, 그러면 달걀이 약간 지나치게 익을 것입니다.

구문 [10행~12행] It's **more** precise and easier to operate **than** *other products* [which only control egg hardness through water volume].
「비교급+than」 구문이 쓰였다. [ ] 부분은 관계대명사절로 선행사 other products를 수식한다.

어휘 description 설명서 capacity 용량 preset 미리 조절[설치]된; 미리 조절[설치]하다 soft boiled 반숙된 hard boiled 완숙된 volume 양 alert 경보 BPA 비스페놀 A ((1950년대부터 플라스틱 제품 제조에 널리 사용돼 온 화학물질)) warranty (품질 등의) 보증(서) *cf.* warrant 보증[보장]하다; 보증서 defect 결함 overcook 너무 익히다

---

7 밑줄 어법 ④

해설 ④ 명사 something을 수식하므로 부사 personally를 personal로 고쳐야 한다.
① make sure의 목적어 자리에 쓰인 명사절을 이끄는 접속사 that으로 뒤에 완전한 절이 나온다.
② '전치사+관계대명사' 형태의 in which는 뒤에 완전한 절을 이끌며 앞의 명사(transactions)를 수식한다.
③ 'to maximize ~ the negative'는 is 동사 다음에 쓰인 보어이다.
⑤ that 다음의 'remaining in a loving relationship'은 동명사 주어이다.

해석 사회적 교환은 사회적 과정의 일반적인 범주로, 조직 내의 사람들이 자원을 거래하고 자신들의 보상이 비용보다 더 크도록 확실히 하려는 시도를 포함한다. 조직에서 일어나는 많은 사회적 상호작용은 한 사람이 다른 사람에게 자원을 제공하고 그 대가로 그 사람으로부터 무언가를 받는 거래로 이루어진다. 거래에는 이익뿐 아니라 수반되는 비용도 있고 교환에 임하는 각 당사자의 동기는 긍정적인 것을 최대화하고 부정적인 것을 최소화하는 것이다. 사회 교환 이론가들은 사람들 사이의 모든 상호작용은, 심지어 사랑과 결혼을 포함하는 것까지도, 사회적 교환이 된다고 제안한다. 사랑처럼 개인적인 것을 이익이 되는 한 계속되는 교환으로 설명하는 것은 냉소적으로 보일 수 있다. 여러분은 사랑하는 관계를 유지하는 것이 보상과 비용으로 축소될 수 없다고 항의하여 말할지도 모른다. 사회적 교환 이론가들은 어떠한 지속적인 관계에서도 그것의 중요한 부분은 상대방과의 거래에서 유리한 대차 대조표를 달성하는 것이라고 말하면서 반박할 것이다.

구문 [1행~4행] Social exchange **is** the general category of social process and **involves** *people in the organization* trading resources and attempting to make sure that their rewards outweigh their costs.
동사 is와 involves가 and로 연결되어 병렬구조를 이룬다. 두 밑줄 친 부분은 동사 involves의 목적어로 병렬구조를 이루며 people in the organization은 두 동명사구의 의미상 주어이다.
[8행~9행] There are *costs* (involved in the transactions) **as well as** *benefits* (involved in the transactions), ~.
'A as well as B'는 'B뿐만 아니라 A도'의 뜻이다. 첫 번째 ( )은 수동의 의미로 costs를 수식하며, benefits 뒤에도 의미상 'involved in the transactions'가 생략

[14행~16행] Explaining something (as personal as love) / **as** *an exchange* [that continues **as long as** it is profitable] **may seem** cynical.

밑줄 친 부분은 동명사 주어이고, 동사는 may seem이다. [ ]은 an exchange를 수식하는 관계사절이고, 조건의 접속사 as long as는 '~하는 한'의 뜻이다. 네모 안의 as는 '~로서'를 의미하는 전치사이다.

어휘 outweigh ~보다 더 크다 transaction 거래 party 당사자 constitute ~이 되다. 구성하다 protest 항의하다; 주장하다 reducible 축소[환원]시킬 수 있는 counter 반박하다 favorable 유리한, 호의적인 balance sheet 대차 대조표

8 밑줄 어휘 ⑤

해설 계절적 출생률과 사망률을 가진 종(즉 거의 모든 동물 종)에서 연령 분포는 해마다의 변동을 겪는다는 내용 다음에는, 그럼에도 이러한 변동을 계절적인 요인을 고려하여 수정하면 연령 분포가 주기성과 예측가능성을 갖게 되어 변동성은 약화될 것이므로, 연령 분포는 불안정 상태가 아니라 안정 상태에 접근하게 될 것이다. 따라서 ⑤의 instability를 stability 등으로 바꿔 써야 한다.

해석 개체군 통계학상의 계층 비율은 집단의 적응도, 그리고 궁극적으로 각 개별 구성원의 적응도에 ① 영향을 미친다. 전적으로 새끼 혹은 노화하는 수컷으로만 구성된 집단은 소멸될 것이다. 확실히 말이다. 비정상성이 ② 덜한 또 다른 집단은 더 높은 생존 확률로 정의될 수 있는 더 높은 적응도를 갖고 있는데, 이는 멸종까지의 더 긴 대기 시간으로 설명될 수 있다. 둘 중 어떤 측정도 길이상의 약 한 세대의 기간에서만 유의미한데, 한 세대에서 몇 세대까지의 기간 동안 번식할 수 있는 비정상적인 개체군이 그 종에 정상인 개체군의 연령 분포를 ③ 복구하는 데 성공할 것이기 때문이다. 그 종이 대단히 기회주의적이지 않다면, 즉 그 종이 빈 서식지에서 대량 서식하고 비교적 단기적인 동안만 그곳을 계속 보유하는 전략을 따르지 않는다면, 연령 분포는 ④ 안정된 상태에 접근하는 경향을 보일 것이다. 계절적 출생률과 사망률을 가진 종. 즉 거의 모든 동물 종에서 연령 분포는 해마다의 변동을 겪을 것이다. 그러나 심지어 그 때조차도 변동은 계절을 고려하여 수정될 때 주기적이고 예측 가능해진다는 의미에서, 연령 분포는 ⑤ 불안정 상태(→ 안정 상태)에 다가간다고 할 수 있다.

구문 [8행~13행] Either measure has meaning / only over periods of time on the order of a generation in length, // because **a deviant population** (allowed to reproduce for one to several generations) **will go far** / to restore *the age distribution of populations* (normal for the species).

because 절에서 a deviant population이 주어이고 will go far가 동사이다. allowed ~ generations는 수동의 뜻을 가지는 과거분사구로 앞의 a deviant population을 수식한다. 형용사구인 normal ~ species는 앞의 the age distribution of populations를 수식한다.

[20행~22행] But even then the age distribution can be said to approach stability, / in the sense that the fluctuation is periodic and predictable / when corrected for season.

that ~ season은 the sense에 대한 동격절이다. when 이하는 분사구문으로 when과 corrected 사이에 it(= the fluctuation) is가 생략되었다.

어휘 fitness 적응도 be comprised of ~로 구성되다 wholly 전적으로, 완전히 perish 소멸되다, 죽다 probability 확률 translate 설명하다; 옮기다, 바꾸다 measure 측정(하다) on the order of 약, 대략 reproduce 번식하다 go far 성공하다 restore 복구[복원]하다 distribution 분포 opportunistic 기회주의적인 colonize 대량 서식하다 hold on to 계속 보유하다 steady 안정된; 변동 없는; 꾸준한 mortality 사망률 fluctuation 변동, 오르내림 periodic 주기적인

9 빈칸 추론 ⑤

해설 지의류는 온기를 찾아서 애쓰지 않고 온도에 맞추어 삶의 속도를 조절한다. 또한 수분을 얻기 위해 물에 의존하지 않고 축축한 날은 수분을 흡수하고 건조한 날에는 수분을 소비하는 것으로 보아 지의류는 적극적으로 환경을 극복하거나 바꾸려 노력하지 않고 환경의 변화에 자연스럽게 스스로를 맞춘다. 자신을 외부에 맞추는 것이 순종(submission)처럼 보일 수 있으나, 실은 순종을 통해 승리하는 삶의 자세를 보여주는 것이라 할 수 있으므로 ⑤ '순종'이 가장 적절하다.
① 성공 ② 희생 ③ 낙관주의 ④ 경계

해석 대부분의 다른 생물들이 겨울에 대비하여 몸을 사릴 때 유연한 생리 기능은 지의류가 생명으로 빛나게 해준다. 지의류는 온기를 찾아서 연료를 태우지 않으며, 대신에 자신의 삶의 속도를 온도계에 맞추어 오르내리게 한다. 그것들은 식물과 동물이 그러하듯이 물에 집착하지 않는다. 지의류의 몸체는 축축한 날에 부풀어 오르고, 그 후 공기가 건조해질 때 주름이 진다. 식물은 냉기로부터 움츠러들며, 봄이 그들을 점차 꾀어낼 때까지 자신의 세포를 꽁꽁 싸놓는다. 지의류의 세포는 깊게 잠들지 않는다. 겨울이 하루 동안 누그러질 때, 지의류는 소생 상태로 쉽게 흘러온다. 이러한 삶에 대한 접근법은 다른 사람들에 의해 독자적으로 발견되었다. 기원전 4세기에 중국의 도교 철학인인 장자는 높은 폭포의 아랫부분에서 혼란 속에 내동댕이쳐진 한 노인에 대한 글을 썼다. 겁에 질린 구경꾼들이 그를 도우러 달려갔지만, 그 남자는 해를 입지 않은 차분한 모습으로 나타났다. 이러한 곤란에서 어떻게 살아남을 수 있었는지 질문을 받았을 때, 그는 대답했다. "저는 물을 제게 맞춘 게 아니라 저 자신을 물에 맞추었어요." 지의류는 이러한 지혜를 도가 사상가들보다 4억 년 전에 알았다. 장자의 비유에 나온 순종을 통한 승리의 진정한 대가들은 폭포 주변의 바위벽에 매달린 지의류였다.

구문 [3행~5행] Lichens burn no fuel in quest of warmth, instead **letting** *the pace of their lives* **rise** and **fall** with the thermometer.

letting 이하는 동시동작을 나타내는 분사구문이다. 'let+O+C'의 구조로 목적격 보어인 rise와 fall이 and로 병렬 연결된다.

[16행~19행] **When** (being) **asked** *how he could survive this hardship*, he replied, "I accommodate myself to the water, not the water to me."

When ~ this hardship은 접속사가 있는 분사구문으로 being이 생략되었다. asked의 목적어로 간접의문문 어순(의문사+주어+동사)의 의문사절이 쓰였다.

어휘 supple 유연한; 순응성이 있는 physiology 생리 기능[현상]; 생리학 lock down ~을 가두다 in quest of ~을 찾아서 thermometer 온도계 cling to ~에 집착하다; ~을 고수하다 swell 부풀다, 팽창하다 damp 축축한, 습기 있는 shrink 움츠러들다; 감소하다 chill 냉기, 한기 pack up (짐 등을) 싸다[챙기다]; 그만두다 coax 부추기다; 달래어 ~하게 하다 ease 누그러지다, 완화하다 float 흘러가다; 부유하다 Taoist 도교(의); 도교 신자(의) turmoil 혼란; 소란 onlooker 구경꾼; 방관자 rush 돌진하다; 성급하게 하다 emerge 모습을 드러내다; 드러나다 accommodate (환경 등에) 맞추다; 적응시키다; 순응하다 allegory 비유; 풍유 sacrifice 희생; 제물 optimism 낙관주의; 낙천관 vigilance 경계; 조심 submission 순종; 굴복; 제출

10 빈칸 추론 ④

해설 빈칸 아래의 내용으로 보아, 인간의 진실성에 영향을 주는 것은 위에 언급된 선을 추구하는 마음이 아니라 '즉각적인 보상을 거둘 것인가, 미래에 예상되는 더 큰 이익을 쌓을 것인가'라는 두 선택지 사이에서의 갈등과 계산이므로 이를 반영하면 빈칸에 들어갈 말로 가장 적절한 것은 ④ '단기적 이득과 장기적 이득'이다.

해석 일반적인 믿음과는 반대로, 진실성은 바뀌지 않는 특질이 아니다. 과거에 공정하고 정직했던 사람이 미래에도 반드시 공정하고 정직한 건 아닐 것이다. 그 이유를 이해하기 위하여, 우리는 먼저 인간이 '선'과 '악'의 충동과 씨름한다는 관념에서 벗어나야 한다. 심

각한 정신병의 경우를 제외하고, 정신은 그런 식으로 작동하지 않는다. 오히려 그것은 두 가지 유형의 이득, 즉 단기적 이득과 장기적 이득에 집중한다. 그리고 일반적으로 어떤 특정 상황에서 진실성에 영향을 주는 것은 그 둘 사이의 선택이다. 예컨대 자신이 하지 않거나 할 수 없는 일을 약속함으로써 신뢰를 깨는 사람들은 즉각적인 보상은 거둘지 몰라도 미래에 그 동일한 파트너(또한 아마도 다른 사람들)와의 교환과 협동으로부터 더 큰 이익을 축적할 가능성은 감소시킨다. 그것은 결정과 관련된 진실성의 핵심이 되는, 즉각적인 보상과 미래의 잠재적 비용에 대한 저울질이며, 이는 상당 부분 상황과 관련 당사자들에 달려 있다.

구문 [9행~11행] And **it's** *the choice between them* **that** typically dictates integrity in any particular situation.
「It is ~ that ...」 강조구문으로, it is와 that 사이의 the choice between them을 의미상 강조하고 있다. them은 two types of gains: short-term and long-term을 지칭한다.

어휘 integrity 진실성 psychopathy 정신병 dictate ~에 영향을 주다; ~을 받아쓰게 하다 diminish 줄어들다; 줄이다 [선택지 어휘] static 고정적인 spatial 공간적인 temporal 시간의; 현세의; 한때의

---

11 빈칸 추론 ⑤

해설 스포츠팬의 기분이 자신의 팀의 승패와 등락을 같이 하고, 자신이 지지하는 정치인의 선거 결과에 따라 기분이 바뀌는 현상은 집단에 대한 개인의 충성을 나타내며, 이를 다르게 표현하면 ⑤ '집단과 자아 간의 경계의 상실'이다.
① 공동의 감정이 가지는 힘
② 집단의 현실에 대한 적응
③ 개인적 정체성의 발달
④ 특정 집단의 사람들과 연관된 가치

해석 스포츠 팀이나 정당과 같이 경쟁 속에서의 집단에 대한 충성은 지배를 향한 우리의 본능을 간접적으로 펼쳐 보이도록 장려한다. Jerry Seinfeld는 한번은 요즘의 선수들이 스포츠 팀을 너무나 빠르게 지나가서 팬이 더 이상 선수들의 집단을 지지할 수 없을 정도라고 말했다. 팬은 그들의 팀 로고와 유니폼을 응원하는 수준으로 전락한다. "일어서서 다른 도시의 옷들을 이기라고 당신의 옷들에게 환호하며 소리치고 있는 거죠." 하지만 우리는 정말로 일어서서 환호한다. 즉, 스포츠팬의 기분은 그의 팀의 운과 등락을 함께 한다. 집단과 자아 간의 경계의 상실은 말 그대로 생화학 실험실에서 관찰될 수 있다. 사람의 테스토스테론 수치는 그들이 레슬링 시합이나 테니스 단식 경기에서 맞수를 개인적으로 무찌를 때 상승하는 것과 꼭 마찬가지로 그들의 팀이 경기에서 맞수 팀을 패배시킬 때 상승한다. 그것은 호감을 받는 정치 후보자가 선거에서 이기거나 질 때도 또한 오르거나 내려간다.

구문 [1행~3행] *Loyalty* to groups in competition, such as sports teams or political parties, **encourages** us **to play out** our instinct for dominance vicariously.
주어는 Loyalty이고 동사는 encourages이다. 'encourage O to-v'는 '…가 ~하도록 장려하다'의 뜻이다.
[4행~6행] Jerry Seinfeld once remarked that today's athletes pass through sports teams **so** rapidly **that** a fan can no longer support a group of players.
'so … that ~'은 '너무 …하여 ~하다'의 뜻이다.
[13행~16행] Men's testosterone level rises when their team defeats a rival in a game, **just as** it rises when they personally defeat a rival in a wrestling match or in singles tennis.
just as는 '~하는 것과 꼭 마찬가지로'의 뜻이다.

어휘 loyalty 충성 political party 정당 play out 펼쳐 보이다 instinct

본능 dominance 지배 remark 말하다 root for 응원하다 yell 외치다 mood 기분 biochemistry 생화학 defeat 패배시키다 favor 호의를 보이다 candidate 후보자

---

12 빈칸 추론   ②

해설 '나는 시간이 빠듯하다'라고 하는 것은 권위의 표현이 될 수 있는데, 이를 역전시켜서 '내 시간의 권리는 온전히 당신의 것이다'라는 전략을 쓰면 상대방의 권위를 높여주고 자발적인 협조를 이끌어낼 수 있다는 내용의 글이므로, 자신의 손목시계를 풀어 시계 앞면이 보이지 않도록 내려놓는(즉 자신의 시간에 대한 소유권을 상대방에게 넘기겠다는) 제스처를 통해 전하고자 하는 뜻은 ② '제 시간은 당신이 필요로 하는 만큼 당신 것입니다'가 가장 적절하다.
① 당신의 시간과 도움을 얻게 되어 기쁩니다
③ 당신의 시간은 제한되어있으니 그것을 회의에 낭비하지 마세요
④ 당신의 시간이 제가 지금 쓸 수 있는 가장 귀중한 것입니다
⑤ 기다리는 것은 제 시간을 결코 쓰고 싶지 않은 행동입니다

해석 시간의 효과적 사용은 심지어 당신에게 권위가 없을 때조차도 권위를 내보일 수 있는 궁극적인 방법 중 하나이다. 대개의 경우 시간을 지배하는 자는 누구든지 상황을 지배한다. 그들은 자신과 만나고 싶어 하는 사람이면 누구에게라도 자신의 시간이 귀중하다는 것을 항상 상기시킬 것이다. 그러나 당신이 빠듯한 시간 사용 전술을 역전시키고 싶을 상황이 있을 수도 있다. 당신과 당신의 동료 중 한 사람이 속한 각 두 부서 간에 발생한 어려운 상황을 논하기 위해 함께 만나기로 동의했다고 해보자. 비록 당신이 당신의 동료에게 당신의 시간이 한정되어있다고 말하긴 했지만, 문제를 해결하기 위해 그녀가 당신에게서 필요로 하는 것보다 당신이 그녀의 도움을 더 많이 필요로 한다. 그녀가 약속된 시간에 당신의 사무실에 들어올 때, 보란 듯이 손목시계를 풀고 시계의 앞면이 책상과 맞닿게 두어라. "제 시간은 당신이 필요로 하는 만큼 당신 것입니다."라고 말하라. 회의의 초반에 동료의 협동 수준이 기하급수적으로 상승하는 것을 지켜봐라. 당신은 그녀로부터 원하는 어떤 것이라도 얻을 수 있을 것이다.

구문 [3행~4행] Whoever controls time **controls** the situation in most instances.
Whoever ~ time이 주어이고 두 번째 controls가 동사이다. whoever는 '~한 사람이면 누구든지'의 뜻이다.
[4행~5행] They will always **remind** anyone [who wants to meet with them] // **that** their time is valuable.
「remind ~ that ....」은 '~에게 …을 상기시키다'의 뜻이다. [ ]는 anyone을 수식하는 주격 관계대명사절이다.

어휘 reverse 역전[반전]시키다; 뒤집다 tactic 전술, 책략 respective 각각의 resolve 해결하다 at the outset 처음에

---

13 흐름 무관 문장   ④

해설 반려동물은 상품과 달리 마음이 바뀌면 쉽게 교체할 수 있는 대상이 아니므로 소유를 결정하기 전에 신중해야 한다는 것이 글의 요지이므로 애완동물을 소유하는 것의 이점을 언급한 ④는 글의 흐름과 무관하다.

해석 중요한 결정에는 시간, 헌신, 그리고 생각이 필요하다. ① 우리가 보통 이런 종류의 결정을 성급하게 내리지는 않지만, 많은 사람들은 충동에 근거하여 반려동물을 선택한다. ② 휴대전화나 자동차는 잘 작동하지 않거나 빨리 흥미가 없어지면 팔거나 웃돈을 주고 새것으로 바꿀 수 있지만, 동물을 상품으로 여겨서는 안 된다. ③ 그리고 우리가 마음이 바뀌면 대학이나 전공을 바꾸는 것과는 달리, 애완동물이 제대로 행동하지 않거나 우

리가 나이가 들면서 흥미를 잃으면 그냥 그것을 버리거나 방치할 수 있다고 생각하는 것은 도리에 맞지 않는다. ④ 보살필 동물을 가진다는 것은 인지 기능에 유익할 수 있는 목적의식을 애완동물 소유자에게 줄 수 있다. ⑤ 동물을 집에 들이는 것은 큰 조치인데 그 일이 일어나기 전에 내려야 하는 매우 중대한 결정들이 있다.

구문 [7행~11행] And unlike switching colleges or majors when we change our minds, / it is not reasonable to assume // that if a pet doesn't perform well or we outgrow our interest, / we can just get rid of it or neglect it.
it은 가주어이고, 진주어는 to assume ~ neglect it이다. that 이하는 to assume의 목적어절이다.

어휘 commitment 헌신, 전념   trade in 거래하다. ~을 웃돈을 주고 신품과 바꾸다
commodity 상품   reasonable 도리에 맞는   get rid of ~을 버리다   neglect (돌보지 않고) 방치하다   beneficial 유익한   cognitive 인식의, 인지의

14 글의 순서   ④

해설 (C) 첫 문장의 them은 주어진 문장의 mechanisms를 지칭하므로 우선 (C)가 나와야 한다. 위험을 감지하면 경계태세에 돌입하는 두뇌의 기제에 대해 논한 (C) 다음에는 But으로 연결되어 언제 경고 신호를 무시할지를 알아야 한다는 (A)가 나와야 한다. 덧붙여 인지적 종결 욕구가 덜 한 사람들이 창의적이라는 연구를 소개한 (A) 다음에는 이에 대해 더 자세히 설명하는 (B)가 나와야 한다.

해석 우리는 우리의 두뇌가 어제 태어난 것이 아님을 이해해야 한다. 우리에게는 오랫동안 작동해왔기에 위협을 경고하고 불안정에 대항하여 지켜주는 기제가 있다.
(C) 그것이 없다면 우리는 지금 여기에 있지 못할 것이다. 어떠한 제정신인 사람이라도 비행기 밖으로 뛰어내리는 것에 대해 염려를 느끼는 것과 마찬가지 방식으로, 우리의 두뇌는 위험이 어렴풋이 나타날 때 그것이 통제하는 유기체가 경계 태세를 취하게 한다.
(A) 그러나 우리는 언제 경고 신호를 무시하고 어쨌든 덜 편안한 길을 택할지 알아야 한다. 미국과 이탈리아 합동 심리학자 팀이 수행한 연구는 '인지적 종결', 즉 애매모호함을 제거하고 명확한 결론에 (때때로 불합리하게) 도달하려는 인간의 욕구에 대한 필요가 덜 한 사람들이 일반적으로 그들의 상대방보다 더 창의적임을 발견했다.
(B) 확실성에 대한 두뇌의 욕구, 즉 안정성을 보존하기 위해 종결의 문을 닫으려는 두뇌의 요구를 지나쳐서 작업할 수 있는 사람들은 더욱 다양한 관점에서 도전과 맞서 싸울 가능성이 더 높다. 그것이 과학적 발견, 기술적 진보와 다양한 다른 인간의 추구를 북돋우는 에너지이다.

구문 [2행~3행] We have *mechanisms* [to **warn** of threats **and** **guard** against instability] ~
[   ]은 mechanisms를 수식한다. warn of는 '~을 경고하다'의 뜻이다. 동사원형 warn과 guard가 병렬구조를 이룬다.
[20행~23행] In *the same way* [that any sane person feels apprehension **about jumping out of an airplane**], **our brain** puts *the organism* [(which[that]) it controls] on alert when danger looms.
첫 번째 [   ]은 the same way를 수식하는 관계부사절이다. 두 번째 [   ]은 앞에 목적격 관계대명사 which[that]가 생략되어 the organism을 수식하며, it은 our brain을 지칭한다.

어휘 mechanism 기제   override 무시하다   joint 합동의   cognitive closure 인지적 종결   ambiguity 애매모호함   counterpart 상대   appetite 식욕, 욕구   engage 교전하다   vantage point 관점   fuel 연료를 공급하다, 부채질하다   a range of 다양한   sane 제정신인   apprehension 걱정, 염려   put ~ on alert ~에게 경계 태세를 취하게 하다

15 글의 순서   ⑤

해설 주어진 글은 질병이 전염되려면 최저한도 이상의 인구 규모가 필요하다는 내용으로 이에 대한 부연설명과 예시가 제시되는 (C)가 바로 뒤이어 나오는 것이 자연스럽고, (B)에서 구체적 사례로 들고 있는 말라리아, 즉 one such disease는 (C)의 numerous diseases중 하나를 가리키므로 (C) 다음에 와야 한다. (A)에서는 부사 similarly를 통해 앞서 나온 것과 유사한 내용이 이어질 것임을 알 수 있는데, (B)에서 수렵, 채집사회보다 인구 밀도가 높은 곳으로 농경 사회를 언급한 뒤에 농경 사회보다 인구 밀도가 높은 곳으로 도시를 언급하는 (A)가 이어지는 것이 자연스럽다.

해설 질병이 계속 전염되는 것을 유지하려면 최저한도의 인구 규모나 (인구) 밀도를 필요로 할지도 모른다.
(C) 따라서 인구의 증가로 우리는 예전의 인구로는 지속될 수 없었던 질병에 노출될 수 있다. 예를 들어, 농업의 도입은 수렵·채집사회에 존재했던 것보다 더 큰 인구 밀도를 요하는 수많은 질병의 확산이라는 결과를 낳았다.
(B) 말라리아는 아마도, 5천 년 전 무렵 아프리카에 정착 농업이 확립되면서 그 치명적인 형태로 발전했을 그러한 질병 중 하나이다. 정착 농업 이전에 아프리카의 수렵·채집사회는 (인구가) 너무 적고 드문드문 떨어져 있어서 말라리아가 존속할 수 없었다.
(A) 도시생활도 이와 비슷하게, 농업 정착지에서 나타나는 것보다 더 높은 인구 밀도를 요하는 무수한 질병의 확산을 돕는다. 그러므로 역사를 통틀어 도시 인구의 증가를 가능케 한 농업의 획기적인 발전에는 항상 전염병의 치명적인 발병이 수반되어왔다.

구문 [4행~6행] Urban life similarly supports *the spread* (of *countless diseases* [that require higher population densities / than found in agricultural settlements]).
관계대명사 that의 선행사는 countless diseases이다. 과거분사인 found 앞에는 population densities가 생략되어 있다.

어휘 density 밀도, 농도   ongoing 계속 진행 중인   transmission 전송; 전염; 전도   urban 도시의, 도회지의   agricultural 농업의, 농사의 *cf.* agriculture 농업   breakthrough 돌파구; (과학 등의) 큰 발전   accompany 동반하다, 동행하다; 수반하다   infectious 전염성의, 전염되는(= contagious)   sustain ~을 살아가게[지탱하게] 하다; ~을 지속하다(= maintain)   numerous 많은

16 문장 넣기   ③

해설 주어진 문장은 강화를 줄수록 보상받는 것에 관심을 잃게 된다는 것으로 이는 ③ 뒤의 That is로 시작하는 문장에 의해 더 자세히 설명되고 있다.

해석 아이들이 금별이나 상, 심지어 금전적 보상에 의해 강화를 받는다면 학교생활을 더 잘할까? 강화 이론에 의하면 보상을 주는 것은 보상받은 행동의 반복을 이끌고, 벌은 반복을 감소시킨다. 대부분의 아이들이 사탕을 대단히 좋아한다는 것을 고려해 볼 때, 강화 이론은 만약 당신이 5분 동안 자신의 의자에 얌전히 앉아 있던 한 아이에게 사탕을 준다면, 그 아이는 항상 얌전히 앉아 있는 것을 빠르게 학습할 것이라고 한다. 강화 이론의 주요 원리에 맞서서, 몇몇 행동주의 과학자들은 사람이 특정한 것을 행하는 것에 대해 강화를 더 주면 줄수록, 그 사람은 보상을 받고 있는 바로 그것에 더 빨리 관심을 잃게 될 것이라 주장한다. 다시 말해, 보상을 받는 것은 활동의 재미를 감소시킨다. 몇몇 연구들은 만약 당신이 분별 있는 행동에 대해 아이들에게 보상한다면, 그들은 그것을 습관화하기보다 그 행동을 '특별한 경우'로 보는 경향이 있다. 그러므로 그들은 보상받지 않은 아이들보다 장기적으로 변화할 가능성이 더 적다.

구문 [2행~5행] ~, / some behavioral scientists argue // that **the more** you reinforce a person for doing a certain thing, / **the faster** that person will lose interest in the very thing that they are being rewarded for.

「The 비교급 ..., the 비교급 ~」은 '…하면 할수록 더 ~하다'의 뜻이다.

어휘 reinforce 강화하다 *cf.* reinforcement 강화 monetary 금전(상)의; 통화 (화폐)의 sensible 분별 있는 make a habit of ~을 습관화하다

17 문장 넣기 ⑤

해설 주어진 문장은 소행성과 지구의 충돌을 기술하고 있으므로 답은 적어도 For example 다음에 운석의 지구 충돌이 예시로 나온 ④ 이후이다. ③ 다음의 문장은 서술이 제약되는 교과서에 관한 내용이고 ④ 다음의 문장은 상세한 기술이 가능한 일반 서적에 관한 내용인데, 주어진 문장의 It은 상세한 연대기적 기술이 가능한 일반 서적을 지칭하므로 주어진 문장은 그 다음 문장 뒤엔 ⑤에 위치해야 한다.

해석 일반 서적은 독자에게 주제에 대한 더 풍부로운 이해를 제공하면서 흥미로운 관찰과 세부사항을 가지고 주제에 활력을 불어넣을 공간을 제공할 수 있다. 교과서는 너무나 많은 주제를 다루어야 하기 때문에 하나의 주제를 조금이라도 깊이 있게 발전시킬 수 없다. 그러므로 교과서는 일반 서적에서 유익한 흥미진진한 종류의 제시를 허용하지 않는 주제들에 대한 넓고 결과적으로 더 얕은 견해를 제공한다. 예를 들어 교과서의 한 구절은 단지 소행성이 지구를 강타할 수 있다고 언급할 뿐이다. 그러나 일반 서적은 소행성의 대기 진입, 그것의 행성과의 충돌, 그리고 25마일 깊이와 100마일의 너비인 분화구의 폭발의 사건을 시간 순으로 기록한다. 그것은 충돌 시점에서의 증발, 지진, 화재, 그리고 암흑과 몹시 낮은 기온이 뒤따르는 강력한 열기의 전 세계적 시기를 유발하는 파편을 매혹적으로 상세히 기술한다. 교과서가 허용하는 한정된 공간 속에 이러한 종류의 세부사항과 통찰력을 독자들에게 제공하기는 어렵다.

구문 [1행~5행] It describes in fascinating detail the vaporization at the impact point, the earthquakes, the fires, and the debris [that caused a worldwide period of *intense heat* (**followed by** darkness and freezing temperatures)].
밑줄 친 부분은 describes의 목적어로 병렬구조를 이룬다. in fascinating detail은 '매혹적으로 상세히'의 뜻이다. [ ]는 the debris를 수식하며 ( )는 intense heat을 수식한다. 「A follwed by B」는 'B가 뒤따르는 A, A 다음에 나오는 B'의 뜻이다.
[20행~22행] It is difficult to provide readers this kind of detail and insight in *the limited space* (allowed by a textbook).
It은 가주어이고 to 이하가 진주어이다. ( )는 the limited space를 수식한다.

어휘 vaporization 증발 intense 강렬한 trade book 보급판, 일반서 bring ~ to life ~에 활기를 불어넣다 consequently 결과적으로 shallow 얕은 allow for ~을 고려[참작]하다, ~을 위해 감안하다 compelling 몹시 흥미로운 passage 구절 entry 입장 collision 충돌 blast 폭발하다 crater 분화구 insight 통찰력

18 요약문 완성 ④

해설 우리의 변연계 뇌는 진화 과정에서 우리의 환경 변화에 맞추어 진화하지 않았기 때문에 불편함이나 두려움을 원시 상황에서처럼 생존의 위협으로 여겨 과도한 반응을 한다는 것이 글의 내용이다. 그러므로 (A)에는 '과잉 반응하다'라는 의미의 overreact가 (B)에는 '부조화'를 의미하는 mismatch가 적절하다.

해석 변연계 뇌는 쾌락과 고통에 의해 활발하게 추진된다. 우리가 원시적인 종이었던 한때에 이것은 확실히 어떤 보존 가치를 지녔다. 그러나 우리가 진화하고 훨씬 더 복잡하고 지적으로 됨에 따라, 이러한 근본적인 충동은 우리와 함께 진화하지 않고, 미묘함에 맞춰진다기보다는 절대적인 상태로 남아있다. 예를 들어 당신이 불편함을 느끼면, 당신의 변연계 뇌는 그것을 당신의 안전이 심각하게 위협받고 있다는 신호로 해석하는데, 그러면 이는 위험을 피하고 당신의 안전을 유지하기 위해 급격한 반응을 촉발시킨다. 당신의 변

연계 뇌는 바로 그 속성상 다양한 정도의 불편함과 두려움을 평가하는 데 그다지 효과적이지 못하다. 그러므로 이러한 원시적인 충동에 휘둘린다는 것은 더욱 복잡한 사회와 문명의 요구와 심하게 충돌하는데, 그곳에서 사람들은 두려움에 대한 그들의 요구에 끊임없이 조치를 취할 수는 없다. 그러나 그것(생존 본능)이 구별을 쉽게 할 수 없고 모든 불편과 두려움을 우리의 생존에 대한 궁극적인 위협으로 여기는 경향이 있다는 점에서 이는 생존 본능이 문제를 제기하는 지점이다.

↓

> 변연계 뇌는 불편함이나 두려움에 (A) 과민 반응하는 경향이 있는데, 왜냐하면 그것은 우리의 현재 환경과 생활 방식에 진화적으로 (B) 부조화를 가지고 있기 때문이다.

구문 [13행~16행] Hence, **being at the mercy of these primary drives** severely *conflicts* with the needs of *a more complex society and civilization*, **in which** people cannot be constantly acting on their needs for fear.
동명사구인 being at ~ primary drives가 주어이고 동사는 conflicts이다. '전치사+관계대명사' 형태의 in which가 이끄는 절은 a more complex society and civilization을 부연 설명한다.
[16행~20행] But this is where the survival instinct poses a problem, **in that** it doesn't easily make distinctions, and tends to view all discomfort and fear as an ultimate threat to our survival.
in that은 '~라는 점에서'의 의미를 가진 접속사이다. in that이 이끄는 절 내에서 두 개의 밑줄 친 동사구가 and로 병렬 연결된다.

어휘 vigorously 활발하게; 발랄하게 drive 추진시키다; 몰아붙이다; 충동 primitive 원시적인; 초기의 preservation 보존, 보호 evolve 진화하다; 발달하다 sophisticated 지적인; 세련된; 정교한 fundamental 근본[본질]적인 attune 맞추다, 조화시키다 subtlety 미묘함; 중요한 세부 요소 interpret 해석하다; 이해하다 threaten 위협[협박]하다 trigger 촉발시키다; 작동시키다 avert 피하다, 방지하다 evaluate 평가[감정]하다 discomfort 불편; 가벼운 통증 at the mercy of ~에 휘둘리는; ~의 처분대로 conflict 충돌하다; 상충하다 civilization 문명 (사회) instinct 본능; 직감 pose (질문을) 제기하다 make a distinction 구별하다 ultimate 궁극적인; 최후의 mismatch 부조화 submit 항복[굴복]하다 overreact 과잉 반응하다

19~20 장문 19 ① 20 ⑤

해설 19. 한 개인에게 사회적 배제는 뇌의 특정 부분이 활성화되며 괴로움을 느끼게 하고 때로는 죽음에 이르기까지 한다는 것이 글의 요지이므로 이를 가장 잘 포괄하고 있는 ① '우리의 가장 큰 두려움은 무엇인가? 배제'가 제목으로 가장 적절하다.
② 사회적 배제: 양날의 검
③ 사회적 배제는 차별의 한 형태이다
④ 소속과 신체 건강의 비밀스러운 상관관계
⑤ 소속의 필요성: 근본적인 생존 기술
20. 사람은 거부당하는 것에 아주 민감하고, 이것은 선천적인 것으로 성격과도 아무 상관이 없다는 내용으로 보아 사회적 배제의 고통은 '자동적'으로 일어나는 것이다. 그러므로 (e)는 automatic으로 바꾸어 써야 적절하다.

해석 어느 날 Purdue 대학의 심리학자인 Kip Williams는 공원에 나가 자기 개를 산책시키다가 프리스비, 즉, 장난감으로 사용되는 플라스틱의 둥근 조각을 등에 맞았다. 그는 그것을 가지고 놀던 두 사내 중 한 명에게 그것을 다시 던졌는데 그는 그것을 Kip에게 다시 던지기 시작했다. 이것은 재미있었지만 약 1분 후 그들은 Kip에게 프리스비를 던지는 것을 그만두었고 서로에게만 주의를 돌렸다. 이제 그들이 Kip을 다시 그들의 게임에 (a) 포함하지 않을 것이 분명해졌다. 그 심리학 교수는 자신이 (그들에게) 완전히 낯선 사람이라는 것을 감안하고도 이러한 배제에 자기가 얼마나 화가 났는지를 알고는 놀랐다. 우리를 다른 사람들에게 (b) 받아들여지도록 강요하는 욕구가 우리 내면의 깊은 곳에 있다는 것을 그는 깨달았다.

Kip은 그 공원에서의 그러한 경험을 가지고 성인 실험 참가자들이 다른 두 명의 놀이 친구들과 공을 주고받아야 하는 게임을 할 때 그들의 뇌를 스캔하는 'Cyberball'이라고 알려진 컴퓨터 시뮬레이션을 개발했다. 프리스비 사건의 경우처럼 Cyberball은 두 다른 사람들이 자기들끼리만 공을 주고받고 뇌 스캐너를 쓴 사람을 (c) 무시하기 시작할 때까지는 순조롭게 진행되고 있었다. 이러한 배제가 분명해졌을 때 사회적 인지에 의해 활성화되는 뇌의 전대상 피질 영역이 활동으로 빛나기 시작했다. 그 게임의 사회적 배제는 감정적인 고통과 관련된 영역을 활성화시켰기 때문에 처음에 괴로움을 유발했다. 여기에서 주목할 만한 것은 우리가 거부당하는 것에 얼마나 (d) 민감한가의 문제이다. 그리고 이 고통은 또한 게임을 하는 사람들의 성격과도 아무 상관이 없었다. 오히려 그것에 대해서는 (e) 의도적인(→ 자동적인) 것이 있다. Kip Williams는 이러한 반응은 분명 타고난 것임이 틀림없다고 주장하고, 다른 많은 사회적 종에서 사회적 배제는 종종 죽음으로 이어진다고 지적한다.

구문 [4행~6행] He threw it back to *one of **the two guys*** [**who** were playing with it] [**who** then began tossing it back to Kip].

두 개의 [ ] 부분은 모두 주격 관계대명사 who가 이끄는 관계사절로 첫 번째 [ ] 부분은 the two guys를, 두 번째 [ ] 부분은 one of the two guys를 수식한다.

[15행~20행] Kip took his experiences from the park and developed *a computer simulation (known as 'Cyberball')* [**where** adult participants had their brains scanned as they played *a game* [**where** they had to toss a ball back and forth between two other playmates]].

( ) 부분은 분사구로 앞에 있는 a computer simulation을 수식한다. 첫 번째 관계부사 where가 이끄는 where adult participants ~ two other playmates는 a computer ~ 'Cyberball'을 수식하고 그 안의 where가 이끄는 [ ]은 선행사 a game을 수식한다.

어휘 Frisbee 프리스비 ((던지기를 하고 놀 때 쓰는 플라스틱 원반)) **toss** 던지다; 흔들리다 **attention** 주의 (집중), 주목; 관심 **exclusion** 배제, 제외 **drive** 욕구, 충동 **compel** 강요[강제]하다 **obvious** 분명한, 명백한 **activate** 활성화[작동]시키다 **cognition** 인지; 인식 **distress** 괴로움, 고통 **personality** 성격; 개성 **intentional** 의도적인, 고의의 **hardwired** 타고나는, 하드웨어에 내장된 **discrimination** 차별; 구별 **correlation** 상관관계 **fundamental** 근본[본질]적인; 핵심[필수]적인

제23회

본문 p.180

| 1 | ④ | 2 | ⑤ | 3 | ④ | 4 | ⑤ | 5 | ④ | | 6 | ⑤ | 7 | ③ | 8 | ④ | 9 | ① | 10 | ① |
| 11 | ③ | 12 | ③ | 13 | ③ | 14 | ④ | 15 | ③ | | 16 | ② | 17 | ③ | 18 | ④ | 19 | ② | 20 | ④ |

---

1 글의 목적 　　　　④

해설 쇼핑몰 건설 계획에 대한 사설을 작성한 사람에게 쓴 글이다. 쇼핑몰 건설을 반대하는 이유를 설명하고 마지막에 We hope that you will reconsider your position이라고 하였으므로 글의 목적으로 가장 적절한 것은 ④이다.

해석 Ervin 씨께

Augusta 시내의 주차 요금 징수기를 반대하는 귀하의 사설에는 동의하지만, 저희는 귀하의 10월 18일 자 사설에는 동의하지 않습니다. 저희의 노면을 보수하여 쇼핑몰로 만드는 것은 시내의 업체들에 돌이킬 수 없는 손해를 끼칠 것입니다. 도시 공학자들은 쇼핑몰 계획으로 인해 최소 1년을 꽉 채운 기간 동안 점포들에 지장을 줄 것이라고 추정합니다. 많은 시내 점포들은 지금 생존을 위해 분투하고 있으며, 쇼핑몰 계획은 그들에게 종말의 조짐이 될 것입니다. 저희는 시내 상업 지구를 쇼핑몰 같은 지역으로 바꾸는 데 무슨 가치가 있다는 건지 모르겠습니다. 게다가 완공되면 저희 고객을 위한 주차 공간이 50% 더 적어질 것입니다. 아마 시내 지역에 성형수술이 정말 필요할지도 모르겠지만, 지역 경제를 파괴하는 때는 그렇지 않을 겁니다. 저희의 반대를 이해해주셔서 감사합니다. 귀하의 입장을 재고해주실 것을 희망합니다.

진심을 담아,

Marvin Quackenbush 드림

구문 [2행~5행] Although we agree with *your previous editorials* (opposing parking meters in downtown Augusta), we are not in agreement with your editorial on October 18.

( )은 your previous editorials를 수식하는 분사구이다.

[15행~17행] Perhaps the downtown area **does** need cosmetic surgery, **but not** when it devastates the area's economy.

does는 동사 need를 강조하는 강조용법으로 쓰였다. but not은 'but the downtown area does not need cosmetic surgery'를 함축한다.

어휘 editorial 사설; 편집의 **parking meter** 주차 요금 징수기 **in agreement with** ~와 일치하여 **resurface** 표면 처리를 다시 하다 **irreversibly** 되돌릴 수 없게 **disrupt** 중단시키다, 방해하다 **cosmetic surgery** 성형 수술 **devastate** 완전히 파괴하다, 황폐시키다 **position** (특정 주제에 대한) 입장[태도]; 위치, 장소

---

2 필자 주장 　　　　⑤

해설 미디어의 정보 편향은 의도적이라기보다는 불가피한 것이라 없앨 수는 없으며, 이에 대항할 수 있는 방법은 가능한 한 여러 출처에서 정보를 얻는 것이라는 내용의 글이므로 필자의 주장으로 가장 적절한 것은 ⑤이다.

해석 텔레비전, 인터넷, 라디오와 인쇄물의 정보는 총괄하여 '대중 매체'로 칭해지며 현대 사회에 담뿍 스며들어있다. 몇몇 비평가들에 따르면 매체는 기자와 미디어 소유주가 특정 집단이나 이익을 지지하여 뉴스 기사를 편향되게 제시할 수 있게 하는 다수의 정교하고 세련된 기법을 사용할 수 있다. 편향은 뉴스 기사의 초점을 특정 방향으로 돌리는 미묘한 성향 혹은 관점이다. 많은 기자들은 참된 객관성은 불가능하며, 편향이 사실 제시에 실제로 영향을 미칠 수 있지만 편향된 미디어는 해로운 의도를 가지고 만들어지는 것은 아니라고 주장한다. 어느 정도의 편향은 불가피하다는 견해를 갖고 있는 기자들은 편향을 제거하기보다는 제한하고 가능한 한 균형 잡힌 견해를 제시할 것을 목표로 한다. 미디어 편향에 대한 최고의 방어는 폭넓고 다양한 출처에서 정보를 얻는 것이다. 정보를 얻기 위해 하나의 미디어 출처에만 의존하는 것은 잘못된 정보를 받게 되는 파국의 길이라는 것은 머리를 안 써도 알 만한 문제이다.

구문 [12행~15행] *Journalists* (holding <u>the view</u> that some degree of bias is inevitable) / aim <u>to limit</u> **rather than** eliminate bias <u>and</u> to present as **balanced a view as possible**.

주어는 Journalists이고 동사는 aim이다. ( )는 Journalists를 능동의 의미로 수식하는 형용사구이다. that~inevitable은 the view에 대한 동격절이다. aim 다음에 to

---

limit와 to present가 and로 연결되어 병렬구조를 이룬다. 「A rather than B」는 'B 라기보다는 A'의 뜻이다. as balanced a view as possible에서 「as ~ as possible」은 '가능한 한 ~한'의 뜻이며, as 다음에는 「as 형용사 a 명사 as」의 어순을 따른다.

[17행~19행] It's a no-brainer **that** relying on one media source for information *is* a slippery slope to being misinformed.
It은 가주어이고 that 이하가 진주어이다. that절에서 relying on ~ information은 동명사 주어이고 is가 동사이다.

어휘 collectively 총괄하여, 집합적으로 **term** 칭하다; 기간; 학기 saturate 스며들게 하다; 포화시키다, 흠뻑 적시다 **employ** 사용하다 elaborate 정교한 sophisticated 세련된 an array of 다수의 in favor of ~을 지지[찬성]하여 bias 편향 subtle 미묘한 leaning 성향 intent 의도, 의향 inevitable 불가피한 no-brainer 쉬운 문제 slippery slope 파멸에 이르는 길; 미끄러운 비탈길 misinformed 잘못된 정보를 받은

3 밑줄 함의   ④

해설 많은 사람들이 큰 노력 없이 갑자기 유명해져서 많은 돈을 벌고 행복한 결말을 맺는 작가들이 있다고 믿지만, J.K. Rowling이나 Amanda Hocking의 경우처럼 책이 나오기까지는 오랜 시간과 노력이 들어간다는 것이 글의 요지이다. 그러므로 우리가 믿지 말아야 할 '가장 큰 글쓰기의 신화'는 ④ '어떤 작가들은 큰 노력 없이 하룻밤 사이에 성공한다.'이다.
① 작가의 슬럼프에 대한 단 하나의 치료법은 없다.
② 작가가 해야 할 일은 책을 출판하는 것뿐이다.
③ 작가들은 출판 시장에 의해 영향을 받는다.
⑤ 유명해지기 전에 작가는 작문에 시간을 들인다.

해석 갑자기 유명해져서 책으로 수백만 달러를 벌고 전설적 이야기의 행복한 결말을 맺는 작가들이 있는 것 같다. 그런 일은 아이디어와 약간의 노력만이 필요하다고 생각하는 것은 솔깃한 일이다. 사실 정말 솔깃하다. 그러나 책을 쓰는 것은 시간, 몇 달, 때로는 몇 년이 걸리는데, 아마도 당신이 출판한 첫 번째 책이 이때까지 쓴 첫 번째 책은 아닐 것이다. 당신의 기술을 완벽하게 익히고, 글쓰기를 속속들이 배우고, 문체를 발전시키고, 탄탄한 줄거리를 쓰는 법을 배운 다음, 당신이 작품을 완성했을 때 모든 것을 판매하기 위한 적절한 방법을 알게 되는 데는 시간이 걸린다. J.K. Rowling은 수년 동안 'Harry Potter'를 세심히 기획하고 집필했으며 출판되기 전에 수십 건의 거절을 받았다. Amanda Hocking 또한 자기 출판계에서 크게 성공하기 전에 자신의 기술을 익히고 출판하려고 애쓰면서 몇 년을 보냈다. 그러한 명단은 계속된다. 가장 큰 글쓰기의 신화를 믿지 마라.

구문 [5행~8행] But writing a book takes time — months, sometimes years — and chances are (that) *the first book* [**that** you publish] won't be *the first book* [(that) you ever write].
접속사 and가 앞뒤로 두 개의 절을 연결한다. and 다음에 나오는 절의 보어로 생략된 접속사 that이 이끄는 명사절이 나온다. 관계대명사 that이 이끄는 두 개의 [ ] 부분은 각각 선행사 the first book을 수식하고 두 번째 [ ] 안의 관계대명사 that은 생략되었다.

[8행~11행] It takes time to perfect your craft, to learn the ins and outs of writing, to develop your writing style and (to) learn how to write a solid plot and then (to) learn *the proper way* (**to market** it all when you've finished).
굵게 표시된 it은 가주어이고, 진주어인 밑줄 친 to부정사구를 콤마(,)와 and가 병렬 연결한다. to market 이하는 형용사적 용법으로 앞에 있는 명사 the proper way를 수식한다.

어휘 come out of nowhere (무명에서) 갑자기 유명해지다[입신하다] ride off into the sunset 행복한 결말을 맺다 tempting 솔깃한; 유혹[매력]적인 chances are 아마

도 ~일 것이다 craft 기술, 기교: 공예 ins and outs 구석구석: 여당과 야당 solid 탄탄한; 견고한; 고체의 plot 줄거리; 음모 market 판매하다; 시장에 내다; 시장 dozens of 수십의, 많은 make it big 크게 성공하다 self-publishing 자기 출판 ((원고 집필부터 편집·인쇄·배본까지 모든 것을 스스로 하여 자신의 책을 출판하는 일)) writer's block 작가의 슬럼프, 글 길 막힘 overnight 하룻밤 사이의; 갑자기

4 글의 제목   ⑤

해설 3차 산업 혁명에 이르면서 지식 노동자들이 더 중요한 집단이 되고 경영진과 투자자가 가진 권한을 그들과 점차 공유하게 되었다. 일부 산업에서는 지적 재산권이 더 중요하고 지식 독점이 시장에서의 성공을 보장한다면서 자금 조달은 부차적인 것이 된다고 했으므로 글의 제목으로는 ⑤ '3차 산업 혁명에서 지식과 아이디어의 힘'이 가장 적절하다.
① 산업에서 지적 재산권 대 노동자의 영향력
② 산업 혁명에서 왜 노동자가 중요하게 되었는가?
③ 3차 산업 혁명에서 어떻게 지식이 습득되는가
④ 초기 산업 시대의 경제 성장에서 노동자의 역할

해석 초기 산업 시대에서 금융 자본과 생산 수단을 통제했던 사람들은 경제의 운용에 있어 거의 전적인 지배력을 행사했다. 지난 세기의 중반 몇십 년 동안에 잠깐, 그들은 그 힘의 일부를 노동자와 공유해야 했는데, 생산에서 그들(노동자들)의 중대한 역할은 사업하는 방식과 수단 그리고 이익의 분배 양쪽 모두를 지배하는 결정에서 노동자에게 어느 정도의 영향력을 보장했다. 이제 노동자의 영향력이 현저히 감소하면서, 지식 노동자들이 경제 방정식에서 더 중요한 집단이 되었다. 그들은 3차 산업 혁명의 촉매제이고 최첨단 기술 경제를 지속시키는 데 책임이 있는 사람들이다. 그 때문에, 최고 경영진과 투자자들은 자신들의 권한 중 최소한 일부를 지적 재산의 창작자들, 즉 첨단 정보 사회에 연료를 공급하는 지식과 아이디어를 가진 남녀와 점점 더 공유해야 했다. 그러므로 일부 산업에서 지적 재산권이 금융보다 훨씬 더 중요해진 것은 당연하다. 지식과 아이디어에 대한 독점권을 갖는 것은 경쟁력 있는 성공과 시장 지위를 보장한다. 그 성공을 위한 자금 조달은 거의 부차적인 것이 된다.

구문 [4행~9행] For a while, during the mid-decades of the past century, / they had to share some of that power with *labor*, // **whose** critical role in production assured it some clout in *decisions* (governing both the ways and means of doing business and the distribution of profits).
계속적 용법으로 쓰인 소유격 관계대명사 whose가 이끄는 절은 앞에 나온 labor를 보충 설명한다. ( )는 decisions를 수식하는 분사구이다.

[11행~14행] They are the catalysts of the Third Industrial Revolution ⎡and⎤ *the ones* (responsible **for keeping** the high-tech economy **running**).
( )는 the ones를 수식하는 형용사구이다. 전치사 for 다음에는 「keep O v-ing」가 쓰여 'O가 계속 v하게 하다'를 의미한다.

어휘 era 시대 finance 금융, 자금; 자금을 조달하다 capital 자금; 자산; 대문자 means of production 생산 수단 exercise (영향력 등을) 행사하다 working 운용, 작동 labor (자본가·기업에 대하여) 노동자, 노동 계급 assure 보장[보증]하다 govern 지배[좌우]하다 distribution 분배 diminish 감소하다, 줄어들다 equation 방정식; 평형 상태 high-tech 최첨단의 intellectual property 지적 재산 fuel ~에 연료를 공급하다[활기를 불어넣다] it is no wonder that ~은 당연하다[전혀 놀랄 일이 아니다] competitive 경쟁력 있는; 경쟁의 secondary 부차[이차]적인

----

5 도표 이해 ④

해설 2018년 방문객 평균 지출 1위인 두바이 바로 다음 도시는 싱가포르($272)가 아닌 파리($296)이다.

해석 2018년 세계 10대 행선지 도시
위 표는 국제 숙박 여행 방문객과 하루당 평균 지출로 본 2018년 세계 10대 행선지 도시들을 보여준다. ① 2018년 10대 도시의 인기 순위에서 세 도시인 방콕, 두바이, 싱가포르는 2017년과 순위 변동이 없었다. ② 2018년에 방콕은 최고의 행선지였으며, 파리와 런던이 그 뒤를 이었고, 두바이와 싱가포르가 각각 4위와 5위 자리로 마무리했다. ③ 안탈리아는 2017년에서 2018년까지 방문객 수에서 10대 도시 중 가장 큰 증가를 보였던 반면 런던은 감소를 보였다. ④ 하루당 평균 지출의 측면에서 보면 두바이가 미화 553달러로 세계 10대 도시에서 선두를 달렸고, 이 뒤를 바로 잇는 곳은 싱가포르로 미화 272달러였다(→ 파리, 미화 296달러). ⑤ 반면에 10대 도시 중에서 안탈리아는 2018년 국제 숙박 여행 방문객이 가장 적은 돈을 지출한 도시였다.

구문 [5행~8행] In 2018, Bangkok was the top destination, **followed by Paris and London**, with <u>Dubai and Singapore</u> **wrapping up** the fourth and fifth spots respectively.
followed by Paris and London 수동의 의미의 분사구문이며 followed by는 '뒤이어[잇달아] ~가 나온다'는 의미이다. 「with+O+v-ing」 분사구문은 'O가 v한 채로[v하면서/v하여]'의 뜻이다.

어휘 overnight (짧은) 숙박 여행용의; 밤을 새는 wrap up 마무리 짓다 respectively 각각

6 내용 불일치 ⑤

해설 마지막 문장에서 Melville은 사후에야 비로소 미국 문학계에 영향력을 가지게 되었다는 진술이 나오므로, 노년에 명성을 떨쳤다는 ⑤가 일치하지 않는다.

해석 Herman Melville은 〈Moby Dick〉이라는 이름의 걸작으로 가장 잘 알려진 미국 작가였다. 그는 또한 평생 많은 단편소설, 시, 그리고 수필을 저술했다. 그는 1819년 뉴욕 시에서 태어났다. 1826년에 Herman Melville의 아버지가 예상치 못한 병으로 사망했고, 그 해 그는 성홍열에 걸려서 시력이 영구적으로 손상되었다. 12살부터 그는 점원과 농장 일꾼으로 일했다. 1841년에 22세의 나이로 Herman Melville은 남양으로 향하는 뉴잉글랜드 포경선인 Acushnet호에 승선하여 출항했다. 이것과 몇몇 그 이후의 항해의 경험은 〈Moby Dick〉을 포함한 여섯 편의 해양 소설에 대한 기반으로서의 역할을 하게 되었다. Herman Melville은 1891년에 72세의 나이로 사망했다. 그의 가장 유명한 작품들은 그의 사후에야 비로소 문학에 중대한 영향을 미치게 되었다.

구문 [15행~16행] His most famous pieces of work / did **not** have a significant impact on literature **until** after his death.
「not A until B」는 'B하고서야 비로소 A하다'의 뜻이다.

어휘 masterpiece 걸작 author 저술하다 contract (병에) 걸리다 permanently 영구적으로 farmhand 농장 일꾼 set sail 출항하다 aboard ~에 타고 whaler 고래잡이 배, 포경선 the South Seas 남양 subsequent 그 다음의 voyage 항해 serve as ~의 역할을 하다 basis 기반 literature 문학

7 밑줄 어법 ③

해설 ③ 분사 navigating을 그대로 두면 앞에 나온 명사 a teacher를 수식하게 되어 문장 전체의 주어 역할을 하는 명사절인 how절에 동사가 없게 된다. navigates

---

로 고치면 How ~ situations가 주절이 되고 문장의 동사는 is, 보어는 significant가 되어 쓰임이 적절하다.
① 주어가 단수형의 명사구 The pedagogical tradition이므로 단수형의 동사 has의 쓰임이 적절하다.
② 주격관계대명사 which가 이끄는 절이 turn-taking을 수식하는 구조로서 쓰임이 적절하다.
④ 의미상의 주어가 it이므로 수동형을 표시하는 과거분사 done의 쓰임이 적절하다. If it is thoughtlessly done의 분사 구문으로 이해하면 이해가 쉽다. 이때 it은 학생들에게 손을 들라고 하는 상황에서 교사가 처리하는 방식을 뜻한다.
⑤ 앞의 to ensure와 as well as로 연결되는 병렬구조로서 to가 생략된 형태이다. both 이하가 목적어이다.

해석 수업에서 학생들에게 손을 들게 하는 교육적 전통은 교실의 질서를 세우고, 질문에 대답하는 것에 도움이 되는 규율 바른 분위기를 유지함으로써 학생들의 수업내용의 이해도를 검증하고, 그룹 토론을 촉진시키는 분명한 도구적인 목적을 가지고 있다. 그러나, 도덕적으로, 그것은(= 손을 들게 하는 것은) 공정성, 타인 존중, 인내심 그리고 자제력이란 이슈와 명확히 관련되는, 교대로 하는 것을 억제한다. 교사가 그런 늘 일어나는 상황(학생들에게 손을 들게 하는 상황)에서 어떻게 처리하는지가 윤리적으로 중요하다. 생각 없이 행해지면 차별하거나, 편들거나, 아니면 그저 학생들에게 신경을 쓰지 않는 교사의 이미지를 보이게 될지 모른다. 신중하게 행해지면, 교대로 하는 것은 교사로 하여금 다정하고 친절한 격려가 필요할 수 있는 목소리를 덜 내는 학생들과 목소리를 더 내어서 그들을 싫어하게 되어 다른 학생들의 괴롭힘의 대상이 될 수 있는 학생들 모두를 보호할 수 있게 할 뿐 아니라 공정한 참여도 확실히 할 수 있게 해 줄 수 있다.

구문 [13행~18행] [**Thoughtfully carried out**], turn-taking may enable the teacher to ensure fair participation as well as protect **both** {the less vocal **students** who may need some gentle and kindly encouragement} **and** {the more vocal **ones** who may become targeted for abuse by other students who grow to resent them}.
[ ] 부분은 분사구문으로 If it(= turn-taking) is thoughtfully carried out으로 바꾸어 쓸 수 있다. 두 개의 { } 부분은 '~과 … 둘 다'라는 뜻의 'both ~ and …' 구문으로 각각 A와 B에 해당이 된다. 두 번째 { } 부분에서 ones는 첫 번째 { }의 students를 대신하는 복수형 표시의 대명사이다.

어휘 instrumental 도구적인, 중요한 comprehension 이해, 이해력 content 내용 disciplined 규율 바른, 통제가 잘 된 facilitate 촉진시키다, 용이하게 하다 morally 도덕적으로 regulate 규제하다 turn-taking 교대로 하는 것, 순서 주고받기 inevitably 어쩔 수 없이, 필연적으로 fairness 공정성 navigate (힘들거나 복잡한 상황을) 처리하다, 다루다 routine 일상적인 ethically 윤리적으로 thoughtlessly 생각 없이 project 보여 주다, 나타내다 discriminate 차별하다 favour (부당하게) 편들다 abuse 괴롭힘, 학대 resent 싫어하다, 분개하다

8 밑줄 어휘 ④

해설 똑똑한 사람도 어리석게 행동할 수 있고, 한 분야에서 지적이라고 평가받는 사람이 다른 분야에서는 그렇지 못할 수 있다는 내용으로 보아 지능을 구성하는 다양한 주요 능력의 발달은 고르지 못하므로 ④는 uneven이나 inconsistent 등으로 바꾸어 써야 적절하다.

해석 이제부터 낮은 지능을 가진 보통 사람들의 행동을 생각해 보자. 우리는 그런 사람들을 ① 어리석다고 부르는 경향이 있다. 물론 그들이 우리보다 더 높은 지위를 차지하고 있는 것이 아닐 경우에 말이다! 그들은 우리의 관심을 받을 만한데, 그들이 때때로 중요한 사건들의 과정에 발휘하는 영향 때문에, 그리고 또한 정신의 가장 가치 있는 특성은 그것의 ② 결핍을 배경으로 했을 때만 온전히 인식되고 평가될 수 있기 때문이다. 게다가, 높은 수준의 지능이 보통인 사람조차도 때때로 피로나 격렬한 감정과 같은 요인의 영향 하

에 ③ 어리석은 방식으로 행동할 것이다. 지능을 구성하는 다양한 주요 능력의 발달은 대체로 ④ 일관된(→ 고르지 못한) 것으로 또한 알려져 있다. 그러므로 유창한 화술과 재치로 인해 똑똑하다고 평가받는 사람이 수와 관련된, 또는 지각과 관련된 자료를 다루는 것에 있어서는 그다지 영리하다고 판명되지 못할 수도 있으며 그 반대도 마찬가지이다. 그런 이유로 전형적인 '어리석은' 행동에 대한 이해가 교육과 독학에서 실제로 ⑤ 중요할지도 모르는 것이다.

구문 [4행~6행] They deserve our attention because of *the influence* [(which[that]) they sometimes exert on the course of vital events], ~.

[ ] 부분은 생략된 목적격 관계대명사 which 또는 that이 이끄는 관계사절로 the influence를 수식한다.

[12행~15행] **It** is also known **that** the development of *various primary abilities*, **which** make up the intelligence, is largely uneven.

It은 가주어, that 이하가 진주어이다. which는 계속적 용법의 관계대명사로 which가 이끄는 절이 various primary abilities를 부연 설명한다.

어휘 intelligence 지능 occupy 차지하다: 점유하다 deserve ~을 받을 만하다: ~을 (당)해야 마땅하다 exert 발휘하다, 미치다 appreciate 평가하다: 이해하다: 감사(감상)하다 deficiency 결핍, 결함 fatigue 피로 primary 주요한: 기본적인 make up ~을 구성하다 consistent 일관된: 변함없는: 일치하는 on account of ~로 인해 [때문에] eloquence 유창한 화술, 웅변 numerical 수와 관련된 perceptual 지각(력)의 typical 전형적인, 대표적인 self-education 독학

9 빈칸 추론 ①

해설 동일한 음료에 대해 고지방 고칼로리 음료라고 인지하고 마셨을 때와 저지방 저칼로리 음료라고 인지하고 마셨을 때, 식욕 조절 호르몬인 그렐린의 수치와 패턴에 변화가 있었으므로 음식에 대한 믿음은 ① '생명 작용'에도 영향을 미치는 것이라고 할 수 있다.

② 행동   ③ 정체성
④ 건강   ⑤ 몸무게

해석 음식에 대한 우리의 믿음은 우리가 내리는 선택뿐만 아니라 우리의 생명 작용에도 영향을 미친다. 예일대 연구자들은 실험 참가자들에게 두 개의 셰이크를 주었다. 하나는 고지방, 620칼로리 '탐닉하는' 셰이크라는 라벨이 붙어있었고, 다른 하나는 저지방, 130칼로리 '합리적인 셰이크'라는 라벨이 붙어있었다. 사실 그 두 셰이크는 동일했다. 그러나 하나는 탐닉(라벨에서 언급하기를 '병 속의 천국')이고 반면에 다른 하나는 더 건강한 선택이라는 참가자들의 믿음은 셰이크에 대한 그들의 신체 반응에 강력한 영향을 미쳤다. 식욕을 자극하는 호르몬인 그렐린의 수치가 '탐닉하는' 셰이크를 마신다는 기대로 가파르게 상승했다가 그 후에 급격하게 떨어졌는데, 이는 그 음료가 만족스러웠음을 나타냈다. '합리적인' 셰이크로는 그렐린 수치가 상대적으로 평탄한 상태로 남아있거나 기대로 겨우 약간만 상승했고, 그 후에 가파르게 떨어지지 않았는데, 이는 그 음료가 만족스럽지 않았다는 것을 나타냈다. 셰이크의 내용물은 같았지만, 참가자들의 믿음이 그들의 식욕 조절 호르몬을 변화시켰다.

구문 [6행~10행] Yet the participants' belief that one was an indulgence — "heaven in a bottle," the label noted — while the other was a healthier choice / had powerful effects on their bodies' response to the shakes.

밑줄 친 두 부분은 동격 관계이다.

[10행~14행] Levels of ghrelin, *a hormone* [that stimulates appetite], **rose** steeply / in anticipation of drinking the "indulgent" shake / and then **fell** sharply afterward, / **indicating** that the drink was satisfying.

ghrelin과 a hormone ~ appetite는 동격 관계이다. [ ]는 관계사절로 a hormone을 수식한다. 동사 rose와 fell은 and로 연결되어 병렬구조를 이룬다. indicating 이하는 분사구문이며 indicating의 의미상 주어는 앞 문장 전체이다.

어휘 identical 동일한   note 언급하다   stimulate 자극하다   appetite 식욕   steeply 가파르게   anticipation 기대: 예상   sensible 합리적인. 분별력 있는   regulation 조절

10 빈칸 추론 ①

해설 인간은 사용하지 않으면 닳아버리는 기계라거나, 인간의 에너지는 사용함으로써 존재한다는 등의 표현을 통해 우리 인간은 ① '에너지를 사용함으로써 에너지를 얻는다'는 결론을 내릴 수 있다.

② 만약을 대비해 에너지를 비축한다
③ 정기 검진을 받아야 한다
④ 휴식을 통해서 정신적 안정을 얻는다
⑤ 운동하는 습관을 들여야 한다

해석 인간은 사용하지 '않으면' 닳아버리는 기계 같은 것이다. 물론 신체적 한계가 있고 우리는 건강에 유익한 휴식과 이완을 '정말로' 필요로 하지만, 대부분 우리는 에너지를 사용함으로써 에너지를 얻는다. 흔히, 신체적 피로의 최상의 치료법은 30분의 유산소 운동이다. 마찬가지로, 정신적 그리고 영적인 무관심은 결연한 행동, 또는 행동하려는 명백한 의도에 의해 치료되는 경우가 자주 있다. 우리는 고등학교 물리 시간에 운동 에너지가 움직임의 면에서 측정된다고 배운다. 그와 동일한 것이 인간의 에너지에도 적용된다. 즉, 인간의 에너지는 사용함으로써 존재하게 되는 것이다. 당신은 그것을 비축해 둘 수 없다. 게슈탈트 심리 요법의 창시자인 Frederich S. Perls는 "나는 저장되고 싶지 않다. 나는 '쓰이고' 싶다."고 말하곤 했다. 아마도 우리 모두는 우리가 이용하기를 바라는 것보다 더 많은 엄청난 양의 잠재 에너지를 가지고 있을 것이다.

어휘 wear out ~을 지치게 하다; 닳대[낡다] *cf.* weariness 권태, 피로   aerobic 유산소 운동의, 에어로빅의   spiritual 정신적인, 영적인; 종교적인   indifference 무관심, 무심   decisive 결정적인, 결단력 있는   kinetic 운동의, 운동에 의해 생기는   in terms of ~의 면에서, ~에 관하여   come into existence 생기다, 나타나다   stockpile 비축량; ~을 비축하다   may well 아마도[틀림없이] ~일 것이다; ~하는 것도 당연하다
[선택지 어휘] a rainy day 비 오는 날; 만일의 경우, 궁할 때   check-up 건강 진단

11 빈칸 추론 ③

해설 음향 시설에서 울리는 소리는 울림이 너무 적어도, 또 너무 많아도 가청도에 좋지 않은 영향을 주므로, 음향 디자인에서 가장 중요한 것은 ③ '이러한 울림이 완전히 잦아드는 데 걸리는 시간'이 되어야 한다.

① 특정 방이나 공간의 계획된 목적
② 공간 속에서 만들어질 음량
④ 모든 가청 소리의 완벽한 제거
⑤ 울리는 소리가 청중과 얼마나 많이 상호작용하는가

해석 거의 모든 사람들이 어떤 종류의 라이브 음악을 듣는 것을 즐긴다. 하지만 우리들 중에서 콘서트홀과 강의실의 음향 시설 디자인에 투입되는 복잡한 과정을 알고 있는 사람은 거의 없다. 소리의 가청도가 주된 고려 사항인 어떠한 건물의 디자인에서라도, 건축가는 그들이 사용하는 공간과 재료를 장소의 의도된 목적에 주의 깊게 맞추어야 한다. 한 가지 문제는 소리의 강도가 밀폐된 공간에서 너무 빠르게 쌓일지도 모른다는 것이다. 또 다른 문제는 우리가 어떤 큰 방이나 강당에서 듣는 소리의·오직 일부만이 음원으로부터 직접 나온다는 것이다. 그것의 많은 양은 그것이 울리는 소리(벽, 천장과 바닥으로부터 튀어서 반사된 후 청자에게 오게 되는 소리)로서 벽, 천장과 바닥으로부터 튀어서 반사된 지 1초의 몇 분의 1 후에 우리에게 도달한다. 각각의 방이 소리를 얼마나 많이 울릴지는 그것의 규모와 그것의 내용물이 소리를 흡수하는 능력에 달려있다. 너무 적은 울림은 음악을 가늘고 허약하게 들리게 할 수 있다. 너무 많은 울림은 하나의 음표가 어디에서 끝나고 다음 음표는 어디에서 시작되는지에 대한 청자의 감각을 흐리게 할 수 있다. 결과적으로 음

향 디자인의 가장 중요한 요소는 이러한 울림이 완전히 잦아드는 데 걸리는 시간이다.

구문 [4행~7행] In the design of *any building* [where audibility of sound is a major consideration], architects have to carefully **match** ***the space and materials*** [(which[that]) they use} **to** the intended purpose of the venue.

[ ]은 any building을 수식한다. 'match A to B'는 'A를 B에 맞추다'의 뜻이다. { }은 앞에 목적격 관계대명사 which[that]가 생략되어 the space and materials 를 수식한다.

[9행~11행] Another problem is **that** only part of *the sound* [(which[that]) we hear in any large room or auditorium] **comes** directly from the source.

that절의 주어는 only part이고 동사는 comes이며, [ ]은 앞에 목적격 관계대명사 which[that]가 생략되어 the sound를 수식한다.

[15행~17행] [How much each room reverberates] *depends* upon **both** its size **and** **the ability of its contents to absorb** sound.

[ ]은 주어이고 depends가 동사이다. 'both A and B'는 'A와 B 둘 다'의 뜻이다. 'the ability of A to-v'는 '~할 수 있는 A의 능력'의 뜻이다.

어휘 acoustics 음향 효과   audibility 가청도   venue 장소   intensity 강도   enclose 봉하다   auditorium 강당   fraction 부분, 분수   ceiling 천장   absorb 흡수하다   blur 흐리게 하다   note 음표   acoustic 음향의

12 빈칸 추론   ③

해설 실생활 속에서 학습하는 어린이들은 다양한 정보를 습득하고 대응 전략도 풍부하게 갖춰놓을 수 있지만, 텔레비전으로만 학습한 어린이들은 TV에서 보이는 단일한 모형만을 습득하고 활용할 수 있어서 실생활에서 활용할 수 있는 대응 전략이 부족해진다. 이렇게 텔레비전이 아동 발달에 부정적인 영향을 미치는 결정 요인은 실생활 학습과 비교하여 압도적으로 부족할 수밖에 없는 ③ '어린이가 축적해 온 정보나 경험의 양'이다.
① 어린이들을 교육하기 위해 고안된 다양한 교육 전략
② 어린이가 속한 사회적, 문화적, 정치적 상황
④ 학교가 책임을 맡아야 하는 사회 목표
⑤ 학교와 교실 수준에서 소셜 미디어 학습의 증가

해석 텔레비전의 사회적 영향에 있어서 발달상의 차이의 한 가지 결정 요인은 어린이가 축적해 온 정보나 경험의 양이다. 어린이들이 발달함에 따라 그들은 다양한 사람들, 행동 그리고 규범에 노출된다. 이것은 그들이 수행하거나 의견을 말할 기회가 있을 때 다양한 선택을 제공한다. 예를 들어, 'Sesame Street'에서만 푸에르토리코 사람과 마주치는 어린이들은 그들과의 상호작용이 항상 화기애애하다고 학습하고, 그것을 실제 푸에르토리코 사람과의 첫 만남을 위한 모델로 사용할 것이다. 대조적으로, 푸에르토리코 소수 민족 거주지 가까운 곳에서 성장하는 어린이는 푸에르토리코 사람들과 교류할 수 있는 다양한 방법에 대해 훨씬 더 많이 이해할 것이다. 바라건대, 'Sesame Street'가 이 어린이에게도 정보를 제공해 주겠지만, 그 정보는 상호작용을 위한 단일 모델을 제공하기보다는 다른 관련 정보와 함께 나와야 존재를 인정받을 것이다.

구문 [10행~13행] In contrast, *a child* [who grows up close to a Puerto Rican enclave] **will understand** much more about *the variety of ways* [in which he or she could interact with Puerto Ricans].

첫 번째 [ ]은 관계대명사 who가 이끄는 관계사절로 주어 a child를 수식하며 문장의 동사는 will understand이다. 두 번째 [ ]은 '전치사+관계대명사'형태의 in which 가 이끄는 관계사절로 the variety of ways를 수식한다.

[14행~17행] Hopefully, *Sesame Street* will provide information for this child too, but the information will take its place alongside other relevant information **rather than** providing the single model for interaction.

「A rather than B」는 'B라기보다는 차라리 A'의 뜻인데, 의미상 A는 'alongside ~ information'부분에, B는 'providing ~ interaction'부분에 대응된다.

어휘 determinant 결정 요인   mature 발달하다, 성숙하다; 성숙한   norm 규범   a range of 다양한   encounter 우연히 마주치다   cordial 화기애애한, 다정한   hopefully 바라건대, 잘만 되면   take one's place 존재를 인정받다   alongside ~와 함께; ~와 나란히   assume (책임을) 맡다; 추정하다

13 흐름 무관 문장   ③

해설 모바일 크라우드 센싱이 낯선 곳을 여행하는 관광객에게 유용할 수 있다는 내용의 글인데, ③은 기기를 인터넷에 연결한다고 기기의 정보가 공유되는 것은 아니라는 내용이므로, 정보 공유가 이롭게 사용되는 경우를 소개한 나머지 글의 내용과 맞지 않다.

해석 스마트 시티를 위한 모바일 크라우드 센싱은 도시 환경 속에서 효율적이고 안전하며 친환경적인 이동성을 지원해 줄 수 있다. ① 전 세계 사람들이 가지고 다니는 모바일 기기가 도처에 있다는 것을 고려해 보면, 사물인터넷을 통한 소셜 모바일 크라우드 센싱에 의해 관광객들은 목적지에서 벌어지는 인기 있는 행사들에 대해 알 수 있고, 다른 장소에 있는 다른 관광객들과의 상호 피드백을 제공할 수 있으며, 특정한 시간에 가기에 가장 좋은 장소, 지역 일기 예보, 그리고 예상 이동 시간을 하루 종일 보여줄 수 있다. ② 여기서 크라우드 소싱은 사람들에게 대안 경로를 찾아야 할지, 언제 관광지나 식당에 도착하는 것이 가장 좋은지, 여행 중에 불쾌한 뜻밖의 일을 어떻게 피해야 할지, 어디에 주차해야 할지, 그리고 어떤 대중교통 방법이 가장 좋을지에 대해 알려 줄 수 있다. ③ 가장 중요한 것은, 인터넷에 기기를 연결하는 것이 그것의 정보가 보편적으로 이용 가능해지고 공유된다는 것을 의미하진 않는다는 점이다. ④ 환경 센서들은 또한 공기나 소음 공해의 정도를 알려줄 수도 있다. ⑤ 이것은 낯선 장소에 있는 관광객들이 아는 바가 많은 현지인들이 내릴 수 있는 것보다 훨씬 더 나은 결정을 할 수 있게 한다.

구문 [3행~10행] **Given** the ubiquity of *mobile devices* (carried by people worldwide), social mobile crowd sensing through the IoT can allow tourists to know about popular events in a destination, provide interactive feedback with other tourists at different locations, reveal {the best places to be at a certain time}, {local weather forecasts}, and {expected travel times} throughout the day.

'Given ~,'은 분사구문으로 '~을 고려하면'의 뜻이다. ( )은 수동의 의미로 mobile devices를 수식하고, 조동사 can 다음에 밑줄 친 세 부분의 동사구가 병렬구조를 이룬다. 세 번째 밑줄 친 부분에서 세 개의 동사구 { }은 다시 병렬구조를 이루며 reveal의 목적어 역할을 한다.

[19행~21행] This **enables** *tourists* (in unfamiliar places) **to make** even better decisions than well-informed locals might take.

「enable+목적어+to-v(목적어가 v하는 것을 가능하게 하다)」의 SVOC 구조로, 목적어 tourists를 전명구 ( )가 수식한다.

어휘 mobility 이동성   given ~을 고려하면   ubiquity 도처에 있음   IoT(Internet of Things) 사물인터넷 ((여러 사물에 정보통신기술이 융합되어 실시간으로 데이터를 인터넷으로 주고받는 기술))   alternative route 대안 경로, 우회 도로   attraction 명소   noise pollution 소음 공해   well-informed 잘 알고 있는, 박식한

14 글의 순서 ④

해설 나이 든 벌들의 뇌가 꼭 좋은 쪽으로 변하는 것은 아니라는 주어진 글 다음에는 그 내용을 예시로 든 (C)가 나와야 한다. (C)의 한 달간의 공백(a month-long gap)이 어떤 의미인지를 상술하는 (A)가 이어지는데, 이때 (C)의 새로운 여왕벌(a new queen)을 the new queen으로 받는다. 나이 든 벌들이 돌아와 양성소 일벌의 일을 한다는 내용의 (A) 이후에 그 벌들의 뇌가 젊은 뇌처럼 작동한다는 내용의 (B)가 마지막으로 오는 것이 적절하다.

해석 더 나이 든 벌들이 벌집 밖에서 꿀과 꽃가루를 모으기 시작하면, 그것들의 뇌가 변화하는데, 꼭 좋은 쪽으로 변하는 것은 아니다.
(C) 예를 들어, 그것들이 벌집의 주변을 외운 후에는, 새로운 것을 학습하는 능력을 잃는다. 보통은 그것들은 죽을 때까지 그렇게 지낸다. 그렇지만 가끔 '정상적인 것'이 중단되기도 하는데, 예를 들어 한 벌집에 사는 벌떼들이 새로운 여왕벌을 키워야 한다면, 새로운 벌들이 부화하기 전까지는 한 달간의 공백이 생길 수 있다.
(A) 보통 그것은 새로운 여왕벌이 낳은 유충들이 자신들을 돌볼 수 있을 양성소의 젊은 일벌을 갖지 못해서 죽게 된다는 것을 의미한다. 그런 경우, 들판으로 나간 몇몇 벌들이 돌아와 양성소 일벌의 일을 한다.
(B) 여기에서 흥미로워지는데, Arizona 주립 대학의 연구자들은 유충을 기르는 일로 돌아가는 것은 그것들의 늙은 뇌를 젊은 뇌처럼 다시 작동하게 하여 그것들의 정신적인 민첩성과 학습 능력을 회복시킨다는 것을 발견했다.

구문 [4행~6행] Normally, that would **mean** (that) *the larvae* (from the new queen) wouldn't have *young nursery workers* (available to take care of them), and they'd die.
동사 mean의 목적어로 생략된 접속사 that이 이끄는 절이 쓰였다. from the new queen은 전명구로 the larvae를, available ~ them은 형용사구로 young nursery workers를 수식한다.
[9행~13행] ~ researchers from Arizona State University *discovered* **that** going back to larvae-rearing **makes** *their old brains* **work** again like young brains, **restoring** their mental agility and ability to learn.
discovered의 목적어로 쓰인 that이 이끄는 절 내에서 「사역동사(makes)+목적어(their old brains)+원형부정사(work)」의 구조가 쓰였다. restoring 이하는 that절의 내용에 대해 부가적인 설명을 하는 분사구문이다.

어휘 nectar 꿀 pollen 꽃가루 hive 벌집; (한 벌집에 사는) 벌떼 nursery 양성소; 육아실; 보육 학교 rear 기르다, 양육하다 restore 회복하다 surroundings 주변, (주위) 환경 disrupt 중단시키다; 방해하다 gap (시간적) 공백; 틈 hatch 부화하다

15 글의 순서 ③

해설 통계가 유의미하려면 집단 크기가 중요하다는 도입 내용과 함께 20명 크기의 집단을 예로 든 주어진 글에 이어 However로 시작하여 작은 표본으로 조사할 때의 문제점에 대해 언급한 (B)가 와야 하고, 이와 대조가 되는 집단의 표본 크기가 클 때의 내용이 시작되는 (A)가 그 다음에 와야 하며, (A)에 대한 추가적인 설명이 이어지는 (C)가 마지막에 오는 것이 자연스럽다.

해석 통계적 유의미성에 관한 한, 비교되고 있는 집단의 크기가 중요하다. 예를 들어, 10명의 운동을 잘하는 친구들과 10명의 소파에 앉아 TV만 보며 많은 시간을 보내는 친구들에 대한 조사가 당신에게 무릎의 질환이 운동의 참여와 관련이 있었는지에 대한 약간의 통찰력을 줄 수 있을 것이다.
(B) 그러나 다섯 명의 운동선수와 두 명의 소파에 앉아 TV만 보며 많은 시간을 보내는 사람들이 무릎 통증을 호소한다면, 이것은 무릎 통증이 운동 참여와 관련이 있다는 충분한 증거가 될 것인가? 실제로는 그렇게 작은 집단의 크기로는 그 차이가 쉽사리 우연에 의

해 생겼을 수도 있기 때문에 그렇지 않을 수도 있다.
(A) 반면에, 1,000명의 운동선수와 1,000명의 소파에 앉아 TV만 보며 많은 시간을 보내는 사람들이 무작위로 선택되어 조사되었고, 운동선수 500명과 운동하지 않는 사람 200명이 무릎 통증이 있다면, 이것은 무릎 통증과 운동 참여 사이에 상관관계가 존재한다는 훨씬 더 강력한 증거가 될 것이다.
(C) 이렇게 큰 표본 크기가 있으면, 50퍼센트/20퍼센트 통계치는 더 작은 집단에서 그랬으리라고, 그 결과를 잘못된 방향으로 이끄는 소수의 특이한 사람들 때문일 수는 없을 것이다.

구문 [10행~12행] ~ this would be much stronger evidence // that a correlation existed between knee pain and participation in sports.
evidence와 that ~ in sports는 서로 동격을 이룬다.
[19행~22행] With such a large sample size, / the 50 percent/20 percent statistic could not be / due to *a few unusual people* (throwing off the result), // **as** could have been the case with the smaller group.
( )는 형용사구로 앞의 a few unusual people을 수식한다. 접속사 as 뒤에 주어와 동사가 도치되었다. as가 '~처럼'의 의미로 쓰일 경우, 선택적으로 주어와 동사의 도치가 일어날 수 있다.

어휘 when it comes to A A에 관한 한 statistical 통계(상)의 *cf.* statistic 통계(치) significance 유의미성; 중요성 poll (여론) 조사; 조사하다; 투표 athletic 운동의; (몸이) 탄탄한, 건강한 *cf.* athlete 운동선수 couch potato 소파에 앉아 TV만 보며 많은 시간을 보내는(사람) be associated with ~와 관련이 있다 evidence 증거(물) by chance 우연히 correlation 상관관계, 연관성 throw off ~을 잘못된 방향으로 이끌다; ~을 털어내다[벗어 던지다]

16 문장 넣기 ②

해설 주어진 문장의 This가 차가운 침묵, 소란스러운 무례한 행동으로 나타난다고 하였으므로 이에 해당하는 내용은 ② 앞의 문장에서 설명된 회의 참여자들의 저항이다.

해석 대개 회의는 갈등을 해결하는 탁월한 방법이다. 그러나 참여자들이 안건, 절차 혹은 결과를 강하게 혐오하며, 진행되고 있는 일에 아무런 발언권을 갖지 못하는 것처럼 느낀다면 그들은 완강한 저항을 계속할 것이다. 이것은 회의를 진행하는 동안 차가운 침묵이나 소란스러운 무례한 행동으로, 혹은 정해진 결정에 대해 뒤에 고의적으로 무시하는 것으로 나타날 것이다. 그러므로 회의에서는 반드시 참여자들(의 말)이 경청되고 있다고 느끼게끔 하라. 논란이 될 만한 주제에 대해서라면 회의를 하기 전에 언제나 핵심 참여자들과 연락하라. 그들의 견해를 구하고, 당신의 목적을 설명하고 공정한 결과가 나오도록 당신이 헌신하겠다고 그들에게 확신을 심어주라. 무엇보다, 모든 사람이 자신에게 필요한 것을 얻게 하도록 '이것 아니면 저것'의 결과가 아니라 '둘 다, 함께'의 결과를 추구하라.

구문 [13행~15행] Most of all, / make sure / **that** you seek a "Both/And" result instead of an "Either/Or" result // **so that** everyone gets what they need.
that 이하는 make sure의 목적어 역할을 하는 명사절이며 so that은 '목적(~할 수 있도록)'을 나타내는 접속사로 쓰였다.

어휘 misbehavior 무례한 행동 deliberate 고의의, 의도적인 disregard 무시(하다) resolve 해결하다 say 발언권; 말하다 put up[offer] ~ resistance (~하게) 저항하다 stubborn 완강한, 고집스러운 get in touch with ~와 연락하다, 접촉하다 controversial 논란이 많은 assure A (that) A에게 (~라고) 장담하다 be dedicated to A A에 헌신하다 outcome 결과

17 문장 넣기 ③

해설 주어진 문장은 Wagner가 최고의 야구 선수였음에도 불구하고 소수의 야구 카드만 발매된 것에 대한 이유이며, did this는 ③ 앞에 있는 denied the tobacco companies the right to use his image를 가리킨다. 그리고 이보다 더 그럴듯한 이유가 ③ 다음에 이어지고 있으므로 주어진 문장은 ③에 들어가는 것이 적절하다.

해석 전 세계에서 가장 유명하고 가치가 높은 야구 카드는 T206 Honus Wagner 카드이다. 그것은 Wagner가 Pittsburgh Pirates에서 아직 선수 생활을 하고 있었던 1900년대 초반에 담뱃갑 속에 증정품으로 들어 있었다. Wagner는 역사상 가장 위대한 야구 선수 중 한 명이었지만, 그가 담배회사에 자신의 이미지를 사용하는 권리를 주지 않았기 때문에 극소수의 카드만이 발매되었다. (그 이유에 대한) 일반적인 이야기는 Wagner가 그 카드들이 어린 소년들의 흥미를 끌어서 그들이 흡연을 하도록 부추긴다는 것을 인식한 후에 이렇게 했다는 것이다. 보다 가능성 있는 이야기는 이전에 담배와 다른 담배 제품들을 홍보했던 Wagner가 회사에서 제공받은 보상에 만족하지 못했다는 것이다. 이유야 어쨌든, 약 40여 장의 카드만이 존재하는 것으로 알려져 있고, Wagner의 선수로서의 엘리트적 지위와 결합된 이 희소성이 그 카드를 야구 카드 수집가들의 성배로 만들었다. 그래서 최상의 상태인 카드 샘플들은 아마도 오늘날 경매나 개인 간의 거래에서 백만 달러 또는 그 이상의 가치가 나갈 수도 있다.

구문 [15행~18행] **Whatever** the reason (is), / about 40 of the cards are known to exist, // and this scarcity, / combined with Wagner's elite status as a player, / has made the card the holy grail of baseball card collectors.
No matter what(무엇이든지 간에)의 의미로 쓰이고 있는 Whatever가 부사절을 이끌며, 동사 is가 생략되어 있다. 삽입된 combined ~ player는 분사구문으로 앞에 있는 this scarcity를 보충 설명해 준다.

어휘 giveaway 증정품, 경품 issue 발매[발행]하다; 주제, 안건; 문제 deny 주지 않다, 거부하다; 부인하다 legend (전해오는) 이야기, 전설 appeal to ~의 흥미를 끌다, ~에게 매력적이다 encourage 부추기다, 조장하다; 격려[고무]하다 previously 이전에 promote 홍보하다; 촉진하다 compensation 보상(금) scarcity 희소성; 부족, 결핍 combined with ~와 결합된 status 지위; 신분, 자격 auction 경매; 경매로 팔다 private 개인의, 개인적인; 사적인 deal 거래(하다); 다루다

18 요약문 완성 ④

해설 실험에 따르면 피실험자들은 사건의 원고 측과 피고 측을 모의로 변호하도록 임의 배정되었을 때, 합당한 합의금에 대하여 각각 자신이 변호한 측에 유리한 금액을 제시했다. 즉 아무리 임의 배정된 것일지라도 자신이 어느 편에 소속(belonging)되었는지에 따라 편향된(biased) 판단을 내렸다.
① 공정함 - 통제된 ② 공정함 - 공정한
③ 소속 - 상호적인 ⑤ 책임 - 단순화된

해석 한 실험에서 연구자들은 피실험자들에게 사건에 관한 문서를 주었는데, 이것은 자신과 충돌한 자동차 운전자를 고소 중이던 부상당한 오토바이 운전자와 관련된 것이었다. 피실험자들은 실제 사건에서 판사가 원고에게 0달러에서 10만 달러 사이의 금액을 지급하는 판정을 내렸다고 들었다. 그들은 그러고 나서 모의 협상에서 한 측 혹은 다른 측을 임의로 대변하도록 배정되었다. 연구자들은 피실험자들에게 그 협상의 성공에 기반하여 지불을 받을 것이라고 말했다. 그러나 이 연구에서 가장 흥미로운 부분은 다음에 나왔다. 피실험자들은 판사가 원고에게 실제로 얼마의 지급 판정을 내렸는지를 5천 달러 이내로 맞출 수 있다면 현금 보너스를 벌 수 있을 거라고 들었다. 그들은 공정했을 지불금을 평가할 수 있다면 현금 보너스를 획득할 최고의 기회를 얻게 될 터였다. 평균적으로 원고 측을 대변하도록 배정된 피실험자들은 판사가 거의 사만 달러의 합의를 명령할 거라고 추정했던 반면 피고를 대변하도록 배정된 피실험자들은 그 숫자를 겨우 2만 달러 정도로 두

어

(우측 단)

었다. 올바르게 맞춰야 재정적 보상을 받는 것이었음에도 불구하고, 그들 간의 불일치는 그래도 상당했다.

↓

> 실험에 따르면 피실험자들의 (A) 소속감은 그들이 (B) 편향된 방식으로 정보를 평가하게 만들기 쉽다.

구문 [16행~20행] On average, / the subjects (assigned to represent the plaintiff's side) **estimated** // that the judge would dictate a settlement of nearly $40,000, // while the subjects (assigned to represent the defendant) **put** that number at only around $20,000.
( ) 부분은 각각 바로 앞의 the subjects를 수동의 의미로 수식한다. 앞에 나온 the subjects에 상응하는 동사는 estimated이며, while절의 the subjects에 상응하는 동사는 put이다.
[20행~22행] **Despite** the financial reward [(which[that]) they were offered for guessing correctly], / the disagreement between them was still significant.
전치사 Despite(~에도 불구하고)는 명사 the financial reward를 목적어로 한다. [ ]는 앞에 목적격 관계대명사 which[that]가 생략되어 the financial reward를 수식한다.

어휘 regarding ~에 관하여 sue 고소하다 collide 충돌하다 award 지급 판정을 내리다; 수여하다 assign 배정하다 mock 모의의, 가짜의 negotiation 협상 payout 지불금 dictate 명령하다, 지시하다 settlement 합의; 해결; 지불; 정착

19~20 장문 19 ② 20 ④

해설 19. 감정과 의식의 관계를 생각해볼 때, 감정은 의식의 영역 밖에서 모르는 사이에 생겨나 압도적인 위용을 떨치는 것 같지만, '감정이 정체성이 아닌 정신과 신체의 일시적인 상태라는 인식'을 가지면 감정에 휘둘리는 잘못된 행동을 막을 수 있다는 내용의 글이므로 제목으로 가장 적절한 것은 ② '우리는 감정이 아니다. 우리는 감정을 소유한다'이다.
① 집중하는 상태를 유지하기 위해 감정을 관리하라
③ 감정이 의식에 미치는 부정적인 영향들
④ 감정은 우리의 정신보다 우리의 건강에 더 많은 영향을 준다
⑤ 감정은 지배될 수는 없지만 키워질 수는 있다
20. (d)가 있는 문장에서 우리에게 적절한 도움이 되는 것은 더욱 광범위한 선택지들을 고려함과 동시에, 충동을 조성하는 것이 아니라 충동에 저항하는 행위일 것이다. 따라서 (d)의 fostering을 resisting 등으로 바꿔 써야 한다.

해석 감정은 셀 수 없이 많은 방식으로 중요하다. 그것은 우리에게 잠재적인 기회와 위기에 대해 경고한다. 그것은 우리가 의식적인 숙고라는 너무나도 더 느린 과정에 의존할 필요 없이 여러 출처에서 나온 막대한 양의 데이터를 동시에 빠르게 처리하게 해준다. 그리고 그것은 인간의 경험을 헤아릴 수 없을 정도로 (a) 풍요롭게 해준다. 기쁨 없이, 혹은 슬픔 없이 살아간다는 건 어떠하겠는가?
감정과 의식 간의 관계는 복잡하다. 우리는 확실히 우리의 느낌에 대해 숙고할 능력을 가지고 있고 우리의 감정적 상태에 영향을 끼칠 다른 의도적인 행동을 한다. 그러나 감정은 일반적으로 (b) 모르는 사이에, 의식의 창 밖에서 생성되며, 느낌이 우리의 의식적인 정신에 나타날 때쯤에는 그것은 완전히 에워싸고 모든 것을 아우르는 것처럼 보일 수 있다. 이는 부분적으로 우리의 심박동수와 혈압을 바꾸는 것에서부터 우리가 '(불안으로 인한) 배 아픔' 혹은 '가라앉는 느낌'으로 묘사하는 다양한 표현에 이르는 감정의 (c) 생리적 차원에 기인한다.
우리의 감정 반응의 압도적인 성질은 우리가 신속하고 결단력 있게 행동하도록 준비시켜 줌으로써 필수적인 도움이 된다. 그러나 때때로 그것은 바로 정확히 잘못된 행동이며, 우리가 그러한 충동을 (d) 조성하고(→ (충동에) 저항하고) 더욱 광범위한 선택들을 고려함으로써 더 나은 도움을 받는다. 이러한 과정은 감정이 정체성이 아닌 정신과 신체의 (e) 일

시적인 상태라는 인식과 더불어 시작된다. "화난다!"보다는 "난 지금 분노의 경험을 겪고 있어"라고 말하는 건 바보같이 느껴질 수 있다. 그러나 우리는 둘 사이의 구별에 대한 인식 수준을 높임으로써 적절한 도움을 받는다. 아마 "난 지금 분노하고 있는 중이야"가 합리적인 타협이 될 것이다.

- -

구문 [13행~17행] But emotions are typically generated involuntarily, / outside the window of consciousness, // and **by the time** a feeling registers in our conscious mind // **it** can seem thoroughly immersive and all-encompassing.
by the time ~ mind는 접속사 by the time(~할 때쯤)이 이끄는 부사절이다. 주어 it은 a feeling을 지칭한다.

[17행~21행] In part this is due to the physiological dimension of emotion, / **from** altering our heart rate and blood pressure **to** *the various expressions* [(which[that]) we describe / as a "pit in the stomach," or a "sinking feeling."]
「from A to B(A부터 B까지)」 구문이 쓰였다. [ ]는 앞에 목적격 관계대명사 which[that]가 생략되어 the various expressions를 수식한다.

[27행~29행] This process starts with an awareness that the emotion is a transitory state of mind and body, not an identity.
that 이하는 an awareness에 대한 동격절이다.

- -

어휘 alert 경고하다 in parallel 동시에 deliberation 숙고, 숙의 *cf.* deliberate 의도적인, 고의의; 신중한; 숙고하다 immeasurably 헤아릴 수 없을 정도로 reflect on 숙고하다 involuntarily 모르는 사이에, 부지불식간에 register (감정이) 나타나다; 등록하다 thoroughly 완전히, 철저히 immersive 에워싸는 듯한, 몰입형의 all-encompassing 모든 것을 아우르는 physiological 생리적인 dimension 차원 pit in the stomach (두려움 혹은 불안으로 인해) 배가 아픈 느낌 overpowering 압도적인, 강한 serve a purpose 도움[소용]이 되다 prime 준비시키다; 주된, 주요한; 최고의 foster 조성하다 impulse 충동 transitory 일시적인 compromise 타협[절충](하다); 위태롭게 하다

제24회
본문 p.188

1	④	2	③	3	⑤	4	⑤	5	③	6	③	7	④	8	④	9	②	10	③
11	④	12	②	13	④	14	③	15	④	16	③	17	④	18	②	19	②	20	④

1 심경 변화 ④

해설 Laura는 심한 폭풍우가 치는 와중에 두 시간 전에 왔어야 할 아버지가 오지 않아 걱정하던(worried) 중에 아버지로부터 자신이 안전하며 곧 도착한다는 전화를 받아서 안도했으므로(relieved) ④가 정답이다.
① 우울한 → 후회하는 ② 신이 난 → 지루해하는
③ 외로운 → 차분한 ⑤ 궁금한 → 속상한

- -

해석 폭풍우가 다가오고 있다는 뉴스를 들었을 때, Laura는 창문을 내다보았다. 비는 도랑을 흘러넘치게 하며 심하게 퍼붓고 있었고, 그동안 맹렬한 바람이 뒷마당의 나뭇가지들 속으로 거칠게 불며, 그것들을 활 모양으로 비틀고 있었다. Laura는 아버지가 점심 식사 후 전화를 건 때부터 아무것도 할 수 없었다. 아버지는 두 시간 전에 집에 오셔야 했는데, 그녀는 점점 더 걱정하며 생각했다. 주의를 다른 데 돌리려는 필사적인 마음에 그녀는 TV를 켰다. 뉴스 진행자는 주가 20년 동안 봤던 것 중 가장 큰 허리케인이라고 말하고 있었다. 뉴스 진행자의 목소리는 파괴의 현장을 떠다녔다. 다리는 파괴되었고, 집들은 조각으로 무너졌고, 도로는 거대한 나무의 부러진 밑동과 가지 아래에 파묻혔다. Laura는 TV를 끄고 다시 창밖을 내다보았다. 그녀가 다시 앉은 바로 그때 전화가 울렸다. 그녀의 아버지였다. 아버지는 안전하며 한 시간 내에 집에 갈 것이라고 말했다. 그녀는 한숨을 쉬며 소파에 앉았다.

- -

구문 [9행~11행] The newscaster was saying // (that) it was *the biggest hurricane* [(that) the state had seen in twenty years].
saying 다음에 명사절을 이끄는 접속사 that이 생략되었다. [ ]는 관계대명사 that이 생략된 관계사절로 선행사 the biggest hurricane을 수식한다.

- -

어휘 in sheets (비·안개 등이) 심하게; 얇은 판으로 펴서 ditch 도랑; 수도 fierce 맹렬한; 사나운 rip through ~ 속으로 거칠게 들어가다 bow 활; 곡선 desperate 필사적인; 몹시 갖고 싶어 하는 distraction 기분 전환; 주의 산만 devastation 파괴; 황폐 splinter 깨진 조각; 파편 trunk 나무의 몸통; 동체 massive 크고 무거운 sigh 한숨 (쉬다); 탄식

2 밑줄 함의 ③

해설 러다이트들은 기계 그 자체를 반대한 것이 아니라 기계의 도입으로 초래된 변화(노동에서의 자율성 상실, 자신의 의사와 관계없는 피고용인으로서의 예속, 가족과 공동체에 미치는 악영향)를 반대했던 것이다. 이를 통해 '그들이 알게 된 것'은 그들이 기계의 지배와 영향을 받는 존재로 전락했다는 깨달음이라는 것을 유추할 수 있고, 그래서 정답은 ③ '장인이 기계를 통제하는 것이 아니라 기계에 의해 통제되었다.'이다.
① 장인은 노동조합이 없으면 공장 소유주에게 저항할 수 없었다.
② 특별한 기술이 없는 노동자는 고등 교육을 받은 노동자로 대체될 것이다.
④ 장인의 파업은 그들이 의도한 것과 반대의 결과를 가져왔다.
⑤ 새로운 기계류의 파괴는 오직 숙련된 장인들의 기반만 약화시켰다.

- -

해석 오늘날 '러다이트'는 기술에 반대하거나 조심스럽게 비판적인 사람을 지칭하는 데 쓰이는 폄하하는 용어이다. 하지만 원래의 러다이트들은 사실 기술 그 자체를 반대하지 않았다는 것을 기억하는 것이 중요하다. 러다이트들이 두려워하고 반발한 것은 기계 그 자체가 아니었다. 오히려 그들은 기술이 인간을 돕도록 의도된 것이지 그 반대가 아니라는 것을 이해했다. 러다이트는 기술 자체에 이의를 제기한 것이 아니라 기계에 의해 생겨난 새로운 경제 현실에 반대하고 있었다. 이전에 장인들은 그들 자신의 속도로 일하고 자신의 물건에 그들 자신의 가격을 매길 수 있었다. 하지만 산업화와 대량 생산이 시작되면서 장인들은 어려운 시기를 경험하게 되었고 증오하는 공장에 고용될 것을 점점 더 강요받았다. 갑자기 그들은 그들 자신에게가 아니라 공장 소유자에게 설명을 해야 하는 입장이 됐고, 자율성을 포기하거나 굶주려야 했다. 그들은 기계가 자신들의 생계, 자신들의 삶, 자신들의 가족, 그리고 자신들의 공동체에 무엇을 의미하는지를 알게 되었다. 그리고 그들은 자신들이 알게 된 것이 맘에 들지 않았다.

- -

구문 [5행~6행] **It was** not the machines themselves **that** the Luddites feared and reacted against.
'~한 것은 바로 …이다'는 뜻의 「It was ... that ~」 강조구문이 쓰여 not the machines themselves를 강조한다.

[18행~20행] They saw what the machines meant <u>to their livelihood</u>, <u>to their lives</u>, <u>to their families</u>, <u>and</u> <u>to their communities</u>.
밑줄 친 네 부분이 콤마(,)와 and로 연결되어 병렬구조를 이룬다.

어휘 be opposed to ~을 반대하다　cautiously 조심스럽게　react against 반발하다　the other way around 반대로, 거꾸로　bring about 초래하다　craftsman 장인　mass production 대량 생산　fall on 경험하다, 직면하다　answerable 설명을 해야 하는, 책임을 져야 하는　autonomy 자율성, 자치권　livelihood 생계　labor union 노동조합　strike 파업　undermine (기반을) 약화시키다

3 글의 요지　⑤

해설 칼로리 섭취가 많은 사람은 노화가 가속되는 현상을 겪게 되며 노화는 체중이나 체질량 지수보다 칼로리 섭취량과 더 큰 관계가 있는데, 이는 노화의 원인이 되는 활성산소의 양이 체중이 아니라 섭취하는 칼로리의 양과 관련이 있기 때문이다. 이를 정리하면 글의 요지로 가장 적절한 것은 ⑤이다.

해석 과학자들은 단지 우리가 섭취하는 음식과 칼로리의 양을 줄임으로써 노화와 그것에 동반되는 모든 못된 것들을 무기한 연기할 수 있다는 것을 언젠가 의심의 여지 없이 확립하기를 바란다. 알츠하이머병을 예방하는 데 이상적인 체중을 유지하는 것이 충분하지 않을 수 있다는 것에 주목하라. 연구들은 알츠하이머병의 위험이 체중이나 체질량 지수(BMI)보다 칼로리 섭취와 더 밀접히 연관되어 있다는 것을 보여주었다. 이것은 체중이 늘어나지 않게 해주는 높은 신진대사율을 가진 복을 받은 정크 푸드 마니아들이 기억력 문제가 생길 위험이 여전히 더 높을 수 있다는 것을 의미한다. 칼로리 제한이 신체와 정신에 어떻게 이로운 영향을 발휘하는지를 설명하는 논리를 고려해 보면, 이 말은 정말 일리가 있다. 우리의 식단에서 생성되는 노화를 가속하는 활성산소의 양은 우리의 몸무게가 아니라 우리가 섭취하는 칼로리의 양과 관련이 있다. 따라서 더 많은 칼로리를 섭취하는 높은 신진대사율을 지닌 사람이 더 느린 신진대사율을 지닌 사람보다 실제로는 더 많은 해로운 형태의 산소를 만들고 있을지도 모른다.

구문 [1행~4행] Scientists hope to someday *establish* beyond a doubt that **aging** and *all the nefarious things* [that go with *it*] can be indefinitely postponed simply by reducing the amount of food and calories we consume.
밑줄 친 부분이 establish의 목적어이고, [ ]은 all the nefarious things를 수식하는 관계사절이다. 이때 go with it의 it은 aging을 지칭한다.
[9행~12행] This means that *a junk food junkie* [who is blessed with *a high metabolic rate*] [that keeps her from gaining weight] **may still be** at a higher risk for developing a memory problem.
means의 목적어 역할을 하는 that절의 주어는 a junk food junkie이고 동사는 may (still) be이다. 첫 번째 [ ]은 a junk food junkie를 수식하고, 두 번째 [ ]은 a high metabolic rate를 수식한다.

어휘 indefinitely 무기한으로　take note 주목하다　intake 섭취　body mass index 체질량 지수　junkie 마니아; 마약 중독자　metabolic rate 대사율　restriction 제한　exert 발휘하다, 가하다　make sense 이치에 맞다

4 글의 주제　⑤

해설 '~라면 어떨까'와 같은 질문은 이미 내린 결정의 가치를 훼손하고, 우리가 결정의 가장 좋은 결과에 도달하는 데 도움이 되지 않는다고 했으므로 주제로 가장 적절한 것은 ⑤ '반사실적인 질문이 내려진 결정에 미치는 부정적 효과'이다.
① 성공적인 결정을 이끄는 핵심 요소들
② 결정을 내리는 것에 만족을 키우는 방법들

③ 다른 사람을 대신해서 결정을 내리는 것의 어려움
④ 사람들이 지나치게 많은 '~라면 어떨까'라는 질문을 하는 이유

해석 우리 모두는 우리가 가진 이용 가능한 정보를 고려하여 가능한 가장 좋은 결정을 내린다. 하지만 그 다음은 어떻게 되는가? 여러분의 결정으로부터 여러분이 경험하는 만족은 그 결정의 결과뿐만 아니라 여러분이 반사실적인 시나리오를 고려하면서 보내는 시간의 양에도 근거한다. 우리는 때때로 "내가 이 직업을 가지지 않았다면 무슨 일이 일어났을까?" 또는 "내가 학교에서 다른 학위를 해나갔다면 어땠을까?"와 같은 질문을 스스로에게 한다. 이러한 질문은 여러분에게 아무것도 확실하지 않으며 모든 대답이 여러분의 상상에 의해서 결정될 수 있는 추상적인 세상에 대해 생각하도록 하기 때문에, 이런 방식으로 생각하는 것은 일련의 무한정한 '했을 수 있는데'로 이어질 수 있다. 반사실적인 질문에 시간을 보내는 행위는 여러분이 처음에 내린 결정의 가치를 훼손할 수 있다. '~라면 어떨까' 질문은 우리의 흥미를 돋우는데, 무엇이 다를 수 있는지를 상상하는 것은 끝없이 아주 재미있을 수 있지만, 가정에 기반한 질문들은 우리가 이미 내린 결정에 대해 가능한 가장 좋은 결과에 도달하도록 기여하거나 도와주지 않는다.

구문 [9행~13행] Because these questions invite you to think about *an abstract world* [in which <u>nothing is certain</u> and every answer can be determined / by your imagination], // **thinking this way can lead** to an infinite series of could-have-beens.
[ ]는 '전치사 + 관계대명사'로 시작되는 관계사절로 an abstract world를 수식하며, in which는 관계부사 where로 바꾸어 쓸 수 있다. 동명사구 thinking this way가 주절의 주어이고 can lead가 동사이다.

어휘 outcome 결과　counterfactual 반(反)사실(적)인　abstract 추상적인　infinite 무한정한, 무한한　undermine 훼손하다, 약화시키다　intrigue ~의 흥미를 돋우다　endlessly 끝없이, 무한하게　fascinating 아주 재미있는; 매력적인　**[선택지 어휘]** on behalf of ~을 대신[대표]하여　adverse 부정적인; 반대의

5 글의 제목　③

해설 첫 문장에 글 전체의 요지가 담겨 있으며, 전체적으로 같은 내용의 부탁이라도 오른쪽 귀에 대고 했을 때 상대방이 훨씬 더 부탁을 잘 들어준다는 것을 밝혀낸 실험에 관한 글이므로 글의 제목으로는 ③ '부탁할 것이 있으세요? 오른쪽 귀에 대고 부탁하세요!'가 가장 적절하다.
① 시끄러운 클럽이 귀가 안 들리게 한다!
② 흡연이 청력에 끼치는 악영향
④ 왼쪽 귀로 듣는 것에 대한 선호
⑤ 뇌의 각 반구(좌뇌와 우뇌)의 다른 역할

해석 대부분의 사람들은 그들의 왼쪽 귀로 부탁을 받을 때보다 오른쪽 귀로 받을 때 호의를 베풀 가능성이 더 높다고 새로운 연구는 보여준다. 이탈리아 Chieti에 있는 Gabriele d'Annunzio 대학의 Luca Tommasi와 Daniele Marzoli는 시끄러운 나이트클럽에서 사회적 상호 작용이 일어나는 동안 귀의 선호성을 관찰했다. 연구자들은 176명의 클럽에 온 사람들에게 담배 한 대를 부탁할 때 의도적으로 그들의 오른쪽 귀 또는 왼쪽 귀에 대고 말을 했다. 그들은 클럽에 온 사람들의 오른쪽 귀에 이야기할 때 왼쪽 귀(에 이야기할 때)와 비교하여 확실하게 더 많은 담배를 얻었다. 그 결과는 언어적 자극을 들을 때 오른쪽 귀가 더 우세하다는, 잘 알려진 인간의 비대칭성을 확인시켜준다. 좌뇌가 언어를 처리함에 있어 더 많이 참여하고 있으며, 이는 일상적인 상황에서 듣기를 위해 오른쪽 귀를 우선적으로 사용하는 것에 정당한 이유가 된다.

구문 [13행~16행] *The brain's left hemisphere is more involved in language processing*, / **which justifies the preferential use of the right ear for listening in everyday situations**.
여기서 관계대명사 which가 이끄는 절은 앞 문장 전체(The brain's ~ language

processing)를 보충 설명한다.

어휘 do a favor 호의를 베풀다 *cf.* favor 부탁, 청; 호의, 친절 preference 선호(성) *cf.* preferential 우선의; 선택적인, 차별적인 interaction 상호 작용 intentionally 의도적으로, 일부러 address 말을 하다[걸다]; 연설하다; 주소 asymmetry 비대칭성, 불균형 dominance 우세; 지배; 우월 stimulus ((복수형 stimuli)) 자극(제) hemisphere (뇌의) 반구 justify 정당한 이유가 되다, 정당화하다; 옳음[타당함]을 보여주다 **[선택지 어휘]** deafen 안 들리게 하다; 귀머거리로 만들다

6 안내문 불일치 ③

해설 에세이 제출은 이메일과 우편 말고도 직접 방문하여 전달하는 방법도 있다. 따라서 ③은 내용과 일치하지 않는다.

해석 엄마가 나에게 갖는 의미 에세이 대회
〈Green Life〉 잡지

당신의 엄마를 최고로 만드는 것을 우리에게 얘기해주는 에세이로 당신의 사랑을 보여주세요. 당신의 에세이는 진심 어린 것일 수도 있고 혹은 재밌는 것이어도 됩니다!

세부사항:
– 에세이는 350단어를 넘지 않아야 합니다.
– 에세이에는 글만 담겨야 하며 첨부 사진 혹은 그림은 어떤 것도 있어서는 안 됩니다.
– 에세이 마감일: 4월 30일 금요일
– 제출물을 보내실 수 있는 곳: editor@greenlifemagazine.com 혹은 우편으로는 P.O.Box 10, Green City, MI 48035로 보내실 수 있으며 혹은 Green City의 1007 Avenue K로 가져오셔도 됩니다.

* 〈Green Life〉의 편집자들이 선발하여 저희의 6월호에 우승작 에세이를 게재할 것입니다.
* 우승자는 몇몇 매우 관대한 〈Green Life〉의 광고주들의 제공으로 특별한 미용 패키지를 받을 것입니다. 콜라겐 페이셜 마사지(Christine's Spa)와 변신 컷, 염색, 스타일링(Fiaz Salon) 그리고 300달러의 상품권(Luna Boutique)입니다.

구문 [3행~4행] Show your love in *an essay* [that tells us what makes your Mom the best].
[ ]는 an essay를 수식하는 주격 관계사절이다. tells 다음에 us는 간접목적어, what makes your Mom the best는 직접목적어이다.

어휘 heartfelt 진심 어린 exceed 초과하다 submission 제출(물) courtesy of ~이 제공한, ~의 호의로 makeover 변신, 단장 gift certificate 상품권

7 밑줄 어법 ④

해설 ① what sociologists call the "weak tie"는 have mastered의 목적어이고, what은 sociologists call 다음의 목적어이다. what은 명사절을 이끄는 관계대명사로서 이 두 역할을 수행하기에 적절히 쓰였다.
② ~ 56 percent of people [he talked to] found their jobs ~
[ ]은 앞에 whom[that]이 생략되어 people을 수식하며, 주어는 56 percent of people이고 동사는 found이다.
③ 'Nothing surprising here.'는 원래 'There is nothing surprising here.'이던 문장을 간단히 쓴 것이라 볼 수 있다. '놀랍게 하는' 것이 없다는 의미이므로 능동의 의미를 가지는 형용사 surprising을 잘 사용했으며, 동사의 자리가 아닌 것에 주의한다. (동사는 생략된 is.)
④ 의미상 '당신이 알지 못하는 것'이라는 뜻의 대동사가 되어야 하므로 don't로 고

쳐 써야 하며, 여기서 don't는 'don't know'를 나타낸다.
⑤ 문맥상 '당신이 알지 못하는 영역'이 아니라 '당신이 알려지지 못한 영역'이라는 의미로서 you와 know가 수동 관계이므로 수동의 형태를 잘 사용하였다.

해석 조직 생존자들은 사회학자들이 '약한 유대'(친밀하지만 무심한 사회적 관계)라 칭하는 것에 통달했다. 사회학자 Mark Granovetter는 자신이 대화한 56%의 사람들이 인맥을 통해 자신의 직업을 찾았음을 발견했다. 여기에는 놀라울 것이 없다. 그러나 그러한 인맥 중 대부분은 '약한 유대'('오직 가끔만' 혹은 '좀처럼 안' 보는 사람들)로 묘사된다. 새로운 일자리, 새로운 정보 혹은 어떠한 종류의 새로운 생각을 찾는 것에 관한 한, 약한 유대가 강한 유대보다 항상 더 중요하다. 결국 당신의 친구들은 당신과 같은 세상을 점유하고 있지 않은가. 여러분의 지인들은 정의상 매우 다른 세상을 점유하는 사람들이며 당신이 모르는 것을 알 가능성이 더 높다. 이러한 역설을 포착하기 위하여 Granovetter는 '약한 유대의 힘'이라는 놀라운 용어를 만들었다. 지인들은 '사회적 힘'의 원천을 나타내어, 당신의 명성을 다른 경우라면 알려지지 않을지도 모르는 영역으로 확장시켜준다. 더 많은 지인이 있으면 있을수록, 당신은 더 강해진다. (그리고 더 눈에 띈다.)

구문 [11행~12행] Your friends, after all, occupy *the same world* [that you **do**].
[ ]은 the same world를 수식하며, do는 occupy를 나타내는 대동사이다.
[19행~20행] **The more** acquaintances you have, **the more** powerful (and visible) you are.
'The 비교급, the 비교급'은 '…하면 할수록 더 ~하다'의 뜻이다.

어휘 casual 무심한, 태평한 occasionally 때때로 rarely 좀처럼 ~ 않다 when it comes to v-ing ~하는 것에 관한 한 occupy 점유하다, 차지하다 acquaintance 지인 by definition 정의상 paradox 역설 coin 신조어를 만들다

8 밑줄 어휘 ④

해설 연구 목적으로 만든 소비자 인력풀에서 포커스 그룹의 참여자들이 참여의 혜택을 즐기기 위해 진행자를 만족시키는 데 주력하여 믿을 만한 피드백을 제공하지 않는다. 따라서 포커스 그룹 패널로부터 얻은 자료의 많은 부분이 가치가 없는 것이 되므로 ④의 worthwhile은 worthless로 바꾸어 써야 적절하다.

해석 포커스 그룹은 마케팅에서 흔하게 사용되지만 어떤 나라에서는 그들에게 아주 실질적인 문제가 있다. 포커스 그룹에 들어갈 무작위의 사람들을 모집하는 것은 ① 어렵기 때문에, 연구 기관들은 촉박한 통보에도 포커스 그룹에 기꺼이 참여할 큰 소비자 인력풀을 개발했다. 그러나 문제는 이런 소비자 중 많은 사람들이 너무 ② 적극적이라는 것이다. 많은 소비자가 보수, 무료 음식, 그리고 전문가가 되는 경험을 즐기고, 정기적으로 다시 초대를 받기 위해 진행자를 만족시키는 데 주력한다는 것이 연구를 통해 밝혀졌다. 안타깝게도, 바로 그 인간적인 진행자를 만족시키는 방식은 브랜드에 대한 ③ 진정한 통찰력을 그들에게 제공하는 것이라기보다는 그들이 듣고 싶어 하는 말을 알아내는 것으로 보인다. 이것은 포커스 그룹 패널로부터 얻은 자료의 많은 부분을 ④ 가치 있게(→ 가치 없게) 만든다. 기관들은 이 문제를 알고 있고, 그들을 ⑤ 새롭게 유지하기 위해 그룹 내에서 참가 중단율을 확실히 하고 있지만, 소비자들은 그 인력풀에 남아 있으려고 여러 이름을 사용함으로써 이것을 피한다.

구문 [3행~6행] Since **it** is difficult **to recruit** random people to be in focus groups, research agencies have developed *large pools of consumers* (willing to take part in focus groups at short notice).
it은 가주어, to recruit 이하가 진주어이다. ( ) 부분은 형용사구로 large pools of consumers를 수식한다.
[14행~16행] This **makes *much of the data*** (gained from focus-group **panels) worthless**.
「makes+목적어(much of ~ panels)+목적격보어(worthless)」의 구조이다. ( ) 부분은 much of data를 수식하는 분사구이다.

어휘 recruit 모집하다　random 무작위의　agency 기관; 단체, 대리(업)　pool 인력 풀; 물웅덩이　willing 기꺼이 하는, 적극적인　take part in ~에 참여하다　at short notice 촉박하게, 예고 없이　moderator 진행자　work out ~을 알아내다　genuine 진정한; 진짜의　panel 패널; 심사단; 판　worthwhile 가치[보람] 있는　ensure ~을 확실하게 하다[보장하다]　get around ~을 피하다

9　빈칸 추론　②

해설　서구 문화권에서 수면이 어떠한 특징을 지니는지 찾아야 한다. 글 중반부에서 대부분의 서구화되지 않은 문화권에서 토착민들은 어린이와 함께 잠을 잔다고 언급했고 이는 서구화된 문화권에서의 수면과 반대되는 특징이다. 따라서 서구 문화권의 특징으로는 수면을 공동의 일로 보는 것과 반대되는 ② '사적인'이 빈칸에 들어가는 것이 가장 적절하다.
① 격식을 차리는　③ 이국적인　④ 전통적인　⑤ 예측할 수 있는

해석　서로 다른 문화 사이의 수면 관습에 대한 2002년의 중대한 보고서에서 인류학자 Carol Worthman과 Melissa Melby는 보통 서구화된 후기 산업 사회 국가의 잠을 자는 사람들은 직장이나 학교에 순응하기 위해 규칙적인 시간에 잠을 자고 일어나는 반면, 전통적인 서구화되지 않은 국가의 잠을 자는 사람들은 하루 중 잠자리에 들거나 나오는 더 유동적인 수면 스케줄이 있다는 것을 알아냈다. 그들은 또한 전 세계 대부분의 문화권(아시아, 아프리카, 중남미, 남유럽, 스칸디나비아 일부)에서 토착민들이 혼자 자는 수면 방식을 발전시킬 것을 촉진하기 위한 식민지의 노력에도 불구하고, 어린이들이 다른 가족 구성원의 손이 닿는 곳 안에서 잠을 자는 것을 발견했는데, 인류학자들은 이를 곁잠이라고 칭한다. 그들이 반드시 같은 침대에서 잠을 자는 것은 아니지만, 움직임을 관찰하고 소리, 심지어는 낮춘 소리도 들을 수 있을 만큼 서로 충분히 가까이 있다. 오직 북유럽 본토와 아메리카의 사회 그리고 어느 정도까지 그 강대국들이 식민지로 만든 곳에서만, 수면은 확실하게 한 차례의 지속 시간으로 압축되어 왔고 취침 시간 의식을 필요로 하는 <u>사적인</u> 일이 되었다.

구문　[6행~8행] ~, while traditional, non-Westernized sleepers have more fluid sleep schedules, **moving** in and out of sleep in the course of a day.
moving 이하는 분사구문으로 의미상 주어는 traditional, non-Westernized sleepers이다.
[18행~23행] Only in the societies of Northern mainland Europe and America, and to some extent the places (colonized by those powers), **has** sleep **been** both reliably compressed into a single stretch of time and become a private affair (necessitating bedtime rituals).
Only를 포함한 부사구가 문두에 나와 「조동사(has)+주어(sleep)+p.p.(been)」의 어순으로 도치되었다. colonized by those powers는 the places를 수식하는 분사구이고, necessitating bedtime rituals 또한 분사구로 a private affair를 수식한다.

어휘　seminal 중대한　anthropologist 인류학자　postindustrial 후기 산업 사회의　accommodate 순응하다; 수용하다　fluid 유동적인　within arm's reach 손이 닿는[가까운] 곳에　term (~라고) 칭하다[부르다]　co-sleeping 곁잠 ((부모가 아이와 함께 자는 것))　colonial 식민지의　solitary 혼자의　arrangement 방식; 배치; 정리, 정돈　colonize 식민지로 만들다; 대량 서식하다　reliably 확실하게, 분명히　compress 압축[요약]하다　affair 일; 사건　necessitate 필요로 하다　ritual 의식(의)

10　빈칸 추론　③

해설　눈송이는 춥고 건조한 대기에서 단순한 육각기둥으로 탄생하지만, 생장하고 떨어지는 동안 각기 다른 온기와 습기를 경험하며 독특한 결정 모양을 발달시키는데, 단순한 육각기둥 형태를 질서(order)로, 눈송이가 지나온 온도와 습기의 변화로

인해 갖게 되는 독특한 결정 형태를 다양성(diversity)으로 볼 수 있다. 이를 반영하면 모두 다른 모습을 한 눈송이는 역사의 우연적 사건들이 ③ '질서와 다양성 간의 긴장을 만들어낸' 결과물이다.
① 아주 비슷한 것 같은 패턴을 형성한다
② 정교하고 기하학적인 총체를 만든다
④ 쉽고 빠르게 각각의 육각형 구조를 안정화한다
⑤ 대기의 습기 차로 촉발되는 춤을 공연한다

해석　눈송이의 기본적인 육각형 모양은 얼음 결정이 자랄 때 다양한 방법으로 정교하게 만들어지고 대기의 온도와 습도가 최종 형태를 결정짓는다. 육각기둥은 매우 춥고 건조한 대기에서 형성된다. 온도가 상승함에 따라, 간단한 육각형의 얼음 결정 생장이 불안정해 지기 시작한다. 매우 축축한 대기에서는 팔이 눈송이의 여섯 개의 모서리로부터 자라나, 새로운 육각형 판으로 변하거나 대기가 충분히 따뜻하다면 더 많은 부속물을 길러낸다. 온도와 습도의 다른 조합들은 텅 빈 각기둥, 바늘 혹은 주름진 판의 성장을 유발한다. 눈송이가 떨어지는 동안, 바람은 공기의 셀 수 없이 많은 경미한 온도와 습도 변화 속을 통과하도록 그것들을 내던진다. 어떠한 두 개의 눈송이도 완전히 동일한 순서를 경험하지 않으며, 이러한 분기하는 역사가 각각의 눈송이를 구성하는 얼음 결정의 독특함에 반영된다. 따라서 역사의 우연적 사건들이 결정 생장의 법칙에 층층이 쌓여 있고, 우리의 미적 감각을 그토록 즐겁게 해주는 <u>질서와 다양성 간의 긴장을 만들어낸다</u>.

구문　[2행~4행] ~ **with** the temperature and humidity of the air **determining** the final shape.
「with+O+v-ing」는 '…가 ~한 채로'라는 의미의 분사구문이다.
[14행~17행] No two flakes experience exactly the same sequence, and these divergent histories are reflected in the uniqueness of the ice crystals [that make up each snowflake].
[　]는 앞의 the ice crystals를 수식하는 관계대명사절이다.
[17행~20행] Thus, the chance events of history are layered over the rules of crystal growth, **producing** the tension between order and diversity [**that** so pleases our aesthetic sense].
producing 이하는 부대상황을 나타내는 분사구문이다. 관계대명사 that이 이끄는 [　] 부분은 the tension ~ and diversity를 수식한다.

어휘　snowflake 눈송이　elaborate 정교하게 만들어 내다; 갈고 다듬다　humidity 습도, 습기　prism 각기둥　straightforward 간단한　destabilize 불안정해지다　sprout (자라)나다; 발아하다　appendage 부속물　hollow 텅 빈　innumerable 셀 수 없이 많은　variation 변화, 차이　sequence 순서; 연속　divergent 분기하는, 갈라지는　layer 층층이 쌓다　aesthetic 미적인　match 아주 비슷하다; 어울리다　sophisticated 정교[복잡]한; 도시적인　geometric 기하학적인　ensemble 총체; 합주단, 앙상블　trigger 촉발[유발]하다; 쏘다

11　빈칸 추론　④

해설　빈칸 뒷부분에 유아들조차 일을 일으킬 때 기뻐하는 모습을 보이며, 사회적인 기대가 인간의 노동 경향성을 강화시킨다는 내용이 나오므로 인간은 노동을 지향하도록, 즉 ④ '생산적으로 되는 것에 의존하도록' 프로그램 되어 있다는 것을 유추할 수 있다.
① 세상에 대해 궁금해하도록
② 협업이 가능하도록
③ 게으름의 위험성을 알도록
⑤ 그들의 사회적 관계에 전념하도록

해석　통념에 따르면, 노동은 사람들이, 주말과 휴일을 갈망할 때조차도 필요상 져야 하는 부담이다. 하지만 1980년대 초, 미국인들에게 할 수 있다면 퇴직할 것인지를 질문했을 때, 약 80퍼센트는 그렇게 하지 않을 것이라고 했다. 사실, 인간은 <u>생산적으로 되는 것에</u>

의존하도록 두 번 프로그램 되어 있는데, 한 번은 유전자에 의해서이고, 그러고 나서는 사회적 기대가 주는 압력에 의해서이다. 생후 일 년이 지나지 않은 유아들도 벌써 수도꼭지를 틀 때나 공놀이를 할 때처럼 일을 일으킬 때 기뻐하는 모습을 보인다. 적절하게 자극적이며 구조화된 환경에서 아이들은 집중적인 노력을 즐기는 것을 익힌다. 사실, 우리 종 대부분은 노동에 대한 애호를 발전시키지 않았더라면 생존하지 못했을 것이다. 그리고 물론, 인간 공동체는 공익에 기여하지 못하는 사람들에게 창피를 주고 그런 사람들을 외면함으로써 이런 경향을 강화시킨다.

구문 [1행~3행] ~ work is *a burden* [(which[that]) people must endure out of necessity], / even as they long for weekends and holidays.

people must ~ of necessity는 문장의 보어인 a burden을 수식하는 절로 앞에 목적격 관계대명사 which[that]가 생략되어 있다.

[13행~14행] Indeed, our species **would not have survived** // if most of us **had not developed** a taste for work.

가정법 과거완료 구문 「If + S´ + had p.p. ~, S + 조동사 과거형 + have p.p. ... (만약 ~했더라면 …했을텐데)」이 쓰여 과거 사실을 반대로 가정하는 내용이다.

12 빈칸 추론

해설 옥시토신을 흡입한 사람들은 '신뢰' 게임에서 신탁자에게 자유재량으로 쓸 수 있는 돈을 더욱 많이 지급했고, 수령자의 반응을 고려하는 '최후통첩' 게임에서는 더욱 관대한 모습을 보였지만, 수령자의 반응을 고려하지 않는 '독재자' 게임에서는 그렇지 않았다. 그러므로 옥시토신은 '② 다른 사람들의 믿음과 욕망에 대해 공감하는 반응'과 관련된다고 할 수 있다.

① 유쾌한 정서적 상태와 불쾌한 정서적 상태를 모두 유도하는 것
③ 개인이 자기방어를 위해 속한 상황을 이해하는 것
④ 감정적인 얼굴 작용, 신체 자세와 음성 표현을 취하는 것
⑤ 자신의 의견을 표현하기 전에 상대방의 반응을 고려하는 것

해석 행동 경제학 분야의 더욱 이상한 실험들 중 하나에서 Ernst Fehr와 그의 협업자들은 사람들이 '신뢰' 게임을 하도록 했는데, 여기에서 그들은 돈을 신탁자에게 건네주었고, 그는 그것을 크게 불린 후 자신이 원하는 어떤 양이라도 참가자에게 돌려준다. 참가자들 중 절반은 옥시토신이 담긴 코 분무기를 흡입했는데, 이는 코에서 뇌로 침투할 수 있다. 나머지 절반은 위약을 흡입했다. 옥시토신을 흡입한 사람들은 처음 만난 사람(= 신탁자)에게 그들의 돈을 더 많이 내어주었다. 다른 실험들은 옥시토신을 코로 들이마시는 것이 사람들을 '최후통첩' 게임(여기에서 그들은 수령자의 반응을 예상하며 총합을 나누는데, 수령자는 그들 둘 다에 대해 거래를 거부할 수 있다)에서 더욱 관대하게 만들어준다는 것을 보여주었지만, '독재자' 게임(여기에서 수령자는 그것을 받거나 놔둬야 하며, 제안자는 그의 반응을 고려할 필요가 없다)에서는 그렇지 않았다. 옥시토신 연결망이 <u>다른 사람들의 믿음과 욕망에 대해 공감하는 반응</u>에 중요한 기폭제일 가능성이 있는 것으로 보인다.

구문 [2행~5행] ~ Ernst Fehr and his collaborators **had** *people* **play** a Trust game, in which they hand over money to a trustee, who multiplies it and then **returns** [*however* much he feels like] to the participant.

'have O 동사원형'은 '…가 ~하게 하다'라는 뜻의 사역동사 구문이다. who 다음의 동사 multiplies와 returns는 병렬구조를 이룬다. [ ]은 returns의 목적어 역할을 하는 명사절이며, however는 '어떤 정도라도'의 뜻으로 사용되었다.

[10행~14행] Other experiments have shown that sniffing oxytocin makes people more generous in an Ultimatum game ~, but not in a Dictator game ~.

not in a Dictator game은 'does not make people more generous in a Dictator game'으로 볼 수 있다.

어휘 behavioral economics 행동 경제학　collaborator 협업자　hand over 건네다　trustee 신탁자　multiply 배가시키다　inhale (숨을) 들이쉬다　nasal spray 코 분무기　penetrate 침투하다　turn over 내어주다　sniff (코를 킁킁대

며) 들이마시다　ultimatum 최후통첩　anticipate 예상하다. 고대하다　recipient 수령인　veto 거부하다　dictator 독재자　take ~ into account ~을 고려하다

13 흐름 무관 문장

해설 부모, 형제자매 간의 관계와 친구 관계의 차이점을 제시하고, 마지막에서 친구관계의 강화와 유지를 위해 많은 노력이 필요하다고 했으므로 자녀의 성격 형성에 미치는 영향 때문에 부모가 항상 자녀의 친구 관계를 예의 주시해야 한다는 ④는 글의 흐름과 무관하다.

해석 친구와의 관계는 부모, 형제자매 간의 관계와는 매우 다르다. 가족 관계, 특히 어른과 아이 간의 관계와는 다르게, 또래 관계는 관계자들 간의 어느 정도의 평등을 기반으로 하고 있다. 이는 관계의 조건에 대한 더 많은 협상을 가능하게 한다. ① 또한, 골라서 선택할 수 없는 가족 관계와는 달리, 또래 관계는 비교적 쉽게 형성될 수 있고 그만큼 쉽게 깨질 수 있다. ② 우리 부모와 형제자매는 그들이나 우리가 좋든 싫든 간에 보통 함께해야 한다. ③ 하지만 친구들은, 만약 우리가 그들에게 상처를 주거나 짜증나게 하는 어떤 것을 말하거나 행한다면, '나는 이제 네 친구가 아니야.'라고 선언할 위험성이 항상 있다. ④ 또래 관계는 아이들의 인격 형성에 매우 중대한 영향을 끼쳐서 부모는 항상 그것들에 세심한 주의를 기울여야 한다. ⑤ 그러므로 아이들은 그 점 때문에 그들의 형제자매와 부모와의 관계보다, 혹은 다른 어떤 어른과의 관계보다, 또래와의 관계를 강화하고 유지하기 위해 훨씬 더 많은 노력을 할 필요가 있다.

구문 [1행~2행] *Our relationships* (with friends) / are very different from ***those*** (with parents and siblings).

수식받는 대명사가 단수일 때는 that, 복수일 때는 those로 받는다. 여기서 those는 our relationships를 지칭한다.

어휘 sibling(s) 형제자매　peer 또래; 동료　equality 평등; 균등　participant 참가자　negotiation 타협; 교섭　be stuck with ~에 들러붙다　declare 선언하다　exert (영향력을) 가하다　strengthen 강화하다

14 글의 순서

해설 법과 도덕률은 다르다고 제시한 주어진 문장 다음에는 이를 상술(도덕에는 판사가 존재하지 않으며 정식 의사 결정 절차가 없으며 완전한 성문화가 불가능함)한 (B)가 나온다. 완전한 성문화가 불가능한 바로 그 지점에 도덕적 책임이 시작된다는 (C)가 그 다음에 오고 (C)의 마지막에 도덕적 책임의 예로 든 납세 문제에 이어서 (A)가 납세자의 재량에 대해 서술하는 것이 자연스럽다.

해석 도덕률은 법 제도와 매우 흡사한 공적 제도이며, 행동을 지배하는 규준을 포함하고 있고, 이는 차례로 다른 사람들에게 영향을 준다. 법과는 달리 도덕률은 비공식적인 제도이다.

(B) 도덕적 갈등을 결정하는 권위를 부여받은 판사는 없으며, 모든 도덕적 질문에 단 하나의 명확한 답을 제공하는 정식 의사 결정 절차는 존재하지 않는다. 공적 도덕과 윤리적 책임은 법에 부분적으로 성문화되어있지만, 법 제도는 공적 도덕을 결코 속속들이 성문화할 수는 없을 것이다.

(C) 도덕적 책임은 행동이 법에 의해 완전히 결정되지 못하는 바로 그 지점에서 시작된다. 즉 선택의 자유는 책임을 수반하며, 예컨대 세금 규정을 이용하는 것은 필연적으로 그 책임을 다하는 문제이다.

(A) 납세자들은 규정에 순응할 수 있지만 또한 자신의 납세 의무를 최소화하는 방식으로 자신의 일을 구성할 수도 있다. 이러한 행위자들이 내리는 선택은 세금 제도의 온전함. 분배적 정의와 지속 가능한 사회적 협력에 영향을 줄 수 있는데, 즉 이것들을 향상시키거나 약화시킬 수 있다.

구문 [7행~10행] *The choices* (made by these actors) **may affect, i.e., enhance or undermine**, the integrity of the tax system, distributive justice and sustainable societal cooperation.

( )는 수동의 의미로 주어 The choices를 수식하는 과거분사구이며 동사는 may affect, i.e., enhance or undermine이다. 세 밑줄 부분은 동사의 목적어로서 and로 연결되어 병렬구조를 이룬다.

[11행~14행] There are no *judges* (authorized to decide moral conflicts), and there exist no *formal decision-making procedures* [that provide unique and definite answers to all moral questions].

( )는 수동의 의미로 앞의 judges를 수식하는 과거분사구이다. [ ]는 앞의 formal decision-making procedures를 수식하는 관계사절이다.

어휘 morality 도덕(률) norm 규준 in turn 차례로 informal 비공식의 comply with 순응하다 affair 일 enhance 향상시키다 undermine 약화시키다 integrity 온전함; 진실성 distributive 분배의 sustainable 지속 가능한 societal 사회의 authorize 권한을 부여하다 procedure 절차 codify 성문화하다 exhaustively 속속들이, 철저하게 precisely 바로, 꼭 inevitably 필연적으로 exercise responsibility 책임을 다하다

15 글의 순서 ④

해설 부동산과 동산의 개념을 설명한 주어진 글 다음에는 같은 냉장고라도 부동산과 동산으로 취급되는 각 경우를 구별하여 설명한 (C)가 나온다. 집에 부착된 물건은 부동산으로 간주되어 집과 '함께' 판매된다는 (C) 다음에는 집에 부속된 물건을 가져가는 것은 계약 위반이 된다는 (A)가 나오고 그럼에도 불구하고 이사를 나가는 사람이 물건을 가져가고자 한다면 상당한 금전적 대가를 치러야 한다는 내용의 (B)가 마지막으로 나온다. (B)의 such a thing은 (A)에 나온 '집에 부속된 물건 가져가기'를 지칭한다.

해석 여러분의 재산을 파는 과정에서, 여러분은 '부동산'과 '동산'이라는 말을 들을 수 있다. 부동산은 고정되고 부착되어 있다. 동산은 대개 이동 가능하고 부착되어 있지 않다. 이것이 나올 가능성이 있는 지점은 여러분의 재산 내에 있는 항목들과 관련해서다. (C) 굴려서 이동하고, 플러그를 뽑아, 여러분이 가져갈 수 있는 대부분의 냉장고는 동산으로 간주된다. 냉장고가 (붙박이 모델과 같이) 어떤 식으로든 집에 영구적으로 부착되어 있다면, 그것은 부동산이며 그대로 남는다. 재산을 팔 때, 여러분은 모든 부동산을 파는 것으로 추정된다. (A) 고정된 설비로부터 난간, 벽난로 등의 물건을 뜯어내어 그것들을 가져가는 것은 교양 없는 행동일 뿐만 아니라, 필시 매매 계약을 위반하는 행위가 될 것이다. 그것들을 옮기는 것이 가능하다 하더라도, 구매자는 모든 부동산이 자신의 것이라고 가정한다. (B) 물론 어떤 것도 협상이 가능하지만, 내가 구매자이고 혹시라도 여러분에게 그런 일을 하도록 허용한다면(아마도 그러진 않겠지만), 여러분이 아마도 "됐어요."라고 말하게 될 정도로, 나는 이전에 협상된 매매 가격에서 상당한 금전적인 대가를 요구할 것이다. 구매자로서, 나는 여러분이 떠나면서 그 부동산을 엉망으로 만드는 것을 원하지 않는다.

구문 [12행~17행] ~ but if I **were** a buyer and I **allowed** you to do such a thing at all (which I most likely wouldn't), I **would demand** significant financial consideration off the previously negotiated sales price, *so much so that* you would most likely say, "Forget it."

「If+S+과거동사 ~, S+would+동사원형(demand)....」의 가정법 과거 구문으로 '~하면 …할 것이다'의 의미(현재의 사실을 반대로 가정)이고 if절에서 밑줄 친 두 개의 절이 병렬구조를 이룬다. 'so much so that ~'은 '매우 그러하여 ~하다'의 뜻이다.

[23행~24행] When selling a property, **it** is assumed **that** you are selling all real property.

밑줄 친 부분은 접속사가 생략되지 않은 분사구문이다. it은 가주어이고 that 이하

가 진주어이다.

어휘 property 재산 real property 부동산 personal property 동산 in regard to ~에 관하여 rip 뜯어내다 contract 계약(서); 계약하다 granted 맞아, 인정한다 negotiable 협상의 여지가 있는 *cf.* negotiate 협상하다 consideration 대가; 고려 somehow 어떻게든, 왠지 built-in 붙박이의

16 문장 넣기 ③

해설 변화가 광범위하여 이동이 유기체의 능력을 넘어설 때 멸종이 발생할 가능성이 있다는 주어진 문장은 동물 종이 이동하기 쉬워 서식지가 덜 적합해지면 다른 새 지역으로 이동해간다는 내용 다음에 오는 것이 적절하다. 또한 주어진 문장 다음에도 주요 멸종사건이 세계적인 재난이어서 탈출이 불가능했을 것이라는 내용이 오는 것이 적절하므로 ③이 정답이다.

해석 왜 식물계에는 대규모 멸종이 일어나지 않았는가? 이 질문에 대한 답변은 식물의 가전성(可轉性)에 관한 것과 식물이 그토록 성공적인 이유를 드러낸다. 대부분의 동물종은 매우 이동하기 쉬워서 서식지가 생존에 덜 적합해지면, 단순히 새로운 지역으로 이동해 갈 수 있다. 하지만 변화가 광범위하면 그 압박이 가해지는 서식지를 넘어 이동해 가는 것이 유기체의 능력 내에 있지 않을 수 있고, 그래서 죽음 혹은 멸종이 발생할 가능성이 있다. 이러한 주요한 멸종 사건은 모두 세계 기후의 주요한 변화를 야기한 세계적인 재난이었을 것이며, 따라서 탈출은 불가능했을 것이다. 하지만 식물은 항상 이동할 수 없는 불편을 견뎌야 했고, 그 결과 그것은 지역적 재난에서 살아남기 위해 적응할 수 있도록 진화했다. 이 생존 방법은 매우 효과적이었던 것처럼 보여 세계적 재난 이후에 조차도 식물들이 매우 신속하게 회복해 온 것처럼 보인다.

구문 [10행~13행] These major extinction events are all likely **to have been** global disasters resulting in major changes in the world's climate; therefore, escape **would have been** impossible.

완료부정사 to have been은 동사의 시제보다 이전에 일어난 사건을 표시하는 것으로 '(과거에) ~이었을 것이다'라는 뜻이다. 「would have p.p.」는 '(과거에) ~했을 것이다'와 같이 과거의 일을 가상적으로 표시한다.

[16행~19행] These survival mechanisms *appear* **to have been so** effective // **that** even after global disasters plants appear to have bounced back very rapidly.

appear의 보어로 나온 완료부정사 to have been은 '(과거에) ~이었을 것이다'라는 뜻으로 주절의 동사 이전의 일을 나타낸다. '너무 ~해서 …하다'라는 뜻의 「so ~ that ....」 구문이 쓰였다.

어휘 organism 유기체 far-reaching 광범위한 capacity 능력 habitat 서식 장소 extinction 멸종, 사멸 plant kingdom 식물계 mobile 이동하기 쉬운, 가동성의 disaster 재해, 재난 tolerate 참다, 견디다 evolve 진화하다 adaptable 적응할 수 있는 mechanism 방법, 메커니즘 bounce back (곧) 회복하다

17 문장 넣기 ④

해설 주어진 문장의 '십 대의 가족과 친구들이 십 대가 선정한 요소에 대해서만 언급할 수 있는' 상황은 ④ 앞 문장에서 '십 대가 소셜 네트워크에 올리는 게시물로 인해 그의 삶의 특정 측면만 드러낼 수밖에 없는' 상황에서 기인한다. ④ 이후의 두 문장은 이러한 상황에 대한 예(즉 십 대가 동물 보호소에 대한 글을 게시하지 않았더니 결국 동물 구조에 대한 영역이 그의 정체성 영역에서 밀려나는 상황)로 응집력 있게 전개되므로 주어진 문장은 ④에 위치해야 한다.

해석 일부 십 대들에게, 스크린 사용은 정체성 발달 부진의 원인이 되어 왔다. 그들은 게임하는 것과 '친구들'과 연결된 상태로 있는 것에 너무 많은 시간을 쏟고 있을 수 있어서 자신의 정체성을 신장시키고 굳건하게 할 흥미를 넓히거나 새로운 기술을 배울 시간이나 욕구가 없다. 또한 기술이 많은 것을 더 용이하게 해주기 때문에, 그들은 자주 자신들의 다양한 능력과 인격 발달 증진에 꼭 필요한 인내력, 근면성, 그리고 학습 능력이 결핍될 수도 있다. 소셜 네트워크에 게시하는 것은 그 게시물이 그들의 삶의 특정 측면만을 인정하는 경향이 있기 때문에 정체성 발달을 제한할 수 있다. <u>그것은 친구들과 가족이 오직 그 요소들, 즉 십 대들이 보여주기로 선택한 요소들에 대해서만 언급하거나 질문할 수밖에 없다는 것을 의미한다.</u> 예를 들어, 그들은 자주 자신들의 음악적 관심사에 대해서는 언급하고 자신들이 동물 보호소에서 자원봉사를 한다는 것은 절대 언급하지 않을 수도 있다. 시간이 흐르고 어떤 친구도 동물 구조에 대한 그 십 대의 관심을 인정하거나 지지하지 않을 때, 그 십 대는 그 관심을 평가 절하하여 관심이 시들해지도록 내버려 두기 시작할 수도 있다.

구문 [5행~9행] They may be **devoting** so much time **to** *gaming* and *staying* connected with "friends" that they don't have *time or desire* (to broaden their interests or learn new skills), **which** would grow and solidify their identity.

「devote O to v-ing」는 'O를 v하는 데에 바치다[헌신하다]'의 뜻이다. to 다음에 gaming과 staying이 병렬구조를 이룬다. 「so … that ~ (너무 …해서 ~하다)」 구문이 사용되었고, ( )는 형용사적 용법으로 쓰인 to부정사로 time or desire를 수식한다. 관계대명사 which가 이끄는 절이 선행사 time or desire를 보충 설명한다.

[13행~16행] {Posting on social networks} **can limit** identity development because the tendency is for posts to acknowledge only certain aspects of their lives.

{ }가 주어이고 can limit이 동사이다. for posts는 to acknowledge에 대한 의미상 주어이다.

어휘 underdeveloped 발달이 불충분한　broaden 넓히다　solidify 굳히다　perseverance 인내(력)　teachability 학습 능력　skill set 다양한 능력　character 인성　acknowledge 인정하다　devalue 평가 절하하다

18 요약문 완성 ②

해설 주변이 잘 정돈되어 있을 때 표지판에서 요구하는 도덕적인 사회적 규범을 잘 지켰다는 것이 실험의 주요 내용이므로 빈칸 (A)에는 '정돈된'의 뜻을 나타내는 orderly가 (B)에는 '(규범에) 따르다'라는 conform이 들어가야 가장 적절하다.
① 정돈된 - 반대하다 ③ 인공적인 - 반대하다
④ 인공적인 - 따르다 ⑤ 도시의 - 맞추다

해석 세 명의 네덜란드인 연구자들은 네덜란드 사람들이 자전거를 두는 암스테르담의 골목길을 하나 골라 자전거 손잡이마다 광고 전단을 붙였다. 통근자들은 자전거를 타기 전에 전단을 떼어내야 했는데 연구자들이 쓰레기통을 모두 치워서 전단을 집에 가져가거나 땅에 던져 버리려 했다. 자전거 위에는 낙서를 금지하는 눈에 두드러지는 경고문이 붙어 있었고, 벽은 실험자들이 일부러 낙서로 뒤덮어 놓았거나(실험조건), 깨끗한 상태에 있거나(대조조건) 둘 중 하나였다. 불법 낙서가 있을 때는 통근자들은 전단을 땅에 버리는 경우가 두 배 더 많았다. 또 다른 실험에서 행인들은 속에 5유로 지폐가 든 것이 뻔히 보이는 우편함에 툭 튀어나오게 꽂아둔 주소가 제대로 적힌 봉투에 유혹을 받았다. 이때 우편함이 낙서로 덮여있거나 주위가 쓰레기로 둘러싸여 있을 때 행인의 4분의 1이 그것을 훔쳤다. 우편함이 깨끗할 때는 그것의 반(8분의 1)만이 훔쳤다.

↓

실험에 의하면 (A) 정돈된 환경은 사람들이 자신도 모르게 주위 환경에 맞는 규범에 (B) 따르게 만든다.

구문 [7행~11행] Above the bicycles was a prominent sign prohibiting graffiti and *a wall* [that the experimenters had either covered in graffiti (the experimental condition) or left clean (the control condition)].
(C) (V) (S)

주어가 길어 부사구가 앞으로 나와 「부사(구)+V+S」로 도치되었다.

어휘 alley 골목　attach 붙이다　flyer (광고·안내용) 전단　handlebar (자전거의) 핸들　commuter 통근자　detach 떼어내다　prominent 두드러진, 돌출한　prohibit 금지하다　graffiti 낙서　illegal 불법의　protrude 튀어나오다　visible 눈에 보이는　litter 쓰레기

19~20 장문　　　　19 ② 20 ④

해설 19. 인간의 피부색은 밝은색에서 어두운색까지 연속성을 보이므로 분리된 범주로 나뉠 수 있는 집합체가 아님에도 인간은 피부색에 따라 서로를 분류하는데, 한 실험에서 한 사람의 사진을 제시하고 그를 흑인으로 명명했을 때와 백인으로 명명했을 때 동일한 사람에 대한 인식이 확연히 달라진다는 것을 증명했다. 이를 통해 인종은 피부색이라는 물리적 특성에 의하여 나누어진 것이 아니라 사회적으로 만들어진 경계 짓기와 그로 인한 인식의 편향에 의해 발생된 개념임을 알 수 있다. 그러므로 글의 제목으로 가장 적절한 것은 ② '인종은 단지 피부색 차이 이상인가?'이다.
① 민족 정체성: 형성과 그것의 영향
③ 어떻게 피부색의 범주가 민족 정체성을 흐리는가
④ 인종에 대한 우리의 인식은 시간이 흐르며 변하는가?
⑤ 색깔 꼬리표는 민족 정체성을 더욱 중요하게 만든다

20. 실험 결과 학생들이 정확히 동일한 사진을 보고 있었지만, 연구자가 제공한 인종적 꼬리표로 편향된 렌즈를 통해 이미지를 인식했다고 했다. 그러므로 사진의 남자가 흑인이라고 들은 사람들은 흑인이라는 편향된 렌즈를 통해 그의 '전형적인 흑인의' 특징을 최소화하는 것이 아니라 과장하여(exaggerate) 그렸을 것을 추론할 수 있다.

해석 오래전에 인간들은 서로에게 꼬리표를 붙이기 시작했다. 결국 피부색이 더 옅은 사람들은 '백인'이 되었고, 피부색이 더 어두운 사람들은 '흑인'이 되었으며, (a) 중간 피부 톤을 가진 사람들은 '황인', '붉은 피부', '갈색 피부'가 되었다. 이러한 꼬리표는 현실을 충실히 반영하지 못하며, 전 세계에서 온 무작위로 선별된 1,000명의 사람들을 줄 세운다면, 그들 중 완전히 동일한 피부 톤을 공유하는 사람들은 아무도 없을 것이다. 물론 피부 톤의 연속성이 인간이 서로를 '흑인'과 '백인' 같은 (b) 분리된 범주, 즉 생물학적으로는 어떤 근거도 없으나 그럼에도 불구하고 그 구성원의 사회적, 정치적, 경제적 행복을 계속하여 결정짓는 범주에 배정하는 것을 막아주진 못했다. 이러한 인종적 꼬리표는 무한히 복잡한 사회 세계에 경계와 범주를 부과하지만, 일단 자리를 잡으면 이러한 경계는 사라지기 대단히 힘들다. 사람들은 인종적 꼬리표에 의존함으로써 인종의 애매모호함을 해결하는 경향이 있다.

스탠퍼드 대학 연구에서 한 실험자가 백인 학생들에게 얼굴의 특징으로 인해 백인인지 흑인인지 결정하기가 (c) 어려운 젊은 남자의 사진을 보여주었다. 학생들 절반에게는 그 남자가 '백인'이라 분류됐고 나머지 절반에게 그는 '흑인'이라 분류됐다. 학생들은 가능한 한 정확하게 자기 앞에 놓인 사진을 그려보라는 요청을 받았다. 거래를 즐겁게 하기 위하여 가장 정확한 그림을 그린 학생은 20달러의 상금을 약속받았다. 그 남자가 흑인이라고 들은 사람들은 그의 '전형적인 흑인의' 특징을 (d) 최소화하는(→ 과장하는) 경향을 보인 반면 그가 백인이라고 들은 사람들은 정확히 반대로 행했다. 비록 학생들이 정확히 동일한 사진을 보고 있었지만, 그들은 연구자가 실험 초반에 제공한 인종적 꼬리표로 (e) 편향된 렌즈를 통해 이미지를 인식했다.

구문 [20행~23행] In a Stanford University study, an experimenter showed white students a picture of *a young man* [**whose** facial features made *it* difficult **to determine** whether he was white or black].

[ ] 부분은 소유격 관계대명사 whose가 이끄는 관계사절로 a young man을 수식한다. 관계사절 내에서 it은 가목적어, to determine 이하가 진목적어이다. 밑줄 친

문장은 whether가 이끄는 명사절로 to determine의 목적어로 쓰였다.

[32행~36행] Although the students were looking at exactly the same photograph, they perceived the image through *a lens* [**that** was biased with *the racial label* [**that** the researcher provided earlier in the experiment]].

that was biased ~ in the experiment는 주격 관계대명사 that이 이끄는 관계사절로 a lens를 수식하고, 그 안의 [ ] 부분은 목적격 관계대명사 that이 이끄는 관계사절로 the racial label을 수식한다.

어휘 label ~에 꼬리표를 붙이다; (라벨을 붙여서) 분류하다; 라벨, 딱지, 꼬리표 **intermediate** 중간[중급]의; 중급자 **faithfully** 충실히, 정확히; 충직하게 **continuity** 연속[연관]성; 지속성 **assign** 배정[배치]하다; 부여하다 **discrete** 분리된, 별개의 **go on to-v** 계속해서 v하다, 이어서 v하기 시작하다 **racial** 인종[민족](간)의 **impose** 부과하다; 도입하다; 강요하다 **dissolve** 사라지다; 녹다; 끝내다 **be apt to-v** v하는 경향이 있다, v하기 쉽다 **resolve** 해결하다; 다짐하다 **ambiguity** 애매모호함 **resort to** ~에 의지하다[기대다] **ethnic identity** 민족 정체성 **blur** 흐릿하게 하다; 흐릿한 것 **perception** 인식, 지각

제25회

본문 p.196

| 1 ⑤ | 2 ② | 3 ② | 4 ⑤ | 5 ④ | | 6 ⑤ | 7 ④ | 8 ⑤ | 9 ② | 10 ④ |
| 11 ③ | 12 ② | 13 ③ | 14 ② | 15 ④ | | 16 ③ | 17 ⑤ | 18 ② | 19 ② | 20 ③ |

1 글의 목적   ⑤

해설 학교 행사의 의의에 이어, 이 행사를 도와준 봉사자들의 활동 내용을 나열하고 이에 감사하다는 표현(sincerely appreciated)으로 글을 맺고 있으므로 정답은 ⑤이다.

해석 학부모님들께.

학부모님들께서 가을 날씨를 즐기고 계시기를 바랍니다. 지난 금요일, 여러분께서 알고 계시듯이, Maple Valley High는 또 하나의 성공적인 Youth Enrichment Day를 개최했습니다. 학생들은 광범위한 직업에 관한 세부 정보들을 보았고, 현재 종사 중인 전문가들의 연설을 직접 듣는 기회를 가졌습니다. 저희는 이것이 학생들에게 엄청나게 소중한 기회였다는 것을 압니다. 저희는 또한 이것이 학부모님들의 도움 없이는 가능하지 않았다는 것을 알고 있습니다. 여러분과 같은 봉사자분들께서 점심을 나눠주시고, 행사를 조직하시고, 참가자들을 맞이하시고, 그리고 학생들에게 자신만의 조언도 해주셨습니다. 여러분의 공헌을 진심으로 감사드리며, 내년에 다시 뵙기를 고대한다는 것을 알아주십시오.

교감 Samantha Lord

구문 [4행~7행] Students were **shown** / the details of a wide range of professions, // 和 (were) **given** the opportunity / to listen directly to speeches / by current working professionals.

shown ~ professions와 given ~ professionals는 and로 연결되어 병렬구조를 이루고, given 앞에 were가 중복되어 생략되었다. to listen ~ working professionals는 the opportunity와 동격 관계이다.

어휘 a wide range of 광범위한, 넓은 범위의 **profession** 직업, 직종; 전문직 *cf.* **professional** 전문가, 전문직 종사자; 전문적인 **current** 현재의, 지금의; 통용되는 **incredibly** 엄청나게, 믿을 수 없을 정도로 **recognize** (공로를) 인정[표창]하다; 알아보다[알다] **distribute** (사람들에게) 나누어주다, 분배[배부]하다 **greet** 맞다, 환영하다 **participant** 참가자 **contribution** 공헌, 기여; 기부, 기증 **look forward to A** A를 고대하다

2 필자 주장   ②

해설 일을 제때에 완수하지 못하는 것에 대해 자책하는 대신 완수할 수 있던 것에 대해 스스로를 인정하는 것이 훌륭한 시간 관리 방법이라고 언급하므로, 필자의 주

장으로 가장 적절한 것은 ②이다.

해석 가끔 당신이 생각하기에 거의 힘이 들지 않을 것 같은 프로젝트가 매우 어렵고 진을 빼는 것으로 드러난다. 관계의 문제나 질병처럼 당신이 집중하지 못하게 할 수 있는 상황들이 있다. 가장 최악의 것은 모든 것을 끝내지 못한 것에 대해, 주기적으로 미루는 것에 대해, 또는 때때로 느긋해지는 것에 대해 스스로를 자책하는 것이다. 당신이 죄책감을 느끼는 데 쓰는 시간과 에너지가 덜 생산적인 아침을 덜 생산적인 하루로 연장시킬 수 있다. 심지어 가장 활력이 넘치고 효율적인 사람들도 가끔 일이 잘 안 되는 날이 있다. 그들을 훌륭한 시간 관리자로 만드는 것은 그들이 이러한 것들(일이 잘 안 되는 날)이 삶의 일부분인 것을 깨닫는다는 것이다. 그들은 자신을 용서하고, 자신들의 일정에 맞게 필요한 조정을 하고, 계속 나아간다. 당신이 성취하지 못한 것을 깊이 생각하는 것 대신, 당신이 할 수 있던 것에 대해 자신의 공로를 인정하라.

구문 [1행~3행] Sometimes, *a project* [that (you thought) would be almost effortless] turns out to be very difficult and draining.

[ ]는 주격 관계대명사가 이끄는 관계사절이며, you thought가 삽입되었다.

[11행~13행] *The thing* [that **makes** them good time managers] is **that they realize these are a part of life**.

첫 번째 that절은 주격 관계대명사가 이끄는 관계사절로 The thing을 수식하고, [ ] 안에서 목적어와 목적격 보어의 관계는 동격이다. 두 번째 that절은 명사절로 문장에서 보어 역할을 한다.

어휘 turn out ~인 것으로 드러나다[밝혀지다] **drain** (힘, 돈 등을) 소모시키다; 물을 빼다 **circumstance** 상황, 사정; 환경 **distract** 집중이 안 되게 하다; (주의를) 딴 데로 돌리다 **beat oneself up** 자책하다 **periodically** 주기[정기]적으로 **from time to time** 때때로, 이따금 **guilty** 죄책감이 드는; 유죄의 **extend** 연장시키다; 확장하다 **occasionally** 가끔 **off day** 일이 잘 안 되는[컨디션이 좋지 않은] 날; 비번[쉬는] 날 **adjustment** 조정, 조절; 적응 **dwell on** ~을 깊이 생각하다 **give A credit for B** B에 대해 A의 공로를 인정하다

3 밑줄 함의   ②

해설 외계 문명이 존재한다고 믿는 과학자들이 외계 문명과의 만남을 기다리고 있으며, 이러한 외계 문명과 연락하기 위해 필요한 모든 기술이 확보되어 있고, 외계 문명 또한 상당히 발달된 기술을 개발했을 수 있다고 했다. 따라서 밑줄 친 '중대한 발걸음을 내딛으려는 문턱'이라는 말은 ② '외계 문명과의 첫 번째 접촉'을 뜻한다.

----

① 주요한 천문학 자료 자산의 통합
③ 지구와 비슷한 행성들로 여행 가는 것의 실현 가능성
④ 우주의 신비를 밝힐 절대 진리
⑤ 인간 문명의 통신 기술에서의 발전

해석 우리 인간의 문명보다 더 발달한 문명이 있는가? 성간 통신을 이루어내고 우리의 은하 전체에 걸쳐서 연결된 사회 네트워크를 구축한 문명이 있는가? 이러한 질문은 오랫동안 신학과 사변 소설의 독점적인 영역이었다. 하지만, 이러한 질문들은 이제 실험 과학의 영역으로 들어갔고, 과학자들은 다른 문명들과의 만남을 간절하게 기다리고 있다. 여기 지구에서 생명체가 생긴 과정에 대한 지식으로, 과학자들은 유사한 과정들이 우주 전체에 걸쳐서 상당히 보편적임에 틀림없다고 믿는다. 지능과 기술은 높은 생존 가치를 지니기 때문에, 다른 별의 행성에서 원시 생명체가 수십억 년에 걸쳐 진화하면서 이따금 지능, 문명, 그리고 첨단 기술을 개발했을 것처럼 보인다. 게다가, 우주 깊은 곳에 있는 다른 문명들과 소통하는 데 필요한 모든 기술이 확보되어 있다. 정말로, 우리는 지금 중대한 발걸음을 내딛으려는 문턱에 서 있는 것일 수 있다.

구문 [12행~17행] Since intelligence and technology have a high survival value, // it seems likely that primitive life forms on the planets of other stars, / evolving over many billions of years, / would occasionally develop intelligence, civilization, and a high technology.
since는 '~ 때문에'라는 의미의 부사절을 이끄는 접속사이다. it은 가주어이고, that 이하가 진주어이다. evolving ~ years는 분사구문이 삽입된 것이다.

어휘 interstellar 성간의, 행성 간의　exclusive 독점적인; 배타적인　province 영역, 분야　theology 신학　speculative fiction 사변 소설(초현실적인 문학 작품)　realm 영역, 범위　anxiously 간절하게, 애타게　await 기다리다　encounter 만남, 접촉　arise 발생하다　primitive 원시적인　secure 확보하다; 안전하게 하다　threshold 문턱, 문지방　momentous 중대한　[선택지 어휘] integration 통합　astronomical 천문학(상)의　asset 자산　extraterrestrial 외계의　cf. terrestrial 지구(상)의; 육지의　feasibility 실현 가능성　uncover 밝히다, 발견하다

---

4 글의 제목 ⑤

해설 걱정은 미래를 예측하고 대비하게 해 주어 생존 가능성을 높여주는 순기능도 있는 반면, 일어나지 않을 미래의 일로 불안해하도록 우리를 붙잡아두는 역기능도 있다는 내용의 글이므로, 글의 제목으로 가장 적절한 것은 ⑤ '두 얼굴의 걱정: 우리의 보호자이자 우리의 적'이다.
① 걱정을 멈추고 삶을 시작하는 방법
② 걱정을 두려움과 다르게 하는 것은 무엇인가
③ 지나간 나날에 대해 걱정해봤자 소용없다
④ 고도 불안을 지닌 사람들의 지능이 더 높다

해석 걱정은 우리가 미래에 일어날지 모르는 가능한 위험 혹은 불쾌한 가능성을 곰곰이 생각해보고 불안해하기 시작하는 지점이다. 그리고 이것은 관련된 부차적 신체 반응을 수반할 수 있다. 걱정은 인간이 특히 초기에 생존을 위한 전투에서 다른 형태의 행동의 가능한 결과를 계산할 수 있게 해주는 진화이다. 우리를 동물과 구별시켜주는 것은 바로 이러한 능력인데, 왜냐하면 우리는 가능한 결과를 예상할 수 있고, 이는 우리에게 진화적 이점을 주기 때문이다. 그러나 실제로 결코 일어나지 않을 많은 상황에 대해 우리가 결국 걱정하고 불안해할 수 있다는 잠재적 불리함이 이러한 이점과 함께 한다. 많은 사람들에게 걱정은 그들의 삶을 장악할 수 있고, 그들은 항상 잠재적인 미래의 시나리오 속에서 살고 있기 때문에 결국 현재를 즐기지 못하게 될 수 있다.

구문 [8행~10행] It is this capacity that distinguishes us from animals, // as we can anticipate possible outcomes, which gives us an evolutionary advantage.

「It is ... that ~」은 '~한 것은 바로 …이다'라는 뜻의 강조구문이며, 이 문장에서는 this capacity가 강조되고 있다. 「distinguish A from B」는 'A를 B와 구별하다'의 뜻이다. which는 앞의 어구를 의미하는데, 의미적으로는 having the capacity to anticipate possible outcomes이다.
[10행~13행] But with this advantage comes the potential disadvantage **that** we may end up **worrying** and anxious about *many situations* [that in practice will never occur].
동사는 comes이고 주어는 the potential disadvantage인 도치 구문이다. that 이하는 the potential disadvantage에 대한 동격절이다. end up 다음의 worrying과 anxious는 병렬구조를 이룬다. [ ]는 many situations를 수식한다.

어휘 reflect on 곰곰이 생각해보다; ~을 반성하다　secondary 이차적인, 부차적인　work out ~을 계산[산출]하다　anticipate 예상하다　evolutionary 진화의　take over 인수하다, 장악하다　[선택지 어휘] it is no use v-ing v해도 소용없다　bygone 지나간, 옛날의

---

5 도표 이해 ④

해설 성인을 위한 프로그램이 더 나이 든 집단에게 10% 포인트 더 중요했고, 또한 청년을 위한 프로그램에서도 더 젊은 집단보다 9% 포인트 더 중요했다. 그러므로 청년을 위한 프로그램은 더 젊은 집단에게 9% 포인트 더 중요했다는 ④의 진술은 도표의 내용과 일치하지 않는다.

해석 어떤 공공 도서관 서비스를 '매우 중요하다고' 생각하나요?
위 그래프는 사람들에게 그들이 어떤 공공 도서관 서비스를 '매우 중요하다고' 생각하는지에 대해 질문한 설문조사의 결과를 보여준다. ① 30세 이상의 사람들에 대해서는, 가장 큰 비율의 응답자들이 도서관이 제공하는 책과 매체를 높이 평가했다. ② 이것은 또한 16세에서 29세 사이의 사람들 사이에서도 인기가 있었고, 더 나이 어린 집단에서 가장 많이 선택된 응답인 '조용하고 안전한 장소 구비'에 겨우 3% 뒤쳐진 결과로 나온 것이다. ③ 한편, '구직, 일자리 지원 도움'은 30세 이상인 사람들의 29%와 30세 미만인 사람들의 32%에게 매우 중요했다. ④ 흥미롭게도, 성인을 위한 프로그램이 더 나이 든 집단에게 10% 포인트 더 중요했고 청년을 위한 프로그램은 더 젊은 집단에게 9% 포인트 더 중요했다. ⑤ 30세 이상의 사람들 중 절반이 넘는 사람들이 '책과 매체' 그리고 '조용하고 안전한 장소 구비'와 같은 서비스가 자신에게 매우 중요하다고 말했다.

구문 [1행~3행] The graph above shows the results of *a survey* (asking people about which *public-library services* they consider to be "very important.")
a survey는 현재분사 asking이 이끄는 (　)의 수식을 받는다. 밑줄 친 부분은 전치사 about의 목적어로 쓰인 명사절이다. 여기서 which는 public-library services를 수식하는 형용사이다. to be very important는 consider의 목적보어 역할을 한다.
[7행~8행] ~, coming in just 3% behind "having a quiet, safe place," the most chosen response from the younger group.
밑줄 친 두 개의 명사구는 동격 어구로 뒤의 어구가 앞의 어구를 보충 설명하고 있다.

어휘 apply for ~에 지원하다　survey 조사　respondent 응답자

---

6 내용 불일치 ⑤

해설 두 편의 전기가 쓰였다는 것은 맞지만, Stanislavski가 사망하기 전이 아닌 사망한 후에 쓰였다고 나와 있으므로 ⑤가 일치하지 않는다.

해석 Stanislavski는 연극의 연습과 준비 그리고 리허설을 위한 유명한 시스템의 발명가였을 뿐만 아니라, 러시아의 배우이자 연출가였다. 어린 시절, 그는 발레와 서커스에 흥미

가 있었다. 그는 나중에 연기에 관심을 갖게 되어 33세까지 아마추어로서 연기를 하고 연출을 했는데, 그때 그는 세계적으로 유명한 모스크바 예술 극단을 Vladimir Nemirovich-Danchenko와 공동으로 창단했다. 그 극단의 인기 있는 제작물인 1898년의 'The Seagull'과 1911년의 'Hamlet'은 Stanislavski의 재능을 전 세계의 관객들에게 선보였다. 불행하게도, Stanislavski는 공연 도중 무대에서 심장마비를 일으켰다. 하지만, 그는 1938년 75세의 나이로 사망할 때까지 계속해서 연기를 감독하고, 가르치고, 연기에 대한 글을 썼다. 사망하기 전에, 그는 한편의 자서전을 집필했으며, 그가 사망한 후 그 이래로 그의 생애에 대한 두 편의 영어로 된 전기(傳記)가 쓰였다.

구문 [4행~8행] He later became interested in acting / and performed and directed as an amateur / until *the age of 33*, // when he co-founded the world-famous Moscow Art Theatre company / with Vladimir Nemirovich-Danchenko. when이 이끄는 관계부사절이 선행사 the age of 33 시기에 대한 부연설명을 하고 있다.

[8행~10행] Its popular productions of *The Seagull* in 1898 and Hamlet in 1911 / **showed** Stanislavski's talent / to audiences around the world.
앞의 밑줄 친 두 부분은 전치사 of로 연결된 동격관계이며, 동사는 showed이다.

어휘 director 연출가, 감독 *cf.* direct 연출[감독]하다; 직접적인; 명령[지시]하다; 직행의 co-found 공동 창단[창립]하다 production 제작[저작]물, 작품; (연구의) 결과; 생산 suffer 고통받다; (안 좋은 일을) 겪다 autobiography 자서전 biography (인물의) 전기, 일대기

7 밑줄 어법 ④

해설 ④ 접속사 because가 이끄는 부사절의 주어 the engine's idling frequency에 호응하는 동사가 있어야 하므로 to be를 is로 바꾸어야 한다.
① '재생되는'이라는 뜻으로 앞에 있는 명사 the sound wave를 수식하는 과거분사 played가 올바르게 쓰였다.
② 절의 주어 the amplitude of the vibration과 동일하여 생략된 분사구문의 주어와 분사가 '진동의 진폭이 도달하는' 능동의 관계이므로, 현재분사 reaching이 올바르게 쓰였다.
③ '심하게, 격렬하게' 라는 뜻으로 동사 shake를 수식하는 부사 violently가 올바르게 쓰였다.
⑤ '~도 마찬가지이다'라는 뜻의 「so + 동사 + 주어」 구문의 동사 자리이다. 복수 주어 designers가 왔고 앞 문장의 동사가 일반동사 try를 대신하므로 조동사 do가 올바르게 쓰였다.

해석 종을 치면 그것이 만들어내는 소리가 '고유 진동수'로 음이 될 것이다. 이제 음향 스피커를 그 종에 부착하고, 이를 통해서 재생되는 음파의 진동수를 점진적으로 증가시켜라. 종은 이 소리에 반응하여 진동할 것이고 진동의 진폭은 증가할 것인데, 종의 진동수가 고유한 진동수와 일치할 때 최고점에 도달하게 되며, 이것이 상대적으로 작은 진폭의 투입에 의해 야기되는 큰 진폭의 진동을 의미하는 공명의 사례이다. 공명은 엔진 공회전을 하는 자동차가 엔진의 회전 속도가 더 빠르게 올라갈 때보다 훨씬 더 큰 진동을 겪으면서 심하게 흔들릴 수 있는 이유이다. 이는 엔진의 공회전 진동수, 즉 1초당 엔진이 만들어내는 회전의 수가 차체의 고유한 진동수와 가깝기 때문에 발생한다. 엔지니어들은 공명 진동의 진폭을 제한해서 공명의 효과를 제한하려 한다. 그리고 지진 지역에서 높은 건물을 담당하는 디자이너들도 마찬가지이다.

구문 [10행~13행] Resonance is *the reason* [why a car with its engine idling can shake violently, / experiencing vibrations **much** larger than when the engine is revving faster].
[ ]는 the reason을 수식하는 관계부사절이다. much는 a lot, far, still, even 등과 같이 비교급을 수식하는 부사로 '훨씬'을 의미한다.

어휘 note 음(표) frequency 진동수, 주파수 attach 붙이다, 부착하다 sound wave 음파 vibrate 진동하다, 떨다 in response to A A에 반응하여 resonance 공명, 울림 relatively 상대적으로 revolution 회전 in charge of ~을 담당하는

8 밑줄 어휘 ⑤

해설 앞의 내용은 유대가 긴밀하고 공동체 전체에 대한 책임 의식이 높으면 범죄를 신고하려는 마음과 범죄에 개입할 가능성을 높여 경찰 순찰대의 필요성을 방지할 수도 있다는 것이다. 따라서 강력한 사회적 유대는 감시를 강화한다는 문맥이 자연스러우므로 ⑤ 'weaken'은 reinforce(강화하다)로 고쳐야 한다.

해석 유대가 긴밀한 공동체는 길거리 범죄의 문제를 최소화할 수 있다. 그러나 비공식적인 사회 통제가 강력 범죄는 ① 억제할 수 있을지 몰라도, 그것은 또한 다원적 사회에 존재하는 행동의 다양성에는 위협을 제기한다. 하지만 공동체 주민 간의 교류가 더 ② 빈번하다면, 그리고 사회적 유대가 더 강하다면 길거리 범죄는 감소할 것이다. 다른 시민들과 공동체 전체에 대한 책임 의식은 범죄를 경찰에 기꺼이 신고하려는 개인의 마음과 일어나고 있는 범죄에 그들이 ③ 개입할 가능성을 높여 줄 것이다. 더 기꺼이 범죄를 경찰에 신고하려는 공동체 주민들의 마음은 또한 민간 경찰 순찰대의 필요성을 ④ 방지할 수도 있다. 공공장소에서의 더 많은 교류와 보도에서 사람들의 더 많은 왕래는 현재 사람들이 가기 두려워하는 장소에 대한 감시를 증가시킬 것이다. 더 강력한 사회적 유대는 범죄자에 대항하여 기꺼이 조치를 취하려는 마음과 더불어 감시를 ⑤ 약화할(→ 강화할) 것이다.

구문 [8행~12행] A sense of responsibility for other citizens and for the community as a whole / would increase <u>individuals' willingness to report crime to the police</u> and <u>the likelihood of their intervention in a crime in progress</u>.
동사 increase의 목적어로 밑줄 친 두 개의 명사구가 and로 연결되었다.

[14행~17행] *More interaction* (in public places) and *human traffic* (on the sidewalks) / would increase surveillance of *the places* [where people now fear to go].
밑줄 친 부분은 문장의 주어로 in public places는 More interaction을 수식하고 on the sidewalks는 human traffic을 수식한다. [ ]는 관계절로 the places를 수식한다.

어휘 tight-knit 유대가 긴밀한 pose a threat to ~에 위협을 제기하다 pluralistic 다원적인; 다민족인 curb 억제하다 bond 유대; 끈 intervention 개입 civilian 민간(인)의 traffic (사람·차의) 왕래 intense 강렬한 take action 조치를 취하다 offender 범죄자

9 빈칸 추론 ②

해설 인간은 만물의 척도라는 자부심을 가지고 스스로를 동물들과 차별화하는 경향이 있는데, 이러한 태도는 동물과 인간이 겉모습과 일부 측면만 제외하면 얼마나 많은 유사점들을 공유하고 있는지를 보지 못하게 작용한다. 즉 인간으로 하여금 많은 것을 ② '간과하게(overlook)' 한다.
① 정당화하게 ③ 공감하게 ④ 관리하게 ⑤ 조사하게

해석 기원전 5세기에, 그리스의 철학자 Protagoras는 "인간이 만물의 척도이다."라고 선언했다. 다시 말해서, 우리는 세상을 향해 "너는 무슨 쓸모가 있느냐?"라고 물어볼 자격이 있다고 느낀다. 우리는 우리가 세상의 기준이라고, 즉 모든 것이 우리에게 비교되어야 한다고 여긴다. 그런 추정은 우리가 많은 것을 간과하게 한다. '우리를 인간으로 만들어 준다고' 말해지는 능력들, 즉 공감, 의사소통, 슬픔, 도구 제작 등은 우리와 세상을 공유하는 다른 지적 존재들에게도 다양한 정도로 모두 존재한다. 척추동물(어류, 양서류, 파충류, 조류, 포유류)은 모두 동일한 기본 골격, 장기, 신경계, 호르몬, 행동을 공유한다. 다양한 자동차의 모델들이 각각 엔진, 동력 전달 체계, 네 개의 바퀴, 문, 좌석을 가지는 것과 마찬

가지로, 우리는 주로 우리의 외면의 윤곽과 몇 가지 내부적인 변경 면에서 다르다. 하지만 순진한 자동차 구매자들처럼, 대부분의 사람들은 오직 동물들의 다양한 겉모습만을 본다.

구문 [7행~10행] *Abilities* (said to "make us human" ― empathy, communication, grief, toolmaking, and so on ―) all **exist** to varying degrees among *other minds* (sharing the world with us).

첫 번째 ( )는 수동의 의미를 나타내는 분사구로 주어 Abilities를 수식하며 동사는 exist이다. 두 번째 ( )는 능동의 의미로 other minds를 수식한다.

[14행~17행] **Just as** different models of automobiles each have an engine, drive train, four wheels, doors, and seats, // we differ mainly in terms of our outside contours and a few internal tweaks.

Just as는 '~하는 것과 마찬가지로'의 의미의 부사절 접속사이다. 밑줄 친 명사(구)는 콤마와 and로 병렬 구조를 이룬다.

어휘 pronounce 선언하다; 발음하다   measure 척도; 치수; 측정[판단]하다   entitle 자격[권리]을 부여하다   vary 다양하다   amphibian 양서류   reptile 파충류   drive train 동력 전달 체계   in terms of ~면에서[관점에서]   contour 윤곽(선); 윤곽을 그리다   naive 순진한   exterior 외부

10 빈칸 추론   ④

해설 아이에게 말할 때 원하지 않는 바를 강조하지 말고 원하는 바를 표현하라고 하면서 문을 닫는 것을 예로 들어 설명하고 있다. 원하는 바를 이야기할 때 아이는 비로소 시각적 이미지를 가진다고 했으므로 빈칸에는 이렇게 언급된 말이 ④ '요청과 잘 들어맞고'가 적절하다.

① 여러 의미를 가지고
② 약간 강조될 수 있고
③ 부정적 함축을 가지고
⑤ 비언어적 행동과 일치하고

해석 아이와 말할 때 여러분이 원하지 않는 바를 강조하기보다는 원하는 바를 표현하는 것을 배우라. 아이들은 자기들이 받는 메시지에 매우 즉각적으로 반응을 보인다. 어른이 "문을 쾅 닫지 마라."고 말하면 그 말을 듣는 아이는 앞에 '…하지 마라'라는 단어가 있는 '문을 쾅 닫다'라는 어구를 듣게 된다. 그 아이는 문을 쾅 닫는 것이 바람직하지 않은 행동임을 이해해야 하는데, 그것은 특히 어린 아이들에게는 이해하기가 어렵다. 아이로부터 성공적인 반응이 나올 가능성은 어른이 "문을 부드럽게 닫아 주렴."이라고 말할 때 극적으로 증가한다. 이제 그 아이는 따라야 하는 시각적 이미지를 갖는다. 언급된 그 말은 요청과 잘 들어맞고, 그것은 이해하는 것을 훨씬 더 쉽게 해준다.

구문 [13행~15행] *The words* (spoken) fit together well with the request, // which makes **it** much easier *to understand*.

과거분사인 spoken은 주어진 The words를 수식한다. 관계대명사절에서 it은 가목적어이고 진목적어는 to understand이고 easier는 목적보어로 쓰였다.

어휘 put emphasis on ~을 강조하다   responsive 즉각적으로 반응하는   slam (문 따위를) 탕 닫다   phrase 어구   figure out ~을 이해하다   undesirable 바람직하지 않은   comprehend 이해하다   dramatically 극적으로   **[선택지 어휘]** connotation 함축, 암시   fit together well 잘 들어맞다   consistent 일치하는, 조화된

11 빈칸 추론   ③

해설 앞에 제시된 세 가지 예에서는 공통적으로, 미래를 예측할 때 과거의 수치를

기준으로 삼아 과거와 달라진 상황을 고려하여 미래에 대한 수치를 조정하는 전략이 제시되어 있다. 이를 반영하여 빈칸에 들어갈 알맞은 말은 ③ '처음의 고정값으로 출발해서 그 다음에 그것을 조정함'이다.

① 우선 관련 자료를 분석하여 그것의 정확성을 추론함
② 상황을 근거로 알려진 사실과 비교함
④ 옳다고 입증될 때까지 그 숫자를 반복적으로 계산함
⑤ 특별한 경우의 결과를 예측하는 능력을 과대평가함

해석 삶은 인간이 불확실한 양을 추정할 것을 요구한다. 학기 보고서를 완성하는 데 얼마나 오래 걸릴 것인가? 5년 후에 주택 담보 대출 금리는 얼마나 높아질 것인가? 군인이 해외의 군사적 개입에서 죽을 확률은 얼마인가? 그러한 질문들에 답하기 위해 노력하는 여러 가지 방법들이 있다. 사람들은 다음의 판단 전략을 사용하는 경향이 있다. "내가 지난 번 보고서를 작성하는 데는 일주일이 걸렸지만, 이번 것은 더 까다로우니까 아마 2주가 합당한 추정이겠지." "주택 담보 대출 금리는 역사에 남을 만한 수준으로 낮으니까 아마 5년 후에는 두세 번 더 고점을 찍겠지." "지난번 전쟁에서의 사망률은 1.5%였지만, 우리의 적들이 기술적으로 따라잡고 있어. 다음 번 충돌에서는 아마 4%가 더 그럴 듯한 수치일 거야." 이 모든 예들이 공유하는 점은 개인들이 그들의 최종 판단에 도달하기 위한 의사 결정의 그 다음 과정 동안 처음의 고정값에서 출발해서 그 다음에 그것을 조정함으로써 수적 규모를 추산한다는 것이다.

구문 [2행~3행] How long will **it take to complete** a term paper?

「It takes (시간) to-v」는 'v하는 데 (시간)이 걸리다'의 뜻이다.

[4행~5행] What is the probability of *a soldier* dying in a military intervention overseas?

밑줄 친 두 부분은 of로 연결된 동격 관계이다. a soldier는 동명사 dying의 의미상 주어이다.

어휘 mortgage rate 주택 담보 대출 금리   probability 확률, 개연성   intervention 조정, 중재   overseas 해외에서   strategy 전략   demanding 까다로운   historic 역사에 남을 만한   fatality rate 사망률   catch up 따라잡다   figure 숫자   gauge 추산하다   subsequent 차후의, 그 다음의

12 빈칸 추론   ②

해설 현대에는 열대보다 온대 지역의 경제가 훨씬 발전해 있기 때문에 기후 혹은 지리와 경제적 성공 간에 연관이 있다고 생각해볼 수도 있겠지만, 콜럼버스의 아메리카 대륙 정복기에는 오히려 열대 지역의 문명이 온대 지역보다 훨씬 발달했기 때문에 그러한 연관관계를 실증할 수 없다는 내용의 글이다. 그러므로 빈칸을 완성하면 ② '기후나 지리와 경제적 성공 간에' 연관이 없다가 된다.

① 지정학적 세력과 무역에 대한 개방성 간에
③ 세계 어느 지역에서나 인종과 지능 간에
④ 교육 부문의 투자와 경제 성장 간에
⑤ 천연 자원의 매장량과 국가의 부 간에

해석 역사는 기후나 지리와 경제적 성공 간에 단순한 혹은 오래가는 연관이 없음을 실증한다. 콜럼버스의 아메리카 대륙 정복기에 오늘날 멕시코, 중앙아메리카, 페루와 볼리비아를 포함하는 지역은 위대한 아즈텍과 잉카 문명을 보유했다. 이 제국들은 정치적으로 중앙집권화되어 있었고 복잡했으며, 도로를 건설했고, 기근 구제를 제공했다. 아즈텍 족에게는 돈도 있었고 글도 있었으며, 잉카 족은 막대한 양의 정보를 매듭진 밧줄에 기록했다. 완전히 대조적으로, 아즈텍 족과 잉카 족의 시대에, 아즈텍 족과 잉카 족이 거주하던 지역의 북쪽과 남쪽은 오늘날 미국, 캐나다, 아르헨티나와 칠레를 포함하고 있는데, 대개 이러한 기술이 없는 석기 시대 문명에 의해 거주되었다. 아메리카 대륙의 열대 지역은 따라서 온대 지역보다 훨씬 부유했다. 오늘날의 미국과 캐나다의 더 거대해진 부는 유럽인들이 도착했던 때에 존재하던 것에 비하여 부의 극명한 역전을 나타낸다.

구문 [6행~8행] These empires <u>were</u> politically centralized and complex, <u>built</u> roads, <u>and</u> <u>provided</u> famine relief.

과거동사 were, built, provided가 and로 연결되어 병렬구조를 이룬다.

[11행~15행] ~ **the north and south of** *the area* (inhabited by the Aztecs and Incas), // which today includes the United States, Canada, Argentina, and Chile, / **were** mostly **inhabited** by *Stone Age civilizations* (lacking these technologies).

첫 번째 ( )는 the area를 수식하는 과거분사구이다. which ~ Chile는 the north and south of the area에 대한 추가적인 정보를 제시한다. 주어는 the north and south of the area이고 동사는 were inhabited이다. 두 번째 ( )는 Stone Age civilizations를 수식하는 현재분사구이다.

어휘 illustrate 실증하다 enduring 오래가는, 지속되는 conquest 정복 empire 제국 centralize 중앙집권화하다 famine relief 기근 구제 knot 매듭을 매다 inhabit 거주하다 mostly 대개 temperate zone 온대 stark 엄연한, (차이가) 극명한 reversal 역전

13 흐름 무관 문장 ③

해설 첫 문장에서 '치료는 오랜 역사를 가지고 있다'는 것이 주제임을 알 수 있고, 이것에 대한 구체적인 사례들이 열거되고 있는데, ③은 과거의 의학이 원시적이어서 경미한 부상이 사망으로 자주 이어졌다는 내용이므로, 글 전체의 흐름과 무관하다.

해석 치료는, 생각의 집합체인 동시에 관행의 연속으로서, 확실히 인간 문화의 가장 오래되고 지속적인 요소들 중의 하나이다. ① 선사시대의 유적에서 나온 물질적인 유물은 우리의 먼 조상들이 질병은 원인을 가지고 있으며 누군가는 아픈 사람을 돕기 위해 그 지식을 사용할 수 있다고 생각했다는 것을 분명하게 보여준다. ② 인간의 유해는 이 사람들이 부러진 뼈를 고치고 심지어는 살아 있는 사람의 두개골에 구멍을 뚫을 수도 있었다는 것을 보여준다. ③ 의학은 원시적이어서 사람들은 오늘날에는 경미한 것으로 간주되고 간단한 살균제로 효과적으로 치료할 수 있었던 부상이나 감염으로 죽었다. ④ 기원전 2700년경에 이탈리아와 오스트리아 사이에 있는 Tisenjoch의 알프스 고산지대의 산길에서 죽은 '얼음인간'은 자신의 마지막이자 치명적인 여행을 떠나기 오래전에 이미 여러 개의 부러진 갈비뼈에서 회복된 적이 있었고, 그는 또한 자신의 여행 장비에 질병과 부상을 치료하는 건조시킨 자작나무 버섯을 지니고 다녔다. ⑤ 의학은 비록 언덕만큼 오래되지는 않았지만, 적어도 언덕을 넘어가려는 인간의 야심만큼은 오래된 것이다.

구문 [3행~7행] *Material remains* (from prehistoric sites) clearly show // that our distant ancestors thought / <u>that disease had a cause</u> <u>and</u> that someone could use that knowledge / to help the sick person.

( )의 수식을 받는 Material remains가 문장의 주어이고, show가 동사이다. that our ~ sick person은 동사 show의 목적어로 쓰인 명사절이며, 그 명사절 안에서 동사 thought의 목적어로 that절 두 개가 and로 연결되어 병렬구조를 이루고 있다.

어휘 collection 집합(체); 수집(품) sequence 연속, 연쇄 practice 관행, 관례; 실행, 실천 ancient 아주 오래된; 고대[옛날]의 persistent 지속적인, 영속적인 material 물질적인; 재료, 원료 remains 유물, 유해; 남은 것, 나머지 prehistoric 선사시대의 indicate 보이다, 나타내다; 가리키다 skull 두개골 primitive 원시적인; 초기의 infection 감염 set out on a journey 여행[여정]을 떠나다 fateful 치명적인; 운명을 결정하는 wound 부상, 상처; 부상[상처]을 입히다 ambition 야심, 의욕; 야망, 포부

14 글의 순서 ②

해설 이야기에 대한 청중의 관심을 받는 것이 힘든 것이며, 그 이유에 대해 관심을 스포트라이트에 비유해 설명하고자 한다는 주어진 글 다음으로 스포트라이트의 특징을 부연 설명하는 (B)가 이어진다. 그리고 이와 유사한 인간이 관심을 아껴서 사용한다는 것에 대한 예로 고속도로에서 운전하는 동안 특정한 것에 관심을 쏟지 않고 다양한 정보를 흡수하는 상황을 설명하는 (A)가 이어진다. 그렇게 흐려진 관심의 스포트라이트가 앞차의 급제동으로 인한 사고를 피하기 위해 초점이 맞추어지는 것처럼, 스토리텔링에서도 지속적으로 긴장감을 유지해야 청중의 관심을 유지할 수 있다고 결론짓는 (C)가 오는 것이 자연스럽다.

해석 하나의 이야기를 효과적으로 만드는 것은 무엇일까? 어떤 할리우드 작가든 관심은 희귀한 자원임(주목받기 매우 힘들다는 것)을 당신에게 말해줄 것이다. 과학자들은 관심을 스포트라이트에 비유한다.

(B) 우리는 그것(스포트라이트)을 좁은 곳에만 비출 수 있을 뿐이다. 만약 그곳이 다른 곳보다 덜 흥미롭게 보인다면, 우리의 관심은 배회하게 된다. 사실 자신의 관심 스포트라이트를 사용하는 것은 신진대사적으로 비용이 많이 들어서(몸이 힘들어서) 우리는 그것을 아껴서 사용한다.

(A) 그래서 당신이 고속도로를 달리며 전화 통화를 하거나 음악을 듣는 일을 동시에 할 수 있는 것이다. 당신의 관심 스포트라이트가 흐릿해서 당신은 다양한 정보의 흐름을 흡수할 수 있다.

(C) 당신은 앞의 차가 급하게 브레이크를 밟아서 당신의 관심 스포트라이트가 사고를 피하는 데 도움이 될 수 있게 완전히 비출 때까지 이것(다양한 정보의 흐름을 흡수하는 것)을 할 수 있다. 스토리텔링의 관점에서 보자면 청중의 관심을 유지하는 방법은 그 이야기에서 지속적으로 긴장을 증가시키는 것이다.

구문 [12행~14행] You can do this // **until** *the car* (in front of you) jams on its brakes / <u>and</u> your attentional spotlight illuminates fully to help you avoid an accident.

시간의 부사절을 이끄는 접속사 until(~할 때까지)이 쓰였고, 부사절 내에서 두 개의 절이 and로 연결되어 병렬구조를 이룬다.

[14행~16행] From a story-telling perspective, / *the way* (to keep an audience's attention) **is** to continually increase the tension in the story.

( )는 to-v의 형용사적 용법으로 the way를 수식하고, to continually increase the tension in the story는 to-v의 명사적 용법으로 문장의 보어 역할을 한다.

어휘 scarce 희귀한, 드문; 부족한 liken A to B A를 B에 비유하다 dim 흐릿한, 희미한 absorb 흡수하다; 받아들이다; 몰두시키다 multiple 다양한; 많은 stream 흐름; 줄기; 개울 wander 배회하다, 돌아다니다; 방황하다 metabolically 신진대사적으로, 대사 작용으로 costly 비용이 많이 드는, 값비싼 sparingly 아껴서; 절약하여; 조금만 illuminate 비추다, 밝게 하다; 분명히 하다[밝히다] perspective 관점; 전망; 원근법 tension 긴장 (상태), 긴장감

15 글의 순서 ④

해설 (C)에 제시된 예들은 주어진 문장의 '동물 행동의 목적성과 정확성'에 대한 것이므로, (C)가 처음에 나와야 하고, 첫 문장에 however가 있는 (A)는 (C)의 뒷부분에 나와 있는 '동물이 이성이나 지혜를 가지고 있을 가능성'에 대해서 반박하는 내용의 시작 부분이므로, (C) 다음에 (A)가 나와야 한다. (B)의 첫 문장의 instinctive (본능적인)는 (A)에서 말하고 있는 동물 행동의 특징인 rigid and innate nature(융통성 없고 타고난 본성), automatic manner(자동적인 방식)와 관계가 있으므로, (B)는 (A) 다음에 오는 것이 적절하다.

해석 우리는 몇몇 동물들이 자기 자신과 자신의 종의 보존을 목표로 할 때 그 (동물들의)

행동의 목적성과 정확성에 자주 놀란다.

(C) 둥지 만들기, 겨울을 위한 식량 저장, 몇몇 종의 물고기와 새들이 완주하는 긴 여행, 그리고 곤충들이 알에게 적절한 영양분을 확실히 주기 위해 알을 배치하는 것은 인간이 항상 이런 동물들에게 어떤 종류의 이성이나 지혜가 있다고 생각하게 해 왔던 행동 방식의 예들이다.

(A) 하지만, 이 현상에 대한 좀 더 자세한 연구는 그것의 융통성 없고 타고난 특성을 드러내어 주었다. 즉, 비록 그것들이 유용하고 목적을 보여주기는 하지만, 그런 행동들은 동물에게 있어서 통찰력을 수반하지 않으며, 자동적인 방식으로 행해진다.

(B) 이런 종류의 행동은 본능적이라고 불리게 되었다. 본능은 동물이 주어진 형태의 환경에 대단히 정확하게 적응할 수 있게 해 준다. 본능적인 행동의 융통성 없고 틀에 박힌 특성 때문에, 환경 속에서의 예상치 못한 어떠한 변화도 그런 행동을 효과 없게 만들 수 있다.

구문 [15행~20행] Nest construction, / food storage for winter, / *the long journeys* (accomplished by some species of fish and bird), / and the placing of eggs by insects / to ensure for them adequate nutrition, / **are** examples of *the type of behavior* [which has always led man to ascribe some kind of reason or wisdom to these animals].

동사 are에 대해 밑줄 친 주어 4개가 열거되어 있다. ( )는 과거분사 accomplished가 이끄는 형용사구로 the long journeys를 수식한다. [ ]는 주격 관계대명사 which가 이끄는 형용사절로 the type of behavior를 수식한다.

어휘 purposefulness 목적성 precision 정확성 preservation 보존, 보호 phenomenon 현상 rigid 융통성 없는, 완고한 innate 선천적인, 타고난 be accompanied by ~을 수반하다 insight 통찰력; 이해, 간파 automatic 무의식적인, 반사적인 instinctive 본능적인; 본능[직감]에 따르는 *cf.* instinct 본능; 직감 owing to A A 때문에 inflexible 융통성 없는 stereotyped 틀에 박힌, 상투적인 storage 저장(고) ensure 확실히 하다, 보장하다 adequate 적절한, 적합한; 충분한 nutrition 영양 (섭취) reason 이성, 지성; 이유

16 문장 넣기 ③

해설 For example 이하는 Neill의 그 운동이 교육의 실행에 큰 영향을 미친 구체적인 사례에 해당하므로 주어진 문장은 ③에 들어가는 것이 가장 적절하다.

해석 A. S. Neill이 그의 영향력 있는 책 'Summerhill'에서 썼듯이 "어린이는 선천적으로 지혜롭고 현실적이다. 어떤 종류의 어른의 지도도 없이 혼자 남게 될 때 아이는 자신이 발달할 수 있는 만큼 발달할 것이다." 1960년대와 1970년대에 Neill과 그의 동료들은 학교가 시험, 성적, 교육과정, 심지어 책도 없어야 한다고 믿었다. 그렇게 극단적으로까지 행했던 학교는 거의 없었으나 그 운동은 교육의 실행에 큰 영향을 미쳤다. 예를 들어, 총체적 언어라고 알려진 읽기 교육 방법에서 아이들은 어떤 철자가 어떤 소리와 상응하는지를 배우는 것이 아니라 읽기 능력이 자발적으로 발현될 것으로 예상되는, 책이 풍부한 환경에 빠져들게 된다. 구성주의라고 알려진 수학 교육의 철학에서는 아이들은 산수 표를 가지고 반복 훈련하는 것이 아니라 모둠에서 문제를 해결함으로써 수학적 진리를 스스로 재발견하도록 지시를 받는다. 두 방법 모두 학생들의 학습이 객관적으로 평가될 때 잘 되지 않지만, 그러한 방법의 옹호자들은 표준화된 시험을 거부하는 경향이 있다.

구문 [14행~18행] In *the philosophy of mathematics instruction* [known as constructivism], / children are **not** drilled with arithmetic tables / **but** are enjoined to rediscover mathematical truths on their own / by working out problems in groups.

'known as constructivism'은 앞의 the philosophy of mathematics instruction을 수식한다. 「not A but B」 (A가 아니라 B) 구문이 사용되었다.

어휘 innately 선천적으로 abandon 버리다; 그만두다 be immersed in ~에 몰두하다 spontaneously 자발적으로, 자연스럽게 constructivism 구성주의 drill 반복 연습 시키다 arithmetic 산수 enjoin 명하다, 지시하다 advocate 지지하다; 옹호자 disdain 무시하다; 거부하다

17 문장 넣기 ⑤

해설 주어진 문장은 연결사 Furthermore(게다가)로 이어지고 있으므로 이 문장 앞에도 박물관의 긴 줄이 의미하는 부정적인 측면이 언급되어야 한다. 그러므로 박물관의 긴 줄은 당신을 기다리게 해서 바람직한 요인이 아니라는 내용이 나온 다음인 ⑤에 들어가는 것이 적절하다.

해석 소비자 행동은 구매, 사용, 처분 행위로 나누어진다. 자극에 대한 소비자들의 반응이 그들이 단일 제품이나 서비스를 구매하고 있는지, 사용하고 있는지, 또는 처분하고 있는지에 따라 달라질 수 있기 때문에 행위의 유형에 따라 소비자 행동을 분류하는 것은 유용하다. 예를 들어, 구매하려 할 때, 박물관 밖의 긴 줄은 그 박물관을 평가하는 데 있어 긍정적인 요인이다. 긴 줄은 모든 사람들이 그곳에 가기를 원해서 그 박물관이 아마도 매우 좋을 것이라는 것을 의미한다. 하지만 당신이 티켓을 구매하고 나서, 그 긴 줄은, 당신이 들어가기 위해 조바심 내며 기다려야 하기 때문에, 더 이상 바람직한 요인이 아니다. 게다가, 일단 당신이 문에 도착하면, 당신 앞에 있는 그 긴 줄은 그 박물관이 지나치게 붐벼서 훨씬 덜 매력적이라는 것을 암시한다. 그러므로 이러한 예로부터, 행위들이 구매하기 전에 일어나는 것인지 사용하는 동안에 일어나는 것인지에 따라 그것들을 분류하는 것이 어떻게 소비자의 반응이 어떤 상황에서 상당히 변화할 수 있는지를 보여준다.

구문 [5행~9행] Categorizing consumer behavior by type of activity is useful // because consumers' responses to stimuli may differ / depending **on** whether they are purchasing, using, or disposing of a single product or service.

전치사 on의 목적어로 접속사 whether가 이끄는 명사절이 사용되었다.

[16행~20행] So, (from this example,) / categorizing activities / by whether they occur prior to purchase versus during use / **shows** how consumer responses can change significantly within a situation.

categorizing activities ~ during use가 주어이고 shows가 동사이다. how가 이끄는 명사절이 동사 shows의 목적어로 사용되었다.

어휘 break down 나누다; 고장 나다 disposal 처분, 처리; 배치 *cf.* dispose 처분하다; 배치 [배열]하다 categorize 분류하다 stimuli 자극((stimulus의 복수형)) evaluate 평가[감정]하다 imply 암시하다; 의미하다 desirable 바람직한, 호감 가는 impatiently 조바심 내어, 초조하게 make it to A A에 도착[도달]하다 crowded 붐비는, 복잡한 appealing 매력적인; 호소하는 prior to A A전에[앞서]

18 요약문 완성 ②

해설 '자기 점수를 정확하게 예측하는 사람들은 돈을 받을 것'을 통해서 정확한 예측을 하면 경제적 이익(benefit)을 얻는다는 것을 알 수 있고, (B)는 실제로 사람들이 한 행동을 가리키므로, predicted higher results를 통해서 부풀려진(inflated) 예측을 했다는 것을 알 수 있다.

① 이익 - 축소된 ③ 안정 - 비관적인
④ 손해 - 자의적인 ⑤ 손해 - 일관된

해석 Duke 대학의 교수 Dan Ariely는 한 기발한 실험을 설명한다. 한 집단의 사람들이 지능 검사를 받게 되지만, 그들 중 절반은 응답지를 '우연히' 보게 되고, 이것이 그들로 하여금 자기 자신의 답을 기입하기 전에 정답을 찾을 수 있게 한다. 말할 필요도 없이, 그들은 나머지보다 더 높은 점수를 받는다. 그다음, 모든 사람이 나중의 지능 검사에서 자기 점수를 예측하도록 요청받는데, 그 검사에서는 부정행위용 종이가 절대로 없을 것이며, 정확하게 예측 하는 사람들은 돈을 받을 것이다. 놀랍게도, 부정행위용 종이로 더 높은 점

수를 받은 그룹의 절반이 다음 검사에 대해 더 높은 결과를 예측했다. 부정행위자들은 성공에 대한 부정확한 예측이 자신들에게 돈을 잃게 할지라도, 자신이 매우 똑똑하다고 믿고 싶어 했다.

↓

> 정확한 예측이 그들에게 경제적 (A) 이익을 가져다줄 때조차, 부정행위로 더 높은 점수를 받은 사람들은 자신들의 능력에 대해 (B) 부풀려진 예측을 하는 경향이 있었다.

구문 [2행~5행] A group of people are given an intelligence test, // but half of them are "accidentally" shown a response sheet, / **allowing them to look up correct answers** / **before recording their own.**

allowing 이하는 결과를 나타내는 분사구로서 which allows ~로 바꿔 쓸 수 있다.

[6행~9행] Next, / everybody is asked to predict their grades / on *the next IQ test,* / **in which there will be absolutely no cheat sheets** — and *those* [who predict correctly] / will get paid.

in which ~ sheets는 앞의 the next IQ test를 보충 설명한다. [ ]는 주격 관계대명사 who가 이끄는 관계사절로 앞의 those를 수식한다.

어휘 intelligence test 지능 검사   accidentally 우연히, 뜻밖에   needless to say 말할 필요도 없이   score 점수(를 받다), 득점(하다)   absolutely (부정의 의미를 강조할 때) 전혀, 전적으로, 틀림없이   cheat sheet 부정행위용 종이 *cf.* cheater 부정행위자; 사기꾼 *cf.* cheat 부정행위 하다; 속이다   accurate 정확한   [선택지 어휘] deflate 축소하다; (타이어·풍선 등의) 공기를 빼다(↔ inflate 부풀리다, 과장하다; 부풀다)   stability 안정(성), 안정감   arbitrary 자의적인, 임의의   consistent 일관된

19~20 장문   19 ② 20 ③

해설 **19.** 이 글의 첫 단락은 식물이 주변 세상의 시각, 후각, 촉각, 중력, 그들의 과거를 예민하게 인식한다는 내용이고, 두 번째 단락은 이러한 식물들의 인식과 인간이 인식하는 것의 차이점을 나타내는 내용이다. 그러므로 ② '식물이 인식하는 것은 우리가 인식하는 것이 아니다'가 제목으로 가장 적절하다.
① 식물은 20억 년 동안 진화해왔다
③ 신비한 식물의 사고: 식물 생명의 철학
④ 식물은 눈, 귀, 입이 없이 남을 의식한다
⑤ 식물이 알고 있는 것: 식물의 인지와 의사소통

20. 정원사들과 식물학자들이 식물을 의인화해서 인식하지만 식물은 그런 방식으로 사람들을 인식하지 않는다고 했으므로 식물과 인간과의 관계는 쌍방 교류하는 것이 아닌 일방적인 관계이다. 그러므로 (c) two-way는 one-way나 unidirectional 등으로 바꿔 써야 적절하다.

해석 식물들은 자신들 주변의 세상을 예민하게 인식한다. 그것들은 자신의 (a) 시각적 환경을 인식한다. 적색, 청색, 자외선을 구별하고 그에 따라 반응한다. 식물들은 자신을 둘러싼 향을 인식하고, 공기 중에 풍기는 극미한 양의 휘발성 화합물에도 반응을 보인다. 식물들은 무언가가 자신을 만지고 있는 것을 알고 다른 (b) 촉각들과 구분할 수 있다. 식물들은 중력을 인식한다. 그것들은 싹이 위로 자라고 뿌리가 아래로 자라는 것을 확실하게 하려고 자신의 모양을 바꿀 수 있다. 그리고 식물들은 자신의 과거를 인식한다. 그것들은 과거에 감염되었던 일과 견뎌 낸 상황을 기억하고, 그 기억들을 바탕으로 현재 자신의 생리 기능을 수정한다.

식물이 인식한다면 이것은 그 녹색 세상과 우리의 상호작용에 관해서 우리에게 어떤 의미가 있을까? 식물은 주변 환경을 인식하고, 사람은 이 환경의 일부이다. 그러나 식물은 자신들이 그 식물과 개인적인 관계라고 생각하는 것을 발전시키는 무수히 많은 정원사들과 식물학자들을 인식하지 않는다. 이런 (개인적인) 관계는 돌보는 이에게는 의미가 있을지 모르지만, 그것들은 어린아이와 아이의 상상 속 친구의 관계와 다르지 않다. 그 의미의 흐름이 (c) 양방향(→ 일방적)이다. 나는 세계적으로 유명한 과학자들과 학부 연구생들이 흰곰팡이가 식물 잎사귀를 장악했을 때 식물이 '별로 즐거워 보이지 않는다'고 하거나, 식물에게 물을 준 다음에 식물이 '만족스러워' 보인다와 같이 자신의 식물을 묘사할 때 한결같이 멋대로 의인화하는 것을 들은 적이 있다. 이런 용어들은 감정이 없는 것이 확실한 식물의 생리적 상태에 대한 우리의 (d) 주관적 평가를 나타낸다. 식물과 사람이 인식하는 모든 풍부한 감각적 입력 정보들에 대해서, 오직 인간만이 이러한 입력 정보를 (e) 감정적 풍경으로 만든다.

구문 [4행~6행] They <u>are</u> aware of *aromas* (surrounding them) and <u>respond to</u> minute quantities of *volatile compounds* (wafting in the air).

두 개의 ( )는 모두 분사구로 각각 바로 앞의 aromas와 volatile compounds를 수식한다. 문장의 동사로 are와 respond to가 접속사 and로 병렬 연결되었다.

[18행~21행] But it's not aware of *the myriad gardeners and plant biologists* [who **develop** what they consider to be personal relationships with their plants].

[ ]는 who가 이끄는 관계사절로 the myriad gardeners and plant biologists를 수식하며, [ ] 내에서 develop의 목적어로 what이 이끄는 관계사절이 쓰였다.

어휘 acutely 예민하게, 날카롭게; 몹시   differentiate 구별하다; 구분 짓다   accordingly 그에 맞춰; 그래서   minute 미세한; 사소한; 자세한   volatile 휘발성의; 변덕스러운; 불안한   compound 화합[혼합]물; 합성하다   waft 퍼지다, 퍼지게 하다   tactile 촉각[촉감]의   shoot (새로 돋아난) 싹[순]   infection 감염, 전염(병)   condition 날씨; 조건; 상태   weather 견뎌 내다, 뚫고 나가다   modify 수정[조정]하다   physiology 생리 기능; 생리학   myriad 무수한; 무수히 많음   caretaker 돌보는 사람; 관리인   alike 한결같이; 마찬가지로   with abandon 멋대로, 아무렇게나   take over 장악[탈취]하   decidedly 확실히, 분명히; 단호히   input 입력   render ~을 만들다, 되게 하다   billion 10억(의)   vegetal 식물(성)의   self-conscious 남을 의식하는; 자의식이 강한

MEMO

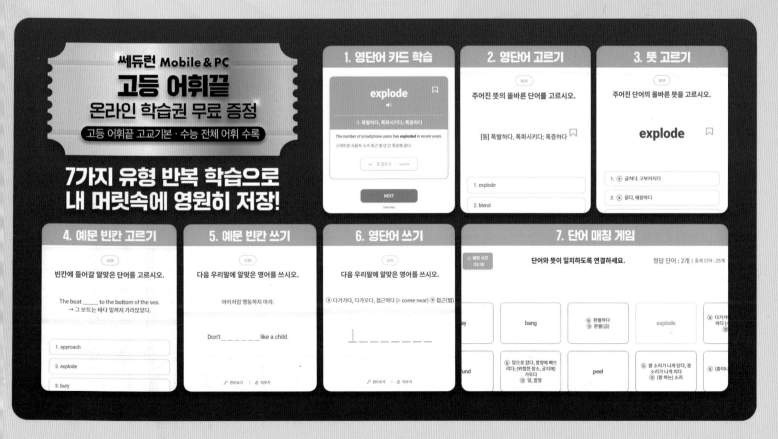

쎄듀 초등 커리큘럼

	예비초	초1	초2	초3	초4	초5	초6
구문				초등코치 천일문 SENTENCE 1001개 통문장 암기로 완성하는 초등 영어의 기초			
문법					초등코치 천일문 GRAMMAR 1001개 예문으로 배우는 초등 영문법		
문법			신간 왓츠 Grammar Start 시리즈 초등 기초 영문법 입문				
문법					신간 왓츠 Grammar Plus 시리즈 초등 필수 영문법 마무리		
독해				신간 왓츠 리딩 70 / 80 / 90 / 100 A / B 쉽고 재미있게 완성되는 영어 독해력			
어휘				초등코치 천일문 VOCA & STORY 1001개의 초등 필수 어휘와 짧은 스토리			
어휘		패턴으로 말하는 초등 필수 영단어 1 / 2 문장 패턴으로 완성하는 초등 필수 영단어					
ELT	Oh! My PHONICS 1 / 2 / 3 / 4 유·초등학생을 위한 첫 영어 파닉스						
ELT		Oh! My SPEAKING 1 / 2 / 3 / 4 / 5 / 6 핵심 문장 패턴으로 더욱 쉬운 영어 말하기					
ELT		Oh! My GRAMMAR 1 / 2 / 3 쓰기로 완성하는 첫 초등 영문법					

쎄듀 중등 커리큘럼

	예비중	중1	중2	중3
구문		신간 천일문 STARTER 1 / 2		중등 필수 구문 & 문법 총정리
문법		천일문 GRAMMAR LEVEL 1 / 2 / 3		예문 중심 문법 기본서
문법		GRAMMAR Q Starter 1, 2 / Intermediate 1, 2 / Advanced 1, 2		학기별 문법 기본서
문법		잘 풀리는 영문법 1 / 2 / 3		문제 중심 문법 적용서
문법		GRAMMAR PIC 1 / 2 / 3 / 4		이해가 쉬운 도식화된 문법서
문법			1센치 영문법	1권으로 핵심 문법 정리
문법+어법			첫단추 BASIC 문법·어법편 1 / 2	문법·어법의 기초
문법+쓰기		EGU 영단어&품사 / 문장 형식 / 동사 써먹기 / 문법 써먹기 / 구문 써먹기		서술형 기초 세우기와 문법 다지기
문법+쓰기				올쏨 1 기본 문장 PATTERN 내신 서술형 기본 문장 학습
쓰기		거침없이 Writing LEVEL 1 / 2 / 3		중등 교과서 내신 기출 서술형
쓰기		개정 중학 영어 쓰작 1 / 2 / 3		중등 교과서 패턴 드릴 서술형
어휘		어휘끝 중학 필수편 중학 필수어휘 1000개	어휘끝 중학 마스터편 고난도 중학어휘 +고등기초 어휘 1000개	
독해		Reading Relay Starter 1, 2 / Challenger 1, 2 / Master 1, 2		타교과 연계 배경 지식 독해
독해		READING Q Starter 1, 2 / Intermediate 1, 2 / Advanced 1, 2		예측/추론/요약 사고력 독해
독해전략			리딩 플랫폼 1 / 2 / 3	논픽션 지문 독해
독해유형			Reading 16 LEVEL 1 / 2 / 3	수능 유형 맛보기 + 내신 대비
독해유형			첫단추 BASIC 독해편 1 / 2	수능 유형 독해 입문
듣기	Listening Q 유형편 / 1 / 2 / 3			유형별 듣기 전략 및 실전 대비
듣기		쎄듀 빠르게 중학영어듣기 모의고사 1 / 2 / 3		교육청 듣기평가 대비